Indexes:

In addition to the General Index, also use the special indexes to find the best markets for your poetry.

Chapbook Index: *Lists publishers of chapbooks.*

Geographical Index: *Lists publications/presses by state or country.*

Subject Index: *Indexes listings by specialization, e.g., a specific form, style or theme.*

General Index: *Lists all titles in the book and includes cross-references.*

For more information about submitting your poetry for publication, read:

1995
Poet's Market

Where & how to publish your poetry

Edited by

Christine Martin

WRITER'S DIGEST BOOKS

Cincinnati, Ohio

If you are a poetry publisher and would like to be considered for a listing in the next edition of Poet's Market, *please request a questionnaire from* Poet's Market—*QR, 1507 Dana Ave., Cincinnati, Ohio 45207.*

Distributed in Canada by McGraw-Hill,
300 Water Street
Whitby Ontario L1N 9B6.
Also distributed in Australia by Kirby Books,
Private Bag No. 19, P.O. Alexandria NSW 2015.

Managing Editor, Market Books Department:
Constance J. Achabal;
Supervising Editor: Michael Willins;
Production Editor: Chantelle Bentley.

This 1995 hardcover edition of Poet's Market *features a "self-jacket" that eliminates the need for a separate dust jacket. It provides sturdy protection for your book while it saves paper, trees and energy.*

International Standard Serial Number
0883-5470
International Standard Book Number
0-89879-677-6

Cover Photo: Guildhaus Photographics

Contents

Resources

Indexes

From the Editor

Welcome to the tenth edition of **Poet's Market**! What you are now holding in your hands is more than just a directory of poetry publishers—and far more than the result of months of continuous work. What you are holding is a detailed map to help you find your way in the world of poetry publishing. And it is the culmination of more than a decade of effort put forth by a variety of individuals, including a number of our readers.

While directory publishing has long been a staple of Writer's Digest Books (beginning with our parent publication, **Writer's Market**), it was the late poet Judson Jerome who first suggested we create an annual resource for those primarily interested in publishing poetry. Before long, Jud and members of our staff were hard at work developing the first edition, which appeared in 1986.

When Jud founded this directory, his main premise was that you shouldn't have to pay to see your poetry in print. That's why, even today, we are selective when it comes to listing publishers. In this edition you will find 1,700 markets for your poetry—including small circulation newsletters, mass circulation magazines, literary journals, small presses and trade book publishers. Approximately 300 of these markets are new to this edition. And while many cannot offer money as payment for your work, they typically provide free copies of the volumes in which your poetry appears.

Deciphering the best markets

Yet, what we have created is much more than just a directory of poetry publishers who offer some form of return for your work. Jud also initiated (and we continue to refine) what he called a "system of market classification," a legend, so to speak, to help you decipher which are the best markets for your poetry. By referring to the Roman numeral(s) in each listing, you can determine which publishers are **(I)** most receptive to the work of beginners, **(II)** expect you to be familiar with literary publications, **(III)** limited, **(IV)** specialized, or **(V)** currently closed to submissions.

By far the most useful classification is the fourth one. Publishers which are "specialized" seek poetry written in certain forms (such as haiku) or by certain groups of people (such as senior citizens) or about certain subjects (such as social issues). All of these publishers are listed according to their specialization in the Subject Index at the back of this book. This year we have both added and refined a number of specialization categories so you can more quickly locate appropriate markets. Read How to Use Your **Poet's Market** and the Publishers of Poetry introduction for details.

Whether you narrow down potential markets by using the Subject Index, Geographical Index or Chapbook Publishers Index (which was added in 1989 at the suggestion of our readers), you will discover that our listings include up-to-date information about the poetry needs and submission policies of publishers. And, as in years past, we have added new information to further guide your submission efforts. For example, this year we asked editors whether they publish theme issues and whether they send pre-publication galleys. We have also noted which publications have work included in recent editions of **The Best American Poetry**.

Outlining submission steps

We would certainly be remiss, however, if we just told you whether editors send prepublication galleys, for instance, without outlining the steps you should take to get your poetry accepted in the first place. Even in the very first edition, Jud provided details on how to go about submitting your work. In later years, this became a standard article called The Business of Poetry.

Now we offer you a brand new piece: Charting Your Path to Poetry Publication. In this article we provide a step-by-step approach to every aspect of the submission process. We not only discuss accepted procedures (such as how many poems to submit and how they should be typed), but we also point out—and analyze—the crossroads (in such areas as simultaneous submissions and book publishing) where only you can decide which route to take. And we include information on such topics as writing cover letters and keeping records.

Also new this year—and prompted by a suggestion from one of our readers—is a special sidebar entitled Evaluating Anthologies. Written by Amy Holman, associate director of information at Poets & Writers, this article proposes eight questions to consider when evaluating anthology publications. It also supplies details about the Poets & Writers "help line," which you can call when you need specific answers about publishing opportunities.

Illustrating community diversity

Another important and long-standing feature of this directory is the "Close-up" interview. Each year we talk to a number of poets and editors in the field and share their publishing stories. The resulting articles not only illustrate the diversity of the poetry publishing community, but they are also sources of inspiration and advice.

In this edition, you'll hear from poets Maggie Anderson, Kelly Cherry, Lucille Clifton and Molly Peacock, president of the Poetry Society of America. You'll also hear from folks with seats on both sides of the editorial desk, including poet David Breeden, who is also editor of ***Context South***; Canadian poet and editor David Green; and Theodore and Renée Weiss, who have been involved in poetry writing and publishing for more than 50 years. You can learn about haiku and other Japanese forms from Francine Porad, published poet, editor of ***Brussels Sprout***, and past president of the Haiku Society of America. And, rounding out the list, are interviews with Russian poet Yevgeny Yevtushenko and translator Albert C. Todd.

To really develop a sense for what's happening in the world of poetry publishing, however, you must read more than our interviews. In the Publishers of Poetry section, also read the sample lines of poetry to see what is currently being published. Add the information contained in Contests and Awards as well as Conferences and Workshops, Writing Colonies, Organizations, and Publications, and you'll find **Poet's Market** to be a detailed topographical view of poetry publishing trends and activities.

When Mark Donovan granted permission for us to use the cover of his publication, ***Howling Dog***, in this edition, he added, "I remember the years when poetry was just a small section of **Writer's Market** and it impresses me to think of the progress this annual publication has made since that time."

Progress indeed! Over the years, **Poet's Market** has grown from 384 to 552 pages. And it has been shaped much by reader suggestion. In fact, for two editions, poet Michael J. Bugeja helped implement the results of a readers' survey. In many ways, we owe Michael, and all of you, our sincere thanks. With your continued help, we hope to make the next ten years just as interesting.

Christine Martin

How to Use Your Poet's Market

To reap the benefits of **Poet's Market**, you need to know how to use it. After all, this directory not only provides listings of poetry publishers, but it is also designed to help you determine which ones are the best markets for your work.

The first step is to examine your poetry. Do you write poetry that makes a political statement? Poetry about wildlife? religious symbols? other poets? Do you write sonnets? prose poems? About a certain area? In a language other than English?

Maybe you don't write any specific type of poetry. Maybe the answer depends on which one of your works we're talking about. No matter. If you've put craft into your poems, you'll find a place for them.

Start with the indexes

All Publishers of Poetry listings are coded as to the category of poetry they are seeking. Publishers that desire poetry within certain realms—on certain subjects, in certain forms or by certain folks—may be quickly identified by a **IV** and word(s) denoting the specialization(s). For example, ***Tails of Wonder*** is coded **IV-Science fiction/fantasy** because it seeks material with some connection to these genres.

Once you've considered your own poetry, you don't have to comb each page for compatible listings. Turn to the Subject Index beginning on page 508. Here you will find all publishers with **IV** codes divided according to their specializations.

Scan the boldface headings to locate the specialization that matches your work. If you write haiku, for instance, check under **Form/Style**. If you're an older adult who writes about the woods near your home, check under both **Senior Citizen** and **Nature/Rural/Ecology** and write down the names of those publishers that sound interesting.

Publishers may classify themselves as **Regional** in the Subject Index, but checking the Geographical Index is also helpful. Here you'll discover the publishers located in your state or country. While some don't consider themselves "regional" in terms of the poetry they accept, they are often more open to writers from their own areas.

Also useful, particularly if you're trying to publish a small collection of poems, is the Chapbook Publishers Index, which lists publishers who consider chapbook manuscripts (typically 20-25 pages of poetry connected by a theme). You'll find more information about both chapbook and book publishing in Charting Your Path to Poetry Publication.

Check market codes

Once you have a list of possible markets for your work—because of specialization or location or an interest in chapbooks—look up their listings and check the market category codes following their titles to discover how open they are to submissions.

Besides a **IV** code, a publisher may also have **I**, **II**, **III** or **V**. Those with **I** are open to beginners' submissions, so if you're just starting out, try sending to them. Publishers with **II** codes are general markets which expect you to be familiar with literary journals and magazines. Those coded **III** are limited as to the number of submissions they accept, so your chances of publishing with these folks are limited too. Finally, those with **V** are not accepting unsolicited manuscripts. Although you may have picked such a publisher out of the Geographical Index, you can't submit your poetry to it at this time. That's okay. Cross it off your list and move on to the next one.

When you discover publishers with more than one code, read their listings carefully to determine if they're still possible markets for your work. For instance, a publisher may be **I, IV-Religious**, which means it either wants religious material as well as poetry from beginners or religious material only, including poetry from beginners. To learn more about market category codes, see the Publishers of Poetry introduction.

Also, as you read the listings based on the indexes, others will attract your eye. Don't feel limited by those on your list. Many publications don't want to be noted for a specialization and are open to ALL types of work.

Read carefully

When you've narrowed your list of possible markets by using the indexes and checking market categories, read each listing *carefully*. Look for the general purpose of the publisher and statements about its interests in poetry. For example, ***Hellas*** accepts any kind of poetry but especially welcomes poems in meter. In their listing, they say, "We prize elegance and formality in verse, but specifically encourage poetry of the utmost boldness and innovation, so long as it is not willfully obscurantist."

Also, the names of recently published poets and sample lines of poetry will indicate what level of writing an editor is seeking and provide insight into editorial tastes.

Consider the date a publisher was founded as well. Older publishers have more stability, and sometimes more prestige. However, newer publishers, especially those new to this edition (designated by a ‡), are often more receptive to submissions.

Carefully reading the description of a publication's format will help you visualize how your poetry will appear in its pages. Better yet, review sample copies. This is the best way to determine whether your poetry is right for a publication. Sample copies can be ordered from publishers or often found in your library or local bookstore.

However, don't just locate a sample copy, decide your work is appropriate and submit to that market without knowing submission procedures. Inappropriate submissions will not only leave a bad impression of your work, they can also affect a publisher's willingness to accept unsolicited manuscripts from others as well.

If you haven't already done so, read Charting Your Path to Poetry Publication. It offers a step-by-step approach to every aspect of the submission process. Most publishers also include specific submission procedures in their listings. And, many offer guidelines for a SASE. Send for them. The goal, after all, is to increase—not decrease—your chances of acceptance.

Other resources

As you develop your craft, take advantage of the various resources for poets. For support services and feedback from others, for example, join one of the groups listed in Organizations Useful to Poets. If you're searching for a place to get away and write, check Writing Colonies. Or, if you're seeking instruction and marketing tips, attend one of the events in Conferences and Workshops or consult one of the magazines listed in Publications Useful to Poets.

Finally, if you don't recognize a symbol or an abbreviation being used, refer to the Key to Symbols on page 14 or the Glossary on page 494. And, for easy reference, you will find a list of U.S. and Canadian Postal Codes on page 493.

Charting Your Path to Poetry Publication

For many, true joy comes not only from writing poetry but also from sharing it with others – be they family and friends, members of the audience at a poetry reading, or readers of local, regional or national publications. Whether you've just spent the last few months writing (and polishing) your first poems and are anxious to start sending them out to editors and publishers or whether you've been writing poetry for years and have just been convinced by your spouse, sibling or best friend that your poetry deserves a wider audience, you probably have a number of questions about how to properly submit your work.

Let's even say your first question is quite basic, more basic than, for example, whether or not you should engage in simultaneous submissions (which we'll get to later). Perhaps you're really wondering: "Where do I begin?" Well, in many ways, you've come to the right place. Here we'll answer, with up-to-date, detailed information, the most often asked questions about submitting poetry.

Where to begin

So, where *do* you begin to look for editors and publishers that might be interested in your work? The easiest answer of course is in this directory. Included along with listings for contests and awards and resources such as organizations and publications, you'll find about 1,700 publishers of poetry from around the world. And most of these magazine and book publishers specifically indicate what they do and do not want to see in the way of poetry for their pages. The biggest challenge you'll have here is narrowing down our list of markets. (For help on this matter, read both How to Use Your **Poet's Market** and the Publishers of Poetry introduction.)

Yet, if you're just beginning, don't overlook the publications you have right on your living room coffee table. Those small (and often specialized) publications, such as your local church bulletin, the weekly neighborhood newspaper, your inhouse company magazine and/or the regional garden club gazette, are probably not listed within these pages. That's okay. Unless you're strictly out for literary fame, they're considered viable options. After all, the best way to determine whether your poetry is appropriate for a publication is to read several sample issues, and you've been reading these magazines for months, perhaps even years. You're already familiar with their contents and you probably have much in common with their other readers. So even if your weekly newspaper does not have a poetry page, the editor might publish an occasional poem – particularly if it relates to life in your neighborhood.

We should also add that new magazines are founded all the time – even as you're reading these pages. To keep up with new literary journals and small presses, read publications such as ***Poets & Writers Magazine*** or ***Writer's Digest***, both which regularly contain information about new markets. On a more local level, check the notices posted on the bulletin board at your library or nearest bookstore. There you may discover a new publication particularly interested in the work of beginning and/or regional writers.

Appearance is everything

When preparing to submit your work to any publication, however, remember that, as in grade school, neatness counts. Use a typewriter or personal computer with a letter-quality (or at least near letter-quality) printer to type and/or print your poems on good, white, standard-size (generally 8½ × 11) bond paper. Do not handwrite your poems and do not use onion skin or erasable bond. Make sure your equipment has a good dark ribbon so each word of your poem is clear. And proofread your work carefully. Sloppy manuscripts with spelling and/or typographical errors are likely to be returned without comment.

No matter how short your work, most editors prefer that you submit each poem on a separate page with the title centered above it and your name, address and telephone number (typically) in the upper right or left corner. Some editors want poems double-spaced. Others prefer single spacing (with double spacing between stanzas) to give them an idea of how your poem will appear on their page. If your poem carries over to a second sheet, make sure to note whether the lines at the top are a continuation of the same stanza or the start of a new one. Don't leave an editor wondering about such details. In all aspects, submit your work exactly as you would like it printed.

What to send

How many poems should you submit? In general, send only three to five poems to any editor at any given time. A few editors, particularly those who like to "feature" poets, prefer to receive seven or eight poems in a submission. But this is rare. Many of the listings in this directory will note exactly how many poems an editor will consider. You can also avoid irritating an editor with too many (or too few) poems by requesting a copy of the publication's submission guidelines (which may not only indicate how many poems you should send but also exactly how you should type them).

As many editors and publishers have very specific submission policies, it is always a good idea to send a self-addressed, stamped envelope (SASE) to receive a copy of a publisher's guidelines before submitting any work. If you're interested in a magazine or book publisher outside of your own country, send a self-addressed envelope (SAE) and International Reply Coupons (IRCs) which can be purchased from most post offices. If a publisher does not have guidelines or if the guidelines do not indicate the number of poems you should submit, don't worry. Sending three to five poems is considered standard.

Choosing which poems to send—and how they should be arranged—is all up to you. Of course, you want to send work that is appropriate for the publication in question. When it comes to arranging your poetry, however, your goal is simply to entice an editor to continue reading. As poet Molly Peacock indicates in an interview in the Publishers of Poetry section, place the boldest poem first and don't worry about whether the poems have a theme or are too much alike. More than anything else, an editor wants to see your best work.

To copyright or not to copyright

Before you send off the poems that you have spent months perfecting, however, you may be wondering about copyright protection. The good news is that you own the copyright to your work from the moment of creation. And, you can, if you wish, put the copyright symbol (©) on your poetry, followed by the year of creation and your name. Yet, copyright notices are typically considered unnecessary as most editors know you own the copyright to your work and few, if any, will steal your ideas. For some, in fact, copyright notices signal the work of amateurs who are distrustful of editors and publishers.

While the decision is certainly yours, it is important to note that most magazines are copyrighted and book publishers will usually register copyrights in your name. In addition, those who are inclined to "borrow" your ideas will do so whether or not the copyright notice is attached. If you wish to register your copyright, however, or if you would like more information, write to the Copyright Office, Library of Congress, Washington DC 20559.

Cover letters

In the past, poets also had to grapple with the issue of cover letters, that is, should you (or should you not) include a cover letter with your poetry submission? As most editors and publishers did not indicate a preference, this question used to be another one poets had to primarily answer for themselves. Now, however, many editors are specifically indicating a desire for cover letters in both their market listings and submission guidelines.

Overall, a cover letter allows you to personally present yourself—and your work—to specific editors. To do so graciously, you'll not only want to note the titles of the poems you are submitting, but you'll also want to demonstrate some familiarity with the publication in question. Editors, of course, like to know that their contributors are among their readers. Include a few of your most recent publishing credits as well. And what if you haven't published a poem yet? Then note that. Some editors are particularly interested in new writers and have special sections for beginners' work.

Before you compose your cover letter, though, check to see if the editor has requested biographical information for the magazine's contributors' page. If so, add a few lines about your job or hobbies, particularly if they relate to the enclosed poems. Above all, refrain from praising your own work. Let your poems speak for themselves. And, no matter how much information is requested, keep your cover letter strictly to one page.

Finally, address your letter to the person listed as the poetry editor (or the editor if the publication is small). Most of the publications in this directory have a particular individual to whom you should direct your submissions. If there is no one listed, however, check the publication's guidelines or the masthead of a recent copy. If you are still unable to locate a specific name, simply address your letter to "Poetry Editor." Of course, use an acceptable business-style format and make sure your letter is free of misspellings and/or grammatical errors. (For an example, see the Sample Cover Letter on page 9.)

Sign, seal and deliver

Once you have decided which poems you are going to submit, place them together (in whatever order you've chosen) and fold them into thirds. Do not fold your poems individually as the hassle of having to unfold and read each poem is apt to annoy editors, many of whom are already overworked. If you have elected (or are required) to also enclose a cover letter, fold the letter into thirds and place it on top of your batch of poems. Then put all of this material into a business-size (#10, 4⅛×9½) envelope.

To ensure a response from the editor or publisher in question, you must also include a SASE. You can use either a #9 (4×9) envelope or a #10 envelope folded into thirds. If you're submitting your poetry to a publication outside of your own country, include a SAE and IRCs. One IRC, by the way, is usually enough for one ounce by surface mail. For airmail return, you need one IRC for each half-ounce. In either case, make sure your reply envelope contains enough postage to cover the cost of returning your submission. And make sure your outside envelope has enough postage attached to get your poetry to the editor in the first place. (In general, three pages of poetry, a cover letter and a SASE can be mailed for one first-class stamp.)

Keeping records

But don't just send the only copy of your poems winging its way through the wild blue yonder. Always keep extra copies for yourself. In fact, you may want to keep the original typewritten or computer-printed version of your work and submit good, clean photocopies to editors and publishers. After all, you never know when your poetry will end up lost in the mail or somewhere in the heap of other submissions at a publisher's office. If you submit your one-and-only copy of your work and it gets lost in the process, you're simply out of luck.

It's also important to keep a record of which poems you have submitted, where and when. You can record such information on 3×5 cards arranged alphabetically (by poem title) in a metal storage container. Or you can use sheets of paper arranged in file folders (in which you can also keep the original copy of each poem). Or you can create a database on your personal computer. In any case, note the title of each poem, the name of the magazine to which it was submitted and the date your work was mailed. Also note the date of each editor's reply, the outcome of your efforts and any comments that may prove useful when you're next submitting to a particular market (such as information about reading periods or changes in editors or frequency of publication).

Tracking responses

By keeping detailed records of when and where you are submitting your work—and the date of the editor's reply—you are also tracking response times. Most editors and publishers indicate (in their market listings and/or submission guidelines) approximately how long you must wait before you can expect to receive a reply to your submission. If an editor does not specify when you will receive a report, it is generally expected to be within three months. Many times, however, the approximate date (or three-month benchmark) will come and go without a word from the editor or publisher.

What should you do when you haven't heard from an editor within the specified time period? Wait another month, then send a note inquiring about the status of your submission. Note the titles of your poems and the date sent. Ask when the editor anticipates making a decision. And enclose a SASE or self-addressed, stamped postcard for the editor's response. If you still do not hear from a particular market, send a postcard withdrawing your poems from consideration. And then send your submission elsewhere.

By all means, do *not* call editors with questions about submissions. Phone calls are only likely to irritate those who must divide their time between publishing a small press magazine and maintaining a fulltime job and family obligations. And you stand little chance of accomplishing your goal anyway as many editors simply cannot supply such answers over the phone. Why risk having your poems completely dropped from consideration?

Previously published poems

When you submit your poetry to magazine editors and publishers, by the way, they not only assume the work is original (that it is yours and nobody else's), but they also assume the work has not been previously published and is not being simultaneously submitted. There is nothing wrong with sending an editor a poem that has already been published. Some editors, however, are simply not open to such submissions.

SAMPLE COVER LETTER

513 Wrenwood Lane
Huntington WV 25707
(304)273-2128

February 17, 1995

Cecelia Donahue
Poetry Editor
Chicken Noodle Soup Review
369 Arlington Drive
Lancaster PA 17603

Dear Cecelia Donahue:

Enclosed are my poems for your consideration: "Monster in My Mirror," "Where's the Moon?" and "Apples and Bananas." My poetry has recently appeared in *Grasshopper*, *Kidsplay* and *Treehouse Magazine*.

I am currently employed as a Special Education instructor by a local school district. I also volunteer at a center for underprivileged children. These children greatly influence my poetry and I frequently get my ideas from them.

I enjoy your publication tremendously and often use the word games in combination with vocabulary lessons in my classes, and the kids at the center love the craft activities and the stories. It would be an honor to see my poetry in your pages.

Sincerely,

Penelope Gordon

These folks want to be the first to publish new work—not the second. They are looking to acquire first rights to your poetry—not reprint rights. So before you send any previously published material, check market listings and/or submission guidelines to see if the editor or publisher in question is willing to consider such work. If so, note (in your cover letter) where the particular poem(s) first appeared.

. . . and simultaneous submissions

As many editors and publishers take months to reply to submitted work, poets in recent years have responded by sending the same package of poems to several editors at the same time. This is considered simultaneously submitting. And most who engage in this practice believe that a batch of three to five poems submitted to two or more editors has a better chance of resulting in an acceptance. However, if you submit your work simultaneously and an editor accepts one of your poems, you must contact the other editor(s) immediately and withdraw your work from consideration. This is likely to annoy (or even anger) the other editor(s) still in the process of making a decision. And future submissions to these markets may no longer be welcome.

To lessen the risks involved with this practice, you need to tell editors up front (in your cover letter) that you are simultaneously submitting your work. This is not only a way of forewarning them, but it may also prompt an editor to make a more timely decision. However, if you're going to tell editors that you're simultaneously submitting your material, make sure they are actually open to such submissions. If not, it is unlikely they will even consider your work. In addition, simultaneously submitting your work only to those publications open to the practice greatly decreases your chances of irritating any editors in the process. Again, check market listings and/or submission guidelines for specific information.

Yet the question still remains whether you should simultaneously submit your work in the first place. Why rush the process? You certainly don't try to take shortcuts in writing your poems. Why take shortcuts in submitting? After all, if you're just beginning and/or are still perfecting your craft, you're likely to quickly collect rejections. That can be discouraging. And if you're already regularly publishing, you're more likely to garner two acceptances at once—which puts you back at the point of having to contact editors and withdraw your work. The final decision, of course, is yours.

Chapbooks and others

Book publishers, by the way, expect some of the poems in your manuscript to be previously published. And, knowing the difficulty poets face in placing a collection, they are more accepting of the practice of simultaneous submissions. Yet you should only begin to think about book publication once you have gathered a fair number of publication credits in literary or small press magazines. Often, publishing a chapbook is a good middle step.

A chapbook is a small volume of 20-25 pages (or less). As such a volume is less expensive to produce than a full-length book collection (which may range from 48 to 80 pages), a chapbook is usually a safe way for a publisher to take a chance on a lesser-known poet. Most chapbooks are saddle-stapled with card covers. Some are photocopied publications. Others contain professionally printed pages. While chapbooks are seldom noted by reviewers or carried by bookstores, they are good items to sell after readings or through the mail. You'll discover that, in addition to some book publishers, a number of magazine publishers also publish chapbooks (for a complete list, refer to the Chapbook Publishers Index, beginning on page 495).

Whether you're planning to submit your work to either a chapbook or book publisher, however, you should always examine sample copies of their previously published collections. This is not only the best way to familiarize yourself with the press' offerings, but it is also a good way to determine the quality of the product. To solicit a publisher's interest in your own work, the standard procedure is to first query. Send a sampling of your poems (again, three to five, unless a publisher has noted otherwise), with a cover letter including brief biographical information and a few of your more noteworthy publication credits. Also let the publisher know that you are familiar with their other collections. And don't forget to include a SASE (or SAE and IRCs) for the publisher's reply.

Book publishing options

Once you develop an interest in having a collection of your work published, you'll soon discover that publishing arrangements vary. Some, in fact, are more beneficial to poets than others. Consider the following options carefully.

- **Standard publishing.** In a standard publishing contract, the publisher usually agrees to assume all production and promotion costs for your book. You receive a 10% royalty on the retail (or sometimes wholesale) price, though with some small presses you are paid with a percentage of the press run instead. It's important to note, however, that such publishers only release a small number of poetry volumes each year.
- **Cooperative publishing.** This arrangement is exactly that: cooperative. Although the details of such contracts vary, they require some type of investment of either time or money on your part. Some, for instance, require involvement in marketing. Others specify money for production costs. In any case, know what you're signing. While cooperative publishing is respected in the literary and small press world (and many such publishers can bring your work the attention it deserves), some vanity/subsidy presses try to label themselves as "cooperative." True cooperative publishing, however, shares both the risks and the profits.
- **Self-publishing.** This option may be most appealing if your primary goal is to publish a small collection of your work to give to family and friends. Self-publishing is also a good choice for those who prefer complete control over the creative process. In this scenario, you work hand-in-hand with a local printer and invent a name for your "press." Most important is that you pay all the costs but own all the books and net all the proceeds from any sales (which you, of course, must generate). For more detailed information about this option, read **The Complete Guide To Self-Publishing** by Tom and Marilyn Ross (a newly revised edition is now available from Writer's Digest Books).
- **Vanity/subsidy presses.** This is probably the least desirable option. Companies in this category usually advertise for manuscripts, lavishly praise your work, and ask for fees far in excess of costs (compare their figures to those of your local printer for a book of similar size, format and binding). These companies also make a habit of collectively advertising their books, that is, your work will simply receive a line along with 20 or so other books in an ad placed in the general media rather than a specific market. Worse yet, sometimes you own all copies of your book. Sometimes you don't. Though such agreements vary, overall, these presses have little respect in the literary community.

We should also note that many believe some anthology publications fall under "vanity" publishing as you must often pay a tidy sum to purchase the volume containing your work. To learn how to spot such vanity publishers and better evaluate anthologies, read the special sidebar on pages 12 and 13. By the way, whichever course you choose to share your poetry, we wish you luck!

Evaluating Anthologies

Many possible routes are open on the publishing map, and anthologies account for one. Since an anthology is a book, even though you may have only one poem published between its covers, the edition will be readily stocked on shelves in more bookstores than would a literary magazine, and it will be easier to market and to catalog. The charming aspect of anthologies is that they offer selections of poems on themes or about certain subjects, written by poets of particular age-groups, nationalities, cultures, or schools of writing and/or collected from decades of successful magazines or presses. A literary magazine sometimes has these parameters, but mostly offers a selection bound only by the editor's tastes. Anthology editors also judge the work they accept based on its merit.

There are some considerations when confronted with the possibility of having one's poetry published in anthologies. As with all aspects of publishing, research of the market is essential, in part because anthologies are the chief domain of vanity or subsidy presses. Each of us has individual expectations for the presentation of our work, and must, at times, defer to the experience of editors, book designers, production assistants, marketers, distributors and bookstore managers. But, as communicators in the field of literature, we all want to reach the widest possible audience. You can be in the driver's seat while motoring along the anthology route by understanding what it means to publish, as opposed to simply print.

Publishing pays the poet for the work that is included, whether in cash, copies of the anthology or both, and makes an effort to market and distribute the book. The poem has been accepted based on its merit and relevance. Since publishing incorporates all of the above and more (with inclusion of royalty payments for books by one author), vanity or subsidy presses do not actually publish, but rather, print. They require payment to print the poem in the anthology that is neither marketed nor distributed. The anthology might not have a theme or subject, but is almost certainly connected to a contest sponsored by the press.

While some anthologies result from awards, such as the Pushcart Prize, all of the poems within ought to be the works of the winners. A contest fee should be minimal. It is up to you to determine how much to pay in contest fees, but measure it against the prize money when making your decision. Most publishers solicit poetry for publication aside from offering a contest, so paying a fee is not obligatory to being accepted. Vanity or subsidy presses only solicit through contests and tend to offer publication to those whose poems lost the contest, as well as those whose poems won, as a kind of consolation, part of which is the discount price of the anthology offered to the poets. Therefore, poets pay the fee to enter the contest and then pay the price of the anthology resulting from a contest they did not win. When any poems can be included in the prize anthology (and they are), there is no sense of poems being chosen based on their merit and celebrated in the form of publication. Furthermore, the books are not distributed through the normal channels of libraries, bookstores, distributors and mail-order catalogs.

The success in determining which is the best venture for you is in evaluating both what is standard in publishing and what you want from it. So keep these questions in mind as you research the possibilities:

1) Is publication in the anthology due to an open submission?
2) Can you submit poetry to the press when a contest is not being offered?
3) Is publication part of the prize awarded to the winners?
4) Do you get paid?
5) In order to receive a copy, must you pay for it?
6) Does the press release anthologies to bookstores, libraries and/or distributors?
7) Will the book be advertised in literary magazines, newsletters and newspapers?
8) Will the book be reviewed in book review journals and papers?

For successful publishing, you need only answer "no" to the fifth question. But if you seek specific answers or consultation, you can call the Information Center at Poets & Writers, from 11 a.m. to 3 p.m. (EST), Monday through Friday. The number is (212)226-3586. Poets & Writers is a nonprofit, literary service organization for poets, fiction writers and performance writers. As well, **Poets & Writers Magazine** *screens out advertising by vanity or subsidy presses.*

If you don't mind that your readership is limited to the people whose poems appear in the book (and their family and friends) due to a lack of standard distribution, and you simply want your poem in a book (for which you don't mind paying), then send your poems anywhere that captures your attention. If you want to reach an audience you may, in large part, never meet, and want to receive payment for the poetry that is accepted for publication, then do your research to find your readership.

When I'm walking on the city streets and see a graceful fern growing in the damp dark under a sidewalk grate, once in awhile passing its minnowy schools of leaves through the bars, I think of poetry. It survives in a society where it is underappreciated most of the time, politically, socially, educationally and personally. It thrives in small pockets of the culture, quietly substantial, tenacious, insistent, beautiful in its contrast, equal in its summary (if not superior) to journalism, fiction, film and speech. In some cultures, it is at the base of language. It may be that anthologies are the tool that will reintroduce the reflective power of poetry, in its great variety and adaptability to most subjects, to the masses that go without it. Properly publishing with anthologies forms a printed community and is a way to inform the public, and to change awareness through issues and writing styles.

Amy Holman, *the author of this piece, is a poet, fiction writer and lecturer living in New York City. She is also the Associate Director of Information at Poets & Writers (see the listing in Publications Useful to Poets).*

Key to Symbols and Abbreviations

‡—*New listing*
ms—*manuscript;* **mss**—*manuscripts*
b&w—*black & white (photo or illustration)*
p&h—*postage & handling*
SASE—*self-addressed, stamped envelope*
SAE—*self-addressed envelope*
IRC—*International Reply Coupon (IRCs should be sent with SAEs for replies from countries outside your own)*

Important Market Listing Information

- *Listings are based on questionnaires and verified copy. They are not advertisements* nor *are markets necessarily endorsed by the editors of this book.*
- *Information in the listings comes directly from the publishers and is as accurate as possible, but publications and editors come and go, and poetry needs fluctuate between the publication date of this directory and the time you use it.*
- *If you are a poetry publisher and would like to be considered for a listing in the next edition, please request a questionnaire from* **Poet's Market**—*QR, 1507 Dana Ave., Cincinnati OH 45207.*
- **Poet's Market** reserves the right to exclude any listing that does not meet its requirements.

The Markets

Publishers of Poetry

Without a doubt, this section is the heart of **Poet's Market**. It lists page after page of potential markets for your work. It also includes interviews with both poets and editors. And, when read carefully, these 400 or so pages provide a feel for what's happening in both the poetry community and our world. So whether you're a newcomer to the realm of poetry publishing or a longtime reader, get out your stethoscope—you don't want to miss a beat!

In total, this section includes about 1,700 poetry publishing markets—everything from those folks who produce small, stapled newsletters to those colleges and universities who publish perfect-bound paperback journals to those publishing houses who release hardcover books. Approximately 300 of these markets are new to this edition.

You'll often notice information about two or three related markets in one listing. Including all of a publisher's activities in one entry provides a quick overview of the entire operation. The listing for ***Amelia*** is a classic example. If you look up our entry for ***Amelia***, you'll also find information about ***Cicada*** and ***SPSM&H***, two other quarterly magazines edited and published by Frederick Raborg. Yet, that's not all you'll find. The entry also lists the numerous awards offered by this publisher. When all of these activities are placed together in the same listing, it's easy to understand why Raborg's response to your submission may take a bit longer than expected.

Nevertheless, if you're looking for a specific magazine, award or poetry publishing imprint, check the General Index for the appropriate page number. Some publications, such as ***Words of Wisdom***, have simply changed names. In the General Index, however, you'll find ***Words of Wisdom*** cross-referenced to ***Timber Creek Review*** and you'll be given the right page number. If you want to know which listings are new to this edition, watch for the double dagger (‡) preceding the listing title.

Welcome new listings!

As in years past, some new listings are publications that were in earlier editions of **Poet's Market** but not the previous one. For example, we're happy to welcome back ***Chelsea***, ***Hammers***, ***Lynx***, ***Quarterly West***, Australia's ***Southern Review*** and Canada's ***Wascana Review***. (By the way, ***Lynx***, like many of our listings, has undergone some changes. It is now edited by Jane Reichhold, includes tanka in addition to renga, and has an attractive new look.)

Other listings new to this edition are actually "new," that is, they are magazines that started publishing in the last few years. These include ***Byron Poetry Works***, Canada's ***Filling Station***, ***The Imploding Tie-Dyed Toupee***, ***Poems & Plays*** and ***Sophomore Jinx***, all of which were founded in 1993.

We are also delighted to report that we have a number of new listings from outside the United States, including Cacanadadada Press, which is located in Vancouver, British Columbia, and publishes work by Canadian poets; ***Mandrake Poetry Magazine***, which was founded in New York but is now based in Poland; ***Planet: The Welsh Internationalist***; ***Poetry London Newsletter***; and ***Sivullinen***, a zine published in Helsinki, Finland.

Of course, once you start paging through this section you'll not only find other new listings, but you'll also discover that a few publishers you expected to be included are not. The annual ***Black Mountain Review***, for example, notified us that it would cease publication with its January 1995 issue, and both ***Colorado North Review*** and ***New Mexico Humanities Review*** have already stopped publishing. Other presses and magazines simply did not respond to our requests for updated information. You'll find a complete list of all those not listed in this edition under Publishers of Poetry/'94-'95 Changes at the end of this section.

Evaluating trends

Yet, to really get a feel for what's happening in the poetry world—and the world in general—you must notice more than which listings are new and which are no longer included. You have to sift through this information to evaluate trends. Over the last few years, for instance, there has been a gradual increase in the number of publications seeking poetry dealing with the disability experience and/or written by people with disabilities. This year, in fact, we have a new listing for ***Expressions***, a publication solely devoted to work by people with disabilities and/or ongoing health problems.

In addition, we have a new listing for ***Healing Journal***, a forum for health care professionals and patients to dialogue about the illness experience; it seeks work that is health-related or healing-focused. We also have a new listing for ***Mediphors***, a literary journal of the health professions that publishes work related to medicine and health. And though it is always difficult to determine what is and is not a trend, it appears that health-related topics are of interest to at least a handful of specialized publications and possibly some general ones as well.

Of course, the main trend is to create publications which speak to and/or are written by certain groups of people. For a number of years, we have had publications specifically written by women and/or addressing women's issues. Last year we included ***Journeymen***, our first magazine devoted to men's issues. New this year is a similar publication, entitled ***Men As We Are***, which seeks work dealing with some aspect of the male experience. And, to further illustrate how specialized publications can be, we note one other new listing: ***Kuumba***, a poetry journal specifically for the black lesbian and gay community.

Refining the Subject Index

If you write poetry that is in any way specialized—poetry pertaining to a particular group or subject or poetry written in a particular form — refer to the Subject Index at the back of this book. This index lists publishers according to their specialties. For instance, under the heading Children/Teen/Young Adult you'll find a list of publishers who seek poetry written by and/or for children, including two new listings ***Fudge Cake*** and ***Poem Train***. Under the heading Form/Style you'll find publishers who want haiku as well as those who seek sonnets or strictly experimental work.

This year we have refined the specialization categories to help you more easily locate potential markets. Noting an increase in listings seeking cowboy poetry, we have added Cowboy as a category. We have also added Mystery and Writing. And, noticing an increase in horror-only publications, we have separated Horror from Science Fiction/Fantasy. While these may seem like minor changes, they will help you more quickly locate the right market(s) for your poetry. If you're a budding cowboy poet, for instance, you will no longer need to read through the listings under Nature/Rural/Ecology—unless, of course, your cowboy poetry relates to these topics.

In the past, Themes was the catch-all category. Whenever a publication had an overriding focus—or whenever we didn't know where else to list it—it landed under Themes. Now, however, the addition of new categories has lessened the number of entries under this heading. Also, publishers who have a specialty but do not fit into one of our other categories fall under the heading Specialized because they are, after all, very narrow in their focus. ***Juggler's World***, for instance, only uses poems on juggling—now that's specialized! Finally, Themes now simply refers to those publishers or publications that *regularly* publish anthologies or issues on announced themes, such as Papier-Mache Press or ***Thema***.

Publishing theme issues

Speaking of themes, one of the questions we asked editors and publishers this year was whether they ever publish theme issues. While some publish theme issues regularly (and, as noted, fall under Themes in the Subject Index), others simply publish an occasional theme-related anthology or one or two theme-oriented issues a year. When planning to submit your work to a magazine, it is important to know whether the editor is working on a general issue or theme-related one. If you send your poetry about life in Appalachia to the editor of an annual working on a one-shot science fiction issue, don't be surprised if your manuscript comes right back.

While some editors compile theme issues based on the material they receive, others plan theme issues well in advance and include information about upcoming themes within their guidelines. If a listing says the editor publishes theme issues and you can send a self-addressed, stamped envelope (SASE) to receive guidelines and upcoming themes, by all means, do so! Not reading—and following—a publisher's guidelines is one of the quickest routes to that dreaded land of rejection.

Sending prepublication galleys

Let's say, however, that you have taken the other road. You located a listing for a magazine that you believe would be interested in your poetry. You then read several recent issues of the magazine at your local library. (Incidentally, reading sample copies is the best way to determine if your poetry is appropriate for a publication and you can order copies directly from most publishers). Following that, you sent for the magazine's guidelines—just to see if they've changed any of their policies as noted in the listing. Then you mailed three of your poems to the poetry editor. And two were accepted!

Now you're beginning to wonder what the poems will look like when they're typeset. Perhaps you're concerned about the special spacing required in the sixth and seventh lines of your longer poem. While you usually have to rely on the magazine's staff to make sure that your poem appears as you sent it, some publishers will mail you a prepublication galley. This is a typeset version of your work that you may proof and return to the editor with any necessary changes. As this step is important to many poets, this year we have also noted which listings send prepublication galleys.

Of course, you cannot expect to receive prepublication galleys from many of the smaller magazines listed in this section. After all, often the editor is also the typesetter, proofreader, photocopier and the person who mails copies of the publication once they have been stapled together. How could this same individual find time to send prepublication galleys? On the other hand, if you do receive a galley from an editor, your job is to proofread it—not change the wording. And you usually have to return the corrected galley fairly quickly or any error you did catch will go uncorrected.

Determining preferences

In addition to questions about publishing theme issues and sending prepublication galleys, we also asked editors what type of poetry they would like to publish but are not receiving. It came as little surprise that many editors indicated they would like to publish more traditional poetry but receive mostly free verse. Some went so far as to say that they did receive a fair amount of traditional poetry but that the free verse they received was of higher quality. For those who write carefully crafted traditional forms, then, the market is good. On the other hand, not all editors are interested in traditional poetry, and if an editor had specific requests (such as more experimental work from women) we included this information within the listing.

By the way, even if you have used the Subject Index to narrow down markets for your work, we encourage you to read through all the listings. This will give you the best sense of what is of interest to most editors and publishers, and there are many markets which are *not* specialized. Besides reading the bold lines regarding what type of material an editor is seeking, read the sample lines of poetry and names of recently published poets. Each year we ask editors and publishers to update these two areas of their listings. We believe this information not only provides insight into the interests of a particular publisher, but it also helps gauge the pulse of the poetry publishing community and our larger world.

One editor we talked to said that one could almost use **Poet's Market** for a poetry course because there are examples of bad poetry as well as good. While he may be right, what was interesting to note was that he had read most of the poetry samples. Readers who do likewise will discover poems dealing with violence and AIDS among this year's new selections. If you're more interested in knowing who's publishing, check the names of the poets listed. While we don't keep an official tally, Lyn Lifshin is certainly one of the most prolific poets, and her work is typically included in a wide range of publications. There are, of course, other poets whose names appear frequently; and, this year, you'll find a few "new" names cropping up again and again.

Including reply envelopes

Although we didn't specifically ask editors and publishers if they had any complaints about submissions, a number of them mentioned that they are still receiving submissions without SASEs. In the past we have tried to refrain from including statements about sending SASEs within individual listings. The main reason being that, throughout this book, readers are repeatedly instructed to include a SASE or a SAE (self-addressed envelope) and IRCs (International Reply Coupons—for replies from outside your own country) with every submission, query or request for information.

It's simple: If you want to know if any editor accepts or rejects your material, you must include a vehicle for his or her response. Yet poets are still not including SASEs with their submissions, and frustrated editors are taking a stand. As one editor wrote: "In the past two years, I have been receiving more and more submissions without SASEs. This gets to be a terrible drain on a budget that runs in the red as it is. As it stands now, the problem has gotten so bad that I feel I have to include a disclaimer regarding SASEs with my notice."

His disclaimer? "Submissions without a SASE cannot be acknowledged." Other editors, however, are not so kind; they discard submissions without SASEs before the material is even read. Although we have started noting these policies within listings, your best bet is to make a habit of sending a SASE (or SAE and IRCs) with all correspondence. Also, to make sure you're following other standard submission procedures, read Charting Your Path to Poetry Publication, page 5.

Continuing commentary

Over the past few years we have added editorial commentary to listings to help you more accurately gauge the quality of various publications and/or the interests of various publishers. Such comments have included a detailed description of a publication's physical appearance, notes about what types of poetry and/or other materials are usually found inside, and, most recently, what awards and honors have been bestowed on editors and publishers or their magazines and books. You'll find similar information again this year.

For instance, last year we noted which publications had poetry selected for inclusion in the 1992 volume of **The Best American Poetry**, an annual anthology highlighting the best poetry published in periodicals during the previous year. At the time we went to press, the 1993 edition was not yet available. This year, however, we are delighted to not only note which publications had poetry selected for the 1992 and 1993 volumes, but also which publications will have poetry included in 1994!

Thanks to David Lehman, the series editor, and his assistant, Kate Fox Reynolds, we were able to obtain an advance list of those publications that have work included in the 1994 volume, guest edited by A.R. Ammons. As a different guest editor compiles **The Best American Poetry** every year, discovering which publications have work included, especially in all of the last three volumes, may provide keen insight into the type and quality of material such publications are including within their pages.

In addition, **The Best American Poetry** (published by Collier Books, Macmillan Publishing Company, 866 Third Ave., New York NY 10022) can help you develop an overall sense for trends in the field of poetry publishing. The 1994 volume, by the way, is published at the same time as this edition of **Poet's Market**. So, when you're ready to read the poetry that has been selected, check your nearest library or bookstore.

Another list of publications we made reference to last year was the 1993 Poetry 60 compiled by ***Writer's Digest*** magazine. This list includes six categories of poetry markets and ranks the top 10 publications in each category based upon their placement in surveys compiled by the magazine's staff. The categories are: Nontraditional Verse, Traditional Verse, Open Markets (those most open to both free and formal verse), Top Pay, New Poets (those who often publish poets whose work is new to them) and Poets' Pick (those in which poets would most like to see their work published).

Though we have retained comments about where individual publications placed in the 1993 Poetry 60, we encourage you to watch for the June 1995 issue of ***Writer's Digest*** which promises to have a completely updated list. In the meantime, if you are interested in knowing more about how the Poetry 60 is compiled, locate the June 1993 issue of ***Writer's Digest*** at your library or write the magazine directly at 1507 Dana Ave., Cincinnati OH 45207.

Understanding market categories

Finally, all of the listings in this section include one or more Roman numerals in their heading. These "codes," selected by editors and/or publishers, may help you determine the most appropriate markets for your poetry. (For more information, see How to Use Your **Poet's Market** on page 3.) The market category codes and their explanation are as follows:

I. **Publishers very open to beginners' submissions.** For consideration, some may require fees, purchase of the publication or membership in an organization, but they are not, so far as we can determine, exploitative of poets. They publish much of the material received and frequently respond with criticism and suggestions.

II. **The general market to which most poets familiar with literary journals and maga-**

zines should submit. Typically they accept 10% or less of poems received and usually reject others without comment. They pay at least one copy. A poet developing a list of publication credits will find many of these to be respected names in the literary world.

III. Limited markets, typically overstocked. This code is often used by many prestigious magazines and publishers to discourage widespread submissions from poets who have not published elsewhere—although many do on occasion publish relatively new and/or little-known poets.

IV. Specialized publications encourage contributors from a specific geographical area, age-group, sex, sexual orientation or ethnic background or accept poems in specific forms or on specific themes. In most **IV** listings we also state the specialty (e.g., **IV-Translations**). Often a listing emphasizes more than one subject area; these listings are marked with two codes. Again, to quickly locate such markets, refer to the Subject Index which lists publishers according to their specialties.

V. Listings which do not accept unsolicited manuscripts. You cannot submit to these without specific permission to do so. If the press or magazine for some reason seems especially appropriate for you, query with a SASE. But, in general, these folks prefer to locate poets themselves. Sometimes they are just temporarily overstocked; other times they have projects lined up for the next few years.

We have included these listings because it is important to know not only where to send your poetry but also where NOT to send it. In addition, many are interesting publishers, and this book is widely used as a reference by librarians, researchers, publishers, suppliers and others who need to have as complete a listing of poetry publishers as possible.

AARDVARK ENTERPRISES (I), A Division of Speers Investments Ltd., 204 Millbank Dr. SW, Calgary, Alberta T2Y 2H9 Canada, phone (403)256-4639, founded 1982, editor J. Alvin Speers. Aardvark **publishes chapbooks on subsidy arrangements.** They have recently published **The Last Hunt** by Duffy Bebout and **The Irish Time Machine** by Tom McFadden. As a sample the editor selected these lines from his poem "Cultural Quiz":

If writing masters in the past
Had thought like that they could not have cast
Their spell over readers as they did,
At least for me, when I was a kid.

For subsidized chapbook publication, query with 3-5 samples, bio, previous publications. "We publish for hire—quoting price with full particulars. We do not market these except by special arrangement. Prefer poet does that. We strongly recommend seeing our books first. Send SASE for catalog to buy book samples. Please note US stamps cannot be used in Canada." They currently concentrate on books, which include **How To Do-It-Yourself Publish For Low Cost** and **Making Poetry Pay,** both by J. Alvin Speers, and consulting for "Do-It-Selfers." They have also announced publication of ***"Teak" Roundup***, an international quarterly open to the work of subscribers only. The premiere issue was scheduled for October 1994. Send SASE (or SAE and IRC) for details.

ABBEY; ABBEY CHEAPOCHAPBOOKS (II), 5360 Fallriver Row Court, Columbia MD 21044, founded 1970, editor David Greisman. They want **"poetry that does for the mind what that first sip of Molson Ale does for the palate. No pornography or politics."** They have published poetry and artwork by Richard Peabody, Vera Bergstrom, Margot Treitel, Harry Calhoun, Wayne Hogan and Cheryl Townsend. ***Abbey***, a quarterly, aims "to be a journal but to do it so informally that one wonders about my intent." It is magazine-sized, 20-26 pgs., photocopied. They publish about 150 of 1,000 poems received/year. Press run is 200. Subscription: $2. **Sample postpaid: 50¢. Guidelines available for SASE. Reports in 1 month. Pays 1-2 copies.** ***Abbey Cheapochapbooks*** come out 1-2 times a year averaging 10-15 pgs. **For chapbook consideration query with 4-6 samples, bio and list of publications. Reports in 2 months. Pays 25-50 copies.** The editor says he is "definitely seeing poetry from two schools—the nit'n'grit school and the textured/reflective school. I much prefer the latter."

ABIKO QUARTERLY (II, IV-Translations), 8-1-8 Namiki, Abiko, Chiba Japan 270-11, phone 011-81-471-84-7904, founded 1988, poetry editor Jesse Glass, is a literary-style quarterly journal **"heavily influenced by James Joyce's** Finnegan's Wake. **We publish all kinds, with an emphasis on the innovative and eclectic. We sometimes include originals and translations. No 'light verse,' and no religious verse, please! Include two International Reply Coupons with SAE for response. Originals will not be returned."** They have recently published poetry by Kenji Miyazawa, Jon Silkin, Cid Corman, Lew Turco, William Bronk and Edith Shiffert. It is magazine-sized, desktop-published with Macintosh laser printer. Press run is 350 for 150 subscribers of which 10 are libraries, 100 shelf sales. **Sample postpaid: 900 yen. Sometimes sends prepublication galleys. Pays 1 copy.** Open to unsolicited reviews. Poets may also send books for review consideration. The editor says, "Poets are in a hurry to publish. Poets, educate yourselves! Read contemporary poetry. In fact, read all poetry! Work at your craft before you attempt to publish. Please remember U.S. postage does not work in Japan with SAEs!"

ABORIGINAL SF (IV-Science fiction), Box 2449, Woburn MA 01888-0849, founded 1986, editor Charles C. Ryan, appears quarterly. **"Poetry should be 1-2 pgs., double-spaced. Subject matter must be science fiction, science or space-related. No long poems, no fantasy."** The magazine is 116 pgs., with 12 illustrations. Press run is 23,000, mostly subscriptions. Subscriptions for "special" writer's rate: $12/4 issues. **Sample postpaid: $4.95. No simultaneous submissions. Send SASE for guidelines. Reports in 2-3 months, no backlog. Always sends prepublication galleys. Pays $25/poem and 2 copies. Buys first North American serial rights.** Reviews related books of poetry in 100-300 words.

ABRAXAS MAGAZINE (V); GHOST PONY PRESS (III), 2518 Gregory St., Madison WI 53711, phone (608)238-0175, *Abraxas* founded 1968, Ghost Pony Press in 1980, by editor/publisher Ingrid Swanberg, who says "Ghost Pony Press is a small press publisher of poetry books; *Abraxas* is a literary journal (irregular) publishing contemporary poetry, criticism, translations and reviews of small press books. *Do not confuse these separate presses!*" ***Abraxas* no longer considers unsolicited material, except as announced as projects arise.** She is interested in poetry that is **"contemporary lyric, concrete, experimental." Does not want to see "political posing; academic regurgitations."** They have published poetry by William Stafford, Ivan Argüelles, Denise Levertov, César Vallejo and Andrea Moorhead. As a sample the editor selected the final lines of an untitled poem by próspero saíz:

> *the beautiful grief of the moon is my beam of silence*
> *Dawn*
> *the splendor of the moon dies*
> *my lips open to a gentle breeze*
> *she rides a silken yellow scarf into the vanishing clouds*
> *i am still here.*

The magazine is 80 pgs. (160 pgs., double issues), flat-spined, 6×9, litho offset, with original art on its matte card cover, using "unusual graphics in text, original art and collages, concrete poetry, exchange ads only, letters from contributors, essays." It appears "irregularly, 4- to 9-month intervals." Press run is 600, 550 circulation, 300 subscriptions of which 150 are libraries. Subscription: $16/4 issues, $20/4 issues overseas. **Sample postpaid: $4 ($6 double issues). *Abraxas* will announce submission guidelines as projects arise. Publishes theme issues. Themes for 1994-95 include contemporary avant-garde; literature and evil; concrete poetry; and lyric poetry. Pays 1 copy plus 40% discount on additional copies. To submit to Ghost Pony Press, inquire with SASE plus 5-10 poems and cover letter. Previously published material OK for book publication by Ghost Pony Press. Reports on queries in 1-3 months, mss in 3 months. Payment varies per project. Editor sometimes comments briefly on rejections. Send SASE for catalog to buy samples.** They have published **zen concrete & etc.**, a "definitive collection" of poetry by d.a. levy. That book is a 245-page, 8½×11, perfect-bound paperback available for $27.50. They have also published **the bird of nothing & other poems** by próspero saíz. It is a 168-page, 7×10, perfect-bound paperback available for $20 (signed and numbered edition is $35). For either book, add $2 postage and handling.

ACM (ANOTHER CHICAGO MAGAZINE) (II); LEFT FIELD PRESS (V), 3709 N. Kenmore, Chicago IL 60613, founded 1976, poetry editor Barry Silesky. *ACM* is a literary biannual, **emphasis on quality, experimental, politically aware** prose, fiction, poetry, reviews, cross-genre work and essays. The editor wants **no religious verse**. They have published prose and poetry by Albert Goldbarth, Michael McClure, Jack Anderson, Jerome Sala, Nance VanWinkel, Nadja Tesich, Wanda Coleman, Charles Simic and Diane Wakoski. As a sample, the editor selected these lines by Dean Sharet:

> *Just the facts. Forgotten on purpose.*
> This is our land. *Yes, you said, "ours."*
> *A gang of teenagers, too young for the army, too stupid for respect.*

Silesky says *ACM* is digest-sized, 220 pgs., offset with b&w art and ads. Editors appreciate traditional to experimental verse with an emphasis on message, especially poems with strong voices articulating social or political concerns. Circulation 1,500, for 500 subscribers of which

100 are libraries. **Sample postpaid: $7. Submit 3-8 pgs. typed. Simultaneous submissions OK. Reports in 2-3 months, has 3- to 6-month backlog. Sometimes sends prepublication galleys. Pays $5/page and 1 copy. Buys first serial rights.** Reviews books of poetry in 250-500 words. Open to unsolicited reviews. Poets may also send books for review consideration. **They do not accept freelance submissions for chapbook publication.** Work published in *ACM* has been included in **The Best American Poetry** (1992 and 1994) and **Pushcart Prize** anthologies.

‡THE ACORN; EL DORADO WRITERS' GUILD (II, IV-Regional), P.O. Box 1266, El Dorado CA 95623, phone and fax (916)621-1833, founded 1993, editor Taylor Graham, is a quarterly journal of the Western Sierra, published by the El Dorado Writers' Guild, a nonprofit literary organization. It includes "history and reminiscence, story and legend, and poetry." They want **poetry "up to 30 lines long, though we prefer shorter. Focus must be on western slope Sierra Nevada. No erotica, pornography or religious poetry."** They have recently published poetry by Grace Grafton, Michael Meinhoff and Jamie Howland. As a sample the editor selected these lines from her own poem, "When the 1st Seed Catalog Comes":

> . . . *Spring is that simple day*
> *we turn things under:*
> *soil so rich and brown*
> *we forget what makes it sweet*
> *and speak of seeds*
> *as a beginning.*

The editor says ***the Acorn*** is 44 pgs., 5⅛ × 8½, desktop-published on quality paper and saddle-stapled. They receive about 250 poems a year, use approximately 15% (10-12/issue). Press run is 200 for 25 subscribers, 100 shelf sales. Single copy: $3.50; subscription: $12. **Sample postpaid: $4. Submit 3-7 poems at a time. Previously published poems and simultaneous submissions OK, if noted. Cover letter with short (50-word) bio required. Deadlines are February 15, May 15, August 15 and November 15.** Time between acceptance and publication is 1 month. **"Five editors each score poems for content, form and suitability. Poetry consultant selects top group. Graphics editor selects to fit space available." Often comments on rejections. Reports within 3 weeks after deadline. Pays 1 copy. All rights revert to author on publication.** The editor says, "If your poetry is about nature, be accurate with the species' names, colors, etc. If you describe a landscape, be sure it fits our region. Metered rhyming verse had better be precise (we have an editor with an internal metronome!). Slant rhyme and free verse are welcome. Avoid trite phrases."

ACUMEN MAGAZINE; EMBER PRESS (I, II), 6 The Mount, Higher Furzeham, Brixham, S. Devon TQ5 8QY England, phone (0803)851098, press founded 1971, ***Acumen*** founded 1984, poetry editor Patricia Oxley, is a "small press publisher of a general literary magazine with emphasis on good poetry." They want **"well-crafted, high quality, imaginative poems showing a sense of form. No experimental verse of an obscene type."** They have published poetry by Elizabeth Jennings, William Oxley, Gavin Ewart, D.J. Enright, Peter Porter, Kathleen Raine and R.S. Thomas. As a sample Mrs. Oxley selected these lines from "The Green Field" by Dannie Abse:

> *As soft-eyed lovers for the very first time,*
> *turning out the light for the first time,*
> *blot out all detail, all colours,*
> *and whisper the old code-words, 'Love you.'*

Acumen appears in April and October of each year and is 100 pgs., digest-sized, flat-spined, professionally printed with illustrations and ads. Of about 12,000 poems received they accept about 90. Press run is 650 for 400 subscriptions (15 libraries). Subscription: $25. **Sample postpaid: $10. No previously published poems; simultaneous submissions OK, if not to UK magazines. Reports in one month. Pays "by negotiation" and one copy.** Staff reviews books of poetry in up to 300 words, single format or 600 words, multi-book. Send books for review consideration to Glyn Pursglove, 25 St. Albans Rd., Brynmill, Swansea, Wales. Patricia Oxley advises, "Read *Acumen* carefully to see what kind of poetry we publish. Also read widely in many poetry magazines, and don't forget the poets of the past—they can still teach us a great deal."

ADASTRA PRESS (II), Dept. PM, 101 Strong St., Easthampton MA 01027, founded 1980 by Gary Metras, who says, "I publish poetry because I love poetry. I produce the books on antique equipment using antique methods because I own the equipment and because it's cheaper—I don't pay myself a

> ‡ ***The double dagger before a listing indicates that the listing is new in this edition. New markets are often the most receptive to submissions.***

salary—it's a hobby—it's **a love affair with poetry and printing of fine editions**. I literally sweat making these books and I want the manuscript to show me the author also sweated." All his books and chapbooks are **limited editions, handset, letterpress**, printed with handsewn signatures. "Chances of acceptance are slim. About 1 in 200 submissions is accepted, which means I only take 1 or 2 unsolicited mss a year." The chapbooks are in square-spine paper wrappers, cloth editions also handcrafted. He wants **"no rhyme, no religious. Poetry is communication first, although it is art. Long poems and thematic groups are nice for chapbooks. No subjects are tabu, but topics should be drawn from real life experiences. I include accurate dreams as real life."** Poets recently published include Thomas Lux, W.D. Ehrhart, Wally Swist and Miriam Sagan. As a sample the editor selected these lines from "Things We Leave Go" by Greg Joly:

tubers of bearded iris
swim dark into the clouded lawn
seed heavy weeds
come the full solstice moon
grackles wire feet dance
on empty metal silos

1-4 chapbooks are brought out each year. **Author is paid in copies, usually 10% of the print run. "I only read chapbook manuscripts in the month of February, picking one or two for the following year. Queries, with a sample of 3-5 poems from a chapbook manuscript, are read throughout the year and if I like what I see in the sample, I'll ask you to submit the ms in February. I prefer a cover letter and a) samples from a completed chapbook ms or b) a completed chapbook ms. Do not submit or query about full-length collections. I will only be accepting chapbook manuscripts of 12-18 double-spaced pages. Any longer collections would be a special invitation to a poet. If you want to see a typical handcrafted Adastra chapbook, send $5 and I'll mail a current title.** If you'd like a fuller look at what, how and why I do what I do, send check for $11.50 ($10 plus $1.50 postage and handling) and I'll mail a copy of **The Adastra Reader: Being the Collected Chapbooks in Facsimile with Author Notes, Bibliography and Comments on Hand Bookmaking**, published in 1987. This is a 247-page anthology covering Adastra publishing from 1979-1986."

ADRIFT (II, IV-Ethnic), #4D, 239 East Fifth St., New York NY 10003, founded 1980, editor Thomas McGonigle, who says, "The **orientation of the magazine is Irish, Irish-American. I expect reader-writer knows and goes beyond Yeats, Kavanagh, Joyce, O'Brien." The literary magazine is open to all kinds of submissions, but does not want to see "junk."** They have published poetry by James Liddy, Thomas McCarthy, Francis Stuart and Gilbert Sorrentino. *Adrift* appears twice a year and is magazine-sized, 32 pgs., offset on heavy stock, cover matte card, saddle-stapled. Circulation is 1,000 with 200 subscriptions, 50 of which go to libraries. Single copy: $4; subscription: $8. **Sample postpaid: $5. Simultaneous submissions OK. Magazine pays, rate varies; contributors receive 1 copy.** Reviews books of poetry. Open to unsolicited reviews. Poets may also send books for review consideration.

ADVOCACY PRESS (V, IV-Children), P.O. Box 236, Santa Barbara CA 93102, founded 1983, contact William Sheehan, publishes children's books. **"Must have rhythm and rhyme."** They have published 4 books of rhymes for children: **Father Gander Nursery Rhymes** (nonsexist, nonviolent, nonracist version of **Mother Goose**), **Mother Nature Nursery Rhymes, Nature's Wonderful World in Rhyme** and **Tonia the Tree**. Their books are 32-48 pgs., illustrated in full color. **"No present plans for additional books in the Children's Rhymes series. Publish no other poetry at this time." Query with description of concept and sample. SASE required for reply.** "All Advocacy Press books have gender equity, self-esteem themes."

THE ADVOCATE (I), 301A Rolling Hills Park, Prattsville NY 12468, phone (518)299-3103, editor Remington Wright, founded 1987, is an advertiser-supported tabloid appearing bimonthly, 12,000 copies distributed free, **using "original, previously unpublished works,** such as feature stories, essays, 'think' pieces, letters to the editor, profiles, humor, fiction, poetry, puzzles, cartoons or line drawings." They want **"nearly any kind of poetry, any length, but not religious or pornographic. Poetry ought to speak to people and not be so oblique as to have meaning only to the poet. If I had to be there to understand the poem, don't send it."** As a sample the editor selected the opening lines from "You Brought Me Lilacs" by Tilitha Waicekauskas:

I was young and slender, and in your eyes
I was more beautiful than morning skies.
My hair was as black as a raven's wing
And the love in your eyes made my spirit sing.
For I adored you and on my hand
Was your diamond of promise—a platinum band
—And you brought me lilacs.

Sample postpaid: $3. No previously published poems or simultaneous submissions. Publishes accepted material an average of 4-6 months after acceptance. **Editor "occasionally" comments**

on rejections. Reports in 6-8 weeks. Pays 2 copies. Acquires first rights only. Accepts about 25% of poems received. Reviews books of poetry. Open to unsolicited reviews. Poets may also send books to the attention of J.B. Samuels for review consideration. Offers occasional contests. The editor says, "All submissions and correspondence must be accompanied by a self-addressed, stamped envelope with sufficient postage."

AEGINA PRESS, INC.; UNIVERSITY EDITIONS (I, II), 59 Oak Lane, Spring Valley, Huntington WV 25704, founded 1983, publisher Ira Herman, is **primarily subsidy for poetry,** strongly committed to publishing new or established poets. Publishes subsidy titles under the University Editions imprint. Aegina has published non-subsidized poetry as well. **Authors of books accepted on a non-subsidized basis receive a 15% royalty.** "We try to provide a way for talented poets to have their collections published, which otherwise might go unpublished because of commercial, bottom-line considerations. Aegina Press will publish quality poetry that the large publishers will not handle because it is not commercially viable. We believe it is unfair that a poet has to have a 'name' or a following in order to have a book of poems accepted by a publisher. Poetry is the purest form of literary art, and it should be made available to those who appreciate it." Poets published include Kenneth Berry and Ivan Veljanoski. As a sample the editor selected the opening lines of "The Zoo's World of Darkness" in **The Country of Connections** by Rose Rosberg:

Only creatures who see best at night
are lodged here,
those like myself who know the dark
can reveal

"Most poetry books we accept are subsidized by the author (or an institution). In return, the author receives all sales proceeds from the book, and any unsold copies left from the print run belong to the author. Minimum print run is 500 copies. We can do larger runs as well. Our marketing program includes submission to distributors, agents, other publishers, bookstores and libraries." **Mss should be typed and no shorter than 40 pages. There is no upper length limit. Simultaneous submissions OK. Reporting time is 1 month for full mss, 7-10 days for queries. Always sends prepublication galleys.** They publish perfect-bound (flat-spined) paperbacks with glossy covers. **Sample books are available for $5 each plus $1.50 postage and handling.**

AERIAL (V), P.O. Box 25642, Washington DC 20007, phone (202)244-6258, founded 1984, editor Rod Smith, editorial assistants Gretchen Johnsen and Wayne Kline, is a yearly publication. Issue #6/7 was the John Cage issue (available for $15). They have published work by Jackson MacLow, Melanie Neilson, Steve Benson, Phyllis Rosenzweig and Charles Bernstein. Two special issues are in the works, on Barrett Watten and Bruce Andrews, therefore **they're not looking for new work at this time.** As a sample the editor selected these lines from "subtracted words" by P. Inman:

still dollar in its pale
mice sight. Parts of knock
in a river of propellor blade.
Wage sand gist. Keyhole
college, its brink on. An
ush stelm of mind ball

The magazine is 6×9, offset, varies from 180 to 280 pgs. Circulation is 1,000. **Sample postpaid: $7.50.** Also publishes critical/political/philosophical writing.

AETHLON: THE JOURNAL OF SPORT LITERATURE (IV-Sports), Dept. PM, English Dept., East Tennessee State University, Johnson City TN 37614-0683, phone (615)929-4339, founded 1983, general editor Don Johnson, Professor of English, ETSU, poetry editor Robert W. Hamblin, Professor of English, Southeast Missouri State University, Cape Girardeau MO 63701. (Submit poetry to this address.) ***Aethlon*** publishes a variety of sport-related literature, including scholarly articles, fiction, poetry, personal essays and reviews; 6-10 poems/issue; two issues annually, fall and spring. **Subject matter must be sports-related; no restrictions regarding form, length, style or purpose. They do not want to see "doggerel, cliché-ridden or oversentimental" poems.** Poets published include Neal Bowers, Joseph Duemer, Robert Fink, Jan Mordenski, H.R. Stonebeck, Jim Thomas, Stephen Tudor and Don Welch. The magazine is digest-sized, offset printed, flat-spined, with illustrations and some ads, 200 pgs./issue. Circulation is 1,000 of which 750 are subscriptions, 250 to libraries. Subscription is included with membership ($30) in the Sport Literature Association. **Sample postpaid: $12.50. Will accept simultaneous submissions. "Only typed mss with SASE considered." Submissions are reported on in 6-8 weeks and the backlog time is 6-12 months. Contributors receive 5 offprints and a copy of the issue in which their poem appears.**

AFRICA WORLD PRESS (V, IV-Ethnic), Box 1892, Trenton NJ 08607, founded 1983, editor Kassahun Checole, publishes **poetry books by Africans, African-Americans, Caribbean and Latin Americans.** They have published **Under A Soprano Sky** by Sonia Sanchez, **From the Pyramid to the Projects** by

Askia Muhammad Toure and, most recently, **The Time: Poems and Photographs** by Esther Iverem. However, they are currently not accepting poetry submissions. Send SASE for catalog.

AFRICAN AMERICAN REVIEW (IV-Ethnic), Dept. of English, Indiana State University, Terre Haute IN 47809, founded 1967, poetry editors Sterling Plumpp, Thadious M. Davis, Pinkie Gordon Lane and E. Ethelbert Miller, is a "magazine primarily devoted to the analysis of African American literature, **although one issue per year focuses on poetry by African Americans." No specifications as to form, length, style, subject matter or purpose.** They have published poems by Amiri Baraka, Gwendolyn Brooks, Dudley Randall and Owen Dodson. *AAR* is 6×9, 200 pgs. with photo on the cover. They receive about 500 submissions/year, use 50. Individual subscriptions: $24 USA, $31 foreign. **Sample postpaid: $10. Submit maximum of 6 poems to editor Joe Weixlmann. The editors sometimes comment on rejections. Publishes theme issues. Send SASE for guidelines. Reports in 3-4 months. Always sends prepublication galleys. Pays in copies.**

AFRO-HISPANIC REVIEW (IV-Ethnic), Romance Languages, #143 Arts & Sciences, University of Missouri, Columbia MO 65211, founded 1982, editors Marvin A. Lewis and Edward J. Mullen, appears twice a year, in the fall and spring, using some **poetry related to Afro-Hispanic life and issues.** They have published poetry by Manuel Zapata Olivella, Melvin E. Lewis and Antar Al Basir. **Sample copy: $5. Reports in 6 weeks. Pays 5 copies.** Reviews books of poetry in "about 500 words."

‡AGENDA EDITIONS; AGENDA (II), 5 Cranbourne Ct., Albert Bridge Rd., London SW11 4PE England, founded 1959, poetry editors William Cookson and Peter Dale. *Agenda* is a quarterly magazine (1 double, 2 single issues/year). **"We seek poetry of 'more than usual emotion, more than usual order' (Coleridge).** We publish special issues on particular authors such as T.S. Eliot, Ezra Pound, David Jones, Stanley Burnshaw, Thomas Hardy, etc." Some of the poets who have appeared in *Agenda* are Peter Dale, Geoffrey Hill, Seamus Heaney, C.H. Sisson, Patricia McCarthy and W.S. Milne. As a sample the editors selected these lines (poet unidentified):

How will you want the snowy impermanence of ash,
your dust, like grass-seed, flighted over heathland,
drifting in spinneys where the boughs clash,
with matted needles laying waste beneath them.

Agenda is 80 pgs. (of which half are devoted to poetry), 5×7. They receive some 2,000 submissions/year, use 40, have a 5-month backlog. Circulation 1,500-3,000, 1,500 subscriptions of which 450 are libraries. Subscription: individuals US $38, libraries and institutions US $50. **Sample postpaid: £4 ($8). Reports in 1 month. Pays £10/page for poetry.** Reviews books of poetry. Open to unsolicited reviews. Poets may also send books for review consideration. **To submit book ms, no query necessary, "as little as possible" in cover letter. SAE and IRCs for return. Reports within a month. Pays in copies.** The editors say poets "should write only if there is an intense desire to express something. They should not worry about fashion."

AGNI (II), Boston University, 236 Bay State Rd., Boston MA 02215, phone (617)353-5389, founded 1972, editor Askold Melnyczuk. *Agni* is a biannual journal of poetry, fiction and essays "by both emerging and established writers." Editors seem to select readable, intelligent poetry—mostly lyric free verse (with some narrative and dramatic, too)—that somehow communicates tension or risk. They have published poetry by Derek Walcott, Patricia Traxler, Thom Gunn, Maxine Scates, Mark Halliday and Ha Jin. As a sample the editor selected these lines from Rafael Campo's poem, "Grandfather's Will":

I leave you the plantation, and the pain
Of sugar. I leave you even the scattered sins
Of island life: thirst in spite of water
Everywhere, to not escape, and to think
You rose above the sea on purpose. Tanks
Are crushing my body now—the traitors
In our house have come for me. A word of caution:
Remember me. Bury me in the ocean.
Burn me to brown sugar—drink me, a potion
In your coffee. It grows on your plantation.

Agni is typeset, printed offset and perfect-bound with about 40 poems featured in each issue. Circulation is 1,500 by subscription, mail order and bookstore sales. Subscription: $12. **Sample: $7. They will consider simultaneous submissions but not previously published poems. Reads submissions October 1 through April 30 only. Mss received at other times will be returned unread. Reports in 1-4 months. Pays $10/page, $150 maximum, plus 2 copies and one-year subscription. Buys first serial rights.** Work published in *Agni* has been included in **The Best American Poetry** (1992, 1993 and 1994) and **Pushcart Prize** anthologies.

AG-PILOT INTERNATIONAL MAGAZINE (IV-Specialized: crop dusting), P.O. Box 1607, Mt. Vernon WA 98273, phone (206)336-9737, publisher Tom Wood, "is intended to be a fun-to-read, technical, as well as humorous and serious publication for the ag pilot and operator. Interested in **agricultural aviation (crop dusting) related poetry ONLY—something that rhymes and has a cadence."** As a sample we selected these lines from "Freedom" by Jack B. Harvey:

So now I dress in faded jeans
And beat up cowboy boots.
My flying's done on veg'tables,
The row crops, and the fruits.

My wife now drives the flaggin' truck
And marks off all my fields.
She tells me all about the crops
And talks about the yields.

It appears monthly, 48-64 pgs., circulation 8,400. **Buys 1 poem/issue. Pays $10-50.**

THE AGUILAR EXPRESSION (I, II), P.O. Box 304, Webster PA 15087, phone (412)379-8019, founded 1986, editor/publisher Xavier F. Aguilar, appears 2 times/year, and is **"open to all types of poetry, including erotica that is well written."** They have recently published poetry by Dorothea Grossman and Rebecca Charry. As a sample the editor selected the poem "Unnoticed" by Kathleen Lee Mendel:

I am blank paper
kept in the back
of your black leather
address book.

The editor describes it as 6-12 pgs., magazine-sized, circulation 150. **Sample postpaid: $6. Cover letter, including writing background, required with submissions. Reports in 1 month. Pays 1 copy.** Open to unsolicited reviews. **"We are also now seeking poetry manuscripts as we wish to publish 1 or 2 chapbooks in 1994-1995. Send SASE for details."** The editor says, "In publishing poetry, I try to exhibit the unique reality that we too often take for granted and acquaint as mediocre. We encourage poetics that deal with *now*, which our readers can relate to. We also offer a cash prize for an essay relating to the writing of poetics (four typed pages). Guidelines for SASE."

AHSAHTA PRESS; COLD-DRILL; COLD-DRILL BOOKS; POETRY IN PUBLIC PLACES (IV-Regional), English Dept., Boise State University, Boise ID 83725, phone (208)385-1999. Ahsahta Press is a project to publish **contemporary poetry of the American West.** But, say editors Tom Trusky, Orv Burmaster and Dale Boyer, **"Spare us paens to the pommel, Jesus in the sagebrush, haiku about the Eiffel Tower, 'nice' or 'sweet' poems."** The work should **"draw on the cultures, history, ecologies of the American West."** They publish collections (45+ pgs.) of individual poets in handsome flat-spined paperbacks with plain matte covers, with an appreciative introduction, at most 3/year. Occasionally they bring out an anthology on cassette of their authors. And they have published an anthology (94 pgs.) **Women Poets of the West**, with an introduction by Ann Stanford. Some of their poets are Susan Deal, Leo Romero, David Baker, Linda Bierds, Philip St. Clair and Gretel Ehrlich. As a sample here are lines from Gerrye Payne's "Machines," in the collection **The Year-God**:

Machines sit to hand, vortices of possibility.
Under their blank gaze biological life
Flares and dies, is ashamed.
The neighbor's tractor hums, clearing brush,
inventing geometry in random chaparral.

You may submit only during their January 1 through March 31 reading period each year—a sample of 15 of your poems with SASE. They will report in about 2 months. Multiple and simultaneous submissions OK. If they like the sample, they'll ask for a book ms. If it is accepted, **you get 25 copies of the lst and 2nd printings and a 25% royalty commencing with the 3rd. They seldom comment on the samples, frequently on the mss.** Send SASE for their catalog and order a few books, if you don't find them in your library. "Old advice but true: Read what we publish before submitting. **75% of the submissions we receive should never have been sent to us. Save stamps, spirit and sweat."** ***cold-drill*** publishes **"primarily Boise State University students, faculty and staff, but will consider writings by Idahoans—or writing about Idaho by 'furriners.'"** They do some of the most creative publishing in this country today, and it is worth buying a **sample of *cold-drill* for $9** just to see what they're up to. This annual "has been selected as top undergraduate literary magazine in the U.S. by such important acronyms as CSPA, CCLM and UCDA." It comes in a box stuffed with various pamphlets, postcards, posters, a newspaper, even 3-D comics with glasses to read them by. **No restrictions on types of poetry.** As yet they have published no poets of national note, but Tom Trusky offers these lines as a sample, from Patrick Flanagan, "Postcard From a Freshman":

The girls here are gorgeous, studying hard,
many new friends, roommate
never showers, tried to
kill myself, doctor says
i'm getting better

Circulation is 400, including 100 subscribers, of which 20 are libraries. **"We read material throughout the year, notifying only those whose work we've accepted December 15 through January 1. Manuscripts should be photocopies with author's name and address on separate sheet. Simultaneous submissions OK. Payment: 1 copy."** They also publish two 24-page chapbooks and one 75-page flat-spined paperback/year. **Query about book publication.** "We want to publish a literary magazine that is exciting to read. We want more readers than just our contributors and their mothers. Our format and our content have allowed us to achieve those goals, so far." Poetry in Public Places is a series of 8 monthly posters/year "presenting the poets in Boise State University's creative students series and poets in BSU's Ahsahta Press poetry series." These, like all publications emanating from BSU, are elegantly done, with striking art. The posters are on coated stock.

AIM MAGAZINE (IV-Social issues, ethnic), 7308 S. Eberhart Ave., Chicago IL 60619, phone (312)874-6184, founded 1974, poetry editor Henry Blakely, is a magazine-sized quarterly, circulation 10,000, glossy cover, **"dedicated to racial harmony and peace." They use 3-4 poems ("poetry with social significance mainly") in each issue. They ask for 32 lines average length.** They have published poetry by J. Douglas Studer, Wayne Dowdy and Maria DeGuzman. They receive only about 30 submissions/year of which they use half. They have 3,000 subscriptions of which 15 are libraries. Subscription: $10. **Sample postpaid: $4. Simultaneous submissions OK. Reports in 3-6 weeks. Pays $3/poem. You will not receive an acceptance slip: "We simply send payment and magazine copy."** The editor's advice: "Read the work of published poets."

ALABAMA LITERARY REVIEW (II), English Dept., Troy State University, Troy AL 36082, phone (205)670-3286, fax (205)670-3519, poetry editor Ed Hicks, a biannual, **wants poetry that is "imagistic—*but* in motion. Will look at anything," but does not want to see "lyrics sent as poetry. We want serious craft."** They have published poetry by R.T. Smith, Ed Peaco, Joanne M. Riley and Martha Payne. As a sample the editor selected these lines from "Late Fall" by Diane Swan:

It's hard to tell birds
from wind-rushed leaves
as they skirl up in the funnels
of blinking October light

The beautifully printed 100-page, 6×9 magazine, matte cover with art, b&w art and some colored pages inside, receives 300 submissions/year, uses 30, has a 2-month backlog. **Sample postpaid: $4.50. Will consider simultaneous submissions. Reads submissions September 1 through July 31 only. Sometimes comments on rejections. Reports in 2-3 months. Sometimes sends prepublication galleys. Pays copies, sometimes honorarium. Acquires first rights.** Open to unsolicited reviews. Poets may also send books for review consideration.

ALASKA QUARTERLY REVIEW (II), College of Arts and Sciences, University of Alaska Anchorage, 3211 Providence Dr., Anchorage AK 99508, phone (907)786-4775, founded 1981, executive editor Ronald Spatz, poetry editor Thomas Sexton. "A journal devoted to contemporary literary art. **We publish both traditional and experimental fiction, poetry, essays and criticism on contemporary writing, literature and philosophy of literature.**" Editors seem to welcome all styles and forms of poetry with the most emphasis perhaps on voice and content that displays "risk," or intriguing ideas or situations. They publish two double-issues a year, **each using between 18-25 pgs. of poetry**. They receive up to 2,000 submissions each year, accept about 40. They have a circulation of 1,300; 250 subscribers, of which 32 are libraries. Subscription: $8. **Sample postpaid: $4. Manuscripts are *not* read from May 15 through August 15. They take up to 4 months to report, sometimes longer during peak periods in late winter. Pay depends on funding. Acquires first North American serial rights.**

ALBATROSS; THE ANABIOSIS PRESS (II, IV-Nature), P.O. Box 7787, North Port FL 34287-0787, phone (813)426-7019, founded 1985, editors Richard Smyth and Richard Brobst. ***Albatross*** appears in the spring and fall. **"We consider the albatross to be a metaphor for an environment that must survive. This is not to say that we publish only environmental or nature poetry, but that we are biased toward such subject matters. We publish mostly free verse, 200 lines/poem maximum, and we prefer a narrative style, but again, this is not necessary. We do not want trite rhyming poetry which doesn't convey a deeply felt experience in a mature expression with words."** They have published poetry by Simon Perchik, Michael Jennings, Karen Volkman and Elizabeth Rees. As a sample, the editors selected these lines by Polly Buckingham:

Many white birds scatter like

doves in a sand dollar,
and I receive you, my body
a murex, whelk, moonshell.

The magazine is 32-36 pgs., 5½×8½, laser typeset with linen cover, some b&w drawings, and, in addition to the poetry, has an interview with a poet in each issue. Circulation 300 to 75 subscribers of which 10 are libraries. Many complimentary copies are sent out to bookstores, poets and libraries. Subscription: $5/2 issues. **Sample postpaid: $3. "Poems should be typed single-spaced, with name and address in left corner and length in lines in right corner." No simultaneous submissions. Cover letter not required; "We do, however, need bio notes if published." Send SASE for guidelines. Reports in 4-6 months, has 6- to 12-month backlog. Pays 2 copies. Acquires all rights. Returns rights provided that "previous publication in *Albatross* is mentioned in all subsequent reprintings."** Staff reviews books of poetry. Also holds a chapbook contest. **Submit 16-20 pgs. of poetry, any theme, any style. Deadline is March 31 of each year. Include name, address and phone number on the title page. Charges $6 reading fee (check payable to *Albatross*). Winner receives $50 and 25 copies of his/her published chapbook. All entering receive a free copy of the winning chapbook.** "The Anabiosis Press is now a nonprofit organization. Membership fee is $20/year." Comments? "We expect a poet to read as much contemporary poetry as possible."

ALDEBARAN (II), Roger Williams University, 1 Old Ferry Rd., Bristol RI 02809, managing editor Matthew Rossi, publishes a spring and a fall issue. "*Aldebaran* publishes both poetry and fiction in **traditional, contemporary and experimental forms; we are receptive to nearly all styles and topics.** We would like to see more diversity in our magazine and encourage submissions from writers of all genres, from fantasy to dark fiction, science fiction, comedy, horror and drama, as well as classical and contemporary poetry and fiction." The magazine is 50-100 pgs., side-stapled or perfect-bound, digest-sized. Press run is 300. Subscription: $10 for 2 issues. **Sample postpaid: $5. Submit no more than 5 poems at a time. Reads submissions February 1 through April 1 and September 1 through November 1. Student-run publication. Seldom comments on rejections. Send SASE for guidelines. Reports in 6-12 weeks. Sometimes sends prepublication galleys.**

ALICEJAMESBOOKS; BEATRICE HAWLEY AWARD (IV-Regional, women, ethnic), 33 Richdale Ave., Cambridge MA 02140, phone (617)354-1408, founded 1973, is "an author's collective which only publishes **poetry. Authors are exclusively from the New England Area**. We strongly encourage submissions by poets of color." They publish flat-spined paperbacks of high quality, both in production and contents, no children's poetry, and their books have won numerous awards and been very respectably reviewed. "Each poet becomes a working member of the co-op with a two-year work commitment." That is, you have to live close enough to **attend meetings and participate in the editorial and publishing process**. They publish about 4 books, 72 pgs., each year in editions of 1,000, paperbacks—no hardbacks. **Query first, but no need for samples: simply ask for dates of reading period, which is in early fall. Simultaneous submissions OK, but "we would like to know when a manuscript is being submitted elsewhere." Send 2 copies of the ms. Reports in 2-3 months. Pays authors 100 paperback copies.** Offers Beatrice Hawley Award for poets who cannot meet the work requirement due to geographical restraints.

ALIVE NOW!; POCKETS; WEAVINGS (IV-Religious, children, themes); THE UPPER ROOM (V), 1908 Grand Ave., P.O. Box 189, Nashville TN 37202, phone (615)340-7200. This publishing company brings out about 20 books a year and four magazines: ***The Upper Room, Alive Now!, Pockets*** and ***Weavings***. Of these, two use unsolicited poetry. ***Pockets, Devotional Magazine for Children***, which comes out 11 times a year, circulation 68,000-70,000, is for children 6-12, "offers stories, activities, prayers, poems—all **geared to giving children a better understanding of themselves as children of God. Some of the material is not overtly religious but deals with situations, special seasons and holidays, and ecological concerns from a Christian perspective."** It uses 3-4 pgs. of poetry/issue. **Sample free with 7×9 SAE and 4 first-class stamps. Ordinarily 24-line limit on poetry. Send SASE for themes and guidelines. Pays $25-50.** The other magazine which uses poetry is ***Alive Now!***, a bimonthly, circulation 75,000, for a general Christian audience interested in reflection and meditation. **They buy 30 poems a year, avant-garde and free verse. Submit 5 poems, 10-45 lines. Send SASE for themes and guidelines. Pays $10-25. *The Upper Room* magazine does not accept poetry.**

ALLARDYCE, BARNETT PUBLISHERS (V), 14 Mount St., Lewes, East Sussex BN7 1HL England, founded 1982, editorial director Anthony Barnett. Allardyce, Barnett publishes "literature, music, art. **We cannot consider unsolicited manuscripts.**" They have published books of poetry by J.H. Prynne, Douglas Oliver and Veronica Forrest-Thomson. In the US, their books can be obtained through Small Press Distribution in Berkeley, CA, except for music titles which are distributed by North Country-Cadence, Redwood, NY.

ALLEGHENY REVIEW (I, IV-Undergraduate students), Dept. PM, Box 32, Allegheny College, Meadville PA 16335, founded 1983. "Each year *Allegheny Review* compiles and publishes a review of the nation's best **undergraduate literature.** It is entirely composed of and by college undergraduates and is nationally distributed both as a review and as a classroom text, particularly suited to creative writing courses. We will print **poetry of appreciable literary merit on any topic, submitted by college undergraduates. No limitations except excessive length (2-3 pgs.)** as we wish to represent as many authors as possible, although exceptions are made in areas of great quality and interest." They have published poetry by Eric Sanborn, Cheryl Connor, Rick Alley and Kristi Coulter. The *Review* appears in a 6×9, flat-spined, professionally-printed format, b&w photo on glossy card cover. **Sample: $3.50 and 11×18 SASE. Submit 3 to 5 poems, typed. Submissions should be accompanied by a letter "telling the college poet is attending, year of graduation, any background, goals and philosophies that the author feels are pertinent to the work submitted." Reports 1-2 months following deadline. Poem judged best in the collection earns $50-75 honorarium.** "Ezra Pound gave the best advice: 'Make it new.' We're seeing far too much imitation; there's already been a Sylvia Plath, a Galway Kinnell. Don't be afraid to try new things. Be innovative. Also, traditional forms are coming 'back in style,' or so we hear. Experiment with them; write a villanelle, a sestina or a sonnet. And when you submit, please take enough pride in your work to do so professionally. Handwritten or poorly typed and proofed submissions definitely convey an impression—a negative one."

ALLY PRESS CENTER (V), Dept. PM, 524 Orleans St., St. Paul MN 55107, founded 1973, owner Paul Feroe, **publishes and distributes work by Robert Bly, Michael Meade, James Hillman and Robert Moore, including books, cassette tapes and videotapes.** Two to three times a year a complete catalog is mailed out along with information about Bly's reading and workshop schedule. **The press is not accepting unsolicited mss at this time.** Book catalog is free on request.

ALMS HOUSE PRESS (I), P.O. Box 217, Pearl River NY 10965-0217, founded 1985, poetry editors Lorraine De Gennaro and Alana Sherman, holds an **annual poetry competition with $9 entry fee (contestants receive a copy of a chapbook). "We have no preferences with regard to style as long as the poetry is high caliber. We like to see previous publication in the small press, but we are open to new writers. We look for variety and excellence and are open to experimental forms as well as traditional forms. Any topics as long as the poems are not whiny or too depressing, pornographic or religious."** They have published chapbooks by Martin Anderson and Sandra Marshburn. As a sample they selected these lines by Steven Lautermilch:

Fisher, fishwife, hold each to each.
Your children, small fry, grow only to feed
the sighing grave. And your roofs,
like these keels,
are the bed and birth of shells.

Submit 16- to 24-page chapbook including all front matter, title page and table of contents, between March 1 and May 31. Name, address and phone number should appear on title page only. Winner receives 15 copies. Send SASE for current rules. Sample copy postpaid: $4. They offer a critical and editorial service for $25.

ALOHA, THE MAGAZINE OF HAWAII AND THE PACIFIC (IV-Regional), 4th Floor, 720 Kapiolani Blvd., Honolulu HI 96813, editorial director Cheryl Chee Tsutsumi, is a bimonthly (every 2 months) "consumer magazine with Hawaii and Pacific focus. **Not interested in lengthy poetry. Poems should be limited to 100 words or less. Subject should be focused on Hawaii."** As a sample the editorial director selected these lines by Sheri Rice:

Sea touching sand
Licks the silent shore
Footsteps melting into smoothness
Erasing ridges, indentations
As each slap and pull of the ocean
Planned by tides and moonlit nights
Delivers one more day.

Aloha is 64 pgs., magazine-sized, flat-spined, elegantly printed on glossy stock with many full-color pages, glossy card cover in color. They publish 6 of more than 50 poems received/year. Circulation 65,000. **Sample postpaid: $2.95. Ms should be typed, double-spaced, with name, address and phone number included.** Poems are matched to color photos, so it is "difficult to say" how long it will be between acceptance and publication. **Send SASE for guidelines. Reports within 2 months. Pays $30 plus 1 copy (and up to 10 at discount).**

ALPHA BEAT SOUP; ALPHA BEAT PRESS (I, IV-Form/style), 31 A Waterloo St., New Hope PA 18938, founded 1987, poetry editor David Christy, appears irregularly **emulating the Beat literary tradition.** *Alpha Beat Soup* is "an international poetry and arts journal featuring Beat, 'post-Beat independent' and modern writing." Christy says that **25% of each issue is devoted to little known or previously unpublished poets.** They have recently published works by Pradip Choudhuri, Erling Friis-Baastad, Carl Solomon, Haynes/elliott and Charles Bukowski. As a sample the editor selected these lines by Ana Christy:

the alley in its
complacency surrenders
to
morning scavenger birds
squawking an Ornette
Coleman sax.

ABS is 7×8½, 50-75 pgs., photocopied from IBM laser printer, card cover offset, graphics included. They use 50% of poetry received. Press run is 600 for 400 subscribers (11 of them libraries). Single copy: $8; subscription: $15. **Sample postpaid: $10. Simultaneous submissions and previously published poems OK. Cover letter, including "an introduction to the poet's work," required. Editor comments on rejections "only on request." Sometimes sends prepublication galleys. Pays 1 copy.** Reviews books of poetry in approximately 700 words, multi-book format. Open to unsolicited reviews. Poets may also send books for review consideration. **Alpha Beat Press publishes chapbooks and supplements as well as a monthly broadside series featuring unknown poets. They offer cooperative publishing of chapbooks, "as a way to fund our press and also showcase the unknown poet." Write for details.** ***Alpha Beat Soup*** ranked #2 in the "Nontraditional Verse" category of the latest ***Writer's Digest*** Poetry 60 list.

ALTERNATIVE PRESS MAGAZINE (II), P.O. Box 205, Hatboro PA 19040, founded 1989, poetry editor Bob Lennon, co-editor Lynne Budnick-Lennon, appears quarterly using **"experimental, philosophical poetry; open to many subjects and styles. No traditional, religious, or worn-out love poems."** They have published poetry by T.N. Turner, Leslie Parker, Thomas Kretz, Rod Farmer, Robb Allan, Michael Estabrook, Tracy Lyn Rottkamp and Cheryl A. Townsend. As a sample the editor selected these lines from "WELcome 2 my bRAIN" by Lori Steinberg:

WATER on the bRAIN
DUGH!!
BoinK/BoinK!!
where am i??
KANSAS!?
RUFF! RUFF!

APM is photocopied from typescript, digest-sized, 36 pgs. with matte card cover, saddle-stapled. Press run is 500 for about 100 subscribers, and growing. Some shelf sales. Subscription: $10 for 4 issues. **Sample postpaid: $3. Inquire about reduced rates for back issues. "Poets from Canada and overseas should include $1 extra for each issue ordered." Make all checks payable to Bob Lennon. "*Alternative Press* will attempt to print many poems submitted unlike some magazines that print trash and reject most poems. Submit up to 5 poems—remember that we publish a digest-sized mag and longer pieces have a harder time finding a place." Simultaneous submissions and previously published poems OK. Publishes theme issues occasionally. Guidelines available for SASE. Reports within 2 weeks to 2 months. Pays 1-3 copies and "occasionally small sums." Editor comments on submissions "sometimes."** They are "now doing reviews of 'zines, books, chapbooks and music." Open to unsolicited reviews. Poets may also send books for review consideration. "***APM*** is currently not accepting unsolicited mss for our chopbook (that's no typo) series but they are available for $3 postage paid." The editor says, "We like to publish new poets, but they should read at least one copy to see what the magazine is about. Send poetry that comes from inside, not works that conform to outdated modes of writing. Response to this listing has been outstanding, but everyone who submits stands a fair chance at being published. This includes our friends in Europe, Australia and Canada too. We are trying to lose our sanity at ***APM***. The amount of poetry that we receive adds to this but a lot of normal, bland and unfeeling poetry is no help. Remember, no SASE—no reply! Creative people should avoid creative writing courses. I want to see the '90s on fire. Write poetry that will burn in my fingers when I read it."

AMATEUR WRITERS JOURNAL/FOUR SEASONS POETRY CLUB MAGAZINE (I), 3653 Harrison St., Bellaire OH 43906, founded 1967, editor/publisher Rosalind Gill, appears quarterly. Though **you have to buy a copy to see your work in print,** ***AWJ*** "accepts all types of articles, essays, short stories and **poetry of any theme. No avant-garde or pornographic material accepted. Do not want to see material pertaining to raw sex. Prefer material of seasonal nature to be submitted in the season prevalent at the time. Length up to 40 regular lines (no longer than 10 words per line). Rhymed or unrhymed. Also accept haiku, limericks and all types of short poems."** They have published poetry by Robert Lowery, Eleanore M. Barker, Elsie Watkins and Remelda Gibson. As a sample the editor selected the first stanza of "Inspiration" by Donna Dietrich:

In the darkness, words come
prancing across my pillow,
clogging my veins and synapses
tap-dancing across my brain.
I quickly reach for the light switch
blinding my bleary eyes.

AWJ is 38 pgs., magazine-sized, photocopied from typescript, side-stapled with colored paper cover. Press run is 500. Subscription: $8. **Sample postpaid: $2. Submit more than one poem/page, single-spaced, camera-ready if writer has typewriter available. Considers simultaneous submissions. Cover letter required; include names of other publications to which ms has been submitted, if any. Send SASE for guidelines. Reports "upon publication." Backlog varies, but seasonal poetry is published immediately.** Certificates of merit are given for "best of issue." Open to unsolicited reviews. Poets may also send books for review consideration. The editor advises: "Always adhere to editor's guidelines; send seasonal poems in correct season; write or print legibly if you can't send typed material."

AMBER (III), #404, 40 Rose St., Dartmouth, Nova Scotia B3A 2T6 Canada, phone (902)461-4934, founded 1967, editor Hazel F. Goddard, appears 4 times/year (in January, April, July and October). "***Amber*** and its one-page supplement, ***Marsh & Maple***, promote and distribute current work. ***Amber*** is nonprofit, entirely subscription-supported." They want **"free verse, half page, regular line lengths (not over 56 characters preferred), also haiku and occasional sonnet. Any subject, but must be in good taste, *not vulgar*. Original, bright content. No religious verse."** They have published poetry by John D. Engle, Jr., Diana K. Rubin and Tony Cosier. As a sample the editor selected these lines (poet unidentified):

i am a symphony
blazing syllables of light
across each phrase
lengthening like eighth notes
from a phantom violin
to touch the inner ear

The editor says ***Amber*** is 28 pgs., stapled. They receive about 500 poems a year, use roughly 70%. Press run is 100 for 90 subscribers of which 3 are libraries. Single copy: $2.50; subscription: $10. **Sample postpaid: $1. Previously published poems OK; no simultaneous submissions. Every sheet should bear the poet's name. "Prefer poems to be seasonal, if on nature."** Time between acceptance and publication is 1-6 months. **Seldom comments on rejections. "First acceptance paid for with 1 free copy; continuing submissions expected to be covered by a subscription."** The editor says, "I receive many books of poets' poems. If up to an average standard I select from them for publication in my magazine. Most poems are from well-crafted poets, a few new writers. Need not be professional but *must* be good work. When space allows, I list contests poets may like to enter, comment on books poets send and devote centrefold to personal chatting, poets' successes, etc."

AMELIA; CICADA; SPSM&H; THE AMELIA AWARDS (II, IV-Form), 329 "E" St., Bakersfield CA 93304 or P.O. Box 2385, Bakersfield CA 93303, phone (805)323-4064. ***Amelia***, founded 1983, poetry editor Frederick A. Raborg, Jr., is a quarterly magazine that publishes chapbooks as well. Central to its operations is a series of contests, most with entry fees, spaced evenly throughout the year, awarding more than $3,500 annually, but they publish many poets who have not entered the contests as well. Among poets published are Pattiann Rogers, Stuart Freibert, John Millett, David Ray, Larry Rubin, Charles Bukowski, Maxine Kumin, Charles Edward Eaton and Shuntaro Tanikawa. As a sample the editor selected these lines by June Owens:

only what is left
of the woods and I
hear the cold crank
of crows   see an
old moon sitting on
its haunches beside
a large rock   or
the terrible glint
on the saw blade
of this night
jagged as its
murderer heart

They are **"receptive to all forms to 100 lines. We do not want to see the patently-religious or overtly-political. Erotica is fine; pornography, no."** The digest-sized, flat-spined magazine is offset on high-quality paper and usually features an original four-color cover; its circulation is about 1,250, with 522 subscriptions, of which 28 are libraries. Subscription: $25/year. **Sample postpaid: $7.95. Submit 3-5 poems. No simultaneous submissions except for entries to the annual Amelia Chapbook Award. Reports in 2-12 weeks, the latter if under serious consideration. Pays $2-25/poem plus 2 copies. "Almost always I try to comment."** The editor says, "*Amelia* is not afraid of strong themes, but we do look for professional, polished work even in handwritten submissions. Poets should have something to say about matters other than the moon. We like to see strong **traditional pieces as well as the contemporary and experimental. And neatness *does* count.**" Fred Raborg has done more than most other editors to ensure a wide range of styles and forms, from traditional European to Asian, from lyric to narrative. Typically he is swamped with submissions and so response time can exceed stated parameters. ***Amelia*** continues to place in outside surveys as a top market for freelancers, because of editorial openness. Brief reviews are also featured. It may be interesting to note that ***Amelia*** ranked #3 in the "Traditional Verse" category of the latest ***Writer's Digest*** Poetry 60 list. As for Raborg's other publications, ***Cicada*** is a quarterly magazine that publishes **haiku, senryu and other Japanese forms,** plus essays on the form—techniques and history—as well as fiction which in some way incorporates haiku or Japanese poetry in its plot, and reviews of books pertaining to Japan and its poetry or collections of haiku. Among poets published are Roger Ishii, H.F. Noyes, Knute Skinner, Katherine Machan Aal, Ryah Tumarkin Goodman and Ryokufu Ishizaki. These sample lines are by Philip A. Waterhouse:

family sauna
melons lemons -
big and little stems.

They are receptive to experimental forms as well as the traditional. "Try to avoid still-life as haiku; strive for the *whole* of an emotion, whether minuscule or panoramic. Erotica is fine; the Japanese are great lovers of the erotic." The magazine is offset on high quality paper, with a circulation of 600, with 432 subscriptions of which 26 are libraries. Subscription: $14/year. **Sample postpaid: $4.50. Submit 3-10 haiku or poems. No simultaneous submissions. Reports in 2 weeks. No payment, except three "best of issue" poets each receive $10 on publication plus copy. "I try to make some comment on returned poems always."** ***SPSM&H*** is a quarterly magazine that publishes **only sonnets, sonnet sequences,** essays on the form—both technique and history—as well as romantic or Gothic fiction which, in some way, incorporates the form, and reviews of sonnet collections or collections containing a substantial number of sonnets. They are **"receptive to experimental forms as well as the traditional, and appreciate wit when very good."** Among poets published are Margaret Ryan, Harold Witt, Sharon E. Martin, Rhina P. Espaillat and Robert Wolfkill. These sample lines are by Michael J. Bugeja:

She knew the steps, the key. The cadence
When she came to him with another minuet,
Sheeted music in her satchel like a poem:
Heavy, black. But even she could dance
Later as he taught her, timing the duet
With the indifference of a metronome.

Perhaps it may help to know the editor's favorite Shakespearean sonnet is #29, and he feels John Updike clarified the limits of experimentation with the form in his "Love Sonnet" from **Midpoint.** The magazine is offset on high quality paper, with a circulation of 600, for 432 subscribers and 26 libraries. Subscription: $14/year. **Sample postpaid: $4. Submit 3-5 poems. No simultaneous submissions. Reports in 2 weeks. No payment, except two "best of issue" poets each receive $14 on publication plus copy. "I always try to comment on returns."** The following annual contests have various entry fees: The Amelia Awards (six prizes of $200, $100, $50 plus three honorable mentions of $10 each); The Anna B. Janzen Prize for Romantic Poetry ($100, annual deadline January 2); The Bernice Jennings Traditional Poetry Award ($100, annual deadline January 2); The Georgie Starbuck Galbraith Light/Humorous Verse Prizes (six awards of $100, $50, $25 plus three honorable mentions of $5 each, annual deadline March 1); The Charles William Duke Longpoem Award ($100, annual deadline April 1); The Lucille Sandberg Haiku Awards (six awards of $100, $50, $25 plus three honorable mentions of $5 each, annual deadline April 1); The Grace Hines Narrative Poetry Award ($100, annual deadline May 1); The Amelia Chapbook Award ($250, book publication and 50 copies, annual deadline July 1); The Johanna B. Bourgoyne Poetry Prizes (six awards of $100, $50, $25, plus three honorable mentions of $5 each); The Douglas Manning Smith Epic/Heroic Poetry Prize ($100, annual deadline August 1); The Hildegarde Janzen Prize for Oriental Forms of Poetry (six awards of $50, $30, $20 and three honorable mentions of $5 each, annual deadline September 1); The Eugene Smith Prize For Sonnets (six awards of $140, $50, $25 and three honorable mentions of $5 each); The A&C Limerick Prizes (six awards of $50, $30, $20 and three honorable mentions of $5 each); The Montegue Wade Lyric Poetry Prize ($100, annual deadline November 1).

AMERICA; FOLEY POETRY CONTEST (II), 106 W. 56th St., New York NY 10019, phone (212)581-4640, founded 1909, poetry editor Patrick Samway, S.J., is a weekly journal of opinion published by the Jesuits of North America. They primarily publish articles on religious, social, political and cultural themes. **They are "looking for imaginative poetry of all kinds. We have no restrictions on form or subject matter, though we prefer to receive poems of 35 lines or less."** They have published poetry by Howard Nemerov, Fred Chappell, William Heyen and Eve Shelnutt. ***America*** is 24 pgs., magazine-sized, professionally printed on thin stock with thin paper cover, circulation 35,000. Subscription: $33. **Sample postpaid: $1.25. Send SASE for excellent guidelines. Reports in 2 weeks. Pays $1.40/line plus 2 copies.** The annual Foley Poetry Contest offers a prize of $500, usually in late winter. Send SASE for rules. "Poems for the Foley Contest should be submitted between January and April. Poems submitted for the Foley Contest between July and December will normally be returned unread." The editor says, "***America*** is committed to publishing quality poetry as it has done for the past 85 years. We would encourage beginning and established poets to submit their poems to us."

AMERICAN ATHEIST PRESS; GUSTAV BROUKAL PRESS; AMERICAN ATHEIST (IV-Specialized), P.O. Box 2117, Austin TX 78768-2117, phone (512)458-1244, founded 1958, editor R. Murray-O'Hair, publishes the quarterly magazine with 30,000 circulation, ***American Atheist***, and under various imprints some dozen books a year reflecting "concerns of Atheists, such as separation of state and church, civil liberties and atheist news." **Poetry is used primarily in the poetry section of the magazine. It must have "a particular slant to atheism, dealing with subjects such as the atheist lifestyle. Anticlerical poems and puns are more than liable to be rejected. Any form or style is acceptable. Preferred length is under 40 lines."** They have published poetry by Julia Rhodes Pozonzycki, Allan Case and Thomas A. Easton. Of their 17,000 subscriptions, 1,000 are libraries. The magazine-sized format is professionally printed, with art and photos, glossy, color cover. They receive over 20-30 poetry submissions/week, use about 12/year. Single copy: $2.95; subscription: $25. **Sample free. Submit typed, double-spaced mss. Simultaneous submissions OK. Time-dependent poems (such as winter) should be submitted 4 months in advance. Guidelines available for SASE, but a label is preferred to an envelope. Reports within 3-4 months. Pays "first-timers" 10 copies or 6-month subscription or $12 credit voucher for AAP products. Thereafter, $15/poem plus 10 copies. Buys one-time rights. Sometimes comments on rejected mss.** Reviews related books of poetry in 500-1,000 words. They do not normally publish poetry in book form but will consider it.

THE AMERICAN COWBOY POET MAGAZINE (I, IV-Cowboy), Dept. PM, P.O. Box 326, Eagle ID 83616, phone (208)888-9838, founded 1988 as ***The American Cowboy Poet Newspaper,*** magazine format in January 1991, publisher Rudy Gonzales, editor Rose Fitzgerald. ***ACPM*** is a quarterly "about real cowboys" using **"authentic cowboy poetry. Must be clean—entertaining. Submissions should avoid 'like topics.' We will not publish any more poems about Old Blackie dying, This old hat, if this pair of Boots could talk, etc. We do not publish free verse poetry. Only traditional cowboy with rhyme and meter."** They also publish articles including a "Featured Poet," stories of cowboy poetry gatherings and news of coming events. Subscription: $12/year, $15 Canada, $20 overseas. **Sample postpaid: $3. Cover letter required with submissions. Send SASE for guidelines. Editor always comments on rejections.** Staff reviews related books of poetry. Send books for review consideration.

‡AMERICAN LITERARY REVIEW; VASSAR MILLER PRIZE IN POETRY (II), University of North Texas, P.O. Box 13615, Denton TX 76203-3615, co-editors Scott Cairns and Barbara Rodman, is a biannual publishing **all forms and modes of poetry, but "less interested in poetry in the personal mode."** They have published poetry by Penelope Austin, Wendy Barker, Bruce Bond, Kevin Cantwell, David Citino, Wyn Cooper, Elizabeth Dodd, Joseph Duemer, Pattiann Rogers, William Stafford, Lee Upton and Ralph Wilson. As a sample the editors selected these lines from "Double or Nothing" by Jack Myers:

And, now, like an amnesiac trying to feel special on his birthday,
I've decided that death must be what it's like before we're born.
Have I finally broken through? Unafraid of the nothing that's eternal
in favor of the nothing that will pass?

Sample postpaid: $8. Reports in 2 months. Sometimes sends prepublication galleys. Pays copies. Sponsors the Vassar Miller Prize in Poetry. The annual prize awards $500 and publication for "an original, book-length poetry manuscript of 50-80 pages." The winning ms will be published by the University of North Texas Press. Mss accepted December through January. Entry fee: $15. Include #10 SASE for reply. Mss will not be returned. Send SASE for guidelines.

AMERICAN POETRY REVIEW (III), Dept. PM, 1721 Walnut St., Philadelphia PA 19103, phone (215)496-0439, founded 1972, is probably the **most widely circulated (18,000 copies bimonthly) and best-known periodical devoted to poetry in the world.** Poetry editors are Stephen Berg, David Bonanno and Arthur Vogelsang, and they have **published most of the leading poets writing in English and many translations.** The poets include Gerald Stern, Brenda Hillman, John Ashbery, Norman Dubie, Marvin Bell, Galway Kinnell, James Dickey, Lucille Clifton and Tess Gallagher. ***APR*** is a newsprint tabloid with 13,000 subscriptions, of which 1,000 are libraries. The editors receive about 4,000 submissions/year, use 200. This popular publication contains mostly free verse (some leaning to the avant-garde) with flashes of brilliance in every issue. Editors seem to put an emphasis on language and voice. Because ***APR*** is a tabloid, it can feature long poems (or ones with long line lengths) in an attractive format. Translations are also welcome. In all, this is a difficult market to crack because of the volume of submissions. **Sample and price per issue: $3.25. No simultaneous submissions. Reports in 3 months, has 1- to 3-year backlog. Always sends prepublication galleys. Pays $1.25/line.** The magazine is also a major resource for opinion, reviews, theory, news and ads pertaining to poetry. Each year the editors award the Jerome J. Shestack Prizes of $1,000, $500 and $250 for the best poems, in their judgment, published in ***APR***. Poetry published here has also been included in the 1992, 1993 and 1994 volumes of **The Best American Poetry**.

THE AMERICAN SCHOLAR (III), 1811 Q St. NW, Washington DC 20009, phone (202)265-3808, founded 1932, associate editor Sandra Costich, is an academic quarterly which **uses about 5 poems/issue. "We would like to see poetry that develops an image, a thought or event, without the use of a single cliché or contrived archaism. The most hackneyed subject matter is self-conscious love; the most tired verse is iambic pentameter with rhyming endings. The usual length of our poems is 30 lines. From 1-4 poems may be submitted at one time; *no more* for a careful reading."** They have published poetry by Robert Pack, Alan Shapiro and Gregory Djanikian. What little poetry is used in this high-prestige magazine is accomplished, intelligent and open (in terms of style and form). Study before submitting (**sample: $6.50, guidelines available for SASE). Reports in 2 months. Always sends prepublication galleys. Pays $50/poem. Buys first rights only.**

AMERICAN TOLKIEN SOCIETY; MINAS TIRITH EVENING-STAR; W.W. PUBLICATIONS (IV-Specialized, themes), P.O. Box 373, Highland MI 48357-0373, founded 1967, editor Philip W. Helms. There are special poetry issues. Membership in the ATS is open to all, regardless of country of residence, and entitles one to receive the quarterly journal. Dues are $7.50 per annum to addresses in US, $12.50 in Canada and $15 elsewhere. Their journal and chapbooks use **poetry of fantasy about Middle-Earth and Tolkien.** They have published poetry by Thomas M. Egan, Anne Etkin, Nancy Pope and Martha Benedict. ***Minas Tirith Evening-Star*** is magazine-sized, offset from typescript with cartoon-like b&w graphics. They have a press run of 400 for 350 subscribers of which 10% are libraries. Single copy: $3.50; subscription: $7.50. **Sample postpaid: $1.50.** "Please make checks payable to American Tolkien Society." **No simultaneous submissions; previously published poems "maybe." Cover letter preferred. Editor sometimes comments on rejections. Publishes theme issues occasionally. Send SASE for guidelines. Reports in 2 weeks. Sometimes sends prepublication galleys. Pays contributor's copies.** Reviews related books of poetry; length depends on the volume, "a sentence to several pages." Open to unsolicited reviews. Poets may also send books to Paul Ritz, Reviews, P.O. Box 901, Clearwater FL 34617 for review consideration. Under imprint of W.W. Publications they publish collections of poetry 50-100 pgs. **For book or chapbook consideration, submit sample poems. Publishes 2 chapbooks/year.** They sometimes sponsor contests.

THE AMERICAN VOICE (II), 332 W. Broadway, Louisville KY 40202, phone (502)562-0045, founded 1985, editor Frederick Smock, is a literary quarterly publishing North and South American writers. They prefer **free verse, avant-garde, in areas such as ethnic/nationality, gay/lesbian, translation, women/feminism and literary.** They have published poetry by Olga Broumas, Odysseus Elytis, Cheryl Clarke, Marge Piercy and Ernesto Cardenal. As a sample here is one stanza of a long poem, "Mother's Day at the Air Force Museum," by George Ella Lyon:

My son loves the machine guns.
He looks through a sight,
he strafes the still air.
At home, his Lego men
die smiling.

TAV is elegantly printed, flat-spined, 140 pgs. of high-quality stock with matte card cover. Editors seem to prefer lyric free verse, much of it accessible, by well-known and new writers. Issues we have seen also had room for both long and sequence poems. Circulation is 2,500 with 1,000 subscriptions of which 100 are libraries. Subscription: $15/year. **Sample postpaid: $5. No simultaneous submissions. Cover letter requested. Occasionally comments on rejections. Reports in 6**

weeks, has a 3-month backlog. Pays $150/poem and 2 copies. (They pay $75 to translator of a poem.) Open to unsolicited reviews. Poets may also send books for review consideration. ***The American Voice*** has received an ***Utne Reader*** Alternative Press Award and has had work included in the **Pushcart Prize** anthologies.

AMERICAN WRITING: A MAGAZINE; NIERIKA EDITIONS (IV-Form/style), 4343 Manayunk Ave., Philadelphia PA 19128, founded 1990, editor Alexandra Grilikhes, appears twice a year using **poetry that is "experimental and the voice of the loner, writing that takes risks with form, interested in the powers of intuition and states of being. No cerebral, academic poetry. Poets often try to make an experience 'literary' through language, instead of going back to the original experience and finding the original images. That is what we are interested in: the voice that speaks those images."** They have recently published poetry by Ivan Argüelles, Antler, Eleanor Wilner, Diane Glancy and Margaret Holley. As a sample the editor selected these lines from "Coyote" by Shelley M. Miller:

There is pain, Coyote, that you have not known yet.
It is good your legs still carry you
tirelessly away from peace;
that your grin still frightens away false caretakers,
that you long ago ate your own heart to survive.

There is pain ahead, Coyote.
Muscle, cunning, speed? These will never set you free.

AW is digest-sized, flat-spined, 80 pgs., professionally printed, with matte card cover. Press run is 1,000 for 250 subscriptions. Subscription: $10. **Sample postpaid: $6. Guidelines on subscription form. Reporting time varies. "If it's a 'possible,' we may keep it 3 months." Pays 2 copies/accepted submission group.** Since ***American Writing*** began in 1990, 15 of the authors they have published won national awards after publication in the magazine. The editor says, "Many magazines print the work of the same authors [the big names] who often publish 'lesser' works that way. ***AW*** is interested in the work itself, its particular strength, energy and voice, not necessarily in the 'status' of the authors. We like to know *something* about the authors, however."

THE AMICUS JOURNAL (IV-Nature/rural/ecology), 40 W. 20th St., New York NY 10011, is the quarterly journal of the Natural Resources Defense Council. ***Amicus* publishes about 15 poems a year and asks that submitted poetry be "rooted in nature."** They have published poetry by some of the best known poets in the country, including Mary Oliver, Gary Snyder, Denise Levertov, Marvin Bell and William Stafford. As a sample, the editors selected these lines from "In the Labyrinth of Elements" by Duane Niatum:

The painter descends into the world
like the morning sun
on madrona branch, azalea and peony,
follows the gold thread passing stem,
leaf, petal, moss, mushroom and trunk,
twig and stone. . . .

The Amicus Journal is finely-printed, saddle-stapled, on high quality paper with glossy cover, using much art, photography and cartoons. Circulation 170,000. **Sample free with SASE (including $1.44 postage). Pays $25/poem.**

ANACONDA PRESS; FUEL (II), P.O. Box 146640, Chicago IL 60614, editor-in-chief Andy Lowry. Currently publishes ***fuel***, "a wiry, highly energized mini-magazine using lots of cool poetry, art and fiction." Also publishes **3-4 poetry chapbooks/year. "We're looking for daring, eccentric works. No academia allowed!" Send SASE for most recent guidelines. Sometimes sends prepublication galleys. Pays 1-2 copies if published in 'zine. Chapbook payment is negotiable. Rights revert to authors.**

ANALECTA (IV-Students), Dept. PM, Liberal Arts Council, FAC 17, University of Texas, Austin TX 78712, phone (512)471-6563, founded 1974, contact Stephanie Holt and Jennifer Conwell, is an annual of literary works and art by **college/university students and graduate students chosen in an annual contest. No restrictions on type; limited to 5 poems/submission. Submissions cannot be returned.** "Our purpose is to provide a forum for excellent student writing. **Works must be previously unpublished."** As a sample, the editor selected this excerpt from "Jitterbug Puppet" by Alex Traugott:

She dances in the garden
with tiger lilies in her white arm.
like a swarm of clouds before a storm.
Her legs pound down the dirt in time . . .

It is a 150-page magazine, glossy plates for interior artwork in b&w, 7×10, flat-spined, soft cover. Of about 800 submissions received, they publish about 40. Press run is 800 for 700 subscribers, 100 shelf sales. **Sample postpaid: $7.50. Entries must be typed; name should appear on**

cover sheet only. Send SASE for guidelines. Deadline is in mid-October. Prizes in each category. Pays 2 copies and various monetary prizes.

‡ANATHEMA REVIEW (II), P.O. Box 891, Bowling Green OH 43402, founded 1993, editors Scott Gallaway and Chad Rohrbacher, appears approximately 4 times/year. **They want "poetry that is not only well crafted but also *says* something. No poetry without thought, purpose or meaning. Nothing overly sentimental."** They have recently published poetry by Doug Martin, John McKernan, Louise Jaffe and Marcia Cohee. As a sample we selected these lines from "Keeping Track of The River" by William J. Vernon:

In such heavy boots, our legs sweat,
we stumble over rocks. No crayfish
scuds away. No minnows break
surface in panic. What splashes

over us is thick, like swirling ink.
Before us, the bottom is gray,
aluminous, ashen. It stinks
when weight releases it. . . .

AR is 30-40 pgs., 5½×8½, professionally printed and saddle-stapled with card cover, b&w art and photos. They accept less than 5% of poetry received. Press run is 150, 50% shelf sales. Subscription: $10. **Sample postpaid: $3. No previously published poems; simultaneous submissions OK. Cover letter required.** Time between acceptance and publication is up to 5 months. **Send SASE for guidelines. Reports in 2-5 weeks. Pays 1 copy.**

ANHINGA PRESS; ANHINGA PRIZE (II), P.O. Box 10595, Tallahassee FL 32302-0595, phone (904)575-5592, founded 1972, poetry editors Rick Campbell and Van Brock, publishes **"books and anthologies of poetry. We also offer the Anhinga Prize for poetry—$1,000 and publication—for a book-length manuscript each year. We want to see contemporary poetry which respects language. We're inclined toward poetry that is not obscure, that can be understood by any literate audience."** They have recently published poetry by Yvonne Sapia, Judith Kitchen, Ricardo Pau-Llosa, Robert J. Levy, Michael Mott, Will Wells, Gary Corseri, Nick Bozanic, Jean Monahan, Earl S. Braggs and Janet Holmes. As a sample the editors selected these lines from **The Secret Life of Moles** by P.V. LeForge:

The sun migrates across whatever scenes
death can spare:
and we have many of these small reprieves
living within us.
When we die, will life stop again?
And for whom?

Considers simultaneous submissions. Publishes themed collections. Send SASE for upcoming themes. Always sends prepublication galleys. Send a "business size" SASE for catalog. Also send SASE for rules (submissions accepted in January and February) of the Anhinga Prize for poetry, which requires a $15 entry fee. The contest has been judged by such distinguished poets as William Stafford, Louis Simpson, Henry Taylor, Hayden Carruth, Denise Levertov, Marvin Bell and Donald Hall. For the next three years the judge will be Joy Harjo.

ANIMA: THE JOURNAL OF HUMAN EXPERIENCE (II, IV-Women/feminism, spirituality/inspirational), 1053 Wilson Ave., Chambersburg PA 17201, founded 1974, editor Barbara Rotz. *Anima* "celebrates the wholistic vision that emerges from thoughtful and imaginative encounters with the differences between woman and man, East and West, yin and yang—*anima* and *animus*. **Written largely by and about women** who are pondering new experiences of themselves and our world, this equinoctial journal welcomes contributions, verbal and visual, from the known and unknown. We publish very few poems, but they are carefully selected. **We are not interested in simply private experiences. Poetry must communicate. Advise all would-be poets to study the kinds of things we do publish. No restrictions on length, form, or such matters.**" There are 5-10 pages of poetry in each semiannual issue of the elegantly-printed and illustrated 8½" square, glossy-covered magazine, 1,000 subscriptions of which 150 are libraries. Single copy: $5.95. **Sample: $3.95. Slow reporting—sometimes 3-6 months. Payment is offprints with covers.**

ANJOU (V), P.O. Box 322 Station P., Toronto, Ontario M5S 2S8 Canada, founded 1980, edited by Richard Lush and Roger Greenwald, publishes broadsides of poetry. **"We do not wish to receive submissions because we publish only by solicitation."**

ANSUDA PUBLICATIONS; ANSUDA MAGAZINE (II), P.O. Box 158JA, Harris IA 51345, founded 1978, "is a small press operation, publishing independently of outside influences, such as grants, donations, awards, etc. Our operating capital comes from magazine and book sales only." Their magazine, ***Ansuda***, "uses some poetry, and we also publish separate chapbooks of individual poets. We **prefer poems with a social slant and originality—we do *not* want love poems, personal poems that can only be understood by the poet, or anything from the haiku family of poem styles. No limits on length, though very short poems lack the depth we seek—no limits on form or style, but rhyme and meter must make sense. Too many poets write senseless rhymes using the first words to pop into their heads. As a result, we prefer blank and free verse.**" They have published poetry by Ian Lawrence, Paul M. Lamb, Anthony Constantino and Terry Everton. They offer no sample because "most of our poems are at least 25-30 lines long and every line complements all other lines, so it is hard to pick out lines to illustrate." ***Ansuda***, which appears irregularly (1-3 times a year), is a low-budget publication, digest-sized, mimeographed on inexpensive paper, making it possible to print 80 or more pages and sell copies for **$3.75 (the price of a sample)**. Press run is 300 for 130 subscribers, of which 7 are libraries. Each issue has 3-12 pages of poetry, but **"we would publish more if we had it; our readers would like more poetry."** Everything accepted goes into the next issue, so there is no backlog. **Reports immediately to 1 month. Pays 2 copies. Acquires first rights. They also publish 1-2 chapbooks (24-28 pgs.)/year. For these, query with 3-6 sample poems.** "We are *not* interested in past credits, who you studied under, etc. Names mean nothing to us and we have found that the small press is so large that big names in one circle are unknown in another circle. In fact, **we get better material from the unknowns who have nothing to brag about (usually)." Replies to queries immediately, to mss in 1-2 months. Simultaneous submissions OK only if clearly indicated. Pays royalties plus 5 copies for chapbooks**. Daniel Betz adds, "About all I have left to say is to tell the novice to keep sending his work out. It won't get published in a desk drawer. There are so many little mags out there that eventually you'll find homes for your poems. Yes, some poets get published on their first few tries, but I've made first acceptances to some who have been submitting for 5 to 10 years with no luck, until their poem and my mag just seemed to click. It just takes time and lots of patience."

ANTERIOR POETRY MONTHLY; ANTERIOR BITEWING LTD. (I), 7735 Brand Ave., St. Louis MO 63135-3212, founded 1988, editor Tom Bergeron, appears 12 times a year using **"poems of excellence. Submissions welcome from everyone; however, there is a $1 reading fee per poem submitted unless you are a subscriber. The top four poems in each issue receive awards of $25, $15, $10 and $5 respectively. Other poems may be published with no payment to the author. Entries received after the 15th, extra submissions and poems more suited to later seasons are automatically entered in future month's contest."** They have published poetry by J. Alvin Speers, Pearl Bloch Segall and Kathleen Lee Mendel. As a sample the editor selected these lines from "The Light" by Barbara N. Paul-Best:

Cold are the winds that blow,
Cold as December ice and January snow;
Soothing as a blanket of snow-starred down;
Peaceful as the absence of every sound.

It is 20 pgs., digest-sized, desktop-published and saddle-stapled with colored paper cover. Press run 200-300 for 110 subscribers. Subscription: $15. **Sample postpaid: $1. Make checks payable to Anterior Bitewing Ltd. "We like cover letters." Send SASE for guidelines. Buys one-time rights.** Anterior Bitewing Ltd. is an imprint for job printing of newsletters and "magazettes." Send SASE for rate sheet. The editor says, "Always resubmit. There's some editor out there somewhere who will love your work. Take advice, make changes accordingly and keep on resubmitting."

ANTHOLOGY OF MAGAZINE VERSE & YEARBOOK OF AMERICAN POETRY (III, IV-Anthology), ℅ Monitor Book Company, P.O. Box 9078, Palm Springs CA 92263, phone (619)323-2270, founded 1950, editor Alan F. Pater. The annual **Anthology** is a selection of the **best poems published in American magazines during the year and is also a basic reference work for poets.** Alan F. Pater says, "We want poetry that is 'readable' and in any poetic form; we also want translations. **All material must first have appeared in magazines.** Any subject matter will be considered; we also would like to see some rhyme and meter, preferably sonnets." They have published poetry by Margaret Atwood, Stanley Kunitz, Robert Penn Warren, Richard Wilbur, Maxine Kumin and John Updike. Indeed, the anthology is a good annual guide to the best poets actively publishing in any given year. For the most part selections are made by the editor from magazines, but some poets are solicited for their work which has been in magazines in a given year. **Cover letters should include name and date or issue number of magazine in which the poem was originally published.**

ANTIETAM REVIEW (IV-Regional), Washington County Arts Council, Bryan Center, 7 W. Franklin St., Hagerstown MD 21740, an annual founded 1981, poetry editors Crystal Brown and Ann Knox, looks for **"well-crafted literary quality poems. We discourage inspirational verse, haiku, doggerel." Uses poets only from the states of Maryland, Pennsylvania, Virginia, West Virginia, Delaware and District of Columbia. Needs 18 poems/issue, up to 30 lines each.** Poets they have published include Roberta Bevington, Naomi Thiers and Ed Zahniser. The editor chose this sample from "Cold" by David Staudt:

Away from her he becomes solid
once again: his ribs rewind around
his lungs, banding tighter and tighter.
He thinks he must feel to her like wood,
or an old stone statue with a crack
inching the length of its thigh.

AR is 48 pgs., 8½×11, saddle-stapled, glossy paper with glossy card cover and b&w photos throughout. Press run is 1,000. **Sample postpaid: $3.15 back issue, $5.25 current. Do not submit mss from February through August. "We read from September 1 through February 1 annually." Send SASE for guidelines. Sends prepublication galleys, if requested. Pays $20/poem, depending on funding, plus 2 copies. Buys first North American serial rights.** The editors seem open to all styles of poetry, free and formal, as long as the author is from the designated region. Overall, a good read; but poems have to compete with prose. Ones used, however, are featured in attractive boxes on the page. Work published in ***Antietam Review*** has been included in a **Pushcart Prize** anthology, and ***Antietam Review*** received an honorable mention for editorial content as part of the 1993 American Literary Magazine Awards.

THE ANTIGONISH REVIEW (II), St. Francis Xavier University, Antigonish, Nova Scotia B2G 1C0 Canada, phone (902)867-3962, fax (902)867-5153, founded 1970, editor George Sanderson, poetry editor Peter Sanger. This high-quality quarterly "tries to produce the kind of literary and visual mosaic that the modern sensibility requires or would respond to." They want poetry **not over "80 lines, i.e., 2 pgs.; subject matter can be anything, the style is traditional, modern or post-modern limited by typographic resources. Purpose is not an issue." No "erotica, scatalogical verse, excessive propaganda toward a certain subject."** They have published poetry by Milton Acorn, Andy Wainwright, Janice Kulyk-Keefer, M. Travis Lane and Douglas Lochhead. ***TAR*** is flat-spined, 6×9, 150 pgs. with glossy card cover, offset printing, using "in-house graphics and cover art, no ads." They accept about 10% of some 2,500 submissions/year. Press run is 1,100 for 800 subscriptions. Subscription: $18. **Sample postpaid: $3. No simultaneous submissions or previously published poems. Include SASE or SAE and IRCs if outside Canada. Editor "sometimes" comments on rejections. Pays 2 copies.**

THE ANTIOCH REVIEW (III), Box 148, Yellow Springs OH 45387, phone (513)767-6389, founded 1941, poetry editor David St. John, "is an independent quarterly of critical and creative thought . . . **For over 50 years, now, creative authors, poets and thinkers have found a friendly reception . . . regardless of formal reputation**. We get far more poetry than we can possibly accept, and the competition is keen. Here, where form and content are so inseparable and reaction is so personal, it is difficult to state requirements or limitations. Studying recent issues of ***The Review*** should be helpful. **No 'light' or inspirational verse.**" They have published poetry by Ralph Angel, Jorie Graham, Mark Strand, Karen Fish, Michael Collier and Andrew Hudgins. Circulation is primarily to their 4,000 subscribers, of which half are libraries. They receive about 3,000 submissions/year, publish 20 pages of poetry in each issue, have about a 6-month backlog. Subscription: $30. **Sample: $6. Reads submissions September 1 through May 15 only. General guidelines for contributors available for SASE. Reports in 6-8 weeks. Pays $15/published page plus 2 copies.** Reviews books of poetry in 300 words, single format. This is a beautiful journal featuring some of the best poems being written by new and well-known writers. As David St. John says, "I have a policy of publishing a poet only once during my tenure as poetry editor. It may be a dumb policy, but it's one way to help keep the magazine open to new folks. I'd like to think that there's at least one place where new poets feel they have a shot." Consequently, voices here are varied and exciting.

ANTIPODES (IV-Regional), 8 Big Island, Warwick NY 10990, founded 1987, poetry editor Paul Kane, is a biannual of Australian poetry and fiction and criticism and reviews of Australian writing. They want **work from Australian poets only. No restrictions as to form, length, subject matter or style.** They have published poetry by A.D. Hope, Judith Wright and John Tranter. As a sample the editor selected these lines from "Poetry and Religion" by Les Murray:

Religions are poems. They concert
our daylight and dreaming mind, our
emotions, instinct, breath and native gesture
into the only whole thinking: poetry

The editor says ***Antipodes*** is 180 pgs., 8½×11, perfect-bound, with graphics, ads and photos. They receive about 500 submissions a year, accept approximately 10%. Press run is 500 for 200 subscribers. Subscription: $20. **Sample postpaid: $17. No previously published poems or simultaneous submissions. Cover letter with bio note required. The editor says they "prefer submission of photocopies which do not have to be returned." Seldom comments on rejections. Reports in 2 months. Pays $20/poem plus 1 copy. Acquires first North American serial rights.** Staff reviews books of poetry in 500-1,500 words. Send books for review consideration.

ANYTHING THAT MOVES: BEYOND THE MYTHS OF BISEXUALITY (IV-Bisexual, themes), #24, 2404 California St., San Francisco CA 94115, phone (415)703-7977, founded 1991, attention fiction/poetry editor. This quarterly uses **"material only from those who consider themselves bisexual, whether they identify as such or not. Pen names are permissible with written notification, however author's real name and address must accompany submission (not to be published). Include name(s), address and phone number on each page. Submissions need not address bisexuality specifically, but may be on topics/themes/subjects of interest to bisexuals. Special consideration given to people of color, those differently abled, those living with HIV disease or AIDS, and those whose work has been denied/censored/erased in mainstream literary communities and publications."** As a sample the editor selected these lines from "Feminine" by Chocolate Waters:

The word has become hateful.
It reminds you of little girl voices,
clutch purses, ankle bracelets,
clean underwear in case you get hit
by a truck.

It is 64 pgs., professionally printed, magazine-sized with glossy paper cover, saddle-stapled. Press run is 5,000 for 1,000 subscribers of which 100 are libraries, 3,000 shelf sales. Subscription: $25. **Sample: $6. Cover letter required. "Include titles of submission(s) and short (under 30 words) bio." No comments on rejections. Publishes theme issues. Send SASE for upcoming themes. "Accepted material cannot be returned. Do not send original copy. Shorter poems are more likely to be accepted. Notification of use will be in the form of 2-copy payment, although notification of acceptance will be given 6-8 weeks upon receipt of submission.** *ATM* is published by the Bay Area Bisexual Network (BABN), a nonprofit institution, and is distributed nationally, with a small international distribution." Open to unsolicited reviews. Poets may also send books for review consideration.

APALACHEE QUARTERLY; APALACHEE PRESS (II, IV-Themes), P.O. Box 20106, Tallahassee FL 32316, founded 1971, editors Barbara Hamby, Mary Jane Ryals, Kim MacQueen, Bruce Boehrer and Paul McCall, want **"no formal verse."** They have published poetry by David Kirby, Peter Meinke and Jim Hall. ***Apalachee Quarterly*** is 160 pgs., 6×9, professionally printed and perfect-bound with card cover. There are 55-95 pgs. of poetry in each issue, circulation 700, with 350 subscriptions of which 75 are libraries. "Every year we do an issue on a special topic. Past issues include Dental, Revenge, Cocktail Party and Noir issues." Subscription: $15. **Sample postpaid: $5. Submit clear copies of up to 5 poems, name and address on each. Simultaneous submissions OK. "We don't read during the summer (June 1 through August 31)." Sometimes comments on rejections. Send SASE for guidelines. Pays 2 copies.** Staff reviews books of poetry. Send books for review consideration.

APPALACHIA; THE APPALACHIA POETRY PRIZE (II, IV-Nature), 5 Joy St., Boston MA 02108, phone (617)523-0636, founded 1876, poetry editor Parkman Howe, editor-in-chief Sandy Stott, is a "semiannual journal of mountaineering and conservation which describes activities outdoors and asks questions of an ecological nature." **They want poetry relating to the outdoors and nature—specifically weather, mountains, rivers, lakes, woods and animals. "No conquerors' odes."** They have recently published poetry by Reg Saner, Warren Woessner, Susan Lier, Mary Oliver and Thomas Reiter. The editor says it is 160 pgs., 6×9, professionally printed with color cover, using photos, graphics and a few ads. They receive about 200 poems a year, use 10-15. Press run is 10,000. Subscription: $10/year. **Sample postpaid: $5. Submit maximum of 6 poems. "We favor shorter poems—maximum of 36 lines usually." No previously published poems or simultaneous submissions. Cover letter required.** Time between acceptance and publication is 1 year. **Seldom comments on rejections. Send SASE for guidelines. Reports in 4-6 weeks. Pays 1 copy. Acquires first rights.** Staff reviews "some" books of poetry in 200-400 words, usually single format. Offers an annual award, The Appalachia Poetry Prize, given since 1972. The editor says, "Our readership is very well versed in the outdoors—mountains, rivers, lakes, animals. We look for poetry that helps readers see the natural world in fresh ways. No generalized accounts of the great outdoors."

APPALACHIAN HERITAGE; DENNY C. PLATTNER AWARDS (IV-Regional), Hutchins Library, Berea College, Berea KY 40404, phone (606)986-9341, ext. 5260, fax (606)986-9494, founded 1973, editor Sidney Saylor Farr, a literary quarterly with Southern Appalachian emphasis. The journal publishes several poems in each issue, and the editor wants to see **"poems about people, places, the human condition, etc., with Southern Appalachian settings. No style restrictions but poems should have a maximum of 14 lines, prefer 8-10 lines." She does not want "blood and gore, hell-fire and damnation, or biased poetry about race or religion."** She has recently published poetry by Jim Wayne Miller, James Still, George Ella Lyon and Robert Morgan. The flat-spined magazine is 6×9, professionally printed on white stock with b&w line drawings and photos, glossy white card cover with 4-color illustration. Issues we have scanned tended toward lyric free verse, emphasizing nature or situations set in nature, but the editor says they will use good poems of any subject and form. **Sample copy: $6.**

Contributors should type poems one to a page. Simultaneous submissions OK. Requires cover letter giving information about previous publications where poets have appeared. Publishes theme issues occasionally. Mss are reported on in 2-4 weeks. Sometimes sends prepublication galleys. Pays 3 copies. Acquires first rights. Reviews books of poetry. Open to unsolicited reviews. Poets may also send books for review consideration. The Denny C. Plattner Awards go to the authors of the best poetry, article or essay, or short fiction published in the four issues released within the preceding year. The award amount in each category is $200.

APPLEZABA PRESS (III), P.O. Box 4134, Long Beach CA 90804, founded 1977, poetry editor D.H. Lloyd, is "dedicated to publishing modern poetry and distributing to the national market." They publish both chapbooks and flat-spined collections of individual poets and occasional anthologies, about 3 titles/year. **"As a rule we like 'accessible' poetry, some experimental. We do not want to see traditional."** They have published poetry by Leo Mailman, Gerald Locklin, John Yamrus, Toby Lurie and Nichola Manning. These sample lines are from Lyn Lifshin's "Kent State 1970":

The ROTC building
still smoking
the Guard moved in, feet on the
grass. By
Monday just
after noon sirens Blood sinking into warm
ground. Parents picking up phones
that burned
their hands

The books are digest-sized, flat-spined paperbacks with glossy covers, sometimes with cartoon art, attractively printed. **No query. Submit book ms with brief cover letter mentioning other publications and bio. Simultaneous submissions OK. Reports in 3 months. Always sends prepublication galleys. Pays 6-12% royalties and 10 author's copies. Buys all rights, does not return them. Send SASE for catalog to order samples.**

APROPOS (I, IV-Subscribers), RD 4, Ashley Manor, Easton PA 18042, founded 1989, editor Ashley C. Anders, appears 6 times/year, and **publishes all poetry submitted by subscribers (subscription: $25/year) except that judged by the editor to be pornographic or in poor taste. Maximum length 40 lines – 50 characters/line.** As a sample, the editor selected her own "Simple Poem":

If I can write a simple poem
that makes somebody smile,
or wipes away a teardrop,
then my poem will be worthwhile.

It need not win a trophy,
for that would not mean as much,
as knowing that my simple poem
and someone's heart will touch.

It is digest-sized, 80 pgs., plastic ring bound, with heavy stock cover, desktop-published. **Sample postpaid: $3. Simultaneous submissions and previously published poems OK. Publishes theme issues. Send SASE for guidelines and upcoming themes. A Holiday Issue is planned for December 1994 and a Love Poem Issue for February 1995. Each issue awards prizes of $50, $25 and $10. All poems are judged by subscribers.** Special contests for subscribers are also offered throughout the year at no additional fee. Prizes are $25, $10 and $5.

AQUARIUS (II), Room A, Flat 10, 116 Sutherland Ave., Maida-Vale, London W9 England, poetry editor Eddie Linden, is a literary biannual publishing quality poetry. The latest issue (19/20), guest edited by Hilary Davies, contains poetry, fictional prose, essays, interviews and reviews. Single copy: $10. Subscription in US: $50. **Payment is by arrangement.**

ARARAT (IV-Ethnic), Dept. PM, 585 Saddle River Rd., Saddle Brook NJ 07662, phone (201)797-7600, editor-in-chief Leo Hamalian, is a quarterly magazine **emphasizing Armenian life and culture for Americans of Armenian descent and Armenian immigrants. They want any verse that is Armenian in theme. They do not want to see traditional, sentimental love poetry.** Their circulation is 2,400. **Sample copy: $7 plus 4 first-class stamps. Previously published submissions OK. Submit seasonal/holiday material at least 3 months in advance.** Publishes ms an average of 1 year after acceptance.

Reports in 6 weeks. Buys 6 poems/issue. Pays $10. Buys first North American serial rights and second (reprint) rights to material originally published elsewhere.

Who's Afraid of Erin Mouré? [1]
Autumn 1993 $5.00

[1] The cat howls.
The dessert on the table (compote de poires) howls.

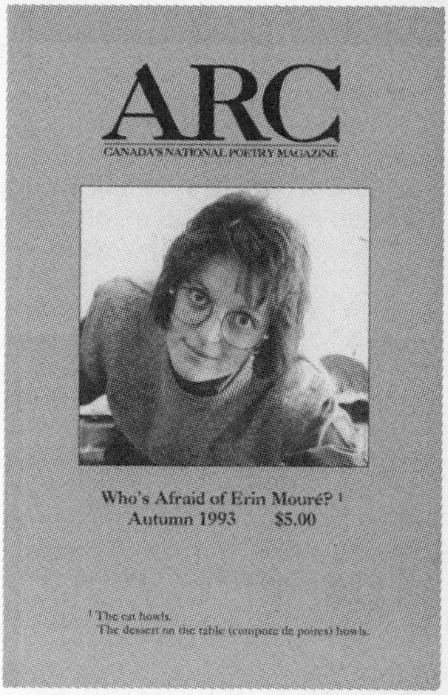

"The sole focus of our publication is poetry," says Nadine McInnis, co-editor of Arc, Ottawa, Ontario's national literary magazine. "And since our debut in 1978, we have consistently offered a quality selection of poetry, poetry-related reviews, criticism and interviews." The biannual publication often includes special features on individual poets. On the cover of this issue is a photograph of featured poet Erin Mouré, an award-winning poet from Montreal. The photograph was taken by the poet herself. "The photo is striking, funny, audacious, just like the featured poet's work," McInnis says. "Our taste is eclectic and we try to represent the poet's aesthetic visually. This makes for a wide range of approaches on the cover." Cover design: Marie Tappin.

ARC; CONFEDERATION POETS PRIZE (II), P.O. Box 7368, Ottawa, Ontario K1L 8E4 Canada, founded 1978, co-editors Nadine McInnis and John Barton, is a biannual of poetry, poetry-related articles, interviews and book reviews. **"Our tastes are eclectic. Our focus is Canadian, but we also publish writers from elsewhere."** They have published poetry by Anne Szumigalski, Heather Spears, Robert Preist and Erin Mouré. *Arc* is 80-88 pgs., perfect-bound, with laminated 2-color cover, artwork and ads. They receive about 400 submissions a year, accept 40-50 poems. Press run is 580 for 200 subscribers of which 30 are libraries, 100 shelf sales. Single copy: $6 Canadian/US; subscription: $18 Canadian/US. **Cost of sample varies. No previously published poems or simultaneous submissions. Cover letter required. Submit 5-8 poems, single spaced, with name and address on each page. Send SASE for guidelines. Reports in 3-6 months. Pays $25 Canadian/page plus 2 copies. Buys first North American serial rights.** "We do not accept unsolicited book reviews." The Confederation Poets Prize is an annual award of $100 for the best poem published in *Arc*.

ARGONAUT (IV-Science fiction/fantasy), P.O. Box 4201, Austin TX 78765, founded 1972, editor/publisher Michael Ambrose, is a **"semiannual magazine anthology of science fiction and weird fantasy, illustrated." They want "speculative, weird, fantastic poetry with vivid imagery or theme, up to 30 lines. Prefer traditional forms. Nothing ultramodernistic, non-fantastic."** They have published poetry by John Grey, David Lunde, Robert R. Medcalf, Jr. and Joey Froehlich. The editor describes it as 64 pgs., digest-sized, typeset. They accept 5-8 of 100-200 poems received. Press run is 750 for 50 subscribers of which 3 are libraries. Subscription: $8. **Sample postpaid: $4.95. Submit no more than 5 poems at a time. Editor comments on submissions "occasionally." Send SASE for guidelines. Reports in 1-2 months. Sometimes sends prepublication galleys. Pays 1 copy.** The editor says, "Too much of what I see is limited in scope or language, and inappropriate for the themes of *Argonaut*. Poets should know what the particular market to which they submit is looking for and not simply shotgun their submissions."

ARIEL, A REVIEW OF INTERNATIONAL ENGLISH LITERATURE (III), English Dept., University of Calgary, Calgary, Alberta T2N 1N4 Canada, phone (403)220-4657, founded 1970, is a "critical, scholarly quarterly with about 5-8 pgs. of poetry in each issue." Though subject matter is open, editors here seem to prefer mostly lyric free verse with attention to form — line, stanza and voice. As a sample here are lines from "Ecstasy!" by Fritz Hamilton:

> *being the*
> *Jackson Pollock of*
> *poetry I*
>
> *dance over the paper in*

the street with
my pen poised to

pour my words of
poetry onto
the world . . .

Ariel is 100 pgs., digest-sized, professionally printed, flat-spined, digest-sized, with glossy card cover. They receive about 300 submissions of poetry/year, use 20-30. Circulation 850, almost all subscriptions of which 650 are libraries. Subscription: $25 institutions; $17 individuals. **Sample postpaid: $6. Prefers 4-8 poems. No long poems. No simultaneous submissions. Cover letter required. Pays 10 offprints plus 1 copy. Editor comments on rejections, "only occasionally and not by request." Canadian postage (or IRCs) required with SAE for return of submissions.**

ARJUNA LIBRARY PRESS; JOURNAL OF REGIONAL CRITICISM (I, II), Space 18, 1025 Garner St. D, Colorado Springs CO 80905, library founded 1963, press founded 1979, editor Joseph A. Uphoff, Jr. "The Arjuna Library Press is avant-garde, designed to endure the transient quarters and marginal funding of the literary phenomenon (as a tradition) while presenting a context for the development of current mathematical ideas in regard to theories of art, literature and performance; photocopy printing allows for very limited editions and irregular format. Quality is maintained as an artistic materialist practice." He wants to see **"surrealist prose poetry, dreamlike, short and long works, not obscene, profane (will criticize but not publish), unpolished work."** He is currently publishing work by Wain Ewing and Victor Pearn. As a sample the editor selected these lines from "Hopeful Romantic" by John Hulse:

he used to
put fresh
pillowcases
on a large
bible
inside his
closet
hoping that
when he
used them
heaven
would bless
his dreams

JRC is published on loose photocopied pages of collage, writing and criticism, appearing frequently in a varied format. Press run: 1 copy each. **Pays "notification." Previously published poems and simultaneous submissions OK. Cover letter preferred; include "biography, intent, discourse (theories, ethics, history). I like ingenuity, legibility, convenience, polish. I expect some sympathy for mathematical, logical and philosophical exposition and criticism. These arguments remain our central ambition."** Reviews books of poetry "occasionally." Open to unsolicited reviews. Poets may also send books for review consideration. "Upon request will treat material as submitted for reprint, one-time rights." Arjuna Library Press publishes 6-12 chapbooks/year, averaging 50 pgs. **To submit to the press, send complete ms, cover letter including bio, publications, "any information the author feels is of value." The press pays royalties "by agreement, if we ever make a profit" and copies. Send $1 for sample.** The editor says, "At a point where the writer has achieved a level of attainment the disparagement of detractors will convince competitors that success is very easy. However, it is too late to defeat the victorious author in regard to the realization of a cherished dream; it will be impossibly difficult to surpass a full scale career from a lax beginning. One should practice every day not to fight or argue but simply to entertain an audience."

THE ARK (V), Dept. PM, 35 Highland Ave., Cambridge MA 02139, phone (617)547-0852, founded 1970 (as BLEB), poetry editor Geoffrey Gardner, publishes books of poetry. **"We are unable to take on new projects at this time."** They have published poetry by David Budbill, John Haines, Joseph Bruchac, Elsa Gidlow, W.S. Merwin, Eliot Weinberger, Kathy Acker, George Woodcock, Kathleen Raine, Marge Piercy and Linda Hogan. The editor selected these lines by Kenneth Rexroth (a translation from the Sanskrit) as a sample:

You think this is a time of Shiva's waking
You are wrong
You are Shiva
But you dream

THE UNIVERSITY OF ARKANSAS PRESS (III); ARKANSAS POETRY AWARD (I, II), 201 Ozark, Fayetteville AR 72701, founded 1980, acquisitions editor Scot Danforth, publishes flat-spined paperbacks and hardback collections of individual poets. Miller Williams, director of the press, says, **"We are not interested in poetry that is obscure or private or self-consciously erudite."** They have published poetry by Frank Stanford, Henri Coulette, Enid Shomer and John Ciardi. As a sample, here is a stanza from "Joy" by William Dickey:

Now I am driving in my small car up the Coast Highway.
The motor is regular, the headlights are dipped and raised
to accommodate other travellers. I am warm and alone
between the dark vigorous sea and the dark mountains.
This is contentment, surely, but it is not joy.

That's from his book **In The Dreaming**, digest-sized, 106 pgs., flat-spined, elegantly printed on eggshell stock with matte 2-color card cover. **Query with 5-10 sample poems. Replies to queries in 2 weeks, to submissions in 2-4 weeks. No replies without SASE. Ms should be double-spaced with 1½" margins. Disks compatible with IBM welcome. Always sends prepublication galleys. Offers 10% royalty contract plus 10 author's copies. Send SASE for catalog to buy samples.** First-book mss are not considered except as submissions for the Arkansas Poetry Award. The Arkansas Poetry Award competition is open to any original ms by a living American poet whose work has not been previously published or accepted for publication in book form. Chapbooks, self-published books, and books produced with the author's subsidy are not considered previously published books. No translations. Submit 50-80 pgs., not more than one poem/page, counting title page in page count. An acknowledgments page listing poems previously published should accompany ms. Author's name should appear on the title page only. $15 reading fee. Postmark no later than May 1. Publication the following spring. A $500 cash advance is part of the award.

ARNAZELLA (II), Bellevue Community College, 3000 Landerholm Circle SE, Bellevue WA 98007-6484, phone (206)641-2373, established 1979, advisor Laura Burns-Lewis, is a literary annual, published in spring, using **well-crafted poetry, no "jingles or greeting card" poetry**. They have published poetry by William Stafford, Judith Skillman and Colleen McElroy. The editor describes this student publication (which uses work from off campus) as 75 pgs., 6×8, offset, using photos and drawings. **They are currently accepting submissions only from poets in Washington, Oregon, Idaho, Alaska and British Columbia.** Of 150-200 poems received/year they use about 30. Press run is 500 for 3 subscriptions, one of which is a library. **Sample postpaid: $5. Submit up to 3 poems. Deadline is usually at beginning of February. Send SASE for guidelines. Reports in 1-4 months. Pays 1 copy.**

‡ARROWSMITH (I, II), P.O. Box 2148, Bellaire TX 77402, founded 1993, editor Keddy Ann Outlaw, is a biannual publication of poetry, short short fiction, b&w photos and collages. **"All styles of poetry considered, as long as well crafted. Length no more than 2 pages per poem. No greeting card doggerel, clichéd statements of self pity, obtuse odes, preachy polemics or Sunday school verse."** They have recently published poetry by Lorenzo Thomas, Chris Woods, F. Dianne Harris, Albert Huffstickler and Carolyn Davis. As a sample the editor selected these lines from "Sleeper's Frost" by R.T. Castleberry:

I have been happiest when day ends,
Darkness closes.
There is something in that mist,
The shadow beneath tree and eave
That both mellows and burns—,
Moves pen to paper, . . .

Arrowsmith is 36-44 pgs., digest-sized, laser printed and saddle-stapled. They currently accept about 1 out of 100 poems received. Press run is 350 for 50 subscribers. Subscription: $8. **Sample postpaid: $4. Submit up to 5 poems at a time. Previously published poems OK by invitation only. Simultaneous submissions OK, if indicated. Cover letter with brief bio preferred.** "Indicate if a yes-or-no reply is sufficient in lieu of poems being returned. **May comment on strong points of poems that almost made it, if time allows." Send SASE for guidelines. Reports in 2-8 weeks. Pays 1 copy. Acquires first-time rights only.** The editor says, "When a poem is finished, sharp and true, it is ready to fly, to pierce its readers with all its singleness, authenticity and intensity. ***Arrowsmith*** is the place such ammunition is gathered, a literary quiver let loose on the world."

‡ARSENAL PULP PRESS (V), 100-1062 Homer St., Vancouver, British Columbia V6B 2W9 Canada, founded 1980, publishes 1 paperback book of poetry/year. They only publish the work of Canadian poets and are **currently not accepting any unsolicited mss.**

ART TIMES: A LITERARY JOURNAL AND RESOURCE FOR ALL THE ARTS (II), P.O. Box 730, Mount Marion NY 12456-0730, phone (914)246-6944, editor Raymond J. Steiner, is a monthly tabloid newspaper devoted to the arts that publishes some poetry and fiction. The editor wants to see **"traditional**

and contemporary poetry no longer than 20 lines but with high literary quality." He does not want to see "poorly written, pointless prose in stanza format." He has published poetry by Helen Wolfert and Anne Mins. ***Art Times*** focuses on cultural and creative articles and essays. The paper is 16-24 pgs., newsprint, with reproductions of artwork, some photos, advertisement-supported. Circulation is 15,000, of which 5,000 are by request and subscriptions; most distribution is free through galleries, theatres, etc. They receive 700-1,000 poems/month, use only 40-50 a year. Subscription: $15/year. **Sample: $1 postage cost. Simultaneous submissions OK. Criticism of mss is provided "at times but rarely." They have a 2-year backlog. Guidelines available for SASE. Reports in 6 months. Pays 6 copies plus 1-year subscription.**

ART-CORE! (I, IV-Themes); APEX (I, IV-Erotica), P.O. Box 49324, Austin TX 78765, founded 1988, publisher/editor Patty Puke, is published 3 times/year **using poems of "one page or less, alternative, underground, off-beat, avant-garde, uncensored—typed or visual layout. No mainstream or lengthy poems."** The editor describes ***Art-Core!*** as 24 pgs., magazine-sized, offset. Press run is 400 for 150 subscribers. They accept about 50 of 300 poems submitted/year. Subscription: $10. **Sample postpaid: $4. Cover letter required with submissions. Publishes theme issues. Themes are comix, flesh art and others. Send SASE for guidelines, upcoming themes and product list. Responds within 3 months. Sometimes sends prepublication galleys. Pays 1 copy.** The editor adds, "We are happy to announce ***APEX***, a poetry publication sponsored by Art-Core and Electric Lord Productions. Our premier issue was a book of erotic poetry. Publication is planned annually. We are searching for a select group of poets and artists to participate. Interested parties should submit a short sample of their work and SASE." **Sample postpaid: $5.** The editor says: "Caution! Everything we print is uncensored. We support anarchy in art. We advise contributors to view a sample copy before submitting. **You must include age statement to participate."**

ARTFUL DODGE (II, IV-Translations), Dept. of English, College of Wooster, Wooster OH 44691, founded 1979, poetry editor Daniel Bourne, is an annual literary magazine that "takes a strong interest in poets who are continually testing what they can get away with successfully in regard to subject, perspective, language, etc., but who also show mastery of current American poetic techniques—its varied textures and its achievement in the illumination of the particular. What all this boils down to is that we require high craftsmanship as well as a vision that goes beyond *one's own* storm windows, grandmothers or sexual fantasies—to paraphrase Hayden Carruth. **Poems can be on any subject, of any length, from any perspective, in any voice, but we don't want anything that does not connect with both the human and the aesthetic. Thus, we don't want cute, rococo surrealism, someone's warmed-up, left-over notion of an avant-garde that existed 10-100 years ago, or any last bastions of rhymed verse in the civilized world.** On the other hand, we are interested in poems that utilize stylistic persuasions both old and new to good effect. We are not afraid of poems which try to deal with large social, political, historical, and even philosophical questions—especially if the poem emerges from one's own life experience and is not the result of armchair pontificating. We often offer encouragement to writers whose work we find promising, but ***Artful Dodge* is more a journal for the already emerging writer than for the beginner looking for an easy place to publish. We also have a sustained commitment to translation, especially from Polish and other East European literatures,** and we feel the interchange between the American and foreign works on our pages is of great interest to our readers. We also feature interviews with such outstanding literary figures as Jorge Luis Borges, W.S. Merwin, Nathalie Sarraute, Stanislaw Baranczak, Omar Pound, Gwendolyn Brooks, John Giorno, William Least Heat-Moon, Cynthia Macdonald, Tim O'Brien, Lee Smith and William Matthews. Recent and forthcoming poets include Naomi Shihab Nye, Charles Simic, Denise Duhamel, Walter McDonald, Lola Haskins, Ron Wallace, Alberta Turner, David Ignatow, Jim Daniels, Peter Wild, William Stafford, Karl Krolow (German), Tomasz Jastrun (Polish), Jorge Luis Borges (Spanish), Mahmud Darwish (Palestinian) and Tibor Zalan (Hungarian)." The digest-sized, perfect-bound format is professionally printed, glossy cover, with art, ads. There are about 60-80 pgs. of poetry in each issue. They receive at least 2,000 poems/year, use 60, and the backlog is 1-12 months between acceptance and publication. Press run is 1,000 for 100 subscribers of which 30 are libraries. **Sample: $5 for recent issues, $3 for others. "No simultaneous submissions. Please limit submissions to 6 poems. Long poems may be of any length, but send only one at a time. We encourage translations, but we ask as well for original text and statement from translator that he/she has copyright clearance and permission of author." Reports in up to 5 months. Pays 2 copies, plus, currently, $5/page honorarium because of grants from Ohio Arts Council.** Open to unsolicited reviews; "query first." Poets may also send books for review consideration; however, "there is no guarantee we can review them!" ***Artful Dodge*** received an Ohioana Library Association Book Award for Editorial Excellence in 1992.

ARTS END BOOKS; NOSTOC MAGAZINE (II), P.O. Box 162, Newton MA 02168, founded 1978, poetry editor Marshall Brooks. **"We publish good contemporary writing. Our interests are broad and so are our tastes.** People considering sending work to us should examine a copy of our magazine and/or our catalog; check your library for the former, send us a SASE for the latter." Their publications are distinguished by excellent presswork and art in a variety of formats: postcard series, posters, pamphlets, flat-spined paperbacks and hardbacks. The magazine appears irregularly in print runs of 300-500, about 30 pgs. of poetry in each, 100 subscriptions of which half are libraries. **Sample postpaid: $4.** They receive a few hundred submissions/year, use 25-30. They offer **"modest payment plus contributor's copies. A cover letter is a very good idea for any kind of submission;** we receive *very* few good, intelligent cover letters. What to include? That's up to the writer, whatever he/she feels important in terms of the work, in terms of establishing a meeting." **Discourages simultaneous submissions. Frequently comments on rejected mss. Tries to report within a few weeks. Always sends prepublication galleys.** Reviews books of poetry "on occasion, length varies." Brooks says, "We try to respond warmly to writers interested in making genuine contact with us and our audience."

ARUNDEL PRESS; MERCER & AITCHISON (V), 8380 Beverly Blvd., Los Angeles CA 90048, phone (213)852-9852, founded 1984, managing editor Phillip Bevis. Arundel Press "publishes only major texts (as we see them) in limited editions printed letterpress. **We no longer consider unsolicited manuscripts.** Most work is illustrated with original graphics. Mercer & Aitchison publishes definitive editions of major (as we see them) works of poetry, literature and literary criticism." They publish about 3 hardbacks/year. Phillip Bevis recommends to beginning poets the Mercer & Aitchison publication, Clayton Eshleman's **Novices: A Study of Poetic Apprenticeship** (paperback, $12.95). He says, "The only thing worth adding to what is said there is that there are only a handful of poets in America (at the most) making a living *as* poets. The majority of even the most prominent must teach or work in other fields to support their poetic endeavors. Poetry must be something you do because you want to – not for the money."

ASCENT (II), P.O. Box 967, Urbana IL 61801, founded 1975, editor Audrey Curley, appears 3 times/year, using **poetry that is "eclectic, shorter rather than longer."** They have recently published poetry by Stuart Friebert, G.E. Murray and Nance Van Winckel. As a sample the editor selected these lines from "Reclamation" by Cynthia Bond:

. . . The tractor
dissipates the building, knocks
the keystone of the smoking
stand and singly it falls.
Labor pulls the home from
its mock; we rescue where we live.

The editor describes it as 64 pgs., 6×9, professionally printed with matte card cover. They accept about 5% of 750 poems received/year. Press run is 900 copies for 250 subscribers of which 90 are libraries. Subscription: $6/year. **Sample postpaid: $2. Always sends prepublication galleys. Pays 3 copies.** This continues as one of the "best buys" in the literary world for its low price, openness to all forms and styles, and relatively quick and encouraging response times. The editor says, "I am usually the sole reader. Poems are rejected or accepted from 2-8 weeks, usually closer to 2 weeks. Acceptances are usually published within the year." In 1993, both a short story and a poem appearing in ***Ascent*** received Illinois Arts Council Literary Awards. That year the same short story received the Daniel Curley Award for Recent Illinois Short Fiction, an award made possible by Audrey Curley and her family to honor the legacy of Daniel Curley, late writer and ***Ascent*** editor. Poetry published here has also been included in **The Best American Poetry 1994.**

THE ASHLAND POETRY PRESS (V, IV-Anthologies, themes), Ashland University, Ashland OH 44805, founded 1969, editor Robert McGovern, publishes anthologies on specific themes and occasional collections. He has published collections by Harold Witt, Alberta Turner and Richard Snyder. As a sample he selected lines from "Jacqueline Du Pré" by Leonard Trawick:

Jacqueline du Pré, when your muscles came untuned,
wasn't the music still there, all those silent years— —
just as, after the last note, when players poise their bows
triumphant for one still moment before the applause,
the whole quartet hangs perfect in the air?

That poem appears in **80 on the 80's: A Decade's History in Verse** edited by Robert McGovern and Joan Baranow. "Watch publications such as ***Poets & Writers*** **for calls for mss, but don't submit otherwise. We do not read unsolicited mss; anthology readings take quite a bit of time." Considers simultaneous submissions. On collections, poet gets 10% royalty; anthologies, poets are paid stipulated price when sufficient copies are sold. Write for book and price list.**

‡ASIAN PACIFIC AMERICAN JOURNAL; ASIAN AMERICAN WRITERS' WORKSHOP (I, IV-Ethnic/nationality, themes), Suite 2R, 296 Elizabeth St., New York NY 10012, phone and fax (212)228-6718, founded 1992. The ***APA Journal*** is a biannual published by the AAWW, a not-for-profit organization. It is **"dedicated to the best of contemporary Asian-American writing."** They have recently published poetry by Amy Uyematsu and R. Zamora Linmark. As a sample the editor selected these lines from "Sound among Sounds" by Koon Woon:

And so because the leaves flutter, we know wind from their gaps.
While the thought of wind is tame, yet by it,
One room inflates, another deflates; one world inflates, another deflates.

APA Journal is 130-160 pgs., digest-sized, typeset and perfect-bound with 2-color cover and ads. They receive submissions from about 80 poets/year, accept about 30%. Press run is 1,500 for 50 subscribers of which 5 are libraries, 800 shelf sales. Single copy: $10; subscription: $16. **Sample postpaid: $12. Submit 4-6 poems at a time. Previously published poems and simultaneous submissions OK. Cover letter with phone and fax numbers and 1- to 4-sentence biographical statement required. Submissions on 3.5 Macintosh disk (or IBM, if necessary) welcome. Deadlines are usually May 15 and December 15 for October 1 and April 1 issues, respectively. Often comments on rejections. "We will work with authors who are promising." Send SASE for guidelines and upcoming themes. Reports in 3 months. Pays 2 copies. Acquires one-time rights.** The AAWW offers creative writing workshops, a newsletter, a bookselling service, readings and fellowships to young Asian-American writers. Write for details.

‡ASKING THE QUESTION (IV-Social issues), P.O. Box D-96356-IN36U, San Quentin CA 94974, founded 1994, editors Paul Truttman and Marjorie Talarico, appears twice a year, in the spring and fall. **They occasionally use poetry but concentrate on "not-more-than" 500-word articles and essays challenging accepted norms pertaining to religion, traditional values and society.** "Analysis should be studious, educated, explorative, objective, or experiential and persuasive, while not offending in its presentation. We seek to promote human evolution not contribute further to its deterioration." The editors say *ATQ* is 8-10 pgs., digest-sized, professionally printed and free, "pending establishment as a literary review." **Prefers original, unpublished material. Submit with SASE to Paul Truttman at the above address. Reports "asap upon receipt." Pays copies.** Marjorie Talarico says, "Paul is in prison and is also interested in networking philosophical discussion through pen friends and/or letters. It is expected that anyone writing for this publication will be open-minded and . . . asking the question!"

ASYLUM (II, IV-Form, translations), P.O. Box 6203, Santa Maria CA 93456, founded 1985, editor Greg Boyd, is "an annual literary anthology with emphasis on short fiction, **the prose poem and poetry. No restrictions on form, subject matter, style or purpose, though we are especially receptive to prose poems, absurdist writing and contemporary modes of surrealism and Dada."** They have published poetry by Thomas Wiloch, Russell Edson, Edouard Roditi and Robert Peters. As a sample, the editor selected these lines from "Twenty Shores" by Cynthia Hendershot:

I dream of a tree with razors
instead of fruit. Every word
that falls from your orange tongue
falls on my palm like a drop of blood.

Asylum is 160-200 pgs., 8½ × 11, perfect-bound, professionally printed with varnished stock cover. They accept about 1% of submissions. Press run is 2,500 for 200 subscriptions of which 20 are libraries. Subscription: $10. **Sample postpaid: $7.95. Put name and address on each page. No simultaneous submissions. Reports in 2 weeks to 6 months. Always sends prepublication galleys. Pays 2 copies. Acquires first North American serial rights.** Regarding reviews of books of poetry, "authors should query before submitting material."

ATHENA INCOGNITO MAGAZINE (I), 1442 Judah St., San Francisco CA 94122, founded 1980, editor Ronn Rosen, is an annual of experimental writing and other arts. They want **poetry that is "experimental, surrealist, Dada, etc. 3 pgs. max. No greeting card verse, overly religious poetry or epics."** They have recently published poetry by Greg Wallace, Michael McClellan and Steven Saxonberg. As a sample the editor selected these lines (poet unidentified):

Arrow strikes
Swims out
Narrow gap lapped up that vulture
Heron heron heron
Of summer brambled.

The editor says the magazine is usually 20-30 photocopied pgs. They receive about 50 poems a year, use approximately 15%. Press run is 200 for 50 subscribers of which 2 are libraries, 50 shelf sales. **"All people submitting poetry *must* buy a sample copy—$5 postpaid." Previously published poems and simultaneous submissions OK. "Name and address required on all pages. SASE also required." Often comments on rejections. Reports in 1-2 months. Pays 1 copy.** The editor says, "Be well read in world poetry, surrealism and Dada, and get inspired."

THE ATLANTEAN PRESS REVIEW; THE ATLANTEAN PRESS (II, IV-Specialized: Romantic poetry, translations), P.O. Box 361116, Milpitas CA 95036, founded 1990, publisher Patricia LeChevalier.

The Atlantean Press was founded to publish Romantic fiction, drama and poetry, beginning with republication of work by Victor Hugo that is out-of-print. ***The Atlantean Press Review***, published quarterly, includes a small amount of poetry as well as fiction, drama and essays. **"We are looking for intelligent, thoughtful, preferably rhyming poems (in traditional forms) that address human values and aspirations."** As a sample the publisher selected these lines from "Icarus" by Moira Russell:

I still refuse to believe that he ever fell: the gold
which ran down his bronze shoulders was gold,
not wax. Why else should it be told
and told again, how he flew, and be told
so often that the story is swallowed in his name,
Icarus and foolish flight the same?

Often comments on rejections. Send SASE for guidelines. Reports in 2 months. Always sends prepublication galleys. Pays up to $2/line plus copies. Buys one-time rights. "We'd be very interested in competent translations of Victor Hugo's poetry."

THE ATLANTIC (II), Dept. PM, 745 Boylston St., Boston MA 02116, phone (617)536-9500, founded 1857, poetry editor Peter Davison, assistant poetry editor Steven Cramer, publishes 1-5 poems monthly. **Some of the most distinguished poetry in American literature** has been published by this magazine, including work by William Matthews, Mary Oliver, Stanley Kunitz, Rodney Jones, May Swenson, Galway Kinnell, Philip Levine, Red Hawk, Tess Gallagher, Donald Hall and W.S. Merwin. The magazine has a circulation of 500,000, of which 5,800 are libraries. They receive some 75,000 poems/year, of which they use 35-40 and have a backlog of 6-12 months. **Sample postpaid: $3. Submit 3-5 poems with SASE. No simultaneous submissions. Publishes theme issues. Always sends prepublication galleys. Pays about $3/line. Buys first North American serial rights only.** Wants "to see poetry of the highest order; we do *not* want to see workshop rejects. **Watch out for workshop uniformity. Beware of the present indicative. Be yourself."** Poetry published here has been included in the 1992 and 1993 volumes of **The Best American Poetry**. In addition, ***The Atlantic*** ranked #9 in the "Poets' Pick" category of the latest ***Writer's Digest*** Poetry 60 list. This category ranks those publications in which poets said they would most like to see their work published.

‡ATOM MIND (II); MOTHER ROAD PUBLICATIONS (V), P.O. Box 22068, Albuquerque NM 87154, first founded 1968-70, reestablished 1992, editor Gregory Smith. ***Atom Mind*** is a quarterly journal of "alternative literature, mostly influenced by the Beats, Steinbeck, John Fante and Bukowski. **Narrative, free verse, 20-80 lines preferred, although length restrictions are not set in stone. No light verse, inspirational poetry, doggerel, 'moon-spoon-June' rhyming verse."** They have recently published poetry by Lawrence Ferlinghetti, Charles Plymell and Wilma Elizabeth McDaniel. As a sample we selected these lines from "good stuff" by Charles Bukowski:

beer from China.
think of it.
this is some a.m.
Caesar and Plato hulk in the
shadows and I love you all
for just a
moment.

The editor says ***AM*** is 100 pgs., 8½ × 11, offset, with illustrations and photographs. They receive approximately 2,000 submissions annually, publish perhaps 5%. Press run is 1,000 for 750 subscribers of which 25 are libraries. Subscription: $16. **Sample postpaid: $5. Prefers to consider submissions of 5-8 poems at a time, rather than 1 or 2 poems. Previously published poems OK; no simultaneous submissions.** Time between acceptance and publication 8-12 months. **"*Atom Mind* is very much a one-man operation; therefore, submissions are subject to the whims and personal biases of the editor only." Often comments on rejections. Send SASE for guidelines. Reports in 2-4 weeks. Pays copies, number varies. Acquires first or one-time rights.** Mother Road Publications also publishes 2 paperback and 2 hardback collections of poetry/year. **"Book-length poetry manuscripts considered by invitation only." Send SASE for catalog.**

ALWAYS include a self-addressed, stamped envelope (SASE) when sending a ms or query to a publisher within your own country. When sending material to other countries, include a self-addressed envelope and International Reply Coupons (IRCs), available for purchase at most post offices.

‡ATTITUDE PROBLEM (I, II), P.O. Box 2354, Prescott AZ 86302, founded 1987, literary editor Jody Cordova, is a "multipurpose nonconformist rag" appearing 3 times/year. "We explore creative alternatives and issues relevant to youth counterculture. Contents range from articles, interviews, music reviews and zine reviews to artwork, poetry and fiction. **We look for poetry that speaks with passion and clarity about the realities of life. We do not want to see indecipherable academic masturbations. No sweetness and light."** As a sample the editor selected these lines from "The Dance of the Blackjacks and the Pricks Who Batter Brains to a Pulp" by JAK:

I had just been pistol whipped seventeen times
about the head and shoulders for
two dollars and a bag of dope
That's what happens when life becomes cheaper than the means
to escape it.

AP is a 16-page, b&w broadsheet including graphics, photos and ads. They receive 300-500 submissions/year, use about 20. Press run is 6,000 for 100 subscribers, 100 shelf sales; 5,000 distributed free. Subscription: $10 for 4 issues. **Sample postpaid: $3. No previously published poems; simultaneous submissions OK.** Time between acceptance and publication is 1-6 months. **Reports in 1-6 months. Pays 2 copies. Acquires one-time rights.** "We do short reviews of other zines"—only using staff-written reviews. The editor says, "We strongly recommend reading our zine before submitting. Advice for beginners: Write from your gut. Be real."

‡THE AVANT-GARDEN (II), P.O. Box 1342, Interlachen FL 32148, phone (904)481-0020, founded 1993, "avant-gardian" James Valvis, is a biannual publication designed "to breathe life into a dying art." **They are open to all forms, lengths, subject matter and styles of poetry, but they do not want to see "rhymed, nonsense, academia."** They have recently published poetry by Shannon Frach, Robert W. Howington, C.F. Roberts, Cheryl Townsend and Lyn Lifshin. As a sample the editor selected these lines by Ron Androla:

ah fuck. who i suppose is the manager comes
in behind the bar with a bagful of zucchini
shakes one like a big, green cock at the amused
barmaid. "in yr dreams!" she yells.

The editor says ***The Avant-Garden*** is 30-40 pgs., 8½×11, side-stapled. They accept about 5% of the poetry received. Press run is 100-250 for 15 subscribers, 50 shelf sales. Single copy: $5; subscription: $10. "It should go without saying: Always make the check out to the editor not to the magazine." **No previously published poems or simultaneous submissions. Cover letter required. Seldom comments on rejections. Reports in 1 week to 2 months. Pays 1 copy. Acquires first-time rights.** Valvis reviews a few chapbooks and other magazines very briefly. Poets may send books for review consideration. He also hopes to begin publishing 1-2 chapbooks/year. The editor adds, "I don't care who you are until you show me that you can write poetry. There are so few left. Let your words be my thoughts."

BABY SUE (I), P.O. Box 1111, Decatur GA 30031-1111, founded 1985, editor/publisher Don W. Seven, appears twice a year publishing politically incorrect humor for the extremely open-minded and not easily offended. **"We are open to all styles, but prefer short poems." No restrictions.** They have recently published poetry by Edward Mycue, Susan Andrews, Stephen Fievet and Barry Bishop. The editor says ***baby sue*** is 20 pgs., offset. "We print prose, poems and cartoons. We usually accept about 5% of what we receive." Single copy: $1.50; subscription: $8 for 4 issues. **Sample postpaid: $2. Previously published poems and simultaneous submissions OK. Deadlines are March 30 and September 30 of each year. Seldom comments on rejections. Reports "immediately, if we are interested." Pays 1 copy.** "We do occasionally review other magazines." The editor adds, "We have received no awards, but we are very popular on the underground press circuit and sell our magazine all over the world."

THE BACON PRESS (V), #2, 4228 Rt. 212, Lake Hill NY 12448, founded 1990, editor T.S. Paul, is a "sporadic" journal of poetry and art, usually appearing 2-3 times/year. **Due to "overwhelming response," they are *not* accepting unsolicited mss at this time.** They have published poetry by Mikhail Horowitz and N. Hartigan. As a sample the editor selected these lines from his own poem, "Building The House":

Her old lovers stir in their beds
Like iron filings
They will shift and gather in moonlight
To stalk this dream of building
Stalk it with beams and sweat and money
While she sleeps.

The Bacon Press is 16 pgs., 5½×8½, saddle-stapled with occasional graphics/b&w art. They receive 1,000 poems a year, accept approximately 24. Press run is 100 for shelf sales in local bookstores. **Sample postpaid: $2.** The editor says, "I find the current 'scene' to be very uplifting for poets. I would encourage beginners to read in public as often as possible, and submit as widely as possible."

BAD ATTITUDE (I, IV-Lesbian, erotica), P.O. Box 390110, Cambridge MA 02139, founded 1984, contact Jasmine Sterling, is a lesbian sex magazine appearing 4-6 times/year. They want **"lesbian erotic poetry."** Press run is 5,000. Subscription: $30/year. **Sample postpaid: $6. No previously published poems; simultaneous submissions OK. Cover letter required. Seldom comments on rejections. Reports "immediately." Pays 2 copies.** Reviews books of poetry. Open to unsolicited reviews. Poets may also send books for review consideration.

BAD HAIRCUT (II, IV-Social issues), P.O. Box 2827, Olympia WA 98507, founded 1987, poetry editors Kimberlea and Ray Goforth, is a "small press magazine with world-wide distribution. Publication schedule varies. **Progressive politics, human rights and environmental themes. Free verse is preferred. Don't want to see anything by bad poets in *love*.**" They have published poetry by M.C. Alpher and T.L. Toma. As a sample the editors selected these lines by Richard Curtis:

on a dark road my friend and I
spoke thoughts and things,
He felt that life is a balancing. . . .
That the universal leger balances.
And I thought of ghettos and death camps
. . . of plague and cribdeath.
And I voiced not a word of my views of the world—
There being disillusion enough, as it is.

Their object is "to inform and inspire others to work for a better world in their own individual ways." ***Bad Haircut*** is digest-sized, using some art and ads. Of thousands of poems received each year, they say, they use 25. Press run is 1,000 for 300 subscribers (3 libraries), and it is carried by 4 stores. Subscription: $14. **Sample postpaid: $4. No simultaneous submissions. Previously published poetry OK. Cover letter—including "what people do in their lives, why they wrote to us, etc."—required. Rejections in 1 day; acceptances can take up to 6 months. Editors comment on rejections "always—as poets ourselves, we learned to hate form rejections." Publishes theme issues. Send SASE for guidelines and upcoming themes. Sometimes sends prepublication issues. Pays 1 copy. Acquires first North American serial rights.** Open to unsolicited reviews. Poets may also send books for review consideration. They also publish a line of poetry postcards.

THE BAD HENRY REVIEW; 44 Press (III), Box 831, Hudson NY 12534, founded 1981, poetry editors Evelyn Horowitz, Michael Malinowitz and Mary du Passage. They have published poetry by John Ashbery, Gilbert Sorrentino, Stephen Sandy and William Matthews. ***The Bad Henry Review*** is an annual publishing quality poetry and is 64 pgs., digest-sized. Press run is 500-1,000 for 200 subscriptions of which 15 are for libraries; 200-300 for shelf sales. Single copy: $6; subscription: $12/2 issues. **Sample: $5. Submit no more than 5 poems with SASE. No simultaneous submissions. No previously published poems unless advised. Rarely comments on rejected mss. Publishes theme issues. Pays 1 copy with half price discount for contributors.** The editor comments, "We've done one issue of long poems and we are doing an issue on photography in 1995."

BAGMAN PRESS (I), P.O. Box 81166, Chicago IL 60681-0166, founded 1989, publisher Bill Falloon, publishes 1 paperback/year—**"emphasis is on 'new' writers who can create powerful first impressions."** They have published poetry by J.J. Tindall and fiction by award-winning novelist Stephen Dueweke. **Submit complete ms with SASE. Previously published poems OK; no simultaneous submissions. Cover letter required. Seldom comments on rejections. Replies to queries in 2 weeks, to submitted mss in 6 months or less. Pays 5-10% royalties and 30 author's copies.** "Inland Book Co. and Small Press Distribution are our primary distributors." The editor says this is "an alternative press that would publish a fish, so long as he or she writes well. We try to read everything with an open mind."

BAKER STREET PUBLICATIONS; FULL MOON PUBLICATIONS; THE HAUNTED JOURNAL; BAKER STREET GAZETTE; HORIZONS BEYOND; MIXED BAG; PEN & INK; REALM OF DARKNESS; REALM OF THE VAMPIRE; THE SALEM JOURNAL; SLEUTH JOURNAL; HOLLYWOOD NOSTALGIA; JACK THE RIPPER GAZETTE; SOUTHWEST JOURNAL; WESTERN SKIES (I, IV-Horror, science fiction, fantasy, mystery, western, writing, themes), P.O. Box 517, Metairie LA 70004-0517, phone (504)733-9138, founded 1983, poetry editors Sharida Rizzuto, Frances Nordan and Ann Hoyt. All of these magazines, chapbooks, perfect-bound paperbacks, and newsletters use poetry. **"No strict requirements on form, length or style. Must be suitable for horror, mystery, science fiction, fantasy, movie nostalgia, western or literary."** They have recently published poetry by Kim Elizabeth, John Youril, Mary Winters, Lyn Lifshin and Richard David Behrens. As a sample the editors selected the poem "On the Canvas of the Night" by Leilah Wendell:

Between the towering obelisks

lies a land of shade and acolytes,
where twilight bleeds in amethyst
and lampshade glows with cool, blue lights.

The editor says, "Most zines are 40-100 pgs., magazine-sized or digest-sized; chapbooks and paperbacks vary. All publications include artwork and graphics inside and on covers. All have ads in the back. Their press runs average 1,000 for each magazine. **Send SASE for guidelines. Sample copies are $4-7.90. Submissions are "preferably typewritten. Author should include a bio sheet." Simultaneous submissions OK, as are previously published poems that are "very good and haven't been published in over 2 years."** Time between acceptance and publication is 2-4 months. **Reports in 2-6 weeks. Pays "mainly in copies but fees negotiable." For book publications send 3-5 sample poems, bio and publication credits. Simultaneous submissions OK. Responds to queries in 2-6 weeks, to mss in 1-2 months. Pays 50% royalties after costs are covered and 10-15 copies. Publishes 4-6 chapbooks/year. Same submission requirements as for other publications.** Sharida Rizzuto advises, "Just be yourself; don't try to imitate anyone else. Respect helpful criticism."

BAKUNIN (II), P.O. Box 1853, Simi Valley CA 93062-1853, founded 1990, editor Jordan Jones, is an annual publication. **"We are looking for poems that challenge accepted pieties and norms. We are also interested in powerful personal poems."** They want **"avant-garde and mainstream poetry of humor, pathos and social comment. No trite or hackneyed verse; no poem that uses but does not earn the word love."** They have published poetry by Sandra McPherson, Dennis Schmitz, Benjamin Saltman and William Stafford. As a sample the editor selected the opening lines of "The Aqueduct" by Dorianne Laux:

We played there on hot L.A. summers, kids poking through
the slick algae and bloated tires, the delicate rafts
of mosquito eggs. Open boxcars pulled gray squares
of sky overhead as we took apples and crackers
from our pockets and ate, watched the cursing workers
from the can factory gathering at the silver lunch truck

Bakunin is 200 pgs., 6×9, offset on acid-free recycled paper, perfect-bound, with laminated cover, b&w artwork and some ads. They receive about 500 submissions a year, publish approximately 5%. The free verse is mostly lyric, and the poems tend to be one-page. Press run is 1,000 for 100 subscribers, 450 shelf sales. Subscription: $8, $10 for institutions. **Sample postpaid: $5. No previously published poems; simultaneous submissions OK, "if the author indicates they are such." Cover letter required.** Time between acceptance and publication is 6-12 months. **Seldom comments on rejections. Send SASE for guidelines. Reports in 2 weeks to 3 months. Pays 2 copies. Acquires first North American serial rights.** "We publish 250- to 750-word reviews of single books, magazines or whole presses." The editor says, "***Bakunin*** is a magazine for the dead Russian anarchist in all of us."

‡BANGTALE INTERNATIONAL (II), P.O. Box 83984, Phoenix AZ 85071-3984, founded 1989, editor William Dudley, appears twice a year. **They want "contemporary poetry of any form and subject, quality in language & imagery, unique presentation & style – Experimental High Energy/Beat Culture/Avant-Garde Poetry."** They have recently published poetry by B.Z. Niditch, Rod Farmer, Lyn Lifshin and John M. Bennett. As a sample the editor selected this complete poem, "Unheard Lights," by Timothy Hadar:

Moths of stars
Eat their way
Into black wool.
They nibble on darkness,
Leaving a hole big enough
For the dawn to crawl through.

Bangtale is 44 pgs., digest-sized, offset and saddle-stapled, glossy card cover with b&w art. Press run is 500. Subscription: $8. **Sample: $4. Sometimes sends prepublication galleys. Pays 1 copy.** The editor says, "We would like to see some humorous poetry and also any b&w artwork."

THE BANK STREET PRESS; THE PORT AUTHORITY POETRY REVIEW (V), 24 Bank St., New York NY 10014, phone (212)255-0692, founded 1985, poetry editor Mary Bertschmann. A small group of poets meet at the Bank Street home of Mary Bertschmann and publish their poetry annually in a series of flat-spined paperbacks called ***The Port Authority Poetry Review***. **Sample: $7 including postage and handling.** The Bank Street Press also publishes solo collections of poetry. They have published **Goslings on the Tundra** ($20 including postage and handling) and **52 Sonnets** ($12 including postage and handling), both limited, fine print volumes by Mary York Sampson. Their most recent title is **The Golden Falcon**, a make-believe story for children of all ages, set at the time of King Arthur. Also written by Mary York Sampson, with illustrations by Harry Bertschmann, the book has 48 cantos and

112 pages ($22.50, including postage and handling). As a sample the editor selected these lines:

As they ascended, the moon bathed them in pale, milky light,
Then the boy and the hippogriff plunged into the night.
The land rushed away beneath them for many an hour,
They strode that vault of heaven and tasted of its power.
The snorting of the beast and the wind against its wings
Made a mighty music like a universe that sings.

BANTAM DOUBLEDAY DELL PUBLISHING GROUP (V), 1540 Broadway, New York NY 10036, phone (212)354-6500, **accepts mss only from agents.**

BAPTIST SUNDAY SCHOOL BOARD; CHRISTIAN SINGLE (IV-Religious, themes); HOME LIFE (IV-Religious); MATURE LIVING (IV-Religious, senior citizen), 127 Ninth Ave. N., Nashville TN 37234, the publishing agency for Southern Baptists. "We publish magazines, monthlies, quarterlies, books, filmstrips, films, church supplies, etc., for Southern Baptist churches. **We want poetry with a message to inspire, uplift, motivate, amuse."** ***Christian Single***, founded in 1979, assistant editor Leigh Neely, is a monthly magazine for single adults, ages 25-45. **"We need inspirational poetry targeted to single adults. Poetry that is happy, positive and shows people living single successfully. This will be thought-provoking, spiritual poetry to tie in with monthly themes."** ***Christian Single*** is magazine-sized, 50 pgs., with a circulation of 70,000. Uses 12 to 20 poems/year. **Previously published poems OK; prefers not to receive simultaneous submissions. For sample, send 9×12 SAE with 4 first-class stamps.** Publishes 6-12 months after acceptance. **Reports in 2 months. Pays upon acceptance; payment varies.** The biggest of the monthlies is ***Home Life***, which began in 1947. Circulation 600,000; 20,000 subscriptions. It is a magazine-sized, saddle-stapled, slick magazine, 60 pgs., illustrated (no ads). Its editor, Charlie Warren, says he wants **"religious poetry; poetry treating marriage, family life and life in general from a Christian perspective. We rarely publish anything of more than 25 lines." Sample: $1 to authors with 9×12 SASE! Submit no more than 6 poems at a time. Query unnecessary. Send SASE for guidelines. Reports in 6-8 weeks. Pays $15-24.** ***Mature Living: A Christian Magazine for Senior Adults***, founded in 1977, is a monthly mass circulation (360,000) magazine providing **"leisure reading for senior adults. All material used is compatible with a Christian life-style." The poetry they use is of Christian content, inspirational, about "nature/God," rhymed, 8-24 lines. You do not have to be a senior citizen to submit.** ***Mature Living*** is magazine-sized, 52 pgs., saddle-stapled, using large print with color art. They "receive hundreds" of poems/year, use about 50-100. Most of their distribution is through churches who buy the magazine in bulk for their senior adult members. **For sample, send 9×12 SAE and 85¢ postage. Reports in 6-8 weeks, but there might be a 3-year delay before publication. Pays $13-25.**

‡BARE WIRE (I, II), P.O. Box 825, Azusa CA 91702-0825, founded 1993, editor/publisher d. ray, is an annual. **They want "poetry that breathes life into the pages, kicks, screams or sobs quietly." No "ordinary" poetry.** The editor simply says ***bare wire*** is 7×8½, photocopied. Press run is 150. "Hopefully many distributed free." **Inquire about cost of sample and guidelines. Previously published poems and simultaneous submissions OK. Cover letter required.** Time between acceptance and publication is about a year, "less with luck." **Seldom comments on rejections. Reports in 1 month or less. Pays 1 copy. "Please note *bare wire* when published elsewhere."** Reviews books of poetry. Open to unsolicited reviews. Poets may also send books for review consideration.

E.W. BARHAM PUBLISHING (III), P.O. Box 5, Bowling Green OH 43402, founded 1992, editor Wayne Barham, plans to publish 1-3 paperbacks, 0-1 hardbacks and **1-3 chapbooks/year.** He wants **"poetry that uses evocative imagery, has a sense of the music of words, has a consistent voice and presents the reader with the world renewed. No so-called L-A-N-G-U-A-G-E poetry."** The first book of poetry he published was "the complete works of a completely unknown poet named Mahlon F. Scott" (released in June 1993), though he says it isn't characteristic of what he expects to be publishing in the future. **Query first with list of magazine (and book, if applicable) publications and a sample of 10-12 pages of poetry. Previously published poems and simultaneous submissions OK. Replies to queries in 2-3 weeks, to mss in 1-3 months.** "All final decisions will be made by the poetry contact person in consultation with other local poets." **Seldom comments on rejections. Pays 12½ to 15% royalties, $150 honorarium and 10 author's copies. Query regarding availability of sample books or chapbooks.** The editor says, "While we're told (mostly by big commercial publishers) that there is no market (i.e. audience) for poetry, we need to be careful that we are not making that claim a self-fulfilling prophesy. There is an audience, but poets have to create it. Give readings at every opportunity. Listen to your listeners; learn from them what still stirs the human soul."

WILLIAM L. BAUHAN, PUBLISHER (V, IV-Regional), P.O. Box 443, Old County Rd., Dublin NH 03444, phone (603)563-8020, founded 1959, editor William L. Bauhan, publishes poetry and art, especially New England regional books. **Currently accepts no unsolicited poetry.** They have recently published books of poetry by Sarah Singer, Anne Marx, Phoebe Barnes Driver and May Sarton.

BAY AREA POETS COALITION (BAPC); POETALK (I), P.O. Box 11435, Berkeley CA 94701-2435, founded 1974, editor Blaine Hammond. Coalition sends monthly poetry letter, ***Poetalk***, to over 400 people ("considering going to a bimonthly format"). They also publish an annual anthology (15th–148 pgs., out in February 1994), giving one page to each member of BAPC for over 6 months who has had work published in of ***Poetalk*** during the prior year. ***Poetalk*** publishes approximately 45 poets in each issue. BAPC has 160 members, 70 subscribers, but ***Poetalk*** is open to all. **"Rhyme must be well done."** Membership: $15 for 12 months of ***Poetalk***, copy of anthology and other privileges; extra outside US. Also offers a $50 patronage which includes a subscription and anthology for another individual of your choice; a $25 beneficiary/memorial, which includes membership plus subscription for friend; and subscriptions at $6/year. As a sample the editor selected this complete poem, "Cezanne," by Marine Robert Warden:

a paintbrush could explode
a mountain
then put it together again

Poetalk is 3 legal-sized pgs., photocopied and folded in half to make 12 pgs. total. **Write (with SASE) for a free copy. Each poem should be 3×4″ maximum, 4 to a page. Typewritten, single-spaced OK. Simultaneous and previously published work OK. "All subject matter should be in good taste." Send 4 poems (on 1 page) with SASE every 6 months. Response time is 2 weeks to 4 months. You'll get copy of *Poetalk* in which your work appears.** BAPC holds monthly readings, yearly contest, etc.; has mailing list open to local members; a PA system members may use for a small fee. People from many states and countries have contributed to ***Poetalk*** or entered their annual contests. The editor says, "We are different from many publishers in that we are very actively involved in working with the poets to make their poems publishable. We try to help people get to the point where we can publish their work, i.e., we make editorial comments on almost everything we reject. If you don't want suggested revisions you need to say so clearly in your cover letter."

BAY WINDOWS (IV-Gay/lesbian), 1523 Washington St., Boston MA 02118, fax (617)266-5973, founded 1983, poetry editors Rudy Kikel and Patricia A. Roth. ***Bay Windows* is a weekly gay and lesbian newspaper** published for the New England community, regularly using **"short poems of interest to lesbians and gay men. Poetry that is 'experiential' seems to have a good chance with us, but we don't want poetry that just 'tells it like it is.' Our readership doesn't read poetry all the time. A primary consideration is giving *pleasure*. We'll overlook the poem's (and the poet's) tendency not to be informed by the latest poetic theory, if it *does* this: pleases. Pleases, in particular, by articulating common gay or lesbian experience, and by doing that with some attention to form. I've found that a lot of our choices were made because of a strong image strand. Humor is *always* welcome–and hard to provide with craft. Obliquity, obscurity? Probably not for us. We won't presume on our audience."** They have recently published poetry by Stewart Aycock, Chocolate Waters, Jeffery Beam, Elspeth Leech, Rondo Mieczkowski and Michele Spring Moore. As a sample Rudy Kikel selected these lines from "Name It" by Roy Gonsalvez:

Since words have power
I name this curse a blessing
These lesions a sign
To eat brown rice instead of sugar. . .
I rename AIDS
Acquired Intelligence
Dream Success.

"We try to run four poems (two by lesbians, two by gay men) each month." They receive about 300 submissions/year, use 1 in 6, have a 3-month backlog. Press run is 13,000, 700 subscriptions of which 15 are libraries. Subscription: $40; per issue: 50¢. **Sample postpaid: $2. Submit 3-5 poems, "5-25 lines are ideal; include short biographical blurb." Poems by men should be sent care of Rudy Kikel, *Bay Windows*, at the address above; by women, care of Patricia Roth Schwartz, Weeping Willow Farm, 1212 Birdsey Rd., Waterloo NY 13165. Reports in 1-2 months. Pays copies. Acquires first rights. Editors "often" comment on rejections.** They review books of poetry in about 750 words–"Both single and omnibus reviews (the latter are longer)."

‡BEACH HOLME PUBLISHERS; PORCÉPIC BOOKS (II, IV-Regional), 4252 Commerce Circle, Victoria, British Columbia V8Z 4M2 Canada, phone (604)727-6514, fax (604)727-6418, founded 1971, editor Antonia Banyard, publishes 3-4 paperback books of poetry each year under the imprint Porcépic Books. They want **"excellent quality writing–all subjects, cultures, etc.–by Canadian authors."** They have recently published **Wrestling the Angel** by Robin Skelton, **Oedipal Dreams** by Evelyn Lau, **Cocktails at the Mausoleum** by Susan Musgrave and **Love As It Is** by Marilyn Bowering. **Query first, with sample poems and cover letter with brief bio and publication credits. Previously published poems and**

simultaneous submissions OK, if indicated. Time between acceptance and publication is 12-18 months. **Seldom comments on rejections. Replies to queries in 3-4 weeks, to mss (if invited) in 3-4 months. Pays 10% royalties, $250 (Canadian) and 5-10 author's copies. Samples may be ordered directly from Beach Holme Publishers or through a bookstore.** The editor says, "We are open to new authors, although we are most interested in poets who have had individual poems published in magazines, etc., or who have some familiarity with the literary scene. We appreciate authors who are familiar with our recent or backlist titles and our company."

‡BEACON (IV-Regional), Southwestern Oregon Community College, 1988 Newmark Ave., Coos Bay OR 97420, editor changes yearly. ***Beacon*** is a small, college literary magazine that appears twice a year and publishes the work of local writers and artists. **They want poetry only from those who have had their beginnings or currently reside in Southwestern Oregon. No specifications as to form, length, subject matter or style. "Submissions limited to five poems per term, prefer non-saga poems; one story per term, maximum 3,000 words."** The editor says *Beacon* is 50-70 pgs., 8½×11, professionally printed with color cover and b&w art within; no ads. They receive about 400 poems a year, accept approximately 25%. Press run is 300, all shelf sales. Single copy: $2.50. **Sample postpaid: $3. No previously published poems or simultaneous submissions. Cover letter required. Reads submissions December 1 to January 15 and March 1 to April 15.** Time between acceptance and publication is 2 months. **Seldom comments on rejections. Reports "on publication." Pays 1 copy. Acquires first rights.** The editor says, "We encourage poets to visit for readings and bring works to offer for sale. We do not compensate in any way for these readings. The purpose of our magazine is to heighten the value of literature in our community."

BEAR TRIBE'S PUBLISHING; WILDFIRE MAGAZINE (IV-Nature, spirituality, ethnic-nationality), P.O. Box 199, Devon PA 19333, phone (610)352-8882, founded 1965 (the magazine's former name: ***Many Smokes Earth Awareness Magazine***), managing editor Judith Trustone. The magazine uses **short poetry (no more than 55 lines) on topics appropriate to the magazine, such as earth awareness, self-sufficiency, sacred places, native people, etc.** They want a **"positive and constructive viewpoint, no hip or offensive language."** They have published poetry by Gary Snyder, W.D. Ehrhart, P.J. Brown and Evelyn Eaton. The quarterly devotes 2 pgs. to poetry each issue. Press run is 20,000 for 15,000 subscriptions of which 5% are libraries, 5,000 shelf sales. Subscription: $20. **Sample postpaid: $5. Send SASE for guidelines. Poets published receive 4-issue subscription. The press publishes books that incorporate Native American poems and songs, but no collections by individuals.**

‡BEDLAM PRESS (V), Church Green House, Old Church Lane, Pateley Bridge, N. Yorkshire HG3 5LZ England, phone 0423 711508, founded 1982, is a "small press publisher of poetry books, specializing in **long poems or sequences, mainly concerned with public affairs.**" They are **currently not accepting unsolicited mss.**

BEGGAR'S PRESS; THE LAMPLIGHT; RASKOLNIKOV'S CELLAR; BEGGAR'S REVIEW (I), 8110 N. 38th St., Omaha NE 68112, phone (402)455-2615, founded 1977, editor Richard R. Carey. ***The Lamplight*** is a semiannual (more frequent at times) publication of short stories, poetry, humor and unusual literary writings. **"We are eclectic, but we like serious poetry, historically orientated. Positively no religious or sentimental poetry. No incomprehensible poetry."** They have published poetry by Fredrick Zydek and John J. McKernan. As a sample the editor selected these lines (poet unidentified):

Lord, why did you curse me with doubt!
I'm a shot discharged in a wood without trees,
like a scream that began as a shout.
Never too far from famine or mire;
hunger and cold, and all creatures turn bold–
But, Lord, why did you give me desire!

The Lamplight is 40-60 pgs., 8½×11, offset printed and perfect-bound with 65 lb. cover stock. They receive about 600 poems a year, use only 10-15%. Press run is 500 for 300 subscribers of which 25 are libraries. Single copy: $9.50. **Sample: $7 plus 9×12 SASE. No previously published poems; simultaneous submissions OK. Cover letter required–"must provide insight into the characteristics of poet. What makes this poet different from the mass of humanity?"** Time between acceptance and publication is 4-12 months. **Often comments on rejections. Also offers "complete appraisals and evaluations" for $4/standard sheet, double-spaced. Brochure available for SASE. Reports in 2 to 2½ months. Pays 2 copies plus discount on up to 5. Acquires first North American serial rights. *Raskolnikov's Cellar*** is an irregular magazine of the same format, dimensions and terms as ***The Lamplight***. However, it deals in **"deeper psychologically orientated stories and poetry.** It is more selective and discriminating in what it publishes. Guidelines and brochures are an essential to consider this market." **Send SASE and $1 for guidelines. Brochures require only SASE. *Beggar's Review*** is 20-40 pgs., 8½×11, offset printed and saddle-stitched. It lists and reviews books, chapbooks and other magazines. "It also lists and reviews unpublished manuscripts: poetry, short stories, book-length, etc. Our purpose is to offer a vehicle for unpublished work of merit, as well as published material. We like to work with poets and authors who have potential but have not yet been recognized." Lengths of reviews range from a listing or mere caption to 1,000 words, "according to merit." Single copy: $6. Beggar's Press also plans to publish 4-6 paperbacks/year—**some on a subsidy basis. "In most cases, we select books which we publish on a royalty basis and promote ourselves. Borderline books only are author-subsidized." Query first with a few sample poems and a cover letter with brief bio and publication credits. "We also like to know how many books the author himself will be able to market to friends, associates, etc." Replies to queries in 1 month, to mss in 2½ months. Pays 10-15% royalties and 3 author's copies. Terms vary for subsidy publishing. "Depending on projected sales, the author pays from 20% to 60%."** The editor says, "Our purpose is to form a common bond with distinguished poets whose poetry is marketable and worthy. Poetry is difficult to market, thus we sometimes collaborate with the poet in publishing costs. But essentially, we look for poets with unique qualities of expression and who meet our uncustomary requirements. We prefer a royalty arrangement. Beggar's Press is different from most publishers. We are impressed with concrete poetry, which is without outlandish metaphors. Keep it simple but don't be afraid to use our language to the fullest. Read Poe, Burns and Byron. Then submit to us. There is still a place for lyrical poetry."

‡BEGINNER'S MIND PRESS (II), Apt. 2, 1059 27th St., Des Moines IA 50311, founded 1992, editor Christien Gholson, publishes both chapbooks (2/year) and broadsides. **"I want to see poetry that has depth, ideas, music; that can be read out loud. No rhyme (unless blues oriented); no vague introspection; no poetry from the world of TV, suburbia; no academic verse (poetry with the poetry edited out of it)."** They have recently published poetry by David Chorlton, Antler, Jane McCray and Will Inman. As a sample the editor selected these lines from "Seascape in Khaki" in **The Exile House** by Erling Friis-Baastad:

The painting turns khaki. A khaki sail
disappears beyond the old shirt; a khaki
child wanders, morose on the shore.
His future once stretched out ahead
of him but now lies behind. . . .

The chapbooks are generally 16 pgs., digest-sized, printed on plain white paper and saddle-stapled with b&w graphic on paper cover. **"I encourage poets to send the entire manuscript. My chapbooks are, at the most, 16 pages long, so there's no reason to just send samples. I want to see the whole." Previously published poems and simultaneous submissions OK, if indicated as such. Does not read mss in December or June through August. Seldom comments on rejections. Reports in 1 month. Pays copies.** The editor says, "BEgiNNer's MIND was established to publish poetry that hums down to the toes of the soul and circulate it out into the world free-for-postage. I've found the interesting poets are usually interested in what others are doing. Why not read what I've published before you send something (52¢ stamp for chaps, 29¢ stamp for a couple B'sides). Art has very little to do with being published—it's a way of life."

BELHUE PRESS (III, IV-Gay), Suite A1, 2501 Palisade Ave., Riverdale, Bronx NY 10463, founded 1990, editor Tom Laine, is a small press **specializing in gay male poetry**, publishing 3 paperbacks/year—no chapbooks. **"We are especially interested in anthologies, in thematic books, in books that get out of the stock poetry market."** They want **"hard-edged, well-crafted, fun and often sexy poetry. No mushy, self pitying, confessional, boring, indulgent, teary or unrequited love poems—yuch!"** As a sample the editor selected these lines from "Thoth" in the book **Sex-charge** by Perry Brass, which was nominated for a 1991 Lambda Literary Award:

How I lie
in your winding sheet, sleeping
past the wake
of our small end,
a whiter corner in your light,
curled toe to toe
against your parts.

"Poets must be willing to promote book through readings, mailers, etc." Query first with sample poems and cover letter. Previously published poems and simultaneous submissions OK. Time between acceptance and publication is 1 year. **Often comments on rejections. Will request criticism fees "if necessary." Replies to queries and submitted mss "fast." No payment information provided. Write for catalog to order samples.** The editor says, "Poetry, like stand-up comedy, has to do a lot more than just sit on the page and tell us about your hard childhood . . . We're looking for valuable poetry."

BELLFLOWER PRESS (III), Box 87 Dept. WD, Chagrin Falls OH 44022-0087, founded 1974, poetry editor/owner Louise Wazbinski, **publishes poetry *books* 50% of the time on a subsidized basis.** She wants **"poetry that crystallizes the attitudes held by our society." Reports in 1-2 months on mss. "Contract depends upon subvention by author, usually 50%. Often the author will subsidize a small percentage and receive books as payment. In other cases, there is no subsidy and the author receives a royalty based on the specific arrangements made at the time of agreement."**

BELLOWING ARK PRESS; BELLOWING ARK (II), P.O. Box 45637, Seattle WA 98145, phone (206)545-8302, founded 1984, editor Robert R. Ward. ***Bellowing Ark*** is a bimonthly literary tabloid that **"publishes only poetry which demonstrates in some way the proposition that existence has meaning or, to put it another way, that life is worth living. We have no strictures as to length, form or style; only that the work we publish is to our judgment life-affirming."** They do not want **"academic poetry, in any of its manifold forms."** Poets published include B.R. Totten, Irene Culver, Katherine Lewis, Susan McCaslin, Muriel Karr, Teresa Noelle Roberts and Mark Allan Johnson. As a sample the editor selected these lines from "Ancient Poets" by Paula Milligan:

Ancient truth must be the same, then as now.
It endures, for it has no shades

Angels in Hesoid's pastures, luminous;
Sight behind Homer's dark eyes

Light is bright in any age.

The paper is tabloid-sized, 32 pgs., printed on electrobright stock with b&w photos and line drawings. It is a lively publication. Almost every poem is accessible, enjoyable and stimulating. All styles seem to be welcome—even long, sequence poems and formal verse. Circulation is 1,000, of which 200 are subscriptions and 600 are sold on newsstands. Subscription: $15/year. **Sample postpaid: $3. The editors say, "absolutely *no* simultaneous submissions." They reply to submissions in 2-6 weeks and publish within the next 1 or 2 issues. Occasionally they will criticize a ms if it seems to "display potential to become the kind of work we want." Sometimes sends prepublication galleys. Pays 2 copies.** Reviews books of poetry. Send books for review consideration. Bellowing Ark Press publishes collections of poetry by invitation only. Work published in ***Bellowing Ark*** appeared in the 1991 **Pushcart Prize** anthology.

BELL'S LETTERS POET (I), P.O. Box 2187, Gulfport MS 39505, founded 1956 as ***Writer's Almanac***, 1958 as ***Thunderhead for Writers***, 1966 as ***Bell's Letters*** (a play on words), publisher and editor Jim Bell, is a quarterly which **you must buy ($4/issue, $16 subscription) to be included.** The editor says "many say they stay up with it all night the day it arrives," and judging by the many letters from readers, that seems to be the case. **Though there is no payment for poetry accepted, many patrons send awards of $5-20 to the poets whose work they especially like. Subscription "guarantees them a byline each issue." Poems are "4 to 20 lines in good taste."** They have recently published poetry by Eleanore-Melissa Barker, James Cannon, Dawn Zapletal and Patrick Flavin. As a sample of the spirit of ***BL*** poetry the editor chose these lines by Sean Brown:

Oozing violet and
red rays of defiance
the sun sets
like slag iron
in a steel mill

It is digest-sized, 76 pgs., offset from typescript on plain bond paper (including cover). **Sample with guidelines: $3. Ms may be typed or even hand-written. No simultaneous submissions. Previously published poems OK "if cleared with prior publisher." Accepted poems by subscribers go immediately into the next issue. "Our publication dates fall quarterly on the spring and autumn equinox and winter and summer solstice. Deadline for poetry submissions is 3 months prior to publication."** Reviews books of poetry by subscribers in "one abbreviated paragraph." "The Ratings" is a competition in each issue. Readers are asked to vote on their favorite poems, and the ratings are announced in the next issue, along with awards sent to the poets by patrons.

THE BELOIT POETRY JOURNAL; CHAD WALSH POETRY PRIZE (II), Box 154, RFD 2, Ellsworth ME 04605, phone (207)667-5598, founded 1950, editor Marion K. Stocking, is a well-known, long-standing quarterly of quality poetry and reviews. **"We publish the best poems we receive, without bias as to length, school, subject or form.** It is our hope to discover the growing tip of poetry and to introduce new poets alongside established writers. **We publish occasional chapbooks on special themes to diversify our offerings."** They want **"fresh, imaginative poetry, with a distinctive voice. We tend to prefer poems that make the reader share an experience rather than just read about it, and these we keep for up to 3 months,** circulating them among our readers, and continuing to winnow out the best. At the quarterly meetings of the Editorial Board we read aloud all the surviving poems and put together an issue of the best we have." They have recently published poetry by Sherman Alexie, Hillel Schwartz, Jane Mead, Albert Goldbarth and Ursula K. Le Guin. As a sample the editor selected these lines from "Kevin Plays the Goldberg Variations" by Lola Haskins:

A fleet of clouds crosses the skylight.
We are riding the wind of your hands.
Sometimes the jib runs easy in its white
curve. Sometimes we vibrate on little
speedy glitters, that build until we
slap through spray. Then fall,
and we settle on the swells like gulls,
and the sea's so clear I want to cry. . . .

The journal is 48 pgs., digest-sized, saddle-stapled, and attractively printed with tasteful art on the card covers. All styles of verse—providing they articulate ideas or emotions intelligently and concisely—are featured. The editor is also keen on providing as much space as possible for poems and so does not include contributors' notes. They have a circulation of 1,700 for 575 subscriptions of which 325 are libraries. **Sample copy: $4, including guidelines. SASE for guidelines alone. Submit any time, without query, any legible form. *"No simultaneous submissions.* Any length of ms, but most poets send what will go in a business envelope for one stamp. Don't send your life's work."** No backlog: **"We clear the desk at each issue." Pays 3 copies. Acquires first serial rights.** Staff reviews books of poetry in an average of 500 words, usually single format. Send books for review consideration. As of 1993 the journal awards a $2,000 Chad Walsh Poetry Prize to a poem or group of poems published in the calendar year. "Every poem published in 1995 will be considered for the 1995 prize." Poetry published in ***The Beloit Poetry Journal*** has been included in **The Best American Poetry 1994** and **Pushcart Prize** anthologies. The editor says, "We'd like to see more strong, imaginative, experimental poetry; more poetry with a global vision; and more poetry with fresh, vigorous language."

BENEATH THE SURFACE (II), % The Dept. of English, Chester New Hall, McMaster University, Hamilton, Ontario L8S 4S8 Canada, founded 1911, editor changes yearly, is a biannual using **"top quality poetry/prose that achieves universality through individual expression."** They want **"quality poetry; any form; no restrictions." Also interested in short stories. Science fiction and medical themes are most welcome.** They have published poetry by Dorothy Livesky and John Barlow. As a sample the editor selected these lines from "War Monument" by tristanne j. connolly:

a soldier's soul
ascending, but concrete
is heavy to lift
war monument, the cross on top
forgotten til the very last minute

It is 30-50 pgs., professionally printed, saddle-stapled, with cover art, drawings and b&w photographs. They receive about 250 submissions/year, use approximately 10%. Press run is 150 for 8 subscribers of which 3 are libraries, 92 shelf sales. Subscription: $8/year. **Sample postpaid: $4. No previously published poems or simultaneous submissions. Submit 4-6 poems with cover letter, including short bio and summary of previous publications, if any. Reads submissions September through April only. Often comments on rejections. Reports in 4-6 weeks. Sometimes sends prepublication galleys. Pays nothing—not even copies. Acquires first North American serial rights.** Rarely reviews books of poetry, "though we do include literary essays when submitted." The editor says, "Do not get discouraged. Getting work in respectable literary journals takes much love and even more hard work. Be patient and allow your work to evolve and mature."

BENNETT & KITCHEL (IV-Form), P.O. Box 4422, East Lansing MI 48826, phone (517)355-1707, founded 1989, editor William Whallon, publishes 1-3 hardbacks/year of **"poetry of form and meaning. No free verse or blank verse, no sestinas or haiku."** As an example of what he admires, the editor chose these lines by Troxey Kemper:

I think what Jeremiah said,
And add my woes in quiet sums.
A cup of broth, a plate of crumbs,
Are all my meat when mirth is fled:
What does it mean?

Bennett & Kitchel recently published **Lapsing into Grace**, by Rhina P. Espaillat. **Sample postpaid: $8. Simultaneous submissions and previously published poems OK if copyright is clear. Minimum volume for a book "might be 750 lines." If a book is accepted, publication within 9 months. Editor comments on submissions "seldom." Reports in 2 weeks. Terms "variable, negotiable."** He remarks, "To make a bad rhyme not from incompetence but willfully is like stubbing your toe on purpose."

BERKELEY POETRY REVIEW (II), 700 Eshleman Hall, University of California, Berkeley CA 94720, founded 1973, is an annual review "which publishes poems and translations of local as well as national and international interest. **We are open to any form or length which knows how to express itself through that form."** They have recently published poetry by Katherine Harer, Lyn Hejinian, Alice Jones, Jennifer Maiden, Ishmael Reed and Jay Griswold. As a sample the editors selected these lines from "Liz and Monty" by Tim Donnelly:

She cradles the head she thinks is dying
his human blood stains her blue taffeta
Roddy weeps silently
Rock blubbers
in a movie the car would burst into flame
not just hug the tree for solace

The editors describe it as a flat-spined paperback, averaging 150 pgs., circulation 500. Subscription: $10/year. **Simultaneous submissions OK. Reads submissions September through June only. Include SASE; allow 2-6 months for reply. Pays 1 copy.**

BERKELEY POETS COOPERATIVE (WORKSHOP & PRESS) (V), 2642 Dana, Berkeley CA 94704, founded 1969, poetry editor Charles Entrekin (plus rotating staff), is "a nonprofit organization which offers writers the opportunity to explore, develop and publish their works. Our primary goals are to maintain a free workshop open to writers and to publish outstanding collections of poetry and fiction by individual writers." The *New York Times* has called it **"the oldest and most successful poetry co-operative in the country."** Chapbooks have been published by Linda Watanabe McFerrin and Chitra Divakaruni. Charles Entrekin says he prefers **"modern imagist—open to all kinds, but we publish very little rhyme." However, he is currently not accepting unsolicited submissions.** They publish two 64-page chapbooks by individuals each year, for which the **poets receive 50% of the profit and 20 copies. Criticism sometimes provided on rejected mss. Poets elsewhere might consider BPWP as a model for forming similar organizations.**

BIG HEAD PRESS; BIG HEAD PRESS BROADSIDE SERIES (III), P.O. Box 17657, Beverly Hills CA 90209-3657, founded 1991, editor Scott C. Holstad, associate editor Lisa Lundgren. **"As a result of our recent move, we will not be reading any submissions until July 1995. Social commentary preferred. 40 lines max. No love poetry."** They have recently published poetry by Antler, Rod Farmer, Arthur Winfield Knight, Lyn Lifshin and Robert Howington. As a sample the editor selected these lines from "Do You Mind" by Sal Salasin:

Some are born to greatness
and some have greatness thrust
upon them for blowing off the
hands and feet of Nicaraguan
coffee harvesters.
The rest of us are
forced to work.

Broadsides are printed on 4½×8 card stock, with author's photo and bio. Of hundreds of submissions, they say they accept 10-15 poems/year. Press run is 250-500, most distributed free. **Sample broadside: $1. Submit 4-10 poems with b&w photo. Previously published poems and simultaneous submissions OK, if noted. Cover letter with brief bio and phone number required.** Time between acceptance and publication is 6-15 months. **Often comments on rejections. Send SASE for guidelines. Reports in 2 weeks to 3 months. Pays 10-15 copies. Acquires one-time rights. "Due to financial constraints, we currently require full subsidation for chapbooks."** Authors then receive **50% of press run. Sample chapbook: $3.** The editor says they would like to see "more politically didactic material."

BILINGUAL REVIEW PRESS; BILINGUAL REVIEW/REVISTA BILINGÜE (IV-Ethnic/Hispanic, bilingual/Spanish), Hispanic Research Center, Arizona State University, Box 872702, Tempe AZ 85287-2702, phone (602)965-3867, journal founded 1974, press in 1976. Managing editor Karen Van Hooft says they are "a small press publisher of U.S. Hispanic creative literature and of a journal containing poetry and short fiction in addition to scholarship." The journal contains some poetry in each issue; they also publish flat-spined paperback collections of poetry. **"We publish poetry by and/or about U.S. Hispanics and U.S. Hispanic themes. We do not publish translations in our journal or literature about the experiences of Anglo Americans in Latin America. We have published a couple of poetry volumes in bilingual format (Spanish/English) of important Mexican poets."** They have published poetry by Alberto Ríos, Demetria Martínez, Pablo Medina, Marjorie Agosin and Alma Villanueva. The editor says the journal, which appears 3 times a year, is 7×10, 96 pgs., flat-spined, offset, with 2-color cover. They use less than 10% of hundreds of submissions received each year. Press run is 2,000 for 1,200 subscriptions. Subscriptions are $16 for individuals, $30 for institutions. **Sample postpaid: $6 individuals/$10 institutions. Submit "2 copies, including ribbon original if possible, with loose stamps**

for return postage." Cover letter required. Pays 2 copies. Acquires all rights. Reviews books of US Hispanic poetry only. Send books, Attn: Editor, for review consideration. **For book submissions, inquire first with 4-5 sample poems, bio, publications. Pays $200 advance, 10% royalties and 10 copies.** Over the years, books by this press have won five American Book Awards and two Western States Book Awards.

BIRD WATCHER'S DIGEST (IV-Nature), P.O. Box 110, Marietta OH 45750, founded 1978, editor Mary Beacom Bowers, is a specialized but promising market for **poems of "true literary merit" in which birds figure in some way, at least by allusion. 2-3 poems are used in each bimonthly issue.** Some poets who have appeared here include Susan Rea, Nancy G. Westerfield, Suzanne Freemans and William D. Barney. **"Preferred: no more than 20 lines, 40 spaces, no more than 3 poems at a time, no queries." Sample postpaid: $3.50. Reports in 2 months. Pays $10/poem.** They have up to a year's backlog and use 12-20 of the approximately 500 poems received each year.

BIRMINGHAM POETRY REVIEW (II, IV-Translations), English Dept., University of Alabama at Birmingham, Birmingham AL 35294, phone (205)934-8573, founded 1988, co-editors Robert Collins and Randy Blythe. The review appears twice a year using poetry of **"any style, form, length or subject. We are biased toward exploring the cutting edge of contemporary poetry. Style is secondary to the energy, the *fire* the poem possesses. We don't want poetry with cliché-bound, worn-out language.** ***No submissions please between 6/1/94 and 6/1/95."*** They have recently published poetry by Hague, Hopes, McDonald, Richards, Call and Miltner. As a sample the editors selected these lines from "Charisma Revisited" by Brendan Galvin:

Still, there was something to be said
for their peasant reticence, though
it leaves us confounded as to why
the country has been empty
these hundred years.

They describe their magazine as 50 pgs., 6×9, offset, with b&w cover. Their press run is 600 for Fall Issue, 500 for Spring Issue, 275 subscriptions. Subscription: $3. **Sample postpaid: $2. Submit 3-5 poems, "no more. No cover letters. We are impressed by good writing; we are unimpressed by publication credits. It should go without saying, but we receive more and more manuscripts with insufficient return postage. If it costs you fifty-two cents to mail your manuscript, it will cost us that much to return it if it is rejected. Manuscripts with insufficient return postage will be discarded." No simultaneous or multiple submissions, and previously published poems only if they are translations. Editor sometimes comments on rejections. Send SASE for guidelines. Reports in 1-4 months. Pays 2 copies and one-year subscription.** They say, "Advice to beginners: Read as much good contemporary poetry, national and international, as you can get your hands on. Then be persistent in finding your own voice."

BISHOP PUBLISHING CO. (IV-Themes), 2131 Trimble Way, Sacramento CA 95825, professor Roland Dickison, is a "small press publisher of **folklore in paperbacks, including contemporary** and out-of-print."

BITS PRESS (III, IV-Humor), English Dept., Case Western Reserve University, Cleveland OH 44106, phone (216)795-2810, founded 1974, poetry editor Robert Wallace. **"Bits Press is devoted to poetry. We publish chapbooks (and sometimes limited editions) by young as well as well-known poets. Our main attention at present is given to light verse and funny poems."** The chapbooks are distinguished by an elegant but inexpensive format. They have published chapbooks by David R. Slavitt, John Updike and Gerald Costanzo. These sample lines are from Ted Kooser's **Etudes**:

...five small black birds as quick
as quarter notes touched down at once, striking
a perfect chord at the cold, high end of the keyboard,
and it frightened them, and off they flew together.

The few chapbooks they publish are mostly solicited. Send $3 for a sample chapbook. Sometimes sends prepublication galleys. Pays poet in copies (over 10% of run). Acquires one-time rights.

BLACK BEAR PUBLICATIONS; BLACK BEAR REVIEW; POETS ELEVEN . . . AUDIBLE (II, IV-Political, social issues), 1916 Lincoln St., Croydon PA 19021-8026, founded 1984, poetry and art editor Ave Jeanne, review and audio editor Ron Zettlemoyer. ***Black Bear Review*** is a semiannual international literary and fine arts magazine that also publishes chapbooks and holds an annual poetry competition. **"We like well crafted poetry that mirrors real life—void of camouflage, energetic poetry, avant-garde, free verse and haiku which relate to the world today. We seldom publish the beginner, but will assist when time allows. No traditional poetry is used. The underlying theme of *BBR* is social and political, but the review is interested also in environmental, war/peace, ecological and minorities themes. We would like to receive more Native American and current political topics."** Poets recently published in

BBR include Sherman Alexie, C B Follett, Paul Weinman, B.Z. Niditch, Robert S. King and Elliot Richman. ***Poets Eleven . . . Audible*** has released poetry on tape by A.D. Winans, Tony Moffeit, Kevin Zepper and Mike Maggio. As a sample from ***BBR***, the editor selected these lines from "Recovering" by Sean Brendan-Brown:

You are storyteller,
masked in asphalt mist under collapsed bridges,
storm drains echoing tobacco baritones
of exhausted Peach-Chiefs, pipes broken,
warriors cursing atop alluvial plains,
knees sunk in razor gravel,
writing under the jaws and bludgeons
of police dogs, men-in-green who stink
proletariat colognes of gunpowder, alcohol,
faces dark with the greasepaint of legislature.

The magazine is perfect-bound, digest-sized, 64 pgs., offset from typed copy on white stock, with line drawings, collages and woodcuts. Circulation of ***BBR*** is 500, of which 300 are subscriptions; 15 libraries. Price: $5/issue; subscription: $10, $15 overseas. **A sample of *BBR*: $5 postpaid; back copies when available are $4 postpaid. Any number of poems may be submitted, one to a page. "Please have name and address on each page of your submissions." Simultaneous submissions are not considered. "Submissions without SASE will be trashed." Guidelines available for SASE. Submissions are reported on in 2 weeks, publication is in 6-12 months. Pays contributor's copy. Acquires first North American serial rights.** Considers reviews of books of poetry and recent issues of literary magazines, maximum 250 words. Send books for review consideration. The editors explain that ***Poets Eleven . . . Audible*** was started for accommodation of longer poems for the reader to take part in poetry as a listener; **the author may submit up to 10 minutes of original poetry. SASE for return of your tape; sample copies available for $4.50 postpaid. Contributor receives 25% royalties. They also publish two chapbooks/year.** Most recently published **A Destiny Going Sour** by Steve Levi. **Chapbook series requires a reading fee of $5, complete ms and cover letter.** For book publication, they would prefer that "***BBR*** has published the poet and is familiar with his/her work, but we will read anyone who thinks they have something to say." **Author receives one-half print run.** They say, "We appreciate a friendly, brief cover letter. Tell us about the poet; omit degrees or any other pretentious dribble. All submissions are handled with objectivity and quite often rejected material is directed to another market. If you've not been published before—mention it. We are always interested in aiding those who support small press. We frequently suggest poets keep up with **Poet's Market** and read the listings and reviews in issues of ***Black Bear***. Most recent issues of ***BBR*** include reviews on small press markets—current releases of chapbooks and the latest literary magazines. We make an effort to keep our readers informed and on top of the small press scene. Camera-ready ads are printed free of charge as a support to small press publishers. We do suggest reading issues before submitting to absorb the flavor and save on wasted postage. Send your best! Our yearly poetry competition offers cash awards to poets." Annual deadline is November 1. Guidelines available for SASE. "Professional black & white artwork is used regularly in each issue. Submissions are welcomed."

BLACK BOOKS BULLETIN: WORDSWORK; THIRD WORLD PRESS (IV-Ethnic), 7822 S. Dobson, P.O. Box 19730, Chicago IL 60619, phone (312)651-0700, fax (312)651-7286. ***BBB*** is a periodic journal of Black culture, including **"Black literature and current issues facing the African-American community."** They have published poetry by Gil Scott Heron, Brian Gilmore, Sonia Sanchez and Keorapetse Kgositsile. They also publish book reviews, essays, interviews, short stories and literary criticism. **Write, fax or call for further information.**

BLACK BOUGH (II, IV-Form), 7 Park Ave., Flemington NJ 08822, founded 1991, editors Kevin Walker and Charles Easter, is a biannual that publishes "haiku and related forms which demonstrate the distinctiveness of haiku as well as its connection to western traditions in poetry." They want **"haiku, senryu, tanka, haibun (in particular) and sequences. No renga, articles, academic essays or extremely long poems."** They have recently published work by Jean Jorgensen, Francine Porad and Stuart Dybeck. As a sample the editors selected this haiku by Michael Ketchek:

pausing to gaze at
the storm damaged tree
boxer doing road work

bb is 30 pgs., digest-sized, professionally printed, saddle-stitched, with cover art, no ads. They receive about 5,200 poems a year, use 5-10%. Press run is 200 for 100 subscribers. Subscription: $13.50. **Sample postpaid: $5. No previously published poems or simultaneous submissions. "Submit no more than 20 haiku; prefer several haiku/page."** Time between acceptance and publication is 3-6 months. **Comments on rejections "if requested." Reports in 3-4 weeks. Pays $1/verse, up to $4 for a long poem or haiku sequence. Acquires first rights.**

BLACK BUZZARD PRESS; BLACK BUZZARD REVIEW; VISIONS—INTERNATIONAL, THE WORLD JOURNAL OF ILLUSTRATED POETRY; THE BLACK BUZZARD ILLUSTRATED POETRY CHAPBOOK SERIES (II), 1110 Seaton Lane, Falls Church VA 22046, founded 1979, poetry editor Bradley R. Strahan, associate editor Shirley G. Sullivan. "We are an independent nonsubsidized press dedicated to publishing fine accessible poetry and translation (particularly from lesser-known languages such as Armenian, Gaelic, Urdu, Vietnamese, etc.) accompanied by original illustrations of high quality in an attractive format. **We want to see work that is carefully crafted and exciting work that transfigures everyday experience or gives us a taste of something totally new; all styles except concrete and typographical 'poems.' Nothing purely sentimental. No self-indulgent breast beating. No sadism, sexism or bigotry. No unemotional pap. No copies of Robert Service or the like. Usually under 80 lines but will consider longer."** They have recently published poetry by Ted Hughes, Louis Simpson, Marilyn Hacker, James Dickey, Allen Ginsberg and Lawrence Ferlinghetti. Bradley Strahan says that "no 4 lines can possibly do even minimal justice to our taste or interest!" ***Visions***, a digest-sized, saddle-stapled magazine finely printed on high-quality paper, appears 3 times a year, uses 56 pages of poetry in each issue. Circulation 750 with 300 subscriptions of which 50 are libraries. **Sample postpaid: $3.50. Current issue: $4.50.** They receive *well* over a thousand submissions each year, use 150, have a 3- to 18-month backlog. "***Visions*** is international in both scope and content, publishing poets from all over the world and having readers in 48 U.S. states, Canada and 24 other foreign countries." ***Black Buzzard Review*** is a "more or less annual informal journal, dedicated mostly to North American poets and entirely to original English-language poems. In ***BBR***, we are taking a more wide-open stance on what we accept (including the slightly outrageous)." **Sample postpaid: $3.50. Current issue: $4.50.** It is 36 pgs., magazine-sized, side-stapled, with matte card cover. **"Poems must be readable (not faded or smudged) and *not* handwritten. We resent having to pay postage due, so use adequate postage! No more than 8 pages, please." Publishes theme issues. Send SASE for upcoming themes. Reports in 3 days to 3 weeks. Pays copies or $5-10 "if we get a grant." Buys first North American serial rights.** Staff reviews books of poetry in "up to 2 paragraphs." Send books for review consideration. **To submit for the chapbook series, send samples (5-10 poems) and a *brief* cover letter "pertinent to artistic accomplishments." Reports in 3 days to 3 weeks. Pays in copies. Usually provides criticism. Send $4 for sample chapbook.** Bradley Strahan adds that in ***Visions*** "We sometimes publish helpful advice about 'getting published' and the art and craft of poetry, and often discuss poets and the world of poetry on our editorial page."

BLACK RIVER REVIEW; STONE ROLLER PRESS (II, IV-Translations), Dept. PM, 855 Mildred Ave., Lorain OH 44052-1213, phone (216)244-9654, founded 1985, poetry editor Michael Waldecki, editorial contact Deb Gilbert, is a literary annual using **"contemporary poetry, any style, form and subject matter, 50 line maximum (usually), poetry with innovation, craftsmanship and a sense of excitement and/or depth of emotion. Do *not* want Helen Steiner Rice, greeting card verse, poetry that mistakes stilted, false or formulaic diction for intense expression of feeling."** They have published poetry by James Margorian, Adrian Louis, Christopher Franke, Catherine Hammond, Sylvia Foley and Leslie Leyland Fields. As a sample the editor selected these lines from "Drought" by Stephen R. Roberts:

The reptilian trunk of a pine crawls up
to needles as loose as an old man's teeth.
There is a fear of frictions.
Poison ivy slumbers in green smiles,
and the crow's harsh voice
could spark the woodpile.
Everything is burned and older.
Children are telling children,
four more weeks and we all die.

The magazine-sized annual is photocopied from typescript on quality stock, saddle-stapled with matte card cover with art, about 60 pgs., using ads, circulation 400 (sold in college bookstore). **Sample postpaid: $3.50 (back copy); $4 (current issue); $7 (two copies of any issue). No simultaneous submissions. Will consider previously published poems if acknowledged. Submit between January and May 1, limit of 10. Editor may comment on submissions. Send SASE for guidelines. Pays 1 copy.** Reviews books of poetry. Kaye Coller, managing editor, comments, "We want strong poems that show a depth of vision beyond the commonplace. We don't care if a poet is well-known or not, but we don't publish amateurs. An amateur is not necessarily a new poet,

Market categories: (I) Beginning; (II) General; (III) Limited; (IV) Specialized; (V) Closed.

but one who doesn't believe in revision, tends to be preachy, writes sentimental slush, tells the reader what to think and/or concludes the poem with an explanation in case the reader didn't get the point. If we think we can use one or more of a poet's poems, we keep them until the final choices are made in June; otherwise, we send them back as soon as possible. Follow the ms mechanics in **Poet's Market. We are also looking for poems written in Spanish. If selected, they will be published with English translation by either the poet or one of our staff."**

THE BLACK SCHOLAR; THE BLACK SCHOLAR PRESS (IV-Ethnic), P.O. Box 2869, Oakland CA 94609, founded 1969, publisher Robert Chrisman, uses **poetry "relating to/from/of the black American and other 'Third World' experience."** The quarterly magazine is basically scholarly and research-oriented. They have published poetry by Ntozake Shange, Jayne Cortez, Andrew Salkey and D.L. Smith. The editor says it is 64 pgs., 7×10, with 10,000 subscribers of which 60% are libraries, 15% shelf sales. "We only publish one issue every year containing poetry." Single copy: $5; subscription: $30. **Sample back issue: $6. Enclose "letter & bio or curriculum vita, SASE, phone number, no originals." Send SASE for guidelines. Pays 10 copies and subscription.** Reviews books of poetry. They also publish 1-2 books a year, average 100 pgs., flat-spined. **Send query letter. For sample books, send 8½×11 SASE for catalog, average cost $10.95 including postage and handling.** "Please be advised–it is against our policy to discuss submissions via telephone. Also, we get a lot of mss, but read ***every single one,*** thus patience is appreciated."

BLACK SPARROW PRESS (III), 24 Tenth St., Santa Rosa CA 95401, phone (707)579-4011, founded 1966, assistant to the publisher Michele Filshie, publishes poetry, fiction, literary criticism and bibliography in flat-spined paperbacks, hardcovers and deluxe/limited editions (hardback). "We do not publish chapbooks. Our books are 150 pgs. or longer." They have published poetry by Charles Bukowski, Tom Clark, Wanda Coleman, Robert Kelly, Diane Wakoski, John Weiners and Edward Dorn. **Include name and address inside package with ms. Reports in 2 months. Pays 10% maximum royalties plus author's copies.**

BLACK TIE PRESS (III), P.O. Box 440004, Houston TX 77244-0004, phone (713)789-5119, founded 1986, publisher and editor Peter Gravis. "Black Tie Press is committed to publishing innovative, distinctive and engaging writing. We publish books; we are not a magazine or literary journal. We are not like the major Eastern presses, university presses or other small presses in poetic disposition. To get a feel for our publishing attitude, we urge you to buy one or more of our publications before submitting." He is **"only interested in imaginative, provocative, at risk writing. *No rhyme.*"** Published poets include Steve Wilson, Guy Beining, Sekou Karanja, Craig Cotter, Donald Rawley, Dieter Weslowski, Laura Ryder, Toni Ortner and Jenny Kelly. As a sample the editor selected these lines from "Blue Mirror" from **A Game of Rules**, by Harry Burrus:

He thought the white glove
Of her memory would suffocate
By its own flame,
Burning itself out like a suicide,
And she would forget
The amber memories their time imbued.

Sample postpaid: $8. "We have work we want to publish, hence, unsolicited material is not encouraged. However, we will read and consider material from committed, serious writers as time permits. Write, do not call about material. *No reply without SASE.*" Cover letter with bio preferred. Reports in 2-6 weeks. Always sends prepublication galleys. Author receives percent of press run. Peter Gravis says, "Too many writers are only interested in getting published and not interested in reading or supporting good writing. Black Tie hesitates to endorse a writer who does not, in turn, promote and patronize (by actual purchases) small press publications. Once Black Tie publishes a writer, we intend to remain with that artist."

THE BLACK WARRIOR REVIEW (II), P.O. Box 2936, Tuscaloosa AL 35486-2936, phone (205)348-4518, founded 1974. They have published poetry by David Ignatow, Simon Perchik, Christopher Buckley, Ricardo Pau-Llosa, Sherod Santos and Linda Gregg. As a sample the editor selected these lines from "Coleman Valley Road" by Gerald Stern:

The strings are stretched across the sky; one note
is almost endless–pitiless I'd say
except for the slight sagging; one note is
like a voice, it almost has words, it sings
and sighs, it cracks with desire, it sobs with fatigue.
It is the loudest sound of all. A shrieking.

BWR is a 6×9 semiannual of 144 pages. Circulation 2,000. **Sample postpaid: $5. Address submissions to Poetry Editor. Submit 3-6 poems. Simultaneous (say so) submissions OK. Send SASE for guidelines. Reports in 1-3 months. Pays $5-10/printed page plus 2 copies. Buys first rights.**

Awards one $500 prize annually. Reviews books of poetry in single or multi-book format. Open to unsolicited reviews. Poets may also send books for review consideration to Leigh Ann Sackrider, editor. Poetry published in ***BWR*** has been included in **The Best American Poetry 1993**. The editor says, "We solicit a nationally-known poet for a chapbook section. For the remainder of the issue, we solicit a few poets, but the bulk of the material is chosen from unsolicited submissions. Many of our poets have substantial publication credits, but our decision is based simply on the quality of the work submitted."

BLANK GUN SILENCER; BGS PRESS (II), 1240 William St., Racine WI 53402, phone (414)639-2406, founded 1991, editor Dan Nielsen, is "an independent art/lit mag" which appears twice a year "publishing Buk-heads, post Dada freaks and everything in between." They want **poetry that is "tight, concise, startling, funny, honest. Nothing flowery, overly 'poetic,' too academic, rhyming or blatantly pointless."** They have published poetry by Charles Bukowski, Gerald Locklin, Fred Voss and Ron Androla. As a sample the editor selected these lines from "Edge" by Mark Weber:

where are my John Coltrane records?
o, i sold them when
i was a junkie
they sold good
but now i want to hear them
need to hear the cycle of 5ths played backwards
on "Giant Steps"
one of the purest musicians ever

The editor says ***BGS*** is 60-80 pgs., digest-sized, photocopied and saddle-stapled with card stock cover and b&w art. They accept approximately 200 poems a year. Press run is 300 for 50 subscribers of which 7 are libraries. Single copy: $4; subscription: $8. **Sample postpaid: $3. Previously published poems OK, if notified. No simultaneous submissions. Cover letter required.** Time between acceptance and publication is up to 1 year. **Often comments on rejections. Send SASE for guidelines. Reports within 3 months. Pays up to 3 copies. Acquires first or one-time rights.** Reviews books of poetry in up to 3 pages. Open to unsolicited reviews. Poets may also send books for review consideration. BGS Press **publishes 4 chapbooks/year. Query first with sample poems and cover letter with bio and publication credits. Replies to queries in 1 week, to mss within 1 month. Sometimes sends prepublication galleys. Pays 30 copies. For sample chapbook, send $2.**

‡BLIND BEGGAR PRESS; LAMPLIGHT EDITIONS; NEW RAIN (IV-Ethnic, anthology, children), P.O. Box 437, Williamsbridge Station, Bronx NY 10467, phone and fax (914)683-6792, founded 1976, literary editor Gary Johnston, business manager C.D. Grant, publishes **work "relevant to Black and Third World people, especially women." New Rain** is an annual anthology of such work. Lamplight Editions is a subsidiary which publishes "educational materials such as children's books, manuals, greeting cards with educational material in them, etc." They want to see **"quality work that shows a concern for the human condition and the condition of the world—arts for people sake."** They have published work by Judy D. Simmons, A.H. Reynolds, Mariah Britton, Kurt Lampkin, Rashidah Ismaili, Jose L. Garza and Carletta Wilson. As a sample the editor selected the opening lines of Brenda Connor-Bey's "Crossroad of the Serpent":

Like a serpent
splitting open fields
this road always brings me back
to this magical place of healing
to this place of hidden waters

New Rain is a digest-sized, saddle-stapled or perfect-bound, 60- to 200-page chapbook, finely printed, with simple art, card covers. **Sample postpaid: $5**. They also publish about 3 collections of poetry by individuals each year, 60-100 pgs., flat-spined paperback, glossy, color cover, good printing on good paper. **Sample: $5.95. For either the anthology or book publication, first send sample of 5-10 poems with cover letter including biographical background, philosophy and poetic principles. Considers simultaneous submissions. Reads submissions January 15 through September 1 only. Replies to queries in 3-4 weeks, to submissions in 2-3 months. Pays copies (the number depending on the print run). Acquires all rights. Returns them "unconditionally."** Willing to work out individual terms for subsidy publication. Catalog available for SASE.

BLOCK'S POETRY COLLECTION; ALAN J. BLOCK PUBLICATIONS (I, II), 1419 Chapin St., Beloit WI 53511-5601, founded 1993, editor Alan J. Block, is a quarterly. **"Poems of shorter length (two pages or less), high quality and unique perspective have a home here." They do not want erotica or religious verse.** They have recently published poetry by Spencer Wright, Ginger Tait, Joyce Frazeur and Steven Duplij. As a sample the editor selected these lines from "Intervention" by Corrine DeWinter:

Clio lingers over Ambrosia,

Licking the tips of her fingers
As she contemplates
The casualty of time.
The sand convenes
Around her toes.

The editor says ***BPC*** is 25 pgs., 5½×8½, offset, saddle-stapled, with cover art and ads. Press run is 500 for 25 subscribers. Subscription: $18. **Sample postpaid: $5. No previously published poems or simultaneous submissions.** Time between acceptance and publication is 6-8 months. **Always comments on rejections. Reports in 1 month. Pays 3 copies.** The editor says, "I am open to most kinds of poetry. I encourage poets to send comments with their poems telling me what they believe are their strong points—and their weak points. I am currently looking for more humorous and more formal poetry."

BLOODREAMS: A MAGAZINE OF VAMPIRES & WEREWOLVES (I, IV-Specialized), 1312 W. 43rd St., North Little Rock AR 72118, phone (501)771-2047, founded 1991, editor Kelly Gunter Atlas, is a quarterly appearing in January, April, July and October. They primarily publish short fiction, with poetry and artwork used as fillers. **"All styles of poetry (including traditional) are considered, but all poetry *must* relate to vampires or werewolves. We prefer poetry that is 25 lines or less, but will consider longer works if especially well-written. However, we do not accept poems which are longer than one typewritten page, single-spaced, unless solicited by the editor."** They have published poetry by Dirk Roaché, Lisa S. Laurencot, Roy Martin Nottestad and Joan Aver Kelly. As a sample the editor selected these lines from her own poem, "My Phantom Love":

Nostalgia walks in moonlight
and with it, you.
Your shadow dances
along the cold, dark corridors
of my soul,
tempting me to follow.

Bloodreams is 40-50 pgs., 8½×11, computer typeset and photocopied on 20 lb. paper, bound by plastic spiral, with 60 lb. colored paper cover, b&w drawings and 3-5 pgs. of ads. They receive about 60 poems/year, use 4-5/issue. Press run is 100 for 75 subscribers. Subscription: $15/year. **Sample postpaid: $4. Make check or money order payable to Kelly Atlas. Previously published poems and simultaneous submissions OK. Cover letter required. Reads submissions in December, March, June and September. "Poems are accepted or rejected depending on availability of space in the issue and on the impact the poem has on the editor." Seldom comments on rejections. Reports in 1-2 weeks. Pays 1 copy. Acquires one-time rights.** "We have a review column, 'Fang and Claw,' where books, comics and vampire/werewolf-related poetry chapbooks are reviewed. It varies from issue to issue." The editor says, "We look for poetry that has mood, atmosphere and description. Make us feel that we are not merely reading it, but experiencing it."

BLUE LIGHT PRESS (V), P.O. Box 642, Fairfield IA 52556, phone (515)472-7882, founded 1988, partner Diane Frank, publishes 3 paperbacks, 3 chapbooks/year. **"We like poems that are emotionally honest and uplifting. Women, Visionary Poets, Iowa Poets, San Francisco Poets. No rhymed poetry or dark poetry." They are currently accepting work by invitation only.** They have recently published poetry by Rustin Larson, Nancy Berg, Viktor Tichy, Tom Centolella and Meg Fitz-Randolph. As a sample the editor selected these lines from **The Houses Are Covered in Sound** by Louise Nayer:

There was something
moving in a garbage can,
a white light glowing in a spiral.
I thought it was a child,
no the wind, no the part
of myself that glowed.

That book is 60 pgs., digest-sized, flat-spined, professionally printed, with elegant matte card cover: $10. They have also published two anthologies of Iowa poets. They have an editorial board. "We also work in person with local poets. We have an ongoing poetry workshop, give classes and will edit/critique poems by mail—$30 for 4-5 poems."

BLUE UNICORN, A TRIQUARTERLY OF POETRY; BLUE UNICORN POETRY CONTEST (II, IV-Translations), 22 Avon Rd., Kensington CA 94707, phone (510)526-8439, founded 1977, poetry editors Ruth G. Iodice, Harold Witt and Daniel J. Langton, wants **"well-crafted poetry of all kinds, in form or free verse, as well as expert translations on any subject matter. We shun the trite or inane, the soft-centered, the contrived poem. Shorter poems have more chance with us because of limited space."** They have published poetry by James Applewhite, Kim Cushman, Charles Edward Eaton, Patrick

Worth Gray, Joan LaBombard, James Schevill, John Tagliabue and Gail White. As a sample the editors selected these lines from "Komorova" by Joan Swift:

The last time I saw all night on the horizon
the red horse grazing
I was with you,
weary on the bed in Sweden but pulling

your gauzy breath in and out like this fisherman
who casts his net again and again
on the sea while I watched
the roses go on burning at three a.m.

The magazine is **"distinguished by its fastidious editing, both with regard to contents and format."** It is 56 pgs., narrow digest-sized, saddle-stapled, finely printed, with some art. It features 40-50 poems in each issue, all styles, with the focus on excellence and accessibility. They receive over 35,000 submissions a year, use about 200, have a year's backlog. **Sample postpaid: $5. Submit 3-5 poems on normal typing paper. No simultaneous submissions or previously published poems. Send SASE for guidelines. Reports in 1-3 months (generally within 6 weeks), sometimes with personal comment. Pays 1 copy.** They sponsor an annual contest with small entry fee to help support the magazine, with prizes of $100, $75, $50 and sometimes special awards, distinguished poets as judges, publication of 3 top poems and 6 honorable mentions in the magazine. Entry fee: $4 for first poem, $3 for others to a maximum of 5. Write for current guidelines. **Criticism occasionally offered.** The editors add, "We would advise beginning poets to read and study poetry—both poets of the past and of the present; concentrate on technique; and **discipline yourself by learning forms before trying to do without them.** When your poem is crafted and ready for publication, study your markets and then send whatever of your work seems to be compatible with the magazine you are submitting to."

BLUELINE (IV-Regional), Dept. PM, English Dept., Potsdam College, Potsdam NY 13676, founded 1979, editor-in-chief Anthony Tyler, and an editorial board, "is an annual literary magazine dedicated to prose and **poetry about the Adirondacks and other regions similar in geography and spirit." They want "clear, concrete poetry pertinent to the countryside and its people. It must go beyond mere description, however. We prefer a realistic to a romantic view. We do not want to see sentimental or extremely experimental poetry." They usually use poems of 75 lines or fewer, though "occasionally we publish longer poems" on "nature in general, Adirondack Mountains in particular. Form may vary, can be traditional or contemporary."** They have published poetry by Phillip Booth, George Drew, Eric Ormsby, L.M. Rosenberg, John Unterecker, Lloyd Van Brunt, Laurence Josephs, Maurice Kenny and Nancy L. Nielsen. It's a handsomely printed, 112-page, 6×9 magazine with 40-45 pgs. of poetry in each issue. Circulation 400. **Sample copies: $4 for back issues. No simultaneous submissions. Submit September 1 through November 30, no more than 5 poems with short bio.** They have a 3- to 11-month backlog. **Occasionally comments on rejections. Guidelines available for SASE. Reports in 2-10 weeks. Pays copies. Acquires first North American serial rights.** Reviews books of poetry in 500-750 words, single and multi-book format. "We are interested in both beginning and established poets whose poems evoke universal themes in nature and show human interaction with the natural world. We look for **thoughtful craftsmanship rather than stylistic trickery."**

BOA EDITIONS, LTD. (III), 92 Park Ave., Brockport NY 14420, phone (716)637-3844 or (716)473-1896, founded 1976, poetry editor A. Poulin, Jr., **generally does not accept unsolicited mss.** They have published some of the major American poets, such as W.D. Snodgrass, John Logan, Isabella Gardner, Richard Wilbur and Lucille Clifton, and they publish introductions by major poets of those less well-known. For example, Gerald Stern wrote the foreword for Li-Young Lee's **Rose. Query with samples, bio and publication credits. Pays royalties.**

BOGG PUBLICATIONS; BOGG (II), 422 N. Cleveland St., Arlington VA 22201, founded 1968, poetry editors John Elsberg (USA), George Cairncross (UK: 31 Belle Vue St., Filey, N. Yorkshire YO 14 9HU England), Sheila Martindale (Canada: P.O. Box 23148, 380 Wellington St., London, Ontario NGA 5N9 Canada) and Robert Boyce (Australia/New Zealand: 48 Academy Ave., Mulgrave, Victoria 3170 Australia). "We publish ***Bogg*** magazine and occasional free-for-postage pamphlets." The magazine uses a great deal of poetry in each issue (with several featured poets)—**"poetry in all styles, with a healthy leavening of shorts (under 10 lines). Our emphasis is on good work per se and Anglo-American cross-fertilization. We are currently looking for American work with British/Commonwealth themes/references."** This is one of the liveliest small press magazines published today. It started in England and in 1975 began including a supplement of American work; it now is published in the US and mixes US, Canadian, Australian and UK work with reviews of small press publications from all of those areas. It's thick (64 pgs.), typeset, saddle-stitched, in a 6×9 format that leaves enough white space to let each poem stand and breathe alone. They have recently published work by Jon Silkin,

John Millett, Robert Cooperman, Ann Menebroker, Charles Bukowski, Janine Pommy Vega and Laurel Speer. As a sample we selected this complete poem, "New Age Rebel," by Paul Dilsaver:

she thought Woodstock
was a subdivision

They accept all styles, all subject matter. "Some have even found the magazine's sense of play offensive. Overt religious and political poems have to have strong poetical merits—statement alone is not sufficient. Prefer typewritten manuscripts, with author's name and address on each sheet. We will reprint previously published material, but with a credit line to a previous publisher." No simultaneous submissions. Prefers to see 6 poems at a time. There are about 50 pgs. of poetry/issue. Press run is 850, 400 subscriptions of which 20 are libraries. Subscription: $12 for 3 issues. **Sample postpaid: $3.50.** They receive over 10,000 American poems/year and use 100-150. "We try to accept only for next 2 issues. SASE required or material discarded (no exceptions)." **Send SASE for guidelines. Reports in 1 week. Pays 2 copies. Acquires one-time rights.** Reviews books and chapbooks of poetry in 250 words, single format. Open to unsolicited reviews. Poets may also send books to relevant editor (by region) for review consideration. Their occasional pamphlets and chapbooks are by invitation only, the author receiving 25% of the print run, and you can get **chapbook samples free for SASE**. Better make it at least 2 ounces worth of postage. John Elsberg advises, "Become familiar with a magazine before submitting to it. Always enclose SASE. Long lists of previous credits irritate me. Short notes about how the writer has heard about ***Bogg*** or what he or she finds interesting or annoying in the magazine I read with some interest."

‡BOHEMIAN CHRONICLE; BOHEMIAN BOOKETTES (I), P.O. Box 387, Largo FL 34649-0387, founded 1991, editor/publisher Emily Skinner, is a monthly publication "promoting sensitivity in the arts." **They want experimental poetry no longer than one page. No rhyming poetry.** They have recently published poetry by Holly Day and Pamela Portwood. The editor simply describes it as 12 pgs., stapled. They receive about 100 poems a year, use 24. Press run is 500 for 100 subscribers, 400 sent abroad free. Subscription: $12. **Sample: $1 and #10 SASE. Submit 4 poems maximum. No previously published poems; simultaneous submissions OK. Reads submissions January through September only.** Time between acceptance and publication is 6-8 months. **Always comments on rejections. Send SASE for guidelines. Reports in 1-2 months. Pays $2 and 2 copies. Buys all rights or first rights. If all rights, does not return them.** "We select the year's best for our anniversary issue each May and award Bohos (framed certificates) to the best in each category." The editor says, "We are not formula-oriented. We only buy what we like, good or bad. Bohemian Bookettes are short, short books to be released in '95."

BOMB MAGAZINE (III), Suite 1002 A, 594 Broadway, New York NY 10012, founded 1981, managing editor Lawrence Chua, is a quarterly magazine that "encourages a dialogue among artists of various media. **We encourage poetry by people of color and serious poetry by experienced poets; shorter is better. Experiments with form and language are also encouraged. No limericks, inspirational verse, clever or greeting card styles."** They have published poetry by David Mamet, Harold Pinter and A.C. Purcell. As a sample the editors selected these lines by Agha Shahid Ali:

Cries Majnoon:
Those in tatters
May now demand love:
I've declared a fashion
of ripped collars.
The breezes are lost
travellers today,
knocking, asking
for a place to stay.
I tell them
to go away.

BOMB is 96 pgs., saddle-stitched with 4-color cover. "We receive about 100 manuscripts a month; we accept 2 or 3 every 4 months." Press run is 12,000 for 2,000 subscribers of which 600 are libraries. Single copy: $4; subscription: $16/year. **Sample postpaid: $5. No previously published poems; simultaneous submissions OK. Cover letter including name, address, telephone number and previous publications required. "Poetry should be legibly typed."** Time between acceptance and publication is 4-6 months. **Reports in 4 months. Pays $50. Buys first North American serial rights.** ***Bomb Magazine*** ranked #10 in the "Top Pay" category of the latest ***Writer's Digest*** Poetry 60 list.

BONE & FLESH PUBLICATIONS (II), P.O. Box 349, Concord NH 03302-0349 or RR1, Box 228, Antrim NH 03440, founded 1988, co-editors Lester Hirsh and Susan Bartlett. In 1995, there will be one main issue of ***Bone & Flesh*** literary journal and one chapbook featuring the works of a selected poet or prose writer and artist. "We are looking for **quality work from seasoned writers: prose, poems, fiction, essays, reviews and art. Themes vary and tend to focus on the substance of our lives and the links with other lives and times. We do not accept prosaic or fundamentalist materials.** This year we wish to publish a volume: **Symposium on Song. We'd like to see songwriting and works related to songs and their places in modern and ancient times.**" They have recently published works by Kathleen ten Haken, Lyn Lifshin, Darlene Fozard, Rebecca Rule, Don Skiles, David Brooks, T.R. Healy, Robert Cesaretti and Timothy Hodor. As a sample, the editors selected these lines by Lysa James:

I dream you are a sparrow,
a lighted window,
the graceful hands of a Balinese dancer.
You are lunar,
your limbs oriental brush strokes,
head resting on a neck so frail
tendons of silver wire twist
beneath translucent skin.

Bone & Flesh is 50-65 pgs. Subscription: $12. **Sample postpaid: $6. Submissions are accepted February through May only. Editors attempt to comment on rejections and provide encouragement "when appropriate." Reports in 1-3 months. Pays copies. Acquires first North American serial rights. Chapbooks are accepted by solicitation only.** *Bone & Flesh* recently published ***Bone & Flesh #11, Stories and Poems***, which includes stories, poems and select art work.

BOOG LITERATURE; MA!; D.A. LEVY POETRY CONTEST (I, II), P.O. Box 221, Oceanside NY 11572-0221, founded 1991, editor/publisher David Kirschenbaum. BOOG Literature publishes *MA!*, a quarterly zine of poetry, prose and arts reviews, as well as 5-10 chapbooks/year and occasional broadsides. The editor says he **would like to see more "heartfelt, non-manufactured political poetry."** They have recently published poetry by Eileen Myles, Bernadette Mayer, Elliot Richman and Anne Waldman. As a sample the editor selected these lines from "keeping up with the joneses" by Kent Taylor, published in *MA!*:

I wait stunned
in Jammin' Java
for the first shudder
of deliverance
as Caroline
of the fine
bones
dispenses hit
after hit

MA! is 40 pgs., digest-sized, offset printed and saddle-stitched, with card stock cover, art, graphics and small press ads. "We accept 10-15 poems per issue, sometimes more, never less." Press run is 500 for 10 subscribers, 200 shelf sales. Single copy: $2.50; subscription: $9. **Sample postpaid: $3. Make all checks payable to David Kirschenbaum. Submit up to 5 poems; 6 short poems can count as 1 poem or page of poetry. Previously published poems and simultaneous submissions OK. "A friendly cover letter is always appreciated. Most small presses have low circulations, so if your piece was (or may be) published elsewhere, but you think it deserves/needs to be read by more people, send it along (but please tell us when and where it was or will be published)."** Time between acceptance and publication is "usually no more than 3 months." **Often comments on rejections. Send SASE for guidelines. Reports in 6-12 weeks. Pays 1 copy. Acquires first North American serial or reprint rights.** "We welcome and will write reviews of either chaps or mags in 250-1,000 words, single or multi-book format." **For chapbook or broadside publication, query with sample poems and cover letter including brief bio and publication credits. Replies to queries within 2 months, to mss within 3 months. Pays 10% of press run; first printing is 100-200 copies.** Recent chapbooks include ***Models*** by Pat McKinnon and ***a museme*** by Lee Ann Brown. For sample chapbook, "send check or money order for $1.50 to $4.50, and we will select a chap to send in return." Chapbooks are also selected for publication through the d.a. levy poetry contest, named after the late Cleveland poet. Contest entry fee is $5 ($1 of which is earmarked for AIDS charities in Albany, New York). Submissions should include a brief bio, previous publishing credits and credits for all poems included in the chapbook ms. Mss should be 30-40 pgs. in length and have a suggested title. Reading period for the d.a. levy poetry contest is May 1 through July 31 only. The winner receives $25 and 10 copies of the finished chapbook. All entrants receive 1 copy of the winning chapbook. The press also publishes occasional spoken word cassette compilations. Query before sending tapes. The editor says, "The job of the small press is to get the word out. If it's solid, we will publish it. It's quality, not résumé."

BOOTS: FOR FOLKS WITH THEIR BOOTS ON! (I, IV-Cowboy, themes), P.O. Box 766, Challis ID 83226, phone (208)879-4475, founded 1990, editor Ethie Corrigan, is a biannual magazine using **"well-**

crafted cowboy poetry and historical pieces (Western Americana). No modernistic mumbo-jumbo." They look for poetry with humor as well as nature/rural/ecology, regional (Western) and/or inspirational themes. They have published poetry by Wallace McRae, Gwen Peterson, Sandy Seaton and Mike Logan. As a sample we selected these lines from "The Quilted History Book" by Marilyn Diamond:

And see this piece of pale pink
With flecks of green and rose
It's from the dress I wore, the night
Your daddy, he proposed.
And them squares of creamy ivory
There must be ten or more,
They're bits saved from my daddy's shirt
He died when I was four.

Boots is 56 pgs., web press printed, saddle-stitched, with glossy cover, photos and ads. Press run is 3,000 for 1,000 subscribers of which 2 are libraries. Single copy: $4.50; subscription: $8. **Sample postpaid: $2.50. Previously published poems OK; no simultaneous submissions. Submit typed poems January through March for fall issue; April through September for spring. Always comments on rejections. Publishes theme issues. Send SASE for upcoming themes. Themes for September 1994 and January 1995 issues are transportation (for example, railroads, stage coaches, etc.) and women and children, respectively. The September 1995 issue will celebrate their 5th anniversary. Reports "immediately." Pays copies, "exact number depends on length."** Reviews related books of poetry "now and then." Open to unsolicited reviews. Poets may also send books for review consideration. The editor says poets should be careful when "trying to write about the West if they don't know the background, vocabulary, etc."

BORDERLANDS: TEXAS POETRY REVIEW (II, IV-Regional), P.O. Box 49818, Austin TX 78765, founded 1992, appears twice a year publishing "high-quality, outward-looking poetry by new and established poets, as well as brief reviews of poetry books and critical essays. Cosmopolitan in content, but particularly welcomes Texas and Southwest writers." They want **"outward-looking poems that exhibit social, political, geographical, historical or spiritual awareness coupled with concise artistry. We also want poems in two languages, where the poet has written both versions. Please, no introspective work about the speaker's psyche, childhood or intimate relationships."** They have recently published poetry by Ted Kooser, Donald Finkel, Elton Glaser, Pattiann Rogers and Stephen Dobyns. As a sample the editors selected these lines from "Plains Battleground" by Chris Willerton:

Those shrill vengeances. They clatter
like grasshoppers thrashed up out of standing wheat.
Here in the cold they are mute. The words
arrested by the monuments prove
how few words we can keep, and those
for other readers.

Borderlands is 80-120 pgs., 5½ × 8½, offset, perfect-bound, with 4-color cover, art by local artists. They receive about 2,000 poems a year, use approximately 120. Press run is 600. Subscription: $14/year. **Sample postpaid: $8.50. Send a maximum of 5 pgs. No previously published poems; simultaneous submissions OK. No submissions are read in June, July, August or December. Seldom comments on rejections. Reports in 4-6 months. Pays 1 copy. Acquires first rights.** Reviews books of poetry in one page. Also uses 3- to 6-page essays on single poets and longer essays (3,000-word maximum) on contemporary poetry in some larger context (query first). Offers annual cash prizes for best poems and essays. Send SASE for details. They say, "We believe it's possible—though not easy—for poetry to be both involved with the world and high-quality."

BOREALIS PRESS; TECUMSEH PRESS LTD.; JOURNAL OF CANADIAN POETRY (V), Dept. PM, 9 Ashburn Dr., Nepean, Ontario K2E 6N4 Canada, founded 1972. Borealis and Tecumseh are imprints for books, including **collections of poetry, by Canadian writers only, and they are presently not considering unsolicited submissions.** Send SASE (or SAE with IRCs) for catalog to buy samples. Poets published include John Ferns and Russell Thornton. These sample lines are by Fred Cogswell:

Often in dreams, when powerless to wake
Or move and thereby ease my pounding heart,
I have felt like a mouse that cannot squeal
When the sprung trap pins its broken spine or
Like a rabbit mesmerized by a snake's
Unchanging otherness of lidless eyes.

The ***Journal*** is an annual that publishes articles, reviews and criticism, not poetry. **Sample postpaid: $15.95.**

THE BOSTON PHOENIX: PHOENIX LITERARY SECTION (PLS) (III), 126 Brookline Ave., Boston MA 02215, phone (617)536-5390, founded 1966, poetry editor Lloyd Schwartz, is a monthly book review with one poem in almost every issue. Press run is 150,000. Single copy: $1.50. **As "most poetry is solicited," no submission information was provided. Reports in 1 month. Pays $50.** Open to unsolicited reviews. Poets may also send books for review consideration to Robert Sullivan, supplements editor. Poems published in ***PLS*** appear in **The Best American Poetry 1992**.

BOSTON REVIEW (II), 33 Harrison Ave., Boston MA 02111, founded 1975, editor Josh Cohen, is a bimonthly arts, culture and politics magazine which uses about **three pages of poetry/issue, or 12 poems a year**, for which they receive about 700 submissions. Poems in select issues seem to echo or somehow complement the prose, which concerns social or literary affairs. The poetry features lyric and narrative verse with an emphasis on voice, often plaintive-sounding or dream-like in tone. They have a 4- to 6-month backlog. Circulation is 20,000 nationally including subscriptions and newsstand sales. **Sample postpaid: $4. Submit anytime to Kim Cooper, poetry editor, no more than 6 poems, simultaneous submissions discouraged. Cover letter listing recent publications encouraged. Reports in 2 months "if you include SASE." Always sends prepublication galleys. Pay varies. Buys first serial rights.** Reviews books of poetry. Only using *solicited* reviews. Poets may send books for review consideration. Poetry published by this review has been included in **The Best American Poetry 1993**. The editor advises, "To save the time of all those involved, poets should be sure to send only *appropriate* poems to particular magazines. This means that a poet should not submit to a magazine that he/she has not read. Poets should also avoid lengthy cover letters and allow the poems to speak for themselves."

BOTTOMFISH (II), Creative Writing Program, De Anza College, 21250 Stevens Creek Blvd., Cupertino CA 95014, editor Robert Scott. This college-produced magazine appears annually. **"Spare us the pat, generic greeting card phrases. We want sharp, sensory images that carry a strong theme."** They have recently published poetry by Chitra Divakaruni and Edward Kleinschmidt. As a sample here are lines from "Blowout" by Walter Griffin:

> *Suddenly you are there, out by the highway, arm*
> *wrestling the dark with the wheel in your hands*
> *gauging the distance between odometers and stars*
> *that shimmer like ghosts in the falling air*
> *as the wheel comes loose from the column and*
> *your brakeless car rolls toward the cliff*

Bottomfish is 60 pgs., 7×8¼, well-printed on heavy stock with b&w graphics, perfect-bound. Circulation is 500, free to libraries, schools, etc., but **$4/copy to individual requests. "Before submitting, writers are strongly urged to purchase a sample copy; subject matter is at the writer's discretion, as long as the poem is skillfully and professionally crafted." Best submission times: September through February 1. Deadline: February 1 each year. Reports in 2-6 months, depending on backlog. Pays 2 copies.** The editor adds, "Nobody likes the stock rejection letter, but no other response is possible. We do make specific requests for changes, however, if we really want to publish something and it has only minor problems."

BOUILLABAISSE (I, IV-Form/style), % Alpha Beat Press, 31 A Waterloo St., New Hope PA 18938, phone (215)862-0299, founded 1991, editors Dave Christy and Ana Christy, is a biannual using **"poetry that reflects life and its ups and downs."** They want **"modern, Beat poetry; poetry from the streets of life—no limit. No rhythm, Christian or sweet poetry."** They have recently published poetry by Charles Bukowski, Allen Ginsberg, William Haynes/elliott and Erling Friis-Baastad. As a sample the editors selected these lines by Janine Pommy Vega:

> *Archangel Mary falls into the water*
> *killing the bridges, the Tappanzee and*
> *railroad tresks. Her backside against the pier, they promenade*
> *across her, River Edge to Harlem*
> *and time runs out*

The editors say it is 160 pgs., 8½×11, offset, saddle-stitched, with graphics. They receive 200 submissions a year, accept 40%. Press run is 500 for 350 subscribers of which 9 are libraries. Subscription: $15. **Sample postpaid: $10. Previously published poems and simultaneous submissions OK. Cover letter required. Always comments on rejections. Send SASE for guidelines. Reports "immediately." Pays 1 copy.** Reviews books of poetry in 250-500 words. Open to unsolicited reviews. Poets may also send books for review consideration. They also publish 2 paperbacks and 2 chapbooks/year. "We work with each individual on their project." **Replies to queries "immediately," to mss within 3 weeks. Always sends prepublication galleys for chapbooks. Pays author's copies.** Also see listing for ***Alpha Beat Soup***.

BOULEVARD (II), % editor Richard Burgin, P.O. Box 30386, Philadelphia PA 19103, phone (215)568-7062, founded 1985, appears 3 times a year. **"We've published everything from John Ashbery to Howard**

Moss to a wide variety of styles from new or lesser known poets. We're eclectic. Do not want to see poetry that is uninspired, formulaic, self-conscious, unoriginal, insipid." They have published poetry by Amy Clampitt, Molly Peacock, Jorie Graham and Mark Strand. As a sample, editor Richard Burgin selected these lines from "Three Soundings of January Snow" by Stuart Lishan:

Snow arias the ground tonight. It quilts
the house; it sounds like a samba of whispers,
Muffled, like a mitten slipped over love, like guilt.

Boulevard is 175 pgs., digest-sized, flat-spined, professionally printed, with glossy card cover. Poetry herein—mostly free verse but wide-ranging in content, length and tone—is accessible and exciting. Poems have one thing in common: careful attention to craft (particularly line, stanza and voice). Their press run is 2,800 with 700 subscriptions of which 200 are libraries. Subscription: $12. **Sample postpaid: $6. "Prefer name and number on each page with SASE. Encourage cover letters but don't require them. Will consider simultaneous submissions but not previously published poems." Reads submissions October 1 through May 1 only. Editor sometimes comments on rejections. Pays $25-250/poem, depending on length, plus 1 copy. Buys first-time publication and anthology rights.** Open to unsolicited reviews. ***Boulevard*** ranked #5 in the "Top Pay" category of the latest ***Writer's Digest*** Poetry 60 list, and poetry published here has also been included in the 1992, 1993 and 1994 volumes of **The Best American Poetry.** Richard Burgin says, "We believe the grants we have won from the National Endowment for the Arts etc., as well as the anthologies that continue to recognize us, have rewarded our commitment. My advice to poets: 'Write from your heart as well as your head.' "

BRANCH REDD BOOKS; BRANCH REDD REVIEW; BRANCH REDD POETRY BROADSHEETS; BRANCH REDD POETRY CHAPBOOKS (V), 4805 B St., Philadelphia PA 19120, phone (215)324-1462, editor Bill Sherman, is a "small press publisher of poetry" that **discourages unsolicited mss.** He has published poetry by Allen Fisher, Pierre Joris, Asa Benveniste, Eric Mottram, Kate Ruse-Glason and Shreela Ray. As a sample the editor selected these lines (poet unidentified):

Her hair, her blue nightslip, more
Frustration. Earlier
news of Bunting's death.

The ***Branch Redd Review*** appears irregularly in varied formats with a press run of 500. **Pays at least 10 copies.** Staff reviews books of poetry. Send books for review consideration.

GEORGE BRAZILLER, INC. (II), 60 Madison Ave., New York NY 10010, phone (212)889-0909, founded 1955, editor Adrienne Baxter, is a major literary publisher. In 1980 they published **Classic Ballroom Dances** by Charles Simic, from which this sample poem, "Bedtime Story," was selected:

When a tree falls in a forest
And there's no one around
To hear the sound, the poor owls
Have to do all the thinking.

They think so hard they fall off
Their perch and are eaten by ants,
Who, as you already know, all look like
Little Black Riding Hoods.

It is 64 pgs., digest-sized, professionally printed, flat-spined, with glossy card cover, $3.95. **"We consider reprints of books of poetry as well as new poems. If submitting a book for reprint, *all* reviews of the book should be submitted as well. Submit sample of work, never *entire* original pgs." Reports in 1 month or less. Payment varies in each case. Buys all rights.** The editor says, "We are a small publishing house that publishes few books (in general) each year. Still, we have published many well-known authors and are always receptive to new writers of every kind—and from all parts of the world."

THE BRIDGE: A JOURNAL OF FICTION AND POETRY (II), 14050 Vernon St., Oak Park MI 48237, founded 1990, editor Jack Zucker, appears twice a year using **"exciting, largely mainstream poetry."** They have published poetry by Ruth Whitman and Daniel Hughes. It is 192 pgs., digest-sized, perfect-bound. Press run is 700. Subscription: $8. **Sample postpaid: $5.** An editorial board of 3 considers mss; decision made by editor and 1 special editor. **Editor comments on submissions "rarely." Pays 2 copies. Acquires first rights.** Reviews books of poetry and prose in 1-10 pgs. Poetry published in ***The Bridge*** has been selected for inclusion in ***The Best American Poetry 1994***.

‡BROADSHEET MAGAZINE (IV-Feminist, regional), P.O. Box 56147, Aukland, New Zealand, phone 09-8343472, founded 1972, is a quarterly appearing in March, June, September and December. "We are now run as a voluntary concern and **publish limited poetry at present, all by New Zealand women poets and written from a feminist perspective."** They have published poetry by Margaret Berry and

CLOSE-UP

Haiku Expands Horizons

should I paint,
should I write—
in the dream
I stride a sunlit street
wearing one black shoe, one white

Francine Porad

When Francine Porad participated in a program on creativity sponsored by the Seattle branch of the National League of American Pen Women, she had no idea the experience would change her life. Porad, an artist, was asked to write a poem. Poets in the group were asked to create paintings. The premise was that the disciplines of writing and painting were so similar that if you were successful in one, you could be successful in the other.

Porad proved the premise correct. She not only succeeded in writing a poem for the program, but she also spent the next three months doing nothing but writing. "I felt I was foolish to pursue writing when I had been trained in fine art, but I just simply could not stop," she says. "I converted every experience of my life into a poem."

Although she originally wrote rhyming free verse (about humorous art experiences), Porad soon stumbled upon haiku. Driving down the street one day, she saw a gaunt man wearing a woman's fur coat. Struck by the image, she wrote a three-line poem that a friend told her was actually a haiku—defined by Porad as "a Japanese poem recording the essence of a moment keenly perceived, in which nature is linked to human nature."

While it comes as little surprise that an artist would find herself drawn to a form as image-based as haiku, Porad also began exploring related Japanese forms, such as tanka and renga (renku). A tanka is a five-line poem of feelings (such as the above). "Where you really are not supposed to have commentary in haiku, you are allowed commentary in tanka," she says.

A self-proclaimed "talker," Porad also enjoys renga, "a Japanese linked verse created by the collective effort of many poets. The starting verse determines here and now (place/season) from which changes evolve in the expanding poem. The most important features are linking and shifting." It is often written as correspondence between two people over a period of time.

Once Porad began regularly writing and submitting her work, it didn't take long for her to realize that more publications for these forms were needed. So she took over ***Brussels Sprout*** from founder Alexis Rotella, expanded its haiku-only format (and its size) and, naturally, started featuring the work of local artists. Eight years later, Porad and associate Connie Hutchison are still editing this international journal of haiku and art.

Within the pages of any issue, you will find haiku and senryu (structurally similar to haiku but primarily concerned with human nature; it is usually humorous or satiric) as well as tanka, renga and/or haibun (a prose passage that either ends in a haiku or is interspersed with haiku). There are also occasional articles, announcements for new publications and mini book reviews.

In all, Porad and Hutchison include about 200 pieces in each issue. When reading submissions, they primarily focus on, but do not differentiate between, haiku and senryu. They avoid material with excessive vulgarity as well as a series of words strung together to make one word, such as blameetinguilt (where the "me" of blame becomes the beginning of meeting, and the "g" of meeting becomes the beginning of guilt). "I think it defeats the purpose of the moment with too, too much intellectualization," Porad says.

Also likely to receive an instant rejection is material that tries to be—but is obviously not—haiku. Many beginners try the form but strain to fit a formula. And titles are unnecessary with haiku, Porad says. Using a title signals that the work is by someone new to the field. "Haiku is really a poetry of images. Therefore, when it's all epigrams or opinions or uses very poetic language with metaphors or similes, you know they really have not investigated haiku."

For those not familiar with the form, Porad suggests reading **The Haiku Handbook** by William Higginson or **The Haiku Anthology**, edited by Cor van den Heuvel. Porad also recommends purchasing a sample copy of ***Brussels Sprout*** to see what is currently being published. And she believes that becoming a member of a local or national group can be beneficial. "Your work improves when you constantly hear excellent work read and critiqued."

With that in mind, Porad started a group in the Seattle area for those interested in haiku. The group, Haiku Northwest Poets/Readers, meets monthly. One month members gather at Porad's house for critique sessions; the next they give a public reading at a major bookstore. It is one of seven regional groups affiliated with the Haiku Society of America, a national organization with more than 500 members. Porad served as president of HSA in 1993 and 1994.

Besides participating in various group activities, editing and publishing ***Brussels Sprout***, and continuing to paint, Porad writes and submits her own work. She has published material in 260 issues of 60 different publications, including those in the U.S., Canada, England, Japan and Romania. She also has ten collections, most of which are self-published under Vandina Press. Every piece in these collections has been previously published.

Porad says, "My reasons for putting the books together were twofold. One, I wanted a record to give my family of what had been published during the year. And another was the challenge of putting together an artistically pleasing and artistically arranged volume." Self-publishing haiku and related forms is not unusual, and such collections may be reviewed because "the work has already received some form of recognition."

Porad adds that the community of people interested in haiku and other Japanese forms is very vocal and active—and growing. To receive recognition in this field, don't lose heart. "If one editor doesn't accept your work, try another. There's lots of different points of view. If you honestly, sincerely believe in your work, you'll find an editor to publish it."

—Christine Martin

Sue Rifelelt. It is 64 pgs., newsprint. Subscription: $27.50 NZ; overseas: $45 NZ (airmail). **Sample postpaid: $9 NZ. Pays 1 copy.**

BROKEN STREETS (I, IV-Religious), 57 Morningside Dr. E., Bristol CT 06010, founded 1979, editor Ron Grossman, is a **"Christian-centered outreach ministry to poets."** The editor wants **"Christian-centered poetry, feelings, etc., usually 5-15 lines, but also haiku. No more than 5 poems at a time. Not necessary to query, but helpful."** He has published Bettye K. Wray and Naomi Rhoads. The magazine, which appears 2 times a year, is 40-50 pgs., digest-sized, photocopied typescript with card cover. Uses about 300 of the 500 poems submitted/year – by folks of all ages, including children and senior citizens. Press run is 1,000. Subscription: $10 (includes "all mailings and current chapbook"). **Sample postpaid: $4. Reports in 1 week. No pay but copies.** Reviews books of poetry. Open to unsolicited reviews. Poets may also send books for review consideration. ***Broken Streets*** ranked #4 in the "Nontraditional Verse" category of the latest ***Writer's Digest*** Poetry 60 list.

BROOKLYN REVIEW (II), 2900 Bedford Ave., Brooklyn College, Brooklyn NY 11210, founded 1974, editors change each year, address correspondence to poetry editor. They have published such poets as Allen Ginsberg, Elaine Equi, Amy Gerstler, Eileen Myles, Alice Notley, Honor Moore, Ron Padgett and David Trinidad. ***BR*** is an annual, 128 pgs., digest-sized, flat-spined, professionally printed with glossy color cover and art. Circulation 750. **Sample postpaid: $6. "Please send no more than four poems." Cover letter with brief history required. Reads submissions September 1 through December 1 only. Reports in 6 weeks to 6 months. Pays copies.** Poems published in this review have been included in **The Best American Poetry 1992.**

BRUNSWICK PUBLISHING COMPANY (I), Rt. 1, Box 1A1, Lawrenceville VA 23868, founded 1978, poetry editor Walter J. Raymond, is a **partial subsidy publisher. Query with 3-5 samples. Response in 2 weeks with SASE. If invited, submit double-spaced, typed ms. Reports in 3-4 weeks, reading fee only if you request written evaluation. Always sends prepublication galleys. Poet pays 50-80% of cost, gets same percentage of profits for market-tester edition of 500, advertised by leaflets mailed to reviewers, libraries, book buyers and bookstores.** Samples are flat-spined, matte-covered, 54-page paperbacks. **Send SASE for catalog to order samples and "Statement of Philosophy and Purpose," which explains terms.** That Statement says: "We publish books because that is what we like to do. Every new book published is like a new baby, an object of joy! We do not attempt to unduly influence the reading public as to the value of our publications, but we simply let the readers decide that themselves. We refrain from the artificial beefing up of values that are not there. . . . We are not competitors in the publishing world, but offer what we believe is a needed service. We strongly believe that in an open society every person who has something of value to say and wants to say it should have the chance and opportunity to do so."

BRUSSELS SPROUT (I, IV-Form), P.O. Box 1551, Mercer Island WA 98040, phone (206)232-3239, Francine Porad, art and poetry editor since 1988. This magazine of **haiku, senryu, tanka and art** appears each January, May and September. **They want "any format (1-5 lines); subject matter open; seeking work that captures the haiku moment in a fresh way."** They have recently published poetry by Elizabeth St. Jacques, Marlene Mountain, Paul O. Williams, Tom Clausen and Yvonne Hardenbrook. As a sample the editor selected these haiku by John Stevenson and June Hopper Hymas respectively:

discussion
of one word . . .
a spark flies

the turnstone's cry
amidst the autumn beach-wrack
his cinnabar legs

The magazine is 48 pgs., digest-sized, professionally printed, saddle-stapled with matte b&w card cover featuring an artist each issue. **Sample postpaid: $5.50. Submit only original work, 4-12 poems (can be on one sheet), name and address on each sheet. Do not submit mss from May 25 to June 15. No simultaneous submissions or previously published poems. Send SASE for guidelines. Editor sometimes comments on rejections. Reports in 3 weeks. No payment, other than 3 $10 Editor's Choice Awards each issue.** Reviews books of haiku "sometimes, but list those received with a brief comment or sample of work." Poets may send books for consideration. ***Brussels Sprout*** sponsors Haiku Northwest, a group of writers meeting bimonthly to share and critique work, and Haiku Northwest Readers, offering public readings locally. The editor advises, "For the record, no editor enjoys saying 'no.' Keep writing, rewriting and sending out your manuscripts. If you value your work, you will find an editor who feels the same."

BUFFALO SPREE MAGAZINE (II), 4511 Harlem Rd., Buffalo NY 14226, founded 1967, poetry editor Janet Goldenberg, is the quarterly regional magazine of western New York. It has a controlled circulation (21,000) in the Buffalo area, mostly distributed free (with 3,000 subscriptions, of which 25 are libraries). Its glossy pages feature general interest articles about local culture, plus book reviews, fiction and poetry contributed nationally. It receives about 300 poetry submissions/year and uses about

25, which have ranged from work by Robert Hass and Carl Dennis to first publications by younger poets. As a sample the editor selected these lines from "Alien in Spring" by Martha Bosworth:

I am a tall pale animal in boots
trampling forget-me-nots and scaring birds
from the lemon tree: with my long-handled claw
I pull down lemons—tear-shaped, dimpled, round,
bouncing they vanish into vines and weeds.

They use 5-7 poems/issue, **these are selected 3-6 months prior to publication. Sample postpaid: $3.75. Considers simultaneous submissions, "but we must be advised that poems have been or are being submitted elsewhere." Pays $20/poem.**

BYLINE MAGAZINE (IV-Writing), P.O. Box 130596, Edmond OK 73013, founded 1981, editor Marcia Preston, is a **magazine for the encouragement of writers and poets, using 8-10 poems/issue about writers or writing.** As a sample the editor selected these lines from "A Prayer for Words" by John D. Engle, Jr.:

I have had enough
of words that sigh
their meekness
on the margins of the mind.
I want the centered word
that holds a high
degree of mystery
no one can find
explained in any
common dictionary.

Byline is professionally printed, magazine-sized, with illustrations, cartoons and ads. They have about 3,000 subscriptions and receive about 2,500 submissions/year, of which they use 144. **Sample postpaid: $3.50. No more than 4 poems/submission, no reprints. Send SASE for guidelines. Reports within 6 weeks. Pays $5-10/poem. Buys first North American serial rights.** Sponsors monthly poetry contests. Send #10 SASE for details. Marcia Preston advises, "We are happy to work with new writers, but please read a few samples to get an idea of our style. We would like to see more serious poetry about the creative experience (as it concerns writing)."

‡BYRON POETRY WORKS (I, IV-Regional), P.O. Box 221, Yellow Springs OH 45387, founded 1993, editor J.L. Preston, is "a journal of regional poetry" appearing twice a year. **"*BPW* features poetry from Ohio and its bordering states—Indiana, Kentucky, Michigan, Pennsylvania and West Virginia. We are open to all types of poetry. Poems about our region welcome! No extremely long poems (100 lines maximum) or foreign language poems."** They have recently published poetry by Robert Miltner, William J. Vernon and Alice Mackenzie Swaim. As a sample the editor selected these lines from "Jackhammer Writing" by Pamela Steed Hill:

The poet sits down to dance to the rhythm
to think to the rhythm of the black
and the bright. He sits down under
a strobe light. Shudders without moving
a bone. Dreams the big dream: to hum
to the music of the jack.

BPW is 28 pgs., 5½×8½, photocopied and saddle-stapled with card cover, b&w graphics and a few ads. They accepted approximately 30% of submissions for their debut issue (Spring 1994), and their initial press run was 50. Subscription: $4/year. **Sample postpaid: $1. Make checks payable to Terri Howard-Preston, associate editor. No previously published poems or simultaneous submissions. Cover letter not required, "but certainly welcomed and encouraged." Submissions from outside Ohio, Indiana, Kentucky, Michigan, Pennsylvania and West Virginia are not considered, but will be returned. Reads submissions January 1 through April 30 for spring issue and June 1 through September 30 for fall. Often comments on rejections. Send SASE for guidelines. Reports in about 10 weeks. Pays 1 copy. Acquires one-time rights.** The editor says, "Enjoy expressing yourself with poetry. Don't worry so much about being published. Write your best and be true to your vision. Publication will come. There are many 'little magazines' like ours all over the country. It is encouraging to know that publishing is never very far from the average person. Poetry is alive and well in the U.S."

C.L.A.S.S. MAGAZINE (IV-Regional), Dept. PM, 900 Broadway, New York NY 10003, phone (212)677-3055, editor Constance M. Weaver, is a monthly magazine, covering **Caribbean/American/African Third World** news and views. It has a slick full-sized format with full-color glossy paper cover. Circulation 250,000. Subscription: $12.95, $18 overseas. **Sample: $2.75.** Publishes **10-20 poems a year, 22-30 lines, on appropriate themes. Submit maximum of 10 poems. Pays maximum of $10.**

‡CACANADADADA PRESS (II, IV-Regional), 3350 W. 21st Ave., Vancouver, British Columbia V6S 1G7 Canada, founded 1988, director Ronald B. Hatch, publishes 6 flat-spined paperbacks of poetry/ year–**by Canadian poets only.** They have recently published **Phantoms in the Ark** by A.F. Moritz, **The East Wind Blows West** by George Jones, and **Unmarked Doors** by Inge Israel. As a sample we selected the opening lines from "To Richard Ciccimarra" in **Popping Fuchsias** by Robin Skelton:

Ouspensky would have understood your reading him
holed up in your box of an apartment,
face a mask, eyes bloodshot, elegance gone,
having reached a time discounting time,
having pared away all mortal lendings
till mankind had become no more than shadows . . .

Query first, with sample poems and cover letter with brief bio and publication credits. Previously published poems and simultaneous submissions OK. Seldom comments on rejections. Replies to queries in 2 weeks, to mss in 2 months. Pays 10% royalties and 10 author's copies. Write for catalog to purchase sample books. The director adds, "Confessional poetry or even first-person poetry is very difficult to write well."

THE CAFÉ REVIEW (II), c/o Yes Books, 20 Danforth St., Portland ME 04101, phone (207)775-3233, founded 1989, editors Steve Luttrell and Wayne Atherton, is a quarterly which has grown out of open poetry readings held at a Portland cafe. The editors say they aim "to print the best work we can!" They want **"free verse, 'beat' inspired and fresh. Nothing rhyming or clichéd."** They have published poetry by Denise Levertov, Gerard Malanga and Anne Waldman. As a sample the editor selected these lines from "Cream Hidden" by Michael McClure, beginning with lines by Rumi:

"LIKE CREAM HIDDEN IN THE SOUL OF MILK
no-place keeps coming into place."
No-place is where I am at.
My soil is where no toil
will upearth it.

The Review is 50-60 pgs., 5½×8½, professionally printed and perfect-bound with card cover, b&w art, no ads. They receive over 300 submissions a year, accept approximately 25%. Press run is 200 for 50 subscribers of which 8 are libraries, 50-75 shelf sales. Subscription: $16. **Sample postpaid: $4. No previously published poems or simultaneous submissions. Cover letter with brief bio required. "We usually respond with a form letter indicating acceptance or rejection of work, seldom with additional comments." Reports in 2-4 months. Pays 1 copy.** They also publish 1-2 chapbooks/year. For those interested, poetry readings are still held on second Tuesday evenings, September through May. Write for information.

CALAPOOYA COLLAGE; $1,000 CAROLYN KIZER POETRY AWARDS (II), P.O. Box 309, Monmouth OR 97361, phone (503)838-6292, founded 1981, editor Thomas L. Ferte. ***CC*** is a literary annual using **"all kinds" of poetry.** They have published poetry by Robert Bly, Joseph Bruchac, Octavio Paz, Marge Piercy, Etheridge Knight, Vassar Miller, William Stafford, Ursula K. LeGuin, Patricia Goedicke, David Wagoner and David Ray. It is 48 pgs., tabloid-sized. Press run is 1,500 for 250 subscribers of which 16 arc libraries. They accept about 6% of 6,000 poems received annually. **Sample postpaid: $5. Reads submissions September 1 through June 1 only. Best times for submissions are January and February. Reports in 1-2 months. Pays 2 copies.** Reviews books of poetry in 600-1,000 words. Open to unsolicited reviews. Poets may also send books for review consideration. All poems accepted for publication are eligible for annual $1,000 Carolyn Kizer Poetry Awards.

CALDER PUBLICATIONS LTD.; RIVERRUN PRESS INC; ASSOCIATION CALDER (V), 9-15 Neal St., London WC2H 9TU England, phone (071)497-1741, publisher John Calder, is a literary book publisher. On their list are Samuel Beckett, Breyten Breytenbach, Erich Fried, Paul Eluard, Pier Paolo Passolini and Howard Barker. **"We do not read for the public,"** says John Calder, and he wants **no unsolicited mss.** "Any communication which requires a response should be sent with a SAE."

CALLALOO (IV-Ethnic), Dept. PM, Dept. of English, University of Virginia, Charlottesville VA 22093, phone (804)924-6616, founded 1976, editor Charles H. Rowell. Devoted to **poetry dealing with North America, Europe, Africa, Latin and Central America, South America and the Caribbean.** They have published poetry by Rita Dove, Jay Wright, Alice Walker, Yusef Komunyakaa, Aimé Césaire, Nicolás

Use the General Index to find the page number of a specific publisher. If the publisher you are seeking is not listed, check the " '94-'95 Changes" list at the end of this section.

Guillén and Jimmy Santiago Baca. Visually beautiful and well-edited with thematic, powerful poems in all forms and styles, this thick quarterly journal features about 15-20 poems in each issue (along with concise and scholarly book reviews). Circulation 1,400, with 1,400 subscriptions of which half are libraries. Subscription: $25, $50 for institutions. **"We have no specifications for submitting poetry except authors should include SASE." Reports in 6 months. Pays copies.** Poetry published in ***Callaloo*** has been included in the 1992 and 1994 volumes of **The Best American Poetry.**

CALYX, A JOURNAL OF ART & LITERATURE BY WOMEN (IV-Women, lesbian), P.O. Box B, Corvallis OR 97339, phone (503)753-9384, founded 1976, managing editor M. Donnelly, is a journal edited by a collective editorial board, **publishes poetry, prose, art, book reviews and interviews by and about women.** They want **"excellently crafted poetry that also has excellent content."** They have published poetry by Diane Glancy, Robin Morgan, Rebecca Seiferle, Lin Max and Carol Ann Russell. As a sample the editor selected these lines from "Watching My Mother Dress" by Cornelia Hoogland:

She, who loudhosannahed every chore,
cleaned and cared for us while she peeled potatoes,
in one deft spiral paring, who spun rooms
and bottles through her dusting cloth, lingered.

Each issue is 7×8, handsomely printed on heavy paper, flat-spined, glossy color cover, 125-200 pgs., of which 50-60 are poetry. Poems tend to be lyric free verse that makes strong use of image and symbol melding unobtrusively with voice and theme. **Sample for the single copy price: $8 plus $1.50 postage. *Calyx* is open to submissions twice annually: March 1 through April 15 and October 1 through November 15. Mss received when not open to reading will be returned unread. Send up to 6 poems with SASE and short biographical statement. "We accept copies in good condition and clearly readable. We report in 2-6 months." Guidelines available for SASE. Pays copies.** Open to unsolicited reviews. Poets may also send books for review consideration. In past years ***Calyx*** has received Bumbershoot Small Press Best Literary Journal Awards, the CCLM Literary Magazine Editors Award for Excellence, and an American Literary Magazine Award for best cover design and honorable mention for editorial content. They say, "Read the publication and be familiar with what we have published."

CAMELLIA; CAMELLIA PRESS INC. (II), P.O. Box 417, Village Station, New York NY 10014-0417, editor Tomer Inbar. ***Camellia*** is a biannual poetry magazine "currently available for free in the San Francisco/Oakland Bay area, Madison, Seattle, Ithaca and D.C., or by sending a 52¢ SASE. **We publish poetry in the W.C. Williams tradition. The poetry of things, moment and sharpness. We encourage young writers and like to work with the writers who publish with us (i.e., publishing them again to widen the forum or exposure of their work). Our main goal is to get the poetry out. We do not want to see poetry where the poem is subordinate to the poet or poetry where the noise of the poetic overshadows the voice. We look for poetry that is honest and sharp and unburdened."** As a sample the editor selected this poem, "Eyes Gray," by David Gonsalves:

No, it's all
static really . . . you
could measure the length
and width of your

street. Or walk
through a cloud
of it, singing

there. She was thinking
about you and this.

Camellia is 20-24 pgs., digest-sized, desktop-published. The first thing that catches your eye is the design. The editors make up for this modest-looking, stapled publication with creative typesetting inside, featuring lively avant-garde or imagistic free verse with titles in large points and varied fonts. "We receive approximately 300-350 poems/issue and publish about 20." Press run is 500-900. Subscription: $5/year, $7 overseas. **Sample: 52¢ SASE. Simultaneous submissions and previously published poems OK. Reports "ASAP." Pays 2 copies. Editor comments on submissions "if asked for or if I want to see more but am not satisfied with the poems sent.** We currently publish two regular issues per year and are instituting a series of special project issues. The first, a chapbook of poems by Jerry Mirskin entitled **Picture A Gate Hanging Open And Let That Gate Be The Sun**, is now available for $5 from Camellia Press Inc." **They send prepublication galleys only for chapbooks. *Camellia*** is supported, in part, by a multi-year grant from the New York State Council on the Arts.

CANADIAN AUTHOR; CANADIAN AUTHORS ASSOCIATION (III), Suite 500, 275 Slater St., Ottawa, Ontario K1P 5H9 Canada, poetry editor Sheila Martindale. ***Canadian Author***, a quarterly, is magazine-sized, 28 pgs., professionally printed, with paper cover in 2 colors. It contains articles useful to writers at all levels of experience. **Sample postpaid: $4.50. Buys 40 poems a year. "The trend is toward thematic issues and profiles of featured poets, so query letters are recommended." Pays $15 plus one copy.** (See also Canadian Authors Association Literary Awards in the Contests and Awards section.)

CANADIAN DIMENSION: THE MAGAZINE FOR PEOPLE WHO WANT TO CHANGE THE WORLD (IV-Political), Dept. PM, 707-228 Notre Dame Ave., Winnipeg, Manitoba R3B 1N7 Canada, phone (204)957-1519, founded 1964, editorial contact Brenda Austin-Smith, appears 6 times/year, using **"short poems on labour, women, native and other issues. Nothing more than one page."** They have published poetry by Tom Wayman and Milton Acorn. It is 48-56 pgs., magazine-sized, slick, professionally printed, with glossy paper cover. Press run is 3,500 for 2,600 subscribers of which 800 are libraries, 1,000 shelf sales. Subscription: $30.50 US ($24.50 Canadian). **Sample postpaid: $1.50. Simultaneous submissions OK. Editor comments on submissions "rarely." Publishes theme issues. Reports in 1 month. Pays 5 copies.** Reviews books of poetry in 750-1,200 words, single or multi-book format.

CANADIAN LITERATURE (IV-Regional), 2029 West Mall, University of British Columbia, Vancouver, British Columbia V6T 1Z2 Canada, phone (604)822-2780, founded 1959, editor W.H. New, is a quarterly review which publishes **poetry by Canadian poets. "No limits on form. Less room for long poems."** They have published poetry by Atwood, Ondaatje, Layton and Bringhurst. As a sample the editor selected these lines from "Subtexts" by Susan Ioannou:

Imagine words are snow we crawl under
and scratch at matted ice for crocuses.

Or, flattened on our backs in white,
that words fan angel wings.

And how could we forget
that clouds are words too?

Each issue is professionally printed, digest-sized, flat-spined, with 176 pgs., of which about 10 are poetry. They receive 100-300 submissions/year, use 10-12. Circulation 1,500, two-thirds of which are libraries. **Sample for the cover price: $15 Canadian plus postage and GST. No simultaneous submissions or reprints. Reports within the month. "Accepted poems must be available on diskette." Pays $10/poem plus 1 copy. Buys first rights.** Reviews books of poetry in 500-1,000 words, depending on the number of books.

CANADIAN WRITER'S JOURNAL (IV-Writing); WIND SONGS (IV-Form/style), Gordon M. Smart Publications, P.O. Box 6618, Depot 1, Victoria, British Columbia V8P 5N7 Canada, is a small quarterly, publishing mainly short "how-to" articles of interest to writers at all levels. They use a few **"short poems or portions thereof as part of 'how-to' articles relating to the writing of poetry and occasional short poems with tie-in to the writing theme."** The Wind Songs column of *CWJ* accepts **unpublished poems including haiku, senryu, tanka, sijo, one-liner renga and sequences. Maximum 15 lines. Submit 5 poems or less (identify each form)** to Elizabeth St. Jacques, Poetry Editor, 406 Elizabeth St., Sault Ste. Marie, Ontario P6B 3H4 Canada. **Include SASE ("U.S. postage accepted; do not affix to envelope"). Token payment.** Subscription: $15 for 1 year, $25 for 2 years. **Sample: $4.** The magazine runs an annual poetry competition with closing date June 30. Send SASE for current rules.

CANDLESTONES (V), P.O. Box 10703, St. Petersburg FL 33733, founded 1990, editor Ann Blain, is a biannual literary arts magazine. "The purpose is to encourage artists and poets who have not been published and share creativity with people who usually do not buy poetry." They publish poetry, b&w art and photos, and short stories. **"I want poetry the poet is proud of. Some long poems are accepted and I always need short poems. No poems containing profanity. No pornographic poetry."** As a sample the editor selected these lines by Holly Blain:

Sun-dappled kisses
Echo off my skin to you
Caught in the web of our love.
We stare
and understand.

"We accept simultaneous submissions and previously published works. We like cover letters just because they are interesting reading. However, at this time we are overstocked." Seldom comments on rejections. Reports in 3 months. Pays 3 copies. The editor says, "*Candlestones* is an outgrowth of a monthly coffee house held in my home. Most contributors are under 30. Its twofold purpose is to give people a chance to have their creative efforts viewed by others and show the general populace (people who would never buy a book of poetry) the artistic achievement around them. It has been distributed in gas stations, factories, bookstores, record stores and beauty parlors. My advice is to submit. If one place rejects it, submit somewhere else. One poet I know wrote a poem in 1922. When it was submitted in 1990, it was printed. Don't wait so long. But be patient with the small press."

THE CAPE ROCK (II), Department of English, Southeast Missouri State University, Cape Girardeau MO 63701, founded 1964, appears twice yearly and consists of **64 pgs. of poetry and photography, with a $200 prize for the best poem in each issue and $100 for featured photography. "No restrictions on subjects or forms. Our criterion for selection is the quality of the work. We prefer poems under 70 lines; no long poems or books, no sentimental, didactic or cute poems."** They have published poetry by Stephen Dunning, Joyce Odam, Judith Phillips Neeld, Lyn Lifshin, Virginia Brady Young, Gary Pacernik and Laurel Speer. As a sample the editor selected these lines from "At The Rodin Museum, Stanford" by Fred D. White:

The lovers unleash their passion on the hot
summer grass of the sculpture garden,
surrounded by metal longing.

They drop wild desires into each other's mouths
like mother birds.

It's a handsomely printed, flat-spined, digest-sized magazine. Their circulation is about 500, with 200 subscribers, of whom half are libraries. **Sample: $3. Guidelines available for SASE.** They have a 2- to 8-month backlog and **report in 1-3 months. Do not submit mss in May, June or July. Pays 2 copies.** This is a solid publication that features a wide selection of forms and styles, leaning in recent years toward free verse that establishes a mood or milieu.

CAPERS AWEIGH MAGAZINE (I, IV-Regional), P.O. Box 96, Sydney, Nova Scotia B1P 6G9 Canada, founded 1992, publisher John MacNeil, is a quarterly of **poetry and short fiction "of, by and for Cape Bretoners at home and away." They want work by Cape Bretoners only. Nothing profane.** The publisher says it is 50-60 pgs., 5×8, desktop-published, stapled, including computer graphics and trade ads. Press run is 500. Subscription: $20. **Sample postpaid: $5. No simultaneous submissions. Cover letter required. Seldom comments on rejections. Pays 1 copy.**

‡THE CAPILANO REVIEW (III), 2055 Purcell Way, North Vancouver, British Columbia V7J 3H5 Canada, phone (604)984-1712, fax (604)984-4985, founded 1972, editor Robert Sherrin, is a literary and visual media review appearing 3 times/year. **They want avant-garde, experimental, previously unpublished work, "poetry of sustained intelligence and imagination."** *TCR* comes in a handsome digest-sized format, 150 pgs., flat-spined, finely printed, semi-glossy stock with a glossy full-color card cover. Circulation: 1,000. **Sample: $9 prepaid. Do not submit mss during June and July. No simultaneous submissions. Reports in up to 6 months. Sometimes sends prepublication galleys. Pays an honorarium plus 2 copies.**

CAPPER'S (I, IV-Nature, inspirational, religious, humor), 1503 SW 42nd St., Topeka KS 66609-1265, founded 1879, editor Nancy Peavler, is a biweekly tabloid (newsprint) going to **370,000 mail subscribers, mostly small-town and farm people. Uses 6-8 poems in each issue. They want short poems (4-10 lines preferred, lines of one-column width) "relating to everyday situations, nature, inspirational, humorous."** They have published poetry by Helen Harrington, Emma Walker, Sheryl Nelms, Alice Mackenzie Swaim, Ralph W. Seager and Ida Fasel. As a sample we selected these lines from "Out West" by Jeannine Thyreen:

I want to see mountains etched in
the distance,
where God stretches the land and
stars,
holding the ends with His
fingertips, arms opened wide.

Send $1 for sample. Not available on newsstand. "Most poems used in *Capper's* are upbeat in tone and offer the reader a bit of humor, joy, enthusiasm or encouragement. Short poems of this type fit our format best." Submit 4-6 poems at a time. No simultaneous submissions. Now returns mss with SASE. Reports within 4-5 months. Pays $3-6/poem. Buys one-time rights. The editor says "Poems chosen are upbeat, sometimes humorous, always easily understood."

THE CARIBBEAN WRITER (IV-Regional), University of the Virgin Islands, RR 02, P.O. Box 10,000, Kingshill, St. Croix, USVI 00850, phone (809)778-0246, founded 1987, editor Dr. Erika Waters, is an annual literary magazine **with a Caribbean focus. The Caribbean must be central to the literary work or the work must reflect a Caribbean heritage, experience or perspective.** They have recently published poetry by Derek Walcott, Phillis Gershator and Ian McDonald. As a sample the editor selected the opening lines of "Nineteen Ninety-Two" by Howard Fergus:

Dawns 1992 a magic landfall

on a brand new world of gold
in Europe. Columbus makes a second
coming after five hundred years
not to violate virgin peoples
but to carnival God for earlier conquests

The magazine is handsomely printed on heavy pebbled stock, flat-spined, 160 pgs., 6×9, with glossy card cover, using advertising and b&w art by Caribbean artists. Press run is 1,000. Single copy: $9 plus $1.50 postage; subscription: $18 for 2 years. **Sample: $5 plus $1.50 postage. Send SASE for guidelines. (Note: postage to and from the Virgin Islands is the same as within the United States.) Simultaneous submissions OK. Blind submissions only: name, address, phone number and title of ms should appear in cover letter along with brief bio. Title only on ms. Deadline is September 30 of each year.** The annual appears in the spring. **Pays 2 copies. Acquires first North American serial rights.** Reviews books of poetry and fiction in 500 words. Open to unsolicited reviews. Poets may also send books for review consideration. The magazine annually awards the Daily News Prize of $250 for the best poem or poems.

CARLETON ARTS REVIEW (II), Box 78, 18th Floor, Davidson Douton Tower, Carleton University, Ottawa, Ontario K1S 5B6 Canada, phone (613)567-3525, founded 1982, is a 60-page biannual publishing poetry, prose, graphics, reviews and criticism. **"All kinds of poetry accepted and encouraged."** They have published poetry by Stan Regal, Brian Burke, Calvin White and Alan Packwood. They receive 200-300 poems a year, publish about 10%. Press run is 400 for 50 subscribers most of which are libraries, 150 shelf sales. Subscription: $7. **Sample postpaid: $3.50. No previously published poems or simultaneous submissions. "Please include a short biography and list of publications." Submit in September or December. Often comments on rejections. Reports in 1-2 months. Pays 2 copies.**

CARNEGIE MELLON MAGAZINE (II, IV-Specialized: university affiliation), Carnegie Mellon University, Pittsburgh PA 15213, phone (412)268-2132, editor Ann Curran, is the **alumni magazine** for the university and **limits selections to writers connected with the university.** As a sample the editor selected these lines from "Raw October" by Jim Daniels, an associate professor of English:

We toss eggs
at cars, houses,
Crazy Eddie chases
us down the street
Larry rips
his shirt on a fence . . .

Direct submissions to Gerald Costanzo, poetry editor. No payment. Only uses staff-written reviews.

CAROLINA WREN PRESS (II, IV-Women, ethnic, gay/lesbian, social issues), 120 Morris St., Durham NC 27701, phone (919)560-2738, founded 1976, poetry editor Maria Lee, publishes 1 book/year, **"primarily women and minorities, though men and majorities also welcome."** They have recently published poetry by Jaki Shelton Green, Mary Kratt and Steven Blaski. **Send book-length mss only. Reports in 2-4 months. Pays 10% of print run in copies. Send 9½×12 SASE for catalog and guidelines (include postage for 3 ounces).**

‡CARPENTER PRESS (V), P.O. Box 14387, Columbus OH 43214, founded 1973, primarily to publish fiction, editor Bob Fox, publishes **an occasional full-length collection of poems, flat-spined. No unsolicited mss. Query, no samples.** They have published poetry by Steve Kowit and David Shevin. **Pays 10% royalties, 10% of press run in copies. Send $1 p&h for illustrated catalog to purchase samples.**

THE CARREFOUR PRESS (V), Box 2629, Cape Town, South Africa 8000, phone (021)6856259, founded 1988, managing editors Douglas Reid Skinner and Dee Murch, is a "small press specializing in poetry, fiction, criticism, philosophy," accepting **"manuscripts by invitation only."** They have published poetry by Basil Du Toit, Douglas Livingstone and Israel Ben Yosef. They publish about 6 paperbacks a year averaging 80 pgs. Poets they publish **"should have an established reputation, primarily through magazines." Query with cover letter including previous publication details. Pays 7½-10% royalties and 20 copies.** About a third of their books are subsidized, and the poet "must assist in obtaining sponsorship."

CAT FANCY (IV-Specialized, children), P.O. Box 6050, Mission Viejo CA 92690, phone (714)855-8822, founded 1965, editor Debbie Phillips-Donaldson. *Cat Fancy* is a magazine-sized monthly that uses **poems on the subject of cats. "No more than 30 short lines; open on style and form, but a conservative approach is recommended. In our children's department we occasionally use longer, rhyming verse that tells a story about cats. No eulogies for pets that have passed away."** They have published poetry by Lola Sneyd and Edythe G. Tornow. Press run is 368,575 for 303,328 subscribers,

37,502 shelf sales. Subscription: $23.97. **Sample postpaid: $5.50. Submit ms with name and address "in upper left-hand corner." Editor sometimes comments on submissions, "especially if the ms is appealing but just misses the mark for our audience." Reports in 6-8 weeks. Pays $20/poem plus 2 copies.** She says, "We have an audience that very much appreciates sensitive and touching work about cats. As for advice – get input from knowledgeable sources as to the marketability of your work, and be open to learning how your work might be improved. Then send it out, and hang on. Rejection may not mean your work is bad. We are able to accept very few submissions, and the competition is fierce. Timing and luck have a lot to do with acceptance, so keep trying!"

CATALYST: A MAGAZINE OF HEART AND MIND (I, II, IV-Themes), Suite 400, 236 Forsyth St., Atlanta GA 30303, phone (404)730-5785, founded 1986, editor Pearl Cleage, is a biannual designed "to stimulate readers and writers and move people to see the world differently." **They are "open to all types" of poetry. However, each issue also has a special theme/focus.** They have published poetry by Sonia Sanchez, Haki Madhubuti, Mari Evans and Amiri Baraka. As a sample we selected these lines from "Log" by Michael Blaine Guista:

Three 6-packs down and I'm only 16, practicing
my father's stupor. Words thick as pines
press through the gauzed air
and my walk is familiar, like an old tic.
I'm here and not here and watch myself
like a ghost or the son of a ghost

The above is from the issue about "The Plague Years" which tries "to tell the truth that emerges during times of great pain and sorrow and even greater confusion." *Catalyst* is 90-120 pgs., 7¾ × 10¾, newsprint, saddle-stapled with glossy cover, limited photographs, no ads. They receive 1,200-1,500 poems a year, accept 125-150. Press run is 5,000 for 1,500 subscribers of which 500 are libraries, 500 shelf sales. Single copy: $2.50; subscription: $10 for 2 years. **Sample: $2.50 and 9 × 12 SAE with 40¢ postage. Previously published poems and simultaneous submissions OK. All submissions must be typed, double-spaced. Include name and address on every page along with a 5-line biographical statement. Send SASE to the above address for theme and guidelines. Send submissions to: *Catalyst*, Atlanta/Fulton Public Library, 1 Margaret Mitchell Square NW, Atlanta GA 30303. "Immediate acknowledgement will be made of work received but large volume submissions and very small staff mean that final decisions are not made for five to six months after submission." Pays $10-50. "Contributors also receive 2 complimentary copies upon publication of their work."**

CATAMOUNT PRESS (II, IV-Anthology), 2519 Roland Rd. SW, Huntsville AL 35805, founded 1992, editor Georgette Perry, publishes 1-2 chapbooks and 1 anthology/year. **During 1995 Catamount will concentrate on broadsides and chapbook-size "mini-anthologies." Query (with SASE) for themes.** Poets recently published include Bruce Berger, Marilyn Krysl and David Mason. As a sample the editor selected these lines from "Nanday" by Gabrielle Dempsey:

I soothe him with a hissing cassette
of rainfall, from the bookstore.
I tell him little birds are sewing the canopy.
tell how slowly the leaves fall
from these improbable trees; their ravelings
make a deep place, sunless, soft, where fulgid beetles
furrow and bumble, clicking like big coins

That is from the anthology **Witnessing Earth,** poems on nature and the sacred, $6 postpaid. The editor says, **"The best chance for publication is to submit 3-5 poems on appropriate anthology theme." Shorter poems preferred, 2-page limit. Previously published poems OK if author holds copyright. Cover letter with SASE required. Reports in 1 month. Sometimes sends prepublication galleys. Pays copies.**

THE CATHARTIC (II), P.O. Box 1391, Ft. Lauderdale FL 33302, phone (305)967-9378, founded 1974, edited by Patrick M. Ellingham, "is a **small poetry magazine devoted to the unknown poet** with the understanding that most poets are unknown in America." He says, "While there is no specific type of poem I look for, **rhyme for the sake of rhyme is discouraged. Any subject matter except where material is racist or sexist in nature. Overly-long poems, over 80 lines, are not right for a small magazine normally. I would like to see some poems that take chances with both form and language.** I would like to see poems that get out of and forget about self ['I'] and look at the larger world and the people in it with an intensity that causes a reader to react or want to react to it. I am gravitating toward work that looks at the darker side of life, is intense and uses words sparingly." **Considers sexually explicit material.** Recently published poets include Joy Walsh, Holly Day, Frank Cioffi and James Langdon. It's a modest, 28-page pamphlet, offset printed from computer-generated text, MSWord and Pagemaker, consisting mostly of poems and appearing twice a year. He receives over

1,000 submissions/year, uses about 60. No backlog. **Sample postpaid: $3. Submit 5-10 poems. Simultaneous submissions OK. Guidelines available for SASE. Reports in 1 month. Contributors receive 1 copy.** Uses reviews of small press books as well as some artwork and photography. Send books for review consideration. He advises, "The only way for poets to know whether their work will get published or not is to submit. It is also essential to read as much poetry as possible–both old and new. Spend time with the classics as well as the new poets. Support the presses that support you–the survival of both is essential to the life of poetry."

CAT'S EAR (II), P.O. Box 946, Kirksville MO 63501, founded 1992, editor Tim Rolands, appears annually publishing both poetry and fiction. They want **"poetry that shows an understanding of music and metaphor."** They have recently published poetry by Diane Wakoski, Charles Edward Eaton, X.J. Kennedy and Denise Levertov. As a sample the editor selected these lines from "Homeland" by Ioanna-Veronika Warwick:

Yet my deepest bond has not been
to any country.
The homeland of the mind
has no boundaries.
Books stand open like houses.
Nobody is foreign.

Cat's Ear is 64 pgs., digest-sized, offset and perfect-bound with cover photo. They receive about 1,000 poems a year, use approximately 10%. Subscription: $5 individuals, $10 institutions. **Sample postpaid: $5. No previously published poems or simultaneous submissions. Seldom comments on rejections. Reports "usually in 1-3 months." Pays 2 copies. Acquires first North American serial rights.**

CATS MAGAZINE (IV-Specialized), P.O. Box 290037, Port Orange FL 32129, phone (904)788-2770, fax (904)788-2710, editor Tracey Copeland, is a monthly magazine **about cats, including light verse about cats,** for cat enthusiasts of all types. **Sample copy and writer's guidelines for $2 (postage and handling). All submissions or requests must have SASE. Publishes theme issues. Pays $5-30/poem on publication.**

‡CAVEAT LECTOR (III), 5546 Fulton St., San Francisco CA 94121, phone (415)668-3239, founded 1989, editors Christopher Bernard, James Bybee, Gordon Phipps and Andrew Towne, appears 3 times/year. "*Caveat Lector* is devoted to the arts and to cultural and philosophical commentary. We publish visual art and music as well as literary and theoretical texts." **They want poetry that is "technically polished and deeply felt–if humorous, actually funny. Classical to experimental. 200-line limit."** They have recently published poetry by Ivan Arguelles, Toby Lurie, Jack Foley, Lyn Lifshin and Alfred Robinson. As a sample the editors selected these lines from "Matthew, do you ride?" by Zoon:

How can you rule a god
who doesn't speak your language?
Why? When the shadow of god's passage touches you
you don't deny the awful unanticipated call –
you rise.

The editors say ***CL*** is 28-32 pgs., 6½×8½, offset and saddle-stitched. They receive approximately 100 poems a year, accept less than 10%. Press run is 500 for 100 subscribers of which 20 are libraries, 350 shelf sales. Single copy: $2.50; subscription: $10 for 4 issues. **Sample postpaid: $3. Simultaneous submissions OK.** Time between acceptance and publication is 6 months. **Often comments on rejections. Reports in 1 month. Pays 5 copies. Acquires first publication rights.** Christopher Bernard says, "The two rules of writing are: 1. Rewrite it again. 2. Rewrite it again. The writing level of most of our submissions is pleasingly high. A rejection by us is not always a criticism of the work, and we try to provide comments to our more promising submitters."

WM CAXTON LTD. (I, IV-Regional), 12037 Hwy. 42, Ellison Bay WI 54210, phone (414)854-2955, founded 1986, publisher K. Luchterhand. **"About 50% of our books involve an author's subvention of production costs with enhanced royalties and/or free copies in return," and the publisher acquires all rights.** They want **"any serious poetry, not children's or doggerel." Poetry must have Northern Midwest author or subject.** They have recently published books of poetry by David Koenig, Marilyn Taylor, William Olson and Caroline Sibr. Write or call to purchase sample copies.

‡CENCRASTUS (II, IV-Ethnic), One Abbeymount Techbase, Edinburgh EH8 8EJ Scotland, phone (031)661-5687, founded 1979, editor Raymond Ross, is a quarterly magazine **"to create the intellectual and imaginative conditions for a new Scottish nation" which uses "no light verse; long poem a specialty; open as to form."** They have published poetry by Edwin Morgan, Kenneth White, Sorley Maclean, Gael Turnbull, Douglas Dunn and international poets. As a sample we selected these lines from "A Legacy" by Irene Evans:

Because I believe she is
there still listening. From within
the cellar of herself
she hands me something
to take away from here.
To keep.

There are 3-8 pages of poetry in each issue. They receive over 600 submissions/year, use 30, have a 1- to 2-issue backlog. Circulation to 1,000 subscriptions of which a fourth are libraries. **Sample: £2 postpaid from USA. Submit 4-8 poems, typed, no query. Reports in 1-2 months. Sometimes sends prepublication galleys. Pays £10/poem or £30/page.** Reviews books of all kinds, including poetry. You have to become familiar with this magazine before sending to it because it is an international journal of literature, arts and affairs. Poems are few, but powerful (with focus on image and idea rather than on feelings and personal experience).

THE CENTENNIAL REVIEW (II), 312 Linton Hall, Michigan State University, East Lansing MI 48824-1044, phone (517)355-1905, founded 1957, editor R.K. Meiners, appears 3 times/year. They want **"that sort of poem which, however personal, bears implications for communal experience."** They have published poetry by David Citino and Dimitris Tsaloumas. As a sample the editor selected these lines from "Those Who Claimed We Hated Them" by Sherri Szeman:

. . . We clicked tongues in sympathy
at the blue-black scratchings on their forearms.

But we had all suffered during the war.
We suffered, as they did. We had only

feigned gaiety at their misfortunes, to
convince our oppressors to spare our homes.

It is 240 pgs., 6×9, desktop-published, perfect-bound, with 3-color cover, art, graphics and ads. They receive about 500 poems a year, accept about 2%. Press run is 1,000 for 800 subscribers. Subscription: $10/year. **Sample postpaid: $5. No previously published poems or simultaneous submissions. Seldom comments on rejections. Publishes theme issues. Send SASE for guidelines and upcoming themes. Reports in about 2 months. Pays 2 copies plus 1-year subscription. Acquires all rights. Returns rights "when asked by authors for reprinting."**

CENTER PRESS; MASTERS AWARD (III), Box 16452, Encino CA 91416-6452, founded 1980, editor Jana Cain. Center Press is "a small press presently publishing approximately 6-7 works per year including poetry, photojournals, calendars, novels, etc. We look for quality, freshness and that touch of genius." In poetry, **"we want to see verve, natural rhythms, discipline, impact**, etc. We are flexible but **verbosity, triteness and saccharine make us cringe."** They have published books by Bebe Oberon, Walter Calder, Exene Vida, Carlos Castenada, Claire Bloome and G.G. Henke. Their tastes are for poets such as Charles Bukowski, Sylvia Plath, Erica Jong and Bob Dylan. **"We have strong liaisons with the entertainment industry and like to see material that is media-oriented and au courant." Sample postpaid: $8. Query first, with 2-3 poems and brief bio material or curriculum vitae. If invited to submit, send double-spaced, typed ms. "No manuscripts will be read without SASE." Simultaneous submissions OK. Criticism offered on rejected mss. (Note: Fee charged if criticism requested.) Replies "ASAP." Offers 20% royalty contract, 10-50 copies, advance or honorarium depending on grants or award money.** "We sponsor the Masters Awards, established in 1981, including a poetry award with a $1,500 grand prize annually plus each winner (and the five runners up in poetry) will be published in a clothbound edition and distributed to selected university and public libraries, news mediums, etc. There is a one-time only $10 administration and reading fee per entrant. Further application and details available with a #10 SASE." The editor says, "Please study what we publish before you consider submitting. Also, querying first is a must! We do not return unsolicited mss!"

UNIVERSITY OF CENTRAL FLORIDA CONTEMPORARY POETRY SERIES (II), % English Dept., University of Central Florida, Orlando FL 32816-1346, phone (407)823-2212, founded 1968, poetry editor Judith Hemschemeyer, publishes **two 50- to 75-page hardback or paperback collections each year.** They have recently published poetry by Don Stap, William Hathaway and John Woods. As a sample we selected these lines from "Disease Without a Name" in **Aid and Comfort** by Greg Johnson:

For in fact you are no disease, or so
they tell us, merely an absence
of polite health that welcomes all manner
of bonafide ills, like unruly relatives,
lets them come barreling in. The body's
alibi, glancing the other way. Baby
sitter stone drunk on the job.

Submit complete ms. Previously published poems and simultaneous submissions OK. "Please send a reading fee of $7, a SASE for return of ms and a self-addressed postcard for acknowledgment of receipt of ms." Reads submissions September through April. Reports in 3 months. Time between acceptance and publication is 1 year.

‡CHAMPION BOOKS, INC.; NEW SHOES SERIES (II), P.O. Box 636, Lemont IL 60439, phone (800)230-1135, fax (800)827-7415, founded 1993, president Rebecca Rush, publishes 3-12 flat-spined paperback books of poetry/year through their New Shoes Series. They say, "In their prime, Kerouac, Ginsberg and Burroughs were never literary stars; they were the unknown and the unheard, speaking their minds and breaking new literary ground. But, now, decades after their heyday, they have become the pantheon for the mainstream of our generation. They are rapidly gaining an audience larger than what used to be that of an underground cult following, and they are also 'inspiration' for contemporary wanna-be Beat authors. **Our New Shoes Series seeks obscure and unrenowned authors interested not in following in the footsteps of others, but in creating their own new shoes to walk in."** As a sample the editor selected "Nature" from **Allergic Reactions** by David Nitka II:

Puberty makes rapists of young men,
wanting kisses on the first date,
challenging young women.

Query first, with sample poems, cover letter with brief bio and publication credits. Previously published poems and simultaneous submissions OK. Replies to queries in 1-3 weeks. Always comments on rejections. Pays 7-10% royalties and about 4 author's copies. Write for catalog to order samples. Rebecca Rush says, "Champion Books works with the author to produce a book that is enjoyable and provoking for the audience as well as rewarding and satisfactory to the author."

CHANTRY PRESS (III), P.O. Box 144, Midland Park NJ 07432, founded 1981, poetry editor D. Patrick, publishes **perfect-bound paperbacks of "high quality" poetry. No other specifications.** They have recently published work by Laura Boss, Anne Bailie, Ruth Lisa Schechter, Susan Clements and Joanne Riley. These sample lines are from **Winter Light** by Maria Gillan:

Remember me, Ladies,
the silent one?
I have found my voice
and my rage will blow
your house down.

That's from an 80-page book (usually books from this press are 72 pgs.), flat-spined, glossy cover, good printing on heavy paper, author's photo on back, $5.95. **Send SASE for catalog to order sample. Don't send complete ms. Query first, with 5 sample poems, no cover letter necessary. Submission period October through April. Replies to queries in 4 months, to submissions in 4 months. Simultaneous submissions OK. Always sends prepublication galleys. Pays 15% royalties after costs are met and 10 author's copies. Very short comment "sometimes" on rejected mss.** The editor advises: "Do not be rude in inquiring about the status of your manuscript."

‡CHANTS (II), RR1 Box 1738, Dexter ME 04930, founded 1989, editor Terrell Hunter, appears twice a year. The editor says their goal is "to publish the best poetry we can find." They want **"strong, serious, good poetry: any style. Open to traditional forms, longer poems, translations. No greeting card, clichéd, sappy or trendy poetry."** They have recently published poetry by Bill Shields, Eugene Brooks and Rane Arroyo. As a sample the editor selected this poem, "During Great Pain," by Sheri Reynolds:

My fingers are nuns.
I gnaw the flesh
around their wimples,
watch them blush and bleed.
Eight sisters kneel in prayer
for me. Fistfuls of heaven—
Their faces shoved downward,
I nibble at ankles and knees.
Hot breath up their habits,
I whisper, I plead, Intercede.

Chants is 64 pgs., digest-sized, professionally printed, flat-spined, with photo or graphic on cover but no inside art. It features narrative, lyric, dramatic (and even erotic) free verse. They accept about 10% of poems received. Press run is 500. Single copy: $4. **Sample: $4 plus $1 postage. No previously published poems or simultaneous submissions.** Time between acceptance and publication is up to 6 months—occasionally longer. **Sometimes comments on rejections. Reports in 1-3 months. Pays 2 copies.** The editor says, "Send for a back issue. Proofread. In most cases, avoid academic language or situations—they're usually boring!"

"Poetry is all we publish, it's the whole journal," says Editor Terrell Hunter of his biannual publication Chants. "Our goal is to publish the best poetry we can find." They are open to traditional forms, free verse and translations, as well as longer poems. "Since many small magazines seem to loath devoting space to longer poems, we thought we'd try to fill that void regularly," he says. The cover photograph (taken by Hunter) is of a canoeing scene in Maine where the journal is published. "Like poetry, it's relatively timeless," says Hunter. "Canoeing is quiet but exciting, adventurous, exploratory, all eyes and ears. Canoeing is like writing, and like life in general." Cover layout: Michael Fournier.

CHAPMAN (IV-Ethnic); CHAPMAN PRESS (V), 4 Broughton Place, Edinburgh EH1 3RX Scotland, phone (031)557-2207, fax (031)556-9565, founded 1970, editor Joy Hendry, "provides an outlet for new work by **established Scottish writers and for new, up-and-coming writers also,** for the discussion and criticism of this work and for reflection on current trends in Scottish life and literature. But *Chapman* is not content to follow old, well-worn paths; it throws open its pages to new writers, new ideas and new approaches. In the international tradition revived by MacDiarmid, ***Chapman* also features the work of foreign writers and broadens the range of Scottish cultural life."** They have recently published poetry and fiction by Alasdair Gray, Liz Lochhead, Sorley MacLean, T.S. Law, Edwin Morgan, Willa Muir, Tom Scott and Una Flett. As a sample the editor selected these lines from Judy Steel's poem "For Nicole Boulanger" who, Steel says, "was born in the same year as my daughter and died in the Lockerbie air disaster of 1988":

You died amongst these rolling Border hills:
The same our daughters played and rode and walked in -
They make a nursery fit to shape and mould
A spirit swift as water, free as air.

But you, west-winging through the Christmas dark
Found them no playground but a mortuary -
Your young life poised for flight to woman's years
Destroyed as wantonly as moorland game.

Chapman appears 4 times a year in a 6×9, perfect-bound format, 104 pgs., professionally printed in small type on matte stock with glossy card cover, art in 2 colors. Press run is 2,000 for 900 subscribers of which 200 are libraries. They receive "thousands" of poetry submissions/year, use about 200, **have a 4- to 6-month backlog. Sample: £2.50 (overseas). Cover letter required. No simultaneous submissions. Reports "as soon as possible." Always sends prepublication galleys. Pays £8/page.** Staff reviews books of poetry. Send books for review consideration. **Chapman Press is not interested in unsolicited mss.** The editor says poets should not "try to court approval by writing poems especially to suit what they perceive as the nature of the magazine. They usually get it wrong and write badly." Also, they are interested in receiving poetry dealing with women's issues and feminism.

THE CHARITON REVIEW PRESS; THE CHARITON REVIEW (II), Northeast Missouri State University, Kirksville MO 63501, phone (816)785-4499, founded 1975, editor Jim Barnes. ***The Chariton Review*** began in 1975 as a twice yearly literary magazine and in 1978 added the activities of the press, producing "limited editions (not chapbooks!) of **full-length collections . . . for the purpose of introducing solid, contemporary poetry to readers.** The books go free to the regular subscribers of ***The Chariton Review***; others are sold to help meet printing costs." The poetry published in both books and the magazine is, according to the editor, **"open and closed forms—traditional, experimental, mainstream. We do not consider verse, only poetry in its highest sense, whatever that may be. The sentimental and**

the inspirational are not poetry for us. Also, no more 'relativism': short stories and poetry centered around relatives." They have published poets such as Michael Spence, Neil Myers, Sam Maio, Andrea Budy, Charles Edward Eaton, Wayne Dodd and Harold Witt. There are 40-50 pages of poetry in each issue of the ***Review***, a 6×9, flat-spined magazine of over a hundred pages, professionally printed, glossy cover with photographs, circulation about 600 with 400 subscribers of which 100 are libraries. They receive 7,000-8,000 submissions/year, of which they use 35-50, with never more than a 6-month backlog. **Sample postpaid: $2.50. Submit 5-7 poems, typescript single-spaced. No simultaneous submissions. Do *not* write for guidelines. Always sends prepublication galleys. Pays $5/printed page. Buys first North American serial rights. Contributors are expected to subscribe or buy copies.** Open to unsolicited reviews. Poets may also send books for review consideration. ***The Chariton Review*** continues to be a lively magazine open to all styles and forms with only one criterion: excellence. Moreover, response times here are quick, and accepted poems often appear within a few issues of notification. **To be considered for book publication, query first—samples of books $3 and $5. Payment for book publication: $500 with 20 or more copies. Usually no criticism is supplied.**

‡CHARLOTTE MAGAZINE (III), P.O. Box 11048, Charlotte NC 28220, phone (704)366-5000, fax (704)366-6144, founded 1974, publisher Bob Dill, is a bimonthly city magazine, 64 pgs., 8½×11, offset and saddle-stitched. Press run is 13,000 for 6,000 subscribers of which 100 are libraries, 3,000 shelf sales. Single copy: $2.95; subscription: $12/year. **Sample postpaid: $5. Previously published poems and simultaneous submissions OK.** Time between acceptance and publication is 4 months. **Seldom comments on rejections. Pay is negotiable; copies a possibility. Buys one-time rights.** Reviews books of poetry in 300-600 words. Open to unsolicited reviews. Poets may also send books for review consideration.

THE CHATTAHOOCHEE REVIEW (II), DeKalb College, 2101 Womack Rd., Dunwoody GA 30338, phone (404)551-3166, founded 1980, editor-in-chief Lamar York, poetry editor (Mr.) Collie Owens, is a quarterly of poetry, short fiction, essays, reviews and interviews, published by DeKalb College. **"We publish a number of Southern writers, but *CR* is not by design a regional magazine. In poetry we look for vivid imagery, unique point of view and voice, freshness of figurative language, and attention to craft. All themes, forms and styles are considered as long as they impact the whole person: heart, mind, intuition and imagination."** They have published poetry by Peter Meinke, David Kirby, Allan Peterson, Bin Ramke, Peter Wild and Cory Brown. As a sample the editors selected these lines from "A Good Date" by David Staudt:

We walked onto the ice dams after supper,
cool floors powdered for a two-step.
Snowfall we couldn't see hissed like sparks
doused on our wet faces. Under the cliffs,
reliefers from Packerton drank and howled,
and domes of visible flakes, thick as glitter
in souvenirs from the Poconos,
flickered over cans of sterno or sticks
where fishermen hunkered in lawnchairs
over blue slots routered in the ice.

The Review is 6×9, professionally printed on white stock with b&w reproductions of artwork, 90 pgs., flat-spined, with one-color card cover. Its reputation as a premiere literary magazine continues to grow. Recent issues feature a wide range of forms and styles augmenting prose selections. Circulation is 1,000, of which 500 are complimentary copies sent to editors and "miscellaneous VIP's." Subscription: $15/year. **Sample postpaid: $4. Writers should send 1 copy of each poem and a cover letter with bio material. No simultaneous submissions. Publishes theme issues. Send SASE for guidelines. Queries will be answered in 1-2 weeks. Reports in 2 months and time to publication is 3-4 months. Pays 2 copies. Acquires first rights.** Staff reviews books of poetry and short fiction in 1,500 words, single or multi-book format. Send books for review consideration.

‡CHELSEA; CHELSEA AWARD COMPETITION (III, IV-Translations), P.O. Box 5880, Grand Central Station, New York NY 10163, founded 1958, editor Sonia Raiziss, associate editors Richard Foerster, Alfred de Palchi, Caila Rossi and Andrea Lockett, is a long-established, high-quality literary annual aiming to promote intercultural communication. **"We look for intelligence and sophisticated technique in both experimental and traditional forms. We are interested primarily in free verse and in translations of contemporary poets. Length: 5-7 pgs. per submission. Although our tastes are eclectic, we lean toward the cosmopolitan avant-garde. We would like to see more poetry by writers of color. Do not want to see 'inspirational' verse, pornography or poems that rhyme merely for the sake of rhyme."** They have recently published poetry by John Ashbery, Carolyn Stoloff, Robert Polito and Julia Alvarez. The editors say ***Chelsea*** is "125-160 pgs., flat-spined, 6×9, offset, cover art varies, occasional use of photographs, ads." Circulation: 1,300, 600 subscriptions of which 200 are libraries. Subscription:

$13 domestic, $17 foreign. **Sample: $6 or more depending on issue. Send SASE for a brochure describing all past issues. 5-7 pgs. of poetry are ideal; long poems should not exceed 10 pgs.; must be typed; include brief bio; no simultaneous submissions. "We try to comment favorably on above-average mss; otherwise, we do not have time to provide critiques." Reports immediately to 3 months. Always sends prepublication galleys. Pays $5/page and 2 copies. Buys first North American serial rights.** Guidelines for their annual Chelsea Award Competition (deadline December 15), $500 for poetry, available for SASE to P.O. Box 1040, York Beach ME 03910. Work published in ***Chelsea*** has been included in the 1993 and 1994 volumes of **The Best American Poetry**. Richard Foerster, associate editor, comments: "Beginners should realize that a rejection often has more to do with the magazine's production schedule and special editorial plans than with the quality of the submission. They should also realize that editors of little magazines are always overworked (and almost invariably unpaid) and that it is necessary haste and not a lack of concern or compassion that makes rejections seem coldly impersonal."

CHICAGO REVIEW (III, IV-Themes, translations), 5801 S. Kenwood, Chicago IL 60637, founded 1946, poetry editor Angela Sorby. **"We publish high quality poetry. About 50% of the work we select is unsolicited; the remainder is solicited from poets whose work we admire. Translations are welcome, but please include a statement of permission from the original publisher if work is not in the public domain."** They have published poets as diverse as Kathleen Spivack, Billy Collins, Cesare Pavese, Turner Cassity, Michael Donaghy, Meena Alexander and Adrian C. Louis. "Out of the 1,500 submissions we receive each year, we accept around 50." Editors seem to prefer lyric free verse—some of it leaning toward avant-garde and some quite accessible—with emphasis on voice and content (depicting tense or intriguing topics or situations). Circulation 2,500. **Sample postpaid: $5. New submissions read October through June. Publishes theme issues. Send SASE for upcoming themes. Reports in 4-6 months, longer in some cases. Sometimes sends prepublication galleys. Pays in copies and one-volume subscription.** Occasionally reviews books of poetry. Open to unsolicited reviews.

CHICKADEE MAGAZINE; THE YOUNG NATURALIST FOUNDATION (IV-Children, nature), Suite 500, 179 John St., Toronto, Ontario M5T 3G5 Canada, founded 1979, editor Lizann Flatt, is a magazine **for children 3-9 about science and nature** appearing 10 times/year. They want **"evocative poetry; poems that play with words; humorous poetry; no longer than 50 lines. Nothing religious, anthropomorphic; no formal language; no poetry that is difficult to understand."** As a sample they selected these lines from "The Lunch Bunch" by Gwen Molnar:

The dining room wall to wall
With birds and beasts and fish,
The whole menagerie looked on
As I downed every dish.

It is 32 pgs., magazine-sized, professionally printed in full-color, with paper cover. They accept 1-2% of every 500 poems received. Circulation: 25,800 within US and 100,000 within Canada. Subscription: $14.95 US. **Sample postpaid: $3.75. Simultaneous submissions considered. Send SASE for writers' guidelines. Pays $10-75/poem plus 2 copies. Buys all rights. "*Chickadee* is a** 'hands-on' science and nature publication designed to entertain and educate 3- to 9-year-olds. Each issue contains photos, illustrations, an easy-to-read animal story, a craft project, puzzles, a science experiment and a pullout poster." The magazine received the 1992 EDPress Golden Lamp Honor Award and Parents' Choice Golden Seal Awards.

CHILDREN'S BETTER HEALTH INSTITUTE; BENJAMIN FRANKLIN LITERARY AND MEDICAL SOCIETY, INC.; HUMPTY DUMPTY'S MAGAZINE; TURTLE MAGAZINE FOR PRESCHOOL KIDS; CHILDREN'S DIGEST; CHILDREN'S PLAYMATE; JACK AND JILL; CHILD LIFE (IV-Children), 1100 Waterway Blvd., P.O Box 567, Indianapolis IN 46206-0567. This publisher of magazines stressing health for children has a **variety of needs for mostly short, simple poems.** For example, ***Humpty Dumpty* is for ages 4-6; *Turtle* is for preschoolers, similar emphasis, uses many stories in rhyme—and action rhymes, etc.; *Children's Digest* is for preteens (10-13); *Jack and Jill* is for ages 7-10. *Child Life* is for ages 9-11. *Children's Playmate* is for ages 6-8.** All appear 8 times a year in a 6½×9, 48-page format, slick paper with cartoon art, very colorful. **Sample postpaid: $1.25. Send SASE for guidelines. Reports in 8-10 weeks. Pays $15 minimum.** Staff reviews books of poetry. Send books for review consideration. The editors suggest that writers who wish to appear in their publications **study current issues carefully.** "We receive too many poetry submissions that are about kids, not for kids. Or, the subject matter is one that adults think children would or should like. We'd like to see more humorous verse."

CHIPS OFF THE WRITER'S BLOCK (I, IV-Writing); CATHARSIS (I), P.O. Box 83371, Los Angeles CA 90083, founded 1986, editor Wanda Windham. ***Chips*** is a bimonthly 16-page, magazine-sized newsletter offering "motivation and preparation for the published and soon-to-be-published writer" and using "**occasional poetry related to writing**, that is, the writing world of your personal muse, ups and downs of writing life, etc." ***Catharsis*** is a 40-page, digest-sized, quarterly poetry journal using **"poetry of all genres with lengths from 1-40 lines. Poems should be meaningful, expressing your deepest emotions.**

No forced rhymes. Also no personal journal-type poetry." As a sample we selected this poem, "Seizing the Moment," by Barbara Grant Richardson:

You come to me in the darkness
of the night.
Seizing the moment of fulfillment
and reaching the extremity of my soul.
Where no other has gone
in the darkness of the night.

Sample postpaid: $3 for *Chips*, $4 for *Catharsis*. Previously published poems and simultaneous submissions OK. Always comments on rejections. Send SASE for guidelines. Reports in 3-6 weeks. Pays 1 copy. Send books for review consideration. ***Catharsis*** also sponsors ongoing poetry contests. Send SASE for details. ***Catharsis*** ranked #9 in the "Open Markets" category of the latest ***Writer's Digest*** Poetry 60 list. This category ranks those publications most open to both free and formal verse.

CHIRON REVIEW; CHIRON BOOKS; CHIRON REVIEW POETRY CONTEST (I, II), 522 E. South Ave., St. John KS 67576-2212, founded 1982 as ***Kindred Spirit***, editor Michael Hathaway, assistant editor Jane Hathaway, contributing editor (poetry) Gerald Locklin, is a tabloid quarterly using photographs of featured writers. **No taboos.** They have recently published poetry by Charles Bukowski, Marge Piercy, Antler, Andrew Demcak and Will Inman. As a sample the editor selected "Up" by Rachel Kubie:

All night I watched the bright slow suicide of moths
till morning shuddered in its cold corner of heaven
and my nerves were gone.
Don't you come home now.

Each issue is 24-32 pgs. and "contains dozens of poems." Their press run is about 1,000. **Sample postpaid: $3 ($6 overseas or institutions). Send 5 poems "typed or printed legibly." No simultaneous submissions or previously published poems. Very seldom publishes theme issues. "None are planned; they are sort of spontaneous. We published a Vietnam Vets' issue in 1991 and a gay poets' issue in 1992." Send SASE for guidelines and upcoming themes. Reports in 2-4 weeks. Pays 1 copy. Buys first-time rights.** Reviews books of poetry in 500-900 words. Open to unsolicited reviews. Poets may also send books for review consideration. **For book publication submit complete ms.** They publish 1-3 books/year, flat-spined, professionally printed, **paying 25% of press run of 100-200 copies.** Their annual poetry contest offers awards of $100 plus 1-page feature in Winter issue, $50, and 5 free subscriptions and a Chiron Press book. Entry fee: $1/poem.

THE CHRISTIAN CENTURY (II, IV-Religious, social issues), Dept. PM, 407 S. Dearborn St., Chicago IL 60605, phone (312)427-5380, founded 1884, named ***The Christian Century*** 1900, founded again 1908, joined by ***New Christian*** 1970, poetry editor Dean Peerman. This "ecumenical weekly" is a liberal, sophisticated journal of news, articles of opinion and reviews from a generally Christian point-of-view, **using approximately one poem/issue, not necessarily on religious themes but in keeping with the literate tone of the magazine. "No pietistic or sentimental doggerel, please."** They have published poetry by Robert Beum, Joan Rohr Myers, Ida Fasel, Jill Baumgaertner, David Abrams, Catherine Shaw and J. Barrie Shepherd. As a sample the editor selected this poem, "Grain Silos," by James Worley:

Cathedrals of the oldest preached religion,
towers erected to the oldest useful god
(the one now worshiped three times every day
by those who can, invoked by those who can't)
these cylinders of homage (oblong praise)
project a plenty that is its own reward,
a yearning that has grown its own response:
the deity whom these raised prayers rise to laud
resides (when crops are good) in grateful guts.

The journal is magazine-sized, printed on quality newsprint, using b&w art, cartoons and ads, about 30 pgs., saddle-stapled. **Sample postpaid: $2. No simultaneous submissions. Submissions without SASE or SAE and IRCs will not be returned. Pays usually $20/poem plus 1 copy and discount on additional copies. Acquires all rights. Inquire about reprint permission.** Reviews books of poetry in 300-400 words, single format; 400-500 words, multi-book.

THE CHRISTIAN SCIENCE MONITOR (II), The Home Forum Page, 1 Norway St., Boston MA 02115, phone (617)450-2474, founded 1908, an international daily newspaper. **Poetry used regularly in The Home Forum, editor Alice Hummer. They want "finely crafted poems that celebrate the extraordinary in the ordinary. Seasonal material always needed. Especially interested in poems about life in the**

city. No violence, sensuality or racism. Short poems preferred." They have recently published work by William Stafford and Diana der-Hovanessian. As a sample the editor selected these lines from "Working in the Rain" by Robert Morgan:

My father loved more than anything to
work outside in wet weather. Beginning
at daylight he'd go out in dripping brush
to mow or pull weeds for hog and chickens.

Submit no more than 5 poems at a time. SASE must be included. Publishes "theme issues." Upcoming themes unavailable. "Theme pages are put together from poetry already in hand." Usually reports within 1 month. Pays varying rates, upon publication.

‡THE CHRISTIAN WAY (IV-Religious, inspirational, subscription), #4, 8131 Lemon Ave., La Mesa CA 91941-6451, founded 1984, editor/publisher Kae Carter Jaworski, is a monthly subscribers-only newsletter using **poems up to 16 lines that are "inspirational, uplifting. Christian verse accepted, seasonal verse. Purpose is to uplift Christianity, build self-esteem and encourage new and professional poets: nature, inspirational, love, family, friends, people. No porno, meaningless verse, profanity-type."** They have recently published poetry by Mary Bourdeau, Rudy Zenker, Ethel Plum, Dr. James W. McMillan, Esther Burkholder and Sylvia Roberts. As a sample the editor selected these lines (poet unidentified):

Desolate, neglected and all alone
Marilyn claims the streets of
Santa Monica as home.
At night she beds down in
doorways of old houses, or on the ground.
Oblivious to a world who rejects her kind.
It's too late now—oh, the wasted years
No one sees the woman's falling tears . . .
The mind is gone—but no one cares . . .
About the Bag Lady . . . who sits alone and stares.

The newsletter is magazine-sized, 10 pgs. The editor says she receives more than 300 pieces each month and "I accept 85% of it, keep some for future issues." Press run is 320 for 300 subscribers. Subscription: $12. **Sample: $2. *Contributors must subscribe.* Simultaneous submissions and previously published poems OK. "I am touchy about misspelled words and sloppy work." Editor usually comments on rejections. Reports within 2 days. Pays 1 copy.** She says, "Subscribe to as many good magazines as you can, observing how well-known or widely published poets work. Join poetry clubs and write and rewrite your poems until they are as near perfect as you can make them. Do not get discouraged when you get rejection slips. Always send SASE for reply. Do a professional job and you will be published. It is wise to order a sample copy before submitting poetry."

THE CHRISTOPHER PUBLISHING HOUSE (II), 24 Rockland St., Commerce Green, Hanover MA 02339, phone (617)826-7474, fax (617)826-5556, managing editor Nancy Lucas, who says **"We will review all forms of poetry." Submit complete ms. Always sends prepublication galleys.**

THE CHRONICLE OF THE HORSE (IV-Specialized), P.O. Box 46, Middleburg VA 22117, phone (703)687-6341, founded 1937, assistant editor Tricia Booker, is a weekly magazine using **short poetry related to horses "the shorter the better. No free verse."** The magazine is devoted to English horse sports, such as horse shows and steeplechasing. It averages 68 pgs., magazine-sized. Subscription: $42. **Sample postpaid: $2. No simultaneous submissions. Summer "is not a good time" to submit. 1-3 editors read poems. Reports in 4-6 weeks. Pays $15/poem. Buys first North American rights.** "We review books submitted to us but do not accept reviews for publication."

CHRYSALIS: JOURNAL OF THE SWEDENBORG FOUNDATION (II, IV-Spirituality, themes), Rt. 1 Box 184, Dillwyn VA 23936, founded 1985, editor Carol Lawson, poetry editor Phoebe Loughrey. ***Chrysalis***, appearing 3 times/year, is a "journal that draws upon diverse traditions to engage thought on questions that challenge inquiring minds. Each issue addresses a topic from varied perspectives using literate and scholarly fiction, essays and poetry dealing with spiritual aspects of a particular theme." They want **poetry that is "spiritually related and focused on the particular issue's theme.**

The Subject Index, located before the General Index, can help you narrow down markets for your work. It lists those publishers whose poetry interests are specialized.

Nothing overly religious or sophomoric." They have recently published poetry by Kate Cheney Chappell and Joan Payne Kincaid. As a sample the editor selected these lines from "Burning the Long Boat" by Robert F. Lawson:

We stand on the flagstones.
Such a small opening for a big man to disappear into.
Alone in the dark, he broke down the coffee table,
in his haste to save his heart;
the vial of pills showed its teeth
just out of reach at the top of the chest.

Chrysalis is 80 pgs., 7½ × 10, professionally printed on archival paper, perfect-bound with coated stock cover, illustrations, photos and ads for other literary publications. They receive about 120 poems a year, use 8-10%. Press run is 3,500 for 3,000 subscribers. Subscription: $20, outside US $25. **Sample postpaid: $6. No previously published poems or simultaneous submissions. Submit no more than 6 poems at one time.** Time between acceptance and publication is 18 months maximum. **Seldom comments on rejections. Send SASE for themes and guidelines. Themes for Spring 1995, Summer 1995 and Autumn 1995 issues are Windows, Play, and The Good Life, respectively. Reports in 2 months. Always sends prepublication galleys. Pays $25 and 5 copies. Buys first-time rights. "We like to be credited for reprints."**

THE CHURCH-WELLESLEY REVIEW; XTRA! (IV-Gay/lesbian), Box 7289, Station A, Toronto, Ontario M5W 1X9 Canada. ***The Church-Wellesley Review*** is the annual spring supplement for ***XTRA! Magazine*** **(Canada's largest gay/lesbian newspaper.) "We want wild humour, fast-paced drama, new takes on old themes, gays and lesbians in other contexts. Our aim is always quality, not style. Although we prefer non-traditional poetry,** we have in the past published a contemporary 30-line 'up-dating' of Chaucer called 'Provincetown Tales.' **Amaze us or amuse us, but just don't bore us."** They have published Patrick Roscoe, Jane Rule, Timothy Findley, Chocolate Waters and David Watmough. The magazine receives over 1,000 submissions/year. Press run is of 24,000 and is distributed free. **Poetry can be any length ("no epics, please"), but no more than 10 poems per writer per year. Mss should include poems with name on every page, daytime phone number and 50-word bio. Submissions are accepted January 1 through March 31. "We do not respond at other times. We report as soon as possible, definitely by publication in April." Payment made in Canadian funds within one month of publication.** Staff reviews books of poetry. Send books for review consideration to the attention of Fiction Editor. ***Xtra***, the review's parent magazine, has received several community awards as well as a journalism award for a column on Living with AIDS.

CIMARRON REVIEW (II), 205 Morrill Hall, Oklahoma State University, Stillwater OK 74078-0135, founded 1967, poetry editors Thomas Reiter, Jeff Kersh and Sally Shigley, is a quarterly literary journal. **"We emphasize quality and style. We like clear, evocative poetry (lyric or narrative) controlled by a strong voice. No obscure poetry. No sing-song verse. No quaint prairie verse. No restrictions as to subject matter, although we tend to publish more structured poetry (attention to line and stanza).** Also, we are conscious of our academic readership (mostly other writers) and attempt to accept poems that everyone will admire." Among poets they have published are Robert Cooperman, James McKean, David Citino, Tess Gallagher and Albert Goldbarth. This magazine, 6 × 9, 100-150 pgs., perfect-bound, boasts a handsome design, including a color cover and attractive printing. Poems lean toward free verse, lyric and narrative, although all forms and styles seem welcome. There are 15-25 pages of poetry in each issue, circulation 500, mostly libraries. Subscription rates: $3/issue, $12/year ($15 Canada), $30 for 3 years ($40 Canada), plus $2.50 for all international subscriptions. **Submit to Poetry Editor, anytime, 3-5 poems, name and address on each typed, single- or double-spaced. No simultaneous submissions. Reports within 3 months. Pays $15 for each poem published. Buys all rights. "Permission for a reprinting is granted upon request."** Reviews books of poetry in 500-900 words, single-book format, occasionally multi-book. All reviews are assigned.

CINCINNATI POETRY REVIEW; CINCINNATI WRITERS' PROJECT (II, IV-Regional), Humanities Dept., College of Mount St. Joseph, 5701 Delhi Rd., Cincinnati OH 45233, founded 1975, editor Jeffrey Hillard, "attempts to set local poets in a national context. Each issue includes **a quarter to a third of work by local poets (within about 100 miles of Cincinnati)**, but most are from all over." They use **"all kinds" of poetry** and have recently published such poets as Enid Shomer, Lynne Hugo de-Courcy, Pat Mora, Eve Shelnutt, David Citino, Jeff Worley, Harry Humes, Walter Pavlich and Yusef Komunyakaa. Publishes one issue/year, usually a fall/winter issue. ***CPR*** is handsomely printed, flat-spined, 80 pgs., digest-sized, all poems, art on the glossy card cover. They use about 40-60 of 2,000 submissions/year. Circulation is about 1,000, with 92 subscriptions, 20 of which are libraries. Subscription: $9 for 4 issues. **Sample: $2. Submit typed mss with address on each poem. "Occasionally" publishes theme issues.** Theme for a special section of ***CPR*** **#25** is Cuban poetry and includes an interview with Cuban poet Julia Calzadilla. **Note, however, that the editor solicits material for special sections. Reports in 1-3 months. Pays 2 copies.** Each issue offers a poetry contest for poems of all types. The poems judged best and second in each issue receive cash awards of $150 and $50. ***CPR*** is published by the Cincinnati Writers' Project. Other publications include **The Shadow Family** by Jeffrey Hillard; **The Kansas Poems** by Dallas Wiebe, **Dismal Man** by Jon Christopher Hughes, **River Dwellers – Poems on the Settling of the Ohio River** by Jeffrey Hillard and **Down the River – A Collection of Fiction & Poetry on the Ohio River Valley**, edited by Dallas Wiebe. Jeffrey Hillard received the 1993 Post-Corbett Award for "Literary Artist" for his collections of poems and for editorship of ***Cincinnati Poetry Review***.

THE CINCINNATI POETS' COLLECTIVE (II), 27 Pleasant Ridge Ave., Ft. Mitchell KY 41017, founded 1988, editor Rebecca Mitchell Sullivan, is an annual poetry magazine. **"I am looking for fresh poetry that takes risks. I would like to see more poetry written about current issues from a conservative or politically incorrect point of view, however no subject is taboo. I do not want overly-didactic or ambiguous poetry; no soapbox material professing to be a poem. I am open to extensively published poets and to those who deserve to be but are not."** Poets recently published include Claire Donohue Roof, Richard Stansberger and J. Patrick Kelly. As a sample the editor selected these lines from "Coup de Grace" by Mg:

You gave me your darkness
that I have now enshrined
in the Crypt of Most Cherished Memory,
the heathen crypt,
where nothing dead ever rises.

TCPC is digest-sized, saddle-stapled. Circulation is approximately 150 through bookstore sales and subscriptions. **Submit up to 5 poems at a time. No previously published poems. Simultaneous submissions OK, if noted. Submit mss October 1 through April 1 only. Send SASE for guidelines. Reports in 4-6 months. Pays 1 copy.**

CITY LIGHTS BOOKS (III), 261 Columbus Ave., San Francisco CA 94133, phone (415)362-1901, founded 1955, edited by Lawrence Ferlinghetti and Nancy J. Peters, is a paperback house that achieved prominence with the publication of Allen Ginsberg's **Howl** and other **poetry of the "Beat" school.** They publish **"poetry, fiction, philosophy, political and social history. Simultaneous submissions OK. Reports in 4-6 weeks. Payment varies.**

THE CLASSICAL OUTLOOK (IV-Specialized, translations), Classics Dept., Park Hall, University of Georgia, Athens GA 30602, founded 1924, poetry editors Prof. David Middleton (original English verse) and Prof. Jane Phillips (translations and original Latin verse), "is an internationally circulated quarterly journal (4,000 subscriptions, of which 250 are libraries) for high school and college Latin and Classics teachers, published by the American Classical League." **They invite submissions of "original poems in English on classical themes, verse translations from Greek and Roman authors, and original Latin poems. Submissions should, as a rule, be written in traditional poetic forms and should demonstrate skill in the use of meter, diction and rhyme if rhyme is employed. Original poems should be more than mere exercise pieces or the poetry of nostalgia. Translations should be accompanied by a photocopy of the original Greek or Latin text. Latin originals should be accompanied by a literal English rendering of the text. Submissions should not exceed 50 lines."** They have published work by Francis Fike and Roy Fuller. As a sample we selected these lines from "Rectius Vives" (Horace, *Carmina* 2.10) by Michael J. Kraus:

Whoever firm pursues the golden mean
Is safe; no crumbling house, unkempt, unseen
Impends about his ears, no splendid hall
Arouses envy, sober not at all.

There are 2-3 magazine-sized pgs. of poetry in each issue, and they use 55% of the approximately 150 submissions they receive each year. They have a 6- to 12-month backlog, 4-month lead time. **Submit 2 anonymous copies, double-spaced. Receipt is acknowledged by letter. Poetry is refereed by poetry editors. Guidelines available for SASE. Reports in 3-6 months. Pays 2 complimentary copies. Sample copies available from the American Classical League, Miami University, Oxford OH 45056 for $7.50.** Reviews books of poetry "if the poetry is sufficiently classical in nature." ***The Classical Outlook*** ranked #7 in the "Traditional Verse" category of the latest ***Writer's Digest*** Poetry 60 list.

CLEANING BUSINESS MAGAZINE; WRITERS PUBLISHING SERVICE CO. (IV-Specialized), 1512 Western Ave., P.O. Box 1273, Seattle WA 98111, phone (206)622-4241, fax (206)622-6876, founded 1976, poetry editor William R. Griffin. ***CBM*** is "a quarterly magazine **for cleaning and maintenance professionals" and uses some poetry relating to their interests. "To be considered for publication in *Cleaning Business*, submit poetry that relates to our specific audience – cleaning and self-employment."** He has published poetry by Don Wilson, Phoebe Bosche, Trudie Mercer and Joe Keppler. The editor says it is 100 pgs., 8½×11, offset litho, using ads, art and graphics. Of 50 poems received, he uses about 10. Press run is 5,000 for 3,000 subscriptions (100 of them libraries), 500 shelf sales. Single copy: $5; subscription: $20. **Sample postpaid: $3. Send SASE and $3 for guidelines. Simultaneous submissions OK; no previously published poems. Pays $5-10 plus 1 copy.** Writers Publishing Service Co. is an imprint for subsidized publication of poetry (author's expense) and other services to writers. William Griffin suggests that "poets identify a specific market and work to build a readership that can be tapped again and again over a period of years with new books. Also write to a specific audience that has a mutual interest. We buy poetry about cleaning, but seldom receive anything our subscribers would want to read."

CLEVELAND STATE UNIVERSITY POETRY CENTER; CSU POETRY SERIES (II); CLEVELAND POETS SERIES (IV-Regional), Cleveland State University, Cleveland OH 44115, phone (216)687-3986, director Nuala Archer, editors Leonard Trawick, David Evett, Nuala Archer and Ted Lardner. The Poetry Center was founded in 1962, first publications in 1971. **The Poetry Center publishes the CSU Poetry Series for poets in general and the Cleveland Poets Series for Ohio poets. "Open to many kinds of form, length, subject matter, style and purpose. Should be well-crafted, clearly of professional quality, ultimately serious (even when humorous). No light verse, devotional verse or verse in which rhyme and meter seem to be of major importance."** They have recently published poetry by Thylias Moss, Richard Jackson, Jan Freeman and Susan Firer. As a sample Nuala Archer selected these lines from **Hurdy-Gurdy** by Tim Seibles:

> *Let's say you're black and you walk in*
> *this restaurant and as you take your seat you*
> *realize you're the only one there darker*
> *than blue—the waiters and waitresses, the hostess*
> *and customers, even the cooks; all of them*
> *could walk into a snowy field and vanish—so*
> *you think* No big deal, it's cool, no need to
> get into a Frederick Douglass kinda thing . . .
> *But soon the peekaboo sets in*

Books are chosen for publication from the entries to the CSU Poetry Center Prize contest. (Write for free catalog and sampler of some 65 Poetry Center books.) Deadline: March 1. Entry fee: $10. The winner receives $1,000 and publication. They publish some other entrants in the Poetry Series, providing 50 copies (of press run of 1,000) and 10% royalty contract. The Cleveland Poets Series (for Ohio poets) offers 100 copies of a press run of 600. To submit for all series, send ms between December 1 and March 1. Reports on all submissions for the year by the end of July. Mss should be for books of 50-100 pgs., pages numbered, poet's name, address and phone number on cover sheet, clearly typed. Poems may have been previously published (listed on an acknowledgement page). Send SASE for guidelines. The Center also publishes other volumes of poetry, including chapbooks (20-30 pgs.), with a **$5 reading fee for each submission (except for Ohio residents).**

THE CLIMBING ART (IV-Specialized: mountaineering), Fairfield Communications, P.O. Box 1378, Laporte CO 80535, phone (303)221-9210, founded 1986, editor Scott Titterington, is a quarterly magazine **"read mainly by mountain enthusiasts who appreciate good writing about mountains and mountaineering. We are open to all forms and lengths. The only requirement is that the work be fresh, well-written and in some way of interest to those who love the mountains. If in doubt, submit it."** They have recently published poetry by Terry Gifford, Allison Hunter, Paul Willis and Denise K. Simon. As a sample we selected "Our Mission" by John Grey:

> *The mountain has size on its side,*
> *the sense that things that big*
> *need not have opinions*
> *or make peace with the world.*
> *We, on the other hand,*
> *are at the bottom,*
> *suburbs, impossible affairs,*
> *promotions missed.*

It is 32 pgs., magazine-sized, professionally printed on heavy stock with glossy card cover. Press run is 3,000 for 1,800 subscribers of which 10 are libraries, 1,200 shelf sales. They use 4-10 poems/issue of 100-200 submissions received/year. Subscription: $18. **Sample postpaid: $4. Simultaneous submissions and previously published poems OK. Reports in 2 months. Sometimes sends prepublication galleys. Pays 3 copies and subscription. Acquires one-time rights.** Reviews books of poetry only if they concern mountains. Open to unsolicited reviews. They also sponsor an annual poetry contest; first prize: $100.

CLOCKWATCH REVIEW (I, II), Dept. of English, Illinois Wesleyan University, Bloomington IL 61702, phone (309)556-3352, founded 1983, editor James Plath, associate editors Lynn Devore, James

McGowan and Pamela Muirhead. "We publish a variety of styles, leaning toward poetry which goes beyond the experience of self in an attempt to SAY something, without sounding pedantic or strained. We like a **strong, natural voice**, and lively, unusual combinations in language. **Something *fresh, and that includes subject matter as well. It has been our experience that extremely short/long poems are hard to pull off*.** Though we'll publish exceptions, we prefer to see poems that can fit on one published page (digest-sized) which runs **about 32 lines or less.**" They have published Peter Wild, Martha Vertreace, John Knoepfle, Rita Dove and Peter Meinke. Asked for a sample, the editors say "trying to pick only four lines seems like telling people what detail we'd like to see in a brick, when what we're more interested in is the design of the *house*." The 80-page, semiannual ***CR*** is printed on glossy paper with colored, glossy cover. They receive 2,080 submissions/year, use 20-30. They use 7-10 unsolicited poems in each issue, with 1 featured poet. Circulation is 1,400, with 150 subscribers, of which 25 are libraries. They send out 300 complimentary copies and "the balance is wholesale distribution and single-copy sales." **Sample postpaid: $4. Prefers batches of 5-6 poems. "We are not bowled over by large lists of previous publications, but brief letters of introduction or sparse mini-vitas are read out of curiosity. One poem per page, typed, single-spacing OK."** No backlog. **Comments on rejections "if asked, and if time permits." Reports in 2-3 months. Pays 3 copies, and, when possible, small cash awards—currently $5/poem.** Only uses staff-written or solicited reviews. Send books for review consideration if not self-published.

CLOUD RIDGE PRESS (V), 815 13th St., Boulder CO 80302, founded 1985, editor Elaine Kohler, is a "literary small press for unique works in poetry and prose." They publish letterpress and offset books in both paperback and hardcover editions. In poetry, they want **"strong images of the numinous qualities in authentic experience grounded in a landscape and its people."** The first book, published in 1985, was **Ondina: A Narrative Poem** by John Roberts. The book is 6×9¼, handsomely printed on buff stock, cloth bound in black with silver decoration and spine lettering, 131 pgs. 800 copies were bound in Curtis Flannel and 200 copies bound in cloth over boards, numbered and signed by the poet and artist. This letterpress edition, priced at $18/cloth and $12/paper, is not available in bookstores but only by mail from the press. The trade edition was photo-offset from the original, in both cloth and paper bindings, and is sold in bookstores. The press plans to publish 1-2 books/year. **Since they are not accepting unsolicited mss, writers should query first. Queries will be answered in 2 weeks and mss reported on in 1 month. Simultaneous submissions are acceptable. Royalties are 10% plus a negotiable number of author's copies. A brochure is free on request; send #10 SASE.**

CLUBHOUSE; YOUR STORY HOUR (I, IV-Children, teens), Dept. PM, P.O. Box 15, Berrien Springs MI 49103, poetry editor Elaine Trumbo. The publication is printed in conjunction with the **Your Story Hour** radio program, founded 1949, which is designed to teach the Bible and moral life to children. The magazine, ***Clubhouse***, started with that title in 1982, but as ***Good Deeder***, its original name, it has been published since 1951. Elaine Trumbo says, **"We do like humor or mood pieces. Don't like mushy-sweet 'Christian' poetry. We don't have space for long poems. Best—16 lines or under."** They have published poetry by Lillian M. Fisher, Audrey Osofsky, Sharon K. Motzko, Bruce Bash and Craig Peters. As a sample the editor selected these lines from "Nurses Office" by Eileen Spinelli:

And it hurts behind my ear,
And I've got a cut right here,
And a rash between my toes,
And a pimple on my nose.
Ouch, my knee feels sore and tender-
Bumped it on my bike's back fender.
I can't tell you all I've got.
Where's the aspirin?
Bring the cot!
I need T.L.C. and rest.

Too bad I'll miss that spelling test!

"***Clubhouse*** has been downscaled to 8 pages from 32—to make it possible to print on inhouse equipment. However, the number of issues per year has increased to 12." The magazine has a circulation of 6,000, with 6,000 subscriptions of which maybe 5 are libraries. Subscription: $5 for 12 issues/year. **Sample: 3 oz. postage. Submit mss in March and April. Simultaneous submissions OK. The "evaluation sheet" for returned mss gives reasons for acceptance or rejection. Writer's guidelines available for SASE. Pays about $12 for poems under 24 lines plus 2 contributor's copies. Negotiates rights.** The editor advises, "Give us poetry with freshness and imagination. We most often use mood pieces and humorous poems that appeal to children."

CLUTCH (II), #4, 132 Clinton Park, San Francisco CA 94103, founded 1991, editors Dan Hodge and Lawrence Oberc, is a biannual "alternative/underground literary review." They want **"poetry which explores or reveals an edge, societal edges especially. *Take chances.* Academic, overly studied poems**

are not considered." They have published poetry by Charles Bukowski, Lorri Jackson, Todd Moore and Robert Peters. As a sample, the editors selected these lines from "1492" by Mitchel Cohen:

and the syringe is the size of a lover, O yes!
and the kisses, and the bodies,
and the fleshy zipless hallucinations
that pass for lovers
are no cure, no cure at all . . .

The editors describe ***Clutch*** as 60-70 pgs., approximately 5½ × 8½. "Printing, binding and graphics vary with each issue. We receive approximately 200 unsolicited submissions a year, but we accept less than 10% of unsolicited material. The majority of material is solicited." Press run is 300 for 25 subscribers of which 2 are libraries, 50 shelf sales. Subscription: $10. **Sample postpaid: $5. Make checks payable to Dan Hodge. Previously published poems and simultaneous submissions OK. Cover letter required. Now reads submissions throughout the year. Seldom comments on rejections. Reports in 1-4 months. Pays 1 copy. Rights revert to authors.** "Open to publishing reviews of books/magazines from underground press." Poets may also send books for review consideration. The editors say, "We advise obtaining a sample copy or otherwise becoming familiar with the kind of poetry we've previously published before considering a submission."

COACH HOUSE PRESS (II, IV-Regional), Suite 107, 50 Prince Arthur St., Toronto, Ontario M5R 1B5 Canada, phone (416)921-3910, fax (416)921-4403, founded 1964, poetry editors Michael Ondaatje, Christopher Dewdney, Frank Davey and Lynn Crosbie, publishes **"mostly living Canadian writers of poetry and fiction, drama and literary criticism."** They have published finely-printed flat-spined paperback collections by such poets as Phyllis Webb, Michael Ondaatje, Robin Blaser, Diana Hartog and Dionne Brand. They **"lean toward experimental." Query with 10 samples. Cover letter should include bio and publication history. Reports in 3-4 months. Contract is for 10% royalties, 10 copies.** Catalog sent on request. **"We expect poets to be familiar with the Coach House flavor and to have a few journal publication credits to their name.** You don't have to be famous, but you do have to be good. Make the effort to do a little research on us, and save yourself time and postage. No SASE, no reply . . . and Canada Post does not accept American postage."

THE COE REVIEW (II), Coe College, 1220 First Ave. NE, Cedar Rapids IA 52402, phone (319)399-8660, founded 1972, poetry editor Kitty O'Day, is "an annual little literary magazine with **emphasis on innovative and unselfconscious** poetry and fiction. We are **open to virtually any and all subject matter."** They have published poetry by James Galvin and Jan Weissmiller. The annual is 100-150 pgs., flat-spined, digest-sized with matte card cover. "Each issue includes 4-8 reproductions of works of art, usually photographs, lithography and etched prints." Circulation is about 500. **Sample postpaid: $4. No simultaneous submissions. Accepted work appears in the next issue, published in Spring. Include "brief cover letter with biographical information. Submissions between April 1st and September 30th will go unanswered, as we only accept from October 1st through March 31st due to the academic school year." Send SASE for guidelines. Reports in 6-8 weeks. Pays 1 copy.** The editor says, "We are supportive in the endeavors of poets whose material is original and tasteful. We are eclectic in our publication choices in that variety of subject matter and style make ***The Coe Review*** exciting."

COFFEE HOUSE PRESS (III), Dept. PM, Suite 400, 27 N. Fourth St., Minneapolis MN 55401, phone (612)338-0125, founded 1984, editorial assistant David Caligiuri, publishes 10 paperbacks/year, 4 of which are poetry. They want poetry that is **"challenging and lively; influenced by the Beats, the NY School or Black Mountain. No traditional or formalistic; nothing that relies on conventional assumptions like rhyme and meter."** They have published poetry collections by Victor Hernandez Cruz, Anne Waldman, Andrei Codrescu and Linda Hogan. As a sample the editor selected these lines from "Heading North" by Steve Levine:

The family that eats together
eats together and eats together, rides a
tiny Honda together, two of them, huge
matching bellies heading north

Previously published poems OK; no simultaneous submissions. Cover letter required. "Please include a SASE for our reply and the return or your ms." Seldom comments on rejections. Replies to queries in 1 month, to mss in 6 months. Always sends prepublication galleys. Pays 8% royalties, $500 honorarium and 15 author's copies. Send SASE for catalog to order sample. The editor says, "We'd like to see more books by writers of color."

COFFEEHOUSE POETS' QUARTERLY (I, II), 3412 Erving, Berthoud CO 80513, founded 1990, editors Ray Foreman and Barbara Teel. They focus exclusively on **"free verse narrative poetry, prose poems and short shorts that are imaginative and clear with opening lines that hook the reader."** They have recently published poetry by Albert Huffstickler, Marc Swan, Ray Dickson, Errol Miller and Terry

Everton. As a sample the editors selected the first lines of "My Father Speaks, Sometimes In Tears" by Ray Roberts:

The frosty bottle of schnapps moves hand to hand
among the three old friends from the Europe days who can't
remember what they had for breakfast, but have no trouble
remembering long dead familiar voices and conversations;
more so lately that advanced years irritate their lives.
Only three remain from the ten who left that winter day;
today is Passover, a hard day, time is a luxury.

It is 40 pgs. Press run is 300 for 180 subscribers, balance sample copies. They accept about 10% of 3,000 poems submitted/year. "We showcase well-crafted narrative work from known and unknown poets and promote contact between writers through the Poets' Dialogue Network." Subscription: $8. **Sample, with guidelines, postpaid: $3. Submit up to 5 poems. "However, please send SASE for guidelines *before* submitting." Reports in about 2 weeks. Pays "with discount on copies."** The editors say, "Good poems convey experience in language, image and psychological clarity in a fresh package. Our readers are writers that have read yesterday's newspaper."

COKEFISH; COKEFISH PRESS (I), 31 Waterloo St., New Hope PA 18938, founded 1990, editor Ana Christy, is an irregular journal **with an entry fee of $1/3 poems. "I want to see work that has passion behind it. From the traditional to the avant-garde, provocative to discreet, trivial to the significant. Am interested in social issues, alternative, avant-garde, erotica and humor for people with nothing to hide."** They have recently published poetry by Charles Bukowski, Herschel Silverman, Dale Russell, Frank Moore and Mike Costanzo. As a sample the editor selected these lines from "Contortionist" by Albert Huffstickler:

The hardest parts the recovery
Unkinking limbs locked into place
Till distortions become the truer way
There's pain and exposure in realignment . . .
And a blood-deep sorrow you can't account for

The format is 60 pgs., side-stapled on heavy paper with a cover printed on both sides on colored photocopy paper. Press run is 300 for 150 subscribers. Subscription: $15. **Sample postpaid: $4. Accepts 30% of mss received. Note entry fee: $1/3 poems, additional $1 for additional poems. Simultaneous submissions and previously published poems OK. Cover letter "explaining why the poet chose *Cokefish*" required. Send SASE for guidelines. Reports in 1 week. Sometimes sends prepublication galleys. Pays 1 copy.** "We publish a mostly poetry broadside and will work with poets on publishing their chapbooks and audiotapes through Cokefish Press. Manuscript length up to 40 pages—$5 reading fee." Cokefish Press also publishes cooperative chapbooks. Write for details. ***Cokefish*** ranked #1 in the "Nontraditional Verse" category of the latest ***Writer's Digest*** Poetry 60 list. The editor advises, "Spread the word; don't let your poems sit and vegetate in a drawer. Send me stuff that will make my hair stand up on end."

CO-LABORER MAGAZINE; WOMAN'S NATIONAL AUXILIARY CONVENTION (IV-Religious), P.O. Box 5002, Antioch TN 37011-5002, founded 1935, editor Melissa Riddle, is "a bimonthly publication **that addresses the concerns of today's Christian woman. We're interested in poetry that reflects daily Christian living, personal evangelism and missions-mindedness."** As a sample the editor selected these lines from "Grownups" by Debbie Payne Anderson:

"Debbie— —ee!"
The cry swells as I climb from the
Car and slam the door behind me.
They press as close as they dare.

Sweet urchins
With their little bloated tummies
And grimy hands extending in welcome.
An inquisitive girl reaches out
To stroke the soft material of my
Dress and pat my pale skin.

The 32-page magazine uses at least three poems/issue, circulation 15,000. **Sample postpaid: $1. Cover letter including name, address and short bio required. Pays copies.**

COLLAGES & BRICOLAGES, THE JOURNAL OF INTERNATIONAL WRITING (II, IV-Translations, feminist, political, social issues, themes), P.O. Box 86, Clarion PA 16214, founded in 1986, editor Marie-José Fortis. ***C&B*** is a "small literary magazine with **a strong penchant for literary, feminist, avant-garde work.** Strongly encourages poets and fiction writers, as well as essayists, whether English-speaking or foreign. (Note: **Writers sending their work in a foreign language must have their ms**

accompanied with an English translation.) We are presently looking for **poetry that is socially aware—politically engaged. No sexism, racism or glorification of war. We are going towards focus-oriented issues."** As a sample the editor selected these lines by C. Payne Brunty:

I am accused of acting strange
but no python lies coiled
in my pocket full of accusations.
No hatchet lies buried
in the bone of my bewildered skull.

The annual is 100 pgs., magazine-sized, flat-spined, with card cover. They accept 5% of 250 poetry submissions/year. Press run is 800. **Sample postpaid: $7.50, 50% off for back issue. Reads submissions August 15 through November 30 only. Publishes theme issues. Reports in 1-3 months. Always sends prepublication galleys. Pays 2 copies. Acquires first rights.** "It is recommended that potential contributors order a copy, so as to know what kind of work is desirable. **Enclose a personalized letter**. Be considerate to editors, as many of them work on a voluntary basis and sacrifice much time and energy to encourage writers." Marie-José Fortis says, "Show me that you write as if nothing else mattered."

COLLEGE & CAREER PUBLISHING; CALIFORNIA WORK WORLD (I, IV-Children/teen/young adult, students), P.O. Box 900, Ontario CA 91762-8900, founded 1989. ***California Work World*** is a "monthly newsletter/workbook to help junior high and high school students learn about college and jobs as well as how to be a good citizen in our world and cope with problems encountered along the way." They want **"rhyming poems with messages for teenagers; 5-40 lines. No non-rhyming, free-form verse."** As a sample the editor selected these lines by Beverly Bassler:

Success with life's struggles begins with one's self,
Jump in, get your feet wet, get off the shelf!
We're all in this world on a stage, in a play;
Each person's unique in his style and his way.
Find something of value . . . stay focused . . . begin,
To reach for your goals by the power from within!

CWW is 16 pgs., glue bound, with puzzles and illustrations. Press run is 10,000. **Sample postpaid: $1. Previously published poems and simultaneous submissions OK.** Time between acceptance and publication is 3-4 months. "Poems are tested with groups of teenagers, and they choose favorites." **Often comments on rejections. "If comments are desired, poet must include SASE." Send SASE for guidelines. Reports in 2-3 months. Pays $30 and 20 copies.**

COLLEGE ENGLISH; NATIONAL COUNCIL OF TEACHERS OF ENGLISH (II), Dept. of English, University of Massachusetts-Boston, 100 Morrissey Blvd., Boston MA 02125-3393, phone (617)287-6733, editor Louise Z. Smith, poetry editors Helene Davis and Thomas Hurley. This journal, which is sent 8 times/year to members of the National Council of Teachers of English (membership: $40, includes subscription to *CE*), is a scholarly journal for the English discipline, but includes poetry by such poets as Beth Kalikoff, Peter R. Stillman and E.M. Schorb. It is 100 pgs., perfect-bound, with matte card cover, 7½×9½, circulation 18,000. Poems tend to be wide-ranging in style, form and content. **Sample postpaid: $6.25, from NCTE, 1111 W. Kenyon Rd., Urbana IL 61801-1096. Submit a "letter-quality copy" of each poem with cover letter including titles of poems submitted. Reports in 4 months maximum, except for summer submissions. Pays 2 copies.**

COLOR WHEEL; COLOR WHEEL REVIEW; 700 ELVES PRESS (II, IV-Nature/ecology, spiritual), RR 2, Box 806, Warner NH 03278, founded 1990, editor Frederick Moe, associate editor Carol Edson, appears approximately 2 times/year. **"*Color Wheel*** uses high quality prose and **poetry related to spiritual, ecological and mythological themes. We want poetry that explores more deeply and intensely our relationships with the earth and one another. All forms of poetry are welcome, including longer poems (2-4 pages). No rhymed verse."** They have recently published poetry by Devon Vose, Lynn Kozma, David Sparenberg and Walt Franklin. The editor says it is 32-40 pgs., 8×11, flat-spined, with heavy cover stock, cover art, graphics and line drawings. They receive about 300 submissions a year, use an average of 5%. Press run is 300 for 30 subscribers of which 4 are libraries, 100 shelf sales. Single copy: $6; subscription: $14 (3 issues). **Sample back issue postpaid: $5. Make checks payable to Frederick Moe. No simultaneous submissions. Cover letter required—include "something that does not keep the writer 'anonymous'!" Reads submissions January 1 through July 31 only. Comments on "close" rejections. Publishes theme issues. Send SASE for guidelines and upcoming themes. Reports in up to 1 month. Pays in copies.** Staff reviews books of poetry. Send books for review consideration to Frederick Moe at the above address. Send Northwest area submissions to Carol Edson at 1804 NE 50th, Seattle WA 98105. "We also publish ***Color Wheel Review***, an occasional supplement of poetry, reviews and essays related to small press culture. The ***Review*** is sent free to subscribers. **700 Elves Press publishes 2 chapbooks/year.** "Some 700 Elves Press chapbooks are thematic anthologies including various writers. I have published chapbooks on elemental poems and plan other thematic chapbooks and occasional individual collections." **Poets should first be published in *Color Wheel*. Replies to queries and mss in 1 month. Pays "negotiable" number of author's copies. For sample chapbooks "send SASE for our small, homespun catalog."** Frederick Moe says, "*Color Wheel* is esoteric yet focused in content. Poets should be familiar with the evolution of the magazine and type of material we publish before sending work. I encourage 'new' voices and appreciate creative approaches to the material. I am annoyed by poets who enclose postcards for response rather than a SASE and expect me to recycle their manuscript. I do not respond to such submissions. Inclusion of a SASE allows me to return press information with response and demonstrates concern on the part of the writer for their work. It is worth the extra expense! I would also like to note that we would appreciate audio submissions of poetry/music/performance/creative work for a potential audio tape issue or anthology."

COLORADO REVIEW (II, IV-Translations, themes), Dept. of English, 359 Eddy Bldg., Colorado State University, Ft. Collins CO 80523, phone (303)491-5449, fax (303)491-5601, founded 1955 as ***Colorado State Review***, resurrected 1977 under "New Series" rubric, renamed ***Colorado Review*** 1985, editor David Milofsky, poetry editor Jorie Graham. ***Colorado Review*** is a journal of contemporary literature which appears twice annually; it combines short fiction, poetry, interviews with or articles about significant contemporary poets and writers, articles on literature, culture and the arts, translations of poetry from around the world and reviews of recent works of the literary imagination. **"We're interested in poetry that explores experience in deeply felt new ways; merely descriptive or observational language doesn't move us. Poetry that enters into and focuses on the full range of experience, weaving sharp imagery, original figures and surprising though apt insight together in compressed precise language and compelling rhythm is what triggers an acceptance here."** They have published poetry by Tess Gallagher, James Galvin and Brendan Galvin. They have a circulation of 1,500, 300 subscriptions of which 100 are libraries. They use about 10% of the 500-1,000 submissions they receive/year. Subscription: $15/year. **Sample postpaid: $8. Submit about 5 poems. Reads submissions September 1 through May 1 only. "When work is a near-miss, we will provide brief comment and encouragement." Publishes theme issues. Send SASE for upcoming themes. Reports in 3-6 months. Always sends prepublication galleys. Pays $10/printed page for poetry. Buys first North American serial rights.** Reviews books of poetry, both single and multi-book format. Open to unsolicited reviews. Poets may also send books for review consideration. Poetry published in ***Colorado Review*** has been included in the 1993 and 1994 volumes of **The Best American Poetry**. They say, "Our attitude is that we will publish the best work that comes across the editorial desk. We see poetry as a vehicle for exploring states of feeling, but we aren't interested in sentimentality (especially metaphysical)."

COLUMBIA: A MAGAZINE OF POETRY & PROSE (II), Dept. PM, 404 Dodge Hall, Columbia University, New York NY 10027, phone (212)854-4391, founded 1977, poetry editors Mary Jo Bang and Kimberly Taylor, is a literary semiannual using "quality short stories, novel excerpts, translations, interviews, nonfiction and **poetry, usually no longer than 2 pgs."** They have recently published poetry by Yusef Komunyakaa, Rachel Hadas and Amy Gerstler. As a sample the editors selected these lines from "November" by Sophie Cabot Black:

Hoarse crows keen through unalterable sky.
Leaves sink and wheel,
Braiding themselves to ground.

Haybale, scarecrow, frozen lamb: the saved
Break down, restless. I gather what remains
For the witness of a warm wind, that vital day.

It is a digest-sized, approximately 180 pgs., with coated cover stock. They publish about 12 poets each issue from 400 submissions. **Sample postpaid: $7. Submit double-spaced mss. "Very brief comments at editor's discretion." Send SASE for guidelines. Reports in 1-3 months. Pays up to 2 copies.**

COLUMBIA UNIVERSITY TRANSLATION CENTER; TRANSLATION; TRANSLATION CENTER AWARDS (IV-Translations), 412 Dodge, Columbia University, New York NY 10027, phone (212)854-2305, founded 1972, director Frank MacShane. "Translation Center publishes only foreign contemporary literature in English language translations and also gives annual awards and grants to translators. ***Translation*** magazine publishes **contemporary foreign poetry/literature in English language translations.** (Note: We do no reviews.)" They have published translations of poetry by Silvina Ocampo, Luis Cernuda, Nina Cassian, Eva Toth and Faiz Ahmed Faiz. As a sample we selected these lines from "Body" by Eugénio de Andrade, translated from the Portuguese by Alexis Levitin:

The sea—whenever I touch
a body the sea is what I feel
wave after wave
against the palm of my hand.

Translation is a biannual, circulation 2,000. Subscription: $18. **Sample postpaid: $9. "All submis-**

sions should be preceded by a query. Each issue is specialized to one language and consequently all unsolicited manuscripts have to be limited to that language." Send SASE for guidelines and descriptions of the various award programs they administer. Columbia University Translation Center Awards are grants to a translator for an outstanding translation of a substantial part of a book-length literary work. Awards range from $250-2,500 and are designed mainly to recognize excellence. Translations from any language into English are eligible, and specific awards exist for translations from the French Canadian, Dutch, Portuguese and Italian. All applications will automatically be considered for all awards for which they are eligible. The Center generally discourages applicants who are retranslating a work unless a special reason exists.

COMMONWEAL (III, IV-Religious), 15 Dutch St., New York NY 10038, phone (212)732-0800, poetry editor Rosemary Deen, appears every 2 weeks, circulation 20,000, is a general-interest magazine for college-educated readers **by Catholics. Prefers serious, witty, well-written poems of up to 75 lines. Does not publish inspirational poems.** As a sample the editor selected these lines from "One is One," a sonnet by Marie Ponsot:

Heart, you bully, you punk, I'm wrecked, I'm shocked
stiff. You? you still try to rule the world—though
I've got you: identified, starving, locked
in a cage you will not leave alive . . .

In the issues we reviewed, editors seemed to favor free verse, much of it open with regard to style and content, appealing as much to the intellect as to the emotions. **Sample: $3. Considers simultaneous submissions. Reads submissions September 1 through June 30 only. Pays 50¢ a line. Buys all rights. Returns rights when requested by the author.** Reviews books of poetry in 750-1,000 words, single or multi-book format.

COMMUNICATIONS PUBLISHING GROUP; COLLEGE PREVIEW, A GUIDE FOR COLLEGE-BOUND STUDENTS; DIRECT AIM; A GUIDE TO CAREER ALTERNATIVES; JOURNEY, A SUCCESS GUIDE FOR COLLEGE AND CAREER-BOUND STUDENTS; VISIONS, A SUCCESS GUIDE FOR NATIVE AMERICAN STUDENTS; FIRST OPPORTUNITY, A GUIDE FOR VOCATIONAL TECHNICAL STUDENTS (IV-Youth, themes, ethnic), Dept. PM, #250, 106 W. 11th St., Kansas City MO 64105-1806, phone (816)221-4404, editor Georgia Clark. These five publications are 40% freelance written. All are designed to inform and motivate their readers in regard to college preparation, career planning and life survival skills. All except *First Opportunity*, which is quarterly, appear in spring and fall. ***College Preview* is for Black and Hispanic young adults, ages 16-21.** Circ. 600,000. ***Direct Aim* is for Black and Hispanic young adults, ages 18-25.** Circ. 500,000. ***Journey* is for Asian-American high school and college students, ages 16-25.** Circ. 200,000. ***Visions* is for Native American students and young adults, ages 16-25.** Circ. 100,000. ***First Opportunity* is for Black and Hispanic young adults, ages 16-21.** Circ. 500,000. **Sample copy of any for 9×12 SAE with 4 first class stamps. Simultaneous and previously published submissions OK. Submit seasonal/holiday material 6 months in advance. "Include on manuscript your name, address, phone and Social Security numbers." They use free verse. Each magazine buys 5 poems/year. Submit up to 5 poems at one time. Length: 10-25 lines. Writer's guidelines for #10 SASE. Reports in 2 months. Pays $10-50/poem. All these magazines pay on acceptance.**

COMMUNITIES: JOURNAL OF COOPERATIVE LIVING (IV-Social issues), 1118 Round Butte Dr., Fort Collins CO 80524, phone (303)490-1550, founded 1972, managing editor Diana Christian, is a "quarterly publication on **intentional communities, cooperatives, social and global transformation," using poetry relevant to those themes.** It is magazine-sized, professionally printed on recycled white stock with 2-color glossy paper cover, 56 pgs., saddle-stapled. **Previously published poems and simultaneous submissions OK. No comment on rejections. Pays 3 copies.** They also publish a directory of international communities.

A COMPANION IN ZEOR (IV-Science fiction/fantasy), 307 Ashland Ave., McKee City NJ 08232, phone (609)645-6938, founded 1978, editor Karen Litman, is a **science fiction, fantasy fanzine appearing *very* irregularly (last published issue December 1990; hopes to publish again this year). "Material used is now limited to creations based solely on works (universes) of Jacqueline Lichtenberg. No other submission types considered. Prefer nothing obscene. Homosexuality not acceptable unless very relevant to the piece. Prefer a 'clean' publication image."** As a sample, we selected these lines from "Fire Also Purifies" by Lisa Calhoun:

A death is a birth, and the reverse is true,
out of the turmoil emerges something new.

It is magazine-sized, photocopied from typescript. Press run is 100. **Send SASE for guidelines. Cover letter preferred with submissions; note whether to return or dispose of rejected mss. Sometimes sends prepublication galleys. Pays copies. Acquires first rights. "Always willing to work with authors or poets to help in improving their work."** Reviews books of poetry. Open to unsolicited reviews. Poets may also send books for review consideration.

COMPENIONS; THE WRITER'S CLUB OF STRATFORD (I), P.O. Box 2511, St. Marys, Ontario N4X 1A3 Canada, founded 1983, president Marco Balestrin, is a quarterly publication of The Writer's Club of Stratford. "We print works by the members of the W.C.S. but would like to expand our mandate to include poetry and short fiction by other writers." They want **"original, sincerely-written poetry of any form, 30 lines maximum. No cliched or trite poetry. No pornography."** They have recently published poetry by Jerry Penner, Susan Chapman-Bossence and Carol Lease. As a sample Marco Balestrin selected these lines from "Songs of Minoa" by Gerald George:

When spring comes,
does the snow melt ecstatically?
does ice rejoice?

Persios, dear heart,
what is ice?
what is snow?

Compenions is 14-20 pgs., 8½×11, photocopied, side-stapled, with computer graphics. They receive about 40 poems a year, use approximately 90%. Press run is 16 ("will increase after further submissions are received"). **Sample postpaid: $4. Submit up to 6 poems at a time *with $3.50 reading fee*. Previously published poems and simultaneous submissions OK. Cover letter required. "Please include a SASE (if within Canada) or SAE and 2 IRCs (if outside Canada)." Reads submissions September 1 through June 30 only. "Two to three members read over submissions and choose suitable poems." Often comments on rejections. Publishes theme issues. Send SASE for upcoming themes. Reports in 1 month. Pays 2 copies.** Balestrin says, "We would like to be a forum providing writers (especially beginners) the opportunity to get published, thereby also exposing ourselves to what is going on 'out there,' in other words, to have a literary relationship beneficial to both parties!"

CONCHO RIVER REVIEW; FORT CONCHO MUSEUM PRESS (IV-Regional), 213 E. Ave. D, San Angelo TX 76903, phone (915)657-4441, founded 1984, poetry editor Gerald M. Lacy. "The Fort Concho Museum Press is entering another year of publishing *Concho River Review*, a literary journal published twice a year. **Work by Texas writers, writers with a Texas connection and writers living in the Southwest preferred. Prefer shorter poems, few long poems accepted; particularly looking for poems with distinctive imagery and imaginative forms and rhythms. The first test of a poem will be its imagery."** Short reviews of new volumes of poetry are also published. *CRR* is 120-138 pgs., flat-spined, digest-sized, with matte card cover, professionally printed. They use 35-40 of 600-800 poems received/year. Press run is 300 for about 200 subscriptions of which 10 are libraries. Subscription: $12. **Sample postpaid: $4. "Please submit 3-5 poems at a time. Use regular legal-sized envelopes—no big brown envelopes; no replies without SASE. Type must be letter-perfect, sharp enough to be computer scanned." Publishes theme issues. Send SASE for upcoming themes. Reports in 1-2 months. Pays 1 copy. Acquires first rights.** The editor says, "We're always looking for good, strong work—from both well-known poets and those who have never been published before."

‡CONFLUENCE; OHIO VALLEY LITERARY GROUP (II), P.O. Box 336, Belpre OH 45714, phone (614)373-2999, founded 1983 as *Gambit*, 1989 as *Confluence*, editor Barbara McCullough-Cress. *Confluence* is an annual "credible platform for outstanding student work complemented by established/emerging authors. This literary magazine is published at Marietta College, Marietta, Ohio, and was named to represent the merging of the Ohio and Muskingum Rivers as well as the collaboration of the Ohio Valley Literary Group with Marietta College." **As for poetry, they want "truths retold in vital, economical language. Nothing cliché, sentimental, same old ax to grind."** They have recently published poetry by Lyn Lifshin, Joel Lipman, Grace Butcher and Penelope Schott. As a sample the editor selected these lines from "The breathtaking indigo of their clothes" by Brigitte Oleschinski, translated by Gary Sea:

Fissures, footprint, shingles.
On the stones spreads a topography of weather
of time, Thirst
and questions. You
wonder over torrent-scarred rock onto
rivers of sand, sun-blanched clefts, stumbling—hear
the barometer's dispatch like
a saxophone and all things blue
are oceans in your head.

Confluence is 96-112 pgs., digest-sized, professionally printed and perfect-bound with 2-color matte card cover and b&w graphics. They receive 800-1,000 submissions a year, accept approximately 2%. Press run is 500 for 300 subscribers of which 10 are libraries, about 150 shelf sales. Single copy: $5. **Sample: $3 plus $1.25 postage. No previously published poems or simultaneous submissions. Cover letter with brief bio required. Reads submissions September 1 to December**

1 only. Time between acceptance and publication is 6 months. **Always comments on rejections. Send SASE for guidelines. Reports in 3 months. Pays 1-3 copies. Returns rights upon publication.**

CONFLUENCE PRESS (II, IV-Regional), Lewis-Clark State College, Lewiston ID 83501, phone (208)799-2336, founded 1975, poetry editor James R. Hepworth, is an "independent publisher of fiction, poetry, creative nonfiction and literary scholarship. **We are open to formal poetry as well as free verse. No rhymed doggerel, 'light verse,' 'performance poetry,' 'street poetry,' etc. We prefer to publish work by poets who live and work in the northwestern United States."** They have published poetry by John Daniel, Greg Keeler, Nancy Mairs and Wendell Berry. They print about 2 books a year. **"Please query *before* submitting manuscript." Query with 6 sample poems, bio, list of publications. Replies to queries in 3 weeks. Pays $100-500 advance and 10% royalties plus copies. Buys all rights. Returns rights if book goes out of print. Send SASE for catalog to order samples.**

CONFRONTATION MAGAZINE (II), English Dept., C.W. Post Campus of Long Island University, Brookville NY 11548-0570, founded 1968, editor-in-chief Martin Tucker, is "a semiannual literary journal with **interest in all forms. Our only criterion is high literary merit.** We think of our audience as an educated, lay group of intelligent readers. **We prefer lyric poems. Length generally should be kept to 2 pages. No sentimental verse."** They have published poetry by Karl Shapiro, T. Alan Broughton, David Ignatow, Philip Appleman, Jane Mayhall and Joseph Brodsky. As a sample the editor selected these lines from "Imagination" by Scott Thomas:

He builds things in my cellar. He fashions things
From wood and glass, flesh and bone, green eyes
And dirt. One day while I was down there washing
Bedclothes, he was at his workbench tinkering
With a small electric motor. "Rewiring
A soul," he said.

Confrontation is 190 pgs., digest-sized, professionally printed, flat-spined, with a circulation of about 2,000. A visually beautiful journal, and well-edited, each issue features about 30-40 poems of varying lengths. The magazine is recommended not only for its "showcase" appeal, but also for the wide range of formal and free styles, displaying craft and insight. They receive about 1,200 submissions/year, publish 150, have a 6- to 12-month backlog. **Sample postpaid: $3. Submit no more than 10 pgs., clear copy. Do not submit mss June through August. "Prefer single submissions." Publishes theme issues. Send SASE for upcoming themes. "We are interested in 'self-censorship' theme for an upcoming supplement in 1995." Reports in 6-8 weeks. Sometimes sends prepublication galleys. Pays $5-50 and copy of magazine**. Staff reviews books of poetry. Send books for review consideration. Basically a magazine, they do on occasion publish "book" issues or "anthologies." Their most recent "occasional book" is **Phantom Pain**, story and drawings by Alfred Van Loen.

CONJUNCTIONS (III), Dept. PM, Bard College, Annandale-on-Hudson NY 12504, founded 1981, managing editor Dale Cotton, editor Bradford Morrow, is an elegant journal appearing twice/year. **"Potential contributor should be familiar with the poetry published in the journal."** They have recently published poetry by John Ashbery, Robert Kelly, Charles Stein, Michael Palmer, Ann Lauterbach and Fanny Howe. As a sample here are lines from "Paulownia" by Barbara Guest:

ravenous the still dark a fishnet—
robber walk near formidable plaits
a glaze—the domino overcast—
violet. shoulder.

Like ***The Quarterly***, this publication is distributed by Random House. It is 400 pgs., 6×9, flat-spined, professionally printed. Issues reviewed feature mostly lyric free verse with occasional sequences and stanza patterns (some leaning toward the avant-garde). Poems compete with prose, with more pages devoted to the latter. Press run is 5,500 for 600 subscribers of which 200 are libraries. Subscription: $18. **Sample postpaid: $10. Pays $100-175.**

THE CONNECTICUT POETRY REVIEW (II), P.O. Box 818, Stonington CT 06378, founded 1981, poetry editors J. Claire White and Harley More, is a "small press that puts out an annual magazine. **We look for poetry of quality which is both genuine and original in content. No specifications except length: 10-40 lines."** The magazine has won high praise from the literary world; they have published such poets as Chen Jingrong, Robert Peters, Peter Wild and Linda Pastan. Each issue seems to feature a poet. As a sample the editors selected these lines by Odysseus Elytis (translated by Jeffrey Carson):

Maybe I'm still in the state of a medicinal
herb or of a cold Friday's snake
Or perhaps of one of those sacred beasts
with its big ear full of heavy sounds
and metallic noise from censers.

The flat-spined, large digest-sized journal is "printed letterpress by hand on a Hacker Hand Press from Monotype Bembo." Most of the 45-60 pgs. are poetry, but they also have reviews. Editors seem to favor free verse with strong emphasis on voice (and judicious use of image and symbol). They receive over 1,200 submissions a year, use about 20, have a 3-month backlog. Press run is 400 for 80 subscribers of which 35 are libraries. **Sample postpaid: $3.50. Reports in 3 months. Pays $5/poem plus 1 copy.** The editors advise, "Study traditional and modern styles. Study poets of the past. Attend poetry readings. And write. Practice on your own."

CONNECTICUT RIVER REVIEW; NATIONAL FALL POETRY CONTEST; BRODINE CONTEST; CONNECTICUT POETRY SOCIETY (II), Dept. PM, 327 Seabury Dr., Bloomfield CT 06002, founded 1978, appears twice yearly, editor Ben Brodinsky. They want poetry that has **"depth of emotion, the truly seen (imaginary or actual), in which sound and sense are one. All forms are welcome, except haiku. We look for high quality, well-crafted poems. We accept poetry from all over the world."** They have published poetry by Joseph Bruchac, Donald Jenkins, Simon Perchik, Viola Shipley and Paul Zimmer. Each of the plain but attractively printed, digest-sized issues contains about 40 pgs. of poetry, has a circulation of about 500, with 175 subscriptions of which 5% are libraries. They receive about 2,000 submissions/year, use about 70. Subscription: $10. **Sample postpaid: $5. Submit no more than 3-5 poems. No simultaneous submissions. Poems over 40 lines have little chance of acceptance, unless exceptional. Deadlines: February 15 and August 15. Guidelines available with SASE. Rejections within 2 weeks, acceptances could take 2 months. Pays 1 copy.** The National Fall Poetry Contest has a $2 entry fee/poem and prizes of $250, $100 and $50. Send SASE for rules. The Brodine Contest, % Norman Kraeft, 86 Bellamy Lane, Bethlehem CT 06751-1203. Guidelines available in February; send SASE. Deadline is July 31, $2 fee/poem. Three cash awards plus publication in the ***Connecticut River Review***.

‡CONSCIENCE (III), CFFC, Suite 301, 1436 U St. NW, Washington DC 20009-3997, founded 1980, poetry editor Andrew Merton, is a quarterly newsjournal of prochoice Catholic opinion, published by Catholics for a Free Choice. **They want poetry up to 45 lines maximum. "We're topically broad and broadminded. However, no polemics (about abortion/choice/religion) nor poems in conflict with a prochoice—albeit not stiflingly politically correct—organization."** They have recently published poetry by Mekeel McBride and Romana Huk. As a sample the editor selected these lines from "Blues" by Sarah Patton:

Black as the dark
of the moon
is the percussion
of her thighs,

the drum
of her belly,
the pump
of her hips.

Conscience is 48 pgs., 8×10½, web press newsprint, saddle-stitched with some b&w art, photos and ads. They accept less than 10% of poetry received. Press run is 15,000. Single copy: $3.50; subscription: $10/year. **Sample: $3 for an issue published within the past year, $1 for earlier issues, and 9×12 SASE. Submit 3-5 poems at a time. No previously published poems; simultaneous submissions OK, if noted.** Time between acceptance and publication is 1-8 months. **Seldom comments on rejections. Reports in 2 months. Pays $10 and 5 copies. Buys first serial rights.** Interested poets are strongly urged to read a few issues of this publication before submitting. The editor says, "***Conscience*** explores ethical and social policy dimensions of sexuality and reproductive health and decision-making, church-state dynamics and related topics. CFFC is a non-profit educational organization that shapes and advances sexual and reproductive ethics that are based on justice, reflect a commitment to women's well-being, and respect and affirm the moral capacity of women and men to make sound and responsible decisions about their lives."

‡CONSERVATIVE REVIEW (II), Room #203, 1307 Dolley Madison Blvd., McLean VA 22101, phone (703)893-7302, fax (703)893-7273, founded January 1990, poetry editor Mattie F. Quesenberry, is a bimonthly magazine that includes "political articles, political statistics, political cartoons and especially strong articles on foreign affairs. **We want to see poetry of any form exploring our relationship to the natural world, especially poems exploring the impact of 20th century science and technology on traditional values. We do not want to see any political poetry. Poetry should transcend political divisions because it should capture universal experiences."** They have recently published poetry by Barbara N. Ewell and Jim Minick. As a sample the editor selected these lines from Ewell's poem, "The Sistine Adam":

The Sistine Adam with incredible
Silence, with brute force, strains in heel and thigh

CLOSE-UP

Make Your Work Speak for Itself

First we learn "Every keg must sit
on its bottom," then we learn that
this is true, then that
it's the law, and so stop
trusting it again. So we're left
with a little time left.
If we believe a little something,
if we are kind a little bit,
if we make a little something,
if we believe in nearly nothing,
we can be happy a little while.

(from "Summarizing Santayana")

David Breeden

"When I pick up a poem, I'm looking for Art. Art with a big A," says editor and publisher David Breeden. "I'm looking for a piece of writing that shows an awareness of the tradition, where we are in the poetic discourse of the ages, but a piece that is [also] totally fresh and different from anything currently being done. I want to find that piece of work and get it out to as many people as possible."

Breeden, a poet himself, began publishing ***Context South*** in 1988. He started the biannual magazine because he wanted to be a good editor, "one who read manuscripts in a timely manner, one who disregarded the fame or obscurity of the writer and just read the work. I wanted to treat poets better than I had been treated. No one ever encouraged me to write; I just kept hacking away in the dark."

From writing jingles and parodies in high school, Breeden went to writing long imitations of Jim Morrison and T.S. Eliot. He attended his first creative writing class as a senior in college but continued to get most of his inspiration from the work of authors such as Allen Ginsberg, William S. Burroughs, William Carlos Williams and Ezra Pound. "I had, I suppose, the privilege of discovering the Modernists completely on my own with no clues from professors or critics about what they were doing."

Breeden, who gets his ideas through observation, keeps a notebook handy at all times. "I read somewhere that the Germans have a word, *gelassenheit*, which means that the small things, the insignificant ones, save us. I like that." He writes poems (in longhand) when he can find the time, which is not often due to the demands of publishing ***Context South***. "So I write and leave the poems in big heaps. That's been healthy for my work," he says.

Before becoming an editor, Breeden submitted his poems regularly. In the past ten years, three books of his poetry have been published: **Picnics** (Black Buzzard Press, 1985); **Hey, Schliemann** (Edwin Mellen Press, 1990); and **Double-Headed End Wrench** (Cloverdale Press, 1992). Now he rarely submits his work, but when he does he only sends his best. "I believe in only sending off work that I know is good. If all poets did the same, then the problems of the editor would be solved tomorrow and every literary magazine would be a shining crystal."

With this in mind, Breeden advises beginning poets to keep the faith and to only go into poetry out of love for it. "There really aren't very many rewards out there, besides the satisfaction of once in a while tapping into that transcendent moment of beauty . . . the joy of creating art. That's a personal joy. Poetry is not too likely to get you applause or even free drinks. But if you have to [go into poetry], there's lots of folks out there to encourage and help you."

In publishing ***Context South***, Breeden uses poetry of all forms, lengths and subjects, and is open to poets from all regions. He suggests poets read ***Context South*** before submitting their work. Blind submissions are often a problem for magazines because many of the poets who want to be published are not willing to support the magazines they submit their work to, he says. "The main frustration of my job is seeing all the poems written just because the author wants to be published for some reason. I get very tired after seeing a string of those."

However, Breeden says the submissions he has received since being listed in **Poet's Market** have been consistently good. "Before, I would get flurries of submissions that were either imitations of 'magazine' poets or half-baked Victorian verse. But now, with the quality of submissions I get, I could make ***Context South*** a monthly magazine with no loss of artistic quality."

His plans for the future are not only to keep publishing despite the lack of money, but to expand his publishing with the addition of a more instant type of magazine. He is thinking of calling it ***Out of Context***. It would be a newsletter photocopied from submissions right off his desk. "I often feel that the time span involved in doing a better production ruins the joy of the moment," he says.

Breeden recommends attending readings and workshops as a great way of sharing work with others. "But, don't go to something sponsored by a university and leave feeling untalented or stupid. Being successful enough to participate in a reading or workshop has nothing to do with intelligence or artistic ability. Trust your muse whatever anyone says."

Ever mindful of his own beginnings as a poet, Breeden challenges every editor to publish only on literary merit. "I've often failed at that out of sheer overload, but I keep the goal in sight: being an editor who reads with an unjaundiced eye the work a poet has done."

His final advice for aspiring poets is to trust the work to speak for itself and "be nice to editors—most of them went into the business to help others."

—Chantelle Bentley

To touch his Father. That regrettable

Space. One mere stroke of absent brush. They lie,
The reversal of their coordinate.

CR is 40 pgs., 8½×11, offset printed and saddle-stitched with glossy card cover. They use one page of poetry in each issue. Press run is 950 for 810 subscribers of which 170 are libraries. Subscription: $28/year. **Sample postpaid: $5. Previously published poems and simultaneous submissions OK. "Unsolicited manuscripts must be accompanied by a letter certifying the material is the original work of the author and involves no contravention of copyright or unauthorized use of another author's material."** Time between acceptance and publication is up to a year. **Often comments on rejections. Reports in 1-2 months. Pays 3 copies. Acquires all rights. Returns rights upon request.** "We will review books and chapbooks and print short critical essays." Open to unsolicited reviews. Poets may also send books for review consideration. The editor says, "There is no real division between poetry and our twentieth century science and technology. Even the most specialized specialists live their lives with consciences housed in flesh and blood. Even our most unscientific writers and poets must live and react in the modern world."

CONTEXT SOUTH (III), #4504, 2100 Memorial Blvd., Kerrville TX 78028, founded 1988, editor/publisher David Breeden, appears twice a year using **"any form, length, subject matter. Looking for strong rhythms, clear vision. Nothing sentimental."** They have published poetry by Andrea Hollander Budy, Simon Perchik and Peter Drizhal. As a sample the editor selected these lines by Dean Taciuch:

The myth remains with us even after the land
has emptied itself into shallow basins our faces
stare back through waves and fields where
the water ran and covered our heads in song.

It is 65 pgs., digest-sized, saddle-stapled, using fiction, criticism and book reviews as well as poetry. They accept less than 1% of poems received. Press run is 500 for 60 subscribers of which 6 are libraries. **Sample: $5. Simultaneous submissions OK. Reads submissions January 1 through March 31 only. Publishes theme issues. Pays 1 copy. Acquires first serial rights.** Reviews books of poetry in 500 words maximum. Open to unsolicited reviews. Poets may also send books for review consideration. The editor advises, "Read every poem you can find from the beginning of time. Every poem encapsulates the tradition."

COPPER BEECH PRESS (III), P.O. Box 1852, English Dept., Brown University, Providence RI 02912, phone (401)863-3744, founded 1973, poetry editor Randy Blasing, publishes **books of all kinds of poetry**, about three 64-page, flat-spined paperbacks a year. They have recently published Christopher Buckley, Margaret Holley, Robert B. Shaw and Kay Ryan. **Query with 5 poems, biographical information and publications. Considers simultaneous submissions. Do not submit queries from Memorial Day to Labor Day. Replies to queries in 1 month, to mss in 3 months. Always sends prepublication galleys. Pays 10% of press run. For sample books, call or write for free catalog.**

‡COPPER CANYON PRESS (III), P.O. Box 271, Port Townsend WA 98368, founded 1972, editor Sam Hamill, publishes 8 paperback books of poetry/year, one of which is through the National Poetry Series Annual Open Competition (for details, write National Poetry Series at P.O. Box G, Hopewell NJ 08525). They have recently published books of poetry by Lucille Clifton, Hayden Carruth, Carolyn Kizer and Olga Broumas. **Query first with sample poems and cover letter with brief bio and publication credits. Replies to queries and mss (if invited) in 1 month.** Time between acceptance and publication is 2 years. **Write for catalog to order samples.**

CORNERSTONE (IV-Religious), Jesus People USA, 939 W. Wilson, Chicago IL 60640, phone (312)989-2080, submissions editor Jennifer Ingerson, is a mass-circulation (50,000), low-cost ($2/copy) publication appearing 2-4 times/year, **directed at young adults (20-35), covering "contemporary issues in the light of Evangelical Christianity." They use avant-garde, free verse, haiku, light verse, rarely traditional—"no limits except for epic poetry. (We've not got the room.)"** As a sample the editor selected these lines from an untitled poem by Bruce Bitmead:

I am white
and have no history
I come from
Nowhere, in particular
My people
Hail from down the street.

Buys 10-50 poems/year, uses 1-2 pgs./issue, has a 2- to 3-month backlog. Sample: $2. Submit maximum of 5 poems. Cover letter required. Send SASE for guidelines. Pays $10 for poems having 1-15 lines, $25 for poems having 16 lines or more. Buys first or one-time rights. Open to unsolicited reviews. Poets may also send books for review consideration. In past years, ***Corner-***

stone has received numerous awards from the Evangelical Press Association (including second place for poetry) as well as a Medal of Distinctive Merit from the Society of Publication Designers and a 1993 Certificate of Design Excellence from ***Print*** magazine.

CORNFIELD REVIEW (II), Dept. PM, Ohio State University–Marion, 1465 Mt. Vernon Ave., Marion OH 43302-5695, phone (614)389-2361, fax (614)389-6786, founded 1974, is an annual of poetry, artwork, short fiction and personal narrative. **"We are open to all forms of high quality poetry, and we are interested in new talent."** It is 6×9, flat-spined, printed on heavy slick stock with b&w graphics, glossy cover with art, approximately 40-48 pgs. Their press run is about 500. **Sample postpaid: $5. No simultaneous submissions or previously published poems. Send no more than 5 poems with brief cover letter. Submissions should be typed. Reports within 2-5 months. Pays 3 copies. Copyright reverts to contributor.**

CORONA (II), Dept. of History and Philosophy, Montana State University, Bozeman MT 59717, phone (406)994-5200, founded 1979, poetry editors Lynda and Michael Sexson, "is an interdisciplinary occasional journal bringing together reflections from those who stand on the edges of their disciplines; those who sense that insight is located not in things but in relationships; those who have deep sense of playfulness; and those who believe that the imagination is involved in what we know." In regard to poetry they want **"no sentimental greeting cards; no slap-dash."** They have published poems by Wendy Battin, William Irwin Thompson, Frederick Turner and James Dickey. In the spring of 1995 the editors are planning a special issue on the subject of the "book." Journal is perfect-bound, 125-140 pgs., professionally printed. They use about 20-25 pgs. of poetry/issue. Press run is 2,000. **Sample postpaid: $7. Submit any number of pages. No simultaneous submissions. Reports in 1 week to 9 months. Payment is "nominal" plus 2 contributor's copies.** The editors advise, "Today's poet survives only by the generous spirits of small press publishers. Read and support the publishers of contemporary artists by subscribing to the journals and magazines you admire."

COSMIC TREND; PARA*phrase (I, IV-Themes, love/romance/erotica), Sheridan Mall Box 47014, Mississauga, Ontario L5K 2R2 Canada, founded 1984, Cosmic Trend poetry editor George Le Grand, ***PARA*phrase*** editor Tedy Asponsen. Cosmic Trend publishes 2 chapbook anthologies and narrated music cassettes a year of **"New Age mind-expanding material of any style, short or medium length; also: humorous, unusual or zany entries (incl. graphics) with deeper meaning. We ignore epics, run-of-a-mill romantic and political material. Would like to publish more free verse."** They have recently published poetry by Jay Bradford Fowler, Jr., Joanna Nealon, Thea Vanderplaats and Iris Litt. As a sample the editor selected these lines by Jiri Jirasek:

When your living flower
opens for my love
I would starve my hunger
half the way to heaven
just to see you bloom
while carving petals
with my tongue . . .

PARA*phrase—Newsletter of Cosmic Trend (irregular: 2-3 times a year)—publishes "poetry related to our major anthologies advertised there." **Submit poems with name and address on each sheet. They will consider simultaneous submissions and previously published poems "with accompanied disclosure and references." Publishes theme issues. Send $1 for guidelines and upcoming themes or $5 for sample publication, guidelines and upcoming themes.** Brief guidelines: $1 for each two poems submitted, plus $1 for postage. Minimum fee $2 plus postage ("No US postal stamps, please.") **Response time is usually less than 3 weeks. Editor "often" comments on submissions. Pays 1 copy/published project. Rights revert to authors upon publication.** Reviews books of poetry. Open to unsolicited reviews. Poets may also send books for review consideration, attn. Tedy Asponsen. Cosmic Trend publishes electronic music cassette tapes in addition to their poetry/music anthology accompaniments. They say, "Share your adventure of poetry beyond the usual presentation! Cosmic Trend can choose your poems for narration with music and inclusion into our cassette accompaniments to our illustrated anthologies."

COSMOPOLITAN (IV-Women), 224 W. 57th St., New York NY 10019, founded 1886, is a monthly magazine "aimed at a female audience 18-34," part of the Hearst conglomerate, though it functions independently editorially. They want **"freshly-written free verse, not more than 25 lines, either light or serious, which addresses the concerns of young women. Prefer shorter poems, use 1-4 poems each issue. Poems shouldn't be too abstract. The poem should convey an image, feeling or emotion that our reader could perhaps identify with. We do publish mostly free verse, although we're also open to well-crafted rhyme poems. We cannot return submissions without SASE."** They have a circulation of 2,987,970. **Buy sample at newsstand. Reports in 3-5 weeks. Pays $25.** "Please do not phone; query by letter if at all, though queries are unnecessary before submitting."

COTEAU BOOKS; THUNDER CREEK PUBLISHING CO-OP; WOOD MOUNTAIN SERIES (II, IV-Regional, children), 401-2206 Dewdney Ave., Regina, Saskatchewan S4R 1H3 Canada, phone (306)777-0170, fax (306)522-5152, founded 1975, managing editor Shelley Sopher, is a "small literary press that publishes poetry, fiction, drama, anthologies, criticism, children's books – **only by Canadian writers."** They have recently published poetry by Nancy Mattson, Kim Morrissey, Anne Szumigalski, Patrick Lane, Louise Halfe, Paul Wilson, Judith Krause, Barbara Klar and Dennis Cooley and 2 anthologies of Saskatchewan poetry. **"We publish theme anthologies occasionally." However, writers should submit 30-50 poems "and indication of whole ms," typed; simultaneous and American submissions not accepted. Cover letter required; include publishing credits and bio and SASE or SAE with IRC if necessary. Queries will be answered in 2-3 weeks and mss reported on in 2-4 months. Always sends prepublication galleys. Authors receive 10% royalty; 10 copies.** Their attractive catalog is free for 9×12 SASE, or SAE with IRC, and sample copies can be ordered from it. The editor says: "Membership has changed through the years in the Thunder Creek Publishing Co-op, but now stands at eight. Each member has a strong interest in Canadian writing and culture. Generally, poets would have published a number of poems and series of poems in literary magazines and anthologies before submitting a manuscript." However, the imprint Wood Mountain Series is for first collections, reflecting their commitment to publishing new writers. The press has had two books nominated for The Lampbert Memorial Award and one nominated for The Governor-General's Award for Poetry.

COTTONWOOD; COTTONWOOD PRESS (II, IV-Regional), Box J, 400 Kansas Union, University of Kansas, Lawrence KS 66045, founded 1965, poetry editor Philip Wedge. **The press "is auxiliary to *Cottonwood Magazine* and publishes material by authors in the region. Material is usually solicited." For the magazine they are looking for "strong narrative or sensory impact, non-derivative, not 'literary,' not 'academic.' Emphasis on Midwest, but publishes the best poetry received regardless of region. Poems should be 60 lines or less, on daily experience, *perception.*"** They have published poetry by Rita Dove, Allen Ginsberg, Walter McDonald, Patricia Traxler and Ron Schreiber. The magazine, published 3 times/year, is 112 pgs., 6×9, flat-spined, printed from computer offset, with photos, using 15-20 pages of poetry in each issue. They have a circulation of 500-600, with 150 subscriptions of which 75 are libraries. They receive about 2,000 submissions/year, use about 30, have a maximum of 1-year backlog. Single copy: $6.50. **Sample postpaid: $4. Submit up to 5 pgs. No simultaneous submissions. Sometimes provides criticism on rejected mss. Reports in 2-5 months. Pays 1 copy.** The editors advise, "Read the little magazines and send to ones you like."

COUNCIL FOR INDIAN EDUCATION (I, IV-Ethnic, cowboy), 517 Rimrock Rd., Billings MT 59102, phone (406)252-7451, founded 1963, poetry editor Sally Old Coyote, is a nonprofit corporation publishing material (small paper-bound books) to use in schools with Indian students. "We publish one poetry book per year. All content is approved by an intertribal editorial board." They want **"poetry on Native American life, ideas and values or cowboy poetry. No vulgarity, sex, prejudice or complaining. Receive many times what we can publish."** As a sample the editor selected these lines:

Eyes on the sunrise: nature's way
Rhythm of the Indian's great new day
Dance to the rhythm
Chant and hum
Never loose the rhythm of the rawhide drum.

Previously published poems and simultaneous submissions OK. Often comments on rejections. Replies to mss in 2-12 months. Sends prepublication galleys "only when whole book is by one author." Pays author's copies. Write for catalog.

COUNTRY JOURNAL (II), P.O. Box 8200, Harrisburg PA 17105, phone (717)657-9555, editor Peter V. Fossel, is a bimonthly magazine featuring country living **for people who live in rural areas or who are thinking about moving there. They use free verse and traditional.** Average issue includes 6-8 feature articles and 10 departments. They have published poetry by Mary Oliver and Wendell Berry. As a sample the editor selected these lines from "The Springs Under the Lake" by Kate Barnes:

The rest of the way
I didn't talk. I could almost hear the words

combining in her mind, the lines gathering
inside her head like butter when it suddenly
starts to come, when it clumps up thick in the churn.

Of 1,000 poems received each year, they accept 10-12. Circulation 200,000. Subscription: $24. **Sample postpaid: $4. Submit seasonal material 1 year in advance. Reports in 1-2 months. Editor comments on submissions "seldom." Pays $50/poem on acceptance. Buys first North American serial rights.**

COUNTRY WOMAN; REIMAN PUBLICATIONS (IV-Women, humor), P.O. Box 643, Milwaukee WI 53201, founded 1970, managing editor Kathy Pohl. *Country Woman* "is a bimonthly magazine dedicated to the lives and interests of country women. Those who are both involved in farming and ranching and those who love country life. In some ways, it is very similar to many women's general interest magazines, and yet its subject matter is closely tied in with rural living and the very unique lives of country women. **We like short (4-5 stanzas, 16-20 lines) traditional rhyming poems that reflect on a season or comment humorously or seriously on a particular rural experience. Also limericks and humorous 4- to 8-line filler rhymes. No experimental poetry or free verse. Poetry will not be considered unless it rhymes. Always looking for poems that focus on the seasons. We don't want rural putdowns, poems that stereotype country women, etc. All poetry must be positive and upbeat. Our poems are fairly simple, yet elegant. They often accompany a high-quality photograph."** They have published poetry by Hilda Sanderson, Edith E. Cutting and Ericka Northrop. *CW* is magazine-sized, 68 pgs., glossy paper with much color photography. Subscription: $16.98/year, $2/copy. They receive about 1,200 submissions of poetry/year, use 40-50 (unless they publish an anthology). Their backlog is 1 month to 3 years. "We're always welcoming submissions." **Sample postpaid: $2. Submit maximum of 6 poems. Photocopy OK if stated not a simultaneous submission. Reports in 2-3 months. Pays $10-25/poem plus copy. Buys first rights (generally) or reprint rights (sometimes).** They hold various contests for subscribers only. One of their anthologies, **Cattails and Meadowlarks: Poems from the Country**, is 90 pgs., saddle-stapled with high-quality color photography on the glossy card cover, poems in large, professional type with many b&w photo illustrations. The editor says, "Any poem that does not have traditional rhythm and rhyme is automatically passed over."

THE COUNTRYMAN (IV-Rural), Sheep St., Burford, Oxon OX18 4LH England, phone 0993 (Burford) 822258, founded 1927, editor Christopher Hall, is a bimonthly magazine "on rural matters." The editor wants **poetry on rural themes, "accessible to general readership but not jingles."** As a sample the editor selected this complete poem, "January omen," by Jane A. Mares:

At the cold birth of the year
I saw what was better unseen:
The Raven or Grimcrag, the grief-bringer,
With his tone of ill-tidings,
A-top the tall stone,
Wiping his bill clean.

It is a handsome, flat-spined, digest-sized magazine, 200 pgs., using popular articles and ads. **Submissions should be short. Reporting time is "within a week usually," longer if from outside the country. Time to publication is "3 months to 3 years." Pays a maximum of £20/poem. Buys all rights "but we stipulate never to refuse permission to reprint at author's wish."** Staff reviews books of poetry in "25 words upwards." Send books for review consideration. The editor says, "Not all our poems are *about* birds or flowers or animals. Personal reaction to rural experience is valued if it comes in a form to which our readers (high-income, quiet not violently green British for the most part) can relate. We get quite a few American submissions which I always read with much interest, not least because of my own love of the few American landscapes I know. Too often these submissions are too obviously American (because of tell-tale species or phrases) and I generally rule these out because 95% of my readers expect a British mag."

‡THE COVENANT COMPANION; COVENANT PUBLICATIONS (II, IV-Religious), 5101 N. Francisco Ave., Chicago IL 60625, phone (312)784-3000, founded 1923, executive secretary of publications James R. Hawkinson, is a monthly designed to "gather, stimulate and enlighten the church it serves—The Evangelical Covenant Church—on the way to promoting Christ's mission in the world." **They want brief poems with Christian viewpoint. Nothing sing-songy.** The editor says it is 40 pgs., 8×10, some 4-color, some 2-color, some b&w, with self cover, pictures, graphics and ads. They receive about 200 poems a year, use 10-20. Press run is 21,000 for about that many subscribers. Subscription: $26. **Sample postpaid: $2.25. Previously published poems and simultaneous submissions OK.** Time between acceptance and publication is 3 months. **Seldom comments on rejections. Reports on submissions "as we get around to them." Pays $10-15 and 3 author's copies. Buys first or one-time rights.** Occasionally reviews books of poetry in 1,000 words. Open to unsolicited reviews. Poets may also send books for review consideration. Covenant Publications also publishes 3-6 flat-spined paperbacks of poetry/year. **Query first with sample poems and a cover letter with brief bio and publication credits. Replies to**

queries in 3-4 months, to mss (if invited) in 3 months. Pays 5-10% royalties and 4 author's copies. Also offers subsidy arrangements on a case-by-case basis.

COVER MAGAZINE (II), P.O. Box 1215, Cooper Station, New York NY 10276, phone (212)673-1152, founded 1986, contact editor/publisher Jeffrey C. Wright, poetry editor Joe DiMattio, is a "broad-based arts monthly covering all the arts in every issue, a 40-page tabloid sold on newsstands and in select bookstores nationwide." They want **"shorter poems—2-24 lines generally, modern, favoring new romantic work. Nothing stodgy or simplistic."** They have recently published poetry by John Ashbery, Lawrence Ferlinghetti, Allen Ginsberg, Robert Creeley and Molly Peacock. As a sample we selected these lines from "Notes From My Pockets" by Ira Cohen:

"I Left three days ago
but no one seems to know
I'm gone."
popular song

Having left yet still here
perhaps the poem can sustain me
still yearning for your touch
I'm afraid it will burn me. . .

Cover tries "to reach a cutting edge/front-line audience in touch with the creative fields." They receive about 1,000 poems a year, accept approximately 50. Entirely supported by subscriptions, sales and ads. Press run is 20,000 for 3,400 subscribers (20 of them libraries), 4,000 shelf sales. Two-year subscription: $15. **Sample postpaid: $5. Submit 4-5 poems with cover letter.** Time between acceptance and publication is 4-6 months. **Editor often comments on submissions. Reports in 4 months. Pays nothing, not even a copy.** Open to unsolicited reviews. Poets may also send books for review consideration. Offers annual poetry contest, for subscribers only.

COWBOY MAGAZINE (IV-Cowboy), P.O. Box 126, La Veta CO 81055, founded 1990, editor Darrell Arnold, is a quarterly "for people who value the cowboy lifestyle." They want **"authentic poetry about the life of cowboys/ranchers. Don't even try if you don't know about cowboys."** They have published poetry by Red Steagall, Baxter Black and Mike Logan. The editor says *Cowboy Magazine* is 48 pgs., 9×11, stapled. They receive about 100 poems a year, "can use about 5%." Press run is 12,000 for 8,000 subscribers of which 10 are libraries, 4,000 shelf sales. Single copy: $4; subscription: $16. **Sample postpaid: $4.50. Previously published poems OK; no simultaneous submissions. Cover letter required.** Time between acceptance and publication is 1 year. **Seldom comments on rejections. Reports on submissions "as soon as I can get to them." Pays $20. Buys one-time rights.** Staff reviews related books of poetry. Send books for review consideration. The editor says, "The best cowboy poetry is written by people who have worked on ranches as cowboys. If you have no such experience, you shouldn't try to write for us. We prefer *highly polished work* that is perfectly rhymed and metered."

COYOTE CHRONICLES: NOTES FROM THE SOUTHWEST (I, II, IV-Political, regional), Suite #9, 222 W. Brown Rd., Mesa AZ 85201, founded 1993, editor Jody Namio, is a "small press publisher of fiction, poetry, nonfiction and scholarly publications, publishing a biannual literary journal. Limited subsidy publishing services offered to selected authors." She wants **"poetry with emphasis on progressive political themes and ideas, ecology etc. No religious, fantasy or 'scenery' poetry."** They have published poetry by Norman German, John Grey, Mark Maire and Richard Davignon. As a sample she selected these lines (poet unidentified):

Last night I went to bed intoxicated again. You watched
"Ghandi," repressing violence.
Today, I am drinking too much coffee,
smoking too many cigarettes.
You say you'll be late . . .

CC is 80 pgs., 8½×11, professionally printed on recycled paper, saddle-stitched. They accept 10-15% of 1,000 poems received a year. Subscription: $12. **Sample postpaid: $4. Guidelines available for SASE. They consider simultaneous submissions and previously published poems. Submit with cover letter and bio.** "Backlog of submissions at this time." **Editor sometimes comments on rejections, "more substantial critiques on request." Reports in 6-8 weeks. Pays 5 copies. "Contributors encouraged to buy additional copies."** Publishes several chapbooks a year averaging 64 pgs. **For chapbook consideration either query or send ms with cover letter and bio. Reports in 12-14 weeks. "Large backlog at this time, but we welcome all submissions." Payment "varies with author."** Send SASE for catalog to buy samples.

CRAB CREEK REVIEW (V, IV-Anthology, themes), 4462 Whitman Ave. N., Seattle WA 98103, phone (206)633-1090, founded 1983, editor Linda J. Clifton. Previously a biannual publication, ***CCR*** will now appear once every 2 years as a theme-based anthology. ***Crab Creek Review: Anniversary Anthology***, the first of these will highlight the "Best of our Past," and "New Work." They publish **poetry which is "free or formal, expresses complex notions through clear imagery, has wit and a voice that is interesting, energetic and gives a strong sense of the individual; accessible to the general reader rather than full of very private imagery and obscure literary allusion."** They have published poetry by Elizabeth Murawski, Maxine Kumin, William Stafford and Eastern European, Japanese, Chinese and Latin American writers. The editor says ***CCR*** is a 160-page, perfect-bound paperback. **Sample postpaid: $10. Not accepting unsolicited submissions. Poets can check *Poets & Writers* for themes and reading periods.** Back issues of the biannual publication are available for $3.

CRAZYHORSE (II), Dept. PM, Dept. of English, University of Arkansas at Little Rock, Little Rock AR 72204, phone (501)569-3161, founded 1960, managing editor Zabelle Stodola, poetry editor Ralph Burns, fiction editor Judy Troy, is a highly respected literary magazine appearing twice a year. They have published poetry by Alberto Rios, Mark Jarman, Bill Matthews and Yusef Komunyakaa. As a sample, here are the closing lines from "For Victor Jara: Mutilated and Murdered, the Soccer Stadium, Santiago, Chile" by Miller Williams (see listing for University of Arkansas Press):

> *Would we have stayed to an end or would we have folded our faces?*
> *Awful and awful. Good friend. You have embarrassed our hearts.*

It is 145 pgs., 6×9, offset. Press run is 900. Subscription: $10. **Sample postpaid: $5. No submissions May through August. Reports in 1-2 months. Pays $10/printed page plus 2 copies. Offers two $500 awards for best poem and best story.** Reviews books of poetry. To get a sense of the quality of the magazine, see the anthology, **The Best of Crazyhorse** (University of Arkansas Press, 1990).

CRAZYQUILT QUARTERLY (II), P.O. Box 632729, San Diego CA 92163-2729, founded 1986, editor Jackie Ball, is a literary quarterly which has published poetry by B.Z. Niditch, Judson Jerome, Charles B. Dickson and Alan Seaburg. As a sample the editor selected these lines from "Road with Cypress and Star" by Charles Fishman:

> *Earlier, the trees are earth,*
> *then water and flame—but here*
> *they are smoke, dark green smoke*
> *. . . turrets of blue wind.*

CQ is 90 pgs., digest-sized, saddle-stapled, professionally printed on good stock with matte card cover. Circulation 200. Subscription: $14.95 (2 years for $25). **Sample: $4.50 plus $1 postage; back issue: $2.50. Submit one poem to a page. Previously published poems and simultaneous submissions OK. Reports in 10-12 weeks, time to publication is 12-15 months. Pays 2 copies. Acquires first rights.**

CREAM CITY REVIEW (II), P.O. Box 413, Dept. of English, University of Wisconsin at Milwaukee, Milwaukee WI 53201, phone (414)229-4708, editors-in-chief Mark Drechsler and Brian Jung, poetry editors Kristin Terwelp and Cynthia Belmont, is a nationally distributed literary magazine published twice a year by the Creative Writing Program. The editors will consider **any poem that is well-crafted and especially those poems that "have a voice, have place or play with the conventions of what poetry is. We get very little humor or parody, and would enjoy getting more."** They have recently published poetry by Albert Goldbarth, Audre Lorde, Marge Piercy, May Sarton, Philip Dacey, Amiri Baraka, Tess Gallagher, Cathy Song, Mary Oliver and Philip Levine. They do not include sample lines of poetry; "We prefer not to bias our contributors. We strive for variety—vitality!" ***CCR*** is 5½×8½, perfect-bound, averaging 300 pgs., with full-color cover on 70 lb. paper. This journal is fast becoming a leader in the literary world. It's lovely to look at—one of the most attractive designs around—with generous space devoted to poems, all styles (but favoring free verse). Press run is 2,000, 400 subscriptions of which 25 are libraries. **Sample postpaid: $5. "Include SASE when submitting (mss without SASE will not be considered) and please submit no more than 5 poems at a time." Simultaneous submissions OK when notified. Editors sometimes comment on rejections. Send SASE for guidelines. Reports in 2 months, longer in summer. Payment varies with funding and includes choice of 2 copies or 1-year subscription. Buys first rights.** Reviews books of poetry in 1-2 pgs. Open to unsolicited reviews. Poets may also send books to the poetry editors for review consideration. **"We give an award of $100 to the best poem published in *Cream City Review* each year."** This magazine ranked #6 in the "Nontraditional Verse" category of the latest ***Writer's Digest*** Poetry 60 list. The editors add, "We are always looking for strong poems on any subject."

CREATIVE WITH WORDS PUBLICATIONS (C.W.W.); SPOOFING (IV-Themes); WE ARE WRITERS, TOO (I, IV-Children, seniors), P.O. Box 223226, Carmel CA 93922, founded 1975, poetry editor Brigitta Geltrich, **offers criticism for a fee.** It focuses "on furthering **folkloristic tall tales** and such; creative writing abilities in **children** (poetry, prose, language-art); creative writing in **senior citizens** (poetry and prose)." The editors publish on a wide range of themes relating to human studies and the environment that influence human behaviors. **$5 reading fee/poem, includes a critical analysis.**

The publications are anthologies of children's poetry, prose and language art; anthologies of special-interest groups such as senior citizen poetry and prose; and ***Spoofing: An Anthology of Folkloristic Yarns and Such***, which has an announced theme for each issue. **"Want to see: folkloristic themes; poetry for and by children; poetry by senior citizens; special topic (inquire). Do not want to see: too mushy; too religious; too didactic; expressing dislike for fellowmen; political; pornographic; death and murder poetry." Guidelines and upcoming themes available for SASE.** *Spoofing!* and *We are Writers, Too!*, are low-budget publications, photocopied from typescript, saddle-stapled, card covers with cartoon-like art. **Submit 20-line, 40 spaces wide maximum, poems geared to specific audience and subject matter.** They have recently published poetry by Mandy Laughtland, Stephanie Schwartz and Mark Domanski. As a sample the editor selected these lines by Jennifer Treheanne:

. . . And she was up
To study and learn.
The test was science
And Jen was all flustered
Her desk was messy . . .

"Query with sample poems, short personal biography, other publications, poetic goals, where you read about us, for what publication and/or event you are submitting." They have "no conditions for publication, but C.W.W. is dependent on author/poet support by purchase of a copy or copies of publication." They offer a 20% reduction on any copy purchased. The editor advises, "Trend is proficiency. Poets should research topic; know audience for whom they write; check topic for appeal to specific audience; should not write for the sake of rhyme, rather for the sake of imagery and being creative with the language. Feeling should be expressed (but no mushiness). Topic and words should be chosen carefully; brevity should be employed. We would like to receive more positive and clean, family-type poetry."

THE CREATIVE WOMAN (IV-Women, feminist, themes), Suite 288, 126 E. Wing, Arlington Hts. IL 60004, phone (708)255-1232, founded 1977, editor Margaret Choudhury, is a quarterly publishing nonfiction articles, fiction, poetry and book reviews. **"We focus on a special topic in each issue, presented from a feminist perspective."** They want poetry **"recognizing, validating, celebrating women's experience, especially fresh and original style."** They have published poetry by Marge Piercy and Larissa Vasilyeva. As a sample the editor selected these lines from "Custom as a Veil" by Carol Ciavonne:

Women do not cry at weddings,
they grieve with open ears.
Let there be compensation they say,
let it be beautifully phrased.

The Creative Woman is 52 pgs., magazine-sized, saddle-stapled, professionally printed with b&w photos, graphics and ads. They use about 5% of several hundred poems received each year. Press run is 2,000 for 600 subscriptions (65 libraries). Subscription: $16, $26 outside US. **Sample postpaid: $5. Mss should be double-spaced, name and address on each page. No simultaneous submissions or previously published poetry. Cover letter required. Send SASE for upcoming themes. Theme for Autumn 1994 issue: "Latin American Women," for Winter 1994: "Women in Classical Music," for Spring 1995: "Quilting" and for Summer 1995: "Female Flyers." Reports in up to 1 year. Pays 4 copies and opportunity to purchase more at half price.** Staff reviews related books of poetry. Send books for review consideration.

CREATIVITY UNLIMITED PRESS; ANNUAL CREATIVITY UNLIMITED PRESS POETRY COMPETITION (I), 30819 Casilina, Rancho Palos Verdes CA 90274, phone (213)541-4844, founded 1989, editor Shelley Stockwell, publishes annually a collection of poetry submitted to their **contest, $4 fee for 1-5 poems; prizes of $300, $150 and $75 in addition to publication. Deadline: December 31. "Clever spontaneous overflows of rich emotion, humor and delightful language encouraged. No inaccessible, verbose, esoteric, obscure poetry. Limit 3 pgs. per poem, double-spaced, one side of page."** As a sample the editor selected her own "Freeway Dilemma":

Of all enduring questions
A big one I can't answer;
How come, whenever I change lanes,
The other lane goes faster?

They also accept submissions for book publication. Query first. "Poems previously published will be accepted provided writer has maintained copyright and notifies us." Editor comments on submissions "always. Keep it simple and accessible." Publishes theme issues. Send SASE for upcoming themes. Sometimes sends prepublication galleys. The editor says, "We are interested in receiving more humorous poetry."

CREEPING BENT (III), Dept. PM, 433 W. Market St., Bethlehem PA 18018, phone (610)866-5613, founded 1984, editor Joseph Lucia, a literary magazine that focuses on serious poetry, fiction, book reviews and essays, with very occasional chapbooks published under the same imprint. **"Please note that during much of 1995 we will be accepting very little (possibly no) unsolicited material. We publish only work that evidences a clear awareness of the current situation of poetry. We take a special interest in poems that articulate a vision of the continuities and discontinuities in the human relationship to the natural world." The editor does not want "any attempt at verse that clearly indicates the writer hasn't taken a serious look at a recent collection of poetry during his or her adult life."** They have published work by Turner Cassity, Charles Edward Eaton, Renée Ashley, Brigit Kelly, Walter McDonald, Donald Revell, Harry Humes and Patricia Wilcox. As a sample, the editor selected these lines from Mark Stevick's "Idiom":

The language of objects is not
unknown to us. What they mean
they articulate to our eyes and
our hands; we listen and learn
from them as we can, make them
our ambassadors. You, listening
in your room, will recognize
your debt to their reliable idiom,
though they are not yours, nor you.

Creeping Bent is digest-sized, nicely printed on heavy stock with some b&w artwork, 48-64 pgs., saddle-stapled with glossy white card cover printed in black and one other color. It appears at least once a year, sometimes more often. Circulation is 250, of which 175 are subscriptions, 25 go to libraries, and 25 are sold on newsstands. Subscription: $6/year. **Sample postpaid: $3. "Absolutely no simultaneous submissions!" Guidelines for SASE. Reporting time is usually 2-3 weeks and time to publication is 6 months at most. Pay is 2 copies plus a 1-year subscription.** The editor says, "Before submitting to any magazine published by anyone with a serious interest in contemporary writing, make certain you understand something about the kind of work the magazine publishes. Be familiar with current styles and approaches to poetry, even if you eschew them."

CRESCENT MOON PUBLISHING; PASSION (II, IV-Anthology, gay/lesbian, love/romance/erotica, occult, religious, spirituality, women/feminism), 18 Chaddesley Rd., Kidderminster, Worcestershire DY10 3AD England, founded 1988, editor Jeremy Robinson, publishes about 25 books and chapbooks/year **on arrangements subsidized by the poet.** He wants **"poetry that is passionate and authentic. Any form or length." Not "the trivial, insincere or derivative.** We are publishing a new quarterly magazine, ***Passion*** ($6 each, $22 subscription). It will feature poetry, fiction, reviews and essays on feminism, art, philosophy and the media. Many American poets are to be featured, as well as British poets such as Jeremy Reed, Penelope Shuttle, Alan Bold, D.J. Enright and Peter Redgrove. **Contributions welcome. We are also publishing two anthologies of new American poetry per year."** They have recently published studies of Rimbaud, Rilke, Cavafy, Shakespeare, Beckett, German Romantic poetry and D.H. Lawrence. As a sample the editor selected these lines from Peter Redgrove's poem "Starlight":

Her menstruation has a most beautiful
Smell of warm ripe apples that are red,
And an odour of chocolate, a touch of poppy,
And bed-opiums roll from her limbs
Like the smokes of innumerable addicts between the sheets . . .

The above is from the book **Sex-Magic-Poetry-Cornwall: A Flood of Poems**, by Peter Redgrove, 76 pgs., flat-spined, digest-sized. Anthologies now available ($15 each): **Pagan America: An Anthology of New American Poetry, Love in America: An Anthology of Women's Love Poetry, Mythic America: An Anthology of New American Poetry and Religious America: An Anthology of New American Poetry. Recent themes include love and/or erotic poetry for Desire in America: An Anthology of Women's Love Poetry (March 1995). Inquiries welcome. Cover letter with brief bio and publishing credits required with submissions ("and please print your address in capitals"). Send SASE (or SAE and IRCs) for upcoming anthology themes. Replies to queries in 1 month, to mss in 2 months. Sometimes sends prepublication galleys.** The editor says, "Generally, we prefer free verse to rhymed poetry."

CRICKET; SPIDER, THE MAGAZINE FOR CHILDREN; LADYBUG, THE MAGAZINE FOR YOUNG CHILDREN (IV-Children), P.O. Box 300, Peru IL 61354, ***Cricket*** founded 1973, ***Ladybug*** founded 1990, ***Spider*** founded 1994, editor-in-chief Marianne Carus. *Cricket* (for ages 9-12) is a monthly, circulation 120,000, **using "serious, humorous, nonsense rhymes, limericks" for children. They do not want "forced or trite rhyming or imagery that doesn't hang together to create a unified whole." They sometimes use previously published work.** The attractive 8×10 magazine, 64 pgs., saddle-stapled, color cover and full-color illustrations inside, receives over 1,000 submissions/month, uses 10-12, and has up to a 2-year backlog. ***Ladybug***, also monthly, circulation 120,000, is similar in format and requirements but is aimed at younger children (ages 2-6). ***Spider***, also monthly, is a brand new magazine for children ages 6-9; premier issue published January 1994. Format and requirements similar to ***Cricket*** and ***Ladybug***. **Do not query. Submit no more than 5 poems—up to 100 lines (2 pgs. max.) for *Cricket*; up to 20 lines for *Spider* and *Ladybug*, no restrictions on form. Sample of any: $4. Guidelines available for SASE. Reports in 3-4 months. Payment for all is up to $3/line and 2 copies. "All submissions are automatically considered for all three magazines."** ***Cricket*** holds poetry contests for children ages 5-9 and 10-14. Current contest themes and rules appear in each issue. ***Cricket*** has received Parents' Choice Awards every year since 1986. The magazine also ranked #2 in the "Top Pay" category of the latest ***Writer's Digest*** Poetry 60 list. ***Ladybug***, launched in 1990, has received Parents' Choice Awards every year since 1991.

THE CRITIC (II), 6th Floor, 205 W. Monroe St., Chicago IL 60606, founded 1940, is a Catholic literary and cultural quarterly. **"Poetry is a minor aspect of the publication. No word games, doggerel, light verse or haiku."** They have published poetry by Samuel Hazo and Martha Vertreace. The editor says ***The Critic*** is 128 pgs., 7×10, perfect-bound, no ads. Press run is 2,500 for 2,000 subscribers of which about 200 are libraries. Subscription: $20 for 1 year, $32 for 2 years. **Sample postpaid: $6. No previously published poems or simultaneous submissions. Cover letter required. Seldom comments on rejections. Reports in 1-3 months. Pays $25-50. Buys first serial rights.**

CROSS-CULTURAL COMMUNICATIONS; CROSS-CULTURAL REVIEW OF WORLD LITERATURE AND ART IN SOUND, PRINT, AND MOTION; CROSS-CULTURAL MONTHLY; CROSS-CULTURAL REVIEW CHAPBOOK ANTHOLOGY; INTERNATIONAL WRITERS SERIES (II, IV-Translations, bilingual), Dept. PM, 239 Wynsum Ave., Merrick NY 11566-4725, phone (516)868-5635, fax (516)379-1901, founded 1971, Stanley H. and Bebe Barkan. Stanley Barkan began CCC as an educational venture, a program in 27 languages at Long Island University, but soon began publishing collections of poetry translated into English from various languages—some of them (such as Estonian) quite "neglected"—in bilingual editions. During the 70s he became aware of Antigruppo (a group against groups), a movement with similar international focus in Sicily, and the two joined forces. **CCR** began as a series of chapbooks (6-12 a year) of collections of poetry translated from various languages and continues as the **Holocaust, Women Writers, Latin American Writers, African Heritage, Asian Heritage, Italian Heritage, International Artists, Art & Poetry, Jewish, Israeli, Cajun, Dutch, Turkish,** and **Long Island** and **Brooklyn Writers Chapbook Series** (with a number of other permutations in the offing)—issued simultaneously in palm-sized and regular paperback and cloth-binding editions and boxed and canned, as well as audiocassette and videocassette. **All submissions should be preceded by a query letter with SASE. The Holocaust series is for survivors. Send SASE for guidelines. Pays 10% of print run.** In addition to publications in these series, CCC has published anthologies, translations and collections by dozens of poets from many countries. As a sample the editor selected the beginning of a poem by Pablo Neruda, as translated by Maria Jacketti:

Quartz opens its eyes in the snow
and covers itself with thorns,
slides into whiteness,
becomes its own whiteness:

That's from the bilingual collection **Heaven Stones**, the second in the **Cross-Cultural Review International Writers Series** published in 1992. It is 80 pgs., digest-sized, smythe-sewn paper and cloth, professionally printed 10pt. chromecoat cover, photo of the Chilean poet on the back—$15 (paperback), $25 (cloth). **Sample chapbook postpaid: $7.50.** ***Cross-Cultural Monthly*** focuses on bilingual poetry and prose. Subscription: $36. **Sample postpaid: $5. Pays 1 copy.** CCC continues to produce the International Festival of Poetry, Writing and Translation with the International Poets and Writers Literary Arts Week in New York and recently co-produced the 1993-1994 Multicultural Poetry Series at the Barnes & Noble flagship superstore in NYC, currently (1994-) at Borders Books & Music in Westbury, Long Island.

CRUCIBLE; SAM RAGAN PRIZE (I, II), Barton College, College Station, Wilson NC 27893, phone (919)399-6456, founded 1964, editor Terrence L. Grimes, is an annual using **"poetry that demonstrates originality and integrity of craftsmanship as well as thought. Traditional metrical and rhyming poems are difficult to bring off in modern poetry. The best poetry is written out of deeply felt experience which has been crafted into pleasing form. No very long narratives."** They have published poetry by Robert Grey, R.T. Smith and Anthony S. Abbott. As a sample the editor selected these lines from "Toward Short Off Mountain" by Mary C. Snotherly:

So dense the fog, each man trudged alone,
accompanied only by a stumble of boots,
slap of laurel, by his own separate breathing,
and like thunder roll, the barks resounding.

It is 100 pgs., 6×9, professionally printed on high-quality paper with matte card cover. Good type selection and point sizes highlight bylines and titles of poems. Press run is 500 for 300 subscribers of which 100 are libraries, 200 shelf sales. **Sample postpaid: $5. Send SASE for guidelines for contests (prizes of $150 and $100), and the Sam Ragan Prize ($150) in honor of the Poet Laureate of North Carolina. Submit between Christmas and mid-April. Reports in 3 months or less. "We require 3 unsigned copies of the manuscript and a short biography including a list of publications, in case we decide to publish the work."** Editor leans toward free verse with attention paid particularly to image, line, stanza and voice. However, he does not want to see poetry that is "forced."

CUMBERLAND POETRY REVIEW; THE ROBERT PENN WARREN POETRY PRIZE (II, IV-Translations), Dept. PM, P.O. Box 120128, Acklen Station, Nashville TN 37212, founded 1981, is a biannual journal presenting poets of diverse origins to a widespread audience. "Our aim is to support the poet's effort to keep up the language. We accept special responsibility for reminding American readers that not all excellent poems in English are being written by U.S. citizens. We have published such poets as Laurence Lerner, Donald Davie, Richard Tillinghast, Emily Grosholz and Rachel Hadas." As a sample the editorial board selected these lines by Seamus Heaney:

When Dante snapped a twig in the bleeding wood
a voice sighed out of blood that bubbled up
like sap at the end of green sticks on a fire.

CPR is 75-100 pgs., 6×9, flat-spined. Circulation 500. **Sample postpaid: $7. Submit poetry, translations or poetry criticism with SASE or SAE with IRC. Cover letter with brief bio required. Reports in 6 months. Acquires first rights. Returns rights "on request of author providing he acknowledges original publication in our magazine."** They award The Robert Penn Warren Poetry Prize annually. Winners receive $500, $300 and $200. For contest guidelines, send SASE.

‡CURMUDGEON; BUT(T) UGLY PRESS (I, II), #112, 2921 Alpine Rd., Columbia SC 29223, phone (803)736-1449, founded 1991, editor Erik C. McKelvey, is a biannual of "reality." **As for poetry, they want "reality. Stuff that can be seen. All forms. No surrealism. I'm not a big fan of reading for the way the words are on the page. I like a meaning to grab me."** They have recently published poetry by John M. Bennett, Ana Christy and Robert Howington. As a sample the editor selected these lines from "Karma dances a Zen movement" by elliott:

at the foot of my brass bed
My past lives devour my false guilt
I pin the spider beneath my weight
Her taut web drawing me to her
My juices, her venom, sing
We recreate Eden.

The editor says ***Curmudgeon*** is 40-60 pgs., 8½×11, folded, photocopied with color cover, art and ads. They receive about 200 poems a year, accept approximately 25%. Press run is 100 for 20 subscribers. Subscription: $6. **Sample postpaid: $3. Previously published poems and simultaneous submissions OK. Cover letter, "telling us where the poet found our name," required.** Time between acceptance and publication is 6 months. **Seldom comments on rejections. Offers criticism for a fee. "A short, or critical spiel is free; but if there needs to be more, terms can be worked out between the individual and the editors." Send SASE for guidelines. Reports in 2-3 weeks. Pays 1 copy.** Reviews books and chapbooks of poetry in 500 words. Open to unsolicited reviews. Poets may also send books for review consideration. The editor adds, "I want reality. I frown on surrealism. We like new poets for every issue of the magazine."

CUTBANK; THE RICHARD HUGO MEMORIAL POETRY AWARD (II), English Dept., University of Montana, Missoula MT 59812, phone (406)243-5231, founded 1973, co-editors C.N. Blakemore and Francesca Abbate, is a biannual publishing "the best poetry, fiction, reviews, interviews and artwork available to us." Offers 2 annual awards for best poem and piece of fiction, The Richard Hugo Memorial Poetry Award and The A.B. Guthrie, Jr. Short Fiction Award. Winners announced in spring issue. They have recently published poetry by James Tate, James Galvin and Greg Pape. As a sample the editors selected these lines from "Faces" by Mark Levine:

We can't make the faces go away
The bodies are not such a problem
We pull them apart with chemicals and stretch them out
Along the cracked surface of the old freeway.

There are about 50 pgs. of poetry in each issue, which has a circulation of about 500, 250 subscriptions of which 10-20% are libraries. Single copy: $6.95; subscription: $12/two issues. **Sample postpaid: $4. Submission guidelines for SASE. Submit 3-5 poems, single-spaced. Simultaneous submissions OK if informed. Reads submissions August 15 through February 1 only. Reports in 2 months. Pays copies. "All rights return to author upon publication."** Staff reviews books of poetry in 500 words, single or multi-book format.

CWM (II, IV-Themes), % Ge(of Huth), 875 Central Pkwy., Schenectady NY 12309-6005, (or % David Kopaska-Merkel, 1300 Kicker Rd., Tuscaloosa AL 35414, phone (205)553-2284), founded 1990, co-geologians Ge(of Huth) and David Kopaska-Merkel. (These "geologians" also edit dbqp press publications and ***Dreams and Nightmares***, but ***CWM*** has no relation to their other imprints.) This magazine, published annually on **set themes, is "not tied down by ideas of proper style, form or substance, and presents work for the person of divergent tastes. The only considerations will be length and quality (as we see it). Extremely long poems will be at a disadvantage. Poems must be on the theme of the issue. The theme for the 1995 issue is 'Archaeology of the Soul.'** Unusual pieces of any kind are welcome, and should be submitted in whatever form the author deems most suitable." As a sample the geologians chose these lines from "The Drowned" by Jonathan Brannen:

Once boatloads of pilgrims
arrived to worship
the drowned children
whose bodies miraculously whole
and uncorrupted were on display

Press run is 100. **Send SASE for guidelines. Reports within 6 weeks. Pays "at least one copy."** Staff reviews books of poetry and poetry journals. Send books for review consideration.

‡CYPHERS (III), 3 Selskar Terrace, Dublin 6 Ireland, founded 1975, appears 2-3 times yearly. They have published poetry by Pearse Hutchinson, Paul Durcan, Medbh McGuckian and P.J. Kavanagh. The editor says it is 52 pgs., A5. Press run is 650 for 250 subscribers of which 20 are libraries. Subscription: $20 US for 3 issues. **Sample postpaid: $6. No previously published poems or simultaneous submissions. Seldom comments on rejections. Reports in 3-4 months. Pays £7/page.**

DAGGER OF THE MIND; K'YI-LIH PRODUCTIONS; SMART PRODUCTIONS (IV-Science fiction/fantasy, horror), 1317 Hookridge Dr., El Paso TX 79925, phone (915)591-0541, founded 1989, executive editor Arthur William Lloyd Breach, assistant editor Sam Lopez, wants **"poetry that stirs the senses and emotions. Make the words dance and sing, bring out the fire in the human soul. Show flair and fashion. No four-letter words, nothing pornographic, vulgar, blasphemous, obscene and nothing generally in bad taste."** They have published poetry by Jessica Amanda Salmonson. The quarterly ***DOTM*** is magazine-sized, saddle-stapled, with high glossy covers. They use about 50 of 100-150 poems received/year. Press run is 4,000-5,000 with 100 subscribers. Subscription: $8/half year, $16/year. **Sample postpaid: $3.50. "Send in batches of 10. I will consider simultaneous submissions only if told in advance that they are such. Include cover letter with published credits, a very brief bio and kinds of styles written. Length is open as is style. Be creative and try to reflect something about the human condition. Show me something that reflects what is going on in the world. Be sensitive but not mushy. Be intelligent not sophomoric. Don't try to carbon copy any famous poet. You lead the way—don't follow. I don't like the trend toward blood and gore and obscenity. Report back in 1 month tops." Pays $1-5/poem plus 1 copy. Buys first North American serial rights and reprint rights. "*DOTM*** is devoted to *quality* horror. The key word is quality. ***DOTM*** is a publication under the division of K'yi-Lih Productions." The editor will evaluate work and review books of poetry for a fee, depending on length and quantity. Send books for review consideration. He says, "I'm planning an anthology of Lovecraftian related material. The paperback will be predominantly Cthulhu Mythos fiction, but I do intend to publish some poetry."

DAILY MEDITATION (V), Box 2710, San Antonio TX 78299, editor Ruth S. Paterson, is a **nonsectarian** religious quarterly that publishes **inspirational poems up to 14 lines, but is currently not accepting poetry submissions. Sample postpaid: $1.**

THE DALHOUSIE REVIEW (II), Suite 314, Sir James Dunn Bldg., Halifax, Nova Scotia B3H 3J5 Canada, founded 1921, phone (902)494-2541, is **a prestige literary quarterly preferring poems of 40 lines or less.** As a sample the editor selected these lines from "My Father, Carving" by Tom Chandler:

The idea of what the wood will be
drifts down his thoughts,
passes through the tip of his hand
and into the sweetpine shape.

all of it framed
in a slice of white light
oblique to the darkness
that swallows the walls.

The review is 144 pgs., 6×9, professionally printed on heavy stock with matte card cover. Relatively few poems are featured in each issue, but ones that are tend to be free verse with emphasis on image and voice. Individual copies range in cost from $6.50-25. Subscription: $19/year within Canada, $28/year outside Canada (both in Canadian dollars). **Contributors receive $3 for a first**

poem. For each poem after (in the same issue) he or she will receive $2/poem, 2 complimentary copies of issue and 15 offprints.

DAM (DISABILITY ARTS MAGAZINE) (IV-Specialized), 10 Woad Lane, Great Coates, Grimsby DN37 9NH Great Britain, phone/fax 0472-280031, founded 1991, editor Roland Humphrey, is a quarterly that "has two primary concerns: access to the arts and the promotion of disability arts—disability as subject for art rather than merely metaphor." They want **any poetry where disability is the theme. "Nothing thoughtless."** As a sample the editor selected these lines from "Roll" by Michael McNeilley:

I am not a man with wheels,
although it is the wheels you see
when I roll in.

I am not a chair that speaks.
Still, you are surprised to hear
a voice come from this chair . . .

DAM is 72 pgs., 6⅞×9¹¹⁄₁₆, perfect-bound, with full-color laminated card cover and photos, "designed to be kept." Press run is 1,500 for 1,000 subscribers of which 100 are libraries. Single copy: £2 (£6 international); subscription: £12 (£20 outside E.E.C.). **No previously published poems or simultaneous submissions. Seldom comments on rejections. Reports in 3 months maximum. Sometimes sends prepublication galleys. Pays disabled people only—£5 a poem (variable)—£15 a page.**

‡DAMAGED WINE (II, IV-Form), P.O. Box 722, Palos Park IL 60464-0722, founded 1993 (first issue spring 1994), editor-in-chief Daniel A. Scurek, appears 3 times a year. "***Damaged Wine***'s purpose is to publish the finest free verse poetry received and to help give greater definition and respect to the much (and often deservedly) maligned form. **We seek only high-quality free verse. Length, subject matter, style and content are open, though we encourage poets to stay clear of self-indulgent writing, a problem typical in free verse. No metered poetry, overtly experimental poetry, poems that extend obviously into prose.**" They have recently published poetry by Richard Calisch, Effie Mihopoulos and John Dickson. The editor says ***DW*** is 50 pgs., 4¼×11, laser typeset, saddle-stapled with card cover and artwork (mostly line drawings). They receive about 1,500 poems a year, accept approximately 10%. Press run is about 300. Single copy: $3.50; subscription: $9. **Sample postpaid: $4.50. "All submissions must be typed; only one poem per page; name and address on each. Send no fewer than 2 poems and no more than 6. Please include a short bio note listing previous credits." Previously published poems and simultaneous submissions OK, if notified upon submission. Cover letter welcome but not required.** Time between acceptance and publication is 6 months. **Seldom comments on rejections ("unless requested"). Send SASE for guidelines or order a sample copy as guidelines are printed in each issue. Reports in 4 months. Pays 2 copies. Acquires one-time rights.** "We do accept books and chapbooks for review, provided they are books of free verse poetry. Reviews run from 5-10 pages and are typically but not exclusively in single-book format. We are not open to unsolicited reviews, but poets may send books for review consideration." The editor adds, "Free verse has defined modern poetry, not always in the most flattering way. We look to give free verse a stronger distinction and more defined quality. We feel that strongly experimental and prose poetry, for example, are fine stylistically, and may even define the poetry of the future, but are, in form, different from free verse. Free verse doesn't necessarily mean absence of meter, absence of logic or absence of internal flow. Poets should concentrate on the strengths of quality free verse: strong visual imagery and a sense of rhythm. Remember, good free verse is actually more difficult to write than metered poetry. We'd even suggest that poets analyze some of the masters of meter (be it Pope or Frost) as well as the masters of free verse (from Williams to Plath)."

DANCE CONNECTION (IV-Specialized), #603, 815 First St. SW, Calgary, Alberta T2P 1N3 Canada, phone (403)237-7327, founded 1983, editor Heather Elton, appears 5 times a year and uses **poems about dance—"contemporary poetry dealing with 'issues' rather than lyrical poetry about young ballerinas. Something tough/challenging that deals with the body in a postmodern context."** It is magazine-sized, 60 pgs., desktop-published, saddle-stapled. Press run is 5,000 for 3,000 subscribers of which 35 are libraries, 1,500 newsstand sales. Subscription: $19 individuals, $29 institutions. **Sample postpaid: $4. Deadline for their literary issue is May 1. Reports in 3 months. Sometimes sends prepublication galleys. Pays 3 copies and "occasional honorarium." Acquires all rights. Returns rights.** The editor says they "very occasionally publish poetry. When we get larger we will publish more, but now space is a precious commodity for review/calendars/news/columns and feature departments."

‡DANCING SHADOW PRESS; DANCING SHADOW REVIEW (I), P.O. Box 28423, Baltimore MD 21234, phone (410)557-0110, founded 1992, editors Alan C. Reese and Bernie Wenker. ***Dancing Shadow Review*** is a biannual "dedicated to publishing outstanding poetry and fiction without regard for political, ideological, social or stylistic constraints." **They want "poetry in which the form and**

language hammer home the poet's vision. We want to see it all, but tend to shy away from preachy or sentimental claptrap." They have recently published poetry by Clarinda Harriss Raymond and Diane Scharper. As a sample the editors selected these lines from Clarinda Harriss Raymond's "Seven Haiku":

No one forgets how to swim
but all summer
my body wouldn't float.

I waded to the waist
in water so cold it split me
like a worm. . . .

DSR is 80-100 pgs., digest-sized and perfect-bound with glossy card cover and b&w artwork. Press run is 500 for 100 subscribers, 50 shelf sales. Single copy: $5.95; subscription: $14. **Sample postpaid: $7. Previously published poems OK; no simultaneous submissions. Send 3-5 poems with a biographical sketch. Reads submissions September 1 through June 30. Often comments on rejections. Pays 1 copy.** Dancing Shadow Press also publishes 2-4 chapbooks/year. **Query first with sample poems and cover letter with brief bio and publication credits. Replies to queries in 4-6 weeks, to mss in 2-4 months. Pays author's copies, 10% of the press run.** They have recently published **Songs of Blynde Nightingales** by Rick Morrow, a collection described as "American haiku for the global community." It is 36 pgs., digest-sized, professionally printed on cream-colored paper and saddle-stapled with forest green matte card cover with silver type. It includes illustrations by Baltimore artists and is available from the press for $6 (postpaid).

DANDELION (II); BLUE BUFFALO (IV-Regional), The Alexandra Centre, 922-9th Ave. SE, Calgary, Alberta T2G 0S4 Canada, phone (403)265-0524, founded 1975, poetry editor Jenine Werner-King, managing editor Bonnie Benoit, appears twice a year. They want **"quality—We are open to any form, style, length. No greeting card verse."** They have published poetry by Claire Harris, Susan Ioannou and Robert Hilles. As a sample the editor selected these lines by Roger Nash:

On Sabbath evenings, a slow hand
tuned the guitar. A fast hand
moved the shifting stars. And, somewhere,
while we were growing up, there was a street still
made of gold of tin of slush

Dandelion is 102 pgs., 6×9, with full-color cover, professionally printed and bound. They accept about 10% of 600 mss received. Press run is 750. **Sample postpaid: $7. Submit in January through March and July through September for issues in June and December. Cover letter with bio required. Send SASE for a short statement of their needs. Reports in 4-6 weeks. Pays honorarium plus 1 copy. Acquires one-time rights.** Reviews books of poetry in 500-1,200 words; preference is for books by Alberta writers. Open to unsolicited reviews. Poets may also send books for review consideration to Reviews Editor. ***blue buffalo*** is a magazine which falls under the Dandelion Magazine Society umbrella. ***blue buffalo*** is also published twice yearly, but **submissions are accepted *only* from Alberta writers.**

JOHN DANIEL AND COMPANY, PUBLISHER; FITHIAN PRESS (II), a division of Daniel & Daniel, Publishers, Inc., P.O. Box 21922, Santa Barbara CA 93121, phone (805)962-1780, founded 1980, reestablished 1985. John Daniel, a general small press publisher, specializes in literature, both prose and poetry. Fithian Press is a subsidy imprint open to all subjects. **"Book-length mss of any form or subject matter will be considered, but we do not want to see pornographic, libelous, illegal or sloppily written poetry."** He has recently published books by Max Brand, Daniel Green and Jeanne M. Nichols. As a sample John Daniel selected "Go Little Book" from the book **Mind and Blood** by John Finlay:

Go little book to the party,
But hide your moral crumb.
Be cunning. Act as if to say,
I'm hungry, Sir, and dumb.

He publishes 10 flat-spined paperbacks, averaging 64 pgs., each year. **For free catalog of either imprint, send #10 SASE. To submit material send 10 sample poems and bio. Reports on queries in 2 weeks, on mss in 2 months. Simultaneous submissions and disks compatible with Macintosh OK. Always sends prepublication galleys. Pays 10-75% of net receipts royalties. Buys English-language book rights. Returns them upon termination of contract. Fithian Press books (50% of his publishing) are subsidized, the author paying production costs and receiving royalties of 50-75% of net receipts. Books and rights are the property of the author, but publisher agrees to warehouse and distribute for one year if desired.** John Daniel advises, "Poetry does not make money, alas. It is a labor of love for both publisher and writer. But if the love is there, the rewards are great."

"For the cover of this issue, we asked Emile Ferris, a Chicago-based artist, to create a piece in black & white which would be representational of our theme," says Cathi Falsani, assistant editor of* Daughters of Sarah, *a quarterly magazine published in Chicago, Illinois. "The theme of this particular issue was 'Crossing Cultural Boundaries: Interreligious Dialogue.' The women presented in the woodblock print are conversing with each other and are multiculturally represented."* DOS *publishes poetry in almost every issue. "The poetry we choose is strong enough and complete enough in its own ideas and images to stand alone," says Falsani. "We do not use poetry as filler. It is treated as equal to our prose pieces and articles."

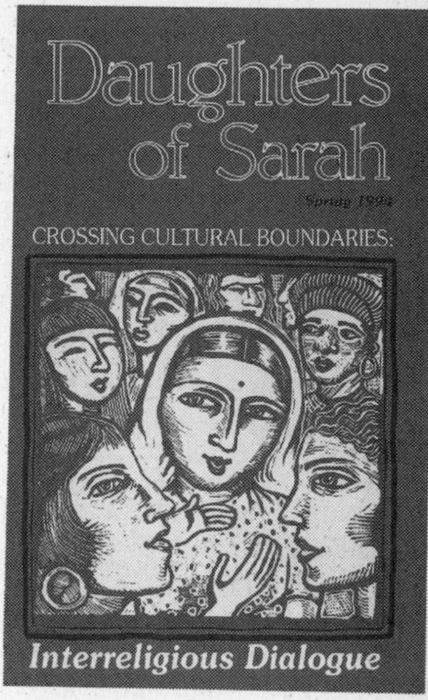

DAUGHTERS OF SARAH (IV-Feminist, religious, social issues, themes), 2121 Sheridan Rd., Evanston IL 60201, phone (708)866-3882, founded 1974, editor Reta Finger, is a quarterly magazine "integrating feminist philosophy with biblical/Christian theology and making connections with social issues." The magazine includes only "occasional" poetry. The editor says, **"Please no rhymed couplets; must be short enough for one 5½×8½ page, but prefer less than 20 lines. Topics must relate to Christian feminist issues, but prefer specific to abstract terminology."** She does not want **"greeting card type verse or modern poetry so obscure one can't figure out what it means."** As a sample the editor selected these lines by Ann Bailey:

> *Who would lay her head on stone,*
> *Would crush the dark to dust?*
> *What dreamstruck one will hurl herself toward holiness*
> *and fight for her own blessings?*
> *Who here would risk her life to wrestle with the Lord?*

The magazine is digest-sized, 64 pgs., with photos and graphics, web offset. Its circulation is 4,500, of which 4,400 are subscriptions, including about 250 libraries; bookstore sales are 50. Single copy: $4.50; subscription: $18/year. Back issues available for $3.50. **Considers simultaneous submissions. Prefers shorter poems. Submit no more than two at once to Cathi Falsani, assistant editor.** Time to publication is 3-18 months. **Publishes theme issues. Send SASE for guidelines and upcoming themes. Themes for 1994-95 include: 20th Anniversary Issue (Fall '94); Our Spiritual Mothers (Winter '95); Women and AIDS (Spring '95); Contemplative Life (Summer '95). Reports in 2-3 months.** ***Daughters of Sarah* pays $15-30/poem plus 2-3 copies. Buys one-time rights.** *Daughters of Sarah* recently received the Associated Church Press Honorable Mention for Poetry and Chicago Women in Publishing's 2nd Place Award for Literature. The editor says, **"Write first for list of upcoming themes, since we usually choose poetry to fit with a particular theme."**

DBQP; ALABAMA DOGSHOE MOUSTACHE; A VOICE WITHOUT SIDES; &; HIT BROADSIDES; THE SUBTLE JOURNAL OF RAW COINAGE; DBQPRESCARDS (IV-Form), 875 Central Pkwy., Schenectady NY 12309-6005, founded 1987, poetry editor Ge(of Huth). "dbqp is the name of the overall press. ***Alabama Dogshoe Moustache*** publishes **language poetry (usually very short) & visual poetry.** ***A Voice Without Sides*** is an occasional magazine in very small runs (about 24 copies) and in strange formats (in jars, as earrings, etc.); it uses the same type of poetry as ***ADM***. **&** is a series of leaflets each featuring a single poem. ***Hit Broadsides*** is a broadside series. ***The Subtle Journal of Raw Coinage*** is a monthly that publishes coined words but occasionally will publish an issue of *pwoermds* (one-word poems such as Aram Saroyan's 'eyeye') or poems written *completely* with neologisms. ***dbqprescards*** is a postcard series publishing mostly poetry. These publications are generally handmade magazines, leaflets, broadsides and objects of very small size. **I am interested only in short language poetry and visual poetry. No**

traditional verse or mainstream poetry." They have published poetry by John M. Bennett, Bob Grumman and Jonathan Brannen. As a sample the editor selected this complete poem by damian lopes:

the small boy walks
like turning pages
& runs like an alphabet
without vowels

Their major poetry magazine is ***Alabama Dogshoe Moustache***, which appears in various formats up to 15 pgs., magazine-sized, held together with thread, staples, fasteners, or packaged inside containers. Its press run is 100-125 with 10 subscriptions. Single copy: 40¢-$2.50. **Sample: $1 or $2 postpaid. Make checks payable to Geof Huth. Catalog available for SASE. Reports within 2 weeks. Pays "at least 2 copies."** Staff occasionally reviews books of poetry. Send books for review consideration. The editor says, "Most of the poetry I reject is from people who know little about the kind of poetry I publish. I don't mind reading these submissions, but it's usually a waste of time for the submitters. If you are familiar with the work of the poets I publish, you'll have a much better idea about whether or not I'll be interested in your work."

DE YOUNG PRESS; THE NEW CRUCIBLE (I), Rt. 1 Box 76, Stark KS 66775, founded 1964, publisher Mary De Young. ***The New Crucible*** is an environmental magazine appearing 8 times/year. They publish environmental, political, free-thought, health, rural farm/garden and general interest articles. **They are open to all forms and styles of poetry but nothing epic-length. Also, no religious poetry, explicit sex or obscene language.** They have published poetry by Alan Rickard and Branley Branson. As a sample the editor selected these lines from Branson's "Ruminations on Raking Leaves":

What color windrows itself in the lurch
Of cycles on the sleepy grass I've wooed
All summer to grow. The leaves cannot lie
Where they fall for their inner stuff will taint
The soil and next year's hairy rootlets will die
(All this comes by way of word of mouth) . . .

The editor says ***The New Crucible*** is approximately 30 pgs., 8½×11, perfect-bound, with b&w cover. Subscription: $50/12 issues. **Sample postpaid: $5. No previously published poems; simultaneous submissions OK. Cover letter required.** Time between acceptance and publication is 6 months. **Publishes theme issues. Send SASE for upcoming themes. Reports within 2 weeks if SASE included. Always sends prepublication galleys. Pays 2 copies. Rights remain with author.** De Young Press **is a subsidy publisher. "Authors should write for particulars. Can be flexible with arrangements."**

THE DEAD REBEL NEWS; CONTEMPORARY AESTHETICS (IV-Form/style), 421 Park St., Oxford PA 19363, founded 1990, "non-editor" Robert Nagler. Both ***TDRN*** and ***CA*** are irregularly published literary newsletters using **very short ("flash" and minimal) fiction and experimental literature of all types. They are especially interested in L-A-N-G-U-A-G-E poetry.** ***TDRN*** has published R. Kostelanetz, J.M. Bennett, S. Murphy, G. Huth, Malok, Musicmaster and R. Howington. As a sample the editor chose these lines from his own work, "She Turns the Ceramic Dogs in, Toward the Living Room, Meaning: My Husband is Here":

The energy of the stroke derives from the quick pivoting of
the waist, the motion of the back downward, and the full
force of the arm, elbow bent.

TDRN and ***CA*** are single-sheet, double-sided, photocopied leaflets with few graphics. Subscription and **samples are available for one business-size SASE.** The editor adds, "The answer to a frequent query: Our title, 'The Dead Rebel', is taken from the name of a tattoo parlor in Germany."

‡DEATHREALM (IV-Horror, fantasy), 3223-F Regents Park, Greensboro NC 27455, founded 1987, editor Mark Rainey, is a quarterly using **"mostly tales of horror/dark fantasy. Small amount of poetry in each issue. No poetry reviews. Poems may be any style or length, though epic-scale pieces are *not* recommended. Rhyme or freestyle OK."** They have recently published poetry by Ardath Mayhar, Jessica Amanda Salmonson, Michael Arnzen and Chad Hensley. It is 64-72 pgs., magazine-sized, saddle-stapled, color covers. They accept 10-12 of 200-300 poems received/year. Press run 3,000 for 500 subscribers, 2,500 shelf sales. Subscription: $15.95. **Sample postpaid: $4.95. Orders *only* to publisher: TAL Publications, P.O. Box 1837, Leesburg VA 22075. Send SASE for guidelines. Reports in 6-9 weeks. Pays $4-8 plus 1 copy. Buys first North American serial rights.**

‡DEFINED PROVIDENCE; DEFINED PROVIDENCE PRESS (II), P.O. Box 16143, Rumford RI 02916, founded 1992, editor Gary J. Whitehead. ***Defined Providence*** is a biannual which aims to publish "new and unknown poets alongside some of those poets considered to be the best in America." They want **"well-crafted lyrical or narrative poems grounded in experience, up to 3 pages long. No overly abstract,**

surreal or 'language' poetry. No overly religious or pornographic; singsong or conspicuous rhyme. Nothing long." They have recently published poetry by Robert Morgan, David Citino, Neal Bowers and Mark Anderson. As a sample the editor selected these lines from "Evening Walk by Eric Trethewey:

The stars, haphazard in their swarming,
blink on—remote, precise in themselves,
as though to pinpoint anew the aim
of each impossible longing.

DP is an average of 56 pgs., digest-sized, offset from laserprint and perfect-bound with color card cover, and contains b&w art and exchange ads. "We receive about 1,500 poems per year and accept about 60 of them." Press run is 400 for 45 subscribers of which 2 are libraries, 30 shelf sales. Single copy: $4; subscription: $8. **Sample postpaid: $2 for Volume 1, $3 for Volume 2. Submit no more than 5 poems at a time, single-spaced, with name and address. No previously published poems or simultaneous submissions. Cover letter with brief bio required. Often comments on rejections. Send SASE for guidelines. Reports in 1-6 weeks. Pays 1 copy. Acquires first rights.** The magazine also includes essays on poetry or poetics, interviews with well-known poets and book reviews of recent poetry collections (in both single and multi-book format). Open to unsolicited reviews—in MLA style, 600-1,500 words. Poets may also send books for review consideration. Defined Providence Press publishes 1-2 chapbooks/year. **"A query with sample poems is a good idea, but entire manuscripts are considered without queries." $10 reading fee required. Replies to queries in 1 week, to submitted mss in 2-4 weeks. Pays $25 and 25 copies. Poets are expected to help sell books by furnishing mailing lists, giving readings, etc. For sample chapbooks, send $4 and 98¢ stamp.** The press holds an annual contest for individual poems (up to 3 poems, $3/poem fee, 3 prizes) in odd years, for chapbooks (40-48 pgs., $10 fee, $25 and 25 copies) in even years. Send SASE for details. The editor says, "I see too much poetry that is hurried and uninteresting. I like to see poems that are surprising in their use of language, that are not predictable, that leave me changed. Those submitting are encouraged to read a copy prior to submitting to get a better idea of what we publish. I also remind poets that small mags stay alive through subscriptions."

‡DELAWARE VALLEY POETS, INC. (IV-Membership, anthology), P.O. Box 6203, Lawrenceville NJ 08648, publications director Donna Gelagotis. "We publish contemporary anthologies and broadsides of **poetry by invitation to submit and books or chapbooks by members who are ready to publish."** They have published poetry by Maxine Kumin, Theodore Weiss, Lois Marie Harrod and Jana Harris. As a sample, they selected these lines from "Mr. Kurtz, I Presume" by John Falk:

and a blue mantle of water unclasps,
Slides down from the clouds and reclothes
The worn and broken armature of stones.

They publish 1-3 books/year averaging 90 pages. **Members submit 6 samples, bio, publications. Reports in 6 months. "For anthologies, poets must have some connection with the basic organization.** Anthologies are paid for by DPV, Inc., and all sales go to the organization. Individual authors pay printing costs; individual editorial services and distribution are provided by DVP. All sales go to the author." They add, "Poets serious about their work need to read all the poetry they can find, write poetry, attend poetry readings and find someone to trade poetry and criticism with. If there is no workshop available, start one."

DENVER QUARTERLY (II), Dept. of English, University of Denver, Denver CO 80208, phone (303)871-2892, founded 1965, editor Donald Revell, is a quarterly literary journal that publishes fiction, poems, book reviews and essays. **There are no restrictions on the type of poetry wanted.** Poems here (mostly free verse) focus on language and lean toward the avant-garde. Length is open, with some long poems and sequences also featured. They have recently published poetry by John Ashbery, Ann Lauterbach and Marjorie Welish. ***Denver Quarterly*** is 6×9, handsomely printed on buff stock, average 130 pgs., flat-spined with two-color matte card cover. Press run is 1,000 for 600 subscribers (300 to libraries) and approximately 300 shelf sales. Subscription: $15/year to individuals and $18 to institutions. **Samples of all issues after Spring 1985 are available for $5 postpaid. No submissions read between May 15 and September 15 each year. Publishes theme issues. Send SASE for guidelines and upcoming themes. Reports in 2-3 months. Sometimes sends prepublication galleys. Pays 2 copies and $5/page.** Reviews books of poetry. Poetry published in ***Denver Quarterly*** has been included in **The Best American Poetry 1992.**

‡ ***The double dagger before a listing indicates that the listing is new in this edition. New markets are often the most receptive to submissions.***

DESCANT (III, IV-Regional), Box 314, Station P, Toronto, Ontario M5S 2S8 Canada, founded 1970, editor-in-chief Karen Mulhallen, is "a quarterly journal of the arts committed to being the finest in Canada. **While our focus is primarily on Canadian writing we have published writers from around the world.**" Some of the poets they have published are Lorna Crozier, Stephen Pender and Libby Scheier. As a sample the editor selected these lines from "Isla Grande" by Lake Sagaris:

I had caught children in my womb like clams
watched them pried open and consumed and tossed away
and still I was young.

It is an elegantly printed and illustrated flat-spined publication with colored, glossy cover, oversized digest format, 140 pgs., heavy paper, with a circulation of 1,200 (800 subscriptions, of which 20% are libraries). They receive 1,200 unsolicited submissions/year, of which they use less than 10, with a 2-year backlog. **Sample postpaid: $8. Guidelines available for SASE. Submit typed ms, unpublished work not in submission elsewhere, name and address on first page and last name on each subsequent page. Include SASE with Canadian stamps or SAE and IRCs. Reports within 4 months. Pays "approximately $100." Buys first-time rights.** Karen Mulhallen says, "Best advice is to know the magazine you are submitting to. Choose your markets carefully."

DESCANT: TEXAS CHRISTIAN UNIVERSITY LITERARY JOURNAL (II), English Dept., Box 32872, Texas Christian University, Fort Worth TX 76129, phone (817)921-7240, founded 1956, editors Betsy Colquitt, Stan Trachtenberg, Harry Opperman and Steve Sherwood, appears twice a year. They want **"well-crafted poems of interest. No restrictions as to subject matter or forms. We usually accept poems 40 lines or fewer but sometimes longer poems."** They have published poetry by Walter McDonald and Lyn Lifshin. It is 6×9, 92 pgs., saddle-stapled, professionally printed, with matte card cover. Poems in issues we read tended to be lyric free verse under 50 lines with short line lengths (for added tension). "We publish 30-40 pgs. of poetry per year. We receive probably 4,000-5,000 poems annually." Their press run is 500 for 350 subscribers. Single copy: $6; volume: $12, $18 foreign. **Sample postpaid: $4. No simultaneous submissions. Reports in 6-8 weeks, usually no more than 8 months until publication. Pays 2 copies.**

THE DEVIL'S MILLHOPPER PRESS; THE DEVIL'S MILLHOPPER; KUDZU POETRY CONTEST; SAND RIVER POETRY CONTEST (II), University of South Carolina at Aiken, 171 University Parkway, Aiken SC 29801, founded 1976, editor Stephen Gardner, assistant editor JoAnn Biga, publishes one magazine issue of ***The Devil's Millhopper*** each year and one chapbook, winner of an annual competition. **They want to see any kind of poetry, except pornography or political propaganda, up to 100 lines.** Some of the poets they have published are Susan Ludvigson, Ann Darr, Lynne H. deCourcy, Ricardo Pau-Llosa, Katherine Soniat, Walt McDonald, R.T. Smith, Dorothy Barresi and Richard Frost. The magazine is 32-40 pgs., digest-sized, saddle-stapled, printed on good stock with card cover and using beautiful b&w original drawings inside and on the cover. The print run of ***Devil's Millhopper*** is 500. The annual chapbook has a print run of 600, going to 375 subscribers of which 20 are libraries. **Sample postpaid: $3.50. Send regular, non-contest submissions September and October only. They want name and address on every page of submissions; simultaneous submissions acceptable. Sometimes the editor comments on rejected mss. Reports usually in 2 months. Sometimes sends prepublication galleys. Pays copies. Acquires first North American serial and reprint rights. Rights automatically revert to author upon publication.** Send SASE for their annual Kudzu Poetry Contest rules (prizes of $50, $100 and $150, $3/poem entry fee), annual Sand River Contest for poetry in traditional fixed forms (prizes of $250, $150 and $50, $3/poem entry fee), chapbook competition rules, and guidelines for magazine submissions. Send Kudzu Contest submissions September 1 to October 31; Sand River Contest submissions June 1 to July 31; chapbook contest submissions January 1 to February 28. Chapbook competition requires either $5 reading fee or $9 subscription for 2 years. Pays $50 plus 50 copies. The editor advises, "There is no substitute for reading a lot and writing a lot or for seeking out tough criticism from others who are doing the same."

JAMES DICKEY NEWSLETTER (III), DeKalb College, 2101 Womack Rd., Dunwoody GA 30338, founded 1984, editor Joyce M. Pair, a biannual newsletter devoted to critical articles/studies of James Dickey's works/biography and bibliography. They **"publish a few poems of *high* quality. No poems lacking form or meter or grammatical correctness."** As a sample here are the opening lines from "Haft Blossom" by R.T. Smith:

Long-sleeping, I rose in the morning
and opened the door to sunlight.
Trough water woke me with sunlight,
dark and the other stars having
yielded their power . . .

It is 30 pgs. of ordinary paper, neatly offset (back and front), with a card back-cover, stapled top left corner. The newsletter is published in the fall and spring. Single copy: $3.50; subscription to individuals: $5/year, $10 to institutions. **Sample available for $3.50 postage. Contributors**

should follow MLA style and standard ms form, sending 1 copy, double-spaced. Cover letter required. Pays 5 copies. Acquires first rights. Reviews "only works on Dickey or that include Dickey." Open to unsolicited reviews. The editor's advice is: "Acquire more knowledge of literary history, metaphor, symbolism and grammar, and, to be safe, the poet should read a couple of our issues."

‡THE DIDACTIC (II), 11702 Webercrest, Houston TX 77048, founded 1993, editor Charlie Mainze, is a monthly publishing **"only, only didactic poetry. That is the only specification. Some satire might be acceptable as long as it is didactic in spirit."** The editor says he is still experimenting with the format of the magazine but planning a press run of 500. **Previously published poems and simultaneous submissions OK.** Time between acceptance and publication is about a year. "Once it is determined that the piece is of self-evident quality and is also didactic, it is grouped with similar or contrasting pieces. This may cause a lag time for publication." **Reports "as quickly as possible." Pay is "nominal." Buys one-time rights.** Considering a general review section, only using staff-written reviews. Poets may send books for review consideration.

DIEHARD (III), 3 Spittal St., Edinburgh EH3 9DY Scotland, phone (031)229-7252, founded 1990, editors Ian King and Sally Evans, publishes 6 hardbacks and 1-2 chapbooks/year. **They want "the heavyweight stuff, no fractured prose, politics and pious piffle."** As examples of poets recently published the editor lists Keats, Oscar Wilde, Tony Rees and John Skelton. "A book is a book. Write me a book rather than ply me with a heap of scraps from magazines. **No reply unless interested, do not send SAE. Use your own name, keep it accurate, keep it legible." Reporting is "slow." Usually sends prepublication galleys. They pay 5% royalties plus 6 copies.** The editor says, "Anyone attempting subsidy will be booted out the door that fast and it might cause an international incident. We are actually quite a major antiquarian bookshop (Grindles of Edinburgh) with a bindery and letterpress printing facilities (for shop use only). As most of our staff are writers or former publishers of some description, we like to keep Diehard going as a sideline where quality of production really matters."

A DIFFERENT DRUMMER (II, IV-Ethnic, translations); SONGS OF THE CITY ANNUAL POETRY CONTEST (II, IV-Themes); CHEAP JAKE ANNUAL CHAPBOOK CONTEST (II), 84 Bay 28th St., Brooklyn NY 11214, founded 1989, editor/publisher Nicholas Stix. *ADD*, a magazine of literature, art and ideas, appears 6 times a year. **"I am promiscuous in my likes (style and theme-wise) and don't want to discourage someone from submitting an excellent poem written in a generally undistinguished genre. I do not expect poetry to toe a political line. Spare me impostors, masquerading as poems: incoherent fragments, uninspiring prose set in short 'poetry-like' lines and literal statements of the writer's moral superiority or love of another person, place or thing. Also: no poems that explain themselves through a preface or epilogue, or poems on the difficulties of writing poetry, unless extremely witty." They lean toward work that is "urban, ethnic (Jewish and black)."** They have published poetry by Stewart David Ikeda, Paul J. Hamill, Damienne Real and Barbara M. Simon. As a sample the editor selected these lines from "Style" by William Russell:

"I told the nigger,
I told the nigger,"
And he stiff-fingers the air
to defy God—
out loud,
in the open;
his words clearly spoken for the bronze beauty at his side,
Because the pay phone he pretends to talk in
is broken.

ADD is 52 pgs., 8×11, flat-spined, professionally printed, with glossy cover. Press run 20,000 for about 2,000 subscriptions, about 2,500 shelf sales. Subscription: $15. **Sample postpaid: $5. Do not submit mss in October, November or December, except for contests. Send SASE for guidelines. Pays a minimum of 5 copies. "Allow 4-6 months for a response. I read all submissions, screening out approximately 98% and discussing the rest with my editors. There are no requirements, but potential contributors are expected to read *ADD* before submitting work." They use translations with original works (author must secure rights of work not in public domain.)** Open to unsolicited reviews. Poets may also send books for review consideration. Their annual Songs of the City Contest (Prizes of $100, $75, $50, plus publication in *ADD* and copies; entry fee: $5/poem; deadline February 1) is for **poems on urban themes.** The Cheap Jake Chapbook contest (Prize of $150, plus publication and copies; entry fee: $10/ms; 24-page limit; deadline February 1; each entrant receives a copy) **has no thematic or stylistic restrictions. Send SASE for rules of either contest.** The editor says, "Don't be a slave to the muse, forcing all of your thoughts and feelings into a 'poetic' form. Work in as many forms of prose and poetry as possible. That way you are more likely to find the style appropriate to your expression. Be your own toughest critic. Proofread and analyze your work carefully. Never rush out a poem before its time. Avoid the company of poets. Above all, do as I say, not as I do."

THE DISABILITY RAG & RESOURCE (IV-Specialized), P.O. Box 145, Louisville KY 40201, founded 1980, fiction/poetry editor Anne Finger, appears 6 times a year and "is the nation's leading disability rights magazine." **The editors have no restrictions as to form, length or style of poetry. "We are interested in material by disabled writers or about the disability experience. Nothing sappy, sentimental, stereotyped or clichéd."** They have recently published poetry by K. Middleton and Susan McBride. As a sample we selected these lines from McBride's "Thanksgiving Day Feast":

Like a wishbone
I am tucked in the V of white bed
my arms sprouting tubes.
Television
spoons up Desert Storm battalions,
soldiers gnawing turkey;
hot gangrene tents.

The editor says ***DR*** is approximately 40 pgs., 8×10⅝, b&w graphics on newsprint, glossy color cover, some advertising. They receive about 100 poems a year, accept approximately 10%. Press run is 5,000 for 4,500 subscribers of which approximately 10% are libraries, 350 shelf sales. Single copy: $3.95; subscription: $17.50 individuals, $35 institutions, $42 international. **Sample postpaid: $4.50. Previously published poems OK, "provided they have not appeared in a publication that circulates to the disabled community." No simultaneous submissions. Cover letter required.** Time between acceptance and publication is 6-12 months. **Often comments on rejections. Send SASE for guidelines. Reports within 2 weeks. Pays $25/poem plus 2 copies. Buys first North American serial rights.** "We do publish reviews of disability-related poetry collections; our reviews run approximately 250-500 words." In 1993 ***The Disability Rag*** won an ***Utne Reader*** Alternative Press Award for best special interest publication.

DJINNI (II), (formerly *Nahant Bay*), #2, 29 Front St., Marblehead MA 01943, founded 1990, editors Kalo Clarke and Kim Alan Pederson, is an annual international magazine publishing contemporary poetry, short fiction, short drama, essays and drawings by well-knowns and new talent. **The editors are especially interested in work that explores new directions. *Djinni*** is published (with help from the Massachusetts Cultural Council) "when sufficient quality material has been selected—usually late fall or early winter." The handsome magazine is 60-100 pgs., digest-sized, professionally printed and perfect-bound with matte card cover. Subscription or **sample: $5. Reads submissions May through November only. Reports in 1-3 months. Pays 1 copy.**

DOC(K)S; EDITIONS NEPE; ZERROSCOPIZ; ANTHOLOGIES DE L 'AN 2.000; LES ANARTISTES (II, IV-Bilingual/foreign language), Le Moulin de Ventabren, 13122 Ventabren, France 13122, uses **"concrete, visual, sound poetry; performance; mail-art; metaphysical poetry," not "poesie à la queue-leu-leu" . . . whatever that means.** They have published work by J.F. Bory, Nani Balestrini, Bernard Heidsieck, James Koller, Julien Blaine and Franco Beltrametti. The magazine ***Doc(k)s*** is published 4 times a year and has a circulation of 1,100, of which 150 are subscriptions. It is an elegantly produced volume, 7×10, over 300 pgs., flat-spined, using heavy paper and glossy full-color card covers. Most of it is in French. "We cannot quote a sample, because concrete poetry, a cross between poetry and graphic art, requires the visual image to be reproduced." **There are no specifications for submissions. Pay for poetry is 5 copies.** Nepe Editions publishes collections of poetry, mostly in French.

DOLPHIN LOG (IV-Children, themes), Suite 402, 870 Greenbrier Circle, Chesapeake VA 23320, phone (804)523-9335, founded 1981, editor Elizabeth Foley, is a bimonthly educational publication for children offered by The Cousteau Society. "Encompasses all areas of science, ecology and the environment as they relate to our global water system. Philosophy of magazine is to delight, instruct and instill an environmental ethic and understanding of the interconnectedness of living organisms, including people." They want to see **"poetry related to the marine environment, marine ecology or any water-related subject matter to suit the readership of 7- to 13-year-olds and which will fit the concept of our magazine. Short, witty poems, thought-provoking poems encouraged. No dark or lengthy ones (more than 20 lines). No talking animals."** The editor excerpted these sample lines from "Garbage Pirates" by Marianne Dyson:

Their treasure bags ready
The garbage pirates three,
Set sail in a wagon boat
Upon the Sidewalk Sea.

They steer around bottle fish
With broken, jagged teeth,

And pinch their noses at the smell
Of trash on Driveway Beach.

It is magazine-sized, 20 pgs., saddle-stapled, offset, using full-color photographs widely throughout, sometimes art, no advertising. It circulates to 80,000 members, approximately 860 library subscriptions. Membership: $28/year for a Cousteau Society family membership, $10/year for *Dolphin Log* only. **Sample: $2 plus 9×12 SAE with 75¢ postage. Prefers double-spaced submissions. Publishes theme issues. Reports within 2 months. Always sends prepublication galleys. Pays $25-100 on publication and 3 copies. Rights include one-time use in *Dolphin Log*, the right to grant reprints for use in other publications, and worldwide translation rights for use in other Cousteau Society publications.** The editor advises, "Become familiar with our magazine by requesting a sample copy and our guidelines. We are committed to a particular style and concept to which we strictly adhere and review submissions consistently. We publish only a very limited amount of poetry each year. We are looking for longer poetry about entire ecosystems rather than one specific animal. For example, a poem about the wetlands or tidepools would be great."

DOLPHIN-MOON PRESS; SIGNATURES (II, IV-Regional), P.O. Box 22262, Baltimore MD 21203, founded 1973, president James Taylor, is **"a limited edition (500-1,000 copies) press which emphasizes quality work (regardless of style), often published in unusual/'radical' format."** The writer is usually allowed a strong voice in the look/feel of the final piece. "We've published magazines, anthologies, chapbooks, pamphlets, perfect-bound paperbacks, records, audio cassettes and comic books. **All styles are read and considered, but the work should show a strong spirit and voice. Although we like the feel of 'well-crafted' work, craft for its own sake won't meet our standards either."** They have published work by Michael Weaver, John Strausbaugh, Josephine Jacobsen and William Burroughs. They have also previously published a collection by the late Judson Jerome, **The Village: New and Selected Poems**, $10.95 paperback, $15.95 hardcover. **Send SASE for catalog and purchase samples or send $10 for their 'sampler' (which they guarantee to be up to $20 worth of their publications). To submit, first send sample of 6-10 pgs. of poetry and a brief cover letter. Replies to query in 2-4 weeks, to submission of whole work (if invited) in 2-4 weeks. Always sends prepublication galleys. Pays in author's copies. Acquires first edition rights.** Three of the books published by this press have been nominated for the Pulitzer Prize and another for a National Book Award. "Our future plans are to continue as we have since 1973, publishing the best work we can by local, up-and-coming and nationally recognized writers–in a quality package."

THE DOMINION REVIEW (II), Bal 220, English Dept., Old Dominion University, Norfolk VA 23529-0078, phone (804)683-3991, founded 1982, faculty advisor Janet Sylvester, Creative Writing, says, **"There are no specifications as to subject matter or style, but we are dedicated to the free verse tradition and will continue to support it."** They have recently published poetry by Donald Morrill, Ioanna-Veronika Warwick and Peter Spiro. *TDR* is flat-spined, 80 pgs., digest-sized, professionally printed, and appears each spring. They have 300 subscriptions. **Sample: $3. They will not consider previously published poems. Cover letter and brief bio requested. Submissions read from September 1 through December 7; allow to March 15 for replies. Sometimes sends prepublication galleys. No pay. Acquires first North American serial rights.**

‡DOUBLE-ENTENDRE (II), P.O. Box 781408, Wichita KS 67278-1408, founded 1993, editor Joshua Friend, is a biannual which contains poetry, short fiction and b&w line art. In regard to poetry, they are **open to all forms, lengths, subjects, etc. However, they do not want "that which is melodramatic, overly abstract or propagandizing."** They have recently published poetry by BJ Ward and Charles Rafferty. As a sample the editor selected these lines from Ward's "Anima":

we've got a date–we're meeting for dinner,
where we'll negotiate once again our separate needs,
trade secrets, decide how to walk perfectly, no tripping,
almost a ballet of silent touchings and consequence.
I'm bringing the wine, she's bringing everything
she knows I'll be lacking.

The editor says it is 50-60 pgs., 5½×8½, desktop-published and staple bound, no ads. Press run is 100-200. Single copy: $4; subscription: $8. **Submit 4-7 poems. No previously published poems or simultaneous submissions. Cover letter with brief bio required.** Time between acceptance and publication is up to 8 months. **Seldom comments on rejections. Reports in 3-6 weeks. Pays 2 copies. Rights remain with authors.** The editor says, "Believe in your work. Sometimes great works get rejected many times, and the only things that will keep the possibility of publication alive are your continued faith in yourself and your persistence in submitting."

DRAGON'S TEETH PRESS; LIVING POETS SERIES (III), El Dorado National Forest, 7700 Wentworth Springs Rd., Georgetown CA 95634, founded 1970, poetry editor Cornel Lengyel. Published poets include Francis Weaver, Marcia Lee Masters and Stanley Mason. As a sample, the editor selected the beginning lines of "Not Just By Word of Mouth Alone" from **The Thirteenth Labor** by Ronald Belluomini:

My sole being elliptic
I have now and anciently dreamt in
the treasuries of hope about
a scheme to elude delusion's wrath,
but I have broken
my egg-shaped dream with collusion's fact.

Dragon's Teeth Press "**subsidy publishes 25% of books** if book has high literary merit, but very limited market"—which no doubt applies to books of poetry. They publish other books on 10% royalty contract. **Simultaneous submissions OK. Reports in 2 weeks on queries, 1 month on mss.**

DREAM INTERNATIONAL QUARTERLY (I, IV-Specialized), % Tim Scott, Apt. 2B, 4147 N. Kedvale Ave., Chicago IL 60641, founded 1981, senior poetry editor Tim Scott. **"Poetry must be dream-inspired and/or dream-related. This can be interpreted loosely, even to the extent of dealing with the transitory as a theme. Nothing written expressly or primarily to advance a political or religious ideology."** They have recently published poetry by Ursula K. LeGuin, Karen Alkalay-Gut and Phil Winter. As a sample the editor selected these lines from "She" by Ralph Bellantoni:

She waits for me on
the corner: green-eyed and blonde,
strong and lithesome as
a leopard . . .

DIQ is 84-94 pgs., 8½×11, with vellum cover and drawings. "Also offer a deluxe edition with protective plastic overlay and toothcomb binding for $2 more." They receive about 150 poems a year, accept about 20. Press run is 300 for 200 subscribers of which 4 are libraries. Subscription: $25 for 1 year. **Sample postpaid: $8. Previously published poems and simultaneous submissions OK. Cover letter including publication history, if any, and philosophy of creation required. "As poetry submissions go through the hands of two readers, poets should enclose one additional first-class stamp, along with the standard SASE." Do not submit mss between Halloween and New Year's.** Time between acceptance and publication is 1 year. **Comments on rejections if requested. Send SASE for guidelines. Reports in 1-4 weeks. Sometimes sends prepublication galleys. Pays 1 copy, "less postage." Also, from time to time, "exceptionally fine work has been deemed to merit a complimentary subscription." Acquires first North American serial or reprint rights.** Staff considers reviewing books of poetry "if the poet is a former contributor to ***DIQ***. Such reviews usually run to about five hundred words." Tim Scott says, "Don't get discouraged. Discouragement is the beginning writer's biggest enemy. If you are good at your craft, you will eventually find an outlet for it. Know your literary predecessors and the tradition in which you are working. Read everything from Shakespeare and Donne to Baudelaire and Rimbaud, from Crane and Hopkins to Plath and Sexton."

THE DREAM SHOP; VERSE WRITERS' GUILD OF OHIO; OHIO HIGH SCHOOL POETRY CONTESTS (IV-Membership, students), 233 E. North St., Medina OH 44256, founded 1928, editor J.A. Totts. The Verse Writers' Guild of Ohio (Amy Jo Zook, treasurer, 3520 St. Rte. 56, Mechanicsburg OH 43044) is a state poetry society open to members from outside the state, an affiliate of the National Federation of State Poetry Societies. ***The Dream Shop*** is their poetry magazine, appearing two times a year. **Only members of VWG may submit poems. They do not want to see poetry which is highly sentimental, overly morbid or porn—and nothing over 40 lines. "We use beginners' poetry, but would like it to be good, tight, revised. In short, not first drafts. Too much is sentimental or prosy when it could be passionate or lyric. We'd like poems to make us think as well as feel something."** They have published poetry by Yvonne Hardenbrook, Frankie Paino and Bonnie Jacobson. The editor selected these sample lines from "Portrait of Daruma (Hakuin Ekaku, 1685-1768)" by Jim Brooks:

How is it the word "tango"
follows me into this corner
of shaped light, follows me
among sacred statues—wooden,
bronze and sandstone eyes
closed or half-closed on faces
full of quiet, full of almost
too remote tranquility? . . .

"Ours is a forum for our members, and we do use reprints, so new members can get a look at what is going well in more general magazines." Annual dues including ***The Dream Shop***: $15. Senior (over 65): $12. Single copies: $2. The magazine is computer typeset, digest-sized, 52 pgs., with matte card cover. **"All rights revert to poet after publication."** The Verse Writers' Guild sponsors an annual contest for unpublished poems written by high school students in Ohio with categories of traditional, modern, and several other categories. March deadline, with 3 money awards in each category. For contest information write Verse Writers' Guild of Ohio, 1798 Sawgrass Dr., Reynoldsburg OH 43068.

‡THE DREAMBUILDING CRUSADE; THE IDEA CO. (I, IV-Spirituality/inspirational), P.O. Box 995, La Mirada CA 90637, founded fall 1992, editor and publisher Art Garcia. ***The Dreambuilding Crusade*** is a bimonthly newsletter promoting spiritual growth through motivation and inspiration. **They want "short, simple poems relating to spirituality, motivation and inspiration. No sad or negative poetry."** They have recently published poetry by Ludema Garza, Alicen Boyer and Yvonne Carrie. As a sample the editor selected this poem, "Heaven-bound," by Connie Goodman:

When the day comes
for you to arrive,
it may not amount
to where you have been,
but what you will leave behind.

The newsletter is 4 double-sided, 8½ × 11 pages, corner-stapled. It includes announcements and "recognitions," poetry, and information on pen pal networking and networking newsletters. "We accept 80% of submitted poetry." Press run is 100 for 50 subscribers. Single copy: $2; subscription: $12. **Sample postpaid: $3. Previously published poems and simultaneous submissions OK.** Time between acceptance and publication is 2-6 months. **No reply or return of rejections. Rather, the authors of the accepted poems simply receive the issues in which their poems are included. Pays 1 copy, "more only on request."** The editor adds, "We would appreciate any donation of monies or stamps to help defer cost. Make checks payable to The Idea Co."

DREAMS AND NIGHTMARES (IV-Science fiction/fantasy), 1300 Kicker Rd., Tuscaloosa AL 35404, phone (205)553-2284, founded 1986, editor David C. Kopaska-Merkel, is published quarterly. The editor says, **"I want to see intriguing poems in any form or style under about 60 lines (but will consider longer poems). All submissions must be either science fiction, fantasy or horror (I prefer supernatural horror to gory horror). Nothing trite or sappy, very long poems, poems without fantastic content, excessive violence or pointless erotica. Sex and/or violence is OK if there is a good reason."** He has published poetry by Lisa Kucharski, Robert Frazier, Donna Zelzer, Ed Mycue, D.F. Lewis, Wendy Rathbone and Thomas Wiloch. As a sample he selected these lines from "In Green Shadows" by Anastasia Andersen:

stranger things than this have happened
in the moment between breaths
and so we will wait for your return

our captain of the stone

It has 20 pgs., digest-sized, photocopied from typescript, saddle-stapled, with a colored card stock cover and b&w illustrations. They accept about 80 of 1,000-1,500 poems received. Press run is 200 for 70 subscriptions. Subscription: $10/6 issues. Lifetime subscription: $50 (includes available back issues). **Samples: $2. Send SASE for guidelines. No simultaneous submissions. "Rarely" uses previously published poems. Reports in 2-10 weeks. Pays $3/poem plus 2 copies. Buys first North American serial rights.** The editor reviews books of poetry "for other magazines; I do not publish reviews in ***DN***." Send books for review consideration. ***Dreams and Nightmares*** received an award from the Professional Book Center for "advancing the field of speculative poetry." The editor says, "There are more magazines publishing fantastic poetry than ever before, and more good fantastic poetry is being written, sold for good money and published. The field is doing very well."

‡DROP FORGE; JADE MOON PUBLICATIONS (I, IV-Form/style), P.O. Box 7237, Reno NV 89510, founded 1992, editor Sean Winchester, appears 3-4 times/year. ***Drop Forge*** is a "forum of individual forays into two-dimensional forms of divinity. **Experimental, visual, otherstream poetry. I want results from a series of personal discoveries in creativity. I do not want to see most established and widely accepted formats, in fact, anything that would fit a format developed by another."** They have recently published poetry by Chris Dew and David Starkey. As a sample the editor selected these lines by Jake Berry:

(tertiary sheath) disclosed:
36.639 xPE. (or) fisile infraquark
vault perenially violated

The editor says the format of ***Drop Forge*** varies. The issue we received is 24 pgs., 5½ × 8½, saddle-stapled with paper cover, hand-drawn and rubber-stamped cartoons and art, and ads. He hopes to increase the number of pages and move to an 8½ × 11 format. They accept 10-15% of the poetry received. Press run is 200-500; most distributed free. Subscription: $8. **Sample postpaid: $2.50. "Purchase of sample copy is advised, but by no means required." No previously**

published poems or simultaneous submissions. Cover letter encouraged. "Please include explanation of motive for the less perspicacious, if necessary." Time between acceptance and publication varies. **Often comments on rejections. Reports in 2 weeks to 2 months. Pays 1-3 copies. Acquires first rights. Rights revert to author upon publication.** The editor says his editorial process is "extremely whimsical, though I always look for integrity, personality, dedication to and exploration of language—and its realities. As for the current literary scene, pay it little attention."

DRY CRIK REVIEW (IV-Cowboy, nature/rural/ecology), P.O. Box 44320, Lemon Cove CA 93244, founded 1991, editor John C. Dofflemyer, is a quarterly **of contemporary cowboy poetry.** "The function of *Dry Crik Review* is to inspire and communicate not only within the range livestock culture but to enhance an understanding of the people and dilemmas facing this livelihood with the urban majority, honestly. **Well-crafted expression must demonstrate insight gained from experience within this rural culture. Topics range from pastoral to political, humorous to serious. Poetry should be purposeful and accessible. No slapstick doggerel or barnyard-pet poetry, please! Prefer shorter unpublished works."** They have recently published poetry by Wilma Elizabeth McDaniels, Keith Wilson, Art Cuelho, Sue Wallis, Neil Meili and Linda Hussa. As a sample the editor selected this poem, "Baby of the Dustbowl," by Barbara Shirk Parish:

Daughter—
stillborn—
1938—
buried in the ravaged earth
of this weary state:
her stone reads simply, BABY—
(She was our first.)—
because we dared not
give our grief
a name.

It is 60 pgs., digest-sized, photocopied from typescript on quality textured paper with matte card cover and perfect-bound. It features free and formal verse with a distinct Western flavor. This magazine is lively and engaging with a sense of humor and social commitment to the land and environment—a rare combination. Press run is 800 for 400 subscribers of which 25 are libraries, 20% shelf sales. Subscription: $20. **Sample postpaid: $7, some back issues more. No simultaneous submissions. Submission quantity 1-5. Cover letter preferred with first submission. Publishes theme issues. Send SASE for guidelines. Reports within 3 months. Always sends prepublication galleys. Pays 2 copies. Acquires one-time rights.** Staff reviews books of poetry in 350-400 words, single format. Send books for review consideration. The editor says, "I am looking for an individualistic perspective that creatively dares contemporary subject matter that may not only serve a function today, but might possibly last as an art/tool."

DUCKABUSH JOURNAL (II), P.O. Box 390, Hansville WA 98340-0390, founded 1988, editors Gary Parks and Tom Snyder, appears annually. **"We consider all types of writing as long as it's correctly edited and spell-checked. No greeting card verse."** They have published poetry by James Bertolino, Alice Derry and Tim McNulty. As a sample the editors selected these lines by Gloria Boyer:

Everything was a sensation she could never place:
night dragging its thin fingers across the glass,
a leaf bug clicking the beads of its abacus.
Already winter was coming and her body curled

It is 70 pgs., digest-sized, flat-spined, with matte card cover. Press run is 350 for 25 subscribers of which 3 are libraries, 250 shelf sales. They accept about 10% of poetry received. Subscription: $10. **Sample postpaid: $4. Reports within 6 weeks. Pays 2 copies.** Staff reviews books of poetry. Tom Snyder says, "We read everything. The two editors have very different styles and ranges of taste. Anything is possible."

DUENDE PRESS (IV-Specialized), P.O. Box 571, Placitas NM 87043, founded 1964, editor Larry Goodell, is interested in **poetry by older underpublished poets. "I will publish your work if you publish mine. Inquiries welcome."**

DUST (FROM THE EGO TRIP); CAMEL PRESS (IV-Specialized), HC 80, Box 160, Big Cove Tannery PA 17212, phone (717)573-4526, founded 1981, poetry consultant Katharyn Howd Machan, publisher James Hedges, who describes himself as "editor/printer of scholarly and scientific journals, does occasional poetry postcards and chapbooks for fun." ***Dust (From the Ego Trip)*** is "an intermittent journal of personal reminiscences." For it he wants **"autobiographical material (can address any subject, but written from the viewpoint of an active participant in the events described). Mss should be between 1,000 and 2,500 words and can be one long poem or a collection of related shorter poems.**

Any style OK, including haiku, and any language using the roman alphabet. No religious (evangelizing) material or other material written primarily to advance a point of view. Any topic is OK, and coarse language is OK, but only if used artistically." As a sample James Hedges selected these lines from "Absent Geese" by Glenn Coats:

Winter washes shoreline
clean of footprints

Old nests jut onto the stream
like the bows of boats.

Bleached brush.

He publishes 1-2 chapbooks a year under the Camel Press imprint, average 20 pgs. **Query with "a few sample poems." Cover letter not required, "but I like the personal contact and the show of sincere interest." No bio or publications necessary because, "we judge on material only, status of poet is irrelevant." Simultaneous submissions and previously published material OK. Reports in 10 days. Always sends prepublication galleys. Pays 50 copies plus half of net after production costs are recovered.** He is open to subsidy publishing poetry of "artistic merit." To buy samples, request catalog. He says, "I always write a cover letter, but I'm not a poetry critic, just a considerate publisher. I do a bit of poetry because I want to encourage the art and broaden my catalog. Everything I publish is handset in metal type and letterpress printed on fine paper. The authors are expected to do most of the promotion. Press run is normally 500, and I give away about 400 copies to friends, plus 50 for the author. The author can order more copies in advance if he expects to sell a large number. Financial arrangements are negotiable."

‡DWAN (I, IV-Gay/lesbian, translations), Box 411, Bellefonte PA 16823, founded 1993, editor Donny Smith, appears every 2 to 3 months. ***Dwan*** is a "queer poetry zine; some prose; some issues devoted to a single poet or a single theme ('Jesus' or ' Mom and Dad,' for instance)." The editor wants **"poetry exploring gender, sexuality, sex roles, identity, queer politics, etc. If you think Charles Manson is cool—or even Charles Bukowski—you might not feel welcome at *Dwan*."** They have recently published poetry by B.Z. Niditch and Stephanie Weckler. As a sample the editor selected these lines from "A House of Cornstalks" by Ed Chaberek:

. . . You said: "Dancing
darkly at the edge can be
only this, lover, only this. Diffuse
cornstalks make our house
only this . . . only this . . ."

Dwan is 12 pgs., 5½×8½, photocopied on plain white paper, and unstapled. They receive 400-500 pgs. of poetry/year ("that's no exaggeration!"), accept less than 10%. Press run is 75. **Sample available for 58¢ in stamps. Submit poems typed "in black on white please, no colored paper, no blue ink." Previously published poems and simultaneous submissions OK. Cover letter required.** Time between acceptance and publication is 6-18 months. **Often comments on rejections. Reports in 1-3 months. Pays copies.** The editor reviews books, chapbooks and magazines usually in 25-150 words. Send books for review consideration. "Heterosexuals always welcome."

THE EAGLE (IV-Ethnic), Eagle Wing Press, Inc., P.O. Box 579MO, Naugatuck CT 06770, phone (203)729-0035, founded 1981, poetry editor Randy Whitehead, is an **American Indian newspaper** appearing every other month. **Poems must be on American Indian themes or written by American Indians. "Try to avoid 'typical' pieces that try to sound 'Indian.' We are looking for clear, concise, strong poetry."** They have published poetry by Marcella Taylor and John Fox. As a sample the editor selected lines from the poem "We the Criminals" by Sean Lawrence:

selling white lies
in a blind man's trade
sorting through beads
in a timeless charade
of meaningless treaties
and the money we made.

The newspaper is tabloid-sized, about 28 pgs., unstapled, with graphics and ads, circulation 4,000 with 1,500 subscriptions of which 120 are libraries, about 600 shelf sales. Subscription: $10/year 3rd class, $15/year 1st class. **Sample postpaid: $2.50. Requires cover letter with biographical information, including tribal affiliation(s) if any. Pays 5 copies, up to 5 more on request. "Rights revert to author after publication, with *Eagle* reserving right to reprint."** Reviews books of poetry by Native Americans. Send books for review consideration.

EAGLE'S FLIGHT; EAGLE'S FLIGHT BOOKS (I, IV-Translations), #822, 2501 Hunter's Hill, Enid OK 73703, phone (405)233-1118, founded 1989, editor and publisher Shyamkant Kulkarni, is a quarterly "platform for poets and short story writers—new and struggling to come forward." **They want "well-crafted literary quality poetry, any subject, any form, including translations. Translations should have permission of original poets."** They have published poetry by Mike Cluff and Kent Clair Chamberlain. As a sample the editor selected these lines from "The Last Straw" by Lisa Eastwood:

> *. . . We hope*
> *This last straw, this last flake of*
> *cotton wool, this last grain of wheat*
> *and golden dust meant to do the last*
> *job comes handy to someone needy like*
> *these ants crawling over my body*
> *getting cold.*

Eagle's Flight is 8-12 pgs., 7×8½, printed on colored paper and saddle-stapled, including simple art, few ads. They receive about 50 poems/year, accept 10%. Press run is 200 for 100 subscribers. Subscription: $5. **Sample postpaid: $1. No previously published poems or simultaneous submissions. Cover letter required. Reads submissions January 1 to June 30.** Time between acceptance and publication is 1 year. **Seldom comments on rejections. Send SASE for guidelines. Reports in 2-3 months. Pays 2 copies or 1-year subscription. Acquires first publication rights.** Reviews books of poetry in 250-750 words, single format. Under Eagle's Flight Books, they publish 1 paperback/year. "Up to now we have been publishing our own books, but **if somebody wants to share publishing cost, we can help or undertake publishing a book/anthology. We don't have selling organizations. Anybody interested in this may enquire." Replies to queries in 1 month.** "We also plan to organize a contest and publish anthologies of poetry. Award depends on our enthusiasm at that time and availability of funds." The editor says, "We expect poets to be familiar with our publication and our expectations and our limitations. To be a subscriber is one way of doing this. Everybody wants to write poems and, in his heart, is a poet. Success lies in getting ahead of commonplace poetry. To do this one has to read, to be honest, unashamed and cherish decent values of life in his heart. Then success is just on the corner of the next block."

EARTH'S DAUGHTERS: A FEMINIST ARTS PERIODICAL (IV-Women/feminism, themes), P.O. Box 41, Central Park Station, Buffalo NY 14215, phone (716)837-7778, founded 1971. The "literary periodical **with strong feminist emphasis**" appears 3 times a year, irregularly spaced. Its "format varies. Most issues are flat-spined, digest-sized issues of approximately 60 pgs. We also publish chapbooks, magazine-sized and tabloid-sized issues. Past issues have included broadsheets, calendars, scrolls and one which could be assembled into a box." **Poetry can be "up to 40 lines (rare exceptions for exceptional work), free form, experimental—we like unusual work. All must be strong, supportive of women in all their diversity. We like work by new writers, but expect it to be well-crafted. We want to see work of technical skill and artistic intensity. We rarely publish work in classical form, and we never publish rhyme or greeting card verse."** They have published poetry by Christine Cassidy, Rose Romano, Lyn Lifshin, Helen Ruggieri, Joan Murray, Susan Fantl Spivack, "and many fine 'unknown' poets, writers and artists." They publish poetry by men if it is supportive of women. As a sample the editor selected ***#36 Over the Transom*** "A Shape Soft Enough to Wear" by Lynn Martin:

> *. . . Two women can talk the night*
> *into a shape soft enough to wear*
> *one more time. It's almost as if*
> *The same onion planted over & over,*
> *never decays, grows like a prayer . . .*

"Our purpose is to publish primarily work that otherwise might never be printed, either because it is unusual, or because the writer is not well known." Subscription: $14/3 issues for individuals; $22 for institutions. **Sample postpaid: $4. Simultaneous submissions OK. "Per each issue, authors are limited to a total of 150 lines of poetry, prose or a combination of the two. Submissions in excess of these limits will be returned unread. Business-size envelope is preferred, and use sufficient postage—we do not accept mail with postage due." Send SASE for guidelines. Some issues have themes, which are available for SASE after April of each year. Length of reporting time is atrociously long if ms is being seriously considered for publication, otherwise within 3 weeks. Pays 2 copies and reduced prices on further copies. Editor comments "whenever we have time to do so—we want to encourage new writers."** The collective says: "Once you have submitted work, please be patient. We only hold work we are seriously considering for publications, and it can be up to a year between acceptance and publication. If you must contact us (change of address, notification that a simultaneous submission has been accepted elsewhere), be sure to state the issue theme, the title(s) of your work and enclose SASE."

EASTERN CARIBBEAN INSTITUTE (I, IV-Regional), P.O. Box 1338, Frederiksted, U.S. Virgin Islands 00841, phone (809)772-1011, founded 1982, editor S.B. Jones-Hendrickson, editorial contact Cora Christian, is a "small press publisher with plans to expand," **especially interested in poetry of the**

Caribbean and Eastern Caribbean. As a sample the editor selected these lines from "The AIDS Watch" in **Of Mask and Mysteries** by Lillian Sutherland:

Today I watched a mother
just sitting there and crying
Today I watched a mother
just sitting there and dying
Today I watched a mother
put her husband in his grave

Their books are softcover, averaging 60 pgs. Sample copies available for purchase. **Submit 5 sample poems, cover letter with bio and previous publications. Simultaneous submissions and previously published poems OK. Reads submissions January to May only. Reports in 1 month. Pays 50 copies.** The editor says, "In our part of the world, poetry is moving on a new level. People who are interested in regional poetry should keep an eye on the Caribbean region. There is a new focus in the Virgin Islands."

EDICIONES UNIVERSAL (IV-Ethnic, foreign language, regional), 3090 SW Eighth St., Miami FL 33135, phone (305)642-3234, founded 1964, general manager Marta Salvat-Golik, is a small press subsidy publisher of **Spanish language books. "We specialize in Cuban authors and themes."** They have published books of poetry by Olga Rosalo and Amelia del Castillo. **Poets "must be able to purchase in advance 75% of the copies, due to the fact that poetry does not sell well." Poets receive the copies they paid for. Submit sample, bio, publications. Reports in 1 month.**

‡EDINBURGH REVIEW (II, IV-Translations), 22 George Sq., Edinburgh EH8 9LF Scotland, founded 1969, is a literary quarterly, which uses **quality poetry. Especially interested in non-metropolitan work, translations, aphorisms, philosophy for the generalist and interviews with lesser known writers. Also interested in poetry with ethnic/nationality, gay/lesbian, political and women/feminism themes.** The *Review* is a 160-page paperback. Circulation 2,500. **Sample: £4.95 for back issues, £6.95 for current issues, plus 50p. postage and handling. Publishes theme issues. Always sends prepublication galleys. Pays.** Reviews books of poetry.

EIDOS MAGAZINE: SEXUAL FREEDOM AND EROTIC ENTERTAINMENT FOR WOMEN, MEN & COUPLES (IV-Erotica, women), P.O. Box 96, Boston MA 02137, founded 1982, poetry editor Brenda Loew Tatelbaum. "Our press publishes erotic literature, photography and artwork. Our purpose is to provide an alternative to women's images and male images and sexuality depicted in mainstream publications like ***Playboy, Penthouse, Playgirl***, etc. We provide a forum for the discussion and examination of two highly personalized dimensions of **human sexuality: desire and satisfaction. We do not want to see angry poetry or poetry that is demeaning to either men or women. We like experimental, avant-garde material that makes a personal, political, cultural statement about sensu-sexuality."** They have recently published poetry by Pamela Hughes, Tracy Henley, Connie Meredith, Sara White and Pete Lee. As a sample we selected these lines from "Byron 12" by Michael Dmytryk:

Sex is a moment I can trust.
Whether it becomes a cornfield of grace
Or a grim rockfield of pain,
It is a moment of ecstasy—
Like the blooming dawn,
quietly smiling its welcome,
Or the lasting storm,
huge in its confusion,
Or the music of winding tree limbs,
playing with the thick wind.

Eidos is a professionally printed, newsprint tabloid, with fine photography and art, **number of poems/issue varies**, print run 10,000, over 7,000 subscriptions. They receive hundreds of poems/year, use about 100. No backlog right now. **Sample postpaid: $15. Only accepts sexually explicit material. 1 page limit on length, format flexible, simultaneous submissions OK. Comment or criticism provided as often as possible. Guidelines available for SASE. Reports in 1 month. Pays 1 copy. Acquires first North American serial rights.** Open to unsolicited reviews. Poets may also send books for review consideration. In 1993, Brenda Loew Tatelbaum received an award from The Lifestyles Organization "In recognition of her courageous and continuing efforts to provide a forum for all eroto-sexual orientations and to protect and promote our human and civil rights as guaranteed by the Constitution." She advises, "There is so much poetry submitted for consideration that a rejection can sometimes mean a poet's timing was poor. We let poets know if the submission was appropriate for our publication and suggest they resubmit at a later date. Keep writing, keep submitting, keep a positive attitude."

‡1812 (III), Box 1812, Amherst NY 14226, founded 1993, editors Dan Schwartz and Richard Lynch, is an annual literary arts publication **"looking for material with a *bang*."** The editor says *1812* is 100 pgs., 6×9, with glossy cover and b&w art. They receive about 1,000 poems a year, accept 1-3%. **Previously published poems OK; no simultaneous submissions. Cover letter required.** Time between acceptance and publication is 6-12 months. **Seldom comments on rejections. Send SASE for guidelines. Payment is "arranged." Buys one-time rights.** Open to unsolicited reviews. Sponsors the Overture Award for poetry. Entry fee is $5 for first poem, $2 for each additional poem. Award is $100 and publication. Send SASE for guidelines.

THE EIGHTH MOUNTAIN PRESS; EIGHTH MOUNTAIN POETRY PRIZE (IV-Women, feminist), 624 SE 29th Ave., Portland OR 97214, founded 1985, editor Ruth Gundle, is a "small press publisher of **feminist literary works by women.**" They have published poetry by Karen Mitchell, Irena Klepfisz, Maureen Seaton and Lori Anderson. They publish 1 book of poetry every other year, averaging 128 pgs. **"We now publish poetry *only* through the Eighth Mountain Poetry Prize." Pays 8-10% royalties. Buys all rights. Returns rights if book goes out of print.** The Eighth Mountain Poetry Prize is a biennial award of a $1,000 advance and publication for a ms of 50-120 pgs. written by a woman, no restrictions as to subject matter. Send SASE for rules. **Submit during January in even numbered years; postmark deadline: February 1.** Entry fee: $15. "The selection will be made anonymously. Therefore, the ms must have a cover sheet giving all pertinent information (title, name, address, phone number). No identifying information except the title should appear on any other ms page. The contest will be judged by a different feminist poet each year, whose name will be announced after the winning ms has been chosen." Previous judges have included Andre Lorde, Linda Hogan, Marilyn Hacker, Judy Grahn and Lucille Clifton.

EL BARRIO; CASA DE UNIDAD (V, IV-Ethnic, regional), Dept. PM, 1920 Scotten, Detroit MI 48209, phone (313)843-9598, founded 1981, poetry editor Marta Lagos. They publish **poetry from Latino residents of the SW Detroit area concerning life, family, politics, repression, etc., but do not normally accept unsolicited material. Query first.** They have published poetry by Lolita Hernandez, Gloria House and Jose Garza. As a sample the editor selected these lines from "Let Us Stop This Madness" by Trinidad Sanchez, Jr.:

Let us destroy the factories
that make the guns
that shoot the bullets
that kill our children.
Let us take a stand
to share life,
to break bread
with each other.

El Barrio is published "to keep the Latino people of the SW Detroit area informed, to give them an opportunity to speak to the community." It appears 3-4 times a year, is magazine-sized, about 28 pgs., professionally printed with commissioned art on the matte card cover, using up to 3 poems/issue. Their press run is 5,000, $3/issue, $12 for a subscription. **"Please call for a sample copy." They sometimes use previously published poems. Sometimes publishes theme issues.** The press has published 2 anthologies: **Detroit: La Onda Latina en Poesía—Latin Sounds in Poetry,** Vols. I and II ($6 each).

‡THE ELEVENTH MUSE; POETRY WEST (II, IV-Regional), P.O. Box 2413, Colorado Springs CO 80901, coordinating editor Ceil Malek. Poetry West is a nonprofit organization of poets and supporters of poetry in the Pikes Peak region. It publishes work from all parts of the country in its literary journal, ***the eleventh MUSE***, and **"is especially interested in well-crafted and striking visions that are rich in detail."** They have published poetry by Lois Hayna, Janice Hays and Tony Moffeit. As an example "of the richness of detail preferred (many styles are acceptable)," the editor selected these lines from "The Best Hamburgers" by Holly Hildebrand:

The best hamburgers
are made in 1962
in mock turtle's old cottage
on redman road
and eaten while we watch
errol flynn die with his boots on

The editor says ***the eleventh MUSE*** is printed with matte card cover and saddle-stapled. It's a solid small press product, featuring a wide selection of verse, from lyric and narrative to beat. Subscription (2 issues): $7/year. **Sample postpaid: $4. Submit up to 5 poems. No previously published poems or simultaneous submissions. Reports within 6-8 weeks. Sometimes sends prepublication galleys. Pays 1 copy. Acquires first North American serial rights.** Poetry West is also committed to developing regional artists. Each month it sponsors readings and workshops in local galleries, coffeehouses and colleges. Membership is $20/year and includes 2-3 newsletters and 2 issues of ***the eleventh MUSE***. Poets may also apply to read by sending 10 poems and a brief bio. Payment varies.

11TH ST. RUSE; BIG FISH (I), #23, 322 E. 11th St., New York NY 10003, phone (212)475-5312, founded 1987, editor Lucid. ***11th St. Ruse*** appears every 3 months, 4 pgs. mimeo, wants **poems "short, without subterfuge, preferably written very quickly. Especially interested in humorous, religious and feminist poetry."** They have published poetry by Teres d' Compagnie and Richard Kostelanetz. As a sample the editor selected these lines from "Why I Hate Violins" by Antimony:

I hate violins because you
Need to take a stick and
Teach them to behave.

Press run is 250. Single copy: 33¢. **Sample postpaid: 50¢. Make checks payable to Ellen Carter. Reports in 1 day to 3 months. Pays 1 copy.** Open to unsolicited reviews. Poets may also send books for review consideration. "I have another magazine, ***Big Fish***, and I am currently seeking poems in foreign languages without translations. I'd like to publish more Yeatsian poetry (great poetry) also Langston Hughes-type and poetry by minorities."

ELF: ECLECTIC LITERARY FORUM (ELF Magazine) (II), P.O. Box 392, Tonawanda NY 14150, founded 1990, editor C.K. Erbes, is a quarterly. **"Subject matter and form are open, but we are looking for well-crafted poetry. We prefer poems of 30 lines or less, but will consider longer poems. No trite, hackneyed, ill-crafted effluvia."** They have recently published poetry by Gwendolyn Brooks, Joyce Carol Oates, John Dickson, Martha Vertreace, David Romtvedt, John Tagliabue, William Stafford, Michael Bugeja and R.T. Smith. As a sample the editor selected these lines from "The Blessing Way" by David C. Meyer:

This blue expanse of time here,
with us and them and only the wind between,
becomes a blessing way
that keens among the stones
making us, whole and broken, one

Elf is 52-56 pgs., magazine-sized, with semi-gloss cover, professionally printed, saddle-stapled. They use approximately 140 poems/year. Circulation 6,000. Subscription: $16. **Sample postpaid: $5.50. Send SASE for guidelines. "Accepted writers are asked to submit a bio of 25 words or less." Poems are circulated to an editorial board of professional poets and writers. Editor comments when possible. Reports in 4-6 weeks. Sometimes sends prepublication galleys. Pays 2 copies. Acquires first North American serial rights.** Staff reviews books of poetry. Publishers only may send books for review consideration. They also sponsor the Ruth Cable Memorial Prize for Poetry (annual deadline March 31). Send SASE for guidelines.

ELK RIVER REVIEW (V), 606 Coleman Ave., Athens AL 35611-3216, founded 1991, editor John Chambers, is a semiannual review of poetry and short fiction. **"Open to all types of poetry, no line limit. We want poems that are well-crafted, musical, provocative. However, we are currently overstocked through 1996."** They have recently published poetry by Helen Norris, Peter Huggins, Robert Parham, Stephen Forster, R.T. Smith, Sue Scalf, Sue Walker and Anne George. As a sample we selected these lines from "Snowflakes and Satellites" by Bettye Cannizzo:

One delights the eye like a baby's smile,
tickles the tongue like a Margarita.
The other jolts the imagination like poetry,
stimulates the mind like philosophy.

ERR is 62-84 pgs., 7×9, offset, saddle-stitched, with 80 lb. glossy cover with b&w photo and b&w line drawings inside. Press run is 600 of which 25 go to libraries. Subscription: $12. **Sample postpaid: $6.50. Submit 3-5 poems at a time; name, address and phone number on each page. No previously published poems. Cover letter required. Include "succinct biographical facts and publishing credits (if any)." Often comments on rejections. Send SASE for guidelines. Reports in 2-4 months. Always sends prepublication galleys. Pays 1 copy. Acquires first rights.** Reviews novels and poetry collections (including chapbooks) of regional interest. Open to unsolicited reviews; query first. Poets may also send books for review consideration. Sponsors Marjorie Lees Linn Poetry Award, an annual contest that awards a $750 grand prize and a $250 prize split by second and third places. "All winners will be published in an issue of ***ERR***, receive 3 copies of the issue and receive a free book of poetry by Marjorie Lees Linn." Submit 2 copies each of as many poems as desired; open length, form and subject matter. Entry fee: $10 for 1-3 poems; $2 each additional. "Those submitting 5 or more poems will receive a free subscription." Judge changes every year. Send SASE for details.

ELLIPSE (V, IV-Translations, bilingual), C.P. 10, FLSH Université de Sherbrooke, Sherbrooke, Quebec J1K 2R1 Canada, phone (819)821-7000, founded 1969, editors M. Grandmangin and C. Bouchara, **publishes Canadian poetry in translation.** That is, on facing pages appear either poems in English and a French translation or poems in French and an English translation. **Currently they are not accepting unsolicited mss.** They have recently published poetry by Michael Ondaatje, Margarer Avison and Anne Hébert. As a sample, the editors selected these lines from "La Malemer" by Rina Lasnier:

> *Malemer, mer stable et fermée à la foudre comme à l'aile—*
> *mer prégnante et aveugle à ce que tu enfantes,*
>
> *emporte-moi loin du courant de la mémoire—et de la longue flottaison des souvenirs;*

translated by D.G. Jones:

> *Malemer, firm sea impervious to the lightning as to the*
> *whispering wing—pregnant and oblivious to your generation,*
>
> *bear me far away from the currents of memory—and the long*
> *hulls cargoed with recollection;*

The magazine appears twice yearly in an elegant, flat-spined, 6×9 format, professionally printed, 120 pgs. Subscription: $12. **Sample postpaid: $5.**

ELLIPSIS MAGAZINE (II), Westminster College of Salt Lake City, 1840 S. 1300 East, Salt Lake City UT 84105, phone (801)488-4158, founded 1967, appears twice a year using **"all kinds of good poetry. Limited on space."** They have published work by William Stafford, William Kloefkorn, Lyn Lifshin and Ron Carlson. The editor describes it as 80-112 pgs., digest-sized, flat-spined. Subscription: $18/year. **Sample postpaid: $10. Send ms with SASE and contributor notes. Responds within 6 months. Pays $10/poem, $20/story, plus 1 copy.**

EMBERS (II), P.O. Box 404, Guilford CT 06437, phone (203)453-2328, founded 1979, poetry editors Katrina Van Tassel, Charlotte Garrett and Mark Johnson, a "poetry journal of talented new and occasional well-known poets." The editors say, **"no specifications as to length, form or content. Interested in new poets with talent; not interested in lighter way-out verse, porn or poetry that is non-comprehensible."** As a sample, the editors selected these lines from "The Time Change: April" by Lynn deCourcy:

> *Soon the time will change*
> *and change ahead, advancing*
> *into summer's wild and heady growth,*
> *but tonight this cold rain is ringing*
> *through my skull, the tension*
> *of straining rivers rising in me. . .*

Embers is digest-sized, nicely printed on white stock with an occasional b&w photograph or drawing, 52 pgs., flat-spined with one-color matte card cover handsomely printed in black; it appears twice a year—spring/summer and fall/winter. Single copy: $6; subscription: $11/year. **Sample postpaid: $3. Submissions must be typed, previously unpublished, with name, address and brief bio of poet. Deadlines: "basically March 15 and October 15, but we read continuously." Cover letter preferred. Pay for acceptance is 2 copies. Rights revert to author after publication.** They sponsor a chapbook contest. Deadline: December 15. Winner is reported by March 1. Write for details. Editors' advice is "Send for sample copies of any publication you are interested in. Be patient. Most editors read as quickly as they can and report likewise. If a poet sends in work at the beginning of a reading time, or long before a deadline, he/she will have to wait longer for answers. ***Embers*** editors are interested in the poet's voice and would like to read up to five submissions showing variety of subject, form, etc."

EMERALD COAST REVIEW; WEST FLORIDA LITERARY FEDERATION; FRANCIS P. CASSIDY LITERARY CENTER; THE LEGEND; BACK DOOR POETS; WISE (WRITERS IN SERVICE TO EDUCATION) (IV-Regional), P.O. Box 1644, Pensacola FL 32597, located at WFLF/Cassidy Literary Center, Pensa-

ALWAYS include a self-addressed, stamped envelope (SASE) when sending a ms or query to a publisher within your own country. When sending material to other countries, include a self-addressed envelope and International Reply Coupons (IRCs), available for purchase at most post offices.

cola Cultural Center, 402 S. Jefferson St., Pensacola FL 32501. The WFLF was founded in 1987 and began the Cassidy Literary Center, a regional writers' resource and special collection library. One of their programs is WISE, which provides over 50 area writers who volunteer their time to share their writing and writing experiences with local students. They sponsor a Student Writers Network for students in grades 9-12 and scholarships for area college student writers. They publish ***The Legend***, a newsletter bringing literary arts news to 800-1,000 area writers and their supporters. Back Door Poets, one of their subgroups, conducts open microphone poetry readings the third Saturday of each month. Also, WFLF hosts a writing workshop the first Sunday of every month. Membership in WFLF ranges from $10/year for students to $500 and up for life-time memberships. The ***Emerald Coast Review*** is an **annual limited to Gulf Coast regional writers. Sample postpaid: $12. Send SASE for guidelines. Submit with required form (included in guidelines) May 1 to July 31. Pays copies.**

THE EMSHOCK LETTER (IV-Subscribers), P.O. Box 411,Troy ID 83871-0411, phone (208)835-4902, founded 1977, editor Steve Erickson, appears 3-12 times a year, occasionally with **poetry and other writings by subscribers. It is "a philosophical, metaphysical, sometimes poetic expression of ideas and events. It covers a wide range of subjects and represents a free-style form of expressive relation. It is a newsletter quite unlike any other."** The editor describes it as magazine-sized, 5-7 pgs., photocopied from typescript on colored paper. Subscription: $25. **"Poets (who are subscribers) should submit poetry which contains some meaning, preferably centering on a philosophic theme and preferably 50 lines or less. Any good poetry (submitted by a subscriber) will be considered for inclusion and will receive a personal reply by the editor, whether or not submitted material is published in *The Emshock Letter*. Editor will promptly discard any and all material submitted by nonsubscribers. Poets must become subscribers prior to submitting any material!"** Reviews books of poetry only if written by subscribers.

‡EN PLEIN AIR (I, II, IV-Translations), Tagetlistrasse 11, 3072 Ostermundigen, Switzerland, founded 1993, editor Aida Ghanim, appears 3 times/year. ***En Plein Air*** is a poetry journal "emphasizing imagery and timely insight and accepting material in all languages, with English translations." **They want "surrealist prose and English translations of contemporary, timely, significant poetry with dreamlike imagery and insight. Nothing sentimental or biased. No unnecessary raw language."** As a sample the editor selected these lines (poet unidentified):

Daylight is too easy
He wants
the difficult moonlight, an
atmosphere of indications: a dancer pulls
on her silks, all tissued with flames.

The editor says ***En Plein Air*** is offset with linen card cover, art and photos, "ecologically friendly but economically limited." Press run is 300 for 200 subscribers. **Sample: $5 plus $4 (in US cash) for airmail. No previously published poems or simultaneous submissions. Send SAE plus $4 (in US cash) for return postage and comments. Do not submit mss in August. Reports in 3-6 weeks. Pays 2 copies.** Sponsors an annual contest. "Send SAE and postage money for details."

ENCODINGS: A FEMINIST LITERARY JOURNAL (IV-Women/feminism), P.O. Box 6793, Houston TX 77265, founded 1989, co-editors Jacsun Shah and Lazette Jackson. ***Encodings*** appears "randomly, twice a year," using **"high quality poetry with a feminist perspective; especially interested in women's ways of knowing, women's invention and use of language."** As a sample the editor selected these lines from "The Anthropologist" by Jill Hammer:

Her scarf,
the color of tea leaves and faded buttercups,
becomes the mantle of an archer,
a hunter of generalizations.
Garnets hang from her ears,
and girls hang from her words . . .

Encodings is 40-60 pgs., 7×8½, photocopied from typescript and saddle-stapled with glossy card cover. Press run is 300 for 60 subscribers of which 1 is a library. Subscription: $9. **Sample postpaid: $4.50. Submit up to 5 poems at a time. Cover letter with brief bio preferred. Send SASE for guidelines. Editor "occasionally" comments on rejections. Reports in 2-3 months. Pays 2 copies.**

ENITHARMON PRESS (V), 36 St. George's Ave., London N7 0HD England, phone (071)607-7194, fax (071)607-8694, founded 1969, poetry editor Stephen Stuart-Smith, is a publisher of fine editions of poetry and literary criticism in paperback and some hardback editions, about 12 volumes/year averaging 80 pages. They have published books of poetry by John Heath-Stubbs, Phoebe Hesketh, David Gascoyne, Jeremy Hooker, Frances Horovitz, Ruth Pitter, Edwin Brock and Jeremy Reed.

"Substantial backlog of titles to produce, so no submissions possible before 1995." Interested poets should query.

ENVOI (II), 44 Rudyard Rd., Biddulph Moor, Stoke-on-Trent, Staffs ST8 7JN United Kingdom, founded 1957, editor Roger Elkin, appears 3 times/year using poetry, articles about poetry and poets, and reviews. "1) ***Envoi*** does not subscribe to any one particular stable, school or style of contemporary poetry writing and has catholic tastes; 2) To be selected, **poetry must be sincere in its emotional and intellectual content, strongly integrated in form and contemporary in its subject matter—while a poem may be set in classical times or depend heavily on mythic archetypes, its overall 'texture' must have contemporary relevance;** 3) ***Envoi*** **requires writing that is daring in its subject matter and challenging in its expressive techniques— in short, work that takes risks with the form, the language and the reader;** 4) ***Envoi*** **is, however, still interested in traditional verse structures (the villanelle, pantoum, sonnet) but these must subscribe to the points listed in 2);** and 5) ***Envoi*** is looking for writing that sustains its creative strengths over a body of poems, or sequence. These criteria are prescriptive, rather than proscriptive; gates rather than hurdles. The over-riding concern is the creation of access for writers and readers to as wide a variety of contemporary poetry as space will allow." ***Envoi*** is 120 pgs., digest-sized, perfect-bound, professionally printed with matte card cover. "The emphasis is on giving space to writers so that the reader can begin to assess the cumulative strengths of any one author over a body of work. This means that competition for space is very keen. I handle between 250 and 300 poems per week and can only feature the equivalent of 100 poems three times a year!" Press run is 1,000 including 20 library subscriptions. Subscription: £10 or $25 ("preferably in bills rather than checks because of the high cost of conversion rates") or equivalent number of IRCs. Single copy: £3 ($7). **Sample: £2 ($5 bills). Submit no more than 6 poems, or a long poem of up to 6 sides; each poem on a separate page, bearing name and address; an accompanying SAE with 3 IRCs for return. Reports in 1-2 months. Pays 2 copies.** Roger Elkin says "***Envoi*** presents the work of any one poet by a group of poems, up to six. Space is given to long(er) poems and short sequences, or extracts from longer sequences. We have a First Publication Feature for writers who have not appeared in national publications previously, and each issue contains a 'reading' of a modern poem or an article on poetic style, as well as an Editors' Backlist which draws attention to poetry collections that readers may have overlooked in the past. The Review section has been expanded in length to feature more comprehensive articles. Each issue also features a competition with prizes totalling £200; prize-winning poems are published along with a full adjudicator's report. We also feature poems in collaboration, as well as translations."

‡THE EPIGRAMMATIST (II, IV-Form, translations), P.O. Box 828, Davis CA 95617-0828, e-mail 72330.3175@cis.com or epigram@aol.com, founded 1990, editor Nancy Winters. ***The Epigrammatist*** appears 3 times a year, in April, August and December. ("The August issue has traditionally been devoted to a single author by invitation.") **"We publish exclusively epigrams as understood by the tradition, which is not to say that innovation and variation are not permissible. Writers should be very familiar with the genre. There is no restriction as to subject. Translations, especially with original texts, are welcome."** They have recently published epigrams by Donald Hall, Janet Lewis, Carolyn Kizer and X.J. Kennedy. As a sample we selected this epigram, "Health Bulletin," by Patricia Wilcox:

Whatever you're chewing
Will prove your undoing.

The Epigrammatist is 24 pgs., 4¼×5½, offset and saddle-stitched with card cover. They receive approximately 500 submissions a year, accept about 25%. Press run is 300 for 80-100 subscribers of which 10-15 are libraries. Single copy: $3; subscription: $10 individuals, $15 institutions. **No previously published poems or simultaneous submissions. "Electronic submissions welcomed. Please, not more than 6-10 at a time without querying first."** Time between acceptance and publication is 6-12 months. **Send SASE for guidelines. Reports "depend on when submissions are made. I try to be reasonably prompt, but sometimes need to hold work for some weeks." Pays 5 copies. Rights remain with the writer.** Includes occasional quotes from collections of related interest. "Review copies may be sent, but will not necessarily be used."

EPOCH; BAXTER HATHAWAY PRIZE (III), 251 Goldwin Smith, Cornell University, Ithaca NY 14853, phone (607)255-3385, founded 1947, has a distinguished and long record of publishing **exceptionally fine poetry** and fiction. They have published work by such poets as Ashbery, Ammons, Eshleman, Wanda Coleman, Molly Peacock, Robert Vander Molen and Alvin Aubert. The magazine appears 3 times a year in a professionally printed, 6×9, flat-spined format with glossy color cover, 100 pgs., which goes to 1,000 subscribers. They use less than 1% of the many submissions they receive each year, have a 2- to 12-month backlog. Mostly lyric free verse, with emphasis on voice and varying content and length, appears here (and, occasionally, avant-garde or "open" styles)—some of it quite powerful. **Sample postpaid: $5. "We *don't read* unsolicited mss between April 15 and September 15." Reports in 2 months. Occasionally provides criticism on mss. Pays $5-10/page. Buys first serial rights.** The annual Baxter Hathaway prize of $1,000 is awarded for a long poem or, in alternate years, a novella. Write for details. Poetry published in ***Epoch*** has also been included in the 1992 and 1993 volumes of **The Best American Poetry**. The editor advises, "I think it's extremely important for poets to read other poets. I think it's also very important for poets to read the magazines that they want to publish in. Directories are not enough."

‡EQUILIBRIUM [10]; EAGLE PUBLISHING PRODUCTIONS (I, IV-Specialized), Box 162, Golden CO 80402, founded 1982, publisher Gary S. Eagle. **"We are not responsible for any mail being received without our $3 processing fee for all submissions.** We publish everything and I mean everything **dealing with equilibrium: balance, opposites, pairs, equality, opposite and equal reactions, etc." They are open to "all types, lengths and styles. Very lenient!" on themes given above.** The following sample is from "The Supposition of Opposition" by Caral Davis:

The sun rises, just to fall.
It's all for one and one for all.
It rains on the rich and on the poor,
The rich get richer and the poor get poorer.
Winter withers summer away, only to revive
another day.

The quarterly is striking in appearance, photocopied on pocket-edition 4¼ × 8½ sheets of various colors, about 70 pgs., saddle-stapled with glossy b&w paper cover, using many photos, drawings and cartoons throughout. One page is devoted to "Poems," each with an illustration. Circulation 10,000. Single copy: $4. **Sample: $4 plus 5 (regular) stamps. Backlog 1-12 months. "We prefer to hold in files until needed!" Editor sometimes comments on rejections. Reports in 6 months. Pays $15 and up plus 1 copy.** He says, "We prefer for poets to keep a photocopy and send us the original for our files. They may be handwritten if you wish for your poem printed as such. It is best for the poet (even youngsters) to include art, pictures, etc., too. Letter and queries arriving at our office will become the property of our company and material may and will be published 'as-is.' "

EQUINOX PRESS (V); BRITISH HAIKU SOCIETY; BLITHE SPIRIT (IV-Form/style, translations), Sinodun, Shalford, Braintree Essex CM7 5HN England, phone 0371-851097, founded 1990, c/o Mr. David Cobb. Equinox publishes poetry (mainly haiku and senryu), 1-2 volumes/year. **They have a waiting list at present and are unable to consider submissions.** BHS publishes a quarterly journal, ***Blithe Spirit***, a quarterly newsletter and other occasional publications (pamphlets, folios). ***Blithe Spirit* publishes mainly haiku, senryu and tanka sent in by society members,** but one section, "The Pathway," accepts **originals in any language plus a translation in one of English, French or German, and is open to non-members.** As a sample the Equinox editor selected this haiku (poet unidentified):

a cloudless sky
painters stretch ladders
to their farthest rungs

Staff reviews books of poetry. Send books for review consideration. The Museum of Haiku Literature, Tokyo, gives a quarterly best-of-issue award (£50). In addition, BHS administers the annual James W. Hackett Haiku Award (currently £60). Rules of entry are available annually in the spring. Send SASE (or SAE and IRC from outside England).

ESSENCE (V, IV-Women, ethnic), 1500 Broadway, New York NY 10036, phone (212)642-0649, founded 1970, poetry editor Angela Kinamore. "***Essence*** caters to the **needs of today's Black women." They publish poetry with humor or poetry dealing with love/romance, politics, religion, social issues or spirituality.** They have published poetry by Margaret Walker Alexander and Pinkie Gordon Lane. As a sample the editor selected these lines from "Ode to My Sons" by Mari Evans:

I am the vessel from whence you came
the lode filled with imaginings
aside from dreams my longing cannot
touch your reaching nor can I direct
your quest . . .

Essence is a mass-circulation consumer magazine with an upscale tone. It is 140 pgs., slick stock with full-color art, photos and ads. **They are currently not accepting poetry submissions.**

EUROPEAN JUDAISM (IV-Religious, ethnic), Kent House, Rutland Gardens, London SW7 1BX England, phone (071)584-2754, founded 1966, poetry editor Ruth Fainlight, is a "twice-yearly magazine with emphasis on European Jewish theology/philosophy/literature/history, with **some poetry in every issue. It should preferably be short and have some relevance to matters of Jewish interest."** They have recently published poetry by Linda Pastan, Jenny Joseph, Ted McNulty and Dannie Abse. As a sample the editor selected these lines from a poem by Micheline Wandor:

we scions of the wooden spoon
must spit the coal dust

and the tailor's chalk
and wipe
the black and the white
from the corners
of our mouths.

It is a glossy, elegant, 7×10, flat-spined magazine, rarely art or graphics, 68 pgs. They have a press run of 950, about 50% of which goes to subscribers (few libraries). Single copy: $9; subscription: $18. **Sample can be obtained gratis from Pergamon Press, Headington Hill Hall, Oxford, England 0X3 OBW. Pays 1 copy.**

EVENT (II, IV-Themes), Douglas College, P.O. Box 2503, New Westminster, British Columbia V3L 5B2 Canada, founded 1971, editor Dale Zieroth, is "a literary magazine publishing **high-quality contemporary poetry**, short stories and reviews. **All good-quality work is considered.**" They have published poetry by Tom Wayman, Elisabeth Harvor and Richard Lemm. These sample lines are from "Poetry" by Don Domanski:

is it a side street or a cat's jaw?
cerecloth or the body's flesh?
I've named it the heart's pillow
wind in a mirror   cloud-rope
lighthouse on the edge of a wound
beadwork   the mote's halo   wolf-ladder

Event appears three times a year. It is 128 pgs., 6×9, flat-spined, glossy-covered and finely printed with a circulation of 1,000 for 700 subscribers, of which 50 are libraries. **Sample postpaid: $6. They comment on some rejections. Reports in 3-4 months. Pays honorarium. Sometimes they have special thematic issues, such as: work, feminism, peace and war, coming of age.**

THE EVERGREEN CHRONICLES (IV-Gay/lesbian), P.O. Box 8939, Minneapolis MN 55408, is "a semiannual journal of arts and cultures dedicated to presenting the best of lesbian and gay literary and visual artists. **The artistry presented is not limited to 'gay' or 'lesbian' themes, but extends to life, in all its dimensions.**" Subscription: $15. **Sample: $7.95 plus $1 postage. "Send 4 copies of your work, up to 10 pgs. of poetry. Please include cover letter with short biographical paragraph describing yourself and your work. Deadlines: July 1 and January 1." Pays 1 copy. Acquires first-time rights.** Staff reviews books of poetry in 500 words, single format. Send books for review consideration.

‡EVIL DOG (II), P.O. Box 20181, Cincinnati OH 45220, founded 1992, editor-in-chief Steve Libbey, is a quarterly of strange, offbeat fiction, poetry, narrative art and photography. **They want "offbeat, grotesque, wild, weird, wonderful poetry. No mainstream, conventional poetry."** They have recently published poetry by Aralee Strange, Ken Ehrman, David Siders and Ashu Misingi. The editor says *ED* is 40-50 pgs., 7×8½, newsprint, matte cover. Press run is 500, mostly shelf sales. Single copy: $1; subscription: $10. **Sample postpaid: $2.25. "Please send no more than five poems at a time." No previously published poems; simultaneous submissions OK. Cover letter required.** Time between acceptance and publication is 1-3 months. **Send SASE for guidelines. Reports in 1-2 months. Pays 2 copies. Acquires first North American serial rights.** Reviews books of poetry. Poets may also send books for review consideration. The editor says, "***Evil Dog*** is drawn to the strange and offbeat. We are open to all formats of poetry, but the individual work must stand on its own. We welcome art along with poetry submissions."

EXIT 13 (IV-Specialized: geography/travel), % Tom Plante, 22 Oakwood Ct., Fanwood NJ 07023, phone (908)889-5298, founded 1987, editor Tom Plante, is a "contemporary poetry annual" using **poetry that is "short, to the point, with a sense of geography."** They have recently published poetry by Ruth Moon Kempher, Gerard Coulombe, Lenore Baeli Wang, Richard Mezo and Pat Hutchings. As a sample the editor selected these lines by Madeline Tiger:

Poetry is more important than anything in my life,
but I will forget this when I get in the car
and drive north and feel weary and think
about calling the roofer.

Exit 13, #6, was 60 pgs. Press run is 300. **Sample postpaid: $6, *payable to Tom Plante*. They accept simultaneous submissions and previously published poems. Reads submissions March 1 through November 30 only. Send SASE for guidelines. Reports in 3 months. Pays 1 copy. Acquires first-time and possible anthology rights.** Staff reviews books of poetry and magazines in a "Publications Received" column, using 25-30 words/listing. Send books for review consideration. The editor advises, "Write about what you know. Study geography. ***Exit 13*** looks for adventure. Every state and region is welcome. Send a snapshot of an 'Exit 13' road sign and receive a free copy of the issue in which it appears."

EXPEDITION PRESS (II, IV-Love, religious), #2306, 105 E. Walnut St., Kalamazoo MI 49007-5253, publisher Bruce W. White, publishes chapbooks of **love poems and religious poems. "I dislike violence."** He likes to see **"experimental, fresh new approaches, interesting spatial relationships, as well as quality artwork. We dislike political diatribes."** He has published poetry by J. Kline Hobbs, Jim DeWitt, Martin Cohen and C. VanAllsburg. As a sample the publisher selected this haiku of his own:

a tree by a lake.
the same tree in winter.
a harvest moon over the lake.

Submit ms of 20-30 pgs. and brief bio. Simultaneous submissions OK. Ms on cassette OK. Reports in 1 month. Sometimes sends prepublication galleys. Pays 100 copies. Bruce White provides "much" criticism on rejected mss.

EXPLORATIONS (II), UAS, 11120 Glacier Highway, Juneau AK 99801-8761, phone (907)789-4418, founded 1980, editor Professor Art Petersen, is the annual literary magazine of the University of Alaska, Southeast. **"The editors respond favorably to 'language really spoken by men and women.' Standard form and innovation are encouraged as well as appropriate and fresh aspects of imagery (allusion, metaphor, simile, symbol . . .)."** As a sample the editor selected these lines from "Seven come eleven" by Charles Bukowski:

I've never ever quite met
anybody
like myself—
living with deadly calm
inside this hurricane of hell.

Explorations is digest-sized, nicely printed, with front and back cover illustration in one color, saddle-stapled. The editors tend to go for smaller-length poems (with small line breaks for tension) and often print two on a page—mostly lyric free verse with a focus on voice. In 1994, they offered first prizes of $500 for poetry and prose and published the best of the submissions received. Each year a prominent poet or writer serves as judge (1994: James B. Hall). **An entry/reading fee is required: $2/poem (up to 5, 60 lines maximum), $4/story (up to 2, 3,000 words maximum); those paying reader/contest entry fees of $4 or more will receive a copy of the publication. Mss must be typed with name and address on the back. Simultaneous submissions OK. Submit entries with 3- or 4-line biography January through March. Mss are not returned. Send SASE for guidelines. Submissions are reported on in May, publication is annual, out in May or June. Pays 2 contributor copies. Acquires one-time rights.**

EXPLORER MAGAZINE; FLORY LITERARY FOUNDATION (I, IV-Inspirational, nature, love), P.O. Box 210, Notre Dame IN 46556, phone (219)277-3465, founded 1960, editor and publisher Raymond Flory, a semiannual magazine that contains **short inspirational, nature and love poetry** as well as prose. The editor wants **"poetry of all styles and types; should have an inspirational slant but not necessary. Short poems preferred—up to 16 lines—the shorter the better. Good 'family' type poetry always needed. Seasonal material also welcome. No real long poetry or long lines; no sexually explicit poetry or porno."** He has recently published poetry by Cheryl A. Lavender, Vladimir N. Orlov, Linda Koffel, Yolanda Gallardo and Wanda Sawatzky. As a sample the editor selected "White Dogwoods" by Jill Zimba-Dybka:

In the afternoon's
Tilted last light,
Springtime lace cascades
Down the dusky mountainside.
Twilight blossoms.

Explorer is 44 pgs., digest-sized, photocopied from typed copy in a variety of fonts (some of it dot-matrix) and saddle-stapled with card cover. Their most recent issue contains the work of 60 authors from 8 different countries. Circulation is 300. Subscription: $6/year. **Sample available for $3, guidelines for SASE. Subscribers vote for the poems or stories they like best and prizes are awarded; four prizes each issue: $25, $20, $15 and $10; first-prize winner in each issue receives a plaque along with the cash prize. In addition to the regular cash prizes, there is also an editor's choice award, the Joseph Flory Memorial Award, named after the editor's late father. Award is $10 and a plaque.** Recent winner: "The Postcard" by Kimberly Snow. **Writers should submit 3-4 poems, typed, camera-ready. Material must be previously unpublished; no simultaneous submissions. Reporting time is 1 week and time to publication 1-2 years. Pays 1 copy only to those appearing in the magazine for the first time.** The editor says, "Over 90% of the poets

CLOSE-UP

Curiosity and Intrigue Inspire Poetry

"night vision"

the girl fits her body in
to the space between the bed
and the wall. she is a stalk,
exhausted. she will do some
thing with this. she will
surround these bones with flesh.
she will cultivate night vision.
she will train her tongue
to lie still in her mouth and listen.
the girl slips into sleep.
her dream is red and raging.
she will remember
to build something human with it.

(from **The Book of Light**, 1993, reprinted by permission of Copper Canyon Press)

Photo by Michael Glaser, St. Mary's College of Maryland

Lucille Clifton

Although Lucille Clifton has been a published poet for 25 years, she emphasizes that she has been writing poetry for 40. It is a significant distinction, pointing to the intimate nature of her relationship to her craft and the fact that she has never been fueled by the goal of publication.

At an early age, this poet, who has since written eight books of poetry and twice been nominated for the Pulitzer Prize, experienced poetry as something that was powerful and accessible, more of a visceral expression than an intellectual one. "I had a mother who recited poetry a lot, and this mother didn't graduate from elementary school, mind you," she says.

At the core of Clifton's early love for poetry was language, which, she says, "I have always been able to feel almost – the possibilities, the mysteries, the music of it." But language, she notes, is only a part of poetry, "the circumstance" of its expression. For her its root lies in who she is and is inspired by curiosity and intrigue. "I think of poetry as something that comes from the human condition. I write poetry not because I know something but because I wonder something. It's a way to try to explore or discover or understand. I've always been able to see and feel connections. I think that as much as anything is what fuels my poetry."

Her first published poem appeared in ***Negro Digest***. It was an occasion, she says, which inspired neither greater nor lesser faith in herself as a poet. "The writing of poems mattered to me so much that I have always been more interested in writing a poem than in being a poet. I never thought about publishing first. I only thought about writing. It has never been a career choice for me. I certainly had never seen anyone like myself who was a published poet."

Clifton attended but did not graduate from college, did not take creative writing courses, and did not have a lot of time on her hands as the mother of six children who from oldest to youngest are only six and a half years apart. Nor has she ever been able to write in longhand. Yet she was both focused and determined. "My family was my first priority and then writing," she says. "Like anybody with children, I learned how to do several things at once" and learned to "work and do a lot of revision inside myself before ever sitting down at a typewriter."

The fact that she did not develop her talents in an academic "workshopping" atmosphere has actually been to her advantage because it has allowed her the freedom to develop faith in her intuition as much if not more than her intellect. It has also enabled her to develop a good feel for her own work, the importance of which she tries to impart to her graduate school students, many of whom refer to her as their "personal mentor."

She has taught at universities around the country and is currently Distinguished Professor of Humanities at St. Mary's College of Maryland. "In the classroom, I model a life of commitment, both an intellectual and passionate commitment, to something other than myself," she says. She tries to encourage her students to "take risks, come out of their heads so completely, pay attention, and think about all of the possibilities of language." Every so often she assigns them the exercise of taking a day during which "everything they look at, they should say, 'Isn't that odd?,' " illustrating that "metaphors are everywhere."

Clifton, who is also an award-winning children's book author, acquired an agent 25 years ago. Since that time her agent has represented her as both a writer of children's books and as a poet. As a result, Clifton's interaction with editors and publishers has been kept to a minimum. Although several of her poetry collections have been published by small presses specializing in poetry, including **quilting: poems 1987-1990** (BOA Editions, 1991) and **The Book of Light** (Copper Canyon Press, 1993), her work has also been published by large houses and university presses.

"Major publishers tend not to be particularly interested in what does not make a lot of money," she acknowledges, "and poetry doesn't. So they say things like, 'Well, we already have our poet.' " However, Clifton does feel poetry is flourishing with the multitude of small magazines publishing it. But "it's not as though there has ever been a golden time when everyone was reading poems," she says.

She advises those who want to get published to keep trying and warns that publishers' reactions to one's poetry should have nothing to do with whether one writes it or not. "Write poetry because you want to write poetry not because you want to be published. For one thing, that gets in the way of your work and you're thinking of yourself instead of the poem."

—Lauri Miller

submitting poetry to ***Explorer*** have not seen a copy of the magazine. Order a copy first—then submit. This will save poets stamps, frustration, etc. This should hold true for whatever market a writer is aiming for!"

‡**EXPRESSIONS (I, IV-Specialized: people with disabilities/ongoing health problems)**, P.O. Box 16294, St. Paul MN 55116-0294, phone (612)451-1208, fax (612)552-1209, founded 1993, editor Sefra Kobrin Pitzele, is a semiannual, subtitled "Literature and Art by People with Disabilities and Ongoing Health Problems," designed "to provide a place for talented people to be published." **They are open to any topic provided poetry is written by people with disabilities and/or ongoing health problems. "No limericks or corny 'rhymes.'"** They have recently published poetry by James Syndal, Tara Allen and Geoffrey Cook. As a sample the editor selected these lines from "Montana Wind" by Sheryl L. Nelms:

it rushes up
through dry grass
pushes the antelope
over the ridge

drops off
the limestone cliff . . .

Expressions is 56-72 pgs., 5½×8½, perfect-bound with 60 lb. glossy card cover. They publish about 25% of the poetry received. Press run is 650 for 120 subscribers. Subscription: $10 US, $15 foreign and institutions. **Sample postpaid: $6. Submit each poem with $2 reading fee. "$10 gets submitter a one-year subscription." Previously published poems and simultaneous submissions OK. Cover letter with 4- to 5-line bio and statement of ownership required. Do not submit mss from December 15 to January 15.** "Five others read each submission and grade it—independently—from 1 to 5. Most 5's are published." **Often comments on rejections. Send SASE for guidelines. Reports in 2-4 months. Pays 2 copies. Acquires one-time rights.** "At the end of each issue, we print book reviews appropriate to our audience. We only review informational books on disability or illness." However, they are open to unsolicited reviews of such materials.

EXPRESSIONS FORUM REVIEW (I), 2837 Blue Spruce Lane, Wheaton MD 20906, founded 1991, is a semiannual of poetry, **"any kind, any form, 20 lines maximum. No sex-related matters, no obscenity." They are currently looking to receive more traditional forms of poetry.** Single copy: $3; subscription: $12. **Submit 1-4 poems with $3 reading fee. Previously published poems and simultaneous submissions OK. Typewritten poems preferred; do not send original copies. Seldom comments on rejections. Send SASE for guidelines. Reports in 3 months. Pays 1 copy.** Open to unsolicited reviews. Poets may also send books for review consideration. Reading fee includes entry into spring and fall poetry contests. 1st prize: $100; 2nd: $50; 3rd: $25 (and 25 honorable mentions). The editor says, "Speak from the heart and soul."

EXQUISITE CORPSE (II), P.O. Box 25051, Baton Rouge LA 70894, founded 1983, editor Andrei Codrescu (whom you can often hear in commentary segments of "All Things Considered," The National Public Radio news program). This curious and delightful monthly ($20/year), when you unfold it, is 6″ wide and 16″ long, 20 pgs., saddle-stapled, professionally printed in 2 columns on quality stock. The flavor of Codrescu's comments (and some clues about your prospects in submitting here) may be judged by this note: "A while ago, alarmed by the number of poems aimed at the office—a number only the currency inflation and Big Macs can hold candles to—we issued an edict against them. Still they came, and some even came live. They came in the mail and under the door. We have no poetry insurance. If we are found one day smothered under photocopy paper, who will pay for the burial? The ***Corpse*** wants a jazz funeral. Rejections make poets happy. Having, in many cases, made their poems out of original, primal, momentary rejections, the rejection of these rejections affirms the beings forced to such deviousness." He has published poetry by Carol Bergé, Charles Plymell, Lawrence Ferlinghetti, Alice Notley and many others. You'll find all styles and forms here, even short light verse. Most examples are freestyle, leaning toward expressionism (effective use of symbol), and accessible, too. Translations also seem welcome. **Payment: "Zilch/Nada." You take your chances inserting work into this wit machine. As of 1990 this is their policy: ". . . we are abolishing the SASE-based privacy system . . . Your submissions will be answered directly in the pages of our publication. Look for your name and for our response to your work in the next *Corpse*. We will continue returning your submissions by SASE if you wish, but as to what we think of your *écriture*, please check 'Body Bag,' our new editorial column. Please rest assured that your work will receive the same malevolently passionate attention as before. Only now we are going to do it in public."** Here's an example: "We were excited by 'The Wind Got Excited' until the puppy-hero got too excited and leapt off the 13th floor. That was cruel . . ." Comments you want, comments you get! Poetry published in this magazine has been included in **The Best American Poetry 1992.**

FABER AND FABER, INC. (V), 50 Cross St., Winchester MA 01890, phone (617)721-1427, editor Betsy Uhrig, has a distinguished list of poetry publications but is **not accepting mss.**

FAMILY EARTH (I, IV-Ecology), 129 W. Lincoln Ave., Gettysburg PA 17325, managing editor Denise Weldon-Siviy, founded 1990, is a family-oriented annual focusing on the environment, using poetry that **"must deal in some way with the environment. Shorter poems, 10-30 lines, are preferred. Cannot consider material over 40 lines due to page layout. All forms and styles are acceptable. No laments abusive to working mothers. I am still receiving a high percentage of negative—world is awful will end any minute—poetry. Anything with a positive attitude has a good chance."** As a sample the editor selected these lines from "Rebirth" by Tippi N. Blevins:

Closer,
You can see the truth:
Green shoots
Pushing through
The burns.

Life is strongest
After the fire.

FE is 28 pgs., digest-sized, photocopied, with colored paper cover. Press run is 300 for 150 subscriptions, 150 shelf sales. They accept about 25% of 100 submissions received/year. Subscription: $3/year. **Sample postpaid: $2.50. Editor always comments on rejections. Publishes theme issues. "1995 will be an all-poetry edition." Send SASE for guidelines. Reports in 2 weeks. Pays $1-3/poem on acceptance plus 1 copy. Buys one-time rights.** Reviews books of poetry if they deal with the environment, conservation, etc. Open to unsolicited reviews. Poets may also send related books for review consideration.

FARMER'S MARKET; MIDWEST FARMER'S MARKET, INC. (II), P.O. Box 1272, Galesburg IL 61402, founded 1981, editors Jean C. Lee, John Hughes, Lisa Ress, Tracy Rose and Romayne Rubinas, is a biannual seeking **poems that are "tightly structured, with concrete imagery, reflective of the clarity, depth and strength of Midwestern life. Not interested in highly abstract work or light verse."** They have recently published poetry by Larry Starzec, Melanie Richards, Philip Dacey, Edward C. Lynskey and Marjorie Maddox. As a sample, they offer these lines from "Everything Changes to Beauty" by Kathryn Burt Winogrod:

The clear skimming line of my father's fishing pole
rides its twinned self off the brightening pond,
a lifting rain of light returning to light,
and beneath, where fish round their mouths
like moons to swallow it, the lure
tiny and shimmering, make-believe.

FM is digest-sized, 100-200 pgs., perfect-bound with card cover, handsomely printed with graphics and photos. The poems are almost always accessible . . . clear, crafted lyric free verse. All in all, this is an enjoyable read. Circulation 700 for 200 subscribers, of which 25 are libraries. They receive about 1,500 submissions/year, of which they use 50-60, have a 6-month backlog. **Sample: $4.50 plus $1 postage and handling. Submit up to 10 pages, typed. Would rather not have simultaneous submissions. Comments on rejections, "only if we think the work is good." Reports in 6-8 weeks (summer replies take longer). Pays 2 copies. Acquires one-time rights.** This publication has received numerous Illinois Arts Council Literary Awards.

FARRAR, STRAUS & GIROUX/BOOKS FOR YOUNG READERS (II, IV-Children), 19 Union Square W., New York NY 10003, phone (212)741-6900, founded 1946, contact Editorial Dept./Books for Young Readers. They publish one book of children's poetry "every once in awhile," in both hardcover and paperback editions. **They are open to book-length submissions of children's poetry only.** They have published collections of poetry by Valerie Worth and Deborah Chandra. As a sample the editor selected "Suspense" from Chandra's book **Balloons**:

Wide-eyed
the sunflowers
stare and catch their summer
breath, while I pause, holding basket
and shears.

Query first with sample poems and cover letter with brief bio and publication credits. Poems previously published in magazines and simultaneous submissions OK. Seldom comments on rejections. Send SASE for reply. Replies to queries in 1-2 months, to mss in 1-4 months. "We pay an advance against royalties; the amount depends on whether or not the poems are illustrated, etc." Also pays 10 author's copies.

FAT TUESDAY (II), RD2 Box 4220, Manada Gap Rd., Grantville PA 17028, founded 1981, poetry editors F.M. Cotolo, Kristen von Oehrke, B. Lyle Tabor, Thom Savion and Lionel Stevroid, is an annual which calls itself "**a Mardi Gras of literary and visual treats featuring many voices, singing, shouting, sighing and shining, expressing the relevant to irreverent.** On Fat Tuesday (the Tuesday before Ash Wednesday, when Lent begins) the editors hold The Fat Tuesday Symposium. In over ten years no one has shown up." They want **"prose poems, poems of irreverence, gems from the gut. Usually shorter, hit-the-mark, personal stuff inseparable from the voice of the artist. Form doesn't matter. Also particularly interested in hard-hitting 'autofiction.'"** They have published poetry by Mark Cramer, Mary Lee Gowland, Chuck Taylor, Patrick Kelly, Charles Bukowski, Gerald Locklin and Kilgore Rimpdu. As a sample they offer these lines by John Quinnett:

It is enough to be alive,
To be here drinking this cheap red wine
While the chili simmers on the stove
& the refrigerator hums deep into the night.

The digest-sized magazine is typeset (large type, heavy paper), 36-50 pgs., saddle-stapled, card covers, (sometimes magazine-sized, unbound) with cartoons, art and ads. Circulation 200 with 20-25 pgs. of poetry in each issue. They receive hundreds of submissions each year, use 3-5%, have a 3- to 5- month backlog. **Sample postpaid: $5. No previously published material. "Handwritten OK; we'll read anything." Reads submissions August 1 through December 22. Reports in 1-2 weeks. Pays 1 copy. Rights revert to author after publication.** The editors say, "Our tip for authors is simply to be themselves. Poets should use their own voice to be heard. Publishing poetry is as lonely as writing it. We have no idea about current trends, and care less. We encourage all to buy a sample issue to see what they have which best fits our style and format, and also to help support the continuation of our publication. We rely on no other means but sales to subsidize our magazine, and writers should be sensitive to this hard fact which burdens many small presses."

FEELINGS: AMERICA'S BEAUTIFUL POETRY MAGAZINE; ANDERIE POETRY PRESS; QUARTERLY EDITOR'S CHOICE AWARDS (I, II), P.O. Box 85, Easton PA 18044-0085, phone (610)559-9287, founded 1989, editors Carl and Carole Heffley, a quarterly magazine, uses **"high-quality (free, blank or rhymed), understandable poems on any aspect of life, no more than 25 lines. Likes traditional as well as hard-biting poetry."** They have recently published poetry by Ronald G. Ribble, Esther Palmenteri and Paul A. Eckhardt. As a sample here are the opening lines from "Borrowed Intrigue" by Terry Fitterer:

A stolen moment has no right
to choose a preference – day or night,
it's built from seconds, here or there,
and races by without a care . . .
rewards are few and far too slight.

Feelings is magazine-sized, saddle-stapled with heavy paper cover, professionally printed on lightweight paper, using "photography appropriate to the season or subject." Subscription: $24. **Sample postpaid: $6.50. Cover letter with background, credits ("something about the writer") required with submissions. Send SASE for guidelines. Reports in 6 weeks. Pays $10 for 3 Editor's Choice Awards in each issue. Acquires first rights.** Also runs several contests throughout the year with prizes ranging from $10 to $50. **"We publish chapbooks, info/price list upon request with SASE."** Mss on "how-to" write, publish poetry welcome. Payment for articles varies.

FEH! A JOURNAL OF ODIOUS POETRY (IV-Humor), #603, 147 Second Ave., New York NY 10003-5701, founded 1986, editor Morgana Malatesta, appears twice a year, using **"silliness and nonsense, but *good* silliness and nonsense. We want well-executed, humorous verse *without* sexist or racist themes!"** They have published poetry by Jerm Boor and Vassar W. Smith. As a sample the editor selected these lines by Ferdinand "Skeet" Giaclepousse:

I believe in God and Bigfoot
and the right to worship as I please.
I've seen angels, demons and the Virgin Mama
in the midst of my D.T.'s

It is 36 pgs., 8½ × 11, with photocopied paper cover. Their press run is 200 with about 35 subscriptions, and sales through bookstores. **Sample postpaid: $2. Considers simultaneous submissions and previously published poems. Editor sometimes comments on rejections, if asked. Send SASE for guidelines. Reports within 6 weeks. Pays 1 copy. Acquires one-time rights.**

FEMINIST STUDIES (IV-Women), %Women's Studies Program, University of Maryland, College Park MD 20742, founded 1969, poetry editor Alicia Ostriker, **"welcomes a variety of work that focuses on women's experience, on gender as a category of analysis, and that furthers feminist theory and consciousness."** They have published poetry by Janice Mirikitani, Paula Gunn Allen, Cherrie Moraga,

Audre Lorde, Judith Small, Milana Marsenich, Lynda Schraufnagel, Valerie Fox and Diane Glancy. The elegantly-printed, flat-spined, 250-page paperback appears 3 times a year in an edition of 8,000, goes to 7,000 subscribers, of which 1,500 are libraries. There are **4-10 pgs. of poetry in each issue. Sample postpaid: $10. Manuscripts are reviewed twice a year, in May and December. Deadlines are May 1 and December 1. Publishes theme issues. Authors will receive notice of the board's decision by June 30 and January 30. Always sends prepublication galleys. No pay.** Commissions reviews of books of poetry. Poets may send books to Claire G. Moses for review consideration.

THE FIDDLEHEAD (II, IV-Regional, students), Campus House, University of New Brunswick, P.O. Box 4400, Fredericton, New Brunswick E3B 5A3 Canada, founded 1945, poetry editors Robert Gibbs, Robert Hawkes and Don MacKay. From its beginning in 1945 as a local little magazine devoted mainly to student writers, **the magazine retains an interest in poets of the Atlantic region and in young poets** but prints poetry from everywhere. It is **open to good work of every kind, looking always for vitality, freshness and surprise.** Among the poets whose work they have recently published are Eric Ormsby, Patrick Moran and Coral Hull. As a sample, the editor chose a stanza by Carole Chambers:

Corallina, Iridaea, Rhodomela,
the seaweed are called
beautiful mermaid names:
Zostera, Constantinea, Leathesia.
Dulse is their word
for skin touching,
floccosa for scale tails entwining.
Kissing under water is fucus, and
ulva the word for congress
with the sea lions.

The Fiddlehead is a handsomely printed, 6 × 9, flat-spined paperback (120 pgs.) with b&w graphics, colored cover, paintings by New Brunswick artists. Circulation is 1,000. Subscription: $18/year plus $4 postage (US). **Sample: $7 (US). They use less than 10% of submissions. Reporting time 2-6 months, backlog 6-18 months. Pay is $10-12/printed page.** Reviews books by Canadian authors only.

FIELD; FIELD TRANSLATION SERIES; CONTEMPORARY AMERICAN POETRY SERIES; O.C. PRESS (II, IV-Translations), Rice Hall, Oberlin College, Oberlin OH 44074, phone (216)775-8408, founded 1969, editors Stuart Friebert and David Young, is a literary journal appearing twice a year with "emphasis on poetry, translations and essays by poets." They want the **"best possible" poetry.** They have published poetry by Thylias Moss, Seamus Heaney, Charles Simic and Sharon Olds. The handsomely printed digest-sized journal is flat-spined, has 100 pgs., rag stock with glossy card color cover. Although most poems fall under the lyrical free verse category, you'll find narratives and formal work here on occasion, much of it sensual, visually appealing and resonant. Circulation 2,500, with 800 library subscriptions. Subscription: $12 a year, $20 for 2 years. **Sample postpaid: $6. Reports in 2 weeks, has a 3- to 6-month backlog. Always sends prepublication galleys. Pays $20-30/page plus 2 copies.** They publish books of translations in the Field Translation Series, averaging 150 pgs., flat-spined and hardcover editions. **Query regarding translations. Pays 7½-10% royalties with some advance and 10 author's copies.** They have also inaugurated a Contemporary American Poetry Series with the publication of a collection of new and selected poems by Dennis Schmitz. This series is by invitation only. Write for catalog to buy samples. Work published in ***Field*** has also been included in the 1992, 1993 and 1994 volumes of **The Best American Poetry.** Stuart Friebert says they would like to see more poetry from "minority" poets "of any and all cultures."

FIGHTING WOMAN NEWS (IV-Women, specialized: martial arts), 6741 Tung Ave. W., Theodore AL 36582, founded 1975, poetry editor Debra Pettis, provides "a communications medium for **women in martial arts, self-defense, combative sports."** They want **poetry "relevant to our subject matter and nothing else."** They have published poetry by Dana Ridgeway. As a sample the editor selected these lines from "Practice" by Cathy Drinkwater Better:

become
the moment
concentrate
be one
with the impact
timing
is all

Fighting Woman News appears quarterly in a magazine-sized, saddle-stapled format, 24 pgs. or more, finely printed, with graphics and b&w photos. Circulation 3,500. **Sample postpaid: $3.50, "and if you say you're a poet, we'll be sure to send a sample with poetry in it." Uses only 1 or 2 poems in each issue. "If your poem *really* requires an audience of martial artists to be appreci-**

ated, then send it." Simultaneous submissions OK. Cover letter required. Poets should include "who they are and possibly why submitting to *FWN*." Replies "ASAP." Sometimes sends prepublication galleys. Pays copies. Acquires one-time rights. Open to unsolicited reviews. Poets may also send books for review consideration. "Because our field is so specialized, most interested women subscribe. It is not a requirement for publication, but **we seldom publish a nonsubscriber**." The editor advises, "Read first; write later. To guarantee publication of your poem(s), submit a hard-core martial arts nonfiction article. Those are what we really need! Fighters who are also writers can have **priority access to our very limited poetry space by doing articles**. Please do not send any poems if you have not read any issues of *FWN*."

THE FIGURES (V), 5 Castle Hill Ave., Great Barrington MA 01230-1552, phone (413)528-2552, founded 1975, publisher/editor Geoffrey Young, is a small press publishing poetry and fiction. They have published poetry by Lyn Hejinian, Clark Coolidge, Ron Padgett and Christopher Dewdney. **They pay 10% of press run. However, they currently do not accept unsolicited poetry.**

‡FILLING STATION (II), P.O. Box 22135, Bankers Hall, Calgary, Alberta T2P 4J5 Canada, founded 1993, appears 3 times/year (January, May and September). ***Filling Station*** is a magazine of contemporary writing featuring poetry, fiction, interviews, reviews and other literary news. **"We are looking for all forms of contemporary writing. No specific objections to any style."** They have recently published poetry by George Bowering, Fred Wah, Nicole Markatic and Su Croll and say, "as an editorial collective, to pick one specific example goes against our objective of representing many different voices." *FS* is 48 pgs., 8½×11, saddle-stapled with card cover and includes photos, artwork and ads. They receive about 100 submissions for each issue, accept approximately 10%. Press run is 500 for 50 subscribers, 150 shelf sales. Subscription: $15/1 year, $25/2 years. **Sample postpaid: $6. Submit typed poems with name and address on each page. No previously published poems; simultaneous submissions OK. Cover letter required. Deadlines are November 15, March 15 and July 15. Seldom comments on rejections. Send SASE for guidelines. Reports in 3 months. Pays 2 copies. Acquires first North American and second reprint rights.** Reviews books of poetry in both single and multi-book format. Open to unsolicited reviews. Poets may also send books for review consideration. The magazine sponsors a contest each issue for short poetry/fiction centered around a specific theme, $2 entry fee, $100 in cash and prizes. Send SASE (or SAE and IRC if outside Canada) for latest contest information. Here's what the collective has to say about ***Filling Station*** and the philosophy behind this publication: "You stop between these 'fixed' points on the map to get an injection of something new, something fresh that's going to get you from point to point. . . . We want to be a kind of connection between polarities: a link. We'll publish any poem or story that offers a challenge: to the mind, to the page, to writers and readers."

FINE MADNESS (II), P.O. Box 31138, Seattle WA 98103-1138, founded 1982, president Louis Bergsagel. ***Fine Madness*** is a biannual magazine. **They want "contemporary poetry of any form and subject. We look for highest quality of thought, language and imagery. We look for the mark of the individual: unique ideas and presentation; careful, humorous, sympathetic. No careless poetry, greeting card poetry, poetry that 10,000 other people could have written."** They have published poetry by Tess Gallagher, David Young and Caroline Knox. As a sample the editor selected these lines from "Natural History of an Idea" by Melinda Mueller:

Ice is over with quickly, while a knife, say, keeps happening,
long after skin has healed. And the mind that thinks this—
this is strangely consoling—is another event among the rest.

Not that that's the end of it. There's the phone
that rings, the avalanche of lights on that suburban hill
across the lake, the incessant evening . . .

Fine Madness is 64 pgs., digest-sized, perfect-bound, offset with color card cover. Their press run is 800 for 100 subscriptions of which 10 are libraries. They accept about 40 of 1,000 poems received. Subscription: $9. **Sample postpaid: $4. Guidelines available for SASE. Submit 3-5 poems, preferably originals, not photocopy, 1 poem/page. No previously published poems or simultaneous submissions. Reports in 2-3 months. Pays 1 copy plus subscription.** Open to unsolicited reviews. Poets may also send books for review consideration to John Malek. They give 2 annual awards to editors' choice of $50 each. ***Fine Madness*** has had poetry selected for inclusion in the 1992, 1993 and 1994 volumes of **The Best American Poetry**. Coeditor Sean Bentley says, "If you don't read poetry, don't send us any."

FIREBRAND BOOKS (IV-Feminist, lesbian, ethnic), 141 The Commons, Ithaca NY 14850, phone (607)272-0000, founded 1984, editor and publisher Nancy K. Bereano, "is a **feminist and lesbian** publishing company committed to producing quality work in multiple genres by ethnically diverse women." They publish both quality trade paperbacks and hardbacks. As a sample, here is a stanza of a sestina, "great expectations," from the book **Living As A Lesbian** by Cheryl Clarke:

dreaming the encounter intense as engines
first me then you oh what a night
of rapture and risk and dolphin
acrobatics after years of intend-
ing to find my lesbian sources in the window
of longing wide open in me

The book is 94 pgs., flat-spined, elegantly printed on heavy stock with a glossy color card cover, a photo of the author on the back, $7.95. **Simultaneous submissions acceptable with notification. Replies to queries within 2 weeks, to mss within one month. Pays royalties.** Send for catalog to buy samples.

FIREWEED: A FEMINIST QUARTERLY (IV-Women), P.O. Box 279, Station B, Toronto, Ontario M5T 2W2 Canada, phone (416)504-1339, founded 1978, edited by the Fireweed Collective, is a feminist journal of writing, politics, art and culture that **"especially welcomes contributions by women of color, working-class women, native women, lesbians and women with disabilities."** As a sample we selected the opening lines of "These Military Men" by Joy Hewitt Mann:

My husband was
a military man.
Dinner
5:30
sharp.
No give.   No take.

It is 88 pgs., 6¾ × 9¾, flat-spined, with 3- or 4-color cover. Poems tend to be freestyle lyrics leaning toward avant-garde, with some room for rhymed verse and stanza patterns. Press run is 2,000. Subscription: $18 individuals, $27 institutions in Canada, $24 individuals, $36 institutions in US. **Sample postpaid: $6 in Canada, $7 in US. Simultaneous submissions OK. Editor comments on submissions "occasionally." Reports in 6-9 months. "Please include SAE and IRC for reply." Pays $30 for first printed page, $5-10 for remaining full or partial printed page.**

FIREWEED: POETRY OF WESTERN OREGON (IV-Regional), 1330 E. 25th Ave., Eugene OR 97403, founded 1989, is a quarterly publishing the work of **poets living in Western Oregon or having close connections to the region. However, poems need not be regional in subject; any theme, subject, length or form is acceptable.** They have published poetry by Vern Rutsala, Barbara Drake, Lisa Steinmann and Lex Runciman. As a sample they selected these lines from "Fault" by Barbara La Morticella:

Quick hold me;
for once, let me hold you.

Our children's suitcases are packed,
and even the hills move in waves.

Fireweed is 44 pgs., digest-sized, laser printed and saddle-stapled with card cover. "We receive several hundred poems and publish about ¼ or ⅕ of them." Press run is 250 for 180 subscribers of which 20 are libraries, 25 shelf sales. Subscription: $10. **Sample postpaid: $2.50. No previously published poems; simultaneous submissions OK. Cover letter with brief bio required. Often comments on rejections. They do not publish guidelines for poets but will answer inquiries with SASE. Reports in 2-4 months. Pays 1 copy. Acquires first North American serial rights.** Reviews books of poetry by Oregon poets in 500-750 words, single format. Open to unsolicited reviews. Oregon poets may also send books for review consideration. ***Fireweed*** received a 1992 publisher's grant from the Oregon Institute of Literary Awards. They add, "We occasionally have special issues organized by theme, compiled by a guest editor or focused on newcomers to ***Fireweed***. Support your local magazines by sending work and buying subscriptions! Submit to the smaller little publications *first*!"

‡1ST & HOPE (I), P.O. Box 36A27, Los Angeles CA 90036, founded 1994 (first issue December 1994 or January 1995), editor Mike Bucell, is an annual designed to publish "the highest quality work we receive. It is also our wish to publish new and emerging talent that gets 'crowded out' of the 'prestige' markets. **We want poetry that is crisp, concise, vivid and carefully, thoughtfully written. Any subject and style is welcomed. Poets should send us the poems that made them sweat blood as they worked on them. Poems should be neither too obscure nor too obvious. If the poem has to be explained in the cover letter, it probably shouldn't be sent.** The editor says ***1st & hope*** will be 60-80 pgs., 6 × 9, professionally printed from laser-printed camera-ready copy and perfect-bound. Estimated press run is 500. **Previously published poems OK, "provided the author retains rights and affirms this in his or her cover letter to us." No simultaneous submissions. Cover letter required. Often comments on rejections. Send SASE for guidelines. Reports in 1-2 months. Pays 1 copy/poem published. Acquires first or one-time rights.** The editor says, "We read year-round. However, response time may be longer in November and December as we will be preparing the current issue for press during those months. Also, it will not be possible for us to return material if the poet provides insufficient postage."

FIRST HAND (IV-Gay, subscribers), Box 1314, Teaneck NJ 07666, phone (201)836-9177, founded 1980, poetry editor Bob Harris, is a **"gay erotic publication written mostly by its readers."** The digest-sized monthly has a circulation of 70,000 with 3,000 subscribers of which 3 are libraries and uses 1-2 pgs. of poetry in each issue. They have published poetry by Michael Swift and Robert Patrick. As a sample the editor selected these lines from "To a Model" by Karl Tierney:

I assure you, I mean no
disrespect when I discover,
beyond sex and half asleep,
you deflate to only half the monster
and will be that much easier
to battle out the door at dawn.

Submit poems no longer than 1 typed page. No queries. Editor Bob Harris sometimes comments on rejected mss. Reports in 6 weeks. Pays $25/poem. Reviews books of poetry. The editor advises, "Make sure what you're writing about is obvious to future readers. **Poems need not be explicitly sexual, but must deal overtly with gay situations and subject matter."**

FIRST TIME; NATIONAL HASTINGS POETRY COMPETITION (I, II), Burdett Cottage, 4 Burdett Place, George St., Hastings, East Sussex TN34 3ED England, phone 0424-428855, founded 1981, editor Josephine Austin, who says the biannual magazine is **open to "all kinds of poetry—our magazine goes right across the board—which is why it is one of the most popular in Great Britain."** The following lines are from "Why a Poet?" by R.M. Griffiths:

Of all types of people
and all their differences in depth,
the poet is the deepest,
Or is it just the most vacuous?

The digest-sized magazine, 24 pgs., saddle-stapled, contains several poems on each page, in a variety of small type styles, on lightweight stock, b&w photographs of editor and 1 author, glossy one-color card cover. Subscription: £5. **Sample: £1 plus postage. "Please send dollars." Poets should send 10 poems. Poems submitted must not exceed 30 lines, must not have been published elsewhere, and must have name and address of poet on each. Cover letter required. Maximum time to publication is 2 months. "Although we can no longer offer a free copy as payment, we can offer one at a discounted price of £1.50." The annual National Hastings Poetry Competition for poets 18 and older offers awards of £100, £50 and £50, £1/poem entry fee.** Editor Josephine Austin has received The Dorothy Tutin Award "for services to poetry." She advises, "Keep on 'pushing your poetry.' If one editor rejects you then study the market and decide which is the correct one for you. Try to type your own manuscripts as longhand is difficult to read and doesn't give a professional impression. Always date your poetry — ©1995 and sign it. Follow your way of writing, don't be a pale imitation of someone else—sooner or later styles change and you will either catch up or be ahead."

FISHDRUM (II), 626 Kathryn Ave., Santa Fe NM 87501, founded 1988, editor Robert Winson, women's and Brooklyn editor Suzi Winson, #2D, 40 Prospect Park W., Brooklyn NY 11215, is a literary magazine appearing 2-4 times a year. **"I love West Coast poetry, the exuberant, talky, often elliptical and abstract 'continuous nerve movie' that follows the working of the mind and has a relationship to the world and the reader. Philip Whalen's work, for example, and much of** Calafia, The California Poetry, **edited by Ishmael Reed. Also magical-tribal-incantatory poems, exemplified by the future/primitive** Technicians of the Sacred, **ed. Rothenberg.** ***FishDrum*** **has a soft spot for schmoozy, emotional, imagistic stuff. Literate, personal material that sings and surprises, OK?"** They have published poetry by Philip Whalen, Joy Harjo, Arthur Sze, Nathaniel Tarn, Alice Notley, John Brandi, Steve Richmond, Jessica Hagedorn, Leo Romero and Leslie Scalapino. As a sample the editor selected these lines from "Glossolalia" by Kate Bremer:

Everywhere I look I see amino acids on the ground.
When I close my eyes, I see molecules and pieces of Sanskrit:
I hear syllables and alphabets.

FD is 80 pgs., perfect-bound, professionally printed. "Of 300 or so unsolicited submissions last year, accepted fewer than twenty." Press run is 500 for 100 subscribers of which 10 are libraries, 400 shelf sales. Subscription: $20 for 4 issues. **Sample postpaid: $5. Publishes theme issues. Reports quickly. Sometimes sends prepublication galleys. Pays 2 copies. In addition, contributors may purchase advance copies at $3 each. Acquires first serial rights.** Reviews books or chapbooks of poetry in long essays and/or capsule reviews. Open to unsolicited reviews. Poets may also send books for review consideration. Robert Winson adds, **"We're looking for New Mexico authors,** also prose: fiction, essays, what-have-you, and artwork, scores, cartoons, etc.—

just send it along. **We are also interested in poetry, prose and translations concerning the practice of Zen. We publish chapbooks, but solicit these from our authors.** '*FishDrum Magazine* On The Air' is a monthly radio show that plays reasonably high audio quality cassettes, live and studio, submitted to us, and provides playlists. We will interview some authors as they come through town—drop us a note."

5 AM (III), 1109 Milton Ave., Pittsburgh PA 15218, founded 1987, editors Patricia Dobler, Lynn Emanuel, Ed Ochester and Judith Vollmer, is a poetry publication that appears twice a year. They are **open in regard to form, length, subject matter and style. However, they do not want poetry that is "religious or naive rhymes."** They have published poetry by Rita Dove, Elton Glaser, Alicia Ostriker and Alberto Rios. The editors describe ***5 AM*** as a 24-page, offset tabloid. They receive about 3,000 poems a year, use approximately 2%. Press run is 1,000 for 550 subscribers of which 22 are libraries, about 300 shelf sales. Subscription: $10 for 4 issues. **Sample postpaid: $3. No previously published poems or simultaneous submissions. Each editor chooses 25% of the magazine. Seldom comments on rejections. Reports within 3 months. Pays 2 copies. Acquires first rights.**

FIVE FINGERS REVIEW; FIVE FINGERS PRESS (III, IV-Themes, translations), P.O. Box 15426, San Francisco CA 94115, founded 1984, editors John High, Thoreau Lovell and Michelle Murphy, is a literary biannual publishing **"diverse, innovative and challenging writing by writers of various aesthetics."** Some of the better-known poets they have published are Kathleen Fraser, John Yau, Rosmarie Waldrop and Leslie Scalapino. As a sample the editors selected these lines from "When She Was Dying" by Fanny Howe:

On the green seat heading everyone
Home, time was credible but rupture now
The problem to figure out.

Five Fingers Review is 150 pgs., 6×9, nicely printed on buff stock, flat-spined with one-color glossy card cover. Circulation is 1,000 copies, 25% of which go to libraries. Single copy: $9; subscription: $15/year. **Sample postpaid: $7. Simultaneous submissions OK. Reporting time is 3-6 months and time to publication is 4 months. Pay is 2 copies.** Open to unsolicited reviews. Poets may also send books for review consideration. Five Fingers Press also publishes a perfect-bound book series. The advice of the editors is: "Pick up a copy of the magazine. Be committed to craft and to looking at the world in fresh, surprising ways."

FLIPSIDE (II), Dixon Hall, California University of Pennsylvania, California PA 15419, founded 1987, poetry editor L.A. Smith, is a literary tabloid appearing twice a year **using poetry. "Sentimentality is forbidden."** They have published poetry by Charles Bukowski and Arthur Winfield Knight. As a sample the editor selected the poem "Mother Lover" by Michael Bagamery:

Make-up on that face
Like rubble.
Ivy won't run up a building
Unless it stands.

The tabloid is 48 pgs., professionally printed. Press run is 5,000, distributed free to the public, libraries, writing schools, colleges, advertisers, poets, etc. They accept less than 5% of hundreds of poems submitted. **Sample postpaid: $2. Send SASE for guidelines. Reports in 2 months. Pays as many copies as you want.**

THE FLORIDA REVIEW (II), Dept. of English, University of Central Florida, Orlando FL 32816, phone (407)823-2038, founded 1972, editor Russ Kesler, is a "literary biannual with emphasis on short fiction and poetry." They want **"poems filled with real things, real people and emotions, poems that might conceivably advance our knowledge of the human heart."** They have published poetry by Knute Skinner, Elton Glaser and Walter McDonald. It is 128 pgs., flat-spined, professionally printed, with glossy card cover. Press run is 1,000 for 400 subscribers of which 50 are libraries, 150 shelf sales. **Sample postpaid: $4.50. Submit no more than 6 poems. Simultaneous submissions OK. Editor comments on submissions "occasionally." Send SASE for guidelines. Reports in 1-3 months. Always sends prepublication galleys. Pays 3 copies, small honorarium occasionally available. Acquires all rights. Returns rights "upon publication, when requested."** Reviews books of poetry in 1,500 words, single format; 2,500-3,000 words, multi-book. Send books for review consideration. The editor says they would like more formal verse.

Market categories: (I) Beginning; (II) General; (III) Limited; (IV) Specialized; (V) Closed.

FLUME PRESS (II), 773 Sierra View, Chico CA 95926, phone (916)342-1583, founded 1984, poetry editors Casey Huff and Elizabeth Renfro, publishes poetry chapbooks. **"We have few biases about form, although we appreciate control and crafting, and we tend to favor a concise, understated style, with emphasis on metaphor rather than editorial commentary."** They have published chapbooks by Tina Barr, Randall Freisinger, Leonard Kress, Carol Gordon, Gayle Kaune, Luis Omar Salinas and Judy Lindberg. As a sample, the editors selected these lines from "Touch Pool" by Pamela Uschuk:

Around and around
the holding pool, rays soar
like squadrons of angels, now and then lifting
a wing to test the edge
as if they would swim through the glass to the sea

Chapbooks are chosen from an annual competition, March 1 through June 30. $6 entry fee. Submit 20-24 pgs., including title, contents and acknowledgments. Name and address on a separate sheet. Considers simultaneous submissions. "Flume Press editors read and respond to every entry." Sometimes sends prepublication galleys. Winner receives $100 and 25 copies. **Sample: $5 plus $1.50 postage and handling.**

FOLIO: A LITERARY JOURNAL (II), Dept. of Literature, Gray Hall, The American University, Washington DC 20016, phone (202)885-2973, founded 1984. Editors change annually. It is a biannual. They have published poetry by Jean Valentine, Henry Taylor and William Stafford. There are 12-20 poems published in each 64- to 72-page issue. It is 6×9, perfect-bound, neatly printed from typeset. **Sample postpaid: $5. Submit up to 6 pgs. with brief bio/contributor's note from August to March 1. Considers simultaneous submissions. Reads submissions September 1 through March 1 only. Pays 2 copies. Acquires first rights.** They also sponsor a contest open to all contributors with a $75 prize for the best poem of the fall and spring issue. A poem published by this journal was selected for inclusion in **Editor's Choice III.**

FOOLSCAP (I, II), 78 Friars Rd., East Ham, London E6 1LL England, phone 081-470-7680, founded 1987, editor Judi Benson, appears twice yearly (summer and winter). **"We are looking for poetry which surprises as well as informs. We look for confidence and a sense of humor, though veer away from flippancy and trite over-used rhyme. We like our poetry to reflect today's world and the issues that concern us all without laborious political banner waving. In other words, we are looking for craft as much as statement."** They have published poetry by Ian Duhig, Frances Wilson and Sal Salasin. As a sample the editor selected "Filmclip: Leningrad, October, 1935" by Ken Smith:

Dark comes early, and wet snow.
The citizens hurry from work,
scarfed, buttoned, thinking of supper,
the tram clanking and squealing
in whose glass an arm has wiped
a V of lit space wherein smoke,
old and young wrapped for winter,
eyes focussed somewhere ahead,
dreaming perhaps of a sausage,
of bread, coffee, a warm bed,
a bullet in the back of the brain.
Then they're gone. Next comes
the future. It looks like the past.

The editor describes ***Foolscap*** as approximately 80 pgs., A4, camera-ready photocopying, with b&w illustrations. "No ads, no reviews, no frills, though we do include short prose pieces and welcome good translations." They accept about 120 of 1,200 poems received/year. Press run is between 150-200 for 150 subscribers. "Copies also sold at poetry readings, bookshops, libraries and to universities." Subscription: $16/£6. **Submit "no more than 6 poems at a time. Cover letter indicating whether or not to return ms required. Best if overseas not to have to return. Allow ample IRCs and 1-2 months for response. Publication could take as long as a year due to backlog of accepted material." Pays 1 copy.** The editor says,"We accept a wide range of styles from both unpublished poets as well as well-known poets from all geographical locations. We advise people to get a copy of ***Foolscap*** before submitting and suggest 'new' poets share their work with others before submitting."

FOOTWORK: THE PATERSON LITERARY REVIEW; HORIZONTES; ALLEN GINSBERG POETRY AWARDS; THE PATERSON POETRY PRIZE; PASSAIC COUNTY COMMUNITY COLLEGE POETRY CENTER LIBRARY (II, IV-Regional, bilingual/foreign language), Poetry Center, Passaic County Community College, Cultural Affairs Dept., College Blvd., Paterson NJ 07505-1179. A wide range of activities pertaining to poetry are conducted by the Passaic County Community College Poetry Center, including the annual literary magazine ***Footwork***, founded 1979, editor and director Maria Mazziotti

Gillan, using **poetry of "high quality" under 100 lines.** They have published poetry by David Ray, Diane Wakoski, William Stafford, Sonia Sanchez, Laura Boss and Marge Piercy. ***Footwork: The Paterson Literary Review*** is magazine-sized, 160 pgs., saddle-stapled, professionally printed with glossy card 2-color cover, using b&w art and photos, circulation 1,000 with 100 subscriptions of which 50 are libraries. **Sample postpaid: $5. Simultaneous submissions OK. Send no more than 5 poems/submission. Reads submissions September through January only. Reports in 1 year. Pays 1 copy. Acquires first rights.** ***Horizontes***, founded in 1983, editor José Villalongo, is an annual Spanish language literary magazine using **poetry of high quality no longer than 20 lines. Will accept English translations, but Spanish version must be included.** They have published poetry by Nelson Calderon, Jose Kozer and Julio Cesar Mosches. ***Horizontes*** is magazine-sized, 120 pgs., saddle-stapled, professionally printed with full color matte cover, using b&w graphics and photos, circulation 800 with 100 subscriptions of which 20 are libraries. **Sample postpaid: $4. Accepts simultaneous submissions. "On occasion we do consider published works but prefer unpublished works." Reads submissions September through January only. Reports in 3-4 months. Pays 2 copies. Acquires first rights.** Staff reviews books of poetry. Send books for review consideration. The Poetry Center of the college conducts The Allen Ginsberg Poetry Awards Competition each year. Entry fee: $5. Prizes of $150, $25 and $10. Deadline: March 1. Send SASE for rules. They also publish a **New Jersey Poetry Resources** book, the **PCC Poetry Contest Anthology** and the **New Jersey Poetry Calendar**. The Paterson Poetry Prize of $1,000 is awarded each year (split between poet and publisher) to a book of poems published in the previous year. Publishers should write with SASE for application form to be submitted by February 1. Passaic County Community College Poetry Center Library has an extensive collection of contemporary poetry and seeks small press contributions to help keep it abreast. The Distinguished Poetry Series offers readings by poets of international, national and regional reputation. Poetryworks/USA is a series of programs produced for UA Columbia-Cablevision.

FOREST BOOKS (V, IV-Translations), 20 Forest View, Chingford, London E4 7AY United Kingdom, phone 081-529-8470, founded 1984, director Brenda Walker, publishes 15-20 paperbacks/year. They have published **Enchanting Beasts: An Anthology of Modern Women Poets in Finland**, a handsomely printed flat-spined book of 126 pgs, **but their list is full for the next 2 years.** Samples may be purchased through Dufour Editions, P.O. Box 449, Chester Springs PA 19425.

THE FORMALIST; HOWARD NEMEROV SONNET AWARD (II, IV-Form, translations), 320 Hunter Dr., Evansville IN 47711, founded 1990, editor William Baer, appears twice a year, **"dedicated to *metrical* poetry written in the great tradition of English-language verse."** This is one of a handful of magazines that publish formal (metered, rhymed) poetry *exclusively*. The poems here are among the best in the genre—a joy to read—tastefully edited so that each verse plays off the other. They have recently published poetry by Richard Wilbur, Donald Justice, Mona Van Duyn, John Updike, Maxine Kumin, James Merrill, Karl Shapiro, X.J. Kennedy, May Swenson, W.S. Merwin, W.D. Snodgrass and Louis Simpson. As a sample the editor chose the opening stanza from "The Amateurs of Heaven" by Howard Nemerov:

Two lovers to a midnight meadow came
High in the hills, to lie there hand in hand
Like effigies and look up at the stars,
The never-setting ones set in the North
To circle the Pole in idiot majesty,
And wonder what was given them to wonder.

"We are interested in metrical poetry written in the **traditional forms, including ballads, sonnets, couplets, blank verse, the Greek forms, the French forms, etc. We will also consider metrical translations of major formalist non-English poets—from the Ancient Greeks to the present. We are not, however, interested in haiku (or syllabic verse of any kind) or sestinas. Although we do publish poetry which skillfully employs enjambment, we have a marked prejudice against excessive enjambment. Only rarely do we accept a poem over 2 pages, and we have no interest in any type of erotica, blasphemy, vulgarity or racism.** Finally, like all editors, we suggest that those wishing to submit to ***The Formalist*** become thoroughly familiar with the journal beforehand." Subscription: $12. **Sample postpaid: $6.50. *The Formalist* considers submissions throughout the year, 3-5 poems at one time. No simultaneous submissions, previously published work, or disk submissions. A brief cover letter is recommended** and a SASE is necessary for a reply and return of ms. **Reports within 2 months. Pays 2 copies. Acquires first North American serial rights.** The Howard Nemerov Sonnet Award offers $1,000 and publication in ***The Formalist*** for the best unpublished *sonnet*. The final judge for 1994 was Richard Wilbur. Entry fee: $2/sonnet. Postmark deadline: May 31. Send SASE for guidelines. See also the contest listing for the World Order of Narrative and Formalist Poets. Contestants must subscribe to ***The Formalist*** to enter. ***The Formalist*** was listed in the "Traditional Verse" category of the latest ***Writer's Digest*** Poetry 60 list, and work published in ***The Formalist*** appears in **The Best American Poetry 1992.**

THE FOUR DIRECTIONS; SNOWBIRD PUBLISHING COMPANY (IV-Ethnic), P.O. Box 729, Tellico Plains TN 37385, phone (615)982-7261, founded 1991, publisher William Meyer. ***The Four Directions*** is an American Indian literary quarterly designed to further American Indian literature. **All authors must be of American Indian heritage, and they want poetry that reflects or touches commom/uncommon American Indian concerns.** They have recently published poetry by Susan Clements and Shirley Hill Witt. The editor says it is 60-68 pgs. with approximately 54 pgs. of poetry, short stories, articles and reviews. They receive about 200 poems a year, use approximately 48. Press run is 2,000 for 180 subscribers of which 90 are libraries, 1,800 shelf sales. Subscription: $21, $25 institutions. **Sample postpaid: $7. Previously published poems and simultaneous submissions OK. Cover letter required. Often comments on rejections. Publishes theme issues. Send SASE for upcoming themes. Reports in 6-9 weeks. Sometimes sends prepublication galleys. Pays $10 for full-page of poetry. Buys one-time rights.** Accepts reviews of all media, including books of poetry. Reviews range from 200 to 2,000 words. Snowbird Publishing Company publishes books but "so far we have not published any books of poetry." **Query first with sample poems and cover letter with brief bio and publication credits. "Poetry may be previously published or not, but must be of professional quality." Replies to queries and mss in 6-9 weeks. Pays 10-18% royalties and 10 author's copies.** The editor says, "The field of American Indian literature is the fastest growing literary effort in North America. We tend to seek writing that furthers the growth of the Indian spirit. We would like to see more traditional American Indian poetry and poetry in bilingual (American Indian and English or Spanish and English) forms."

FOUR QUARTERS (II, III), La Salle University, 1900 W. Olney, Philadelphia PA 19141-1199, phone (215)951-1700, founded 1951, editor John J. Keenan, is a semiannual cultural magazine which targets the college educated. It includes poetry, fiction, articles and essays. They have published poetry by X.J. Kennedy, David Ignatow, Joyce Carol Oates and William Stafford. As a sample the editor selected the opening lines from "Losing the Farm" by Barbara Daniels:

> *What we had is gone, the stone porch, bright fall*
> *loading trees with light, the sheep that blundered*
> *through the open door. Beyond the thin wall*
> *the old woman thumped her stick and made me wonder . . .*

FQ is 64 pgs., 7×10, professionally printed and designed, flat-spined with card cover. Poems generally appear one to a page. They receive approximately 100 submissions a year, accept 15. Press run is 1,000. Single copy: $4; subscription: $8 for 1 year, $13 for 2 years, $20 for 3 years. **Sample postpaid: $5. Previously published poems ("occasionally") and simultaneous submissions OK. Reads submissions September 1 through May 1 only. Poems are circulated to an editorial board. Seldom comments on rejections. Send SASE for guidelines. Reports in approximately 3-6 months. Sometimes sends prepublication galleys. Pays $2/line. Buys all rights. Returns them.** Open to unsolicited reviews.

FOX CRY (II), University of Wisconsin Fox Valley, 1478 Midway Road, P.O. Box 8002, Menasha WI 54952-8002, phone (414)832-2600, founded 1973, editor Professor Don Hrubesky, is a literary annual using **poems up to 50 lines long, deadline February 15.** They have published poetry by Shirley Anders, Ellen Kort, David Graham, Clifford Wood and Laurel Mills. As a sample, the editor selected these lines (poet unidentified):

> *She was out there with the leaves*
> *the old woman bent but broad of back*
> *In long even pulls, she collected*
> *the detritus of the sun's decline.*

Their press run is 400. **Sample postpaid: $5. Submit maximum of 3 poems from September 1 through February 15 only. Simultaneous submissions considered. Send SASE for guidelines. Pays 1 copy.**

FRANK: AN INTERNATIONAL JOURNAL OF CONTEMPORARY WRITING AND ART (II, IV-Form, translations), Les Amis de la Fonderie Association, 104 rue Edouard Vaillant, 93100 Montreuil France, founded 1983, editor David Applefield. ***Frank*** is a literary semiannual that **"encourages work of seriousness and high quality which falls often between existing genres. Looks favorably at true internationalism and stands firm against ethnocentric values. Likes translations. Publishes foreign dossier in each issue. Very eclectic."** There are no subject specifications, but the magazine **"discourages sentimentalism and easy, false surrealism. Although we're in Paris, most Paris-poems are too thin for us. Length is open."** They have published poetry by Rita Dove, Derek Walcott, Duo Duo, Raymond Carver, Tomas Tranströmer, James Laughlin, Breytenbach, Michaux, Gennadi Aigi, W.S. Merwin, Edmond Jabes, John Berger, and many lesser known poets. The journal is 224 pgs., digest-sized, flat-spined, offset in b&w with color cover and photos, drawings and ads. Circulation is 4,000, of which 2,000 are bookstore sales and subscriptions. Subscription: $30 (individuals), $60 (institutions) for 4 issues. **Sample postpaid: $9 airmail from Paris. Guidelines available for SASE. Poems must be previously unpublished. The editor often provides some criticism on rejected mss. Submissions are re-**

ported on in 3 months, publication is in 3-6 months. Pay is $5/printed page and 2 copies. Editor organizes readings in US and Europe for ***Frank*** contributors. He says, "Send only what you feel is fresh, original, and provocative in either theme or form. Work of craft that also has political and social impact is encouraged."

FREDRICKSON-KLOEPFEL PUBLISHING CO. (F-K BOOKS) (I, IV-Themes), 7748 17th SW, Seattle WA 98106, phone (206)767-4915, "established 1983 as an outlet for J. Fred Blair's poetry and pamphlets, went public 1990," editor John F. Blair, publishes **anthologies on specific themes. He "tries to publish at least one selection from each contributor; 1,000 words max, likes strong viewpoint, vibrant poetics, earthy style.** A collection of poems and short prose on one subject from a myriad of sources establishes a panoramic discourse or Antho-logue. **Wants mss from male and female poets on maleness for 'Hold the Macho.' Also wants positive items about the work-a-day life for 'Our Daily Bread.'** Have a glut of negative things (are poets afraid of work?) already and nothing for counterpoint. Ergo: No dialogue." He has published poetry by Ralph La Charity, Judith Skillman, John Grey and Jeffrey Zable. As a sample the editor selected these lines from "Beyond Games" by Joanne Seltzer:

You tell me to be grateful
for the things I do have.
Two eyes. Twenty eight teeth.
What about my losses?
Hope. Unanswered Valentines.
Snowflakes that melt in my hand.

Reports in 3 months. "After book is completed, contributors may purchase copies at print cost for promotion in their locales. They should make a small profit wholesaling them and get full mark-up on the ones they retail. Any profit I make will be shared across the board with contributors."

FREE FOCUS (I, IV-Women/feminist); OSTENTATIOUS MIND (I, IV-Form/style), P.O. Box 7415, JAF Station, New York NY 10116, ***Free Focus*** founded 1985, ***Ostentatious Mind*** founded 1987, poetry editor Patricia D. Coscia. ***Free Focus*** "is a literary magazine **only for creative women, who reflect their ideas of love, nature, beauty and men and also express the pain, sorrow, joy and enchantment that their lives generate. *Free Focus* needs poems of all types on the subject matters above. Nothing x-rated, please. The poems can be as short as 2 lines or as long as 2 pages.** The objective of this magazine is to give women poets a chance to be fullfilled in the art of poetry, for freedom of expression for women is seldom described in society." They have published poetry by Helen Tzagoloff, Elizabeth Hahn Ph.D., Patricia A. Pierkowski, D.R. Middleton, Crystal Beckner, Elaine F. Powell, Kris Anderson, Carol L. Clark and Mary Anderson. As a sample the editor selected these lines from "A Woman I Once Knew" by Maura Schroeder:

She sleeps in the desert alone,
Carving ancestral bone,
from waking mountains.
She sleeps in the desert alone,
Wading in salt-soaked rivers,
with wounds unfolded.

Ostentatious Mind "is a co-ed literary magazine **for material of stream of consciousness and experimental poems. The poets deal with the political, social and psychological."** They have published poetry by Paul Weinman, Rod Farmer, L. Mason, Dr. John J. Soldo, Carl A. Winderl, James W. Penha and Joe Lackey. As a sample the editor selected this poem, "Poetic Wax," by Sheryl L. Nelms:

comes in 1.5 liter

bottles

at Majestic
Liquors

Both magazines are printed on 8×14 paper, folded in the middle and stapled to make a 10-page (including cover) format, with simple b&w drawings on the cover and inside. The two magazines appear every 6-8 months. **Sample of either is $3.50 postpaid. Poems should be typed neatly and clearly on white typing paper. Submit only 3 poems at one time. Simultaneous submissions and previously published poems OK. Publishes theme issues. Send SASE for guidelines and upcoming themes. Reports "as soon as possible." Sometimes sends prepublication galleys. Pays 1-2 copies.** The editor says, "I think that anyone can write a poem who can freely express intense feelings about their experiences. A dominant thought should be ruled and expressed in writing, not by the spoken word, but the written word."

FREE LUNCH (II), P.O. Box 7647, Laguna Niguel CA 92607-7647, founded 1988, editor Ron Offen, is a **"poetry journal interested in publishing whole spectrum of what is currently being produced by American poets.** Also features a 'Mentor Series,' in which an established poet introduces a new, unpublished poet. Mentors have included Maxine Kumin, James Dickey, Lucille Clifton, Kenneth Koch and Stephen Dunn. **Especially interested in experimental work and work by unestablished poets. Hope to provide all serious poets living in the US with a free subscription. For details on free subscription send SASE. No restriction on form, length, subject matter, style, purpose. Don't want cutsie, syrupy, sentimental, preachy religious or aggressively 'uplifting' verse. No aversion to form, rhyme."** Poets recently published include Thomas Carper, Billy Collins, David Ray, Paul Violi and Peter Wild. As a sample the editor selected these lines from "These Heart Hammers, These Small Xylophone Joys" by Peter Bakowski:

These hearthammers, these small xylophone joys,
Keep the taste of fire
burning in my mouth
and my hands fill with
rubies, wise sparrows, the moth's dizzy haunting
of candles and schemes,
and I sit here eating corn off the cob
as if I were tasting
the petals of the sun.

FL is published 3 times a year. It is 32-40 pgs., saddle-stapled, digest-sized, attractively printed and designed, featuring free verse that shows attention to craft with well-knowns and newcomers alongside each other. Press run is 1,200 with 150 subscriptions of which 10 are libraries. Subscription: $12 ($15 foreign). **Sample postpaid: $5 ($6 foreign). "Submissions must be limited to 3 poems and are considered only between September 1 and May 31. Submissions sent at other times will be returned unread. Although a cover letter is not mandatory, we like them. We especially want to know if a poet is previously unpublished, as we like to work with new poets." They will consider simultaneous submissions. Editor usually comments on rejections and tries to return submissions in 2 months. Send SASE for guidelines. Pays 1 copy plus subscription.** Work published in ***Free Lunch*** has been included in ***The Best American Poetry 1993***. He quotes Archibald MacLeish, " 'A poem should not mean/ But be.' Poetry is concerned primarily with language, rhythm and sound; fashions and trends are transitory and to be eschewed; perfecting one's work is often more important than publishing it."

FRENCH BROAD PRESS (III), Dept. PM, The Asheville School, Asheville NC 28806, phone (704)255-7909, founded 1989, publishers Jessica Bayer and J.W. Bonner, publishes 20- to 40-page chapbooks. **"Any style or form welcome. Considers sexually explicit material."** They have recently published poetry by Thomas Meyer, Jeffrey Beam, Jonathan Williams and Jonathan Greene. **"We're slow. May take 6 months to respond to a ms and up to 2 years before publication. Always sends prepublication galleys. Many of our poets have paid 'in kind': typesetting mss and covers on disks or pasting up the book for printing." Pays 10% of press run.** Write to buy samples or order from The Captain's Bookshelf, 31 Page Ave., Asheville NC 28801.

FRIENDS JOURNAL (II, IV-Specialized: Quakerism), 1501 Cherry St., Philadelphia PA 19102, phone (215)241-7277, founded 1827 as ***The Friend***, 1844 as ***Friends Intelligencer,*** 1955 as ***Friends Journal,*** appears monthly, magazine-sized, circulation 9,500. Subscription: $21/year. **"We seek poetry that resonates with Quakerism and Quaker concerns, such as peace and nonviolence, spiritual seeking, the sanctuary movement, the nuclear freeze." No multiple or simultaneous submissions. Pays 2 copies/ poem.**

FRITZ (I), P.O. Box 170694, San Francisco CA 94117, founded 1991, editor Lisa McElroy, is a biannual publication open to new writers/artists "that is accessible and soulful. **I'm open to all kinds of poetry. However, because of limited space we may occasionally be overstocked."** They have published poetry by Rane Arroyo and Nancy Bonnell-Kangas. As a sample the editor selected these lines from Arroyo's "Thinking of AIDS, That Treblinka Just Blinks Away":

"I will be buried
wearing the red shoes

of the sun on my death
day." The test results:
I'm negative. Love,
I won't be smoke up

your criminal chimney.

Fritz is 24 pgs., 8½ × 11, offset, saddle-stitched, with line drawings and b&w photos. They receive under 150 poems a year, use approximately 5%. Press run is 300 for 100 shelf sales. Single copy: $2. **Sample postpaid: $3. Previously published poems and simultaneous submissions OK. Cover letter with short bio required. "I only publish twice a year if possible and there's no set publishing time. I mull over my choices for a month or so and when I have a reasonable amount of material, I decide if things fit together well. Since *Fritz* is only 24 pages long, I try to make its content 'gel.' " Send SASE for guidelines. Reports in 1-2 months. Pays 3 copies. Acquires one-time rights.** The editor says, "I encourage purchasing a sample issue so the writer will have some idea of what he/she is submitting to. I mostly publish fiction, but I always reserve 3 to 4 pages in the back for poetry. I feel it's important to keep those pages open to poets because there's so few outlets in the U.S. for new authors to publish. Although the magazine is small, it's been well-received in the U.S. and overseas. Distribution ranges from the Western U.S. to New York City to Australia and I'm hoping to expand."

FROGMORE PAPERS; FROGMORE POETRY PRIZE (III), 42 Morehall Ave., Folkestone, Kent CT19 4EF England, founded 1983, poetry editor Jeremy Page, is a biannual literary magazine with emphasis on new poetry and short stories. **"Quality is generally the only criterion, although pressure of space means very long work (over 100 lines) is unlikely to be published."** They have recently published poetry by Geoffrey Holloway, Myra Schneider, Frances Wilson, Linda France, Pauline Stainer, R. Nikolas Macioci and John Latham. As a sample the editor selected these lines by Elizabeth Garrett:

I rock on my heels and test
My breath's spillage on the air.
I shall fold it with the weather
For safe keeping, in a camphor chest.

The magazine is 38 pgs., saddle-stapled with matte card cover, photocopied in photoreduced typescript. They accept 5% of poetry received. Their press run is 250 with 100 subscriptions. Subscription: £5 ($10). **Sample postpaid: £1 ($3). (US payments should be made in cash, not check.) Considers simultaneous submissions. Editor rarely comments on rejections. Reports in 3-6 months. Pays 1 copy.** Staff reviews books of poetry in 2-3 sentences, single format. Send books for review consideration to Sophie Hannah, reviews editor, 127 Horton Rd., Manchester M14 7QD England. They also publish ***Crabflower*** pamphlets and have published collections by Geoffrey Holloway, Robert Etty, David Lightfoot and Sophie Hannah as well as several anthologies. Write for information about the annual Frogmore Poetry Prize. The editor says, "My advice to people starting to write poetry would be: Read as many recognized modern poets as you can and don't be afraid to experiment."

FROGPOND: QUARTERLY HAIKU JOURNAL; HAIKU SOCIETY OF AMERICA; HAIKU SOCIETY OF AMERICA AWARDS/CONTESTS (IV-Form, translation), % Japan Society, 333 E. 47th St., New York NY 10017, has been publishing ***Frogpond*** since 1978, now edited by Elizabeth Searle Lamb, and **submissions should go directly to her** at 970 Acequia Madre, Santa Fe NM 87501. ***Frogpond*** is a saddle-stapled quarterly of 48 pgs., 5½ × 8½, of haiku, senryu, sequences, linked poems (renga/renku), haibun, tanka and haiku translations. It also contains essays and articles, book reviews, some news of the Society, contests, awards, publications and other editorial matter—a dignified, handsome little magazine. Poets should be familiar with modern developments in English-language haiku as well as the tradition. **Haiku should be brief, fresh, using clear images and non-poetic language. Focus should be on a moment keenly perceived. Ms. Lamb hopes contributors will be familiar with contemporary haiku and senryu as presented in** The Haiku Handbook **(William J. Higginson) and** The Haiku Anthology **(Cor van den Heuvel, Ed.).** Recent contributors include Kenneth Tanemura, Lenard D. Moore, Michael Dylan Welch, Bruce Ross, Ion Codrescu and Patricia Neubauer. Considerable variety is possible, as these two examples from the magazine illustrate:

a wedge of geese
carries the last patch of sky
into the sunset
—nick avis

abused child
only her doll
still cries
—John J. Dunphy

Each issue has between 25 and 30 pages of poetry. They receive about 8,000 submissions/year and use about 400-450. The magazine goes to about 600 subscribers, of which 15 are libraries, as well as to over a dozen foreign countries. **Sample back issues postpaid: $10 (biannual issues of 1992, 1993); $5 (quarterly issues). Make checks payable to Haiku Society of America. They are flexible on submission format, but Ms. Lamb prefers haiku on 3 × 5 cards or one to a page or half-page. Submissions of 5 to 20 at one time are preferable. No simultaneous submissions. Seasonal material should be submitted 3-4 months before seasonal issue is due; non-seasonal material read anytime. Reports within 6 weeks. They hope contributors will become HSA mem-**

bers, but it is not necessary, and all contributors receive a copy of the magazine in payment. Send SASE for Information Sheet on the HSA and submission guidelines. Poetry reviews usually 1,000 words or less. Open to unsolicited reviews. Poets may also send books for review consideration. Four "best-of-issue" prizes are given "through a gift from the Museum of Haiku Literature, Tokyo." The Society also sponsors The Harold G. Henderson Haiku Award Contest, The Gerald Brady Senryu Award Contest, The Haiku Society of America Renku Contest, The Nicholas A. Virgilio Memorial Haiku Competition for High School Students and gives Merit Book Awards for books in the haiku field.

FRONTIERS: A JOURNAL OF WOMEN STUDIES (IV-Feminist), Room 2142, Mesa Vista Hall, University of New Mexico, Albuquerque NM 87131-1586, founded 1975, is published 3 times a year and **uses poetry on feminist themes.** They have published work by Audré Lorde, Janice Mirikitani, Carol Wolfe Konek and Opal Palmer Adisa. The journal is 200-208 pgs., 6×9, flat-spined. Circulation 1,000. **Sample: $8. No simultaneous submissions. Reports in 3-5 months. Pays 2 copies.** "We are not currently publishing reviews of books, poetry or otherwise. However, we consider review essays, if from a clear theoretical perspective."

‡THE FUDGE CAKE (I, IV-Children/teens), P.O. Box 197, Citrus Heights CA 95611-0197, founded 1994, editor/publisher Jancarl Campi, is a bimonthly children's newsletter designed to showcase the work of young writers. They want **poetry and short stories written by children ages 6-14. "Any form is fine. Open to any style or subject matter. Poetry: 30 lines or less. Short stories: 150 words."** As a sample we selected this poem, "Super Hero," by Ben Wade, age 9:

I know a super hero.
He has more friends than zero.
Lasers come out of his hands.
He can bury people in the sand.
He's stronger than titanium.
He can speed through a gymnasium.
He doesn't need a bed.
All he says is, "Nuff said!"

The Fudge Cake is 20 pgs., 5½×8½, desktop-published and saddle-stapled with colored paper cover and computer-generated graphics. Press run is 200 for 25 subscribers; 150 distributed free to libraries and bookstores. Subscription: $10 US, $12 Canada. **Sample postpaid: $2.50. "Submissions should be typed or neatly printed on 8½×11 white paper." Previously published poems and simultaneous submissions OK. Cover letter required. Often comments on rejections or suggests revisions. Send SASE for guidelines. Reports in 1 month. Pays 2 copies. Authors retain all rights.** Holds bimonthly contests. Winners are published in the winners' section of the next edition. The editor adds, "We value the work of today's children and feel they need an outlet to express themselves."

FUGUE (I), Room 200, Brink Hall, University of Idaho, Moscow ID 83843, founded 1991, is a biannual literary digest of the University of Idaho. **They have "no limits" on type of poetry. "We're not interested in trite or quaint verse. Nothing self-indulgent or overly metaphoric to the point of being obscure."** They have published poetry by Ricardo Sanchez and Maria Theresa Maggi. As a sample the editor selected these lines from Maggi's "The Appointment":

. . . the conceptual warble of arms and legs
caught me in cold waves
at the isinglass window, slicing
its heavy and not quite
willing prisoners, my parents
and all parents, in a tide
of dulled longing and shadows.

The editor says ***Fugue*** is 48-52 pgs., digest-sized, saddle-stapled. They receive 100-200 poems/semester, use 10-15 poems/issue. Press run is 200 for 30-50 subscribers of which 2 are libraries. **Sample postpaid: $3. No previously published poems or simultaneous submissions. Reads submissions September 15 through April 15 only. Seldom comments on rejections. Send SASE for guidelines. Reports in 1-3 months. Pays roughly $5-10 plus one copy. Buys first North American serial rights.** The editor says, "Proper manuscript format and submission etiquette is expected; submissions without proper SASE will not be read or held on file."

‡FURRY CHICLETS: A LAWPOETS CREATION (I, IV-Themes), 269 Nepal Rd., Ashland OR 97520, founded 1990, editors Charles Carreon and Tom Brill, an annual, wants **"unaffected poems that take the shortest route to the reader's mind, deliver a message worth getting, and leave no academic aftertaste. Poems: 1 page."** As a sample the editors selected these lines from "Here Comes The Guy In The Wheelchair" by Hank Roth:

They saw him coming in his wheelchair
and it made them nervous . . .
In the lounge in some beer joint,
he called me. Said
at gun point, he was being held prisoner
by a tall blonde. He said
"Do you know what she wants?"
I said I didn't know.
He says, "She wants my body."

FC consists of 30-40 photocopied pages stapled at the top to a blue matte backing. **Back issues available for $5. Make checks payable to Charles Carreon. "Our poets are in travail. They struggle with a love/hate relationship with life, death, themselves and others. Some speak with dried tongues and cracked voices; others come bearing freshest flowers of flame, ice and flesh; all are smitten with yearning." Editors often comment on submissions. They try to respond in 3 months.**

FUTURIFIC MAGAZINE (IV-Specialized), Foundation for Optimism, Terrace 3, 150 Haven Ave., New York NY 10032, phone (212)297-0502, founded 1976, publisher Balint Szent-Miklosy, is a monthly newsmagazine dealing with **current affairs and their probable outcomes. "We pride ourselves on the accuracy of our forecasting. No other limits than that the poet try to be accurate in predicting the future." They want to see "positive upbeat poetry glorifying humanity and human achievements."** *Futurific* is magazine-sized, 32 pgs., saddle-stapled, on glossy stock, with b&w photos, art and ads, circulation 10,000. Subscription: $140; for students and individuals: $70. **Sample postpaid: $10. Pays 5 copies.** The editor says, "*Futurific* is made up of the words Future-Terrific. Poets should seek out and enjoy the future if they want to see their work in *Futurific*."

G.W. REVIEW (II, IV-Translations), Marvin Center Box 20B, George Washington University, Washington DC 20052, phone (202)994-7288, founded 1980, editor Merrell K. Maschino, appears 2 times a year. "The magazine is published for distribution to the university community, the Washington, D.C. metropolitan area and an increasing number of national subscribers." They have published poetry by William Stafford, Jean Valentine, Carol Muske, Jeffrey Harrison and Richard Peabody. It is 64 pgs., perfect-bound with cover photograph. They receive about 3,300 poems a year and accept 50-60. Their annual press run averages 4,000 copies. Subscription: $5/year, $8/2 years. **Sample postpaid: $3. They consider simultaneous submissions but not previously published poems. Cover letter, including present career and recent publications, required. The staff does not read manuscripts from May 15 through August 15. Editor sometimes comments on rejections when the staff likes the work but thinks it needs to be revised. Reports in 1-3 months. Pays 5 copies.**

GAIA: A JOURNAL OF LITERARY & ENVIRONMENTAL ARTS; WHISTLE PRESS, INC. (II, IV-Political, social issues), P.O. Box 709, Winterville GA 30683, phone (706)549-1810, founded 1992, editor-in-chief Robert S. King, associate editor for poetry Charles Fishman, is a quarterly. **"Poetry may explore any subject; other work should center on environmental, social or political themes. We seek a riveting blend of intellect, emotion and beautiful language. No poetasters please."** They have recently published poetry by E.G. Burrows, Helen Frost, Mary Scott and R.T. Smith. As a sample the editor selected these lines from "If" by Gale Warner:

Stumble back to the meadow, swim
in the stream, grasp at brambles,
burrow in the earth, begging
forgiveness, tearing our flesh, worshipping
the astonishingly harmless lives
of the beasts.

Gaia is 54 pgs., 8½×11, offset, saddle-stapled, with b&w art and photos, no ads. Press run is 500 for 102 subscribers of which 7 are libraries, 250 shelf sales. Subscription: $9. **Sample postpaid: $4. Submit up to 10 poems. Previously published poems OK; no simultaneous submissions. Often comments on rejections. Send SASE for guidelines. Reports within 3 months maximum. Sometimes sends prepublication galleys. Pays 2 copies and 4-issue subscription. Acquires all rights. Returns rights upon written request of the author.** Whistle Press, Inc. **publishes 3 chapbooks/year. Chapbooks are selected from annual competitions. Send SASE for complete guidelines.** They are also planning to sponsor several poetry contests beginning this year. Entries will require a small fee. Query for details.

GAIN PUBLICATIONS (V), P.O. Box 2204, Van Nuys CA 91404, phone (818)786-1981, founded 1982. **Currently does not accept unsolicited poetry.**

GAIRM; GAIRM PUBLICATIONS (IV-Ethnic, foreign language), 29 Waterloo St., Glasgow G2 6BZ Scotland, editor Derick Thomson, founded 1952. ***Gairm*** is a quarterly, circulation 2,000, which uses **poetry in Scottish Gaelic only.** It has published the work of all significant Scottish Gaelic poets, and much poetry translated from European languages. An anthology of such translations, **European Poetry in Gaelic**, is available for £7.50 or $15. ***Gairm*** is 96 pgs., digest-sized, flat-spined with coated card cover. **Sample: $3.50. Reads submissions October 1 through July 31 only.** Staff reviews books of poetry in 500-700 words, single format; 100 words, multi-book format. Occasionally invites reviews. Send books for review consideration. **All of the publications of the press are in Scottish Gaelic.** One of them, **Uirsgeul Myth,** poems in Gaelic with English translations, by Christopher Whyte, received a Saltire Literary Award for a First Book.

‡GALAXY PRESS (II), 71 Recreation St., Tweed Heads, N.S.W. 2485 Australia, phone 075-361997, founded 1979, editor Lance Banbury, is a small press publisher of short modernist to deconstructionist poems in chapbooks. He wants **"post-modernist short to medium-length verse, or didactic blank verse. No poetry of an anecdotal type."** As a sample he chose these lines from "Dickens in Jail" by Phyllis Crockett:

He arrived at J.F.K., and had only been five minutes,
In the country, 'fore the brightly smart N.Y.P.D.,
Placed Charles in course with jail-linnets,
Who each confirmed the view that Newgate's seedy.

Query with 5 samples. Reports in 2 months. Always sends prepublication galleys. Pays 2 copies. Lance Banbury says, "I would like to receive more ideological poetry."

GAZELLE PUBLICATIONS (V), 1906 Niles-Buchanan Rd., Niles MI 49120, founded 1976, editor Ted Wade, is a publisher for home schools and compatible markets including **books of verse for children but is not currently considering unsolicited manuscripts.**

GENERATOR; GENERATOR PRESS (V), 8139 Midland Rd., Mentor OH 44060, founded 1987, poetry editor John Byrum, is an annual magazine "devoted to the presentation of **language poetry and 'concrete' or visual poetic modes."** They have recently published poetry by Susan Smith Nash, Jessica Grim, Jane Reavill Ransom, Deborah Meadows, Liz Waldner and Carla Bertola. As a sample the editor selected these lines by W.B. Keckler:

or char ds of
st one or cha
r ds of st one
who looks through sad pylons
roasted in belief. ripe river lotus. lotioned.
  flax seed asphalt in a constant mash
bee technology, ham radio, cream pink feet
  crocodile colors in eyes in silky glass

Generator is magazine-sized, side-stapled, using b&w graphics, photocopied, with matte card cover. Press run is 200 copies for 25 subscriptions of which 20 are libraries. **Sample postpaid: $8.** Generator Press also publishes the **Generator Press chapbook series. Approximately 2-4 new titles/year. They are not currently accepting unsolicited manuscripts for either the magazine or chapbook publication.** Together with Score (see listing in this section), Generator Press has published **CORE: A Symposium on Contemporary Visual Poetry,** described as "an international survey of the methods, opinions and work of over 75 contemporary visual poets" ($7 postpaid individuals, $11 institutions). The editor adds, "Worthwhile writers do not need advice and should not heed any but their own."

‡THE GENTLE SURVIVALIST (I, IV-Ethnic, nature, inspirational), Box 4004, St. George UT 84770, founded 1991, editor/publisher Laura Martin-Bühler, publishes "11 issues over a 13-month period" (not published in February and August). ***The Gentle Survivalist*** is a newsletter of "harmony–timeless truths and wisdom balanced with scientific developments. For Native Americans and all those who believe in the Great Creator." They want poetry that is **"positive, inspirational, on survival of body and spirit, also man's interconnectedness with God and all His creations. Nothing sexually oriented, occult, negative or depressing."** They have recently published poetry by Keith Moore and C.S. Churchman. As a sample the editor selected these lines from Moore's poem, "A Line in Motion":

Little else pleases like
Seven-o'clock downing sun
On the faces and flanks of beasts,
An hour of crisp clarity and
The highest flattery in nature

TGS is 8 pgs. (two 11 × 17 sheets folded in half). The issue we received warns readers about the dangers of aluminum and formaldehyde and offers natural remedies for winter colds as well as money-saving tips. "We print two poems average per issue." Press run is 200. Subscription: $20. **Sample postpaid: $2. Previously published poems and simultaneous submissions OK. Cover letter required; "just a note would be fine. I find noteless submissions too impersonal."** Time between acceptance and publication is 3-4 months. **Often comments on rejections. Send SASE for guidelines. Reports within 2 months. Pays 2 copies.** The editor says, "To succeed, one must not seek supporters, but seek to know whom to support."

"Our magazine tries to strike a balance between fiction and poetry," says Steven Carter, editor of Georgetown Review, a biannual literary journal based in Georgetown, Kentucky. "We generally publish 20-30 poems per issue and we look for honest, quality work," Carter says. "For the cover of our premiere issue, we thought it would be fitting to use the work of a Kentucky artist. We admire the work of Wallace Kelly and thought his woodblock print 'Snow Angel' would make an attractive cover. We also felt the woodblock print was a modern interpretation of a classical theme. And that's what we're all about here at the Georgetown Review." The cover layout was done by Art Director Stephen Gullette.

GEORGETOWN REVIEW (II), Box 227, 400 E. College St., Georgetown KY 40324, founded 1992 (first issue Spring 1993), is a biannual literary journal publishing fiction and poetry—no criticism or reviews. **They want "honest, quality work; not interested in tricks."** They have recently published poetry by John Tagliabue, William Greenway, Elton Glaser, X.J. Kennedy, Peter Wild, Michael Cadhum and Alan Feldman. *GR* is 100-120 pgs., 5½×8½, perfect-bound, with heavy stock cover with art. They receive about 1,000 submissions a year, "take maybe 10%." Press run is 1,000. Subscription: $10/year. **Sample postpaid: $5. Submit no more than 5 poems at a time. No previously published poems; simultaneous submissions OK. Reads submissions September 1 through May 1 only. Poems are read by at least 3 readers. Sometimes comments on rejections. Reports in 2-4 months. Always sends prepublication galleys. Pays 2 copies. Acquires all rights. Returns rights provided "our name is mentioned in any reprint."** Sponsors annual poetry contest. $150 1st prize; runners-up receive publication and subscription. Entry fee: $2.50/poem. Winner and runners-up announced in fall issue each year.

GEORGIA JOURNAL (IV-Regional), P.O. Box 27, Athens GA 30603-0027, phone (404)354-0463, poetry editor Janice Moore. *Georgia Journal* is a quarterly magazine, circulation 15,000, covering the state of Georgia. **They use poetry "mostly from Southern writers but not entirely. It should be suitable for the general reader."** They have published poetry by former President Jimmy Carter, Stephen Corey, Blanche Farley, Michael Chitwood and June Owens. As a sample Janice Moore selected these lines from "Next Door" by John Stone:

of a sudden
with no fanfare
but much finesse

the gingko that
has blazed all month
has acquiesced

Georgia Journal is 80 pgs., 8½×11, saddle-stapled and professionally printed on glossy paper with color cover. Recent issues feature accessible narrative and lyric free verse. Content is genuinely open and varied, from nature and personal poems to war and meditative verse. About 8-10 poems appear in each issue. **Sample: $3. Submit maximum of 3-4 poems, maximum length 30 lines. "A brief cover letter with previous publications is fine, but keep it brief." Send SASE for guidelines. Reports in 2-3 months. Pays copies. Acquires first rights.** Staff selects books by Georgia authors to review.

UNIVERSITY OF GEORGIA PRESS; CONTEMPORARY POETRY SERIES (II), 330 Research Dr., University of Georgia, Athens GA 30602, phone (706)369-6140, press founded 1938, series founded 1980, series editor Bin Ramke, publishes four collections of poetry/year, **two of which are by poets who have not had a book published,** in simultaneous hardcover and paperback editions. They have recently published poetry by Martha Collins, Marjorie Welish, Arthur Vogelsang and C.D. Wright. As a sample the editor selected these lines from "The Sciences Sing a Lullabye" by Albert Goldbarth:

Physics says: go to sleep. Of course
you're tired. Every atom in you
has been dancing the shimmy in silver shoes
nonstop from mitosis to now.
Quit tapping your feet. They'll dance
inside themselves without you. Go to sleep.

That is from the book **Heaven and Earth: A Cosmology** for which Goldbarth won the 1992 National Book Critics Circle Award. **"Writers should query first for guidelines and submission periods. Please enclose SASE." There are no restrictions on the type of poetry submitted,** but "familiarity with our previously published books in the series may be helpful." **$10 submission fee required.** Manuscripts are *not* returned after the judging is completed. **Always sends prepublication galleys.** The book **Empirical Evidence** by Steve Kronin received honorable mention from the Great Lakes Colleges Association's 24th Annual New Writers Awards Competition.

THE GEORGIA REVIEW (II), The University of Georgia, Athens GA 30602-9009, phone (706)542-3481, founded 1947, editor Stanley W. Lindberg, associate editor Stephen Corey. They have published poetry by Galway Kinnell, Yusef Komunyakaa, Pattiann Rogers, Gerald Stern, Lisel Mueller, Seamus Heaney, Linda Pastan, Albert Goldbarth, Rita Dove and Charles Simic. "Also have featured first-ever publications by many new voices over the years, but encourage all potential contributors to become familiar with past offerings before submitting." As a sample, Stephen Corey selected "Wave and Particle" by Laura Fargas:

Herons hunt at the marsh edge,
lacking the mind to desire abstractions.
What I take boating in the bright fog
is my need to be seen by them, to feel
the ice of the moon melting on my palms.
Round as a kiss, sharp as a bullet,
light soaks the slow event.

This is a distinguished, professionally printed, flat-spined quarterly, 200 pgs., 7×10, glossy card cover. They use 60-70 poems a year, less than one-half of one percent of those received. Circulation: 7,000. Subscription: $18/year. **Sample postpaid: $6. No submissions accepted during June, July and August. Rarely uses translations. Submit 3-5 poems. No simultaneous submissions. Publishes theme issues occasionally. Reports in 1-3 months. Always sends prepublication galleys. Pays $3/line. Buys first North American serial rights.** Reviews books of poetry. "Our poetry reviews range from 500-word 'Book Briefs' on single volumes to 5,000-word essay reviews on multiple volumes." ***The Georgia Review*** is one of the best literary journals around. It respects its audience, edits intelligently and has won or been nominated for awards in competition with such slicks as ***The Atlantic, The New Yorker*** and ***Esquire***. Work appearing here has also been included in **The Best American Poetry 1992.** In addition, ***The Georgia Review*** ranked #3 in the "Poets' Pick" category of the latest ***Writer's Digest*** Poetry 60 list. This category ranks those publications in which poets said they would most like to see their work published. Needless to say, competition here is extremely tough. All styles and forms are welcome, but response times can be slow during peak periods in the fall and late spring. Yet the editor says they would like to receive, "the very best work from an even wider slate of poets."

GEPPO HAIKU WORKSHEET; HAIKU JOURNAL MEMBERS' ANTHOLOGY; YUKI TEIKEI HAIKU SOCIETY (I, IV-Form, membership), 20711 Garden Place Court, Cupertino CA 95014, ***Geppo*** founded 1977 and first published by the Yuki Teikei Haiku Society, editor Jean Hale. ***Geppo*** is devoted to haiku and haiku criticism; contest winners and **"members' haiku only are published here."** It is a bimonthly offset newsletter for members using **haiku, especially traditional haiku: 17 syllables with a KIGO."** Press run is 200. ***HJ*** appears every 2 years and "contains the winning haiku voted on in *Geppo*." The editor describes ***HJ*** as "around 60 pgs., 5½×8½, nicely printed on heavy paper, card stock cover." Press run is 300 for 100 subscriptions of which 10 are libraries. Membership in the Yuki Teikei Haiku Society is $15/year and includes 6 issues of ***Geppo***. **Sample of *Geppo* available for SASE. Sample of *HJ* postpaid: $4.50. Send SASE for guidelines. Simultaneous submissions and previously published poems OK.** They have an annual contest in the spring. Send SASE for rules.

THE GETTYSBURG REVIEW (II), Gettysburg College, Gettysburg PA 17325, phone (717)337-6770, founded 1988, editor Peter Stitt, is a multidisciplinary literary quarterly considering **any poetry except**

that which is "badly written." Include SASE with submission. They accept 1-2% of submissions received. As a sample the editor selected these lines by Kirsten Smith:

There's a way to pander to a woman
and not actually harm her.
It starts with the lies you tell,
the way you call her into a glib fable
and let her float there.

Press run is 4,500 for 2,000 subscriptions. **Sample postpaid: $7. Publishes theme issues occasionally. Pays $2/line.** Essay-reviews are featured in each issue. They are open to unsolicited essay-reviews. Poets may also send books for review consideration. Editor Peter Stitt, a leading literary critic and reviewer, has created a well-edited and -respected journal that features a tantalizing lineup of poems in all styles and forms. Competition is keen, and response times can be slow during heavy submission periods, especially in the late fall. Work appearing in ***The Gettysburg Review*** has been included in **The Best American Poetry** (1993 and 1994) and **Pushcart Prize** anthologies. The review itself ranked #4 in the "Top Pay" category of the latest ***Writer's Digest*** Poetry 60 list. As for its editor, Peter Stitt won the first PEN/Nora Magid Award for Editorial Excellence.

GINGER HILL (II), c/o English Dept., Room 314, Spotts World Cultures Building, Slippery Rock University, Slippery Rock PA 16057, phone (412)738-2043, founded 1963, is an annual literary magazine using **"academic poetry, with preference for excellent free verse, but all forms considered. 27-line limit. No greeting card verse, no sentimentality, no self-serving or didactic verse."** They have published poetry by Elizabeth R. Curry, B.Z. Niditch and Robert Cooperman. It is digest-sized, "varies in format and layout every year," perfect-bound, with 2,000 distributed free. **Submissions must be postmarked on or before December 1 of each year. Send SASE for guidelines. Pays 2 copies.** They say, "We choose about 5-10% of all submissions. Excellence is stressed."

GIORNO POETRY SYSTEMS RECORDS; DIAL-A-POEM POETS (V), 222 Bowery, New York NY 10012, phone (212)925-6372, fax (212)966-7574, founded 1965, poetry editor John Giorno, "star of Andy Warhol's movie, *Sleep* (1963)," who publishes a poetry magazine in three formats: LP record, compact disc and cassette; and a videopak series. He originated Dial-A-Poem in 1968, installing it in many cities in the United States and Europe. He says he has published poetry on the surface of ordinary objects: Matchbook Poems, T-Shirt Poems, Cigarette Package Poems, Window Curtain Poems, Flag Poems, Chocolate Bar Poems, and Silk-Screen and Lithograph Poem Prints. He started the AIDS Treatment Project in 1984. **No submission information provided.**

GLB PUBLISHERS (III, IV-Gay/lesbian/bisexual), P.O. Box 78212, San Francisco CA 94107, phone (415)243-0229, founded 1990, associate editor John Hanley. "We are **cooperative publishers. Founded for gay, lesbian and bisexual writers. Authors share cost of printing and promotion but have much control over cover design, typefaces, general appearance."** They publish 2-4 paperbacks and 1-2 hardbacks/year. They want **"book-length collections from gay, lesbian or bisexual writers. Nothing antagonistic to gay, lesbian or bisexual life-styles."** They have published poetry by Robert Peters, Paul Genega and Thomas Cashet. **Previously published poems OK; no simultaneous submissions. Cover letter required. "Author should explain intention for poems and expectations for sales of books." Often comments on rejections. Replies to queries in 10 days, to mss in 1 month. Always sends prepublication galleys. Pays 15-25% royalties and 20 author's copies. Check bookstores for samples.**

GLOBAL TAPESTRY JOURNAL; BB BOOKS (II), Spring Bank, Longsight Rd., Copster Green, Blackburn, Lancs. BB1 9EU United Kingdom, founded 1963, poetry editor Dave Cunliffe. **"Experimental, avant-garde—specializing in exciting high-energy new writing. Mainly for a bohemian and counterculture audience. Poetry in the Beat tradition. Don't want contrived, traditional, pompous and academic or pretentious mainstream." Also considers sexually explicit material.** In addition to the magazine, *Global Tapestry Journal*, BB Books publishes chapbooks. "We want honest, uncontrived writing, strong in form and content. We don't want 'weekend hobby verse' and poetry without energy." They have published poetry by David Tipton, Joy Walsh, Belinda Subraman, Ellen Zaks and Jim Burns. As a sample the editor selected these lines by Lisa Kucharski:

the system doesn't fit where our
body's going to
we make square corners
and walk around them in curves

GTJ is 9×6, 72 pgs., saddle-stapled, typeset in a variety of mostly small sizes of type, rather crowded format, casual pasteup, with b&w drawings, photos, collages, display and classified ads, with a 2-color matte card cover. Circulation 1,150 with 450 subscriptions of which 50 are libraries. Subscription: £8 sterling for 4 issues mailed seamail to USA. Subscription (4 issues): $20. **Sample postpaid: $3. Considers previously published poems. Cover letter, with clear address, telephone**

number and short publishing history, required. Send SASE (or SAE and IRC) for guidelines. Responds "soon," has an 18-month backlog. Pays 1 copy. Open to unsolicited reviews. Poets may also send books for review consideration. **BB Books publishes about 4 chapbooks of poetry/year. To submit for chapbook publication send 6 samples and cover letter giving publication credits. Pays 10% of press run in copies. Send SASE (SAE with IRCs if foreign) for catalog to buy samples.** David Cunliffe comments, "The United Kingdom has a limited number of magazines and small press ventures publishing poetry from unknowns. Many little mags are self-publishing cliques or small-time vanity operations. Simultaneous submissions and simultaneous publication are often resented. There is much readership crossover among the non-poet subscribers and they resent seeing the same work in many magazines over a short period. We typeset for a few United Kingdom mags and publishers and we see this in the setting jobs we do every week. Many of the editors circulate poet blacklists to help prevent this tendency from spreading."

DAVID R. GODINE, PUBLISHER, Horticultural Hall, 300 Massachusetts Ave., Boston MA 02115. Prefers not to share information. **"Our poetry program is completely filled through 1996, so we are not accepting any unsolicited materials at this time."**

GOLDEN ISIS MAGAZINE; AGE OF AQUARIUS; GOLDEN ISIS PRESS; POEM OF THE YEAR CONTEST (I, IV-Mystical/Occult), P.O. Box 525, Fort Covington NY 12937, founded 1980, editor Gerina Dunwich. "*Golden Isis* is a mystical literary magazine of poetry, magick, pagan/Egyptian artwork, Wiccan news, occult fiction, letters, book reviews and classified ads. **Occult, Egyptian, cosmic, euphonic and Goddess-inspired poems, mystical haiku and magickal chants are published. We are also interested in New Age spiritual poetry, astrological verses and poems dealing with peace, love and ecology. All styles considered; under 60 lines preferred. We do not want to see pornographic, Satanic, sexist or racist material."** They have published poetry by H.L. Prosser, Eileen Kernaghan and Timothy Kevin Perry. As a sample the editor selected these lines from "Full Circle" by Mary Shifman:

The Goddess steps inside my heart
To share me with Her dance
The Horned God plies his minstrel art
And all the world enchants

The magazine is 15-20 pgs., digest-sized, desktop-published, saddle-stapled with paper cover. International circulation is 5,000. Single copy: $3; subscription: $10/year. "No postal money orders, please." **Submit 1 poem/page, typed single-spaced, name and address on upper left corner and the number of lines on upper right corner. Previously published poems and simultaneous submissions OK. Occasionally comments on rejected material. Reports within 2-3 weeks. No payment or free copies. "We can no longer afford it." All rights revert to author upon publication.** Reviews books of poetry, "length varies." Open to unsolicited reviews. Poets may also send books for review consideration. ***Age of Aquarius*** is a digest-sized "psychedelic journal of 60s counter-culture in the 90s." Sample: $3. Circulation: 3,600. Golden Isis Press **currently accepts mss for chapbook publication. Send complete ms and $5 reading fee. "Please make checks payable to Golden Isis. We offer a small advance, 10 free copies of the published work, and 10% royalty on every copy sold for as long as the book remains in print." Sample chapbook (Circle of Shadows by Gerina Dunwich): $3.95.** The magazine sponsors an annual "Poem of the Year" contest that offers cash prizes. Entry fee: $1/poem. Deadline: December 1. No limit on number of poems entered. Poems should be up to 60 lines, any form, with author's name and address on upper left corner of each page. Free guidelines and contest rules for SASE. ***Golden Isis*** is a member of W.P.P.A. (Wiccan/Pagan Press Alliance).

GOLDEN QUILL PRESS (I), P.O. Box 2327, Manchester Center VT 05255, phone (802)362-5066, publishes a great deal of poetry on a "cooperative" basis. **"Funds returned when guarantees are met." Call or write for detailed brochure before submitting complete ms. Reports in 2 weeks on queries, 1 month on submissions. Pays maximum 10% royalties.**

GOOD HOUSEKEEPING (II, IV-Humor, women), Hearst Corp., 959 Eighth Ave., New York NY 10019, poetry editor Andrea Krantz, is a women's magazine, circulation 5,000,000, which uses up to 3 poems/issue. **Light verse and traditional. "We look for poems of emotional interest to American women. Must be wholesome, clever, upbeat or poignant."** As a sample the editor selected the first stanza of "Autumn Chill" by Betty Bunts:

The last red rose
crowns the browning bush
its bud unfolding
in rubescent mystery,
a suppliant
to the sun.

Submit up to 10 poems; maximum length: 25 lines. Cover letter with name, address and credits

required. Send seasonal material 6-12 months before publication date. "Poets whose work interests us will hear from us within 4-5 weeks of receipt of a manuscript. We ask that poets send inexpensive copies of their work, and do *not* enclose SASEs or postage. We no longer return or critique manuscripts." Pays $10/line. "Light Housekeeping" no longer accepts unsolicited submissions. *Good Housekeeping* ranked #1 in the "Top Pay" category of the latest ***Writer's Digest*** Poetry 60 list.

GOOSE LANE EDITIONS (V, IV-Regional), 469 King St., Fredericton, New Brunswick E3B 1E5 Canada, phone (506)450-4251, fax (506)459-4991, managing editor S. Alexander, founded 1956, a small press publishing Canadian fiction, poetry and literary history. **Writers should be advised that Goose Lane considers mss by Canadian poets only.** They receive approximately 400 mss/year, publish 10-15 books yearly, 3 of these being poetry collections. Writers recently published include Claire Harris and Eric Trethewey. As a sample the editor selected these lines from "Civil Servant," published in **In This House are Many Women** (1993) by Sheree Fitch:

Some nights still
I wake up
having dreamt
people swivel by my desk
in turn-stile fashion
my voice is a recorded message

Can I have your sin?
Can I have your sin?

Not reading submissions before January 1995. After that date, unsolicited Canadian mss considered if individual poems have been previously published in literary journals. Cover letter required; include name and address and where work was previously published. SASE essential (IRCs or Canadian postage stamps only). Reports in 3-4 months. Always sends prepublication galleys. Authors may receive royalty of up to 10% of retail sale price on all copies sold. Copies available to author at 40% discount.

GOSPEL PUBLISHING HOUSE; PENTECOSTAL EVANGEL (V); LIVE; HICALL; JUNIOR TRAILS (IV-Religious, children/teens), The General Council of the Assemblies of God, 1445 Boonville, Springfield MO 65802, phone (417)862-2781. ***Pentecostal Evangel*** is a weekly magazine containing **inspirational articles and news of the Assemblies of God for members of the Assemblies and other Pentecostal and charismatic Christians**, circulation 280,000. **"Presently, the *Pentecostal Evangel* is not accepting poetry due to lack of readership interest."** ***Live*** is a weekly **for adults in Assemblies of God Sunday schools**, circulation 200,000. **Traditional free and blank verse, 12-20 lines. "Please do not send large numbers of poems at one time." Submit seasonal material 1 year in advance; do not mention Santa Claus, Halloween or Easter bunnies. Sample copy and writer's guidelines for 7×10 SAE and 2 first-class stamps. Letters without SASE will not be answered. Pays 25¢/line on acceptance. Buys first and/or second rights.** ***HiCall*** is a weekly magazine of **Christian fiction and articles for teenagers, 12-17**, circulation 78,000. **Free verse, light verse and traditional, 10-40 lines. Buys 50 poems/year. Submit seasonal/holiday material 18 months in advance. Simultaneous and previously published submissions OK if typed, double-spaced, on 8×11 paper. Sample copy and writer's guidelines for 8×11 SAE and 2 first-class stamps. Reports in 6 weeks. Pays 25¢/line for first rights, 15¢/line for second rights; minimum of $2.50.** ***Junior Trails*** is a weekly tabloid covering **religious fiction and biographical, historical and scientific articles with a spiritual emphasis for boys and girls ages 10-11**, circulation 75,000. **Free verse and light verse. Buys 10-15 poems/year. Submit seasonal/holiday material 15 months in advance. Simultaneous and previously published submissions OK. Sample copy and writer's guidelines for 9×12 SAE and 2 first-class stamps. Reports in 2-4 weeks. Pays 20¢/line on acceptance. Buys first and/or second rights.** "We like poems showing contemporary children positively facing today's world."

GOTTA WRITE NETWORK LITMAG; MAREN PUBLICATIONS (I, II, IV-Science fiction/fantasy, subscription), 612 Cobblestone Circle, Glenview IL 60025, fax (708)296-7631, founded 1988, editor/publisher Denise Fleischer, is a desktop-published, semiannual, saddle-stapled, 64-page magazine featuring "general poetry, articles, short stories and market listings. *GWN* now spans 40 states, Canada and England. Half of the magazine is devoted to science fiction and fantasy in a section called 'Sci-

Use the General Index to find the page number of a specific publisher. If the publisher you are seeking is not listed, check the " '94-'95 Changes" list at the end of this section.

Fi Galleria.' **A short checklist of what I look for in all poems and stories would be: drawing the reader into the protagonist's life from the beginning; presenting a poem's message through powerful imagery and sensory details; and language that is fresh and dynamic. I prefer free verse. Would also like to receive experimental, multicultural, feminist, humor, contemporary and translations."** She has recently published poetry by Lynda S. Silva, Lyn Lifshin, Mary Winters and J. Blaire Hudson. As a sample the editor selected these lines from "Epiphany" by Christine Swanberg:

Because twenty years ago I walked
in Red Square, stood in long lines
for Lenin's Corpse, and oranges,
because I too know the disappointment
of too much thought and theory
and have found church doors locked
in my own country, because I wait
as the eagle dies in the desert,
I need to proclaim this epiphany
with bells, I am burdened, . . .

"***Gotta Write Network*** subscribers receive more than a magazine. In subscribing, they become part of a support group of both beginners and established poets. I offer critiques at request, will even retype a poem to point out spelling errors and suggest other appropriate markets. Readers are from all walks of life: housewives, religious persons, seniors, nursing home residents. Five reside in prisons." Press run is 200. "I'm striving to give beginners a positive starting point (as well as promote the work of established writers and editors) and to encourage them to venture beyond rejection slips and writer's block. Publication can be a reality if you have determination and talent. There are over a thousand U.S. litmags waiting for submissions. So what are you waiting for?" Subscription: $12.75. **Sample postpaid: $5. Include a cover letter and SASE with submissions. Reports in 2-4 months. Sometimes sends prepublication galleys. Pays 1 copy. Acquires first North American serial rights.** Pays $5 for assigned by-mail interviews with established paperback authors and small press editors. Maren Publications now offers both typesetting and a "news service." She adds, "Write the way you feel the words. Don't let others mold you into another poet's style. Poetry is about personal imagery that needs to be shared with others."

GRAFFITI OFF THE ASYLUM WALLS (IV-Humor, erotica, fetishes), P.O. Box 1603, Nashville AR 71852-1603, founded 1991, "curator" BrYan Westbrook, is an "illiterary journal published whenever I receive enough suitable material." He wants **"stuff you would be afraid to show your mother, priest and/or shrink; also anything that can make me laugh. No formal poetry; no pro-religious or animal rights poetry; nothing boring."** They have published poetry by Cheryl Townsend, Belinda Subraman, harland ristau and Scott C. Holstad. As a sample the editor selected these lines from "Cheap Date" by Richard Cody:

His hands played over her fine young body,
seeking to unleash forbidden pleasures.
"You better enjoy this . . ." he whispered.
"You're going back to the graveyard tomorrow."

GOTAW is 8½ × 11, stapled with colored paper cover, drawings and cartoons. Press run varies. Subscription: $10 for 4 issues. **Sample postpaid: "$3 (checks made out to BrYan Westbrook) or will trade copies with other editors." Previously published poems and simultaneous submissions OK. Cover letter required. "I do not want to just see a list of previous publications. I want to know who you are more than where you've been." Often comments on rejections. Reports "usually next day, rarely more than 3 months." No payment, but offers contributors unlimited copies at discount price of $2. Acquires one-time rights.** Staff will review "*anything* someone wants to send me. Length varies with how much I think needs to be said." Sponsors annual chapbook contest. There is a $3 reading fee and 24-page limit. Deadline: September 17. Winner receives 27 copies; all others receive a copy of winning chapbook. BrYan Westbrook says, "Throughout history the preserved literature of any period has mainly been what the people of that time actually enjoyed. Scholars have placed these works upon lofty pedestals and declared them the only true art. It's time we stop trying to imitate what others have considered entertainment and get on with creating the art we really want for ourselves. ***GOTAW*** is my contribution to this endeavor."

GRAHAM HOUSE REVIEW (II, IV-Translations), Box 5000, Colgate University, Hamilton NY 13346, phone (315)824-1000, ext. 262, founded 1976, poetry editors Peter Balakian and Bruce Smith, appears yearly. "We publish contemporary poetry, poetry in translation, essays and interviews. **No preferences for styles or schools, just good poetry.**" They have published poems by Seamus Heaney, Marilyn Hacker, Maxine Kumin, Michael Harper and Carolyn Forché. ***GHR*** is digest-sized, flat-spined, 120 pgs., professionally printed on heavy stock, matte color card cover with logo, using 100 pgs. of poetry in each issue. They receive about 2,000 submissions of poetry/year, use 20-50. One of the best "reads" in the literary world, this publication features well-crafted free verse depicting emotionally tense or intellectually stimulating ideas and themes. It welcomes translations and has an "international" flavor. Circulation 500, with 300 subscriptions of which 50 are libraries. **Sample postpaid: $7.50. Reports in 2 months or less. Pays 2 copies.**

GRAIN; SHORT GRAIN CONTEST (II), Box 1154, Regina, Saskatchewan S4P 3B4 Canada, phone (306)757-6310, is a literary quarterly. "*Grain* strives for artistic excellence and seeks material that is accessible as well as challenging to our readers. Ideally, a ***Grain* poem should be well-crafted, imaginatively stimulating, distinctly original.**" They have published poetry by Evelyn Lau and Jay Meek. The editor selected as a sample the opening of "The Children" by Patrick Lane:

The children are singing.
Hear them as they rise out of the deep hollows,
the tangles of wildwood and wandering vines.
They are lifting from the shadows
where the black creek water flows
over mud and stones. They have left behind
the green whip of a snake
thrown like a thin necklace into the trees . . .

Grain is digest-sized, professionally printed with chrome-coated cover, 144 pgs., circulation 1,800, with 1,300 subscriptions of which 100 are libraries. They receive about 700 submissions of poetry/year, use 80-140 poems. Subscription: $19.95 (Canadian), $23.95 for US, $25.95 for other foreign destinations. **Sample: $5 plus IRC (or 80¢ Canadian postage). They want "no poetry that has no substance." Submit maximum of 8 poems. Cover letter required. Include "the number of poems submitted, address (with postal or zip code) and phone number." Send SASE for guidelines. Reports in 3-4 months. Pays $30+/poem. Buys first North American serial rights.** Holds an annual Short Grain Contest. Entries are either prose poems (a lyric poem written as a prose paragraph or paragraphs in 500 words or less) or postcard stories (also 500 words or less). Prizes in each category, $250 first, $150 second, $100 third and honorable mentions. All winners and honorable mentions receive regular payment for publication in *Grain*. Entry fee of $20 (Canadian) allows up to two entries in the same category, and includes a one-year subscription. Additional entries are $5 each. Entries are normally accepted between January 1 and April 30. The editor comments, "Only work of the highest literary quality is accepted. Read several back issues.

‡GRAND STREET (III), Room 906, 131 Varick St., New York NY 10013, is an attractive quarterly publishing poetry, fiction and nonfiction. **"We have no writer's guidelines, but publish the most original poetry we can find."** Work published in *Grand Street* has been included in the 1992, 1993 and 1994 volumes of **The Best American Poetry.**

GRASSLANDS REVIEW (I, II), Dept. of English, P.O. Box 13827, Denton TX 76203-3827, phone (817)565-2127, founded 1989, editor Laura B. Kennelly, is a magazine **"to encourage beginning writers and to give creative writing class experience in editing essays, fiction, poetry; using any type of poetry; shorter poems stand best chance."** They have recently published poetry by Albert Huffstickler, Allison Joseph, Al Cardinale, Lenore Sills, Michael McNeilley, Elizabeth Creamer and Jan Seale. As a sample the editor selected these lines from "Small Bird with a Chest of Red" by Helen Frost:

The window, the time to look through it,
grace of the trees, snow weight on branches.
Small red glow of a bird, settling
flying, lending its weight to the changing
colors of one, no two, sharp points
of light in the snow, on the tree.

GR is 80 pgs., digest-sized, professionally printed, photocopied, saddle-stapled with card cover. They accept 20-40 of 400 submissions received. Press run is 300. Subscription (2 issues): $8 for individuals, $20 institutions. **Sample postpaid: $3. Submit only during October and March, no more than 5 poems at a time. Editor comments on submissions "sometimes." Reports in 10-12 weeks. Sometimes sends prepublication galleys. Pays 2 copies.**

GRAYWOLF PRESS (V), Suite 203, 2402 University Ave., Saint Paul MN 55114, phone (612)641-0077, founded 1975, **does not read unsolicited mss.** They have published poetry by Tess Gallagher, Linda Gregg, Jack Gilbert, Chris Gilbert, John Haines, D. Nurkse and William Stafford. **Sometimes sends prepublication galleys. Pays 7½-10% royalties, 10 author's copies, advance negotiated.**

GREAT RIVER REVIEW (II), 211 W. Seventh, Winona MN 55987, founded 1977, poetry editor Orval Lund, is published twice a year. They want **"high quality contemporary poetry that uses image as the basis for expression. Suggested submission: 4-6 poems."** They have recently published poetry by Jack Myers, Rich Broderick, Jim Daniels, Margaret Hasse, Pam Harrison and Tom Hennen. *GRR* is 6×8, elaborately printed, with a featured poet in each issue. They use about 50 poems/issue, receive about 500, use 5-10%. Press run is 750 for 300-400 subscribers of which 30-50 are libraries, and 200-300 newsstand or bookstore sales. Subscription: $10 for two issues. **Sample postpaid: $6. Simultaneous submissions discouraged. Editor "sometimes" comments on rejections. Reports in 4-10 weeks, 4-12 months between acceptance and publication. Pays 2 copies.** Reviews books of poetry.

GREEN FUSE (III, IV-Political, ecology, social issues), 3365 Holland Dr., Santa Rosa CA 95404, phone (707)544-8303, founded 1984, editor Brian Boldt, is published in April and October. **"We are looking for accessible free verse—with strong concrete details and images—that celebrates earth's beauty, the harmony in diversity, and poetic sanity and truth in an age of prosaic lies and madness. We no longer accept simultaneous submissions and previously published work (unless, of course, you've written the perfect *Green Fuse* poem). Sentimental and religious work, poems submitted without SASE and work stinking of nicotine will be folded into origami."** They have recently published poetry by Antler, Barbara Crooker, Doug Dorph, Dorianne Laux, Denise Levertov, Laurel Speer and Elliot Richman. As a sample the editor selected these lines from "No Loving Beyond" by G.W. Kroeker:

There is no loving beyond
the earth . . . no
love of body free from
a passion for the rank
tangle of river bottoms . . .
no sex except it share the puffed
lips of lupine and the deep
honeyed throat of hibiscus
no musk free of leaf-mold
and the slow, hushed rot
of wood in ancient forests.

Green Fuse is 56 pgs., digest-sized, offset, perfect-bound, with b&w illustrations on the cover and throughout. They receive 3,000 poems a year and accept about 80. Press run is 600 for subscriptions, shelf and reading sales. Subscriptions: $14 for 3 issues, $18 for 4. **Sample postpaid: $4. "Please submit no more than three poems—or 70 lines or less." Do not submit mss February through March and August through September. Editor "sometimes" comments on rejections. Send SASE for guidelines. Reports within 3 months. Pays 1 copy, more to featured poets. Acquires first rights.**

GREEN MOUNTAINS REVIEW (II), Johnson State College, Johnson VT 05656, phone (802)635-2356, founded 1975, poetry editor Neil Shepard, appears twice a year and includes poetry (and other writing) by well-known authors and promising newcomers. They have published poetry by Denise Levertov, William Stafford, Hayden Carruth, Theodore Weiss, Roger Weingarten and Amy Clampitt. ***GMR*** is digest-sized, flat-spined, 150-200 pgs. Of 300 submissions they publish 30 authors. Press run is 1,200 for 200 subscriptions of which 30 are libraries. Subscription: $8.50/year. **Sample postpaid: $5. Submit no more than 5 poems. No simultaneous submissions. Cover letter with greetings and personal information required. Reads submissions September 1 through May 15 only. Editor sometimes comments on rejection slip. Send SASE for guidelines. Reports in 2-3 months. Pays 1 copy plus 1-year subscription. Acquires first North American serial rights.** Send books for review consideration. Poetry published in ***GMR*** has been selected for inclusion in ***The Best American Poetry 1994***.

GREENHOUSE REVIEW PRESS (V), 3965 Bonny Doon Rd., Santa Cruz CA 95060, founded 1975, publishes a series of poetry chapbooks and broadsides. **"Unsolicited mss are not accepted."** Send SASE for catalog to buy samples.

GREEN'S MAGAZINE (I, II); CLOVER PRESS (V), P.O. Box 3236, Regina, Saskatchewan S4P 3H1 Canada, founded 1972, editor David Green. ***Green's Magazine*** is a literary quarterly with a balanced diet of short fiction and poetry; Clover Press publishes chapbooks. They publish **"free/blank verse examining emotions or situations." They do not want greeting card jingles or pale imitations of the masters.** They have published poetry by Sheila Murphy, Mary Balazs, Robert L. Tener, B.Z. Niditch, Ruth Wildes Schuler and Kit Knight. As a sample the editor selected these lines from "Silhouette" by R.L. Cook:

She dreams tomorrows crowding like a flock
Of unborn children through her fallow womb.
Bearing a harvest ripe with memories
And, as she sighs, a presence fills the room.
Leave her alone, she is the ghost of youth:
Leave her to sleep, the ghost of love her groom.

The magazine is digest-sized, 100 pgs., with line drawings. A sample chapbook is also digest-sized, 60 pgs., typeset on buff stock with line drawings, matte card cover, saddle-stapled. Circulation is 400. Subscription: $12. **Sample postpaid: $4. Guidelines available for SASE. (IRCs for US queries and/or mss.) The editor prefers typescript, complete originals. Submissions are reported on in 2 months, publication is usually in 3 months. Pays 2 copies. Acquires first North American serial rights.** Occasionally reviews books of poetry in "up to 150-200 words." Send books for review consideration. **Unsolicited submissions are accepted for the magazine but not for books; query first on latter. Comments are usually provided on rejected mss.** "Would-be contributors are urged to study the magazine first."

THE GREENSBORO REVIEW; GREENSBORO REVIEW LITERARY AWARDS; AMON LINER POETRY AWARD (II), English Dept., University of North Carolina, Greensboro NC 27412, phone (910)334-5459, founded 1966, editor Jim Clark. ***TGR*** appears twice yearly and showcases well-made verse in all styles and forms, though shorter poems (under 50 lines) seem preferred. They have recently published poetry by Thomas Lux, Jeanne Larson, Stuart Friebert and Edward Kleinschmidt. As a sample the poetry editor selected these lines from "Guide" by Christine Garren:

The sun was out to show me

how dark, halcyon current
pulled you past the arched branches

and left your boat in the silver river
with its prow beating against the pine and boulder.

And you came up without me

The digest-sized, flat-spined magazine, 120 pgs., colored matte cover, professional printing, uses about 25 pgs. of poetry in each issue. Circulation 500 for 300 subscriptions of which 100 are libraries. Uses about 2.5% of the 2,000 submissions received each year. **Sample postpaid: $4. "Submissions (of no more than 5 poems) must arrive by September 15 to be considered for the Winter issue (acceptances in December) and February 15 to be considered for the Summer issue (acceptances in May). Manuscripts arriving after those dates will be held for consideration with the next issue." No simultaneous submissions. Cover letter not required but helpful. Include number of poems submitted. Reports in 2-4 months. Always sends prepublication galleys. Pays 3 copies. Acquires first North American serial rights.** They offer the Amon Liner Poetry Award for the best poem appearing in the magazine. They also sponsor an open competition for the Greensboro Review Literary Awards, $250 for both poetry and fiction each year. Deadline: September 15. Send SASE for guidelines.

GROVE ATLANTIC (V), 841 Broadway, New York NY 10003. Grove Press and Atlantic Monthly Press merged in February 1993. **They currently do not accept unsolicited mss.**

GRUE MAGAZINE (IV-Horror), Box 370, New York NY 10108, founded 1985, editor Peggy Nadramia, is a horror fiction magazine "with emphasis on the experimental, offbeat, rude." The editor wants **"poems of any length, including prose poems, with macabre imagery and themes. Not interested in Poe rip-offs (although we'll look at rhyming poems if subject is weird enough), 'straight' vampire, ghost or werewolf poems."** She has recently published poetry by Robert Frazier, G. Sutton Breiding, Denise Dumars, Todd Mecklem, John Grey and Jonathan Yungkans. As a sample she selected these lines from "And Die In Her Eyes" by Wayne Allen Sallee:

the night is her world
a heaving narcopolis,
its lodgers cramped in the most distant
of outposts, or trapped
with a nuclear awareness
in urban townhouse isolation

The magazine is digest-sized, 96 pgs., offset, with a glossy b&w cover, "sharp" graphics, and "a centerfold that is unique." It appears 3 times a year and has a press run of 3,000, of which 500 are subscriptions and 1,000 are newsstand sales. Subscription: $13/year. **Sample postpaid: $4.50. Submit up to 5 poems at a time. The editor usually provides criticism of rejected mss. Guidelines are available for SASE. Submissions are reported on in 3 to 6 months and time to publication is 12 to 18 months. Poets receive 2 copies plus $5/poem upon publication to a maximum of $5/ issue.** Her advice is: "We like poems that go for the throat, with strong, visceral controlling images. We're also interested in poems that comment upon, or challenge the conventions of, the horror genre itself."

GUERNICA EDITIONS INC.; ESSENTIAL POET SERIES, PROSE SERIES, DRAMA SERIES; INTERNATIONAL WRITERS (IV-Regional, translations, ethnic/nationality), P.O. Box 117, Toronto, Ontario M5S 2S6 Canada, founded 1978, poetry editor Antonio D'Alfonso. "We wish to bring together the

CLOSE-UP

Arresting Poems Are Those With Freshness

The prof sits in his muse.
He mews? The prof mews;
softly he speaks,
keeps his claws corked,
to be unstopped on paper.
But is it his purpose
to shred us there?
Where's all the humor then?
His scratches scar my ego.

(from "June Twilight")

David Green

Back in 1972 Canadian David Green was teaching creative writing at Oakland University in Rochester, Michigan, when he decided to start his own magazine. He was discouraged by trends in fiction writing at the time. "It was a time when good short fiction might be written but not find a home, that being an era when everything had to be oozy sex, a spell broken only to become sex and violence." Not that he wanted to produce a publication that was fastidious or highly moral; instead he hoped to "encourage writings that dealt with life without having to wallow through sex scenes imposed for their own sakes."

Green is a journalist by profession who also writes both fiction and poetry. His poems have been published in a number of small magazines including the British journal ***Envoi*** and the American publication ***Hyacinths and Biscuits*** (no longer in publication). Although he started ***Green's Magazine*** as a fiction magazine, it was not long before he was including poetry. "The first came from a Detroit colleague whose work was just too good to leave out. Today, poems take up about half the average magazine. Their use is no longer chance, but a most important part of each issue."

When Green returned to Regina, Saskatchewan, to teach journalism, he took his magazine with him. It's now a 100-page quarterly publication with about 40 poems in each issue. A quick look at the contributors' page reveals that the magazine draws work from poets living in the United States, Scotland and England as well as Canada. Green says Canada offers its poets a lot of publishing opportunities.

"Canada is blessed with a wide variety of poetry publications, a number of which have acquired solid international reputations," he says. While Canadian poets are fortunate to have so many opportunities, he warns them not to expect to be published in these magazines simply because they are Canadian. Magazines still look for quality over geography. On the other hand, Green says Canadian poets should never feel self-conscious about nationality or hesitant about expressing national pride.

To American poets and others interested in being published by Canadian magazines, he says keep in mind that you must use International Reply Coupons when requesting your material be returned from another country and avoid chauvinistic themes such as the Fourth of July. "Nor should your 1964 visit to Banff [Alberta] be regarded as a credential for 'knowing' Canada. . . . As with any other submissions, your work should seek the universality that poetry, like music, can convey."

Green directs his publication with John Hammond and Bill Matthew and he relies on help from outside readers as well. In reading poetry, Green is assisted by author James Mossman. Mossman has had stories and poetry published in the magazine and recently agreed to help screen submissions.

In addition to the magazine, Green also publishes an occasional (solicited) chapbook under the name Clover Press. In 1992 the press published **A Mind in the Square**, a collection of poetry by Canadian poet and short story writer L.A.A. Harding. The poet, who died that year, had helped Green for several years as an outside reader and contributor to the magazine. The collection was published as a tribute.

For the magazine, Green likes to see four to six poems in a submission to indicate the poet's scope. All submissions are read at least once; those that interest him are read a number of times. "Most of my readers like to read poetry aloud—it adds a dimension, even though the selections are made only on their printable merit." He doesn't like to restrict the magazine to any particular style or theme, but he is not interested in "greeting card jingly stuff" unless it is so skillfully done as to be a parody of the genre.

"The poems that arrest are those with freshness," Green says. "Consider the generations that have lived, yet each child awakens to the world as though it is new. The poetic experience has to convey that, not just for the 'child' but for the gnarled, saw-toothed old cynics."

Featuring new writers is one of the biggest joys of publishing his own magazine, says Green. It's all about "discovery—discovering a new talent or even a delicious new phrase," he says. He advises beginners to know and draw from the past, but write with their own voice and vision.

"The world's best explorations through language still are those of the Greeks, Romans and Mr. Shakespeare. However, your own view of life is still distinctive and so deserves to be expressed. Choose a model, but don't try to be a latter-day Tennyson or Ogden Nash; rather, study what made their works so appealing to you, borrow from their techniques, but make your work your own. Accept criticism without flinching or giving up. Write for yourself, but with the idea that it completes its circuit of communication only when it is published, so make it publishable."

—Robin Gee

different and often divergent voices that exist in Canada and the U.S. We are interested in translations. We are mostly interested right now in translated poetry and essays on pluriculturalism." They have published work by Gérald Godin, Anne Dandurand and Clément Marchand (Quebec); Mario Luzi, Antonio Porta and Giorgio Caproni (Italy); Marco Fraticelli and Antonino Mazza (Canada); and Diane Raptosh, Giose Rimanelli and Anthony J. Tamburri (USA). **Query with 1-2 pgs. of samples. Send SASE (Canadian stamps only) or SAE and IRCs for catalog.** The editor comments, "We are interested in promoting a pluricultural view of literature by bridging languages and cultures. Besides our specialization in international translation, we also focus on the work of Italian, Italian/Canadian and Italian/American writers."

GUILD PRESS; FULL CIRCLE SERIES (I, IV-Ethnic), Dept. PM, P.O. Box 22583, Robbinsdale MN 55422, founded 1978, senior editor Leon Knight, **"the leading publisher of minority authors in Minnesota," wants poems to 40 lines max., nothing sexually graphic.** They have recently published poetry by George Clabon, Hazel Clayton Harrison and Nancy Ellen Williams (Big Mama). As a sample the editor selected these lines (poet unidentified):

I thought poetry
made a difference
...
But photography
doesn't alter sunsets:
poetry does not
restrain the wind

The Full Circle Series are **annual anthologies of 35-50 poets. Individual collections are published "by invitation only" to poets who have appeared in the "open-invitation" anthologies. Send SASE for guidelines. Pays copies.**

GULF STREAM MAGAZINE (II), English Dept., Florida International University, North Miami Campus, North Miami FL 33181, phone (305)940-5599, founded 1989, editor Lynne Barrett, associate editors Chris Gleason and Blythe Nobleman, is the biannual literary magazine associated with the creative writing program at FIU. They want **"poetry of any style and subject matter as long as it is of high literary quality."** They have published poetry by Gerald Costanzo, Judith Berke and Naomi Shihab Nye. The handsome magazine is 90 pgs., digest-sized, flat-spined, printed on quality stock with glossy card cover. They accept less than 10% of poetry received. Press run is 750. Subscription: $7.50. **Sample postpaid: $4. Submit no more than 5 poems. No simultaneous submissions. Reads submissions September 15 through April 30 only. Editor comments on submissions "if we feel we can be helpful." Publishes theme issues. Send SASE for guidelines. Reports in 2-3 months. Pays 2 free subscriptions. Acquires first North American serial rights.**

GUT PUNCH PRESS (III), P.O. Box 105, Cabin John MD 20818, founded 1987, editor Derrick Hsu, publishes 1-2 paperbacks/year. They want **"free verse with an innovative edge and possibly a sense of humor. No language school or formal narrative style."** They have published poetry collections by Richard Peabody and Sunil Freeman and an anthology of African-American poetry edited by Alan Spears. They recently published **Difficult Weather**, a collection by Rose Solari. **Query first with sample poems and cover letter with brief bio and publication credits. No poems previously published in book form or simultaneous submissions.** Time between acceptance and publication is 1 year. **Often comments on rejections. Replies to queries in 1 month, to mss (if invited) in 3 months. Pays royalties ("determined on an individual basis") and 50 author's copies. For sample books, send SASE for list and order form.** Most books are $7.95 postpaid. **Fingering the Keys** by Reuben Jackson won the 1992 Columbia Book Award, awarded by the Poetry Committee of the Greater Washington DC Area.

GUYASUTA PUBLISHER (I), The Sterling Building, 440 Friday Rd., Pittsburgh PA 15209, phone (412)821-6211, fax (412)821-6099, founded 1988, owner Cynthia Shore-Sterling. **"Guyasuta offers both straight and co-op publishing. We publish approximately 25 collections of poetry each year.** Our line has been expanded to trade paperback, self-help and quality short fiction." As a sample the owner selected these lines from Sheila Fiscus' poem "Thoughts From The Throne" from her book **Just A Housewife:**

As I sit naked on the porcelain throne,
My life files by, a procession of household care products.
But what of my heart, my soul, my joy of living?
Are they to be flushed into the sewer
By consummate daily tasks?

They will consider simultaneous submissions and unsolicited mss of 25-60 poems throughout the year. For further information, send SASE for catalog and guidelines. Sample: $5.95 (includes shipping). They are presently developing Guyasuta Writers and Artists Colony.

GYPSY (II); VERGIN PRESS (V), % Belinda Subraman and S. Ramnath, 10708 Gay Brewer, El Paso TX 79935, founded 1984 (in Germany), general editor Belinda Subraman, publishes poetry, fiction, interviews, articles, artwork and reviews. She wants **poetry that is "striking, moving, but not sentimental, any style, any subject matter."** They have recently published poetry by Maggie Jaffe, Elisavietta Ritchie, Jennifer Lagier and James Bertolino. As a sample she selected these lines by Cher Holt-Fortin:

Black oil and steel bent beyond the rim of purpose,
turned to a farmer's frame of use,
the urge of life outweighing
phantoms of death,
swords into plowshares.

Gypsy appears twice a year, with subscribers and contributors from the U.S., Canada, England, Europe and other countries. It is 56-90 pgs., magazine-sized, offset, usually with a hard spine. Circulation is 1,000 for 300 subscriptions of which 40 are libraries, about 80 shelf sales. Single copy: $8; subscription: $14/year. **Sample postpaid: $7. Editor sometimes comments on rejections. Reports in 1-3 months. Pays 1-3 copies.** Open to unsolicited reviews. Poets may also send books for review consideration. She publishes **2-3 books/year under the Vergin Press imprint but at present is not accepting unsolicited submissions for these.** New writers establish themselves with her by acceptance in *Gypsy*. Belinda Subraman says, "This is not a place for beginners. I'm looking for the best in all genres. Although I don't have anything against work of total self-absorption (guess I write some of that myself), I am just about fed up with it. I'd like to see work with a more universal appeal, a searching to connect, an understanding or a trying to understand other peoples in the universe. Please do not submit blindly. **We are planning a series of paperback anthologies on important issues. Send SASE for details.** Also please be advised that poetry is only about ⅕ (or less) of our focus these days. We value other forms of expression equally (if not more)."

HAIGHT ASHBURY LITERARY JOURNAL (II, IV-Social issues, themes), 558 Joost Ave., San Francisco CA 94127, phone (415)221-2017, founded 1979-1980, editors Joanne Hotchkiss, Alice Rogoff and Will Walker, is a newsprint tabloid that appears 1-3 times a year. They use **"all forms and lengths, including haiku. Subject matter sometimes political, but open to all subjects. Poems of background—prison, minority experience—often published, as well as poems of protest and of Central America. Few rhymes."** They have recently published poetry by Joyce Odam, Jack Micheline, Edgar Silex, Leticia Escamilla, Bill Shields and Ina Cumpiano. As a sample the editors selected these lines by Elliot Richman (which also appear in **Shrapnel in the Heart: Letters & Remembrances from the Vietnam Veterans Memorial)**:

I'd like to love you as I did in Nam
holding your hand on the last evening
of your life. Helping you die
is more intimate than sex,
more intimate than the children I bore.

The tabloid has a photo of its featured poet on the cover, uses graphics, ads, 16 pgs., circulation 2,000-3,000. $35 for a lifetime subscription, which includes 3 back issues. $12 for 4-issue subscription. **Sample postpaid: $3. Make checks payable to Alice Rogoff. Submit up to 6 poems or 8 pgs. "Please put name and address on every page and include SASE." Each issue changes its theme and emphasis. Send SASE for guidelines and upcoming themes. Reports in 2-3 months. Pays 3 copies.**

HAIKU HEADLINES: A MONTHLY NEWSLETTER OF HAIKU AND SENRYU (IV-Form), 1347 W. 71st, Los Angeles CA 90044, founded 1988, editor/publisher David Priebe, uses **haiku and senryu only. The editor prefers the 5/7/5 syllabic discipline, but accepts minimalist haiku which display pivotal contrast and appropriate imagery.** They have published haiku by Matthew Louviere, Dorothy McLaughlin, Mark Arvid White and Yvonne Hardenbrook. As a sample here are two haiku by Rengé/David Priebe:

whatever language
random objects speak: the rain
speaks it fluently

carnival balloon
rising up . . . and up . . . fading
into the darkness

The newsletter is 8 pgs., 8½×11, corner-stapled and punched for a three-ring notebook. They accept about 10% of submissions. Their press run is 300 with 185 subscriptions of which 3 are libraries. Subscription: $18. **Sample postpaid: $1.50. Haiku may be submitted with up to 10/single page. Submissions are "answered with proof sheets of acceptances, suggested revisions sheets, with occasional notes on originals—within 4-6 weeks." Publishes theme issues. Pays 1 copy with SASE, or free extra copy to subscribers.** Monthly Readers' Choice Awards: The Awards Kitty (average $50—contributions of postage stamps by the voters) is divided half for the 1st place winner; two runners-up share the other half. *HH* sponsors an annual contest (prizes

$100, $75, $50) and publishes the results in a calendar book, **Timepieces: Haiku Week At-A-Glance,** which the selected contributors can purchase at half the market price. The contest is open to the public and accepts entries from April 1 through July 31. Write for details.

HALF TONES TO JUBILEE (II), English Dept., Pensacola Junior College, 1000 College Blvd., Pensacola FL 32504, phone (904)484-1400, founded 1986, faculty editors Walter Spara and Allan Peterson, is an annual literary journal featuring poetry and short fiction. They have published poetry by R.T. Smith, Sue Walker, Larry Rubin and Simon Perchik. As a sample we selected these lines from "Penpal Who Has Not Written" by Andrea Hollander Budy:

> *You are the one I've never met who*
> *wrote so splendidly when I needed you*
> *and I am the one who, after awhile, let*
> *years grow like a row of taverns*
> *between receiving and giving*
> *back. . .*

HTTJ is 100 pgs., digest-sized, perfect-bound with matte card cover, professionally printed. Press run is 500. They receive 1,000 submissions/year, use 50-60. Subscription: $4. **Sample: $4. No previously published work, no simultaneous submissions, SASE mandatory. Cover letter with bio and/or publication history preferred. Reads submissions August 1 through May 15 only. Reports in 2-3 months, faster when possible. Pays 2 copies. Acquires first rights.** ***HTTJ*** sponsors an annual poetry competition, $300 first prize, $200 second, $100 third. Entry fee: $2/poem. Send SASE for rules, deadlines. In addition to numerous awards from the Florida Press Association, ***Half Tones to Jubilee*** has received two national awards, a first place with merit from the American Scholastic Press Association, and first place, Southern division, literary magazine competition, Community College Humanities Association.

‡HAMMERS; DOUBLESTAR PRESS (II), #203, 1718 Sherman, Evanston IL 60201, founded 1989, editor Nat David. ***Hammers***, "an end of millennium irregular poetry magazine," appears at least twice a year. Many of the poets they have published are from the Chicago area, although each issue also includes the work of poets from a variety of other geographical regions. They want **"honest, well-written poetry from the depths of the poet's universe and experience, which is cognizant of our interconnectedness."** They have recently published poetry by Rane Arroyo, John Grey, Nancy Peters Hastings, Albert Huffstickler and T. Kilgore Splake. As a sample we selected these lines from "At the Grocery" by Hal J. Daniel III:

> *Ninety or so,*
> *confused about the one-way direction*
> *of the check out lane,*
> *she pushes her cart east*
> *rather than with the slow westward flow.*

Hammers is 88 pgs., 6⅞ × 8½, professionally printed and saddle-stapled with matte card cover. Single copy: $5; subscription: $15 for 4 issues. **Sample postpaid: $6. Editor seldom comments on submissions. Reports ASAP. Pays 1 copy.** In 1999, the editor intends to publish in book form **The Best of Hammers**.

‡HANDSHAKE EDITIONS (V); CASSETTE GAZETTE (II), Atelier A2, 83 Rue de la Tombe-Issoire, Paris, France 75014, phone 4327-1767, founded 1979. ***Cassette Gazette*** is an audiocassette issued "from time to time." They are interested in **humorous poetry and poetry dealing with love/romance, political/social issues and women/feminism themes.** Poets recently published include Ted Joans, Yianna Katsoulos, Judith Malina, Elaine Cohen, Amanda Hoover, Jayne Cortez, Roy Williamson, Mary Guggenheim and Susi Wyss. **Pays in copies. Handshake Editions does not accept unsolicited mss for book publication.** Jim Haynes, publisher, says, "I prefer to deal face to face."

HANGING LOOSE PRESS (V); HANGING LOOSE (I, II, IV-Teens/students), 231 Wyckoff St., Brooklyn NY 11217, founded 1966, poetry editors Robert Hershon, Dick Lourie, Mark Pawlak and Ron Schreiber. **The press does not accept unsolicited book mss, but welcomes work for the magazine,** which appears 3 times/year. The magazine has published poetry by Paul Violi, Donna Brook, Kimiko Hahn, Ron Overton, Jack Anderson and Frances Phillips. ***Hanging Loose*** is 96 pgs., flat-spined, offset on heavy stock with a 2-color glossy card cover. One section contains **poems by high-school-age poets. The editor says it "concentrates on the work of new writers." Sample postpaid: $6.50. Submit 4-6 "excellent, energetic" poems. No simultaneous submissions. "Would-be contributors should read the magazine first." Reports in 1-12 weeks. Pays small fee and 3 copies.** Poetry published in ***Hanging Loose*** has been included in **The Best American Poetry 1993**.

HANGMAN BOOKS (IV-Regional), 2 May Rd., Rochester, Kent ME1 2HY England, founded 1982, editor Jack Ketch, publishes selected books of poetry on a cooperative basis. Jack Ketch says, "We receive no grant, **therefore we expect the writers to put their money where their mouth is. We don't advertise this fact as we are not a vanity press. We only approach a writer with this proposal if we are sufficiently impressed with their work and want to help them (this is very rare)." They want "personal" poetry, "none rhyming, none political, bla bla bla."** They have published poetry by Chris Broderick, Neil Sparkes and Billy Childish. As a sample the editor selected these lines from **May My Piss Be Gentle** by Mark Lowe:

all those tears
all that madness and grief
in that big old house of ours
and i think back
and it's like i'm drowning
in a whole fucking river
of unnecessary sadness

That is from a handsomely printed flat-spined book of 110 pgs. **Editor always sends prepublication galleys. 60% of press run belongs to poet.**

HANSON'S SYMPOSIUM (II), P.O. Box 4490, Annapolis MD 21403, founded 1988, is an annual using **"all forms, styles, subjects and points of view reflective of intelligence and a sense of beauty."** As a sample the editor selected these lines from "Sometimes I Just Tip Over" by George Kempis:

You wonder at these moods of mine;
how I seem such a monster of self-enraged will;
as do I, looking out from the cage of my soul,
wondering why must I rage and pull at my line.
Why can't I lie here so peaceful and still,
licking the water from out of my bowl?

It is magazine-sized, 75-100 pgs., saddle-stapled with matte card cover. Press run is 3,000 for 1,500 subscriptions including 2 library systems. "We receive thousands of poems per year, publish about 30-40." **Sample postpaid: $6. Editor seldom comments on submissions. Reports in 2 months. Pays $25-50 plus 1 copy. Buys first North American serial rights. "Previous publication is not a prerequisite. We'd rather see honest, careful art, than a resume."** The editor adds, "Due to the limited space in our publication, and due to its unique nature, we require that all writers interested in being published in ***Hanson's Symposium*** review a sample copy before submitting work."

HARCOURT BRACE & COMPANY; HB CHILDREN'S BOOKS; GULLIVER BOOKS; BROWNDEER PRESS; JANE YOLEN BOOKS (IV-Children), Suite 1900, 525 B St., San Diego CA 92101, phone (619)699-6810. HB Children's Books, Gulliver Books, Browndeer Press and Jane Yolen Books publish hardback and trade paperback books for children. They have published books of children's poetry by Jane Yolen, Arnold Adoff, James Dickey, e.e. cummings, Lee Bennett Hopkins and Carl Sandburg. **Submit complete ms. Always sends prepublication galleys. Pays favorable advance, royalty contract and copies. Send SASE for guidelines and book catalog.**

HARD ROW TO HOE; MISTY HILL PRESS (I, IV-Nature/rural/ecology), P.O. Box 541-I, Healdsburg CA 95448, phone (707)433-9786. ***Hard Row to Hoe,*** taken over from Seven Buffaloes Press in 1987, editor Joe E. Armstrong, is a "book review newsletter of literature from rural America with a section reserved for short stories (about 2,000 words) and **poetry featuring unpublished authors. The subject matter must apply to rural America including nature and environmental subjects. Poems of 30 lines or less given preference, but no arbitrary limit. No style limits. Do not want any subject matter not related to rural subjects."** As a sample the editor selected "Cheers" by Donna Kalchik:

No one told them
When they set out
To be farmers
That some years
They would lean
Over glasses of whiskey
Celebrating harvest
Like a wake.

HRTH is magazine-sized, 12 pgs., side-stapled, appearing 3 times a year, 3 pgs. reserved for short stories and poetry. Press run is 300. Subscription: $7/year. **Sample postpaid: $2. Send SASE for guidelines. Editor comments on rejections "if I think the quality warrants." Pays 2 copies. Acquires one-time rights.** Reviews books of poetry in 600-700 words. Open to unsolicited reviews. Poets may also send books for review consideration. ***Hard Row to Hoe*** was selected by ***Small Press Review*** as one of the 10 best newsletters in the US.

HARP-STRINGS; EDNA ST. VINCENT MILLAY AWARD; ELIZABETH B. BROWNING SONNETS AWARD; ROBERT FROST BLANK VERSE AWARD (II), P.O. Box 640387, Beverly Hills FL 34464, founded 1989, editor Madelyn Eastlund, appears 3 times/year. **They want poems of "14-70 lines, narratives, lyrics, ballads, sestinas, rondeau, redouble, blank verse. Nothing 'dashed off,' trite, broken prose masquerading as poetry."** They have published poetry by Barbara Nightingale, Robert Cooperman, Robin Shectman and Anne Marx. As a sample we selected these lines from "Standing on the South Rim of the Grand Canyon" by Lucille Morgan Wilson:

The shuffle of my feet
dislodges a pebble, sends it over the edge
toward the turbulent river. From this distance
I cannot tell if it breaks the water's surface,
but I claim the instant of its descent.

It is 40 pgs., digest-sized, saddle-stapled, professionally printed in colored ink on quality colored matte stock with matte card cover. She accepts 5-10% of poems received. Press run is 100 for 75 subscribers. Subscription: $12. **Sample postpaid: $5 for previous year, $6 for current year. Pays 1 copy. Acquires one-time rights. "I am interested in seeing poems that have won awards but have not been published."** Sponsors 3 contests each year: Elizabeth B. Browning Sonnets Award (Shakespearean or Petrarchan Sonnet, deadline March 15); Edna St. Vincent Millay Award (narrative from 36 to 80 lines, deadline July 15); Robert Frost Blank Verse Award (deadline November 15). Entry fee for each contest: $2/poem, $5/3 poems. Cash awards of $10-40 and publication. "Stanley Kunitz once said, 'Poetry today has become easier to write but harder to remember.' ***Harp-Strings*** wants poetry to remember, poetry that haunts, poetry the reader wants to read again and again."

THE HARTLAND POETRY QUARTERLY; HARTLAND PRESS (I, II, IV-Children, themes), Dept. PM, 168 Fremont, Romeo MI 48065, phone (313)752-5507, founded 1989, contact David Bock. **"Prefer 24 lines or less; no style restrictions; no pornography—none—nada—nil! Looking for serious poems by Viet Nam veterans and I mean serious—don't send the one-and-only angry poem—I got that stuff coming out of my ears. Very, very open to good children's poems written only by children under 15 for a special 'coming out' part of the magazine."** They have published poetry by Loriann Zimmer, T. Kilgore Splake and Laurence W. Thomas. Their quarterly is digest-sized, spine-stapled, 25-30 pgs. They accept about 15% of 300-500 poems received/year. Press run is 500 for 70 subscribers of which 15 are libraries, 300 shelf sales. Subscription: $8. **Sample postpaid: $1. Include bio with submission. Publishes theme issues occasionally. Upcoming theme: "Coming Home Again," for a special Viet Nam issue in fall 1995. Reports in 8-10 weeks. Sometimes sends prepublication galleys. Pays 2 copies.** Reviews books of poetry. **They publish 2 chapbooks/year of poets already published in the quarterly. Pays 20 copies.** The editor says, "Write about what you have lived. Read, read, write, write—repeat cycle 'till death. Support as many small publications as you can afford."

THE HARVARD ADVOCATE (IV-Specialized: university affiliation), Dept. PM, 21 South St., Cambridge MA 02138, phone (617)495-0737, founded 1866, is a quarterly literary magazine, circulation 4,000, that publishes **poetry, fiction and art only by those affiliated with Harvard University; open to outside submissions of essays. Sample: $4. In submitting state your exact relationship to Harvard. Does not pay.** Reviews books, including poetry.

HAUNTS (IV-Science fiction/fantasy, horror), Nightshade Publications, P.O. Box 3342, Providence RI 02906, phone (401)781-9438, is a "literary quarterly geared to those fans of the 'pulp' magazines of the 30s, 40s and 50s, with tales of **horror, the supernatural and the bizarre. We are trying to reach those in the 18-35 age group.**" Circulation: 1,000. **Sample: $4.25 plus $1 postage. Uses free verse, light verse and traditional, about 12-16 poems a year. Send a maximum of 3 poems. Cover letter including "brief introduction of the writer and the work submitted" required. Send SASE for guidelines. Pays $3/poem.**

HAWAII PACIFIC REVIEW (II), 1060 Bishop St., Honolulu HI 96813, founded 1986, editor Elizabeth Fischel, is an annual literary journal "publishing quality poetry, short fiction and personal essays from writers worldwide. **Our journal seeks to promote a world view that celebrates a variety of cultural themes, beliefs, values and viewpoints. Although we do publish beginning poets on occasion, we do not publish amateurish poetry. We wish to further the growth of artistic vision and talent by encouraging sophisticated and innovative poetic and narrative techniques."** They have recently published poetry by Robert Cooperman and Mary Kay Rummel. As a sample the editor selected these lines from Rummel's "Stations of the Cross":

As I type through rivers of pulp
The desktop meets me at the waist.
I am the vertical shaft.

We finish our crosses. A poor place
to hang a life whether with yeasted strips
of bread, cotton pieces or a plastic pen-
to hang so long and miss the resurrection.

HPR is 80-120 pgs., 6×9, professionally printed on quality paper, perfect-bound, with coated card cover; each issue features original artwork. Mostly free verse, poems here tend to be insightful, informative and well-made with an emphasis on cultural diversity. They receive 800-1,000 poems, accept 30-40. Press run is approximately 1,000 for 200 shelf sales. Single copy: $5-6. **Sample postpaid: $4. No previously published poems; simultaneous submissions OK. Cover letter with 5-line professional bio including prior publications required. Seldom comments on rejections. Send SASE for guidelines. Reports within 3 months. Pays 2 copies. Acquires first North American serial rights.** The editor says, "We'd like to receive more experimental verse. Many of the poems we receive are more personal therapy than true art. Good poetry is eye-opening; it investigates the unfamiliar or reveals the spectacular in the ordinary. Good poetry does more than simply express the poet's feelings; it provides both insight and unexpected beauty."

HAWAI'I REVIEW (I, II), % Dept. of English, University of Hawai'i, 1733 Donaghho Rd., Honolulu HI 96822, phone (808)956-3030, editor-in-chief Michelle Viray, poetry editors Sam Gonzalez and Annie Fanning. "We are interested in **all sorts of poetry, from free verse to formal lyricism, rhyme and meter; heroic narrative, haiku, light verse, satire and experimentation; we're also interested in poems translated from other languages; and while *Hawai'i Review* has published poets with established reputations like Eric Chock and W.S. Merwin, the beginner is also welcome."** They have published poetry by Lyn Lifshin, Lois-Ann Yamanaka and Tony Quagliano, and translations by Carolyn Tipton and Alexis Levitin. As a sample the editors selected the poem "The Pearl" by Cai Qi-Jiao, translated by Edward Morin and Dennis Ding:

The wound inside
The oyster's tender body
Expands into a hard, rough obstruction.
Month by month, year after year,
Wrapped in layer upon adhesive layer,
It becomes mellow and smooth.
Here you see crystaline grief and sea tears,
Yet all humankind treasures it!
I sense that it still wears the salt smell of the ocean,
That its glistening teardrops bear
The laments of sun, moon, stars, and clouds.

HR appears 3 times yearly and is 160 pgs., 6½×9½, flat-spined, professionally printed on heavy stock with b&w or color cover, 150 subscriptions of which 40 are libraries. Up to 1,800 are used by University of Hawai'i students. Subscription: $15/one year; $25/two years. **Sample: $5. Send SASE for guidelines. "Artwork to accompany poetry is welcomed." Editors rarely comment on rejections. Reporting time: 3-4 months.** Publication 9-12 months thereafter. **Pays $10-60 plus 2 copies "to anyone with a Social Security number. Anyone without a Social Security number is paid in copies." Buys first North American serial rights.** Does not normally review books, but "authors can query" or send books for review consideration to Michelle Viray. The editorial staff rotates each year, so content varies. Sometimes one staff rejects work that has "come close" and suggests sending the same manuscript in the next year to see what the new editors think. ***Hawai'i Review*** ranked #8 in the "New Poets" category of the latest ***Writer's Digest*** Poetry 60 list. This category ranks those markets who often publish poets whose work is new to their publication. The editors say, "Good poetry shows more than pseudo-literary erudition; it will, as Anthony Wallace says, *sing* and *mean*."

HAYDEN'S FERRY REVIEW (II), Box 871502, Arizona State University, Tempe AZ 85287-1502, phone (602)965-1243, founded 1986, managing editor Salima Keegan, is a handsome literary magazine appearing twice a year. They have published poetry by Dennis Schmitz, Maura Stanton, Ai, and David St. John. ***HFR*** is 6×9, 120 pgs., flat-spined with glossy card cover. Press run is 1,000 for 100 subscribers of which 30 are libraries, 500 shelf sales. They accept about 3% of 2,800 submissions annually. Subscription: $10. **Sample postpaid: $6. "No specifications other than limit in number (6) and no simultaneous submissions. We would like a brief bio for contributor's note included." Submissions circulated to two poetry editors. Editor comments on submissions "often." Send SASE for guidelines. Reports in 8-10 weeks of deadlines. Deadlines: February 28 for Spring/Summer issue; September 30 for Fall/Winter. Contributors receive galley proofs. Pays 2 copies.**

‡HEALING JOURNAL (III, IV-Specialized), Suite 150, 1050 Fulton Ave., Sacramento CA 95825, founded 1992, managing editor Katrina Middleton, is an attractive quarterly magazine "about communication, a forum for healthcare professionals and patients to dialogue about the illness experience through art, poetry, interviews/profiles and personal essays." **They want "avant-garde, free verse or traditional poetry that is health related or 'healing' focused. Humor OK, but no limericks or puns."** As a sample the editor selected these lines from "After My Stroke" by Margaret Robison:

My right side feels lonely for my left side.
The two sides of my body
are like husband and wife
who stay together for the sake of the children.
My left arm no longer listens
to my brain. It has gone to sleep . . .

HJ is 36 pgs., 8½ × 11, professionally printed on matte-coated recycled paper and saddle-stapled with color cover, art and b&w photos. They publish 10-20 poems/year. Press run is 5,500. Single copy: $3, subscription: $30/year. **Previously published poems OK; no simultaneous submissions. Submit no more than 5 poems at a time.** Time between acceptance and publication is 4 months to 1 year. **Reports in 1 month. Pays 5 copies. Acquires one-time rights.**

HEAVEN BONE PRESS; HEAVEN BONE MAGAZINE (II, IV-Spiritual, nature/rural/ecology), P.O. Box 486, Chester NY 10918, phone (914)469-9018, founded 1986, poetry editor Steve Hirsch, publishes poetry, fiction, essays and reviews with **"an emphasis on spiritual, metaphysical, esoteric and ecological concerns."** They have published poetry and fiction by Charles Bukowski, Marge Piercy, Kirpal Gordon and Hart Sprager. As a sample the editor chose "Five-Petaled Regular Corolla Rose" by Edward Mycue:

has surrounding fingers that play
with your nose from the inner en-
velope. This is not the Rose of
Sharon. That spindling hollyhock
is as near to a rose as a hemlock.
The rosary has five sacred mysteries
and five decades of Ave Marias, &
each begins with a paternoster, ends
with a Gloria, repeated in formula
like a prayer or/and magic-mystic
charm: more of a path than pastime.
Rose, you single step, pilgrimage,
you Rose, of colored hope, chafe.
You are window, compass, pleasantly
rote: I know you now, know you not.

Heaven Bone is 64 pgs., magazine-sized, saddle-stapled, using b&w art, photos and ads, on recycled bond stock with glossy 4-color recycled card cover. They have a press run of 2,500. Of 250-350 poems received they accept 18-30. Subscription: $16.95. **Sample postpaid: $6. Submit 3-10 poems. Simultaneous submissions and previously published poems OK "if notified." Occasionally publishes theme issues. Send SASE for upcoming themes. Reports in 2 weeks to 6 months, up to 8 months until publication. Sometimes sends prepublication galleys. Pays 2 copies. Acquires first North American serial rights.** Reviews books of poetry. Open to unsolicited reviews. Poets may also send books for review consideration. The press offers an annual chapbook contest. 1992 winner: **Red Bracelets**, by Janine Pommy-Vega. Send SASE for guidelines. Editor advises, "Please be familiar with the magazine before sending mss. We receive too much religious verse. Break free of common 'poetic' limitations and speak freely with no contrivances. No forced end-line rhyming please. Channel the muse and music without being an obstacle to the poem."

HELICON NINE EDITIONS (V); MARIANNE MOORE POETRY PRIZE (II), P.O. Box 22412, Kansas City MO 64113, phone (913)722-2999, founded 1977, editor Gloria Vando Hickok. Helicon Nine, formerly a literary magazine, is a publisher of books of poetry as well as fiction, creative nonfiction and anthologies. **"Our one requirement is excellence; nothing pedestrian."** They have published poetry by Joyce Carol Oates, Grace Paley, Ellen Gilchrist and James Dickey. As a sample the editor selected these lines from "The instruction of Clotilde" by Regina deCormier from her new book, **Hoofbeats on the Door:**

Dragging his reluctant shadow, Francois
leaves the stone paved courtyard of his house
at dawn. His cloak lifts with the wind
of his step, the long toes of his shoes
curl, and point to Heaven. Light is
just beginning to spool off the face
of Our Lady of Paris and a bronze cock

is crowing goodbye. Evening will find him
fifteen kilometres southeast of Paris,
a blue rug over his knees.

"Payment varies, but we're in the publishing business to *help* poets and authors, not to hinder them or take advantage. We publish *beautiful* books and try to get them into the hands of readers. We have national distributors making sure our books are made available throughout the States. We also aggressively pursue new markets and book reviews and advertise in many trade publications as well as exhibit at the ABA, etc." **They are currently not accepting poetry submissions, other than annual contest entries.** The Marianne Moore Poetry Prize, $1,000 for an unpublished poetry ms of at least 50 pgs., is awarded each year and includes publication by Helicon Nine Editions. Send SASE for guidelines. Helicon Nine received the Kansas Governor's Arts Award in 1991 for making "a significant contribution" to the arts in that state.

HELIKON PRESS (V), 120 W. 71st St., New York NY 10023, founded 1972, poetry editors Robin Prising and William Leo Coakley, **"tries to publish the best contemporary poetry in the tradition of English verse."** As a sample the editors selected these lines from **Selected Poems & Ballads** by Helen Adam:

Towers of atoms fall and rise
Where gigantic Adam lies.

"We read (and listen to) poetry and ask poets to build a collection around particular poems. We print fine editions illustrated by good artists. Unfortunately we cannot encourage submissions."

HELLAS: A JOURNAL OF POETRY AND THE HUMANITIES; THE HELLAS AWARD (II, IV-Form), 304 S. Tyson Ave., Glenside PA 19038, phone (215)884-1086, fax (215)884-3304, e-mail 73564.1037@compuserve.com, founded 1988, editor Gerald Harnett. ***Hellas*** is a semiannual that wants poetry of **"any kind but especially poems in meter. We prize elegance and formality in verse, but specifically encourage poetry of the utmost boldness and innovation, so long as it is not willfully obscurantist; no ignorant, illiterate, meaningless free verse or political poems."** They have recently published poetry by Hadas, Steele, Moore, Butler, Kessler, Gioia and many others. As a sample we selected these lines from "Seed" by Charley Custer:

Within the hard damp dark, marooned
in rot between dead root and weed
through every bitter winter wound
and solstice, is the seed.

It is 172 pgs., 6×9, flat-spined, offset, using b&w art. Press run is 750. Subscription: $14. **Sample postpaid: $8.75. Send SASE for guidelines. They will not consider simultaneous submissions or previously published poems. Reports in 3-4 months. Editor comments on rejections "happily if requested. If I don't understand it, I don't print it. On the other hand, we don't want obvious, easy, clichéd or sentimental verse." Pays 1 copy. Acquires first North American serial rights.** The ***Hellas*** Award ($200) is open to ***Hellas*** subscribers only and is awarded annually to the finest poem entered in the contest. Poems may be submitted to both ***Hellas*** and the contest simultaneously at any time throughout the year, but the annual deadline is December 31. Winner is published in spring issue of ***Hellas***. Enclose SASE if submission is to be returned. They also sponsor the ***Hellas*** readings, held at various locations in Philadelphia, New York and elsewhere. Send SASE for guidelines. In its first years, ***Hellas*** was voted one of the "Best New Journals of 1991" by the Conference of Editors of Learned Journals. Their flyer says, **"*Hellas*** is a lively and provocative assault on a century of modernist barbarism in the arts. A unique, Miltonic wedding of *paideia* and *poiesis*, engaging scholarship and original poetry, ***Hellas*** has become the forum of a remarkable new generation of poets, critics and theorists committed to the renovation of the art of our time . . . **Meter is especially welcome, as well as rhymed and stanzaic verse. We judge a poem by its verbal artifice and its truth. Lines should not end arbitrarily, diction should be precise: we suggest that such principles can appear 'limiting' only to an impoverished imagination. To the contrary: we encourage any conceivable boldness and innovation, so long as it is executed with discipline and is not a masquerade for self-indulgent obscurantism. . . . We do not print poems about Nicaragua, whales or an author's body parts. We do specifically welcome submissions from newer authors."**

The Subject Index, located before the General Index, can help you narrow down markets for your work. It lists those publishers whose poetry interests are specialized.

HEN'S TEETH (V), P.O. Box 689, Brookings SD 57006, founded 1988, editor Janice H. Mikesell, expects to publish a book every 2 years but **will not be open for submissions. "I publish material that I have written or co-edited only. Unsolicited material, unless accompanied by a SASE, will not be returned."** She has published **Women Houses & Homes: an anthology of prose, poetry and photography,** $8 postage paid, a 52-page, saddle-stapled book, cut with a roof-line top, professionally printed with a cover photograph of a "painted lady" Victorian house and now in its fifth printing. As a sample the editor selected these lines from **A Survivor's Manual: a book of poems:**

I ask you this
remember me
I used to be your wife

be sure that I'll remember you
as the man who
stole my life

That book is a 52-page, perfect-bound paperback with an arresting cover photo (also $8 postage paid).

HERESIES (IV-Women/feminism, lesbian, themes), P.O. Box 1306, Canal St. Station, New York NY 10013, founded 1977, editorial collective, is a "feminist publication on art and politics." **Poetry "must be by women and fit into the specific issue theme."** They have published poetry by Adrienne Rich, Alice Walker and Margaret Randall. ***Heresies***, one of the oldest and best-known feminist publications, appears 1-2 times a year in a 96-page, flat-spined, magazine-sized format, offset with half-tones, 2-color glossy card cover, using nonprofit, book related exchange ads. They accept about 5 out of 100 submissions. Mostly free verse lyrics are featured here, though all of them accessible. Press run is 5,000 for 1,500 subscriptions of which a fourth are libraries, 1,500 shelf sales. Single copy: $8; subscription: $27/4 issues. **Sample back issue postpaid: $6. Simultaneous submissions OK. Mss should be submitted in duplicate. Send SASE for issue themes and guidelines before submitting work. "Nonthematic work cannot be considered." Reports in 8-12 months. Pays small honorarium plus 3 copies.**

HERSPECTIVES MAGAZINE (I, IV-Women, feminism), Box 2047, Squamish, British Columbia V0N 3G0 Canada, phone (604)892-5723, founded 1989, editor Mary Billy, uses **"poetry that expresses women's lives in a positive experiential way—open to almost anything by, for or about women. Nothing obscure. Short poems have a better chance. Will accept almost anything with intelligent humor."** As a sample the editor selected these lines by Gert Beadle:

When they have closed
The windows where I fled
And gave the empty house
to fire
Will they remember how
I loved a mystery

Herspectives appears quarterly in a 40- to 50-page stapled format. Uses 4-6 poems/issue. Press run is 250 for 125 subscribers of which 2 are libraries. Subscription: $22-35 ($35-45 US); $40-50 for businesses and organizations. **Sample postpaid: $6. "No checks from outside Canada; send cash or money order in Canadian funds, please." Simultaneous submissions and previously published poetry OK. Cover letter required. Publishes theme issues. Editor often comments on rejections. Pays 1 copy.** Reviews books of poetry in 500-750 words. Open to unsolicited reviews. Poets may also send books for review consideration. They also use short, short fiction and other writing. **"We are mainly interested in giving new writers exposure. I don't like poetry that is so obscure only the mentally defective can understand it. We are about openness and ideas, about women's creative expression, wherever that may lead them.** The name says it all: HER-spectives. We don't print material by men although they are welcome as subscribers."

HIGH PLAINS LITERARY REVIEW (III), Suite 250, 180 Adams St., Denver CO 80206, phone (303)320-6828, founded 1986, editor Robert O. Greer, associate poetry editor Ray Gonzalez, appears 3 times/year using **"high quality poetry, fiction, essays, book reviews and interviews."** The format is 135 pgs., 70 lb. paper, heavy cover stock. Subscription: $20. **Sample postpaid: $4. Pays $10/published page for poetry.**

HIGH PLAINS PRESS (IV-Regional), P.O. Box 123, Glendo WY 82213, phone (307)735-4370, founded 1985, poetry editor Nancy Curtis, considers books of **poetry "specifically relating to Wyoming and the West, particularly poetry based on historical people/events. We're mainly a publisher of historical nonfiction, but do publish a book of poetry about every other year."** They have published poetry by Peggy Simson Curry, Robert Roripaugh and Mary Alice Gunderson. As a sample she quoted these lines from the book **No Roof But Sky** by Jane Candia Coleman. The poem is "Geronimo photographed at Ft. Sill (1905)":

Bring me the elusive images
of my life, and I will smile for you—
over and over—an exchange of illusions
like the dying change into light.

Reports in 2 months, publication in 18-24 months. Always sends prepublication galleys. Pays 10% of sales. Buys first rights. Catalog available on request; sample chapbooks: $5. No Roof But Sky won the Wrangler Award for "accuracy and literary merit in portraying the West" in the poetry category from the National Cowboy Hall of Fame.

HIGH/COO PRESS; MAYFLY (IV-Form), 4634 Hale Dr., Decatur IL 62526, phone (217)877-2966, founded 1976, editors Randy and Shirley Brooks. High/Coo is a small press publishing nothing but **haiku in English.** "We publish haiku poemcards, minichapbooks, anthologies and a bibliography of haiku publications in addition to paperbacks and cloth editions and the magazine *Mayfly*, evoking emotions from contemporary experience. We are not interested in orientalism nor Japanese imitations." They previously published the **Midwest Haiku Anthology** which included the work of 54 haiku poets. **They publish no poetry except haiku.** They have published haiku by Virgil Hutton, Lee Gurga and Wally Swist. As a sample the editors selected this haiku by Bill Pauly:

country field—
home run rolling
past the headstones

Mayfly is 16 pgs., saddle-stapled, 3×5, professionally printed on high-quality stock, one haiku/page. It appears in January and August. They publish 32 of an estimated 1,800 submissions. Subscription: $8. **Sample postpaid: $4. A Macintosh computer disk of haiku-related stacks is available for $10 postpaid. Guidelines available for SASE. Submit no more than 5 haiku/issue. No simultaneous submissions or previously published poems. Pays $5/poem and no copies.** High/Coo Press **considers mss "by invitation only."** Randy Brooks says, "Publishing poetry is a joyous work of love. We publish to share those moments of insight contained in evocative haiku. We aren't in it for fame, gain or name. We publish to serve an enthusiastic readership. **Please note that we have changed our policy of requiring contributors to be subscribers, so submissions are open from all writers."**

HIGHLIGHTS FOR CHILDREN (IV-Children), 803 Church St., Honesdale PA 18431, phone (717)253-1080, founded 1946, appears every month using **poetry for children ages 2-12. They want "meaningful and/or fun poems accessible to children of all ages. Welcome light, humorous verse. Rarely publish a poem longer than 16 lines, most are shorter. No poetry that is unintelligible to children, poems containing sex, violence or unmitigated pessimism."** They have published poetry by Nikki Giovanni, Aileen Fisher, John Ciardi, A.A. Milne, Myra Cohn Livingston and Langston Hughes. As a sample they selected "Where Is the Night Train Going?" by Eileen Spinelli:

Oh where is the night train going?
Please may I go along?
I'd like to see the mountains
And sing a mountain song.
I'd like to ride past cities
Past sleepy, shadowed farms.
I'd like to see the whole wide world
From within the night train's arms.

It is generally 44 pgs., magazine-sized, full-color throughout. They purchase 6-10 of 300 submissions/year. Press run is 3.3 million for approximately 3 million subscribers. Subscription: $21.95 (one year; reduced rates for multiple years). **Submit typed ms with very brief cover letter. Please indicate if simultaneous submission. Editor comments on submissions "occasionally, if ms has merit or author seems to have potential for our market." Reports "generally within 1 month." Always sends prepublication galleys. Payment: "money varies" plus 2 copies. Buys all rights.** The editor says, "We are always open to submissions of poetry not previously published. However, we purchase a very limited amount of such material. We may use the verse as 'filler,' or illustrate the verse with a full-page piece of art. Please note that we do not buy material from anyone under 16 years old."

HILLTOP PRESS (V, IV-Science fiction), 4 Nowell Place, Almondbury, Huddersfield, West Yorkshire HD5 8PB England, founded 1966, editor Steve Sneyd, publishes books of **"mainly science fiction poetry nowadays," but does not accept unsolicited mss. Query with proposals for relevant projects.** Publications include **War of the Words**, an anthology of humorous science fiction verse from the 30s to the 70s, including John Brunner, A. Vincent Clarke and C.S. Yond (John Christopher); and **The Fantastic Muse**, reprinting a 1938 article and 1939 poem by science fiction giant Arthur C. Clarke. From that poem, "The Twilight of A Sun," come these representative lines:

The Intellect, pure, unalloyed, on courage eternally

buoyed,
Will span the vast gulfs of the void and win a new planet's
fair face.
For one day our vessels will ply to the uttermost depths
of the sky,
And in them at the last we shall fly, ere the darkness
sweeps over our race.

The ongoing Data Dump series, up to #7 at the end of 1993, gives bibliographical information on science fiction poetry collections and anthologies. 4 pgs. A5 each. The set to date costs £2.50 or $5 postpaid. (Checks payable to S. Sneyd. US orders: will also accept $ bills or small denomination, unused US stamps). "My advice for beginning poets is (a) persist—don't let any one editor discourage you. 'In poetry's house are many mansions,' what one publication hates another may love; (b) be prepared for the possibility of long delays between acceptance and appearance of work—the small press is mostly self-financed and part time, so don't expect it to be more efficient than commercial publishers; (c) *always* keep a copy of everything you send out, and put your name and address on *everything* you send."

HIPPOPOTAMUS PRESS; OUTPOSTS POETRY QUARTERLY; OUTPOSTS ANNUAL POETRY COMPETITION (II, IV-Form), 22 Whitewell Rd., Frome, Somerset BA11 4EL England, ***Outposts*** founded 1943, Hippopotamus Press founded 1974, poetry editor Roland John, who explains, "***Outposts*** is a general poetry magazine that welcomes all work either from the recognized or the unknown poet. **The Hippopotamus Press is specialized, with an affinity with Modernism. No Typewriter, Concrete, Surrealism.** The press publishes 6 full collections per year." They have published in ***OPQ*** poetry by John Heath-Stubbs, Peter Dale and Elizabeth Jennings. ***Outposts*** is digest-sized, 70-100 pgs., flat-spined, litho, in professionally set small type, using ads. Of 120,000 poems received he uses about 300. Press run is 3,000 for 2,800 subscriptions of which 10% are libraries, 2% of circulation through shelf sales. Subscription: $24. **Sample postpaid: $8. Simultaneous submissions and previously published poems OK. Cover letter required. Reports in 2 weeks plus post time. Sometimes sends prepublication galleys. Pays $8/poem plus 1 copy. Copyright remains with author.** Staff reviews books of poetry in 200 words for "Books Received" page. Also uses full essays up to 4,000 words. Send books for review consideration, attn. M. Pargitter. The magazine also holds an annual poetry competition. Hippopotamus Press publishes 6 books a year, averaging 80 pgs. **For book publication query with sample poems. Simultaneous submissions and previously published poems OK. Reports in 6 weeks. Pays 10% royalties plus 20 paper copies, 6 cloth. Send for book catalog to buy samples.**

HIRAM POETRY REVIEW (I, II), P.O. Box 162, Hiram OH 44234, founded 1967, poetry editors Hale Chatfield and Carol Donley, is a semiannual with occasional special supplements. **"We favor new talent—and except for one issue in two years, read *only* unsolicited mss." They are interested in "all kinds of high quality poetry"** and have recently published poetry by Grace Butcher, David Citino, Michael Finley, Peter Wild, Jim Daniels, Peter Klappert and Harold Witt. As a sample they offer these lines from "Three Musics" by William Johnson:

Grief has a sound
the way snow ticks
and falls away
from the metal light pole.

There are 30 pgs. of poetry in the professionally printed, digest-sized, saddle-stapled magazine (glossy cover with b&w photo). It has a circulation of 400, 250 subscriptions of which 150 are libraries. They receive about 7,500 submissions/year, use 50, have up to a 6-month backlog. Although most poems appearing here tend to be lyric and narrative free verse under 50 lines, exceptions occur (a few longer, sequence or formal works can be found in each issue). Single copy: $4; subscription: $8. **Sample: free! No simultaneous submissions. "Send 4-5 fresh, neat copies of your best poems." Reports in 2-6 months. Pays 2 copies plus year's subscription. Acquires first North American serial rights; returns rights upon publication.** Reviews books of poetry in single or multi-book format, no set length. Send books for review consideration.

HOB-NOB (I), 994 Nissley Rd., Lancaster PA 17601, phone (717)898-7807, founded 1969, poetry editor Mildred K. Henderson, is a small literary semiannual with certain "family" emphasis. About ¼ poetry, ¾ prose. **They publish "poetry preferably up to 16-line limit, light or humorous verse, serious poetry on vital current themes, people, nature, animals, etc. Religious poetry is also acceptable. No erotica, horror, suicide, excess violence, murder, overly depressing themes, especially utter hopelessness."** They have published poetry by Effie Mihopoulos, C. David Hay and Patrick J. Cauchi. As a sample Mildred Henderson selected these lines from "The Fence Post" by Cathryn Hoellworth:

Wrinkled and leaning,
rails gone,
still it stands

Proud settler
staking a claim
to fertile dreams.

Hob-Nob is 84 pgs., magazine-sized, saddle-stapled, offset, on 20 lb. bond and heavier cover, printed from photoreduced typescript. It offers free ads to subscribers and exchange publications. About 20 new poets are featured in each issue. Press run is 500. Subscription: $6. **Sample postpaid: $3.50. Send SASE for guidelines. Pays 1 copy for first appearance only. After that you have to subscribe to be accepted. She accepts submissions only in January and February of each year, 2-year wait for first-time contributors. Material received at other times will be returned unread. She prefers not to have simultaneous submissions. The editor comments on rejections "especially if I can think of a way a rejected item can be salvaged or made suitable to submit elsewhere." Reports in 2 months. Acquires first rights only.** The Readers Choice contest, every issue, pays $10 for first prize, lesser amount for other place (unless special prizes are offered by readers). Awards are on the basis of votes sent in by readers. The editor advises, "Poets and would-be poets should read contemporary poetry to see what others are doing. Most of what I receive does not seem to be rhymed and metered anymore, and unless a poet is extremely skilled with rhyme and meter (few are), he will find free verse much easier to deal with. I told one poet recently that the content is vital. Say something new, or if it's not new, say it in a new way. Nobody wants to see the same old 'June-moon-spoon' stuff. Patterns can be interesting, even without formal rhyme and meter. Take an unusual viewpoint. Notice the imagery in the poem quoted above, for an example. Let your imagination soar!"

HOLIDAY HOUSE, INC. (V, IV-Children), Dept. PM, 425 Madison Ave., New York NY 10017, phone (212)688-0085, founded 1936, editor-in-chief Margery Cuyler, is a trade children's book house. They have published hardcover books for children by Myra Cohn Livingston. They publish 3 books a year averaging 32 pages. **However, they are currently not accepting poetry submissions.**

THE HOLLINS CRITIC (II), P.O. Box 9538, Hollins College, Roanoke VA 24020-1538, phone (703)362-6317, founded 1964, editor John Rees Moore, appears 5 times yearly, publishing critical essays, poetry and book reviews. **They use a few short poems in each issue, interesting in form, content or both.** They have recently published poetry by Scott T. Hutchison, Glenna Holloway, H.R. Cousen, Susan Rea and Tom Hansen. As a sample the editor selected these lines from "Tokens of Living" (for Doug) by Mattie F. Quesenberry:

You palm water lily bulbs
and pronounce new words:

Marliac Carnea, Chromatella,
Sulphuria, Braziella.

You hang the rosewood mirror
in which I will dress our daughter.

You give gifts worth giving,
tokens of living.

The Hollins Critic is 20 pgs., magazine-sized. Circulation 500. **Sample: $1.50. Submit up to 5 poems, none over 35 lines, must be typewritten. Cover letter preferred. Reports in 6 weeks (slower in the summer). Pays $25/poem plus 5 copies.** Open to unsolicited reviews. Poets may also send books for review consideration. Traditionally, verse here has been open as to form and style with poems that please the mind, eye and senses. As the magazine is occasionally overstocked, your best bet is to send for a sample copy and inquire as to whether editors are reading unsolicited submissions.

HOLMGANGERS PRESS; KESTREL CHAPBOOK SERIES (V), 95 Carson Ct., Shelter Cove, Whitethorn CA 95589, phone (707)986-7700, founded 1974, editor Gary Elder, was "founded primarily to bring out **young or unjustly ignored 'older' poets.** We have since published collections of fiction, novels, history, graphic art and experimental works as well." **Holmgangers Press is currently not accepting unsolicited mss. Replies to queries in 3-4 days, to mss (if invited) in 1 month. Sometimes sends prepublication galleys.**

HENRY HOLT & COMPANY (V), 115 W. 18th St., New York NY 10011, **accepts no unsolicited poetry.**

HOME PLANET NEWS (II), Dept. PM, P.O. Box 415, Stuyvesant Station, New York NY 10009, phone (718)769-2854, founded 1979, editors Enid Dame and Donald Lev, is a tabloid (newsprint) journal, appearing 3-4 times a year presenting a "lively, eclectic and comprehensive view of contemporary literature." They want **"honest, well-crafted poems, open or closed form, on any subject, but we will**

not publish any work which seems to us to be racist, sexist, ageist, anti-semitic or has undue emphasis on violence. Poems under 30 lines stand a better chance. We lean somewhat toward poetry with urban sensibility but are not rigid about this." They have published poetry by Alicia Ostriker, Tuli Kupferberg, Denise Duhamel, Will Inman, Andrew Glaze, Robert Peters, Carl Solomon and Rose Romano. As a sample the editors selected these lines from "Clotheslines" by Robbie Casey:

Clothes on a rope
gallop in the wind
freer than the bodies they cover
will ever be

They use approximately 13 full 11×16 pgs. of poetry in each 24-page issue. Circulation 1,000 with 400 subscriptions of which 8 are libraries. Of 1,200 submissions/year, they use about 50-60. Publication could take one year from acceptance. Subscription: $8/year. **Sample postpaid: $3. Submit 3-6 poems typed double-spaced, with SASE. Reports within 3 months. Pays 4 copies and year's subscription.** Reviews books of poetry. Open to unsolicited reviews. Poets may also send books for review consideration. "We cosponsor 'Day of the Poet,' a poetry festival and contest which takes place each October in Ulster County, New York." Poetry by Daniel Berrigan published in ***Home Planet News*** appeared in the **Pushcart Prize** anthology.

HONEST ULSTERMAN (II, IV-Regional), 14 Shaw St., Belfast BT4 1PT United Kingdom, founded 1968, editor Tom Clyde, is a literary magazine appearing 3-4 times a year using **"technically competent poetry and prose and book reviews. Special reference to Northern Irish and Irish literature. Lively, humorous, adventurous, outspoken."** They have published poetry by Seamus Heaney, Paul Muldoon, Gavin Ewart, Craig Raine, Fleur Adcock and Medbh McGuckian. The editor describes it as "75-100 pgs., A5 (digest-sized), photolithographic, phototypeset, with photographs and line drawings. Occasionally color covers." Press run is 1,000 for 300 subscriptions. Subscription: $28. **Sample postpaid: $7. "Potential contributors are strongly advised to read the magazine before submitting two copies of their work." Editor comments on submissions "occasionally." Publishes theme issues. Send SASE (or SAE and IRCs) for upcoming themes. Pays "a nominal fee" plus 2 copies.** Reviews books of literary and cultural interest in 500-1,000 words, single or multi-book format. Open to unsolicited reviews. Poets may also send books for review consideration. They also publish occasional poetry pamphlets.

HOPEWELL REVIEW (IV-Regional), Suite 701, 47 S. Pennsylvania St., Indianapolis IN 46204-3622, is an annual publication using poems and short stories **by residents of Indiana. "Writers should send no more than three poems and/or one short story with a manuscript-sized SASE and a brief biography. Poems of 40 lines or less will stand best chance of publication." Simultaneous submissions OK if so noted. Deadline: March 4. Send SASE for guidelines. Pays $35 for each accepted poem.** One poem will be selected by Daniel Halpern, editor of ***Antaeus***, for a $500 cash award of excellence.

HOPSCOTCH: THE MAGAZINE FOR GIRLS (IV-Children), P.O. Box 164, Bluffton OH 45817-0164, phone (419)358-4610, founded 1989, editor Marilyn B. Edwards, is a bimonthly magazine for **girls 6-12. "No length restrictions. In need of short traditional poems for various holidays and seasons. Nothing abstract, experimental."** They have recently published poetry by Lois Grambling, Judy Nichols, Leila Dornak, Judith Harkham Semas and Maggie McGee. As a sample we selected these lines from "First Frost" by Glenn DeTurk:

The sugary white glaze
Glistens in the morning sun.
The whole world seems to be waiting,
For a new season has begun.

The editor describes ***Hopscotch*** as "full-color cover, 50 pgs. of 2-color inside, 7×9, saddle-stapled." They use about 30-35 of some 2,000 poems received/year. Press run is 9,000 for 8,200 subscribers of which 7,000 are libraries, 200 to inquiring schools and libraries. Subscription: $15. **Sample postpaid: $3. Submit no more than 6 poems/submission. Cover letter preferred; include experience and where published. Publishes theme issues. Send SASE for upcoming themes. Theme for December 1994/January 1995 issue: Dolls, for February/March: Cats, for April/May: Twins, for June/July: Summer and The Ocean, and for August/September: Handicaps. Reports in 2-4 weeks. Pays $10-40. Buys first American serial rights.** The few poems in this children's magazine occasionally address the audience, challenging young girls to pursue their dreams. To see how, order a sample copy (or check one out at the library) because it is too easy for poets who write children's verse to forget that each magazine targets a specific audience . . . in a specific way. ***Hopscotch*** received the Parents Choice Gold Medal Award for 1992 and an EDPress Award for "Best in Educational Publishing for One Theme Issue," in June 1993.

HOUGHTON MIFFLIN CO. (V), 222 Berkeley St., Boston MA 02116, founded 1850, poetry editor Peter Davison. Houghton Mifflin is a high-prestige trade publisher that puts out both hardcover and paperback books, but **poetry submission is by invitation only and they are not seeking new poets at present.** They have recently issued poetry books by Donald Hall, May Swenson, Rodney Jones, Geoffrey Hill, Galway Kinnell, Thomas Lux, Erica Funkhouser, William Matthews, Margaret Atwood and Andrew Hudgins. **Always sends prepublication galleys. Authors are paid 10% royalties on hardcover books, 6% royalties on paperbacks (minimum), $1,000 advance and 12 author's copies.**

HOUSE OF MOONLIGHT (I), 15 Oakwood Rd., Bracknell, Berkshire RG12 2SP United Kingdom, founded 1981, editor John Howard, publishes 4-page leaflets of poems by individual poets at irregular intervals. **"Poems on love, death and the universe—common themes expressed in an uncommon way. Long poems up to 100 lines only."** They have published poetry by Steve Sneyd and John Francis Haines. **Sometimes sends prepublication galleys. Pays 5 copies. Acquires all rights. Returns rights if "acknowledgment that I published first."** The editor says, "I would like long pieces (as noted above) but very often receive short pieces—which are a waste of time and money to send! I am happy to receive submissions/inquiries from the United States—but only ones enclosing International Reply Coupons can be responded to. Checks payable to 'House of Moonlight' and/or in US currency are not acceptable. Also if poetry is to be regarded as a 'disposable ms' then it should be marked as such."

HOUSEWIFE-WRITER'S FORUM (IV-Women, humor), P.O. Box 780, Lyman WY 82937, phone (307)786-4513, founded 1988, editor/publisher Diane Wolverton, is a magazine of "prose, poetry, information and open forum communication for and by housewives or any woman or man who writes while juggling a busy schedule. **We have no specifications as to form, subject, style or purpose. Length maximum 30 lines. We publish both serious poetry and humorous. Nothing pornographic, but erudite expression is fine."** As a sample she selected these lines from "Off Limits" by Katherine H. Brooks:

I used to save a lot of stuff.
Till Mother hollered "That's enough!"
And made me have, all day, a fear
That something nice would disappear.
I hurried home from school, to see
What damage had been done to me,
And when I went to find the rocks
I'd hidden underneath my socks,
I saw it—almost in a flash—
That all my things were in the trash.

Diane Wolverton describes the magazine as "a small market for women who aspire to write for larger women's markets or support each other in the quest for finding time and energy to write." It is 48 pgs., desktop-published, using some art, graphics and ads, appearing bimonthly. Press run is 1,500. **Sample postpaid: $3. "Simultaneous submissions are OK." Send SASE for guidelines. Reports in 2 months. Pays 1 copy plus $1-2/poem. Buys first-time rights.** She holds an annual contest with $4/poem fee, June 1 deadline. ***Housewife-Writer's Forum*** received a 1st place award for magazine editing from Wyoming Media Professionals. The editor adds, "I like to see poems that have a strong central purpose and use the language to express it beautifully, powerfully. I also like to see poems that make me laugh."

HOWLING DOG (II), 2913 Woodcock, Rochester MI 48306, founded 1985, poetry editor Wipee Zippie, is a literary journal of "letters, words and lines." The editor likes **"found poetry, graphically interesting pieces, humorous work, avant-garde, Experimental, fun and crazy. All forms. All subjects, but we tend to have a light satirical attitude towards sex and politics."** He has recently published poems by Keith Wilson, John Sinclair, Laurel Speer, Larry Goodell and M.L. Liebler. As a sample the editor selected these lines by Karl E. Francis:

And so it probably seemed less of
a big deal to Johnny than it did to me,
his cutting his feet off.
They froze, as feet can do out there
and they started to rot.

Howling Dog appears 2 times a year. It is 64 pgs., digest-sized, flat-spined, offset. Press run 500 for 100 subscriptions of which 3 are libraries. They receive some 4,000 submissions/year, use maybe 150. Subscription: $20/4 issues. **Sample postpaid: $4. Send SASE for guidelines. Submit 3-4 poems with name and address on each page. Use regular #10 business-size envelopes. "We don't use much rhyme or poems under 10 lines." Simultaneous submissions OK. Previously published poems OK "but let us know." Reporting time is 6-12 months, "longer if we like it." Pays with copies and discount. Acquires first-time rights.** Reviews books of poetry in 200 words, single format. Open to unsolicited reviews. Poets may also send books for review consideration. **They are not presently considering book mss.** Wipee says, "We produce an effect similar to the howl of a dog with its foot caught in the fence. Something that may not be pleasant or permanent, yet still heard by everyone in the neighborhood. Don't send anything unless you've seen a copy."

"I chose this particular cover photo because it shows the more smooth and subtle side of art, almost as a diversion to set the reader off guard before he or she turns the page and is blasted by the work available inside," says Mark Donovan, publisher of the Michigan-based journal* Howling Dog. *Poetry is the major portion of this semiannual publication which has generally been "a wild, irreverent, radical and humorous magazine." Donovan says, "This photo seems similar to the images used on the covers of many of the more conventional literary journals, so I felt it could catch the interest of readers attracted to those journals and recruit them to read the diversity within the pages of* Howling Dog." *Cover photo: Steven E. Gross, Chicago IL.

‡HQ: THE HAIKU QUARTERLY; THE DAY DREAM PRESS (II), 39 Exmouth St., Kingshill, Swindon, Wiltshire SN1 3PU England, phone 0793-523927, founded 1990, editor Kevin Bailey, is "a platform from which new and established poets can speak and/or experiment with new forms and ideas." They want **"any poetry of good quality."** They have recently published poetry by Peter Redgrove, Alan Brownjohn, James Kirkup and Cid Corman. As a sample the editor selected these lines from "Copenhagen" by Tom Lowenstein:

It was winter in Europe.
I thump up the pillows and
lay Rilke on the bedside table.
The snow drifts at random
through the aspen branches.

The editor says ***HQ*** is 48-64 pgs., A5, perfect-bound with art, ads and reviews. They accept approximately 5% of poetry received. Press run is 500-600 for 500 subscribers of which 30 are libraries. Subscription: £8. **Sample postpaid: £2.40. No previously published poems or simultaneous submissions. Cover letter and SASE (or SAE and IRCs) required.** Time between acceptance and publication is 3-6 months. **Often comments on rejections. Reports "as time allows." Pays 1 copy.** Reviews books of poetry in about 1,000 words, single format. Open to unsolicited reviews. Poets may also send books for review consideration.

HRAFNHOH (IV-Form, religious), 32 Strŷd Ebeneser, Pontypridd, Wales via GB, phone 0443 492243, founded 1987, editor Joseph Biddulph, is a small press magazine **seeking "metrical verse."** They use **"poetry in traditional verse forms with a Christian inspiration and purpose, with an active concern for metrical technique and conveying a serious message in an evocative and entertaining style."** They have published poetry by John Waddington-Feather, M.A.B. Jones, Joe Keysor and many others. The editor describes ***Hrafnhoh*** as digest-sized, 24 pgs., typeset, illustrated with carefully-researched heraldic illustrations and other sketches. He accepts about 1 of 6-10 poems received, but is not always able to publish even if accepted. Press run is 100-500. **Sample postpaid: £3 outside Europe. Simultaneous submissions and previously published poems OK. Publishes theme issues. Reports as soon as possible. Pays "in free copies as required."** The editor says, "Almost all unsolicited manuscripts are in one form—free verse—and without substance, i.e., without a definite purpose, message or conclusion. I am anxious to obtain verse with a strong technique, particularly on Pro-life and Christian subjects."

HUBBUB (II), 5344 SE 38th Ave., Portland OR 97202, founded 1983, editors L. Steinman and J. Shugrue, appears twice a year (except on rare occasions is a single "double issue"). ***Hubbub*** is designed "to feature a multitude of voices from interesting contemporary American poets. **We look for poems that are well-crafted, with something to say. We have no single style, subject or length requirement and, in particular, will consider long poems. No light verse."** They have published poetry by Madeline DeFrees, William Matthews, Carolyn Kizer, Agha Shahid Ali and Alice Fulton. The editors describe ***Hubbub*** as 35-45 pgs., 5½×8½, offset, saddle-stitched, cover art only, usually no ads. They receive about 800 submissions/year, use approximately 10%. Press run is 350 for 100 subscribers of which 12 are libraries, about 150 shelf sales. Single copy: $2.50; subscription: $5/year. **Sample postpaid: $2.65 (volumes 1-8), $3.15 (volumes 9, 11 and following), $6.25 (volume 10 only). Submit 3-6 typed poems (no more than 6). No previously published poems or simultaneous submissions. Send SASE for guidelines. Reports in 1-2 months. Pays 2 copies. Acquires first North American serial rights.** "We review one to two poetry books a year in short (3-page) reviews; all reviews are solicited. We do, however, list books received/recommended." Send books for consideration. Outside judges choose poems from each volume for three awards: Vi Gale Award ($100), Adrienne Lee Award ($50) and Walter Hall Award ($25). There are no special submission procedures or entry fees involved.

THE HUDSON REVIEW; THE BENNETT AWARD (III), 684 Park Ave., New York NY 10021. ***The Hudson Review*** is a high-quality, flat-spined quarterly, considered one of the most prestigious and influential journals in the nation. Editors welcome all styles and forms. However, competition is extraordinarily keen, especially since poems compete with prose. **Sample postpaid: $7. Non-subscribers may submit poems only between April 1 and September 30. Reports in 6-8 weeks. Always sends prepublication galleys. Pays 50¢ a line for poetry.** They also sponsor the Bennett Award, established in memory of Joseph Bennett, a founding editor of ***HR***. Every other year $15,000 is given to honor a writer "of significant achievement, in any literary genre or genres, whose work has not received the full recognition it deserves, or who is at a critical stage in his or her career—a stage at which a substantial grant might be particularly beneficial in furthering creative development. There are no restrictions as to language or nationality. **The Bennett Award is not open to nominations, and *The Hudson Review* will not accept nominations or applications in any form.**" Work published in this review has been included in the 1993 and 1994 volumes of **The Best American Poetry**.

THE HUMAN QUEST (IV-Political), 1074 23rd Ave. N., St. Petersburg FL 33704, editor Edna Ruth Johnson, is a "humanistic monthly dealing with society's problems, especially peace. We use practically no poetry." It is magazine-sized, appears 9 times a year, circulation 10,000, of which 1,000 go for library subscriptions. **Send for free sample. Pays copies.**

THE HUNTED NEWS; THE SUBOURBON PRESS (I), P.O. Box 9101, Warwick RI 02889, founded 1990, editor Mike Wood. ***The Hunted News*** is a biannual "designed to find good writers and give them one more outlet to get their voices heard." As for poetry, the editor says, **"The poems that need to be written are those that need to be read." They do not want to see "the poetry that does not need to be written or which is written only to get a reaction or congratulate the poet."** As a sample the editor selected these lines (poet unidentified):

Birds who strike window panes with
a heavy thud
are misinformed.
They've been sabotaged by outmoded
weather charts
In miniscule and mugging ways
they resemble our finest actors
Bury them in sand . . .
and wait.

The editor says ***THN*** is 25-30 pgs., 8½ × 11, photocopied, unstapled. "I receive over 200 poems per month and accept perhaps 10%." Press run is 150-200. **Sample free with SASE. Previously published poems OK; no simultaneous submissions. Always comments on rejections. Send SASE for guidelines. Reports in 1 month. Pays 1 copy, more on request.** "I review current chapbooks and other magazines and do other random reviews of books, music, etc. Word count varies." The Subourbon Press publishes 2 chapbooks/year. **Query first with a few sample poems and cover letter with brief bio and publication credits. Replies to both queries and mss in 1 month. Pays 15-20 author's copies. "No subsidies unless given voluntarily." Send SASE for information about samples.** The editor says, "I receive mostly beginner's poetry that attempts to be too philosophical, without much experience to back up statements, or self-impressed 'radical' poems by poets who assume that I will publish them because they are beyond criticism. I would like poets to send work whose point lies in language and economy and in experience, not in trite final lines, or worse, in the arrogant cover letter."

HURRICANE ALICE (IV-Feminist), Lind Hall, 207 Church St. SE, Minneapolis MN 55455, founded 1983, acquisitions editor Toni McNaron, is a quarterly feminist review. Poems should be **"infused by a feminist sensibility (whether the poet is female or male)."** They have recently published poetry by Alice Walker, Ellen Bass, Patricia Hampl, Nellie Wong, Pauline Brunette Dauforth and Marcella Taylor. The magazine is a "12-page folio with plenty of graphics." Circulation is 500-1,000, of which 350 are subscriptions and about 50 go to libraries. Single copy: $1.95; subscription: $10 (or $8 low-income). **Sample postpaid: $2.50. Considers simultaneous submissions. Reports in 3-4 months and**

time to publication is 3-6 months. Pays 5-10 copies. Reviews books of poetry. The editor says, "Read what good poets have already written. If someone has already written your poem(s), listen to the message. Spare the trees."

HYACINTH HOUSE PUBLICATIONS; BROWNBAG PRESS; PSYCHOTRAIN (II), P.O. Box 120, Fayetteville AR 72702-0120, founded 1989, contact Shannon Frach. ***Brownbag Press*** and ***PsychoTrain*** are both semiannual magazines. ***Brownbag Press*** seeks "forceful writing full of spark and vigor for a widely diverse, intelligent, fairly left-of-center audience." ***PsychoTrain*** uses "bizarre, avant-garde material with a delightfully psychotic edge. Heady and chaotic." The editors want **poetry that is "avant-garde, confessional, contemporary, erotic, experimental, gay/lesbian, pagan/occult or punk. Also Dada, surrealism and decadent writing at its best. Stop sending us rhyming poetry, mainstream poetry, academic poetry. We are interested in free verse. Don't send traditional 'horror' or vampire poetry. We're looking for what would typically be considered 'underground' or 'alternative' writing. People who send us material that isn't in some way twisted, bizarre or weird are wasting both our time and theirs. We're seeing far too much 'straight' writing. Be bold. Morbid humor is always a plus here. We prefer two-fisted, dynamic, very intense poetry. Don't be afraid to show us street language from any culture."** They have recently published poetry by Tom Caufield, James Valvis, Kirsten Fox, C.F. Roberts, Stephen Fried and Belinda Subraman. As a sample the editors selected these lines from "Spontaneous Abortion" by Carolyn Ann Schirmbeck Campbell:

A gremlin stretched my cervix like stockings.
A fetus projected like a champagne cork:

I stuffed it back in denial.
A light shone in my uterus:

O where O where did my dead baby go?
The gremlin swallowed and smiled.

Brownbag is 24 pgs. and ***PsychoTrain*** is 20 pgs., magazine-sized. Both are photocopied and stapled with card covers. Press run for each is 300 for 100 subscribers, 125 shelf sales. **Sample postpaid: $4 for *Brownbag*, $4 for *PsychoTrain*. "Make checks out to Hyacinth House Publications. Cash is also OK." Previously published poems and simultaneous submissions OK.** Time between acceptance and publication is 1 year or more. **Often comments on rejections. Send SASE for guidelines. Reports in "2 weeks to 8 months—depends on the backlog." We do not pay. Acquires one-time rights.** "Please, *always* tell us whether or not your submissions are disposable. It's best to send 5-10 poems. That way, we have a better overview of your material, but are not overwhelmed. We'd prefer to see each poem on a separate sheet. Don't send us long poems; if a poem runs over a single standard-sized page, the chances of its acceptance diminish dramatically. Finally, always include a SASE. We are getting an alarming number of submissions arriving without return postage—submissions which are promptly used for kindling, as are any queries or correspondence arriving without the courtesy of an enclosed SASE." Hyacinth House also has **a chapbook series. "Presently we're using solicited material only**—please don't send us unsolicited chapbook mss at this time. We will be doing approximately seven chapbooks this year, all from authors who have first appeared in our magazines. We don't take chapbook submissions 'out of the blue'—we like to know who we're working with." Hyacinth House Publications also sponsors the Richard A. Seffron Memorial Poetry Prize. "This is an ongoing competition with an annual deadline of May 1. Winners receive chapbook copies and a small cash prize. Send SASE for details and any queries concerning the Seffron Prize. Do not even *think* about submitting without first acquiring guidelines." The editors say, "We may end up having to reject your submissions, but we'll still respect you in the morning. We encourage both new and established 'name' writers to submit here. Anyone sending us material should be aware that we don't like pretentious, windy, overly-serious poetry; we also dislike smarmy, trite rhymes about God and family. Send those to your hometown newspaper, not us. Also, please be aware that when you submit to one Hyacinth House publication, you're submitting to them all. If you submit to ***Brownbag***, but the piece would work better in ***PsychoTrain***, that's where it's going."

ICE COLD WATERMELON (IV-Ethnic, erotica, gay/lesbian), 2394B Adina Dr., Atlanta GA 30324, founded 1990 as ***Mots Et Images: Press-Work Project***, editors M.C. Young and Simoné, appears annually (usually around October/November). **"Want to see brave poetry, with an edge, that gives us a look into any facet of being African-American in America. Want to see poetry with voice and character using fresh imagery. Erotica/gay/lesbian writings especially encouraged. Prejudiced toward the more economical poem but will consider longer poems if they show promise. Do not want to see anything that tries too hard. No academic or 'selfish' personal poetry. Nothing trite or mundane."** As a sample the editors selected these lines from "Act of Freedom Right On" by M.C. Young:

personally
i find my

slightly
nappy
tresses
to be
exquisite
however unarresting

The editors describe it as 30-50 pgs., digest-sized, professionally printed, saddle-stapled, with card cover. They accept about 45 of 400 submissions received annually. Press run is 200 with 5 library subscriptions. "Most copies distributed free to other editors, publishers and writing institutions." Subscription: $10 for 2 years. **Submit 5 poems, typed. Send SASE for guidelines. Reports in 2-4 weeks, up to 18-month backlog. Pays 3 copies. Editors often comment on rejections.** They say, "What we want is the unusual and extraordinary. We want fresh new slants on life in the U.S.A. for the African-American. In your writing, we want you to have no qualms about telling the truth as you know it and allowing us to explore the dimensions with you."

ICON; HART CRANE AWARD (II), English Dept., Kent State University, Trumbull Campus, 4314 Mahoning Ave. NW, Warren OH 44483, phone (216)847-0571, founded 1966, faculty advisor Dr. Robert Brown, appears twice a year. **"We prefer experimental poetry, poetry that takes risks in terms of form and subject matter, but will consider anything well-written. No religious, sentimental, formulaic or prosaic poetry."** They have recently published poetry by Gay Brewer, William Greenway, Rane Arroyo and Laurie MacDiarmid. As a sample the editor selected these lines from "To an Abused Wife" by Mark Fitzpatrick:

The gods will grow plankton
Around their faces, green-
spotted, like a tombstone . . .

It is digest-sized, 40-80 pgs., saddle-stapled, with matte card cover. Poems and a few illustrations/photos grace the pages of this professionally printed and designed magazine. Artwork is especially attractive, not so much illustrating poems as lending a mood to the entire issue. They accept 5% of 1,000 poems submitted. Press run is 1,000 for 50 subscribers of which 10 are libraries. Distributed free to students and faculty. Subscription: $6. **Sample postpaid: $3. Submit September 1 through March 1 only. Reports in 1-3 months. Pays 2 copies.** The Hart Crane Award of $100 for poetry is given annually.

THE ICONOCLAST (I, II), 1675 Amazon Rd., Mohegan Lake NY 10547, founded 1992, editor/publisher Phil Wagner, is a general interest literary publication appearing 8 times/year "for those who find life absurd and profound." **They want "poems that have something to say—the more levels the better. Nothing sentimental, religious, obscure or self-absorbed."** ***The Iconoclast*** is 16 pgs., 8½×11, double-stapled, typeset and photocopied on 20 lb. white paper, with b&w art, graphics and ads. They receive about 400 poems a year, use between 5-10%. Press run is 500 for 225 subscribers. Subscription: $12 for 8 issues. **Sample postpaid: $1.50. Previously published poems and simultaneous submissions OK, though they say "previously published and simultaneous submissions must be demonstrably better than others."** Time between acceptance and publication is 2-4 months. **"Poems are subject to the extremely fallible judgements of the editor-in-chief." Often comments on rejections. Reports in 2-4 weeks. Pays 1 copy, 40% discount on extras. Acquires one-time rights.** Reviews books of poetry in 250 words, single format.

IHCUT (I), P.O. Box 612, Napavine WA 98565, founded 1989, contact Larry L. Randall, is an inexpensively produced newsletter appearing every other month. **"I would love to see some positive poetry, something with some answers and hope. I would rather not see rhyming poetry."** They have recently published poetry by Dawn Zapletal and Judy Saxon. As a sample the editor selected the last lines of "Three Fleeting Moments" by Julie Brinson Yopp:

I've Come Down
I've Left the Trees.
I'm on the Ground
No More Flying for Me.

It is 15-20 pgs., photocopied, side-stapled on ordinary paper. Press run is 20. **Sample postpaid: $2. Previously published poems and simultaneous submissions OK. Cover letter including "likes and dislikes, personal stuff" required.** "It annoys me when a poet does not include a cover letter, which to me is a poem in itself." **Publishes theme issues. Send SASE for guidelines and upcoming themes. "Love issue will come out just before Christmas of 1994 and the positivity issue will be out at the end of February 1995." Reports in 1 week. Pays 1 copy.**

UNIVERSITY OF ILLINOIS PRESS (III), 1325 S. Oak St., Champaign IL 61820, phone (217)333-0950, founded 1918, poetry editor Laurence Lieberman, publishes **collections of individual poets, 65-105 pgs. Submissions by invitation only.** They have published collections of poetry by Mark Doty, Debora

Greger, Alice Fulton, Len Roberts and Michael Harper. **Also publishes thematic collections, "for which letters of inquiry should be addressed to Richard L. Wentworth, editor-in-chief." Offers royalty contract and 10 copies.** Mark Doty's **My Alexandria** was a 1993 National Book Award Finalist and winner of the Los Angeles Times 1993 Book Prize for a Work of Poetry.

THE ILLINOIS REVIEW; ILLINOIS WRITERS, INC. (II), 4240/English Dept., Illinois State University, Normal IL 61790-4240, phone (309)438-7705, founded 1992, first issue fall 1993, editor Jim Elledge. *The Illinois Review* appears twice a year and supersedes ***Illinois Writers Review***. **"We're open to any 'school'—experimental to traditional, alternative to mainstream—by recognized, unknown and marginalized poets. Translations and prose poems are acceptable.** Selection for publication is based on excellence of poems not reputation of poets. **We look for poetry that reveals control of language and form, that engages the intellect and emotions simultaneously, and that is honest. No specifications as to length, etc. We do not want to see poetry that is sentimental, religious, filled with abstractions, or 'self-therapy.' "** They have published poetry by Gary Soto, Lisa Ress, Rochelle Ratner, David Trinidad, Kelly Cherry, Albert Goldbarth, Alison Stone and William Matthews. As a sample the editor selected these lines from "Nightfall" by Yusef Komunyakaa:

> *Every Saturday night someone new*
> *Is on his arm, her low-cut gown*
> *A school of angelfish.*

The editor says the review is 72 pgs., 5½×8½, perfect-bound, offset, with b&w cover art. Press run is 500 for 300 subscribers of which 10 are libraries. Subscription: $10. **Sample postpaid: $6. No previously published poems or simultaneous submissions. Reads submissions August 1 through May 1 only.** "Because we have a very large backlog of material and because we publish only twice a year, accepted work may not appear in print for a year or longer." **Seldom comments on rejections. Reports in 1-2 months. Pays 2 copies and year's subscription. Acquires all rights. Returns rights upon publication. "However, we ask contributors to notify us if they reprint their work from the *Review* and to acknowledge the *Review* when reprinting."** Reviews books of poetry "but only those of Illinois authors or presses." Query first. Individuals or institutions interested in becoming members of Illinois Writers, Inc., which includes a one-year subscription to both ***The Illinois Review*** and the ***I.W.I. Newsletter***, may also send SASE for membership rates. The editor says, "While ***The Illinois Review*** is published by Illinois Writers, Inc., an organization dedicated to supporting in-state writers, it is not a regional nor a 'members only' journal but publishes work by poets throughout the U.S. and elsewhere, as well as by Illinois residents. It is truly eclectic. Potential contributors are advised to buy a sample before submitting, but this is not a requirement."

IMAGO: NEW WRITING; CITY OF BRISBANE POETRY AWARD (II, IV-Regional), School of Communication and Organisational Studies, Q.U.T., GPO Box 2434, Brisbane 4001 Queensland, Australia, phone (07)864-2976, founded 1988, appears three times a year, publishing "the best **Australian writing, placing particular emphasis on Queensland writing and culture, but also welcoming submissions from overseas. Poems preferably short—up to about 50 lines, most from 12-25 lines. Our main criterion is good writing."** They have recently published poetry by Tom Shapcott, Bruce Dawe and Robert Adamson. As a sample the editor selected these lines from "Far and Near" by David Malouf:

> *. . . We are held*
> *by this; the coins in our pockets, amalgam fillings,*
> *gold that laps a finger gravely compliant*
> *as the magnet tilts and tugs us*
> *down. A flair for technology and faith is what keeps us*
> *above earth's instant muddle, but never far and not for long.*

It is 108 pgs., digest-sized, with glossy card cover. They accept about 10% of 500 poems from about 150 writers. Press run is 1,000 for 450 subscribers of which 36 are libraries. Subscription: $A21 in Australia. **Sample postpaid: $A9.50. Comments if requested. Reports in 1-6 months. Never sends prepublication galleys "unless specifically asked for by contributor." Pays $A30-40 plus 1 copy. Buys first Australian serial rights. They publish the winning poems of the City of Brisbane Poetry Award (annual).** Reviews books of poetry in 600 words—"usually commissioned. Unsolicited reviews would have to be of books relevant to ***Imago*** (Queensland or writing)." Send books for consideration.

‡THE IMPLODING TIE-DYED TOUPEE; BURNING LLAMA PRESS (II, IV-Form/style), 100 Courtland Dr., Columbia SC 29223-7148, founded 1993, editors Keith Higginbotham and Tracey R. Combs, is a biannual outlet "for people who dare to take language to its outer limits. We prefer sounds and juxtapositions of images over 'meaning.' " **They want "Dada, surrealism, experimental, visual poetry, found poetry, collaborative poetry—anything unusual. No traditional poetry, light verse, blood and guts, academic, confessional or inspirational poetry."** They have recently published poetry by Guy R.

Beining, Richard Kostelanetz, Sheila E. Murphy and Dan Raphael. As a sample the editors selected "Hilt" by John M. Bennett:

Better lamping's what I
need or your face
pillowed a conference of
hair like the phone's
dust my pants just billowed

Lace hanging like my speech milk

The Imploding Tie-Dyed Toupee is 40 pgs., digest-sized, photocopied and saddle-stapled with card stock cover and bizarre graphics coupled with intriguing visual poems. "On the average, we accept one poem per 200 received." Press run is 200 for 20 subscribers, various shelf sales. Subscription: $13 for 4 issues. **Sample postpaid: $3.50. No previously published poems or simultaneous submissions. "A cover letter isn't required, but we cringe when we don't get one. The poetry had better knock our socks off."** Time between acceptance and publication varies. **Seldom comments on rejections. Send SASE for guidelines. Reports within 2 months. Pays 1 copy. Acquires first North American serial rights.** "Open to short reviews of magazines; surreal reviews of TV shows." Poets may also send books for review consideration. The editors add, "Salvador Dali once said, 'So little of what could happen actually does happen. When I order lobster, why doesn't the waiter bring me a telephone book on fire?' Bring us that telephone book. Do the unexpected with language."

IMPLOSION PRESS; IMPETUS (I, II, IV-Erotica, women), 4975 Comanche Trail, Stow OH 44224, phone (216)688-5210, founded 1984, poetry editor Cheryl Townsend, publishes ***Impetus***, a quarterly literary magazine, chapbooks, special issues. The editor would like to see **"strong social protest with raw emotion. No topic is taboo. Material should be straight from the gut, uncensored and real. Absolutely no nature poetry or rhyme for the sake of rhyme, oriental, or 'Kissy, kissy I love you' poems. Any length as long as it works. All subjects okay, providing it isn't too rank. *Impetus* is now publishing annual erotica and all female issues. Material should reflect these themes."** They have published poetry by Ron Androla, Kurt Nimmo and Lonnie Sherman. As a sample the editor selected these lines from "Gun-shy" by B. Arcus Shoenborn:

Instead,
I hid in my bedroom.
Soaked between blooded sheets,
I explored immaculate concepts.
Then my white heart severed;
It gushed rivers of angry rapists.
One flagged a revolver;
he held it to my head and said,
I'd live, but couldn't tell.

The 7½×9 magazine is photocopied from typescript, saddle-stapled. Press run is about 500, with 300 subscriptions. Generally a 3-month backlog. **Sample postpaid: $4; make check payable to Cheryl Townsend. The editor says, "I prefer shorter, to-the-point work." Include name and address on each page. Previously published work OK if it is noted when and where. Send SASE for guidelines. Usually reports within 2 months. Pays 1 copy. Acquires first rights.** In her comments on rejections, the editor usually refers poets to other magazines she feels would appreciate the work more. Reviews books of poetry. Open to unsolicited reviews. Poets may also send books for review consideration. She says, "Bear with the small press. We're working as best as we can and usually harder. We can only do so much at a time. Support the small presses!"

IMPROVIJAZZATION NATION (I), HQ, 19th Supcom, Unit 15015, P.O. Box 2879, APO AP 96218-0171, founded 1991, editor Dick Metcalf, who is currently stationed in Korea. ***Improvijazzation Nation*** is a quarterly "devoted to networking; prime focus is tape/music reviews, includes quite a bit of poetry." **They want "experimental, visual impact and non-establishment poetry, no more than 15 lines. No hearts and flowers, shallow, epic."** They have published poetry by John M. Bennett, Joan Payne Kincaid and Anthony Lucero. The editor says *IN* is 20 pgs., 8½×11, photocopied, no binding. They receive 50-100 poems a year, use approximately 50%. Press run is 100. Single copy: $2.25 or 8 first-class stamps; subscription: $8 for 4 issues. **Sample postpaid: $2.50 Previously published poems and simultaneous submissions OK. Often comments on rejections. Reports within a week or two. "No payment, no contributor's copies, no tearsheets; poets must buy the issue their work appears in."** Reviews books of poetry. Also accepts short essays/commentary on the use of networking to void commercial music markets, as well as material of interest to musical/artist improvisors.

‡IN YOUR FACE! (I), P.O. Box 6872, Yorkville Station, New York NY 10128, founded 1992, editor Gina Grega, is a quarterly that publishes art, poetry, essays and reviews, "whatever strikes my fancy and knocks the wind out of me." **They want "anything bold, risky and/or risqué, funny, political, personal, sexual, honest, real-life language. No PC multicultural whinings, phony pseudo-emotionalism, rhyming poems, unintelligible manifestos filled with 50-cent words. No women-hating spewage."** They have recently published poetry by Mary Panza, Laurel Speer, Eugenia Hepworth-Jenson and Lou Ferrante. As a sample we selected this poem, "The Ex," by G. Marault:

When I dream of him
I have to bear in mind
how I dreamt of cigarettes
for years after I quit smoking.

IYF! is 50 pgs., 5½×8½, saddle-stapled, with colored card cover, b&w art and ads. They receive about 1,500 pieces a year, accept 10-15%. Press run is 350 for 100 subscribers. Subscription: $12. **Sample postpaid: $3. Submit no more than 5 pgs. at a time. Previously published poems and simultaneous submissions OK. "Be friendly, drop me a note, not a pretentious bio!" Often comments on rejections. Send SASE for guidelines. Publishes an annual women's issue. Reports in 1-2 months. Pays 1-2 copies.** Reviews books, chapbooks, 'zines, "whatever else I can get my hands on," in roughly 75-100 words each. Open to unsolicited reviews. Poets may also send books for review consideration. The editor says, "***In Your Face!*** isn't afraid to offend. I look for gut-punching work—not big names. I especially encourage beginners as they haven't been polished by the cold, impersonal 'name' magazines and are usually still humble enough to send a 'hi' with their submission. We *recommend* that contributors see a copy of our publication, but this is not a requirement."

INDIA CURRENTS (IV-Ethnic, regional), P.O. Box 21285, San Jose CA 95151, phone (408)274-6966, founded 1987, editor Arvind Kumar, is a monthly magazine about Indian culture in the U.S. They want **"poetry that offers an insight into India, Indians, Indian Americans; very brief works stand a better chance of acceptance." They do not want "poetry that exploits mystery or exoticism about India or long poems (over 300 words). Readership is 70% Indian, 30% non-Indian."** They have published poetry by Chitra Divakaruni. It is 136 pgs., 8½×11, offset, newsprint, saddle-stitched. They receive 50-75 submissions a year, "accept fewer than 12." Press run is 27,000 for 9,000 subscribers. Rest distributed free at stores, restaurants and libraries. Single copy: $1.95; subscription: $19.95. **Sample postpaid: $3. Previously published poems and simultaneous submissions OK. Cover letter with brief bio and background required.** Time between acceptance and publication is 6-12 months. **Send SASE for guidelines. Reports in 3 months.** Reviews books of poetry in 300 words maximum. Open to unsolicited reviews. Poets may also send books for review consideration. The magazine received a Cultural Awareness through Journalism Award from the Federation of Indo-American Associations in 1991. The editor says, "***India Currents*** has a heavy tilt in favor of arts. We feel that arts can contribute to global understanding and peace by bringing it about at a personal level. America needs to learn about India just as India needs to learn about America."

INDIANA REVIEW (II), 316 N. Jordan Ave., Indiana University, Bloomington IN 47405, founded 1982, is a biannual of new fiction and poetry. "In general the ***Review* looks for fresh, original poems of insight, poems that are challenging without being obtuse. We'll consider all types of poems—free verse, traditional, experimental. Reading a sample issue is the best way to determine if *IR* is a potential home for your work. Any subject matter is acceptable if it is written well."** They have recently published poetry by Philip Levine, Ramola Dharmaraj, Mark Levine, Diane Glancy and Michael Evans. As a sample, the editor selected these lines from "Jouissance" by Stephen Runkle:

The coax of gravity relaxed across the curvature of Europe.
The moon shellacked the ocean into scallops.
The soldier rubbed the roughness of his lover's elbows, and when they kissed
they kissed with tongues, stealing oranges
in a dark that bloomed a beautiful sickness
everyone stole from everyone else.

The magazine uses about 40-60 pgs. of poetry in each issue (6×9, flat-spined, 200 pages, color matte cover, professional printing). The magazine has 1,000 subscriptions of which 120 are libraries. They receive about 8,000 submissions/year of which they use about 60. **Sample postpaid: $7. Submit no more than 4-5 pgs. of poetry. "Please indicate stanza breaks on poems over 1 page. Simultaneous submissions very strongly discouraged." Publishes theme issues. "*Possible* spirituality issue for spring 1995." Pays $5/page when available ($10 minimum/poem), plus 2 copies and remainder of year's subscription. Buys first North American serial rights only. "We try to respond to manuscripts in two to three months. Reading time is often slower during summer months."** This magazine's reputation continues to grow in literary circles. It is generally accepted now as one of the best publications, featuring all styles, forms and lengths of poetry (much of it exciting or tense). Brief book reviews are also featured in some issues. Send books for review consideration.

INFINITY LIMITED: A JOURNAL FOR THE SOMEWHAT ECCENTRIC (II), P.O. Box 2713, Castro Valley CA 94546, phone (510)581-8172, founded 1988, editor-in-chief Genie Lester, is a "literary quarterly dedicated to presenting emerging talent attractively illustrated. Staff artists illustrate most work, but we encourage writer-artists to submit their own illustrations." They want poetry that **"deals in an original way with concerns common to all of us. Poetry with less agony, more joy would be delightful."** They have recently published poetry by William Nesbit, Norman Kraeft, Norman Kirk, Mary De Maine and Kenneth Johnson. As a sample the editor selected the first lines of "The Buddhas of Borobudur" by I.B. Nelson:

The Buddhas of Borobudur
stare in ageless silence
the patience of stone.
The carved maidens and young men
a reverie in frozen dance
broken only by crackling grit echoes
of curious slow foot steps

It is magazine-sized, "printed on 60 lb. bond with parchment cover (2-3 color)" and appears "more or less quarterly, 4 times a year. We receive about 40 submissions per week, use about 25 poems per issue." Press run is 1,000 for 250 subscribers. Subscription: $10. **Sample postpaid: $3.95. Simultaneous submissions and occasionally previously published poems OK. "Bio info is helpful if work accepted." Reads submissions January 1 through June 1 and September 1 through November 15. Publishes theme issues. Send SASE for guidelines and upcoming themes. Theme for Autumn 1994 is formal verse. Reports within 6 months, "but we read everything." Editor comments on submissions "if writing or art shows promise." Always sends prepublication galleys. Pays 2 copies. Acquires one-time or first reprint rights.** Open to unsolicited reviews. Poets may also send books for review consideration. The editor says, "We are small but growing rapidly, probably because we are willing to work with our writers and artists and we make an effort to present material attractively."

‡INKSLINGER (I, IV-Subscription), 8661 Prairie Rd. NW, Washington Court House OH 43160, founded 1993, publisher/editor Nancy E. Martindale, appears 3 times/year (in March, July and November) to "provide an additional market for poets and to further the poetic arts." **They want poetry from subscribers only. Any subject, any format, no longer than 30 lines. "No porn or erotica. Also no translations or foreign language poetry."** They have recently published poetry by Anthony R. Arment, Ken MacDonnell, Geraldine Zeigler and Terri Warden. As a sample, we selected the last two stanzas of "Radish" by Katherine H. Brooks, one of the poems named Editor's Choice in *Inkslinger*'s premiere issue:

Rejected by robins, who'd rather wreck fruit,
no bearer of runners, but wearing a root,
It's rampant in summer, and racy to munch,
and readily wrenched from the ground in a bunch.

Try rearing the radish. You'll hardly go wrong.
It's crispy, unwrinkled, produced for a song,
And a riot for diners, who crunch it in blobs,
in order to rouse the repugnance of snobs.

Inkslinger is 20 pgs., digest-sized, saddle-stapled with colored paper cover. They receive 60-75 poems a year, accept 54 or more if short in length. Subscription: $10.60/year. **Sample postpaid: $4. "Purchase of a 1-year subscription is required to submit." Send no more than 3 poems at a time. Previously published poems OK if author still owns copyright; no simultaneous submissions.** Time between acceptance and publication is 1 month. "Poems arriving too late for one issue will be held for the next issue's consideration. Poems are judged according to imagery, style, creativity, originality and sincerity (5 points each). Poems with most points are accepted. One(s) with the highest named 'Editor's Choice' (but no cash award)." **Seldom comments on rejections. Send SASE for guidelines. Reports in 5 months maximum. Pays no money at present, "but hoping to pay soon." Poets retain all rights.** The editor says, "Novices and experienced poets welcome. We're small, but open. *Always read guidelines first*. Failure to meet even one will result in unread, returned manuscripts."

INKSTONE: A MAGAZINE OF HAIKU (IV-Form), 20 Bloor St. E., P.O. Box 75009, Hudson Bay Ctr, Toronto, Ontario M4W 3T3 Canada, founded 1982, poetry editors Keith Southward, Marshall Hryciuk and J. Louise Fletcher, "is a publication dedicated to the development of a distinctive English language haiku and to the craft of writing as it relates to haiku. Submissions reflecting these concerns are welcomed. We publish haiku and related forms, plus reviews and articles related to haiku. **Poems must be haiku or related but we use a very liberal definition of haiku."** They have published haiku by Carol Montgomery, Alexis Rotella, Akira Kowano and Guy Beining. There are roughly 20 pgs. of poetry and reviews/articles in the digest-sized format, 40 pgs., offset from typescript, matte card cover. Circulation 100. They accept "perhaps 10%" of the poems submitted each year. Poems appear as space permits, usually in the next issue after acceptance. **Sample postpaid: $5.50. Submit any number of poems, preferably 1 per 5½ × 8½ sheet, typewritten. Editor "occasionally" comments on rejections. Reports within 6 weeks. Pays 1 copy. Acquires first serial rights.** Reviews books of poetry in 1 to 3 pgs., single or multi-book format. Open to unsolicited reviews. Poets may also send books for review consideration "with an indication that it is a review copy."

INKY BLUE (I), 3200 North Rd., Greenport NY 11944, founded 1989 by Cat Spydell, editor as of December 1992 is Yvonne Lieblein, appears semiannually. In 1993, Yvonne Lieblein moved production from San Francisco to the East Coast where she continues her predecessor's quest for **"thought-provoking poetry, with a tendency to avoid the mundane. No sexist, red-necked-beer-bellied-middle-American-women-are-only-good-if-they-have-flat-heads poetry."** She has recently published poetry by John Richard Williams, Lyn Lifshin, Larry L. Randall, Daniel Langton and Gloria Good. As a sample the editor selected these lines from "Trying Godiva" by Mari Niescior:

. . . Bright TV-babies
turn me on; got me stepping
through flowerbeds to be with you. Wish
my legs were made of slinky
just to feel your second-story
love . . .

The magazine averages 100 pgs. and is digest-sized with matte card cover. Press run is 500-1,000 depending on funding. The editor accepts 30% of submissions. Subscription: $10/year. **Sample: $5 plus $1 postage and handling. Previously published poems and simultaneous submissions OK. Poems without a SASE or without the poet's name and address on each page will not be considered. Pays 1 copy. Rights revert to poet after publication.** Sponsors the Blue Plate Special Annual Contest, cash prizes, new theme each year. Deadline: April 15. Send SASE for details. ***Inky Blue*** ranked #10 in the "New Poets" category of the latest ***Writer's Digest*** Poetry 60 list. This category ranks those markets who often publish poets whose work is new to their publication. The editor says, "We might have dark circles under our eyes and be delirious from lack of sleep, but we're sticking to our original goal: No poet will receive a form letter rejection. We give poets feedback and that's what makes us tick. We're accepting less poetry, but it's being drawn from a wide base of new poets. My advice: Send 3 to 5 poems, a short cover letter and a SASE. While most editors would consider a 4-page bio, 100 pages of poetry and a photo of the poet *sans* pet octopus fodder for the verticle file, we still read everything so have pity on us."

INNISFREE MAGAZINE (II), P.O. Box 277, Manhattan Beach CA 90266, phone (310)545-2607, fax (310)546-5862, founded 1981, editor Rex Winn, appears every other month with many short stories and **poetry. "Items of merit: Entertainment value—humor, fright, emotional experience; Something for the reader to take away—inspiration, enlightenment, interesting information; Writing craft—structure, style and technique."** They have published poetry by William Doreski, Barry Sheinkopf and Josephine C. Radai. As a sample, the editor selected these lines by Arlene Joffee Pollack:

My impulses ride herd on me
And I, astonished,
Powerless, stare
At the world around me
Through a beggar's eyes,
Rattling the empty beggar cup
And yet ashamed to own the cup
At all.

It is 42 pgs., magazine-sized, saddle-stapled, professionally printed. They accept about 3% of poetry received. Press run is 300 for 150 subscribers of which 3 are libraries. Subscription: $20. **Sample postpaid: $5. Previously published poems and simultaneous submissions OK. Reads submissions February 1 through September 30. Send SASE for guidelines. Pays "splattered awards" but no copies. Acquires first rights. "If a person asks, I will comment. Sometimes I can't resist anyway!"** Reviews books of poetry. Send books for review consideration.

INSECTS ARE PEOPLE TOO; PUFF 'N' STUFF PRODUCTIONS (I, IV-Specialized), P.O. Box 146486, Chicago IL 60614, phone (312)772-8686, founded 1989, publisher H.R. Felgenhauer, an infrequent publication focusing solely on **"poems about insects doing people things and people doing insect things."** The first issue was a collection of the publisher's own poems. The second edition, scheduled for release this past summer, contains "better than 50 poems by 40 poets, one short story and one novella." As a sample the publisher selected these lines from a poem of his own, "Resist and You Will be Destroyed":

Geometrical abstraction of space-vehicle-ness sprouts conquest.
Inferior species succumb to superior weapons, transport and
communication systems blistering through onion skinned civilizations.
They were bigger and better and all around us; we expanded right
into their hoary mouths, razor sharp venom spouting ruin . . .

Insects is 8½×11, stapled down the side, with card cover, b&w art and graphics. Press run is 400. Single copy: $3. **Sample postpaid: $4. Previously published poems and simultaneous submissions OK. Often comments on rejections. Reports "immediately." Pay varies.** Open to unsolicited reviews. Poets may also send books for review consideration. **Puff 'N' Stuff Productions publishes 1 chapbook/year. Replies to queries and mss in 10 days. Pay is negotiable.** H.R. Felgenhauer says, "Hit me with your best shot. Never give up—editors have tunnel-vision. The *BEST* mags you almost *NEVER* even hear about. Don't believe reviews. Write for yourself. Prepare for failure, not success."

‡INSIGHT PRESS (V), P.O. Box 25, Drawer 249, Ocotillo CA 92259, founded 1983, publishers John and Merry Harris. The Harrises publish short poetry chapbook anthologies containing the work of **"pre-selected writers (no submissions without invitation, please)." The work published must be "short, non-academic poetry for the layman—clarity and lucidity a must. Prefer humorous, inspirational poetry."** They have published poems by L.C. Dancer, Elizabeth Lee, Jack Adler, Falling Blossom (Cherokee) and Merry Harris. The chapbooks are paperback, flat-spined, 40-50 pgs. "We sell our chapbooks at cost and send out at least 50 of first run for promotion of our poets, who are then widely reprinted." **Sample: $3 for "Laughter: a Revelry."** Merry Harris advises, "1) Join an amateur press association, as I did 40 years ago, to learn basics while being published. Amateur does NOT mean 'Amateurish.' AMAT = LOVE! 2) Join a local writers' co-op. 3) *Avoid those who exploit writers.* 4) As for technique, keep it simple, avoid erudite phrasing and pseudo-intellectualism. We do not publish other people's books. We publish ***Merry-Go-Round, Contest Carousel*** and ***Roadrunner***, literary newsletters containing essays on writing (by Merry)."

INSOMNIA & POETRY (I), P.O. Box 0431, Murrieta CA 92564-0431, founded 1991, publishes irregularly, "but at least four times a year. This publication was started to give poets more opportunity to express themselves without the pressures of editorial intimidation (cover letters, guidelines, etc.). **Please send us your most poignant poetry—as the publication's title suggests. We try not to discriminate."** They have recently published poetry by Emil P. Dill, Ben Ohmart and Tracy Lyn Rottkamp. As a sample the editor selected these lines by Katerina Papadopoulos:

eyes green as leaves
yet, closed now, like a flower
the life gone from them

Insomnia & Poetry is 8 pgs., 8½×11, photocopied with occasional photographs accompanying poems. Press run is 250, all distributed free—left in libraries, bookstores and at colleges. **Sample postpaid: $1 (no checks). Previously published poems and simultaneous submissions OK. Reports ASAP. Usually pays 1 copy. "Please type name, address and the number of lines on every poem submitted."** The editor says, "We don't think poetic expression is some privilege to be 'crafted' by only a select bunch. We think of it as human expression that can be shown by anyone—a cathartic endeavor for all."

INTERIM (II), Dept. of English, University of Nevada, Las Vegas, Las Vegas NV 89154, phone (702)739-3172, magazine, founded in Seattle, 1944-55, revived 1986. Editor and founder A. Wilber Stevens, associate editors James Hazen, Joseph B. McCullough and Timothy Erwin, English editor John Heath-Stubbs. Member CLMP, New York. Indexed in **Index of American Periodical Verse.** Appears twice a year, **publishing the best poetry and short fiction it can find, no specific demands in form, new and established writers.** They have published poetry by William Stafford, Richard Eberhart, Diane Wakoski, Stephen Stepanchev and Anca Vlasopolos. As a sample we selected these lines from "Winter's Tale" by Charlotte F. Otten:

Her voice is silent now,
sunk deep into the tap root of her brain.
A stroke that struck her throat
blizzarded all sound.
Words swirl around her like an early snow

clinging to unfallen leaves.

Interim is 48 pgs., 6×9, professionally printed and saddle-stapled with coated card cover. Press run is 600. Individual subscription: $8 one year, $13 two years, $16 three years; libraries: $14/year. **Sample copy: $5. Submit 4-6 poems, SASE and brief biographical note. No simultaneous submissions. Decision in 2 months. Sometimes sends prepublication galleys. Pays 2 contributor's copies and a 2-year subscription. *Interim* acquires copyright. Poems may be reprinted elsewhere with a permission line noting publication in *Interim*.** Starting short poetry review. Send books for review consideration.

INTERNATIONAL BLACK WRITERS; BLACK WRITER MAGAZINE (I, IV-Ethnic), P.O. Box 1030, Chicago IL 60690, founded 1970, contact Mable Terrell, executive director. ***BWM*** is a "quarterly literary magazine to showcase new writers and poets and provide educational information for writers. **Open to all types of poetry.**" The editor describes it as 30 pgs., magazine-sized, offset printing, with glossy cover, circulation 1,000 for 200 subscriptions. Subscription: $19/year. **Sample postpaid: $1.50. Reports in 10 days, has 1 quarter backlog. Pays 10 copies. For chapbook publication (40 pgs.), submit 2 sample poems and cover letter with short bio. Simultaneous submissions OK. Pays copies. For sample chapbook send SASE with bookrate postage.** They offer awards of $100, $50 and $25 for the best poems published in the magazine and present them to winners at annual awards banquet. ***IBW*** is open to all writers.

‡INTERNATIONAL OLYMPIC LIFTER (IOL) (IV-Specialized), P.O. Box 65855, Los Angeles CA 90065, founded 1973, poetry editor Dale Rhoades, is a bimonthly "for the serious weight lifter, coach, administrator and enthusiast." They want **poetry about olympic-style weight lifting—occasionally use poetry about nature, the environment or health. "We prefer balanced meter, rhyming 10-16 lines."** Press run is 3,000 for 2,700 subscribers of which approximately 5% are libraries. Subscription: $25. **Sample postpaid: $4.50. No previously published poems; simultaneous submissions OK. Reports "immediately." Pays $10-25.** The editor says, "Know your market. Often we get poems on body building, power lifting, running or aerobics which are all foreign to olympic lifting. Purchase a copy to understand our requirements."

INTERNATIONAL POETRY REVIEW (II, IV-Translations), Dept. of Romance Languages, UNC-Greensboro, Greensboro NC 27412, phone (909)334-5655, fax (909)334-5404, founded 1975, editor Mark Smith-Soto, is a biannual primarily publishing **translations of contemporary poetry with corresponding originals (published on facing pages) as well as original poetry in English.** They have recently published work by Jasha Kessler, Lyn Lifshin, Pureza Canelo, Jaime Sabines and Olga Orozco. As a sample the editor selected these lines from "Poema de Invierno" by Chilean poet Jorge Teillier:

En la casa ha empezado la fiesta.
Pero el niño sabe que la fiesta está en otra parte,
y mira por la ventana buscando a los desconocidos
que pasará toda la vida tratando de encontrar.

translated as "Winter Poem" by Mary Crow:

In the house the party has begun.
But the child knows the party is somewhere else,
and he looks out the window searching for the strangers
he will spend his whole life trying to find.

IPR is 84 pgs., 5½×8½, professionally printed and perfect-bound with 2-3 color cover. "We accept 10% of original poetry in English and about 80% of translations submitted." Press run is 500 for 200 subscribers of which 100 are libraries. Subscription: $10 individuals, $15 institutions. **Sample postpaid: $5. Submit no more than 10 pages of poetry. No previously published poems; simultaneous submissions OK. Seldom comments on rejections. Send SASE for guidelines. Reports in 1 month. Pays 1 copy. All rights revert to authors and translators.** Occasionally reviews book of poetry. Open to unsolicited reviews. Poets may also send books for review consideration. The editor says, "We strongly encourage contributors to subscribe. We get too much original poetry and not enough translation. We prefer poetry in English to have an international or cross-cultural theme."

INTERNATIONAL POETS ACADEMY; INTERNATIONAL POETS (I, IV-Membership), 5, Mohamed Hussain Khan Lane, Royapettah, Madras 600-014, India, founded 1981, poetry editor Prof. Syed Ameeruddin. The Academy publishes books by members (for a price) and brings out special numbers of ***International Poets***, their quarterly journal publishing poetry by members, "highlighting the poems of selected poets with detailed bio-data and with a scholarly critical article focusing the main features of the selected poet's poetry to the world audience, with a photograph of the poet published on the front cover." **Membership is $40 a year. Life fellow membership is $100.** They have recently published poetry by Naomi F. Faust (USA), Eda Howink (USA), David Moe (USA), Maria Do Carmo Gaspar De Oliveira (Brazil), Daisak Ikeda (Japan), Frances Hockney (Australia) and Rhee Han Ho (South

Korea). The editor describes the quarterly as 5¼ × 8½, perfect-bound; printed in Madras. Reviews books of poetry. They also publish 3 chapbooks/year subsidized by the poets. For details contact the Academy.

‡**INTERNATIONAL QUARTERLY (II, IV-Translations)**, P.O. Box 10521, Tallahassee FL 32302-0521, phone (904)224-5078, fax (904)224-5127, founded 1993, editor-in-chief Van K. Brock. **"We welcome outstanding writing in all genres, in original English and in translation, quality work that transcends cultural givens. No one-dimensional views of people or place, work that is amateurish or lacks complexity."** They have recently published work by Peter Meinke, Jayanta Mahapatra and Bei Dao. As a sample the editor selected these lines by Anna Akhmatova, translated by Judith Hemschemeyer:

I came here without a child, without a knapsack,
Without so much as a walking stick
Accompanied only by the ringing voice
of yearning.

IQ is 200 pgs., 7½ × 10, offset, perfect-bound, with full-cover artwork on the coated card cover and an 8-page, 4-color insert. They receive about 500 mss/year, accept a quarter to a third. Press run is 5,000 for 1,000 shelf sales. Single copy: $8; subscription: $19/year. **Sample postpaid: $6. Submit no more than 8 poems, name on each. No previously published poems; simultaneous submissions OK. Cover letter welcomed.** Time between acceptance and publication is 3-9 months. Poems go from multiple readers to poetry editor to editorial board and editor-in-chief. **Often comments on rejections. Reports within 4 months. Pays 2 copies. Acquires first serial rights.** Reviews books of poetry. Open to unsolicited reviews; query first. Poets may also send books for review consideration. The editor says, "Writers who have not published elsewhere are welcome to submit, but rarely have the polish necessary to be published in ***IQ***."

INTERTEXT (V, IV-Translations), 2633 E. 17th Ave., Anchorage AK 99508-3207, founded 1982, editor Sharon Ann Jaeger, publishes "full-length collections by poets of demonstrated achievement" and is "devoted to producing lasting works in every sense. We specialize in poetry, translations and short works in the fine arts and literary criticism. **We publish work that is truly excellent—no restrictions on form, length or style. Cannot use religious verse. Like both surrealist and realist poetry, poetry with intensity, striking insight, vivid imagery, fresh metaphor, musical use of language in both word sounds and rhythm. Must make the world—in all its dimensions—come alive."** To give a sense of her taste she says, "I admire the work of Sarah Kirsch, Louise Glück, William Stafford, António Ramos Rosa and Rainer Maria Rilke." They have recently published **Elegy for Dan Rabinowitz**, a collection of poems by George Estreich. As a sample the editor chose these lines by James Hanlen from **17 Toutle River Haiku**:

I would paint a black
cloud tied to roots; river rock
floating on sunlight.

She says, **"Because we are 'booked up,' Intertext will not be looking at any unsolicited mss in the foreseeable future." Query first with 3 samples only and SASE. "Cover letter optional—the sample poems are always read first—but no form letters, please. If sample poems are promising, then the complete ms will be requested." Simultaneous queries OK. Always sends prepublication galleys. Pays 10% royalty after costs of production, promotion and distribution have been recovered.** The editor says, "We would like to receive higher-quality poetry than is usually sent to us. Intertext is not grant-supported, and each poet published represents a heavy investment of time, money and life moments on the part of the staff."

‡**INTREPID; MYTH BROTHERS (I)**, 11712 Monte Vista, Chino CA 91710, phone (909)590-3560, founded 1993, editor Anthony Rivera. ***Intrepid*** is a bimonthly that publishes poetry only, **all types, styles and subjects. No pornography. They want "experimental, upbeat poetry not too long. Also, we would like to see poems from children."** The editor says ***Intrepid*** is 32-40 pgs., 5½ × 8½, laser printed and photocopied, saddle-stapled with card cover, sometimes illustrated. They currently accept about 75% of poetry received. Press run is 300 for 120 subscribers of which 2 are libraries, 80 shelf sales. Subscription: $10. **Sample: $2 and 6 × 9 SAE with 52¢ postage. Previously published poems and simultaneous submissions OK. Do not submit mss in November and December.** Time between acceptance and publication is 6 weeks to 4 months. **Often comments on rejections. Send SASE for guidelines. Reports in 2-6 weeks. Pays 1 copy. Acquires one-time rights.** Myth Brothers also **publishes 4 chapbooks/year, usually on a subsidized basis. "Poets pay portion of expenses ($100-250) and receive 25 copies."** Also considering a chapbook contest. The editor says, "We want poets to be intrepid—boldly going where no one has gone before. Give us something that'll knock us off our feet."

INTRO (IV-Students), AWP, Old Dominion University, Norfolk VA 23529-0079, phone (804)683-3839, founded 1970, publications manager D.W. Fenza. See Associated Writing Programs in the Organizations Useful to Poets section of this book. **Students in college writing programs belonging to**

AWP may submit to this consortium of magazines publishing student poetry, fiction and plays. They are open as to the type of poetry submitted except they do not want "non-literary, haiku, etc." As to poets they have published, they say, "In our history, we've introduced Dara Wier, Carolyn Forché, Greg Pope, Norman Dubie and others." Circulation 9,500. **All work must be submitted by the writing program. Programs nominate *Intro* works in the fall. Ask the director of your writing program for more information.**

INVERTED-A, INC.; INVERTED-A HORN (I), 401 Forrest Hill, Grand Prairie TX 75051, phone (214)264-0066, founded 1977, editors Amnon Katz and Aya Katz, a very small press that evolved from publishing technical manuals for other products. "Our interests center on justice, freedom, individual rights and free enterprise." ***Inverted-A Horn*** is a periodical, magazine-sized, offset, usually 9 pages, which appears irregularly; circulation is 300. **Submissions of poetry for *Horn* and chapbooks are accepted. They publish 1 chapbook/year. The editors do not want to see anything "modern, formless, existentialist."** As a sample, they quote the following lines by Leslie Fish:

Come bring the clouds from the skies of the sea.
Roll to the mountains and set the snow free.
Come draw the winds with the storms in their wake.
Unleash the waters, and let the air shake.

Queries are reported on in 1 month, mss in 4 months. Simultaneous submissions are OK. Pay is one free copy and a 40% discount on further copies. Samples: "A recent issue of the *Horn* can be had by merely sending a SASE (subject to availability)." The editor says "I strongly recommend that would-be contributors avail themselves of this opportunity to explore what we are looking for. Most of the submissions we receive do not come close."

IOTA (II), 67 Hady Crescent, Chesterfield, Derbyshire S41 0EB Great Britain, phone +44246-276532 (UK: 0246-276532), founded 1988, editor David Holliday, is a quarterly wanting **"any style and subject; no specific limitations as to length, though, obviously, the shorter a poem is, the easier it is to get it in, which means that poems over 40 lines can still get in if they seem good enough. No concrete poetry (no facilities) or self-indulgent logorrhea."** They have recently published poetry by Michael Hatwell, Paul Greene, Sophie Hannah, David Starkey and Diane Engle. As a sample the editor selected these lines by David Wheatley:

First they blew the chimney up,
and then the stump
and then the pile.

Now all that's standing is the hole.

Iota is printed from typescript, saddle-stapled, 36 pgs., with colored paper cover. They publish about 200 of 4,000 poems received. Their press run is 400 with 200 subscriptions of which 6 are libraries. Subscription: $8 (£5). **Sample postpaid: $2 (£1.25) "but sometimes sent free." The editor prefers name and address on each poem, typed, "but provided it's legible, am happy to accept anything." He considers simultaneous submissions, but previously published poems "only if outstanding." First report in 1-3 weeks (unless production of the next issue takes precedence) but final acceptance/rejection may take up to a year. Pays 2 copies. Acquires first British serial rights only. Editor usually comments on rejections, "but detailed comment only when time allows and the poem warrants it."** Reviews books of poetry in about 200 words, single or multi-book format. Open to unsolicited reviews. Poets may also send books for review consideration. He says, "I am after crafted verse that says something; self-indulgent word-spinning is out. All editors have their blind spots; the only advice I can offer a beginning poet is to find a sympathetic editor (and you will only do that by seeing their magazines) and not to be discouraged by initial lack of success. Keep plugging!"

‡UNIVERSITY OF IOWA PRESS; THE IOWA POETRY PRIZES (III), Iowa City IA 52242-1000. The University of Iowa Press offers annually The Iowa Poetry Prizes **for book-length (50-120 pgs.) mss by poets who have already published at least one full-length book in edition of at least 750 copies. Two awards are given each year of $1,000 plus publication with standard royalty contract.** (This competition is the only way in which this press accepts poetry). **Mss are received annually in February and March only. First judging is done by press editors. All writers of English are eligible, whether citizens of the US or not. Poems from previously published books may be included only in mss of selected or collected poems, submissions of which are encouraged. Simultaneous submissions OK if press is immediately notified if the book is accepted by another publisher. No reading fee is charged, but stamped, self-addressed packaging is required or mss will not be returned.** "These awards have been initiated to encourage poets who are beyond the first-book stage to submit their very best work."

THE IOWA REVIEW (II), Dept. PM, 308 EPB, University of Iowa, Iowa City IA 52242, phone (319)335-0462, founded 1970, editor David Hamilton (first readers for poetry and occasional guest editors vary), appears 3 times a year in a flat-spined, 200-page professionally printed format. The editor says, "We simply look for poems that at the time we read and choose, we admire. **No specifications as to form, length, style, subject matter or purpose**. There are around 30-40 pgs. of poetry in each issue and currently we like to give several pages to a single poet." They receive about 5,000 submissions/year, use about 100. Editors of this influential journal do seem open to all styles and lengths, with most poems falling into the lyric free verse category. Diction, for the most part, is accessible although some examples show degrees of experimentation with form. In all, poems evoke intriguing situations or ideas. Circulation 1,200-1,300 with 1,000 subscriptions of which about half are libraries. Subscription: $18. **Sample postpaid: $6. Reads submissions September 1 through May 1 only. Their backlog is "around a year. Sometimes people hit at the right time and come out in a few months." Occasional comments on rejections or suggestions on accepted poems. Reports in 1-4 months. Pays $1 a line, 2-3 copies and a year's subscription. Buys first North American serial rights.** Poetry published in ***The Iowa Review*** has also been included in the 1992, 1993 and 1994 volumes of **The Best American Poetry.** The editor advises, "That old advice of putting poems in a drawer for 9 years was rather nice; I'd at least like to believe the poems had endured with their author for 9 months."

IOWA WOMAN (IV-Women), P.O. Box 680, Iowa City IA 52244, phone (319)277-8077, founded 1979, poetry editor Sandra Adelmund. "We are a literary quarterly publishing fiction, essays and poetry of interest to women. It is a literary magazine that has received national recognition for editorial excellence. We are publishing work **by women, about women and for women. Prefer contemporary poetry that is clear and concise. Prefer narrative and lyric. No greeting card verse."** They have recently published poetry by Lyn Lifshin, Alice Friman and Enid Shomer. As a sample the editor selected these lines by Maria S. Wickwire:

She forgot and forgot, releasing
small things with infinite patience and love
gently pulling threads from the tapestry she had kept so long in place.

As she forgot the foxes, they came out from the trees
and leaned their soft noses into her palms.
All the forgotten birds came down in a flock, returning their wordless songs.

Iowa Woman is elegantly printed, 48 pgs., magazine-sized, 4-color cover with "original cover art and illustrations." Of 2,000 poems received "I accept about 30." Press run is 2,500 for subscriptions and national newsstand sales. **Sample postpaid: $6. No simultaneious submissions. Guidelines available for SASE. Pays 2 copies and $5/poem. Acquires first-time rights.** Reviews books of poetry in 500-1,000 words. Open to unsolicited reviews. Poets may also send books to Book Editor for review consideration. "No guarantee that books sent will be reviewed; this is at the discretion of our reviewers." They hold an annual poetry contest with first place prize of $300. $10 entry fee, 3 poems, for non-subscribers. Last year's judge was Pinkie Gordon Lane. Contest guidelines available after May. Deadline: December 31. The editor says, "We would like to receive more poetry from minority women about their life experiences."

ISRAEL HORIZONS (IV-Ethnic), Suite #403, 224 W. 35th St., New York NY 10001, founded 1952, editor Ralph Seliger, poetry consultants Rochelle Ratner and Jon Shevin. A quarterly Socialist-Zionist periodical which **uses poetry reflecting Israeli and Jewish culture and concerns.** ***Israel Horizons*** reflects the Israeli left and the Zionist peace camp in Israel, including but not exclusively *Mapam* and the National Kibbutz (*Artzi*) Federation; it deals with current challenges to Israeli Society and the world Jewish community from a Socialist-Zionist perspective and examines questions confronting democratic socialism in our day. It includes editorial comments, regular columns on various topics and book and film reviews. It has an international readership with readers in the U.S., Israel, Canada and 22 other countries. The publication is 8½ × 11, 32-40 pgs. Press run is 5,000. Subscription: $15/year. **Sample: $3 and SASE.**

ITALIAN AMERICANA (IV-Ethnic), URI/CCE, 199 Promenade St., Providence RI 02908-5090, founded 1974, editor Carol Bonomo Albright, poetry editor Dana Gioia, appears twice a year using **2-4 poems "on Italian-American subjects, no more than 3 pgs. No trite nostalgia; no poems about grandparents."** As a sample the editor selected these lines from "Inside the Inside of the Moon" by Brian McCormick:

Armstrong's hop from module videos
To earth: Mom Vecchio lays down a heart.
She asks, "When is he going to go in?"
This puts a stop to the conversation.

CLOSE-UP

Master Many Techniques

"Song About Creation"

Trees are the clear bass line;
their leaves, the complication.
Deer are grace notes.
And so forth, if I define creation
as bringing into view what was previously only heard,
God's word.
On the seventh day, he listened to a little night music.

(from **God's Loud Hand**, 1993, reprinted by permission of Louisiana State University Press)

Photo by Meg Theno

Kelly Cherry

"I like moving around in all forms of writing," says poet Kelly Cherry. "I can explore the same themes through different forms. I don't see the forms as a hierarchy, however. I like to think of them as concentric circles. If I look at the forms that way, for me poetry is at the center, at the heart."

Cherry, who is also a fiction writer, essayist and translator as well as a professor of English at the University of Wisconsin in Madison, has published work in more than 350 magazines and anthologies. And her books—collections of short stories, poetry and novels—have received praise and recognition from a variety of sources.

In some ways, she says, each type of work is closely connected, often inspiring another or helping her explore different aspects of the same subject matter. Her very personal memoir, **The Exiled Heart**, published in 1991 by Louisiana State University Press, recounts her relationship with a Latvian composer and their difficulties with the Soviet government. Two of her poetry collections, **Natural Theology** (L.S.U. Press, 1988) and **God's Loud Hand** (L.S.U. Press, 1993), draw from this same experience.

When Cherry began writing, poetry seemed a natural place to start, but her first experiences with creative expression came from music. "My parents were string quartet violinists and their particular love was the late Beethoven string quartets. I grew up listening to this music, and long before I could even read, I knew I wanted to make something beautiful like that."

Cherry says she finds all forms of writing to be musical. "I remember being simply swept away by the music of language, and I had that response not only to poetry but to other forms of literature. I remember one of the earliest pieces of literature I encountered and fell in love with was **A Midsummer Night's Dream**. I think fiction like **Moby Dick** is a kind of music too. I've felt possessed by the idea that a line of prose could be full of melody but at the same time intellectually rigorous."

"Intellectual" has often been the word used to describe Cherry's poetry. "I've been told that my approach is more cerebral than a lot of other poets' and I don't mind that word, but I want my poems also to be filled with feeling. The ideal poem is one that contains both intellect and emotion."

Although some of her poems have been inspired by her experiences or people she's known, she says, "a lot come from thinking about ideas. To give a specific example, one evening I was at the dinner table at a writers' colony when someone brought up a question about the theological concept of grace. Later I wrote a sonnet about grace that is now in **God's Loud Hand**. That sonnet didn't come from anything that happened to me—it's simply an attempt to answer this interesting question posed at the dinner table."

Cherry admits she was "serious" about her writing long before she learned all the skills that come with being a professional, published writer. "I was working on my MFA before I began to understand what being a professional writer was all about—thinking about sending things out and trying to get paid for it."

She published a number of poems and stories in literary journals early in her writing career (her first when she was 16), but the experience that stands out most to her was the publication of her long poetic work, "Benjamin John," in the ***Carolina Quarterly***. "I don't recall if they paid me any money for it, but it was exciting to see a whole piece like that [more than 30 pages] in a literary journal. The first big sale I had was in fiction. I sold a short story to ***Commentary*** magazine that then came out in **Best American Short Stories**. I think I still have the check stub for that somewhere."

Cherry tends to be a slow writer, she says, so to complete projects constantly she's worked out a system. "I tend to work on a poem, story or novel for a period of time, then stop and switch to some other kind of material. While I'm working on the second thing, the first is simmering, waiting for me to get back to it. It usually takes a very long time to complete any given piece of work this way, but after you've been working like this for a very long time, there's usually some piece of work nearing completion."

Taking breaks to work on other material and then returning allows Cherry to do extensive revision. She says it took 15 years to write **The Exiled Heart**, which she estimates she revised at least once every 18 months. Yet Cherry is a very consistent writer, working almost every day on something. "Paradoxically, I find poetry requires more of my time than short stories or even, sometimes, novels. With poetry I need a certain amount of emotional space."

The most difficult task for a poet, or any writer, she says, is to learn to read your own work with a critical eye. "The writer's view of the page is to some degree blinkered by the writer's intention, memory of the experience, and even the memory of what was written yesterday. The writer has to get past these obstacles to see clearly where the poem, story or novel wants to go."

Beyond reading extensively, Cherry advises beginning writers not to be afraid to be clumsy or make mistakes. "The writer has to give herself the freedom to attempt anything that occurs to her. I would also advise writers to master as many techniques as possible. The point of this is freedom. The more command you have of techniques, the freer you are to do with them whatever you want."

—*Robin Gee*

It is 150-200 pgs., 6×9, professionally printed, flat-spined. Press run is 1,000 for 900 subscribers of which 175 are libraries, the rest individual adult subscribers. Subscription: $15. **Sample postpaid: $7.50. Cover letter not required "but helpful." Name on first page of ms only. Do not submit mss in July, August or September. Occasionally comments on rejections. Reports in 4-6 weeks. Acquires first rights.** Reviews books of poetry in 600 words, multi-book format. Poets may send books for review consideration to Prof. John Paul Russo, English Dept., University of Miami, Coral Gables FL 33124. The editor says, "Single copies of poems for submissions are sufficient."

ITALICA PRESS (IV-Translations), #605, 595 Main St., New York NY 10044-0047, phone (212)935-4230, founded 1985, publishers Eileen Gardiner and Ronald G. Musto, is a small press publisher of **English translations of Italian works** in Smyth-sewn paperbacks, averaging 175 pgs. They have published **Guido Cavalcanti, The Complete Poems**, a dual language (English/Italian) book with English translation and introduction by Marc Cirigliano. Forthcoming: **Selected Poems** by Gaspara Stampa, edited and translated by Laura Anna Stortoni and Mary Prentice Lillie. **Query with 10 sample translations of important 20th Century or medieval and Renaissance Italian poets. Include cover letter, bio and list of publications. Simultaneous submissions OK, but translation should not be "totally" previously published. Reports on queries in 3 weeks, on mss in 3 months. Always sends prepublication galleys. Pays 7-15% royalties plus 10 author's copies. Buys English language rights. Sometimes comments on rejections.**

‡JACARANDA REVIEW (III), Dept. of English, University of California at Los Angeles, Los Angeles CA 90024-1530, phone (310)825-3429, founded 1984, editor Bruce Kijewski, is a literary journal appearing twice a year. **"We publish all kinds, from poems by poets who publish in the *New Yorker* to L.A. Beat poets, to translations from the Japanese. Subject matter and style are open. No inspirational verse, etc."** They have recently published poetry by Carolyn Forché, Alfred Corn, Charles Bukowski, Wanda Coleman and Heather McHugh. The editor describes it as digest-sized, 100-124 pgs., with 2- or 4-color covers, no art inside the magazine, 4-6 ads/issue. They accept 40-50 of 750-1,000 poems received a year. Press run is 1,000 for 100 subscribers (25 of them libraries), about 400 shelf sales. Subscription: $10. **Sample postpaid: $5. No simultaneous submissions. Editor often comments on promising rejections. Publishes theme issues. Reports in 4-6 weeks. Sometimes sends prepublication galleys. Pays 3 copies plus 20% discount on additional copies.** The editor says, "We'd like to see more emotionally adventurous poetry, poetry which could but chooses not to hide behind its technical proficiency. We receive too many workshop poems. We want poetry that matters, that changes the way people think and feel by the necessity of their vision. That's a lot to ask, but good poets deserve demanding readers."

JACKSON'S ARM (III), % Sunk Island Publishing, Box 74, Lincoln LN1 1QG England, founded 1985, editor Michael Blackburn, is a small press publisher of poetry chapbooks and translations. **"No specifications as to subject or style. The poetry I want to publish should be vigorous and imaginative, with a firm grasp of everyday realities. Nothing bland, safe or pretentious."** The press publishes occasional chapbooks, books, cards and cassettes. However, the editor says **he does not usually accept unsolicited submissions. Pays in copies: 10% of print run.** Mr. Blackburn advises, "Read everything you can, in particular *contemporary* poets and writers. Get hold of all the 'small' poetry magazines you can, as well as the more commercial and prestigious."

JAPANOPHILE (IV-Form, ethnic), P.O. Box 223, Okemos MI 48864, phone (517)349-1795, founded 1974, poetry editor Earl R. Snodgrass, is a literary quarterly about Japanese culture (not just in Japan). Issues include articles, art, a short story and **poetry. They want haiku or other Japanese forms or any form if it deals with Japan, Japanese culture or American-Japanese relations. (Note: karate and ikebana in the US are examples of Japanese culture.)** They have published poetry by Linda McFerrin, Elizabeth St. Jacques, Alexis Rotella, Glenna Holloway, David Carroll, Mimi Hinman and reprints of Basho. There are 10-15 pgs. of poetry in each issue (digest-sized, about 56 pgs., saddle-stapled). They have a circulation of 500 with 100 subscriptions of which 30 are libraries. They receive about 500 submissions a year, use 70, have a 2-month backlog. **Sample postpaid: $4. Summer is the best time to submit. Cover letter required; include brief bio and credits if any. Send SASE for guidelines. Reports in 2 months. Pays $1 for haiku and up to $15 for longer poems.** Open to unsolicited reviews. Poets may also send books for review consideration, attn. Vada L. Davis. They also publish books under the Japanophile imprint, but so far none have been of poetry. Query with samples and cover letter (about 1 pg.) giving publishing credits, bio. The editor says, "This quarterly is out as each season begins. Poems that name or suggest a season, and are received two or three months before the season, get a good look."

JEWISH CURRENTS (V), Suite 601, 22 E. 17th St., New York NY 10003-1919, phone (212)924-5740, founded 1946, editor Morris U. Schappes, is a magazine appearing 11 times a year that publishes

poetry on Jewish themes, including translations from the Yiddish and Hebrew (original texts should be submitted with translations). **"We have been forced to declare a temporary moratorium on all poetry acceptances owing to the size of our backlog of material already accepted and awaiting publication in this category."** The editor says it is 48 pgs., 5×8, offset, saddle-stapled. Press run is 2,700 for 2,600 subscribers of which about 10% are libraries. Subscription: $20/year. **Sample postpaid: $2. Always sends prepublication galleys. Pays 6 copies.** Reviews books of poetry. Open to unsolicited reviews. Publishers may also send books of poetry for review consideration.

JEWISH SPECTATOR (IV-Religious), 4391 Park Milano, Calabasas CA 91302, phone (818)591-7481, founded 1935, editor Robert Bleiweiss. ***Jewish Spectator*** is a 68-page Judaic scholarly quarterly that **welcomes poetry on Jewish themes.** Subscribers: 1,200. **No simultaneous submissions or previously published poems. Cover letter with brief bio (2-3 lines) required. Reports in 6 weeks. Returns mss only with SASE. Pays 2 copies.** Open to unsolicited reviews. Poets may also send books for review consideration.

‡JEWISH VEGETARIANS NEWSLETTER; JEWISH VEGETARIANS OF NORTH AMERICA (I, IV-Religious, specialized), 6938 Reliance Rd., Federalsburg MD 21632, phone (410)754-5550, founded 1983, editor Eva R. Mossman. ***Jewish Vegetarians Newsletter*** is a quarterly publication of the Jewish Vegetarians of North America, a nonprofit organization. It is designed to promote vegetarianism within the Judaic tradition and includes various articles, recipes and short book reviews. **They want poetry that is "'Jewish related and/or about vegetarianism, veganism, animal rights and/or the environment."** The newsletter is 32 pgs., 8½×11, printed on recycled paper and saddle-stapled. Press run is 2,000 for 1,500 subscribers. Subscription: $12/year. **Sample available free with #10 SAE and 2 first-class stamps. Previously published poems and simultaneous submissions OK. Cover letter required. "Please include permission to print." Often comments on rejections. Reports in no more than 3 months. "We do not pay for literary contributions." However, copies are available free for the cost of postage and all poetry remains the property of the author.** The editor says, "We encourage everyone to obtain a sample issue."

THE JOURNAL (III), Dept. of English, Ohio State University, 164 W. 17th Ave., Columbus OH 43210, founded 1972, co-editors Kathy Fagan and Michelle Herman, appears twice yearly with reviews, essays, quality fiction and poetry. **"We're open to all forms; we tend to favor work that gives evidence of a mature and sophisticated sense of the language."** They have published poetry by David Baker, T.R. Hummer, Cynthia Ozick and Carol Frost. The following sample is from the poem "The Helmet of Mambrino" by Linda Bierds:

> *I would know that tumble often, that*
> *explorer's slide, belief to belief, conviction*
> *to its memory, to conviction. Once I placed*
> *my marker-coin on Mt. Whitney's double, lost in a mist,*
> *convinced I had climbed to the highest land. Once*
> *I charted a lake from opal air.*

The Journal is 6×9, professionally printed on heavy stock, 80-100 pgs., of which about 40 in each issue are devoted to poetry. They receive about 4,000 submissions/year, use 200, and have a 3- to 6-month backlog. Press run is 1,500. Subscription: $8. **Sample: $5. On occasion editor comments on rejections. Pays copies and an honorarium of $25-50 when funds are available. Acquires all rights. Returns rights on publication.** Reviews books of poetry. Contributing editor David Citino advises, "However else poets train or educate themselves, they must do what they can to know our language. Too much of the writing that we see indicates that poets do not in many cases develop a feel for the possibilities of language, and do not pay attention to craft. Poets should not be in a rush to publish—until they are ready." (Also see Ohio State University Press/*The Journal* Award in Poetry.)

JOURNAL OF ASIAN MARTIAL ARTS (IV-Specialized), 821 W. 24th St., Erie PA 16502, phone (814)455-9517, fax (814)838-7811, founded 1991, editor-in-chief Michael A. DeMarco, is a quarterly "comprehensive journal on Asian martial arts with high standards and academic approach." They want **poetry about Asian martial arts and Asian martial art history/culture. They have no restrictions provided the poet has a feel for, and good understanding of, the subject. They don't want poetry showing a narrow view. "We look for a variety of styles from an interdisciplinary approach."** As a sample we selected the opening lines from "Kensei" by Berrien C. Henderson:

> *He approaches last.*
> *A zephyr gusts and swirls about him.*
> *His gi flaps and pops in the wind.*
> *Brow furrowed and jet hair shining, he stands*
> *As tranquil as a distant mountain*
> *While his topknot swings ever so gently.*

The editor says the journal is 128 pgs., 8½ × 11, perfect-bound, with soft cover, b&w illustrations, computer and hand art and ads. Press run is 5,000 for 1,000 subscribers of which 50 are libraries, the rest mainly shelf sales. Single copy: $9.75; subscription: $32 for 1 year, $55 for 2 years. **Sample postpaid: $10. Previously published poems OK; no simultaneous submissions. Cover letter required. Often comments on rejections. Send SASE for guidelines. Reports in 1-2 months. Sometimes sends prepublication galleys. Pays $1-100 and/or 1-5 copies on publication. Buys first and reprint rights.** Reviews books of poetry "if they have some connection to Asian martial arts; length is open." Open to unsolicited reviews. Poets may also send books for review consideration. The editor adds, "We offer a unique medium for serious poetry dealing with Asian martial arts. Any style is welcome if there is quality in thought and writing."

JOURNAL OF NEW JERSEY POETS (II, IV-Regional), English Dept., County College of Morris, Randolph NJ 07869, phone (201)328-5471, founded 1976, editor Sander Zulauf. This biannual periodical uses poetry from **current or former residents of New Jersey. They want "serious work that is regional in origin but universal in scope." They do not want "sentimental, greeting card verse."** Poets published include Lesley Choyce, Alfred Starr Hamilton, Phebe Davidson and Joe Weil. As a sample, the editor selected the following excerpt from " 'For May Is the Month of Our Mother' " by Cat Doty:

Next, I played Nelson Eddy "Ave Maria." Her one inch of face
held too much sadness to bear. To cheer her up,
I played "Rum and Coca Cola" The Andrews Sisters, and our souls
were so open from all that ave maria that we threw ourselves
into the rhythm, and jumped on the bed, and I beat Mary
like a maraca in my palm, her burden of black beads clacking
thick and loud, until one slap too many cracked her right in half,
and her beads flung themselves to the floor, where they lay
like intestines.

The journal is published in March (spring) and October (autumn), digest-sized, offset, with an average of 64 pgs. Press run is 900. Subscription: $7/year. **Sample: $4. There are "no limitations" on submissions; SASE required, reporting time is 3-6 months and time to publication within 1 year. Pays 2 copies/published poem. Acquires first North American serial rights.** Only using solicited reviews. Send books for review consideration. "We plan to offer brief reviews of 100-150 words. An annual 'Books Received' list is slated for Spring."

JOURNAL OF POETRY THERAPY (IV-Specialized), Dept. PM, Human Sciences Press, 233 Spring St., New York NY 10013-1578, phone (212)620-8471, founded 1987. **Poetry mss should be sent to journal editor,** Dr. Nicholas Mazza, School of Social Work, Florida State University, Tallahassee FL 32306-2024. They use **"poems that could be useful in therapeutic settings, prefer relatively short poems; no sentimental, long poems."** They have published poetry by Ingrid Wendt and Virginia Bagliore. As a sample the editor selected these lines from "all too often, love " by Elaine Preston:

like our hunger
in the house where we warmed our fingers
and laughed against cracks in walls
long since plastered shut against the cold

"The ***Journal*** is devoted to the use of the poetic in health, mental health education and other human service settings." The quarterly is 64 pgs., flat-spined, digest-sized, using 3-6 pgs. for poetry. They accept approximately 10% of 100 poems received. There are 500 subscriptions. Subscription: $38 (US), $46 (international) for individuals; $125 (US), $145 (international) for institutions. **Write publisher for free sample. Submit maximum of 3 poems, 4 copies of each with name on only 1 of them. Include SASE. Editor "occasionally" comments on rejections. Pays 1 copy.**

JOURNAL OF THE AMERICAN MEDICAL ASSOCIATION (JAMA) (II, IV-Themes), 515 N. State, Chicago IL 60610, phone (312)464-2417, founded 1883, associate editor Charlene Breedlove, has a "Poetry and Medicine" column and publishes **poetry "in some way related to a medical experience, whether from the point-of-view of a health care worker or patient, or simply an observer. No unskilled poetry."** They have published poetry by Diane Ackerman and Daisy Aldan. As a sample the editor selected these lines from "Healing Powers" by Floyd Skloot:

I have come to learn
the body belongs to the self
in the same way light belongs
to time, the way death
belongs to life, which must explain
why I have also come to
treasure whatever lies within
the dark vigilant nights.

JAMA, magazine-sized, flat-spined, with glossy paper cover, has 360,000 subscribers of which 369 are libraries. They accept about 7% of 550 poems received/year. Subscription: $66. **Sample free. Publishes theme issues. Theme for issue in late 1994 or early 1995 is cancer. Pays up to 3 copies. "We ask for a signed copyright release, but publication elsewhere is always granted free of charge."**

JOURNEYMEN (II, IV-Specialized: men's issues), 513 Chester Turnpike, Candia NH 03034, founded 1991, editor Paul S. Boynton, is a quarterly described as "one of the men's movement's leading magazines, featuring interviews with prominent movement leaders and feature stories and columns on modern men and the issues they face in a changing world. Our purpose is to serve as a means for opinions and perspectives among men to be communicated, pooled and used to shed light upon a long silent topic: being male. **Unless you are familiar with current men's movement trends and/or 'men's issues,' don't submit to us. Themes must be applicable to men in modern world. No rhyming poetry unless excellent. 10-45 lines or thereabouts. No haiku. Our audience is men, so we want poetry that will speak to men. Suggested themes: fatherhood, sons, substance abuse, power/powerlessness, mythopoetic/gay/legal issues, leisure, or anything else men experience."** The editor says *Journeymen* is 32 pgs., 8½ × 11, printed and stapled with color photo cover. "We're growing better and bigger with every issue. We get over 1,000 poems a year, use only 4-10." Press run is 4,000 for 3,000 subscribers, 500 shelf sales. Single copy: $4.95; subscription: $18/year. **Sample postpaid: $5.50. Send no more than 6 poems. No previously published poetry; simultaneous submissions OK. Cover letter required.** Time between acceptance and publication is up to a year. **Seldom comments on rejections. Reports in 2 months. Sometimes sends prepublication galleys. Pays 1 copy. Rights revert to poet.** The editor says, "You should be familiar with the flavor of our magazine before submitting. If you're not, it'll probably show. Send for a sample. We prefer male poets because *Journeymen* is a forum for men."

JUGGLER'S WORLD (IV-Specialized), % Ken Letko, College of the Redwoods, 883 W. Washington Blvd., Crescent City CA 95531-8361, phone (707)464-7457, founded 1982, literary editor Ken Letko, is a quarterly magazine, **using poems about juggling. "Only restriction is that all content is focused on juggling."** They have published poetry by Robert Hill Long, Barbara Goldberg and Margo Wilding. As a sample the editor selected these lines from "Street Mime" by Ann B. Knox:

> *. . . a girl*
> *smiles, the man bows to her, then*
> *spreads his hands wide and silver*
> *balls lift in an arc high*
> *over his head. Faces pivot*

JW is 40 pgs., magazine-sized, saddle-stapled, professionally printed on glossy stock with 2-color glossy paper cover. Press run is 3,500, circulated to more than 3,000 jugglers in more than 20 countries. They receive 50-100 poetry submissions/year, use 4-8 poems. Subscription: $18. **Sample: "$2 or $3 depending on issue." They will consider previously published poems. Editor sometimes comments on rejections, suggesting some revision. Reports in 1-4 months. Pays 1 copy. Acquires first or one-time rights.** The editor urges poets to "provide insights."

‡JUNIPER PRESS; NORTHEAST; JUNIPER BOOKS; THE WILLIAM N. JUDSON SERIES OF CONTEMPORARY AMERICAN POETRY; CHICKADEE; INLAND SEA SERIES; GIFTS OF THE PRESS (III, IV-Form), 1310 Shorewood Dr., La Crosse WI 54601, founded 1962, poetry editors John Judson and Joanne Judson, is one of the oldest and most respected programs of publishing poetry in the country. *Northeast* is a semiannual little magazine, digest-sized, saddle-stapled. **"Poets published in our books have first appeared in *Northeast* and are invited to submit mss. Any other book mss sent will be returned without being read." Reports in 2-4 months.** A subscription to *Northeast*/**Juniper Press** is $33/year ($38 for institutions), which brings you 2 issues of the magazine and the Juniper Books, Chickadees, WNJ Books and some gifts of the press, a total of about 5-8 items. (Or send SASE for catalog to order individual items. **Sample postpaid: $2.50.**) The Juniper Books are perfect-bound books of poetry; the WNJ Books are letterpress poetry books by one author; Chickadees are 12-24 pgs. each, in wrappers; Inland Sea Series is for larger works; Gifts of the Press are usually given only to subscribers or friends of the press. "Please read us before sending mss. It will aid in your selection of materials to send. If you don't like what we do, please don't submit."

‡ ***The double dagger before a listing indicates that the listing is new in this edition. New markets are often the most receptive to submissions.***

‡**JUST ABOUT HORSES (I, IV-Specialized)**, 34 Owens Dr., Wayne NJ 07470-2300, founded 1975, editor Stephanie Macejko, is a magazine which appears 5 times/year and provides information about both the model horse hobby and real horses. **"Our magazine deals with model horses and real horses. Any style of poetry will be read as long as the style suits the subject matter."** ***Just About Horses*** is 32 pgs., digest-sized, saddle-stapled, professionally printed on glossy paper with b&w and color photos. Press run is 12,000 for 9,000 subscribers. Subscription: $9. **Sample postpaid: $2.50. No previously published poems or simultaneous submissions. Pays $25 plus 2 copies.**

KAIMANA: LITERARY ARTS HAWAII; HAWAII LITERARY ARTS COUNCIL (III, IV-Regional), P.O. Box 11213, Honolulu HI 96828, founded 1974, editor Tony Quagliano. ***Kaimana***, a semiannual, is the magazine of the Hawaii Literary Arts Council. **Poems with "some Pacific reference are preferred—Asia, Polynesia, Hawaii—but not exclusively."** They have published poetry by Howard Nemerov, John Yau, Reuben Tam, Robert Bly, Joe Balaz, Ursule Molinaro, Lyn Lifshin, Haunani-Kay Trask, Anne Waldman and Joe Stanton. As a sample the editor selected "Next Time" by Naomi Shihab Nye:

Gingko trees live 1,000 years.
Eating the leaves will clear your brain.
When I heard about them, I thought of my mother,
how much I would like to sit under one with her
in the ancient shade, nibbling
the flesh, the stem, the central vein.

It is 64-76 pgs., 7½ × 10, stapled, with high-quality printing. Press run is 1,000 for 600 subscribers of which 200 are libraries. Subscription: $12. **Sample postpaid: $5. Cover letter with submissions preferred. Sometimes comments on rejections. Reports with "reasonable dispatch." Pays 2 copies.** The editor says, "Hawaii gets a lot of 'travelling regionalists,' visiting writers with inevitably superficial observations. We also get superb visiting observers who are careful craftsmen anywhere. ***Kaimana*** is interested in the latter, to complement our own best Hawaii writers."

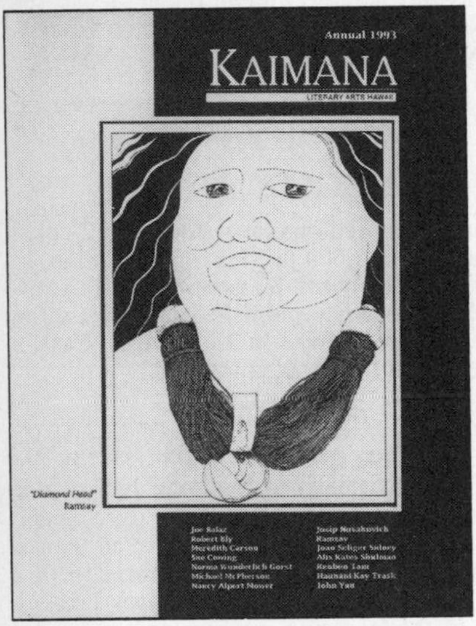

"Poetry is Kaimana's primary content," says Editor Tony Quagliano. The semiannual magazine is published by the Hawaii Literary Arts Council, and intends to honor and promote indigenous Hawaiian culture as well as contemporary artistic and literary activity in Hawaii. "The India ink cover illustration of a strong and regal Hawaiian woman evokes, for me, the strength and endurance of Hawaiian culture," says Quagliano. "I like to think that with courage and luck, local poets and artists can help preserve Hawaiian and Pacific culture." The cover art is by Ramsay, a longtime resident of Honolulu.

‡**KALDRON: AN INTERNATIONAL JOURNAL OF VISUAL POETRY AND LANGUAGE ART (IV-Form)**, P.O. Box 7164, Halcyon CA 93421-7164, phone (805)489-2770, editor and publisher Karl Kempton. ***Kaldron*** is a "journal of visual poetry and language art interested only in works which are a true wedding of language/poetry/literature and the other arts. This is a journal which publishes works from around the world." Mr. Kempton says, **"A visual poem is a poem which takes the patterns and densities of language and molds them with other art forms, mainly the visual arts in such a way that without either element the work falls apart, that is to say the entire image is what is on the page."** It is handsomely printed in an oversized magazine format. The "poems" are graphic, using little verbal text, and can be reproduced only photographically. It is impossible to quote works from the magazine without photographing them; contributors include Doris Cross, Scott Helmes, Alan Satie, Hassan Moussady, Paula Hocks, Shoji Yoshizawa and Giovanni Fontana. ***Kaldron*** appears "irregularly" and has a circulation of 800. Single copy: $10 (issue 20/21). **Sample postpaid: $5. Contributors receive 2 to 10 copies. The only instruction for contributors is: "no image should be larger than 10¼ × 16."**

Submissions will be reported on in "one day to one month," and time to publication "varies, but contributor kept informed of any delays." Criticism will be given "if submissions are accompanied with a cover letter." Mr. Kempton says, "Visual poetry and language art published in ***Kaldron*** may be considered examples of an ongoing development of an international meta-language/poetic/artistic gesturing which attempts to express what language is unable to express. Such concerns have created a strong international dialogue. The roots of this expression are ancient; the modern roots are found in movements like futurism and dadaism in the early part of this century and the more contemporary roots are found in the concrete poetry movement of the 50's and 60's, a poetry held by many to be the first true international poetic expression. Around 100 serious visual poets and language artists are at work in this country and hundreds more at work around the globe."

KALEIDOSCOPE: INTERNATIONAL MAGAZINE OF LITERATURE, FINE ARTS, AND DISABILITY (IV-Specialized, themes), 326 Locust St., Akron OH 44302, phone (216)762-9755, founded 1979, editor-in-chief Dr. Darshan C. Perusek, consulting poetry editor Christopher Hewitt. ***Kaleidoscope*** is based at United Disability Services, a nonprofit agency. **Poetry should deal with the experience of disabilty but not limited to that when writer has a disability. "*Kaleidoscope* is interested in high-quality poetry with vivid, believable images and evocative language. Works should not use stereotyping, patronizing or offending language about disability."** They have recently published poetry by Laura Hershey, Lee Steuer and Barbara Seaman. As a sample, they offer these lines from "Apraxia" by Margaret Robison:

I search for music to unlock
my damaged speech, some
rhythm I can ride
like birds' wings ride the wind.

Circulation 1,500, including libraries, social service agencies, health-care professionals, universities and individual subscribers. Single copy: $5; subscription: $9 individual, $14 agency. **Sample: $4. Submit photocopies with SASE for return of work. Limit 5 poems/submission. All submissions must be accompanied by an autobiographical sketch. Deadlines: March and August 1. Publishes theme issues. Send SASE for upcoming themes. Themes for 1995 and 1996 are as follows: "Disability and the Abuse of Children"—July 1995 (deadline March 1995), "Disability and Violence in the Family"—January 1996 (deadline August 1995), and "Disability and Travel"—July 1996 (deadline March 1996). Reports back in 3 weeks, acceptance or rejection may take 6 months. Pays $10-125. Rights return to author upon publication.** Staff reviews books of poetry. Send books for review consideration to Gail Willmott, senior editor.

KALLIOPE, a journal of women's art (IV-Women, translations, themes), 3939 Roosevelt Blvd., Jacksonville FL 32205, phone (904)381-3511, founded 1978, editor Mary Sue Koeppel, a literary/visual arts journal published by Florida Community College at Jacksonville; the emphasis is on women writers and artists. The editors say, **"We like the idea of poetry as a sort of artesian well—there's one meaning that's clear on the surface and another deeper meaning that comes welling up from underneath. We'd like to see more poetry from Black, Hispanic, Native American women, and more translations. Nothing sexist, racist, conventionally sentimental. We will have one special theme issue each year. Write for specific guidelines."** Poets recently published include Elisavietta Ritchie, Marge Piercy, Kathryn Machan Aal, Enid Shomer and Sue Daniel Elkind. As a sample, the editor selected the following lines by Ruth Moon Kempher:

But I sail hot, sail cold, depending
not on externals, but on that queer greed
driving, from sea to street
on to dark hedgerows
shadowed alleys, like a creature
chased, like Cinderella
shoes in hand.

Kalliope calls itself "a journal of women's art" and publishes fiction, interviews, drama and visual art in addition to poetry. The magazine, which appears 3 times a year, is 7¼×8¼, flat-spined, handsomely printed on white stock, glossy card cover and b&w photographs of works of art. Average number of pages is 80. Poems here are lively, celebratory and varied in form, style and length. The circulation is 1,250, of which 400-500 are subscriptions, including 100 library subscriptions, and 600 are copies sold on newsstands and in bookstores. Subscription: $12.50/year or $22/2 years. **Sample: $7. Poems should be submitted in batches of 3-7 with brief bio note, phone number and address. Because all submissions are read by several members of the editing staff, response time is usually 3-4 months. Publication will be within 6 months. Criticism is provided "when time permits and the author has requested it." Send SASE for guidelines and upcoming themes. Pays 3 copies. Acquires first publication rights.** Reviews books of poetry, "but we prefer groups of books in one review." Open to unsolicited reviews. Poets may also send books for review consideration. They sponsor the Sue Saniel Elkind Poetry Contest, judged last year by Carolyn Forché. First prize: $1,000; runners up published in ***Kalliope***. Deadline:

November 1. Send SASE for details. The editor says, "***Kalliope*** is a carefully stitched patchwork of how women feel, what they experience, and what they have come to know and understand about their lives . . . a collection of visions from or about women all over the world. Send for a sample copy, to see what appeals to us, or better yet, subscribe!"

KANGAROOS AND BEANS (V), P.O. Box 40231, Redford MI 48240, phone (313)537-9425, founded 1989, editor Gregg Nannini, appears twice a year. **They publish "poetry that excites or strikes a philosophical chord." However, they are currently overstocked and not accepting any poetry submissions.** They have published poetry by Jeanette Picardi and Kathleen Meade. As a sample the editor selected these lines from Meade's "Attempts to Enter a Pastoral Painting":

Her fingers press the oil,
extract lanolin from sheep.
Her tongue searches the Italian Vale.

It is 20 pgs., 8½ × 11, photocopied from typescript and corner-stapled. Press run is 500. Subscription: $4. **Sample postpaid: $2. Make check payable to Gregg Nannini.**

KANSAS QUARTERLY; KANSAS ART COMMISSION AWARDS; SEATON AWARDS (II, IV-Regional, themes), The English Dept., Kansas State University, Manhattan KS 66506, phone (913)532-6716, founded 1968 as an outgrowth of ***Kansas Magazine,*** editors Ben Nyberg, John Rees and G.W. Clift, is "a magazine devoted to the culture, history, art and writing of mid-Americans, but not restricted to this area." It publishes poetry in all issues. They say, **"We are interested in all kinds of modern poetry except limericks, extremely light verse or book-length mss."** They have recently published poetry by David Ray, Tom Hansen, Bruce Cutler, Deborah Pierce Nichols, F.D. Reeve, Harold Witt, Anthony Sobin, David Citino, Peter Cooley and David Kirby. There are an average of 80 pgs. of poetry in each creative issue. They receive 10,000 submissions/year, use 300-400. There is at least a 12- to 18-month backlog unless a poem fits into a special number – then it may go in rapidly. Circulation 1,150-1,350 with 721 subscriptions of which 50% are libraries. **Sample postpaid: $6 ($8 for double number). Submit "enough poems to show variety (or a single poem if author wishes), but no books. Typed, double-spaced, OK. No queries. We consider, reluctantly, simultaneous submissions." Reports in 1-3 months. Pays 2 copies and yearly awards of up to $200/poet for 6-10 poets.** The ***Kansas Quarterly***/Kansas Art Commission Awards are $200 (1st prize), $150 (2nd), $100 (3rd), $75 (4th) and up to 5 honorable mentions ($50). There are also similar prizes in the Seaton Awards (to native-born or resident Kansas poets). The editors **often comment on rejections, even at times suggesting revision and return.** An excellent market, this magazine has been known on occasion to pack the work of more than 60 poets in its 200 pages/issue. All styles are welcome, but response times can be slow. Editors say, "Our only advice is for the poet to *know* the magazine he is sending to: consult in library or send for sample copy. Magazines need the support and their published copies should provide the best example of what the editors are looking for. We believe that we annually publish as much generally good poetry as nearly any other U.S. literary magazine – between 250 and 400 poems a year. Others will have to say how good it really is."

KARAMU (II), Dept. of English, Eastern Illinois University, Charleston IL 61920, phone (217)581-5614, founded 1966, editor Peggy Brayfield, is an annual whose "goal is to provide a forum for the best contemporary poetry and fiction that comes our way. We especially like to print the works of new writers. **We like to see poetry that shows a good sense of what's being done with poetry currently. We like poetry that builds around real experiences, real images and real characters and that avoids abstraction, overt philosophizing and fuzzy pontifications. In terms of form, we prefer well-structured free verse, poetry with an inner, sub-surface structure as opposed to, let's say, the surface structure of rhymed quatrains. We have definite preferences in terms of style and form, but no such preferences in terms of length or subject matter. Purpose, however, is another thing. We don't have much interest in the openly didactic poem. If the poet wants to preach against or for some political or religious viewpoint, the preaching shouldn't be so strident that it overwhelms the poem. The poem should first be a poem."** They have published poetry by David Bond, Mary McDaniel, Pamela Donald and Karen Subach. As a sample the editor chose these lines from "We Begin Here" by Steven Blaski:

Your death broke into you as if it were a door
of glass that you smashed your body through.
Still, each night I followed you to the rooms
of my ravaged childhood, where you wore
the hellish body that performed in the freak show
of intensive care . . .

The format is 120 pgs., 5 × 8, matte cover, handsomely printed (narrow margins), attractive b&w art. The most recent issue carries 60 pgs. of poetry. They have also published a special oversized issue of ***Karamu*** on the theme "Looking Back at the Sixties" available for $7.25 postpaid. They have a circulation of 350 with 300 subscriptions of which 15 are libraries. They receive submissions from about 300 poets each year, use 40-50 poems. Never more than a year – usually 6-7 months—between acceptance and publication. **Sample: $4; 2 recent issues: $5. Poems—in batches of no more than 5-6—may be submitted to Peggy Brayfield. "We don't much care for simultaneous submissions. We read September 1 through June 30 only, for fastest decision submit February through May. Poets should not bother to query. We critique a few of the better poems. We want the poet to consider our comments and then submit new work." Pays one contributor's copy. Acquires first serial rights.** The editor says, "Follow the standard advice: Know your market. Read contemporary poetry and the magazines you want to be published in. Be patient."

KATYDID BOOKS (V), 1 Balsa Rd., Santa Fe NM 87505, founded 1973, editors/publishers Karen Hargreaves-Fitzsimmons and Thomas Fitzsimmons, publishes 3 paperbacks and 1 hardback/year. "We publish three series of poetry: Asian Poetry in Translation, European Writing in Translation, and American Poets." They have published poetry by Makoto Ooka, Shuntaro Tanikawa and Ryuichi Tamura. **However, they are currently not accepting submissions.**

KAWABATA PRESS; SEPIA POETRY MAGAZINE (I, II, IV-Anthology), Knill Cross House, Millbrook, Torpoint, Cornwall, United Kingdom, founded 1977, poetry editor Colin David Webb, publishes **"non-traditional poetry, prose and artwork (line only), open to all original and well thought-out work. I hate rhymes, traditional poems and dislike 'genre' stories. I want original and thought-provoking material."** They have recently published poetry by A. Lipkind and S. Sneyd. ***Sepia*** is published 3 times a year in an inexpensively produced, digest-sized, 32-page, saddle-stapled format, photoreduced from typescript, with narrow margins and bizarre drawings. They receive 250 submissions/year, use 50-60. Press run is 150 for 75 subscribers of which 5-6 are libraries. Subscription: £1.50 ($3) a year. **Sample: 50p. ($1). Submit 6-10 pgs., typed. Simultaneous submissions OK. Reports in 10 days. Sometimes sends prepublication galleys. Pays free copy.** Reviews books of poetry in 50-100 words. Open to unsolicited reviews. Poets may also send books for review consideration. Under the imprint of Kawabata Press, Colin Webb also publishes anthologies and collections. **However publication of these has been temporarily suspended. Query with 6-10 poems and "maybe a brief outline of intent." Poet gets 50% of profits (after cost of printing is covered) and 4 copies.** A book catalog of Kawabata Press publications is on the back of ***Sepia***, for ordering copies. The editor **always comments on rejections** and advises, "Strike out everything that sounds like a cliché. Don't try any tricks. Work at it, have a feeling for what you write, don't send 'exercise' pieces. Believe in what you send."

KELSEY REVIEW (IV-Regional), Mercer County Community College, P.O. Box B, Trenton NJ 08690, phone (609)586-4800, founded 1988, editor-in-chief Robin Schore, is an annual published by Mercer County Community College. It serves as "an outlet for literary talent **of people living and working in Mercer County, New Jersey only."** They have **no specifications as to form, length, subject matter or style, but do not want to see poetry about "kittens and puppies."** As a sample we selected these lines from "The Cricket Player" by Mukul Pandya:

Electric memories thrill through fingers
that tighten; not around willow
but Sunoco's nozzle.
"There's money here," he says, "nothing else."

A few dollars here, a new lifestyle there.
A taxi-ride home; silk sarees;
children shrilling at Nintendo;
appliances; friendly envy . . .
that's why he came.

Kelsey Review is 64 glossy pgs., 7 × 11, with paper cover and line drawings; no ads. They receive about 50 submissions a year, accept 6-10. Press run is 1,500. All distributed free to contributors, area libraries and schools. **No previously published poems or simultaneous submissions. Submit no more than 6 poems, typed, under 2,000 words. Deadline: May 1. Always comments on rejections. Reports in May of each year. All rights revert to authors.**

KENNESAW REVIEW (II), English Dept., Kennesaw State College, P.O. Box 444, Marietta GA 30061, phone (404)423-6297, founded 1987, poetry editor Don Russ, editor Robert W. Hill, appears twice a year. **"Open to any form, style or subject; we are looking for high-quality, finely crafted contemporary poetry of all kinds."** They have published poetry by David Bottoms, Malcolm Glass, Larry Rubin, Eve Shelnutt, R.T. Smith and Lewis Turco. As a sample the editor selected these lines from "Raising the Dead" by Ron Rash:

The quick left weeks ago, most voluntarily.
Those who remain are brought up, row by row,
into the fading light
of this November afternoon.

It is 100 pgs., 6×9, flat-spined, professionally printed, with embossed matte card cover. They accept about 20 of 2,000 poems received. Press run is 1,000. Subscription: $5. **Sample postpaid: $1. Submit no more than 5 poems. Reports within 3 months. Pays 5 copies.**

THE KENYON REVIEW (III), Dept. PM, Kenyon College, Gambier OH 43022, phone (614)427-3339, founded 1939, editor Marilyn Hacker, associate editor for poetry Eleanor Bender, is a quarterly review containing poetry, fiction, criticism, reviews and memoirs. It is **one of the country's leading literary publications.** Under Marilyn Hacker's editorship, this magazine continues to blossom, featuring all styles and forms, lengths and subject matters—a real openness. But this market is more closed than others because of the volume of submissions typically received during each reading cycle. Issues contain work by such poets as Cyrus Cassells, Judith Ortiz Cofer, Joy Harjo, Richard Howard, Josephine Jacobsen, Alicia Ostriker, Sherod Santos and Quincy Troupe. The elegantly printed, flat-spined, 7×10, 180-page review has a circulation of 4,000 with 3,200 subscriptions of which 1,100 are libraries. They receive about 3,000-4,000 submissions a year, use 50-60 (about 50 pgs. of poetry in each issue), have a 1-year backlog. The editor urges poets to read a few copies before submitting to find out what they are publishing. **Sample postpaid: $8. Unsolicited submissions are read from September 1 through March 31 *only*. Reports in 3 months. Pays $15/page for poetry, $10/page for prose. Buys first North American serial rights.** Reviews books of poetry in 2,500-7,000 words, single or multi-book format. "Reviews are primarily solicited—potential reviewers should inquire first." Poetry published in ***The Kenyon Review*** was also selected for inclusion in the 1992, 1993 and 1994 volumes of **The Best American Poetry.** In addition, ***The Kenyon Review*** ranked #8 in the "Poets' Pick" category of the latest ***Writer's Digest*** Poetry 60 list. This category ranks those publications in which poets said they would most like to see their work published.

KEYSTROKES; COMPUWRITE ANNUAL POETRY CONTEST; WRITERS ALLIANCE (IV-Writing), 12 Skylark Lane, Stony Brook NY 11790, founded 1981, executive director of Writers Alliance, Kiel Stuart. Writers Alliance sponsors, in addition to its triannual newsletter ***Keystrokes***, workshops and other activities devoted to building a "dedicated arts community." Membership: $10. You needn't be a member to enter its annual poetry contest (poems about writing with a computer, prize of computer software with a retail value of at least $100, subscription to and publication in the newsletter, January 15 deadline) or to submit poetry to the newsletter **"up to 10 lines on the subject of writing or using a computer or word processing system. 4-6 lines works best. We don't want anything that strays from the subject matter of writers, writing and using computers for that task."** They have published poetry by Karen Elizabeth Rigley and Margaret Park Bridges. As a sample the editor selected this poem, "Dilemma," by Beatrice G. Davis:

Free-lancer—hyphenated
Freelancer—compounded
Free lancer—separated

Which am I?
That's a typesetter's decision
It would seem.

Keystrokes is 16 pgs., desktop-published (on folded sheets of 8½×11 paper). "Receive about a dozen poems a year; room for 8-10 but less than 50% accepted." Subscription: $15 (with membership). **Sample postpaid: $3.50. "All checks are payable to Kiel Stuart. This is essential." Previously published poems OK if they did not appear in a competing magazine or more recently than 6 months. Editor frequently comments on rejections. Send SASE for guidelines. Reports in 6-8 weeks. Pays 2 copies. Acquires one-time rights.** Reviews books of poetry in 250 words, single format. The editor says more "well-done humor" is needed. The editor also advises, "Treat your craft with respect. Learn the business aspects of being a poet and adhere to those rules. Sloppiness or failure to stick to standard ms format or (worst of all) failure to enclose SASE with ANY communication does NOT indicate an artistic soul."

‡KINGFISHER (V, IV-Anthologies, children), Elsley House, 24-30 Great Titchfield St., London W1P 7AD United Kingdom, is the children's imprint of Larousse plc and publishes very little poetry. "We currently have five titles in print, anthologies of verse for children either on particular themes or for particular age-groups, compiled by leading British poets. Our **Poems For The Very Young**, compiled by Michael Rosen, was the Gold Medal Winner of The National Parenting Publications Awards. The anthologies contain published work except in a few rare instances. **Because our anthologies are compiled by outside editors we do not accept unsolicited poetry."**

KIOSK (II), 306 Clemens Hall, SUNY, Buffalo NY 14260, founded 1985, editor Mary Obropta, poetry editor A.M. Allcott, is an annual literary magazine using **poetry of "any length, any style, especially experimental."** They have published poetry by Raymond Federman, Sheila Murphy and Charles Bernstein. As a sample the editor selected these lines by Seth Frechie:

The intent
to say it without awkwardness,
"I __________________"
A grave uttering,
the gravity—

The editor describes *Kiosk* as flat-spined, digest-sized. Of 400 poems they accept 10-15. **Free sample (if available) with SAE and 4 first-class stamps. Submit poems in batches of five. Cover letter not required, "but we suggest one be included." Reads submissions September 1 through April 30 only. Reports within 2 months. Pays 1 copy.**

KITCHEN TABLE: WOMEN OF COLOR PRESS (V, IV-Women, lesbian, ethnic), P.O. Box 908, Latham NY 12110, phone (518)434-2057, fax (518)434-0905, founded 1981, is "the only publisher in North America committed to producing and distributing the **work of Third World women of all racial/cultural heritages, sexualities and classes.**" They publish flat-spined paperback collections and anthologies. **"Unfortunately, because we are severely undercapitalized and understaffed, we receive far more manuscripts than we can respond to and cannot, at this time, give the manuscripts the attention they deserve."** They publish an average of one book of poetry every other year and have published three anthologies, two of which contain poetry. All books are published simultaneously in hardback for library sales. **Write for catalog to purchase samples.** The editors say, "We are particularly interested in publishing work by women of color which would generally be overlooked by other publishers, especially work by American Indian, Latina, Asian-American and African-American women who may be working class, lesbian, disabled or older writers."

ALFRED A. KNOPF (V), 201 E. 50th St., New York NY 10022, poetry editor Harry Ford. Over the years Knopf has been one of the most important and distinguished publishers of poetry in the United States. **"The list is closed to new submissions at this time."**

KRAX; RUMP BOOKLETS (II, IV-Humor), 63 Dixon Lane, Leeds, Yorkshire LS12 4RR England, founded 1971, poetry editors Andy Robson et al. *Krax* appears twice yearly, and they want poetry which is **"light-hearted and witty; original ideas. Undesired: haiku, religious or topical politics, $1,000 bills." 2,000 words maximum. All forms and styles considered.** As a sample the editor chose these lines from "Overheard On A Bus" by Howard Frost:

. . . He snores a lot, but singers do—he says—, and he should know,
It's all to do with breathing deep and where the dust must go.
I tell him it's his smoking, that and all the beer he drinks,
That and all those smelly curries—why, his bedroom sometimes stinks! . . .

Krax is 6×8, 48 pgs. of which 30 are poetry, saddle-stapled, offset with b&w cartoons and graphics. They receive up to 1,000 submissions/year of which they use 6%, have a 2-3 year backlog. Single copy: £1.50 ($3); subscription: £6 ($12). **Sample: $1 (75p). "Submit maximum of 6 pieces. Writer's name on same sheet as poem. SASE or SAE with IRC encouraged but not vital." Reports within 2 months. Pays 1 copy.** Reviews books of poetry (brief, individual comments; no outside reviews). Send books for review consideration. ***Rump Booklets*** are miniature format, 3×4, 16-page collections. **Query with "detailed notes of projected work." Send SASE for catalog.** The editor says, "Sadly banks will not accept checks made payable to the magazine but for convenience we can take IRCs, dollar bills and postage stamps."

KUMQUAT MERINGUE; PENUMBRA PRESS (I, II), P.O. Box 5144, Rockford IL 61125, phone (815) 968-0713, founded 1990, editor Christian Nelson, appears approximately 2 times/year using **"mostly shorter poetry (under 20 lines) about the small details of life, especially the quirky side of love and sex. Not interested in rhyming, meaning of life or high-flown poetry."** They have recently published works by Gina Bergamino, Antler, Cheryl Townsend, Lynne Douglass and Ianthe Brautigan. As a sample the editor selected these lines from "Leaping Lizards" by Emile Luria:

After we made love . . . Kate said,
"You're so weird, really,
Even weirder than I thought."
And I thought, could she taste the salt,
Feel the sea lapping on my back?
I went to sleep wondering
About dinosaurs and lungfish
And the deepest reaches of the sea

It is digest-sized, 32-36 pgs., "professionally designed with professional typography and nicely printed." Press run is 500 for 250 subscribers. Subscription: $8 (3 issues). **Sample postpaid: $4. "We like cover letters but prefer to read things about who you are, rather than your long list of publishing credits. Previously published and simultaneous submissions are OK, but please let us know." Often comments on submissions. Send SASE for guidelines. Usually reports in 50**

days. Pays 1 copy. Acquires one-time rights. The magazine is "dedicated to the memory of Richard Brautigan." The editor advises, "Read ***Kumquat Meringue*** and anything by Richard Brautigan to get a feel for what we want, but don't copy Richard Brautigan, and don't copy those who have copied him. We just want that same feel. We also have a definite weakness for poems written 'to' or 'for' Richard Brautigan. When you get discouraged, write some more. Don't give up. Eventually your poems will find a home. We're very open to unpublished writers, and a high percentage of our writers had never been published anywhere before they submitted here."

‡KUUMBA (IV-Ethnic, gay/lesbian), Box 83912, Los Angeles CA 90083-0912, phone (310)410-0808, fax (310)410-9250, founded 1991, editors G. Winston James and Terri L. Jewell, is a biannual poetry journal of the black lesbian and gay community. **They want subject matter related to black lesbian and gay concerns.** "Among the experiences of interest are: coming out, interacting with family and/or community, substance abuse, political activism, oral histories, AIDS and intimate relationships." **They do not want to see "gay only subjects that have no black content, or black only subjects with no gay content."** They have recently published poetry by David Frechette, Assotto Saint, Sabrina Sojourner and Eric S. Booth. As a sample we selected these lines from "The Sweetest Taboo" (for Gene) by Richard D. Gore:

Forbidden,
But I loved you anyway
Dark, smouldering, and sweet
Luminous Black skin and Sloe-eyes. . .

Kuumba is 48 pgs., 8½×11, offset and saddle-stitched, with b&w cover drawing and ads. They accept about 25% of the poetry received. Press run is 1,000 for 100 subscribers, 500 shelf sales. Subscription: $7.50/year. **Sample postpaid: $4.50. No previously published poems; simultaneous submissions OK, if notified. Seldom comments on rejections. Send SASE for guidelines. Reports in 6 weeks. Pays 2 copies. Acquires first North American serial rights and right to anthologize.** The editors add, "Named for one of the Nguzo Saba (Seven Principles) which are celebrated at Kwanzaa, Kuumba means creativity." This poetry journal is not only dedicated to the celebration of the lives and experiences of black lesbians and gay men, but it is also intended to encourage new and experienced writers to develop their poetic craft.

KWIBIDI PUBLISHER; KID'S PLAYYARD; GREAT ADVENTURES FOR YOUNG PEOPLE; THE JOURNAL OF THE NATIONAL SOCIETY OF MINORITY WRITERS AND ARTISTS; THE WRITERS' AND ARTISTS' AID (I, IV-Ethnic, children, membership), P.O. Box 3424, Greensboro NC 27402-3424. Kwibidi founded 1979, ***JNSMWA*** 1981, ***KP*** 1986. Editor Dr. Doris B. Kwasikpui. Kwibidi Publisher **"needs poems, one-act plays, short stories, articles, art, jokes, book reports, research papers and how-to-do and make, for books, *Kid's Playyard* (a biannual magazine for kids of all ages), *GAYP* (a biannual containing short stories, poetry and articles about nature, travel, science and history) and *JNSMWA*." Publication limited to minorities.** As a sample the editor selected this poem (poet unidentified):

Poems are desperate screams of drowning thoughts
sinking faster with every word,
Bellowing verses of pain and despair
to surface buoyantly and to be heard.

Reads submissions January 1 through August 30 only. Publishes much of the material received and often responds with suggestions. Send SASE for guidelines. Reports in about 3 weeks. Upon acceptance, requires membership in the National Society of Minority Writers and Artists ($15/year). Pays in copies.

LACTUCA (II, IV-Translations), P.O. Box 621, Suffern NY 10901, founded 1986, editor/publisher Mike Selender, appears 1-3 times a year. **"Our bias is toward work with a strong sense of place, a strong sense of experience, a quiet dignity and an honest emotional depth. Dark and disturbing writings are preferred over safer material. No haiku, poems about writing poems, poems using the poem as an image, light poems or self-indulgent poems. Readability is crucial. We want poetry that readily transposes between the spoken word and printed page. First English language translations are welcome provided that the translator has obtained the approval of the author."** They have recently published poetry by Sherman Alexie, Joe Cardillo, Christy Beatty and Kathleen ten Haken. As a sample the editor selected these lines from "The Jaws of Factory" by Peter Bakowski:

In war or prison there is fear,
here it is the slow death:
Danny's lost an arm last week,
David's got crow's feet under his eyes
and he's only 24. . .

Lactuca is 72 pgs., digest-sized, saddle-stapled, laser printed or offset on 24 lb. bond with matte card cover, no ads. They receive "a few thousand poems a year of which less than 5% are accepted." Circulation 500 for 100 subscriptions, 200 stores. Subscription: $10/3 issues, $17/6 issues. **Sample postpaid: $4. "We do not print previously published material. We comment on rejections when we can. However the volume of mail we receive limits this." Reports within 3 months, "usually within one." Always sends prepublication galleys. Pays 2-5 copies "depending on length." Acquires first rights.** Reviews books of poetry. Open to unsolicited reviews. Poets may also send books for review consideration. He says, "The purpose of ***Lactuca*** is to be a small literary magazine publishing high-quality poetry, fiction and b&w drawings. Much of our circulation goes to contributors' copies and exchange copies with other literary magazines. ***Lactuca*** is not for poets expecting large circulation. Poets appearing here will find themselves in the company of other good writers."

‡THE LAMP-POST (I, II, IV-Religious, form/style), 29562 Westmont Court, San Juan Capistrano CA 92675, founded 1977, editor James Prothero, is the quarterly publication of the Southern California C.S. Lewis Society and "echoes his thoughts in scholarly essays, informal essays, fiction and poetry as well as reviews. **We look for (1) formal, (2) literary quality poetry with an (3) orthodox Christian slant. Will look at free verse, but prefer formal."** They have recently published poetry by Paul Willis and Joe Christopher. As a sample the editor selected these lines from "Still, to Be Neat" by John J. Brugaletta:

The lion's muzzle is a mess of blood;
The rain's a blessing here but there a flood:
A faith that's based on neatness with not last.

When God sees neatness, he begins to blast
Away at it with rounds of circumstance,
Demolishing our plans with gifts of chance . . .

The Lamp-Post is 32 pgs., digest-sized, professionally printed and saddle-stapled with card cover and b&w line drawings. They receive 20 poems a year, use about 6. Press run is 300 for 250 subscribers of which 5 are libraries. Subscription: $12, $8 students, seniors and libraries. **Sample postpaid: $3. For subscriptions and sample back issues, write to Edie Dougherty, managing editor/secretary, 1212 W. 162nd St., Gardena CA 90247. Previously published poems accepted "cautiously." No simultaneous submissions. Cover letter not required, "but we like them." No SASE, no reply.** Time between acceptance and publication is about 6 months. **Sometimes comments on rejections. Send SASE for guidelines. Reports in 6-8 weeks. Pays 3 copies. Acquires first serial or reprint rights.** Reviews books of poetry "if the poet is a Lewis scholar or the poetry has some connection to C.S. Lewis." Open to unsolicited reviews. Poets may also send books for review consideration to M.J. Logsdon, book review editor, 119 Washington Dr., Salinas CA 93905. The editor says, "We exist to echo the thought of C.S. Lewis in contemporary writing. Quality, literary poetry only, please. Read John Donne, George Herbert, Gerard Manley Hopkins and Francis Thompson and give us that sort of formal, literary and Christian quality—no 'inspirational' please; inspire us with quality and depth."

PETER LANG PUBLISHING, INC. (IV-Translations), 62 W. 45th St., New York NY 10036, phone (212)302-6740, fax (212)302-7574, publishes primarily scholarly monographs in the humanities and social sciences. List includes **critical editions of great poets of the past. Submit descriptive cover letter and *curriculum vita.***

LANGUAGE BRIDGES QUARTERLY (I, IV-Ethnic, foreign language), P.O. Box 850792, Richardson TX 75085, founded 1988, editor Eva Ziem, "is a **Polish-English bilingual forum for Polish matters. One of its purposes is to introduce the English-speaking reader to Polish culture. The subject is Poland and the Polish spirit:** a picture of life in Poland, mainly after World War II, with emphasis on the new and ponderous Polish emigration problems." **For more information send SASE.**

L'APACHE: AN INTERNATIONAL JOURNAL OF LITERATURE & ART (I, IV-Ethnic), P.O. Box 71, Wheeler OR 97147, founded 1986, editor Kathryn Vilips, appears twice a year. **"We prefer short fiction, articles and poetry on the Indians, or any ethnic group. One way to get an immediate rejection is to include sex, drugs or violence. You can allude to love without descriptive scenes or four-letter words. Although we prefer typewritten double-spaced submissions on 8 × 11 paper, *L'Apache* will not reject a poem simply because a writer does not have access to a typewriter. All we ask is that you print or write legibly."** They have published poetry by Barbara Jennings and Elizabeth Brooks Preddy. As a sample the editor selected these lines from "I Wonder and Wait" by Noel De Luca:

The tides roll in . . .
and I have waited, along lonely shores . . .
but that which you love so dearly
never returns . . .

The editor describes ***L'Apache*** as 6×9, "full-color cover. Drawings suitable for framing, high gloss, varnished heavy covers, 144 pgs., each journal a collector's edition." Their press run is 5,000 with most subscribers being libraries. Subscription: $18. **Sample: $5 plus SAE and 94¢ postage. No simultaneous submissions or previously published poems. Editor sometimes comments on rejections. Guidelines available for SASE. Pays $5-10/poem.**

LATEST JOKES NEWSLETTER (IV-Humor), P.O. Box 023304, Brooklyn NY 11202-0066, phone (718)855-5057, editor Robert Makinson. ***LJN*** is a monthly newsletter of humor for TV and radio personalities, comedians and professional speakers. **They use light (humorous) verse from 2-8 lines.** Circulation 250. **Sample: $3 and 1 first-class stamp. Submit maximum 3 poems at one time. Submit seasonal/holiday material 3 months in advance. Reports in 3 weeks. Pays 25¢/line.**

THE LAUREATE LETTER (I), 899 Williamson Trail, Eclectic AL 36024-9275, founded 1993, editor Brenda Williamson, is a monthly newsletter open to submissions of poetry, short-short-short stories, articles on writing, artwork and other short miscellaneous writings or creative works. It will also periodically contain markets, contests, reviews and other items of interest to writers. **As for poetry, they want "any form, but prefer titled, 20 lines maximum. Any subject or style. However, no jibberish or extremely mushy garbage."** As a sample the editor selected these lines by Robert E. Rouge:

I was a babe, babe in her arms,
she held me tight and true,
she sheltered me, she loved me,
unlike so many could not do.

They receive 1,500-2,000 poems a year, accept 25%. Press run is 250. Single copy: $2. **Sample postpaid: $2 plus #10 SASE. Previously published poems and simultaneous submissions OK.** Time between acceptance and publication is 1-2 months. **Send SASE for guidelines. Reports in 1-4 weeks "most of the time." No pay in cash or copies, but no fee required for publication. Acquires one-time rights.** "Reviews any published material that is only poetry related." Poets may also send books for review consideration. The editor says, "This is a new publication, but space is limited. Much material will be passed up because of length, so length needs to be a top priority."

LAUREL REVIEW (III); GREENTOWER PRESS (V), Dept. of English, Northwest Missouri State University, Maryville MO 64468, phone (816)562-1265, founded 1960, co-editors William Trowbridge, David Slater and Beth Richards. ***LR*** is a literary journal appearing twice a year using **"poetry of highest literary quality, nothing sentimental, greeting card, workshop, spit and whistle."** They have published poetry by George Starbuck, Marcia Southwick, Albert Goldbarth, David Citino and Pattiann Rogers. This handsome journal (128 pgs., 6×9) features excellent poems—usually more than 20 each issue—in all styles and forms. Press run is 800 for 400 subscribers of which 53 are libraries, 100 shelf sales. Subscription: $8/year. **Sample postpaid: $5. Submit 4-6 poems/batch. Reads submissions September 1 through May 31 only. Editor "does not usually" comment on submissions. Reports in 1 week to 4 months. Always sends prepublication galleys. Pays 2 copies plus 1-year subscription. Rights revert to author upon publication. Greentower Press accepts no unsolicited mss.**

THE LEADING EDGE (I, IV-Science fiction/fantasy), 3163 JKHB, Provo UT 84602, phone (801)378-2456, executive editor Michael Carr. ***The Leading Edge*** is a magazine appearing 3 times a year. They want **"high quality poetry related to science fiction and fantasy, not to exceed 3-4 typewritten, double-spaced pages. No graphic sex, violence or profanity."** They have recently published poetry by Michael Collings, Thomas Easton and Bruce Boston. As a sample the editors selected these lines from "An Astronaut Discusses a Black Hole Binary System" by Russell W. Asplund:

It looks like a sink
A cosmic drainhole slightly clogged in
Some cosmic downpour
The star a carelessly dropped
Bar of soap slowly dissolving
In God's shower

The editors describe the magazine as 6×9, 140 pgs., using art. They accept about 15 out of 150 poems received/year. Press run is 500, going to 100 subscribers (10 of them libraries) and 300 shelf sales. Single copy: $2.95; subscription: $8. **Sample postpaid: $3.50. Submit with no name on the poem, but with a cover sheet with name, address, phone number, length of poem, title and type of poem. Simultaneous submissions OK, but no previously published poems. Send SASE for guidelines. Reports in 3-4 months. Always sends prepublication galleys. Pays $10/typeset page plus 2 copies. Buys first North American serial rights.** Open to unsolicited reviews. Poets may also send books for review consideration. They say, "We accept traditional science fiction and fantasy poetry, but we like innovative stuff. If a poet has a good idea, go with it."

THE LEDGE POETRY AND FICTION MAGAZINE (II), 64-65 Cooper Ave., Glendale NY 11385, founded 1988, editor-in-chief Timothy Monaghan, appears twice a year and "searches for **high-quality poetry that is gritty, arresting and/or provocative in nature, though we will publish a great poem even if it doesn't meet these criteria. We suggest poems not exceed 60 lines in length, though again, we will publish the long poem if it so impresses us."** Recent contributors include Robert Cooperman, Barbara Hamby, Elliot Richman, Cris Mazza, Tony Gloeggler and Evan Zimroth. As a sample the editor selected this stanza from "Blind Spot" by Steve Leto:

When she finally took her two sons
and ran for it,
while you punched in to another nightshift,
I couldn't guess that you'd load guns and ammo
into the back seat, track her down,
then point-blank bullets into her chest
until she died slumped
over her baby boys.

The Ledge is 80 pgs., digest-sized, typeset and perfect-bound with glossy cover. They accept 2% of poetry submissions. Circulation is 600, including 100 subscribers. Subscription: $15 for 2 years, $9 for 1 year. **Sample postpaid: $5. Send up to 5 poems at a time. "We do not consider previously published work, though we will consider simultaneous submissions, if so informed." Reports in 1 month, longer if under serious consideration. Pays 1 copy. Acquires one-time rights. Sponsors annual poetry chapbook contest. Submit 20-24 pgs., including title page, bio and credits. Winner receives $50 and 100 copies of professionally printed chapbook. $10 reading fee includes copy of winning chapbook. Deadline: April 30.** ***The Ledge*** also sponsors annual poetry and fiction contests. Send SASE for details. The editor says, "Poets should take as much consideration in the presentation of their work as they expect the editor to take in the reading of the work."

LEFT CURVE (II, IV-Social issues), P.O. Box 472, Oakland CA 94604, phone (510)763-7193, founded 1974, editor Csaba Polony, appears "irregularly, about every 10 months." They want **poetry that is "critical culture, social, political, 'post-modern,' not purely formal, too self-centered, poetry that doesn't address in sufficient depth today's problems."** They have published poetry by Jack Hirschman, Sarah Menefee and Etel Adan. As a sample the editor selected these lines by HM:

my unfriend the machine awakens me
to a world one step removed
from the dark, from the grave

The editor describes it as "about 100 pgs., offset, flat-spined, Durosheen cover." Press run is 1,200 for 150 subscribers of which 50 are libraries, 800 shelf sales. Subscription: $20/3 issues (individuals). **Sample postpaid: $7. Cover letter stating "why you are submitting" required. Publishes theme issues. Send SASE for upcoming themes. Reports in 3-6 months. Pays 3 copies.** Open to unsolicited reviews. Poets may also send books for review consideration.

LEGEND: AN INTERNATIONAL "ROBIN OF SHERWOOD" FANZINE (I, IV-Fantasy), Dept. PM, #75, 75 Melville St., Abington, North Hampton NN14HX England, founded 1989, editor Janet P. Reedman, appears approximately once a year. She wants **"fantasy poetry dealing with/based on episodes of the British TV series 'Robin of Sherwood.' Length is open. No porn or dull poetry about mundane matters."** She has published poetry by Julianne Toomey, Frances Quinn and Steve Sneyd. The magazine is 170 pgs., spiral-bound, photocopied from typescript, uses much b&w art. Press run is 130. Accepts **80-90% material from 2 dozen or so. "Will help with rewrites; prefer to outright rejection." Sample: send for cost. No previously published poems. Typed or handwritten mss acceptable. Reports in 1-10 weeks, usually sooner. Nearly always comments on rejections. Send SAE and IRCs with US submissions/inquiries. Pays: "a substantial discount." Acquires first serial rights.**

L'EPERVIER PRESS (V), 1326 NE 62nd, Seattle WA 98115, founded 1977, editor Robert McNamara, is a "small press publisher of contemporary American poetry in perfect-bound and casebound books." **Currently not accepting submissions.** He has published books by Bruce Renner, Linda Bierds, Frederic Will and Paul Hoover. The press publishes 2 poetry books each year, 6×9 with an average page count of 64, some flat-spined paperbacks and some hardcovers. **Second Sun** by Bill Tremblay, is handsomely printed on heavy buff stock, 81 pgs., with glossy card cover in grey, yellow and white; there is a b&w landscape photo on the front cover and a photo of the author on the back; the book is priced at $6.95.

LIBIDO: THE JOURNAL OF SEX AND SEXUALITY (I, IV-Erotica, humor, gay/lesbian), P.O. Box 146721, Chicago IL 60614, founded 1988, editors Marianna Beck and Jack Hafferkamp, is a quarterly. **"Form, length and style are open. We want poetry of any and all styles as long as it is erotic and/or erotically humorous. We make a distinction between erotica and pornography. We want wit not dirty words."** They have recently published poetry by Stuart Silverman, Alan Isler, Lani Kaahumanu, Anne

MacNaughton, Chocolate Waters, Robert Perchan, Bruce Lennard and Bill Vickers. As a sample the editors selected these lines by Ralph Tyler:

'Twas brillig in that cheap hotel
The looking glass had cataracts
All mimsey were the bureau drawrs
The paper was a glimpse of hell
"Come to my arms, my beamish boy"
Her scarlet mouth invited him.

It is 88 pgs., digest-sized, professionally printed, flat-spined, with 2-color varnished card cover. They accept about 5% of poetry received. Press run is 9,500 for 3,500 subscribers, 3,500 shelf sales and 1,500 single issues by mail. Subscription: $26 in US, $36 outside. **Sample postpaid: $7. Cover letter including "a one-sentence bio for contributors' page" required with submission. "Please, no handwritten mss." Reports in 4-6 months. Pays $0-25 plus 2 copies.** Send books for review consideration "only if the primary focus is love/eroticism."

LIBRA PUBLISHERS, INC. (I), Suite 383, 3089C Clairemont Dr., San Diego CA 92117, phone (619)571-1414, poetry editor William Kroll, publishes two professional journals, ***Adolescence*** and ***Family Therapy***, plus books, primarily in the behaviorial sciences but also some general nonfiction, fiction and poetry. "At first we published books of poetry on a standard royalty basis, paying 10% of the retail price to the authors. Although at times we were successful in selling enough copies to at least break even, we found that we could no longer afford to publish poetry on this basis. Now, unless we fall madly in love with a particular collection, **we offer professional services to assist the author in self-publishing."** They have published books of poetry by Martin Rosner, William Blackwell, John Travers Moore and C. Margaret Hall. **Prefers complete ms but accepts query with 6 sample poems, publishing credits and bio. Replies to query in 2 days, to submissions (if invited) in 2-3 weeks. Ms should be double-spaced. Sometimes sends prepublication galleys. Send 9×12 SASE for catalog. Sample books may be purchased on a returnable basis.**

LIFTOUTS MAGAZINE; PRELUDIUM PUBLISHERS (V), Dept. PM, 1503 Washington Ave. S., Minneapolis MN 55454, phone (612)333-0031, founded 1971, poetry editor Barry Casselman, is a "publisher of **experimental literary work and work of new writers in translation from other languages." Currently accepting no unsolicited material.** ***Liftouts*** appears irregularly. It is 5½×8, offset, 50-150 pgs. Press run is 1,000. Reviews books of poetry.

LIGHT (II), Box 7500, Chicago IL 60680, founded 1992, editor John Mella, is a quarterly of **"light and occasional verse, satire, wordplay, puzzles, cartoons and line art." They do not want "greeting card verse, cloying or sentimental verse."** As a sample the editor selected "The Cow's Revenge" by X.J. Kennedy:

Obligingly, the mild cow lets us quaff
The milk that she'd intended for her calf,
But takes revenge: In every pint she packs
A heavy cream to trigger heart attacks.

The editor says ***Light*** is 32 pgs., stapled, including art and graphics. Single copy: $4; subscription: $12. **No previously published poems or simultaneous submissions. Submit one poem on a page with name, address, poem title and page number on each page. Seldom comments on rejections. Publishes theme issues. Send SASE for guidelines and upcoming themes. Reports in 3 months or less. Sometimes sends prepublication galleys. Pays 2 copies to domestic contributors, 1 copy to foreign contributors.** Open to unsolicited reviews; query first. Poets may also send books for review consideration.

LIGHT AND LIFE MAGAZINE (IV-Religious), Dept. PM, Free Methodist Church of North America, P.O. Box 535002, Indianapolis IN 46253-5002, phone (317)244-3660. ***Light and Life*** is a religious monthly magazine. Guidelines available. **"Poems are used only as they relate to an article in the magazine. No 'fillers' or descriptive poems are used."** They also conduct annual writing contests with varying rules and prizes (send SASE for rules December through March). **"We are looking for short, well-written devotional or inspirational pieces and poetry . . . offering unique insights into the great themes of the Bible. Poems should rhyme and flow with a recognizable rhythm pattern. Avoid obscure allusions and unfamiliar language. Maximum length: 20 lines. Each submission should be typed on plain white paper, double-spaced, at least 1" margin on all sides, no erasable bond, name, address and telephone number on each ms, each submission on a separate sheet of paper, even if they are short pieces." Response time 4-6 weeks. Pays $7.50-10. Buys first rights.**

LILITH MAGAZINE (IV-Women, ethnic), Suite 2432, 250 W. 57th St., New York NY 10107, phone (212)757-0818, founded in 1976, editor-in-chief Susan Weidman Schneider, poetry editor Alicia Ostriker, "is an independent magazine with a Jewish feminist perspective" which uses **poetry by Jewish**

women "about the Jewish woman's experience. Generally we use short rather than long poems. Run 4 poems/year. Do not want to see poetry on other subjects." They have published poetry by Irena Klepfisz, Lyn Lifshin, Yael Messinai, Sharon Neemani, Marcia Falk and Adrienne Rich. It is glossy, magazine-sized. "We use colors. Page count varies. Covers are very attractive and professional-looking (one has won an award). Generous amount of art. It appears 4 times a year, circulation about 10,000, about 5,000 subscriptions." Subscription: $16 for 4 issues. **Sample postpaid: $5. Send no more than 3 poems at a time; advise if simultaneous submission. Editor "sometimes" comments on rejections. Send SASE for guidelines. Reports in 2-3 months.** She advises: "(1) Read a copy of the publication before you submit your work. (2) Be realistic if you are a beginner. The competition is *severe*, so don't start to send out your work until you've written for a few years. (3) Short cover letters only. Copy should be neatly typed and proofread for typos and spelling errors."

LILLIPUT REVIEW (II, IV-Form), 207 S. Millvale Ave. #3, Pittsburgh PA 15224, founded 1989, editor Don Wentworth, is a tiny (4½×3.6 or 3½×4¼) 12- to 16-page magazine, appearing irregularly and **using poems in any style or form no longer than 10 lines.** They have recently published poetry by Albert Huffstickler, Lonnie Sherman, Lyn Lifshin, Vogn, and Carl Jablonski. As a sample the editor selected "Postcard" by Bart Solarczyk:

> *A light wet snow*
> *waters the back yard.*
> *I watch from the sofa.*
> *I miss your small hands.*

LR is printed from typescript on colored paper and stapled. Press run is 225. **Sample: $1 or SASE. Submit no more than 3 poems. Currently, every fourth issue is a broadside featuring the work of one particular poet. Send SASE for guidelines. Reports usually within 2 months. Pays 2 copies/poem. Acquires first rights. Editor comments on submissions "occasionally—always at least try to establish human contact."** He says, "For a magazine that publishes only short poems, ***LR*** receives surprisingly little haiku. We are always open to this and any other short Eastern forms."

LIMBERLOST PRESS; THE LIMBERLOST REVIEW (II), HC 33, Box 1113, Boise ID 83706, phone (208)344-2120, founded 1976, co-editors Richard and Rosemary Ardinger. Limberlost Press publishes poetry, fiction and memoirs in letterpressed chapbooks, flat-spined paperbacks and other formats. ***Limberlost Review*** appears "fairly regularly. **We want the best work by serious writers. No restrictions on style or form."** They have published poetry by William Stafford, Lawrence Ferlinghetti, Charles Bukowski, Allen Ginsberg, John Clellon Holmes, Nancy Stringfellow, Robert Creeley and Gino Sky. The editor describes ***LR*** as digest-sized ("varies. One issue has been devoted to a series of 20 letter-pressed poem postcards."). **Issues through 1995 will be devoted to letterpressed chapbooks.** It has a press run of 500-1,000. **Sample postpaid: $10. No simultaneous submissions. For chapbook submission, submit samples, bio and prior publications. Editor sometimes comments on rejections. Reports on queries in 1 week, on submissions in 1-2 months. Pays a varied number of author's copies. "We like interested poets to be familiar with our press work."**

LIMESTONE: A LITERARY JOURNAL (II), Dept. of English, 1215 Patterson Office Tower, University of Kentucky, Lexington KY 40506-0027, phone (606)257-6976, founded as ***Fabbro*** in 1979, as ***Limestone*** in 1986, editor Tim Dunn, is an annual seeking **"poetry that matters, poetry that shows attention to content and form. We're interested in all poetics, but we do watch for quality of thought and a use of language that will wake up the reader and resonate in his/her mind."** They have published poetry by Wendell Berry, Guy Davenport, Michael Cadnum, Noel M. Valis and James Baker Hall. It is 6×9, perfect-bound, offset. They accept 5-10 of 100-150 poems submitted annually. Press run is 500 for 30 subscriptions (20 of them libraries). **Sample postpaid: $3. Simultaneous submissions and previously published poems OK. Submit 1-10 pgs. Reports in 3-6 months. Pays 3 copies.** "If you're considering publication," the editor advises, "read as much poetry as possible. Listen carefully. Work over your poems till you're sick of them. The lack of such care shows up in many of the mss we receive."

LIMITED EDITIONS PRESS; ART: MAG (III), P.O. Box 70896, Las Vegas NV 89170, phone (702)734-8121, founded 1982, editor Peter Magliocco, "have become, due to economic and other factors, more limited to a select audience of poets as well as readers. We seek to expel the superficiality of our factitious culture, in all its drive-thru, junk-food-brain, commercial-ridden extravagance—and stylize a magazine of hard-line aesthetics, where truth and beauty meet on a vector not shallowly drawn. Conforming to this outlook is an operational policy of **seeking poetry from solicited poets primarily, though unsolicited submissions will be read, considered and perhaps used infrequently. Sought from the chosen is a creative use of poetic styles, systems and emotional morphologies other than banally constricting."** They have recently published poetry by Michael Estabrook, Gina Bergamino, Duane Locke, Alan Catlin, the mag man and others. As a sample the editor selected these lines from "What Mag Man Said" by James Purdy:

I was me from the beginning
and today more so.
I had no peaceful intentions
with reference to salvation,
yet I saved myself & opened the tent flap
for others.

ART: MAG, appearing in 1-2 large issues of 100 copies/year, is limited to a few poets. Occasionally publishes chapbooks (such as **Rungs in the Ladder**, by Susan Smith Nash), "along with other possibly 'aesthetic surprises' (such as original art sketchbooks for patrons, etc.), but these aren't strictly scheduled." **Sample copies are the price of a regular issue, $3.50 or more, postpaid. Submit up to 5 poems. No previously published poems; simultaneous submissions OK. Sometimes comments on rejections. Publishes theme issues. Send SASE for guidelines and upcoming themes. Reports within 3 months. Pays 1 copy. Acquires first rights.** Staff occasionally reviews books of poetry. Send books for review consideration.

LINCOLN SPRINGS PRESS (II), P.O. Box 269, Franklin Lakes NJ 07417, founded 1987, editor M. Gabrielle, publishes 1 paperback and 1 hardback book of poetry each year. They have published poetry by Maria Mazziotti Gillan, Justin Vitiello and Abigail Stone. **Query first with sample poems and cover letter with brief bio and publication credits. No previously published poems; simultaneous submissions OK. Seldom comments on rejections. Replies to queries in 2-4 weeks, to mss in 2-3 months. Always sends prepublication galleys. Pays 15% royalties.**

LINES N' RHYMES (I), 5604 Harmeson Dr., Anderson IN 46013, phone (317)642-1239, founded 1989, editor Pearl Clark, appears every other month using **"some poetry to 40 lines—use some 4 lines, most between 12-20 lines. I like poems concerning life, belief in God's guidance. Nothing pornographic or occult."** They have recently published poetry by Ainsley Jo Phillips, Ruth E. Cunliffe, Rosina Clifford, Dr. Harry Snider and Kaec Jaworski. As a sample the editor selected these lines from "The Wilding" by C. David Hay:

You bloom and die in solitude
Beyond the touch of care.
Your shining was not wasted—
God surely put you there.

It is photocopied on 6 legal-sized colored sheets, sometimes 5. Press run is 50. 3-5 shelf sales. Subscription: $5/6 issues. **Sample: $1. "I receive 170 poems/year—accept 70%. I pay nothing for poetry used. I award 'Editor's Choice' to 2 poets/issue at $1. I give preference to subscribers. However, I also use poetry from non-subscribers." Previously published poems OK.** Reviews books of poetry and comments in current issue. Open to unsolicited reviews. Poets may also send books for review consideration. She holds a contest for humorous poetry (4-6 lines) each September with 3 prizes of $5 each, open only to subscribers.

LINES REVIEW (III, IV-Regional), Edgefield Rd., Loanhead, Edinburgh EH20 9SY Scotland, phone (031)440-0246, founded 1952 ("the oldest continuing Scottish literary magazine"), editor Tessa Ransford. *LR* is a quarterly which **gives priority to poets living in Scotland** and, the editor says, "is generally receiving too much from elsewhere at present. **I like to accept from 4-6 poems in traditional page format, though with energy and intelligence in use of language, form and content. No unusual typography, concrete, sensation-seeking, nostalgic, dully descriptive or fanatically political poetry."** They have recently published poetry by David Grubb, Martin Bennett, Alan Riach, Jenni Daiches and Robin Fulton. Press run is 750 for 500 subscribers of which 100 are libraries, 100 shelf sales. **Sample postpaid: £2.32. Cover letter required with submissions; include information relevant to the poems. "Double spacing helps, and clear indication whether a page break is or is not also a stanza break, and careful attention to punctuation—that it is as it will be printed." Reports in 2-3 weeks. Pays £10/page plus 1 copy.** Includes "good review section." *LR* often has special issues devoted, for example, to poetry from Glasgow, Japan, America and Canada, and an Italian issue is forthcoming. They also publish translations. Tessa Ransford is also director of Scottish Poetry Library (see listing under Organizations) and offers a School of Poets and Critical Service through the library.

ALWAYS include a self-addressed, stamped envelope (SASE) when sending a ms or query to a publisher within your own country. When sending material to other countries, include a self-addressed envelope and International Reply Coupons (IRCs), available for purchase at most post offices.

LINQ (II), c/o English Dept., James Cook University, Townsville, Queensland 4811 Australia, phone (077)814336, founded 1971, secretary Ms. M. Miles. ***LiNQ*** is a 100-page biannual which "aims to publish works of a high literary standard, encompassing a wide and varied range of interest." They have recently published poetry by Sally Sleinis, Kevin Irie, Sue Moss, Alan Peter Kelly, Justin Macdonnell and David Reiter. As a sample we selected these lines from "vibrations" by Ted Nielsen:

would we believe those mechanisms
until more than the walls buckle
(sleight of money makes the cables discreet)
even as we lead and follow pas de deux
i watch the air reviving
a tender documentary

They receive about 250 poems a year, use approximately 10%. Press run is 350 for 160 subscribers of which 30 are libraries, 180 shelf sales. Single copy: $8; subscription: $20 individual (within Australia), $25 institution (within Australia), $30 overseas (for individual and institution). Since the journal is published in May and October, all subscriptions are due by April 30. **Sample back issue postpaid: $3 (Australian). No previously published poems or simultaneous submissions. "*LiNQ* rotates its editors. Each volume is the responsibility of an individual editor, with occasional co-editorial advice." Often comments on rejections. Reports "ASAP." Payment is subject to grant funding. Author retains copyright.** Reviews books of poetry in 1,000 words. Open to unsolicited reviews. Poets may also send books for review consideration. The editors say, "***LiNQ*** aims for a broadly based sympathetic approach to creative work, particularly from new and young Australian writers." The secretary adds, "Attention to presentation is a very important criteria taken into consideration by editors. Intending contributors should take note of this."

LINTEL (II), P.O. Box 8609, Roanoke VA 24014, phone (703)982-2265, founded 1977, poetry editor Walter James Miller, who says, **"We publish poetry and innovative fiction of types ignored by commercial presses. We consider any poetry except conventional, traditional, cliché, greeting card types, i.e., we consider any artistic poetry."** They have published poetry by Sue Saniel Elkind, Samuel Exler, Adrienne Wolfert and Edmund Pennant. As a sample the editor selected these lines by Nathan Teitel:

loneliness
is a Mexican earring
and fear
a crushed cigarette

The book from which this was taken, **In Time of Tide**, is 64 pgs., flat-spined, digest-sized, professionally printed in bold type, hard cover stamped in gold, jacket with art and author's photo on back. Walter James Miller asks that you **query with 5 sample poems. Reads submissions January and August only. He replies to the query within a month, to the ms (if invited) in 2 months. "We consider simultaneous submissions if so marked and if the writer agrees to notify us of acceptance elsewhere." Ms should be typed. Always sends prepublication galleys. Pays royalties after all costs are met and 100 copies. Buys all rights. Offers usual subsidiary rights: 50%/50%. To see samples, send SASE for catalog and ask for "trial rate" (50%).** The editor says,"Form follows function! We accept any excellent poem whose form—be it sonnet or free verse—suits the content and the theme. We like our poets to have a good publishing record in literary magazines, before they begin to think of a book."

LINWOOD PUBLISHERS (II), P.O. Box 371819, Decatur GA 30037-1819, phone (404)408-6082, founded 1982, poetry editor Bernard Chase, was "organized as an independent small press, primarily to publish the poetry of known, unknown and little known poets." They have recently published in both paper and hardback editions. The editor says he is interested in **"quality poetry of any form."** They have recently published poetry by Simon Perchik, Carl Lindner, Barbara Unger, T.S. Wallace, George Gott, Isabella Pupurai Matsikidze, Barbara Crooker, Betty Schilling, Gary Fort and Steve Wilson. As a sample the editor selected these lines from **Touch The Concrete** by Anthony Grenek, Jr.:

When dark clouds appear
And again we doubt our goal,
We search for ways to salvage
Our heart, our mind, and soul.

We realize in trying
There has to be some pain,
But once we see the rainbow,
We've made it through the rain

They will consider unsolicited submissions of book mss. **It is your option whether to query first, send samples or complete mss. Your cover letter should give publication history and bio. They try to reply to queries within 1 month, to mss within a year. They prefer typed mss. Simultaneous**

submissions OK. Contracts are for 5-10% royalties and author's copies (negotiated). Send 7×10 SASE with 3 ozs. postage for catalog. "Sample copies of our publications can be purchased directly from the publisher." Bernard Chase advises, "Feel no intimidation by the breadth, the depth of this craft of which you have chosen to become a part. Although we are very open to beginners, we do not as a rule respond with comments, suggestions or criticisms."

‡LIPS (III), Box 1345, Montclair NJ 07042, founded 1981, poetry editor Laura Boss, "is a quality poetry magazine that is published twice a year and takes pleasure in publishing previously unpublished poets as well as the most established voices in contemporary poetry. **We look for quality work: the strongest work of a poet; work that moves the reader; poems take risks that work. We prefer clarity in the work rather than the abstract. Poems longer than 6 pages present a space problem."** They have published poetry by Michael Benedikt, Gregory Corso, Allen Ginsberg, Richard Kostelanetz, Lyn Lifshin, Theodore Weiss, Marge Piercy, Warren Woessner, Maria Gillan, Nicholas Christopher, Diana Chang, Stanley Barkan, David Ignatow and Ishmael Reed. The editor selected these sample lines by Chocolate Waters from "Confessions of an Ex Feminist-Malarkist (that's a person who's one-fourth feminist, three-fourth's malarkey)":

> *It was Easter Sunday morning.*
> *I woke up with an ugly hangover*
> *and an even uglier man.*

Lips is 70 pgs. (average), digest-sized, flat-spined. They receive about 8,000 submissions/year, use less than 1%, have a 6-month backlog. Circulation 1,000, 200 subscriptions, approximately 100 are libraries. **Sample postpaid: $6. Poems should be submitted between September and March, 6 pgs., typed, no query necessary. She tries to respond in 1 month but has gotten backlogged at times. Sometimes sends prepublication galleys. Pays 2 contributor's copies. Acquires first rights. Send SASE for guidelines.** Her advice to poets is, "Remember the 2 T's: Talent *and* Tenacity."

LITE MAGAZINE: THE JOURNAL OF SATIRE AND CREATIVITY; THE LITE CIRCLE, INC.; LITE CIRCLE BOOKS (I), P.O. Box 26162, Baltimore MD 21210, phone (410)719-7792, founded 1989, editor/publisher David W. Kriebel. ***Lite***, Baltimore's literary monthly, is a "general literary publication including humorous columns, reviews and perspective pieces and one interview in each issue." **They want "creative, thoughtful, beautiful poetry, generally 1 page or less in length. No overly-erotic, exploitative or dogmatic poetry. Also, no political or preachy religious poems."** The editor says *Lite* is generally 40 pgs., 8×10, newsprint with b&w photos, original art and ads. They receive about 150 poems a year, accept 20-25%. Press run is 10,000 for 100 subscribers, the rest distributed free to colleges, writing groups and art galleries. Subscription: $13 (includes membership in Lite Circle, Inc.) **Sample free with SAE and 2 first-class stamps. Previously published poems and simultaneous submissions OK. Cover letter required. Seldom comments on rejections—"Only when authors ask for it." Send SASE for guidelines. Reports in 3-6 months. Pays 5 copies. Acquires one-time rights.** Reviews books of poetry. Lite Circle Books publishes 2 paperbacks/year. "We are just getting into book publishing. **Right now we operate as a subsidy press. Terms are settled on a contract-by-contract basis."** Their first two books, **The Laughing Ladies** and **Stations In a Dream**, are each available as a sample for $6.95 plus postage. The Lite Circle, Inc. sponsors poetry readings and offers an annual contest with $75 first prize, $45 second. Send SASE for information. The editor says, "Be persistent. The market is tight, but if you are willing to work with the small presses, they will work with you. ***Lite*** is very kind to new writers."

LITERARY FOCUS POETRY PUBLICATIONS; ANTHOLOGY OF CONTEMPORARY POETRY; INTERNATIONAL POETRY CONTESTS: FALL CONCOURS, SPRING CONCOURS, SUMMER CONCOURS (I, IV-Anthology), P.O. Box 36242, Houston TX 77236-0242, phone (713)781-7724, founded 1988, editor-in-chief Adrian A. Davieson. **Purchase of anthology may be required of poets accepted for publication.** Literary Focus publishes anthologies compiled in contests, 3 times/year, with prizes of $200, $100 and $50, plus "Distinguished Mention" and "Honorable Mention." **"Contemporary poetry with no restriction on themes. 20-line limit. Maximum submission 15 poems, minimum 3 poems. No abusive, anti-social poetry."** As a sample the editor selected these lines from his own poem, "Delayed Journey":

> *I saw the footsteps retracing to*
> *A lost moment, then there was a*
> *Whisper of ancient sorrows long*
> *Left in the trail of endless*
> *Struggles.*

The digest-sized anthologies are either flat-spined or saddle-stapled, 70 pgs., typeset. **Previously published poems and simultaneous submissions OK. "In order to evaluate serious entries, a $5 entry fee is now required for the first three poems. Poems are evaluated on an individual basis by a panel of five editors chaired by editor-in-chief. Poets are notified of acceptance two weeks**

after deadlines." Send SASE for guidelines. Reviews books of poetry.

‡**LITERARY FRAGMENTS (I)**, P.O. Box 751, Beaverton OR 97075, e-mail SIP@EPUB.RAIN.COM, founded 1980, editor Susan Roberts, is a printed and electronic quarterly "contemporary authors showcase" **open to all forms, lengths, styles and subjects of poetry as well as short stories.** As a sample the editor selected this poem, "Essentials," by Diana Watanabe:

The pierced heart
The pulsating pain
The provoked waves of poignant feelings
Mental polarity struggling for identity
Searching for trust. . . a trust in the process.

The editor says *LF* is 24-80 pgs., 5½×8, saddle-stitched, with b&w art/graphics and display ads. They receive approximately 1,500 poems a year. Press run is 3,500, largely distributed free to various distant points. **Sample postpaid: $5 for current issue and guidelines. Send SASE for guidelines alone. Submit poems with $10 reading fee. Previously published poems and simultaneous submissions OK. Prefers electronic submissions.** Time between acceptance and publication is 6 months. **Usually comments on rejections. Reports in 3-6 months. Pays $5 and up. Acquires one-time rights. "Poems of notable merit are also published in 'Best of' anthology."** Reviews books of poetry in 350-1,200 words, single or multi-book format. Open to unsolicited reviews. Poets may also send books for review consideration.

LITERARY OLYMPICS, INC. (IV-Anthology, translations, children), Suite 250, 4411 Morena Blvd., San Diego CA 92117, phone (619)273-1652, founded 1984, president and editor Elizabeth Bartlett, is an international organization "to encourage and promote public interest in poetry by honoring leading contemporary poets from all over the world on the occasion of the Olympics every four years. The newest anthology, **Literary Olympians 1992**, contains poems by 132 poets from 66 countries in 55 languages, including English translations. **We favor poems that have a universal appeal.**" They have published poetry by Maxine Kumin, Josephine Jacobsen, Octavio Paz and Odysseus Elytis. As a sample the editor selected these lines from "Horse Play" by Ayyappa Panikar:

The one-legged horse
said to the others:
the time for dance has come,
Sweet friends,
let's dance on a single hoof!
All of them liked the idea
and the dance began.
The four-legged horse fainted outright,
the three-legged horse slipped and fell,
the two-legged horse limped to a fall:
only the one-legged one
danced on and on.

Qualified, nationally recognized poets may submit English poems up to 30 lines, with cover letter, in 1994 and 1995 for Literary Olympians 1996. Most will be invited by the Associate Editors in charge of various countries. **Only unpublished poems may be considered. Each poet and translator receives a copy of the anthology.** "Besides appearing in the anthology, poets are candidates for gold, silver and bronze medals awarded by a jury of literary scholars. We also hope to raise enough funds to clear expenses and then pay each contributor an additional honorarium. We now have a contest for **original poems by children age 5-12**. Winners will receive honorary certificates as Junior Poets and have their poems included in a supplement to the anthology. We hope to reach primary grade teachers and children's librarians to attract young contestants to poetry." **Literary Olympians 1992** was published by Ford Brown & Co. ($22.95 paperback, $29.95 hardcover plus postage and handling). To date they have included seven Nobel Laureates among their contributors. The editor says, "We rely heavily on qualified translators to obtain poems and permissions to translate and publish. Poets familiar with **Literary Olympians** can best judge the quality of our selection."

THE LITERARY REVIEW: An International Journal of Contemporary Writing (III), Fairleigh Dickinson University, 285 Madison Ave., Madison NJ 07940, phone (201)593-8564, founded 1957, editor-in-chief Walter Cummins, a quarterly, seeks **"work by new and established poets which reflects a sensitivity to literary standards and the poetic form." No specifications as to form, length, style, subject matter or purpose.** They have published poetry by Robert Cooperman, Gary Fincke, José Bergamin, Tomasz Jastrun and R.S. Thomas. The magazine is 6×9, flat-spined, 128 pgs., professionally printed with glossy color cover, using 20-50 pgs. of poetry in each issue, circulation 2,500, 900 subscriptions of which one-third are overseas. They receive about 1,200 submissions/year, use 100-150, have 6-12 months backlog. Poems appearing here show careful attention to line, image and form—largely lyric free verse. Editors of recent issues also seem particularly open to translations. **Sample postpaid: $5, request a "general issue." Submit no more than 5 poems at a time, clear typing, simultaneous submissions OK. At times the editor comments on rejections. Publishes theme issues. Send SASE for upcoming themes. An "Iranian Exile" issue is scheduled for Summer 1995 and a "Portuguese" issue for Fall 1995. Reports in 2-3 months. Always sends prepublication galleys. Pays copies. Acquires first rights.** Reviews books of poetry in 500 words, single format. Open to unsolicited reviews. Poets may also send books for review consideration. ***The Literary Review*** ranked #10 in the "Nontraditional Verse" category of the latest ***Writer's Digest*** Poetry 60 list, and one of the poems published in this review was selected for inclusion in **Editor's Choice III**. They advise, "Read a general issue of the magazine carefully before submitting."

LITERATURE AND BELIEF (II, IV-Religious), 3076-E Jesse Knight Humanities Building, Brigham Young University, Provo UT 84602, phone (801)378-3073, founded 1981, editor Jay Fox, is the "annual journal of the Center for the Study of Christian Values in Literature." **It uses "affirmation poetry in the Judeo-Christian tradition."** They have published poetry by Ted Hughes, Donnel Hunter, Leslie Norris and William Stafford. It is handsomely printed, flat-spined. Single copy: $5 US, $7 outside US. They conduct an annual contest with $150 first prize for poetry.

LITTLE RIVER PRESS (V), 10 Lowell Ave., Westfield MA 01085, phone (413)568-5598, founded 1976, editor Ronald Edwards, publishes **"limited editions of poetry collections, chapbooks and postcards of New England poets."** They have published poetry by Steven Sossaman, Wanda Cook and Frank Mello. **However, they currently do not accept unsolicited submissions.**

LIVING POETS SOCIETY (I, IV-Ethnic), P.O. Box 8555, New York NY 10116-4654, founded 1991, editor-in-chief Gabrellar Jordan, is a bimonthly newsletter of "inspirational writing and poetry and community news and development." The editor wants **poetry with "style, creativity and substance" from African-Americans but will also accept poems from other groups. No "poems that most people will not understand."** As a sample the editor selected these lines (poet unidentified):

Out of the confinement
of our stuffy apartment
we huddled
on chipped marble stairs
smooth cooling slabs

The newsletter is 6-8 double-sided pgs., side-stapled, with some drawings. Press run is 75 to 100. Both 4- and 6-issue subscriptions are offered, $4 and $6 respectively. **Previously published poems and simultaneous submissions OK. Bio requested.** Time between acceptance and publication is 3 months. **No pay at the present time. "Poets have all rights to their work."** The editor says, "You don't have to buy the newsletter to contribute, but it would be helpful to the continuation of the newsletter."

‡THE LIZARD'S EYELID (IV-Form/style), P.O. Box 109, Gainesville FL 32602-0109, founded 1990, "editor supreme" Sterling Sandow, is a quarterly, left wing, punk rock music fanzine, featuring articles about and interviews with bands and individuals involved in the punk rock scene. **They want "short, witty, shocking, bizarre poetry (about sex, drugs, punk rock, death, etc.). No hallmark variety poetry or pop psychology inspired self therapy poems."** The editor says *The Lizard's Eyelid* is approximately 32 pgs., 8½ × 11, newsprint with extensive artwork, intense graphics, very few ads. They receive approximately 750 mss a year, accept about 5%. Press run is 7,000 for 150 subscribers, 500 shelf sales; 2,500 distributed free to record, book and tattoo shops in Florida. Single copy: $2; subscription: $7.50. **Sample postpaid: $2.90. Make checks payable to S. Sandow. Previously published poems and simultaneous submissions OK. Cover letter required.** Time between acceptance and publication is 2-5 months. **"Poems are chosen on a basis of need, depending on recent theme or upcoming feature." Seldom comments on rejections. Reports in 2-4 weeks. Pays 20 copies.** Staff reviews books of poetry. Send books for review consideration to Claudia Park, reviews coordinator. The editor says, "We are looking for poetry that would be censored or misunderstood in conventional publications."

LMNO PRESS (V), P.O. Box 862, Westminster MD 21158, founded 1991, editor Laurie Precht. ***LMNO Press*** publishes yearly in July. It accepts **concrete, narrative poetry under 100 lines and short stories. However, they are currently not accepting submissions.** As a sample the editor selected these lines from "Los Angeles is Beirut, 1992" by Wendy Deal:

Violence spreads
through the senses
an angry whispering rush.
Accept the wildfire of the mind.
Fall into it like loving
in a black hole.

LMNO Press is digest-sized, 40 pgs. Press run is 200. It is distributed through subscription and at poetry readings, local bookshops and literary fairs. Subscription or **sample copy postpaid: $3. "Don't send cash; please send check or money order made out to Laurie Precht."** She advises, "Go deeply into your writing. Draw on your experiences; let the reader live what you know. And don't dawdle on the same worn topics—pick something new and go!"

LODESTAR BOOKS (V, IV-Children/teen), 375 Hudson St., New York NY 10014, phone (212)366-2627, affiliate of Dutton's Children's Books, a division of Penguin USA, founded 1980, editorial director Virginia Buckley, is a trade publisher of **juvenile and young adult nonfiction, fiction and picture books. "We are not currently accepting unsolicited submissions."**

LONDON MAGAZINE (II), 30 Thurloe Place, London SW7 England, founded 1954, poetry editor Alan Ross, is a literary and art monthly using **poetry "the best of its kind."** Editors seem open to all styles and forms, including well-made formal works. Some of the best poems in England appear here. It is a 6×8½, perfect-bound, elegant-looking magazine, with card cover, averaging about 150 pages six times a year. They accept about 150 of 2,000 poems received each year. Press run is 5,000 for 2,000 subscribers. Subscription: £28.50 or $67. **Sample postpaid: £4.75. Cover letter required with submissions. Reports "very soon." Pays £20/page. Buys first British serial rights.** Reviews books of poetry in up to 1,200 words. Open to unsolicited reviews. Poets may also send books for review consideration. Alan Ross says, "Quality is our only criterion."

‡LONDON REVIEW OF BOOKS (III), 28/30 Little Russell St., London WC1A 2HM England, founded 1979, editor Mary-Kay Wilmers, is published 24 times a year, mostly reviews and essays but some poems. They have published some of the most distinguished contemporary poets, such as Ted Hughes, Tony Harrison, James Fenton, Frederick Seidel and Thom Gunn. As a sample we selected the opening stanza of "The Metronomic Moon" by Michael Young:

In other years I would say, how pretty they are,
The cherries outside our house.
This autumn I see the first leaves
Writhe from the green into the yellow and
From the yellow into what seems a frantic red
Before they corkscrew to their conclusion
When the morning wipers scrape them from the windscreens
To drop them in the dog shit on the pavement
Their beauty has not brought them mercy.

The paper has a circulation of 17,000 with 14,000 subscriptions. **Sample: £2.10 in United Kingdom, $2.95 in US and Canada – excluding postage. Considers simultaneous submissions. Always sends prepublication galleys. Pays £50/poem.**

LONG ISLAND QUARTERLY (IV-Regional), P.O. Box 114, Northport NY 11768, founded 1990, editor and publisher George Wallace, is a quarterly using **poetry by people on or from Long Island. "Surprise us with fresh language. No conventional imagery, self-indulgent confessionalism, compulsive article-droppers."** They have recently published poetry by Edmund Pennant, David Ignatow and William Heyen. As a sample here are lines from "Summer" by Claire Nicolas White:

The wind on its great wings erases sound,
wipes out all desire, all preconceived notion
of pleasure with the music on the panes
and the leafy branches sweeping out there,
shaking their green hair.

LIQ is a handsome publication whose clean design (28 pgs., digest-sized, saddle-stapled, professionally printed on quality stock with matte card cover) enhances the image-based, mostly lyric free verse inside. Most contributions show attention to craft and structure. Press run is 250 for 150 subscribers of which 15 are libraries, 50-75 shelf sales. Subscription: $12. **Sample postpaid: $3. Cover letter including connection to Long Island region required. Name and address on each page. Submissions without SASE not returned. Responds in 3 months. Sometimes sends prepublication galleys. Pays 1 copy.** Sponsors a semiannual open poetry competition with deadlines of March 31 and August 31. The winner and runners up are awarded cash prizes. Entrants may send up to 5 original, unpublished poems for consideration. No restrictions on theme or length. Entry fee: $5. No mss will be returned. Winners announced 2 months after closing date. For competition results, include SASE. Send submissions to: Long Island Quarterly Poetry Prize at the above address. The editor advises: "(1) Go beyond yourself; (2) Don't be afraid to fictionalize; (3) Don't write your autobiography – if you are worth it, maybe someone else will."

LONG ISLANDER; WALT'S CORNER (II), 313 Main St., Huntington NY 11743, phone (516)427-7000, fax (516)427-5820, founded 1838 by Walt Whitman, poetry editor George Wallace, is a weekly newspaper, 25,000 circulation, using **unrhymed poetry up to 40 lines "grounded in personal/social matrix, no haiku, inspirational."** They have published poetry by David Ignatow, David Axelrod and R.B. Weber. As a sample the editor selected these lines from "The Gleaners" by L. Dellarocca:

They bend, clutch earth by its
straw season and sing
while we loosen our belts.

It is "48 pgs., newsprint." They use 52 of about 1,000 poems submitted each year. Subscription: $18. **Sample postpaid: $2.50. Simultaneous submissions OK. Editor "normally" comments on rejections. Pays 1 copy.** Staff reviews books of poetry. Send books for review consideration.

LONG SHOT (II), P.O. Box 6238, Hoboken NJ 07030, founded 1982, published by Danny Shot, edited by Jack Wiler, Jessica Chosid, Tom Polhamus, Nancy Mercado and Erik LaPrade, is, they say, "writing from the real world." They have recently published poetry by Charles Bukowski, Miguel Algarin, Pedro Pietri, Allen Ginsberg, Amiri Baraka and June Jordan. It is 144 pgs., flat-spined, professionally printed with glossy card cover using b&w photos, drawings and cartoons. It comes out twice a year. Press run is 1,500. Subscription: $22 for 2 years (4 issues). **Sample: $7. Simultaneous submissions OK. Reports in 2 months. Pays 2 copies.** Unlike other publishers, Danny Shot says they receive "too many requests for writer's guidelines. Just send the poems."

LONGHOUSE (II); SCOUT (V); ORIGIN PRESS (V), Green River R.F.D., Brattleboro VT 05301, founded 1973, editor Bob Arnold. ***Longhouse*** is a literary annual using **poems "from the serious working poet" from any region in any style.** They have published poetry by Hayden Carruth, Janine Pommy-Vega, Bobby Byrd, Sharon Doubiago, George Evans, Lorine Niedecker, Tim McNulty and Alan Lau. Its format is unusual: a thick packet of looseleaf 8½×14 sheets, photocopied from typescript, in a handsomely printed matte cover. Press run 200. **Sample postpaid: $5. Pays 2 copies.** Reviews books of poetry. **They publish chapbooks and books (manuscripts solicited only) under the imprints of Longhouse and Scout.** "We are also a bookshop and mail-order business for modern first editions and modern poetry and small presses. We encourage poets and readers looking for collectible modern first editions and scarce–and not so scarce–books of poetry and small press magazines to send a donation for our catalog; whatever one can afford." Bob Arnold says, "Origin Press is best known as Cid Corman's press. One of the quiet giants in American poetry/plus the wide scope of international work. Established in the early 1950s in Boston, it has moved around as Cid went with his life: France, Italy, Boston, for many years now in Kyoto, Japan. Cid has merged with Longhouse in that we now edit and publish a few items together. He continues to edit, translate and publish from Kyoto. His own books are heavily based in our bookshop and mail order catalog."

LOOM PRESS (II), P.O. Box 1394, Lowell MA 01853, founded 1978, editor Paul Marion, is a small press publisher of books and chapbooks. Poets published include William O'Connell, Ann Fox Chandonnet and Jane Brox. Books are perfect-bound, 6×9, with an average page count of 64. The chapbooks are saddle-stitched, 6×9, with an average page count of 20. **Writers should query first for book and chapbook publication, sending credits, 5 sample poems and bio. Queries will be answered in 1 month, mss reported on in 2 months. Simultaneous submissions will be considered.** Time to publication is 6-12 months. **The editor comments on mss "when time allows." Always sends prepublication galleys. Pays royalties of 10% on books and chapbooks, plus 5% of print run. Samples are available at $5 each.** He says, "Please support the small publishers who make poetry available."

LOONFEATHER; LOONFEATHER PRESS (I, IV-Regional), P.O. Box 1212, Bemidji MN 56601, phone (218)751-4869, founded 1979, poetry editors Betty Rossi, Elmo Heggie and Marshall Muirhead, is a small press publisher of the literary magazine ***Loonfeather*** appearing 2 times a year, **"primarily but not exclusively for Minnesota writers. Prefer short poems of not over 42 lines, accepts some traditional forms if well done, no generalizations on worn-out topics."** They have recently published poetry by Mark Vinz, Stephen Van Buren and Kathleen Heideman. As a sample the editors selected these lines from "Looking at a Storm, Remembering Childhood" by Donna Turner:

How difficult life is
with the reds gone out of the world,
with all the little flower hearts
shut tight, and the earth so closed
a hammer could not shatter it.

Loonfeather is 5½×8½, 48 pgs., saddle-stapled, professionally printed in small type with matte card cover, using b&w art and ads. Subscription: $7.50/year; single copy current issue: $5 (Fall '88 through current year); back issues: $2.50. **Submission deadlines January 31 and July 31 for May and November publications. Publishes theme issues occasionally. Send SASE for upcoming themes. Pays 2 copies.** Loonfeather Press publishes a limited number of quality poetry books. **Query with 2-3 sample poems, cover letter and previous publications. Replies to queries in 3 months.** Time between acceptance and publication is 1-1½ years. **Pays 10% royalties.**

LORIEN HOUSE (I), P.O. Box 1112, Black Mountain NC 28711-1112, phone (704)669-6211, founded 1969, editor David A. Wilson, is a small press publishing many books under the Lorien House imprint (poetry on a subsidy basis). The press also regularly published the ***Black Mountain Review***, but has decided to cancel that annual after the January 1995 issue ("On Carl Sandburg"). **Query regarding**

subsidized book publication. Editor comments on submissions "occasionally," and offers "full analysis and marketing help" for $1/typed page of poetry.

LOTHROP, LEE & SHEPARD BOOKS (V), 1350 Avenue of the Americas, New York NY 10019, founded 1859, editor-in-chief Susan Pearson. **"We do not accept unsolicited mss."**

LOTUS POETRY SERIES (II); NAOMI LONG MADGETT POETRY AWARD (IV-Ethnic), P.O. Box 21607, Detroit MI 48221, phone (313)861-1280, fax (313)342-9174, founded 1972, editor Naomi Long Madgett, distributed by Michigan State University Press. "With one exception of a textbook, we publish books of **poetry by individual authors,** although we have published three anthologies. We occasionally sponsor readings. **Most, but not all, of our authors are black."** Their most recent anthology is **Adam of Ifé: Black Women in Praise of Black Men.** They have recently published poetry by Oliver LaGrone, May Miller, Robert Chrisman, James A. Emanuel and Selene de Medeiros. As a sample the editor selected these lines by Monifa Atungaye:

my last swim
and final push into this whiteness
your bright roundness
peering through narrow wooden bars . . .
marks the beginning of me.

Query. Response is usually within 6 weeks. Pays 25 author's copies; others may be ordered at a discount. Poets are not expected to contribute to the cost of publication. "Copies may be ordered from our catalog, which is free upon request. We do not give samples." The editor adds, "The Hilton-Long Foundation held its first annual Naomi Long Madgett Poetry Award in 1993. The winner for 1993 was Adam David Miller. The award goes to a manuscript by an African-American poet who is 60 years of age or older. Interested persons may write for details."

LOUISIANA LITERATURE; LOUISIANA LITERATURE PRIZE FOR POETRY (II, IV-Regional), SLU-792, Southeastern Louisiana University, Hammond LA 70402, editor David Hanson, appears twice a year. They say they **"receive mss year round although we work through submissions more slowly in summer. We consider creative work from anyone though we strive to showcase our state's talent. We appreciate poetry that pays attention to line, movement, musicality and resonant imagery."** They have recently published poetry by Sue Owen, Catharine Savage Brosman, Diane Wakoski, Claire Bateman, Kate Daniels, Elton Glaser, Sandra Nelson and Gray Jacobik. The editor chose these sample lines from "Four Coffees" by Jody Bilyeu:

In his grandparents' shallow, ancient pond
he discovered among cattails
and swamped Sudan grass a hundred baby
fish and yanked some into a kitchen strainer,
rapt by their slippery blackness,
their writhing, the fact that some had legs.

The magazine is a large (6¾×9¾) format, 100 pgs., flat-spined, handsomely printed on heavy matte stock with matte card cover (using engravings). Subscription: $10 for individuals, $12.50 for institutions. Single copies: $5 for individuals. **Publishes theme issues. Send SASE for upcoming themes. Sometimes sends prepublication galleys.** Open to unsolicited reviews. Poets may also send books for review consideration; include cover letter. The Louisiana Literature Prize for Poetry offers a $400 award. Send SASE for guidelines. ***Louisiana Literature*** received honorable mention for editorial content from the 1993 American Literary Magazine Awards. The editor says, "It's important to us that the poets we publish be in control of their creations. Too much of what we see seems arbitrary."

LOUISIANA STATE UNIVERSITY PRESS (V), P.O. Box 25053, Baton Rouge LA 70894-5053, phone (504)388-6294, founded 1935, poetry editor L.E. Phillabaum, is a highly respected publisher of collections by poets such as Lisel Mueller, Margaret Gibson, Fred Chappell and Henry Taylor. **Currently not accepting poetry submissions; "fully committed through 1996."**

THE LOUISVILLE REVIEW (II, IV-Children/teen), Dept. PM, 315 Bingham Humanities, University of Louisville, Louisville KY 40292, phone (502)852-6801, founded 1976, faculty editor Sena Jeter Naslund, appears twice a year. **They use any kind of poetry except translations, and they have a section of children's poetry (grades K-12).** They have published poetry by Richard Jackson, Jeffrey Skinner, Maura Stanton, Richard Cecil, Roger Weingarten and Greg Pape. ***TLR*** is 200 pgs., flat-spined, 6×8¾. They accept about 10% of some 700 pieces received a year. **Sample postpaid: $4. "Poetry by children must include permission of parent to publish if accepted. In all of our poetry we look for the striking metaphor, unusual imagery and fresh language. We do not read in summer. Poems are read by 3 readers; report time is 1-2 months and time to publication is 2-3 months." Pays 1 copy.**

LOW-TECH PRESS (V), 30-73 47th St., Long Island City NY 11103, founded 1981, editor Ron Kolm, has published work by Hal Sirowitz, John Yau and Jennifer Nostrand. As a sample the editor selected these lines (poet unidentified):

They firebombed
the dinner table
taking us completely
by surprise.

"I am only interested in short poems with clear images. Since almost nobody gets paid for their work, I believe in multiple submissions and multiple publishings. Even though we only publish solicited mss, I respond right away to any mail the press receives."

LUCIDITY; BEAR HOUSE PUBLISHING (I), Route 2, Box 94, Eureka Springs AR 72632-9505, founded 1985, editor Ted O. Badger. *Lucidity* is a quarterly of poetry. **Submission fee required—$1/poem for "juried" selection by a panel of judges or $2/poem to compete for cash awards of $15, $10 and $5. Other winners paid in both cash and in copies. In addition, the editor invites a few guest contributors to submit to each issue. Contributors are encouraged to subscribe or buy a copy of the magazine.** The magazine is called *Lucidity* because, the editor says, "I have felt that too many publications of verse lean to the abstract in content and the obscure in style." They are **"open as to form. 40-line limit due to format. No restriction on subject matter except that something definitive be given to the reader." Purpose: "to give a platform to poets who can impart their ideas with clarity." He does not want "religious, nature or vulgar poems."** Recently published poets include Joyce Frazeur, Buck Allen, Janice Braud and Grant Perry. As a sample of the type of verse sought, the editor offers these lines by Nancy E. Martindale:

I have learned womanly secrets
by eavesdropping, listening at the doors
of my sisters, peering
into closets and diaries.

The magazine is photocopied from typescript, digest-sized, saddle-stapled, 72 pgs. with matte card cover. It's a surprisingly lively small press magazine featuring accessible narrative and lyric poetry, with almost equal space given to free and formal verse. Press run is 310 for 190 subscribers. Subscription: $10. **Sample postpaid: $2.50. Simultaneous submissions OK. Send SASE for guidelines. Reports in 2-3 months, a 3-month delay before publication. Buys one-time rights.** Bear House Press is a self-publishing arrangement by which poets can pay to have booklets published in the same format as *Lucidity*, prices beginning at 50 copies of 32 pgs. for $140. Publishes 10 chapbooks/year. The editor says, "The only poets who never get reject slips are those not submitting. But they don't get published, either."

LULLWATER REVIEW (II), Box 22036, Emory University, Atlanta GA 30322, phone (404)727-6184, founded 1989, editor revolves, appears 2 times/year. They want **"original, imaginative treatment of emotional and intellectual topics. No mere wordplay. Ideas and concepts should be emphasized."** They have recently published poetry by Turner Cassity, Colette Inez, Mark Svenvold, Eve Shelnutt and Ioanna-Veronika Warwick. As a sample the editor selected this poem, "Seven Lean Cows," by Aurel Rău, translated by Adam J. Sorkin and Liviu Bleoca:

Every day becomes a gift to the wise man.
O, if only these stupid days had traveled on,
these seven lean cows. The man of wax
and the woman of wax
and the emperor of wax
that gleam in the wax museum of all the capitals
they knew they knew not

Lullwater Review is a handsome, 6×9, flat-spined magazine, 96 pgs. Press run is 2,000. Subscription: $12. **Sample postpaid: $5. Will consider simultaneous submissions. Reads submissions August 1 through May 31 only. Send SASE for guidelines. Reports in 2 months or less. Pays 3 copies. All rights revert to author upon publication.** "*Lullwater* places no limits on theme or style; the sole criterion for judging submitted work is its excellence. While much of the poetry we publish is free verse, we hold in high regard well-crafted formal poems. We expect our contributors to be acquainted with the broad field of contemporary poetry and able to find within that field a voice uniquely their own."

LUNA BISONTE PRODS; LOST AND FOUND TIMES (IV-Style), 137 Leland Ave., Columbus OH 43214, founded 1967, poetry editor John M. Bennett, may be the zaniest phenomenon in central Ohio. John Bennett is a publisher (and practicioner) of **experimental and avant-garde writing**, sometimes sexually explicit, and art in a bewildering array of formats including the magazine, ***Lost and Found Times***, postcard series, posters, chapbooks, pamphlets, labels and audiocassette tapes. You can get a **sampling of Luna Bisonte Prods for $5. Numerous reviewers have commented on the bizarre *Lost***

and Found Times, "reminiscent of several West Coast dada magazines"; "This exciting magazine is recommended only for the most daring souls"; "truly demented"; "Insults . . . the past 3,000 years of literature," etc. Bennett wants to see **"unusual poetry, naive poetry, surrealism, experimental, visual poetry, collaborations—*no* poetry workshop or academic pablum."** He has recently published poetry by I. Argüelles, G. Beining, B. Heman, R. Olson, J. Lipman, B. Porter, C.H. Ford, P. Weinman, E.N. Brookings, F.A. Nettelbeck, D. Raphael, R. Crozier, S. Sollfrey, M. Andre, N. Vassilakis, S.E. Murphy, T. Taylor and S.S. Nash. As a sample the editor selected part of a poem by Jack A. Withers Smote:

Unable to furnish your Mister Thigh
with a normal sexual outlet,
the limp clevered over, nudged a smile.
From the social standpoint, your delusion makes you a
wind over the stretched-out hose, and a smouldering styrofoam cup,
as if you had kinda seeped and felt pleasure as never before.

The digest-sized, 52-page magazine, photoreduced typescript and wild graphics, matte card cover with graphics, has a circulation of 350 with 75 subscriptions of which 30 are libraries. **Sample postpaid: $5. Submit anytime—preferably camera-ready (but this is not required). Reports in 1-2 days. Pays copies. All rights revert to authors upon publication.** Staff reviews books of poetry. Send books for review consideration. **Luna Bisonte also will consider book submissions: query with samples and cover letter (but "keep it brief"). Chapbook publishing usually depends on grants or other subsidies and is usually by solicitation.** He will also consider subsidy arrangements on negotiable terms. The editor says, "I would like to see more experimental and avant-garde material in Spanish and Portuguese, or in mixtures of languages."

LUNA NEGRA (I), (formerly listed as *The New Kent Quarterly—Luna Negra*), Box 26, Student Activities, English Dept., Kent State University, Kent OH 44240, is a student-run, biannual literary and art magazine of the KSU main campus, **open to all forms of poetry.** The editor says it is 40-50 pgs., 5½×8½, with art and photography throughout. They receive 400-450 poems a year, accept 40 or 50. Press run is 2,000, most distributed to KSU students. **Simultaneous submissions OK. Reads submissions September 1 through March 30 only. Seldom comments on rejections. Reports in 1 month or so ("depending on school calendar"). Pays 1 copy. "All rights revert to author immediately after publication."** The editor adds, "We are also interested in any b&w reproducible artwork or photographs."

THE LUTHERAN JOURNAL (IV-Religious), Dept. PM, 7317 Cahill Rd., Edina MN 55439, phone (612)941-6830, editor The Rev. Armin U. Deye, is a family quarterly, 32 pgs., circulation 136,000, for Lutheran Church members, middle age and older. They use **poetry "related to subject matter," traditional, free verse, blank verse. Sample free for SASE. Simultaneous submissions OK. Pays.**

‡LYNX, A JOURNAL FOR LINKING POETS (IV-Form), AHA Books, P.O. Box 1250, Gualala CA 95445, founded as ***APA-Renga*** in 1986, later the name was changed to ***Lynx*** "to link an endangered species of poetry with an endangered animal and to inspire the traditional wit of renga," says editor Jane Reichhold. ***Lynx***, published 3 times a year (February, June and October) "is **based on the ancient craft of renga, linked verse with origins in Zen and Japanese culture, and now publishes both renga and tanka.** A renga is a non-narrative series of linked images as a group effort. Tanka is the most popular poetry form in Japan and the oldest continued form." As a sample the editor selected this renga excerpt by Jane Reichhold, T.B., Kenneth C. Leibman and Tundra Wind:

panty hose   as she crosses her legs   she whispers
from the back room   a sigh
on the table   her letter punctuated   with a teardrop
from the apartment upstairs   a lullaby

Lynx is 60-80 pgs., 4½×11, neatly printed and comb-bound with card cover. It also publishes essays, book reviews, articles, interviews, experimental linked forms, linked prose, art, commentaries and "whatever encourages poets to link ideas." They currently have 300 subscribers. Subscription: $15 US and Canada, $20 elsewhere. **Sample postpaid: $4, includes guidelines. Please make checks payable to AHA Books. *Lynx* encourages submissions by those experienced and experimenting with collaborative forms. Subscribers participate in ongoing rengas, start trends and otherwise determine the content. All submissions should include a brief bio with the title of the work. "Please send us copies that do not need to be returned." Include SASE for reply. Editor responds to all who submit. Reports in 3 months.**

THE LYRIC; LYRIC ANNUAL COLLEGE POETRY CONTEST (II, IV-Form, students), 307 Dunton Dr. SW, Blacksburg VA 24060-5127, founded 1921 ("the oldest magazine in North America in continuous publication devoted to the publication of **traditional poetry**"), poetry editor Leslie Mellichamp, uses about 65 poems each quarterly issue. **"We use rhymed verse in traditional forms, for the most part, with an occasional piece of blank or free verse. 40 lines or so is usually our limit. Our themes are varied, ranging from religious ecstasy to humor to raw grief, but we feel no compulsion to shock,**

embitter or confound our readers. We also avoid poems about contemporary political or social problems—grief but not grievances, as Frost put it. Frost is helpful in other ways: If yours is more than a lover's quarrel with life, we're not your best market. And most of our poems are accessible on first or second reading. Frost again: Don't hide too far away. Poems must be original, unpublished and not under consideration elsewhere." They have recently published poetry by Anne Barlow, John J. Brugaletta, Michael J. Bugeja, Rhina P. Espaillat, Barbara Loots, Irene Warsaw, Alfred Dorn, Sharon Kourous, Gail White, Neill Megaw and Alice Mackenzie Swaim. The editor selected these sample lines by Joseph Harris:

Old griefs come at noon
Up from twilight caves;
They gibber in my ear
Like ghosts from deserted graves.

It is digest-sized, 36 pgs., professionally printed with varied typography, matte card cover, has a circulation of 850 with 800 subscriptions of which 290 are libraries. They receive about 5,000 submissions/year, use 250, have an average 3-month backlog. Subscription: $10 US, $12 Canada and other countries (in US funds only). **Sample postpaid: $3. Submit up to 5 poems. Send SASE for guidelines. Reports in 1 month (average). Pays 1 copy, and all contributors are eligible for quarterly and annual prizes totaling over $800.** ***The Lyric*** also offers an annual poetry contest in traditional forms for fulltime undergraduate students enrolled in any American or Canadian college or university, prizes totaling $500. Send SASE for rules. ***The Lyric*** ranked #1 in the "Traditional Verse" category of the latest ***Writer's Digest*** Poetry 60 list. Leslie Mellichamp comments, "Our *raison d'être* has been the encouragement of form, music, rhyme and accessibility in poetry. We detect a growing dissatisfaction with the modernist movement that ignores these things and a growing interest in the traditional wellsprings of the craft. Naturally, we are proud to have provided an alternative for over 70 years that helped keep the true roots of poetry alive."

M.A.F. PRESS; THIRTEEN POETRY MAGAZINE (I, IV-Form), Box 392, Portlandville NY 13834-0392, phone (607)286-7500, founded 1982, poetry editor Ken Stone. ***Thirteen Poetry Magazine*** **"publishes only 13-line poetry; any theme or subject as long as in 'good' taste. We would like to see more foreign language poetry with English translations. We seek to publish work that touches the beauty of this life."** They have published poetry by Pamela Portwood, Ida Fasel, Will Inman, Stan Proper, Janet Carncross Chandler and Marion Cohen. As a sample the editor selected "Leaving" by John Craig:

And still the memory
of you standing, waving good-bye.
I should have turned around then
for the sadness of your eye.

Thirteen appears quarterly in a magazine-sized, 40-page, saddle-stapled format, photocopied from typescript, matte card cover with b&w cartoon. Circulation is 350 for 130 subscribers of which 20 are libraries. Ken Stone accepts about 100 of the 300 submissions he receives each year. **Sample postpaid: $2.50. Submit 4-6 poems. No reprint material. "We have even taken hand-written poems. As to queries, only if 13 lines gives the poet problems." Comments on rejections "especially if requested." Send SASE for guidelines. Reports "immediately to 2 weeks." Pays 1 copy.** The editor advises, "Send more poetry, less letters and self-promotion. Read the 'want lists' and description listings of magazines for guidelines. When in doubt request information. Read other poets in the magazines and journals to see what trends are. Also, this is a good way to find out what various publications like in the way of submissions."

M.I.P. COMPANY (IV-Foreign language, erotica), P.O. Box 27484, Minneapolis MN 55427, founded in 1984, contact Michael Peltsman, publishes 3 paperbacks/year. **They only publish Russian erotic poetry written in Russian.** They have published poetry collections by Mikhail Armalinsky and Aleksey Shelvakh. **Previously published poems and simultaneous submissions OK. Replies to queries in 1 month. Seldom comments on rejections.**

MACFADDEN WOMEN'S GROUP; TRUE CONFESSIONS; TRUE ROMANCES; TRUE LOVE; TRUE STORY; SECRETS; MODERN ROMANCES (I), Dept. PM, 233 Park Ave. S., New York NY 10003, phone (212)979-4800. **Address each magazine individually; do not submit to Macfadden Women's Group.** Each of these romance magazines uses poetry—usually no more than 1 poem/issue. **Their requirements vary; readers should study them individually and write for guidelines.** These mass-circulation magazines (available on newsstands) are a very limited market, yet a possible one for beginners—especially those who like the prose contents and are tuned in to their editorial tastes.

THE MACGUFFIN (II), Schoolcraft College, 18600 Haggerty Rd., Livonia MI 48152, phone (313)462-4400, ext. 5292, founded 1983, editor Arthur Lindenberg, who says, "***The MacGuffin*** is a literary magazine which appears three times each year, in April, June and November. We publish the best poetry, fiction, nonfiction and artwork we find. We have no thematic or stylistic biases. **We look for**

well-crafted poetry. Long poems should not exceed 300 lines. Avoid pornography, trite and sloppy poetry." They have published poetry by Kathleen Ripley Leo, Stephen Dunning and Daniel James Sundahl. As a sample the editor selected these lines from "Neruda" by Peter Brett:

The women pass like calendar days
leaving in mind the aftertaste of
mango, papaya days with high fore-
heads and astonished eyes . . .

The MacGuffin is 144 pgs., digest-sized, professionally printed on heavy buff stock, with matte card cover, flat-spined, with b&w illustrations and photos. Circulation is 600, of which 140 are subscriptions and the rest are local newsstand sales, contributor copies and distribution to college offices. Single copy: $4.50; subscription: $12. **Sample postpaid: $4. "The editorial staff is grateful to consider unsolicited manuscripts and graphics." Writers should submit no more than 6 poems of no more than 300 lines; poems should be typewritten. Publishes theme issues. Send SASE for upcoming themes. Themes for 1995 will include Humor and Parody (for June issue). Mss are reported on in 8-10 weeks and the publication backlog is 6 months. Pays 2 copies,** "occasional money or prizes." The magazine also sponsors an annual contest with a $100 first prize for Michigan poets only; they hope to be able to sponsor a national competition soon. ***The MacGuffin*** ranked #8 in the "Traditional Verse" category of the latest ***Writer's Digest*** Poetry 60 list. The editor says, "We will always comment on 'near misses.' Writing is a search, and it is a journey. Don't become sidetracked. Don't become discouraged. Keep looking. Keep traveling. Keep writing."

MACMILLAN PUBLISHING CO.; CHARLES SCRIBNER'S SONS; ATHENEUM; COLLIER, 866 Third Ave., New York NY 10022. Prefers not to share information.

MAD RIVER PRESS (V), State Road, Richmond MA 01254, phone (413)698-3184, founded 1986, editor Barry Sternlieb, publishes 3 broadsides and 1 chapbook/year, **"all types of poetry, no bias," but none unsolicited.** They have recently published poetry by Gary Snyder, Hayden Carruth, W.S. Merwin, Louise Glück, Linda Gregg and Richard Wilbur. Call or write for information.

THE MADISON REVIEW; FELIX POLLAK PRIZE IN POETRY (II), Dept. of English, Helen C. White Hall, University of Wisconsin, 600 N. Park St., Madison WI 53706, founded 1978, poetry editors Christine Grimando and Joshua Moses, want **poems that are "smart and tight, that fulfill their own propositions. Spare us: love poems, religious or patriotic dogma, light verse. We'd like to see poetry in ethnic/nationality, form/style, gay/lesbian, humor (not light verse, though), political, social issues and women/feminism categories."** They have published work by Lise Goett, Lisa Steinman and Richard Tillinghast. As a sample the editors selected these lines from "Gulls" by Jerry Mirskin:

Now it's the sharp and damp smell of gasoline
and now the sun, the full theater of the sun
torching the town, so the windows
of the houses along the shore burn like glasses of tea.

The Madison Review is published in May and December, with 15-20 poems selected from a pool of 750. **Sample back issue postpaid: $2.50. Submit maximum of 6 poems. No simultaneous submissions. Usually reports in 4 months, may be longer in summer. Pays 2 copies. "We do appreciate a concise cover letter with short bio information."** The Felix Pollak Prize in Poetry is for $500 and publication in ***TMR***, for "the best group of three unpublished poems submitted by a single author." Send SASE for rules before submitting for prize or see announcement for guidelines in ***AWP*** or ***Poets & Writers*** magazines. Submissions must arrive during September—winner announced December 15. ***The Madison Review*** ranked #10 in the "Traditional Verse" category of the latest ***Writer's Digest*** Poetry 60 list. The editors say, "Contributors: Know your market! Read before, during and after writing. Treat your poems *better* than job applications!"

THE MAGAZINE OF SPECULATIVE POETRY (IV-Science fiction), Box 564, Beloit WI 53512, founded 1984, editors Roger Dutcher and Mark Rich, a quarterly magazine that publishes **"the best new speculative poetry. We are especially interested in narrative form, but interested in variety of styles, open to any form, length (within reason), purpose. We're looking for the best of the new poetry utilizing the ideas, imagery and approaches developed by speculative fiction and will welcome experimental techniques as well as the fresh employment of traditional forms."** They have published poetry by Brian Aldiss, Jane Yolen, William Stafford, Ron Ellis and S.R. Compton. As a sample Roger Dutcher chose these lines from "Time Machines" by Steve Rasnic Tem:

The Big Bang tide sends us chasing
each of our moments through space
trying to escape the collapse
and our own heat-death
when all time runs backward

CLOSE-UP

Russia's "Spiritual Newspaper" Lives On

You're a brave man
they tell me.
It's not true.
I've never been courageous.
I only thought it an unworthy act
to degrade myself to cowardice as others did.

I didn't shake any foundations.
I no more than laughed at the pompous
and the false.
I wrote verses.
Never denunciations.
I tried to say what I had thought.

(from "Talk," translated by Albert C. Todd and published in **The Collected Poems, 1952-1990**, Henry Holt & Company, 1991)

Photo by Michael R. Barwell

Yevgeny Yevtushenko

There is something indescribably boyish about Russian poet Yevgeny Yevtushenko. Tall and lanky, the 61-year-old Siberian radiates energy and enthusiasm. His poetry readings are dramatic affairs, even by Russian standards. He paces the stage, leaps into the audience, his voice ranging from a shout to a caress. Yevtushenko has survived a World War, a Cold War, and decades of literary censorship to become an internationally known poet, filmmaker, and tireless advocate of literary and political freedom.

There was no organized dissident movement in the Soviet Union in the 1950s, when Yevtushenko began writing. Solzhenitsyn was in a northern prison camp, and Sakharov was still an unknown nuclear scientist when Yevtushenko and his contemporaries began to speak out against chauvinism and intolerance in Soviet society. "I am very happy that I belong to a generation of poets who declared their thirst for freedom," he says.

During the brief thaw after the death of Stalin, many poets were able to write relatively freely. Few were as popular as Yevtushenko, who published his first book at age 19 and was a national star at 22. "Our safeguard, our protection, was our popularity," he says. Poetry readings were commonly held in stadiums and large halls. "Even Russian bureaucrats, who didn't like us troublemakers in politics, knew by heart many of our poems."

Poetry has always played an important role in Russian society, Yevtushenko notes. Even before the Russian Revolution there was strict censorship on political expression, and poets were "the ambassadors of freedom which did not exist.

"A poet in Russia is more than a poet," he says, and poetry "is the spiritual newspaper," saying what others cannot say. Yevtushenko has always seen himself as a part of that tradition of poet as rebel and truth-sayer. In his own straightforward, intensely personal poetry, he has challenged hypocrisy and intolerance of governments on both sides of the Iron Curtain. He protested the invasion of Czechoslovakia and the war in Vietnam with equal fervor and has traveled widely, trying to get to know the people behind the governments. He was an early champion of glasnost in Russia and served a term as a member of Parliament for the Ukrainian town of Kharkov.

Ironically, Yevtushenko is ambivalent about the impact of Western literature and culture on Russia. "We idealized freedom when we were fighting for it," he says. "We thought freedom had only one face and that face was beautiful. But we discovered that freedom has many faces." He says the collapse of the state printing system has meant that many serious writers, especially ethnic writers from states like Georgia and the Ukraine, are no longer able to publish. Censorship has been replaced, he says, by the dictatorship of the marketplace, and cheap, Western-style novels have supplanted more traditional literature. He jokingly refers to this as the "McDonaldization of Russian culture."

Yevtushenko continues to publish poetry, both in Russia and abroad. He has turned to other creative forms as well, including filmmaking. The film **Stalin's Funeral**, which he wrote and directed, has been shown in Russia and America. Inspired by one of his poems, "Lies," the film describes a critical turning point in Yevtushenko's own history, when he and other Russians began to question their blind obedience to the state and to challenge the authorities.

Yevtushenko has also continued to champion other Russian poets. He recently compiled a massive collection of Russian poetry from the last 100 years, **Twentieth Century Russian Poetry: Silver and Steel: An Anthology** (Doubleday, 1993), a selection of poets from the Golden Age of turn-of-the-century poets to modern poets born after World War II. He says this is the first collection that has drawn together poets from the left and the right, both romantic and political writers. Unfortunately, while the volume has been released in English, Yevtushenko is still looking for a publisher to release it in Russian.

Yevtushenko is philosophical about the future of poetry in Russia. "I think we will survive," he says with a smile. "In the land of Tolstoy and Pushkin, I think literature will continue to grow." Forms may change, but the need for poetry, the "spiritual newspaper," will always exist in Russia. "Full optimism is a lack of information," he says. "Full pessimism is lack of imagination."

–Alison Holm

"A poet in Russia is more than a poet. . . . [Poetry] is the spiritual newspaper . . ."

—Yevgeny Yevtushenko

and we leap from our graves

The digest-sized magazine, 20-24 pgs., is offset from professional typesetting, saddle-stapled with matte card cover. They accept less than 10% of some 500 poems received/year. Press run is 100-200, going to nearly 100 subscribers of which 4 are libraries. Subscription: $11. **Sample postpaid: $3.50. No previously published poems or simultaneous submissions. Prefer double-spaced. Editor comments on rejections "on occasion." Send SASE for guidelines. Reports in 1-2 months. Pays 3¢/word, minimum $3 plus copy. Buys first North American serial rights.** Reviews books of speculative poetry. Query on unsolicited reviews. Send speculative poetry books for review consideration.

MAGIC CHANGES (IV-Themes), P.O. Box 658, Warrenville IL 60555-0658, phone (708)416-3111, founded 1978, poetry editor John Sennett, is published every 18 months, in an unusual format. Photocopied from typescript on many different weights and colors of paper, magazine-sized, stapled along the long side (you read it both vertically and horizontally), taped flat spine, full of fantasy drawings, pages packed with poems of all varieties, fiction, photos, drawings, odds and ends—including reviews of little magazines and other small press publications. It is **intended to make poetry (and literature) fun—and unpredictable. Each issue is on an announced theme. "*Magic Changes* is divided into sections such as 'The Order of the Celestial Otter,' 'State of the Arts,' 'Time,' 'Music' and 'Skyscraper Rats.' A magical musical theme pervades."** They have recently published poetry by Sue Standing, Caleb Bullen, Hugh Ogden, Brian Shaw, Chris Robbins, Kaela Sennett, Patricia A. Davey and Walt Curtis. As a sample the editor selected these lines from "Satchmo" by Roberta Gould:

Satchmo's teeth gleam
like the diamond "LA"
on his ring
and his cheeks shine
like the sun he
lifts in his horn

There are about 100 pgs. of poetry/issue, circulation 500, 28 subscriptions of which 10 are libraries. **Sample postpaid: $5. Submit 3-5 poems anytime. Send SASE for upcoming themes. The editor sometimes comments on rejections and offers criticism for $5/page of poetry. Reports in 2-4 months. Pays 1 or 2 copies. Acquires first North American serial rights.** Reviews books of poetry in "usually about 500 words." Open to unsolicited reviews. Poets may also send books for review consideration.

THE MAGIC MOUNTAIN (I, II), P.O. Box 7161, Syracuse NY 13261, founded 1993, editor Greg Carter, is a quarterly forum for individual thought, subtitled "The Syracuse Quarterly of Growth and Expression." They want to see **"the work of individuals, poetry related to individual growth and experience. My only criteria are strength and uniqueness of vision. No politically correct mush."** They have recently published poetry by Tom Eaton and Charlene Mary-Cath Smith. The editor says it is approximately 20 pgs., 5½×8½, newsletter format. Press run is 150. Subscription: $8/year. **Sample postpaid: $2. No previously published poems; simultaneous submissions OK. Often comments on rejections. Reports within 1 month. Pays 1 copy. Acquires one-time rights.** Staff reviews books of poetry. Send books for review consideration. The editor says, "I would like to publish more traditional forms of poetry."

MAGIC REALISM (II, IV-Fantasy), Pyx Press, P.O. Box 620, Orem UT 84059-0620, founded 1990, editors C. Darren Butler and Julie Thomas. *Magic Realism* appears 2-3 times/year using poetry **"of depth and imagination. *Magic Realism* subverts reality by shaping it into a human mold, bringing it closer to the imagination and to the subconscious. Inner reality becomes empirical reality. We always need good short poems of 3-12 lines."** It is typeset, offset or xerographically printed, digest-sized, 80 pgs. with card cover using b&w art. They use 5-15 poems/issue. Press run is 600-800. **Current issue postpaid: $5.95. Send #10 SASE for guidelines. Reports in 2-6 months. Sometimes sends prepublication galleys. Pays $3/magazine page for poetry and 1 copy. Acquires first North American serial or one-time rights *and* non-exclusive reprint rights; also needs worldwide Spanish language rights for translation which appears 1 year after English edition. Editor rarely comments.** He says, "I am looking for literary work based in exaggerated realism. Fantasy should permeate the reality, give it luster. My needs are somewhat flexible. For example, I occasionally publish genre work, or glib fantasy of the sort found in folktales and fables. We review unsolicited books, chapbooks and magazines as space permits; reviews generally run one-fourth to one-half page."

Market categories: (I) Beginning; (II) General; (III) Limited; (IV) Specialized; (V) Closed.

THE MALAHAT REVIEW (II); LONG POEM PRIZES (II, IV-Form), P.O. Box 1700, University of Victoria, Victoria, British Columbia V8W 2Y2 Canada, phone (604)721-8524, founded 1967, editor Derk Wynand, is "a high quality, visually appealing literary quarterly which has earned the praise of notable literary figures throughout North America. Its purpose is to publish and promote poetry and fiction of a very high standard, both Canadian and international. **We are interested in various styles, lengths and themes. The criterion is excellence.**" They have recently published poetry by P.K. Page, Barbara Carey and Wallis Wilde-Menozzi. As a sample the editor selected these lines from "Adagio, K.219" by Jan Zwicky:

Now the sky above New Mexico
is hazy with Los Angeles, what words
will you invent for clarity?
Some things were always nameless:
the heart as rainbarrel,
the ear a long-stemmed glass.

They use 50 pgs. of poetry in each issue, have 1,800 subscriptions of which 300 are libraries. They use about 100 of 2,000 submissions received/year, have no backlog. Topics and length in this handsome publication are particularly open, though editors show a distinct taste for free verse exhibiting craft and focus. Subscription: $20. **Sample postpaid: $7. Submit 5-10 poems, addressed to Editor Derk Wynand. The editors comment if they "feel the ms warrants some attention even though it is not accepted." Send SASE for guidelines. Reports within 3 months. Pays $20 per poem/page plus 2 copies and reduced rates on others.** Reviews books of poetry. The Long Poem Prizes of $400, plus publication and payment at their usual rates, entry fee $20 (which includes a year's subscription), is for a long poem or cycle 5-15 pgs. (flexible minimum and maximum), deadline March 1.

THE MANDEVILLE PRESS (III), Old Hall, Norwich Rd., South Burlingham, Norfolk NR13 4EY England, phone 0493-750-804, founded 1972, editors Peter Scupham and John Mole, publishes hand-set pamphlets of the work of individual poets. They want **"formal poetry, intelligence guiding emotion. No formless poetry, emotion eliminating intelligence."** They have published poetry by Anthony Hecht, Patric Dickinson, Edward Lowbury and Bernard O'Donoghue. **Interested poets may query. Replies to queries in 1 week, to mss (if invited) in 1 month. Pays 10 author's copies. Send SASE for catalog to buy samples.**

‡MANDRAKE POETRY MAGAZINE; THE MANDRAKE PRESS (II), ul. Wielkiej Niedźwiedzicy 35/8, Gliwice 44-117 Poland, founded 1993 in New York, editor and publisher Leo Yankevich, appears twice a year, in April and October. The editor says, **"I'd like to see well-crafted poetry, broadly formalist, with the passion of John the Baptist and the insight of Pythagoras or Plotinus. I have a weakness for Italian sonnets. I prefer masculine rhymes as well as off-rhymes. I think that moon/spoon is much better than pretty/city, but moon/gryphon is even better. Anything with a metaphysical-existential slant, if well done, has a good chance of being accepted. I'm very open to Japanese forms as well as translations. I don't want to see poetry that's trite, hackneyed, banal, nor anything trendy and uninspired that reads like lines from a newspaper."** He has recently published poetry by Stanislaw Grochowiak, Dan Kaderli and Bartlomiej Sokolowicz. As a sample the editor selected these lines from "Cross Purposes" by Leonard Cirino:

The beautiful and the true, both tyrants,
struggle toward an inevitable pitch.
Some things are unlike themselves forever.

A star or flower, what is the difference?
moon or mountain, light eclipses them all.

Mandrake Poetry Magazine is 20-32 pgs., digest-sized, photocopied from ink-jet typeset copy and glue bound with white card cover. The editor says he accepts about 15% of poetry received. Press run is 200 for 50 subscribers from 3 continents. Single copy: $3 (by airmail); two-year subscription: $12. **Previously published poems and simultaneous submissions OK. Cover letter required. "Keep cover letter terse and informative. Please enclose SAE along with one unattached U.S. (airmail) postage stamp or one IRC for all submissions. Send only copies of your poems, as I do not return poems with my reply." Always comments on rejections. Reports in 1 month. Pays "a brace of free copies." All rights revert to author.** The Mandrake Press also publishes one perfect-bound collection of poems, averaging 36 pgs., each year. "I should at least be familiar with a poet before publishing a book. If he's published poems in magazines and has a modest readership, it certainly helps." **Query first with sample poems and cover letter with brief bio and publication credits. Replies to queries and mss in 1 month. Pays 50 copies out of a press run of 100. "More copies can be purchased at the cost of production, usually $1.80 a book."** Poets may obtain a sample copy of Leonard's Cirino's book, **Tinctured Blood,** by sending $3 in unattached US postage stamps or by sending 3 oz. worth of IRCs. The editor says, "My advice to beginners is to understand the mind of a lizard, to possess dark secrets like a gnostic, to cast incantations like a wizard, to see bright sparks like a schizophrenic."

THE MANHATTAN REVIEW (II, IV-Translations), Apt. 45, 440 Riverside Dr., New York NY 10027, phone (212)932-1854, founded 1980, poetry editor Philip Fried, tries "**to publish American and foreign writers, and we choose foreign writers with something valuable to offer the American scene. We like to think of poetry as a powerful discipline engaged with many other fields. We want to see ambitious work. Interested in both lyric and narrative. Not interested in mawkish, sentimental poetry.** We select high-quality work from a number of different countries, including the U.S." They have recently published poetry by A.R. Ammons, Bei Dao, Wistawa Szymborska, Baron Wormser and Penelope Shuttle. As a sample the editor selected these lines by Adam Zagajewski:

The shoes of Auschwitz, in pyramids
high as the sky, groan faintly:
Alas, we outlived mankind, now
let us sleep, sleep:
We have nowhere to go.

The *MR* is now "an annual with ambitions to be semiannual." The magazine is 60 pgs., digest-sized, professionally printed with glossy card cover, photos and graphics. Press run is 500 for 85 subscribers of which 35 are libraries. It is also distributed by Bernhard DeBoer, Inc. and Fine Arts Distributors. They receive about 300 submissions/year, use few ("but I do read everything submitted carefully and with an open mind"). "I return submissions as promptly as possible." Single copy: $5; subscription: $10. **Sample: $6.25 with 6×9 envelope. Submit 3-5 pgs. No simultaneous submissions. Cover letter with short bio and publications required. Editor sometimes comments "but don't count on it." Reports in 10-12 weeks. Pays copies.** Staff reviews books of poetry. Send books for review consideration. Philip Fried advises, "Don't be swayed by fads. Search for your own voice. Support other poets whose work you respect and enjoy. Be persistent. Keep aware of poetry being written in other countries."

MANKATO POETRY REVIEW (II), Box 53, English Dept., Mankato State, Mankato MN 56001, phone (507)389-5511, founded 1984, editor Roger Sheffer, is a semiannual magazine that is "**open to all forms of poetry. We will look at poems up to 60 lines, any subject matter.**" They have published poetry by Edward Micus, Judith Skillman and Walter Griffin. As a sample the editor chose the following lines from a poem by Richard Robbins:

Sage connects to lava rock mile by mile.
West of Atomic City, blue flowers
in the craters of the moon.

The magazine is 5×8, typeset on 60 lb. paper, 30 pgs., saddle-stapled with buff matte card cover printed in one color. It appears usually in May and December and has a circulation of 200. Subscription: $5/year. **Sample postpaid: $2.50. Do not submit mss in summer (May through August). "Please indicate if simultaneous submission, and notify." Send SASE for guidelines. Reports in about 2 months; "We accept only what we can publish in next issue." Pays 2 copies.** The editor says, "We're interested in looking at longer poems—up to 60 lines, with great depth of detail relating to place (landscape, townscape)."

MANNA (I, II), 2966 W. Westcove Dr., West Valley City UT 84119-5940, founded 1978 by Nina Wicker, poetry editors Roger A. Ball, Brad Cutler and Rebecca Bradley, is "a small poetry magazine for the **middle-of-the-road poet. We like humor, short poems with feeling, farm poems and especially quality inspirational poetry; we mostly use free verse, some rhyme. We do not want long poems. Prefer short quality poems with feelings. Images, tone and thoughtful use of language important.**" They have published poetry by Sheryl L. Nelms, Errol Miller, Robert R. Hentz, Michael Estabrook and Patricia Higginbotham. As a sample the editors selected these lines from "November waits quietly" by Susan Noe Rothman:

While waiting for the bread to rise, I wandered
past the barn, coffee mug in hand
I gazed at the mountainside—saw—
empty hairbrushes, rakes, arms thin—bent—shaking
little old men waiting for winter—

The magazine is 35-40 pgs., 7×8½, photocopied from laser printed type and saddle-stapled with card cover, comes out twice a year, using nothing but poetry; circulation 200, with 100 subscriptions. They receive 600 submissions/year, use about 200, and generally have less than a 6-month backlog. Subscription: $6. **Sample postpaid: $3.50. Submit 3-5 poems anytime ("please do not submit a lone poem"). Simultaneous submissions OK. Send SASE for additional guidelines. Reports in 3 weeks or less. "Publication is payment," but they give 3 small prizes ($7, $5 and $3) for the best in each issue. Acquires first North American serial rights.** *Trilobite Broadsides*, included with each issue of *Manna*, use 3-10 published or unpublished poems, printed on a folded 8½×11 sheet. **Sample for a quarter and SASE. "Please provide acknowledgement for previously published works." Reports in less than 6 months. Author receives 25 copies.** They also sponsor an annual chapbook contest between January 1 and April 1. **Submit 24 published or unpublished poems. Entry fee: $7. Prize: 50 "high-quality, *handbound* copies" and $50. Sample postpaid: $6. Send SASE for details before submitting.** The editor advises, "Trust instinct and *write*. Submit poems that give your audience a unique vision. Use language and images worthy of that vision. Don't send sentimental love poetry."

MANNA; MANNA FORTY, INC. (I, IV-Nature/ecology, religion, spirituality/inspirational), Box 548, Rt. 1, Sharon OK 73857, phone (405)995-4906, founded 1986, literary format 1991, editor Richard D. Kahoe. As their "Mission Statement" says: "***manna***, a quarterly literary-professional journal, advances and publishes interests of manna forty, inc., a not-for-profit corporation. ***manna*** promotes ideals of a holistic view of truth and beauty, expressed in poetry, appropriate prose and pen sketches. It focuses on nature (natural living, ecology, environmental issues), religion (Christian and ecumenical) and psychology (and related sciences), and especially the interfaces of these areas." **They are open to all styles of poetry up to 50 lines. They want poetry related to religion, nature and psychology. "Prefer content integrating two or three of these areas. No mushy sentimentality, highly obscure verse or doggerel (except possibly in short humorous context)."** They have recently published poetry by C. David Hay, Marian Ford Park and Sheryl L. Nelms. As a sample the editor selected these lines from "Autumn Promenade" by Lowell Long:

Sumac shimmies without shame,
outrageous in her scarlet gown,
broad Catalpa hangs her head
above her shift of shapeless brown.

manna is 8 pgs., 8½×11, desktop-published and professionally printed on 70 lb. recycled stock, with line drawings. Press run is 400 for 50 subscribers of which 5 are libraries, 250 distributed free to community groups. Subscription: free ("donation encouraged"). **Sample available for 1 first-class stamp. "Contributors who can are asked (but not required) to make donation toward costs, generally $5-10, depending on length of poem." Previously published poems and simultaneous submissions OK. Cover letter required. "Prefer to receive 2-6 poems on separate pages, but we're not picky." Deadlines: February 15, May 15, August 15 and November 15. Publication appears one month later. Often comments on rejections. Publishes theme issues. Send SASE for guidelines and upcoming themes. Reports in 1-4 months. Pays "5 copies direct to poet, 10 we mail to addresses provided by poet. If contributor does not make donation, we reserve rights to 50% of subsequent cash income from the writing."** The editor says, "If the poem seems to fit our subject guidelines, send it to us and we'll give it full consideration. Beginners encouraged, but we prefer poems not to *sound* like beginners. We would like to see more traditional forms and light verse (humor)."

MANOA: A PACIFIC JOURNAL OF INTERNATIONAL WRITING (II), 1733 Donaghho Rd., Honolulu HI 96822, founded 1989, poetry editor Frank Stewart, appears twice a year. **"We are a general interest literary magazine, open to all forms and styles. We are not for the beginning writer, no matter what style. We are not interested in Pacific exotica."** They have published poetry by John Updike, Norman Dubie, Walter Pavlich and Eugene Ruggles. It is 200 pgs., 7×10, offset, flat-spined using art and graphics. They accept about 2% of 3,000 submissions received/year. Press run is 2,000 for 700 subscribers of which 30 are libraries, 700 shelf sales. Subscription: $18/year. **Sample postpaid: $10. Send SASE for guidelines. Reports in 6 weeks. Always sends prepublication galleys. Pay "competitive" plus 2 copies. Seldom comments on rejections.** They review current books and chapbooks of poetry. Open to unsolicited reviews. Poets may also send books for review consideration, attn. reviews editor. This magazine, one of the most exciting new journals in recent years, has become well known for the quality and diversity of its verse. It has also received a Design Excellence Award from the American Association of University Presses and Best Journal of the Year Award from the Council of Editors of Learned Journals. The editor says, "We welcome the opportunity to read poetry submissions from throughout the country. We are not a regional journal, but we do feature work from the Pacific Rim, national and international, especially in our reviews and essays. We are not interested in genre or formalist writing for its own sake, or picturesque impressions of the region."

‡MARK: A LITERARY JOURNAL (II), 2801 W. Bancroft SU2514, Toledo OH 43606, first appeared 1967-69, then resumed 1978, co-editors Carrie Fowler and Mike Donnelly, is an annual journal of fiction, poetry, photographs and sketches. **"We want politically responsible stuff."** As a sample the editors selected these lines from "Children" by Luis Alfredo Arango, translated by Preston Browning:

I saw a dead child buried in a pasteboard box.
(This is true and, oh, I can't forget it.)
On the side of the box
was written this slogan:

"General Electric Company.
Progress is Our Best Product."

Mark is digest-sized, 70 pgs., saddle-stapled, professionally printed, with matte card cover. Single copy: $3. **Reads submissions September 1 through January 31. Editor comments "very rarely." Pays 2 copies. Acquires first serial rights.**

MARYLAND POETRY REVIEW; MARYLAND STATE POETRY AND LITERARY SOCIETY (II), P.O. Drawer H, Catonsville MD 21228, founded 1985, edited by Rosemary Klein, "is interested in promoting the literary arts in Maryland as well as nationally and internationally. **We are interested in strong, thoughtful poetry with a slight bias to free verse. All submissions are read carefully.** ***MPR*** **is open to good poets who have not published extensively as well as to those who have."** They have published poetry by Celia Brown, Elisabeth Stevens, Enid Shomer and Joseph Somoza. As a sample the editor selected these lines from "The Fool's Dark Lantern" by Michael Fallon:

Like a fly that spins
in wounded circles on the sill
his thoughts revolve around a single thought:
there is only so much time
in which to know

MPR is professionally printed in small type on quality eggshell stock, 7×11, 75 pgs., saddle-stapled with a glossy b&w card cover. It appears twice a year in double issues (Spring/Summer and Fall/Winter). In the past they have done special issues on confessional, Irish, Hispanic and Australian poetry. Query about possible future special issues. Subscription and Maryland State Poetry and Literary Society membership is $17 ($12 for students and senior citizens; $20 for member and spouse; $25 for institutions). **Sample postpaid: $7. Submit no more than 5 poems at a time with brief bio. No simultaneous submissions. "We read submissions only in January, April and September but accept all year." Reports in 3-6 months. Pays 1 copy.** Book reviews are generally solicited. Send books for review consideration, attn. Robert Cooperman. MSPLS sponsors the Maryland State Poetry and Literary Society's Annual Poetry and Fiction Contest for poetry of any length and fiction to 2,500 words. Entry fee: $3/poem or four for $10, $3/story. Contest runs from January 1 through May 31. Cash prizes and magazine publication. They also sponsor the Michael Egan Memorial Poetry Contest for poetry of any length. Entry fee: $3/poem. Contest runs from September 1 through October 28. Cash prizes and magazine publication. Send SASE for guidelines.

THE UNIVERSITY OF MASSACHUSETTS PRESS; THE JUNIPER PRIZE (II), P.O. Box 429, Amherst MA 01004-0429, phone (413)545-2217, founded 1964. The press offers an annual competition for the Juniper Prize, in alternate years to first and subsequent books. In 1995 only "first books" will be considered: mss by writers whose poems have appeared in literary journals and/or anthologies but have not been published, or been accepted for publication, in book form. In 1996 the prize is for a subsequent book: mss whose authors have had at least one full-length book or chapbook of poetry published or accepted for publication. **Submissions should be approximately 60 pgs. in typescript (generally 50-55 poems). Include paginated contents page. A list of poems published in literary journals and/or anthologies must also accompany the ms. Such poems may be included in the ms and must be identified. "Mss by more than one author, entries of more than one ms simultaneously or within the same year and translations are not eligible." Entry fee: $10 plus SASE for return of ms or notification. Entries must be postmarked not later than September 30.** The award is announced in April/May and publication is scheduled for spring. The amount of the prize is $1,000 and is in lieu of royalties on the first print run. **Send SASE for guidelines and/or further information.**

THE MASSACHUSETTS REVIEW (II), Memorial Hall, University of Massachusetts, Amherst MA 01003, founded 1959, editors Paul Jenkins and Anne Halley. Mostly free verse, all lengths and topics, appears here, with emphasis in recent issues on narrative work. An interesting feature: Editors run poems with long-line lengths in smaller type, to fit on the page without typographical interruption (as in other journals). They have published poetry by Marge Piercy, Michael Benedikt and Eavan Boland. The editors describe this quarterly as offset (some color used in art sections), 6×9. They receive about 2,500 poems a year, use about 50. Press run is 1,600 for 1,100-1,200 subscribers of which 1,000 are libraries, the rest for shelf sales. Subscription: $15 (US), $20 outside US, $17 for libraries. **Sample postpaid: $5.75. No simultaneous submissions or previously published poems. Read submissions October 1 through June 1 only. Send SASE for guidelines. Reports in 6 weeks. Pays minimum of $10, or 35¢/line, plus 2 copies.**

MATRIX (IV-Regional), Box 100, Ste. Anne de Bellevue, Quebec H9X 3L4 Canada, founded 1975, is a literary publication appearing 3 times a year using **quality poetry by Canadians without restriction as to form, length, style, subject matter or purpose.** They have published poetry by George Elliott Clarke, Joy Kogawa, David McFadden, Carolyn Smart and Douglas Barbour. There are 5-8 pgs. of poetry in each issue. The magazine is 8½×11, 80 pgs., stapled, professionally printed, glossy cover with full-color art and graphics. They receive about 500 submissions/year, use 20-30, have a 6-month backlog. Circulation 2,000. Subscription: $15 Canadian, $20 international. **Sample postpaid: $10 (Canadian funds). Submit 6-10 poems. No simultaneous submissions. Reports in 3 months. Pays $10-40/poem. Editor sometimes comments on rejections.** Reviews books of poetry. Send books for review consideration, marked "Review copy."

‡MATTOID (II), School of Literature & Journalism, Deakin University, Geelong, Victoria, Australia 3217, founded 1977, Dr. Brian Edwards, appears 3 times/year. **"No special requirements but interesting complexity, quality, experimentation. No naive rhyming verse."** They have published poetry by Lauris Edmond, Kevin Hart and Judith Rodriguez. It is 200 pgs., flat-spined with 2-color cover. They publish about 10-15% of 800 poems received/year. Press run is 600 for 400 subscribers of which 10 are libraries, 30-50 shelf sales. **Sample postpaid: $10 overseas. Publishes theme issues. Send SASE (or SAE and IRC) for upcoming themes. Reports in 2-3 months. Pays 2 copies.** Reviews books of poetry in 1,000-2,000 words, single format.

MATURE YEARS (IV-Senior citizen, religious), P.O. Box 801, 201 Eighth Ave. South, Nashville TN 37202, phone (615)749-6292, founded 1954, editor Marvin W. Cropsey, is a quarterly. "The magazine's purpose is to help persons understand and use the resources of Christian faith in dealing with specific opportunities and problems related to aging. **Poems are usually limited to fifteen lines and may, or may not, be overtly religious. Poems should not poke fun at older adults, but may take a humorous look at them. Avoid sentimentality and saccarine. If using rhymes and meter, make sure they are accurate."** As a sample the editor selected these lines by Carole Johnston:

What is winter
but a large and cold
secret that somehow
keeps me warm . . . for
I know where sweet
daffodils lie sleeping.
I know the graves of
six brave crocuses
and the tulip colors
of next spring.

It is 100 pgs., magazine-sized, saddle-stapled, with full-color glossy paper cover. Circulation 80,000. **Sample postpaid: $3.50. Submit season and nature poems for spring during December through February; for summer, March through May; for fall, June through August; and for winter, September through November. Send SASE for guidelines. Reports in 2 months, a year's delay before publication. Pays 50¢-$1/line upon acceptance.**

THE MAVERICK PRESS (II, IV-Regional), Rt. 2 Box 4915, Eagle Pass TX 78852, phone (210)773-1836, founded 1991, editor Carol Cullar, publishes a biannual of "outstanding Texas writers and other mavericks whose works represent the contemporary scene. Each issue is individually named (i.e., the November 1993 issue was titled *Horny Toad*)." They are **looking for "strong, uncluttered figurative language to 100 lines. No diatribes on current events or political posturings, no smut."** They have recently published poetry by Crawdad Nelson, Jeffery DeLotto, Tess Lecuyer and Lois Hershkowitz. As a sample the editor selected these lines from "in what image" by Will Inman:

shaking its flaming seedpods,
its fanged jaws,
chattering with the charged silence
of the great serpent, what muscular river
down the dark tongue of god

The editor says it is 74 pgs., 5½×8½, saddle-stapled. Cover is an original block print by the editor, inside illustrations include b&w line drawings or block prints by contributors. They receive 1,000-2,000 poems a year, accept 4-8%. Press run is 250 for 100 subscribers of which 12 are libraries, 120 shelf sales. Subscription: $13.50. **Sample postpaid: $7.50. No previously published poems; simultaneous submissions OK with notification up front and a phone call if ms is accepted elsewhere. Cover letter with brief bio required. Submit up to 5 poems. "Author's name and address must appear on every page submitted. Prefer standard size paper and envelopes 6×9 or larger."** Time between acceptance and publication is a year and a half maximum. **"All entries are sorted into Texans/Non-Texans, then read impartially. Outstanding pieces are reread and resorted later with slight consideration made to Texas writers. Final selections are made after consultation with Rio Bravo Literary Arts Council." Often comments on rejections. Criticism provided, if requested. Fee negotiated on a job-by-job basis, minimum $25. Publishes one theme issue each year. Send SASE for guidelines and upcoming themes. Theme for November 1994: "Bangs & Whimpers" (endings of all sorts). Title for April 1995: "Wild Turkey." Reports**

in 6-8 weeks. Sometimes sends prepublication galleys. Pays 2 copies. "All rights retained by authors." The editor says, "We are looking for strong, uncluttered, figurative language and prefer free verse, although the exception is considered. I would like to see more poems that 'push the envelope'—test the limits of what is poetic. Main criterion is excellence. Beginners: Presentation is important, but content is paramount."

MAYAPPLE PRESS (III, IV-Regional, women), P.O. Box 5473, Saginaw MI 48603-0473, phone (517)793-2801, founded 1978, publisher/editor Judith Kerman, publishes **"women's poetry, Great Lakes regional poetry"** in chapbooks. They want **"quality contemporary poetry rooted in real experience and strongly crafted. No greeting card verse, sentimental or conventional poetry."** They have published chapbooks by Judith Minty, Evelyn Wexler and Toni Ortner-Zimmerman. **Query with 5-6 samples. Check *Poets & Writers* for open times.** "We are not likely to publish unless poet accepts a *primary* role in distribution. Reality is only poets themselves can sell unknown work." **Usually sends prepublication galleys. Pays 5% of run. Publishes on "cooperative" basis.** "Generally poet agrees to purchase most of the run at 50% of cover price." **Editor "sometimes comments (very briefly)" on rejections.** She says, "Poets must create the audience for their work. No small press 'white knight' can make an unknown famous (or even sell more than a few books!)."

‡MEDIPHORS (I, II, IV-Specialized: medicine/health-related), P.O. Box 327, Bloomsburg PA 17815, founded 1992, editor Eugene D. Radice, M.D. ***Mediphors*** is a biannual literary journal of the health professions that publishes literary work in medicine and health, including poetry, short story, humor, essay, drawing, art/photography. **They want poetry related to medicine and health; 30 lines maximum.** As a sample the editor selected these lines from "The Horn of Africa" by Michael H. Lythgoe:

In the villages, voices long dehydrated,
Grope to compose lyrical lines,
Rumors of virtues among the villainy.
Oral poems trickle as a serum,
Sustaining drips
Of life for skin and bones.

Mediphors is 65 pgs., 8½×11, offset and saddle-stapled with color cover and b&w art, graphics and photos throughout. They receive about 750 poetry submissions a year, accept approximately 100. Press run is 600 for 175 subscribers of which 20 are libraries, 200 shelf sales. Single copy: $6.50; subscription: $12. **Sample postpaid: $5. Submit "2 copies of each poem that we can keep." No previously published poems or simultaneous submissions. Cover letter not required "but helpful."** Time between acceptance and publication is 10-12 months. **Seldom comments on rejections. Send SASE for guidelines. Reports in 1-3 months. Pays 2 copies. Acquires first North American serial rights.** The editor says, "Our goal is to place in print as many new authors as possible, particularly those working within the health/medical fields (such as doctors, nurses, technologists, therapists, etc.). We encourage unsolicited manuscripts."

THE EDWIN MELLEN PRESS (II), P.O. Box 450, Lewiston NY 14092, phone (716)754-2266, founded 1973, poetry editor Patricia Schultz, is a scholarly press. "We do not have access to large chain bookstores for distribution, but depend on direct sales and independent bookstores." **They pay 2 copies, no royalties. "We require no author subsidies. However, we encourage our authors to seek grants from Councils for the Arts and other foundations because these add to the reputation of the volume." They want "original integrated work—living unity of poems, preferably unpublished, encompassable in one reading."** They have published poetry by W.R. Elton and Albert Cook. Their books are 64 pgs., 6×9, softcover binding, no graphics. Price $12.95. **Submit 40 or more sample poems with cover letter including bio, publications. "We do not print until we receive at least 100 prepaid orders. Successful marketing of poetry books depends on the author's active involvement.** We send out up to 15 free review copies to journals or newspapers, the names of which may be suggested by the author. Authors may purchase more copies of their book (above the 2 free copies provided) at the same 20% discount (for quantities of 10 or more) which we allow to bookstores. An author may (but is not required to) purchase books to make up the needed 100 prepublication sales." The editor says, "We seek to publish volumes unified in mood, tone, theme—most poets try to include too much within one volume."

‡MEN AS WE ARE (II, IV-Specialized), P.O. Box 150615, Brooklyn NY 11215-0007, phone and fax (718)499-2829, founded 1991, editor-in-chief Jonathan Running Wind, is a quarterly of fiction, poetry, essays, commentary, art, reviews and photography designed to nurture "self-acceptance and transformation of men. **All forms of poetry welcome. Subject must be some aspect of the male experience, but from any perspective."** They have recently published poetry by Timothy Walsh and David Thorn. As a sample the editor selected these lines from "The Overthrow of Despair" by Jim Sorcic:

Each breath is a rosary
of desire, a prayer

for the overthrow of despair.
There are times
When I breathe, it seems
a small sound, a found voice
erupts, crying for
forgiveness.

The editor says ***Men As We Are*** is 40 pgs., 8¼ × 10⅞ offset, saddle-stitched, self-cover, with lots of art and graphics, 10% ads. They receive about 400 submissions a year, accept approximately 4%. Press run is 1,000 for 200 subscribers, 800 shelf sale. Single copy: $3; subscription: $12. **Sample postpaid: $3.98. Previously published poems and simultaneous submissions OK. Cover letter required; include brief bio and "note where you heard about us."** Time between acceptance and publication is 3-6 months. **Sometimes comments on rejections. Send SASE for guidelines. Reports in 3-6 months. Pays 3-5 copies. Acquires first North American serial or reprint rights and non-exclusive anthology rights.** Reviews books of poetry in 300-500 words. Open to unsolicited reviews. Poets may also send books for review consideration.

MENNONITE PUBLISHING HOUSE; PURPOSE; STORY FRIENDS; ON THE LINE; WITH (IV-Religious, children), 616 Walnut Ave., Scottdale PA 15683-1999, phone (412)887-8500. **Send submissions or queries directly to the editor of the specific magazine at address indicated.** The official publisher for the Mennonite Church in North America seeks also to serve a broad Christian audience. **Each of the magazines listed has different specifications, and the editor of each should be queried for more exact information.** ***Purpose***, editor James E. Horsch, a "monthly in weekly parts," circulation 17,500, is **for adults of all ages, its focus: "action oriented, discipleship living."** It is 5⅜ × 8⅜, with two-color printing throughout. **They buy appropriate poetry up to 12 lines.** ***Purpose*** uses 3-4 poems/week, receives about 2,000/year of which they use 150, has a 10- to 12-week backlog. **Send SASE for guidelines and free sample. Mss should be typewritten, double-spaced, one side of sheet only. Simultaneous submissions OK. Reports in 6-8 weeks. Pays $5-15/poem plus 2 copies.** ***On the Line***, edited by Mary C. Meyer, another "monthly in weekly parts," is **for children 10-14**, a "story paper that reinforces Christian values," circulation 8,500. It is 7 × 10, saddle-stapled, with 2-color printing on the cover and inside, using art and photos. **Sample free with SASE. Wants poems 3-24 lines. Submit "as many as desired, but each should be typed on a separate 8 × 11½ sheet." Simultaneous submissions and previously published poems OK. Reports in 1 month. Pays $5-15/poem plus 2 copies.** ***Story Friends***, edited by Marjorie Waybill, is for **children 4-9**, a "story paper that reinforces Christian values," also a "monthly in weekly issues," circulation 9,000, uses poems **3-12 lines. Send SASE for guidelines/sample copy. Pays $5-10.** ***With***, Editorial Team, Box 347, Newton KS 67114, phone (316)238-5100, is for **"senior highs, ages 15-18,"** focusing on helping "high school youth make a commitment to Christ in the context of the church amidst the complex and conflicting values they encounter in their world," circulation 6,100, uses **poetry dealing with youth in relation to their world, nature and light verse. Poems should be 4-50 lines. Pays $10-25.**

MERLYN'S PEN: THE NATIONAL MAGAZINES OF STUDENT WRITING, GRADES 6-12 (IV-Students, young adults), Dept. PM, Box 1058, East Greenwich RI 02818, phone (800)247-2027, founded 1985, editor R. Jim Stahl, one for grades 6-9, the other ('senior edition') for grades 9-12. Each edition is 40 pgs., magazine-sized, professionally printed with glossy paper, color cover. Press run is 35,000 for 30,000 subscriptions of which 5,000 are libraries. Subscription: $18.95. **Sample postpaid: $3. Send SASE for guidelines. Reports in 3 months. Pays 3 copies.**

METAMORPHOUS PRESS (V), P.O. Box 10616, Portland OR 97210-0616, phone (503)228-4972, founded 1982, publishes and distributes books, cassettes and videotapes on **neurolinguistic programming,** health and healing education, business and sales, women's studies, and children's books. **They currently do not accept unsolicited poetry.**

METRO SINGLES LIFESTYLES (I), Box 28203, Kansas City MO 64118, phone (816)436-8424, founded 1984, editor Robert L. Huffstutter. ***MSL*** is a tabloid publication for women and men of all ages: single, divorced, widowed or never-married. Not a lonely hearts type of publication, but positive and upbeat, it is published 6 times/year and has a circulation of 25,000 (approximately 5,000 subscribers in Kansas City and throughout the USA), newsstand, bookstore sales and limited complimentary copies to clubs, organizations and singles groups. Interested in seeing **"free verse, lite verse, philosophical, romantic, sentimental and Frost-type poetry. All subjects considered."** They have published poetry by Patricia Castle, Milton Kerr and Mary Ann McDonnell. As a sample, the editor selected these lines from "The Women of Cairo" by Phillip Slattery:

Eyes made of the Egyptian night
Sparkling like an oasis pool
Skin the color of the endless sand
Beauty of forgotten goddesses lives on.

Each issue is about 36 pgs. and printed on Webb Offset press. Each issue features at least 12 poems by poets living throughout the USA. "Poets are invited to send a photo and a brief paragraph about their goals, single status and lifestyle. This is optional and does not influence selection of poetry, but does add interest to the publication when space for this extra feature permits." **Sample copy of current issue is $3 postpaid. Ms should be typewritten, double-spaced or written in easy-to-read format. "Prefer to look at original poetry. No simultaneous or previously published work." Reports in 6-8 weeks. Pays from $5/poem or in subscriptions plus complimentary copies.** The editor says, "We do not limit or restrict subject of poems, but insist they convey an emotion, experience or exercise the reader's imagination."

MICHIGAN QUARTERLY REVIEW (III), Dept. PM, 3032 Rackham Bldg., University of Michigan, Ann Arbor MI 48109, phone (313)764-9265, founded 1962, editor-in-chief Laurence Goldstein, is "an interdisciplinary, general interest academic journal that publishes mainly essays and reviews on subjects of cultural and literary interest." They use **all kinds of poetry except light verse. No specifications as to form, length, style, subject matter or purpose.** Poets they have published include Tess Gallagher, Robert Hass, Amy Gerstler and Cathy Song. As a sample the editor chose these lines by Donald Hall:

Daylilies go from the hill; asters return; maples redden again
as summer departs for winter's virtuous deprivation.
When we stroll the Pond Road at nightfall, western sun stripes
down through dust raised by a pickup ten minutes ago:
vertical birches, hilly road, sunlight slant and descending.

The ***Review*** is 6×9, 160 pgs., flat-spined, professionally printed with glossy card cover, b&w photos and art, has a circulation of 2,000, with 1,500 subscriptions of which half are libraries. They receive 1,500 submissions/year, use 30, have a 1-year backlog. Single copy: $5; subscription: $18. **Sample postpaid: $2.50. They prefer typed mss. Publishes theme issues. For example, the Fall 1995/Winter 1996 issue will be a double issue on the "100th Anniversary of Motion Pictures." Reports in 4-6 weeks. Always sends prepublication galleys. Pays $8-12/page. Buys first rights only.** Reviews books of poetry. "All reviews are commissioned." Poetry published in the ***Michigan Quarterly Review*** was also selected for inclusion in the 1992 and 1994 volumes of **The Best American Poetry.** Laurence Goldstein advises, "There is no substitute for omnivorous reading and careful study of poets past and present, as well as reading in new and old areas of knowledge. Attention to technique, especially to rhythm and patterns of imagery, is vital."

MID-AMERICAN REVIEW; JAMES WRIGHT PRIZE FOR POETRY (II, IV-Translations), Dept. of English, Bowling Green State University, Bowling Green OH 43403, phone (419)372-2725, founded 1980, editor-in-chief George Looney, poetry editor Doug Martin, appears twice a year. **"Poetry should emanate from strong, evocative images; use fresh, interesting language; and have a consistent sense of voice. Each line must carry the poem, and an individual vision should be evident. We encourage new as well as established writers. There is no length limit."** They have recently published poetry by Stephen Dunn, Catherine Sasanov, Silvia Curbelo, Mark Doty, Fleda Brown Jackson, Pat Mora, Frankie Paino and Ronald Wallace. The following lines are the closing of "Hopalong Cassidy" by Dionisio D. Martinez:

West, she says, is what you tell
yourself when every word has lost its name.

West is where you go when you run out of sky.

The review is 200 pgs., flat-spined, offset printed, using line drawings, laminated card cover. They receive over 1,000 mss a year, use 60-80 poems. Press run is 1,000. Single copy: $7; subscription: $12. **Sample postpaid: $5. Reads submissions September 1 through May 30 only. Send SASE for guidelines. Sometimes sends prepublication galleys. Pays $10/printed page plus 2 copies. Rights revert to authors on publication.** Reviews books of poetry. Open to unsolicited reviews. Poets may also send books to Andrea Van Vorhis, reviews editor, for review consideration. **They also publish chapbooks in translation. *MAR*** awards the James Wright Prize for Poetry to a ms published in its regular editions, when funding is available.

MIDDLE EAST REPORT (IV-Regional, ethnic, themes), Suite 119, 1500 Massachusetts Ave. NW, Washington DC 20005, phone (202)223-3677, founded 1971, editor Joe Stork, is "a magazine on contemporary political, economic, cultural and social developments in the Middle East and North Africa and U.S. policy toward the region. We occasionally publish **poetry that addresses political or social issues of Middle Eastern peoples."** They have published poetry by Dan Almagor (Israeli) and Etel Adnan (Lebanese). It is 48 pgs., magazine-sized, saddle-stapled, professionally printed on glossy stock with glossy paper cover, 6 issues/year. Press run is 7,500. "We published 9 poems last year, all solicited." Subscription: $25. **Sample postpaid: $6 domestic; $8 airmail overseas. Simultaneous submissions and previously published poems OK. Reports in 6-8 weeks. "We key poetry to the theme**

of a particular issue. Could be as long as 6 months between acceptance and publication." Editor sometimes comments on submissions. Pays 3 copies.

‡MIDLAND REVIEW (II), English Dept., Morrill Hall, Oklahoma State University, Stillwater OK 74078, phone (405)744-9474, founded 1985, is a literary annual that publishes "poetry, fiction, essays, ethnic, experimental, women's work, contemporary feminist." The editors say, **"style and form are open." They do not want "long or religious poetry."** They have recently published poetry by Amy Clampitt, William Stafford, Bill Knott, Tom Lux and Richard Kostelanetz. As a sample, the editors selected these lines by James Doyle:

The pressured houses squat
beneath a black sky. Smoke
passes back and forth between
them down the street. Gilled
animals swim the thin odors
home, calling themselves planets . . .

Midland Review is 100-120 pgs., digest-sized, with photography, artwork and ads. Circulation is 500, of which 470 are subscriptions. Single copy: $6. **Sample postpaid: $5. Writers should submit 3-5 poems, typed ms in any form. "We no longer read during the summer (May 1 through August 31)." Reporting time is 3-6 months and time to publication 6-12 months. Pays 1 copy.**

MIDSTREAM: A MONTHLY JEWISH REVIEW (IV-Ethnic), 110 E. 59th St., New York NY 10022, phone (212)339-6021, editor Joel Carmichael, associate editor M.S. Solow, is a national journal appearing monthly except February/March, June/July and August/September, when it is bimonthly. They want **short poems with Jewish themes or atmosphere.** They have published poetry by Yehuda Amichai, James Reiss, Abraham Sutzkever, Liz Rosenberg and John Hollander. The magazine is 48 pgs., approximately 8½ × 11, saddle-stapled with colored card cover. Each issue includes 4 to 5 poems (which tend to be short, lyric and freestyle expressing cogent ideas). They receive about 300 submissions/year, use 5-10%. Circulation: 10,000. Single copy: $3; subscription: $21. **Reports in 1 month. Pays $25/poem. Buys all rights.**

MIDWEST POETRY REVIEW; MIDWEST POETRY LIBRARY SERIES; RIVER CITY PUBLICATIONS (IV-Subscribers), P.O. Box 4776, Rock Island IL 61201, founded 1980, poetry editors Tom Tilford, Grace Keller and Jillian Roth, is a "subscriber-only" quarterly, with no other support than subscriptions—that is, **only subscribers may submit poetry and/or enter their contests. Subscribers may also get help and criticism on 1 poem/month.** "We are attempting to encourage the cause of poetry and raise the level thereof by giving aid to new poets, to poets who have lapsed in their writing and to poets who desire a wider market, by purchasing the best of modern poetry and giving it exposure through our quarterly magazine. We want **poetry from poets who feel they have a contribution to make to the reader relating to the human condition, nature and the environment. Serious writers only are sought. No jingly verses or limericks. No restrictions as to form, length or style. Any subject is considered, if handled with skill and taste."** They have published poetry by Tom McFadden, John Thomas Baker, B.R. Culbertson, Martin Musick, Nancy Graham and Maude Paro. One of their latest features is The Festival of States salute to poets. Each issue features the poets of a selected state writing about natural beauties, historical features and heroes of that state. Kimberly Courtright, in her poem "Drought," writes of California:

Each slow and
snowless month-to-a-minute
day lies sluggish on
brittle hills where grass no longer
grows (the clouds are
Ebenezer-stingy here).

The digest-sized, saddle-stapled magazine is 52 pgs., professionally printed in various type styles, with matte card cover and some b&w art. They have quarterly and annual contests plus varied contests in each issue, with prizes ranging from $25-500 (the latter for the annual contest), with "unbiased, non-staff judges for all competitions. Paid-up subscribers enter the contests with fees." **Sample postpaid: $5. Subscription fee of $20 ($25 Canadian, $30 foreign, both in US funds) must accompany first submission. Send SASE and $1 for guidelines. Reports in 2 weeks. Pays $5-500/poem. Buys first rights.** Staff reviews books of poetry in 400 words. Send books for review consideration. They are currently embarking on a project to publish subscribers' chapbooks under the auspices of the Midwest Poetry Library Series. They say, "The books will have matching covers, for an attractive shelf display. Poets will retain full editorial control and copyright but may benefit from the advice and help of the editorial staff. Books will be listed for sale in the magazine's register which will appear in each issue." ***Midwest Poetry Review*** ranked #7 in the "Nontraditional Verse" category of the latest ***Writer's Digest*** Poetry 60 list. Tom Tilford advises, "We are interested in serious poets, whether new or published. We will help those who wish to consider serious criticism and attempt to improve themselves. We want to see the poet improve, expand and achieve fulfillment." He has developed a 20-point Self-Analysis Survey to assist poets in analyzing their own work. It is offered free to subscribers.

THE MIDWEST QUARTERLY (II), Pittsburg State University, Pittsburg KS 66762, phone (316)235-4689, founded 1959, poetry editor Stephen Meats, "publishes articles on any subject of contemporary interest, particularly literary criticism, political science, philosophy, education, biography and sociology, and each issue contains a **section of poetry from 10-30 pages in length.** I am interested in **well-crafted, though not necessarily traditional poems that see nature and the self in bold, surrealistic images of a writer's imaginative, mystical experience of the world. 60 lines or less (occasionally longer if exceptional).**" They have recently published poetry by Charles Bukowski, Marguerite Bouvard, Jared Carter, Lyn Lifshin, Jeanne Murray Walker and Greg Kuzma. As a sample the editor selected these lines from "Resurrection" by Andrea Moorhead:

tear the ice from dirt
the arms from stone
electric and cold
when the voice runs along the ground
murmuring in the soil, murmuring along the bent cut wood.

The magazine is 130 pgs., digest-sized, flat-spined, matte cover, professionally printed. A nice mix of poems appears here, most of it free verse with room for an occasional formal or narrative piece. Circulation is 650, with 600 subscriptions of which 500 are libraries. They receive approximately 4,200 poems annually; publish 60. "My plan is to publish all acceptances within 1 year." Subscription: $12. **Sample: $3. Mss should be typed with poet's name on each page, 10 poems or fewer. Simultaneous submissions accepted. Publishes theme issues occasionally. Reports in 1 month, usually sooner. "Submissions without SASE cannot be acknowledged." Pays 3 copies. Acquires first serial rights. Editor comments on rejections "if the poet or poems seem particularly promising."** Reviews books of poetry by *MQ* published poets only. He says, "Keep writing; read as much contemporary poetry as you can lay your hands on; don't let the discouragement of rejection keep you from sending your work out to editors."

MIDWIFERY TODAY (IV-Specialized: Childbirth), P.O. Box 2672, Eugene OR 97402, phone (503)344-7438, founded 1986, editor Jan Tritten, is a quarterly that "provides a voice for midwives and childbirth educators. **We are a midwifery magazine. Subject must be birth or profession related." They do not want poetry that is "off subject or puts down the subject."** As a sample the editor selected these lines by Karen Hope Ehrlich:

you get to keep the baby
not the midwife
she is a fickle lover
merged and passing

MT is 52 pgs., approximately 8½×11, offset, saddle-stapled, with glossy card cover with b&w photo and b&w photos, artwork and ads inside. They use about 1 poem/issue. Press run is 3,000 for 1,500 subscribers, 1,000 shelf sales. Subscription: $30. **Sample postpaid: $7.50. No previously published poems or simultaneous submissions. Cover letter required.** Time between acceptance and publication is 1-2 years. **Seldom comments on rejections. Publishes theme issues. Send SASE for writer's guidelines and upcoming themes. Reports in 2-6 weeks. Pays 2 copies. Acquires first rights.** The editor says, "With our publication *please* stay on the subject."

MILKWEED EDITIONS (II), Suite 400, 430 First Ave. N., Minneapolis MN 55401, phone (612)332-3192, founded 1979, poetry editor Emilie Buchwald. Three collections published annually. **Unsolicited mss are only accepted from writers who have previously published a book-length collection of poetry or a minimum of 10 poems in commercial or literary journals.** One of the leading literary presses in the country, Milkweed publishes some of the best poets composing today in well-made, attractively designed collections. Recent books of poetry include: **The Phoenix Gone, The Terrace Empty** by Marilyn Chin; **Firekeeper** by Pattiann Rogers; and **Paul Bunyan's Bearskin** by Patricia Goedicke. **Unsolicited mss read in June and January; please include return postage.** Catalog available on request, with 74¢ in postage.

MIND IN MOTION: A MAGAZINE OF POETRY AND SHORT PROSE (I, II), P.O. Box 1118, Apple Valley CA 92307, phone (619)248-6512, founded 1985, a quarterly, editor Céleste Goyer, wants **poetry "15-60 lines. Explosive, provocative. Images not clichéd but directly conveyant of the point of the poem. Use of free association particularly desired. We encourage free verse, keeping in mind the essential elements of rhythm and rhyme. Traditional forms are acceptable if within length restrictions. Meaning should be implicit, as in the styles of Blake, Poe, Coleridge, Stephen Crane, Emily Dickinson, Leonard Cohen. Submit in batches of 5-6. Not interested in sentimentality, emotionalism, simplistic nature worship, explicit references."** She has recently published poetry by Robert E. Brimhall, Kenneth Lamb, Michael Swofford, Rose Rosberg and Jennifer E. Balogh. As a sample she selected these lines from "Command Performance" (poet unidentified):

Objects drop up not down
not even a circle is round
donkeys wear the crowns.

Darkness obliterates light
ignorance invades insight
wrongs overpower the right.

MIM is 54 pgs., digest-sized, saddle-stapled, photocopied from photoreduced typescript with a heavy matte cover with b&w drawing. Of approximately 2,400 poems/year she accepts about 200. Press run is 525 for 350 subscribers. Subscription: $14. **Sample postpaid: $3.50 (overseas: $4.50, $18/year). Unpublished works only. Simultaneous submissions OK if notified. "Please have name and address on each poem. We also use dates of composition; it would help if these were provided with submissions." Editor usually comments on rejected mss. Send SASE for guidelines. Reports in 1-6 weeks. Pays 1 copy "when financially possible." Magazine is copyrighted; all rights revert to author.**

MIND MATTERS REVIEW (III), #234, 2040 Polk St., San Francisco CA 94109, founded 1988, editor Carrie Drake, poetry editor Lorraine A. Donfor **(and submissions should be sent directly to her at 2837 Blue Spruce Lane, Silver Spring MD 20906)**, is a **"literary quarterly with emphasis on use of science as a tool for responsible organization of information;** analysis of the role of language in consciousness, knowledge and intelligence; and social criticism particularly of metaphysics. Also includes book reviews, poetry, short stories, art and essays." They want **"short poems for fillers. Would like to see inspirational poetry; but open to satire and contemporary subjects that reflect the struggle between the 'inner voice' and external pressures. Rhythm important, but rhyme isn't."** They have recently published poetry by Terry Williams, Charles Corry, T.N. Turner, Michael Edward Burczynski and Simon Perchik. As a sample the editor selected these lines from "Instant War" by Daniel Green:

History books record too late
the failures of diplomats
battles fought on city streets.
Wars concluded where all are losers.
Few, if any, read the books.

MMR is magazine-sized, desktop-published, includes graphics, sketches, b&w photos. Subscription: $15 US, $20 foreign. **Sample postpaid: $3.50. Poets are encouraged to buy a copy before submitting. Simultaneous submissions and previously published poems OK. Cover letter required; include publishing credits and note if submissions have been previously published or accepted for publication elsewhere. Send SASE for guidelines. Sometimes sends prepublication galleys. Pays 1 copy.** Staff reviews books of poetry. Send books for review consideration to David Castleman, 512 Tamalpais Dr., Mill Valley CA 94941. The editor says, "Poetry should reflect the deeper layers of consciousness, its perceptions, observations, joys and sorrows; should reflect the independence of the individual spirit. Should not be 'trendy' or 'poetic' in a forced way."

THE MINNESOTA REVIEW (II), English Dept., East Carolina University, Greenville NC 27858-4353, phone (919)757-6388, founded 1960, editor Jeffrey Williams, poetry editor Rebecca Wee, is a biannual literary magazine wanting **"poetry which explores some aspect of social or political issues and/or the nature of relationships. No nature poems, and no lyric poetry without the above focus."** As a sample the editors selected these lines from "What Keeps Me Here" by Margaret Lloyd:

What keeps me here is not
the light on leaves outside my window

beautiful as I can see it is,
or the thrumming of crickets

in the wet grass of late summer.
Not adult love, not the past.

But that flesh, that flesh
I put my arm across in bed

this morning, my small son,
and the round face of my daughter.

TMR is 200 pgs., digest-sized, flat-spined, with b&w glossy card cover and art. Mostly free verse (lyric and narrative), poems here tend to have strong themes and powerful content, perhaps to coincide with the magazine's subtitle: "a journal of committed writing." Circulation: 2,500 for

1,500 subscriptions. Subscription: $12 to individuals, $24 to institutions. **Sample postpaid: $7.50. Cover letter including "brief intro with address" preferred with submissions. Publishes theme issues. Send SASE for upcoming themes. Themes for Spring 1995 and Fall 1995 are "The White Issue" and "The Class Story," respectively. Reports in 2-4 months. Pays 2 copies. Acquires all rights. Returns rights upon request.** Reviews books of poetry in single or multi-book format. Open to unsolicited reviews.

MINORITY LITERARY EXPO (IV-Membership, ethnic), 216 Avenue T, Pratt City, Birmingham AL 35214, phone (205)798-9083, founded 1990, editor/publisher Kervin Fondren, is an annual literary professional publication featuring minority poets, novices and professionals. **"Organization membership open to all minority poets nationally. I want poems from minority poets that are holistic and wholesome, less than 24 lines each, no vulgar or hate poetry accepted, any style, any form, any subject matter. Poetry that expresses holistic views and philosophies is very acceptable. Literary value is emphasized. Selected poets receive financial awards, certificates, honorable mentions, critiques and special poetic honors." No fee is charged for inclusion.** As a sample the editor selected these lines from his poem "Rain and Pain":

Do I Dare
As A Man
Dance in My Backyard
In the Rain

An annual national literary expo, implemented in Birmingham, Alabama, features many entertainers, stars, health fairs, health runs, writing and poetry workshops, concerts, etc. Write for details. They also sponsor an annual poetry chapbook contest and an annual "Analyze the Poem" contest. Send SASE for details. ***Minority Literary Expo*** ranked #7 in the "New Poets" category of the latest ***Writer's Digest*** Poetry 60 list. This category ranks those markets who often publish poets whose work is new to their publication.

MINOTAUR PRESS; MINOTAUR (II), #11, 95 Harbormaster Rd., S. San Francisco CA 94080, founded 1974, editor Jim Gove. ***Minotaur*** is a "small press literary quarterly **with emphasis on contemporary and experimental styles. Must be relevant. No rhymed and/or traditional verse."** They have published poetry by Judson Crews, Ed Mycue and Julia Vinograd. As a sample the editor selected these lines from "For Jack Spicer" by William Talcott:

No one listens to poetry
Jack Spicer.
Salt & Pepper
Are just another passida laugh
in the mashed potatoes

The editor describes it as digest-sized, perfect-bound, photocopied, "stock cover—cover graphics—sometimes use interior graphics, but rarely." They publish about 12 of 100 poems received. Press run is 400 for 300 subscribers of which 50 are libraries. Subscription: $18. **Sample postpaid: $3.50. Send SASE for guidelines. Submit 4-8 poems with name and address on each page. Always sends prepublication galleys. Pays 1 copy. "You do not need to subscribe to be published." Editor comments on submissions "if requested only."** Open to unsolicited reviews. Minotaur Press publishes a "Back to Back" chapbook with each issue. **Chapbook mss are selected from regular magazine contributors only. Pays 40 copies.** The editor says, "Subscribe to the magazines that publish your work. Few poetry magazines run in the black. We would like to see more experimental, leading edge, borderline (but no language) poetry."

MIORITA: A JOURNAL OF ROMANIAN STUDIES (IV-Ethnic), Dept. of Linguistics, University of Rochester, Rochester NY 14627, is an irregular scholarly publication, 100 pgs., digest-sized, circulation 200, focusing on **Romanian culture and using some poetry by Romanians or on Romanian themes. Sample: $5. Pays copies.** Reviews books of poetry "occasionally; must be Romanian-connected."

THE MIRACULOUS MEDAL (IV-Religious), 475 E. Chelten Ave., Philadelphia PA 19144-5785, phone (215)848-1010, founded 1928, editor Rev. John W. Gouldrick, C.M., is a religious quarterly. **"Poetry should reflect solid Catholic doctrine and experience. Any subject matter is acceptable, provided it does not contradict the teachings of the Roman Catholic Church. Poetry must have a religious theme, preferably about the Blessed Virgin Mary."** They have published poetry by Gladys McKee. The editor describes it as 32 pgs., digest-sized, saddle-stapled, 2-color inside and cover, no ads. ***The Miraculous Medal*** is no longer circulated on a subscription basis. It is used as a promotional piece and is sent to all clients of the Central Association of the Miraculous Medal. Circulation is 340,000. **Sample and guidelines free for postage. Poems should be a maximum of 20 lines, double-spaced. No simultaneous submissions or previously published poems. Reports in 6 months to 3 years. Pays 50¢ and up/line, on acceptance. Buys first North American rights.**

MIRRORS; AHA BOOKS (IV-Form, subscribers), P.O. Box 1250, Gualala CA 95445 (AHA Books, P.O. Box 767), founded 1987 (out of Humidity Productions, Hamburg, Germany), editor Jane Reichhold. *Mirrors* is a **"subscriber-produced haiku magazine.** Each subscription entitles the author to the use of one 8½×11 page each issue. Each author is totally in control of page for choice of material, layout, artwork, copyrights, taste, quality and readability. **The author should be familiar enough with the form that he/she can publish with the top authors in this field. Beginners are not encouraged. No poetry set into 3 lines and labeled haiku. Haiku is different and the author should know the rules—before breaking them."** They have published poetry by Marlene Mountain, Anne McKay, Joe Nutt and Charles Dickson. As a sample the editor selected this haiku by Penny Crosby:

reflections
in a quiet pool
the room once white

The magazine-sized publication is 90-100 pgs., perfect-bound with matte card cover, appearing biannually. Press run is 300 for 200 subscriptions of which 10 are libraries, about 35 shelf sales. Subscription: $10. **Sample postpaid: $5. Send SASE for guidelines. Submit camera-ready work with 1" gutter for binding on plain white paper with black ink. "Author is responsible for copyrights on artwork or quotes." Simultaneous submissions and previously published poems OK, "but most are new and experimental. Only the timid who cannot trust their own judgment use previously published poems." No report on submissions: "I reject only material that is not haiku or related." Pays nothing, not even copies.** Open to unsolicited reviews. Poets may also send haiku-related books for review consideration. ***Mirrors*** sponsors an annual international tanka contest. Send SASE for guidelines. AHA Books publishes 5 flat-spined paperbacks/year averaging 200 pgs. **They accept submissions for books *only* during October. "Only interested in Japanese genre!"** Two books published by AHA Books have recently received first and third place Merit Book Awards from The Haiku Society of America. **More Light, Larger Vision**, by Geraldine C. Little, received the first place award and **A Dictionary of Haiku**, by Jane Reichhold, received the third place award.

MISNOMER (II), P.O. Box 2115, Oxford MS 38655, founded 1990, editors Eric Cash and Jeff Weddle, appears twice a year. **"We like to see poetry that is vibrant and honest, poetry that communicates the human experience by dancing on the matchhead of reality, yet conveys true human compassion. We want real images, real situations. If your head is in the clouds, leave it there. Send us those poems that you would be afraid to show your mother, poems that scream to the reader. If it's good, we'll publish it. We need good poetry and would like more political and imagist poetry. No religious, light verse, rhymed, overly sentimental pieces about your grandmother, your dog or your grandmother's dog."** They have recently published poetry by Charles Bukowski, Lyn Lifshin, A.D. Winans, B.Z. Niditch, Arthur Winfield Knight and C Ra McGuirt. As a sample the editors selected "abstract and concrete" by Gerald Locklin:

how thick is a line?
can a line be a color?
can a line not be linear?
can a line cast a shadow?

a line may catch a fish.
a line may catch a critic.
refugee families catch fish
to feed their families.
a critic feeds a line to feed his.

The editors describe it as 40-60 pgs., digest-sized, saddle-stapled, photocopied from typescript. They use less than 3% of work submitted. Each issue also features work by an author the editors consider "ground breaking in or vital to the world of contemporary poetry." These "Promethean Poet" selections are not open to solicitation. Press run is 300. Subscription: $9. **Sample postpaid: $5. "Need short bio to be included with cover letter: tell us who you are (no bearing on acceptance)." Pays 1 copy.** Occasionally reviews books, chapbooks and other magazines. Open to unsolicited reviews. Poets may also send books for review consideration. "***misnomer*** runs a yearly chapbook contest. Deadline is August of each year. Entry fee is $10 per manuscript. Manuscript should be from 15-25 pgs. Winner receives 20 copies of chapbook. All entrants receive one copy of winning chapbook." Eric Cash says, "We are always looking for poems that deal with political and social issues, and we can never get enough concrete or imagist poems."

MISSISSIPPI MUD (III), 1336 SE Marion St., Portland OR 97202, phone (503)236-9962, founded 1973, editor Joel Weinstein, is an irregular publication that features fiction, poetry and artwork that "portray life in America at the twilight of the 20th century." As for poetry they want **"lively, contemporary themes and forms, free verse preferred." They do not want "anything stodgy, pathetic or moralistic; the self-consciously pretty or clever; purely formatl exercises."** They have published poetry by Ivan

Arguelles, Christy Sheffield Sanford and Simon Perchik. *MM* is 48 pgs., 11×17, saddle-stitched, with 4-color glossy paper cover, full-page graphics and display ads. They receive 100-200 poems a year, accept less than 10%. Press run is 1,500 for 150 subscribers of which 16 are libraries, 1,000 shelf sales, about 200 distributed free to galleries, museums and critical media. Subscription: $25 for 4 issues. **Sample postpaid: $6. Submit no more than 6 poems at a time. No previously published poems; simultaneous submissions OK.** Time between acceptance and publication is 1 year. **Seldom comments on rejections. Reports in 4-6 months. Pays $25 and 2 copies. Buys first North American serial rights.**

MISSISSIPPI REVIEW (II), University of Southern Mississippi, Box 5144, Hattiesburg MS 39406-5144, phone (601)266-4321, editor Frederick Barthelme, managing editor Rie Fortenberry. Literary publication for those interested in contemporary literature. Poems differ in style, length and form, but all have craft in common (along with intriguing content). **Sample: $8. Does not read manuscripts in summer. Pays copies.**

MISSISSIPPI VALLEY REVIEW (II), English Dept. 11-V, Western Illinois University, Macomb IL 61455, phone (309)298-1588, founded 1973, editors John Mann and Tama Baldwin, is a semiannual literary magazine publishing poetry, fiction and essays **without regard for any special slant or theme. They encourage work by new and unpublished writers as well as experienced ones.** They have recently published poetry by Martha Vertreace, Michael Waters, A.E. Stringer, William Heyen, David Ray, Ronald Wallace, Patricia Henley and Edward Allen. ***MVR*** is handsomely printed, 6×9, perfect-bound, 96 pgs. with glossy 5-color cover. They have about 25 pgs. of poetry in each issue, receive 1,000-2,500 submissions/year, use about 30, and have a 6- to 12-month backlog. Press run is 400. Subscription: $12. **Sample postpaid: $6. Submit 4-8 poems. No simultaneous submissions. *MVR* does not read over the summer. Editor comments on rejections "occasionally, particularly if we are interested in the ms. Send us poems of high quality which speak authentically from human experience." Reports in 3 months. Pays 2 copies and a year's subscription.** Occasionally reviews books of poetry.

UNIVERSITY OF MISSOURI PRESS; DEVINS AWARD (II), 2910 LeMone Blvd., Columbia MO 65201, phone (314)882-7641, founded 1958, editor Clair Willcox. **The press accepts poetry mss from both published and unpublished authors throughout the year. Query first with 5-6 sample poems (not a complete ms), a table of contents and a cover letter stating the ms length.** The Devins Award is given for **an outstanding poetry ms, not necessarily a first book, already accepted for publication by the University of Missouri Press during the year.**

MISSOURI REVIEW (II), 1507 Hillcrest Hall, University of Missouri, Columbia MO 65211, phone (314)882-4474, founded 1978, poetry editor Greg Michalson, general editor Speer Morgan, is a quality literary journal, 6×9, 208 pgs., which appears 3 times a year, **publishing poetry features only—6-12 pages for each of 3 to 5 poets/issue.** By devoting more editorial space to each poet, ***MR*** provides a fuller look at the work of some of the best writers composing today. However, the number of poets whose work appears here has decreased significantly, limiting your chances in a prestigious market where competition has become even keener than in the past. **Sample: $6. No simultaneous submissions. Reports in 8-10 weeks. Sometimes sends prepublication galleys. Pays $125-250/feature. Buys all rights. Returns rights "after publication, without charge, at the request of the authors."** Reviews books of poetry. "Short, inhouse reviews only." Awards the Tom McAfee Discovery Feature once or twice a year to an outstanding young poet who has not yet published a book; poets are selected from regular submissions at the discretion of the editors. Also offers the Editors' Prize Contest in Poetry. Deadline: October 15. $500 first prize and publication. Three finalists named in addition. Write for details. The editors add, "We think we have enhanced the quality of our poetry section and increased our reader interest in this section. We remain dedicated to publishing at least one younger or emerging poet in every issue."

MR. COGITO PRESS; MR. COGITO (II), Pacific University, 2518 NW Savier, Portland OR 97210, founded 1973, poetry editors John M. Gogol and Robert A. Davies. ***Mr. Cogito***, published 2-3 times/year, is a tall, skinny (4½×11) magazine, 24-26 pgs. of poetry. The editors want **"no prose put in lines. Yes: wit, heightened language, craft. Open to all schools and subjects and groups of poets."** They have published poetry by Norman Russell, Ann Chandonnet, John Minczeski, Peter Wild and Zbigniew Herbert. As a sample the editors selected these lines from "ghost poem" by Bill Shields:

I don't think the country is ever going to forgive us

Use the General Index to find the page number of a specific publisher. If the publisher you are seeking is not listed, check the " '94-'95 Changes" list at the end of this section.

for throwing up our hands and dying in Vietnam

They use poems in both English and translation, "preferably representing each poet with several poems." The magazine has a circulation of 400. Subscription for 3 issues: $9. **Sample: $3. Submit 4-5 poems. Simultaneous submissions OK. Reports in 2 weeks to 2 months. Pays copies. Acquires first rights and anthology rights.** Mr. Cogito Press publishes collections by poets they invite from among those who have appeared in the magazine. Send SASE for catalog to buy samples. They also conduct special theme and translation contests with prizes of $50 or $100. The editors advise, "Subscribe to a magazine that seems good. Read ours before you submit. Write, write, write."

MIXED MEDIA (I, II), 33 Aspen Rd., West Orange NJ 07052, founded 1992, executive editor Paul Semel, is an annual "outlet for all forms of expression—poetry, short stories, drama, art, cartoons and photography. They want **poetry up to 50 lines, any style. "Because of the range of taste our editors have—we are all diverse individuals—the magazine has no theme; anything goes."** They have recently published poetry by Henry Rollins, Johnette Napolitano and Kevin Powell. As a sample we selected this poem, "Losing Battle," by Edmund Conti:

In a final desperate attempt
at survival, the sun sets
fire to the western sky.
Overblown say my poet friends
Cute, say my non-poet friends,
what does it mean? How much
will you get paid for it?
asks my nosy neighbor

My father's an astronaut,
my son lies.

Mixed Media is 40 pgs., 8½ × 11, saddle-stapled with card cover. Press run is 200. **Sample postpaid: $3. Submit up to 3 poems, typed, with short bio. Previously published poems and simultaneous submissions OK. Reporting time varies. Pays 1 copy. All rights revert to author upon publication.**

MOBIUS (I, II), P.O. Box 674, St. Clair Shores MI 48080, phone (313)693-4986, founded 1982, editor Jean Hull Herman, assistant editor Joanna Linsalata. They look for "the informed mind responding to the challenges of reality and the expression of the imagination in poetry with intelligence and wit. **Poets should say significant, passionate things about the larger world outside themselves and use all the resources of our language and art. Open to meter, rhyme, dramatic and narrative structures, traditional as well as free verse and all that pleases the ear as well as the soul. General topics include response to art and to nature; the philosophical questions; love and romance; relationships; war; the events of and thoughts about everyday life; science and technology; and humor (for which the editor has a weakness). Shorter poems as well as longer ones will be considered."** They have recently published poetry by John Williams, Michael R. Collings, Robert Cooperman, Michael Estabrook, Diane Albertina, Lenore A. Reiss, Lyn Lifshin and Coral Sutor. As a sample the editor selected these lines from "As June A Day" by Alvah K. Howe:

As June a night as firefly
Could cause to glow with blinking eye,
Or shine, like Chinese lantern, spry
Darting dots that mystify.
As June a night as moonbeam's gloss
Casts on a stalwart spruce tree, joss-
Like spires, whose waves inspire the toss
Of volley-moon, up and across.

Mobius is published twice a year, at Memorial Day and Thanksgiving. It is magazine-sized, 60 pgs., professionally printed, saddle-stapled with matte card cover. Subscription: $12/year. **Sample postpaid: $8. Send SASE for guidelines. "Response time is two weeks to two months, as editor does read submissions all year round. Printed authors receive one copy free. Editor will comment on all rejections."**

MODERN BRIDE (IV-Love/romance), 249 W. 17th St., New York NY 10011, phone (212)337-7000, managing editor Mary Ann Cavlin, a slick bimonthly, occasionally buys **poetry pertaining to love and marriage. Pays $30-40 for average short poem.**

MODERN HAIKU; KAY TITUS MORMINO MEMORIAL SCHOLARSHIP; MARGARET DUFFIELD MEMORIAL SCHOLARSHIP; ANN ATWOOD MEMORIAL SCHOLARSHIP (IV-Form, students), P.O. Box 1752, Madison WI 53701, founded 1969, poetry editor Robert Spiess, "is the foremost international journal of English language haiku and criticism. We are devoted to publishing only the very best haiku being written and also publish articles on haiku and have the most complete review section of haiku books. Issues average over 100 pages." They use **haiku only. No tanka or other forms. "We publish all 'schools' of haiku, but want the haiku to elicit intuition, insight, felt-depth."** They have published haiku by William J. Higginson, James Kirkup, Elizabeth Lamb and Alexis Rotella. As a sample the editor selected this haiku (poet unidentified):

a life near its close—
and still foolishly scribbling
poems of wild plum

The digest-sized magazine appears 3 times a year, printed on heavy quality stock with cover illustrations especially painted for each issue by the staff artist. They receive 16,000-18,000 submissions/year, use 800. There are over 260 poems in each issue, circulation 650. Subscription: $14.25. **Sample postpaid: $5. No simultaneous submissions. Submit on "any size sheets, any number of haiku on a sheet; but name and address on each sheet." Send SASE for guidelines. Reports in 2 weeks. Pays $1/haiku (but no contributor's copy). Buys first North American serial rights.** Staff reviews books of haiku in 350-1,000 words, single format. Send books for review consideration. The Kay Titus Mormino Memorial Scholarship of $500 is for the best haiku by a high school senior, deadline early March. They also offer the Margaret Duffield Memorial Scholarship of $200 and the Ann Atwood Memorial Scholarship of $200. Send SASE for rules. ***Modern Haiku*** ranked #2 in the "New Poets" category of the latest ***Writer's Digest*** Poetry 60 list. This category ranks those markets who often publish poets whose work is new to their publication. As for the journal's editor, Robert Spiess received a third place 1992 Merit Book Award from The Haiku Society of America for his book **The Cottage of Wild Plum**. He says, "Haiku achieve their effect of felt-depth, insight and intuition through juxtaposition of perceived entities, not through intellective comment or abstract words."

MOKSHA JOURNAL; VAJRA PRINTING & PUBLISHING OF YOGA ANAND ASHRAM (IV-Spiritual), 49 Forrest Pl., Amityville NY 11701, phone (516)691-8475, founded 1984, is a "small press publisher **of spiritual and/or philosophical literature, poetry, nonfiction and poetry pertaining to the concept of 'Moksha,' defined by Monier-Williams as a 'liberation, release' (A Sanskrit-English Dictionary, 1899). Perspectives include, but are not limited to: Yoga, various schools of Buddhism, Sufism, Mystical Christianity, etc."** *Moksha Journal* appears twice a year and is 40-55 pgs., 7¼ × 9½, offset, litho. Press run is 400-500 for that many subscribers. Subscription: $8. **Sample: $4. Simultaneous submissions OK. Reports in 4-6 weeks. Pays 2 copies.** The press publishes flat-spined paperbacks.

MONOCACY VALLEY REVIEW (II), Dept. of English, Mount Saint Mary's College, Emmitsburg MD 21727, founded 1985, poetry editor Mary Noel, editor William Heath, is an annual literary review. **Submissions should be received by January 15th.** "In general, we cannot publish longer poems; we also publish short stories, nonfiction prose, book reviews and artwork. **We pride ourselves in being a review that is always local but never provincial. If we have a bias, it is in favor of clarity of vision and eloquence of language. We dislike poems that 'hurt the ear and unfit one to continue.' "** ***MVR*** is magazine-sized, 60 pgs., saddle-stapled, high quality paper. "We reject over 95% of submissions, publish 15-20 poems an issue." Their press run is 500 with 200 subscriptions of which 10 are libraries. Subscription: $8. **Sample postpaid: $5. Include a 50-word or less biographical statement with all submissions. All submissions are judged anonymously and there is no backlog. If mss are sent in December and early January, response time is 6-8 weeks. Pays $10-25/poem plus 2 copies.** The editor says they "prefer reviews of major writers in the area."

THE MONTANA POET MAGAZINE (IV-Cowboy, regional); GOLDEN STAR AWARD FOR POETRY (II), P.O. Box 100, Three Forks MT 59752, founded 1987, editor Don "Cheese" Akerlow. ***TMP*** is a bimonthly publication using **"cowboy poetry and poetry from all walks of life." They are interested in poems about Montana or from poets who live in Montana.** They also use cartoons and philosophies. They have published poetry by Greg Keeler and Sandy Seaton. As a sample the editor selected these lines from his own poem "Want Ads":

I've been writin' poems for some 25 years
Written cowboy poems about shootin', Ridin', and drinkin' beers
Kickin' up my heels and once at the moon I did howl
Guess that Chicken Factory is still with me cause my poems are still just plain foul.

TMP is 16 pgs., magazine-sized, saddle-stapled. Their press run is 1,000. Subscription: $10. **Sample postpaid: $2. Guidelines available for SASE. Submit up to 5 poems at a time, with name and address on each page. Considers simultaneous submissions and previously published poems. Cover letter required; include bio and photo. Reports in 4-6 weeks. Pays $5/poem plus 1 copy upon publication.** The magazine annually sponsors the Golden Star contest, entries accepted January 1 through May 15, entry fee $1/poem, prizes of $50, $25, $15, $10, and 6 honorable mentions. The ***TMP*** Membership offers 1-year subscription plus the ***TMP*** T-shirt (which sells for $10), plus 5 poems entered in the Golden Star competition, for $20. They also sponsor the Montana Poets' Hall of Fame. ***The Montana Poet Magazine*** ranked #5 in the "New Poets" category of the latest ***Writer's Digest*** Poety 60 list. This category ranks those markets who often publish poets whose work is new to their publication. The editor says, "I feel that poetry has too long been enjoyed by a select few. It is the purpose of ***TMP*** to get more people involved in reading and enjoying poetry; to make reading poetry as commonplace as reading any other type of literature. Advice to beginning poet: Don't be discouraged. Believe in your work because, if it comes from within, you are pleasing at least one person, and keep sending your work to editors. I do not judge poetry on perfect grammar or structure but on feeling and that's what I look for when selecting poems for the magazine."

THE MOODY STREET REVIEW (I, II), 205 E. 78th St., New York NY 10021, founded 1988, editor David Gibson, appears once annually, publishes **"poetry with stylistic and/or structural *integrity*. This refers to aspects such as a strong sense of line or sentence rhythm, lyricality, and identity as verse vs. prosaic forms. It is important that poets be familiar with the lyrical and inspirational traditions of the twentieth century, i.e., symbolism, imagism, objectivism, projective verse, beat generation, etc. No out-and-out sexual poetry, no poems disguised as political or religious sermons (or vice versa), very little metered verse, nothing boring."** They have recently published poetry by Arthur Winfield Knight, Joy Walsh, Nicanor Parra, Federico Garcia Lorca, George Bowering and Raymond Radiguet. The editor says ***MSR*** is 60-120 pgs.; 8½×11, saddle-stitched, quality photocopy, with b&w artwork in drawings, linoleum prints and photography. They receive 20-80 submissions of poetry/month, "publish no more than 20% of all material received." Press run is 500. Subscription: $10. **Query to receive sample copies. Previously published poems and simultaneous submissions OK. Cover letter not required, "but make sure return address is clearly indicated on all copies. We like to get an overview of a poet's work, so send at least a half-dozen poems. Also, if there is no SASE, or only a postcard to be filled out, the submission will probably get tossed." Sometimes comments on rejections or recommends other markets. Report in under 6 months, "all bets off after that date. If curious, query for immediate response." Pays 2 copies, more at a discount. Acquires one-time rights.** The editor says, "Persistence is an admirable trait, but know when to stop sending to any one publication. Be educated about poetry. Read, read, read! Blank verse is not the end all, be all. Know the metered forms, if not practice them. Their importance is only in the discipline they teach. Editors will appreciate this self-conscious approach to your craft. We would like to receive more translations from all over the world, especially France, Latin America, Africa and Germany."

WILLIAM MORROW AND CO. (V), 1350 Avenue of the Americas, New York NY 10019, phone (212)261-6500, publishes poetry on standard royalty contracts **but accepts no unsolicited mss. Queries with samples should be submitted through an agent.**

‡MOSTLY MAINE (I), P.O. Box 8805, Portland ME 04104, founded 1992, editor Peter McGinn, poetry editor Vera Smetzer, appears quarterly. **"We want poetry with vivid images. We have no line limit, as such, but the magazine is too small for epic-length poems. No overtly religious poems as opposed to spiritual poems."** They have recently published poetry by Rod Farmer, Carolyn Page and Michael Smetzer. As a sample the editor selected these lines from "In Memory" by Michele Jacques:

susan
how many dreams grew in your company
the paper mache roses that decorated our friendship
crumble in a box in the garage on top of
the 1969 funny papers you used to wrap me a present . . .

MM is 32-40 pgs., digest-sized, photocopied from laser printed original and saddle-stapled, with paper cover and computer graphics. In addition to poetry, fiction and creative nonfiction, it includes a "Feedback File" where readers may comment on material published in the last issue. They currently receive about 80 poems a year, accept 30. Press run is 75 for 25 subscribers, 20 shelf sales. Single copy: $2; subscription: $8. **Sample postpaid: $1.50. Previously published poems and simultaneous submissions OK. Cover letter with brief bio required. "We are not fussy about submissions. Photocopies are fine. Manila envelopes are not required." Always comments on rejections. Send SASE for guidelines. "Guidelines are also in every issue." Reports generally in 1 or 2 months. Pays 1 copy to first-time submitters. "We found early on that authors/poets whose work has appeared more than once have wanted to subscribe to help support the magazine. Extra issues are available at a discount." Acquires one-time rights. All rights revert to author upon publication.** Open to unsolicited reviews. Poets may also send books for review consideration. The editor says, "We hear it again and again: The best course for beginning writers includes writers' conferences, workshops and classes. Writing groups help provide encouragement and deadlines. This is why ***Mostly Maine*** tries to be a writer's group by mail."

(m)ÖTHÊR TØÑGUÉS (II, IV-Translations), RR#2 Alders C-14, Ganges, British Columbia V0S 1E0 Canada, founded 1990, editor/publisher Mona Fertig, is a little international literary magazine of poetry, fiction and essays appearing nearly twice a year. She wants **"unpublished, new, volatile, well-written poetry; particularly interested in translations (poetry) to and from mother tongue. Also work-sheets, dreams, lyrics with music."** *MT* is 50 pgs., 7×8, photocopied. Press run is 500. Subscription: $12 Canadian, $14 USA, $18 international. **Sample postpaid: $7. Include "Writer's Notes" (and SAE with IRCs) with submissions. Reports in 3-5 months. Pays 1-year subscription.**

‡MOVING OUT: A FEMINIST LITERARY AND ARTS JOURNAL (IV-Women/feminist), Box 21249, Detroit MI 48221, founded 1970, co-editor Margaret Kaminski, is an annual magazine with poetry, fiction, nonfiction and artwork **by and about women. Submit "at least 6 poems, no special length. We especially like thematic groupings by poets. We also like work which develops a feminist/women's aesthetic, or that of a particular minority or ethnic group. Nothing that is sexist or pornographic."** They have published poetry by Marge Piercy, Margaret Atwood, Susan Fromberg Schaeffer and Ursula K. LeGuin. As a sample the editor selected the poem "Questions for Karen Silkwood" by Nancy Weber:

Was it long enough
to see him rifle through your purse
and grab your notebook?
Did you have time to ask him
why the cancer wasn't enough?

The editor describes ***Moving Out*** as 50-100 pgs., magazine-sized, offset, glossy cover, with b&w high-contrast photos and graphics, using commercial and exchange ads, with a circulation of 500-1,000, with 300 subscriptions of which 250 are libraries, selling for $9. **Sample: $6 plus $1 postage. No simultaneous submissions or previously published work. Reports in 6-12 months, 6- to 12-month delay before publication. Pays 1 copy.**

MOVING PARTS PRESS; MUTANT DRONE PRESS (V), 70 Cathedral Dr., Santa Cruz CA 95060, phone (408)427-2271. Moving Parts founded 1977, Mutant Drone, 1982. Poetry editor Felicia Rice says they are a "fine arts literary publisher using letterpress printing and printmaking to produce handsome and innovative books, broadsides and prints in limited editions." Moving Parts has recently published books of poetry by Francisco X. Alarcón, Elba Rosario Sánchez and Henri Michaux. Mutant Drone "the One-&-Only-Wholly-Owned Subsidiary, is free to laugh and throw punches at the whole predicament," and has published books by Charles Bukowski and Nick Zachreson. As a sample here are the opening lines of "On a Darkening Road" by Robert Lundquist from **Before-the-Rain,** Moving Parts Press:

This evening the tide is low,
Ducks walk through bunched beds of kelp
Looking for insects.

They do not accept unsolicited mss. Pay 10% of the edition in copies. In 1993 the book **De Amor Oscuro/Of Dark Love** (Moving Parts Press) received one of 18 international design awards from among the "600 Best Designed Books in the World" exhibit mounted by Stiftung Buchkunst at the Leipzig Book Fair.

MS. MAGAZINE (V), 7th Floor, 230 Park Ave., New York NY 10169, founded 1972, is a bimonthly "feminist source of national and international news, politics, arts, scholarship and book reviews." **They are currently not accepting unsolicited poetry.** They have published poetry by Alice Walker, Maya Angelou and May Swenson. Circulation is 150,000. Single copy: $5 (available on newsstands); subscription: $30. They say, "Due to the volume of the material received, we cannot accept, acknowledge or return unsolicited poetry or fiction. We cannot discuss queries on the phone and cannot be held responsible for manuscripts sent to us."

MUDFISH; BOX TURTLE PRESS (I, II), 184 Franklin St., New York NY 10013, phone (212)219-9278, founded 1983, editor Jill Hoffman. ***Mudfish,*** published by Box Turtle Press, is a journal of poetry and art that appears once a year and is looking for **"energy, intensity, and originality of voice, mastery of style, the presence of passion." Considers sexually explicit material.** They have recently published poetry by Charles Simic, Gerrit Henry, Nicholas Kolumban, Denise Duhamel and John Ashbery. As a sample the editor selected these lines from "AIDS" by Shelley Stenhouse:

I couldn't help thinking about your penis,
that deflated party balloon, that old thin
dachshund hanging behind the dark curtain of
your pants. I knew I should have been thinking
how sad it is I have to lift you into a cab,
wearing a turtleneck in the middle of summer

Press run is 1,500. Single copy: $10. **Sample copies are available, include $2.50 shipping and**

handling. They will not consider simultaneous submissions or previously published poems. Reports from "immediately to 3 months." Sometimes sends prepublication galleys. Pays 1 copy.

MUSE PORTFOLIO (II), Unit Box 8, 25 Tannery Rd., Westfield MA 01085, founded 1992, editor Haemi Balgassi, appears 2-4 times a year. ***Muse Portfolio*** is a "casual magazine for sincere, eloquent, earnest writers who crave forum to share work with others." They want **poetry of "any structure, formal or free, 50 lines maximum. Poetry with writing themes welcome. No forced rhymes, nothing profane.** We also publish short stories and nonfiction, as well as cartoons and art sketches." They have recently published poetry by Paul A. Hanson and Michael Hemmingson. As a sample the editor selected these lines from "You Are an Author" by Delma Luben:

A writer will grow old
austerely regimenting his
short allotted days—all
for a temporary season of
praise: Author, author.

Muse Portfolio is 40 pgs., 5½×8½, saddle-stapled, printed on 20 lb. paper with heavier stock cover, b&w artwork, occasional ads. They receive about 150 poems/year, accept 10%. Press run is 150 for 100 subscribers. Subscription: $5. **Sample postpaid: $2.50. Previously published poems OK; no simultaneous submissions. Cover letter required. "Include a biographical paragraph—need not list published credits if author prefers to write something else." Seldom comments on rejections. Send SASE for guidelines. Reports in 2 months. Pays 1 copy. Acquires one-time rights.** The editor says, "Remember the three P's: Be professional, persistent and patient."

MUSICWORKS (IV-Themes), 179 Richmond St. W., Toronto, Ontario M5V 1V3 Canada, phone (416)977-3546, founded 1978, editor Gayle Young, is a triannual journal of contemporary music. The editor says, **"The poetry we publish only relates directly to the topics discussed in the magazine or relates to contemporary sound poetry—*usually* it is poetry written by the (music) composer or performers we are featuring."** Poets published include bpnichol, Colin Morton and Jackson Mac Low. The magazine is 64 pgs., 8½×11, with b&w visuals, b&w photography, some illustrative graphics and scores and accompanied by 60-minute cassette. Circulation is 1,600, of which 500 are subscriptions. Price is $5/issue or $15 for the magazine plus CD. **Sample postpaid: $10 for magazine and CD. Considers simultaneous submissions. They report on submissions within 2 months, and there is no backlog before publication. The magazine pays Canadian contributors $20-50/contribution plus 2-3 free copies.**

‡THE MUSING PLACE (IV-Specialized: poets with a history of mental illness), 2700 N. Lakeview, Chicago IL 60614, phone (312)281-3800, ext. 2465, fax (312)281-8790, founded 1986, editor Linda Krinsky, is a biannual magazine **"written and published by people with a history of mental illness. All kinds and forms of poetry are welcome."** As a sample the editor selected these lines from "Why Must I Be Poor?" by Gracian Vital:

Wrapped in elegance,
I was born
Queenly to behold
But when you see my
Pocketbook
I fold.

The editor says ***The Musing Place*** is 32 pgs., 8½×11, typeset and stapled with art also produced by people with a history of mental illness. They receive about 100 poems/year, publish about 40. Press run is 1,000. Single copy: $2. **No previously published poems; simultaneous submissions OK. Cover letter required. "Poets must prove and explain their history of mental illness."** Time between acceptance and publication is 6 months to 1 year. **"The board reviews submissions and chooses those that fit into each issue of the publication. All submissions are kept for possible publication in future issues." Seldom comments on rejections. Reports within 6 months. Pays "negotiable" number of contributor's copies.**

MY LEGACY (I); OMNIFIC (I); FELICITY (I, IV-Themes); THE BOTTOM LINE, HC-13, Box 21-AA, Artemas PA 17211-9405, phone (814)458-3102, editor/publisher Kay Weems. ***My Legacy*** is a quarterly of poetry and short stories using **36-line, sometimes longer, poems, "anything in good taste" with an Editor's Choice small cash award for each issue. No contributor copies.** Subscription: $12/year; $3.50/copy. ***Omnific,*** **a "family-type" quarterly publishes poetry only, 36 lines, sometimes longer; readers vote on favorites, small cash award or copy to favorites. Send SASE for guidelines. No contributor copies.** Subscription: $12/year; $3.50/copy. ***Felicity,*** founded 1988, is a bimonthly newsletter for contests only, 30-40 pgs. They offer 10 contests/flyer including a bimonthly theme contest, 36 lines. Other contests may be for theme, form, chapbook, etc. Entry fees vary. Send SASE for guidelines and upcoming themes. Payment for contest winners is small cash award and/or publication. No work is returned. They consider simultaneous submissions and previously published poems. All winning entries including honorable mentions are printed in the newsletter which also publishes market and other contest listings. Subscription: $15/year; $2.50/copy. She also publishes an annual **Christmas anthology. Poetry only, published/unpublished, 36 lines maximum, Christmas themes. Address to "Christmas Anthology." Deadline: August 31.** ***The Bottom Line,*** founded 1988, is a monthly newsletter listing over 50 publications and contests for writers, reproducing guidelines of still others. Information is presented in chronological order by deadline date, and then in alphabetical order. Circulation 200-300. Subscription: $21/year; $2.50/copy.

MYSTERY TIME (I, IV-Mystery); RHYME TIME (IV-Subscribers), P.O. Box 2907, Decatur IL 62524, poetry editor Linda Hutton, founded 1983, is an semiannual containing 1-2 pages of **humorous poems about mysteries and mystery writers** in each issue. As a sample the editor selected the poem, "Writer's Block" by Elizabeth R. Crummer:

A pox on that loathsome curse,
Watching the departing hearse;
Widows wail a mournful cry,
Again the arsenic in the pie.

Mystery Time is 44 pgs., digest-sized, stapled with heavy stock cover. They receive up to 15 submissions a year, use 4-6. Circulation 100. **Sample: $3.50. Does not read mss in December. Guidelines available for #10 SASE. Pays $5 on acceptance.** Hutton's other publication ***Rhyme Time***, is a quarterly newsletter **publishing only the work of subscribers. No length limit or style restriction.** Subscription: $20. **Sample: $3.50. Submit 3 poems, "typed in proper format with SASE."** Cash prize of $5 awarded to the best poem in each issue. She also sponsors an annual poetry contest that awards a $10 cash prize for the best poem in any style or length. Submit typed poem with SASE. No entry fee; one entry/person. Deadline: November 1.

THE MYTHIC CIRCLE; THE MYTHOPOEIC SOCIETY (II, IV-Fantasy), P.O. Box 6707, Altadena CA 91001, editor Tina Cooper. ***The Mythic Circle*** is a "writer's workshop in print," appearing 2-3 times a year, publishing fantasy short stories and poems. They want **"poetry, particularly traditional poetry, with a mythic or fairy-tale theme."** They have published poetry by Angelee Anderson and Gwyneth Hood. They receive approximately 100 poetry submissions/year, accept 10%. Press run is 230 for 200 subscribers. Subscription: $18/year for non-members of sponsoring organization, The Mythopoeic Society; $13/year for members. **Sample postpaid: $6.50. No previously published poems or simultaneous submissions.** Time between acceptance and publication is 2 years. **Seldom comments on rejections. Send SASE for guidelines. Reports in 2-4 months. Pays 1 copy for 3 poems.** The editor says, "Subscribers are heavily favored, since they provide the critical review which our authors need in their letters of comment."

NADA PRESS; BIG SCREAM (II, IV-Form/style, bilingual), 2782 Dixie SW, Grandville MI 49418, phone (616)531-1442, founded 1974, poetry editor David Cope. ***Big Scream*** appears annually and is **"a brief anthology of mostly 'unknown' poets.** We are promoting a **continuation of objectivist tradition begun by Williams and Reznikoff. We want objectivist-based short works; some surrealism; basically short, tight work that shows clarity of perception and care in its making. Also poems in Spanish—*not* translations."** They have recently published poetry by Antler, James Ruggia, Richard Kostelanetz, Andy Clausen, Allen Ginsberg, John Steinbeck, Jr., Jim Cohn and Marcia Arrieta. ***Big Scream*** is 35 pgs., magazine-sized, xerograph on 60 lb. paper, side-stapled, "sent gratis to a select group of poets and editors." They receive "several hundred (not sure)" unsolicited submissions/year, use "very few." Press run is 100. Subscription to institutions: $6/year. **Sample postpaid: $6. Submit after July. Send 10 pgs. No cover letter. "If poetry interests me, I will ask the proper questions of the poet." Simultaneous submissions OK. Comments on rejections "if requested and ms warrants it." Reports in 1-14 days. Sometimes sends prepublication galleys. Pays as many copies as requested, within reason.** The editor advises: "Read Pound's essay, 'A Retrospect,' then Reznikoff and Williams; follow through the Beats and NY School, especially Denby & Berrigan, and you have our approach to writing well in hand. I expect to be publishing ***BS*** regularly 10 years from now, same basic format."

NASHVILLE HOUSE (III, IV-Cowboy, science fiction/fantasy, horror), P.O. Box 60072, Nashville TN 37206, founded 1991, publishes books**, including poetry, relating to the South, Old West and Civil War.** They have published **Toreros** by John Gawsworth, selected by Richard Aldington, introduced by Roy Campbell. They are **also interested in science fiction, fantasy and horror poetry** and have published **Poems of the Divided Self** by Gothic poet and scholar Gary William Crawford, introduced by Joey Froehlich. **Query with letter only.** As a sample the director, Steve Eng, selected these lines from one of Crawford's poems, "My Thoughts Conceive":

Days pass, infinitely stretching my
Brain cells to the rings of Saturn.
Forever travelling in the emptiness of Time,

I see a grain of dust floating
and never settling.

NASSAU REVIEW (II), English Dept., Nassau Community College, Garden City NY 11530, phone (516)572-7792, founded 1964, managing editor Dr. Paul A. Doyle, is an annual "creative and research vehicle for Nassau College faculty and the faculty of other colleges." They want **"serious, intellectual poetry of any form or style. No light verse or satiric verse." Submissions from adults only. "No college students; graduate students acceptable."** They have recently published poetry by Patti Tana, Dick Allen, Louis Phillips, David Heyen and Simon Perchik. As a sample the editor selected these lines from "Chekhov, For Beginners" by Barbara Novack:

Chekhov said
throw out the first three pages;
it takes that long
to get to the beginning.

And I may say
put aside the first three decades
sweep away their debris
cast off versions of the self . . .

NR is about 150 pgs., digest-sized, flat-spined. They receive 550-600 poems/year, use approximately 20-25. Press run is 1,000 for about 1,000 subscribers of which 600 are libraries. **Sample free. No previously published poems or simultaneous submissions. Submit only 3 poems at a time. Reads submissions October 1 through March 1 only. Reports in 2-3 months. Pays copies.** They sponsor occasional contests with $100 or $200 poetry awards, depending on college funding. Well-edited and visually appealing, ***Nassau Review*** tends to publish free verse emphasizing voice in well-crafted lyric and narrative forms.

THE NATION; LEONORE MARSHALL/NATION PRIZE FOR POETRY; DISCOVERY/THE NATION POETRY CONTEST (III), 72 Fifth Ave., New York NY 10011, founded 1865, poetry editor Grace Schulman. ***The Nation*'s only requirement for poetry is "excellence,"** which can be inferred from the list of poets they have published: Marianne Moore, Robert Lowell, W.S. Merwin, Maxine Kumin, Donald Justice, James Merrill, Richard Howard, May Swenson, Garrett Hongo and Amy Clampitt. The editor chose this sample from a poem in ***The Nation***, 1939, by W.B. Yeats:

Like a long-legged fly upon the stream
His mind moves upon silence.

Pay for poetry is $1/line, not to exceed 35 lines, plus 1 copy. The magazine co-sponsors the Leonore Marshall/Nation Prize for Poetry which is an annual award of $10,000 for the outstanding book of poems published in the US in each year; and the "Discovery"/The Nation Poetry Contest ($200 each plus a reading at The Poetry Center, 1395 Lexington Ave., New York NY 10128. Deadline: mid-February. Send SASE for application). Poetry published in ***The Nation*** has been included in **The Best American Poetry 1993.**

NATIONAL ENQUIRER (II, IV-Humor), Lantana FL 33464, assistant editor Michele Cooke, is a weekly tabloid, circulation 4,550,000, which uses **short poems, most of them humorous and traditional rhyming verse. "We want poetry with a message or reflection on the human condition or everyday life. Avoid sending obscure or 'arty' poetry or poetry for art's sake. Also looking for philosophical and inspirational material. Submit seasonal/holiday material at least 3 months in advance." Requires cover letter from first-time submitters; include name, address, social security and phone numbers. Pays $25 after publication; original material only. Buys first rights.**

NATIONAL FORUM (III), 129 Quad Center, Mell St., Auburn University AL 36849-5306, phone (205)844-5200, founded 1915, editor James P. Kaetz, is the quarterly of Phi Kappa Phi using **quality poetry, no "profanity, brutality, love poems."** They have published poetry by William Stafford, Bin Ramke, Mary Oliver and Marge Piercy. As a sample the editor selected these lines from "In Spite of Everything, the Stars" by Edward Hirsch:

Like a stunned piano, like a bucket
of fresh milk flung into the air
or a dozen fists of confetti
suddenly thrown hard at a bride
stepping down from the altar, the stars
surprise the sky.

NF is 48 pgs., magazine-sized, professionally printed, saddle-stapled, with full-color paper cover. They publish about 20 poems of 300 received a year. Their press run is 118,000 with 115,000 subscriptions of which 600 are libraries. Subscription: $25. **Sample postpaid: $2.75. Submit 3-5 poems. Reads submissions January and September only. Reports in 4-6 weeks, publishes within**

9-12 months. Pays "small honorarium" and 10 copies. The editor advises, "Do not send out work that has not been proofread by a couple of helpfully critical friends. Enclose a biographical sketch with recent publications. We do not include comments on rejected work."

NAUGHTY NAKED DREAMGIRLS; COMIC UPDATE (I, IV-Erotica, science fiction, humor), Suite 253, 5960 S. Land Park Dr., Sacramento CA 95822, phone (916)429-8522, founded 1986, publisher Andrew L. Roller, editor William Dockery (and submissions should be sent directly to him at P.O. Box 3663, Phenix City AL 36868). These newsletters appear "approximately monthly." They want **erotic poetry.** Also willing to look at **"weird, occult or science fiction, or humorous poetry (political or comics related)."** They have recently published poetry by Peter Layton, Sharon Jones, Lyn Lifshin, E.B. Brewton and Juliet Cook. As a sample the publisher selected these lines by William Dockery:

Sassanna was painting the back porch,
in the early afternoon.
I opened the window, hot air flowed in.
Carried the smell of both soup
and nearby garbage.
Singing and pissing on a bluebricked wall,
Lit by moonlight.

The newsletters are saddle-stitched, 8 pgs. Press run is 500 for 20 subscribers of which 2 are libraries. **Sample postpaid: $1 US or free for a SASE from William Dockery at his address above ("greeting card SASE preferred"), $2 Canada, $3 foreign. "Poems should be well typed for camera ready reproduction." Reports "at once." Pays 1 copy ("2 for regulars"). Acquires first North American serial rights.** Reviews loose poetry, books of poetry and zines in ***Comic Update.*** Open to unsolicited reviews. Poets may also send chapbooks for review consideration to William Dockery. Send loose poetry for review consideration to Monty Milne at 7 Salisbury Lane, Malvern PA 19355. The editor says, "As for poetry submissions, **don't send me more than a few pages of poems.** I'm getting more poems than I can handle right now. I prefer to send 'rejected' poems on to other potential publishers and respond with an informative letter on self-publishing."

NAZARENE INTERNATIONAL HEADQUARTERS; STANDARD; WONDER TIME; LISTEN; BREAD; TEENS TODAY; HERALD OF HOLINESS (IV-Religious, children), 6401 The Paseo, Kansas City MO 64131, phone (816)333-7000. Each of the magazines published by the Nazarenes has a separate editor, focus and audience. ***Standard***, circulation 177,000, is a weekly **inspirational "story paper" with Christian leisure reading for adults. Send SASE for free sample and guidelines. Uses a poem each week. Submit maximum of 5, maximum of 50 lines each. Pays 25¢ a line.** ***Wonder Time***, editor Lois Perrigo, a publication of the Children's Ministries Department, Church of the Nazarene, **"is committed to reinforcement of the Biblical concepts taught in the Sunday School curriculum, using poems 4-8 lines, simple, with a message, easy to read, for 1st and 2nd graders. It should not deal with much symbolism."** This weekly 4-page leaflet is magazine-sized, newsprint, circulation 37,000. **Send SASE for free sample and guidelines. Reports in 2-3 weeks. Pays minimum of $3—25¢/line—and 4 contributor's copies. For *Listen, Bread, Teens Today* and *Herald of Holiness*,** write individually for guidelines and samples.

NCASA JOURNAL (NEWSLETTER OF THE NATIONAL COALITION AGAINST SEXUAL ASSAULT) (IV-Specialized, social issues, women/feminism), Suite 500, 123 S. Seventh, Springfield IL 62701, founded 1986, editor Becky Bradway. Appears 3 times/year using **"well-written poetry by survivors of rape, child sexual abuse and incest. Poems may deal with aspects of the sexual assault experience or recovery from sexual assault."** It is 16 pgs., magazine-sized, professionally printed, with matte card cover, saddle-stapled. Press run is 700 for 600 subscribers. Subscription: $12; or with NCASA membership: $25. **Sample postpaid: $4. Previously published poems and simultaneous submissions OK. Pays 3 copies. Acquires first rights.** Accepts reviews of books relevant to feminism and the anti-rape movement—up to 1,000 words. Poets may also send books relating to sexual assault for review consideration. The editor says, "***NCASA Journal*** is a nationally circulated magazine. Its 'Voices of Survivors' section includes poetry and fiction by survivors of sexual assault."

NEBO: A LITERARY JOURNAL (II), English Dept., Arkansas Tech University, Russellville AR 72801-2222, phone (501)968-0256, founded 1982, poetry editor Michael Ritchie, appears in May and December. Regarding poetry they say, **"We accept all kinds, all styles, all subject matters and will publish a longer poem if it is outstanding. We are especially interested in formal poetry."** They have published poetry by Jack Butler, Turner Cassity, Wyatt Prunty, Charles Martin, Julia Randall and Brenda Hillman. ***Nebo*** is digest-sized, 50-70 pgs., professionally printed on quality matte stock with matte card cover. Press run "varies." **Sample postpaid: $6. Simultaneous submissions OK. "Please no onion skin or offbeat colors." Cover letter with bio material and recent publications required. Do not submit mss between May 1 and August 15 of each year. Editor comments on rejections "if the work has merit but requires revision and resubmission; we do all we can to help." Reports at the end of November and**

February respectively. Pays 1 copy. Staff reviews books of poetry. Send books for review consideration.

THE NEBRASKA REVIEW; TNR AWARDS (II), ASH 212, University of Nebraska, Omaha NE 68182-0324, phone (402)554-2771, founded 1973, co-editor Art Homer, is a semiannual literary magazine publishing fiction and poetry with occasional essays. The editor wants **"lyric poetry from 10-200 lines, preference being for under 100 lines. Subject matter is unimportant, as long as it has some. Poets should have mastered form, meaning poems should have form, not simply 'demonstrate' it." He doesn't want to see "concrete, inspirational, didactic or merely political poetry."** They have published poetry by Patricia Goedicke, Mary Swander, Roger Weingarten and Billy Collins. As a sample, he selected these lines from "The Twins Visit a Farm" by Mary Crow:

The heavy black bulk of the draft horse
lay in the heat, circled by lime. Too huge
to bury, it was left for flies, night animals.
We walked around the gleaming hill
of its flanks, the tulip-blue nostrils,
the tiny terrain of the pink gums,
the belly mushrooming sweetness.

The magazine is 6×9, nicely printed, 60 pgs., with flat-spined, glossy card cover. It is a publication of the Writer's Workshop at the University of Nebraska. Some of the most exciting, accessible verse is published in this magazine. All styles and forms are welcome here, although relatively few long poems are used. Circulation is 400, of which 260 are subscriptions and 80 go to libraries. Single copy: $3.50; subscription: $9/year. **Sample postpaid: $2. "Clean typed copy strongly preferred." Reads submissions August 15 through March 31 only. Reporting time is 3-4 months and time to publication 3-6 months. Pays 2 copies and 1-year subscription. Acquires first North American serial rights.** The TNR Awards of $300 each in poetry and fiction are published in the spring issue. Entry fee: $7, includes discounted subscription. You can enter as many times as desired. Deadline: November 30. The editor says, "Your first allegiance is to the poem. Publishing will come in time, but it will always be less than you feel you deserve. Therefore, don't look to publication as a reward for writing well; it has no relationship."

NEGATIVE CAPABILITY; NEGATIVE CAPABILITY PRESS; EVE OF ST. AGNES COMPETITION (II), 62 Ridgelawn Dr. E., Mobile AL 36608-2465, founded 1981, poetry editor Sue Walker. ***Negative Capability*** is a tri-quarterly of verse, fiction, commentary, music and art. The press publishes broadsides, chapbooks, perfect-bound paperbacks and hardbacks. They want **both contemporary and traditional poetry. "Quality has its own specifications—length and form."** They have published poetry by John Brugaletta, Rita Dove, Richard Moore, Marge Piercy, William Stafford and John Updike. As a sample Sue Walker selected these lines from "Flakey Blake" by Dorothy Moseley Sutton:

I asked Billy Blake
to come out and play with me
and while we was out there playin'
he said he seen a buncha angels
settin' up in a tree.
There wasn't no angels
settin' up in a tree.
I ain't playin with that flakey Blake no more.

The editor says, "Reaching irritably after a few facts will not describe ***Negative Capability***. Read it to know what quality goes to form creative achievement. Shakespeare had negative capability, do you?" In its short history this journal has indeed achieved a major prominence on our literary scene. It is a flat-spined, elegantly printed, digest-sized format of 130 pgs., glossy card color cover with art, circulation 1,000. About 60 pgs. of each issue are devoted to poetry. They receive about 1,200 unsolicited submissions/year, use 350. Subscription: $15; single copy: $5. **Sample postpaid: $4. Reads submissions September 1 through May 30 only. Send SASE for guidelines. Reports in 6-8 weeks. Pays 2 copies. Acquires first rights. For book publication, query with 10-12 samples and "brief letter with major publications, significant contributions, awards. We like to know a person as well as their poem." Replies to queries in 3-4 weeks, to submissions (if invited) in 6-8 weeks. Payment arranged with authors. Editor sometimes comments on rejections.** Reviews books of poetry. They offer an Annual Eve of St. Agnes Competition with major poets as judges. ***Negative Capability*** ranked #3 in the "New Poets" category of the latest ***Writer's Digest*** Poetry 60 list. This category ranks those markets who often publish poets whose work is new to their publication.

NEW COLLAGE MAGAZINE (II), 5700 N. Tamiami Trail, Sarasota FL 34243-2197, phone (813)359-4360, founded 1970, poetry editor A. McA. Miller. ***New CollAge*** provides "a forum for contemporary poets, both known and undiscovered. We are **partial to fresh slants on traditional prosodies and poetry with clear focus and clear imagery. No greeting card verse. We prefer poems shorter than five**

single-spaced pages. We like a maximum of 3-5 poems per submission." They have published poetry by Peter Meinke, Yvonne Sapia, Lola Haskins, J.P. White, Peter Klappert, Peter Wild, Stephen Corey and Malcolm Glass. The editor selected these sample lines from "The Palm at the Edge of the Bay" by Daniel Bosch:

I would need a ship to moore here, really,
if I were to earn this girth of fibrous hemp,
round-waisted, tall, leaning a head
into the corner a cross-breeze walls itself against . . .

The magazine appears 3 times a year, 28-32 pgs. of poetry in each issue, circulation 500 with 200 subscriptions of which 30 are libraries. They receive about 5,000 poems/year, use 90. Subscription: $6. **Sample: $2. Simultaneous submissions are not read. Publishes theme issues. Send SASE for upcoming themes. Reports in 6 weeks. Pays 2 copies. Editor sometimes comments on rejections.** "We review books and chapbooks in 1,000-2,000 words." Editor "Mac" Miller advises, "Sending a ms already marked 'copyright' is absurd and unprofessional. Mss may be marked 'first North American serials only,' though this is unnecessary. Also, quality is the only standard. Get a sample issue to see our taste."

THE NEW CRITERION (III), The Foundation for Cultural Review, Inc., 850 Seventh Ave., New York NY 10019, poetry editor Robert Richman, is a monthly (except July and August) review of ideas and the arts, which uses poetry of high literary quality. They have published poetry by Donald Justice, Andrew Hudgins, Elizabeth Spires and Herbert Morris. It is 90 pgs., 7×10, flat-spined. Poems here truly are open, with structured free verse and formal works highlighted in the issues we critiqued. Much of it was excellent, and book reviews were insightful. **Sample postpaid: $4.75. Cover letter required with submissions. Reports in 2-3 months. Pays $2.50/line ($75 minimum).** Poetry published in this review was selected for inclusion in the 1992 and 1994 volumes of **The Best American Poetry**, and ***The New Criterion*** ranked #3 in the "Top Pay" category of the latest ***Writer's Digest*** Poetry 60 list. The editor says, "To have an idea of who we are or what we stand for aesthetically, poets should consult back issues."

NEW DELTA REVIEW; THE EYSTER PRIZE (II), English Dept., Louisiana State University, Baton Rouge LA 70803-5001, poetry editor Brook Haley, writes, **"We publish works of quality, many of them by young writers who are building their reputations."** They have recently published poetry by Robert Brown, Janet Bowdan, Timothy Geiger and Ioanna-Veronika Warwick. As a sample, the editor selected these lines from "Those Tattooed" by Allan Peterson:

Bodies are gangs of ourselves;
there is a heap of us in our organs
and the edge of us may hold messages.
Diagnostic spiders and roses come like fish
to the surface, the names of those women
surely wronged have come up on the arms
once around them. . .

NDR appears twice a year, 6×9, flat-spined, 90-120 pgs., typeset and printed on quality stock with glossy card cover with art. Press run is 500, with 100 subscriptions, 20 of which are from libraries; the rest are for shelf sales. Subscription: $7. **Sample postpaid: $4. No simultaneous submissions or previously published poems. Cover letter with biographical information required. Mss read in summer. Poetry editor sometimes comments on rejections, often suggesting possible revisions. Reports in 1-2 months. Sometimes sends prepublication galleys. Pays 2 copies. Acquires first North American serial rights.** Reviews books of poetry in no more than 2,000 words, single or multi-book format. Open to unsolicited reviews and interviews. Poets may also send books to poetry editor for review consideration. The Eyster Prize of $50 is awarded to the best story and best poem in each issue. The editor says, "Our only criterion is quality: work that has obviously resulted from much care and respect for the poetic arts. We consider all work that we accept innovative, because even formal verse is an inexhaustible source of new, beautiful poems."

NEW DIRECTIONS PUBLISHING CORPORATION (V, IV-Translations), 80 Eighth Ave., New York NY 10011, founded 1936, poetry editor Peter Glassgold. New Directions is "a small publisher of 20th-Century literature with an emphasis on the experimental," publishing about 36 paperback and hardback titles each year. **"We are looking for highly unusual, literary, experimental poetry. We can't use traditional poetry, no matter how accomplished. However, we are not accepting submissions at this time."** They have published poetry by William Carlos Williams, Ezra Pound, Denise Levertov, Jerome Rothenberg, Robert Creeley, Michael McClure, Kenneth Rexroth, H.D., Robert Duncan, Stevie Smith, David Antin, Hayden Carruth, George Oppen, Dylan Thomas, Lawrence Ferlinghetti, Jimmy Santiago Baca, Rosmarie Waldrop and Gary Snyder. **To see samples, try the library or purchase from their catalog (available), local bookstores or their distributor, W.W. Norton.** New Directions advises, "Getting published is not easy, but the best thing to do is to work on being published in the magazines and journals, thus building up an audience. Once the poet has an audience, the publisher will be able to sell the poet's books. Avoid vanity publishers and read a lot of poetry."

NEW EARTH PUBLICATIONS (IV-Spiritual, political, translations), 1921 Ashby Ave., Berkeley CA 94703, phone (510)549-0176, founded 1990, editors Clifton Ross and Dave Karoly, publishes **"books (up to 96 pgs.; query if longer) dealing with the struggle for peace and justice, revolutionary anarchism, quality poetry, prose and translations. Some publications are author subsidized."** They publish 1-2 paperbacks, 2-3 chapbooks/year. **Reports on queries in 2 weeks, on mss in 6 weeks. Sometimes sends prepublication galleys. Pays 10% royalties or 10% of press run.** Also publishes ***Utopian Worker***, an annual magazine of revolutionary spiritual culture.

NEW ENGLAND REVIEW (II), Middlebury College, Middlebury VT 05753, phone (802)388-3711, ext. 5075, founded 1978, acting editor David Huddle, associate editor William Lychack. ***New England Review*** is a prestigious literary quarterly, 6×9, 160 pgs., flat-spined, elegant make-up and printing on heavy stock, glossy cover with art. All styles and forms are welcome in this carefully edited publication. Poets published include Toi Derricotte, Albert Goldbarth, Norman Dubie, Philip Booth and Carol Frost. Subscription: $18. **Sample postpaid: $4. Response times can be exceptionally slow here, far exceeding published limits of 6-8 weeks. Always sends prepublication galleys. Pays.** Also features essay-reviews. Publishers may send books for review consideration. Work published in this review was included in the 1992, 1993 and 1994 volumes of **The Best American Poetry.** In addition, ***New England Review*** ranked #7 in the "Poets' Pick" category of the latest ***Writer's Digest*** Poetry 60 list. This category ranks those publications in which poets said they would most like to see their work published.

NEW ERA MAGAZINE (I, IV-Religious, teen/young adult), 50 E. North Temple St., Salt Lake City UT 84150, phone (801)240-2951, founded 1971, managing editor Richard M. Romney, appears monthly. ***New Era*** is an "official publication for youth of The Church of Jesus Christ of Latter-day Saints; it contains feature stories, photo stories, fiction, news, etc." They want **"short verse in any form, particularly traditional—must pertain to teenage LDS audience (religious and teenage themes). No sing-songy doggerel, gushy love poems or forced rhymes."** As a sample the editor selected these lines from "Walls" by Dorothy Karen Patterson:

All those walls,
See how they crumble
At the touch of the hand
Of love.

Like sandcastles,
Melted by the kiss of the sea,
My fortress falls
With each warm word
And gentle look.

New Era is 52 pgs., approximately 8×10½, 4-color offset, saddle-stitched, quality stock, top-notch art and graphics, no ads. They receive 200-300 submissions, purchase 2-5%. Press run is 220,000 for 205,000 subscribers, 10,000 shelf sales. Single copy: 75¢; subscription: $8/year. **Sample: 75¢ plus postage. No previously published poems or simultaneous submissions. Send no more than 5 poems at one time.** Time between acceptance and publication is a year or longer. "We publish one poem each month next to our photo of the month." **Sometimes comments on rejections. Publishes 1-2 theme issues each year, one of which is geographically themed (LDS youth in one country). Theme for the October 1994 issue: LDS Youth in Australia; for March 1995: Leadership; for September 1995: LDS Youth in New Zealand. Send SASE for writer's guidelines. Reports in 6-8 weeks. Sometimes sends prepublication galleys. Pays $10 minimum. Buys all rights. "LDS church retains rights to publish again in church publications—all other rights returned."** They also offer an annual contest—including poetry—for active members of the LDS church between ages 12-23. Poetry entries should consist of one entry of 6-10 different original poems (none of which exceeds 50 lines) reflecting LDS values. Deadline: January. Winners receive either a partial scholarship to BYU or Ricks College or a cash award. Send SASE for rules. The editor says, "Study the magazine before submitting. We're a great market for beginners, but you must understand Mormons to write well for us. Just because a subject is noble or inspirational doesn't mean the poetry automatically is noble or inspirational. Pay attention to the craft of writing. Poetry is more than just writing down your thoughts about an inspirational subject. Poetry needs to communicate easily and be readily understood—it's too easy to mistake esoteric expression for true insight."

NEW HOPE INTERNATIONAL (II), 20 Werneth Ave., Gee Cross, Hyde, Cheshire SK14 5NL United Kingdom, founded 1969, editor Gerald England, includes **"*NHI Writing*, publishing poetry, short fiction, translations, artwork, literary essays and reports. All types of poetry from traditional to avant-garde, from haiku to long poems. *NHI Review* carries reviews of books, magazines, cassettes, CDs, records, PC software, etc. Special Edition Chapbooks with a theme or individual collections also included."** They have recently published poetry by Steven Duplij, Eric Forsberg, Elizabeth Hillman, D.F. Lewis, Gordon Mason, tolek and Maureen Weldon. As a sample the editor selected these lines from "The Couple" by B.W. Beynon:

I celebrate the invisible embrace
feeding the relationship of atmosphere
which crackles with warm moods
A flame of relish for making pleasure,
the art of untamed bodies which hotly caress
residing as one within hidden spaces.

The digest-sized magazine, 36-40 pgs., is printed offset-litho from computer typesetting, saddle-stapled, color card cover, using b&w artwork. Press run is 600 for 300 subscribers of which 25 are libraries. $30 for 6 issues (***NHI Writing*, *NHI Review*** and **S.E. Chapbooks** as published). **Sample postpaid: $5 cash (add $5 to cover bank charges if paying by check). Put name and address on each sheet; not more than 6 at a time; simultaneous submissions *not* encouraged. Cover letter required. Translations should include copy of original. Full guidelines available for IRC (3 for airmail). Send 1 IRC for reply if return of mss not required. Publishes theme issues. Themes for 1995 include computer poetics. Reports "usually fairly prompt, but sometimes up to 4 months." Always sends prepublication galleys. Pays 1 copy. Acquires first British serial rights.** Staff reviews books of poetry. Send books for review consideration. **For chapbooks, query first.** The editor advises, "Long lists of previous publications do not impress; perceptive, interesting, fresh writing indicative of a live, thinking person makes this job worthwhile."

NEW HORIZONS POETRY CLUB (II, IV-Membership), Box 5561, Chula Vista CA 91912, phone (619)474-4715, founded 1984, poetry editor Alex Stewart. This organization offers poetry contests of various sorts for experienced writers, publishing winners in an anthology. They also offer newsletters and critiques and publish anthologies of members' poetry. Membership (includes 4 newsletters): $10/year. They have published poetry by Alice Mackenzie Swaim, Glenna Holloway, Pegasus Buchanan and Thelma Schiller. Prizes in their Annual Poetry Day Contest are "$250 and down. We offer other cash awards, prizes and trophies, and certificates for honorable mentions. 'Mini-manuscript' winners are offered trophies, cash prizes and free anthologies." Entry fees are $5/2 poems, $10/5 poems. **"We expect poets to know technique, to be familiar with traditional forms and to be able to conform to requirements regarding category, style and length and to show originality, imagery and craftsmanship. Nothing amateurish, trite or in poor taste."** Alex Stewart offers critiques at reasonable rates. (Discounts on critiques and books to members.) She says, "Poets need to study technique before *rushing to get published!* (*Where* is what counts!) The current trend seems to be a healthy blend of traditional forms and comprehensible free verse." NHPC publishes 3 books annually, 2 in the NHPC Poets' Series (4 poets/book) and 1 anthology of prizewinning and selected poems from the semiannual contests. (Book list, including **The Poet's Art**, the editor's complete handbook on the craft of poetry writing, available on request.)

THE NEW LAUREL REVIEW (II, IV-Translations), 828 Lesseps St., New Orleans LA 70117, founded 1971, editor Lee Meitzen Grue, "is an annual independent nonprofit literary magazine dedicated to fine art. Each issue contains poetry, translations, literary essays, reviews of small press books, and visual art." They want **"poetry with strong, accurate imagery. We have no particular preference in style. We try to be eclectic. No more than 3 poems in a submission."** They have published poetry by Jane McClellan, Kalamu Ya Salaam, Melody Davis, Sue Walker and Keith Cartwright. As a sample the editor selected these lines by Quo Vadis Gex-Breaux:

She had a kind of classy coarseness
like raw silk
a kind of open earthiness

The Subject Index, located before the General Index, can help you narrow down markets for your work. It lists those publishers whose poetry interests are specialized.

without being dirt
a way of saying things
that made them seem something
more than she meant
(sometimes a little less)

The ***Review*** is 6×9, laser printed, 115 pgs., original art on cover, accepts 30 poems of 300 mss received. It has a circulation of 500. Single copy: $9. **Sample (back issue) postpaid: $7. Accepts simultaneous submissions. Submit 3-5 poems with SASE and a short note with previous publications. Reads submissions September 1 through May 30 only. Guidelines for SASE. Reports on submissions in 3 months, publishes in 8-10 months. Pays contributor's copies. Acquires first rights.** Reviews books of poetry in 1,000 words, single or multi-book format. The editor advises, "Read our magazine before submitting poetry."

"Poetry is a matter of life," says Robert Stewart, managing editor of* New Letters. *"It comprises about a third of our content." The quarterly magazine, published by the University of Missouri-Kansas City, includes the work of both established writers and new talents. "We are dedicated to publishing the best poetry, short fiction, photography and artwork available," Stewart says. "We choose art that is fresh, lively and sophisticated, without regard for theme or philosophy." The artwork on this cover is entitled "Wall Eye" and is by Arizona artist James G. Davis.

NEW LETTERS; NEW LETTERS POETRY PRIZE (II), University of Missouri-Kansas City, Kansas City MO 64110, phone (816)235-1168, founded 1934 as ***University Review***, became ***New Letters*** in 1971, managing editor Bob Stewart, editor James McKinley, "is dedicated to publishing the best short fiction, best contemporary poetry, literary articles, photography and artwork by both established writers and new talents." They want **"contemporary writing of all types—free verse poetry preferred, short works are more likely to be accepted than very long ones."** They have published poetry by Joyce Carol Oates, Hayden Carruth, John Frederick Nims, Louise Glück, Louis Simpson, Vassar Miller and John Tagliabue. The flat-spined, professionally printed quarterly, glossy 2-color cover with art, 6×9, uses about 65 (of 120) pgs. of poetry in each issue. Circulation 1,845 with 1,520 subscriptions of which about 40% are libraries. They receive about 7,000 submissions/year, use less than 1%, have a 6-month backlog. Poems appear in a variety of styles exhibiting a high degree of craft and universality of theme (rare in many journals). Subscription: $17. **Sample postpaid: $5. Send no more than 6 poems at once. No simultaneous submissions. "We strongly prefer original typescripts and we don't read between May 15 and October 15. No query needed." Reports in 4-10 weeks. Pays a small fee plus 2 copies. Occasionally James McKinley comments on rejections.** The New Letters Poetry Prize of $750 is given annually for a group of 3-6 poems, entry fee $10 (check payable to New Letters Literary Awards). Send SASE for entry guidelines. Deadline: May 15. They also publish occasional anthologies, selected and edited by McKinley. Work published in ***New Letters*** appeared in **The Best American Poetry 1992.**

‡NEW METHODS: THE JOURNAL OF ANIMAL HEALTH TECHNOLOGY (IV-Specialized: animals), P.O. Box 22605, San Francisco CA 94122-0605, phone (415)664-3469, founded as ***Methods*** in 1976, poetry editor Ronald S. Lippert, AHT, is an irregular 4-page newsletter "a networking service in the animal field, active in seeking new avenues of knowledge for our readers, combining animal professionals under one roof." They want poetry which is "**animal related but not cutesy, two pages maximum.**" They receive about 50 poems a year, accept 5. Press run is 5,000 for 4,000 subscribers of which 100 are libraries. Subscription: $29. **Sample: $2.90. A listing of all back issues and the topics covered is**

available for $5, and there is a 20% discount on an order of 12 or more mixed copies. No previously published poems; simultaneous submissions OK. Dated cover letter required. Everything typed, double space with one-inch margins. Often comments on rejections. Send SASE for guidelines. Reports in 2-4 weeks. Pays negotiable number of copies. Reviews books of poetry "pertaining to our subject matter."

NEW ORLEANS POETRY JOURNAL PRESS (III), 2131 General Pershing St., New Orleans LA 70115, phone (504)891-3458, founded 1956, publisher/editor Maxine Cassin, co-editor Charles deGravelles. **"We prefer to publish relatively new and/or little-known poets of unusual promise or those inexplicably neglected—'the real thing.' " They do not want to see "cliché or doggerel, anything incomprehensible or too derivative, or workshop exercises. First-rate lyric poetry preferred (not necessarily in traditional forms)."** They have published books by Vassar Miller, Everette Maddox, Charles Black, Raeburn Miller and Martha McFerren. Their most recent book is **Illuminated Manuscript** by Malaika Favorite. As a sample the editor selected these lines from "Missing Z and Nola" in **Hanoi Rose** by Ralph Adamo:

Nobody owns the bright blue dawn for long.
You can be there day after day, raking it in,
and still there'll be a palm under your token,
and the palm won't be yours. And the animal
you traded power with will contrive to be
given away. In the barracks where the last
detachment waits, beauty won't show her face.

Query first. They do not accept unsolicited submissions for chapbooks, which are flat-spined paperbacks. **The editors report on queries in 2-3 months, mss in the same time period, if solicited. Simultaneous submissions will possibly be accepted. Sometimes sends prepublication galleys. Pay is in author's copies, usually 50-100.** Ms. Cassin does not subsidy publish at present and does not offer grants or awards. For aspiring poets, she quotes the advice Borges received from his father: "1) Read as much as possible! 2) Write only when you *must*, and 3) Don't rush into print!" As a small press editor and publisher, she urges poets to read instructions in **Poet's Market** listings with utmost care! She says, "No poetry should be sent without querying first! Publishers are concerned about expenses unnecessarily incurred in mailing manuscripts. *Telephoning is not encouraged.*"

NEW ORLEANS REVIEW (II), Box 195, Loyola University, New Orleans LA 70118, phone (504)865-2295 or 865-2286, founded 1968, editor Ralph Adamo. They have recently published poetry by Jimmy Carter. It is 100 pgs., perfect-bound, elegantly printed with glossy card cover using a full-color painting. Poems are set off from prose with plenty of white space in this 8½×11 magazine and tend toward free verse establishing a milieu and appealing to the senses (via voice). Circulation is 750. **Sample postpaid: $10. Reports in 3 months. Acquires first North American serial rights.**

THE NEW POETS SERIES, INC.; CHESTNUT HILLS PRESS (II); STONEWALL SERIES (IV-Gay/lesbian/bisexual), 541 Piccadilly, Baltimore MD 21204, phone (301)830-2863 or 828-0724, founded 1970, editor/director Clarinda Harriss Raymond. The New Poets Series, Inc. brings out **first books by promising new poets. They want "excellent, fresh, nontrendy, literate, intelligent poems. Any form (including traditional), any style."** Provides 20 copies to the author, the sales proceeds going back into the corporation to finance the next volume (usual press run: 1,000). "It has been successful in its effort to provide these new writers with a national distribution; in fact, The New Poets Series was named an Outstanding Small Press by the prestigious Pushcart Awards Committee, which judges some 5,000 small press publications annually." Chestnut Hills Press publishes author-subsidized books—"High quality work only, however. CHP has achieved a reputation for prestigious books, printing only the top 10% of mss CHP and NPS receive." The New Poets Series has published books by Nuala Archer, Richard Fein, Shelley Scott, Carole Glasser Langille, Peter Wessel, Charles Stuart Roberts, Elaine Erickson, Jan-Mitchell Sherrill, Gail Wronsky and Tony Esolen. Clarinda Harriss Raymond selected "Calling Canada," a complete poem by Irish writer Medbh McGuckian, as a sample:

I talk to the darkness as if to a daughter
Or something that once pressed from inside
Like a street of youth. My striped notebook
Is just a dress over my body, so I will waken
At a touch, or for no reason at all. In it
I learn how to cut into other people's dreams,
How to telephone them Paris-style and how
Like sunshine, a tenderness roughened
Because there was so little time for snow-months
To paint my woman's walls into sea.

Send a 50- to 55-page ms, $10 reading fee and cover letter giving publication credits and bio. Simultaneous submissions OK. Editor sometimes comments briefly on rejections. Reports in 6

weeks to 8 months. Mss "are circulated to an editorial board of professional, publishing poets. NPS is backlogged, but the best 10% of the mss it receives are automatically eligible for Chestnut Hills Press consideration," a subsidy arrangement. **Send $5 for a sample volume.** Stonewall Series offers a chapbook contest whose winner is published by NPS. Send 20-25 poems with $20 entry fee. Stonewall is for gay, lesbian and bisexual writers.

THE NEW PRESS LITERARY QUARTERLY; THE NEW PRESS POETRY CONTEST (II), 53-35 Hollis Ct. Blvd., Flushing NY 11365, founded 1984, poetry editors Evie-Ivy and Francine Witte, is a quarterly magazine using **poems "less than 200 lines, accessible, imaginative. No doggerel, sentimentality."** They have recently published poetry by Allen Ginsberg, Lawrence Ferlinghetti, Les Bridges and Gina Bergamino. As a sample the editor selected these lines by R. Nikolas Macioci:

a conversation he has
with himself as he thinks now
of hinges he must oil
before old doors will open
quietly onto another year's
garden and the scent
of newly spaded soil.

It is magazine-sized, 40 pgs., desktop-published, with glossy cover, saddle-stapled. They accept about 10% of 700 poems received/year. Press run is 1,600 for 275 subscribers of which 3 are libraries, 1,100 shelf sales. Subscription: $15. **Sample postpaid: $4. "Include name and address on the top of each page." Publishes theme issues. Send SASE for upcoming themes. Reports in 3 months. Always sends prepublication galleys. Pays 3 copies. Acquires first-time rights.** The New Press Poetry Contest is semiannual, deadlines are January and July 1, entry fee of $5 for up to 3 poems or 200 lines, has prizes of $150, $75 and ten 2-year subscriptions. Also sponsors quarterly essay and short story contests. Send 10 and 22 double-spaced pgs. maximum with entry fee of $5 and SASE. Prize is $100.

THE NEW QUARTERLY (II, IV-Regional), ELPP University of Waterloo, Waterloo, Ontario N2L 3G1 Canada, phone (519)885-1211, ext. 2837, founded 1981, managing editor Mary Merikle, is a "literary quarterly – new directions in Canadian writing." For the poetry they want, the editors have **"no preconceived conception – usually Canadian work, poetry capable of being computer typeset – 4½" line length typeset lines. No greeting card verse."** The editor describes it as 120 pgs., flat-spined, 6×8½, with a photograph on the cover, no graphics or art, some ads. Of 2,000 poems received/year, they use 100. Press run is 600 for 300 subscriptions (10 of them libraries) and additional shelf sales. Subscription: $15 (add $2 for US or overseas subscriptions). **Sample postpaid: $4 Canadian, $4 US. Submit no more than 5 poems at a time. Cover letter with short bio required. Send SASE for guidelines. Reports in 3-6 months. No comments on rejections of poetry. Pays $20/poem plus 3 copies.**

‡THE NEW RENAISSANCE (II, IV-Translations, bilingual), 9 Heath Rd., Arlington MA 02174, founded 1968, poetry editor Stanwood Bolton. ***the new renaissance*** is "intended for the 'renaissance' person, the generalist rather than the specialist. Seeks to publish the best new writing, to offer a forum for articles of public concern, to feature established non-mainstream as well as emerging visual artists, and to highlight interest in neglected writers and artists in its essay/review section. **We are open to traditional as well as other types of poetry and usually receive samples of every kind during our submission periods.**" They have recently published poetry by Richard Holinger, Robert Parham, Frank Finale and Fr. Benedict Auer and translations by Ruth Feldman (Gina Labriola), Marek Labinski (Halina Poswiatowska), Alexis Levitin (Eugenio de Andrade) and Don Mager (Jaroslav Seifet). As a sample of the poetry they're publishing, the editor selected these lines from "Rumors" by Jay Griswold:

And the man who lives alone,
what will they say about him?
A killer inhabits each of his hands;
a reptile is coiled inside his pulse.
A man who writes poetry must defend himself.
He's not called Ulysses when the sirens
sing, when his poetry falls on its own sword.
He prefers seagulls and foreign towns.

tnr is flat-spined, professionally printed on heavy stock, glossy, color cover, 144-206 pgs., using 20-40 pgs. of poetry in each issue. They receive about 650 poetry submissions/year, use 20-26, have about a 3-year backlog. Usual press run is 1,600 for 710 subscribers of which approximately 132 are libraries. Subscriptions: $19.50/3 issues US, $21 Canada, $23 all others. **"We're an unsponsored, independent small litmag. Contributors are expected to help the magazine by sending in, with their submissions, a check for $10, for which they may receive any combination of the following: 2 back issues or 1 back issue and a 1980s issue or a current issue.** ***Exceptions to this***

rule: **All current subscribers and all writers who have bought an issue or two since July 1, 1992. For guidelines, send $5 and we'll send an '82 issue and copy of guidelines. We will be reading manuscripts from January 2 through March 2, 1995." Reports in 3-6 months. Pays $13-20, more for the occasional longer poem, plus 1 copy. Buys all rights. Returns rights provided *tnr* retains rights for any *tnr* collection, anthology, etc.** Reviews books of poetry in 4-5 pgs., single book; 5-11 pgs., multi-book. "We believe that poets should not only be readers but lovers of poetry. We're looking for 'literalists of the imagination—imaginary gardens with real toads in them.' **Our range is from traditionalist poetry to post-modern, experimental (the latter only occasionally, though) and street poetry. We also like the occasional 'light' poem and, of course, we have an emphasis on translations. We're especially interested in the individual voice. We aren't interested in greeting card verse or prose set in poetic forms."**

THE NEW REPUBLIC (II), 1220 19th St. NW, Washington DC 20036, phone (202)331-7494, founded 1914, poetry editor Mary Jo Salter. ***The New Republic***, a weekly journal of opinion, is magazine-sized, printed on slick paper, 42 pgs., saddle-stapled with 4-color cover. Subscription: $69.97/year. **Back issues available for $3.50 postpaid. Include SASE with submissions. Always sends prepublication galleys. They provide no payment information.** Poetry published in ***The New Republic*** has also been included in the 1993 and 1994 volumes of **The Best American Poetry.**

NEW RIVERS PRESS; MINNESOTA VOICES PROJECT, INC. (II, IV-Regional, translations), Suite 910, 420 N. Fifth St., Minneapolis MN 55401, founded 1968, publishes collections of poetry, translations of contemporary literature, collections of short fiction, and is also involved in publishing **Minnesota regional literary material. Write for free catalog or send SASE for guidelines/inquiries. New and emerging authors living in Iowa, Minnesota, North and South Dakota and Wisconsin are eligible for the Minnesota Voices Project. Book-length mss of poetry,** short fiction, novellas or familiar essays are all accepted. **Send SASE for entry form. Winning authors receive a stipend of $500 plus publication by New Rivers. Second and subsequent printings of works will allow 15% royalties for author.**

NEW VIRGINIA REVIEW (II), 2A, 1306 E. Cary St., Richmond VA 23219, phone (804)782-1043, founded 1978, poetry editor Margaret Gibson, appears 3 times a year publishing both fiction and poetry. They want **"seriously written poetry addressing any subject matter, in any variety of styles. No greeting card verse or haiku."** They have published poetry by Mona Van Duyn, Mary Oliver, Philip Booth and Norman Dubie. ***NVR*** is 160 pgs., 6¾×10, offset, perfect-bound, with color cover, no graphics. They receive over 6,000 mss a year, accept approximately 10%. Press run is 2,500 for 1,500 subscribers of which 20% are libraries, 250 shelf sales. Subscription: $15. **Sample postpaid: $6. No previously published poems; simultaneous submissions OK. Reads submissions September 1 through May 31 only. Seldom comments on rejections. Send SASE for guidelines. Reports in 3-6 weeks. Pays $25/poem on publication, plus $10 for additional printed pages. Buys first North American serial rights.**

NEW VOICES IN POETRY AND PROSE; NEW VOICES SPRING/FALL COMPETITIONS (I), P.O. Box 52196, Shreveport LA 71135, founded 1990, editor Cheryl White, is a semiannual that publishes new poets and writers and reviews collected works. **"All types of poetry welcome. However, prefer poetry that makes a statement about the emotions of the writer."** The editor says it is 12-16 pgs., 8½×11. Press run is approximately 250 for 100 subscribers. Subscription: $8. **Sample postpaid: $5. Seldom comments on rejections. Send SASE for guidelines. Reports in approximately 1 month. Pays 1 copy.** Offers semiannual poetry and short fiction competitions. Small entry fees. Cash prizes.

NEW WRITER'S MAGAZINE (I, II, IV-Humor, writing), P.O. Box 5976, Sarasota FL 34277, phone (813)953-7903, founded 1986, editor George J. Haborak, is a bimonthly magazine "for aspiring writers, and professional ones as well, to exchange ideas and working experiences." **They are open to free verse, light verse and traditional, 8-20 lines, reflecting upon the writing lifestyle. "Humorous slant on writing life especially welcomed." They do not want poems about "love, personal problems, abstract ideas or fantasy."** As a sample the editor selected this poem, "Lucky Who?" by Vera Koppler:

> *I wish I were Anonymous*
> *When I send out a rhyme*
> *For lucky old Anonymous*
> *Gets published all the time.*

NWM is 28 pgs., 8½×11, offset, saddle-stapled, with glossy paper cover, b&w photos and ads. They receive about 300 poems a year, accept approximately 10%. Press run is 5,000. Single copy: $2; subscription: $14 for 1 year, $25 for 2 years. **Sample postpaid: $3. Submit up to 3 poems at a time. No previously published poems or simultaneous submissions.** Time between acceptance and publication is 1 year maximum. **Send SASE for guidelines. Reports in 1-2 months. Pays $5/poem. Buys first North American serial rights.** Each issue of this magazine also includes an interview with a recognized author, articles on writing and the writing life, tips and markets.

NEW YORK QUARTERLY (II), P.O. Box 693, Old Chelsea Station, New York NY 10113, founded 1969, poetry editor William Packard, appears 3 times/year. They seek to publish "a cross-section of the best of contemporary American poetry" and, indeed, **have a record of publishing many of the best and most diverse of poets**, including W.D. Snodgrass, Gregory Corso, James Dickey and Judson Jerome. It appears in a 6×9, flat-spined format, thick, elegantly printed, glossy color cover. Subscription: $15 to 305 Neville Hall, University of Maine, Orono ME 04469. (This address is for subscriptions *only*. Poetry mss should be submitted to above New York address.) **Submit 3-5 poems. Reports within 2 weeks. Pays copies.** This magazine is sponsored by The National Poetry Foundation. See listing under Organizations Useful to Poets.

THE NEW YORKER (III, IV-Translations, humor), 20 W. 43rd St., New York NY 10036, founded 1925, poetry editor Alice Quinn, circulation 640,000, uses **poetry of the highest quality (including translations). Sample: $2.50 (available on newsstands). Mss are not read during the summer. Replies in 6-8 weeks. Pays top rates.** Seven poems appearing in *The New Yorker* were selected for inclusion in the 1992, 1993 and 1994 volumes of **The Best American Poetry**. In addition, *The New Yorker* itself ranked #2 in the "Poets' Pick" category of the latest *Writer's Digest* Poetry 60 list. This category ranks those publications in which poets said they would most like to see their work published.

NEWSLETTER INAGO (I), P.O. Box 26244, Tucson AZ 85726-6244, phone (602)294-7031, founded 1979, poetry editor Del Reitz, is a monthly newsletter, 4-5 pgs., corner-stapled. **"Free verse preferred although other forms will be read. Rhymed poetry must be truly exceptional (nonforced) for consideration. Due to format, 'epic' and monothematic poetry will not be considered. Cause specific, political or religious poetry stands little chance of consideration. A wide range of short poetry, showing the poet's preferably eclectic perspective is best for *NI*. No haiku, please."** They have recently published poetry by Steve Fay, Paul D. McGlynn, Ian Westbrook, Robert E. Sharp, Michel Fortier, Evelyn Elster, Angie Dixon, Maureen Weldon, Kimberly Swanson and Deborah Forbes. The editor says, "Since editorial taste in poetry especially is such a subjective and narrow thing," a short selection cannot be chosen "with any fairness to either that taste or the poet whose material might be quoted." However, as a sample the editor selected these lines by Patricia M. Mahon:

Field flies made their last dance
In a luminous bath of light.
A black horned slug crawled
Down a wet wall
To the cover of grass.
Four plump nuns passed.

Their press run is approximately 200 for that many subscriptions. **No price is given for the newsletter, but the editor suggests a donation of $3 an issue or $17 annually ($3 and $20 Canada, £7 and £20 U.K.). Guidelines available for SASE. They consider simultaneous submissions and previously published poems. Editor sometimes comments on rejections. Reports ASAP (usually within 2 weeks). Pays 4 copies.**

NEXUS (II), 006 University Center, Wright State University, Dayton OH 45435, phone (513)873-5533, founded 1967, editor J.S. Ampleforth. **"*Nexus*** is a student operated magazine of mainstream and street poetry; also essays on environmental and political issues. **We're looking for truthful, direct poetry. Open to poets anywhere. We look for contemporary, imaginative work."** Issues have featured themes on Japan and American West. *Nexus* appears 3 times a year—fall, winter and spring, using about 40 pgs. of poetry (of 80-96) in each issue, circulation 1,000. They receive 1,000 submissions/year, use 30-50. **For a sample, send a 10×15 SAE with 5 first-class stamps and $5. Submit up to 6 pgs. of poetry, with bio, September through May. Simultaneous submissions OK. Editor sometimes comments on rejections. Send SASE for guidelines. Reports in 10-12 weeks except summer months. Pays 2 copies. Acquires first American serial rights.**

NIGHT OWL'S NEWSLETTER (I, IV-Specialized: living by night, themes), (formerly listed under Julian Associates), P.O. Box 488, La Porte TX 77572-0488, phone (713)470-8748, editor Robin Kendle Parker. *NON*, a quarterly newsletter, uses **poetry relevant to their overall theme only: living by night. "Anything with a clear message. No limitations on style. Humor is a plus! Poems that are all image and no clear meaning waste our time."** They have published poetry by Lynn Bradley. *NON* is magazine-sized, corner-stapled. Press run is 250-300. **Sample postpaid: $3.50. Previously published poems and simultaneous submissions OK, but tell the editor about them. Publishes theme issues. Send SASE for guidelines and upcoming themes. Possible future themes: Drugs and Sleep, Sleep Clinic Therapies, Insomniac or Owl: Which Are You?. Reports in 2 months. Pays at least $1 plus at least one copy. Buys one-time rights.**

NIGHT ROSES (I, IV-Teen/young adult, love/romance, nature, students, women/feminism); MOONSTONE BLUE (I, IV-Anthology, science fiction/fantasy), P.O. Box 393, Prospect Heights IL

60070, phone (708)392-2435, founded 1986, poetry editor Allen T. Billy, appears 2-4 times a year. "*Moonstone Blue* is a science fiction/fantasy anthology, but we have no set dates of publication. We do an issue every 14-24 months as items, time and funds allow. We look for women/feminism themes for our ***Bikini*** series." For ***Night Roses*** they want **"poems about dance, bells, clocks, nature, ghost images of past or future, romance and flowers (roses, wildflowers, violets, etc.). Do not want poems with raw language."** They have recently published poetry by Judith Beckett, M. Riesa Clark, Joan Payne Kincaid, Lyn Lifshin and Alice Rogoff. As a sample the editor selected these lines from "Blue Notes" by Cynthia C. Bergen:

A funky sax wails
on a violet evening
in the square.

Night Roses is 44 pgs., saddle-stapled, photocopied from typescript on offset paper with tinted matte card cover. Press run is 200-300. Subscription: $10 for 3 issues. **Sample postpaid: $3.50 for *Night Roses*, $3 for *Moonstone Blue*. "Desire author's name and address on all sheets of ms. If previously published—an acknowledgment must be provided by author with it." No simultaneous submissions; some previously published poems used. "I prefer submissions between March and September." Reports in 6-12 weeks. "Material is accepted for current issue and 2 in progress." Sometimes sends prepublication galleys. Pays 1 copy. Acquires first or reprint rights.** Staff reviews books of poetry. Send books for review consideration. The editor says, "We are more interested in items that would be of interest to our teen and women readers and to our readership in the fields of dance, art and creative learning. We are interested in positive motives in this area."

NIGHT SONGS (IV-Horror), 4998 Perkins Rd., Baton Rouge LA 70808-3043, founded 1991, editor Gary William Crawford, is a quarterly newsletter that publishes "supernatural horror poetry in the great tradition of supernatural verse. Poems that modernize themes explored in the poetry of Poe, Baudelaire, H.P. Lovecraft." They want **"horror poetry in a variety of forms. However, not interested in strict imitations of such poets as Edgar Allan Poe or H.P. Lovecraft. In general, themes of terror and darkness, madness and death should be present. Poems that explore the underlying horror of civilization."** They have published poetry by Bruce Boston, Lisa Lepovetsky, Keith Allen Daniels and Joey Froehlich. As a sample the editor selected these lines from "The Morning of Interment" by June Miller:

The human step creeps closer, almost silent
but at first tread great wings outspread,
three glittering jet projectiles shoot the sky
soaring, arcing over shore and ocean,
black against the sun.

Night Songs is 6 pgs., 8½×11, neatly photocopied with line drawings and stapled at the corner. They receive about 30 poems/month, use approximately 5. Press run is 75 for 45 subscribers. Subscription: $3/year. **Sample postpaid: $1. No previously published poems or simultaneous submissions.** Time between acceptance and publication is 6 months. **Often comments on rejections. Reports in 2 weeks. Always sends prepublication galleys. Pays $1/poem. Buys first rights.**

NIGHTSUN (II), Dept. of English, Frostburg State University, Frostburg MD 21532, founded 1981, editor Douglas DeMars, is a literary annual of poetry, fiction and interviews. **They want "highest quality poetry." Subject matter open. Prefers poems not much longer than 40 lines. Not interested in the "extremes of sentimental, obvious poetry on the one hand and the subjectless 'great gossamer-winged gnat' school of poetry on the other."** They have recently published poetry by William Stafford, Linda Pastan, Marge Piercy, Diane Wakoski, Dennis Brutus, Philip Dacey and Walter McDonald. Interviews include Carolyn Forché, Grace Cavalieri, Lucille Clifton, Sharon Olds, Galway Kinnell and Stephen Dobyns. As a sample the editor selected these lines from "Adultery" by Michael Cadnum:

We swim quietly so no one wakes,
chlorine stinging our eyes.
Beyond the city limit
the gullies fall away to oleander.

Nightsun is 54 pgs., 6×9, printed on 100% recycled paper and saddle-stapled with card cover, b&w photo on front. This attractive journal features well-known poets alongside relative newcomers. Editors take free verse mostly with attention paid to line, stanza and shape of poem. They accept about 1% of poetry received. **Subscription/sample postpaid: $6.50. Do not submit mss during summer months. "Contributors encouraged to subscribe." Reports within 2-3 months. Pays 2 copies. Acquires first rights.**

NIMROD INTERNATIONAL JOURNAL OF CONTEMPORARY POETRY AND FICTION; RUTH G. HARDMAN AWARD: PABLO NERUDA PRIZE FOR POETRY (II), 2210 S. Main St., Tulsa OK 74114, phone (918)584-3333, founded 1956, poetry editor Fran Ringold, "is an active 'little magazine,' part of the movement in American letters which has been essential to the development of modern literature. *Nimrod* publishes 2 issues per year: an awards issue in the fall featuring the prize winners of our national competition and a thematic issue each spring." They want **"vigorous writing that is neither wholly of the academy nor the streets, typed mss."** They have recently published poetry by Pattiann Rogers, Denise Levertov, Willis Barnstone, Alvin Greenberg, Francois Camoin, Tess Gallagher, Mekeel McBride, Bronislava Volek, Josephine Jacobsen, Janette Turner Hospital, William Stafford and Ishmael Reed. The 6×9, flat-spined, 160-page journal, full-color glossy cover, professionally printed on coated stock with b&w photos and art, uses 50-90 pgs. of poetry in each issue. It is an extraordinarily lovely magazine with one of the best designs in the lit world. Poems in non-award issues range from formal to freestyle with several translations. They use about 1% of the 2,000 submissions they receive each year, have a 3-month backlog. Circulation 3,500, 500 subscriptions of which 100 are public and university libraries. Subscription: $10/year plus $1.50 inside USA; $3 outside. **Sample postpaid: $6.90 for a recent issue, $5 for an issue more than 2 years old. Reports in 3 weeks to 4 months. Pays $5/page up to $25 total/issue. "Poets should be aware that during the months that the Ruth Hardman Awards Competition is being conducted, reporting time on non-contest manuscripts will be longer."** Send business-sized SASE for guidelines and rules for the Ruth G. Hardman Award: Pablo Neruda Prize for Poetry ($1,000 and $500 prizes). Entries accepted January 1 through April 1 each year with $10 entry fee for which you get one copy of ***Nimrod.*** This annual poetry contest is considered one of the most prestigious in the publishing world, and your material is still considered for publication if you lose in the contest!

NINETY-SIX PRESS (V, IV-Regional), Furman University, Greenville SC 29613, founded 1991, editors William Rogers and Gilbert Allen, publishes 1 paperback book of poetry/year. "The name of the press is derived from the old name for the area around Greenville, South Carolina—the Ninety-Six District. The name suggests our interest in the writers, readers and culture of the region. In 1994, we published an anthology of South Carolina poetry, including the work of more than 40 poets. **We currently accept submissions by invitation only. At some point in the future, however, we hope to be able to encourage submissions by widely published poets who live in South Carolina."** They have published poetry by William Aarnes and Bennie Lee Sinclair. As a sample the editors selected these lines from "Who Can Show the Child as She Is?" in Aarnes' book, **Learning to Dance**:

Truth is, she's just too ridiculous,
my daughter standing naked in her pool,
her swimming suit tossed into the grass,
and over her head the tilted hose spouting
a putto's wing. She commands, imperious:
"Take your *shorts off; take them off* now!"

That book is 58 pgs., 6×9, professionally printed and perfect-bound with coated stock cover. **For a sample, send $10.**

9TH ST. LABORATORIES; MODOM; THE EXPERIODDICIST (IV-Form), P.O. Box 3112, Florence AL 35630, phone (205)760-0415, founded 1986, "front man" Jake Berry. "***9th St. Laboratories*** is a noncommercial enterprise publishing *experimental* poetry, fiction, graphics and audio material in broadsheets, booklets, postcards, objects, chapbooks and audiotapes. ***MODOM*** is an ongoing series of any of the above. ***The Experioddicist*** is a newsletter of poetry, deviant theory and graphics. **The key words are *experiment* and *explore*. Poetry that breaks new ground for the poet personally, that comes from the commitment to a vision. Also graphic poetry. Poetry using devices other than straight linear narrative, that makes use of things otherwise considered nonsensical or absurd."** They have published poetry by Jack Foley, Chris Winkler, Malok, Richard Kostelanetz, Mike Miskowski and John M. Bennett. As a sample the editor selected these lines by Harry Polkinhorn:

to challenge your balance drastic yet nuclear ocean
urgent to implement an unwilling shifty murder victim
subject I say a minister question of what she meant

MODOM and ***The Experioddicist*** appear irregularly: "something appears 4 times a year." They use about 10 of 150 submissions received a year. Press run is 100-200. **Sample postpaid: $4. "All checks or money orders should be made out to Jake Berry, not the name of the mag and not to *9th St. Laboratories." No simultaneous submissions. They use some previously published work. Considers submissions January 1 through October 31 only. They pay 1 copy. They publish chapbooks by invitation only. Pay 15-20 copies. Editor sometimes comments on rejections.*** He says, "We publish as much as we can as often as we can, attempting to expand the area of poetic, visionary concentration. Going to the mailbox to find it full of work that ignores conventional limitations and is highly involved with exploring new ideas, provoking unusual insights, is what makes us happy. We would especially like to receive more experimental poetry by women."

NOCTURNAL LYRIC (I), P.O. Box 77171, San Francisco CA 94107-7171, phone (415)621-8920, founded 1987, editor Susan Moon, is a quarterly journal "featuring bizarre fiction and poetry, primarily by new writers." They want **"poems dealing with the bizarre: fantasy, death, morbidity, horror, gore, etc. Any length. No 'boring poetry.'"** They have recently published poetry by Tracy Lyn Rottkamp and Randall Rogers. As a sample the editor selected these lines from "Tastee Freeze" by Greg M. Nannini:

death smells like a carnival
bullet blasted through bone
crack of busted wood blood bathes
the white walls like a strawberry sundae

NL is 40 pgs., digest-sized, photocopied, saddle-stapled, with trade ads and staff artwork. They receive about 140 poems a year, use approximately 70%. Press run is 250 for 40 subscribers. Subscription: $8. **Sample postpaid: $1.50 through December 1992, $2 for more recent issues. "Make checks payable to Susan Moon." Previously published poems and simultaneous submissions OK. Seldom comments on rejections. Reports in 3 months. Pays 50¢ "discount on subscription" coupons. Acquires one-time rights.** The editor says, "Please send us something really wild and intense!"

NOMAD'S CHOIR (II), % Meander, P.O. Box 232, Flushing NY 11385-0232, founded 1989, editor Joshua Meander, is a quarterly. **"No curse words in poems, little or no name-dropping, no naming of consumer products, no two-page poems, no humor, no bias writing, no poems untitled. 9-30 lines, poems with hope. Simple words, careful phrasing. Free verse, rhymed poems, sonnets, half-page parables, myths and legends, song lyrics. Subjects wanted: love poems, protest poems, mystical poems, nature poems, poems of humanity, poems with solutions to world problems and inner conflict."** They have published poetry by Brenda Charles, Joseph Gourdji, Dorothy Wheeler and Jeff Swan. As a sample the editor selected these lines from "Loves Giant Piano" by Connie Goodman:

Walk a giant piano . . .
Destination, the stars
Along love's entrancing melody;
The night, it is ours.

Nomad's Choir is 10 pgs., 8½×11, typeset and saddle-stapled with 3 poems/page. They receive 150 poems/year, use about 50. Press run is 400, all distributed free. Subscription $5; **per copy $1.25. Make check payable to Joshua Meander. Reports in 6-8 weeks. Pays one copy.** The editor says, "Stick to your guns; however, keep in mind that an editor may be able to correct a minor flaw in your poem. Accept only minor adjustments. Go to many open poetry readings. Respect the masters. Read and listen to other poets on the current scene. Make pen pals. Start your own poetry journal. Do it all out of pure love."

NOMOS PRESS INC.; NOMOS: STUDIES IN SPONTANEOUS ORDER (IV-Political), 9400 S. Damen, Chicago IL 60620, phone (312)233-8684, poetry editor John Enright. *Nomos* is a quarterly magazine **"dedicated to individual freedom and responsibility." One page of each issue is devoted to poetry up to 24 lines, "although longer pieces are considered. Poetry must promote individual freedom and responsibility, skepticism toward government solutions for economic and social ills and/or celebrate the human condition. Clarity of meaning and direct emotional appeal are paramount; form should contribute to, not detract or distract from these."** They have recently published poetry by James Henderson and Roger Donway. As a sample John Enright selected these lines of his own:

Into the distance
run at full speed.
Something bright glistens—
Something you need.

"*Nomos*' purpose is to call attention to the erosion of civil and economic rights, much of which erosion has government as its catalyst." The editor describes it as magazine-sized, generally 40 pgs. in length, offset, matte cover occasionally printed 2-color. Ad copy, line art for cover and article illustrations are solicited. It has a circulation of 1,000 with 450 subscriptions of which 10 are libraries, 300 sent out to potential subscribers. Subscription: $18. **Sample postpaid: $4.50. Submit poems with name on each page. Reporting time varies, up to 1 year to publication. Pays 3 copies.**

‡THE NORTH; THE POETRY BUSINESS; SMITH/DOORSTOP PUBLISHING (II), 51 Byram Arcade, Westgate, Huddersfield HD1 1ND England, phone 0484-434-840, founded 1986, editors Peter Sansom and Janet Fisher, is a small press and magazine publisher of contemporary poetry. **"No particular restrictions on form, length, etc. But work must be contemporary, and must speak with the writer's own authentic voice. No copies of traditional poems, echoes of old voices, poems about the death of poet's grandfather, poems which describe how miserable the poet is feeling right now."** They have recently published poetry by Robert Hershon, Paul Violi, Joan Jobe Smith and John Harvey. As a sample, the editors selected these lines from "Swimming the English Channel" by Susan Bright:

I did not intend to be a theater.
I do not like the man in the basement who controls me.

I do not want to be a house, a hotel, a car.
I do not like being exposed!

The North is "⅔ A4 format, 48-52 pgs., offset litho, graphics, ads, colored card cover, staple-bound." It appears 2 times/year. Press run is 600 for 400 subscriptions. Subscription: £10 (£12 US rate). **Pays 2 copies.** Smith/Doorstop publishes 6 perfect-bound paperbacks/year. **For book consideration, submit 6 sample poems, cover letter, bio, previous publications. Responds to queries in 1 month, to mss in 3 months. Pays 20 copies.** They hold an annual book (perfect-bound, laminated) competition. Write for full details. The editors say, "Read plenty of poetry, contemporary and traditional. Attend workshops, etc., and meet other writers. Keep submitting poems, even if you fail. Build up a track record in magazines before trying to get a book published."

‡NORTH AMERICAN REVIEW (III), University of Northern Iowa, Cedar Falls IA 50614, phone (319)273-6455, founded 1815, poetry editor Peter Cooley, is a slick magazine-sized bimonthly of general interest, 48 pgs. average, saddle-stapled, professionally printed with glossy full-color paper cover, **publishing poetry of the highest quality.** They have recently published poetry by Francine Sterle, Cynthia Hogue and Marvin Bell. The editor says they receive 15,000 poems a year, publish 20-30. Press run is 6,400 for 2,200 subscribers of which 1,100 are libraries, some 2,800 newsstand or bookstore sales. Subscription: $18. **Sample postpaid: $4. No simultaneous submissions or previously published poems. Publishes theme issues. Send SASE for guidelines. Reports in 1-2 months, as much as a year between acceptance and publication. Always sends prepublication galleys. Pays 50¢/line and 2 copies.** Work published in the ***North American Review*** has been included in **The Best American Poetry 1992.**

NORTH DAKOTA QUARTERLY (III), Box 7209, University of North Dakota, Grand Forks ND 58202, phone (701)777-2703, fax (701)777-3650, founded 1910, poetry editor Jay Meek, is a literary quarterly published by the University of North Dakota that includes material in the arts and humanities—essays, fiction, interviews, poems and visual art. **"We want to see poetry that reflects an understanding not only of the difficulties of the craft, but of the vitality and tact that each poem calls into play."** Poets recently published include Martín Espada, Albert Goldbarth and Maura Stanton. As a sample, the poetry editor selected lines from "Dog Days" by Mark Vinz:

The apartment swells with August heat,
an old jazz man on the radio—
we climb the slippery stairs of each piano riff
and wonder out loud if some day
we'll ever do anything that well.

The poetry editor says ***North Dakota Quarterly*** is 6×9, about 250 pgs., perfect-bound, professionally designed and often printed with full-color artwork on the white matte card cover. You can find almost every kind of poem here—avant-garde to traditional. Typically the work of about 10 poets is included in each issue. Circulation of the journal is 850, of which 650 are subscriptions. Subscription: $15/year. **Sample postpaid: $5. No simultaneous submissions. Reporting time is 4-6 weeks and time to publication varies. Always sends prepublication galleys. Pays 2 copies and a year's subscription.** Reviews books of poetry in 500-5,000 words, single or multi-book format. The press does not usually publish chapbooks.

NORTHEAST ARTS MAGAZINE; BOSTON ARTS ORGANIZATION, INC. (III), P.O. Box 6061, J.F.K. Station, Boston MA 02114, founded 1990, editor/president Mr. Leigh Donaldson, is a biannual using **poetry that is "honest, clear, with a love of expression through simple language, under 30 lines. Care for words and craftsmanship are appreciated."** They have published poetry by Otto Laske, Meleta Murdock Baker, Jennifer Smith and Win Travassos. As a sample the editor selected this poem, "How I Gained Knowledge of the World," by Thomas Wiloch:

So I traded an eye for a drink of
water, Then she told me, go ahead,
pick one of those apples too.

It is digest-sized, 32 or more pgs., professionally printed with 1-color coated card cover. They accept 20-25% of submissions. Press run is 500-1,000 for 150 subscribers of which half are libraries, 50 to arts organizations. An updated arts information section and feature articles are included. Subscription: $10. **Sample postpaid: $4.50. Reads submissions September 1 through May 30 only. "A short bio is helpful." Send SASE for guidelines. Reports in 1-2 months. Pays 2 copies. Acquires first North American serial rights.**

NORTHEAST JOURNAL (II, IV-Regional), P.O. Box 2321, Providence RI 02906, founded 1969, editor Henry Gould, is a literary annual published by The Poetry Mission, a nonprofit literary arts organization. The journal is **"open to conventional-experimental poetry."** They have recently published poetry by Edwin Honig and Janet Gray. As a sample the editor selected these lines from "The Surface and Depths of Southern Friendship" by Janet McCann:

I wait, Alice poised
on the giant chair, an obedient child.
Men in brown suits discuss the Kuwait War
and problems with their software. I don't
snicker.

The purpose of *NJ* is "to encourage local (state and area) writers while remaining open to national submissions." They are currently experimenting with a new design format. Circulation is 500, with 200 subscriptions of which 100 are libraries. **Sample postpaid: $6. Reports in 3-6 months. Sometimes sends prepublication galleys. Pays 1 copy.** Reviews books of poetry.

NORTHEASTERN UNIVERSITY PRESS; SAMUEL FRENCH MORSE POETRY PRIZE (III), Northeastern University, 360 Huntington Ave., Boston MA 02115. The Samuel French Morse Poetry Prize, % Prof. Guy Rotella, Editor, Morse Poetry Prize, English Dept., 406 Holmes, Northeastern University, Boston MA 02115, for book publication (ms 50-70 pgs.) by Northeastern University Press and an **award of $500. Entry fee: $10. Deadline of August 1 for inquiries, September 15 for single copy of ms. Ms will not be returned. Open to US poets who have published no more than 1 book of poetry.**

THE NORTHERN CENTINEL (II), Suite 8B, 115 E. 82nd St., New York NY 10028-0833, founded 1788, poetry editors Ellen Rachlin and Lucie Aidinoff, is a newspaper appearing 6 times/year focusing on "political/cultural essays and analyses on matters of national interest." **They publish 2 poems each issue.** They have recently published poetry by Molly Peacock and Allen Ginsberg. It is 16-24 pgs., 11×17, offset on newsprint, with b&w artwork, photos, engravings, woodcuts, political cartoons and ads. Press run is 18,000. Subscription: $15. **Sample postpaid: $2.50. No previously published poems; simultaneous submissions OK. Cover letter with SASE required.** Time between acceptance and publication is up to a year. **Seldom comments on rejections. Reports within 3 months. Pays $40 plus 1 copy.**

NORTHWEST REVIEW (II), 369 PLC, University of Oregon, Eugene OR 97403, phone (503)346-3957, founded 1957, poetry editor John Witte. They are "seeking excellence in whatever form we can find it" and use **"all types" of poetry.** They have published poetry by Alan Dugan, Olga Broumas, William Stafford and Richard Eberhart. *NR*, a 6×9, flat-spined magazine, appears 3 times/year and uses 25-40 pgs. of poetry in each issue. They receive 3,500 submissions/year, use 4%, have up to a 4-month backlog. Press run is 1,300 for 1,200 subscribers of which half are libraries. **Sample postpaid: $3. Submit 6-8 poems clearly reproduced. No simultaneous submissions. The editor comments "whenever possible" on rejections. Send SASE for guidelines. Reports in 8-10 weeks. Pays 3 copies.** Poetry published in this review has been included in **The Best American Poetry 1994.** The editor advises poets to "persist."

NORTHWOODS PRESS; DAN RIVER PRESS; NORTHWOODS JOURNAL: A MAGAZINE FOR WRITERS; C.A.L. (II), P.O. Box 298, Thomaston ME 04861-0298, phone (207)354-0998, Northwoods Press founded 1972, Dan River Press 1978, C.A.L. (Conservatory of American Letters) 1986 and *Northwoods Journal* 1993. *Northwoods Journal* is a quarterly literary magazine, incorporating a brief version of the C.A.L. newsletter. **"The journal is interested in all poets who feel they have something to say and who work to say it well. We have no interest in closet poets, or credit seekers. All poets seeking an audience, working to improve their craft and determined to 'get it right' are welcome here. Please request submission guidelines (with SASE) before submitting."** Subscription: $10/year, free to C.A.L. members. **Sample: $4. Deadlines are the 1st of April, July, October and January for seasonal publication. Reports within 2 weeks after deadline, sometimes sooner. Pays $5/page, average, on acceptance.** "Northwoods Press is designed for the excellent *working poet* who has a following which is likely to create sales of $3,000 or more. Without at least that much of a following and at least that level of sales, no book can be published. Request 15-point poetry program. **Northwoods Press will pay a minimum of $250 advance on contracting a book.** C.A.L. is a nonprofit tax-exempt literary/educational foundation; up to 4 anthologies of poetry and prose are published each year. **There is a $1 (cash—no checks) reading fee for each poetry submission to their anthologies, which goes to readers, not to the publisher. Poets are paid $5/page on acceptance, shorter poems pro-rata page rate. Payment is advance against 10% royalties on all sales we can attribute to the influence of the author."** Robert Olmsted regards his efforts as an attempt to face reality and provide a sensible royalty-contract means of publishing many books. He says, **"If you are at the stage of considering book publication, have a large number of poems in print in respected magazines, perhaps previous book publication, and are confident that you have a sufficient following to insure very modest sales, send 8½×11 SASE (3 oz. postage) for descriptions of the Northwoods Poetry Program and C.A.L."** His advice is, **"Poetry must be non-trite, non-didactic. It must never bounce. Rhyme, if used at all, should be subtle. One phrase should tune the ear in preparation for the next. They should flow and create an emotional response." Query with cover letter dealing with publication credits and marketing ideas. Submit "entire ms as desired for final book form." No simultaneous submissions; no previously published poems. Pays 10% royalties. Bob Olmsted "rarely" comments on rejections, but he offers commentary for a fee, though**

he says he "strongly recommends *against* it." Query. Membership in C.A.L. is $24 a year, **however, membership is not required.** Members receive the quarterly ***Northwoods Journal*** plus 10% discount on all books and have many services available to them. C.A.L. sponsors an annual writers' conference with no tuition, only a $20 registration fee. Dan River Press, which publishes books of prose, also publishes an annual **Dan River Anthology,** using short fiction and **poetry. Pays $5/page on acceptance.**

‡W.W. NORTON & COMPANY, INC. (III), 500 Fifth Ave., New York NY 10110, phone (212)354-5500, founded 1925, poetry editor Jill Bialosky. W.W. Norton is a well-known commercial trade publishing house that publishes only original work in both hardcover and paperback. They want **"quality literary poetry" but no "light or inspirational verse."** They have recently published books by Ellen Bryant Voigt, Rosanna Warren, Stephen Dunn and Eavan Boland. W.W. Norton publishes approximately 10 books of poetry each year with an average page count of 64. They are published in cloth and flat-spined paperbacks, attractively printed, with two-color glossy card covers. **Unsolicited submissions are accepted, but authors should query first, sending credits and 15 sample poems plus bio. Simultaneous submissions will be considered if the editor is notified. Norton will consider only poets whose work has been published in quality literary magazines. They report on queries in 2-3 weeks and mss in 4 months. Royalties are 10%, but there are no advances. Catalog is free on request.**

NOSTALGIA: A SENTIMENTAL STATE OF MIND (II), P.O. Box 2224, Orangeburg SC 29116, founded 1986, poetry editor Connie Lakey Martin, appears spring and fall using **"nostalgic poetry, style open, prefer *non* rhyme, but occasional rhyme OK, relatively short poems, never longer than one page, no profanity, no ballads."** *Nostalgia* is digest-sized, 24 pgs., saddle-stapled, offset typescript, with matte card cover. Press run is 1,000. Subscription: $5. **Sample postpaid: $3. "Most poems selected from contest." Guidelines available for SASE.** There are contests in each issue with award of $100 and publication for outstanding poem, publication and 1-year subscription for Honorable Mentions. Entry fee of $3 reserves future edition, covers 3 entries. Deadlines: June 30 and December 31 each year. **"Previously published poems OK *with credits*, but prefer no simultaneous submissions." Sometimes sends prepublication galleys. All rights revert to author upon publication.** Reviews books of poetry. Open to unsolicited reviews. Poets may also send books for review consideration. Connie Martin says, "I offer criticism to most rejected poems and feature a poet each edition as 'Poet of the Season.' I suggest sampling before submitting. I receive a wide variety of poems but most poets don't seem to take time to read what's really accepted in literary magazines. Many are more interested in publication, rather than sampling for preferred use."

NOSUKUMO (V), GPO Box 994-H, Melbourne, Victoria 3001 Australia, founded 1982, editor Javant Biarujia, publishes 1-2 chapbooks/year. **"We publish language-oriented and experimental poetry, but not exclusively so. We are particularly interested in prose poems. However, our program is fully committed for the foreseeable future."** Their products are characterized by elegant printing on quality paper in sewn chapbooks. Send SASE (or SAE and IRCs if outside Australia) for catalog.

NOW AND THEN (IV-Regional, themes), P.O. Box 70556, ETSU, Johnson City TN 37614-0556, phone (615)929-5348, founded 1984, poetry editor Jo Carson, is a regional magazine that deals with Appalachian issues and culture. **The editor does not want any poetry not related to the region. Issues have themes—previous issues have focused on Appalachian veterans, working Cherokees, blacks, children, rural life, media, Scottish-Appalachian connection, sports and recreation, and education. "No haiku or sentimental, nostalgic, romantic or religious poems."** They have published poetry by Fred Chappell, Michael McFee, Michael Chitwood, Jim Wayne Miller and George Ella Lyon. As a sample the editor selected these lines from "Field Trip to Montgomery, 1965" by William Miller:

Back on the bus most of the kids slept,
faces smeared with the moonpie and grape drink
we brought for a snack, the long ride home.
But a few listened, thought the gun part
was neat and wondered how many men it killed.

Now and Then appears three times a year and is 48 pgs., magazine-sized, saddle-stapled, professionally printed, with matte card cover. Its press run is 2,000 for 900 subscriptions of which 200 are libraries. Of 200 poems received they accept 6-10 an issue. Subscription: $15. **Sample: $4.50 plus $1.50 postage. They will consider simultaneous submissions but "not usually" previously published poems. Submit up to 5 poems, with cover letter including "a few lines about yourself for a contributor's note and whether work has been published or accepted elsewhere." Deadlines: March 1, July 1 and November 1. Publishes theme issues. Send SASE for guidelines and upcoming themes. Reports in 3-4 months. Sometimes sends prepublication galleys. Pays 2 copies plus subscription. Acquires one-time rights.** Reviews books of poetry in 750 words. Open to unsolicited reviews. Poets may also send books for review consideration to Pat Arnow, editor.

THE OAK (I); THE ACORN (I, IV-Children); THE GRAY SQUIRREL (I, IV-Senior citizens), 1530 Seventh St., Rock Island IL 61201, phone (309)788-3980, poetry editor Betty Mowery. *The Oak*, founded 1991, is a "publication for writers with short articles, poetry, fiction (no more than 500 words) and writers conferences." They want poetry **"no more than 32 lines. No restrictions as to types and style, but no pornography."** *The Oak* appears 6 times/year. They take more than half of about 100 poems received each year. Press run is 200, with 10 going to libraries. Subscription: $10. **Sample: $2. Simultaneous submissions and previously published poems OK. Reports in 1 week. "The Acorn does not pay in dollars or copies but you need not purchase to be published." Acquires first or second rights.** *The Acorn* is a "newsletter for young authors and teachers or anyone else interested in our young authors. **Takes mss from kids K-12th grades or from adults if it is slanted to grades K-12. Poetry no more than 32 lines.** It also takes articles and fiction, no more than 500 words." It appears 6 times/year and **"we take well over half of submitted mss."** Press run is 100, with 6 going to libraries. Subscription: $10. **Sample postpaid: $2. Simultaneous submissions and previously published poems OK. Reports in 1 week. "*The Acorn* does not pay in dollars or copies but you need not purchase to be published." Acquires first or second rights. Young authors, submitting to *The Acorn*, should put either age or grade on manuscripts. *The Gray Squirrel* takes poetry of no more than 20 lines only from poets 60 years of age and up.** Press run is about 50. Six issues: $10. **Sample: $2. Make checks for *Squirrel* payable to *The Oak*. Pays copy. *The Oak*** holds an Orange Blossom Poetry Contest February 1 through August 1. ***The Gray Squirrel*** sponsors the Minnie Chezum Memorial Contest December through May. Editor Betty Mowery advises, "Beginning poets should submit again as quickly as possible if rejected. Study the market: don't submit blind. Always include a SASE or rejected manuscripts will not be returned."

OBLATES (IV-Religious, spirituality/inspirational), Missionary Association of Mary Immaculate, 15 S. 59th St., Belleville IL 62223-4694, phone (618)233-2238, editor Christine Portell, is a magazine circulating free to 500,000 benefactors. **"We use well-written, perceptive traditional verse, average 16 lines. Avoid heavy allusions. Good rhyme and/or rhythm a must. We prefer a reverent, inspirational tone, but not overly 'sectarian and scriptural' in content. We like to use seasonal material. We like traditional poetry (with meter) and are always on the lookout for good Christmas poetry."** They have published poetry by Raymond A. Schoeder, Joy Lee Holman and Claire Puneky. ***Oblates*** is 20 pgs., digest-sized, saddle-stapled, using color inside and on the cover. **Sample and guidelines for SAE and 2 first-class stamps. Considers simultaneous submissions.** Time to publication "is usually within 1 to 2 years." **Editor comments "occasionally, but always when ms 'just missed or when a writer shows promise.' " Reports within 4-6 weeks. Pays $30 plus 3 copies. Buys first North American serial rights.** She says, "We are a small publication very open to mss from authors—beginners and professionals. We do, however, demand professional quality work. Poets need to study our publication, **and to send no more than one or two poems at a time. Content must be relevant to our older audience to inspire and motivate in a positive manner."**

OBSIDIAN II: BLACK LITERATURE IN REVIEW (IV-Ethnic), Box 8105, North Carolina State University, Raleigh NC 27695-8105, phone (919)515-4153, founded 1975, editor Gerald Barrax, is a biannual publication "for the study and cultivation of creative works in English **by Black writers worldwide,** with scholarly critical studies by all writers on Black literature." They are **open as to subject matter but want poetry (as well as fiction and drama) from Black writers only.** The editor says *Obsidian II* is 126 pgs., 6×9. Lyric and narrative free verse appear here for the most part and, typically, several poems by each author are featured. Press run is 700 for 500 subscriptions of which an eighth are libraries. Subscription: $12; single issue: $5. **Sample postpaid: $11. Submit double-spaced ms on 8½×11 paper. Send SASE for guidelines. "See copy of journal for more detailed submission guidelines." Reports in 3-4 months. Pays 2 copies and 1-year subscription.**

ODRADEK (II), (formerly *Pendragon*), Dept. of English, VSC Box 7110, Valdosta GA 31698, founded 1983, is a biannual literary publication of Valdosta State College. **"We publish the best fiction and poetry we can find. No particular preferences. Send your best. No more than 3 pages usually. No poorly-crafted work."** They have published poetry by Trent Busch, Marvin Evans and Susan Ludvigson. As a sample the editor selected these lines from "Georgia Evening" by Faye Altman:

Light the fire.
There will be time tonight for neighbors

and guitar picking.
Someone will tell a story of their childhood

Odradek is about 85 pgs., digest-sized, perfect-bound and publishes approximately 15% of poetry received. Press run is 700. Subscription: $8. **Sample postpaid: $4. No previously published poems or simultaneous submissions. Cover letter with brief bio required. Reads submissions September 15 through June 15. Seldom comments on rejections. Reports in 2-3 months. Pays 2 copies. Acquires first rights.** The editors award an annual $50 prize for the best poetry of the year. Contributions here are not only from English departments but also from poets with varied careers and backgrounds (i.e. counselors, political scientists, journalists). The work is appealing because the authors focus on a number of critical concerns, including racism and diversity, from differing viewpoints.

OFFICE NUMBER ONE (I), 1708 S. Congress Ave., Austin TX 78704, founded 1988, editor Carlos B. Dingus, appears 4 times/year. ***ONO*** is a "zine of news information and events from parallel and alternate realities." In addition to stories, they want **"haiku, limericks and quatrains mostly. However well-crafted poetry of other kinds also acceptable. Poems should be short (2-12 lines), make a definite point, have meter and rhyme. No long rambling poetry about suffering and pathos. Need more poetry that is technically perfect."** As for a sample, the editor says, "No one poem will provide a fair sample of what I accept." ***ONO*** is 12 pgs., 8½×11, computer set in 10 pt. type, saddle-stitched, with graphics and ads. They use about 20 poems a year. Press run is 2,000 for 75 subscribers, 50 shelf sales, 1,600 distributed free locally. Single copy: $1.85; subscription: $8.82/6 issues. **Sample postpaid: $2. Previously published poems and simultaneous submissions OK. "Will comment on rejections if comment is requested." Publishes theme issues occasionally. Send SASE for guidelines and upcoming themes. Reports in 1 month. Pays "23¢" and 1 copy. Buys "one-time use, and use in any *ONO* anthology."** The editor says, "Say something that has the power to change someone's life. Know who that person is, the change you seek, and how what you write can accomplish this."

THE OGALALA REVIEW (II), (formerly *Epiphany*), P.O. Box 628, Guymon OK 73942, founded 1990, editors Gordon Grice and Tracy Hiatt Grice, is a semiannual journal of poetry, fiction, creative nonfiction and translation, **interested in all styles of poetry. "We'd especially like to see more long poems (up to 600 lines or so) and formal work."** They have recently published poetry by Enid Shomer and Trent Busch. As a sample the editors selected these lines from " 'Large Bear Deceives Me' " by David Citino:

He could turn even a song

against you, rearing suddenly
as you open wide as night
to life's final surprise,
the sweet delicate meat of you.

The Ogalala Review is about 120 pgs., digest-sized, perfect-bound, with glossy cover. They receive about 2,000 poems a year, use about 4%. Subscription: $10. **Sample postpaid: $5. Include name and address on each poem. Simultaneous submissions OK, "but writers must notify us promptly of acceptance elsewhere. We do not normally consider previously published work." For translations, include written permission from copyright holder or statement that the work is in public domain. Reports in 2 months or less. Pays 2 copies. Acquires first serial rights only.** "We are phasing out our review section, but will list all books received." The editors add, "Because the magazine is under new staff, we suggest people who haven't seen it recently order a sample or a subscription."

THE OHIO REVIEW (II); OHIO REVIEW BOOKS (V), 209C Ellis Hall, Ohio University, Athens OH 45701-2979, phone (614)593-1900, founded 1959, editor Wayne Dodd, attempts "to publish the best in contemporary poetry, fiction and reviews" in the ***Review*** and in chapbooks, flat-spined paperbacks and hardback books. They use **"all types"** of poetry and have published poems by David Baker, William Matthews, Lynn Emanuel and Robin Behn. As a sample the editor selected these lines from "Alba" by Pamela Kircher:

The lovers rise from bed and leave
the fire banked in ashes,
stars dim and disappearing
as night unpins and drops
its faded cloth.

The ***Review*** appears 3 times/year in a professionally printed, flat-spined format of 140 pgs., matte cover with color and art, circulation 2,000, featuring about 18 poets/issue. One of the respected "credits" in the literary world, this magazine tends to publish mostly lyric and narrative free verse with an emphasis on voice. Content, structure and length seem open, and voices tend to complement each other, evidence of careful editing. Moreover, you'll find top-name writers appearing with relative newcomers. They receive about 3,000 submissions/year, use 1% of them, and have a 6- to 12-month backlog. Subscription: $16. **Sample postpaid: $4.25. Reads submissions September 1 through June 30 only. Editor sometimes comments on rejections. Send SASE for guidelines. Reports in 1 month. Always sends prepublication galleys. Pays $1/line for poems and $5/page for prose plus copies. Buys first North American serial rights.** Reviews books of poetry in 5-10 pgs., single or multi-book format. Send books to Robert Kinsley for review consideration. **They are not presently accepting unsolicited submissions of book mss. Query with publication credits, bio.** Work published in ***The Ohio Review*** has been included in **The Best American Poetry** (1992 and 1993) and **Pushcart Prize** anthologies.

OHIO STATE UNIVERSITY PRESS/JOURNAL AWARD IN POETRY (II), 180 Pressey Hall, 1070 Carmack Rd., Columbus OH 43210-1002, phone (614)292-6930, poetry editor David Citino. Each year ***The Journal*** (see that listing) selects for publication by Ohio State University Press for the Ohio State University Press/Journal Award **one full-length (at least 48 pgs.) book ms submitted during September, typed, double-spaced, $15 handling fee (payable to OSU).** Send SASE for return of ms; self-addressed, stamped postcard for notification of ms receipt. **Some or all of the poems in the collection may have appeared in periodicals, chapbooks or anthologies, but must be identified. Along with publication, *The Journal* Award in Poetry pays $1,000 cash prize from the Helen Hooven Santmyer Fund "in addition to the usual royalties."** Each entrant receives a subscription (2 issues) to ***The Journal.***

OLD HICKORY REVIEW (I), P.O. Box 1178, Jackson TN 38302, founded 1969, president Becky Gooch, poetry editor Edna Lackie, is a "literary triannual publishing 2-4 short stories and approximately 75-80 poems each issue. **No more than 24-30 lines, any form, any subject.** We publish poets from Maine to California and several foreign countries." It is digest-sized, 120 pgs., professionally printed with matte card cover. Press run is about 450 for 400 subscribers of which 17 are libraries. Subscription: $12/year. **Sample postpaid: $3.50. Guidelines available for SASE. Pays 1 copy/poem.** Poets may send books for review consideration, but *must query first.*

THE OLD RED KIMONO (I, II), P.O. Box 1864, Rome GA 30162, phone (706)295-6312, founded 1972, poetry editors Ken Anderson and Jon Hershey, a publication of the Humanities Division of Floyd College, has the "sole purpose of putting out a magazine of original, high-quality poetry and fiction. ***ORK* is looking for submissions of 3-5 short poems. Poems should be very concise and imagistic. Nothing sentimental or didactic."** They have published poetry by Walter McDonald, Peter Huggins, Kim Thomas, Kathleen Condon, Paul Rice and David Huddle. As a sample the editors selected these lines by T. Sheehan:

Wet leaves
at the bottom
of a leaf pile
shine
like new shoes.

The magazine is an annual, circulation 1,400, 8½×11, 72 pgs., professionally printed on heavy stock with b&w graphics, colored matte cover with art, using approximately 40 pgs. of poetry (usually 1 or 2 poems to the page). They receive 1,000 submissions/year, use 60-70. **Reading period is September 1 through March 1. Reports in 3 months. Pays copies. Acquires first publication rights.**

THE OLIVE PRESS PUBLICATIONS (V), Box 99, Los Olivos CA 93441, phone (805)688-2445, founded 1979, editor Lynne Norris, is a general small press publisher for whom "poetry is an incidental effort at this time. We specialize in local and family history." They have previously published **It Don't Hurt to Laugh**, a collection of cowboy poetry by Jake Copass.

OLYMPIA REVIEW; OLYMPIA REVIEW PRESS; ORVILLE BABCOCK MEMORIAL POETRY PRIZE (II), Suite A-6254, 3430 Pacific Ave. SE, Olympia WA 98501, founded 1992, editor Michael McNeilley, managing editor Stephanie Brooks, appears at least twice annually, publishing "the best available contemporary writing, without regard for rules, conventions or precedent. **No taboos, beyond reasonably good taste; style and talent, significance and artistry are our only criteria. Seldom use rhyme. Nothing incidental, religious or sentimental. Prefer poems under 50 lines or so."** They have recently published poetry by Charles Bukowski, Ronald Wallace, Hayley R. Mitchell, Mary Harrison, Albert Huffstickler, Errol Miller, Virgil Hervey, Antler, Greg Perry and Lyn Lifshin. As a sample the editor selected this poem by Thomas Wiloch:

the water and the light
upon the water,
how they dance

like lovers in the sunset

rippling
slow together

as the boat rocks

The editor says ***OR*** is 60-100 pgs., digest-sized, flat-spined, with 2-color coated card cover, art, graphics, photos and ads. Press run is 750-1,000. Subscription: $12.95 for 4 issues. **Sample postpaid: $4.50. Submit up to 6 poems at a time. Previously published poems ("tell us where") and simultaneous submissions OK. Cover letter and short bio required. Seldom comments on rejections. Send SASE for guidelines. Reports in 1-2 months. Pays 1 copy. Acquires first North American serial or one-time rights.** Reviews books of poetry and magazines in up to 700 words, single or multi-book format. Olympia Review Press publishes 1-2 chapbooks/year in varied formats; authors selected from those published in ***OR***. They also publish a bimonthly broadside "using work representative of the quality found in the ***Olympia Review***." Pays 3 copies. ***OR*** also sponsors the annual Orville Babcock Memorial Poetry Prize. Maximum 36 lines. Entry fee: $2/poem; 3 poems for $5. Deadline: December 1. Winners receive publication in annual contest issue, free subscription and a percentage of proceeds. Entries cannot be returned. Send SASE for list of winners. The editor advises poets to "start with the classics, to see where poetry has been. Then read more poetry, and fiction, in the little magazines, where today's writing is found. Develop your own voice, write a clean line, edit mercilessly and you may help determine where poetry is going. We look for poetry, prose and things between that illuminate archetypal hopes, fears, dreams and understandings. We want every issue of ***OR*** to connect with every reader, in as visceral a way as possible. Read an issue, see firsthand what we're up to, then submit."

ONCE UPON A WORLD (IV-Science fiction/fantasy), Route 1, Box 110A, Nineveh IN 46164, founded 1988, editor Emily Alward. **"All poetry submitted should relate to science fiction or fantasy in concept and/or imagery. This does not mean it has to be 'about' space travel or dragons. None with a nihilistic outlook, extremely avant-garde style or formats."** They have published poetry by John Grey, W. Gregory Stewart and Laura Vess. As a sample the editor selected these lines by Mark L. Ridge:

Flashing swords,
and dented shields,
what our blood and bodies build.

Once Upon A World is magazine-sized, 80-100 pgs. with heavy card stock colored covers, spiral-bound. They accept 5-10 of 50 submissions received. Press run is 120. **Sample postpaid: $8. Checks payable to Emily Alward. Reports in 1-4 months. Pays 1 copy. "We strongly recommend purchase of a copy before submitting both to give some idea of the content and tone and to help keep the magazine solvent. But this is not a requirement."** The editor says, "Our major interest is in presenting science fiction and fantasy *short* stories with well-worked-out alternate world settings and an emphasis on ideas and/or character interaction. We use poetry for fillers. Where possible we try to match a poem with an adjacent story that it somewhat resembles in subject matter or tone. As the editor's major interest is fiction, she does not feel qualified to give in-depth critiques of poetry."

ONE EARTH: THE FINDHORN FOUNDATION & COMMUNITY MAGAZINE (II, IV-Spiritual/inspirational, ecology), The Park, Findhorn, Forres, Morayshire 1V36 0TZ Scotland, phone (03094)574, founded 1974, contributing editor Vidura LeFeuvre, is a quarterly which "reflects awakening of consciousness throughout the world and also developments and life of the spiritual community at Findhorn." They want **poetry that is "spiritual, inspirational, about personal/social awakening, or ecological. Not overly long—15 lines maximum. Nothing sentimental, negative or partisan; no poetry that is *too* subjective."** As a sample the editor selected these lines by Dana Finch:

Will my death leave a trace
in the world
Will the invisible be shattered
into fragments of sight.

One Earth is 48 pgs., A4, offset litho, saddle-stapled, with full-color cover, recycled paper throughout, line art and photos; 20% ads. They receive about 50 poems a year, accept approximately 30%. Press run is 4,000 for 1,700 subscribers of which 10 are libraries, 2,300 shelf sales. Single copy: $4.50; subscription: $20 surface, $26 airmail. **Sample postpaid: $3, surface mail. Previously published poems and simultaneous submissions OK. Cover letter required.** Time between acceptance and publication is 2-6 months. **Comments on rejections "only if asked." Publishes theme issues. Sometimes sends prepublication galleys. Pays 2 copies.** The editor says, "Please include IRC with SAE, *not* U.S. stamps."

ONIONHEAD; ARTS ON THE PARK, INC. (THE LAKELAND CENTER FOR CREATIVE ARTS); WORD-ART, THE NATIONAL POETS COMPETITION; ESMÉ BRADBERRY CONTEMPORARY POETS PRIZE

(II), 115 N. Kentucky Ave., Lakeland FL 33801-5044, phone (813)680-2787. Arts on the Park founded 1979; ***Onionhead*** founded 1988. ***Onionhead*** is a literary quarterly. **"Our focus is on provocative political, social and cultural observations and hypotheses. Controversial material is encouraged. International submissions are welcome. We have no taboos, but provocation is secondary to literary excellence. No light verse please."** They have published poetry by Jessica Freeman, Arthur Knight, Lyn Lifshin, B.Z. Niditch and A.D. Winans. As a sample we selected these lines from "Paying Back Karma" by Jo Ann Lordahl:

> *This bed I made*
> *will haunt me*
>
> *Until I burn it*
> *bury it, or defuse it.*

The magazine is 40-50 pgs., digest-sized, photocopied from typescript, saddle-stapled with glossy card cover. They use 100 of 2,500 submissions received/year. Press run is 250. Complimentary distribution to universities, reviews and libraries worldwide. Subscription: $8 US, $16 other. **Sample postpaid: $3. Poet's name and title of poems should appear on the upper right-hand corner of each page. Poem "should be submitted exactly as you intend it to appear if selected for publication." Editor comments on rejections "rarely."** Poems are reviewed by an Editorial Board and **submissions are reported on within 2 months. If accepted, poems will normally appear within one year. Pays 1 copy.** WORDART, The National Poets Competition, established 1983, is open to all American authors. Cash awards, "including the prestigious Esmé Bradberry Contemporary Poets Prize and chapbook, are announced at a reading and reception during the first part of March." $8 reading fee. For guidelines and specific dates send SASE to the sponsoring organization, Arts on the Park, Inc., at the above address.

ONTARIO REVIEW; ONTARIO REVIEW PRESS (V), 9 Honey Brook Dr., Princeton NJ 08540, founded 1974. The ***Ontario Review*** appears twice a year. They have published poetry by William Heyen, Alicia Ostriker, Albert Goldbarth and Jana Harris. ***OR*** is 112 pgs., 6×9, offset, flat-spined. Press run is 1,200 for 650 subscribers of which 450 are libraries, 250 shelf sales, 75 direct sales. Subscription: $12. **Sample postpaid: $6.** Poetry published in this review has been included in **The Best American Poetry 1993. Currently not accepting unsolicited poetry. Ontario Review Press is also not currently considering new poetry mss. They publish 1-2 hardbacks and that many paperbacks/year, paying 10% royalties plus 10 copies.**

ONTHEBUS; BOMBSHELTER PRESS (II), 6421 ½ Orange St., Los Angeles CA 90048, founded 1975, ***ONTHEBUS*** editor Jack Grapes, Bombshelter Press poetry editors Jack Grapes and Michael Andrews. ***ONTHEBUS*** uses **"contemporary mainstream poetry—no more than 6 poems (10 pgs. total) at a time. No rhymed, 19th Century traditional 'verse.'"** They have published poetry by Charles Bukowski, Albert Goldbarth, Ai, Norman Dubie, Kate Braverman, Stephen Dobyns, Allen Ginsberg, David Mura, Richard Jones and Ernesto Cardenal. As a sample Jack Grapes selected these lines from "A Significant Poet" by Michael Andrews:

> *Tu Fu knew what I found out—*
> *a poet that leaves his poems to unborn children*
> *is planting dandelions on his grave.*
> *Pissing on your grave won't make the roses grow.*
> *For all the difference the poem will make*
> *it is better to dig an honest trench.*

ONTHEBUS is a magazine appearing 2 times/year, 275 pgs., offset, flat-spined, with color card cover. Press run is 3,500 for 600 subscribers of which 40 are libraries, 1,200 shelf sales ("500 sold directly at readings"). Subscription: $28 for 3 issues; Issue #8/9, special double issue: $15. **Sample postpaid: $12. Guidelines are printed on the copyright page of each issue. Simultaneous submissions and previously published poems OK, "if I am informed where poem has previously appeared and/or where poem is also being submitted. I expect cover letters with list of poems included plus poet's bio." Do not submit mss between November 1 and March 1 or between June 1 and September 1. Submissions sent during those times will be returned unread. Reports in "anywhere from 2 weeks to 2 years." Pays 1 copy. Acquires one-time rights. No comments on rejections.** Reviews books of poetry in 400 words (chapbooks in 200 words), single format. Open to unsolicited reviews. Poets may also send books for review consideration. This exciting journal seems a cross between ***The Paris Review*** and ***New York Quarterly*** with a distinct West Coast flavor that puts it in a league of its own. Editor Jack Grapes jampacks each issue with dozens upon dozens of poems, mostly free verse (lyric, narrative, dramatic)—some tending toward avant-garde and some quite accessible—that manages somehow to reach out and say: "Read Me." Poetry published in ***ONTHEBUS*** has been included in **The Best American Poetry 1993.** Bombshelter Press publishes 4-6 flat-spined paperbacks and 5 chapbooks/year. **Query first. Primarily interested in Los Angeles poets. "We publish very few unsolicited mss." Reports in 3 months.**

Pays 50 copies. Jack Grapes says, "My goal is to publish a democratic range of American poets and insure they are read by striving to circulate the magazine as widely as possible. It's hard work and a financial drain. I hope the mag is healthy for poets and writers, and that they support the endeavor by subscribing as well as submitting."

OPEN HAND PUBLISHING INC. (V), P.O. Box 22048, Seattle WA 98122, phone (206)323-2187, fax (206)323-2188, founded 1981, publisher P. Anna Johnson, is a "literary/political book publisher" bringing out flat-spined paperbacks as well as cloth cover editions designed "to promote understanding between the world's people." They have published **Puerto Rican Writers at Home in the USA**, "an anthology of seventeen of the most well-known Puerto Rican writers," and **Where Are the Love Poems for Dictators?** by E. Ethelbert Miller. **They do not consider unsolicited mss. Send SASE for catalog to order samples.**

ORACLE POETRY; ASSOCIATION OF AFRICAN WRITERS; RISING STAR PUBLISHERS (I, IV-Ethnic), 2105 Amherst Rd., Hyattsville MD 20783, phone (301)422-2665, founded 1989, editorial director Obi Harrison Ekwonna. ***Oracle Poetry*** and ***Oracle Story*** appear quarterly using works **"mainly of African orientation; must be probing and must have meaning—any style or form. Writers must have the language of discourse and good punctuation. No gay, lesbian or erotic poetry."** As a sample the editor selected these lines from "War of 1968" by Greggette Soto:

Twenty-three years ago
A son went off to war
It wasn't to fight
Communism in Vietnam
But to fight
Racism in his own backyard.

Membership in the Association of African Writers is $20/year. The editor describes ***Oracle Poetry*** as digest-sized, saddle-stapled, print run 500. Subscription: $20/year. **No previously published poems or simultaneous submissions. Reports in 4-6 weeks. Pays copies. Acquires first North American serial rights.** Reviews books of poetry. The editor says, "Read widely, write well and punctuate right."

ORBIS: AN INTERNATIONAL QUARTERLY OF POETRY AND PROSE (II), 199 The Long Shoot, Nuneaton, Warwickshire CV11 6JQ England, founded 1968, editor Mike Shields, considers **"all poetry so long as it's genuine in feeling and well executed of its type."** They have published poetry by Sir John Betjeman, Ray Bradbury, Seamus Heaney and Naomi Mitchison, as well as a US issue including Bukowski, Levertov, Piercy, Stafford and many others, "but are just as likely to publish absolute unknowns." The quarterly is 6×8½, flat-spined, 64 pgs., professionally printed with glossy card cover. They receive "thousands" of submissions/year, use "about 5%." Circulation 1,000 with 600 subscriptions of which 50 are libraries. Single copy: £3.95 ($8); subscription: £15 ($30). **Sample postpaid: $2 (or £1). Submit typed on 1 side only, one poem/sheet. No bio, no query. Enclose IRCs for reply, not US postage. Reports in 1-2 months. Pays $10 or more/acceptance plus 1 free copy automatically. Each issue carries £50 in prizes paid on basis of reader votes. Editor comments on rejections "occasionally—if we think we can help. *Orbis*** is completely independent and receives no grant-aid from anywhere."

ORCHISES PRESS (II), P.O. Box 20602, Alexandria VA 22320-1602, founded 1983, poetry editor Roger Lathbury, is a small press publisher of literary and general material in flat-spined paperbacks. **"Although we will consider mss submitted, we prefer to seek out the work of poets who interest us." Regarding poetry he states: "No restrictions, really; but it must be sophisticated—i.e., no religious versification, arty nonsense, etc. I find it increasingly unlikely that I would publish a ms unless a fair proportion of its contents has appeared previously in respected literary journals."** He has recently published poetry by Fred Dings, Greg Kuzma and Richard Foerster. Asked for a sample, he says, "I find this difficult, but . . ." (from Franz Baskett's "The Workers"):

Blank and unjealous,
They tend the larval souls
With no sense of pleasure or longing.
Those white cells
Recede in every direction
In limitless perspective, time, and space.

He publishes about 4 flat-spined paperbacks of poetry a year, averaging 96 pgs., and some longer casebound books. **When submitting, "tell where poems have previously been published." Reports in 1 month. Pays 36% of money earned once Orchises recoups its initial costs.** Roger Lathbury says, "Real poets persist and endure."

ORE (III, IV-Psychic/occult, spirituality/inspirational), 7 The Towers, Stevenage, Hertfordshire SG1 1HE England, founded 1955, editor Eric Ratcliffe, a magazine that appears 2-3 times/year. They want work that is or relates to **"folk, legend, Celtic, Arthurian, fairy, spiritual, religious. No obscenities or too much materialism."** They have recently published poetry by Peter Russell, Jay Ramsay and James Kirkup. As a sample the editor selected these lines (poet unidentified):

Ashurnasipal worships the sun-god Shamash
in front of the Sacred Tree
priest of Ashur
beloved of Anu and Dagan
son of Tukulti-Ninurta.

They receive about 1,000 poems/year, accept 5%. **Sample: £2.15 (surface mail) or 6 IRCs. Simultaneous submissions OK. Brief cover letter noting "items forwarded and successes elsewhere" required. Editor "always" comments—"no curt rejection slips." Pays 1 copy, others at half price.** Staff reviews books of poetry. Send books for review consideration. Query regarding unsolicited reviews. He advises: "1.) Realize what your type of interest is and your educational and expression limits. 2.) Read lots of poetry consistent with 1. Dwell internally on imagery, etc. 3.) Write poetry when something comes in the head—don't intend to write first. 4.) Put it away for a week and rewrite it."

OREGON EAST (II, IV-Regional), Hoke Center, Eastern Oregon State College, La Grande OR 97850, founded 1950, editor changes yearly, is the "literary annual of EOSC, 50% of magazine open to off-campus professional writing." Their preferences: **"Eclectic tastes in poetry with the only requirement being literary quality work for off-campus submissions. Chances of publication are better for short poems (one page) than longer ones. Northwest themes welcome. No 'greeting card' verse."** They have recently published poetry and fiction by Felicia Mitchell, Mark Shadle, Jessica Mills, David Reimer and Kari Sharp Hill. It is flat-spined, book format, typeset, with end papers, 6×9, approximately 100 pgs., using graphics and b&w art. Circulation 1,000 (300 off-campus) with 100 subscriptions of which 30-40 are libraries. Content tends toward free verse lyrics. Editors try to give readers an overview of art in each issue, from poetry to prose to graphics. "We also publish short one-act plays." Single copy: $5. Special 35-year issue available for $9.95 (256 pgs.). "Over 35-year anthology includes work by William Stafford, Ursula K. LeGuin, George Venn and Vern Rutsala." **Submit only 3-5 poems. No simultaneous submissions. All submissions must be accompanied by SASE and cover letter with brief bio and phone number. Reads submissions September 1 through March 1 only. Notification by June. Sometimes sends prepublication galleys. Pays 2 copies. Acquires all rights. Returns rights "with condition that *Oregon East* may reprint in any upcoming anthology."** The editor says, "When I read poetry, I look for original images that address the senses in startling new ways. We're always on the lookout for new voices that are exploring the human experience in an inventive fashion."

‡OREGON REVIEW; THE BACCHAE PRESS; THE BACCHAE PRESS CHAPBOOK CONTEST (II), 985 Hyde-Shaffer Rd., Bristolville OH 44402, founded 1992, editor/publisher Robert Brown, is a nationally distributed biannual magazine of poetry, fiction, art and reviews. **"We publish writers from all over the world but give special attention to those from the Pacific Northwest. We're open to all types of poetry. We want poems that surprise and delight us. We'd like to see more good language and experimental poems. No didactic, badly rhymed, overly sentimental poems written by beginners who haven't practiced their craft."** They have recently published poetry by Robert Wrigley, Heather McHugh, William Greenway and Vern Rutsala. As a sample the editor selected these lines from "Personal History" by Julia Wendell:

From my midnight balcony
I see a tiny figure teasing the moonlight
at the edge of the wood. Darting
from tree to shadowy tree, he glances up
and smiles at me,
having once been banished from my body.

The ***Oregon Review*** is 92 pgs., 6×9, professionally printed and flat-spined. The issue we received featured a b&w photo on the coated card cover. They receive about 10,000 poems a year, publish approximately 1%. Press run is 1,000 for 300 subscribers of which 50 are libraries, 500 shelf sales. Subscription: $9. **Sample postpaid: $5. Send clean copies of poems with name and address on each. No previously published poems; simultaneous submissions OK. Cover letter preferred.** Time between acceptance and publication is "no more than" a year. **Seldom comments on rejections. Reports in 1-6 months. Pay depends on grant money but always includes 1 copy. Buys first North American serial rights.** Reviews books and chapbooks of poetry by Northwest writers in 300-500 words. "We also review books by ***Oregon Review*** contributors." Open to unsolicited reviews. Poets may also send books for review consideration, attn. review editor. The Bacchae Press also publishes 2 paperback books of poetry and 2 chapbooks each year. **Query first with sample poems and cover letter with brief bio and publication credits. Replies to queries in 2 months, to mss in 6 months. Pays 10% royalties and 20 author's copies. Send $8 for a sample book, $5 for a chapbook.** One of the two chapbooks is selected for publication through an annual contest. Chapbook mss should be 16-24 pgs. and should be submitted with a brief bio, acknowledgements and $8 entry fee. Winner receives 50 copies. Send SASE for more information.

ORIEL BOOKSHOP (IV-Regional), The Friary, Cardiff, Wales CF2 5AT United Kingdom, phone 0222-395548, founded 1974, head of bookshop Peter Finch, publishes **Anglo-Welsh poetry, nothing else.** They have published poetry by Dylan Thomas, T. Harri Jones and R.S. Thomas. As a sample the editor selected these lines from Dannie Abse's "Return to Cardiff":

No sooner than I'd arrived the other Cardiff had gone,
smoke in the memory, these but tinned resemblances,
where the boy I was not and the man I am not
met, hesitated, left double footsteps, then walked on.

That poem is handsomely printed on a large color poster.

ORTALDA & ASSOCIATES (V), 1208 Delaware St., Berkeley CA 94702, phone (510)524-2040, fax (415)527-3411, founded 1985, poetry editor Floyd Salas, director/editor Claire Ortalda, publishes quality flat-spined paperbacks of poetry but **is not accepting submissions at this time.** They have published poetry by Czeslaw Milosz, Robert Hass, Ishmael Reed, Gary Soto, Jack Micheline and Carolyn Kizer. As a sample Claire Ortalda selected these lines by Floyd Salas:

There is no honor among thieves
He will bleed me down to serum for his vein
and pop me into his arm
He will sell me to the fence
at the corner grocery store

OSIRIS, AN INTERNATIONAL POETRY JOURNAL/UNE REVUE INTERNATIONALE (II, IV-Translations, bilingual), P.O. Box 297, Deerfield MA 01342, founded 1972, poetry editor Andrea Moorhead, is a 6×9, saddle-stapled, 40-page semiannual that **publishes contemporary poetry in English, French and Italian without translation and in other languages with translation, including Polish, Danish and German.** They also publish graphics and photographs. They want poetry which is **"lyrical, non-narrative, multi-temporal, well crafted. Also looking for translations from non-IndoEuropean languages."** They have recently published poetry by Dieter Weslowski, Ingrid Swanberg, Yánnis Kondós (Greece) and Robert Marteau (France). As a sample the editor selected this poem, "To Waken," by Eugenio de Andrade, translated from the Portuguese by Alexis Levitin:

Is it a bird, is it a rose,
is it the sea that wakens me?
Bird or rose or sea,
all is fire, all desire.
To awake is to be rose of the rose,
song of the bird, water of the sea.

There are 15-20 pgs. of poetry in English in each issue of this intriguing publication. They have a print run of 500 and send 50 subscription copies to college and university libraries, including foreign libraries. They receive 50-75 unsolicited submissions/year, use 12. Single copy: $5; subscription: $10. **Sample postpaid: $3. Include short bio with submission. Reports in 1 month. Sometimes sends prepublication galleys. Pays 5 copies.** If you translate poems from other countries or want to gain an international perspective on the art, you should send for a sample copy. Two poems published in ***Osiris*** have received Honorable Mentions from **The Pushcart Prize.** The editor advises, "It is always best to look at a sample copy of a journal before submitting work, and when you do submit work, do it often and do not get discouraged. Try to read poetry and support other writers."

THE OTHER SIDE MAGAZINE (II, IV-Political, religious, social issues), 300 W. Apsley St., Philadelphia PA 19144, phone (215)849-2178, founded 1965, poetry editor Rod Jellema, is a "magazine (published 6 times a year) concerned with **social justice issues from a Christian perspective. The magazine publishes 1-2 poems per issue. We will consider no more than 4 poems at one time from the same author. Submissions should be of high quality and must speak to and/or reflect the concerns and life experiences of the magazine's readers. We look for fresh insights and creative imagery in a tight, cohesive whole. Be warned that only 0.5% of the poems reviewed are accepted. Seldom does any published poem exceed 40-50 lines. We do not want to see pious religiosity, sentimental schlock or haiku."** They have published poetry by Eric Ormsby, Elisabeth Murawski, Nola Garrett and Mark Mitchell. ***The Other Side*** is magazine-sized, professionally printed on quality pulp stock, 64 pgs., saddle-stapled, with full-color paper cover, circulation 13,000 to that many subscriptions. Subscription: $29.50. **Sample postpaid: $4.50. No simultaneous submissions. Previously published poems rarely used. Editor "sometimes" comments on rejections. Send SASE for guidelines (material pertaining to poetry is quoted above). Pays $15 plus 4 copies and free subscription.**

OTTER (IV-Regional), Parford Cottage, Chagford, Devon TQ13 8JR United Kingdom, founded 1988, editor Christopher Southgate, appears 3 times/year **using poetry by contributors associated with the County of Devon, "poems concerned with local community and with issues—social, political, religious. Like poems in strict forms."** They have published poetry by Lawrence Sail, Ron Tamplin, Harry Guest and Jane Beeson. As a sample, here are lines from "The Yellow and Green Daughter" by Sandra McBain:

She dances like a daffodil
or wind driven forsythia
like a petal whirled in water

It is digest-sized, 48 pgs., stapled with glossy card cover, professionally printed. They accept about 25% of 400-500 poems/year. Press run is 400 for 70 subscribers of which 5 are libraries. Subscription: £5. **Sample postpaid: £2 (or $5 US; dollar checks OK). "Those not resident in Devon should indicate in their cover letter their connection with the county." Editor always comments on rejections. Reports within 3 months. Pays 1 copy.**

OUR FAMILY (IV-Religious), Box 249, Battleford, Saskatchewan S0M 0E0 Canada, phone (306)937-7771, fax (306)937-7644, founded 1949, editor Nestor Gregoire, o.m.i., is a monthly religious magazine **for Roman Catholic families. "Any form of poetry is acceptable. In content we look for simplicity and vividness of imagery. The subject matter should center on the human struggle to live out one's relationship with the God of the Bible in the context of our modern world. We do not want to see science fiction poetry, metaphysical speculation poetry, or anything that demeans or belittles the spirit of human beings or degrades the image of God in him/her as it is described in the Bible."** They have published poetry by Nadene Murphy and Arthur Stilwell. ***Our Family*** is magazine-sized, 40 pgs., glossy color paper cover, using drawings, cartoons, two-color ink, circulation 13,500 of which 48 are libraries. Single copy: $1.95; subscription: $15.98 Canada/$21.98 US. **Sample postpaid: $2.50. Send SASE or SAE with IRC or personal check (American postage cannot be used in Canada) for writer's guidelines. Will consider poems of 4-30 lines. Simultaneous submissions OK. Reports within 1 month after receipt. Pays 75¢-$1/line.** The editor advises, "The essence of poetry is imagery. The form is less important. Really good poets use both effectively."

OUTERBRIDGE (II), English A324, The College of Staten Island, 2800 Victory Blvd., Staten Island NY 10314, phone (718)982-3651, founded 1975, editor Charlotte Alexander, publishes "the most crafted, professional poetry and short fiction we can find (unsolicited except special features—to date rural, urban and Southern, promoted in standard newsletters such as ***Poets & Writers, AWP, Small Press Review***), interested in newer voices. **Anti loose, amateurish, uncrafted poems showing little awareness of the long-established fundamentals of verse; also anti blatant PRO-movement writing when it sacrifices craft for protest and message. Poems usually 1-4 pgs. in length."** They have published poetry by Craig S. Brown, Kay Murphy and Naomi Rachel. As a sample the editor selected these lines from "How to Imagine Deafness" by Kim Roberts:

Darken your ears until the tunnels
with their intricate clockwork
are sheathed in pitchy calm.
Hum a little blue, to yourself,

but keep it secret.

The digest-sized, flat-spined annual is 100 pgs., about half poetry, circulation 500-600, 150 subscriptions of which 28 are libraries. They receive 500-700 submissions/year, use about 60. **Sample postpaid: $5. Submit 3-5 poems anytime except June and July. Include name and address on each page. "We dislike simultaneous submissions and if a poem accepted by us proves to have already been accepted elsewhere, a poet will be blacklisted as there are many good poets waiting in line." Cover letter with *brief* bio preferred. Reports in 2 months. Pays 2 copies (and offers additional copies at half price). Acquires first rights.** The editor says, "As a poet/editor I feel magazines like ***Outerbridge*** provide an invaluable publication outlet for individual poets (particularly since publishing a book of poetry, respectably, is extremely difficult these days). As in all of the arts, poetry—its traditions, conventions and variations, experiments—should be studied. One current 'trend' I detect is a lot of mutual backscratching which can result in very loose, amateurish writing. Discipline!"

OUTREACH: FOR THE HOUSEBOUND, ELDERLY AND DISABLED (IV-Senior citizens, specialized: disabled, religious), 7 Grayson Close, Stocksbridge, Sheffield S30 5BJ England, editor Mike Brooks, founded 1985, is a quarterly using **"semi-religious poetry and short articles. This is a magazine for the housebound, elderly and disabled who need cheering up, not made more depressed or bored!"** As a sample, here are lines from "Stairs to God" by Helen S. Rice:

Prayers are the stairs
We must climb every day,

If we would reach God
There is no other way.

Outreach is photocopied from typescript on ordinary paper, folded and saddle-stapled.

OUTRIDER PRESS (II, IV-Women), Suite C-3, 1004 E. Steger Rd., Crete IL 60417, founded 1988, president Phyllis Nelson, publishes 1-2 chapbooks/year. They want **"poetry dealing with the terrain of the human heart and plotting inner journeys; growth and grace under pressure. No bag ladies, loves-that-never-were, please."** As a sample the editor selected these lines from "Elegy" in **Listen to the Moon** by Whitney Scott:

He slipped
Away,
Gently as the rustle of silk
He so favored in his shirts.

That chapbook is 16 pgs., digest-sized, photocopied from typescript with matte card cover, $4. **Responds to queries in 3 months, to submissions in 6 months. Sometimes sends prepublication galleys. Pay is negotiable.** The editor notes, "Outrider Press published its first original trade paper novel, **Dancing to the End of the Shining Bar**, by Whitney Scott, in January, 1994."

OUTSIDE LINING DEATH BATCH (I, IV-Political), (formerly *Unsilenced Voice*), #29, 9333 N. Lombard, Portland OR 97203, founded 1990, editor Clint C. Wilkinson, is a monthly of "politically left (anarchist) and experimental art/literature." They want **"anarchist free verse poetry of one page or less. Nothing else."** They have published poetry by Jon Brann. As a sample the editor selected these lines (poet unidentified):

Single raindrop falls
from a cloudless blue heaven
maybe it was spit

The editor says ***OLDB*** is a 4-page, photocopied newsletter. They receive about 5 poems/issue, accept 1-2. Press run is for 8 subscribers. Subscription: $8/year. No single copy sales. **Previously published poems and simultaneous submissions OK. Often comments on rejections. Send SASE for guidelines. Reports in 1 month. Pays 1 copy. Acquires one-time rights.** The editor says, "Put your heart into your work and throw it at the world. If it's good, it'll stick. One sure way to know what I want is to read us for a while. By all means, subscribe; don't act like you don't want to."

THE OVERLOOK PRESS; TUSK BOOKS (V), 149 Wooster St., New York NY 10012, phone (212)477-7162, founded 1972, are trade publishers with about 8 poetry titles. They have published books of poetry by David Shapiro and Paul Auster. Tusk/Overlook Books are distributed by Viking/Penguin. **They publish on standard royalty contracts with author's copies. They "are no longer accepting poetry submissions."**

‡OVERVIEW LTD. POETRY (I, II), P.O. Box 211, Wood-Ridge NJ 07075, founded 1990, editor Joseph Lanciotti, is a biannual publication of **"plain good poetry, 10-40 lines."** They have recently published poetry by Rose Romano, Thomas Lin and Lyn Lifshin. As a sample we selected the opening lines of "Life List" by Edward Johnson:

We glided easily downstream,
in eighteen feet of aluminum,
our every turn controlled by his
subtle commands from the stern,

While, at the bow, my mother sat,
her paddle across her lap
binoculars and a bird guide
for pinning wood ducks in the reeds.

Overview Ltd. is 24 pgs., digest-sized, professionally printed and saddle-stapled with matte card cover. Press run is 500 for 150 subscribers, 250 shelf sales. **Sample postpaid: $5. No previously published poems; simultaneous submissions OK. Cover letter required. Send SASE for guidelines "*before* submitting." Reports in 1 month. Pays 1 copy.** The editor says, "***Overview Ltd.*** is published only when a sufficient amount of good poetry has been submitted. It has no board of directors, or committees, or budget. We exist from day to day to supply a base for honest poets to take root. There are unheard voices out there and we know it. Send us a message and we will listen, and if everything else goes well, we will publish it."

OWL CREEK PRESS; OWL CREEK POETRY BOOK AND CHAPBOOK COMPETITIONS (II), 1620 N. 45th St., Seattle WA 98103, founded 1979, poetry editor Rich Ives. "Owl Creek Press is a nonprofit literary publisher. Selections for publication are based solely on literary quality." They publish full-length poetry books, chapbooks, anthologies. **"No subject or length limitations. We look for poetry**

that will endure." They have published poetry by Angela Ball, Art Homer and Laurie Blauner. As a sample here are the opening lines of "Ordinance on Returning" by Naomi Lazard:

We commend you on your courage.
The place you have chosen to revisit
is as seductive as ever.
It has been in that business for centuries.

Owl Creek Press accepts books and chapbooks for publication only through its annual contests for each. The *book* competition selects 1-3 books for publication. Mss should be a minimum of 50 typed pages and should include an acknowledgments page for previous publications. Deadline: February 15; entry fee: $15; winners receive 100 copies of published book. The *chapbook* competition chooses 1-3 chapbooks for publication. Mss should be under 40 pages and should include an acknowledgments page for previous publications. Deadline: August 15; entry fee: $10; winners receive 50 copies of published chapbook and a cash prize of $500 as an advance against royalties. Additional payment for reprinting. Send SASE for information on Owl Creek Poetry Book and Chapbook Contests. The editor says, "It is clear that many would-be poets do not read enough. A hungry mind is a valuable asset. Feed it."

OXALIS; STONE RIDGE POETRY SOCIETY ANNUAL POETRY CONTEST; DAY OF THE POET (II), P.O. Box 3993, Kingston NY 12401, founded contest 1983, ***Oxalis*** (a literary quarterly) 1988. **"We are generally open as to form and subject matter. Usually would not take over 50 lines per poem. No gratuitous sex, violence, ugh types."** They have published poetry by Stephen Dunn, Elizabeth Hahn and Albert Huffstickler. As a sample the editor selected these lines from "Positive Self Images" by Michael S. Smith:

Looking only on the bright side
became so natural
we could walk around in the dark
and feel enlightened.

Oxalis is 40 pgs., magazine-sized, saddle-stapled, desktop-published with matte card cover using some b&w art. Their press run is 300 with 70 subscriptions of which 15 are libraries. They receive about 700 poems a year, use 120. Single copy: $6; subscription: $18 for 3 issues, $14 for members of Stone Ridge Poetry Society. **Sample postpaid: $5. Submit poems double-spaced with cover letter including a brief bio (2 or 3 sentences to use on contributor's page if work is accepted). "We return unread anything that comes without adequate postage. Please send SASE for our reply even if you don't want your poems returned." Send SASE for guidelines and contest rules. Pays 2 copies.** Reviews books of poetry only if poet has already been published in ***Oxalis***. Stone Ridge Poetry Society sponsors weekly poetry readings March through September. They co-sponsor, with ***Home Planet News*** (see separate listing), an annual Day of the Poet in early October, at Ulster County Community College. The day features a poetry reading contest, open readings, a book fair, music and refreshments. They have a paid featured poet for that event, and the $5 entry fees for poets participating in the contest are used for winners' prizes (as well as to benefit ***Oxalis*** and ***Home Planet News***). SRPS also sponsors an annual poetry contest. **NOTE: At press time we were notified that *Oxalis* no longer plans to publish in 1995.**

OXFORD UNIVERSITY PRESS (V), 200 Madison Ave., New York NY 10016, phone (212)679-7300, founded 1478, poetry editor Elizabeth Maguire (U.K.), is a large university press publishing academic, trade and college books in a wide variety of fields. **Not accepting any poetry mss.** "Our list includes Conrad Aiken, Richard Eberhart, Robert Graves, Geoffrey Hill, Peter Porter, M.L. Rosenthal, Stephen Spender, Anne Stevenson and Charles Tomlinson. These indicate our direction."

PABLO LENNIS (I, IV-Science fiction/fantasy), 30 N. 19th St., Lafayette IN 47904, founded 1976, editor John Thiel, appears irregularly, is a **"science fiction and fantasy fanzine preferring poems of an expressive cosmic consciousness or full magical approach. I want poetry that rimes and scans and I like a good rhythmic structure appropriate to the subject. Shorter poems are much preferred. I want them to exalt the mind, imagination, or perception into a consciousness of the subject. Optimism is usually preferred, and English language perfection eminently preferable. Nothing that is not science fiction or fantasy, or which contains morbid sentiments, or is perverse, or does not rime, or contains slang."** They have published poetry by Scott Francis, Paul Humphrey, David Hundley and Anne Valley. As a sample the editor selected these lines from "We are All Travellers Together in Space" by James Musheneaux:

Did you ever sit down, pause and think
Relative to what the universe actually is?
Let us put a few words on this paper
To try to give it some thought, analysis.

Let us begin with our solar system,

With the Sun the center and heartbeat,
A tremendous ball of hot glowing gas,
Source of all Earth's light and heat.

It is magazine-sized, 30 pgs., side-stapled, photocopied from typescript, with matte card cover, using fantastic ink drawings and hand-lettering. "I get maybe fifty poems a year and have been using most of them." Press run is "up to 100 copies." Subscription: $12/year. **Sample postpaid: $1. Reports "at once. I generally say something about why the poetry was not used, if it was not. If someone else might like it, I mention an address." Pays 1 copy, 2 if requested.** Reviews books of poetry if they are science fiction or fantasy. Open to unsolicited reviews. Poets may also send books for review consideration. The editor says, "Poetry is magic. I want spells, incantations, sorceries of a rhythmic and rhyming nature, loftily and optimistically expressed, and I think this is what others want. People buy poetry to have something that will affect them, add new things to their lives. If they want something to think about, they get prose. See how much magic you can make. See how well-liked it is."

PAGE 5 (III), 1455 W. Prospect Ave., Appleton WI 54914, founded 1990, editor and publisher R. Chris Halla, who says ***Page 5*** is an irregular publication designed "to publish what I feel like publishing regardless of the opinions of others. **Nothing poorly written, poorly cultivated, poorly nurtured and poorly harvested.**" They have recently published poetry by Gary Busha, Bruce Taylor, John Judson, Robert Schuler and Tom Montag. ***Page 5*** is one 11×17 sheet, folded twice so the cover is 5½×8½. It usually contains the work of one author. The editor accepts less than 1% of poetry received. Press run is 250-500, all distributed free. **Sample free with 6×9 or larger SASE. Due to format, poets should submit work to fit two 5½×8½ pages and one 11×17 page spread. No previously published poems or simultaneous submissions. Cover letter required. "Submissions unaccompanied by 6×9 SASE or larger will be fed to the perch." Seldom comments on rejections. Publishes theme issues. Send SASE for upcoming themes. Reporting time varies. Sometimes sends prepublication galleys. Pays 25-50 copies. Acquires first and reprint rights.** Staff reviews books of poetry "if something comes in that knocks us out of our saddles." Send books for review consideration.

PAINTBRUSH: A JOURNAL OF POETRY, TRANSLATIONS, AND LETTERS (III), Division of Language & Literature, Northeast Missouri State University, Kirksville MO 63501, phone (816)785-4000, founded 1974, editor Ben Bennani. ***Paintbrush*** appears 2 times/year and is 5½×8½, 64 pgs., using **quality poetry.** Circulation is 500. **Sample: $7. No submissions June, July and August. Send SASE with inquiries and request for samples.** Reviews books of poetry.

‡PAINTED BRIDE QUARTERLY (II), 230 Vine St., Philadelphia PA 19106, phone (215)925-9914, editors Kathy Volk Miller, Brian Brown and Marion Wrenn, founded 1973. **"We have no specifications or restrictions. We'll look at anything."** They have published poetry by Robert Bly, Charles Bukowski, S.J. Marks and James Hazen. ***"PBQ*** aims to be a leader among little magazines published by and for independent poets and writers nationally." The 80-page, perfect-bound, digest-sized magazine uses 40 pgs. of poetry/issue, receiving over 1,000 submissions/year and using under 150. Neatly printed, it has a circulation of 1,000, 850 subscriptions, of which 40 are libraries. Subscription: $16. **Sample postpaid: $5. Submit no more than 6 poems, any length, typed; only original, unpublished work. "Submissions should include a *short* bio." Editors seldom comment on rejections. They have a 6- to 9-month backlog. Pays 1-year subscription and half-priced contributor's copies.** Reviews books of poetry.

PAINTED HILLS REVIEW (II), #411, 2950 Portage Bay West, Davis CA 95616, founded 1990, editors Michael Ishii and Kara Kosmatka, appears 3 times/year using **"well-crafted poetry. Poems must sustain themselves. Rather than abstractly generalizing, make a poem detailed and real—full of 'real' people and 'real' situations. Nothing abstract, general, sloppy and unsustained, trite, 'greeting card' verse, no philosophy or dogmatism."** They have recently published work by Patricia Goedicke, Roland Flint, William Stafford, Ingrid Wendt, and Barry Spacks. As a sample the editors selected these lines from "Swimming After Birds" by Laurie O'Brien:

Over water it is easier to understand. They
need some angle of light on the silver
backs of fish, they must have a line
of descent before the plunge. The child
in the green waves chases every rocking
trough, the fish which spiral and disperse,
the feathers just above foam. The world tilts
and we see her swimming with a little flutter
kick out into the territory of summer air.

PHR is 48-60 pgs., digest-sized, professionally printed and typeset, perfect-bound, with matte card cover, all on recycled paper. Press run is 400. Subscription: $10 (add 7.5% tax in California).

Paintbrush Award Issue
Fall 1993, Number Ten

"Poetry is a strong part of our publication," says Michael Ishii, editor/publisher of Painted Hills Review. "Though we strive to have a balance of poetry and fiction, it just seems there is so much more poetry out there." The California-based publication appears three times a year and uses poems that are detailed and full of real people and situations. Ishii says, "We want poems that sustain themselves." The cover for their annual award issue was chosen for its bold lines, contrast and reproducibility. The cover artist is Elizabeth Gething of Tucson, Arizona.

Sample postpaid: $3 (add 7.5% tax in California). Send no more than 6 poems at a time, no more than 100 lines/poem. "We would also like biographical information on the author." Publishes theme issues. Send SASE for upcoming themes. Reports in 1-2 months. Pays 2 copies. Acquires first North American serial rights. Reviews books of poetry in 250-500 words, single or multi-book format. Open to unsolicited reviews. Poets may also send books (marked attn. Reviews) for review consideration. Sponsors "Paintbrush Award in Poetry," yearly contest. Postmark deadline is June 1. Send SASE for information. Winners receive up to $100 cash prize and are published in ***PHR***. One of the poems published in this review was included in a **Pushcart Prize** anthology. They would like to receive more "poetry that does not reflect 'New Age' or social relativism, poetry that appears retired." The editors advise, "Read other poets; revise and revise again; keep trying."

PAISLEY MOON PRESS; OPEN UNISON STOP (II), (formerly just *Paisley Moon*), P.O. Box 95463, Seattle WA 98145-2463, founded 1990, editors Michael Spring and p. notzka. ***open unison stop*** is an annual magazine publishing poems, short (short) stories, parts-of-novels, essays with a literary bent and reviews from all fronts, quarters, movements and schools writing in English. **"Prefer poems around 35 lines or less, but will consider longer poems if exceptional. Open to all forms/styles. Editors prefer strong imagery, rich language and explorative verse, original twists in vision and metaphor. No didactic, greeting-card, cliché-ridden verse."** They have recently published poetry by Joyce Odam, Judson Crews, Sonya Hess, Peter Desy, Carolyn Stoloff, B.Z. Niditch, Stephen Kessler and Marcia Arrieta. As a sample the editors selected these lines from "Reconciliation" by Susanne Kort:

All it took was time, mainly, & a thousand
Complimentary cups of tea, Sweeta
Stirred in; & blatant flurries

Of kisses where your hair parts
Company from the back of your neck, snuck in
As you went on reading, or maybe deigned

To pick at what
I laid, penitentially,
On the table, on the sackcloth, on the

Ashes, on the old plaid cloth disguised as
Neutral ground.

open unison stop is 20 pgs., 4¼ × 11, photocopied from laser printed master sheets on ordinary paper with b&w illustrations. They accept about 35% of 1,000 poems received/year. Subscription: $10, includes at least 2 issues, as well as any broadsides or chapbooks Paisley Moon Press may publish. **Sample postpaid: $3. No previously published poems or simultaneous submissions. "No SASE sees the submission directly to the door and into the street." Reports in 1 day to 3 months.**

Always sends prepublication galleys. Pays 1 copy. The editors advise, "Read past and present masters (critically); read everything you can on poetry; read enough to know what is and isn't a cliché. Write and rewrite often. Be patient and persistent with your craft and vision. We publish whatever reduces us to confetti. If you're not going to blow our heads off, don't cock the gun. Paisley Moon Press solicits manuscripts for chapbooks from regular contributors of ***open unison stop***."

PALANQUIN/TDM; PALANQUIN POETRY SERIES (II), Dept. of English, University of South Carolina-Aiken, Aiken SC 29801, founded 1989, editor Phebe Davidson. This pamphlet/broadside series is now a ***Devil's Millhopper*** affiliate, but continues to have **an issue every 2 months consisting of 3-5 columns of poetry showcasing a single poet, professionally printed on a folded card. They do not want "sentimental, religious, consciously academic" poetry.** They have recently published poetry by Joe Weil, Dorothy Perry Thompson and Lois Marie Harrod. As a sample the editor selected these lines from "between us" by Alice Brand:

. . . .I can keep myself as blunt
as bedrock. I'll need nothing more
than days to go by faster than nights.

The card we received, featuring poems by Sander Zulauf, is printed on heavy recycled paper. Press run is 100 for 50 subscribers. Subscription: $10. **Sample postpaid: $2. No previously published poems. "I read January through March for the following year." Reports in 2 months. Pays half of press run. *Palanquin* also holds a spring chapbook contest for fall publication. Entry fee: $10 (includes subscription). Winner receives $50 and 50 copies. Contest deadline: April 1. Send SASE for further information.**

PANCAKE PRESS (V), 163 Galewood Circle, San Francisco CA 94131, phone (415)665-9215, founded 1974, publisher Patrick Smith, a small press publisher of hand-bound paperbacks with sewn signatures. **"Current projects are selected. At present we can consider only solicited mss for publication. Unsolicited mss will be returned with brief comment and thanks."** The editor publishes **"poetry aware of its own language conventions, tuned to both the ear and eye, attentive to syntax, honest about its desires, clear about something, spoken or written as a member of the species."** He has published books by John Logan, David Ray and Stephen Dunning.

THE PANHANDLER (II), Dept. PM, English Dept., University of West Florida, Pensacola FL 32514, phone (904)474-2923, founded 1976, editor Dr. Laurie O'Brien, appears twice a year, using **poetry "grounded in experience with strong individual 'voice' and natural language. Any subject, no 'causes.' Length to 200 lines, but prefer 30-100. No self-consciously experimental, unrestrained howling, sophomoric wailings on the human condition."** They have published poetry by Malcolm Glass, Lyn Lifshin, Donald Junkins, David Kirby and Joan Colby. As a sample here is the first stanza of "York, Maine" by Leo Connellan:

Through the Cutty Sark motel room 21 picture window now
the gray waves coming into York Beach like
an invasion of plows pushing snow. Tomorrow
the sun will scratch its chin and bleed along the skyline
but today everything is gray poached in a steam of fog.

The handsomely printed magazine is digest-sized, 64 pgs., flat-spined, large type on heavy eggshell stock, matte card cover with art. Circulation is 500 for 100 subscribers of which 10 are libraries and 200 complimentary copies going to the English department and writing program. Subscription: $5. **Sample postpaid: $2. No simultaneous submissions. Submit maximum of 7 poems, typewritten or letter-perfect printout. Reports in 1-2 months, 6-12 months to publication. Pays 2 copies.** They sponsor a national chapbook competition each year, October 15 through January 15. Submit 24-30 pgs. with $7 reading fee. Send SASE for details. The editor advises: "(1) Take care with ms preparation. Sloppy mss are difficult to evaluate fairly. (2) Send only poems you believe in. Everything you write isn't publishable; send finished work."

PANTHEON BOOKS INC., 201 E. 50th St., New York NY 10022. Prefers not to share information.

THE PAPER BAG (I, II), Box 268805, Chicago IL 60626-8805, phone (312)285-7972 (an answering service), founded 1988, editor M. Brownstein, is a quarterly using **poetry "any kind, any style. We look for strong and original imagery. No love poems at the beach, by water, across from candlelight."** As a sample the editor selected this complete poem, "Road Kill," by Michael Scott:

In the cool light of summer
morning, the possum seems
almost alive, no blood or guts
spilled in the road, white
fur tipped with gray,

looking like the dirty
snow of early spring.

The Paper Bag is 24 pgs., digest-sized, saddle-stapled, photocopied from typescript, with matte card cover. They publish about 30 of 200 poems received/issue. "Our circulation varies from 20-300 and we sell out every issue." Subscription: $12/4-5 issues plus "anything else we publish." **Sample postpaid: $3. Typed mss only, address and phone number on each submission. Cover letter with brief bio required. Editor comments on submissions "always." Send SASE for guidelines. Sometimes sends prepublication galleys. Pays copies.** All checks or money orders should be made out to M. Brownstein. The editor says, "Be persistent. Because we reject one group of submissions does not mean we will reject another batch. Keep trying."

THE PAPER SALAd POETRY JOURNAL (II), P.O. Box 520061, Salt Lake City UT 84152-0061, founded 1990, editor R.L. Moore, is an annual using **"poetry by poets who work rigorously on their poetry, who make every poem an attempt at the 'perfect' poem, and who know that the meaning of a poem is always secondary to the music of the poem."** They have recently published poetry by Richard Cronshey, Glenn Parker, Lyn Lifshin, Robert Nagler, John M. Bennett and Ana Christy. As a sample the editor selected these lines from "Fire Tales" by Michael Poore:

Past the tracks on
fifteenth street,
Phil the taxi man drinks a
whole trashcan of wine.
He changes into a story.

The editor describes it as 80-110 pgs., flat-spined, digest-sized. Press run is 250. **Sample: $6.50 ("An additional dollar will help with postage, but is optional"). Submit no more than 6 poems, one poem to a page, name and address on each. "Submissions without a SASE get tossed." A $1.50/item coupon toward *PAPER SALAd* stuff will be given to each poet who submits work on disk. "All poems in one file, please. IBM compatible, WordPerfect preferred. Please also include a hard copy of each poem." Seldom comments on rejections. Replies within 2 months. Pays 1 copy.** The editor says, "I don't really feel that a poem has to be *about* anything at all. In fact it's often the poem that tries to be *about* something that ends up failing. It starts to feel forced or too intentional. I think it's more important for a poem to draw the reader into a space or situation that is both familiar and yet new. I feel the best poetry helps to draw attention to the tension between the mundane and the ascensional."

PAPIER-MACHE PRESS (IV-Themes, anthologies, women), #14, 135 Aviation Way, Watsonville CA 95076, phone (408)763-1420, fax (408)763-1421, founded 1984, editor Sandra Martz, is a small press publisher of anthologies, poetry and short fiction in perfect-bound and casebound books. **Their anthologies typically "explore a particular aspect of women's experience, e.g., aging, parental relationships, work, sports, etc. Any length of poetry is acceptable for the anthologies."** They have published poetry by Sue Saniel Elkind, Shirley Vogler Meister, Sue Doro, Patti Tana and Janet Carncross Chandler. As a sample the editor selected these lines from **Phases of the Moon**, a collection by Lynn Kozma:

Listening, I hear the unexpected:
Ivy hisses, creeping up defenseless trunks.
New grass pipes through warmed soil.
Leaves whisper old secrets. Moss,
springing between red bricks, hums
long-lost tunes. Ceaseless chatter
of dandelions floods blue air.
Stones chant, hollow as drums.

They publish 1-2 poetry collections each year and one anthology every two years. Poetry collections contain 100-120 poems and are accepted in July and August only. Each anthology contains 30-40 poems, and submissions are accepted only when a particular theme has been announced (watch *Poets & Writers Magazine* for announcements). Send SASE for guidelines. Simultaneous submissions must be identified as such. Cover letter required; include name, address, phone and fax numbers (if available) as well as length and subject of submission. They report on mss in 3-4 months. Always sends prepublication galleys. Royalties, modest advances and several copies are negotiated for both individual collections and work accepted for anthologies. Send SASE for catalog to buy samples, books typically cost $8-14. "*Papier-Mache*'s primary objective is to publish anthologies, poetry and fiction books by, for and about mid-life and older women and about the art of women and men aging. We select well-written, accessible material on subjects of particular importance to women, develop attractive, high quality book formats and market them to an audience that might not otherwise buy books of poetry. We take particular pride in our reputation for dealing with our contributors in a caring, professional manner."

‡PARADISE PUBLICATIONS (I, IV-Cowboy), P.O. Box 7885, Colorado Springs CO 80933, phone (719)636-1734, founded 1992, editor Leah Galligar, publishes 3-4 perfect-bound paperback books of poetry each year. **"We are looking for cowboy poetry and poetry with an old-fashioned, Western flair."** They have recently published poetry by D.L. Chance and Sharon Chance. **Query first with 5 sample poems and cover letter with brief bio and publication credits. No previously published poems; simultaneous submissions OK. Replies to queries in 1 month. Pays 10% royalties and 2 author's copies.** Send $5 for sample copies of their books.

‡PARADOX; PARADOX PUBLICATIONS (II), P.O. Box 643, Saranac Lake NY 12983, founded 1991, editor Rev. Dan Bodah, appears 1-2 times/year. "***Paradox*** thrives on diversity and raw electricity. ***Paradox*** is exempt from stopping at railroad crossings. **I like poetry with *power*, no matter which genre. However, I wish to see no light verse."** They have recently published poetry by Maurice Kenny, John M. Bennett, Rochelle Owens and Susan Smith Nash. As a sample the editor selected these lines from "Resurgence" by Jake Berry:

Suddenly I'm nauseous and run for the door.
Outside and vomiting I see frogs like
crucifixes rising out of the ground, drifting
toward the sun where they explode in a
sweet crimson rain of mother horns.

The editor says ***Paradox*** varies between digest-sized and magazine-sized and is photocopied, hand-assembled, and often individually decorated. "Audiotapes are included with #3 onwards." Press run is 200 for 3 subscribers, 25-50 shelf sales. Single copy: $4; subscription: $15 for 4 issues. **Sample postpaid: $2.50. No previously published poems; simultaneous submissions OK.** Time between acceptance and publication is 6-12 months. **Seldom comments on rejections. Reports in 2-4 weeks. Pays 1-2 copies. Acquires first rights.** Paradox Publications **also publishes 1 chapbook/year. "I can only be swayed to publish unsolicited book mss if they are really good and I feel I can do them justice and/or handle the project. Poets can feel free to send an entire ms without a prior query." Replies in 2-4 weeks. Pays royalties and 10 author's copies. For sample chapbook, send $3.**

PARAGON HOUSE PUBLISHERS (III), Dept. PM, Suite 1700, 70 Lexington Ave., New York NY 10017, phone (212)953-5950, founded 1983, has published books of poetry by Louis Simpson and Leo Connellan.

THE PARIS REVIEW; BERNARD F. CONNORS PRIZE (III), 45-39 171st Pl., Flushing NY 11358, phone (718)539-7085, founded 1952, poetry editor Richard Howard. (**Submissions should go to him at 541 E. 72nd St., New York NY 10021**). This distinguished quarterly (circulation 10,000, digest-sized, 200 pgs.) has published many of the major poets writing in English. Though form, content and length seem open, free verse—some structured, some experimental—tends to dominate recent issues. Because the journal is considered one of the most prestigious in the world, competition is keen and response times can lag. **Sample: $8. Study publication before submitting.** The Bernard F. Connors prize of $1,000 is awarded annually for the best previously unpublished long poem (over 200 lines), submitted between April 1 and May 1. **All submissions must be sent to the 541 E. 72nd St., New York NY 10021 address.** Poetry published in ***The Paris Review*** was selected for inclusion in the 1992, 1993 and 1994 volumes of **The Best American Poetry.** As for the publication itself, ***The Paris Review*** ranked #4 in the "Poets' Pick" category of the latest ***Writer's Digest*** Poetry 60 list. This category ranks those publications in which poets said they would most like to see their work published.

PARIS/ATLANTIC, INTERNATIONAL MAGAZINE OF CREATIVE WORK (II, IV-Translations), 31 Avenue Bosquet, 75007 Paris, France, founded 1982. The magazine appears twice a year, published by the American University of Paris. It includes poetry, prose and b&w artwork. "Recent poets have been from a wide variety of countries—U.S., U.K., France, Ireland, Canada, Russia, the Netherlands and Taiwan, among others. **We encourage both published and unpublished writers and artists."** The magazine is 96 pgs., 6×9. Circulation 1,000. **Submit up to 6 poems, typed. Cover letter with short bio ("30 words or less") required. Sufficient postage for reply—in the form of either French stamps or IRCs—should also be included. Contributors receive 2 copies of the magazine. Copyright reverts to authors after publication.** They say, "We offer a unique bilingual, international medium for publica-

‡ ***The double dagger before a listing indicates that the listing is new in this edition. New markets are often the most receptive to submissions.***

tion and like to establish links with poets from as wide a variety of backgrounds as possible."

PARNASSUS LITERARY JOURNAL (I, II), P.O. Box 1384, Forest Park GA 30051, founded 1975, edited by Denver Stull: "Our sole purpose is to promote poetry and to offer an outlet where poets may be heard. **We are open to all poets and all forms of poetry, including Oriental, 24-line limit, maximum 5 poems.**" They have recently published poetry by Lyn Lifshin, H.F. Noyes, Curtis Nelson, C. David Hay and John Soldo. As a sample the editor selected "Pet Shop Parrot" by David Henson:

Here they come. Faces
that hover like wrinkled
balloons round my perch. Hello
yourself. These bright yellow
feathers you admire and touch. . .
I wish they were flames. I wish
they'd singe your fingers.
Hello yourself. No,
I don't want a cracker.
Give me back
my hole in the cliff.
Pretty bird yourself.

PLJ is 84 pgs., saddled-stapled, photocopied from typescript, with an occasional drawing. They receive about 1,500 submissions/year, of which they use 350. Currently have about a 1-year backlog. The magazine comes out 3 times a year with a print run of 300 copies. Subscribers presently number 200 (5 libraries). Circulation includes: Japan, England, Greece, India, Korea, Germany and Netherlands. **Sample: $4.50** (regularly $5.25/copy, $15/subscription US, $16.50 Canada, $22.50 overseas). **Make checks or money orders payable to Denver Stull. Include name and address on each page of ms. "Definitely" comments on rejections. "We do not respond to submissions or queries not accompanied by SASE." Reports within 1 week. Pays 1 copy. Acquires all rights. Returns rights.** Readers vote on best of each issue. Also conducts a contest periodically. Staff reviews books of poetry by subscribers only. ***Parnassus Literary Journal*** ranked #2 in the "Open Markets" category of the latest ***Writer's Digest*** Poetry 60 list. This category ranks those publications most open to both free and formal verse. The editor advises: "Write about what you know. Study what you have written. Does it make sense? A poem should not leave the reader wondering what you are trying to say. Improve your writings by studying the work of others. Be professional."

PARNASSUS: POETRY IN REVIEW; POETRY IN REVIEW FOUNDATION (V), Room 804, 41 Union Square W., New York NY 10003, phone (212)463-0889, founded 1972, poetry editor Herbert Leibowitz, provides "comprehensive and in-depth coverage of new books of poetry, including translations from foreign poetry. **We publish poems and translations on occasion, but we solicit all poetry. Poets invited to submit are given all the space they wish; the only stipulation is that the style be non-academic.**" They have published work by Alice Fulton, Eavan Boland, Ross Feld, Debora Greger, William Logan, Tess Gallagher, Seamus Heaney and Rodney Jones. They do consider unsolicited essays. In fact, this is an exceptionally rich market for thoughtful, insightful, technical essay-reviews of contemporary collections. However, it is strongly recommended that writers study the magazine before submitting. **Multiple submissions disliked. Cover letter required. Reports on essay submissions within 4-10 weeks (response takes longer during the summer). Pays $25-250 plus 2 gift subscriptions—contributors can also take one themselves. Acquires all rights. Editor comments on rejections—from 1 paragraph to 2 pages.** Send for a sample copy (prices of individual issues can vary) to get a feel for the critical acumen needed to place here. Subscriptions are $23/year, $46/year for libraries; they have 1,100 subscribers, of which 550 are libraries. The editor comments, "Contributors should be urged to subscribe to at least one literary magazine. There is a pervasive ignorance of the cost of putting out a magazine and no sense of responsibility for supporting one."

PARTING GIFTS; MARCH STREET PRESS (II), 3413 Wilshire, Greensboro NC 27408, founded 1987, editor Robert Bixby. **"I want to see everything.** I'm a big fan of Jim Harrison, C.K. Williams, Amy Hempel and Janet Kauffman. If you write like them, you'll almost certainly be published. But that's pretty useless advice unless you're one of those people." He has published poetry by Eric Torgersen, Lyn Lifshin, Elizabeth Kerlikowske and Russell Thorburn. ***PG*** is digest-sized, 72 pgs., photocopied, with colored matte card cover, press run 200, appearing twice a year. Subscription: $8. **Sample postpaid: $4. Submit in groups of 3-10 with SASE. No previously published poems, but simultaneous submissions OK. "I like a cover letter because it makes the transaction more human. Best time to submit mss is early in the year." Send SASE for guidelines. Reports in 1-2 weeks. Sometimes sends prepublication galleys. Pays 1 copy. March Street Press publishes chapbooks; $10 reading fee.**

PARTISAN REVIEW (III, IV-Translations, themes), Dept. PM, 236 Bay State Rd., Boston MA 02215, phone (617)353-4260, founded 1934, editor William Phillips, is a distinguished quarterly literary journal (6×9, 160 pgs., flat-spined, circulation 8,200 for 6,000 subscriptions and shelf sales), using **poetry of high quality.** They have published poetry by Joseph Brodsky, Eavan Boland, W.S. Merwin and C.H. Sisson. **Sample postpaid: $7.50. Submit maximum of 6. No simultaneous submissions. Reports in 2 months. Pays $50 and 50% discount on copies. "Our poetry section is very small and highly selective. We are open to fresh, quality translations but submissions must include poem in original language as well as translation. We occasionally have special poetry sections on specified themes."**

PASQUE PETALS; SOUTH DAKOTA STATE POETRY SOCIETY, INC. (I, IV-Regional, subscribers), 909 E. 34th St., Sioux Falls SD 57105, phone (605)338-9156, founded 1926, editor Barbara Stevens. This is the official poetry magazine for the South Dakota State Poetry Society, Inc., but it is open to non-members. **Those not residents of SD are required to subscribe when (or before) submitting. They use "all forms. 44-line limit, 50-character lines. Count titles and spaces. Lean toward SD and Midwest themes. No rough language or porno—magazine goes into SD schools and libraries."** As a sample the editor chose her poem "The Errol Flynn Look-Alike":

His tongue was as smooth as honey on a spoon.
Went from job to job,
Fooled everyone at first meeting
talked great projects completed by others.
Fooled his wife all the time,
she grew fat and comfortable
He left her
for a size five.

PP appears 10 times a year (no August or November issues) and is digest-sized, 16-20 pgs., using small b&w sketches. Circulation is 250 to members/subscribers (16 to libraries). Subscription: $15/year. **Sample postpaid: $1.50. Submit 3 poems at a time, 1 poem (or 2 haiku)/page, seasonal material 3 months ahead. Editor "always" comments on rejections. Send SASE for guidelines. Reports in 3 months. Has a 2- to 3-month backlog. Pays non-members only 1 copy. Acquires first rights.** Reviews books of poetry by members only. Offers $5 prize for the best poem in every issue. They also sponsor a yearly contest with 10 categories. Entry fees vary. Prizes total $600. Send SASE for details.

PASSAGER: A JOURNAL OF REMEMBRANCE AND DISCOVERY (I, II, IV-Senior citizen, themes), English and Communications Design Dept., University of Baltimore, 1420 N. Charles St., Baltimore MD 21201-5779, phone (410)625-3041, founded 1989, editors Kendra Kopelke and Sally Darnowsky. *Passager* is published quarterly and publishes fiction, poetry and interviews that give voice to human experience. **"We seek powerful images of remembrance and discovery from writers of all ages. One of our missions is to provide exposure for new older writers; another is to function as a literary community for writers across the country who are not connected to academic institutions or other organized groups."** The journal is 8×8, 32 pgs., printed on white linen, saddle-stitched. Includes photos of writers. **Poetry, 30 lines maximum; fiction, 3,000 words maximum. Simultaneous submissions acceptable if notified. No reprints. Do not submit mss in August. Occasionally does special issues. Send SASE for guidelines. Reports in 2 months. Pays 1 year's subscription.** They sponsor an annual poetry contest for poets over 50 years old. Prize is $100 and publication in *Passager*.

PASSAGES NORTH (II), Kalamazoo College, 1200 Academy St., Kalamazoo MI 49006-3295, founded 1979, editor Michael Barrett, poetry editor Conrad Hillberry, is a semiannual magazine containing fiction, poetry, essays, interviews and visual art. **"The magazine publishes quality work by established and emerging writers."** They have published poetry by Mark Halliday, William Matthews, Thomas Lux, Cynthia Huntington, Jo Anne Rawson, Mark Doty, Nancy Eimers and John Rybicki. As a sample the editor selected these lines from "The Waves Roll In" by Susan Wylie:

I lay flat over the engine, the thrum
of the motor in my chest and belly,
the close sun hot on my head,
and memorized the roadside blur:
dried brush and trash, a blue inverted
sky cradling the dunes.

Passages North is 100 pgs., perfect-bound. Circulation is at 1,000 "and growing." Single copy: $5; subscription: $10 for 1 year, $18 for 2 years. **Prefers groups of 4-6 poems, typed single-spaced. Simultaneous submissions OK. Reads submissions September through May only. Reports in 6-8 weeks, delay to publication is 6 months. Pays copies.**

PATH PRESS, INC. (IV-Ethnic), Suite 724, 53 W. Jackson Blvd., Chicago IL 60604, phone (312)663-0167, fax (312)663-5318, founded 1969, president Bennett J. Johnson, executive vice president and poetry editor Herman C. Gilbert, a small publisher of books and poetry primarily **"by, for and about African American and Third World people." The press is open to all types of poetic forms except "poor quality." Submissions should be typewritten in manuscript format. Writers should send sample poems, credits and bio.** The books are "hardback and quality paperbacks."

‡PEACE AND FREEDOM; EASTERN RAINBOW (I), 17 Farrow Rd., Whaplode Drove, Spalding, Lincs PE12 OTS England, phone 0406-330242, editor Paul Rance, founded 1985, is a "small press publisher of poetry, music, art, short stories, reviews and general features," and also is a distributor. *Peace and Freedom* is a magazine appearing 2 times a year. **"We are looking for poems up to 32 lines particularly from U.S. poets who are new to writing, particularly women. The poetry we publish is anti-war, environmental; poems reflecting love; erotic, but not obscene poetry; humorous verse and spiritual, humanitarian poetry. With or without rhyme/metre."** They have recently published poetry by Dorothy Bell-Hall, Chloe Heuch, Matthew Dalby, Indiana Candy, Bernard Shough and Sidney Morleigh. These sample lines are by Katie Bolton:

'I started so I'll finish,' he said.
'It's over.'
'Over what ?' I asked.
'Overrated ? Over ripe ? Overdone ?'
'Overbetweenus.'
'Oh.'

Peace and Freedom has a card cover, normally 16 A4 pages. 50% of submissions accepted. "Poetry is judged on merit, but non-subscribers may have to wait longer for their work to appear than subscribers." **Sample: US $3; £1 and SAE UK. "Sample copies can only be purchased from the above address, and various mail-order distributors too numerous to mention. Advisable to buy a sample copy first. Banks charge the equivalent of $5 to cash foreign cheques in the U.K., so advisable to send bills, preferably by registered post."** Subscription: US $11, U.K. £5 for 4 issues. **No simultaneous submissions or previously published poems. Poets are requested to send in bios. Reads submissions all through the year. Publishes theme issues. Send SAE with IRC for upcoming themes. Replies to submissions normally under a month, with IRC/SAE. "Work without correct postage will not be responded to or returned until proper postage is sent." Pays 1 copy.** Reviews books of poetry. "***Peace and Freedom*** now holds regular contests as does one of our new publications, ***Eastern Rainbow***, which is a magazine concerning 20th century popular culture using poetry up to 32 lines. Subscription: $11/£5 for 4 issues. Further details of competitions and publications for SAE and IRC." The editor says, "Too many writers have lost the personal touch and editors generally appreciate this. It can make a difference when selecting work of equal merit."

THE PEACE FARM ADVOCATE (IV-Social issues), HCR 2 Box 25, Panhandle TX 79068, phone (806)335-1715, founded 1986, editor Mavis Belisle, is a quarterly which promotes peacemaking through information, commentary and reflection. **"We consider only poetry related to peace, environmental and social justice issues."** As a sample the editor selected these lines from "Packing for Saudi Arabia" by Mary Carter Rak:

I stare at the empty green bag
I must fill in the next fifteen minutes
with things most important
to you. Underwear, T-shirts,
your St. Christopher medal
wrapped in tissue.

The Peace Farm Advocate is 40 pgs., 8½×11, printed on recycled paper. Press run is 1,000 for 800 paid subscribers. The rest are distributed free. Subscription: $5. **Previously published poems and simultaneous submissions OK.** Time between acceptance and publication is 3-6 months. **Reports in 6 months. "We do not pay for published poems."** Open to unsolicited reviews. Poets may also send books for review consideration. The editor says, "Because of downsizing, opportunity will be very limited; we do not expect to be able to accept more than 1-2 short to medium-length poems per issue."

THE PEACE NEWSLETTER (IV-Social issues, political), Dept. PM, Syracuse Peace Council, 924 Burnet Ave., Syracuse NY 13203, founded 1936, is magazine-sized, 24 pgs., circulating 12 times a year to 5,000 people mostly in upstate and central NY with news about the peace movement and using **some poetry relating to that movement.** Subscription: $12/year. **Sample free for SASE. Considers simultaneous submissions. Unable to pay.**

PEACEMAKING FOR CHILDREN (V, IV-Children, social issues, themes), 2437 N. Grant Blvd., Milwaukee WI 53210, phone (414)445-9736, founded 1983, editor Jacqueline Haessly, is a magazine appearing 5 times a year, covering **peace education themes *for* children.** "The magazine is highly specialized in this field. **Writers must have a sensitivity to interdependence of justice and peace issues, a commitment to non-violence, and an ability to write for children's level of comprehension." All issues have a single-focus theme such as the environment, handicapped, "all the ways we are family, space exploration vs. exploitation, understanding racism, our Latin friends." They do not want "Bible-related" or avant-garde poetry. Poems 5-20 lines only. However, they are currently not accepting poetry submissions.** Circulation is 10,000 and growing, "includes schools, libraries, churches, families on 6 continents." **Sample: $2.**

PEARL; PEARL CHAPBOOK CONTEST (II), 3030 E. Second St., Long Beach CA 90803, phone (310)434-4523 or (714)968-7530, founded 1974, folded after 3 issues, resurrected in 1987, poetry editors Joan Jobe Smith, Marilyn Johnson and Barbara Hauk, is a literary magazine appearing three times a year. **"We are interested in accessible, humanistic poetry that communicates and is related to real life. Humor and wit are welcome, along with the ironic and serious. No taboos stylistically or subject-wise. Prefer poems up to 35 lines, with lines no longer than 10 words. We don't want to see sentimental, obscure, predictable, abstract or cliché-ridden poetry. Our purpose is to provide a forum for lively, readable poetry that reflects a wide variety of contemporary voices, viewpoints and experiences—that speaks to *real* people about *real* life in direct, living language, profane or sublime."** They have recently published poetry by Mark Weber, Fred Voss, Charles Bukowski, Donna Hilbert, Cherry Jean Vasconcellos and Ann Menebroker. As a sample they selected these lines from "What the Fast Girl Knows" by Lisa Glatt:

I have always been afraid
of my breasts. I was twelve
with my hand in my red nightgown
feeling them, convinced even then
that what they were
was cancer. . .

Pearl is digest-sized, 96 pgs., perfect-bound, offset, with laminated cover. Their press run is 600 with 100 subscriptions of which 7 are libraries. Subscription: $15/year. **Sample postpaid: $6. "Handwritten submissions and unreadable dot-matrix print-outs are not acceptable." No simultaneous submissions or previously published poems. "Cover letters appreciated." Guidelines available for SASE. Reports in 6-8 weeks. Sometimes sends prepublication galleys. Pays 2 copies. Acquires first serial rights.** Each issue contains the work of 60-70 different poets and a special 10- to 15-page section that showcases the work of a single poet. Staff reviews books of poetry. Send books for review consideration to Marilyn Johnson. "We sponsor an annual chapbook contest, judged by one of our more well-known contributors. Winner receives publication, $100 and 50 copies, with an introduction by the final judge. Entries accepted during the months of May and June. There is a $10 entry fee, which includes a copy of the winning chapbook." Send SASE for complete rules and guidelines. Recent chapbooks include **Reflections of a White Bear** by Carolyn E. Campbell, **The Coolest Car in School** by Joan Jobe Smith, **The Old Mongoose and Other Poems** by Gerald Locklin and **Steubenville** by Julie Herrick White. ***Pearl*** ranked #8 in the "Nontraditional Verse" category of the latest ***Writer's Digest*** Poetry 60 list. The editors add, "Advice for beginning poets? Just write from your own experience, using images that are as concrete and sensory as possible. Keep these images fresh and objective, and always listen to the music. . . ."

PECKERWOOD (II), Apt. C-3, 1475 King St. West, Toronto, Ontario M6K 1J4 Canada, phone (416)531-4262, founded 1987, editors Ernie Ourique and Yuki Hayashi, appears 3 or 4 times/year. **"It could be any style you wish, any length. Haiku—yes. Rhymes—yes. Beauty—yes. Ugliness—yes. No clones of good poets, creative writing class crap or poems written by television housewives."** They have recently published poetry by Chris Wood, Libby Scheier, Sheila E. Murphy, Charles Bukowski and Allen Ginsberg. As a sample the editor selected these lines from "bottles" by Coral Hull:

and how his dog branto used to dive down to the rivers centre and bring up fresh water mussels
cracking them between his canine teeth in his frenzy to please
i would feel the black edge of mussel shells between my toes . . .

It is 30-40 pgs., saddle-stapled, photocopied from typescript with matte card cover. They accept about 30% of poems received. Press run is 450 for 160 shelf sales. **Sample: $2 cash. Editors sometimes provide comments on rejections. Pays 5 copies.** Staff reviews books of poetry. Send books for review consideration. Ernie Ourique says, "The poems should have tongues and hearts. No one can teach you how to write poetry. Don't accept the 'masters' of poetry (Pound, Eliot, Yeats) as the greatest. Explore poetry from all over the world. This means reading more than writing. Also get a job that doesn't involve brains: construction, washing toilets. You'll meet the greatest and worst human beings in the working class. Never insult people."

PEGASUS (II), 525 Ave. B, Boulder City NV 89005, founded 1986, editor M.E. Hildebrand, is a poetry quarterly "for serious poets who have something to say and know how to say it using sensory imagery." **Submit 3-5 poems, 3-40 lines. Avoid "religious, political, pornographic themes."** They have published poetry by Stan Moseley, Gayle Elen Harvey, Robert K. Johnson and Elizabeth Perry, who provides the opening lines of "The Meeting Hour" as a sample:

Before Dawn drops
her luminous petals
I wake and listen
for your muted voice
to break the silence
of our worlds
like rustlings
in the deep woods.

Pegasus is 32 pgs., digest-sized, saddle-stapled, offset from typescript with colored paper cover. Publishes 10-15% of the work received. Circulation 200. Subscription: $12.50. **Sample postpaid: $4.50. Previously published poems OK, provided poet retains rights, but no simultaneous submissions. Send SASE for guidelines. Reports in 2 weeks. Publication is payment. Acquires first or one-time rights.**

THE PEGASUS REVIEW (I, II, IV-Themes), P.O. Box 88, Henderson MD 21640-0088, founded 1980, is a 14-page (counting cover) pamphlet entirely in calligraphy, illustrated on high-quality paper, some color overlays. Editor Art Bounds says, "This magazine is a bimonthly, **based on specific themes. Those for 1995 are: January/February – Imagination; March/April – Memories; May/June – Nature; July/August – Freedom; September/October – Autumn; and November/December – Hope. Uses poetry not more than 24 lines (the shorter the better); fiction that is short short (about 2½ pages would be ideal); essays and cartoons. All material must pertain to indicated themes only. Would like to see various forms rather than just free verse."** Poets recently published include Milton Finkelstein, Alix Weisz, Linda Asher and Shirley Vogler Meister. As a sample the editor selected these lines from "After a Broken Engagement" by Bruce Key:

After a while,
one must turn the key,
lock away the memories

but leave the heart ajar,
should it reopen on its own,
again, someday.

Press run is 160 for 150 subscribers, of which 4 are libraries. Subscription: $10. **Sample: $2. Submit 3-5 poems with name and address on each page. Cover letter with brief background and list of publishing credits helpful. "If a beginner – no problem." Query if additional information is needed. Reports within a month, often with a personal response. Pays 2 copies.** Occasional book awards throughout the year. Also issues a writer's calendar – in calligraphy – with motivational sayings and writing advice ($8 plus $2.50 postage and handling). The editor advises, "Try to become familiar with your markets. Publications are available at the library or a sample copy may be purchased. Adhere strictly to the guidelines: If brevity is emphasized, don't send a ten-page submission. Get involved with a local writers' group... or start one! Use the wealth of information in various marketing publications such as **Poet's Market**. Keep on writing."

PELICAN PUBLISHING COMPANY (V, IV-Children, regional), Box 3110, Gretna LA 70054, phone (504)368-1175, founded 1926, editor Nina Kooij, is a "moderate-sized publisher of cookbooks, travel guides, regional books and inspirational/motivational books," which accepts **poetry for "hardcover children's books *only*, preferably with a Southern focus. However, our needs for this are very limited; we do fewer than 5 juvenile titles per year, and most of these are prose, not poetry." They are currently not accepting unsolicited mss. Query first with cover letter including "work and writing backgrounds, plot summary and promotional connections." No simultaneous submissions. Reports on queries in 1 month, on mss (if invited) in 3 months. Always sends prepublication galleys. Pays royalties. Buys all rights. Returns rights upon termination of contract.** These are 32-page, large-format (magazine-sized) books with illustrations. Two of their popular series are prose books about Gaston the Green-Nosed Alligator by James Rice and Clovis Crawfish by Mary Alice Fontenot. They have a variety of books based on "The Night Before Christmas" adapted to regional settings such as Cajun, prairie, and Texas. Typically their books sell for $14.95. **Write for catalog to buy samples.** The editor says, "We try to avoid rhyme altogether, especially predictable rhyme. Monotonous rhythm can also be a problem."

PEMBROKE MAGAZINE (II), Box 60, Pembroke State University, Pembroke NC 28372, founded 1969 by Norman Macleod, edited by Shelby Stephenson, is a heavy (252 pgs., 6×9), flat-spined, quality literary annual which has published poetry by Fred Chappell, Stephen Sandy, A.R. Ammons, Barbara

Guest and Betty Adcock. Press run is 500 for 125 subscribers of which 100 are libraries. **Sample postpaid: $5. Sometimes comments on rejections. Reports within 3 months. Pays copies.** Stephenson advises, "Publication will come if you write. Writing is all."

‡**PEMMICAN (III); PEMMICAN PRESS (V)**, P.O. Box 16374, St. Paul MN 55116, phone (612)698-7710, founded 1992, editor Robert Edwards, is an annual magazine designed to publish "the best poetry of imagery, imagination and political commitment we can find." They want **"political, narrative poetry—anything with imagery and imagination. No workshop minimalist, right wing or fundamentalist poetry; no greeting card verse."** They have recently published poetry by Adrian C. Louis, Margaret Randall and Patrick Stanhope. As a sample the editor selected these lines from "Little Big Man" by Sherman Alexie:

I got eyes, Jack, that can see
an ant moving along the horizon
can pull four bottles shattering
down from the sky and recognize
the eyes of a blind man

Pemmican is 40 pgs., 7×8½, saddle-stitched, card stock cover with original art. They receive 200-300 submissions a year, use less than 10%. Press run is 300 for 50 subscribers of which 15 are libraries, 100 shelf sales. Single copy: $3.50. **Sample postpaid: $2. No previously published poems; simultaneous submissions OK. Cover letter required. "Make sure postage on SASE is adequate for full return of submitted materials." Seldom comments on rejections. Send SASE for guidelines. Reports in 1 week to 6 months. Pays 2 copies. Acquires first North American serial rights.** Editor occasionally writes short (200-word) reviews of books, chapbooks and magazines. Send books for review consideration. Pemmican Press also publishes 1 paperback and 3 chapbooks of poetry each year. Publication is by invitation only. **"I only publish books by poets published in *Pemmican* magazine." Pays 50 author's copies. For sample book, send SASE for flyer.** The editor says, "There are no requirements—however, I hope poets realize the importance of the small presses and put their money where their mouth is. Advice for beginners? Keep writing. Read everything. Don't write to please an editor or to get published. Follow your own voice."

PENNINE PLATFORM (II), Ingmanthorpe Hall Farm Cottage, Wetherby, W. Yorkshire LS22 5EQ England, phone 0937-64674, founded 1973, poetry editor Brian Merrikin Hill, appears 3 times a year. The editor wants **any kind of poetry but concrete ("lack of facilities for reproduction"). No specifications of length, but poems of less than 40 lines have a better chance. "All styles—effort is to find things good of their kind. Preference for religious or sociopolitical awareness of an acute, not conventional kind."** They have published poetry by Elizabeth Bartlett, Anna Adams, John Ward, Ian Caws, John Latham and Geoffrey Holloway. As a sample the editor selected these lines from "A Vision of Cabez De Vaca" by Cal Clothier:

Blanched to a skin manned by bones,
we have blood and our breathing
to prove we are men, and the hungry light
jerking our eyes. We are down to mercy,
gratitude, love, down to humanity.

The 6×8, 48-page journal is photocopied from typescript, saddle-stapled, with matte card cover with graphics, circulation 400, 300 subscriptions of which 16 are libraries. They receive about 300 submissions/year, use about 30, have about a 6-month backlog. Subscription: £7 for 3 issues (£10 abroad; £25 if not in sterling). **Sample postpaid: £2. Submit 1-6 poems, typed. Reports in about a month. No pay. Acquires first serial rights. Editor occasionally comments on rejections.** Reviews books of poetry in 2,500 words, multi-book format. Open to unsolicited reviews. Poets may also send books for review consideration. They would like to see more sociopolitical themes in traditional forms, less free verse. Brian Hill comments, "It is time to avoid the paradigm-magazine-poem and reject establishments—ancient, modern or allegedly contemporary. Small magazines and presses often publish superior material to the commercial hyped publishers."

PENNSYLVANIA ENGLISH (II), Penn State-Erie, Erie PA 16563, phone (814)824-2000, founded 1988 (first issue in March, 1989), poetry editor John Coleman, is "a journal sponsored by the Pennsylvania College English Association." They want poetry of **"any length, any style."** The journal is magazine-sized, saddle-stapled, and appears twice a year. Press run is 300. Subscription: $15, which includes membership in PCEA. **Submit 4-5 typed poems. Do not submit mss in the summer. They consider simultaneous submissions but not previously published poems. Reports in 1 month. Pays 2 copies.**

THE PENNSYLVANIA REVIEW (II), English Dept., 526 CL, University of Pittsburgh, Pittsburgh PA 15260, phone (412)624-0026, founded 1985, editor Julie Parson-Nesbitt. This ambitious semiannual journal was described by *Choice* as "a fine small literary magazine." **There are no restrictions on subject matter, style or length, although they do not want to see "light verse or greeting card verse." They would like to receive more work by "non-mainstream writers (African-American, Latino/a, etc.)."** They have published poetry by Nance Van Winckel, Jim Daniels, Maggie Anderson, Sharon Doubiago, Lawrence Joseph, Debra Bruce, Sonia Sanchez and translations of Karl Krolow by Stuart Friebert. As a sample the editor selected these lines from "Live Remote" by Dorothy Barresi:

. . . Me? I hate myself.
I could be me at thirteen or eighteen
but I am fat, six,
deeply aware that we are given the world and each other
and no wonder we're lonely.

It is a handsome magazine, 7×10, 80 pgs., flat-spined, professionally printed on heavy stock with graphics, art and ads, glossy card cover with b&w illustration. Circulation is approximately 1,000 with 350 subscriptions. Subscription: $10 for 2 issues. **Sample postpaid: $6. Writers should submit 3-6 poems, typewritten only. Cover letter with brief 3-line bio (publishable if work is accepted) required. Do not submit mss between May 1 and September 1. Publishes theme issues occasionally. Reports in 2-3 months. Pays 2 copies.** Staff reviews books of poetry and fiction. Send books for review consideration.

‡**THE PENNY DREADFUL REVIEW (I, IV-Erotica, form/style)**, H-9, 6680 Charlotte Ave., Nashville TN 37209, phone (615)352-3095, founded November 1993, "maximum domineditrix" Ms. Penelope Dreadful, assistant editor C Ra McGuirt, is a monthly where "sex and fear are forced to shake hands by humor." **They want "very, very personal, dark, funny, erotic and/or experimental stuff. Any length under 2 pages. No forced rhyme, dry academic rot, self-congratulatory pabulum or sentimentality."** They have recently published poetry by Lyn Lifshin, Tom House, Gina Bergamino and Todd Moore. As a sample the editors selected "the prophet" by Gerald Locklin:

i have seen the future
and it does not have a penis.

The Penny Dreadful Review is 10 pgs., 8½×11, photocopied and corner-stapled with b&w photos and graphics. Press run is 200. Single copy: 1¢; subscription: $3.60/year. **Sample for "SASE and love offering." Previously published poems and simultaneous submissions OK. Cover letter preferred. "Rather than a SASE, we prefer loose stamps. Penny says: 'Rules were made to be twisted, however.' "** Time between acceptance and publication is 2 weeks to 2 months. **Often comments on rejections. Send SASE for guidelines. "We try for same day response." Pays at least 1 copy. All rights remain with poets.** "We'll review—or think about reviewing—almost anything in our genre." Open to unsolicited reviews. Poets may also send books for review consideration. Penny Dreadful says, "Don't speak *to* us, speak *for* us, but always speak for yourself. Nothing is true; everything is permissible. Do what thou wilt shall be the whole of the law."

THE PENUMBRA PRESS (II), 920 S. 38th St., Omaha NE 68105, phone (402)346-7344, founded 1972, poetry editors Bonnie O'Connell and George O'Connell, publishes "contemporary literature and graphics in the tradition of fine arts printing." Their books are "designed, illustrated (unless otherwise indicated), hand printed from hand-set type, and bound by the proprietor," Bonnie O'Connell. All are limited editions, including hard and soft cover books, chapbooks, postcards and theme anthologies. They have published poetry by David St. John, Sam Pereira, Brenda Hillman, Debora Greger, Peter Everwine, Laura Jensen, Norman Dubie and Rita Dove. As a sample the editor selected these lines from "Cool Dark Ode" by Donald Justice:

When the long planed table that served as a desk
was recalling the quiet of the woods
when the books, older, were thinking farther back,
to the same essential stillness . . .

Query with 5-6 samples, some personal background and publication credits. Simultaneous submissions OK. Editor sometimes comments on rejections. Send SASE for catalog to order samples or inquire at university libraries (special collection) or through the distributor, Nebraska Book Arts Center, 124 Fine Arts Bldg., University of Nebraska-Omaha, Omaha NE 68182.

PEOPLENET (I, IV-Specialized: disabled people, love/romance), P.O. Box 897, Levittown NY 11756, phone (516)579-4043, founded 1987, editor/publisher Robert Mauro, is a newsletter **for disabled people focusing on dating, love and relationships.** The editor wants **"poetry on relationships, love and romance only. The length should remain 10-20 lines. 3 or 4 poems at a time. We publish beginners, new poets. Prefer free verse, a lot of good imagery—and very little rhyme."** As a sample the editor chose these lines from his poem "When All That Blooms Are Roses":

Mornings are not mornings
when all that blooms are roses:

dewy petals opening, blushing
in the wind; a hand
plucks a flower, a finger
touches a bud that didn't
bloom and never will.

Peoplenet appears 3 times a year and is 12-16 pgs., magazine-sized, offset, using graphics and ads. Press run is about 200, with that many subscriptions. Subscription: $25. **Sample copy: $3. Poems should be double-spaced with name and address on each page. No simultaneous submissions. Editor comments on good but rejected mss. Reports "immediately." Pays tearsheets only. Acquires first rights.** (Copies of the newsletter, which contains personal ads, go to subscribers only. Free brochure available.) **He says, "We want to publish poems that express the importance of love, acceptance, inner beauty, the need for love and relationship, and the joy of loving and being loved."**

PEP PUBLISHING; LOVING MORE (I, IV-Specialized: group marriage), P.O. Box 6306, Captain Cook HI 96704-6306, founded 1984, editor Ryam Nearing. ***Loving More*** is a quarterly that "publishes articles, letters, poems, drawings and reviews related to **polyfidelity, group marriage and multiple *intimacy*." They use "relatively short poems, though a quality piece of length would be considered, but topic relevance is essential. Please no swinger or porno pieces. Group marriage should not be equated with group sex."** It is 14 pgs., magazine-sized, few ads. Circulation 500. Subscription: $30 a year. **Sample: $4 to poets. Ms should be "readable." Considers simultaneous submissions. Editor comments on rejections "sometimes – if requested." Responds "ASAP," delay to publication is 2-6 months. Pays 1 copy.** Open to unsolicited reviews. Poets may also send books for review consideration. The editor says, "Writers should read our publication before submitting, and I emphasize no swinger or porno pieces will be published."

PEQUOD: A JOURNAL OF CONTEMPORARY LITERATURE AND LITERARY CRITICISM (III), Dept. of English, New York University, Room 200, 19 University Place, New York NY 10003, contact poetry editor, is a semiannual literary review publishing **quality poetry, fiction, essays and translations**. They have recently published poetry by Sam Hamill, Donald Hall and John Updike. It is professionally printed, digest-sized, 200 pgs., flat-spined with glossy card cover. Subscription: $12. **Sample postpaid: $5. Reads submissions September 15 through April 15 only. Always sends prepublication galleys.** Poetry published in ***Pequod*** has also been included in **The Best American Poetry 1993.**

PERCEPTIONS (IV-Women), #2, 14 Cedar St., Brunswick ME 04011-2309, founded 1982, poetry editor Temi Rose, is a "small prize-winning **women's poetry magazine for the promotion and development of women's consciousness of peace and hope and freedom to be."** They have published poetry by Chocolate Waters, Lyn Lifshin and Edna Kovacs. As a sample the editor selected these lines by Marcia Arrieta:

eyes like birds
and hips for babies
a woman who is
not afraid to wander
into mountains alone

Perceptions is 30 pgs., digest-sized, photocopied from typescript with printed cover and comes out 3 times a year. They publish about 360 of 3,000 poems received/year. Press run is 300 for 50 subscribers of which 3 are libraries. Subscription: $21. **Sample postpaid: $7. They consider simultaneous submissions and previously published poems. Guidelines available for SASE. Reports in 1-3 months. Pays 1 copy. *Perceptions*** ranked #1 in the "Open Markets" category of the latest ***Writer's Digest*** Poetry 60 list. This category ranks those publications most open to both free and formal verse.

PEREGRINE: THE JOURNAL OF AMHERST WRITERS & ARTISTS (II); AWA CHAPBOOK SERIES (V), P.O. Box 1076, Amherst MA 01004, ***Peregrine*** founded 1983, Amherst Writers & Artists Press, Inc., 1987. **Open to all styles, forms and subjects except greeting card verse.** They have published poetry by Jane Yolen, Walter McDonald and Barbara Van Noord. As a sample the editors selected these lines by Rosalie Moore:

The moon wanes,
with all of our vanished powers,
comes to one side of the day
to complete its series. . .

Slight as a memory that once said
"locket" or "silver spoon",
the last of the quarters

vanishes in thin air.

Peregrine is 70 pgs., digest-sized, professionally printed, with matte card cover. Their press run is 500. **Sample postpaid: $4.50. "We may hold poems for several months, so we encourage simultaneous submissions." Pays contributor's copies.**

‡PERIVALE PRESS; PERIVALE POETRY CHAPBOOKS; PERIVALE TRANSLATION SERIES (II, IV-Translations, anthology), 13830 Erwin St., Van Nuys CA 91401-2914, founded 1968, editor Lawrence P. Spingarn, publishes **Perivale Poetry Chapbooks, Perivale Translation Series**, anthologies. The collections by individuals are usually translations, but here are some lines by R.L. Barth from "Da Nang Nights: Liberty Song" in **Forced-Marching to the Styx**:

In sudden light we choose
Lust by lust our bar:
And whatever else we lose,
We also lose the war.

They publish an average of one 20-page saddle-stapled chapbook, one perfect-bound (20-70 pgs.) collection, one anthology per year, all quality print jobs. Send SASE for catalog. Perivale publishes both on **straight royalty basis (10%, 10 author's copies) usually grant supported, and by subsidy, the author paying 100%, being repaid from profits, if any. "Payment for chapbooks accepted is 50 free copies of press run.** Authors should agree to promote books via readings, talk shows, orders and signings with local bookshops. **Contributors are encouraged to buy samples of chapbooks, etc., for clues to editor's tastes." Samples of previous poetry chapbooks: $5 postpaid.** (Barth title out of print.) Latest title: **Going Home** (chapbook) by Sheryl St. Germain. **To submit, query first, with sample of 6-10 poems, cover letter, bio, previous books. Do not submit mss from June 15 to September 1. Always sends prepublication galleys. Spingarn, a well-known, widely published poet, offers criticism for a fee, the amount dependent on length of book. Sponsors a poetry chapbook contest. Send SASE for details. The editor advises, "Contributors should read samples and guidelines thoroughly before submitting. Also, we would like to see poems with less self-involvement (fewer poems that open with 'I') and a wider world view."**

PERMAFROST (II, IV-Regional), Dept. PM, English Dept., University of Alaska, Fairbanks AK 99775, phone (907)474-5237, founded 1977. "Editors change annually." ***Permafrost*** is a biannual journal of poems, short stories, essays, reviews, b&w drawings and photographs. "We survive on both new and established writers, and hope and expect to see your best work (we are not the Siberia of mediocre poetry). **We publish any style of poetry provided it is conceived, written, revised with care; favor poems with strong, unusual images or poems with abstraction backed up by imagery; both must have universal applications. We discourage 'tourist poetry' which rarely works because of its hackneyed imagery and lack of universal theme; encourage poems about Alaska and by Alaskans, but they are works and writers at ease with their setting. We also encourage poems about anywhere and from anywhere. We are not a regional publication, but in order to support contemporary Alaskan literature, we publish reviews only of work by Alaskan authors or publishers."** They have published poetry by Wendy Bishop, Jerah Chadwick, Leslie Leyland Fields, Linda Gregg, Patricia Monaghan, John Morgan, Peggy Shumaker and Kim Stafford. The digest-sized journal is 100 pgs., flat-spined, professionally printed, two-color paper cover with b&w graphics and photos, has a circulation of 500 with 100 subscriptions of which 20 are libraries. Subscription: $7. **Sample postpaid: $4. Submit no more than 5 poems, neatly typed; considers simultaneous submissions but "expects to be told." Does not accept submissions between April 1 and August 1. Deadlines are December 1 and April 1. Editors comment only on mss that have made the final round and then are rejected. Depth of comments vary. Guidelines available for SASE ("although most are listed here"). Return time is 1-3 months; "longer if work was submitted well before deadline and is under serious consideration." Pays 2 copies, reduced contributor rates on others.**

PERMEABLE PRESS; PUCK: THE UNOFFICIAL JOURNAL OF THE IRREPRESSIBLE (III), #15, 900 Tennessee, San Francisco CA 94107-3014, phone (415)648-2175, founded 1984, editor Brian Clark, associate editor Kurt Putnam. ***Puck*** is a triannual designed to "provoke thought, dialog. Contents: reviews, stories, essays, poems." **As for poetry they want "radical reinterpretations of the 'accepted.' No restrictions as to style, length, etc. No love poems."** They have published poetry by B. Subraman and Hugh Fox. As a sample they selected these lines from "Tarot of Nature" by Susan Luzarro:

Yesterday the queen of wands came to me. She was painted with honey-colored locks
to perpetuate the myth that nature, like christ, was blonde. Lay me down, *she said.*
Do not reverse me & I will offer you this sunflower, beneath it—a promise—the
bud of an unknown flower. I spit on the solace of nature, *I said*, give me a happy life.

The editors describe ***Puck*** as 80 pgs., 8½×11, offset and saddle-stapled with color covers. They accept 1% or less of poetry received. Press run is 2,000 for 200 subscribers of which 4 are libraries, 1,000 shelf sales. Single copy: $6.50; subscription: $17/3 issues. **Previously published poems OK; no simultaneous submissions. Cover letter required. "SASE must be big enough to**

accommodate return of all material submitted." Send SASE for guidelines. Reports in 1-4 weeks. Pays 2 copies. Acquires first North American serial or reprint rights. "Subsequent publication should mention *Puck*." They add, "Current issue contains 30 (out of 80) pages of reviews. We review anything, everything." Permeable Press also publishes 6 paperbacks and **3 chapbooks/ year. Query first with sample poems and cover letter with brief bio and publication credits. Replies to queries in 1 month, to mss in 1-2 months. Pays 50 author's copies for chapbooks.**

PERSEA BOOKS (V), 60 Madison Ave., New York NY 10010, phone (212)779-7668, editor Michael Braziller, publishes books of **"serious" poetry.** They have recently published poetry by Thylias Moss, Paul Blackburn and Wayne Koestenbaum. They publish 1-2 books of poetry/year. **However, they are not reading unsolicited mss until November 1995. "We are committed to future books of poets we are already publishing."**

‡PETERLOO POETS (II), 2 Kelly Gardens, Calstock, Cornwall PL18 9SA Great Britain, founded 1977, poetry editor Harry Chambers. They publish collections of poetry under the Peterloo Poets imprint: flat-spined paperbacks, hardbacks and poetry cassettes. **Query with 10 sample poems, bio and list of publications. Considers simultaneous submissions and previously published poems if they have not been in book form. Always sends prepublication galleys. Pays 10% royalties, $100 advance (for first volume, $200 for subsequent volumes) and 12 copies. Editor "normally, briefly" comments on rejections.** Sponsors an annual open poetry competition. First prize: £2,000 sterling; second prize: £1,000 sterling; four other prizes totaling £1,100 sterling. Send IRC for entry form and rules.

PHASE AND CYCLE (II); PHASE AND CYCLE PRESS (V), 3537 E. Prospect, Fort Collins CO 80525, phone (303)482-7573, founded 1988, poetry editor Loy Banks. ***Phase and Cycle*** is a poetry magazine published semiannually. **"We look for short to moderate-length poems of all kinds, especially those that set out 'the long perspectives open at each instance of our lives' (Larkin). We are looking for poetry that will pass technical inspection in the academic community."** They have recently published poetry by David James Sundahl, Ted Genoways, Lawrence Minet, Errol Miller, Simon Perchik, Michael Yots, Mary Rudbeck Stanko and Scott Owens. The magazine is 48 pgs., digest-sized, saddle-stapled. **Sample postpaid: $2.50. Guidelines available for SASE. "A brief bio note may accompany poems." No simultaneous submissions or previously published poems. Editor sometimes comments on rejections. Reports in 5-10 weeks. Pays 2 copies. Acquires first rights only.** Poets may send books for review consideration. Phase and Cycle Press has published two poetry chapbooks, **Breathing In The World** by Bruce Holland Rogers and Holly Arrow and **Out of Darkness** by Mary Balazs. **"At present we accept inquiries only. No book manuscripts."**

PHILOMEL BOOKS (III), 200 Madison Ave., New York NY 10016, phone (212)951-8700, an imprint founded in 1980, editor-in-chief Paula Wiseman. Philomel Books publishes 2-3 paperbacks, 40-45 hardbacks and 5-10 chapbooks/year. They say "since we're a children's book imprint, **we are open to individual poem submissions—anything suitable for a picture book. However, publication of poetry collections is usually done on a project basis—we acquire from outside through permissions, etc. Don't usually use unpublished material."** They have published poetry by Edna St. Vincent Millay and Walt Whitman. **Previously published poems and simultaneous submissions OK. Cover letter—including publishing history—required. Replies to queries in 1 month, to mss in 2. Pay is negotiable.**

PHOEBE (IV-Women/feminism), Women's Studies Dept., S.U.N.Y. College at Oneonta, Oneonta NY 13820, phone (607)436-2014, founded 1988, editor Kathleen O'Mara, is a biannual feminist journal containing scholarly articles, short fiction and poetry, book reviews and occasional artwork. **As for poetry, they have "no specifications vis-a-vis form, length, etc. Seek material describing, either directly or vaguely, women's experiences/realities. Nothing sexist, racist or homophobic."** They have published poetry by Lyn Lifshin, Rita Ann Higgins, Zoe Angelesey, Edith Pearlman and Kyoko Mori. As a sample the editor selected these lines from "Girlfriends" by Wanda Coleman:

we are faced with the irrefutable analyses
no one's gonna pay us for what's left of
our gal youth and out lady beauty

a connection in New York, London or the Vatican
is worth the expense of self-transmission as in
send bio demo-tape shoe size and lock of hair

Phoebe is 120 pgs., approximately 7×9, professionally printed and perfect-bound, coated card cover with artwork. They receive about 220 poems a year, use approximately 18-20%. Press run is 500 for 200 subscribers of which 15% are libraries, 100 shelf sales. Single copy: $7.50; subscription: $15. **Sample postpaid: $5. Previously published poems OK; no simultaneous submissions. Submissions preferred August 15 through April 15. Seldom comments on rejections. Send SASE**

for guidelines. Reports within 3 months. Pays 2 copies. Reviews books of poetry in 500-2,000 words.

‡PHOEBE; THE GREG GRUMMER AWARD (II), George Mason University, 4400 University Dr., Fairfax VA 22030, phone (703)993-2915, founded 1970, poetry editors Jean Donnelly and Kaki Ouzts, is a literary biannual **"looking for imagery that will make your thumbs sweat when you touch it."** They have recently published poetry by C.K. Williams, Mark Doty, Cornelius Eady, Carolyn Forché, Thomas Lux and Bill Knott. As a sample the editor selected these lines from "Semantics of Longing" by Leslie Bumstead:

Was he superb in speech
class? Even at parties with women dangling
hunger on their brilliant clavicles, he must
forever look for the just and longest
word (it's Samson through the trees
of high heels) . . .

Circulation 3,000, with 30-35 pgs. of poetry in each issue. Subscription: $8/year; $4/single issue. *Phoebe* receives 4,000 submissions/year. **Submit up to 5 poems; submission should be accompanied by SASE and a short bio. No simultaneous submissions, no dot-matrix. Reports in 2-3 months. Pays copies.** They also sponsor The Greg Grummer Award, an annual poetry contest. Entry fee: $8. Deadline: October 15. Prize: $500. Send SASE for rules. Work published in ***Phoebe*** was selected for inclusion in **The Best American Poetry 1993.**

PHOENIX BROADSHEETS; NEW BROOM PRIVATE PRESS (II), 78 Cambridge St., Leicester LE 3 0JP England, founded 1968, poetry editor Toni Savage, publishes chapbooks, pamphlets and broadsheets on a small Adana Horizontal Hand Press. The editor wants poetry which is "**descriptive—not too modern, not erotica or concrete, up to 12 lines (for the sheets)**. Also some personal background of the poet." He has recently published poems by Spike Milligan, Sue Townsend, Alix Weisz, Don Carlson, Greg Joly, Paul Humphrey, Roger McGough and Arthur Caddick. As a sample Toni Savage selected this poem, "Verses," by Edward Murch (Phoenix Broadsheet No. 394):

I write my verses underneath the trees
On scrolls of mist, the cormorant my quill.
If I should tell them to the passing breeze
Will it whisper them to you
over the distant hill?

The broadsheets are letterpress printed on tinted paper (about 5×8) with graphics. "Some sheets are hand coloured." **Submit no more than 3 poems with cover letter giving "personal background and feelings." Poet receives 20-30 copies.** "My ***Broadsheets*** are *given* away in the streets. They are given away to Folk Club, Jazz Club and theater audiences. The broadsheets started as a joke and now are up to 400. Now much sought after and collected. This is my hobby and is strictly part-time. Each small booklet takes 1-3 months, so it is impossible to ascertain quantities of publications." ***Phoenix Broadsheets*** may be obtained by sending adequate postage, approximately $1.50 (cash—no cheques) for 5 or more sheets.

PHOENIX PRESS (V), 22 Pintail Dr., Pittsburgh PA 15238, founded 1982, poetry editors Heywood Ostrow and Robert Julian, publishes 2-3 books a year **but accepts no unsolicited mss.** They have published poetry by Robert Julian and Sebastian Barker. As a sample here are the opening lines from **XII** by George Barker:

Ah most unreliable of all women of grace
in the breathless hurry of your leave taking
you forgot, you forgot for ever, our last embrace

‡PIE (POETRY IMAGERY AND EXPRESSION) (V), P.O. Box 739, Parramatta, New South Wales 2124 Australia, founded 1984, compiled by Daryl Wayne Hall and Bill Tibben, is a publication of the poets who attend and participate in **readings sponsored by the group. "The publications are a record of the readings. We will return all unsolicited work without comment.** Our reason for requesting an entry in **Poet's Market** is that we think what we do is a good idea and one worth promoting. The people who come to the readings and who see themselves in print on that night (plus get copies for their friends, etc.) get a good buzz! This is poetry that is happening in the here and now and the day-to-day world!" They publish the poetry in an attractive oversize format, photocopied from typescript, side-stapled with card cover.

PIEDMONT LITERARY REVIEW; PIEDMONT LITERARY SOCIETY (II, IV-Form), Rt. 1, Box 512, Forest VA 24551, founded 1976; poetry editor Gail White, 1017 Spanish Moss Lane, Breaux Bridge LA 70517 (and **poetry submissions should go to her address**). If you join the Piedmont Literary Society, $12 a year, you get the quarterly ***Review*** and a quarterly newsletter containing much market and contest information. Gail White says, **"I consider all types of poems—am partial to rhyme—up to 48 lines. Each issue has a special section for oriental forms with an emphasis on haiku." Each also includes short fiction. She does *not* want: "smut or overly romantic verse."** She has published poetry by Harold Witt, Julie Kane, John Brugaletta and Jared Carter. As a sample the editor selected these lines by Martha Bosworth:

Our lives fall open, all that's left of them,
under the gulls' wing-scattered requiem;
building on waste, for wastrels to destroy,
the landfill cities rise: here is my Troy,
and my Jerusalem.

The quarterly is digest-sized, saddle-stapled, offset from typescript, matte card cover, using b&w graphics, with 40-50 pgs. of poetry in each issue, circulation 300 with 200 subscriptions of which 10 arc libraries. It's a modest-looking publication with well-made formal and free verse poems. **Sample postpaid: $3. Welcomes all submissions. She "sometimes" comments on rejections. Send SASE for guidelines. Reports within 3 months. Pays copies. Acquires first rights.** Briefly reviews "a few" books of poetry, "mostly contributors' books," in accompanying newsletter. They sponsor occasional contests. **NOTE: As this edition of Poet's Market went to press, we were informed of the resignation of Gail White as poetry editor. Write to the Forest, VA address for new publication details.**

PIG IRON; KENNETH PATCHEN COMPETITION (II, IV-Themes), Dept. PM, P.O. Box 237, Youngstown OH 44501, phone (216)747-6932, founded 1975, poetry editor Jim Villani, is a literary annual devoted to special themes. They want **poetry "up to 300 lines; free verse and experimental; write for current themes."** Forthcoming themes: The Family: Tradition & Possibility and Jazz Tradition. **They do *not* want to see "traditional" poetry.** They have published poetry by Wayne Hogan, Laurel Speer, Louis McKee, Lloyd Mills, Marian Steele, Hugh Fox and John Pyros. As a sample the editor selected these lines by Joan Kincaid:

I'm yelling my goose call
bahonk bahonk
to make her laugh
because there are no geese
when we're surprised
by an eerie screech-purr
echoing across the dark water
I bahonk again
and a white swan launches
into the night a song
I've never heard.

Pig Iron is magazine-sized, flat-spined, 128 pgs., typeset on good stock with glossy card cover using b&w graphics and art, no ads, circulation 1,000. They have 200 subscriptions of which 50 are libraries. Single copy: $10.95. Subscription: $9/1 year, $16/2 years. **Sample postpaid: $4. No simultaneous submissions. Send SASE for guidelines. Reports in 3 months, 12-18 months delay to publication. Pays $5/poem plus 2 copies. Buys one-time rights.** They sponsor the annual Kenneth Patchen Competition. Send SASE for details. The editor says, "We want tomorrow's poetry, not yesterday's."

THE PIKESTAFF FORUM; PIKESTAFF PUBLICATIONS, INC.; THE PIKESTAFF PRESS; PIKESTAFF POETRY CHAPBOOKS (II, IV-Children, teens), P.O. Box 127, Normal IL 61761, phone (309)452-4831, founded 1977, poetry editors Robert D. Sutherland, James R. Scrimgeour and James McGowan, is "a not-for-profit literary press. Publishes a magazine of national distribution, ***The Pikestaff Forum***, and a poetry chapbook series." They want **"substantial, well-crafted poems; vivid, memorable, based in lived experience—*Not*: self-indulgent early drafts, 'private' poems, five finger exercises, warmed over workshop pieces, vague abstractions, philosophical woolgathering, 'journal entries,' inspirational uplift. The shorter the better, though long poems are no problem; we are eclectic; welcome traditional or experimental work. We won't publish pornography or racist/sexist material."** They have published poetry by Gayl Teller, J.W. Rivers, Lucia Cordell Getsi, Frannie Lindsay and Fritz Hamilton. ***The Pikestaff Forum*** is an annual newsprint tabloid, 40 pgs., "handsome, open layout. Trying to set a standard in tabloid design. Special features: poetry, fiction, commentary, reviews, young writers (7-17 in a special section), editors' profiles (other magazines), The Forum (space for anyone to speak out on matters of literary/publishing concern)." Circulation 1,100 with 200 subscriptions of which 5 are libraries. They receive 2,000-3,000 submissions/year, use 3%, have a year's backlog. Subscription: $10/6 issues. **Sample postpaid: $2. "Each poem should be on a separate sheet, with author's name and address. We prefer no simultaneous submissions—but if it is, we expect to be informed of it." No more than 6 poems/submission. Send SASE for guidelines. Reports within 3 months. Pays 3 copies.** Reviews books of poetry if published by small presses or self-published. Open to unsolicited reviews.

Poets may also send books to Jim Elledge, Review Editor, Dept. of English, Illinois State University, Normal IL 61761 for review consideration. This is a lively publication and editors typically comment on rejected work that has merit. All forms and styles appear here, but published verse usually displays a high degree of craft that somehow enhances content (always insightful or unusual). **Query with samples and brief bio for chapbook publication. Replies to queries in 2 weeks, to submission (if invited) in 3 months. Always sends prepublication galleys for chapbooks. Pays 20% of press run.** They advise, "For beginners: Don't be in a hurry to publish; work toward becoming your own best editor and critic; when submitting, send only what you think is your very best work; avoid indulging yourself at the expense of your readers; have something to say that's worth your readers' life-time to read; before submitting, ask yourself, 'Why should *any* reader be asked to read this?'; regard publishing as conferring a responsibility."

PIKEVILLE REVIEW (II), Humanities Dept., Pikeville College, Pikeville KY 41501, founded 1987, editor James Alan Riley, who says: **"There's no editorial bias though we recognize and appreciate style and control in each piece. No emotional gushing."** *PR* appears once yearly, accepting about 10% of poetry received. Press run is 500. **Sample postpaid: $3. No simultaneous submissions or previously published poetry. Editor sometimes comments on rejections. Send SASE for guidelines. Pays 5 copies.** They also sponsor contests.

PINCHGUT PRESS (V), 6 Oaks Ave., Cremorne, Sydney, NSW 2090 Australia, founded 1948, publishes **Australian poetry but is not currently accepting poetry submissions. Send SASE for catalog to order samples.**

THE PINEHURST JOURNAL; PINEHURST PRESS (I, II), P.O. Box 360747, Milpitas CA 95036, founded 1990, editor Michael K. McNamara, is a quarterly. **"Generally open, 24-line limit. Some sort of rhyme, meter, assonance, consonance or alliteration is a plus as well as good haiku. No religious, porno or dire despair. Work should be original, no reprints."** They have recently published poetry by Roger Ball, Pearl Bloch Segall and Wilma Elizabeth McDaniel. As a sample the editor selected "End Creation" by Rose Marie Hunold:

Erasure is the day
when the writer throws
his eyes high into the Africanesque
picks a tune that bleats
the starred black net
of eternalizing revelation
as Banama, those who refuse
to serve the master
defied the bowings of others
and stood to the drum sounds
of saying dreams and African
morning dew.

It is magazine-sized, 44 pgs., offset from typescript, saddle-stapled. Of 800 poems/year received they use 120. Press run is 225 for 100 subscribers of which 1 is a library, 20 shelf sales. Subscription: $18. **Sample postpaid: $5. Submit no more than 6 poems at a time. "We feel a cover letter is an asset/vehicle of introduction for all contributors and should be employed. It is not a requirement, however." Send SASE for guidelines. Reports in 6-8 weeks. Pays 1 copy. Acquires one-time rights.** Staff reviews books of poetry. Send books for review consideration.

THE PIPE SMOKER'S EPHEMERIS (I, IV-Specialized), 20-37 120th St., College Point NY 11356, editor/publisher Tom Dunn, who says, "The ***Ephemeris*** is a limited edition, irregular quarterly **for pipe smokers and anyone else who is interested in its varied contents.** Publication costs are absorbed by the editor/publisher, assisted by any contributions—financial or otherwise—that readers might wish to make." **They want poetry with themes related to pipes and pipe smoking.** Issues range from 76-96 pgs., offset from photoreduced typed copy, colored paper covers, with illustrations, saddle-stitched. The editor has also published a collection covering the first 15 years of the ***Ephemeris***. It is 541 pgs.,

ALWAYS include a self-addressed, stamped envelope (SASE) when sending a ms or query to a publisher within your own country. When sending material to other countries, include a self-addressed envelope and International Reply Coupons (IRCs), available for purchase at most post offices.

hardcover. **Cover letter required with submissions; include any credits.** Staff also reviews books of poetry. Send books for review consideration.

PIRATE WRITINGS; PIRATE WRITINGS PUBLISHING (I, II, IV-Science fiction/fantasy, mystery), 53 Whitman Ave., Islip NY 11751, founded 1992, editor and publisher Edward J. McFadden. ***Pirate Writings*** is a biannual "collection of contemporary, energetic, socially relevant, imaginative poems and short stories by 'under' published writers. Our theme is anything from the down deep to the way out." **They want all forms and styles of poetry "within our genres—literary (humorous or straight), fantasy, science fiction, mystery/suspense and adventure. Best chance is 20 lines or less. No crude language or excessive violence. No pornography, horror, western or romance. Poems should be typed with exact capitalization and punctuation suited to your creative needs."** They have recently published poetry by John Sweet, Faith L. Justice, Holly Day and R.H. Yodice. As a sample the editor selected these lines from "Dreams" by Danya' D'Arcy:

Dreams breath fire,
bellow
through caverns gray
A glistening beast
each parlous scale a
memory
harbored in vert.

Pirate Writings is 40-50 pgs., digest-sized and saddle-stapled with a full-color cover and b&w art throughout. They receive about 150 poetry submissions a year, use approximately 15-25 poems. Press run varies. Subscription: $7.25 for 2 issues. **Sample postpaid: $4. Previously published poems accepted from "well established poets only." Simultaneous submissions OK. Cover letter required; include credits, if applicable. Often comments on rejections. Send SASE for guidelines. Reports in 1-2 months. Pays 1-2 copies. Acquires first North American serial rights. Also "reserves the right to print in anthology."** Query regarding reviews of chapbooks. Pirate Writings Publishing **publishes chapbooks through various arrangements.** They have recently published **Moorhaven Fair** by Richard Novak and **Many Tales** by Edward J. McFadden III. **Query first. Replies to queries in 1 month, to mss in 2 months. Poets may have to share publication costs. For sample chapbooks, write for flier.** Pirate Writings Publishing has also published **The Poe Pulpit**, stories and poems in the Poe tradition, and **currently needs poems for children (8-12) with a Christmas theme** for an upcoming children's book. **Pay is $10/poem.**

PITT POETRY SERIES; UNIVERSITY OF PITTSBURGH PRESS; AGNES LYNCH STARRETT POETRY PRIZE (II), 127 N. Bellefield Ave., Pittsburgh PA 15260, founded 1968, poetry editor Ed Ochester, publishes **"poetry of the highest quality; otherwise, no restrictions—book mss minimum of 48 pages." Poets who have previously published books should query. Simultaneous submissions OK. Always sends prepublication galleys.** They have published books of poetry by Richard Garcia, Larry Levis, Sharon Doubiago, Robley Wilson and Liz Rosenberg. Their booklist also features such poets as Peter Meinke, Leonard Nathan, Sharon Olds, Ronald Wallace, David Wojahn and Belle Waring. **"Poets who have not previously published a book should send SASE for rules of the Starrett competition ($12.50 handling fee), the *only* vehicle through which we publish first books of poetry." The Starrett Prize consists of cash award of $2,500 and book publication.**

THE PITTSBURGH QUARTERLY; THE SARA HENDERSON HAY PRIZE (II), 36 Haberman Ave., Pittsburgh PA 15211-2144, phone (412)431-8885, founded 1990, editor Frank Correnti, who says, **"Our first criterion is good writing with the variety of content that is common to a broad community interest. Generally, writing with narrative and real-life elements. We don't want doggerel or most rhyme."** They have published poetry by Marc Jampole, Ellen Smith, Kristin Kovacic, Robert Cooperman and Lynne Hugo de Courcy. As a sample the editor selected these lines from "Tender Meat" by June Hopper Hymas:

. . . the sounds and the smells of the lives of the poet
and the poet's ancestors. I haven't thought

to ask my children if they talk to janitors or sometimes feel
like sawdust: null brown bits, cellulose without form.

Tonight is a hot night; when you hung up on me,
I did not call you back. I am reclaiming myself.

It is digest-sized, 76 pgs., professionally printed, saddle-stapled with matte card cover. Press run is 700 for 250 subscribers of which 10 are libraries, 300 shelf sales. Subscription: $12 ($14 Canadian). **Sample postpaid: $5. "We will reply by letter to queries." Editor often comments on submissions. Reports in 3-4 months. Pays 2 copies. Acquires first North American serial rights.** Published books are reviewed as space is available, 1-2/issue. Accepts reviews of 4-6 pages,

CLOSE-UP

Listen, Read and Make Your own Rules

Most of my walk today was leisure and delight,
no more than the usual cleats of sorrow
attaching to my heart, but even the most beautiful
of late summer days can cramp into a memory, uneasy
attention to what we haven't thought about in years,
like the wrong mother's hand in the shopping line.
We hold it until we feel the strangeness, then
let go, a little frightened, a little embarrassed
to have done this thing, caught off balance,
like the quiet leafy path I just now turned to
and surprised myself by starting to walk down.

(from "Setting Out")

Photo by Katie Warnke

Maggie Anderson

Perhaps the best way to describe Maggie Anderson's poetry is with the title of her most recent book, **A Space Filled With Moving** (University of Pittsburgh Press, 1992). The settledness of her verse, combined with its emotional and intellectual urgency, results in a poetry of wisdom, of truth—and truth has been elemental in Anderson's career.

It was during an open reading at a writers' conference in West Virginia that Gwendolyn Brooks first heard Anderson's work. "Afterwards, she asked me if I had a book and I said yes," Anderson explains. "But actually what I had was a pile of poems. I worked on them for about a week and a half for nearly 24 hours a day. I cut things out and rearranged things, fixed things and made as good a book as I could make. Then I sent it to Gwendolyn Brooks, who sent it to her editor." This led to the publication of Anderson's first book of poetry, **Years That Answer** (Harper and Row, 1980). Brooks later told Anderson that what she saw in her poetry was "something true."

Anderson is understandably reluctant to tell this story for fear that beginning writers will deem it appropriate to send their manuscripts to established poets. Also, the story makes little mention of the years that led up to that pile of poems. "My mother died when I was fairly young," says Anderson. "All my memories of my mother are of her being sick. I spent a lot of time in hospital waiting rooms while my father was visiting her. I think I was a quiet and lonely little kid. Looking back, I must have seemed a bit strange. I remember always carrying my books and papers with me. I sort of made a little world that felt safe to me and that had to do with reading books and writing."

This self-contained world opened up when Louise McNeill came to the small college in town and Anderson heard her read. "That was sort of the beginning of thinking that maybe this was a thing that people could do. My parents were teachers, so I knew grown-ups taught. Also, my mother wrote books—very boring books about constitutional law. So the idea that grown-ups wrote books and even that women wrote books was not outside the range of possibilities for me. But that grown-ups wrote poems—I was still reading dead poets. So when Louise McNeill came to town I thought, here's a woman who's alive, who's also from West Virginia and is writing about our people. That was really important because it opened up the possibility that I could do the same."

The influence of Louise McNeill, and later Gwendolyn Brooks, is one reason Anderson encourages poets to attend readings. "Hear all the poets reading that you can, all the different kinds of poets. Go to poetry slams, go hear formalist poets read, go hear poets on the street corners. The more you hear the language of poetry, the better.

"I went to one of the Marches on Washington and to a Black Arts Festival in Pittsburgh where poets were reading their work. This made me realize that poetry was something that could enter the public arena. Up until then, my own poetry had been something very private. But here were poets who felt their work had something to do with the peripheral life of the country," she says.

In addition to attending readings, Anderson advocates a wide and indiscriminate range of reading. "This is the best thing because then you begin to form your *own* opinions," she says. "What you should read over and over again and learn from are those poets whose words feel like the language of the truth."

Regarding rules for beginning poets, Anderson advises, "Don't start cutting off your options because somebody said so. The best rules are the ones we make ourselves. What you learn from other people's rules is something about your own relationship to rules." Anderson makes this point in the creative writing classes she teaches at Kent State University. "I ask students to try certain exercises, and what they learn is something about their own resistances.

"The thing I've learned is that the process doesn't change. It doesn't get any easier, or any harder either. It's very similar for everybody—you have to find something that seizes you, then you have to get at the core of that idiosyncratic obsession, get it somehow down on the page," she says.

What "seizes" Anderson is landscape and the function of place, both of which are very important to her work. "My parents were educated, but they were exceptions in my family. No one else in the family was educated. They were miners and railroad workers. Because of my mother's illness, and then her death and my father's busyness, I spent a lot of time with those aunts and uncles. So the world I grew up in was fairly nonliterary but very richly metaphorical. I like to write in a language that acknowledges that nonliterary tradition and yet doesn't ignore the fact that I have, by now, read a lot of books and that I've been privileged to have an education."

Anderson's second book, **Cold Comfort** (University of Pittsburgh Press, 1986), pays close attention to her West Virginia origins. "I like to write in a way that the women I knew in the small mining towns would understand, and that includes a world they would have loved to have, if they'd had a chance. However, I don't have an audience in mind—I have a voice in mind. I think all poets create a listener. You write in the truest voice you can write for yourself and pretty soon, if it gets good enough, you feel like someone's listening."

—*Michelle Moore*

double-spaced. Send books for review consideration. "We are responding in part to the network of writers whose crafted creativity made the magazine possible, but also we are attempting to provide a readership that will connect more strongly to the community of poets and writers through this quarterly." ***The Pittsburgh Quarterly*** now sponsors an annual prize for poetry: The Sara Henderson Hay Prize. Entry requires current subscription or renewal and is limited to 3 poems up to 100 lines each. Deadline: July 1. Winner receives a cash award and publication of the winning poem in the fall issue.

PIVOT (II), #23, 250 Riverside Dr., New York NY 10025, phone (212)222-1408, founded 1951, editor Martin Mitchell, is a poetry annual that has published poetry by Philip Appleman, William Matthews, Eugene McCarthy, Craig Raine, W.D. Snodgrass and Robert Wrigley. As a sample the editor selected "January Thaw" by X.J. Kennedy:

Beware. This seamless inverness of ice
Cloaking the brick walk and the treacherous street
Might, in a plot that sweeps you off your feet,
Induce paralysis.

Some gray, malignant growth, it lies immune
To clouded skies till, slicing through the cold,
One ray of sun, inserted, breaks its hold
Like a good scalpel freeing up a brain.

Pivot is a handsome, 6×9, flat-spined, professionally printed magazine with glossy card cover. Press run is 1,200. Single copy: $5. **Reads submissions January 1 through June 1 only. Reports in 2-4 weeks. Sometimes sends prepublication galleys. Pays 2 copies.**

THE PLACE IN THE WOODS; READ, AMERICA! (I, IV-Children), 3900 Glenwood Ave., Golden Valley MN 55422, phone (612)374-2120, founded 1980, editor and publisher Roger A. Hammer, publishes ***Read, America!***, a quarterly newsletter for reading coordinators. They want **"poems for children that are understandable, under 500 words, unusual views of life. Also, foreign-language poems with English translation. Nothing vague, self-indulgent, erotic. No navel introspection."** As a sample we selected these lines from "Circus" by Eugene C. Baggott:

Did you ever watch the bareback riders
As they lovingly groomed their steeds?
Or the trapeze artist practice his catch
While hanging by his knees?

Read, America! is 8 pgs., magazine-sized, professionally printed on yellow paper. "Pages 1-4 are distributed free to some 10,000 programs. Four additional pages go only to readers who support us as subscribers." Most poems appear in the "Subscribers only" insert but poets do not have to be subscribers to submit. Subscription: $20. **No previously published poems; simultaneous submissions OK. Cover letter "optional and appreciated for insight into poet's background and interests or goals." Always comments on rejections. Pays $10 on publication. Buys all rights.**

PLAINS POETRY JOURNAL; STRONGHOLD PRESS (II, IV-Form), P.O. Box 2337, Bismarck ND 58502, founded 1982, editor Jane Greer, publishes **"meticulously crafted, language-rich poetry which is demanding and accessible. We love rhyme and meter and poetic conventions used in vigorous and interesting ways.** I strive to publish unpublished poets as well as old pros. **I do *not* want broken-prose 'free verse' or greeting card-type traditional verse. I want finely-crafted poetry which uses the best poetic conventions from the past in a way that doesn't sound as if it were *written* in the past. No specifications. I'm especially interested in compelling long poems and essays on poetry. Our credo is, 'no subject matter is taboo; treatment is everything.'"** They have recently published poetry by Julia Budenz, Rhina P. Espaillat, Harold McCurdy, Jack Butler, Johnny Wink, Frederick Feirstein and Frederick Turner. As a sample, Jane Greer selected these lines from "Epilogue" by Richard Moore:

As painters might arrange still life,
so I, decades of daughters, wife,
me with them, playing my bit part.
Then it all withered into art.

Plains Poetry Journal is semiannual, digest-sized, 60 pgs. (of which about 57 are poetry), saddle-stapled, professionally printed on tinted paper with matte card cover, graphics, circulation 500, 400 subscriptions of which 50 are libraries. They receive 1,500-2,000 submissions/year, use about 200, seldom have more than a 1-year backlog. Subscription: $9/year, $18/5 issues. **Sample postpaid: $4.50. Submit "not less than 3 poems, not more than 10 at a time. Hand-written and simultaneous submissions OK." Comments on rejections "occasionally, especially if the ms is especially promising or if I think the poet is a child or teen." Send SASE for guidelines. Reports in 1 week to 3 months. Pays copies. Acquires first or reprint rights.** This remains one of the best outlets for formal poetry and otherwise well-crafted free verse displaying verve, energy and insight. If unfamiliar with this publication, request a sample copy. Editor Jane Greer also has a clear vision of what she wants frankly expressed in her writer's guidelines. She comments, "An author is *crazy* not to submit simultaneously. Do enclose SASE, and *don't* enclose an explanation of the poems. Above all understand that a poet never 'gets good,' he or she just keeps *working* at it. If you're willing to do this, I am too."

PLAINSONG (I, II), Box 8245, Western Kentucky University, Bowling Green KY 42101, phone (502)745-5708, founded 1979, poetry editors Frank Steele, Elizabeth Oakes and Peggy Steele, is an occasional poetry journal. "Our purpose is to print the best work we can get, from known and unknown writers. This means, of course, that we print what we like: poems about places, objects, people, moods, politics, experiences. **We like straightforward, conversational language, short poems in which the marriage of thinking and feeling doesn't break up because of spouse-abuse (the poem in which ideas wrestle feeling into the ground or in which feeling sings alone—and boringly—at the edge of a desert). Prefer poems under 20 lines in free verse. No limits on subject matter, though we like to think of ourselves as humane, interested in the environment, in peace (we're anti-nuclear), in the possibility that the human race may have a future."** They have published poetry by William Matthews, Ted Kooser, William Stafford, Del Marie Rogers, Betty Adcock, Julia Ardery and Abby Niebauer. The magazine is 48-56 pgs., 6×9, professionally printed, flat-spined, color matte card cover with photos and graphics. They use about 100 of the 2,000 submissions received each year. Press run is 600 with 250 subscriptions of which 65 are libraries. Subscription: $7. **Sample postpaid: $3.50. "We prefer poems typed, double-spaced. Simultaneous submissions can, of course, get people into trouble, at times." Publishes theme issues occasionally. Send SASE for guidelines. Reports "within a month, usually." Pays copies.** Staff reviews books of poetry. Send books for review consideration to Frank Steele. The editor says, "We receive too many poems in 'the schoolroom voice'—full of language that's really prose. We'd like to see more poems with a voice that feels something without being sentimental or melodramatic."

PLAINSONGS (II), Dept. of English, Hastings College, Hastings NE 68902-0269, phone (402)463-2402, founded 1980, editor Dwight C. Marsh, a poetry magazine that **"accepts manuscripts from anyone, considering poems on any subject in any style."** They have recently published poetry by Don Colburn, Corrine DeWinter, Errol Miller and Nancy G. Westerfield. As a sample the editor selected these lines from "Prayers for William Stafford" by Michael Robbins:

Stay home tonight, on earth, and pray
he has prairie where he's gone,
rivers say his lines, and bison
strain their necks toward dawn.

Plainsongs is 40 pgs., digest-sized, saddle-stapled, set on laser, printed on thin paper with b&w illustrations, one-color matte card cover with black logo. The magazine is financed by subscriptions, which cost $9 for 3 issues/year. **Sample copies: $3. Submit poems with name and address on each page. Ms deadlines are August 15 for fall issue; November 15 for winter; March 15 for spring. Notification is mailed about 3 weeks after deadlines. Pay is 2 copies and a year's subscription, with 3 award poems in each issue receiving small monetary recognition. "A short essay in appreciation accompanies each award poem." Acquires first-time rights.**

‡PLANET: THE WELSH INTERNATIONALIST (III), P.O. Box 44, Aberystwyth, Dyfed, Wales, phone 0970-611255, fax 0970-623311, founded 1970, editor John Barnie, is a bimonthly cultural magazine, "centered on Wales, but with broader interests in arts, sociology, politics, history and science." They want **"good poetry in a wide variety of styles. No limitations as to subject matter; length can be a problem."** They have recently published poetry by Les Murray and R.S. Thomas. As a sample we selected this poem, "The Mating Behaviour of Human Beings," by J.K. Gill:

Puzzled by her hedgehog spikes
his paws uncurl her to
her softest.

Planet is 120 pgs., A5 size, professionally printed and perfect-bound with glossy color card cover. They receive about 300 submissions a year, accept approximately 5%. Press run is 1,400 for 1,150 subscribers of which about 10% are libraries, 200 shelf sales. Single copy: £2.50; subscription: £12 (overseas: £13). **Sample postpaid: £3.56. No previously published poems or simultaneous submissions.** Time between acceptance and publication is 6-10 months. **Seldom comments on rejections. Send SASE (or SAE and IRCs if outside UK) for guidelines. Reports within a month or so. Pays £25 minimum. Buys first serial rights only.** Reviews books of poetry in 700 words, single and multi-book format. Open to unsolicited reviews. Poets may also send books for review consideration.

PLANTAGENET PRODUCTIONS (V), Westridge, Highclere, Nr. Newbury, Royal Berkshire RG 15 9 PJ England, founded 1964, director of productions Miss Dorothy Rose Gribble. Plantagenet issues cassette recordings of poetry, philosophy and narrative (although they have issued nothing new since 1980). Miss Gribble says, "Our public likes classical work . . . We **have published a few living poets, but this is not very popular with our listeners, and we shall issue no more.**" They have issued cassettes by Oscar Wilde, Chaucer and Pope, as well as Charles Graves, Elizabeth Jennings, Leonard Clark and Alice V. Stuart. The recordings are issued privately and are obtainable only direct from Plantagenet Productions; write for list. Miss Gribble's advice to poets is: "If intended for a listening public, let the meaning be clear. If possible, let the music of the words sing."

THE PLASTIC TOWER (II), P.O. Box 702, Bowie MD 20718, founded 1989, editors Carol Dyer and Roger Kyle-Keith, is a quarterly using **"everything from iambic pentameter to silly limericks, modern free verse, haiku, rhymed couplets—we like it all! Only restriction is length—under 40 lines preferred. So send us poems that are cool or wild, funny or tragic—but especially those closest to your soul."** They have published poetry by "more than 325 different poets. It wouldn't be fair to single anyone out!" As a sample we selected these lines from ". . . and here's one for management" by John C. Erianne:

Sometimes I think
it is better to dress
intelligently
than to be intelligent.
shrugged shoulders
puzzled stare
they
only notice
the outfit.

It is digest-sized, 38-54 pgs., saddle-stapled; "variety of typefaces and b&w graphics on cheap photocopy paper." Press run is 200. Subscription: $8/year. Copy of current issue: $2.50. **"We'll send a back issue free for a *large* (at least 6×9) SAE with 75¢ postage attached." Simultaneous submissions OK. Editors comment on submissions "often." Send SASE for guidelines. Reports in 2-3 months. Pays 1-3 copies.** Open to unsolicited reviews. Poets may also send books for review consideration. Roger Kyle-Keith says, "*PT* is an unpretentious little rag dedicated to enjoying verse and making poetry accessible to the general public as well as fellow poets. We don't claim to be the best, but we try to be the nicest and most personal. And we really, genuinely love poetry—just like you! And always remember (never forget?) your poems are important. Rejection and acceptance slips aren't. Don't let those cruddy pieces of paper define your life. Most, ours included, aren't worth the paper on which they're printed. So sing and shout and laugh and cry and stop on by ***The Plastic Tower***."

‡PLEIADES MAGAZINE; PHILAE MAGAZINE; EPIC JOURNAL & CHRONICLE (I, IV-Form), Box 357, Lakewood CO 80215, phone (303)237-3398, founded 1983, editor-in-chief John L. Moravec, poetry editor Hadrian K. Zve, appears twice a year **using "rhyming poetry, any length, on modern subjects."** It is magazine-sized, 75 pgs. Press run 1,200. Subscription: $9. **Sample postpaid: $3. Responds in 2 weeks. Pays copies and cash awards. *Philae Magazine***, founded 1947, editor Cyril Osmond, appears quarterly using **"rhymed poetry only, average length, on any subject."** It is the same size as ***Pleiades***. Subscription: $9. **Sample copy: $3.75. Responds in 2 weeks. Pays in copies, cash awards and trophies. *Epic Journal & Chronicle***, founded 1993, poetry editor Frank Klicpery. As a sister publication of ***Pleiades*** and **Philae**, this publication seeks to publish **"longer poems and literature of a heroic nature or events that may suggest legendary topics and also a tradition which can form the proper subject of an epic whether ancient or modern."** It is 8½×12. Subscription: $12. **Sample postpaid: $3.75. Responds in 1 month. Pays in copies.**

PLOUGHSHARES (III), Emerson College, 100 Beacon St., Boston MA 02116, phone (617)578-8753, founded 1971. **The magazine is "a journal of new writing edited on a revolving basis by professional poets and writers to reflect different and contrasting points of view."** Recent editors have included Carolyn Forché, Gerald Stern, Rita Dove, Chase Twichell and M.L. Rosenthal. They have published poetry by Donald Hall, Li-Young Lee, Robert Pinsky, Brenda Hillman and Thylias Moss. The triquarterly is 5½×8½, 250 pgs., circulation 6,000. They receive approximately 2,500 poetry submissions/year. Since this influential magazine features different editors with each issue, content varies. The issue edited by Carolyn Forché, for example, displays a variety of styles and forms with strong voices and messages. As always with prestigious journals, competition is keen. Response times can be slow because submissions are logged inhouse and sent to outside guest editors. Subscription: $19 domestic; $24 foreign. **Sample postpaid: $8.95 current issue, $6 back issue. "Due to our revolving editorship, issue emphasis and submission dates will vary. We suggest you read a few issues and send a #10 SASE for writer's guidelines (and upcoming themes) before submitting." Simultaneous submissions acceptable. Do not submit mss from April 1 to August 1. Reports in 3-5 months. Always sends prepublication galleys. Pays $20 minimum per poem, $10/printed page per poem, plus 2 contributor copies**

and a subscription. Work published in ***Ploughshares*** appears in the 1992, 1993 and 1994 volumes of **The Best American Poetry**. The magazine itself ranked #10 in the "Poet's Pick" category of the latest ***Writer's Digest*** Poetry 60 list. This category ranks those publications in which poets said they would most like to see their work published.

THE PLOWMAN (I, II), Box 414, Whitby, Ontario L1N 5S4 Canada, phone (416)668-7803, founded 1988, editor Tony Scavetta, appears 3 times/year using **"didactic, eclectic poetry; all forms."** As a sample the editor selected these lines from his own poetry:

The Word of God
Sharper than a two edged sword
Rip and tear
The eyes of your children
Like a fish-hook
Same Holy Spirit
Gives you everlasting Life
Through Jesus Christ
My Lord and Saviour

The Plowman is a 56-page, newsprint tabloid which accepts 70% of the poetry received. Press run is 15,000 for 1,200 subscribers of which 500 are libraries. Single copy: $7.50; subscription: $10. **Sample free. Previously published poems and simultaneous submissions OK. Cover letter required. No SASE necessary. Always comments on rejections. Guidelines available free. Reports in 1 week. Always sends prepublication galleys.** Reviews books of poetry. They offer monthly poetry contests. Entry fee: $2/poem. 1st prize: 50% of the proceeds; 2nd: 25%; 3rd: 10%. The top poems are published. "Balance of the poems will be used for anthologies." **They also publish 125 chapbooks/year. Replies to queries and mss in 1 week. Requires $20 reading fee/book. Pays 20% royalties.**

THE PLUM REVIEW (II), P.O. Box 3557, Washington DC 20007, founded 1990, editors M. Hammer and Christina Daub, appears twice a year. **"We are open to original, high quality poetry of all forms, lengths, styles and subject matters. Our only criterion is excellence."** They have recently published poetry by Robert Bly, Hayden Carruth, Donald Hall, Jane Shore, Rod Jellema, Larry Levis, David Ignatow, Linda Pastan and William Stafford. As a sample the editor selected these lines from "Erythronium Americanum" by Brooks Haxton:

What-was-to-be kept coming back with leaves
to the willow, with late sleet, with a familiar smell
of bark, with mud between the frost and the old ice.

Downed-over scales of pussy willow bud now broke,
first into tatters, then full catkins of white silk,
and all, all that much sooner for it, fell apart.

It is approximately 100 pgs., flat-spined, professionally printed, 6×9. Editors seem to favor well-made free verse, emphasizing voice and line. Press run is 1,000. **Sample postpaid: $6. "Absolutely no simultaneous submissions. Include a brief bio indicating previous publications and/or awards. We do not read in August or December." Seldom comments on rejections. Send SASE for guidelines. Reports in 1-2 months. Pays 1 copy.** They welcome unsolicited reviews (up to 15 pgs., single or multi-book format) of recently published books of poetry and interviews with prominent poets. Poets may also send books for review consideration. They sponsor a reading series and creative writing workshops for the elderly and the handicapped. ***The Plum Review*** also has an annual poetry competition. Deadline: February 28, 1995. Submit up to 5 poems with SASE and $5 entry fee. All entries will be considered for publication. No simultaneous submissions. No previously published poems. This magazine says that it is "so delicious"—a takeoff on William Carlos Williams' famous lyric "This Is Just To Say"?—and it is, too, featuring the best work of top-name poets and relative newcomers. In addition, ***The Plum Review*** was awarded a grant from the Council of Literary Magazines and Presses for outstanding content and design.

POCAHONTAS PRESS, INC.; MANUSCRIPT MEMORIES (V), P.O. Drawer F, Blacksburg VA 24063-1020, phone (703)951-0467, founded 1984, president Mary C. Holliman, publishes chapbook collections of poetry, but is temporarily not considering new mss "because I am trying to finish those already accepted." Inquire before submitting. **"Most of the poetry books I have published have been subsidized to some extent by the author. So far one of those authors' books has sold enough copies that the author has received a significant reimbursement for his investment. We continue to market all of our books as aggressively as possible. The idea is to make a profit for both of us (though we have yet to do so)."** She has published books by Leslie Mellichamp, Lynn Kozma, Mildred Nash, Preston Newman and Elaine Emans. As a sample the editor selected these lines by Cecil J. Mullins:

In the East, time has been divorced

From things. No clocks hem the hours
In, and time, not being firmly forced,
Slops around.

Always sends prepublication galleys. Pays 10% royalties on all sales receipts, 10 free copies of book, and any number of copies at 50% for resale or "whatever use author wishes. If author helps with printing costs, then an additional percentage of receipts will be paid." She offers editorial critiques for $40/hour. Mary Holliman adds, "There's much more good poetry being written than is getting published, and I only wish I could publish more of it. We are trying a new marketing technique—single-fold notecards with one poem from a collection per card, perhaps 3 poem/cards (2 each in a set of 6). The full collection and how to order will be given on the back of each card."

POEM; HUNTSVILLE LITERARY ASSOCIATION (II), English Dept., University of Alabama at Huntsville, Huntsville AL 35899, founded 1967, poetry editor Nancy Frey Dillard, appears twice a year, consisting entirely of poetry. **"We are particularly open to traditional as well as non-traditional forms, but we favor work with the expected compression and intensity of good lyric poetry and a high degree of verbal and dramatic tension. We welcome equally submissions from established poets as well as from less known and beginning poets. We do not accept translations or previously published works. We prefer to see a sample of 3-5 poems at a submission, with SASE. We generally respond within a month. We are a nonprofit organization and can pay only in copy to contributors. Sample copies are available at $5."** They have published poetry by Robert Cooperman, Andrew Dillon and Scott Travis Hutchison. As a sample the editor selected these lines from "Mister Varsey" by Sally Jo Sorensen:

With the myths
his methods excelled:
The Odyssey, *for instance,*
became more than just the same old song
about some guy who'd left his wife and kid
for the guys. Mr. Varsey fetched a bow
out of his great, fabled closet
and asked the gentlemen of the class—
as he called them—to see who might be
Penelope's true suitor. None could
match the task, so he exclaimed
blind Homer walks again!
until I raised my hand

Poem is a flat-spined, 4⅜×7¼, 90-page journal that contains more than 60 poems (mostly lyric free verse under 50 lines) generally featured one to a page on good stock paper with a clean design and a classy matte cover. Circulation is 400 (all subscriptions of which 90 are libraries). Overall, it's a good market for beginners and experienced poets who pay attention to craft.

‡POEM TRAIN (I, IV-Children), P.O. Box 203, Jarrettsville MD 21084, founded 1993, editor Lisa Ancarrow, is a quarterly (seasonal) poetry publication designed to appeal to children from preschool-age through 12 years old. **"We want poetry for children written by adults as well as poetry written by children. We want to see honest, upbeat poems with an imaginative or interesting view. Rhyme is nice but not necessary. We like a mix. Most forms or subjects will be considered. Humor, however, is *always* welcome. Poetry no longer than 25 lines is preferred as space is limited. We don't want to see taboo subjects, abuse of any sort, overly religious or obscure subjects. Remember the audience. Don't be preachy or use an adult tone."** They have recently published poetry by Charles Ghigna and Patricia Crandall. As a sample the editor selected "The Deer" by Jim Roth:

The deer received a letter.
It started with, "Dear deer.
I love you very deer-ly.
I wish that you were here.
You are my deer-est *darling.*
You always bring me luck.
No one is more deer *to me.*
Please marry me."
Signed, "Buck".

Poem Train is 28 pgs., digest-sized and saddle-stapled with colored card cover and b&w illustrations. They receive about 400 submissions a year, use approximately 50%. Press run is 200 for 15 subscribers, 50 shelf sales. Single copy: $3.75; subscription: $12. **Sample postpaid: $2.50. Previously published poems and simultaneous submissions OK, if noted. Cover letter and 6×9 SASE preferred.** Time between acceptance and publication is 3-6 months. **Seldom comments on rejections. Send SASE for guidelines. Reports in 1-2 months. Pays 1 copy. Acquires first or one-time rights.** The editor says, "Read, read, read to your child! Get down to his level and talk with him. If you listen, there will always be ideas for good poems there."

‡POEMS & PLAYS; THE TENNESSEE CHAPBOOK PRIZE (II), English Dept., Middle Tennessee State University, Murfreesboro TN 37132, phone (615)898-2712, founded 1993, editor Gay Brewer, is an annual "eclectic publication for poems and short plays," published in April/May. **They have no restrictions on style or content of poetry.** They have recently published poetry by Ray Bradbury and Charles Bukowski. As a sample we selected the last stanza of "A Poem Should Be Mean" by Kevin Griffith:

A poem doesn't give politely. If you want to write it,
you've got to ask. The poem sits in a dark chair
and listens to your story. And it better be good,
or else, like a book, you're history.

Poems & Plays is 84 pgs., 6×9, professionally printed and perfect-bound with coated color card cover and art. "We received approximately 1,200 poems for our first issue (Spring/Summer 1994), published 40." Press run is 500. Subscription: $9 (2 issues). **Sample postpaid: $5. No previously published poems or simultaneous submissions. Reads submissions October 1 through January 15 only. "Work is circulated among advisory editors for comments and preferences. All accepted material is published in the following issue." Seldom comments on rejections. Reports in 1-2 months. Pays 1 copy. Acquires first publication rights only.** "We accept chapbook manuscripts (of poems or plays) of 24-30 pages for The Tennessee Chapbook Prize. The winner is printed as an interior chapbook in ***Poems & Plays*** and receives 50 copies of the issue. SASE and $10 fee (for two copies of the issue) required. Dates for contest entry are the same as for the magazine (October 1 through January 15)."

POEMS FOR A LIVABLE PLANET (V, IV-Nature/ecology, translations), 1235½ N. Larrabee St., Los Angeles CA 90069, founded 1990, editor Jeffrey Dellin, publishes **"poems dealing with the beauty/peril of the Earth & Her Creatures." Sample postpaid: $3.75.** The ecology theme of this publication is one of the most important of our time. The poetry is insightful and, overall, well-executed; craft does not suffer because of politics. The editor says, "I am taking a sabbatical in Italy for one year and, therefore, **not accepting poetry submissions."**

POET; COOPER HOUSE PUBLISHING INC.; JOHN DAVID JOHNSON MEMORIAL POETRY AWARDS; IVA MARY WILLIAMS INSPIRATIONAL POETRY AWARDS; AMERICAN CHAPBOOK AWARDS; AMERICAN COLLEGE & UNIVERSITY POETRY AWARDS; AMERICAN HIGH SCHOOL POETRY AWARDS; THE AMERICAN LITERARY MAGAZINE AWARDS (I, II), P.O. Box 54947, Oklahoma City OK 73154, founded 1984, managing editor Peggy Cooper, editor Joy Hall, poetry editor Michael Hall. "***Poet*** is one of the largest commercial publishers of poetry in the U.S. and is **open to submissions from writers at all levels of experience. Contributors receive a free copy of the issue in which their work appears."** Michael Hall says, **"I look for poems that display wit, knowledge and skill . . . verse that employs arresting images, poems that make the reader think or smile or even sometimes cry."** They have published poetry by Lewis Turco and H.R. Coursen. As a sample the editor selected the opening stanzas of "Marshwind Song" by Patricia A. Lawrence:

The music of the marsh has my heart pinned
To tidal flats and skittle dancing crabs.
A hanging gull is tossed on beats of wind.

Her lonely mewing, plaintive, swordlike, stabs
Each note that wells to fullness like a tide
Until she streaks the sky. A talon grabs

Another note that haunts me . . .

It is magazine-sized, professionally printed, 56-80 pgs. with glossy cover, saddle-stitched. Of about 7,000-10,000 submissions, they use a little fewer than 5%. Subscription: $20/year. Subscribers receive free the giant "Forms of Poetry" poster. **Sample copy of *Poet*, postpaid: $5.50 or "call your bookstore where you can purchase it for $4 ($5 Canada) if it's in stock." For guidelines, send 2 loose first-class stamps with request. Previously published poems and simultaneous submissions OK. Editor sometimes comments on rejections. Reports within 3-6 months. Pays 1 copy.** Reviews books of poetry. Open to unsolicited reviews. Poets may also send books for review consideration to Joy Hall, P.O. Box 22047, Alexandria VA 22304. They sponsor annual chapbook awards (up to 48 pgs., $30 entry fee, grand prize: publication in book form and 50 copies). John David Johnson Memorial Poetry Awards (prizes of $100, $50, $25, special merit and honorable mention awards, award certificates, publication and a copy of the magazine in which the winning poems appear to all winners. Additionally, all contestants receive the "Forms of Poetry" poster. Entry fee: $5/poem. March 1 and September 1 deadlines). Iva Mary Williams Inspirational Poetry Awards (prizes of $100, $50, $25, special merit and honorable mention awards, award certificates, publication and a copy of the magazine in which the winning poems appear to all winners. Additionally, all contestants receive the master form for a poetry calendar. Entry fee: $5/poem. February 1 and August 1 deadlines). American College & University Poetry Awards (prizes of $100, $50, $25, each divided equally between winning student and teacher, special merit and honorable mention awards, award certificates, publication and copy of the magazine in which the winning poems appear to all winners. Additionally, all teachers receive the "Forms of Poetry" classroom poster. No entry fee. Rules and official entry forms may be requested with 4 loose first-class stamps). American High School Poetry Awards (prizes of $100, $50, $25, each divided equally between winning student and teacher, special merit and honorable mention awards, award certificates, publication and copy of the magazine in which the winning poems appear to all winners. Additionally, all teachers receive the "Forms of Poetry" classroom poster. No entry fee. Rules and official entry forms may be requested with 4 loose first-class stamps). The American Literary Magazine Awards are engraved plaques for Best Overall, Best Editorial Content and Best Cover Design. Special merit and honorable mention award certificates may also be given. The top three winners will also receive free advertising in ***Poet***. All contestants receive an engraved mug. $30 entry fee/title. Deadline: December 31. Send 2 loose first-class stamps with request for rules and entry form.

POET & CRITIC (II), 203 Ross Hall, Iowa State University, Ames IA 50011, phone (515)294-2180, founded 1961, editor Neal Bowers, appears 3 times a year. This is one of the best literary magazines for the money; it is packed with some of the most readable poems being published today—all styles and forms, lengths and subjects. The editor shuns elite-sounding free verse with obscure meanings and pretty-sounding formal verse with obvious meanings. ***Poet & Critic*** is 6×9, 48 pgs., staple bound, professionally printed, matte card cover with color, circulation 400, 300 subscriptions of which 100 are libraries. Subscription: $18. **Sample postpaid: $8. "We don't require a cover letter, but we prefer one." Submit 4-6 poems. "We do not read mss between the end of May and mid-August." Reports in 2 weeks (often sooner). Pays 1 copy. Acquires first rights.** The magazine also includes review-essays usually focusing on the works of one poet. "We assign reviews following a query." Poets may also send books for review consideration.

POET LORE (II), The Writer's Center, 4508 Walsh St., Bethesda MD 20815, founded 1889, managing editor Sunil Freeman, executive editors Philip Jason and Geraldine Connolly, is a quarterly dedicated "to the best in American and world poetry and objective and timely reviews and commentary. We look for **fresh uses of traditional form and devices, but any kind of excellence is welcome. The editors encourage narrative poetry and original translations of works by contemporary world poets."** They have published poetry by Sharon Olds, John Balaban, William Heyen, Walter McDonald, Reginald Gibbons and Howard Nemerov. ***Poet Lore*** is 6×9, 80 pgs., perfect-bound, professionally printed with matte card cover. Circulation includes 600 subscriptions of which 200 are libraries. Editors are open to all styles (as long as the work is well-crafted and insightful), leaning toward lyric and narrative free verse with an emphasis on voice. They receive about 3,000 poems/year, use about 125. Single copy: $4.50 plus $1 postage. Subscription: $15. **Sample postpaid: $4. Submit typed poems, author's name and address on each page. Reports in 3 months. Pays 2 copies.** Reviews books of poetry. Open to unsolicited reviews. Poets may also send books for review consideration. Poetry published in ***Poet Lore*** has also been selected for inclusion in **The Best American Poetry 1994.**

‡POETIC ELOQUENCE (I), Route 5, Box 181-N, Elgin TX 78621, phone (512)281-2222, founded 1992, editor/publisher Doris F. Rodriguez, is a quarterly poetry journal published at the end of February, May, August and November. They want **"any subject (except holiday), any style, 40 lines maximum, 12-24 lines preferred. No profanity or sexually graphic material nor anything that puts crime in a positive light. Each issue highlights two sestinas and one page of tanka and/or haiku."** They have recently published poetry by Marian Ford Park, Phil Eisenberg, Kathleen Wheeler-Bramer and Nancy Watson-Dodrill. The editor says ***Poetic Eloquence*** is 50-60 pgs., 8½×11, typeset and perfect-bound with colored card cover. It includes a featured poet section, a poetry book review column and a biographical section. **"We also feature three writing challenges per issue to stimulate, encourage and awaken the poetic muse sleeping inside us all.** Seeing how others respond to the same challenge is a valuable tool in helping poets stretch beyond their usual style and voice." They publish approximately 75% of the poetry received. Single copy: $6; subscription: $24. **Sample postpaid: $5. Submit up to 10 poems, typed, with name, address and phone number in the top righthand corner of each page. Previously published poems OK; no simultaneous submissions. Include brief (50-word) bio. "Poems will not be returned."** Time between acceptance and publication is 3-6 months. **Sometimes comments on rejections. Send SASE for guidelines. Reports within 3-6 weeks. Pays 1 copy to first-time contributors. Acquires one-time rights.** Offers Editor's Choice awards of $25 each to the top three poems in each issue. Also offers $10 to the top poem for each writing challenge. Promotes books and chapbooks of poetry in 50-100 words. "Send one copy of the book you want promoted. Books will not be returned." The editor says, "Subscriptions are encouraged but not required for publication. We welcome poets who employ knowledge of the craft, skill and imagination in just the right combination to create a poem that displays vivid imagery, powerful feelings and outstanding craftsmanship . . . a poem that fairly dances across the page or transports its reader to another place and time by the skillful use of concise words and creative phrases to create fresh insight on old themes."

THE POETIC KNIGHT: A FANTASY ROMANCE MAGAZINE (I, IV-Fantasy, romance), 110 S. West St., Columbiana OH 44408, founded 1990, editor Michael While, appears 4 times/year. **They want "fantasy poetry that exemplifies the classical romantic in all of us. Accept poetry from haiku to ballad length as well as fiction under 5,000 words. Prefer traditional, but will look at all forms. No profanity or explicit sex. Like to see work based on very human characters. Looking for more poetry with action bent to it and something that tells a specific story."** They have published poetry by Carl Heffley and William Robertson. As a sample the editor selected these lines from "The Ocean Tryst" by Jessica Amanda Salmonson:

There standing in the gate or crack
A damsel clad in green and black
Her eyes half shut, her hair adrift-
Around her brilliant rainbows shift.

It is 40-52 pgs., magazine-sized, laser set with full color cover, saddle-stapled. They accept on a "30 to 1 ratio and we get 50-60 submissions a week." Press run is 300 for 100 subscribers of which 10 are libraries, 150 shelf sales. Subscription: $20/4 issues. **Sample postpaid: $5. Submit 3-5 poems with cover letter. Send SASE for guidelines. Pays 1 copy. Acquires first North American serial rights. Editor "tries to comment on all submissions and make everyone who writes to us feel at home."**

POETIC LICENSE; HATHAWAY-MILLER PUBLICATIONS (I), 13 Cebold Dr., Montgomery IL 60538, phone (708)897-3363, Hathaway-Miller Publications founded 1992, ***Poetic License*** founded 1993, editor/publisher Deena Miller. ***Poetic License*** appears 4 times a year using all kinds of poetry, articles, book reviews, b&w line drawings and ads. It also includes a mailbox section for correspondence. They are **"open to all forms of poetry. Keep it under 40 lines, any genre. 'Make me feel!' Nothing obscene nor anything so abstract that it becomes obscure. I like analytical stuff."** As a sample of the kind of poetry she is seeking, the editor selected these lines from her own poem, "Vulnerable," published in ***Poetic Page***:

Rock me
Gently in your lyings—
Let hypocrisy rest east
On your careless fingertips or
Thrusts of weaknesses and dyings—
Leave my belly soft with white/ Blinding
As an act of birth.

The editor describes ***PL*** as 8½×11, desktop-published and comb bound with cover art and graphics. Press run is 100. Single copy: $5; subscription: $18/year. **Sample back issue postpaid: $4. Submit poems with $1/poem reading fee. Previously published poems and simultaneous submissions OK. Cover letter with brief bio and credits required. Sometimes comments on rejections. For an additional $1/poem the editor will provide "a private written critique containing suggestions and/or offering helpful advice." Send SASE for guidelines. Reports in 4-6 weeks. Sometimes sends prepublication galleys. Pays 1 copy. Acquires first or reprint rights.** Reviews chapbooks of poetry in 250 words or less, single format. Open to unsolicited reviews. Poets may also send books for review consideration. Hathaway-Miller Publications is a chapbook publishing service. **"You pay costs, books are yours." Query first with sample poems and cover letter with brief bio and publication credits. Replies to queries and mss in 4-6 weeks. If interested, write for samples.** The editor says, "Spend time developing your craft. Read as much poetry as you can! Learn the basics. Attend workshops or public readings. Best yet, find a writers group! Writers groups offer support and feedback—two important elements for a writer's growth! I am after quality, not quantity. I watch for depth and conciseness. Make me think and feel! Don't be trite or didactic, ever."

POETIC PAGE (I); OPUS LITERARY REVIEW (II), P.O. Box 71192, Madison Heights MI 48071-0192, phone (313)548-0865, ***Poetic Page*** founded 1989, ***Opus Literary Review*** founded 1993, editor Denise Martinson. ***Poetic Page*** appears bimonthly. **Each issue has a contest, $1/poem fee, prizes of $30, $20 and $10. All poetry published is that of contest winners, and some poets receive invitations to appear on their own page. "All forms are used except explicit sex, violence and crude. 30 lines."** They have recently published poetry by Marian Ford Park, Pearl Bloch Segall, Alice Mackenzie Swaim, T.N. Turner, T. Kilgore Splake, Glenna Holloway and John Grey. As a sample the editor selected her poem "Edward Scissorhands":

He usually cuts pieces from the whole,
reveals hidden hearts and love.

Once he found frozen fragments
laced with confusion. A cold
reminder that truth can sting,
burn a dry-ice awareness
on the verge of his extinction.
But he lives and learns,
continues to shape his world
in whatever form fits illusion.

Poetic Page is 36 pgs., magazine-sized, desktop-published. Press run is 250-350, sent to libraries, universities, editors and subscribers. Subscription: $15. **Sample postpaid: $3. Simultaneous submissions and previously published poems OK. Cover letter required. Send SASE for guidelines. Nonsubscribers receive 1 copy.** The editor says, "We look for poetry that has something to say. No trite rhyme. Only the very best poems are selected each issue. First place is featured on its own page. We now use more articles, tidbits, poet interactions and fillers. We pay copies for articles and cover art, but must be of the highest quality. We ask poets to send us copies of their poetry books for our 'Review' section. Just because we are listed under the I category, does not mean that we are an easy magazine to be published in. We want poetry that is well written, poetry that demands to be read. Send your best." ***Opus Literary Review*** is a biannual that publishes **poetry only. No specifications as to form, length, style, subject matter or purpose.** They have published poetry by Rudy Zenker, Leonard Cirino, Daniel Gallik, John Grey and Patricia A. Lawrence. As a sample, the editor selected these lines from "My Mother's Third Call On A Day Of Sleet And December Falling" by Lyn Lifshin:

as if the whiteness was
gauze wrapped over the
mouth of someone dying
and she had to slash it
with a last word, or
Monday was a blank
sheet of paper only my
words would cling to.

Opus Literary Review is digest-sized, saddle-stitched, desktop-published, with matte cover. Subscription: $10. **Sample postpaid: $5. No previously published poems or simultaneous submissions. Cover letter required. All accepted poets are listed with bio. Editor often comments on rejections. Send SASE for guidelines. Reports in 1 month. Pays 1 copy. Acquires first rights.** The editor says: "We want poetry that will last the ages. Poetry that is intelligent, well thought out. Use strong verbs and nouns and let your reader feel your work by showing, not telling. If you want to write a poem about a flower, go ahead. But make that flower unique—surprise us. Give us your best work; we want to publish it. But beginners beware, no trite rhyme here. However, we will publish a well-written rhyme if the rhyme is the poem, not the word endings. Free verse is what we prefer."

POETIC SPACE: POETRY & FICTION (I), P.O. Box 11157, Eugene OR 97440, founded 1983, editor Don Hildenbrand, is a literary magazine with emphasis on contemporary poetry, fiction, reviews (including film and drama), interviews, market news and translations (Chinese and Spanish). Accepts poetry and fiction that is **"well-crafted and takes risks. We like poetry with guts. Would like to see some poetry on social and political issues. We would also like to see gay/lesbian poetry and poetry on women's issues. Erotic and experimental OK."** They have recently published poetry by Crawdad Nelson, Sesshu Foster, Keith A. Dodson, Simon Perchik, Bill Shields, John M. Bennett, Peter Kime, Wang Jiang Ping, Albert Huffstickler and Arthur W. Knight. As a sample the editor selected these lines by Spenser Reese:

The elm's groins I groom,
my bible-wings
cruising, hustling— —

my wrinkled mouth
masticating
The night's nerves.

The magazine is 8½×11, saddle-stapled, 20-24 pgs., offset from typescript and sometimes photo-reduced. It is published twice a year. They use about 25% of the 200-300 poems received/year. Press run is 800-1,000 with 50 subscriptions of which 12 are libraries. Subscription: $10/one year, $18/two years. **Sample: $3. Send SASE for list of available back issues ($4). No simultaneous submissions or previously published poems. Ms should be typed, double-spaced, clean, name/address on each page. Editor provides some critical comments. Guidelines for SASE. Reports in 2-4 months. Pays 1 copy, but more can be ordered by sending SASE and postage.** Reviews books of poetry in 500-1,000 words. Open to unsolicited reviews. Poets may also send books for review consideration. They have published an **Anthology: 1987-1991 Best of Poetic Space**, $5. Also publishes one chapbook each spring. Their first chapbook is **Truth Rides to Work & Good Girls**, poetry by Crawdad Nelson and fiction by Louise A. Blum, ($5 plus $1.50 p&h). Don Hildenbrand says, "We like poetry that takes risks—original writing that gives us a new, different perspective."

POETICAL HISTORIES (IV-Regional, style), 27 Sturton St., Cambridge CB1 2QG United Kingdom, founded 1985, editor Peter Riley, is a "small press publishing **poetry only." They publish poetry that is "British, modernist," not "concrete, experimental, translated, homely."** They have published poetry by J.H. Prynne, John James, Denise Riley and Nicholas Moore. **They publish 8-10 hand-printed chapbooks/year averaging 8 pgs. each.** *PH* is also a contact address for The Cambridge Conference of Contemporary Poetry, which takes place annually in late April.

POETPOURRI; COMSTOCK WRITERS' GROUP INC.; SUMMER SIZZLER CONTEST (II), 907 Comstock Ave., Syracuse NY 13210, phone (315)475-0339, founded 1987, published by the Comstock Writers' Group, Inc., co-editors Jennifer B. MacPherson and Kathleen Bryce Niles, appears biannually. **They use "work that is clear and understandable to a general readership, that deals with issues, ideas, feelings and beliefs common to us all—well-written free and traditional verse. No obscene, obscure, patently religious or greeting card verse."** They have published poetry by Gayle Elen Harvey, Katharyn Howd Machan, Robert Cooperman, Susan A. Manchester and R. Nikolas Macioci. As a sample they selected these lines from "Now That The Trees Are Dancers" by Sarah Patton:

See how the trees
solicit the sky,

how leaves
flatten themselves
against windowpanes
where white horses sleep.

Poetpourri is 100 pgs., digest-sized, professionally printed, perfect-bound, raised cover. Circulation 550. Subscription: $8. **Sample postpaid: $4. Poems may be submitted anytime for possible publication, 3-6 at a time, name and address on each page, unpublished poems only. Cover letter with short bio of poet preferred. Return time is about 6 weeks. Editors usually comment on returned submissions. Pays copies. Acquires first North American serial rights.** They offer a yearly Summer Sizzler contest with over $400 in prizes, $2/poem fee, 30-line limit.

POETRY; THE MODERN POETRY ASSOCIATION; BESS HOKIN PRIZE; LEVINSON PRIZE; OSCAR BLUMENTHAL PRIZE; EUNICE TIETJENS MEMORIAL PRIZE; FREDERICK BOCK PRIZE; GEORGE KENT PRIZE; UNION LEAGUE PRIZE; RUTH LILLY POETRY PRIZE (III), 60 W. Walton St., Chicago IL 60610, founded 1912, editor Joseph Parisi, "is the oldest and most distinguished monthly magazine devoted entirely to verse," according to their literature. "Founded in Chicago in 1912, it immediately became the international showcase that it has remained ever since, publishing in its earliest years—and often for the first time—such giants as Ezra Pound, Robert Frost, T.S. Eliot, Marianne Moore and Wallace Stevens. *Poetry* has continued to print the major voices of our time and to discover new talent, establishing an unprecedented record. There is virtually no important contemporary poet in our language who has not at a crucial stage in his career depended on *Poetry* to find a public for him: John Ashbery, Dylan Thomas, Edna St. Vincent Millay, James Merrill, Anne Sexton, Sylvia Plath, James Dickey, Thom Gunn, David Wagoner—only a partial list to suggest how *Poetry* has represented, without affiliation with any movements or schools, what Stephen Spender has described as 'the best, and simply the best' poetry being written." Although its offices have always been in Chicago, *Poetry*'s influence and scope extend far beyond, throughout the US and in over 45 countries around the world. Asked to select 4 lines of poetry "which represent the taste and quality you want in your publication" Joseph Parisi selected the opening lines of "The Love Song of J. Alfred Prufrock" by T.S. Eliot, which first appeared in *Poetry* in 1915:

Let us go then, you and I,
When the evening is spread out against the sky
Like a patient etherized upon a table;
Let us go, through certain half-deserted streets . . .

Poetry is an elegantly printed, flat-spined, 5½×9 magazine. They receive over 70,000 submissions/year, use 300-350, have a 9-month backlog. Circulation 7,500, 6,000 subscriptions of which 65% are libraries. Single copy: $2.50; subscription: $25, $27 for institutions. **Sample postpaid: $3.50. Submit no more than 4 poems. Send SASE for guidelines. Reports in 2-3 months—longer for mss submitted during the summer. Pays $2 a line. Buys all rights. Returns rights "upon written request."** Reviews books of poetry in 750-1,000 words, multi-book format. Open to unsolicited reviews. Poets may also send books to Stephen Young, associate editor, for review consideration. This is probably the most prestigious poetry credit in the publishing business. In fact, ***Poetry*** ranked #1 in the "Poets' Pick" category of the latest ***Writer's Digest*** Poetry 60 list. (This category ranks those publications in which poets said they would most like to see their work published.) Consequently, competition here is extraordinarily keen with more poems received in a year than there are people in some cities in your state. Yet Joseph Parisi is one of the most efficient (and discerning) editors around, and he does much to promote poetry. This is a magazine that you can buy straight off the newsstand to get a feel for the pulse of poetry each month. Seven prizes (named in heading) ranging from $100 to $1,000 are awarded annually to poets whose work has appeared in the magazine that year. *Only verse already published in **Poetry** is eligible for consideration and no formal application is necessary.* ***Poetry*** also sponsors the Ruth Lilly Poetry Prize, an annual award of $75,000, and the Ruth Lilly Collegiate Poetry Fellowship, an annual award of $15,000 to undergraduates to support their further studies in poetry/creative writing. Work published in ***Poetry*** was also selected for inclusion in the 1992, 1993 and 1994 volumes of **The Best American Poetry** .

POETRY & AUDIENCE; PELICANS POETRY MAGAZINE; GREAT NORTHERN UNION (I, II), School of English, University of Leeds, Leeds, West Yorkshire LJ2 9JT England, founded 1953, editor Antony Rowland. ***P&A*** and ***PPM*** each appear 2-3 times/year. Both are "general poetry journals accepting work from new and established poets. **We do not discriminate against any form of poetry although there is a general move towards a more lyrical style. This said, we have and will continue to publish even the most obscure poetic forms."** They have published poetry by Carol Ann Duffy, Ian Duhig and Seamus Heaney. As a sample the editor selected these lines from "Recovery Room" by Peter Porter:

There's a record here
I can't bear to play,
It has your tears on it.

No wonder they cut me open,
They were looking for a heart
They didn't think was there.

The editor describes the 2 publications simply by saying "***P&A*** is somewhat larger and more elegant." Both have press runs of 200-300 for 50 subscribers of which 10 are libraries. Subscription for either: £10 (overseas). **Sample: £1.50. "Poetry must be sent either to *P&A* or *PPM*, not both. Indicate on envelope which. Please double or at least use 1.5 spacing for all lines with triple-line spacing of stanzas. Please give birth date and place in any correspondence as well as previous publications, if applicable. No comments on rejections."** ***P&A*** has a small consultative council. ***Pelicans*** is a more personal magazine with rotating or sometimes joint editorship. **Replies for either: 2 months. Pays 1 copy.** Open to unsolicited reviews. Poets may also send books for review consideration. They founded Great Northern Union, "which brings together the university poets of Northern England."

POETRY BREAK; BEING; NAVARRO PUBLICATIONS (V), P.O. Box 1107, Blythe CA 92226-1107. **"Please note that we are no longer accepting unsolicited submissions as we are overstocked and revamping our whole operation."**

POETRY DURHAM (II), English Dept., University of Durham, New Elvet, Durham DH1 3JT England, edited by David Hartnett, Michael O'Neill and Gareth Reeves, founded 1982, appears 3 times a year using **quality poetry and essays on modern poetry.** It is 32 pgs., digest-sized, professionally printed on good stock with glossy card cover. Circulation 300. Subscription: £6 for 3 issues. **All overseas subscriptions by international money order. Pays £12/poem.** Reviews books of poetry.

POETRY EAST (II), Dept. of English, DePaul University, 802 W. Belden Ave., Chicago IL 60614, phone (312)362-5114, founded 1980, editor Richard Jones, "is a biannual international magazine publishing poetry, fiction, translations and reviews. We suggest that authors look through back issues of the magazine before making submissions. **No constraints or specifications, although we prefer open form.**" They have published poetry by Tom Crawford, Thomas McGrath, Denise Levertov, Galway Kinnell, Sharon Olds and Amiri Baraka. The digest-sized, flat-spined journal is 100 pgs., professionally printed with glossy color card cover. They use 60-80 pgs. of poetry in each issue. They receive approximately 4,000 submissions/year, use 10%, have a 4-month backlog. Circulation 1,200, 250 subscriptions of which 80 are libraries. Single copy: $8; subscription: $12. **Sample postpaid: $5. Reports in 4 months. Pays copies. Editors sometimes comment on rejections.** Open to unsolicited reviews. Poets may also send books for review consideration. This is one of the best-edited and designed magazines being published today. Award-winning editor Richard Jones assembles an exciting array of accessible poems, leaning toward lyric free verse with room for narrative and otherwise well-structured poems in all traditions. He occasionally schedules theme issues and selects poems accordingly. Because competition is keen, response times can exceed stated limits, particularly in the spring. Work published in ***Poetry East*** has been included in **The Best American Poetry 1993.** The magazine itself ranked #8 in the

"Open Markets" category of the latest ***Writer's Digest*** Poetry 60 list. This category ranks those publications most open to both free and formal verse.

THE POETRY EXPLOSION NEWSLETTER (THE PEN) (I), P.O. Box 2648, Newport News VA 23609-0648, phone (804)722-7127, founded 1984, editor Arthur C. Ford, is a "quarterly newsletter dedicated to the preservation of poetry." Arthur Ford wants **"poetry—40 lines maximum, no minimum. All forms and subject matter with the use of good imagery, symbolism and honesty. Rhyme and non-rhyme. No vulgarity."** He has published poetry by Veona Thomas and Rose Robaldo. ***The Pen*** is 12-16 pgs., saddle-stitched, mimeographed on both sides. He accepts about 80 of 300 poems received. Press run is 450 for 300 subscribers of which 5 are libraries. Subscription: $12. **Send $3 for sample copy and more information. Submit maximum of 5 poems. Include $1 for reading time. Simultaneous submissions and previously published poems OK. Editor comments on rejections "sometimes, but not obligated." Pays 1 copy.** He will criticize poetry for 15¢ a word. Open to unsolicited reviews. Poets may also send books for review consideration. The editor comments: "Even though free verse is more popular today, we try to stay versatile."

POETRY FORUM (I); THE JOURNAL (IV-Subscription), 5713 Larchmont Dr., Erie PA 16509, phone (814)866-2543 (also fax: 8-10 a.m. or 5-8 p.m.), poetry editor Gunvor Skogsholm, appears 3 times a year. **"We are open to any style and form. We believe new forms ought to develop from intuition. Length up to 50 lines accepted. Would like to encourage long themes. No porn or blasphemy, but open to all religious persuasions."** As a sample the editor selected these lines (poet unidentified):

Is it anger I see in your eyes
When they look at mine?
Because I see no smile or happiness
there—merely a blank stare.
Is it anger I see
Or is it Longing for me?

The magazine is 7×8½, 38 pgs., saddle-stapled with card cover, photocopied from photoreduced typescript. **Sample postpaid: $3. They will consider simultaneous submissions and previously published poems. Editor comments on poems "if asked, but respects the poetic freedom of the artist." Publishes theme issues. Send SASE for guidelines and upcoming themes. Sometimes sends prepublication galleys. Gives awards of $25, $15, $10 and 3 honorable mentions for the best poems in each issue. Acquires one-time rights.** ***The Journal***, which appears twice a year, accepts **experimental poetry of any length from subscribers only. Sample: $3.** Reviews books of poetry in 250 words maximum. Open to unsolicited reviews. Poets may also send books for review consideration. They offer a poetry chapbook contest. Entry fee: $9. Prize is publication and 20 copies. Send SASE for information. The editor says, "I believe today's poets should experiment more and not feel stuck in the forms that were in vogue 300 years ago. I would like to see more experimentalism—new forms will prove that poetry is alive and well in the mind and spirit of the people."

‡POETRY HARBOR; NORTH COAST REVIEW (I, II, IV-Regional), 1028 E. Sixth St., Duluth MN 55805, phone (218)728-3728, fax (218)727-0645, founded 1989. Poetry Harbor is a "nonprofit, tax-exempt organization dedicated to fostering literary creativity through public readings, publications, radio and television broadcasts, and other artistic and educational means." Its main publication, ***North Coast Review***, is a regional magazine appearing 3 times a year with **poetry and prose poems by and about Upper Midwest people, including those from Minnesota, Wisconsin, North and South Dakota, and the upper peninsula of Michigan. "No form/style/content specifications, though we are inclined toward narrative, imagist poetry. We do not want to see anything from outside our region, not because it isn't good, but because we can't publish it due to geographics."** They have recently published poetry by Mark Vinz, Joe Paddock, Susan Hauser and Louis Jenkins. As a sample the editor selected these lines from "Rolling Up Sidewalks" by William Borden:

I imagine the sidewalks rolled to each corner
like sardine can lids
each evening at sundown by old men
underpaid but loyal, in blue uniforms
a bit shabby and threadbare. They start at one corner
and wiggle their calloused fingers into the crack
between curb and cement. No one tries it, so no one knows it's easy.

NCR is 56 pgs., 7×8½, offset and saddle-stapled, paper cover with various b&w art, ads at back. They receive about 500 submissions a year, use 100-150. Press run is 1,000 for 100 subscribers of which 20 are libraries, 300 shelf sales. One-year subscription: $9.50. **Sample postpaid: $3.50. Submit 3-6 pgs. of poetry, typed single-spaced, with name and address on each page. Previously published poems and simultaneous submissions OK, if noted. Cover letter with brief bio ("writer's credits") required. "We read three times a year, but our deadlines change from time to**

time. Write to us for current deadlines for our various projects." Send SASE for guidelines. Reports in 1-5 months. Pays $10 plus copies. Buys one-time rights. Poetry Harbor also publishes 1 perfect-bound paperback of poetry and 4-8 chapbooks each year. One chapbook is selected through an annual contest; send SASE for guidelines. "Others are selected by our editorial board from the pool of poets we have published in ***North Coast Review*** or have worked with in our other projects. **We suggest you send a submission to *North Coast Review* first. We almost always print chapbooks and anthologies by poets we've previously published or hired for readings."** Recent anthologies include **We Are All Living With AIDS, A Rural Experience** and **Poets Who Haven't Moved to St. Paul.** Send SASE for complete publications list. Poetry Harbor also sponsors a monthly reading series ("poets are paid to perform"), a weekly TV program (3 different cable networks regionally), an annual radio series, a prison workshop series and other special events. They say, "Poetry Harbor is extremely committed to cultivating a literary community and an appreciation for our region's literature within the Upper Midwest. There was a vacuum up here when it came to poetry reaching this community. Poetry Harbor projects are in place to change that. Poets are now OK to people up here, and our literary 'scene' is thriving. The general public is proving to us that they *do* like poetry if you give them some that is both readable and rooted in the lives of the community. We strongly believe that to be a greater poet, one must read poetry and attend poetry events as often as possible."

POETRY KANTO (V), Kanto Gakuin University, Kamariya-cho, Kanazawa-Ku, Yokohama 236, Japan, founded 1984, editor William I. Elliott. ***Poetry Kanto*** is a literary annual published by the Kanto Poetry Center, which sponsors an annual poetry conference. It publishes **well-crafted original poems in English and in Japanese.** The magazine publishes **"anything except pornography, English haiku and tanka, and tends to publish poems under 30 lines." They are not reading mss until further notice, however, as "special numbers are planned."** They have published work by Seamus Heaney, Desmond Egan, Shuntaro Tanikawa and Les Murray. As a sample, here is the final stanza from "A Suite . . ." by Serge Gavronsky:

> *Is it perverse to be inspired*
> *by poems when outside*
> *a pine tree*
> *waits*
> *for my pen to move*
> *in a respectful manner?*

The magazine is digest-sized, nicely printed (the English poems occupy the first half of the issue, the Japanese poems the second), 60 pgs., saddle-stapled, matte card cover. Circulation is 700, of which 400 are complimentary copies sent to schools, poets and presses; it is also distributed at poetry seminars. The magazine is unpriced. **Pay is 3-5 copies.** The editor advises, "Read a lot. Get feedback from poets and/or workshops. Be neat, clean, legible and polite in submissions. *SAE with International Reply Coupons absolutely necessary when requesting sample copy.*"

‡POETRY LONDON NEWSLETTER (II), P.O. Box 4LF, London W1A 4LF England, founded 1988, editors Leon Cych, Pascale Petit and Katherine Gallagher, appears 3 times a year. ***Poetry London Newsletter*** is "Southeast England's biggest magazine," including poetry, listings of "every poetry event in the London area," and reviews. They want **"poetry about rites of passage, women's poetry; no experimental or l-a-n-g-u-a-g-e poets!"** They have recently published poetry by Penelope Shuttle, Jo Shapcott, Selima Hill and Moniza Alvi. As a sample the editors selected these lines from "Safeguards" by Ruth Padel:

> *She kept changing. Strong,*
> *mottled, silent, ingesting*
> *Meryl Streep in the Dingo*
> *Baby trial, she was a chameleon*
>
> *that mounted every rainbow*
> *in spitting distance.*

PLN is 40 pgs., A4 size, typeset, saddle-stapled, coated card cover with b&w photo of a poet. They receive about 12,000 poems a year, accept 40. Press run is 500 for 300 subscribers of which 20 are libraries, 200 shelf sales. Single copy: £3.50; subscription: £12 for 3 issues. **Sample postpaid: $10. Submit no more than 6 poems. No previously published poems; simultaneous submissions OK. Cover letter required; "be short and precise with any accompanying information." Seldom comments on rejections. Reports within 1-3 months. Pays £10 *or* 4 copies.** Staff reviews books of poetry in 800-1,500 words, single and multi-book format. Send books for review consideration. They also provide comprehensive critiques for $100 per 25 poems. The editors add, "We list every poetry event, venue, bookshop and library in London – very useful if you're visiting and want to know where to go."

POETRY MOTEL; SUBURBAN WILDERNESS PRESS, BROADSIDES AND CHAPBOOKS (I, II), 1619 Jefferson, Duluth MN 55812, founded 1984, editors Pat McKinnon, Bud Backen and Jennifer Willis-Long aim **"to keep the rooms clean and available for these poor ragged poems to crash in once they are through driving or committing adultery." They want "poems that took longer than 10 minutes to author." No other specifications.** They have recently published poetry by Adrian C. Louis, Robert Peters, Hayley Mitchell, Albert Huffstickler, Susan Hauser, Ligi and Todd Moore. As a sample they selected this poem, "Family Traditions," by Will Lahti:

when great-grandfather was 4 years old
he and his brothers would play funeral.

since matti was the youngest
he had to be the corpse.

he played this role so well that
one day his brothers buried him alive.

Poetry Motel appears "every 260 days" as a 7×8½ digest, with wallpaper cover, circulation 800 (to 600 subscriptions), 52 pgs. of poetry, prose, essays and reviews. They receive about 1,000 submissions/year, take 250, have a 6- to 12- month backlog. **Sample: $5.95. Submit 3-5 pgs., name and address on upper half of each page. Simultaneous submissions OK. Informal cover letter with bio credits required. Reports in 1-3 weeks. Sometimes sends prepublication galleys. Payment varies. Acquires one-time rights.** Reviews books of poetry. Open to unsolicited reviews. Poets may also send books for review consideration. They advise, "Poets should read as much poetry as they can lay their hands on. And they should realize that although poetry is no fraternal club, poets are responsible for its survival, both financially and emotionally. Join us out here—this is where the edge meets the vision. We are very open to work from 'beginners.' "

POETRY NEW YORK: A JOURNAL OF POETRY AND TRANSLATION (II, IV-Translations, themes), P.O. Box 3184, Church Street Station, New York NY 10008, founded 1985, editors Burt Kimmelman, Todd Thilleman and Emmy Hunter, is an annual. They have published poetry by Wanda Coleman, Jerome Rothenberg, Enid Dame, Amiel Alcalay and Ann Lauterbach, and translations of Mallarme, Hesiod and Makoto Ooka. As a sample the editors selected these lines from "The Second Month of Separation" by Corinne Robins:

I don't hear or see,
an ocean and your drugs are
in between.
The beautiful garbage birds fly the island ferry,
and ocean planes criss-cross
while I dream you grow beyond closed doors.

The editors describe it as 6×9, perfect-bound, 80 pgs. They accept about 20% of "blind submissions." Press run is 500 for 300 shelf sales. **Some issues are on themes. "Query us first to see whether we are currently reading manuscripts. If so, send no more than five poems per submission." Editor comments on submissions "at times." Reports in 3-4 months. Pays 1 copy.** They sometimes sponsor readings. Work published in *Poetry New York* has been included in the 1993 and 1994 volumes of **The Best American Poetry.**

POETRY NORTHWEST (II), 4045 Brooklyn NE, Seattle WA 98105, phone (206)685-4750, founded 1959, editor David Wagoner, is a quarterly. The magazine is 48 pgs., 5½×8½, professionally printed with color card cover. It features all styles and forms. For instance, in two recent issues, lyric and narrative free verse was included alongside a sonnet sequence, minimalist sonnets and stanza patterns—all accessible and lively. They receive 10,000 poems/year, use 160, have a 3-month backlog. Circulation 1,500. Subscription: $10. **Sample postpaid: $3. Occasionally comments on rejections. Reports in 1 month maximum. Pays 2 copies. Awards prizes of $100, $50 and $50 yearly, judged by the editors.**

POETRY NOTTINGHAM; LAKE ASKE MEMORIAL OPEN POETRY COMPETITION (II); NOTTINGHAM POETRY SOCIETY; QUEENIE LEE COMPETITION (IV-Membership/subscription), 39 Cavendish Rd., Long Eaton, Nottingham NG10 4HY England, founded 1941, editor Martin Holroyd. Nottingham Poetry Society meets monthly for readings, talks, etc., and publishes quarterly its magazine, ***Poetry Nottingham: The International Magazine of Today's Poetry***, which is open to submissions from all-comers. **"We wish to see poetry that is intelligible to and enjoyable by the intelligent reader. We do**

not want any party politics or religious freaks. Poems not more than 30 lines in length." They have published poetry by Bert Almon, William Davey and Nikolas Macioci from the US. As a sample the editor selected these lines from "Half-Term" by Maurice Rutherford:

And if you've ever wondered what goes on
inside the heads of men who sit on seats
and ogle passers-by, come, sit with me,
it's marvelous . . . fantastic's more the word!
I chose at will, make this one rich, that poor . . .

There are 40 pgs. of poetry in each issue of the 6×8 magazine, professional printing with occasional essays, glossy art paper cover. They receive about 1,500 submissions/year, use 120, usually have a 1- to 3-month backlog. Circulation 325 for 200 subscriptions of which 20 are libraries. Subscriptions: £4 overseas ($60 for 2 years US); per copy: £2 ($8 US). **Sample postpaid: $8 or £1.75. Submit at any time 3 poems, not more than 30 lines each, not handwritten, and previously unpublished. Send SAE and 3 IRCs for stamps. No need to query but requires cover letter. Reports "within 2 months plus mailing time." Pays 1 copy.** Staff reviews books of poetry, but space allows only listings or brief review. Send books for review consideration. **Nottingham Poetry Society publishes collections by individual poets who are members of Nottingham Poetry Society.** The Lake Aske Memorial Open Poetry Competition offers cash prizes, annual subscriptions and publication in ***Poetry Nottingham.*** Open to all. The Queenie Lee Competition is for members and subscribers only, offers a cash prize and publication. The editor says they would like to see "more traditional forms. No disjointed prose under the guise of free verse."

POETRY OF THE PEOPLE (I, IV-Humor, love, nature, fantasy, themes), P.O. Box 13077, Gainesville FL 32604, founded 1986, poetry editor Paul Cohen. ***Poetry of the People*** is a leaflet that appears once a month. **"We take all forms of poetry but we like humorous poetry, love poetry, nature poetry and fantasy. No racist or highly ethnocentric poetry will be accepted. I do not like poetry that lacks images or is too personal or contains rhyme to the point that the poem has been destroyed."** ***Poetry of the People*** is 8-16 pgs., about 5½×4⅛, stapled, sometimes on colored paper. Issues are usually theme oriented. It has a circulation between 300 and 2,300. Copies are distributed to Gainesville residents for 25¢ each. **Samples: $4 for 11 pamphlets. Cover letter with biographical information required with submissions. "I feel autobiographical information is important in understanding the poetry." Poems returned within 3 months. Editor comments on rejections "often." Takes suggestions for theme issues. Sometimes sends prepublication galleys. Pays 5 copies. Acquires first rights.** He advises, "Be creative; there is a lot of competition out there."

POETRY PLUS MAGAZINE; GERMAN PUBLICATIONS (I, IV-Subscribers), Route 1, Box 52, Pulaski IL 62976, founded 1987, publisher/editor Helen D. German. ***PPM*** is a quarterly with articles about poetry, stories and poems. **"We accept all styles. Length should be no more than 24 lines. Poets can write on any subject that offers a meaningful message. We want our poets to write poems that will make the reader really think about what has been said. Reader should not have to guess at what was said. We would like to receive more haiku. We do *not* want any holiday poems, obscene poems or sexual poems. Poems should not be indecent."** As a sample the editor selected these lines by Milo Von Strom:

There are moments in every poet's life when they
Hardly know what to write as they struggle to
Entertain with witty words.

Poems are scribbled onto crumpled paper from
Magical pens, as eternity sits by the hourglass
Of time waiting to record poems from
Empirical thought.

PPM is magazine-sized, 25-35 pgs., photocopied from typescript, bound with tape, paper cover. Subscription: $20 (includes the booklet **Poetry Profits: How to Turn Your Poems into Dollars). Sample postpaid: $3. "Please submit at least 5 poems for consideration." Send SASE for guidelines. Subscribers are paid up to $5 for outstanding poems; no payment to nonsubscribers.** Offers editorial/critique service for $6/poem. Sponsors a poetry contest. $2 reading fee/poem. Prizes are $25 for first, $15 for second, $10 for third. Any style or subject "written in good taste. Poems will be entered in next upcoming contest. Winners will be notified." They also offer two other booklets to poets and writers: **Make and Sell Your Own Line of Greeting Cards** and **How to Operate a Poetry Telegram Service.** Cost is $10 each. The editor says, "***Poetry Plus*** is a fresh magazine that offers poets and writers the opportunity to see their poems in print. We want poems that are written to stimulate the deeper side of the reader. Rhymed or unrhymed, poems should offer a message that is meaningful. They should leave a memorable impression. Always send a large SASE with sufficient postage to return your unused poems. We publish both the work of our subscribers and nonsubscribers. Of course, due to limited space in each issue, subscribers get their poems published first. If you haven't been published yet or if you have, order a sample copy today and see what you've been missing in literary refreshment."

POETRY: USA; NATIONAL POETRY ASSOCIATION (II, IV-Translations, children/teen/young adult), 2569 Maxwell Ave., Oakland CA 94601, founded 1985, editor Jack Foley. ***Poetry: USA*** **publishes a wide range of poetry, including regular features of poetry by the homeless and by prisoners and an international section. "No style or technique of poetry is excluded, and we are actively interested in poetry issuing from every possible ethnic awareness. We want work which manifests intelligence, imagination and risk as well as awareness of the issues facing poetry *now*. A reviewer wrote that *Poetry: USA* 'grounds itself solidly in the everyday world,' though at the same time it 'leans toward' the experimental."** They have recently published poetry by Diane di Prima, Jake Berry, Jerome Rothenberg, Kathleen Fraser, Reginald Lockett, Hank Lazer, Barbara Guest, Michael McClure, James Broughton and Judy Grahn. As a sample the editor selected these lines from "Chicano" by Ivan Arguelles:

I am a pachuco
I am a lowrider   look at the back of my hands, man
those aren't lovebites on my neck, Vato
if you want some king weed
some puffin'-death reefer
man, we are the kings the led Zeppelin of east LA

It is a typeset unstapled tabloid, 28 pgs., with photos, graphics and ads, circulation 4,000, a portion of which is distributed by the homeless. Individual issues: $2. **Sample postpaid: $4. Previously published poems OK (if the editor knows). Pays copies. "Send SASE for guidelines or, better, order a sample copy."**

POETRY WALES PRESS; POETRY WALES (II, IV-Ethnic), Andmar House, Trewsfield Ind. Estate, Tondu Rd., Bridgend, Mid-Glamorgan CF31 4LJ Wales, founded 1965. ***Poetry Wales***, a 72-page, 253×185mm quarterly, circulation 1,000, has a primary interest in **Welsh and Anglo-Welsh poets but also considers submissions internationally. Send submissions (with SAE and IRC) to Richard Poole, editor, Glan-y-Werydd, Llandanwg, Harlech LL46 2SD Wales.** Overseas subscription: £18/year. **Sample: £2.50. One-page cover letter required with submissions; include name, address and previous publications. Publishes theme issues. Send SASE (or SAE and IRC) for upcoming themes. Theme for September 1994 was love and death. Pays.** Staff reviews books of poetry. Send books for review consideration to Amy L. Wack, reviews editor, Andmar House address. The press publishes books of **primarily Welsh and Anglo-Welsh poetry**, also biography, critical works and some fiction, distributed by Dufour Editions, Inc., Box 449, Chester Springs PA 19425. They have received several Welsh Arts Council "Book of the Year" Prizes. The editor says, "We would like to see more formal poetry."

POETRY WLU (I, II), Dept. of English, Wilfrid Laurier University, Waterloo, Ontario N2L 3C5 Canada, phone (519)884-1970, ext. 3308, founded 1979, editorial contact E. Jewinski, is an annual literary magazine (published every March) "with emphasis on *all* poetry and *all* prose *under* 1,000 words. **20-30 lines are ideal; but all kinds and lengths considered."** As a sample the editor selected the opening lines from "Katherine's Eye" by Bruce Bond:

It's the faithfulness that fools us,
how its fine red vein
slips under the living seam

When Katherine lost her glass eye
in the deep-end of her uncle's pool,
her brothers scouted the blue

Poetry WLU is 6½×8, saddle-stapled, typeset, with matte card cover using b&w art. They receive about 100-120 submissions a year, use approximately 15-20%. Press run is 300. **Sample postpaid: $5. Cover letter preferred. Reads submissions September 1 through January 30 only. "When the editorial board has time, comments are made." Reports in 6-8 months. Pays 1 copy.** Staff reviews books of poetry.

POETS AT WORK (I, IV-Subscribers), VAMC 325 New Castle Rd., Box 113, Butler PA 16001, founded 1985, editor/publisher Jessee Poet, **all contributors are expected to subscribe.** Jessee Poet says, **"Every poet who writes within the dictates of good taste and within my twenty-line limit will be published in each issue. I accept all forms and themes of poetry, but no porn, no profanity."** He has published poetry by Jaye Giammarion, Katherine Krebs, James Webb, Phil Eisenberg and Ernestine Gravely. As a sample he selected his poem "An Old Romance":

I almost loved you . . . did you know?
Sometimes you still disturb my dreams.
A summer romance long ago

I almost loved you . . . did you know?
We danced to music soft and low
Just yesterday . . . or so it seems
I almost loved you . . . did you know?
Sometimes you still disturb my dreams.

Poets at Work, a bimonthly, is generally 36-40 pgs., magazine-sized, saddle-stapled, photocopied from typescript with colored paper cover. Subscription: $16. **Sample: $3. Simultaneous submissions and previously published poems OK. Reports within 2 weeks. Pays nothing, not even a copy.** "Because I publish hundreds of poets, I cannot afford to pay or give free issues. Every subscriber, of course, gets an issue. Subscribers also have many opportunities to regain their subscription money in the numerous contests offered in each issue. Send SASE for flyer for my separate monthly and special contests." He also publishes chapbooks. Send SASE for details. Jessee Poet says, "These days even the best poets tell me that it is difficult to get published. I am here for the novice as well as the experienced poet. I consider ***Poets at Work*** to be a hotbed for poets where each one can stretch and grow at his or her own pace. Each of us learns from the other, and we do not criticize one another. The door for poets is always open, so please stop by; we probably will like each other immediately."

‡POET'S FANTASY (I), Dept. PM, 227 Hatten Ave., Rice Lake WI 54868, founded 1991, publisher/editor Gloria Stoeckel, is a bimonthly designed "to help the striving poet see his/her work in print." **They want sonnets, haiku and humorous free verse, 4-16 lines. "I accept good, clean poetry. I also accept some religious poetry if it doesn't portray Jesus Christ—merely religious themes. No profanity or sexual use of words."** They have recently published poetry by Andy Marshall and Ruth E. Cunliffe. As a sample we selected these lines from "Bachelor Diner" by Merle Taliaferro:

I thought he was handsome
His being overweight did not detract
he was interesting, talented, kind
our lives could interact.
At last a man for me
but when I showed my affection
I found myself fenced out
by a big table of confections.

Poet's Fantasy is 26 pgs., digest-sized, computer-generated dot-matrix, photocopied and saddle-stapled with colored paper cover, graphics and ads. They receive approximately 200 poems a year, accept about 90%. Press run is 125 for 100 subscribers. Subscription: $12/year. **Sample postpaid: $2; includes 2 greeting cards. Previously published poems and simultaneous submissions OK. Often comments on rejections. Send SASE for guidelines. Reports within 2 weeks. Pays coupon for $5 off subscription price or greeting card order. (Poets must purchase copy their work is in.) Acquires one-time rights.** "I do book reviews if poet sends a complimentary copy of the book. Reviews are approximately 200 to 300 words in length." She holds a few contests and also creates greeting cards for poets. "They use verse they wrote and can design their own cover." Send SASE for details.

POETS ON: (IV-Themes), 29 Loring Ave., Mill Valley CA 94941, phone (415)381-2824, founded 1976, poetry editor Ruth Daigon, is a poetry semiannual, **each issue on an announced theme (such as *Poets On: Regrets*). "We want well-crafted, humanistic, accessible poetry. We don't want to see sentimental rhymed verse. Length preferably 40 lines or less, or at the very most 80 lines (2-page poems)."** They have published poetry by Marge Piercy, Charles Edward Eaton, Walter Pavlich, Barbara Crooker and Lyn Lifshin. As a sample we selected these lines from "Widow's Walk" by Lisa Lepovetsky in ***Poets On: Remembrance***:

Memory casts me too far adrift
and old currents swallow me deep
in turmoils of damp debris and
dreams, till I'm worn smooth
as a whelk half-buried in sand.
Years bend me leeward, clinging
to the sides of these rocky fists.

Poets On: is 48 pgs., digest-sized, professionally printed, matte card cover with b&w graphics. Circulation is 450, 350 subscriptions of which 125 are libraries. They use about 5% of the 800 submissions they receive each year, have a 2- to 3-month backlog. Daigon tends to accept strong and well-structured lyric free verse, although you are apt to find any style or form with exciting or insightful content. Subscription: $8. **Sample postpaid: $5. Query with SASE for upcoming themes and deadlines. Submit 1-4 poems (40 lines or shorter). No handwritten mss. Include short bio. "It's a good idea to read the magazine before submitting poetry." Submit only September 1 through December 1 or February 1 through May 1. Reports in 2-3 months. Pays 1 copy.**

Editor sometimes comments on rejections. She has designed a rejection slip that has several categories explaining why your work didn't make it into the magazine, and yet she'll often add a comment to encourage good work. Ruth Daigon says, "We are not interested in poetry that is declamatory, sloganeering, bathetic or opaque. Nor are we concerned with poetry as mere word-games or technical exercises."

POETS. PAINTERS. COMPOSERS; COLIN'S MAGAZINE (II), Dept. PM, 10254 35th Ave. SW, Seattle WA 98146, phone (206)937-8155, founded 1984, editor Joseph Keppler, who says "***Poets. Painters. Composers.*** is an avant-garde arts journal which publishes poetry, drawings, scores, criticism, essays, reviews, photographs and original art. **If poetry, music or art is submitted, the work should be exciting, knowledgeable and ingenious."** The journal, which appears once or twice a year, has published such artists as Carla Bertola, Fernando Aguiar, Ana Hatherly and Sarenco and such poets as Carol Barrett, Carletta Wilson and D. Bauer. "We also publish ***Colin's Magazine, A Special Review from Poets. Painters. Composers.*** with a focus on the interface of literature and computer technology." As a sample the editor selected these lines from "Carpenter Mondrian" by Gregory Jerozal:

. . . Forget
Green fields: they are
The summer places of
Regret, forgetfulness,
The past we watch with others
Reassembled on the screen.

The journal is magazine-sized, 86 pgs. Each cover has an original painting on it. Mr. Keppler says, "each odd-numbered issue appears in an 8½×11 format; each even-numbered issue changes format: No. 2, for example, is published as posters; No. 4 appears on cassettes. No. 6 will be an exhibition of sculpture with a catalog and a collection of multiples." Circulation is 300, no subscriptions. Each issue of the magazine carries an individual price tag. A copy of ***Poets. Painters. Composers.*** **No. 5 is $50. Sample of No. 2 available for $10.50 postpaid. Sample of *Colin's Magazine* is available for $7. "Contributors' poetry receives great care. All material is returned right away unless (a) it's being painstakingly examined for acceptance into the journal or (b) it's being considered as right for some other way of publishing it or (c) we died." Contributors receive 1 copy. Acquires one-time rights.** "We prefer short (500-800 word) reviews unless we already have asked for a longer piece from a poet/reviewer because of his or her interest in the book." He expects to publish 3 chapbooks of poetry a year and will accept unsolicited submissions. **For chapbook publication poets should query first "if poet prefers," sending credits, 7 sample poems, bio, philosophy and poetic aims. Pay for chapbooks will be in author's copies, number negotiable ("We're generous"); honorariums are given whenever possible.** Format of the chapbooks is expected to be "small, avant-garde, distinguished, exciting, experimental." Joseph Keppler says, "Poets' work is important work, and poetry is a most difficult art today. We maintain absolutely high standards, yet offer a hopeful critique . . . . We want to develop the avant-garde here and everywhere. We expect to last well into the 21st century and to change the way this culture understands literature. We intend to transform the role of poets in society. Advice for beginning poets? We're all beginning poets today."

POETS PEN QUARTERLY; M&M PUBLISHING (I, IV-Children/teens/young adults), Dept PM, 233 E. Wacker Dr., Chicago IL 60601, phone (312)946-8213, poetry editor Marlena Zohimsky, is a quarterly poetry publication including a Children's Corner and a Featured Poet in each issue. **"Poetry types/form open but no smut or slander. No epics. Children and young writer submittals encouraged."** It is approximately 50-60 pgs., 8½×11, tape-bound with glossy paper cover. **Sample postpaid: $6. No previously published poems. Cover letter with bio and photo preferred. Send SASE for guidelines. Reports within 2 weeks, international takes longer. "No payment for published submittals."**

POET'S REVIEW (I, IV-Subscribers), P.O. Box I, 806 Kings Row, Varnell GA 30756, phone (706)694-8441, founded 1988, publisher Bob Riemke, is a monthly booklet, digest-sized, 28 pgs., photocopied from typescript with paper cover, using **poetry by subscribers** and making cash awards monthly and annually on basis of votes by subscribers. **"Prefer rhyme. Short poems, 44 lines or less. Open to limericks and humor. Any subject. No porn! No foreign languages."** They have published poetry by Helen Webb, Ashley Anders and J. Alvin Speers. Subscription: $36. **Sample postpaid: $4. Publishes theme issues. Send SASE for upcoming themes. Themes for 1995 include Mother's Day, Father's Day and Christmas. "Subscribers are sent a ballot along with their monthly booklet to vote for the poems they believe to be the best." Monthly prizes are $75, $50 and $25, plus 7 honorable mentions. "All $75 winners are presented to the subscribers again at the end of the year and compete for a $500, $250 and $100 prize."** 30-50 poems are printed each month along with the names of winners for the previous month. ***Poet's Review*** ranked #4 in the "Open Markets" category of the latest ***Writer's Digest*** Poetry 60 list. This category ranks those publications most open to both free and formal verse.

POETS' ROUNDTABLE; POETS' STUDY CLUB OF TERRE HAUTE; POETS' STUDY CLUB INTERNATIONAL CONTEST (I, IV-Membership), 826 S. Center St., Terre Haute IN 47807, phone (812)234-0819, founded in 1939, president/editor Esther Alman. Poets' Study Club is one of the oldest associations of amateur poets. It publishes, every other month, ***Poets' Roundtable***, a newsletter of market and contest information and news of the publications and activities of its members in a mimeographed, 10-page bulletin (magazine-sized, stapled at the corner, on colored paper), circulation 2,000. They have also published an occasional chapbook-anthology of poetry by members "but do not often do so." **Dues: $6 a year. Sample free for SASE. Uses short poems by members only. Simultaneous submissions and previously published poems OK.** They offer an annual Poets' Study Club International Contest, open to all, with no fees and cash prizes—a $25 and $15 award in 3 categories: traditional haiku, serious poetry, light verse. Deadline: February 1. Also contests for members only each two months. "We have scheduled criticism programs for members only."

POINT JUDITH LIGHT (IV-Form/style), P.O. Box 6145, Springfield MA 01101, founded 1992, editor Patrick Frank, is a biannual publishing individual haiku/senryu, sequences and essays on Eastern philosophy and creativity theory. They want **haiku/senryu "which explore the relation of the poet to his/her environment and which focus on life as truly lived; 17 syllables maximum."** They have recently published haiku/senryu by H.F. Noyes, Elizabeth St. Jacques and Alexis Rotella. As a sample the editor selected these haiku/senryu by Gloria H. Proscal and the editor respectively:

rain
the billboard girl's
autumn tears

beside the ghetto court
hidden in the weeds—
cricket.

PJL is desktop-published in a newsletter format, 20 pgs. maximum. Press run is 300. Subscription: $6/year. **Sample postpaid: $3. Previously published poems OK; no simultaneous submissions. Send 20 haiku/senryu maximum. Submissions should be typed. Cover letter with bio required.** "I want to have some knowledge of the poet behind the work and publish a brief bio." **Often comments on rejections. Send SASE for guidelines. Reports within 1 month. Pays 1 copy. Acquires first rights.** The editor says, "Focus on the aspects of life that are immediately before you. Be yourself. Follow your intuition and be willing to explore and experiment. With James J.Y. Liu, I see poetry as a vehicle to explore external and internal worlds, as well as the language in which it is written. I am particularly interested in promoting the development of haiku/senryu sequencing in English. I am also exploring the connection between haiku, Eastern philosophy and creativity theory. Children's haiku are welcome. Politically relevant haiku are welcome, if they are imagistic and grounded in concrete experience. I also publish sports-related haiku."

THE POINTED CIRCLE (II), 705 N. Killingsworth, Portland OR 97217, phone (503)244-6111, ext. 5230, founded 1980, advisor Rachel Stevens, is an annual. They want poems **"under 60 lines, mostly shorter. One-page poems on any topic of any form."** They have published poetry by Judith Barrington, William Stafford, Dianne Averill and Barbara Drake. As a sample the editor selected these lines from "Jessie" by Michael Ishii:

She folds her hands like a dry dish towel,
remembers leftover rain from last evening,
unexpected, the smell of wet bark and turned-up
dirt. Her bread drawer, full. She bends over dishes.
The sky out her window is rough like a cutting board;
it opens in anger, each raindrop finding
its target, collecting in drainpipes.

It is 80 pgs., flat-spined, with b&w glossy card cover, professionally printed. Press run is 400. **Sample postpaid: $3.50. Cover letter required. Submit mss from December 1 through February 15 only. "Place name, address, etc., on cover sheet only, listing titles of submissions. Limit 5 poems/poet. All submissions are read anonymously by student editorial staff; notification about June 1 for submissions received by February 15." Send SASE for guidelines. Pays 1 copy. Acquires one-time rights.**

POLYPHONIES (III, IV-Translations), 85, rue de Pa Santé, 75073 Paris, France, founded 1985, editor Pascal Culerrier. Editorial committee: Laurence Breysse, Emmanuelle Dagnaud, Jean-Yves Masson and Alexis Pelletier. Appears twice a year. **"Every case is a special one. We want to discover the new important voices of the world to open French literature to the major international productions. For example, we published Brodsky in French when he was not known in our country and had not yet the Nobel Prize. No vocal poetry, no typographic effects."** They have published poetry by Mario Luzi (Italy), Jeremy Reed (Great Britain), Octavio Paz (Mexico) and Claude Michel Cluny (France). It is about 110 pgs., 6½×9½, flat-spined, with glossy card cover, printed completely in French. Press run is 850 for 300 subscribers. **Uses translations of previously published poems. Pays 2 copies.** The editor says, "Our review is still at the beginning. We are in touch with many French editors. Our purpose is to publish together, side-by-side, poets of today and of yesterday."

"The idea for this 1993 cover originated back in the summer of 1968 when my brother and I were deeply into counter-cultural activities, a.k.a. 'secret hippie stuff,' " says Daniel Struckman, publisher of* The Portable Wall*, a biannual magazine based in Billings, Montana. The cover illustration is a wood engraved self-portrait by Montana artist Dirk Lee. "We have a number of regular contributors such as Dave Thomas, FL Light, Daniel Quinn, Kathleen Taylor, Ivon White and Lyn Lifshin," says Struckman. "They send us letters and poems and we often print both. However, we currently have more poetry than we can publish."

PORTABLE WALL (V), 215 Burlington, Billings MT 59101, phone (406)256-3588, founded 1977, publisher Daniel Struckman. He publishes, as Ezra Pound described, **"words that throw the object on to the visual imagination and that induce emotional correlations by the sound and rhythm of the speech."** He has published poetry by Dave Thomas and Joe Salerno. As a sample he selected these lines by Kathleen Taylor:

Lightning rams down
a cloud-clotted sky;
the red moon is wasted.

PW is published twice a year. It is 40 pgs., saddle-stapled, on heavy tinted stock with 2-color matte card cover. Press run is 200. Subscription: $15 for 2 years. **Sample postpaid: $5. Currently not accepting poetry submissions.** The editor says, "I have more poetry than I can print."

‡PORTLAND REVIEW (II), Box 751-SD, Portland State University, Portland OR 97207, phone (503)725-4533, founded 1954, is a literary annual published by Portland State University 3 times a year. **"Experimental poetry welcomed. No poems over 3 pages. No rhyming poetry."** The annual is magazine-sized, about 128 pgs. They accept about 30 of 300 poems received each year. Press run is 500 for 100 subscribers of which 10 are libraries. **Sample: $5. Simultaneous submissions OK. Send SASE for guidelines. Pays 1 copy.**

POST-INDUSTRIAL PRESS (III), P.O. Box 265, Greensboro PA 15338, founded 1989, publishes 1-3 paperbacks/year. They have published poetry by Georges Perec and Johannes Poethen. **No simultaneous submissions. Replies to queries in 1 month.**

POTATO EYES; NIGHTSHADE PRESS (II), P.O. Box 76, Troy ME 04987-0076, phone (207)948-3427, founded 1988, editors Roy Zarucchi and Carolyn Page, is a semiannual literary arts journal **"with a focus on writers who write about the land and/or quality of life close to the earth. We now accept submissions from throughout the U.S. and Canada, although much of our poetry is from Appalachian states."** They have recently published poetry by Linda L. Harper, Barbara Presnell, Jack Coulehan, Joe Bathanti and Willie James King. As a sample the editors selected these lines from "You Never Get To The Horizon" by Ava Leavell Haymon, published in her new chapbook **Built in Fear of Heat**:

In the delta, you're ringed by horizons.
The great plowed land is flat as Holland
and all the trees were cut down with the Indians.
The taste of dust in your mouth there
is flavored always by cotton poison.
The air must have tasted like that
in Berlin, between the wars.

PE is 5½×8½, 100 pgs., flat-spined, professionally printed, with block cut matte paper cover. Circulation is 800. Subscription: $11 (Canadian $14). **Sample postpaid: $6 (back issue $5), or $7 Canadian. The editors say, "those who submit receive a handwritten rejection/acceptance. We are open to any form other than rhymed, in batches of 3-5, but we tend to favor poetry with concrete visual imagery, solid intensity and compression. We respect word courage and risk-taking, along with thoughtful lineation. We prefer rebellious to complacent poetry. We prefer a cover letter with brief bio along with SASE." Reports in 1-2 months. Pays 1 copy. Acquires first North American serial rights.** Reviews books of poetry. Open to unsolicited reviews. Poets may also send books for review consideration. Nightshade Press is the imprint under which they publish about 10 chapbooks/year, each 24-48 pgs., "usually with block print or pen-and-ink covers, endsheets and recycled 60 lb. text, 80 lb. covers. **Chapbooks are selected from competitions, mainly, but a few may be from poets who appear first in our magazine." Send SASE for catalog and information and/or send $5 for sample chapbook.** They advise, "Beginning poets should devour as much good poetry as possible in order to delineate their own style and voice. Look for a match between substance and sound."

‡POTES & POETS PRESS, INC.; ABACUS (III), 181 Edgemont Ave., Elmwood CT 06110, phone (203)233-2023, press founded in 1981, magazine in 1984, editor Peter Ganick. The press publishes avant-garde poetry in magazine form under the *Abacus* imprint, one writer per 20-page issue. The P+Pinc books are perfect-bound and range from 80-120 pages in trade editions. **In addition to avant-garde, they want experimental or language-oriented poetry, not too much concrete poetry. No "*New Yorker* magazine, *Ploughshares* magazine, mainstream poetry."** They have published poems by Ron Silliman, Jackson Mac Low, Charles Bernstein, Leslie Scalapino, Carla Harryman and Rachel Blau Du Plessis. *Abacus* is magazine-sized, photocopied, no graphics, 12-18 pgs.; it appears every 6 weeks. Circulation is 150, of which 40 are subscriptions and 10 go to libraries. Price per issue is $4, subscription $26/year. **Sample available for $4.50 postpaid. Simultaneous submissions are OK. Pay is 12 copies. Unsolicited submissions are accepted for book publication. Writers should "just send the manuscript." However, they rarely accept mss from authors new to the press.** The press publishes 4 books of poetry/year with an average page count of 100, flat-spined paperbacks.

POTPOURRI (II), P.O. Box 8278, Prairie Village KS 66208, founded 1989, poetry editor Pat Anthony, haiku editor Carl Bettis, is a monthly tabloid "to publish works of writers, **including new and unpublished writers. We want strongly voiced original poems in either free verse or traditional. Traditional work must represent the best of the craft. No religious, confessional, racial, political, erotic, abusive or sexual preference materials unless fictional and necessary to plot or characterization. No concrete/visual poetry (because of format)."** They have published poetry by Bernard Morris, David Ray and Gabriel Neruda. As a sample the editor selected these lines from "Flight 532-Houston to MPLS" by Diane Glancy:

> *You know there's rain that falls so high it dries before*
> *it gets to earth. You see it spill from clouds on a high*
> *flight. And one spook of a cloud with its ladle stirring*
> *a backyard kettle. But you leave it spinning. . .*

It is 32 pgs. Press run is 6,000-10,000 for 550 subscribers of which 20 are libraries, "over 500 distributed to other publications through *Potpourri*'s networking program and the balance distributed free to libraries, bookstores, universities, hospitals, community centers and others." Subscription: $15. **Sample postpaid: $1.50. Submit no more than 3 poems, no more than 1/page, length to 75 lines (approximately 30 preferred). Submit seasonal themes 6 months in advance. Address haiku and related forms to Carl Bettis. "*Potpourri*** publishes reprints of exceptional materials only from submissions by other magazines." **Send SASE for guidelines. Reports in 8-10 weeks at most. Pays 1-20 copies (poet's request). Acquires first North American serial rights.** The David Ray Poetry Award ($100 or more, depending upon grant monies) is given annually for best of volume. They also publish a line of ***Potpourri Petites***, 20-24 pgs., 4×8, set in 9.5 pt. type. "At present, we do not accept unsolicited submissions. New poets can establish themselves for consideration by solid acceptances in ***Potpourri*** and through other credits." ***Potpourri*** recently received the 1994 Governor's Arts Award sponsored by the Kansas Arts Commission in recognition of its "outstanding contribution to the excellence of literary arts in Kansas." The editor advises, "Keep your new poems around long enough to become friends with them before parting. Let them ripen, and, above all, learn to be your own best editor. To borrow from William Carlos Williams, strive to let your particular 'specific' idea or poem be window to universality for your reader. Let them *in* to your work and write *for* an audience in terms of professionality and clarity. Unrequited love, favorite pets and description that seems to be written for its own sake find little chance."

PRAIRIE FIRE (III), Room 423, 100 Arthur St., Winnipeg, Manitoba R3B 1H3 Canada, phone (204)943-9066, founded 1978, editor Andris Taskans, is a quarterly magazine of new writing including fiction, poetry and reviews. They want **"poetry that articulates a connection between language and ethics, an aesthetic of writing 'from the body', and open to the nuances of orality, ethnic and racial differences and feminism. No haiku, sonnets or other rhyming forms, nor political or religious treatises in verse form."** They have recently published poetry by Di Brandt, Elizabeth Brewster and Kristjana Gunnars. As a sample the editor selected these lines from "talking 3 a.m." by Patrick Friesen:

it's 3 a.m. and I remember the fall of white silk from my love's shoulders
the mole on her left arm her slender thighs
remembering again and again what matters losing the rest in small
blowouts of the brain and the radio's noise
I want to say something about love how it's flesh only for a while how
it's words for a long time

Prairie Fire is 128 pgs., 6×9, offset, perfect-bound, glossy card cover, illustrations and ads. They receive 400-500 submissions (average 6 poems each), accept approximately 2%. Press run is 1,700 for 1,100 subscribers of which 100 are libraries, 150 shelf sales. Single copy: $7.95; subscription: $24 Canadian, $28 US. **Sample postpaid: $8 Canadian. No previously published poems or simultaneous submissions. Cover letter required. Include other publications, brief biographical information, list of poems submitted, name, address and phone number. Submissions should be typed, double-spaced, one poem to a page, name and address on each page, no more than 6 poems at a time. Reads submissions September 1 through June 30 only.** Time between acceptance and publication is 1 year. **Seldom comments on rejections. Publishes theme issues. Send SASE (or SAE and IRC) for guidelines and upcoming themes. Reports in 3-4 months. Pays $35 for first page, $20 for each additional page, plus 1 copy. Buys first Canadian serial rights only.** Staff reviews books of poetry in 500-2,000 words, single or multi-book format. Send books for review consideration. The editor says, "Be patient!"

‡THE PRAIRIE JOURNAL (II); PRAIRIE JOURNAL PRESS (IV-Regional, themes), P.O. Box 61203, Brentwood Post Office, 217-3630 Brentwood Rd. NW, Calgary, Alberta T2L 2K6 Canada, founded 1983, editor A. Burke, who wants to see **poetry of "any length, free verse, contemporary themes (feminist, nature, urban, non-political), aesthetic value, a poet's poetry." Does not want to see "most rhymed verse, sentimentality, egotistical ravings. No cowboys or sage brush."** They have published poetry by Mick Burrs, Lorna Crozier, Mary Melfi, Art Cuelho and John Hicks. ***Prairie Journal*** is 7½×8½, 40-60 pgs., offset with card cover, b&w drawings and ads, appearing twice a year. They accept about 10% of the 200 or so poems they receive a year. Press run is 500 per issue, 150 subscriptions of which 60% are libraries. Subscription: $6 for individuals, $12 for libraries. **Sample postpaid: $3. No simultaneous submissions or previously published poems. Guidelines available for postage (but "no U.S. stamps, please"—get IRCs from the post office). "We will not be reading submissions until such time as an issue is in preparation (twice yearly), so be patient and we will acknowledge, accept for publication or return work at that time." Sometimes sends prepublication galleys. Pays 1 copy. Acquires first North American serial rights.** Reviews books of poetry "but must be assigned by editor. Query first." **For chapbook publication, Canadian poets only (preferably from the region) should query with 5 samples, bio, publications. Responds to queries in 2 months, to mss in 6 months. Payment in modest honoraria.** They have recently published **Voices From Earth**, selected poems by Ronald Kurt and Mark McCawley. "We also publish anthologies on themes when material is available. **Prairie Journal Poetry 2**, an anthology of new poetry, was published in 1992." A. Burke advises, "Read recent poets! Experiment with line length, images, metaphors. Innovate."

THE PRAIRIE PUBLISHING COMPANY (III, IV-Regional), Dept. PM, Box 2997, Winnipeg, Manitoba R3C 4B5 Canada, phone (204)885-6496, founded 1963, publisher Ralph E. Watkins, is a "small press catering to regional market, local history, fantasy, poetry and nonfiction," with flat-spined paperbacks. They want **"basically well-crafted poems of reasonable length" and do not want to see "the work of rank amateurs and tentative and time-consuming effort."** They have published collections of poetry by Brian Richardson and Brian MacKinnon. Their books are handsomely produced, 6×9, using b&w photos and art along with the poems, glossy card covers. They publish about 1 a year, 68 pgs. **Samples available at a 20% discount—send SASE or SAE and IRC for catalog. Query with samples. Simultaneous submissions OK. Do not submit mss during summer. Responds to queries in 6 weeks.** Nancy Watkins notes, "Robert E. Pletta's point that most poets need to do more reading is well taken. We would endorse this suggestion."

PRAIRIE SCHOONER; STROUSSE PRIZE; SLOTE PRIZE; FAULKNER AWARD; STANLEY AWARD; READERS' CHOICE AWARDS (II), 201 Andrews, University of Nebraska, Lincoln NE 68588-0334, phone (402)472-3191, founded 1927, editor Hilda Raz; "one of the oldest literary quarterlies in continuous publication; publishes poetry, fiction, personal essays, interviews and reviews." They want **"poems that fulfill the expectations they set up." No specifications as to form, length, style, subject matter or purpose. No simultaneous submissions.** They have published poetry by Carl Dennis, Albert Goldbarth, Sharon Hashimoto, Joan Murray, Alicia Ostriker, David Slavitt and Marcia Southwick. As a sample the editor selected these lines from "How to Get in the Best Magazines" by Eleanor Wilner:

it is time to write
the acceptable poem—
ice and glass, with its splinter
of bone, its pit
of an olive,
the dregs
of the cup of abundance,
useless spill of gold
from the thresher, the dust
of it filling the sunlight, the chum
broadcast on the black waters
and the fish
—the beautiful, ravenous fish—
refusing to rise.

The magazine is 6×9, flat-spined, 176 pgs. and uses 70-80 pgs. of poetry in each issue. They receive about 4,000 mss (of all types)/year from which they choose 300 pgs. of poetry. Press run is 3,100. Subscription: $20/year; $6.45/copy. **Sample postpaid: $3.50. Submit 5-7 poems. "Clear copy appreciated." Publishes theme issues. Send SASE for guidelines. Reports in 2-3 months; "sooner if possible." Always sends prepublication galleys. Pays copies. Acquires all rights. Returns rights upon request without fee.** Reviews books of poetry. Open to unsolicited reviews. Poets may also send books for review consideration. One of the most influential magazines being published today (often named as such in independent surveys of creative writers), this publication is genuinely open to excellent work in any form: lyric, narrative, dramatic, traditional, etc. Send only your best work, as competition is keen. Brief reviews are an excellent way to break into the journal. Editor Hilda Raz also promotes poets whose work has appeared in her pages by listing their continued accomplishments in a special section (even when their work does not concurrently appear in the magazine). The $500 Strousse Prize is awarded to the best poetry published in the magazine each year. The Slote Prize for beginning writers ($500), the Stanley Award for Poetry ($300) and six other ***PS*** prizes are also awarded, as well as the Faulkner Award for Excellence in Writing ($1,000). Also, each year 5-10 Readers' Choice Awards ($250 each) are given for poetry, fiction and nonfiction. Editors serve as judges. ***Prairie Schooner*** ranked #1 in the "New Poets" category of the latest ***Writer's Digest*** Poetry 60 list. This category ranks those markets who often publish poets whose work is new to their publication. Hilda Raz comments, "***Prairie Schooner*** receives a large number of poetry submissions; we're not unusual. We don't have time to comment on mss, but the magazine's reputation is evidence of our careful reading. We've been dedicated to the publication of good poems for a very long time and have published work early in the career of many successful poets."

PRAIRIE WINDS (II), Box 159, Dakota Wesleyan University, 1200 University Ave., Mitchell SD 57301, phone (605)995-2633, editor Joseph M. Ditta, is an annual of poetry, fiction, short essays, photos and art. **They are open to all forms, lengths, styles and subjects of poetry except pornographic.** They have published poetry by Simon Perchik, Aaron Kramer, David Ignatow and Henry Hughes. The editor says ***PW*** is 50-60 pgs., 7½×9¼, offset, bound, gloss litho, no ads. They accept approximately 25% of the poetry received each year. Press run is 500 for 50 subscribers of which 10 are libraries. The rest are distributed free to professors and students. **Sample postpaid: $4. No previously published poems; simultaneous submissions OK. Cover letter required. "We are an annual, published in spring. All submissions must arrive by January 15." Reads submissions January 15 through February 15 only. Seldom comments on rejections. Send SASE for guidelines. Reports by end of February. Pays 1 copy.**

PRAKALPANA LITERATURE; KOBISENA (I, IV-Bilingual, form), P-40 Nandana Park, Calcutta 700034, West Bengal, India, ***Kobisena*** founded 1972, ***Prakalpana Literature*** press founded 1974, magazine 1977, editor Vattacharja Chandan, who says, "We are small magazines which publish only *Prakalpana* (a mixed form of prose and poetry), Sarbangin (whole) poetry, experimental b&w art and photographs, essays on Prakalpana movement and Sarbangin poetry movement, letters, literary news and very few books on Prakalpana and Sarbangin literature. **Purpose and form: for advancement of poetry in the super-space age, the poetry must be really experimental and avant-garde using mathematical signs and symbols and visualizing the pictures inherent in the alphabet (within typography) with sonorous effect accessible to people. That is Sarbangin poetry. Length: within 30 lines (up to 4 poems). Prakalpana is a mixed form of prose, poetry, essay, novel, story, play with visual effect and it is not at all short story as it is often misunderstood. Better send 6 IRCs to read *Prakalpana Literature* first and then submit. Length: within 16 pages (up to 2 prakalpanas) at a time. Subject matter: society, nature, cosmos, humanity, love, peace, etc. Style: own. We do not want to see traditional, conventional, academic, religious, mainstream and poetry of prevailing norms and forms."** They have recently published poetry by Dilip Gupta, Arun Kumar Chakraborty, t. Winter-Damon and Susan Smith Nash. As a sample the editor chose these lines by Richard Frankfother:

Change current Energy Field density and get
Reaction.
←Big Bang—X—Big Bang—X—Big Bang—→
Contraction = Expansion.
And true Vacuum = False.

Prakalpana Literature, an annual, is 120 pgs., 7×4½, saddle-stapled, printed on thin stock with matte card cover. ***Kobisena***, which appears once a year, is 16 pgs., digest-sized, a newsletter format with no cover. Both are hand composed and printed by letterpress. Both use both English and Bengali. They use about 10% of some 400 poems received/year. The press run is 1,000 for each, and each has about 450 subscriptions of which 50 are libraries. **Samples: 15 rupees for *Prakalpana*, 4 rupees for *Kobisena*. Overseas: 6 IRCs and 2 IRCs respectively or exchange of avant-garde magazines. Simultaneous submissions OK. Previously published poetry OK. Cover letter with short bio and small photo/sketch of poet/writer/artist required. Publication within a year. After being published in the magazines, poets may be included in future anthologies with translations into Bengali/English if and when necessary. "Joining with us is welcome but not a pre-condition." Editor comments on rejections "if wanted." Send SAE with IRC for guidelines. No reporting time given. Sometimes sends prepublication galleys. Pays 1 copy.** Reviews books of poetry, fiction and art, "but preferably experimental books." Open to unsolicited reviews. Poets, writers and artists may also send books for review consideration. He says, "We believe that only through poetry, fiction and art, the deepest feelings of humanity as well as nature and the cosmos can be best expressed and conveyed to the peoples of the ages to come. And only poetry can fill up the gap in the peaceless hearts of dispirited peoples, resulted from the retreat of god and religion with the advancement of hi-tech. So, in an attempt, since the inception of Prakalpana Movement in 1969, to reach that goal in the avant-garde and experimental way we stand for Sarbangin poetry. And to poets and all concerned with poetry we wave the white handkerchief saying (in the words of Vattacharja Chandan) 'We want them who want us.' "

THE PRESBYTERIAN RECORD (IV-Inspirational, religious), 50 Wynford Dr., Don Mills, Ontario M3C 1J7 Canada, phone (416)441-1111, founded 1876, is "the national magazine that serves the membership of The Presbyterian Church in Canada (and many who are not Canadian Presbyterians). We seek to stimulate, inform, inspire, to provide an 'apologetic' and a critique of our church and the world (not necessarily in that order!)." They want **poetry which is "inspirational, Christian, thoughtful, even satiric but *not* maudlin. No 'sympathy card' type verse a la Edgar Guest or Francis Gay. It would take a *very* exceptional poem of epic length for us to use it. Shorter poems, 10-30 lines, preferred. Blank verse OK (if it's not just rearranged prose). 'Found' poems. Subject matter should have some Christian import (however subtle)."** They have published poetry by Jean Larsen, Jeanne Davis, Joan Stortz, Marlow C. Dickson, Len Selle and J.R. Dickey. The magazine comes out 11 times a year. Press run is 64,000. Subscription: $11. **Submit seasonal work 6 weeks before month of publication. Simultaneous submissions OK. Poems should be typed, double-spaced. Pays $20-50/poem. Buys one-time rights.** Staff reviews books of poetry. Send books for review consideration. ***The Presbyterian Record*** has won several Canadian Church Press Awards.

‡PRESCOTT STREET PRESS (V, IV-Regional), Box 40312, Portland OR 97240-0312, founded 1974, poetry editor Vi Gale: "**Poetry and fine print from the Northwest.**" Vi Gale says, "Our books and cards are the product of many hands from poet, artist, printer, designer, typesetter to bookstore and distributor. Somewhere along the line the editor/publisher [herself] arranges to pay one and all in the same way. Sometimes we have had grant help from the NEA and also from state and metropolitan arts organizations. But most of our help has come from readers, friends and the poets and artists themselves. Everyone has worked very hard. And we are immodestly pleased with our labors! **We are not a strictly regional press, although the poets I take on are connected with the Northwest in some way when we bring out the books. We are chronically overstocked with poetry.**" Vi Gale publishes a series of postcards, notecards, paperback and hardback books of poetry in various artistic formats with illustrations by nationally known artists. Send SASE for catalog to order copies. As a sample, here are lines by Rolf Aggestam from a postcard:

muttering. cold
hands split fresh kindling
damn
what a life. you are far away.
in the darkness we used to call
each other forth
with fingers and a few small words.
we created a little border
between darkness and darkness.

Considers simultaneous submissions. Sometimes sends prepublication galleys. "We pay all of our poets. A modest sum, perhaps, but we pay everyone something."

THE PRESS OF MACDONALD & REINECKE (II); PADRE PRODUCTIONS (I), P.O. Box 840, Arroyo Grande CA 93421-0840, phone (805)473-1947, founded 1974, poetry editor Lachlan P. MacDonald. Padre Productions prints books on a fee basis, as a book packager. MacDonald & Reinecke **requires the poet to "purchase 200 copies of an edition (at liberal discounts)" but they do not consider themselves subsidy publishers. They publish under the M&R imprint only work they consider of merit and in which they, like the poet, must invest.** "The press is a division of Padre Productions bringing together under one imprint drama, fiction, literary nonfiction and poetry. We publish poetry in broadsides, flat-spined paperbacks, chapbooks and hardcover. We are looking for **poetry of literary merit and also poetry suitable for travel and nature photo books. We are averse to tightly rhymed conventional poetry unless designed to appeal to the general humor market."** They have published Terre Ouwehand's **Voices from the Well**, Steven Schmidt's **Avigation and Other Poems** and Phyllis K. Collier's **Daughters of Cain. Query with 5-6 samples, publication credits, bio. The editor also wants to know "do they give readings or have marketing opportunities? Some authors distribute fliers to build up pre-publication orders sufficient to justify the print order." Replies to queries in 2-4 weeks, to submissions (if invited) in 2-6 months. Simultaneous submissions OK. Ms should be double-spaced. Pays minimum of 4% royalties, 6 copies. The editor "frequently makes brief comments" on rejections. Send 6×9 SASE for catalog.** The editor advises, "Poets who have not published 10 or 20 poems in literary magazines are unlikely to have developed the craft we require. We also prefer books with a unifying theme rather than a sampling reflecting the author's virtuosity."

THE PRESS OF THE NIGHTOWL (V), 320 Snapfinger Dr., Athens GA 30605, phone (706)353-7719, founded 1965, owner Dwight Agner, publishes 1-2 paperbacks and 1-2 hardbacks each year. They have published poetry by Paul Zimmer, Stephen Corey, Mary Anne Coleman and C.K. Williams. **However, they are currently not accepting unsolicited poetry submissions. Pays author's copies. Sample books may be ordered directly from the publisher or located through bookstores.**

THE PRESS OF THE THIRD MIND (IV-Form), #6P, 65 E. Scott St., Chicago IL 60610, phone (312)337-3122, founded 1985, poetry editor Rasta Purina, is a small press publisher of artist books, poetry and fiction in glass bottles, tape measures, paperbacks, broadsides, T-shirts and Tarot cards. **"We are especially interested in the cut-up/fold-in technique, concrete poetry, translations, collaborative *(Exquisite Corpse)* poetry, found poems, Dada, surrealism, etc."** They have published poetry by "Pessoa, Spiro, Cesariny, Mansour and Lamantia." As a sample the editor selected these lines from "Frisco Spleen" by G. Sutton Breiding:

Dark city
I have stripped shadows of
concrete
From your flesh
To find my face

Asked how much poetry they typically receive each year and how much they accept, the editor said, "We get about 6 metric tons and accept it all for fireplace logs." They have a press run of 1,000 with 100 subscriptions of which 38 are libraries. **Sample postpaid: $5. *"No dot matrix!!!"* Simultaneous submissions OK, if noted. Cover letter preferred. They have sometimes used previously published poetry and have simultaneously published with *Exquisite Corpse*. Pay? *"Surely you jest!"* But contributors can have all the copies they can photocopy.** Reviews books of poetry. Press of the Third Mind publishes 2 flat-spined paperbacks, 56 pgs., each year. They most recently published **Concave Buddha and Other Public Disservice Announcements** (paperback). **For book publication submit 20 sample poems, bio and credits. Responds to queries in 1 week, mss in 3 weeks. "Just ask for free samples and include a substantial 'love offering.'" Editor comments on rejections.** His advice: "Absolute zero corrupts absolutely; Absolut Vodka boils at Fahrenheit 491."

PRIMAVERA (II, IV-Women), P.O. Box #37-7547, Chicago IL 60637, phone (312)324-5920, founded 1975, co-editor Ruth Young, is "an irregularly published but approximately annual magazine of poetry and fiction reflecting **the experiences of women. We look for strong, original voice and imagery, generally prefer free verse, fairly short length, related, even tangentially, to women's experience."** They have recently published poetry by Janet McCann, Krystyna Lars, Anna Czekanowicz, Jacqueline Hartwich and Susan Murphy. As a sample the editors selected these lines by Maxine Clair:

She is smiling. She will whirl
among the figures holding tight
onto the clothesline. The sun's light
will change and I will follow her.

The elegantly printed publication, flat-spined, generously illustrated with photos and graphics, uses 30-35 pgs. of poetry in each issue. Circulation is 1,000. They receive over 1,000 submissions of poetry/year, use 32. Single copy: $9. **Sample postpaid: $5. No simultaneous submissions. Submit no more than 6 poems anytime, no queries. Editors comment on rejections "when requested or inspired." Send SASE for guidelines. Reports in 1-2 months. Pays 2 copies. Acquires first-time rights.**

PRINCETON UNIVERSITY PRESS; LOCKERT LIBRARY OF POETRY IN TRANSLATION (IV-Translations, bilingual), 41 William St., Princeton NJ 08540, phone (609)258-4900. "In the Lockert Library series, we publish simultaneous cloth and paperback (flat-spine) editions for each poet. Clothbound editions are on acid-free paper, and binding materials are chosen for strength and durability. Each book is given individual design treatment rather than stamped into a series mold. We have published a wide range of poets from other cultures, including well-known writers such as Hölderlin and Cavafy, and those who have not yet had their due in English translation, such as Ingeborg Bachmann and Faiz Ahmed Faiz. Manuscripts are judged with several criteria in mind: the ability of the translation to stand on its own as poetry in English; fidelity to the tone and spirit of the original, rather than literal accuracy; and the importance of the translated poet to the literature of his or her time and country." The editor says, "All our books in this series are heavily subsidized to break even. We have internal funds to cover deficits of publishing costs. We do not, however, publish books chosen and subsidized by other agencies, such as AWP. **Our series is an open competition, for which the 'award' is publication." Simultaneous submissions OK if you tell them. Cover letter required. Send mss only during respective reading periods stated in guidelines. "We comment on semifinalists only." Send SASE for guidelines to submit. Reports in 2-3 months. Pays royalties (5% or more) on paperback and 12 author's copies.** In 1993 the press published **A Child Is Not a Knife: Selected Poems of Göran Sonnevi**, translated from the Swedish by Rika Lesser, who was awarded the 1992 American-Scandinavian Foundation Translation Prize for her work.

PRISM INTERNATIONAL (I, II), Dept. of Creative Writing, University of British Columbia, Vancouver, British Columbia V6T 1Z1 Canada, phone (604)822-2514, founded 1959, executive editors Shelley Darjes and Gregory Nyte. "***Prism*** is an international quarterly that publishes poetry, drama, short fiction, imaginative nonfiction and translation into English in all genres. We have no thematic or stylistic allegiances: Excellence is our main criterion for acceptance of mss. **We want poetry that shows an awareness of the tradition while reiterating its themes in a fresh and distinctive way. We read everything.**" They have published poetry by Daphne Marlatt, Al Purdy, Diana Hartog, Roo Borson and Bill Bissett. As a sample the editors selected these lines from "Too Much Brightness" by Lorna Crozier:

Now sun finds the lines it carved
from eye to jaw, around my mouth,
above my freckled knees. It seeks
them out like glacial melt
pushing the ancient river beds
closer to the sea. Soon I'll be
all running light and water.

Prism is elegantly printed in a flat-spined, 6×9 format, 80 pgs., original color artwork on the glossy card cover, circulation to 1,000 subscribers of which 200 are libraries. They receive 1,000 submissions/year, use 125, have 1-2 special issues/year, and a 1- to 3-month backlog. Subscription: $16. **Sample postpaid: $5. Submit a maximum of 6 poems at a time, any print so long as it's typed. Cover letter with brief introduction and previous publications required. Send Canadian SASE or SAE with IRCs for guidelines. Reports in 6-12 weeks ("or we write to poets to tell them we're holding onto their work for a while"). Pays $20/printed page plus subscription. Editors often comment on rejections. *Prism International*** is known in literary circles as one of the top journals in Canada. The editors say, "While we don't automatically discount any kind of poetry, we prefer to publish work that challenges the writer as much as it does the reader. We are particularly looking for poetry in translation."

PRISONERS OF THE NIGHT; MKASHEF ENTERPRISES (IV-Psychic/occult, science fiction/fantasy, horror, erotica), P.O. Box 688, Yucca Valley CA 92286-0688, poetry editor Alayne Gelfand. ***Prisoners of the Night***, founded 1987, **focusing on vampire erotica, uses poetry that is "erotic, unique, less horrific and more romantic, non-pornographic, original visions of the vampire."** Poets who have appeared recently in ***POTN*** include Keith Allen Daniels, Charlee Jacob, Ann K. Schwader and Steve Sneyd. As a sample the editor selected these lines from "Chiffon Draped Dreams" by Susan Youssef:

The beasts howl in the night.
Remembering your Kiss.
your glance.
A trance bewitched by a candle.
I go to bed full of flowers you never gave me.

Go to bed in yesterdays you put on me. . .

The intent of ***POTN*** is "to show the erotic, the romantic, rather than the horrific aspects of the vampire." It is 70-90 pgs., magazine-sized, perfect-bound, with color cover, produced by high-speed photocopying. Most poems are illustrated. It appears annually, usually in August. Of over 300 poems received/year they use between 10 and 20. It has an initial press run of 3,000, but each issue is kept in print. **Sample postpaid: $15 each (for #1-4), $12 (#5), $9.95 each (#6-7). Send SASE for guidelines. No more than 6 poems/submission. No simultaneous submissions or previously published poems, "unless they've only appeared in your own chapbook." Reading schedule: September 15 through March 31 annually. Editor sometimes comments on rejections. Reports "within 3 months." Pays $5/poem plus 1 copy. Buys first serial rights. *POTN* wants unusual visions of the vampire, not stereotypical characterizations.** The editor says, "We're *not* looking for your standard run-of-the-mist counts or countesses. The gothic loner in his run-down castle is the exact image we *do not* want. Stretch the boundaries of the vampire myth, let your imagination go! Take the reader some startling place we've never been before!"

PROOF ROCK PRESS; PROOF ROCK (I, II, IV-Humor), Box 607, Halifax VA 24558, founded 1982, poetry editors Serena Fusek and Don R. Conner. "We try to wake up a passive readership. We challenge our writers to search for something new under the sun and improve on the old." They want **"adventure, contemporary, humor/satire, fantasy and experimental poetry. Avoid overt sentimentality. Poems up to 32 lines. All subjects considered if well done."** The digest-sized magazine appears 2-3 times/year, is offset from typescript copy, colored matte card cover, with 30-40 pgs. in each issue. They receive 800-1,000 submissions/year, use 120-150, have a 3- to 6-month backlog. Press run is 300 for 100 subscribers of which 8-10 are libraries. Subscription: $4. **Sample postpaid: $2.50. Submit no more than 6 pieces, year round. No query needed, though some issues are on announced themes. Simultaneous submissions OK. Send SASE for guidelines. Reports "usually within 1 month." Pays 1 copy.** Proof Rock Press publishes an occasional anthology and collections by individuals. **Query with 8-10 samples, bio and publishing credits. Reply to queries in 1 month, to submissions (if invited) in 1-3 months. Simultaneous submissions OK. Pays copies. Send $2.50 for a sample chapbook. Editor sometimes comments on rejections.** His advice is, "Be introspective. Accept the challenge of looking within and write from experience."

PROPHETIC VOICES (II); HERITAGE TRAILS PRESS (V), 94 Santa Maria Dr., Novato CA 94947, founded 1982, poetry editors Ruth Wildes Schuler, Goldie L. Morales and Jeanne Leigh Schuler. "Our goal is to share thoughts on an international level. We see the poet's role as that of prophet, who points the way to a higher realm of existence." They publish ***Prophetic Voices*** twice a year and chapbooks. They want **"poetry of social commentary that deals with the important issues of our time. Poetry with beauty that has an international appeal. Do not want religious poetry or that with a limited scope. Open to any kind of excellent poetry, but publish mostly free verse. Limited number of long poems accepted due to lack of space."** They have published Jack Brooks, Hazel F. Goddard, A. Manoussos, B.Z. Niditch, H.F. Noyes, Gloria H. Procsal and Bo Yang. ***Prophetic Voices*** is digest-sized, 144 pgs., perfect-bound, offset from typescript with matte card cover, colored stock with graphics. They have 100 pgs. of poetry in each issue, circulation to 400 subscribers of which 10 are libraries. They receive 4,000 submissions/year, use 800, have a 5-year backlog. Single copy: $7; subscription: $14; $16 to libraries. **Sample postpaid: $5. Submit 4 poems or less. Reports in 1-8 weeks. Pays 1 copy. "Due to our excessive backlog, Heritage Trails can no longer read unsolicited mss."** The editors advise, "Be aware of what is going on in the world around you. Even the personal poem should have universal appeal if it is to survive the test of time."

THE PROSE POEM (II, IV-Form), 1004 Sycamore, San Marcos TX 78666, phone (512)353-4998, founded 1990, editor Steve Wilson, is an annual using **prose poems only. "I hope and pray the author knows what prose poetry is before submitting to me. For me 'prose poems' run from margin to margin, with no line breaks, and use intense, compact language."** They have published poetry by Linda Nemec Foster, Barry Silesky, Ray Gonzalez, Tom Whalen, Harriet Zinnes, Robert Bly and George Myers, Jr. The editor describes ***TPP*** as 60 pgs., professionally printed with card stock cover, saddle-stapled. Most selections are one paragraph or a few small ones, each about (or under) 200 words. Press run is 200. **Sample postpaid: $3. Publishes theme issues. Send SASE for upcoming themes. "Will read submissions September 1 through November 30, 1995 for 1995 issue. Submissions returned unread if received outside this reading period." Reports by 1 month after deadline. Pays 1 copy. Acquires first**

Use the General Index to find the page number of a specific publisher. If the publisher you are seeking is not listed, check the " '94-'95 Changes" list at the end of this section.

North American serial rights. Staff reviews books of poetry. Send books for review consideration. The editor says, "*TPP* is a journal focusing on one particular genre and publishing only the best work done in that genre. This does not mean an author cannot experiment. I encourage it. It also does not mean I don't want to see work from new writers. Please send, but only your best. I publish this magazine with my own money, so sales are very important. If you think prose poetry matters and like the idea of a journal dedicated to it, please help me keep it going by sending great work and subscribing."

PROSETRY: NEWSLETTER FOR, BY AND ABOUT WRITERS (I), The Write Place, P.O. Box 117727, Burlingame CA 94011, phone (415)347-7613, editor P.D. Steele, founded 1985. ***Prosetry*** is a monthly newsletter featuring "new and newly published poets and prose writers with a 'guest writer' column each month. Includes original poetry, new markets, contests, seminars, workshops and **general poetry potpourri gleaned from our subscribers." 50% freelance. Sample for 52¢ postage. Invites new writers. Send up to 3 poems, no more than 20 lines, English only. No profanity. Requires 2-line bio plus latest credits ("tell us if you've never been published"). Publishes theme issues. Guidelines and upcoming themes available for SASE. Themes for February, May and December are Love, Spring and Holidays, respectively. "All deadlines are first of month." Reports in less than 1 month. Pays one-year subscription. Acquires one-time rights; release required.** Reviews books of poetry in 150 words. Open to unsolicited reviews. "For 'guest writer' column we would prefer information relevant to the beginning or newly published writer/poet." Also publishes "How-to" ***CLIPS©*** for writers, $2.50 each. Free list for SASE. The editor says, "I'd like to receive less morose poetry and more humor."

‡THE PROSPECT REVIEW (V), 557 10th St., Brooklyn NY 11215, founded 1990, editor Peter A. Koufos, appears once a year. **"We no longer accept unsolicited mss."** The review is 85-90 pgs., 6×9, professionally printed, flat-spined, with glossy card cover. Press run is 500. The editor says, "If poets are truly legislators on this planet then the time is here for these artists to cast aside confessional affectations in their work and, in light of social problems now existing, create poetry for a new society."

PROVINCETOWN ARTS; PROVINCETOWN ARTS PRESS (II), 650 Commercial St., Provincetown MA 02657, phone (508)487-3167, founded 1985, editor Christopher Busa, is an elegant, flat-spined annual, 170 pgs., with full-color glossy cover, using quality poetry. "***Provincetown Arts*** focuses broadly on the artists and writers who inhabit or visit the tip of Cape Cod and seeks to stimulate creative activity and enhance public awareness of the cultural life of the nation's oldest continuous art colony. Drawing upon a century-long tradition rich in visual art, literature and theater, ***Provincetown Arts*** publishes material with a view towards demonstrating that the artists' colony, functioning outside the urban centers, is a utopian dream with an ongoing vitality." They have published poetry by Bruce Smith, Franz Wright, Sandra McPherson and Cyrus Cassells. As a sample the editor selected these lines from "Sky of Clouds" by Susan Mitchell:

And after heavy rains, when the egrets
settle on the gardens, cramming
their beaks with the shrill
cries of the frogs, I think
I could do that too, I could be gorgeous and cruel.

Press run is 10,000 for 500 subscribers of which 20 are libraries, 6,000 shelf sales. **Sample postpaid: $7.50. Reads submissions August through February. Reports in 2-3 months. Sometimes sends prepublication galleys. Pays $25-100/poem. Buys first rights.** Reviews books of poetry in 500-3,000 words, single or multi-book format. Open to unsolicited reviews. Poets may also send books for review consideration. The Provincetown Arts Press published 4 volumes of poetry in 1993, including **Rival Heavens** by Keith Althaus and **1990** by Michael Klein. ***Provincetown Arts*** has also had work published in **Pushcart Prize XVIII** and received first place in the 1993 American Literary Magazine Awards for editorial content and design. In addition, two poems by Susan Mitchell ("Sky of Clouds" and "Rapture"), published in ***Provincetown Arts***, have been included in **The Best American Poetry** (1991 and 1993, respectively).

PSYCHOPOETICA (II, IV-Specialized: psychologically-based), Dept. of Psychology, University of Hull, Hull HU6 7RX England, founded 1979, editor Dr. Geoff Lowe, uses **"psychologically-based poetry."** That is not a very narrow category, though many of the poems in ***Psychopoetica*** are explicitly about psychology or psychological treatment. But most good poetry is in some sense "psychologically based," as the editor seems to recognize in these comments (from his guidelines): **"I prefer short, experimental, rhymed and unrhymed, light verse, haiku, etc., (and visual poems). I will read and consider any style, any length, providing it's within the arena of 'psychologically-based' poetry. I'm not too keen on self-indulgent therapeutic poetry (unless it's good and original), nor sweetly inspirational stuff. I like poetry that has some (or all!) of the following: humor, vivid imagery, powerful feelings, guts and substance, originality, creative style, punch or twist, word-play, good craftsmanship, etc."** Recently published poets include Sheila E. Murphy, Wes Magee, R. Nikolas Macioci, Allen Renfro, Vi Vi Hlavsa and John Brander. The magazine appears 3 times/year, circulating to "several hundred and increasing." It is A4, perfect-bound. **Sample: £1.50 ($3). Publishes theme issues. Send SASE for guidelines and upcoming themes. Themes for 1994-95 include Dream Poems, Remembering and Forgetting, and Life Stories. Considers simultaneous submissions. Editor usually comments on rejections. Pays 1 copy.** Occasionally reviews books of poetry in 25 words, single format. Open to unsolicited reviews. Poets may also send books for review consideration. He says, "Careful presentation of work is most important. But I continue to be impressed by the rich variety of submissions, especially work that shifts boundaries. Also, we now welcome interesting juxtapositions of words and graphics."

THE PUCKERBRUSH PRESS; THE PUCKERBRUSH REVIEW (IV-Regional), 76 Main St., Orono ME 04473, phone (207)581-3832, press founded 1971, ***Review*** founded 1978, poetry editor Constance Hunting, is a "small press publisher of a literary, twice-a-year magazine focused on Maine and of flat-spined paperbacks of literary quality." The editor **does not want to see "confessional, dull, feminist, incompetent, derivative" poetry.** They have published poetry by Amy Clampitt, and the editor selected these sample lines from "Not a Navigable River" by Muska Nagel:

flow seaward, seaward
my river, filled to the brink—
(but no king's horses, no more
will ever come to drink).

For book publication, query with 10 samples. Prefers no simultaneous submissions. Offers criticism for a fee: $100 is usual. Pays 10% royalties plus 10 copies.

PUDDING HOUSE PUBLICATIONS; PUDDING MAGAZINE: THE INTERNATIONAL JOURNAL OF APPLIED POETRY; PUDDING WRITING COMPETITIONS; PUDDING HOUSE BED & BREAKFAST FOR WRITERS; OHIO POETRY THERAPY CENTER & LIBRARY (II, IV-Political, social issues), 60 N. Main St., Johnstown OH 43031, phone (614)967-6060, founded 1979, poetry editor Jennifer Welch Bosveld, provides "a sociological looking glass through poems that provide 'felt experience' and shares intense human situations. Speaks for the difficulties and the solutions. Additionally a forum for poems and articles by people who take poetry arts into the schools and the human services." They publish *Pudding* every several months, also chapbooks, anthologies, broadsides. They **"want experimental and contemporary poetry—what hasn't been said before. Speak the unspeakable. Don't want preachments or sentimentality. Don't want obvious traditional forms without fresh approach. Long poems happily considered too, as long as they aren't windy. Interested in receiving poetry on popular culture and rich brief narratives, i.e. 'virtual journalism.' "** They have recently published poetry by Lowell Jaeger, Edward Boccia and Jane Elsdon. The editor selected these sample lines from "Dustbowl Prophet" by Wilma Elizabeth McDaniel:

Like all the men in the Meade family
Uncle John's hands were farmer rough and big as shovels.

***Pudding* is a literary journal with an emphasis on poetry arts in human service.** They use about 80 pgs. of poetry in each issue—5½×8½, 80 pgs., offset composed on IBM 1st choice, circulation 1,500, 1,400 subscriptions of which 50 are libraries. Subscription (3 issues): $15.75. **Sample postpaid: $6. Submit 5-10 poems. No simultaneous submissions. Previously published submissions *respected* but include credits. Likes cover letter. Publishes theme issues. Send SASE for guidelines and upcoming themes. Reports on same day (unless traveling). Pays 1 copy—to featured poet $10 and 4 copies. Returns rights "with *Pudding* permitted to reprint."** Staff reviews books of poetry. Send books for review consideration. **For chapbook publication, no query. $5 reading fee. Send complete ms and cover letter with publication credits and bio. Editor often comments, will critique on request for $3/page of poetry or $50 an hour in person.** Jennifer Welch Bosveld shares, "Editors have pet peeves. I won't respond to postcards or on them. Don't individually-fold rather than group-fold poems. I don't like cover letters that state the obvious." The Pudding Writing Competitions are for single poems (deadline September 30, fee $2/poem) and for chapbook publication (deadline June 30, $9 entry fee). Pudding House Bed & Breakfast for Writers offers "luxurious rooms with desk and all the free paper you can use" as well as free breakfast in large comfortable home ½ block from post office—location of the Ohio Poetry Therapy Center and Library. $65 single or double/night, discounts available. Reservations recommended far in advance. Send SASE for details.

PUEBLO POETRY PROJECT (IV-Regional), Dept. PM, 1501 E. Seventh St., Pueblo CO 81001, phone (719)584-3401, director Tony Moffeit, founded 1979, **publishes poets from the Pueblo area only. If you qualify, inquire.**

PUERTO DEL SOL (II, IV-Translations, regional), Box 3E, New Mexico State University, Las Cruces NM 88003, phone (505)646-3931, founded 1972 (in present format), poetry editors Joseph Somoza and Kathleene West (on alternate years). "We publish a literary magazine twice per year. Interested in poems, fiction, essays, photos, originals and translations from the Spanish. Also (generally solicited) reviews and dialogues between writers. We want **top quality poetry, any style, from anywhere. We are sympathetic to Southwestern work, but not stereotype (cactus and adobe). Anything that is interesting and/or moving. Poetry, of course, not verse (light or otherwise).**" They have published poetry by Bill Evans, Naton Leslie, Anselm Hollo, Philip Garrison, Cecelia Hagen, J.B. Goodenough and Marilyn Hacker. The 6×9, flat-spined, professionally printed magazine, matte card cover with art, has a circulation of 650, 300 subscriptions of which 25-30 are libraries. 40-50 pgs. are devoted to poetry in each 150-page issue, which also includes quite a lot of prose. They use about 60 of the 700 submissions (about 3,500 poems) received each year to fill up the 90 pgs. of poetry two issues encompass. "Generally no backlog." You won't find many literary journals as attractive as this one. It has an award-caliber design (from the selection of fonts to the use of rules and type-size to enhance content). Furthermore, the journal features readable, thought invoking verse in all styles including translations. It's an exceptional publication. One-year subscription (2 issues): $10. **Sample copy: $7. Submit 5-6 pgs., 1 poem to a page. Simultaneous submissions not encouraged. Reports within 10 weeks. Sometimes sends prepublication galleys. Pays copies. Editor comments "on every ms."** They advise: "Be true to yourself rather than worrying about current fashions—but *do* read as much of the best of contemporary poetry as you can find. We're always interested in top quality poems—poems that move the reader and that use language interestingly."

PURDUE UNIVERSITY PRESS; VERNA EMERY POETRY COMPETITION (II), 1532 S. Campus Courts-B, West Lafayette IN 47907-1532, phone (317)494-2038, founded 1960. They select 1 book/year to publish through the Verna Emery Poetry Competition. They have published poetry by Jim Barnes, editor of ***Chariton Review***, and Fleda Brown Jackson, whose book, **Fishing With Blood**, won the GLCA New Writers Award. **There is a reading fee. Those interested are urged to send SASE for guidelines as particulars vary from year to year.**

‡THE PURPLE MONKEY (I, II), 200 E. Redbud Rd., Knoxville TN 37920, founded 1993, editors "and zoo keepers" Brian Ellis and Scott Gilbert, appears 3 times/year "juxtaposing seasoned and fledgling poets, creating a publication of well-crafted material." **They want "challenging work that is dynamic and colorful with a creative emphasis toward style and craft. No pretentious, self-righteous, bad examples of poetic movements or art without craft."** They have recently published poetry by Jeff Daniel Marion and Susan O'Dell Underwood. As a sample the editors selected these lines from "In and Around the Bodega (Huata, Peru)" by Donald Secreast:

and when you do come to shade it is
almost audible   someone slapping shut
a book to get your attention. . .

tpm is 30-40 pgs., 5½×8½, professionally printed and saddle-stapled with card stock cover, some art and graphics, no ads. Interestingly, in the issue we received, unusual animal names were used instead of page numbers, and the last page included definitions of these terms (everything from addax to zibet). Their press run is 100 for 20 subscribers, 50 shelf sales. Single copy: $2; subscription: $6/year. **Sample postpaid: $2.50. Submit 3-5 typed poems. Previously published poems and simultaneous submissions OK, if noted. Cover letter with brief bio required. "Mss without SASE are ignored."** Time between acceptance and publication is 1-5 months. **Seldom comments on rejections. Reports within 2 months. Pays 1 copy. Acquires one-time rights.** Reviews books of poetry. Open to unsolicited reviews. Poets may also send books for review consideration. The editors add, "Poetry is not for the common man. We pay particular attention to craft and skillful editing. Unpolished journal entries are not poetry."

PURPLE PATCH; THE FIRING SQUAD (I, II), 8 Beaconview House, Charlemont Farm, West Bromwich B7I 3PL England, founded 1975, editor Geoff Stevens, a bimonthly poetry and short prose magazine with reviews, comment and illustrations. The editor says, **"All good examples of poetry considered, but prefer 40 lines max. Do not want poor scanning verse, non-contributory swear words or obscenities, hackneyed themes."** They have recently published poetry by Sheila Jacob, Alex Warner, Sam Smith, Dylan Pugh, Jessica Freeman, Peter Hawkins and "Cato." As a sample the editor selected "Ely Cathedral" by Gordon Mason:

Pitched black like a Mogul tent
it hangs its tattered anthems.
It's a raven chimed to the
village green. It's prostrate
Gulliver arched finger-tips
tentering the grass pool-table
tight.

Purple Patch is 14-20 pgs., magazine-sized, offset on plain paper, cover on the same stock with b&w drawing, side-stapled. Circulation "varies." Price is 3 issues for £3 UK; US price is $5/issue (submit dollars). **Cover letter with short self-introduction preferred with submissions. Time to publication is a maximum of 4 months. Publishes theme issues occasionally. Send SASE (or**

SAE and IRCs) for upcoming themes. Reporting time is 1 month to Great Britain, can be longer to US. Overseas contributors have to buy a copy to see their work in print. Acquires first British serial rights. Staff reviews poetry chapbooks, short stories and tapes in 30-300 words. Send books for review consideration. ***The Firing Squad*** is a broadsheet of **short poetry of a protest or complaint nature**, published at irregular intervals. "All inquiries, submissions of work, etc., must include SASE or SAE and IRCs or $1 U.S./Canadian for return postage/reply."

PYGMY FOREST PRESS (II), P.O. Box 591, Albion CA 95410, founded 1987, editor/publisher Leonard Cirino, publishes flat-spined paperbacks. **"Forms of any kind/length to 96 pgs., subject matter open; especially ecology, prison, asylum, Third World, anarchist to far right. Prefer Stevens to Williams. I like Berryman, Roethke, Jorie Graham; dislike most 'Beats.' Open to anything I consider 'good.' Open to traditional rhyme, meter, but must be modern in subject matter."** He has published **From Beirut** by Mahmoud Darwish, translated by Stephen Kessler; **Pagan Fishing & Other Poems** by Walt McLaughlin; **Where the Four Winds Blow** (including epitaphs) by Phillipe Soupault, translated by Pat Nolan; **Light At The Edge** by Devreaux Baker; **The Cat Food Factory** by Jack Evans; and **A Natural History of Mill Towns** by Theresa Whitehill. **Submit 10-15 poems with bio, acknowledgements, publications. Simultaneous submissions and previously published material OK. Reports on queries in 1-3 weeks, submissions in 2-4 weeks. Sometimes sends prepublication galleys. Pays 10% of run—about 30-50 copies. Buys first rights. He comments on "almost every" ms.** Leonard Cirino says, "I am basically an anarchist. Belong to no 'school.' I fund myself. Receive no grants or private funding. Generally politically left, but no mainline Stalinist or Marxist. Plan to publish 3-8 books yearly."

QUARRY MAGAZINE; QUARRY PRESS; POETRY CANADA (II, IV-Regional), P.O. Box 1061, Kingston, Ontario K7L 4Y5 Canada. Quarry Press founded 1952, *Poetry Canada* founded 1979, managing editor Jake Klisiritch, poetry editor Barry Dempster. "Quarry Press is designed to extend the range of material, poetry and prose, generally handled by *Quarry Magazine*—that is, to represent, as accurately as may be, the range of contemporary writing. We publish chapbooks, soft-bound books of stories and poetry collections ranging from 60-150 pgs., in addition to the quarterly *Quarry Magazine*. **We are interested in seeing any and all forms of contemporary verse. *Quarry Magazine* maintains a practical limit on length of submissions—that we cannot consider any single piece or series by one author that would print at more than 10 pages. Quarry Press considers mss on an individual basis."** They have published poetry by Roo Borson, Kim Maltman, Roger Nash, Jane Munro, Fred Cogswell and Don Bailey. *Quarry* is 130 pgs., digest-sized, flat-spined, professionally printed on eggshell stock. There are 40-50 pgs. of poetry in each issue. An interesting mix of poems appears here: rhymed sequences, couplets and lyric free verse—ranging from the accessible to the experimental—all with an emphasis on voice. Press run is 1,000 for 600 subscribers of which 140 are libraries. They use about 70 of over a thousand submissions of poetry received each year. "We are prompt. Very small backlog if any. 3- to 6-month lead time." Single copy: $5.95; subscription: $19. **Sample postpaid: $6. No limit on number or time of submissions; prefers typed (or WP) double-spaced; query not necessary, though it will be answered. Cover letter with any previous publication credits required. Send SASE (or SAE and IRC) for guidelines. Reports in 6-8 weeks. Pays $10/poem plus 1-year subscription. Buys first North American serial rights. For book consideration, query with 6-10 samples, publication credits, brief bio and current projects. "We give priority to Canadians because of our Arts Council funding and our own interest in promoting Canadian writing." Replies to queries in 1 month, to submissions (if invited) in 6-8 weeks. Contract is for 10% royalties, 10 author's copies. Send 5×7 SASE (or SAE and IRCs) for catalog to order samples. Editor "frequently" comments on rejections.** ***Poetry Canada*** is a quarterly magazine featuring interviews, essays, international criticism and comprehensive reviews of every Canadian poetry book published. Each issue features a major Canadian poet on the cover and center spread (issues have featured Marlene Nourbese Philip, Di Brandt and Don McKay). Press run is 1,800 for 600 subscribers, 600 newsstand. Subscription: $18.19/year ($35.85/year institutions). **Sample postpaid: $4.55. Submit average 10 poems with SAE and IRC. Reports within 1-2 months. Pays $100/page of poetry (usually 100 lines). Buys first North American serial rights.**

THE QUARTERLY (II), Suite 2600, 650 Madison Ave., New York NY 10022, phone (212)888-4769, founded 1987, editor Gordon Lish, is a literary quarterly publishing poetry, fiction, essays and humor. They want **poetry of the "highest standards."** They have published poetry by Sharon Olds, Bruce Beasley, Jack Gilbert and Thomas Lynch. It is 256 pgs., digest-sized, flat-spined, with glossy card cover. Circulation: 15,000. Subscription: $40. **"Do not submit a batch of poems folded separately!" Sometimes sends prepublication galleys. Pays contributor's copies.** The editor says, "We would like to receive new writing on the cutting edge."

QUARTERLY REVIEW OF LITERATURE POETRY SERIES; QRL PRIZE AWARDS (II, IV-Subscription, translation), 26 Haslet Ave., Princeton NJ 08540, founded 1943, poetry editors T. Weiss and R. Weiss. After more than 35 years as one of the most distinguished literary journals in the country, ***QRL*** now appears as the ***QRL Poetry Series***, in which 4-6 books, chosen in open competition, are combined in one annual volume, each of the 4-6 poets receiving $1,000 and 100 copies. The resulting 300- to 400-page volumes are printed in editions of 3,000-5,000, selling in paperback for $10, in hardback for $20. Subscription—2 paperback volumes containing 10 books: $20. **Manuscripts may be sent for reading during the months of November and May only. The collection need not be a first book. It should be 50-80 pgs. if it is a group of connected poems, a selection of miscellaneous poems, a poetic play or a work of poetry translation, or it can be a single long poem of 30 pgs. or more. Some of the individual poems may have had magazine publication. Also considers simultaneous submissions. Manuscripts in English or translated into English are also invited from outside the US. Only one ms may be submitted per reading period and must include a SASE. They always send prepublication galleys.** "Since poetry as a thriving art must depend partly upon the enthusiasm and willingness of those directly involved to join in its support, the editors require that **each ms be accompanied by a subscription to the series."**

‡QUARTERLY WEST (II), 317 Olpin Union, University of Utah, Salt Lake City UT 84112, phone and fax (801)581-3938, founded 1976, editor M.L. Williams, poetry editors Sally Thomas and Craig Arnold. *Quarterly West* is a semiannual literary magazine that **seeks "original and accomplished literary verse—free or formal. No greeting card or sentimental poetry."** They have recently published poetry by Philip Levine, John Hollander and Eavan Boland. *QW* is 220 pgs., 6×9, offset with 4-color cover art. They receive 750-1,000 submissions a year, accept less than 1%. Press run is 1,100 for 500 subscribers of which 300-400 are libraries. Single copy: $6.50; subscription: $11 for 1 year, $20 for 2 years. **Sample postpaid: $4.50. No previously published poems; simultaneous submissions OK, with notification. Seldom comments on rejections. Send SASE for guidelines. Reports in 1-6 months. Pays $15-100. Buys all rights. Returns rights with acknowledgement and right to reprint.** Reviews books of poetry in 1,000-3,000 words. Open to unsolicited reviews. Poets may also send books for review consideration.

QUARTOS MAGAZINE (IV-Subscription), BCM-Writer, London WC1N 3XX United Kingdom, founded 1987, editor Suzanne Riley, appears every other month. This is a "creative writers publication which includes reviews usually submitted by subscribers. **Poems included are usually those previously accepted by other editors or competition judges to help other readers establish a clear idea of editorial requirements. Submissions accepted are the work of our readers."** The newsletter is magazine-sized, 28 pgs. folded. Press run is 1,200 for that many subscribers, of which 20 are libraries. Subscription: $25. **Sample postpaid: $2. Pays 1 copy.** "The Writers Handbook lists us as the 'best single source of UK poetry competitions anywhere.' We would accept articles of 800 words on poetry writing from any source." Pays $10.

QUEEN OF ALL HEARTS (IV-Religious), 26 S. Saxon Ave., Bay Shore NY 11706, phone (516)665-0726, founded 1950, poetry editor Joseph Tusiani, is a magazine-sized bimonthly that uses **poetry "dealing with Mary, the Mother of Jesus—inspirational poetry. Not too long."** They have published poetry by Fernando Sembiante and Alberta Schumacher. The professionally printed magazine, 48 pgs., heavy stock, various colors of ink and paper, liberal use of graphics and photos, has approximately 5,000 subscriptions at $15/year. Single copy: $2.50. **Sample postpaid: $3.** They receive 40-50 submissions of poetry/year, use 2/issue. **Submit double-spaced mss. Reports within 3-4 weeks. Pays 6 copies (sometimes more) and complimentary subscription. Sometimes editor comments on rejections.** His advice: "Try and try again! Inspiration is not automatic!"

ELLERY QUEEN'S MYSTERY MAGAZINE (IV-Mystery), 1540 Broadway, New York NY 10036, founded 1941, appears 13 times a year, primarily using short stories of mystery, crime or suspense. **"We also publish short limericks and verse pertaining to the mystery field."** As a sample the editor selected these lines from "Another Grave Tone" by James Holding:

Here lies a hitman, David Stout,
Whose major talent was rubbing out
Whoever you wanted to turn up dead
With a thirty-eight-caliber hole in the head.
David was expert—a pro, of course,
A cold-blooded killer without remorse—

EQMM is 160 pgs., 5×7¾, professionally printed newsprint, flat-spined with glossy paper cover. Subscription: $31. **Sample: $2.50 (available on newsstands). No previously published poems; simultaneous submissions OK. Reports in 3 months. Pays $5-20.**

QUEEN'S QUARTERLY: A CANADIAN REVIEW (II, IV-Regional), Queen's University, Kingston, Ontario K7L 3N6 Canada, phone (613)545-2667, founded 1893, editor Boris Castel, is "a general interest intellectual review featuring articles on science, politics, humanities, arts and letters, extensive book reviews, some poetry and fiction. **We are especially interested in poetry by Canadian writers. Shorter poems preferred."** They have published poetry by Evelyn Lau, Sue Nevill and Raymond Souster. There are about 12 pgs. of poetry in each issue, 6×9, 224 pgs., circulation 3,500. They receive about

CLOSE-UP

Flexibility Is One Key to *Review*'s Longevity

R. & T. Weiss

"If one respects the enterprise [of poetry] beyond one's own little involvement, one should want to support it, just as with any worthy enterprise," says Renée Weiss. The support and enrichment of poetry through publication of the ***Quarterly Review of Literature*** has engaged Renée and her husband, Theodore, for the past 52 years.

From its inception in 1943 as what Theodore describes as "an orthodox 'little' magazine" devoted to stories, poems, articles and reviews, the ***QRL Poetry Series***, as it is now called, has evolved into an annual issue devoted exclusively to books of poetry. Perhaps one of the most exciting aspects of ***QRL***'s success is its staying power, a testament to the editors' willingness to embrace change in the publication. "We have several times through the years made very crucial adjustments based on our sense of what was going on and what was needed," says Theodore.

This sense of "what was going on" in poetry has been sharpened by their personal involvement in its creation. Theodore, an accomplished poet and author of 13 books of poetry (most recently **The Sum of Destructions**, Louisiana State University Press, fall 1994), is quick to note the collaborative nature of their endeavor. "Renée is recently becoming a poet herself," he says. "We've already published several poems together and read from Princeton to Peking. We've been collaborating for over 50 years. Renée has always been my sharpest critic. She knows my work well enough to find its strengths and weaknesses."

Renée adds: "In our early days, even as I was very much involved in Ted's poetry, I was dancing and interested in the combination of dance and poetry." Says Theodore, "It appealed to me, too. When I look back I realize that the main driving force in my work has been the dramatic. This force was helped along by my writing poems for Renée to dance to."

Glancing through a list of ***QRL***'s back issues, one is struck by the publication's involvement in the unfolding of great modern poetry, from publishing works of e.e. cummings, Kenneth Rexroth, Louis Zukofsky and John Ashbery in the 1940s and '50s; to Denise Levertov, Robert Duncan, David Ignatow and James Merrill in the 1960s and '70s; to Frederick Feirstein, Reg Saner, Judith Kroll and Naomi Clark in the present. Theodore's view of contemporary American poetry is hopeful. "American poetry right now is wonderfully varied. It ranges from the personal lyric to the dramatic and the narrative. One of the excitements, and one of the greatnesses, I think, of our recent poetry is precisely that: It is as rich as one could want it to be."

While *QRL*'s list of contributors reads like an index of notable modern and contemporary American poetry, the editors are equally committed to publishing works by poets outside of the U.S. and works in translation. Of the four to six books featured in each annual volume of the *QRL Poetry Series*, usually one quarter are foreign works. Volume XXXI, however, contains work by Israeli poet Dan Pagis, Uruguayan Cristina Peri Rossi and French poet Yves Bonnefoy.

Asked whether they notice any significant disparity in the quality of American and foreign poetry, Theodore says, "We are at a crucial moment now with the changes in Europe and especially Russia. I think American and English poets have always been a little envious of the seriousness with which poetry is taken in these countries." Renée adds, "They have a long tradition of poetry being very important. That's something we're just developing."

They hesitate to offer any hard-and-fast rules about what they are seeking in submissions. "We want to see everything within the limits of what we have set up as our requirements," says Renée. Theodore adds, "Our attempt is to be as open and accepting as possible, to give the poetry a chance to express itself before we assert our opinions." He generally reads through all of the manuscripts as they come in during November and May (the only months they are open to submissions). He puts aside those of interest and then rereads them. And in the last round, he reads them aloud with his wife to decide which to publish.

"Very frequently," says Renée, "we'll see a manuscript that we think has potential but isn't right, and we say so." Manuscripts may be returned to contributors several times. "Sometimes they are printed – sometimes they are not," she says. Thus, a relationship is built with poets whose work shows promise.

Theodore and Renée strongly recommend that potential contributors obtain a copy of the *QRL Poetry Series* catalog, which is available for $1 and contains 40 poems from their entire publishing history, as well as photos and articles. They also ask that each submission be accompanied by a subscription to the series. "We request that people subscribe for their own benefit, pleasure and enlightenment, and in order to help poetry," says Renée.

"That's why we edit," adds Theodore. "It's an act of gratitude, since we feel we've learned and found so much in poetry. It's our duty and pleasure to pay back by helping others to see what's there." Their generosity extends beyond their commitment to editing, for they award each of the four to six poets appearing in every annual issue with $1,000 and 100 copies.

The couple's advice to beginning poets is simple: "Read as carefully as you can, and find a good workshop," says Theodore. "It's a lonely business, writing poetry, and any time one is able to find congenial, serious people available to [review] his work, it's a great gift."

Regarding the importance of networking in the pursuit of publication, Theodore reminds us that great poets of the past had very little involvement with networking. "Of course, you meet poets at their best in their work," he says. "I've been supported all my life by the poets I admire: Browning, Williams, Stevens, Pound, Eliot – they have always been good supports. It's the poets that one loves that become one's constant companions."

– Roseann S. Biederman

400 submissions of poetry/year, use 40. Subscription: $20 Canadian, US subscribers may pay either $20 US or $25 Canadian. **Sample postpaid: $5 US. Submit no more than 6 poems at once. No simultaneous submissions. Reports in 1 month. Pays usually $50 (Canadian)/poem, "but it varies," plus 2 copies.**

RACKHAM JOURNAL OF THE ARTS AND HUMANITIES (RAJAH) (II, IV-Students, themes), 411 Mason Hall, The University of Michigan, Ann Arbor MI 48109, phone (313)763-2351, founded 1971, editor Anna Dalby, is "primarily a forum for the critical and **creative work of graduate students of the University of Michigan**" but each year they include three contributions by others. It is an annual journal with emphasis on criticism, fiction, poetry and translation. **Open to all varieties of poetry, but usually limited to 1-2 pgs. in length. Nothing "pornographic or grotesque."** They have published poetry by Duchess Edmée de la Rochefoucauld and John Ditsky. The editor selected these sample lines by David L. Labiosa:

The small dog makes me think
of our island in Puerto Rico:
confronted with the ponderous
importer, person government . . .

RAJAH is 6×9, professionally printed, 120 pgs., flat-spined, with b&w glossy card cover, using illustrations, photos and ads. Of 50 submissions from non-university graduate students they accept three. Press run is 400 for 200 subscriptions of which 150 are libraries. It sells for $3 to individuals, $6 to institutions. **Sample postpaid: $1.75. Include cover letter with short bio (previous publications), address and telephone number with submissions. No simultaneous submissions, but previously published poems OK. Reports in 4-6 months. Pays 2 copies. Editor sometimes comments on rejections.**

RADCLIFFE QUARTERLY (IV-Specialized: alumnae), 10 Garden St., Cambridge MA 02138, phone (617)495-8608, editor Ruth Whitman, is an alumnae quarterly that **publishes alumnae and college-related poets.** *RQ* is magazine-sized, with glossy full-color paper cover. They receive about 50 poems/year, use 3 poems/issue. Press run is 31,000 for 30,500 subscribers. **Samples free to anyone. No pay.** Reviews books of poetry in 250 words, single format. The Dean's office sponsors a contest for poets, winners printed in the quarterly. Must be a Radcliffe student to enter.

RADDLE MOON (II, IV-Form), Dept. PM, 2239 Stephens St., Vancouver, British Columbia V6K 3W5 Canada or 9060 Ardmore Dr., Sidney, British Columbia V8L 3S1 Canada, founded 1985, editors Susan Clark, Lisa Robertson and Catriona Strang, appears twice a year using **"language-centered and 'new lyric' poetry."** They have recently published poetry by Claude Royet-Journoud, Lyn Hejinian, Rosmarie Waldrop, Norma Cole, Laura Moriarty, Abigail Child, Lise Downe and Leslie Scalapino. The editor describes it as 6×9, flat-spined, 100 pgs. Press run is 700. **Sample postpaid: $6. Reports in 2-3 months. Pays subscription.**

RADIANCE: THE MAGAZINE FOR LARGE WOMEN (I, IV-Women), P.O. Box 30246, Oakland CA 94604, phone and fax (510)482-0680, founded 1984, publisher/editor Alice Ansfield, appears quarterly. **"Keeping in mind that our magazine is geared toward large women, we look for poetry from women of any size and men who don't accept society's stereotypical standards of beauty and weight—but who celebrate women's bodies, sexuality, search for self-esteem and personal growth."** As a sample she quotes "Homage to My Hips" by Lucille Clifton:

these hips are big hips
they need space to
move around in.
they don't fit into little
petty places. these hips
are free hips.
they don't like to be held back.
these hips have never been enslaved,
they go where they want to go
they do what they want to do.
these hips are mighty hips.
these hips are magic hips.
i have known them
to put a spell on a man and
spin him like a top!

Radiance is magazine-sized, professionally printed on glossy stock with full-color paper cover, 60 pgs., saddle-stapled, 2-color graphics, photos and ads, circulation 10,000 to 4,000 subscriptions, 2,500 selling on newsstands or in bookstores, 1,000 sent as complimentary copies to media and clothing stores for large women. Subscription: $20/year. **Sample postpaid: $3.50. Submit double-spaced, typed ms. Editor usually comments on rejections. Send SASE for guidelines.**

Reports in 2-3½ months. Pays $10-30. Buys one-time rights. Reviews related books of poetry in 500-800 words.

RAG MAG; BLACK HAT PRESS (I, II), P.O. Box 12, Goodhue MN 55027, phone (612)923-4590, founded 1982, poetry editor Beverly Voldseth, accepts **poetry of "any length or style. No pornographic SM violent crap."** They have published poetry by Bill Keith, James Lineberger, Laurel Mills and JoAnne Makela. As a sample the editor selected these lines from "Life Here & Hereafter; a Phototropism" by Gayle Nordling:

Looking inside an immense home on a woody,
back-lit lot you see a woman lying
beside the kitchen door. She is slaughtered.
One eye bulges, two gunshot holes in her
skull gleam copper-bright as new pennies.
Her hands lie open—they are unclouded and
turning blue at the edges, like an
advancing morning sky.

Rag Mag, appearing twice a year, is 80-112 pgs., perfect-bound, 6×9, professionally printed in dark type with ads for books, matte colored card cover. The editor says she accepts about 10% of poetry received. Press run is 250 for 80 subscriptions of which 8 are libraries. Subscription: $10. **Sample postpaid: $6. "Send 6-8 of your best with brief bio. Something that tells a story, creates images, speaks to the heart." Pays 1 copy.** Reviews books of poetry. Open to unsolicited reviews. Poets may also send books for review consideration. **They may publish chapbook or paperback collections of poetry under the imprint of Black Hat Press. Query first. Simultaneous submissions and previously printed material OK. Reports in 6 weeks. Detailed comments provided "sometimes." Financial arrangements for book publication vary.** They have published Riki Kölbl Nelson's English/German poems about living in 2 worlds/2 languages, **Borders/Grenzen**, 128 pages plus the author's artwork. In addition, they published **The Book of Hearts**, poems by Karen Herseth Wee in 1993.

RAMBUNCTIOUS PRESS; RAMBUNCTIOUS REVIEW (II, IV-Regional), 1221 W. Pratt, Chicago IL 60626, founded 1982, poetry editors Mary Dellutri, Richard Goldman, Beth Hausler and Nancy Lennon. ***Rambunctious Review*** appears once yearly in a handsomely printed, saddle-stapled, 7×10 format, 48 pgs. They want **"spirited, quality poetry**, fiction, photos and graphics. **Some focus on local work, but all work is considered."** As a sample the editors selected these lines from "I Grew Up in Arles" by Anne Valdez:

I grew up in Arles, South Chicago,
The town where Vincent lived
I never knew the tavern/cafe/bars
But I knew the trees and houses
And people with spider-jointed fingers.

They receive 500-600 submissions a year and use 50-60. They have a circulation of about 500 with 200 subscriptions. Single copy: $3.50. **Sample postpaid: $4. Will consider simultaneous submissions. No submissions accepted June 1 through August 31. No queries. Occasionally comments on mss. Publishes theme issues. Reports in 9 months. Pays 2 copies.** They run annual contests in poetry, fiction and short drama.

RANGER INTERNATIONAL PRODUCTIONS; LION PUBLISHING; ROAR RECORDING (III), P.O. Box 71231, Milwaukee WI 53211-7331, phone (414)332-7474, founded 1969, editor Martin Jack Rosenblum, publishes **"objectivist/projectivist poetry, primarily with action subjects by adventurers—such as the Harley poetry**—in flat-spined paper and hardcover chapbooks." They have published poetry by Karl Young, Howard McCord, Toby Olson and Carl Rakosi. To illustrate the nature of submissions they prefer, the editor selected these lines of his own:

sleep uncovered
by windows letting
light in from snow
skies backlit
it is looking
through an eggshell cracked

They publish about 3 books a year. **Query with cover letter including "something interesting to say regarding your work." Always sends prepublication galleys. Payment "negotiable." Editor comments on submissions "always."** He says, "Poetry has been swept into an academic corner and dusted off of daily living spaces and this is what Ranger International Productions works against: We want to bring poetry out of academics and back into life's daily platform. Write hard, accept no public money and achieve honesty and integrity personally while studying the master poets in school or out. Control of the forms is essential. Control of the life is absolutely required."

RANGER RICK MAGAZINE (III, IV-Children, nature/ecology), 8925 Leesburg Pike, Vienna VA 22184, founded 1967, senior editor Deborah Churchman, is a monthly nature magazine for children aged 6-12. **They want "short, funny verses for children about nature and the environment. Must be accurate. No religious, preachy or difficult poetry."** They have published poetry by John Ciardi and Charles Ghigna. *RR* is 48 pgs., 8×10, saddle-stitched, glossy paper with numerous full color photos. They receive 100-200 submissions/year, "may accept one." Press run is 900,000. Subscription: $15. **Sample postpaid: $2. Previously published poems OK; no simultaneous submissions.** Time between acceptance and publication is 2-5 years. **Seldom comments on rejections. Publishes theme issues. Send SASE for guidelines and upcoming themes. Reports in 2 months. Always sends prepublication galleys. Pays $5/line plus 2 copies. Buys all rights. Return is "negotiable."** The editor says, "Think: Will kids understand these words? Will it hook them? Will an 8-year-old want to read this instead of playing Nintendo?"

‡RANT (I, II), P.O. Box 6872, Yorkville Station, New York NY 10128, founded 1992, editor Alfred Vitale. *Rant*, which appears 3 times/year, is "a journal of fiction, poetry and nonfiction rants, a hybrid of a literary zine and a literary journal, offering real voice, real thought, real humor." **They want "ranting verse: raw, powerful, sharp, witty, radical. Nothing over 3 pages. No romanticism, no technical, academic, crafted, vague, inane, soft, harmless or PC poetry."** They have recently published poetry by Charles Bukowski, Hal Sirowitz, Arthur Nersesian, Gina Grega, Cheryl Townsend and Tuli Kupferberg. As a sample the editor selected these lines from "Meat/Hate/War" by J. Donnelly:

He eats food already fouling de com pos ing
I see it when I'm out among the dumpsters
he says I hate the homeless scum
but I feel the scum he swallows when it runs down the cloth of my workpants
through a break in the plastic bag
I think of him saying hate

Rant is 80 pgs., 5½×8½, perfect-bound, with card cover, b&w graphics and ads. They receive about 3,000 poems a year, publish approximately 60. Press run is 1,000 for 60 subscribers, 430 shelf sales. Single copy: $4.95; subscription: $16 (4 issues). **Sample postpaid: $5. Submit no more than 10 pages of poetry. Previously published poems and simultaneous submissions OK. Often comments on rejections. Send SASE for guidelines. Reports in 2 weeks to 3 months. Pays 1 or 2 copies.** Includes small staff-written zine reviews and listings. The editor says, "Editors know less than you—and their little rejection slips should not bother you—thus, I try to be very humane and believe me, as someone with a shitload of rejections, I *know* what it's like! Have no fear!"

RARACH PRESS (V), 1005 Oakland Dr., Kalamazoo MI 49008, phone (616)388-5631, founded 1981, owner Ladislav Hanka, is a "small bibliophilic press specializing in hand-printing, hand-binding with original artwork. The material is either in Czech or, if English, dealing with environmentalist subject matter." He has printed books of poetry by James Armstrong, Richard Neugebauer, Bennet Mitchell and Rainer Maria Rilke. "Authors tend to be friends, acquaintances or dead. They are given a portion of the books or a portion of sales after the fact. **I do not care to receive unsolicited mss.** I pity the lot of you. I fully expect most of my books to eventually be taken apart and sold for the artwork when they pass from the present collector of bibliophili to some philistine. This means the poetry will be lost . . . I really sell my books for the price of the binding and artwork."

RARITAN QUARTERLY (III), Dept. PM, 31 Mine St., New Brunswick NJ 08903, phone (908)932-7887, founded 1982, editor Richard Poirier. **"We publish very little poetry. We publish *almost* no unsolicited poetry, so it would be misleading to encourage submissions."** They have published poetry by J.D. McClatchy, James Merrill, Richard Howard and Robert Pinsky. It is 6×9, flat-spined, 150 pgs., with matte card cover, professionally printed. The few poems appearing here (including sequences and translations) tend toward free verse. Press run is 4,000 for 3,500 subscribers of which 800 are libraries. Subscription: $16. **Sample postpaid: $5. Pays $100/submission if accepted.** Reviews recent poetry books and chapbooks. Poetry published in this quarterly was included in **The Best American Poetry 1992**.

RASHI (IV-Ethnic), Box 1198, Hamilton, New Zealand, founded 1985, editor Norman Simms, uses poetry on **"Jewish topics in English or any Jewish language such as Hebrew, Yiddish, Ladino, etc." They do not want poetry that is "pompous, self-indulgent nonsense."** They have published poems by Anne Ranasinghe and Simon Lichman. *Rashi* is the literary supplement of the monthly *New Zealand Chronicle.* They accept about 25 of 40 poems received/year. Circulation is over 2,000. Subscription: $30. **Sample postpaid: $4. Subscription "recommended, but not necessary." Cover letter with some background on the author required. Reports in 1 month. Pays 1 copy. Editor comments on rejections**

for $5/page. Open to unsolicited reviews. Poets may also send books for review consideration. He says, "This is a special part of our overall projects. We would like to see multilingualism develop, reinterpretation of ancient and medieval traditions."

‡RAVEN CHRONICLES (II), P.O. Box 95918, University Station, Seattle WA 98145, founded 1990, poetry editors Phoebe Bosché, John E. Smelcer and John Olson, is a literary journal publishing poetry, fiction, essays, art and reviews in three issues a year, **"devoted to promoting contemporary multicultural arts by minority writers and artists."** The editors say *RC* is a beautifully printed, 65-page magazine sometimes using color covers. They use as many as 30 poems/issue. They have a circulation of 2,500 subscribers including some libraries. Subscription: $12. **Submit up to 10 poems with SASE. Editors often comment on rejections. Send SASE for guidelines. Pays 2 copies.** Poets may also send books for review consideration.

RAW DOG PRESS; POST POEMS (II, IV-Humor), 151 S. West St., Doylestown PA 18901-4134, phone (215)345-6838, founded 1977, poetry editor R. Gerry Fabian, "publishes Post Poems annual—a postcard series. **We want short poetry (3-7 lines) on any subject. The positive poem or the poem of understated humor always has an inside track. No taboos, however. All styles considered. Anything with rhyme had better be immortal.**" They have published poetry by ave jeanne, Lyn Lifshin, Philip Miller, Conger Beasley, Jr. and the editor, R. Gerry Fabian, who selected his poem, "Arc Welder," as a sample:

After years of burning
he pressed his lips against hers
and sealed out any doubt.

Send SASE for catalog to buy samples. The editor "always" comments on rejections. Pays copies. Acquires all rights. Returns rights on mention of first publication. Sometimes reviews books of poetry. He says he will offer criticism for a fee; "if someone is desperate to publish and is willing to pay, we will use our vast knowledge to help steer the ms in the right direction. We will advise against it, but as P.T. Barnum said . . . . Raw Dog Press welcomes new poets and detests second-rate poems from 'name' poets. We exist because we are dumb like a fox, but even a fox takes care of its own."

‡REACH MAGAZINE (I, IV-Subscribers), P.O. Box 134, Drawer 194, Pearl Harbor HI 96860-5181, founded March 1993, publisher/editor Jessie Porter. ***REACH Magazine*** (successor to ***Breakthrough!***) is a quarterly **subscribers-only publication** designed to provide a place for "new writers around the world who would otherwise be overlooked by larger publishers. **Range, format and style of poetry is unlimited. No vulgar, sexually lewd and/or hate poems nor poems without social or literary value."** They have recently published poetry by Li Min Hua, Neal E. Desch and Allison Grayhurst. As a sample the editor selected these lines from "Humble Servant" by Barry Elisofon:

Do me a great endeavor,
and sanctify my soul,
let me worship in your spirit,
in an exalted and priestly role,
baptize me in your aura,
surround me with holy air,
train me in your rituals,
be the object of my prayer

REACH is at least 20 pgs., 8½×11, typeset and saddle-stitched with card stock cover and b&w graphics. About 30% of the submissions they receive are poetry and "we accept about 29%." Press run is 600 for 400 subscribers. Single copy: $3; subscription: $11. **Sample postpaid: $2. "Priority is given to our subscribers for publication." Previously published poems OK; no simultaneous submissions. Cover letter required. A 1-page biography is also required for new subscribers. Always comments on rejections. "We provide one-on-one critiques." Send SASE for guidelines. Reports within 2 weeks. Pays 2 copies. Acquires first North American serial or one-time rights.** Staff reviews books of poetry. Send books for review consideration with $10 reading fee. The editor says, "1)Do not insist on sending material which is unacceptable for publication. 2) Be original. Practice the art of rewriting if something does not fit. 3)Write to inspire, not so much gloom."

REAL (RE ARTS & LETTERS) (II, IV-Bilingual, translations, humor), Dept. PM, Box 13007, Stephen F. Austin State University, Nacogdoches TX 75962, phone (409)568-2101, founded 1968, editor Lee Schultz, is a "Liberal Arts Forum" using short fiction, drama, reviews and interviews; contains editorial notes and personalized "Contributors' Notes"; printed in the winter and summer. They "hope to use from 15 to 35 pages of poetry per issue, one poem per page (typeset in editor's office). Last two issues had submissions from thirty-eight states, Great Britain, Italy and Israel." **They receive between 10-35 poems/week. "We presently do not receive enough formal or witty/ironic pieces. We need a better**

balance between open and generic forms. We're also interested in critical writings on poems or writing poetry and translations with a bilingual format (permissions from original author)." As a sample the editor selected these lines from "Within the Womb of This Mountain" by Jenna Fedock:

We will not see him again,
"Lord have mercy,"
but only in the black box wedged in an aisle,
heavy lid crushing our heads. We chant
"Vichnaya pamyat, Vichnaya pamyat, Vichnaya pamyat,"
trying to cast it off—but cannot.

It is handsomely printed, "reserved format," perfect-bound with line drawings and photos. Simply one of the most readable literary magazines published today, ***REAL*** welcomes all styles and forms that display craft, insight and accessibility. Circulation approximately 400, "more than half of which are major college libraries." Subscriptions also in Great Britain, Ireland, Italy, Holland, Puerto Rico, Brazil and Canada. **Sample postpaid: $5. Submit original and copy. "Editors prefer a statement that ms is not being simultaneously submitted; however, this fact is taken for granted when we receive a ms." Writer's guidelines for SASE. They acknowledge receipt of submissions and strive for a 1-month decision. Submissions during summer semesters may take longer. "We will return poems rather than tie them up for more than a one-issue backlog (6-9 months)." Pays copies.** Reviews are assigned, but queries about doing reviews are welcome.

REALITY STREET EDITIONS (V), 4 Howard Court, Peckham Rye, London SE15 3PH United Kingdom, is the joint imprint of Reality Studios and Street Editions, editors Ken Edwards and Wendy Mulford. They publish 2 paperbacks/year. They have published books of poetry by Allen Fisher, Tom Raworth and Stephen Rodefer, but **they currently do not accept unsolicited mss.** Their US distributor is Small Press Distribution, 1814 San Pablo Ave., Berkeley CA 94302.

RECONSTRUCTIONIST (IV-Ethnic), Church Rd. & Greenwood Ave., Wyncote PA 19095, founded 1935, poetry editor Jeremy Garber, is a Jewish cultural and intellectual review published 1-2 times/year. **"We publish about 4 poems per year—either on Jewish themes or in some other way related to Jewish spiritual quests—short poems up to about 30-35 lines."** They have published poetry by Gabriel Preil, Shulamis Yelin and Marcia Falk. As a sample the editor selected these lines (poet unidentified):

Come, share the watermelon I have sliced.
My yearning for the hurricane
fills yawning distance with our pain

Reconstructionist is 32 pgs., magazine-sized, professionally printed on heavy stock with matte card cover, saddle-stapled. Subscription: $20. **Sample postpaid: $3. No simultaneous submissions. Editor sometimes comments on rejections. Reports in 1-2 months, delay to publication 1-2 years. Pays $36/poem plus 5 copies.**

THE RED CANDLE PRESS; CANDELABRUM (II), 9 Milner Rd., Wisbech PE13 2LR England, founded 1970, editor M.L. McCarthy, M.A., administrative editor Helen Gordon, B.A., was "founded to encourage poets working in **traditional-type verse, metrical unrhymed or metrical rhymed.** We're more interested in poems than poets: that is, we're interested in what sort of poems an author produces, not in his or her personality." They publish the magazine, ***Candelabrum***, twice yearly (April and October), occasional postcards, paperbound staple-spined chapbooks and occasional poetry leaflets. For all of these they want **"good-quality metrical verse, with rhymed verse specially wanted. Elegantly cadenced free verse is acceptable. No weak stuff (moons and Junes, loves and doves, etc.) No chopped-up prose pretending to be free verse. Any length up to about 50 lines for *Candelabrum*, any subject, including eroticism (but not porn)—satire, love poems, nature lyrics, philosophical—any subject, but nothing racist or sexist."** They have recently published poetry by Brian McGregor Foxcroft, Michael Axtell, Leo Yankevich, Claire Willow, Alice Evans and Joe Ruggier. The editors offer these lines by Jack Harvey as a sample:

The spider spins her strong and endless thread,
Which neatly ties the apple to the rose.
She reasons with her feet, not with her head,
and tarantella-swift the crochet grows.
An early autumn mist sets on the line,
In beads placed with a faultless keen precision . . .

The digest-sized magazine, staple-spined, small type, exemplifies their intent to "pack in as much as possible, wasting no space, and try to keep a neat appearance with the minimum expense." They get in about 44 pgs. (some 60 poems) in each issue. They receive about 2,000 submissions/year, use approximately 5% of those, sometimes holding over poems for the next year or longer. Circulation: 900 with 700 subscriptions of which 22 are libraries. **Sample: $4 in bills only; checks not accepted. "Submit anytime. IRCs essential if return wished, and please check the weight. Each poem on a separate sheet please, neat typescripts or neat *legible* manu-**

scripts. *Please* no dark, oily photostats, no colored ink (only black or blue). Author's name and address on each sheet, please." No simultaneous submissions. Reports in about 2 months. Pays 1 contributor's copy. Staff occasionally reviews books of poetry in 500 words, single format. Send books for review consideration. The books published by **Red Candle Press "have been at our invitation to the poet, and at our expense. We pay the author a small royalty-advance, but he/she keeps the copyright."** The editor comments, "Traditional-type poetry is much more popular here in Britain, and we think also in the United States, now than it was in 1970, when we founded *Candelabrum*. We **always welcome new poets, especially traditionalists, and we like to hear from the U.S.A. as well as from here at home**. General tip: Study the various outlets at the library, or buy a copy of ***Candelabrum***, or borrow a copy from a subscriber, before you go to the expense of submitting your work. The Red Candle Press regrets that, because of bank charges, it is unable to accept dollar cheques for under $100. However, it is always happy to accept U.S. and Canadian dollar bills."

RED CEDAR REVIEW (II), 17C Morrill Hall, Dept. of English, Michigan State University, East Lansing MI 48824, phone (517)355-7570, editors Laura Klynstra and Jachary Chartkoff, founded 1963, is a literary biannual which uses poetry—**"any subject, form, length; the only requirement is originality and vision." The editors encourage work "beyond animal poems, flora and fauna poems, etc. No pornography."** They have published poetry by Diane Wakoski, Margaret Atwood and Stuart Dybek. As a sample the editors selected these lines by Matt Marinovich:

Beats Times Square, Jeff says,
where once we squeezed into
a sticky peep show booth
to watch a naked woman cry
because it was Christmas Eve
and she was coming down.

The review is 80 pgs., digest-sized. They receive about 400 submissions/year, use 30. Press run is 400 for 200 subscribers of which 100 are libraries. Subscription: $10. **Sample postpaid: $2. Current issue: $5. Submit only previously unpublished works. Reports in 2 months, sometimes longer. Pays 2 copies. Editor sometimes comments on rejections.** Reviews books of poetry. Open to unsolicited reviews. Poets may also send books for review consideration. They offer an annual writing contest. Entry fee: $5/poem, $10/short story. Prizes: $150 poetry, $300 fiction. Winners are published in ***Red Cedar Review***, finalists mentioned. All entrants receive copy. Send SASE for deadline information.

RED DANCEFLOOR (V); RED DANCEFLOOR PRESS (III), P.O. Box 4974, Lancaster CA 93539-4974, founded 1989, editor David Goldschlag, publishes poetry, fiction, interviews, profiles, reviews, photos and art. **"No restrictions on form, length or subject matter. We want poetry that is well thought out—not a first draft. If you send us rhyme it should have a specific purpose and work; would consider a good sestina."** They have published poetry by Michael C Ford, David Lake, Mario René Padilla and Charles Webb. As a sample the editor selected the poem "(Avalanche)" by Laurel Ann Bogen:

(my secret name)

frozen tundra glistens
in moonlight
as precise
            as this
            icicle
while growing
faultlines loom craggy
in these *mountains*
like the Gestapo
outside the window
in the snow
with their dogs

(will you say it?)

He says, **"The magazine will be suspending publication until further notice."** Current issue postpaid: $6.05. **Sample postpaid: $4.50.** Red Dancefloor Press publishes full-length books, chapbooks and poetry audiotapes. "The author may want to get a copy of a book, chap or tape before submitting. **(Send SAE with first-class stamp for catalog.) "We openly accept submissions for books, chaps and tapes, but *please* query first with 10 samples and a cover letter explaining which area of our press you are interested in. Listing credits in a cover letter is fine, but don't go crazy."**

RED HERRING POETS; MATRIX; RED HERRING PRESS; RED HERRING CHAPBOOK SERIES; CHANNING-MURRAY FOUNDATION (IV-Membership), 1209 W. Oregon St., Urbana IL 61801, phone (217)344-1176, founded 1975, director of Red Herring Poets Ruth S. Walker. The Red Herring Poets is a workshop that publishes its members' work, after they have attended at least 5 meetings, in their annual magazine, ***Matrix***, and, for those who have been members for at least 2 years and given 2 public readings, one chapbook/year.

RED RAMPAN' PRESS; RED RAMPAN' REVIEW; RED RAMPAN' BROADSIDE SERIES (V), 4707 Fielder St., Midland TX 79707-2817, phone (915)697-7689, founded 1981, poetry editor Larry D. Griffin. ***RRR*** is an "eclectic review quarterly." The editor says it is 6×9, 48-60 pgs., with a press run of 300, **"presently not accepting poetry** and only using staff-written reviews." The press plans to publish flat-spined paperback collections.

THE REDNECK REVIEW OF LITERATURE (II, IV-Regional), 1326 W. Sheridan Court, Milwaukee WI 53209-5145, phone (414)351-1322, founded 1975, editor Penelope Reedy, is a semiannual magazine publishing poetry, fiction, drama and essays **dealing with the contemporary West. The editor wants to see "any form, length or style." She does not want "ethereal ditties about nothing; obscure."** She has published poetry by R.M. Davis, C. Bukowski, Charlotte Wright, Lawson Inada, Ed Abbey and Suzanne Scollon. As a sample the editor selected these lines by Gary David:

In the middle of cow country
he knows the range
of free expression
to be the gauge
of his Smith & Wesson

The magazine, which appears in the spring and fall each year, is magazine-sized, offset, perfect-bound, some advertising. Circulation is 500, of which 200 are subscriptions and 100-150 are newsstand sales. **Sample postpaid: $7. Writers should submit "2-3 poems at a time, letter quality—don't like simultaneous submissions. Please send SASE with *enough* postage to return mss." Criticism is sometimes given. Rejected mss are reported on immediately, and no accepted mss are held beyond 3 issues. Publishes theme issues. Send SASE for upcoming themes. Themes for fall 1994 and spring 1995 are "Games" and "20th Anniversary Cookbook," respectively. Pays 1 copy.** Reviews books of poetry. The editor says, "Rethink what 'the West' means to American culture—as a concept rather than merely a geographical area."

REDWOOD FAMILY CHAPEL PUBLICATIONS; CHRISTIAN POET (I, II, IV-Religious), (formerly CCR Publications), 2745 Monterey Hwy #76, San Jose CA 95111-3129, founded as Realities Library in 1975, as CCR Publications in 1987, now Redwood Family Chapel Publications, editor and publisher Ric Soos. He has published books of poetry by Ruth Daigon and Ella Blanche Salmi. "Because of economic conditions, we have discontinued our book series. To replace the book series we have started ***Christian Poet***. It will be published as often as we have time, poetry and finances. Seven issues appeared in 1992, 15 issues in 1993." ***Christian Poet*** is one 8½×11 page of colored paper, neatly printed and tri-folded. Subscription: $5 for 12 issues. **Poets may submit up to 15 poems for consideration. Send SASE for guidelines.** The editor says, "Please keep in mind when you contact me that I believe in Jesus Christ, and that anything I publish will be to help further the Gospel if it is for that purpose. **In poetry, I look for items that will not hinder the spread of the Gospel. In other words, the poet need not be Christian, does not need to mention Christ by name, but I will no longer be publishing for shock value."** He publishes those "who support me in some respect . . . Support is not always financial."

REFLECT (IV-Form/style), 3306 Argonne Ave., Norfolk VA 23509, founded 1979, poetry editor W.S. Kennedy. They use **"spiral poetry: featuring an inner-directed concern with sound (euphony), mystical references or overtones, and objectivity—rather than personal and emotional poems. No love poems, pornography, far left propaganda; nothing overly sentimental. (Don't write yourself into the poem.)"** They have published poetry by B.Z. Niditch, Joe Malone, Ruth Wildes Schuler and Stan Proper. As a sample the editor selected these lines from "Euphonies" by Marikay Brown:

The spring wind is a silver flute
Piping lilac-hyacinth
Passionatos of perfume.
The summer wind—a green guitar
Of fluttering leaves and grasses
Strummed on fretted sunlight gold . . .

The quarterly is digest-sized, 48 pgs., saddle-stapled, typescript. Subscription: $8. **Sample postpaid: $2. All submissions should be *single-spaced* and should fit on one typed page. Editor sometimes comments on rejections. Guidelines available for SASE. Reports within a month. No backlog. Pays 1 copy. Acquires first rights.** Occasionally reviews books of poetry in 50 words or more. ***Reflect*** ranked #5 in the "Open Markets" category of the latest ***Writer's Digest*** Poetry 60 list. This category ranks those publications most open to both free and formal verse.

RENDITIONS: A CHINESE-ENGLISH TRANSLATION MAGAZINE (IV-Translations), Research Center for Translation, CUHK, Shatin, NT, Hong Kong, editor Dr. Eva Hung, appears twice a year. **"Contents exclusively translations from Chinese, ancient and modern."** They also publish a paperback series of Chinese literature in English translation. They have published translations of the poetry of Gu Cheng, Shu Ting, Mang Ke and Bei Dao. ***Renditions*** is magazine-sized, 180 pgs., flat-spined, elegantly printed, all poetry with side-by-side Chinese and English texts, using some b&w and color drawings and photos, with glossy card cover. Annual subscription: $20; 2 years: $36; 3 years: $50 (US). **Sample postpaid: $13. Publishes theme issues. Reports in 2 months. Pays "honorarium" plus 2 copies. Use British spelling. They "will consider" book mss, for which they would like a query with sample translations. Books pay 10% royalties plus 10 copies. Mss usually not returned. Editor sometimes comments on rejections.**

RENEGADE (II), P.O. Box 314, Bloomfield Hills MI 48303, phone (313)972-5580, founded 1988, editors Miriam Jones and Michael Nowicki, appears twice a year using stories, essays and poems. **"We are an eclectic publication. There is no preference for form or style; we simply wish to see polished work of good quality. Poems are generally of a length no more than 200 lines, no less than 10 lines. We try to avoid anything that is anarchistic, antifeminist or of a derogatory nature to any group of persons or individuals."** They have recently published poetry by John Sinclair, M.L. Liebler, Linda Nemec Foster, Laurence Pike, S.S. Waters, Mary Rudbeck Stanko and Lyn Lifshin. As a sample the editors selected "Day After Tomorrow" by Kainoa Koeninger:

i'm gonna get up
& dance,
just rise like a phoenix dancing a resurrection dance. . .

With every one watching,
i'm gonna dance like a bright phoenix,

burning a hole in the night

Renegade is 32 pgs., digest-sized, laser-printed, with matte card cover, b&w drawings and graphics. Ads welcome. They accept about 5% of 300 mss of 5 poems or less. Press run is 200 for 20 subscribers, free to libraries and editors of other literary journals, 50 shelf sales. Subscription: $9.90. **Sample postpaid: $5. Editor comments on submissions "often." Reports in 3-6 months. Sometimes sends prepublication galleys. Pays 1 copy, 2 on request. Acquires all rights. Returns rights to author free of charge.** Reviews books of poetry. Open to unsolicited reviews. Poets may also send books for review consideration to the attention of Larry Snell. "We put together Warlords of the Subculture Poetry Contest. People interested should inquire first." They add, "We want poems in any form that speak clearly, metaphorically and imagistically to the reader about pain, or joy."

RESPONSE (IV-Ethnic, students), 9th Floor, 27 W. 20th St., New York NY 10011, phone (212)675-1168, fax (212)929-3459, founded 1966, poetry editor Yigal Schleifer, is a "contemporary Jewish review publishing poetry, fiction and essays **by students and young adult authors." The only specification for poetry is that it be on a Jewish theme and have some significant Jewish content.** They have published poetry by Sharon Kessler, Sue Saniel Elkind and Shulamith Bat-Yisrael. As a sample the editor chose these lines from "Old Nazis Don't Die (They Move To South America)" by Sylvia Warsh:

The jungles of Brazil teem
with a new strain of
European animal, serpents of
such camouflage that their own
Bavarian mothers would not
recognize them,
insects that thrust hard
consonants into a victim's
heart and suck him dry,
then use his shell
for a livingroom.

They look for "creative, challenging and chutzapadik writing" from young writers. The quarterly is 64 pgs., flat-spined, 6×9, professionally printed on heavy stock, with a glossy "varnished" cover with artwork. Circulation 1,600 with 600 subscribers of which 30% are libraries. 1,000 distributed through bookstores and newsstands. Subscription: $16 ($10 for students); $20 for institutions. **Sample postpaid: $4. Cover letter with bio and previous publications required with submissions. Reports in about 2 months. 6 months between acceptance and publication. Pays 2 copies/poem published. Acquires all rights.** Occasionally reviews books of Jewish poetry. Open to unsolicited reviews. Poets may also send books for review consideration.

THE REVIEW (I, II), P.O. Box 3331, Montebello CA 90640, founded 1992, editor Paul Quintero, is a triannual which **"accepts all poetry; open to length, subject matter and style."** They have recently published poetry by Lyn Lifshin, James M. Canon and Carol Frith. As a sample the editor selected these lines from "Perpetuality And The Past" by Timothy Hodor:

And when the night came
To drop death
Into my evening,
I hid within the wind
And the breeze carried me
Into your infinity.

The editor says it is about 30 pgs., photocopied. Subscription: $10. **Sample postpaid: $4. Make checks or money orders payable to the editor. Previously published poems OK; no simultaneous submissions. Submit 3-5 poems. Reports in 1 month. Pays 1 copy. Acquires one-time rights. Rights revert to authors upon publication.** The editor says, "I would really like to start seeing and publishing more lyrics, such as the style of Lyn Lifshin and Timothy Hodor."

REVIEW: LATIN AMERICAN LITERATURE AND ARTS (IV-Ethnic, regional, translations), Dept. PM, 680 Park Ave., New York NY 10021, phone (212)249-8950, ext. 366, founded 1967, managing editor Daniel Shapiro, is a biannual magazine which serves as a "major forum for Latin American literature in English translation and articles on Latin American visual and performing arts." **They want contemporary Latin American poetry.** They have published poetry by Jose A. Mazzotti, Mateo Rosas de Oquendo and Gregorio de Matos. As a sample the editor selected these lines from "The Forest" by Mariela Dreyfus, translated from the Spanish by Alfred J. MacAdam:

Dark, I wander amid the uncertain
I avoid the traces of the human
silence is the king in this forest
here, where only your breath protects me in winter.

It is 100 pgs., 8½ × 11, with b&w photos of Latin American art. They receive 50-100 submissions, accept the work of 1-2 poets. Press run is 10,000 for 6,000 subscribers of which 500 are libraries. Subscription: $16 for individuals, $25 for institutions. **Sample postpaid: $9. Previously published poems and simultaneous submissions OK. Cover letter required. Do not submit mss November 15 through March 1. Seldom comments on rejections. Reports in 2-3 months. Pays $100-300.** Reviews books of poetry by Latin Americans. The ***Review*** is published by the Americas Society, a not-for-profit organization.

RFD: A COUNTRY JOURNAL FOR GAY MEN EVERYWHERE (I, IV-Gay), P.O. Box 68, Liberty TN 37095, founded 1974, poetry editor Steven Riel. ***RFD*** "is a quarterly for gay men with emphasis on lifestyles outside of the gay mainstream—poetry, politics, profiles, letters." They want **poetry with "personal, creative use of language and image, relevant to journal themes, political themes. We try to publish as many poets as we can so tend to publish shorter poems and avoid epics."** They have published poetry by Antler, James Broughton, Gregory Woods and Winthrop Smith. ***RFD*** has a circulation of 3,300 for 1,300 subscriptions. Single copy: $5.50; subscription: $25 first class, $18 second class. **Sample postpaid: $5. Submit up to 5 poems at a time. Simultaneous submissions OK. Send SASE for guidelines. Editor sometimes comments on rejections. Reports in 6-9 months. Pays copies.** Open to unsolicited reviews. The editor says, "***RFD*** looks for interesting thoughts, succinct use of language and imagery evocative of nature and gay men and love in natural settings."

RHINO (II), 8403 W. Normal, Niles IL 60714 or 1808 N. Larrabee, Chicago IL 60614, founded 1976, editors Kay Meier and Don Hoffman, "is an annually published poetry journal. **We seek well-crafted work with fresh insights and authentic emotion by known or new writers, poems which show careful attention to form and contain surprise. Poems no longer than 3 pgs. double-spaced."** They have recently published poetry by John Dickson, Marcellus Leonard and Robert Edwards. The editors chose as a sample the opening lines of "Grandma and the Latch-Key Child" by Carol L. Gloor:

In 1916 my Irish grandma clutches
her needlepoint satchel on the heaving
ferry from Ellis Island. She has escaped

The Subject Index, located before the General Index, can help you narrow down markets for your work. It lists those publishers whose poetry interests are specialized.

the starched convent, and the wheeling
seagull air screams fish, sweat and hope.
She doesn't know in four years she will marry
the Midwest and a man
she doesn't love.

Rhino is a 96-page journal, digest-sized, perfect-bound, matte card cover with art, offset from typescript on high-quality paper. They receive 1,000 submissions a year, use 50-70. Press run is 500 for 200 subscribers of which 10 are libraries. **Sample: $6 plus $1.15 postage. Submit 3-5 double-spaced poems. Submission period begins October, ends in April. Reports in 3-4 months. Pays 1 copy. Acquires first rights only.** They offer an annual ***Rhino*** poetry contest with a $100 prize, a $50 prize and two $25 prizes as well as publication in ***Rhino.***

THE RIALTO (II), 32 Grosvenor Rd., Norwich, Norfolk NR2 2PZ England, founded 1984, poetry editors John Wakeman and Michael Mackmin, wants **"poetry of intelligence, wit, compassion, skill, excellence, written by humans. Potential contributors are strongly advised to read *The Rialto* before submitting."** They have recently published poetry by Fleur Adcock, Jacques Dupin, Carol Rumens, Charles Simic and Pauline Stainer. As a sample the editors selected "Couplet" by Leo de Freyne:

That child is not involved in war,
So close his eyes, bind up his jaw.

The Rialto, which appears 3 times a year, is magazine-sized, 48 pgs., saddle-stapled, beautifully printed on glossy stock with glossy b&w card cover, using b&w drawings. "U.S.A. subscription is now £15 (fifteen pounds sterling). If paying in dollars, please add £3 to cover bank charges, i.e. send dollar equivalent of £18 pounds sterling. **Single issue to U.S.A. is £5 sterling. If paying in dollars, send equivalent of £8 pounds sterling." Submit up to 6 poems with SAE and IRCs. No simultaneous submissions or previously printed poetry. Editor "only rarely" comments on rejections. Reports within 3 months. Pays £10/poem.** They recently received a special grant for "excellence" from the Arts Council of Great Britain. The editors add, "We would like to receive more poetry that confronts contemporary political issues with compassion and art, without hysteria."

RIDGE REVIEW MAGAZINE; RIDGE TIMES PRESS (IV-Regional), Dept. PM, Box 90, Mendocino CA 95460, phone (707)964-8465, founded 1981, poetry editor Nancy Kay Webb, is a "bio-regional quarterly looking at economic, political and social phenomena of the area" which uses **only poets from Northern California.** They have published poetry by Michael Sykes and Judith Tannenbaum. The 7×10 magazine, saddle-stapled, 50 pgs., linen card cover with art, photos and ads with text, circulation 3,500, 1,000 subscriptions, uses about 1 page of poetry/issue. Subscription: $10. **Sample postpaid: $3.85. Considers simultaneous submissions. Reports in about a week. Usually pays $10/poem.**

RIO GRANDE PRESS; SE LA VIE WRITER'S JOURNAL (I, IV-Themes); RIO GRANDE CHAPBOOK CLUB (I, IV-Membership), P.O. Box 71745, Las Vegas NV 89170, founded 1987, editor Rosalie Avara. ***Se La Vie Writer's Journal*** is a quarterly journal with articles and cartoons about poetry and writing and monthly contests in poetry and quarterly contests in poetry, essays and short stories. Prizes are $5-25 for poems, entry fee $5 for 3 poems. Publishes 70% of mss received/quarter, **"dedicated to encouraging novice writers, poets and artists; we are interested in original, unpublished mss that reflect the 'life' theme (La Vie). Poems are judged on originality, clarity of thought and ability to evoke emotional response."** They have recently published poetry by Marian Ford Park, Phil Eisenberg and Doris Benson. ***SLVWJ*** is 64 pgs., digest-sized, photocopied from typescript, with blue cover, saddle-stapled. **Sample postpaid: $4. Publishes theme issues. Send SASE for guidelines and upcoming themes.** Staff reviews books of poetry. Send books for review consideration. Also publishes several poetry/short story anthologies annually. "No fee or purchase necessary to enter contests and be published." Cash prizes. Send SASE for guidelines. Those interested in the Rio Grande Chapbook Club "receive 4 free books for joining, then receive 4 more quarterly—original unpublished/published poems from new and experienced poets." ***Se La Vie Writer's Journal*** ranked #6 in the "Traditional Verse" category of the latest ***Writer's Digest*** Poetry 60 list.

‡RIVER CITY; HOHENBERG AWARD (II), English Dept., Memphis State University, Memphis TN 38152, phone (901)363-4438, founded 1980, editor Sharon Bryan. ***River City*** publishes fiction, poetry, interviews and essays. Contributors have included John Updike, Marvin Bell, Philip Levine, Maxine Kumin, Robert Penn Warren, W.D. Snodgrass, Mary Oliver, Fred Busch, Beth Bentley, Mona Van Duyn and Peter Porter. The biannual is 6×9, perfect-bound, 100 pgs., 40-50 pgs. of poetry in each issue, professionally printed, two-color matte cover. Circulation 1,000. Subscription: $9. **Sample postpaid: $5. Submit no more than 5 poems, none June through August. Reports in 2-12 weeks. Pays 2**

copies (and cash when grant funds available). $100 Hohenberg Award is given annually to best fiction or poetry selected by the staff.

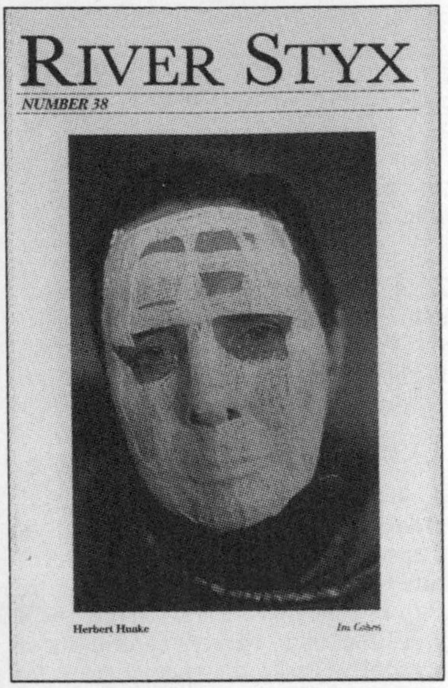

"We chose this particular cover because we thought it fit nicely with the Beat poetry we were featuring in the issue," says Anne Makeever, executive director of* River Styx. *This photograph of Herbert Huncke is from* The Bandaged Poets Series *by Ira Cohen, a photographer and writer living in New York City. Other photos from the series, including pictures of such well-known poets as Allen Ginsberg and William S. Burroughs, are also featured inside. The Missouri-based journal appears "three times a year and seeks excellent, thoughtful poetry. Our magazine is predominantly a poetry magazine," says Makeever. "But we also feature fine art, photography, interviews and short prose, and include work by both award-winning and newly published writers."

RIVER STYX MAGAZINE; BIG RIVER ASSOCIATION (II), 14 S. Euclid, St. Louis MO 63108, founded 1975, executive director Anne Makeever, is "an international, multicultural journal publishing both award-winning and relatively undiscovered writers. We feature fine art, photography, interviews, poetry and short prose." They want **"excellent poetry—thoughtful."** They have published work by Diane Wakoski, Marge Piercy, Simon Ortiz, Toni Morrison and Donald Revell. As a sample the editor selected these lines by Eric Pankey:

Contact and intersection, a communion
With the unrisen moon,
Trouble the sharp doubt that delves and disciplines
His labor and purpose.

River Styx appears 3 times a year. The editor describes it as 90 pgs., digest-sized with b&w cover. They accept less than 10% of 750 mss received a year. **Sample postpaid: $7. Submit 3-5 poems, "legible copies with name and address on each page." Reading period is September 1 through October 31. Guidelines available for SASE. Editor sometimes comments on rejections. Reports in 1 week to 2 months, publication within a year. Pays $8 a page plus 2 copies. Buys one-time rights.** Poetry published in ***River Styx*** has been selected for inclusion in **The Best American Poetry 1994.**

RIVERRUN (II), Glen Oaks Community College, Centreville MI 49032-9719, phone (616)467-9945, ext. 277, founded 1974, poetry editor David Bainbridge, is a literary biannual, using **30-40 magazine-sized pages of poetry in each issue—"no prejudices. We try to give each issue its own distinct, admittedly subjective personality. Best bet is to see the attitude and themes portrayed in the most recent guidelines."** They receive 1,000 poems/month, use up to 240/year. Press run is 850-1,000. **Sample postpaid: $5. Publishes theme issues. Send SASE for upcoming themes. Themes for the Fall 1994 and Spring 1995 issues are "Work Ethic and Leisure Time" and "Horror/Fantasy/Science Fiction," respectively. Reports ASAP (usually 2 weeks to 1 month).** ***Riverrun*** ranked #2 in the "Traditional Verse" category of the latest ***Writer's Digest*** Poetry 60 list. The editor says, "We proudly publish an extremely broad range of individuals well-known to small press circles and beyond (for instance, t. Winter-Damon, Bruce Boston, Stuart Friebert, Philip Miller, Mary Winters and Lyn Lifshin), but we also pride ourselves on devoting occasional space to local poets and as-yet-unpublished poets."

RIVERSIDE QUARTERLY (II, IV-Science fiction/fantasy), Box 958, Big Sandy TX 75755, phone (903)636-5505, founded 1964, editor Leland Sapiro, poetry editor Sheryl Smith **(and submissions should go directly to her at 515 Saratoga #2, Santa Clara CA 95050).** ***Riverside Quarterly*** **is "aimed at the literate reader of science fiction and fantasy.** If you've been reared on 'Startrek,' then ***RQ*** is not for you. **We have no specific subject matter or style preferences. Length: 50 lines maximum. No didactic**

or 'uplifting' verse." They have published poetry by George Gott, Sue Saniel Elkind, Julia Thomas, Edward Mycue and Denise Dumars. As a sample the editor selected these lines from "Ymir's Mirror/ Eiseley's Glass" by Ace Pilkington:

From the skull in the stone
Eye sockets scrape the sky:
Both are wayward worlds
Aglint with stars.
Black, bleak caverns
Where the lightning grows

RQ is 68 pgs., approximately 5 × 8, offset, saddle-stapled with paper cover and b&w art. They receive about 1,100 poems a year, accept approximately 3%. Press run is 1,200 for 550 subscribers of which 200 are libraries. Subscription: $8. **Sample postpaid: $2.50. No previously published poems or simultaneous submissions. Cover letter recommended.** Time between acceptance and publication is 15 months. **Usually comments on rejections. Reports in 10 days. Always sends prepublication galleys. Pays 4 copies. Acquires all rights; rights released to contributor after publication.** "We print reviews of books, movies and magazines—no maximum length." They say, "We advise all contributors (of poetry or prose) to read a copy or two (available at any major public or college library) before sending a ms."

RIVERWIND (II, IV-Regional), General Studies, Hocking College, Nelsonville OH 45764, phone (614)753-3591, ext. 2375, founded 1982, poetry editor J.A. Fuller, is a literary annual publishing **mainly writers from Appalachia.** They want **"work from serious writers. We are most open to work with serious content, though humor may be the vehicle. Do not want to see poetry from those who view it as a 'hobby.' We have not published limericks."** They have published poetry by Naton Leslie, Gloria Ruth, Charles Semones, Walter McDonald, John Haines, John Aber, James Riley and Greg Anderson. ***Riverwind*** is 7 × 7, flat-spined, 80-120 pgs., offset, with 2-color semiglossy card cover. Of 500 poems received they accept approximately 60. Press run is 500. Single copy: $2.50. **Sample back issue postpaid: $1. Submit batches of 3-5, no previously published poems, no simultaneous submissions. Reads submissions September 15 through June 15 only. Submissions received after June 15 will be considered for the following year. Editor comments "particularly if we would like to see more of that person's work." Reports in 1-4 months. Response slow during summer months. Pays 2 copies.** Reviews books of poetry. They hope to begin publishing chapbook collections.

ROANOKE REVIEW (II), Roanoke College, Salem VA 24153, phone (703)389-2351, ext. 367, founded 1968, poetry editor Robert R. Walter, is a semiannual literary review which uses **poetry that is "conventional; we have not used much experimental or highly abstract poetry."** They have published poetry by Peter Thomas, Norman Russell, Alan Seaburg, Mary Balazs and Irene Dayton. ***RR*** is 52 pgs., 6 × 9, professionally printed with matte card cover with decorative typography, using 25-30 pgs. of poetry in each issue, circulation 250-300, 150 subscriptions of which 50 are libraries. They receive 400-500 submissions of poetry/year, use 40-60, have a 3- to 6-month backlog. Subscription: $5.50. **Sample postpaid: $3. Submit original typed mss, no photocopies. Reports in 8-10 weeks. No pay.** The editor advises, "There is a lot of careless or sloppy writing going on. We suggest careful proofreading and study of punctuation rules."

ROCK FALLS REVIEW; AUTHOR'S INK (I), P.O. Box 104, Stamford NE 68977, phone (308)868-3545, founded 1989, editor Diana L. Lambson. ***Rock Falls Review*** is a quarterly that "started as a learning tool for our writer's group. We try to maintain a learning atmosphere. Much of what we publish is by new writers but we still insist on quality work submitted in a professional manner." They **"prefer shorter poems—under 100 lines. Inspirational poetry is okay. No 'doomsday' or 'preachy' verse, though. Also okay: fantasy and science fiction, free verse, humor and traditional forms. No obscure, far out, experimental or pornographic verse. No horror or dark image. No violence. No obscene language! Concrete or shaped verse is nearly impossible for us to use."** They have recently published poetry by R. Nikolas Macioci, Lyn Lifshin, Mary Winters, T. Kilgore Splake and Barbara Crooker. As a sample the editor selected these lines from "Waking Up" by Noel Smith:

Headfirst
I drift down a silken thread
Arms folded like wings.

Voices of grand—
Mothers and children who cannot follow
Echo
From far back at the beginning.

RFR is 14-24 pgs., 8½ × 11, photocopied typescript, side-stapled with colored paper cover, clip art and original b&w line art and ads inside. They receive about 150 poems a year, use 115 to 120. Press run is 50 for 30 subscribers. Single copy postpaid: $3 US, $6 foreign; subscription: $10

US, $22 foreign. **Previously published poems OK with release and proper credits. Simultaneous submissions also OK. "While we do not require a cover letter it is nice to know something about the person submitting." Often comments on rejections. Send SASE for guidelines. Reports in 6-12 weeks "usually." Pays 1 copy.** Reviews books of poetry. Open to unsolicited reviews. Poets may also send books for review consideration; "one of our group will review." The editor says, "We do not require purchase or subscription. However, because of space and funding restrictions, members of Author's Ink or the Great Plains Writer's Club and subscribers will be given first consideration. This should not discourage anyone, however, as 50-75% of our accepted submissions are non-subscribers. We prefer poetry that is *not* obscure. In order for most people to read and enjoy poetry, it should be understandable: something they can relate to."

‡ROCKET LITERARY QUARTERLY (I, II), P.O. Box 672, Water Mill NY 11976-0672, founded 1993, editor Darren Johnson, features "styles and forms definitely for the 21st century." **The editor wants "original ideas expressed in 'a true voice.' I don't want to see hero worship-type poems that drop names. Don't use the words 'poem,' 'love' or 'ode.'"** They have recently published poetry by Leslie Scalapino, Lyn Lifshin and Ana Christy. As a sample we selected these lines from "The Holiday Season Falls" by Cheryl A. Townsend:

like the stock market sending
mass hysteria and emotional
duress out like children to recess
hurry get your shopping done
while the druggers quietly await
in the dark by your car for any
money not already spent . . .

Rocket is 20 pgs., photocopied, saddle-stapled with colored card cover, cartoons and ads for almost anything. They receive about 400 poems a year, accept approximately 10%. Press run is 400 for 100 subscribers of which 2 are libraries, 100 shelf sales. Subscription: $3.96. **Sample postpaid: 99¢. Make checks payable to D. Johnson. Submit 3 pages of poetry (maximum). No previously published poems; simultaneous submissions OK.** Time between acceptance and publication is 1 week to 3 months. **Often comments on rejections. "Subscribers get fuller critiques." Reports in less than 1 month. Pays 1 copy. Acquires one-time rights.** Editor includes his own blurb reviews "of anything cool." Send books for review consideration. The editor says poets published by ***The Rocket*** get full support through community flyers with samples and mailings of interest. His advice: "Write whatever you want! Too many poets 'respect' and 'admire' more established writers, so much so they start writing in the established poet's style—may even refer to them in verse. Sad. Delve into yourself and realize there is no one better to tell your life than you."

THE ROCKFORD REVIEW (I, II), P.O. Box 858, Rockford IL 61105, founded 1971, editor David Ross, is a quarterly publication of the Rockford Writers Guild, **publishing their poetry and prose, that of other writers throughout the country and contributors from other countries. "We look for the magical power of the words themselves, a playfulness with language in the creation of images and fresh insights on old themes, whether it be poetry, satire or fiction."** They have published poetry by Russell King, David Koenig and Christine Swanberg. As a sample the editor selected these lines by Olivia Diamond:

The chill will nip us all in the end
even fragile stems we brace in vases.
The tips of petals curl in and bend
toward the ground in stiff embraces.

TRR is 50 pgs., digest-sized, flat-spined, glossy cover with b&w photos. Circulation 800. Single copy: $5; subscription: $15 (4 issues). **Considers simultaneous submissions. Reports in 4-6 weeks. Pays 1 copy. Acquires first North American serial rights.** They offer Editor's Choice Prizes of $25 for prose, $25 for poetry.

ROCKY MOUNTAIN REVIEW OF LANGUAGE AND LITERATURE (IV-Membership, translations), Boise State University English Dept., Boise ID 83725, phone (208)385-1246, founded 1947, editor Jan Widmayer, poetry editor Marcia Southwick (**and submissions should go directly to her at English Dept., University of Nebraska, Lincoln NE 68588-0333). Contributors to the literary quarterly must be members of Rocky Mountain Modern Language Association. Poetry should be "generally relatively short" and may be in English or other modern languages.** The review has published poetry by Scott P. Sanders and translations of Antonio Cisneros and David Huerta. The 6×9, 276-page, flat-spined quarterly publishes work of interest to college and university teachers of literature and language. Circulation of the review is 1,100-1,200, all membership subscriptions. They accept a few ads from other journals and publishers. **Contributors are not paid and do not receive extra copies; contributors must be RMMLA members. Poets should submit 2 copies, *without author's name*. They report on**

submissions in 1-2 months and publish usually within 6 months but no more than 1 year after acceptance.

THE ROMANTIST (IV-Fantasy, horror), Saracinesca House, 3610 Meadowbrook Ave., Nashville TN 37205, phone (615)226-1890, poetry editor Steve Eng, founded 1977, is a "literary magazine of nonfiction articles on fantasy, horror and romantic literature, using **lyrical poetry—prefer fantasy and horror content. No homespun, gushy, trite verse with forced rhyme."** They have published poetry by Donald Sidney-Fryer, Joey Froehlich, Stephanie Stearns and Gary William Crawford. The annual is magazine-sized. Press run is 300 numbered copies for 150 subscriptions of which 50 are libraries. **Sample postpaid: $10. Contributors may purchase a copy for 50% of its price. They receive tearsheets. Submit no more than 3 poems at a time, double-spaced. Editor sometimes comments on rejections. Reports in 1 month.** Open to unsolicited reviews. Poets may also send books for review consideration; query first. The editor says, "Too much contemporary poetry is easy to write and hard to read. We resist the depressed, carefully jaded tone so often fashionable. We prefer lyric verse that reflects some knowledge of traditions of poetry, though we do not require the slavish adherence to any school."

ROOM OF ONE'S OWN (IV-Women), P.O. Box 46160 Station D, Vancouver, British Columbia V6J 5G5 Canada, founded 1975, is a quarterly using **"poetry by and about women, written from a feminist perspective. Nothing simplistic, clichéd. Short fiction also accepted."** It is 128 pgs., digest-sized. Press run is 1,000 for 420 subscribers of which 50-100 are libraries, 350 shelf sales. Subscription: $20 ($30 US or foreign). **Sample: $7 plus postage or IRCs. "We prefer to receive 5-6 poems at a time, so we can select a pair or group." No simultaneous submissions. Send SASE or SAE with 1 IRC for guidelines. The mss are circulated to a collective, which "takes time." Publishes theme issues. Themes for Fall 1994 and Spring 1995 are "Women and the Body" and "The Geography of Gender," respectively. Reports in 6 months. Pays honorarium plus 2 copies. Buys first North American serial rights.**"We solicit reviews." Send books for review consideration, attn. book review editor.

ROSE SHELL PRESS (I), 5111 N. 42nd Ave., Phoenix AZ 85019 (Northeast branch: 516 Gallows Hill Rd., Cranford NJ 07016, phone (908)276-9479), press originally founded as Merging Media in 1978 by D.C. Erdmann, current editor/publisher Rochelle L. Holt, who says she "will attempt to keep the press alive with Merging Media ideals as I believe there is still a need for presses open to women and a few sensitive men." **They would like to receive poetry dealing with feminism, women's issues, alternative love/lifestyles, the occult; inspirational and ethnic poetry; and poems on New Age/healing.** She has recently published books by Ruth Moon Kempher, Stephen Gill and Sally Hughes. As a sample, she selected these lines from Kempher's book **Mother Goose on Wheels:**

Hey Diddle Diddle
The cat and the fiddle!
Our cow jumped over the moon!

She jumped at the clatter
of a car coming at her
and it wasn't a moment too soon.

Interested poets should query first with 5 sample poems and a cover letter noting "how they heard of us and what they've read of Merging Media in the past." Include SASE and $10 "for criticism and/or suggestions." They also sponsor an annual contest for writers, ages 10-18, who have not had a book published. Submit ms 24-32 pgs. in length. Entry fee: $10, include SASE and bio. Deadline: July 1.

THE ROUND TABLE: A JOURNAL OF POETRY AND FICTION (II), 375 Oakdale Dr., Rochester NY 14618, phone (716)244-0623, founded 1984, poetry editors Alan Lupack and Barbara Lupack. "We publish a journal of poetry and fiction. Currently, one issue a year. **Few restrictions on poetry—except high quality. We like forms if finely crafted. Very long poems must be exceptional. We are tending to focus more on Arthurian poetry and prose and to publish almost exclusively material on this theme."** They have published poetry by Kathleene West, John Tagliabue, Wendy Mnookin and Paul Scott. ***The Round Table*** is 64 pgs., digest-sized, perfect-bound, professionally printed (offset) with matte card cover. Circulation 125, 75 subscribers of which 3 are libraries. Subscription: $7.50. **Sample postpaid: $5. "We like to see about 5 poems (but we read whatever is submitted)." Cover letter required. Simultaneous submissions OK. "But we expect to be notified if a poem submitted to us is accepted elsewhere. Quality of poetry, not format, is most important thing. We try to report in 3 months, but—especially for poems under serious consideration—it may take longer." Pays copies.** "Some years we will publish a volume of Arthurian poetry by one author."

THE RUGGING ROOM; RUGGING ROOM BULLETIN (IV-Specialized: rug hooking), 10 Sawmill Dr., Westford MA 01886, founded as a press in 1983, periodical in 1987, poetry editor Jeanne H. Fallier, publisher of "how-to books **related to traditional rug hooking and related subjects of interest**

to people in fibre crafts." Verses of a philosophical theme or concerning nature are acceptable if they refer to hand works, wool or fibers, the therapeutic value of hand-made fiber crafts, etc. She accepts "very short poems related to fibre arts (especially hooking) crafts—not more than ½ page." Wants more traditional forms. The *Rugging Room Bulletin* is a newsletter, 8-16 pgs., 8½×11, appearing 4 times a year, printed on white stock, with b&w illustrations, ads and graphics. Circulation 300 but widespread, coast to coast. Subscription: $11. **Sample postpaid: $2.50. Simultaneous submissions OK. Cover letter explaining what inspired your poem required. Reports within about 2 weeks. Pays 3 copies plus 1-year subscription. Contributors are also expected to buy 1 copy. Acquires all rights. Returns rights after publication, by arrangement.** Staff reviews related books of poetry. Send books for review consideration.

THE RUNAWAY SPOON PRESS (IV-Form), Box 3621, Port Charlotte FL 33949, phone (813)629-8045, founded 1987, editor Bob Grumman, is a "photocopy publisher of chapbooks of otherstream poetry & illumagery." He wants **"visual poetry, textual poetry mixed with visual matter, verbo-visual collages, burning poodle poetry—or anything insane. No work in which politics is more important than aesthetics. Free verse is way too traditional for my press."** He has recently published poetry by Jefferson Hansen, Michael Basinski and Gregory Vincent St. Thomasino. As a sample the editor selected this poem by Guy R. Beining:

blue-prints of a dream
in red
for the insomniac

The books are usually about 4×5½, printed on good stock with matte card covers. He prints about 10 a year averaging 48 pgs. **"Query is a good idea but not necessary." Simultaneous submissions and previously published poems OK. Editor comments on submissions "always." Sometimes sends prepublication galleys. Pays 25% of first edition of 100. Acquires all rights. Releases rights to author(s) upon publication. Sample books available for $3 apiece.** The editor advises, "Don't let anti-intellectuals convince you the brain is less important than the heart in poetry."

RURAL HERITAGE (I, IV-Rural, humor), 281 Dean Ridge Lane, Gainesboro TN 38562-5039, founded 1975, editor Gail Damerow, **uses poetry related to rural living, Americana. "Traditional meter and rhyme only. Preference is given to poems with a touch of humor or other twist. Please, no comparisons between country and city life and no religious, political or issues-oriented material."** As a sample the editor selected this poem, "I Believe," by William Sowell:

Some people demonstrate their faith
Through church attendance or by deed,
But surely the greatest show of faith
Must be a farmer planting seed.

RH is magazine-sized, bimonthly, using b&w photos, graphics and ads, 4-6 poems/issue. Circulation 3,000. Subscription: $19. **Sample postpaid: $6. Submit no more than 3 poems at a time, one/page.** Time between acceptance and publication is 4-6 months. "We often group poems by theme, for example gardening, quilting, and so forth according to season. Verse is also coupled with an article of similar theme such as maple sugaring, mule teams, etc." **Guidelines available for SASE. Reports ASAP. Pays on publication, $5 and up (depending on length) and 2 copies.** The editor says, "We receive too much modern poetry, not enough traditional, not enough humor. We get too much image poetry (we prefer action) and most poems are too long—we prefer 12 lines or less."

SACHEM PRESS (II, IV-Translations, bilingual), P.O. Box 9, Old Chatham NY 12136, phone (518)794-8327, founded 1980, editor Louis Hammer, a small press publisher of poetry and fiction, both hardcover and flat-spined paperbacks. **No new submissions, only statements of projects, until January 1995. Submit mss January through March.** The editor wants to see **"strong, compelling, even visionary work, English-language or translations."** He has published poetry by Cesar Vallejo, Yannis Ritsos, 24 leading poets of Spain (in an anthology), Miltos Sahtouris and himself. As a sample, he selected the following lines from his book **Poetry at the End of the Mind**:

If the only paper you had
was the flesh on your back
between your shoulder blades
what would you write
with the motion of your body?

The paperbacks average 120 pgs. and the anthology of Spanish poetry contains 340 pgs. Each poem is printed in both Spanish and English, and there are biographical notes about the authors. The small books cost $6.95 and the anthology $11.95. **Royalties are 10% maximum, after expenses are recovered, plus 50 author's copies. Rights are negotiable.** Book catalog is free "when available," and poets can purchase books from Sachem "by writing to us, 33⅓% discount."

ST. ANDREW PRESS (IV-Religious), P.O. Box 329, Big Island VA 24526, phone (804)299-5956, founded 1986, poetry editor Jean Horne, is a "small press publisher of religious material (worship materials, lyrics and music, etc.), **specializing in meditations, lifestyle, church renewal, spirituality, hunger, peace and justice issues." Any form or style up to 64 lines on subjects listed. "No profanity for shock value only; no sickeningly sweet idealism."** They say they will publish 3 chapbooks and flat-spined paperbacks, averaging 64 pgs., each year. **Submit 6 samples, bio, other publications. Simultaneous submissions and previously published poems OK. Reports in 2-4 weeks. Payment usually $10 minimum, averages more.** They will consider subsidy publishing. The editor says, "We are looking forward to doing more with poetry in the next couple of years. The amount we do will be largely determined by quality of submissions we receive. Poetry is not accepted if it is too 'sing-song' with trite rhymes, if it could be rewritten in paragraphs as prose, or if it is so 'stream-of-consciousness' that no one could possibly follow the thought or get any meaning from it."

ST. ANTHONY MESSENGER (IV-Religious), 1615 Republic St., Cincinnati OH 45210-1298, phone (513)241-5615, is a monthly 56-page magazine, circulation 325,000, for Catholic families, mostly with children in grade school, high school or college. In some issues, they have a **poetry page which uses poems appropriate for their readership. Their poetry needs are limited but poetry submissions are always welcomed.** As a sample here is "A Valentine for Darby" by Jean M. Syed:

Why do I love you, my potbellied love?
Not for your pregnant form or shiny pate.
Were these on tender those decades ago,
would I have been so indiscriminate
as to let you win my heart? No princess
from passion ever took a frog to mate.

"Submit seasonal poetry (Christmas/Easter/nature poems) several months in advance. Submit a few poems at a time; do not send us your entire collection of poetry. We seek to publish accessible poetry of high quality." Send regular SASE for guidelines and 9×12 SASE for free sample. Pays $2/line on acceptance. Buys first North American serial rights. ***St. Anthony Messenger*** poetry occasionally receives awards from the Catholic Press Association Annual Competition.

ST. JOSEPH MESSENGER AND ADVOCATE OF THE BLIND (I, IV-Religious), 541 Pavonia Ave., P.O. Box 288, Jersey City NJ 07303, phone (201)798-4141, founded 1898, poetry editor Sister Ursula Maphet, C.S.J.P, is a quarterly (16 pgs., 8×11). They want **"brief but thought-filled poetry; do not want lengthy and issue-filled."** Most of the poets they have used are previously unpublished. They receive 400-500 submissions/year, use 50. There are about 2 pgs. of poetry in each issue. Circulation 20,000. Subscription: $5. **Editor sometimes comments on rejections. Publishes theme issues. Send SASE for guidelines, free sample and upcoming themes. Reports within 2 weeks. Pays $5-20/poem.**

ST. MARTIN'S PRESS, 175 Fifth Ave., New York NY 10010. Prefers not to share information.

SALMAGUNDI (III), Skidmore College, Saratoga Springs NY 12866, phone (518)584-5000, ext. 2302, founded 1965, edited by Peggy Boyers and Robert Boyers, has long been **one of the most distinguished quarterlies** of the sciences and humanities, publishing poets such as Robert Penn Warren, Louise Glück, John Peck, Howard Nemerov and W.D. Snodgrass. Each issue is handsomely printed, thick, flat-spined, priced at $5-10. Editors here tend to use more lyric free verse than any other style, much of it accessible and usually under 50 lines. Although the magazine is hefty, poems compete with prose (with the latter dominating). They use about 10-50 pages of poetry in each issue, receive 1,200 submissions/year, use about 20 and have a 12- to 30-month backlog. Paid circulation is 5,400 with 3,800 subscriptions of which about 900 are libraries. Subscriptions are $15 a year, $25 for two years. **Sample postpaid: $6. Submissions not accompanied by SASE are discarded. Reads mss November through April only. Reports in 3 months. Pays copies.** Send books for review consideration. Work published in ***Salmagundi*** has been selected for inclusion in **The Best American Poetry 1994.**

SALMON RUN PRESS (III), P.O. Box 231081, Anchorage AK 99523-1081, founded 1991, editor/publisher John E. Smelcer, publishes 2-3 paperbacks/year, "only poetry mss by well-known authors." They want **"quality poetry by established poets, any subject, any style. No poetry that is not representative of the highest achievement in the art."** They have recently published Tom Sexton, Joseph Bruchac, John Daniel, Barry Sternlieb, X.J. Kennedy and John Haines. As a sample the editor selected these lines from Daniel's "The Meal":

The meat is before us, the flagons
have been filled, but my father
doesn't rise to speak. His head
is turned toward the spectacled man
who stares at his plate, and I've seen

that sharp white jaw in a picture.

Their books are flat-spined, with "letterpress quality print appearing on heavy, natural-colored paper." **Query first with sample poems and cover letter with brief bio. Previously published poems and simultaneous submissions OK. Usually comments on rejections. Replies to queries within 1-3 weeks, to mss in 1-2 months. Sometimes sends prepublication galleys. Pays 10% royalties and a negotiable number of author's copies.** They also sponsor a pamphlet series and an annual poetry contest for book-length mss of 48-64 pgs. $15 reading fee and SASE required. Entries must be postmarked by November 30. The winning ms will be published in book form, and all contestants will receive a copy of the winning book.

SALT LICK; SALT LICK PRESS; SALT LICK SAMPLERS; LUCKY HEART BOOKS (II), Apt. #15, 1416 NE 21st Ave., Portland OR 97232-1507, phone (503)249-1014, founded 1969, editor James Haining, publishes "new literature and graphic arts in their various forms." They have recently published poetry by Robert Creeley, Charles Olson, Michael Lally, David Searcy, Julie Siegel, Paul Shuttleworth, Wm. Hart, Robert Slater, Gerald Burns and Sheila Murphy. The magazine-sized journal, 66 pgs., saddle-stapled, matte cover, experimental graphics throughout, appears irregularly. They receive 400-600 poems/year, use 1-2%. Press run is 1,000. **Sample postpaid: $6. Reports in 1-6 weeks. Pays copies. To submit for book publication under the Lucky Heart Books imprint, send 20 samples, cover letter "open." Simultaneous submissions OK. Always sends prepublication galleys. Pays copies.**

SAN DIEGO POET'S PRESS; LA JOLLA POET'S PRESS; AMERICAN BOOK SERIES (II), P.O. Box 8638, La Jolla CA 92038. San Diego Poet's Press, a nonprofit press founded 1981 by editor/publisher Kathleen Iddings, has published collections and anthologies that include Galway Kinnell, Carolyn Kizer, Allen Ginsberg, Carolyn Forche, Tess Gallagher and Robert Pinsky, among others. Iddings began publishing individual poets in 1985 and has published approximately 25 poets to date. In 1989, she originated the "American Book Series" wherein she awards the winner $500 and publishes his/her first book of poetry. Past winners include Joan LaBombard, Regina McBride, Charles Atkinson and Michael Cleary. As a sample she selected these lines from "The Pond Near Crematorium Four" in Kevin Griffith's **Someone Had To Live**:

Now, our guide's red dress flaps
as she leads us through
cautioning fields, each long blade
wind bent. She stops, slips
her arm in pond's shallows,
and lifts the bone chips
into my hand
light and delicate as wasps.

Sample of any winning book, postpaid: $11.50. Watch the ***Small Press Review*** or ***Poets & Writers*** for contest information.

SAN FERNANDO POETRY JOURNAL; KENT PUBLICATIONS, INC. (I, IV-Social issues), 18301 Halsted St., Northridge CA 91325, founded 1978, poetry editors Richard Cloke, Shirley Rodecker and Lori Smith. ***San Fernando Poetry Journal*** uses **poetry of social protest.** According to Richard Cloke, "Poetry, for us, should be ***didactic*** **in the Brechtian sense. It must say something, must inform, in the tenor of our time.** We follow Hart Crane's definition of poetry as architectural in essence, building upon the past but incorporating the newest of this age also, including science, machinery, sub-atomic and cosmic physical phenomena as well as the social convulsions wrenching the very roots of our present world." **Send SASE for guidelines which explain this more fully.** For example, we quote this passage for its general usefulness for poets: "In some, the end-line rhyming is too insistent, seeming *forced;* in others the words are not vibrant enough to give the content an arresting framework. Others do not have any beat (cadence) at all and some are simply not well thought out – often like first drafts, or seem like prose statements. Please try reworking again to get some energy in your statement. If your poetry is to succeed in impelling the reader to act, it must electrify, or at least command interest and attention." **They welcome new and unpublished poets.** As a sample the editor selected this poem, "Paradise Lost," by Marian Steele:

Adam trod the earth enraptured
When he was nearly alone on a younger land.
His name was Muir . . . Bartram . . . Burroughs . . .
Audubon.
It was not so long ago.
We have seen to it;
Whether in Saudi desert,
Flaming Brazilian rain forest,
In Detroit's blighted back streets
Or South Bronx alleyways,

In the belches from redbrick smokestack,
Recoilless rifle, naval Big Gun,
Or even Three-Mile-Island-Chernobyl—
We have remodeled our planet
In our own image.

The flat-spined quarterly, photocopied from typescript, uses 100 pgs. of poetry in each issue. They use about 300 of the 1,000 submissions (the editor rightly prefers to call them "contributions") each year. Press run is 400 for 350 subscribers of which 45 are libraries. **Sample postpaid: $2.50. No specifications for ms form. Simultaneous submissions OK. Reports in 1 week. Pays copies.** The press, under its various imprints, also publishes a few collections by individuals. **Query with 5-6 pgs. of samples.**

SAN JOSE STUDIES; CASEY MEMORIAL AWARD (II), San Jose State University, San Jose CA 95192-0090, phone (408)924-4476, founded 1975, poetry editor John Engell. This "journal of general and scholarly interest, featuring critical, creative and informative writing in the arts, business, humanities, science and social sciences" uses poetry of **"excellent quality—with a focus on Bay Area and California cultures. Tend to like poems with something to say, however indirectly it may be communicated. Usually publish 7-12 pgs. of verse in each issue. We like to publish several poems by one poet—better exposure for the poet, more interest for the reader."** They have published poetry by Leonard Nathan, Lyn Lifshin and James Sutherland-Smith. As a sample the editor chose these lines from "Mountain Woman" by Virginia de Araújo:

. . . But place in her is deep root:
hand, brain, nerve, tooth. Planted, she will
spill upward in fern fronds, tight buds and fists.
Overhead, winter and summer secretly will move,
and she remain planted in true place.

SJS appears thrice yearly in a 6×9, flat-spined, 100-page format, professionally printed, matte card cover, using b&w photos, circulation of 500-600 of which 70-75 are libraries. They receive about 200 submissions/year, use 8-10 authors, have a 1-year backlog. Subscription: $12 individuals, $18 institutions. **Sample postpaid: $5. No simultaneous submissions. Reports in 2-3 months. Pays 2 copies. Annual award of a year's subscription for best poetry printed that year and a Casey Memorial Award of $100 for the best contribution in prose or poetry.** Editor Emeritus O.C. Williams comments, "Poetry is both an art and a craft; we are not interested in submissions unless the writer has mastered the craft and is actually practicing the art."

SAN MIGUEL WRITER (II, IV-Bilingual/foreign language), Apdo. 989, San Miguel de Allende, GTO 37700 Mexico, founded 1988, editor Carl Selph, appears twice a year publishing verse, short stories and essays. "About one-third of the magazine is in Spanish." **They want "well-crafted poetry. No effusions submitted in first draft."** They have published poetry by W.D. Snodgrass, Miller Williams and Nicholas A. Patricca. As a sample the editor selected these lines from "Quartering" by Charles Hasty:

Reach where standing skies, like old faces,
Awful floods blaze in Eden,
Amber galleons of the nerve,
In the firm lace of air, downwind.

San Miguel Writer is 110 pgs., 5⅞×8⅜, photo-offset, flat-spined, glossy card cover with drawings. They receive about 150 submissions a year, use approximately 25. Press run is 250. **Sample postpaid: $5. No simultaneous submissions. Cover letter required. Enclose SASE or (from US) stamped return postcard. Mss are circulated and chosen by a two-thirds majority of the editorial board. Often comments on rejections. Reports in 2-3 months. Pays 1 copy.** The editor advises, "Don't submit your 'Mexican experience' unless it is an example of your best work."

SANDBERRY PRESS; DEBROSSE, REDMAN, BLACK & CO. LTD. (IV-Ethnic/nationality, regional, children), P.O. Box 507, Kingston 10, Jamaica, West Indies, founded 1986, managing director Pamela Mordecai, publishes 8 paperbacks and 5 hardbacks/year. **They want to see work from "poets born in the Caribbean or naturalized citizens of a Caribbean country or poets who have lived most of their lives in the region. Nothing racist, sexist or pornographic. Also interested in poetry for children."** They have recently published collections by Judith Hamilton and Elaine Savory. As a sample the director selected these lines from "flame tree time" in Savory's collection of the same name:

flame trees
are death reversed:
they stun your eyes
on those blue days
when the sea already makes you spin

"Previously published poems may form part of a ms submission" but no simultaneous submis-

sions. Cover letter required "to know whether, what and where the author has previously published. Also a brief bio note." Often comments on rejections. Also publishes themed collections. Send SASE (or SAE and IRCs) for upcoming themes. Replies to queries in 2 months, to mss in 6 months. Always sends prepublication galleys. Pays 10% royalties on net receipts, $200 (US) advance and 6 author's copies. Inquire about sample books. The editor says, "We would like to receive more humorous verse."

SANDPIPER PRESS (V), P.O. Box 286, Brookings OR 97415, phone (503)469-5588, founded 1979, is a small press publisher of large print books. They have published **Poems from the Oregon Sea Coast; Unicorns for Everyone,** which includes some poetry; and **Walk With Me,** a book of prayers and meditations. However, **they currently do not accept unsolicited poetry.**

SANSKRIT (I), Cone Center, UNCC, Charlotte NC 28223, phone (704)547-2326, founded 1965, editor Jeff Byers, is a literary annual using **poetry. "No restrictions as to form or genre, but we do look for maturity and sincerity in submissions. Nothing trite or sentimental."** They have recently published poetry by Kimberleigh Luke-Stallings, Stella Hastie and Makyo. As a sample the editor selected these lines by Christy Beatty:

If your father's taking lithium and your nana
won't let the shades up and the caterpillars
in your backyard are ablaze at some slight
fault of your own, if there exists urban
atrocity and decay that don't quite touch you
yet infect your daily media intake
Fight back.
Change your name.

Their purpose is "to encourage and promote beginning and established artists and writers." It is 60-65 pgs., 9×12, flat-spined, printed on quality matte paper with heavy matte card cover. Press run is 3,500 for about 100 subscriptions of which 2 are libraries. **Sample postpaid: $6. Submit no more than 5 poems. Simultaneous submissions OK. Cover letter with biographical information and past publications required. Reads submissions September through October only. Editor comments on submissions "infrequently." Reports in 6-8 weeks. Pays 1 copy.**

SANTA MONICA REVIEW (III), 1900 Pico Blvd., Santa Monica CA 90405, founded 1988, editor Jim Krusoe, appears twice a year publishing fiction and poetry, but is **not interested in traditional forms.** They have recently published poetry by Charles Bernstein, Tom Clark, Norman Dubie, Alicia Ostriker, Maureen Owen and Eileen Myles. Single copy: $7; subscription: $12/year. **No submission information provided.** Poetry published in this review has been included in **The Best American Poetry 1993.**

SANTA SUSANA PRESS (V), CSU Libraries, 18111 Nordhoff St., Northridge CA 91330, phone (818)885-2271, founded 1973, a small press publisher of limited edition fine print books, history, literature and art, some poetry, all hardcover editions. **They do not accept unsolicited submissions of poetry. Poets should query first, and queries will be answered in 2 weeks. Honorariums paid depend on grant money.** The press has published books by George Elliott, Ward Ritchie and Ray Bradbury. Book catalog is free on request; prices are high. For instance, **Reaching: Poems by George P. Elliott,** illustrated, is published in an edition of 350 numbered copies at $35 and 26 lettered copies at $60.

SATURDAY EVENING POST (IV-Humor), 1100 Waterway Blvd., Indianapolis IN 46202, phone (317)636-8881, founded 1728 as the ***Pennsylvania Gazette***, since 1821 as ***The Saturday Evening Post***, Post Scripts editor Steve Pettinga, P.O. Box 567, Indianapolis IN 46206. ***SEP*** is a general interest, mass circulation monthly with emphasis on preventive medicine, using **"*humorous light verse only.* No more than 100 words per poem. Stay away from four-letter words and sexually graphic subject matter. No experimental verse (haiku, etc.) Morally, the *Post* is an anachronism of the early 50s; most of its readers are elderly. Other than that, anything goes, as long as it's in good taste."** Subscription: $13.97. **Payment is $15 for all rights.**

SATURDAY PRESS, INC.; EILEEN W. BARNES AWARD SERIES; INVITED POETS SERIES (V, IV-Women), Box 884, Upper Montclair NJ 07043, phone (201)256-5053, founded 1975, poetry editor

Charlotte Mandel with contest guest editors; these have included Maxine Kumin, Colette Inez, Sandra M. Gilbert, Geraldine C. Little and Rachel Hadas. "Saturday Press, Inc., is a nonprofit literary organization. The press has a **special—though not exclusive—commitment to women's poetry, and by sponsoring the Eileen W. Barnes Award Competition for first books by women over 40 seeks to offer opportunity for new poets who have delayed their writing careers. Selection is by means of open competition or, in alternate years, by editorial board decision. Query for current information.** Not an annual event, the contest is widely posted when announced. The Invited Poets Series offers publication to established or less-known poets. We want **authoritative craft, strong, fresh imagery, sense of imagination and a good ear for syntax, sounds and rhythms. Language should lead the reader to experience a sense of discovery. Any form, content or style, but do not want polemic, jingles or conventional inspiration."** They have published books of poetry by Janice Thaddeus, Jean Hollander, Anne Carpenter, Anneliese Wagner and Doris Radin. As a sample the editor selected these lines from "Legacy" by Dixie Partridge:

Out on the plateau a ground hog,
upright from his burrow, listens
to the world. It is yesterday,
or five centuries ago, and from dugouts
on the hillside come monotones of prophecy
that name us.

"We are fully committed at present." Query first. Enclose 1-3 samples and minimum summary of publications. Replies to queries in 2 weeks. If invited, book ms may be photocopied; simultaneous submissions OK. "Prefer no binder, simple folder or paper clip." Always sends prepublication galleys. Pays 50 copies and possible honorarium ("depends on grants"). Send SASE for catalog to buy samples.

SCAT! (I, IV-Regional), Innis College, 2 Sussex Ave., Toronto, Ontario M5S 1J5 Canada, phone (416)978-2513, founded 1982, editors Claire Thompson, Donald Peters and Aub Glazer, is an annual, with **"dedication to new, wordy, smart poetry, any length, sure of speed and delivery, get to the point! Believe that 'It's all in the delivery.' Poet must be aware of the time and thought s/he's writing in."** They have published poetry by Brian Burke, Robbie Newton Drummond and Debbie Ferst. As a sample the editors selected these lines from "The Altar" by Jonathan Hyman:

It is night, wind
and we storm together.
There is nothing that binds
like fury, nothing as quiet as air,
The other corners
are sunlit,
holy.

Scat! is published annually in the spring. **Sample postpaid: $10. "Stress on Canadian representation and content." Submit maximum of 5 poems. Cover letter required with $15 evaluation fee (*postal money order only*). Editors comment "occasionally." No payment information provided.**

SCAVENGER'S NEWSLETTER; KILLER FROG CONTEST (IV-Science fiction/fantasy, horror, mystery, writing), 519 Ellinwood, Osage City KS 66523-1329, may seem an odd place to publish poems, but its editor, Janet Fox, uses 1-2 every month. The *Newsletter* is a **28-page booklet packed with news about science fiction and horror publications** and printed at a quick printing shop. **Janet prefers science fiction/fantasy, horror and mystery poetry and will read anything that is offbeat or bizarre. Writing-oriented poetry is occasionally accepted but "poems on writing must present fresh ideas and viewpoints. Poetry is used as filler so it must be 10 lines or under."** Published poets include Lin Stein, Jacie Ragan, Steve Eng and Herb Kauderer. As a sample she selected this poem, "Rocky Road," by Jamie Meyers:

The great thing about bloodstains
Is that, when left alone long enough
They look just like chocolate ice cream.

Janet Fox says, "I have added mystery to the genres I cover, so I wouldn't mind seeing some mystery oriented poems in addition to those in the science fiction/fantasy/horror genres." She has around 800 subscribers. Subscription: $14/year; $7/6 months. **Sample copy plus guidelines for $2; guidelines alone for SASE. "I like poems with sharp images and careful craftsmanship." At last report was "accepting about 1 out of 10 poems submitted." Simultaneous submissions OK (if informed)—even reprints if credit is given. "For the past few years, I have been closing in September due to overstock and opening again April 1." No need to query. Reports in 1 month or less. Pays $2 on acceptance plus one copy. Buys one-time rights.** Staff reviews science fiction/fantasy/horror and mystery chapbooks, books and magazines only. Send materials for review to either: Jim Lee, 801 - 26th St., Windber PA 15963 or Steve Sawicki, 186 Woodruff Ave., Watertown CT 06795. "I hold an annual 'Killer Frog Contest' for horror so bad or outrageous it becomes funny. There is a category for horror poetry. Has been opening April 1, closing July 1 of each year. Prizes are $25 each in four categories: poetry, art, short stories and short short stories, plus the 'coveted' Froggie statuette." The last contest had no entry fee but entrants wanting the anthology pay $3 (postpaid). Winners list available for SASE.

SCIENCE FICTION POETRY ASSOCIATION; STAR*LINE (IV-Science fiction, horror); THE RHYSLING ANTHOLOGY (V), %Mike Arnzen, P.O. Box 3712, Moscow ID 83843-1916, for membership information. **For poetry submissions:** Margaret Simon, 1412 NE 35th St., Ocala FL 34479. Founded 1978, the Association publishes ***Star*Line***, a bimonthly newsletter and poetry magazine. The Association also publishes **The Rhysling Anthology**, a yearly collection of nominations from the membership "for the best science fiction/fantasy long and short poetry of the preceding year," along with a Science Fiction Poetry Handbook. The magazine has published poetry by Bruce Boston, Thomas Disch, Denise Dumars, John M. Ford, Robert Frazier and Steve Rasnic Tem. As a sample they selected this poem, "Moonwalking Surtsey," by Ann K. Schwader:

Here too, few traces:
pale shell, gray feather
laid against firebirth's lava image
still warming infant skin

fair warning
of otherness stark as basalt sky/ocean,
alien fragments forged for nothing
further
not even footprints

The digest-sized magazines and anthologies are saddle-stapled, photocopied, with numerous illustrations and decorations. They have 250 subscribers (1 library) paying $13 for 6 issues/year. **Sample postpaid: $2. Submissions to *Star*Line* only.** They receive 200-300 submissions/year and use about 80—**mostly short (under 50 lines).** They are **"open to all forms—free verse, traditional forms, light verse—so long as your poetry shows skilled use of the language and makes a good use of science fiction, science, fantasy, horror or speculative motifs." Send 3-5 poems/submission, typed. Best time to submit is November. No simultaneous submissions, no queries. Publishes theme issues. They have one all-horror issue each year and an occasional prose poetry issue. Reports in a month. Pays 5¢/line plus 1¢/word and a copy. Buys first North American serial rights.** Reviews books of poetry "within the science fiction/fantasy field" in 50-500 words. Open to unsolicited reviews. Poets may also send books for review consideration to William J. Daciuk, 304 N. Scott Ave., Glenolden PA 19036. A copy of **The Rhysling Anthology** is $3.

SCOP PUBLICATIONS, INC. (II, IV-Regional), Box 376, College Park MD 20740, phone (301)422-1930, founded 1977, president Stacy Tuthill, publishes approximately 2 paperbacks/year as well as an occasional anthology. They want **"book-length regional manuscripts. No restrictions as to length or form but want well-crafted modern poetry with vivid imagery and skillful use of language with regard to sense impressions and fresh insights."** They have published poetry by Ann Darr, Barbara Lefcowitz and Elisavietta Ritchie. **For sample book, send $5.** Interested poets should **query with sample poems. Previously published poems and simultaneous submissions OK. Cover letter should include a short biography and recent credits. Seldom comments on rejections. Replies to queries in 6 weeks, to mss in 2-3 months. Pays copies.**

SCORE MAGAZINE; SCORE CHAPBOOKS AND BOOKLETS (II, IV-Form), #B, 125 Bay View Dr., Mill Valley CA 94941-2627, phone (415)388-0578, poetry editors Crag Hill and Laurie Schneider, is a small press publisher of **visual poetry** in the magazine *Score*, booklets, postcards and broadsides. They want **"poetry which melds language and the visual arts such as concrete poetry; experimental use of language, words and letters—forms. The appearance of the poem should have as much to say as the text. Poems on any subject; conceptual poetry; poems which use experimental, non-traditional methods to communicate their meanings."** They don't want **"traditional verse of any kind—be it free verse or rhymed."** They have published poetry by Stephen-Paul Martin, Bruce Andrews, Karl Kempton, Larry Eigner and Bern Porter. They say that it is impossible to quote a sample because "some of our poems consist of only a single word—or in some cases no recognizable words." **We strongly advise looking at a sample copy before submitting if you are not familiar with visual poetry.** *Score* is 18-40 pgs., magazine-sized, offset, saddle-stapled, using b&w graphics, 2-color matte card cover, appearing once a year. Press run is 200 for 25 subscriptions (6 of them libraries) and about 40 shelf sales. **Sample postpaid: $6. No simultaneous submissions. Previously published poems OK "if noted." Send SASE for guidelines. Pays 2 copies.** Open to unsolicited reviews. Poets may also send books for review consideration. **For chapbook consideration send entire ms. No simultaneous submissions. Almost always comments on rejections. Pays 8-16 copies of the chapbook.** They subsidy publish "if author requests it."

SCRATCH (II, IV-Translations), 9 Chestnut Rd., Eaglescliffe, Stockton-on-Tees TS16 OBA England, founded 1989, editor Mark Robinson, appears twice yearly using poetry, reviews (mainly books/chapbooks, some magazines) and some b&w graphics. As for poetry, the editor says, **"We tend to the gritty, but mix styles, tones and subjects."** Recent issues have been "specials," including "Born in the 60s" featuring many leading young writers, such as Simon Armitage, Glyn Maxwell and Helen Kitson, and "Untitled Continent 1992," a European special featuring work in translation. As a sample the editor selected these lines from "Years like leaves" by Bo Carpelan, translated from Finland-Swedish by Anne Born:

It's very possible I used to think
that what I looked for was a "great" simplicity.
Well, when the road wound through encroaching forests,
all manner of ugly cottages strung across the fields,
it was good to go down to the shore
and see how sea and sky reflected each other.

Scratch is 80 pgs., A5 ($5^{11}/_{16} \times 8^{1}/_{4}$), perfect-bound with card cover. Single copy: £3.50 ($10); subscription: £5.50 ($18). **No previously published poems or simultaneous submissions. Seldom comments on rejections. Reports in 2-3 weeks. Pays 2 copies.** Staff reviews books of poetry. Send books for review consideration. They have also started a chapbook series but are not currently accepting unsolicited chapbook mss. The editor says, "**Translations of younger poets especially welcome.** Insufficient IRCs (a common U.S. failing) irk!"

‡SCRIVENER (II), 853 Sherbrooke St. W., Montreal, Quebec H3A 2T6 Canada, founded 1980, is an annual review of contemporary literature and art published by students at McGill University. With a circulation throughout North America, *Scrivener* publishes the best of new Canadian and American poetry, short fiction, criticism, essays, reviews and interviews. **"*Scrivener* is committed to publishing the work of new and unpublished writers."** *Scrivener* uses about 50 of 1,000 submissions received each year. It is a book-sized review, 120 pgs., printed on natural recycled paper and bound with a flat spine and one color matte card cover; all graphics and ads are black & white. Subscription: $10/2 years. **Sample postpaid: $5. January 31 deadline for submissions for April 1st publication; contributors encouraged to submit in early fall. Send 5-10 poems, one poem/page; be sure that each poem be identified separately, with titles, numbers, etc. . . . Editors comment individually on each submission. Reports in 6 months. Pays 2 copies or 2-year subscription.**

SEATTLE REVIEW (II), Padelford Hall GN-30, University of Washington, Seattle WA 98195, phone (206)543-9865, founded 1978, poetry editor Colleen McElroy, appears in the fall and spring using **"contemporary and traditional" poetry.** They have published poetry by William Stafford, Tess Gallagher, Marvin Bell and Walter McDonald. As a sample the editor selected these lines from "Car Mechanic Blues" by Jan Wallace:

He lords his wrench over me like
a magic wand. His ease with grease, the way
he calms the speeding idle should convince
me, this man's got the power. He wants
to show me how the sparks fire. I say,
No thanks, I'll get the book.

The review is professionally printed, flat-spined, 110 pgs., with glossy card cover. Press run is 800 for 250 subscribers of which 50 are libraries, 400 shelf sales. Single copy: $5; subscription: $8. **Sample postpaid: $3. Reads submissions September 1 through May 31 only. Send SASE for guidelines. Reports in 2-6 months. Pay "varies, but we do pay" plus 2 copies.** The editors offer these "practical suggestions: Cover letters with submissions do help. A cover letter provides something about the author and tells where and for what s/he is submitting. And don't let those rejection letters be cause for discouragement. Rejections can often be a matter of timing. The journal in question may be publishing a special issue with a certain theme (we've done a number of themes—'all-fiction,' 'all-poetry,' 'Asian-American,' 'Northwest,' 'science fiction,' etc.). Also, editorial boards do change, and new editors bring their individual opinions and tastes in writing. Good poetry will eventually be published if it is circulated."

SECOND AEON PUBLICATIONS (V), 19 Southminster Rd., Roath, Cardiff CF2 S4T Wales, phone 0222-493093, founded 1966, poetry editor Peter Finch, is a "small press concerned in the main with **experimental literary works."** He has published poetry by Bob Cobbing and himself. **Does not accept unsolicited mss. Pays copies.** Reviews poetry as a freelancer for a broad range of publications.

‡SEEMS (II), P.O. Box 359, Lakeland College, Sheboygan WI 53082-0359, founded 1971, published irregularly (29 issues in 22 years). This is a handsomely printed, nearly square ($7 \times 8^{1}/_{4}$) magazine, saddle-stapled, generous with white space on heavy paper. Two of the issues are considered chapbooks, and the editor, Karl Elder, suggests that a way **to get acquainted would be to order *Seems #14, What***

Is The Future Of Poetry? **for $5**, consisting of essays by 22 contemporary poets, and "If you don't like it, return it and we'll return your $5." There are usually about 20 pgs. of poetry/issue. Elder has recently used poetry by Harry Brody, M.J. Echelberger, Carol Granato, Chris Halla, Robert Nagler and Mark Strand. He said it was "impossible" to select four illustrative lines. The magazine has a print run of 350 for 200 subscriptions (20 libraries) and sells for $4 an issue (or $16 for a subscription—four issues). There is a **1- to 2-year backlog. Reports in 1-3 months. Pays copies. Acquires North American serial rights. Returns rights upon publication.** The editor says, "We'd like to consider more prose poems, especially those with a narrative quality."

SEGUE FOUNDATION; ROOF BOOKS; SEGUE BOOKS (V), 303 E. Eighth St., New York NY 10009, phone (212)674-0199, fax (212)254-4145, president James Sherry, is a small press publisher of poetry, literary criticism, and film and performance texts. Most of their books are flat-spined paperbacks, some hardcover. They have published books by Jackson MacLow, Charles Bernstein, Ron Silliman and Diane Ward, but **they do not consider unsolicited mss. Query first.**

SENECA REVIEW (II, IV-Translations), Hobart and William Smith Colleges, Geneva NY 14456-3397, phone (315)781-3349, founded 1970, editor Deborah Tall. They want **"serious poetry of any form, including translations. No light verse. Also essays on contemporary poetry."** They have published poetry by Seamus Heaney, Rita Dove, Denise Levertov, Stephen Dunn and Hayden Carruth. ***Seneca Review*** is 100 pgs., 6×9, flat-spined, professionally printed on quality stock with matte card cover, appearing twice a year. You'll find plenty of free verse here—some accessible and some leaning toward experimental—with the emphasis on voice, image and diction. All in all, poems and translations complement each other and create a distinct editorial mood each issue. Of 3,000-4,000 poems received they accept approximately 100. Press run is 1,000 for 500 subscribers of which half are libraries, about 250 shelf sales. Subscription: $8/year, $15/2 years. **Sample postpaid: $5. Submit 3-5 poems. No simultaneous submissions or previously published poems. Reads submissions September 1 through May 1 only. Reports in 6-12 weeks. Pays 2 copies.** Poetry published in the ***Seneca Review*** has been selected for inclusion in **The Best American Poetry 1994.**

‡SENSATIONS MAGAZINE (I, IV-Membership/subscription, themes), 2 Radio Ave., A5, Secaucus NJ 07094, founded 1987, founder David Messineo. **Subscription required before submission of material, but this is among the top 10 paying poetry markets in the US.** *Sensations* is an unusual mix of contemporary poetry, contemporary fiction and historical research. **"We encourage diversity: Buy back issue, see types and themes of published poems, and send something different."** As a sample, the founder selected these lines from "Bird and the Sea" (based on a painting by Morris Graves at Montclair Museum) by Moira Bailis:

> *It crouches, waiting*
> *talons grasping a rock*
> *by the moonlit winter sea,*
> *the ominous waves*
> *stretch to the horizon—*
> *the water looks calm*
> *but the paint strokes hint*
> *at a turbulence that's hidden,*
> *menacing.*

Sensations is "desktop-published with elegance and respect for the written word." Subscription: $16 for December 1994 issue; $20 for May 1995 issue; **$10 for back issues. "We send SASE for your poetry submission once you have subscribed, so don't send poetry until *after* you have subscribed. Check (or International Money Order) must be made payable to David Messineo. If you send material without a SASE, you will receive no response. No information requests will be processed between October 15-31, 1994, and March 15-30, 1995." Previously published poems OK. Theme for December 1994 issue is "almost anything goes, 50 lines or less (no profanity)." Deadline: October 31, 1994. Theme for May 1995 issue is the 100th Anniversary of Coney Island's Amusement Parks. Deadline: March 30, 1995. Pays $125/poem. Acquires one-time publication rights.** The founder says, "Funds raised go into costs of publication and research—editors are unpaid volunteers. Have doubts? Name five independent, non-grant-funded publications you submitted to back in 1987 that are still around. We have beaten the odds of failure and are looking forward to our Fifteen Anniversary Issue in 2002 (we even advance planned all issues, deadlines, and themes between now and then). ***Sensations Magazine*** is unlike any other literary magazine you've seen. We will treat you with respect and remarkable courtesy, and ask your professionalism in return by following our submission requirements in full. For those of you who tried us before, we strongly encourage you to revisit. Why not prepare a SASE right now and send it to the address above, while we're on your mind? We look forward to hearing from you, and will respond within a week or two of your inquiry (except for dates noted above)."

SEQUOIA (II), Storke Publications Building, Stanford University, Stanford CA 94305, founded 1892, poetry editor Carlos Rodriguez, appears twice a year. They have published poetry by Susan Howe, Seamus Heaney, Adrienne Rich, Rita Dove and James Merrill. As a sample the editor selected these lines from "The Amish Visit Pella, Iowa" by Keith Ratzlaff:

to be healed of themselves,
the curves their bones take.
They come because the chiropractor
works in the open the way they do:
hard and with his hands.

Sequoia is 80-100 pgs., 6×9, professionally printed, flat-spined, with matte card cover with art. They publish a small percentage of hundreds of unsolicited submissions. Their press run is 500 with 200 subscriptions, of which half are libraries. Subscription: $10. **Sample postpaid: $5. They do not consider simultaneous submissions or previously published poems. Reads submissions September 15 through June 1. Reports in "2 months or more." Pays 2 copies.**

SERPENT & EAGLE PRESS (V), RD#1, Box 29B, Laurens NY 13796, phone (607)432-2990, founded 1981, poetry editor Jo Mish. "Our aim is to print fine limited letterpress editions of titles worth printing in all subject areas." Their chapbooks are elegantly designed and printed on handmade paper with hand-sewn wrappers. **However, they are currently not accepting poetry submissions.**

SEVEN BUFFALOES PRESS; AZOREAN EXPRESS; BLACK JACK; VALLEY GRAPEVINE; HILL AND HOLLER ANTHOLOGY SERIES (IV-Rural, regional, anthologies), Box 249, Big Timber MT 59011, founded 1973, editor Art Cuelho, who writes, "I've always thought that rural and working class writers, poets and artists deserve the same tribute given to country singers." These publications all express that interest. For all of them Art Cuelho wants **poetry oriented toward rural and working people, "a poem that tells a story, preferably free verse, not longer than 50-100 lines, poems with strong lyric and metaphor, not romantical, poetry of the heart as much as the head, not poems written like grocery lists or the first thing that comes from a poet's mind, no ivory tower, and half my contributors are women."** He has published poetry by R.T. Smith, James Goode, Leo Connellan and Wendell Berry. *The Azorean Express* is 35 pgs., 5½×8½, side-stapled. It appears twice a year. Circulation 200. **Sample postpaid: $6.75. Submit 4-8 poems. No simultaneous submissions. Reports in 1-2 weeks. Pays 1 copy.** *Black Jack* is an anthology series on Rural America that uses rural material from anywhere, especially the American West; *Valley Grapevine* is an anthology on central California, circulation 750, that uses rural material from central California; *Hill and Holler*, Southern Appalachian Mountain series, takes in rural mountain lifestyle and folkways. **Sample of any postpaid: $6.75. Seven Buffaloes Press does not accept unsolicited mss but publishes books solicited from writers who have appeared in the above magazines.** Art Cuelho advises, "Don't tell the editor how great you are. This one happens to be a poet and novelist who has been writing for 30 years. Your writing should not only be fused with what you know from the head, but also from what you know within your heart. Most of what we call life may be some kind of gift of an unknown river within us. The secret to be learned is to live with ease in the darkness, because there are too many things of the night in this world. But the important clue to remember is that there are many worlds within us."

SEVENTEEN (V), 850 Third Ave., New York NY 10022, phone (212)759-8100, founded 1944, contact poetry/voice editor, is a slick monthly for teenage girls, circulation 1,750,000. They publish **"all styles of poetry up to 40 lines by writers 21 and under. However, due to a large backlog, *Seventeen* can no longer accept poetry submissions." Purchase sample ($1.75) at newsstands.**

THE SEWANEE REVIEW; AIKEN TAYLOR AWARD FOR MODERN POETRY (III), University of the South, Sewanee TN 37375, founded 1892, thus being our nation's oldest continuously published literary quarterly, editor George Core. Fiction, criticism and poetry are invariably of the **highest establishment standards. Most of our major poets appear here from time to time.** They have published poetry by William Logan, Howard Nemerov and Barry Spacks. Each issue is a hefty paperback of nearly 200 pgs., conservatively bound in matte paper, always of the same typography. Truly a magazine open to all styles and forms, issues we critiqued featured formal sequences, metered verse, structured free verse, sonnets, and lyric and narrative forms—all accessible and intelligent. Circulation: 3,200. **Sample: $5.75. Reports in 1-4 weeks. Pays 70¢/line.** Also includes brief, standard and essay-reviews. The Aiken Taylor Award for Modern Poetry is awarded by ***The Sewanee Review*** and its publisher, the University of the South in Sewanee, TN, "for the work of a substantial and distinguished career." Poetry published in ***The Sewanee Review*** was also selected for inclusion in **The Best American Poetry 1992.**

‡SHADES OF GRAY (I, II), P.O. Box 2806, Merrifield VA 22116-2806, founded 1993, editor Jason A. White, is a quarterly magazine which includes both new and well-published poets. **"We are open to all forms, subjects, lengths. We seek to be eclectic, but our own subconscious preferences inevitably leak through. We really don't want trite, forced rhyme. Make it flow naturally."** They have recently published poetry by Robert Sargent, Lyn Lifshin, Michael Lithgoe and Bradley Strahan. As a sample we selected these lines from "Fusion" by Daniel Laitsch:

To Know
for an instant
the words jumped to life
and rose off the paper
greeting the reader with
smiles and
bidding welcome.

Shades of Gray is 40 pgs., digest-sized, saddle-stapled with light card stock cover and some b&w art. They receive 40 submissions/month, accept about 25%. Press run is 100 for 10 subscribers. Single copy: $3; subscription: $10. **Sample postpaid: $3.75. Submit poetry with name and address on each page. No previously published poems or simultaneous submissions. Cover letter required.** Time between acceptance and publication is 6 months. **Seldom comments on rejections. Reports in 2 months. Pays 1 copy. Acquires first-time rights.** Open to unsolicited reviews. Poets may also send books for review consideration. The editor adds, "We have a 'Future Voices' section, reserved for poets under 18. We also have a 'Featured Poet' each issue and are always looking for well-known, well-published poets for this feature."

SHAMAL BOOKS (IV-Ethnic, anthologies), Dept. PM, GPO Box 16, New York NY 10116, phone (718)622-4426, founded 1976, editor Louis Reyes Rivera. Shamal Books is a small press whose purpose is **"to promote the literary efforts of African-American and Caribbean writers, particularly those who would not otherwise be able to establish their literary credentials as their concerns as artists are with the people."** The press publishes individual and "anthological" books and chapbooks, mostly flat-spined paper texts. They have published poetry by SeKou Sundiata, Sandra Maria Esteves and Rashidah Ismaili. The editor wants to see **"poetry that clearly demonstrates an understanding of craft, content and intent as the scriptural source of the word guiding and encouraging the intellect of the people." He does not consider unsolicited submissions of individual mss, but will look at work only while anthologies are open. How many sample poems should you send? "Two is cool." The cover letter should include a "leaning toward personal goals and poetic principles." Mss of poetry should be "neat and single-spaced." The editor will reply to queries within 2 months. Royalties for book authors are 15%.** The editor says that he will subsidy publish "delicately—depends on resources and interest in work." His projects include "an international anthology; drama; prison anthology; books on language as a weapon; a collectivized publisher's catalog of Third World presses working out of NYC." His advice to poets: "Certainly to study the craft more and to research more into the historical role that has been the hallmark of poetry across class and caste conscious lines that limit younger perspectives. Not to be as quick to publish as to be in serious study, then while looking to publish, looking as well into collective ventures with other poets for publication and distribution. Above all, *read*!"

SHARING THE VICTORY (IV-Spirituality/inspirational, sports), 8701 Leeds Rd., Kansas City MO 64129, phone (816)921-0909, founded 1959, editor John Dodderidge, assistant editor Robyne Baker, managing editor Don Hilkemeier. This monthly magazine is published September through May by the Fellowship of Christian Athletes. **They want free verse on themes of interest to Christian athletes (high school and college, male and female).** As a sample they selected these lines by Aileen L. Myers:

I am more than
skill and conditioning
More because
I am a child of a loving God,
who created me in His spiritual image,
loves me for myself
and promises me the eternal Victory.

They use 2-3 poems/year. Press run is 50,000. **Sample available for $1 with 8½ × 11 SASE (first-class stamps for 3 ozs.). Reads submissions July 1 through March 1 only. Guidelines available free. Reporting time is 2 weeks and time to publication averages 3-4 months. Pays $25-50. Buys first or second rights.**

SHATTERED WIG REVIEW (II), #1, 2407 Maryland Ave., Baltimore MD 21218, phone (410)243-6888, founded 1988, contact Fred Engels, is a semiannual using **"liquid, messy poetry, oozing the stuff of life. No frustrated English professor poetry."** They have published poetry by John M. Bennett, Eel Leonard, Lyn Lifshin and Dan Raphael. As a sample the editor selected these lines by Chris Toll:

A 10,000-year-old white man rules the world
when he needs a new heart,
he murders a 16-year-old boy
His tanks may rumble through the cities

My crack dealers will fight back to back with my crystal healers
Every cell in my body knows the new world is coming

SHW is approximately 70 pgs., 8½×8½, photocopied, side-stapled with card stock covers with original artwork and art and graphics inside. They receive about 10 submissions/week, accept about 20%. Press run is 300 for 100 subscribers of which 10 are libraries, 100 shelf sales. Subscription: $9 for 2 issues. **Sample postpaid: $4. Previously published poems and simultaneous submissions OK. Seldom comments on rejections. Reports within a month. Pays 1 copy. Acquires one-time rights.** Occasionally reviews books of poetry in 100 words. Open to unsolicited reviews. Poets may also send books for review consideration. The editor says there are no requirements for contributors except "that the contributor include us in their nightly prayers."

HAROLD SHAW PUBLISHERS; WHEATON LITERARY SERIES (V), Box 567, Wheaton IL 60189, phone (708)665-6700, founded 1967, Director of Editorial Services Ramona Cramer Tucker, is "small publisher of the Wheaton Literary Series and Northcote Books, **works of Christian and literary merit** including fiction, poetry, literary criticism and original prose" in flat-spined paperback and hardback books. They have published poetry by Madeleine L'Engle, John Leax, Sister Maura Eichner and Luci Shaw. **They publish on a 10/5% royalty basis plus 10 author's copies.** They publish a volume of poetry approximately every 2 years. "Our work reflects **a Christian evangelical world-view**, though this need not be explicit. In the future we may publish an anthology, rather than single poets." **However, they are currently still not accepting poetry submissions.**

SHEILA-NA-GIG (II), 23106 Kent Ave., Torrance CA 90505, founded 1990, editor Hayley R. Mitchell. *Sheila-na-gig* appears once a year as a large general issue using **"all forms (particularly free verse), styles and subject matter—length, I generally don't publish poems over three pages (don't ramble!). No religious or ultra traditional verse, please."** They have recently published work by Michael Estabrook, Lyn Lifshin, Gerald Locklin, Patrick McKinnon, Dan Nielsen, Dan Sicoli, Marc Swan, Cheryl Townsend and Charles Webb. As a sample the editor selected these lines by Lance Dean:

it's butt cold
and the streetbound boys
shiver off their asses tonight.
Jack Frost carries a shiv
to slice throats that sleep on the benches;
and when they wake up dead
they'll be brittle as glass
the snowmen of the gutter kids.

Sheila-na-gig is digest-sized, flat-spined, 100-150 pgs., photocopied from laser prints with matte card cover. Subscription: $7 yearly, $12 for two years. **Sample postpaid: $7 for current issue ($5/$3 for older back issues). Cover letter preferred with submissions. Include brief bio and note whether poems are previously published or simultaneous submissions. 1995 Deadline: May 31. "I'll begin reading these submissions on June 1, and will report in 6-8 weeks. Submit up to 5 poems,** and/or short stories (1-10 pgs.), and/or b&w artwork (5×7 and easy to reproduce)." **Pays copies. Acquires first rights.** For the 3rd Annual Poetry Contest: Submit 3 poems. Include SASE and $5 entry fee. $50 first prize, copies, and publication of runners-up. Deadline: June 1. Work in ***Sheila-na-gig*** has been nominated for inclusion in **Pushcart Prize XIX: Best of the Small Presses (1994-95 edition).** The editor says, "I encourage new poets with new styles and a strong voice, and look especially for poets not afraid to speak out on issues of sexuality, politics, human rights and feminist issues. Looking for poetry on the edge. If in doubt, order a back issue. Please make all checks payable to Hayley R. Mitchell. Thank you for your interest in and support of ***Sheila-na-gig.***"

SHENANDOAH (II), Box 722, Lexington VA 24450, phone (703)463-8765, founded 1950, editor Dabney Stuart, managing editor Lynn Williams. Published at Washington and Lee University, it is a quarterly literary magazine which has published poetry by Conrad Hilberry, Martha McFerren, Robert B. Shaw, Cathy Song and Jeanne Walker. As a sample the editor chose these lines from "The Lake of thc Unconscious" by Geraldine Connolly:

and everything was still,
the deer frozen between two pines

the way the child was caught
between the two worlds, the air

and the bottom of the lake
bobbing there, amazed

The magazine is 6×9, 100 pgs., perfect-bound, professionally printed with full-color cover. Generally, it is open to all styles and forms but leans toward lyric and narrative free verse with an emphasis on voice. Circulation: 1,700. **Sample postpaid: $3.50. All submissions should be typed on one side of the paper only. Your name and address must be clearly written on the upper right corner of the ms. Include SASE. Reads submissions September 1 through May 30. Reports in 3 months. Payment includes a check, one-year subscription and one copy. Buys first publication rights.** Staff reviews books of poetry in 7-10 pages, multi-book format. Send books for review consideration. Some reviews are solicited. Poetry published in ***Shenandoah*** has been included in **The Best American Poetry 1993.**

SHIP OF FOOLS (II); SHIP OF FOOLS PRESS (V), Box 1028, University of Rio Grande, Rio Grande OH 45674, phone (614)245-5351, founded 1983, editor Gina Pellegrino-Pines, assistant editor Jack Hart, review editor James Doubleday, is "more or less quarterly." They want **"coherent, well-written, traditional or modern, myth, archetype, love, odd and/or whimsical poetry—most types. No concrete, incoherent or greeting card poetry."** They have published poetry by Rhina Espaillat, Carolyn Page, Denver Stull and T. Kilgore Splake. As a sample the editors selected these lines from "Following the Reaper" by Nancy Haas:

I am here again;
Gathering the heads
With their wide astonished eyes
And the hands
With their silent fluttering fingers.

They describe ***Ship of Fools*** as digest-sized, saddle-stapled, offset printed with cover art and graphics. Press run is 275 for 36 subscribers of which 6 are libraries. Subscription: $7 for 4 issues. **Sample postpaid: $2. No previously published poems or simultaneous submissions. Cover letter preferred. Often comments on rejections. Reports in 2-4 weeks. "If longer than six weeks, write and ask why." Pays 1 copy.** Reviews books of poetry. Ship of Fools Press publishes chapbooks but does not accept unsolicited mss.

SHOFAR (IV-Children, ethnic, religious), 43 Northcote Dr., Melville NY 11747, founded 1984, publisher/editor Gerald H. Grayson, is a magazine **for American Jewish children 9-13,** appearing monthly October through May (double issues December/January and April/May). It is 32 pgs., magazine-sized, professionally printed, with color paper cover. Their press run is 17,000 with 16,000 subscriptions of which 1,000 are libraries. Subscription: $14.95. **Sample: $1.05 postage and SAE. They will consider simultaneous submissions and "maybe" previously published poems. Send SASE for guidelines. Reports in 6-8 weeks. Pays $25-50/poem.**

SHOOTING STAR REVIEW; SHOOTING STAR WRITING CONFERENCE (II, IV-Themes, ethnic), 7123 Race St., Pittsburgh PA 15208-1424, phone (412)731-7464, founded 1986, publisher Sandra Gould Ford. **"This is an adult-oriented magazine dedicated to the African-American experience. Each issue explores a specific theme."** They have published poetry by Toi Derricotte, Dennis Brutus, Terri Jewell and Pinkie Gordon Lane. As a sample Sandra Gould Ford selected these lines from "Budget Crunch" by Don W. Robinson:

I just lost my job
My unemployment's zeroed out
I'm reduced to eatin' Budget Crunch
This new thing they're talkin' bout!

It's got fat tax raisin's
And little pink slips . . .

SSR is 64 pgs., saddle-stitched, offset with glossy cover and art, "illustrated with significant attention to design and graphics." It appears quarterly. They receive about 1,200 poems a year, accept approximately 40. Press run is 1,500 for 700 subscribers of which 50 are libraries, 350 shelf sales. Single copy: $3; subscription: $10/year. **Sample: $3 plus $1.21 in postage. Submit up to 6 poems/quarter, one poem/page. No previously published poems; simultaneous submissions OK. Seldom comments on rejections. Send SASE for guidelines and upcoming themes. Reports in 3 months. Pays $10, "as funds permit," and 2 copies. Buys first North American serial rights.** The Shooting Star Writers Conference is usually held in the fall. Send SASE for information. The publisher adds, "Work by non-Black writers on the Black experience is welcome."

SIERRA NEVADA COLLEGE REVIEW (I), P.O. Box 4269, Incline Village NV 89450, founded 1990, editor June Sylvester, is an annual literary magazine featuring poetry and short fiction by new writers. They want **"high quality, image-oriented poems that suggest or surprise; no limit on length, style, etc. No light verse, sloppy sentiment, purposeful obscurity, clichés or cuteness."** They have published poetry by Marisella Veiga, Darrell G.H. Schramm, Ted Thompson and Terry Wright. As a sample the editor selected these lines from "Bee Song" by William Powley:

and the bee's open mouth

swallows pollen: it is love
without mistakes,

only sweetness
in a yellow fold,
a bee song.

The editor says ***SNCR*** is approximately 60 pgs., with cover art only, no ads. "We receive approximately 100-200 poems a year and accept approximately 25-35." Press run is 300. Subscription: $5/year. **Sample postpaid: $2.50. No previously published poems; simultaneous submissions OK. Include brief bio. Reads submissions September 1 through April 1. Often comments on rejections. Reports in 2 weeks to 2 months. Pays 1 copy.** The editor says, "We delight in publishing the unpublished or underpublished writer. We look specifically for subtlety and skill."

THE SIGNPOST PRESS; THE BELLINGHAM REVIEW; 49TH PARALLEL POETRY CONTEST (II), 1007 Queen St., Bellingham WA 98226, phone (206)734-9781, founded 1975, editor Knute Skinner, publishes ***The Bellingham Review*** twice a year, runs an annual poetry competition and publishes other books and chapbooks of poetry occasionally. **"We want well-crafted poetry but are open to all styles," no specifications as to form.** Poets they have published recently include Laure-Anne Bosselaar, Gerald Locklin, Joanne McCarthy, Carlos Reyes and Leigh Mcdiarmid. As a sample, the editor selected these lines by Leslie Palmer:

Take a girl we don't know. Film her
in Baghdad, blood-soaked rags limp
in a soldier's bare arms, words we don't
understand, the badly aimed bomb
that tore her from her family.

The ***Review*** is digest-sized, saddle-stapled, typeset, with art and glossy cover. Each issue has about 38 pgs. of poetry. They have a circulation of 700 with 500 subscriptions. **Sample postpaid: $2. Simultaneous submissions OK. Reads submissions September 1 through March 1 only. Reports in 1-4 months. Pays 1 copy plus a year's subscription. Acquires first North American rights.** Staff reviews books of poetry in 500-1,000 words, single or multi-book format. Send books for review consideration also between September 1 and March 1. Send SASE for rules for the next 49th Parallel Poetry Contest and query regarding book publication.

SILVER APPLES PRESS (V), P.O. Box 292, Hainesport NJ 08036, phone (609)267-2758, founded 1982, poetry editor Geraldine Little. "We're a very small press with very limited funds. Published our first chapbook in 1988; open contest for same. We plan to publish randomly, as things turn us on and as funds permit—pamphlets, chapbooks, a set of postcards. **We are over-committed at present. Not currently accepting unsolicited poetry submissions. Watch *Poets & Writers* for announcements."** They publish **"first-class poetry by experienced poets. No greeting card verse, soupy sentimental verse or blatantly religious verse."** They have published **Contrasts in Keening: Ireland** by Geraldine C. Little, **Abandoned House** by Susan Fawcett and **The Verb to Love** by Barbara Horton. As a sample the editor selected these lines from **Keeping Him Alive** by Charlotte Mandel:

We do not cut it down.
In winter,
within the bitter scrabble
of bared, practiced branches,
the dead tree, too, promises.

SILVER WINGS (IV-Religious, spirituality/inspirational), P.O. Box 1000, Pearblossom CA 93553-1000, phone (805)264-3726, founded 1983, published by Poetry on Wings, Inc., poetry editor Jackson Wilcox. "As a committed Christian service we produce and publish ***Silver Wings***, a quarterly poetry magazine. We want **poems with a Christian perspective, reflecting a vital personal faith and a love for God and man. Will consider poems from 3-20 lines. Quite open in regard to meter and rhyme."** They have published poetry by William T. Burke, Andrew Peterson, C. David Hay and Harriett Hunt. As a sample the editor selected these lines from "Rainbow Coronation" by Mary P. Stewart:

Mountains of burgeoning clouds
Race across dark skies.
Tall trees bow low
In the face of howling wind,
Green leaves clutch switching limbs. . . .

The magazine is 32 pgs., digest-sized, offset from typescript with hand-lettered titles on tinted paper with cartoon-like art. They receive 1,500 submissions/year, use 260. Circulation is 450 with 250 subscribers. Subscription: $7. **Sample postpaid: $2. Submit typed ms, double-spaced. Reports in 3 weeks, providing SASE is supplied;** time to publication can be up to 2 years. **Pays $9 in subscription and copy value. Acquires first rights. Rarely comments on rejections.** They hold an annual contest with $200 in prizes and chapbook publication. Deadline: October 1. Send SASE for details. ***Silver Wings*** ranked #10 in the "Open Markets" category of the latest ***Writer's Digest*** Poetry 60 list. This category ranks those publications most open to both free and formal verse. The editor says, "While we will look at any poetry which is submitted, we do want to encourage Christian poets to master the techniques of quality poetry, remembering that this takes time and care. We are glad to look at poetry that has an uplift to it. The ecumenical nature of ***Silver Wings*** is guaranteed by a governing board with members representing six different Christian communions."

SILVERFISH REVIEW; SILVERFISH REVIEW PRESS (II), P.O. Box 3541, Eugene OR 97403, phone (503)344-5060, founded 1979, poetry editor Rodger Moody, is a semiannual, digest-sized, 48-page literary magazine, circulation 750. **"The only criterion for selection of poetry is quality. In future issues *Silverfish Review* also wants to showcase the short short story."** They have recently published poetry by Chelsey Minnis, Denise Duhamel, Dick Allen, Ivan Arguelles, D.M. Wallace, Robert Gregory, Ralph Salisbury, Richard Jones, Floyd Skloot and Susan Cobin. As a sample the editor selected these lines by Lauren Mesa:

This one, the tall boy with brown hair,
the wicker creel's strap slung
across his crest, is Great-Uncle Mickey,
Michelangelo Cipolla, the uncle
who dressed as Santa the years
my mother was a child.

There are 36-48 pgs. of poetry in each issue. The magazine is professionally printed in dark type on quality stock, matte card cover with art. They receive about 1,000 submissions of poetry/year, use 20, have a 6- to 12-month backlog. Subscription for institutions: $15; for individuals: $12. **Sample: $4, single copy orders should include $2 for postage and handling. Submit at least 5 poems to editor. No simultaneous submissions. Reports in about 2-6 months. Pays 2 copies and one-year subscription, plus small honorarium when grant support permits.** Reviews books of poetry. Open to unsolicited reviews. Poets may also send books for review consideration. **Silverfish Review Press will consider mss for poetry chapbook publication and conducts an annual chapbook competition with an award of $100 and 25 copies (with a press run of 750). Send SASE for rules.**

SING HEAVENLY MUSE! (IV-Feminist), Box 13320, Minneapolis MN 55414, founded 1977, editor Sue Ann Martinson, fosters "the work of women poets, fiction writers and artists. The magazine is **feminist in an open, generous sense: We encourage women to range freely, honestly and imaginatively over all subjects, philosophies and styles. We do not wish to confine women to women's subjects,** whether these are defined traditionally, in terms of femininity and domesticity, or modernly, from a sometimes narrow polemical perspective. We look for explorations, questions that do not come with ready-made answers, emotionally or intellectually." For poetry they have **"no limitations except women's writing or men's writing that reflects awareness of women's consciousness."** They have published poetry by Alexis Rotella, Jill Breckenridge and Amirh Bahati. The editor selected these sample lines from "Sons of Soweto" by June Jordan:

Words live in the spirit of her face
and that sound will no longer yield . . .
she will stand under the sun!
She will stay!

The magazine appears once a year in a 6×9, flat-spined, 125-page format, offset from typescript on heavy stock, b&w art, glossy card color cover. They receive 1,500 submissions/year, use 50-60. Press run is 1,000 for 275 subscribers of which 50 are libraries. Single copy: $7; subscription: $14 (2 issues). **Sample postpaid: $4. Submit 3-10 pgs., name and address on each page. No simultaneous submissions. Editors sometimes comment on rejections. Send SASE for guidelines, information about upcoming reading periods and themes. Reports in 4-5 months. Pays "usually $25 plus 2 copies."**

SINGING HORSE PRESS (III), P.O. Box 40034, Philadelphia PA 19106, founded 1976, editor/publisher Gil Ott, publishes an average of 2 new titles/year, primarily poetry. **"We are most interested in work which explores the intersection of poetics and human relation, be that political, cultural or psychological."** Most recent titles: **S*PeRM*K**T** by Harryette Mullen and **Her Angel** by Karen Kelley. Press run is 1,000. Average page count: 48-64. Prices average $6. **Writers should become acquainted with their publications/editorial preferences and query before submitting. "Most work is solicited."**

SINGULAR SPEECH PRESS (V), 10 Hilltop Dr., Canton CT 06019, phone (203)693-6059, founded 1976, editor Don D. Wilson. "Singular Speech Press nonprofitably lives to present *some* fine examples of our many real poets—probably our most unsupported artists. **And so we publish at least 6 mss per**

annum, 40-96 pages. We have few biases, are enamored of both free and formal verse, are gladdened by unknown and well-known poets; we cannot stomach prosaic or confessional poetry." They have recently published William Burns, Charles Fishman, Stephen Smith, four Bulgarian poets and Ron McFarland. As a sample here are six lines from "Poem Written From Memory" in **The Cities We Will Never See** by Michael Cadnum:

This poem takes its place,
as though the casts of bodies
in Pompeii might flesh
and breathe. As though
a sandal found beside a road
begins to dream.

The press is currently not encouraging poetry submissions—"booked up for next 2½ years."

‡SINISTER WISDOM (IV-Lesbian, feminist), P.O. Box 3252, Berkeley CA 94703, founded 1976, editor Elana Dykewomon, is a lesbian feminist journal. The editor says, **"We want poetry that reflects the diversity of lesbian experience—lesbians of color, Third World, Jewish, old, young, working class, poor, disabled, fat, etc.—from a lesbian and/or feminist perspective. No heterosexual themes. We will not print anything that is oppressive or demeaning to women, or which perpetuates negative stereotypes."** The journal has published work by Gloria Anzaldúa, Sapphire and Betsy Warland. As a sample the editor chose the following lines from Minnie Bruce Pratt's poem "#67 To Be Posted on 21st Street, Between Eye and Pennsylvania":

Like a movie, sudden threat
Predictable. I get so tired of this disbelief.
My tongue, faithful in my mouth, said: Yes, we are.
the shout: Lesbians. Lesbians. Trying to curse
us with our name. Me louder: That's what we are.

The editor says the quarterly magazine is 128-144 pgs., digest-sized, flat-spined, with photos and b&w graphics. Circulation is 3,500 of which 1,000 are subscriptions and 100 go to libraries; newsstand sales and bookstores are 1,500. Single copy: $5; subscription: $17 US, $22 foreign. **Sample postpaid: $6.50. No simultaneous submissions. Publishes theme issues. Send SASE for upcoming themes. Reports in up to 9 months and time to publication is 6 months to 1 year. Pays 2 copies.** Reviews books of poetry in 500-1,500 words, single or multi-book format. The editor says they would like "anything *other* than love poetry."

SISTER VISION PRESS (IV-Ethnic, women), P.O. Box 217, Station E, Toronto, Ontario M6H 4E2 Canada, phone (416)533-2184, founded 1985, managing editor Makeda Silvera, publishes 8-10 paperbacks/year. They want **"poetry that reflects our lives as women of color; not restricted by form or length."** They have published poetry by ahdri zhina mandiela and Ramabai Espinet. As a sample the editor selected these lines from "Crebo" in Espinet's book **Nuclear Seasons**:

My hands had wrinkles
But rims grew around my eyes
My skin became ebony and rose
And my tongue grew long beyond words

Previously published poems and simultaneous submissions OK. Cover letter required. Submit a sample of work, to a maximum of 10 pages. Replies to queries in 2 weeks, to mss (if invited) in 2 months. Pays 10% royalties and 10 author's copies. Write for samples. They say, "Know the publisher you are submitting mss to. This saves the poet and publisher time, money and energy."

SISTERS TODAY (II, IV-Spirituality/inspirational), The Liturgical Press, Collegeville MN 56321; send submissions to: 1884 Randolph, St. Paul MN 55105, poetry editor Sister Mary Virginia Micka, C.S.J. *Sisters Today* has been published for about 60 years. Though it is a Roman Catholic magazine, **poetry may be on any topic, but "should clearly be *poems*, not simply *statements* or *prayers*." They want "short (not over 25 lines) poems using clean, fresh images and appealing to the reader's feelings in a compelling way." They do not want poetry that depends "heavily on rhyme and on 'tricks' such as excessive capitalization, manipulation of spacing, etc."** *ST*, appearing 6 times/year, is 80 pgs., 6×9, saddle-stapled, professionally printed with matte card cover. Press run is 9,000 for 8,500 subscribers. They receive about 50 poems/month, accept about 6. Subscription: $16 US; $18 foreign. **Sample postpaid: $3 (Send to: Sister Mary Anthony Wagner, O.S.B., Editor, *Sisters Today*, St. Benedict's Convent, St. Joseph MN 56374). No simultaneous submissions. Original poems much preferred. They require "each poem typed on a separate standard-size typing sheet, and each page must carry complete legal name, address and social security number typed in the upper right corner." Send SASE to poetry editor at St. Paul, MN address (above) for guidelines. Reports within 1-2 months, 6-12 months until publication. Pays $10/poem and 2 copies. Buys first rights.**

‡SIVULLINEN (II), Kaarelantie 86 B 28, 00420 Helsinki, Finland, founded 1985, editor Jouni Waarakangas, is a biannual publication of drawings, graphics, poems and short stories—**open to all kinds of poetry.** They have recently published poetry by Bob Z, Belinda Subraman and Paul Weinman. As a sample we selected these lines from "the real bukowski will do just fine, thank you" by Gerald Locklin:

this guy from l.a. decided to make
a bukowskian reputation for himself
by disrupting the end of the poetry reading,
mainly by kissing everyone, male and female,
against their wishes.

most of us just shoved him away . . .

The editor says *Sivullinen* is offset and varies between 32-40 pgs., A4 size and 28 pgs., A5 size. They accept about 20% of poetry received. Press run is 500. **Sample postpaid: $2-3. Previously published poems and simultaneous submissions OK.** Time between acceptance and publication is 3 months to a year. **Reports in 2-6 weeks. Pays 1 copy.**

SKYLARK (I, II, IV-Themes), Purdue University Calumet, 2200 169th St., Hammond IN 46323, phone (219)989-2262, founded 1972, editor Pamela Hunter, is "a fine arts annual, **one section of which is devoted to a special theme."** They are looking for **"original images, concise presentation and honesty; poems up to 30 lines; narrative poems to 75 lines. No horror, nothing extremely religious, no pornography."** They have recently published poetry by Constance Vogel, Agnes Tatera and Charles Eaton. As a sample the editor selected these lines from "Actaeon in Town" by Hugh Hennedy:

He had no hounds,
she no maidens attendant,
nor pool nor youth nor beauty,
but he saw her naked again,
though cloaked and fixed in gray,
and the old wonder returned

Skylark is magazine-sized, saddle-stapled, 100 pgs., professionally printed, with matte card cover. Press run is 500-1,000 for 50 subscriptions of which 12 are libraries. Single copy: $6. **Sample postpaid: $4. "Typed or computer printout manuscripts OK. No simultaneous submissions. Inquire (with SASE) as to annual theme for special section." The theme for 1995 is "Fire." Do not submit mss between June 1 and November 1. Reports in 4 months. Pays 1 copy. Acquires first rights. Editor may encourage rejected but promising writers.** Over the past three years, *Skylark* has won several awards for individual works from The Columbia Scholastic Press Association. The editor says she would like to receive "more prose poems, narrative poems, tankas and sonnets."

‡SLANT: A JOURNAL OF POETRY (II), Box 5063, University of Central Arkansas, Conway AR 72035, founded 1987, editor James Fowler, is an annual using *only* poetry. They use **"traditional and 'modern' poetry, even experimental, moderate length, any subject on approval of Board of Readers; purpose is to publish a journal of fine poetry from all regions of the United States. No haiku, no translations."** They have recently published poetry by E.G. Burrows, Andrea Budy and Robert Cooperman. As a sample the editor selected these lines from "The Judge" by Doris Henderson:

There's an old raccoon on my back porch.
I can't see him—I never see him,
but I know he's there.
He comes around at night, like worry, like guilt,
fattens on the things we throw out—
our foolishness, our blunders.
He tabulates my worst moments
in the rings of his tail.

Slant is 145 pgs., professionally printed on quality stock, flat-spined, with matte card cover. They publish about 70-80 poems of the 1,500 received each year. Press run is 250 for 70-100 subscribers. **Sample postpaid: $10. Submit no more than 5 poems of moderate length. "Put name and address top of each page." No simultaneous submissions or previously published poems. Editor comments on rejections "on occasion." Allow 3-4 months from November 15 deadline for response. Pays 1 copy.** The editor says, "I would like to see more formal verse."

‡ ***The double dagger before a listing indicates that the listing is new in this edition. New markets are often the most receptive to submissions.***

SLATE & STYLE (IV-Specialized: blind writers), Dept. PM, 2704 Beach Dr., Merrick NY 11566, phone (516)868-8718, editor Loraine Stayer, is a **quarterly for blind writers available on cassette, in large print and Braille,** "including articles of interest to blind writers, resources for blind writers. Membership/subscription $6 per year, all formats. Division of the National Federation of the Blind." **Poems may be "5-30 lines. Prefer contributors to be blind writers, or at least writers by profession or inclination. No obscenities. Will consider all forms of poetry. Interested in new talent."** They have published poetry by Mary McGinnis, Barbara Shaidnagle and Alice Chandler. As a sample the editor selected "Word Picture" by Jodie Hittle:

What if I could paint a picture with words so keen
That I could make color, size and shape be seen?
To say the sun looks like orange juice tastes,
or that polka dots feel like an unshaven face;
That blue is ice and red is fire;
that water is lower and wind is higher. . .

The print version is magazine-sized, 28-32 pgs., stapled, with a fiction and poetry section. Press run is 200 for 160 subscribers of which 4-5 are libraries. Subscription: $6/year. Single copy: $1.25 except Braille. **Sample postpaid: $2.50. No simultaneous submissions. Submit 6-7 poems once a year. Cover letter preferred. Do not submit mss in July. Editor comments on rejections "if requested." Send SASE for guidelines. Reports in "2 weeks if I like it." Pays 1 copy.** Reviews books of poetry. Open to unsolicited reviews. Poets may also send books for review consideration. They offer an annual poetry contest. Entry fee: $5/poem. Deadline: May 1. Loraine Stayer says, "Poetry is one of the toughest ways to express oneself, yet ought to be the easiest to read. Anything that looks simple is the result of much work."

‡SLIGHTLY WEST (I), CAB 320, The Evergreen State College, Olympia WA 98505, phone (206)866-6000, ext. 6879, founded 1985, coordinators Ethan Salter and Gregory A. Nicholl, is a biannual designed "to give beginning poets a place to be published." **They are open to all types, forms and styles of poetry. "No fluff. We are taking only the upper crust of submissions."** They have recently published poetry by Lowell Jaeger, D.M. Kumfermann, Douglas S. Johnson and Michael McNeilley. As a sample the editors selected these lines from "Dear October" by Brian Nadal:

The trees are beginning to fold their leaves
Like hands in prayer

The editors say ***SW*** is 50-60 pgs., 7¼×10½, saddle-stitched with cover and inside artwork. They receive 300-400 submissions a year, accept approximately 15%. Press run is 1,500 for 20 subscribers of which 5 are libraries; 1,000 distributed free to local community. Subscription: $5. **Sample postpaid: $2.50. Previously published poems and simultaneous submissions OK. Cover letter required. Reads submissions September 10 through June 17 only. "We have a selections board of 5-10 poets and writers who critique and comment on submissions." Often comments on rejections. Send SASE for guidelines. Reports in 2-3 months. Pays 1 copy. Acquires one-time rights.** The editors say, "We have been established for 10 years as just a 'school' magazine. Currently we are upgrading our requirements for poetry submissions. We encourage beginners to send poetry. We will return manuscripts with comments only if SASE enclosed."

SLIPPERY WHEN WET (V, IV-Erotica, humor), P.O. Box 3101, Berkeley CA 94703, founded 1991, editor Sunah Cherwin, is a quarterly magazine of "humor, liberation and the best sex I can find in two dimensions." **They publish "2 kinds of poetry: hot and funny. If it's funny, I like it to rhyme and scan. No stream-of-consciousness, politics, romance. If it's not explicitly about sex I will throw it out." Currently not accepting poetry submissions because "so many poets are ignoring my guidelines."** They have published poetry by Trish Thomas, Jackie Weltman and Phil Buff. The editor says it is 48 pgs., saddle-stitched, offset, with art, graphics and ads. Press run is 2,000 for 50 subscribers, 1,600 shelf sales. Subscription: $20. **Sample postpaid: $7 plus an age statement. Interested poets should query.** Reviews "*zines only*" in about 2 paragraphs. The editor says, "Read any magazine before you submit to it. I hope the idea of submitting your work to my magazine is kind of exciting and scary, because if it's not dangerous, I don't want it."

SLIPSTREAM; SLIPSTREAM AUDIO CASSETTES (II, IV-Themes), Box 2071, New Market Station, Niagara Falls NY 14301, phone (716)282-2616 (after 5pm, EST), founded 1980, poetry editors Dan Sicoli, Robert Borgatti and Livio Farallo. ***Slipstream*** is a "small press literary mag, uses about 70% poetry and 30% prose, also artwork. The editors like **new work with contemporary urban flavor. Writing must have a cutting edge to get our attention. Occasionally do theme issues. We like to keep an open forum, any length, subject, style. Best to see a sample to get a feel. Like city stuff as opposed to country. Like poetry that springs from the gut, screams from dark alleys, inspired by experience."** No **"pastoral, religious, traditional, rhyming" poetry.** They have recently published poetry by Fred Voss, Charles Safford, Gerald Locklin, Alan Catlin, Charles Bukowski, Patrick McKinnon, Jennifer

Olds, Marael Johnson, Denise Duhamel and M. Scott Douglass. As a sample the editors selected these lines from "Oh God" by Frank Hart:

YEAH, I could smell death on her.
But it was the smell of her *death*
and none of her odors had exactly
bothered me before.
Why should this one?

Slipstream appears 1-2 times a year in a 7×8½ format, 128 pgs., professionally printed, saddle-stapled, using b&w photos and graphics. More than 100 pgs. are devoted to poetry. The poems are of varying quality; all attempt to be lively with the focus on voice. It contains mostly free verse, some stanza patterns. They receive over 1,500 submissions of poetry/year, use less than 10%. Press run is 300 for 200 subscribers of which 10 are libraries. Subscription: $8.50/2 issues. **Sample postpaid: $5. Editor sometimes comments on rejections. Publishes theme issues. Send SASE for guidelines and upcoming themes. "Working stiff," "erotic," "protest," "night life" and "ethnic" theme issues have been released in the past. Reports in 2-8 weeks, "if SASE included." Pays copies. Also produces an audio cassette series that unfortunately will be inactive through 1995. Query for current needs.** Annual chapbook contest has December 1 deadline. Reading fee: $10. Submit up to 40 pgs. of poetry, any style, previously published work OK with acknowledgments. Winner receives $500 and 50 copies. All entrants receive copy of winning chapbook and an issue of the magazine. Past winners have included Gerald Locklin, Serena Fusek, Robert Cooperman, Kurt Nimmo, David Chorlton, Richard Amidon and Sherman Alexie. Dan Sicoli advises, "Do not waste time submitting your work 'blindly.' Sample issues from the small press first to determine which ones would be most receptive to your work."

SMALL POND MAGAZINE OF LITERATURE (II), P.O. Box 664, Stratford CT 06497, phone (203)378-4066, founded 1964, editor Napoleon St. Cyr, a literary triquarterly that features poetry . . . "and anything else the editor feels is original, important." Poetry can be **"any style, form, topic, except haiku, so long as it is deemed good, but limit of about 100 lines." Napoleon St. Cyr wants "nothing about cats, pets, flowers, butterflies, etc. Generally nothing under 8 lines."** Although he calls it name-dropping, he "reluctantly" provided the names of Marvin Soloman, Deborah Boe, Richard Kostelanetz, Fritz Hamilton and Emilie Glen as poets published. The magazine is digest-sized, offset from typescript on off-white paper, 40 pgs. with matte card cover, saddle-stapled, artwork both on cover and inside. Circulation is 300, of which about a third go to libraries. Subscription: $8 (for 3 issues). **Sample postpaid: $2.50 for a random selection, $3 current. Guidelines are available in each issue. The editor says he doesn't want 60 pages of anything; "dozen pages of poems max." He reports on submissions in 10-45 days (longer in summer), and publication is within 3-18 months. Pays 2 copies. Acquires all rights. Returns rights with written request including stated use. "One-time use per request."** Staff reviews books of poetry. Send books for review consideration. All styles and forms are welcome here. The editor usually responds quickly, often with comments to guide poets whose work interests him. He says, "I would like to receive more good surreal verse."

SMALL PRESS GENRE ASSOCIATION (SPGA); SPGA DIGEST (IV-Membership, science fiction/horror/fantasy/mystery), (formerly Small Press Writers and Artists Organization), 2131 S. 227th Dr., Buckeye AZ 85326-3872, secretary Cathy Hicks, board of trustees Mike Olson, John Rosenman, Joe Morey, Brian Smart and Dana Allen. The association publishes a bimonthly digest with emphasis on aiding members, advice columns, short poetry, art, reviews and short fiction, provides a poetry commentary service for members only; and hopes to publish a yearly anthology of members' work. **They don't want to see "religious, highly sentimental, pornographic, racial or political poetry."** Staff reviews books of poetry in 200-500 words, single format. Cathy Hicks says, "SPGA is new, but developed from the ashes of the Small Press Writers and Artists Organization (SPWAO) which is now defunct. We think SPGA is better because we are planning it, creating it better."

GIBBS SMITH, PUBLISHER; PEREGRINE SMITH POETRY COMPETITION (II), P.O. Box 667, Layton UT 84041, phone (801)544-9800, founded 1971, poetry series established 1988, assistant editor Dawn Valentine Hadlock. **They want "serious, contemporary poetry of merit. No specs except book is only 64 pgs."** They have published books of poetry by David Huddle and Carol Frost. Books are selected for publication through competition for the Peregrine Smith Poetry Prize of $500 plus publication. **Entries are received in April only and require a $15 reading fee and SASE. Always sends prepublication galleys.** The judge and editor for the series is Christopher Merrill.

THE SMITH; THE GENERALIST PAPERS (II), 69 Joralemon St., Brooklyn NY 11201, founded 1964, editor Harry Smith, publishes 3 to 5 books yearly. They have published poetry by Menke Katz, Lloyd Van Brunt, Richard Nason, Glenna Luschei and Karen Swenson. As a sample the editor selected these lines from "Hawk Forever in Mid-Dive" in Lance Lee's **Wrestling with the Angel**:

Her feet on the patio are leaves blown

over flagstones. Aimed at her head,
beak thrust out wings angled severely
a hawk hangs frozen in mid-air,
fanned to permanent fire in her sky.

"Send 3-6 poem sampling with query. No jingles, no standard academic verse. The decision process is relatively slow—about three months—as many mss are offered. Readers' reports are often passed along and the editor often comments." Always sends prepublication galleys. Pays 15% royalties, $500 advance, 10 copies. Write for catalog (free) or send $2 for a "slightly irregular" book ("with bumped corners or a little dust"). ***The Generalist Papers***, appearing 6 times/ year, consists of lively critical commentaries on contemporary writing—more candor than you will find in most reviews. Subscription: $12. **Sample postpaid: $2.** Harry Smith received the 1992 Poor Richard Award, a lifetime achievement award for distinguished contribution to small press publishing from the Small Press Center. He advises, "Revert to earlier models. *Avoid* university wordshops where there are standard recent models leading to standard mod verse. A close reading of **The Pearl Poet** will be more nourishing than all the asparagus of John Ashbery or Robert Bly."

SMITHS KNOLL (I, II), 49 Church Rd., Little Glemham, Woodbridge, Suffolk IP13 0BJ England, founded 1991, co-editors Roy Blackman and Michael Laskey, is a magazine appearing 3 times a year printing **"poems of pity, indignation and celebration,"** with no other restrictions. They have published poetry by Geoffrey Holloway, John Latham, Carole Satyamurti, Myra Schneider, Frances Wilson and Patricia Pogson. As a sample the editors selected this poem by Peter Wyles, called "Image":

Little blond kid
straight out of the Mothercare catalogue.
Tiny trainers, and trendy jeans,
and your smart, dark and shiny jacket . . .

across its back a flag, and a plane,
and the slogan "Born to Kill."

The editors say it is 60 pgs., A5, offset-litho, perfect-bound, with card cover. They receive 3,500-4,000 poems a year, "accept about one in twenty-four." Press run is 400 for 250 subscribers. Single copy: £2.50; subscription: £6.50 for 3 issues (plus postage outside UK). **Sample postpaid: £3. "We would consider poems previously published in magazines outside the U.K." No simultaneous submissions. Poems only. Doesn't commission work. "Constructive criticism of rejections where possible." Tries to report within 1 month (outside UK). Pays £5 plus 1 copy/poem.** Roy Blackman says, "We would like to see more thoughtful and well-crafted poems of indignation."

SNAKE NATION REVIEW; SNAKE NATION PRESS (II), #2, 110 W. Force St., Valdosta GA 31601, phone (912)249-8334, founded 1989, editor Roberta George, appears 4 times a year. **"Any form, length of 60 lines or less."** They have published poetry by Irene Willis and William Fuller. The handsome, 6×9, flat-spined magazine, 100 pgs., matte card cover, has a press run of 1,000 for 200 subscriptions of which 11 are libraries. Subscription: $15. **Sample postpaid: $6. Editor comments on submissions sometimes. Send SASE for guidelines. Reports in 3 months. Pays 2 copies or prizes. Acquires first rights.** Snake Nation Press publishes books of poetry. **Submit 60-page ms with $10 reading fee. Pays $500 on publication.**

SNAKE RIVER REFLECTIONS (I, II), 1863 Bitterroot Dr., Twin Falls ID 83301, phone (208)734-0746, appears 10 times a year using **short poems, up to 20 lines, any topic.** It is 8 pgs., stapled on the side. Press run is 100-200. Subscription: $6.50. **Sample postpaid: 30¢. Send SASE for guidelines. Pays 2 copies. Acquires first rights.** Reviews books of poetry. Send books for review consideration to editor Bill White.

SNOWY EGRET (II, IV-Nature), P.O. Box 9, Bowling Green IN 47833, founded 1922 by Humphrey A. Olsen, editor Philip Repp. **They want poetry that is "nature-oriented: poetry that celebrates the abundance and beauty of nature or explores the interconnections between nature and the human psyche."** As a sample of published poetry they selected the opening lines of "In a Climax Forest" by Conrad Hilberry:

The wooden past grows larger, I grow less
and less convincing in this sullen air
that wants a wind to stir its emptiness.

Snowy Egret appears twice a year in a 48-page, magazine-sized format, offset, saddle-stapled, with original graphics. Of 500 poems received they accept about 20. Their press run is 800 for 500 subscribers of which 50 are libraries. **Sample postpaid: $8. Send #10 SASE for writer's guidelines. Reports in 1 month. Always sends prepublication galleys. Pays $4/poem or $4/page**

plus 2 copies. Buys first North American or reprint rights. Open to unsolicited reviews. Poets may also send books for review consideration.

SOCIAL ANARCHISM (IV-Political, social issues, women/feminism), 2743 Maryland Ave., Baltimore MD 21218, phone (410)243-6987, founded (Vacant Lots Press) 1980, poetry editor Howard J. Ehrlich, is a digest-sized, 96-page biannual, print run 1,500, using about 6 pgs. of poetry in each issue which **"represents a political or social commentary that is congruent with a nonviolent anarchist, antiauthoritarian and feminist perspective."** They have recently published poetry by Earl Coleman, John Sokol, E.C. Archibeque, Richard Ballon, Barbara F. Stout, Deirdre V. Lovecky, Joel Lewis and Steven Hill. As a sample we selected these lines from "The Painted Soldier" by Lynn Olson:

He lay flat on the dirt road
flat where the thick, wide tires of our trucks
had pressed him out thin against the dirt road
flat where the wide treads of our tanks
had pressed him out thinner on the dirt road. . . .

Sample postpaid: $3.50. Submit up to 5 poems. Considers simultaneous submissions. Cover letter with short (3-sentence) bio required. Reports in 4-6 weeks. Pays 3 copies. Query regarding book reviews. The editor says, "We would like to receive more humorous poetry and concrete poetry."

THE SOCIETY OF AMERICAN POETS (SOAP); IN HIS STEPS PUBLISHING COMPANY; THE POET'S PEN; THE POET'S PROGRESS (I, IV-Religious, membership), P.O. Box 120, Reidsville GA 30453, phone (912)557-4265, founded 1984, editor Dr. Charles E. Cravey. ***The Poet's Pen*** is a literary quarterly of poetry and short stories. In His Steps publishes religious and other books and publishes music for the commercial record market. **"Open to all styles of poetry and prose–both religious and secular. No gross or 'X-rated' poetry without taste or character."** They have published poetry by Carlton Cook, Lessie Perry and Joann Saulino. As a sample the editor selected these lines from "Grapevine" by Carol Ann Lindsay:

The withered winter vine
of naked, knotted branches
nailed to man-made fences,
chains the cursing crosses to stolid, silent rows
that betray the bitter sip
of hollow human ways.

The Poet's Pen **uses poetry primarily by members and subscribers.** (Membership: $20/year.) ***The Poet's Progress***, a quarterly newsletter supplement to ***The Poet's Pen*****, also uses poetry by members and subscribers. Publishes seasonal/theme issues. Send SASE for upcoming themes. Sometimes sends prepublication galleys. Query for book publication. 60/40 split of pay. Editor "most certainly" comments on rejections.** Sponsors various contests throughout the year. Editor's Choice Awards each quarter, prizes $25, $15 and $10. President's Award for Superior Choice has a prize of $50; deadline is November 1. They also publish an anthology that has poetry competitions in several categories with prizes of $25-100. ***The Poet's Pen*** ranked #3 in the "Open Markets" category of the latest ***Writer's Digest*** Poetry 60 list. This category ranks those publications most open to both free and formal verse. The editor says, "We're looking for poets who wish to unite in fellowship with our growing family of poets nationwide. We currently have over 850 poets and are one of the nation's largest societies, yet small enough and family operated to give each of our poets individual attention and pointers."

SOJOURNERS (IV-Religious, political), 2401 15th St. NW, Washington DC 20009, phone (202)328-8842, fax (202)328-8757, founded 1975, poetry editor Rose Berger, appears 10 times/year, "with approximately 40,000 subscribers. **We focus on faith, politics and culture from a radical Christian perspective. We publish 1-3 poems/month depending on length. All poems must be original and unpublished. We look for seasoned, well-crafted poetry that reflects the issues and perspectives covered in our magazine. Poetry using non-inclusive language (any racist, sexist, homophobic poetry) will not be accepted."** As a sample the editor selected these lines by David Abrams:

An eagle against a clear sky,
A snake coming off a rock,
A skiff in the center of a lake,
And the Spirit slipping into bodies.

The editor describes ***Sojourners*** as 52 pgs., offset printing. It appears monthly except that there is one issue for August/September and February/March. Of 400 poems received/year, they publish 8-10. Press run is 50,000 for 40,000 subscribers of which 500 are libraries, 2,000 shelf sales. Subscription: $30. **Sample postpaid: $2.75. Submit no more than 3 poems at a time. Cover letter with brief bio required. Editor comments on submissions "sometimes." Publishes theme issues. Send SASE for guidelines and upcoming themes. Reports in 4-6 weeks. Pays $15-25/poem plus**

5 copies. "We assume permission to grant reprints unless the author requests otherwise." Staff reviews books of poetry in 600 words, single or multi-book format.

SOLEIL PRESS (IV-Ethnic), Box 452, RFD 1, Lisbon Falls ME 04252, phone (207)353-5454, founded 1988, contact Denis Ledoux, publishes and distributes **writing by and about Franco-Americans (Americans of French-Canadian and Acadian descent)** in chapbooks and paperbacks. **Not interested in the continental French experience. Submit sample poems with cover letter noting how the material is Franco-North American. Pays copies.**

SOLO FLYER; SPARE CHANGE POETRY PRESS (IV-Regional), 2115 Clearview NE, Massillon OH 44646, Spare Change Poetry Press founded 1979, editor David B. McCoy. ***Solo Flyer*** is a 4-page flyer appearing 2-5 times/year featuring the work of a single poet in each issue. **"Submissions limited to Ohio poets."** They want **poetry using punctuation and capitalization. "Like to see poems with a common theme."** As a sample the editor selected "Absences" by Ruth V. Tams-Fuquen:

Wordless
we walked that hotel's midnight garden.
The blossom you laid on my palm

spoke
for the song you hummed,

suggested
the words you chose
not to sing.

The flyers are folded 8½×11 sheets of colored paper. **Sample free with #10 SASE. Previously published material OK. Pays 20-25 copies.** The editor says, "Submissions without SASE are not read."

SONORA REVIEW (II), Dept. of English, University of Arizona, Tucson AZ 85721, phone (602)626-8383 or 621-1836, founded 1980, address all work to Poetry Editor, is a semiannual literary journal that publishes "non-genre" fiction and poetry. **The editors want "quality poetry, literary concerns. Translations welcome. No dull, well-crafted but passionless poetry or swooping and universal sentiment. Experimental work welcome."** They have recently published poetry by Jane Miller, Christopher Davis, Barbara Cully and Rosmarie Waldrop. As a sample, the editors chose the following lines by Joshua Clover:

Across the tracks her scalp took on the feel
of a cigarette foil's papered side. Snow
hair & boots. The most wasted man around
would persuade his lover to waste him even more
in the pause I woke into.

Sonora Review is a handsome magazine, 6×9, professionally printed on heavy off-white stock, 130 pgs., flat-spined, with 2-color glossy card cover. Recent issues have tended to include lyric and narrative free verse, with some metered poetry, translations and sequences rounding out selections. Circulation is 650, of which 250 are subscriptions and 45 go to libraries. Subscription: $10/year, $18/2 years. **Back issue available for $5 postpaid. Poets should submit typed copy; simultaneous submissions OK. "Brief cover letter helpful but optional." Publishes theme issues. Send SASE for upcoming themes. Reporting time is 2 months and time to publication 6 months. Sometimes sends prepublication galleys. Pays 2 copies.** Send books for review consideration. The magazine sponsors annual poetry awards with prizes of $150 and $50. Send #10 SASE for deadlines and guidelines. In the past, contributors to ***Sonora Review*** have been listed in **Best of the West, Pushcart Prize, O. Henry** and **Best American Poetry** anthologies.

‡SOPHOMORE JINX (I), P.O. Box 770728, Woodside NY 11377-0728, phone (718)507-8360, founded 1993, editors Anne-Marie Mooney and Anthony Rutella, Jr., is a quarterly poetry publication especially open to beginners. **"We would like to see traditional forms as well as free verse and conventional subjects as well as experimental material. Nothing more than 60 lines. No vulgarity."** They have recently published poetry by Lyn Lifshin, Emily Yau, John Grey and T.N. Turner. As for a sample, they say, "We do not feel that any one of our poems/poets exemplifies what we are looking for at ***Sophomore Jinx***. We have published poems ranging from very serious to humorous and free verse to traditional forms." ***SJ*** is about 60 pgs., 5½×8½, desktop-published and saddle-stapled with paper cover. Single copy: $5; subscription: $15 for 1 year, $25 for 2 years. **Sample postpaid: $6. "Please submit no more than 3 poems at a time. The more poems a person submits, the longer the response time." Previously published poems and simultaneous submissions OK. Cover letter required.** Time between acceptance and publication is 3-6 months. **Send SASE for guidelines. Reports within 1 month. Each issue the authors of the top 3 poems (chosen by the editors) are awarded 1 copy and prizes of**

$20, $15 and $10, respectively. Other contributors must order a copy/subscription if they would like to see their work in print. The editors add, "We encourage our submitters to tell us about themselves in their cover letter. We don't mean a formal bio—we want to know who you are so that we can see where you're coming from. And we like to be personal in our replies."

‡SOUNDINGS: A NEWSLETTER FOR SURVIVORS OF CHILDHOOD SEXUAL ABUSE; ECHOES NETWORK, INC. (IV-Specialized), 4370 NE Halsey, Portland OR 97213, founded 1983, executive director Wendy Ann Wood, M.A. Echoes Network is an organization devoted to therapy of victims of childhood sexual abuse. Their quarterly newsletter, ***Soundings***, uses **poetry on the theme of survival of childhood sexual abuse, ritual abuse and multiple personality disorder.** As a sample, here is a complete poem, "Little One," by Lynn:

It hurt to be so small
And have her for the mom
And need a little help
To tie my shoe
To print my name
Or learn a prayer for school.
She was never nice to me.
No one was.

It is 8 pgs., laser printed, "folded left." They use 50% of poems received. Press run is 1,500-2,000 for 1,800 subscriptions. Subscription: $10. **Sample: $2 plus SASE. Editor often comments on rejections. "No SASE, no response." Reports in 6-8 weeks. Pays 2 copies.** Reviews books on related topics, poetry or other subjects. The editor advises, "Focus on what you have *personally* done to heal from the trauma of childhood sexual abuse. Stay present rather than reliving your life story. If your material is past-oriented then include a progress report explaining where you are now in recovery. Read **Triumph Over Darkness** by W.A. Wood and L. Hatton or **Triumph Over Darkness Vol. II** by W.A. Wood [published by Beyond Words Publishing and Echoes Network in 1988 and 1993, respectively] for specific examples."

SOUNDINGS EAST (II), Salem State College, Salem MA 01970, phone (508)741-6270, founded 1973, advisory editor Claire Keyes. "*SE* is published by Salem State College and is staffed by students. We accept short fiction (15 pgs. max) and **contemporary poetry (5 pgs. max).** Purpose is to promote poetry and fiction in the college and beyond its environs. We **do not want graphic profanity.**" They have recently published poetry by Martha Carlson Bradley and Gale Renee Walden as well as a feature section on "Incarcerated Poets." *SE* appears twice a year, 64-68 pgs., digest-sized, flat-spined, b&w drawings and photos, glossy card cover with b&w photo. They receive about 500 submissions/year, use 40-60. Press run is 2,000 for 120 subscribers of which 35 are libraries. **Sample postpaid: $3. Simultaneous submissions OK. Reads submissions September 1 through May 1 only. Fall deadline: November 20; Spring: April 20. Reports within 1-4 months. Pays 2 copies. Acquires all rights. Rights revert to the writers.** "We occasionally, when funding allows, publish an extra spring issue which features only poetry, fiction and artwork by Salem State College students."

SOUTH ASH PRESS (I, II), 2311 E. Indian School Rd., Phoenix AZ 85016, founded 1991, publisher Chuck Hadd Jr., is a monthly poetry magazine sustained and distributed by community advertisers. **They want "well-crafted poems by beginning and established poets. 75 lines maximum."** They have published poetry by Denis Johnson. As a sample the publisher selected these lines from "Traveling Between Storms" by Albino Carrillo:

Thunder is what wakes us all,
the taste like salt and meat
lingering as we pull on our clothes.
And just before the evening's spent
to wander with the gray constellations.
To know this blackness, to know it well.

South Ash Press is 8 pgs., magazine-sized, saddle-stapled with card cover with b&w photo, numerous ads on same pages as poems. They receive about 1,000 poems a year, publish about 200. Each issue includes a number of poems by a "Featured Poet." Press run is 2,000 for 50 subscribers, the rest distributed free through advertisers. Subscription: $20/year. **Sample postpaid: $2. No previously published poems; simultaneous submissions OK. "Three people select submissions. An acceptance by any one of them gets poem included. While we are glad to see work by beginners, we do not provide critiques and/or advice." Reports in 6-8 weeks. Pays 2 copies. Acquires first rights.**

SOUTH CAROLINA REVIEW (II), English Dept., Clemson University, Clemson SC 29634-1503, phone (803)656-3229, founded 1968, editor Richard J. Calhoun, is a biannual literary magazine "recognized by the ***New York Quarterly*** as one of the top 20 of this type." They will consider **"any kind of poetry**

as long as it's good. No stale metaphors, uncertain rhythms or lack of line integrity. Interested in seeing more traditional forms. Format should be according to new MLA Stylesheet." They have published poetry by Pattiann Rogers, J.W. Rivers and Claire Bateman. It is 200 pgs., 6×9, flat-spined, professionally printed and uses about 8-10 pgs. of poetry in each issue. Reviews of recent issues back up editorial claims that all styles and forms are welcome; moreover, poems were accessible and well-executed, too. Circulation is 600, for 400 subscribers of which 250 are libraries. They receive about 1,000 unsolicited submissions of poetry/year, use 10, have a 2-year backlog. Subscription: $7. **Sample postpaid: $5. Do not submit during June, July, August or December. Publishes theme issues. Send SASE for upcoming themes. Reports in 6-9 months. Always sends prepublication galleys. Pays copies.** Staff reviews books of poetry.

SOUTH COAST POETRY JOURNAL (II), English Dept., California State University, Fullerton CA 92634, founded 1986, editor John J. Brugaletta. The twice-yearly (January and June) magazine publishes poetry only. **"We'd like to see poems with strong imagery and a sense that the poem has found its best form, whether that form is traditional or innovative. We prefer poems under 36 lines, but we'll look at others. Any subject matter or style.** We have published Marge Piercy, Mark Strand, X.J. Kennedy and Robert Mezey." As a sample, the editor selected these lines from "Fran's Revenge" by Skip Eisiminger:

Sunday daybreak   no day to die
Fran hauled out the Hoover   hooked up the hose
shoved on the chrome wand   and started to suck
dust from the carpet   crud from the couch
litter from last night   lint from the wash.

Roused from a rough night   rubbing his eyes
Don slouched from the bedroom   in loose boxer briefs . . .

The journal is 60 pgs., digest-sized, perfect-bound, offset, heavy paper cover, some line art. Press run is 700 for 420 subscribers, 25 of which are libraries, 50 shelf sales. Subscription: $10, $6/issue. **Sample postpaid: $4. No simultaneous submissions. Reads submissions September 1 through June 1 only. Every submission is read by at least 3 editors. Guidelines are available for SASE. Reports in 6-8 weeks. Pays 1 copy. Acquires first North American serial rights.** They conduct an annual poetry contest judged by eminent poets. Entry fee is $3/poem. The editor says, "Although we publish free verse, we would like to publish more traditional forms."

SOUTH DAKOTA REVIEW (II, IV-Regional, themes), University of South Dakota, Vermillion SD 57069, phone (605)677-5220 or 677-5966, founded 1963, editor John R. Milton, is a "literary quarterly publishing poetry, fiction, criticism, essays. **When material warrants, an emphasis on the American West; writers from the West; Western places or subjects; frequent issues with no geographical emphasis; periodic special issues on one theme, or one place or one writer. Looking for originality, some kind of sophistication, significance, craft—i.e., professional work. Nothing confessional, purely descriptive, too filled with self-importance."** They use 6-10 poems/issue, "receive tons, it seems." Press run is 650-900 for 450 subscribers of which half are libraries. Subscription: $15/year, $25/2 years. **Sample postpaid: $4. Editor comments on submissions "rarely." Reports in 1-12 weeks. Pays 1 copy/page. Acquires first and reprint rights.** They have a distinct bias against personal or confessional poems, and generally publish free verse with a strong sense of place, a strong voice and a universal theme. Read the magazine—it's attractive and well-edited—to get a feel for the type of poetry that succeeds here. Milton advises, "Find universal meaning in the regional. Avoid constant 'I' personal experiences that are not of interest to anyone else. Learn to be less self-centered and more objective."

SOUTHEASTERN FRONT (II), 565 17th St. NW, Cleveland TN 37311, founded 1985, publisher Robin Merritt, is "an artists' and writers' presentation/representation service; a gallery in a magazine. **No stylistic limitations, substantial human experience is a plus. Nothing devoid of artistic or literary merit, nor strictly commercially designed work."** It is approximately 60 pgs., b&w, glossy, offset print with photos. Press run is 1,000. **Inquire (with SASE) about availability of sample. Previously published poems ("if author retains all rights") and simultaneous submissions OK. Cover letter not required "but often beneficial." Often comments on rejections. Send SASE for guidelines. Reporting time varies. Pays "exposure, publication, referrals." Authors retain rights.** Open to unsolicited reviews "as long as review is accompanied by a copy of the book." Poets may also send books for review consideration. ***Southeastern FRONT*** also offers short-run book printing and manufacturing services to individuals and institutions. "Will print as few as fifty copies of perfect-bound or saddle-stitched books. Perfect for poets, teachers, catalogs, etc. Inquire for more information." They have published **Four Wheeler & Two Legged**, poems by Stephen Wing. "This author's first book was published due to his high quality submissions to our artists' and writers' presentation service. **Four Wheeler & Two Legged** is contemporary poetry with themes on hitchhiking, nature and earth awareness, international human rights and relationships. It is 112 pgs. and is available for $9.95 plus $1.05 postage from ***Southeastern FRONT***." The

CLOSE-UP

Passion and Virtuosity Set Poetry Apart

Photo by Star Black

Molly Peacock

"Friendship With Men"

Is friendship with men like friendship with birds?
Is friendship the way this parrot nestles
beneath my chin, its feathers only disturbed
by the regular wind from my nostrils?

Unexpectedly, another species
and I achieve intimacy: we are
each other's pets; as I imagine the seas
at a great distance are pets of the stars.

(from **Take Heart**, 1989, reprinted by permission of Random House/Vintage Books)

". . . I love the things I've sought," Molly Peacock reads from one of her poems. Her voice rises and falls *with* the poem, *for* the audience, this time in Cincinnati. Before and after each poem, she chats. "When I went to poetry readings, I hated the shufflers [poets rearranging their poems at the podium]," she tells the audience. "Now I shuffle because the order that I'd planned doesn't feel like the atmosphere in the room."

She not only changes the order of her poems, but also offers to read any poem requested. To her, people in the audience matter. They're part of what she loves as a poet and whom she works for as president of the 3,000-member Poetry Society of America.

In both New York City and London, Ontario, Canada, where she lives, Peacock writes fulltime. Her poems have appeared in ***The Paris Review***, ***The Nation*** and dozens of other publications. Her books of poetry include **And Live Apart** (University of Missouri Press, 1980), **Raw Heaven** (Vintage Books, 1984) and **Take Heart** (Vintage Books, 1989). Her latest collection is **Original Love**, to be published by W.W. Norton & Company in the spring of 1995.

Peacock followed two roads to poetry: as a way of processing her emotional life and as "a place for explosive emotion." She also loved language. "I simply loved the idea of making something beautiful with language," she says. "There's another part of me that loves clarity and meaning."

When she writes, "passion and virtuosity" matter. They are the difference, she says, between a mediocre poem and an excellent one. And passion and virtuosity are the criteria she uses in judging her work. Poets must devise their own criteria for what makes an excellent poem, she says.

Part of a poem's "passion and virtuosity" depends on a careful revision that doesn't sap life from the original impulse. Peacock disagrees with the workshop aesthetic that equates revision with deletion. Another way to look at revision is to add and recast lines so the links between the ideas get reprovided for the reader. "The emotional freshness of a poem sometimes dissolves into a kind of obscurity if the writer doesn't concentrate on the syntax of the poem and how the syntax coordinates with the music of the lines."

Poets can learn from fiction writers and "the music of the sentence and how the sentence unfolds," she says. "There is the music of the line [in a poem] which can be quite formal, and then there is the rhythm of the sentence." Some poets look at their lines and not the sentence structure, or they depend on the most simple sentence structure. This oversimplification doesn't allow causality into the poem and into its logic. The poem becomes a still life on one plane. "Complicated syntax gives depth of perspective and depth to ideas."

Peacock works individually with about 50 private students, teaching in person, by mail, fax and electronic mail (whichever outlet a student chooses). Her students live throughout the United States and Canada and as far away as Costa Rica. Some have published books of poetry; many have earned MFA degrees and are looking for further instruction; still others are learning to write.

She advises her students—and all poets—to submit finished poems throughout the year rather than sending 20 packages at a time. When the poet gets back 19 of those packages, there's a tendency to get discouraged. "There is going to be an incredibly high rejection rate," Peacock says. That doesn't mean that you'll get accustomed to having poems returned. "I'm just as hurt by a rejection now as I was when I was 17 years old."

Designing a package of poems to send to each magazine shouldn't be a poet's major concern. Place the boldest poem first, she suggests, and don't worry about whether the poems have a theme or are too much alike. Simply submit your best. "Keep your standards high for yourself but your expectations low," she recommends. "Poet Marianne Moore once said a poem wasn't 'dead' until she'd sent it out 40 times. It's a question of utterly valuing what you do."

Poetry readings and networking can be a solace or learning opportunity for poets awaiting an editor's decision. But, with networking, follow your own instincts as to when and how: in person, letters or electronic mail. "Networking makes a social and literary reality that's important, and it brings you and your work into other people's consciousness." Networking to land a publishing contract or bylines doesn't always work, though. "The opportunities that I've had have come out of genuine bonds that I've had with people."

Poetry readings at universities or community centers can also help poets find an audience. In some cases, poets who read their work have a better chance of selling a book. And the Poetry Society of America sponsors poetry readings and programs throughout the country. The organization also strives to promote poets by sponsoring poetry awards and placing poetry in subways and hotel rooms.

Peacock is amazed at the variety of impulses, energies and styles among today's poets. "The urge of poets to tell the truth of their situations gives this urgency to the fabric of American poetry," she says.

"Listen to yourself," she recommends, whether writing or marketing poems. Follow your instincts. The best poets "dare to say the things they deeply feel."

—*Paula Deimling*

editor says, "*Southeastern FRONT* offers its contributors exposure to selected publishers, reviewers, museums, galleries and individuals actively involved in the fine arts. We do not presently require submission or reading fees from our contributors; however, your purchase of Stephen Wing's excellent new collection of poetry is the most effective way you can help us expedite the completion of our Artists' & Writers' showcase publications."

THE SOUTHERN CALIFORNIA ANTHOLOGY; ANN STANFORD POETRY PRIZES (III), c/o Master of Professional Writing Program, WPH 404, University of Southern California, Los Angeles CA 90089-4034, phone (213)740-3252, founded 1983, is an "annual literary review of serious contemporary poetry and fiction. **Very open to all subject matters except pornography. Any form, style OK."** They have published poetry by Robert Bly, John Updike, Denise Levertov and Peter Viereck. As a sample the editor selected these lines from "The Rivers of Paris" by James Ragan:

The boulevards are the rivers wind owes
to the eyes' reflections, light
to the panes transparent
in the domes of air wind weaves along Sacre Coeur

The anthology is 144 pgs., digest-sized, perfect-bound, with a semi-glossy color cover featuring one art piece. A fine selection of poems distinguish this journal, and it has an excellent reputation, well-deserved. The downside, if it has one, concerns limited space for newcomers. Circulation is 1,500, 50% going to subscribers of which 50% are libraries. 30% are for shelf sales. **Sample postpaid: $5.95. No simultaneous submissions or previously published poems. Submit 3-5 poems between September 1 and January 1. All decisions made by mid-February. Send SASE for guidelines. Reports in 4 months. Pays 3 copies. Acquires all rights.** The Ann Stanford Poetry Prizes ($750, $250 and $100) have an April 15 deadline, $10 fee (5 poem limit), for unpublished poems. Include cover sheet with name, address and titles and SASE for contest results. All entries are considered for publication, and all entrants receive a copy of *SCA*.

SOUTHERN HUMANITIES REVIEW (II, IV-Translations), 9088 Haley Center, Auburn University AL 36849, co-editors Dan Latimer and R.T. Smith, founded 1967, is a 6×9 literary quarterly, 100 pgs., circulation 700. **Interested in poems of any length, subject, genre. Space is limited, and brief poems are more likely to be accepted. "Translations welcome."** This journal continues to gain influence and prestige in the literary world by publishing a wide variety of verse that displays careful attention to image, theme, craft and voice. They have recently published poetry by Eamon Grennan, Donald Hall, Brendan Galvin, Mary Ruefle, Hayden Carruth, Robert Morgan and John Engels. Subscription: $15/year. **Sample: $5. "Send 3-5 poems in a business-sized envelope. Avoid sending faint computer printout." Responds in 1-2 months, possibly longer in summer. Always sends prepublication galleys. Pays 2 copies and $50 for the best poem published during the year. Copyright reverts to author upon publication.** Staff reviews books of poetry in approximately 750-1,000 words. Send books for review consideration. The editors advise, "For beginners we'd recommend study and wide reading in English and classical literature, and, of course, American literature—the old works, not just the new. We also recommend study of or exposure to a foreign language and a foreign culture. Poets need the reactions of others to their work: criticism, suggestions, discussion. A good creative writing teacher would be desirable here, and perhaps some course work too. And then submission of work, attendance at workshops. And again, the reading: history, biography, verse, essays—all of it. We want to see poems that have gone beyond the language of slippage and easy attitudes."

SOUTHERN POETRY REVIEW; GUY OWEN POETRY PRIZE (II), English Dept., University of North Carolina, Charlotte NC 28223, phone (704)547-4309, editor Ken McLaurin, founded 1958, a semiannual literary magazine "with emphasis on effective poetry. **There are no restrictions on form, style or content of poetry; length subject to limitations of space."** They have published work by Linda Pastan, Judith Ortiz Cofer, David Ray, Stephen Sandy, Betty Adcock and Walter McDonald. As a sample the editor selected these lines from "The Last Image" by Heather Burns:

I hold onto it with dissolving hands.
The bed is wet from nightsweating.
A vapor has entered the room.
It smells like ocean foam and salt.
It is warm, like another skin.
Whose face have I touched besides my own?

Southern Poetry Review is 6×9, handsomely printed on buff stock, 78 pgs., flat-spined with textured, one-color matte card cover. Circulation is 1,000. Subscription: $8/year. **Sample available for $2 postpaid; no guidelines, but will answer queries with SASE. Writers should submit no more than 3-5 poems. Reads submissions September 1 through May 31 only. Pays 1 copy. Acquires first-time rights.** Staff reviews books of poetry. Send books for review consideration. This is the type of literary magazine to settle back with in a chair and read, particularly during dry creative spells, to inspire one's muse. It is recommended as a market for that reason. It's a tough sell, though. Work is read closely and the magazine reports in a timely manner. There is a yearly contest, the Guy Owen Poetry Prize of $500, to which the entry fee is a subscription; submission must be postmarked in April.

‡SOUTHERN REVIEW (II), Curtin University, Bentley 6101 Western Australia, founded in the 1960s, poetry editor Anne Brewster, published jointly by University of Adelaide and Curtin University of Technology, appears 3 times a year **using poetry that is not sexist, racist. "Would like to see language poetry."** They have published poetry by John Kinsella and Jeri Kroll. As a sample the editor selected these lines from "He (III)" by Kate Llewellyn:

I cross my legs
playing for time
he won't take tea
There's only one thing
on his mind
and pretty soon
it's on mine too
I pick up my pen

SR is 100 pgs., digest-sized, flat-spined. Press run is 500 for 375 subscribers. **Sample postpaid: A$12. Publishes theme issues. Theme for March 1995 issue: "The Millennium," for September 1995: "Teaching the Postmodern." Reports in 3 months. Pays 1 copy. Acquires first publication rights.** Reviews books of poetry in 1,000 words minimum, single format.

THE SOUTHERN REVIEW (II), 43 Allen Hall, Louisiana State University, Baton Rouge LA 70803, phone (504)388-5108, founded 1935 (original series), 1965 (new series), poetry editors James Olney and Dave Smith, "is a literary quarterly which publishes fiction, poetry, critical essays and book reviews, with emphasis on contemporary literature in the U.S. and abroad, and with special interest in Southern culture and history. Selections are made with careful attention to craftsmanship and technique and to the seriousness of the subject matter." By general agreement this is one of the most distinguished of literary journals. Joyce Carol Oates, for instance, says, "Over the years I have continued to be impressed with the consistent high quality of *SR*'s publications and its general 'aura,' which bespeaks careful editing, adventuresome tastes and a sense of thematic unity. *SR* is characterized by a refreshing openness to new work, placed side by side with that of older, more established, and in many cases highly distinguished writers." The editors say, **"We are interested in any formal varieties of poetry, traditional or modern, that are well crafted, though we cannot normally accommodate excessively long poems (say 10 pgs. and over)."** They have published poetry by Norman Dubie, Margaret Gibson, Susan Ludvigson and Peter Schmitt. The editors selected these sample lines by Mary Oliver:

The story about Jesus in the cave
is a good one,
but when is it ever like that

as sharp as lightning,
or even the way the green sea does everything—
quickly,
and with such grace?

The beautifully printed quarterly is massive: 6¾×10, 240 pgs., flat-spined, matte card cover. They receive about 2,000 submissions of poetry, use 10%. All styles and forms seem welcome, although accessible lyric and narrative free verse appear most often in recent issues. Press run is 3,100 for 2,100 subscribers of which 70% are libraries. Subscription: $18. **Sample postpaid: $5. "We do not require a cover letter but we prefer one giving information about the author and previous publications." Prefers submissions of 1-4 pgs. Send SASE for guidelines. Reports in 2 months. Pays $20/printed page plus 2 copies. Buys first North American rights.** Staff reviews books of poetry in 3,000 words, multi-book format. Send books for review consideration. ***The Southern Review*** ranked #5 in the "Poets' Pick" category of the latest ***Writer's Digest*** Poetry 60 list. This category ranks those publications in which poets said they would most like to see their work published.

SOUTHWEST REVIEW; ELIZABETH MATCHETT STOVER MEMORIAL AWARD (II), 307 Fondren Library West, Box 374, Southern Methodist University, Dallas TX 75275, phone (214)768-1037, founded 1915, editor Willard Spiegelman. ***Southwest Review*** is a literary quarterly that publishes fiction, essays, poetry and interviews. "It is hard to describe our preference for poetry in a few words. We always suggest that potential contributors read several issues of the magazine to see for themselves what we like. But some things may be said: We demand **very high quality in our poems; we accept both traditional and experimental writing, but avoid unnecessary obscurity and private symbolism; we place no arbitrary limits on length but find shorter poems easier to fit into our format than longer ones. We**

have no specific limitations as to theme." They have published poetry by Adrienne Rich, Amy Clampitt, Albert Goldbarth, John Hollander, Molly Peacock and Charles Wright. The journal is 6×9, 144 pgs., perfect-bound, professionally printed, with matte text stock cover. They receive about 1,000 unsolicited submissions of poetry/year, use 32. Poems tend to be lyric and narrative free verse combining a strong voice with powerful topics or situations. Diction is accessible and content often conveys a strong sense of place. Circulation is 1,500 with 1,000 subscriptions of which 600 are libraries. Subscription: $20. **Sample postpaid: $5. No simultaneous submissions, no previously published work. Publishes theme issues. Send SASE for guidelines. Reports within a month. Always sends prepublication galleys. Pays cash plus copies.** The $150 Elizabeth Matchett Stover Memorial Prize is awarded annually for the best poem, chosen by editors, published in the preceding year. Poetry published in *Southwest Review* has been included in the 1993 and 1994 volumes of **The Best American Poetry.**

SOU'WESTER (II), Box 1438, Southern Illinois University, Edwardsville IL 62026, phone (618)692-3190, founded 1960, editor Fred W. Robbins, appears 3 times a year. **"We like poetry with imagery and figurative language that has strong associations and don't care for abstract poetry. We have no particular preference for form or length."** They have recently published poetry by Marnie Bullock, Susan Swartwont and Bruce Guernsey. As a sample the editor selected the final stanzas of "The Gleaners" by William Jolliff:

And even when their too-large coats are soaked
with winter rains, I envy those children,
the birds we were, kicking their buckles

through the muddy dark. It would be a fair trade,
a fair swap, for the work we turn to now,
each grey and brittle season, seeking, digging,

kicking the stalks for a blessing.

There are 25-30 pgs. of poetry in each 6×9, 80-page issue. The magazine is professionally printed, flat-spined, with textured matte card cover, circulation 300, 110 subscriptions of which 50 are libraries. They receive some 2,000 poems (from 600 poets) each year, use 36-40, have a 4-month backlog. Subscription: $10 (3 issues). **Sample postpaid: $5. Simultaneous submissions OK. Rejections usually within 4 months. Pays 2 copies. Acquires all rights. Returns rights. Editor comments on rejections "usually, in the case of those that we almost accept."** He says, "Read poetry past and present. Have something to say and say it in your own voice. Poetry is a very personal thing for many editors. When all else fails, we may rely on gut reactions, so take whatever hints you're given to improve your poetry, and keep submitting."

THE SOW'S EAR POETRY REVIEW (II), 19535 Pleasant View Dr., Abingdon VA 24210-6827, phone (703)628-2651, founded 1988, managing editor Larry Richman, graphics editor Mary Calhoun, is a quarterly. **"We are open to many forms and styles, and have no limitations on length. We try to be interesting visually, and we use graphics to complement the poems. Though we publish some work from our local community of poets, we are interested in poems from all over. We publish a few by school-age poets and occasionally feature a previously unpublished poet."** They have recently published poetry by John Grey, Kerry Shawn Keys and Katharyn Howd Machan. As a sample the editors selected these lines from "The Forbidden" by Lisa Sewell:

I was never his little girl. It is not that simple.
Even when the door is closed I know he's there,
tall in the glowing corridor, beyond the threshold.
He knows which way my dreams are blowing, is waiting
for me to smile, for our sentences to fail and fall away
the way veils might, and the light come shining.
O light that terrifies, place we swore not to enter.

TSE is 32 pgs., 8½×11, saddle-stapled, with matte card cover, professionally printed. They accept about 100 of 2,000 poems submitted. Press run is 600 for 500 subscribers of which 15 are libraries. Shelf sales: 20-40. Subscription: $10. **Sample postpaid: $3.50. No previously published poems; simultaneous submissions OK if you tell them promptly when work is accepted elsewhere. Enclose brief bio. Reports in 3-6 months. Pays 1 copy. Buys first publication rights.** Most prose (reviews, interviews, features) is commissioned. They offer an annual contest for unpublished poems, with fee of $2/poem, $500 prize, and publication for 20-25 finalists. For contest, submit poems in September/October, with name and address on back of each poem. Submissions of 5 poems/$10 receive a subscription. Include SASE for notification. 1993 judge: Josephine Jacobsen. They also sponsor a chapbook contest in March/April with $10 fee, $500 prize and publication. Send SASE for chapbook contest guidelines.

SPARROW: THE SONNET MAGAZINE (IV-Form), 103 Waldron St., West Lafayette IN 47906, editor and publisher Felix Stefanile, publishes "as material permits." They want **"formal sonnets *only*, 4 or 5 per submission. No subject restrictions. We don't publish poems in poor taste."** They have recently published poetry by Karl Shapiro, John Frederick Nims and Annie Finch. As a sample the editor selected these lines by Howard C. Baumgartner:

I love the feel of silky pantyhose
Which hug her soft and smoothly shaven thighs;
And, certainly, I love the way hose shows
Those shapely calves which always hold my eyes.

The editor says *Sparrow* is 9×12, using occasional graphics only by invitation. They receive about 1,000 pieces a year, use less than 1%. Press run is 750 for about 450 subscribers of which about 100 are libraries, 300 shelf sales. **Sample postpaid: $5. No simultaneous submissions. Typed copy only, 8½×11 bond. No material returned without SASE. "We have a very cynical attitude toward long cover letters."** **Seldom comments on rejections. "We are not in the business of offering criticism or advice." Send SASE with all queries. Reports "usually in a week." Sometimes sends prepublication galleys. Pays $3 a sonnet plus 2 copies. Buys first and non-exclusive reprint rights. "We also offer a $25 prize for the best sonnet each issue."** Staff reviews books of poetry. Send books for review consideration. The editor says, "We are now essentially a 'new' magazine with a fine, old name. We pride ourselves on our liveliness and our currency. We also publish scores of musical settings for sonnets, by special arrangement with the composer. We are really not a market for beginners and the MFA degree does not impress us."

SPECTACULAR DISEASES (II), 83B London Rd., Peterborough, Cambridgeshire PE2 9BS United Kingdom, founded 1974, Paul Green editor (various invited poetry editors). "The press presents **experimental writing with bias to the current French scene and to current, and past scenes, in the U.S. and Britain. Most poetry is solicited by the editors.** Long poems will be clearly accepted, if falling in the special categories." They have published poetry by Saúl Yurkievich, Jackson MacLow and Bernard Noël. ***Spectacular Diseases*** is "occasional," 40-60 pgs., digest-sized. **Sample postpaid: £1.75. Query before submitting as most material is invited. Pays copies.** Under the Spectacular Diseases imprint a number of books and anthologies are printed. For book consideration, **query with about 16 samples; letter helpful but not essential. Pays 10% of run. Send postage for catalog to buy samples.**

SPECTRUM (II), Anna Maria College, Box 72-D, Paxton MA 01612, phone (508)849-3450, founded 1985, editor Robert H. Goepfert, is a "multidisciplinary national publication with liberal arts emphasis," presenting 6-8 poems in each 64-page issue: **"poems of crisp images, precise language, which have something of value to say and say it in an authentic voice. Not the self-conscious, the 'workshop poem,' the cliché, the self-righteous."** They have published poetry by William Stafford. ***Spectrum*** appears twice a year in a 6×9, flat-spined format, professionally printed on quality stock with 2-color matte card cover, using b&w photos and art. Press run is 1,000 for 650 subscriptions (200 of them to libraries). Single copy: $4; subscription: $7 for 1 year, $13 for 2 years. **Sample: $3. No previously published poems or simultaneous submissions. Reads submissions September 1 through May 15 only. Editor "occasionally" comments on rejections. Mss returned only with SASE. Reports in 6 weeks. Always sends prepublication galleys. Pays $20/poem plus 2 copies. Buys first North American serial rights.** Open to unsolicited reviews.

SPINDRIFT (II), Shoreline Community College, 16101 Greenwood Ave., Seattle WA 98133, founded 1962, faculty advisor varies each year, currently Carol Orlock, is **open to all varieties of poetry except greeting card style.** They have published poetry by James Bertolino, Edward Harkness and Richard West. ***Spindrift***, an annual, is 125 pgs., handsomely printed in an 8″ square, flat-spined. Circulation 500. Single copy: $6.50. **Sample postpaid: $5. "Submit 2 copies of each poem, 6 maximum. Include cover letter with biographical information. We accept submissions until February 1—report back in March." Send SASE for guidelines. Pays 1 copy. Acquires first serial rights.** The editors advise, "Read what the major contemporary poets are writing. Read what local poets are writing. Be distinctive, love the language, avoid sentiment."

THE SPIRIT THAT MOVES US; THE SPIRIT THAT MOVES US PRESS (II); EDITOR'S CHOICE (IV-Anthology), P.O. Box 720820-PM, Jackson Heights, Queens NY 11372-0820, phone (718)426-8788, founded 1974, poetry editor Morty Sklar. ***"The Spirit That Moves Us*** will be continuing its **Editor's Choice** series biennially and publishing regular issues only occasionally. **Editor's Choice** consists of reprints from other literary magazines and small presses, where our selections are made from nominations by the editors of those magazines and presses." They have recently published poetry by Susan Montez, Darryl Holmes, Yala Korwin, Rhina Espaillat and Rita Dove. As a sample the editor selected these lines from "Just Off The Queen Elizabeth, New York City, 1948" (poet unidentified):

"I called out the only two words
I could think of in English,

'GO AWAY!'
I meant for the children to come,
I was longing to touch them."

They offer **Patchwork of Dreams: Voices from the Heart of the New America**, an anthology in which the above poem appears, as a sample for $8 plus $1 postage (regularly $11 plus $1.50 postage). **Publishes theme issues. Send SASE for upcoming themes and time frames. Sometimes sends prepublication galleys.** The editor's advice: "Write what you would like to write, in a style (or styles) which is/are best for your own expression. Don't worry about acceptance, though you may be concerned about it. Don't just send work which you think editors would like to see, though take that into consideration. Think of the relationship between poem, poet and editor as personal. You may send good poems to editors who simply do not like them, whereas other editors might."

SPITBALL; CASEY AWARD (IV-Sports), 6224 Collegevue Pl., Cincinnati OH 45224, phone (513)541-4296, founded 1981, poetry editor William J. McGill, is "a unique literary magazine devoted to poetry, fiction and book reviews ***exclusively* about baseball.** Newcomers are very welcome, but remember that you have to know the subject. We do and our readers do. Perhaps a good place to start for beginners is one's personal reactions to the game, *a* game, a player, etc. and take it from there." The digest-sized, 96-page quarterly is computer typeset and perfect-bound. They receive about 1,000 submissions/year, use 40–very small backlog. "Many times we are able to publish accepted work almost immediately." Circulation is 1,000, 750 subscriptions of which 25 are libraries. Subscription: $16. **Sample postpaid: $5. "We are not very concerned with the technical details of submitting, but we do prefer a cover letter with some bio info. We also like batches of poems and prefer to use several of same poet in an issue rather than a single poem." Publishes theme issues. Send SASE for upcoming themes. Pays 2 copies.** "We encourage anyone interested to submit to ***Spitball.*** We are always looking for fresh talent. Those who have never written 'baseball poetry' before should read some first probably before submitting. Not necessarily ours. We sponsor the Casey Award (for best baseball book of the year) and hold the Casey Awards Banquet every January. Any chapbook of baseball poetry should be sent to us for consideration for the 'Casey' plaque that we award to the winner each year. We are also sponsoring a big Babe Ruth Poetry Contest to celebrate the 100th birthday of the bambino in 1995." Interested poets should send an original, unpublished poem about Babe Ruth, along with SASE. Deadline: December 31, 1994.

THE SPOON RIVER POETRY REVIEW (III, IV-Regional, translations), 4240/English Dept., Illinois State University, Normal IL 61790-4240, phone (309)438-7906, founded 1976, poetry editor Lucia Getsi, is a "poetry magazine that features newer and well-known poets from around the country and world." Also features **one Illinois poet/issue** at length for the magazine's Illinois Poet Series. **"We want interesting and compelling poetry that operates beyond the ho-hum, so-what level, in any form or style about anything; language that is fresh, energetic, committed, filled with a strong voice that grabs the reader in the first line and never lets go. Do not want to see insipid, dull, boring poems, especially those that I cannot ascertain why they're in lines and not paragraphs; poetry which, if you were to put it into paragraphs, would become bad prose." They also use translations of poetry.** They have recently published poetry by Frankie Paino, Margaret Gibson, Lynn McMahan, Tim Seibles, Walter McDonald, Elaine Terranova, Roger Mitchell and Katharinè Soniat. As a sample Lucia Getsi selected these lines by Kay Murphy:

This is as close as I can come to make what she says true:
Inside, my uncle has his hand inside my aunt's blue dress.
The fields are burning with a want I don't yet understand.
The orchard has simply given up, as my cousin has.

TSRPR has moved to a twice a year, double issue format. It is digest-sized, laser set with card cover using photos, ads. They accept about 2% of 1,000 poems received/month. Press run is 800 for 400 subscriptions (100 of them libraries) and shelf sales. Subscription: $12. **Sample: $8. "No simultaneous submissions unless we are notified immediately if a submission is accepted elsewhere. Include name and address on every poem." Do not submit mss May 1 through September 1. Editor comments on rejections "many times, if a poet is promising." Reports in 2 months. Pays a year's subscription. Acquires first North American serial rights only.** Staff reviews books of poetry. Send books for review consideration. ***The Spoon River Poetry Review*** has received several Illinois Arts Council Awards and is one of the best reads in the poetry-publishing world. Work published in this review has also been included in **The Best American Poetry 1993.** Editor Lucia Cordell Getsi jampacks the journal with poems of varied styles and presents them in a handsome, perfect-bound product. You'll want to order a sample issue to get a feel for this fine publication.

‡THE SQUIB (I), Suite 101, 25 S. Atlantic Ave., Cocoa Beach FL 32931, founded 1993-1994, is a monthly designed to "entertain, inform and share through literature, poetry, art, cartoons and writer's hints. **All types of poetry are accepted with no current line limitation. No highly esoteric poems nor poetry using vile language."** As a sample the editor selected these lines (poet unidentified):

The faces of the idols fleshen
stone bodies come to life
hands joined, they cake-walk around the fire, ever closer
until they, themselves, are sacrificed to the flames.

The Squib is 12 pgs., 8½×11 (actually six 11×17 pgs. folded in half and unbound) with b&w line art and graphics. They receive about 200 poems a year, accept approximately 80%. Press run is 100 for 40 subscribers. Single copy: $2.50; subscription: $13 for 6 issues. **Sample postpaid: $4. Previously published poems and simultaneous submissions OK. Unlike most editors, they say, "We accept and encourage handwritten poetry. Use black felt-tip marker on white paper."** Time between acceptance and publication is 2 months. **Always comments on rejections. Send SASE for guidelines. Reports in 1 month. Pays 3 copies. Acquires one-time rights.** Plans to begin reviewing books of poetry. Open to unsolicited reviews. Poets may also send books for review consideration. The editor says, "We are very open to the unpublished. We aim to encourage *not* discourage. We avoid trite, hackneyed themes!"

STAND MAGAZINE; NORTHERN HOUSE (I, II, IV-Translations), 179 Wingrove Rd., Newcastle on Tyne NE4 9DA England. US Editors: Daniel Schenker and Amanda Kay, Route #2, Box 122-B, Lacey's Spring AL 35754. ***Stand***, founded by editor Jon Silkin in 1952, is a highly esteemed literary quarterly. Jon Silkin seeks more subscriptions from US readers and also hopes "that the magazine **would be seriously treated as an alternative platform to American literary journals." He wants "verse that tries to explore forms. No formulaic verse."** They have published poems by such poets as Peter Redgrove, Elizabeth Jennings and Barry Spacks. ***Library Journal*** calls ***Stand*** "one of England's best, liveliest and truly imaginative little magazines." Among better-known American poets whose work has recently appeared here are Robert Bly, William Stafford, Michael Mott, Angela Ball and Naomi Wallace. Poet Donald Hall says of it, "among essential magazines, there is Jon Silkin's ***Stand***, politically left, with reviews, poems and much translation from continental literature." In its current format it is 6×8, flat-spined, 84 pgs., professionally printed in 2 columns, small type, on thin stock with glossy cover, using ads. Circulation is 4,500 with 2,800 subscriptions of which 600 are libraries. Subscription: $25. **Sample postpaid: $7. Cover letter required with submissions, "assuring us that work is not also being offered elsewhere." Publishes theme issues. Always sends prepublication galleys. Pays £30/poem (unless under 6 lines) and 1 copy (⅓ off additional copies). Buys first world serial rights for 3 months after publication. If work(s) appear elsewhere *Stand*/Northern House must be credited.** Reviews books of poetry in 3,000-4,000 words, multi-book format. Open to unsolicited reviews. Poets may also send books for review consideration. Northern House (19 Haldane Terrace, Newcastle on Tyne NE2 3AN England) "publishes mostly small collections of poetry by new or established poets. The pamphlets often contain a group of poems written to one theme. Occasionally larger volumes are published, such as the full-length collection by Sorley Maclean, translated by Iain Crichton Smith."

STAPLE (I, II), Gilderoy East, Upperwood Rd., Matlock, Bath DE4 3PD United Kingdom, phone 0629-583867 and 0629-582764, founded 1982, co-editor Bob Windsor. This literary magazine appears 4 times a year including supplements. **"Nothing barred: Evidence of craft, but both traditional and modernist accepted; no totally esoteric or concrete poetry."** They have recently published poetry by Elizabeth Bartlett, Adrienne Brady, Geoffrey Holloway, Christine McNeill and David Winwood. As a sample they selected these lines from "A Swarm of Bees" by John Powell Ward:

And helmeted men, gold at midnight,
The opponent team in blazing white
Like light, like intellectual light

That Dante saw, too bright to see.
Still from our loaded apple tree
Pure gold dripped from the honey bee.

Staple is professionally printed, flat-spined, 80 pgs., with card cover. Of 10,000 poems received/year they accept about 2%. Their press run is 600 with 300 subscriptions. Subscription: £15 (sterling only). **Sample postpaid: £3. They do not consider simultaneous submissions or previously published poems. Cover letter preferred. Editors sometimes comment on rejections. Submission deadlines are end of February, June and November. Response in up to 3 months. Sometimes sends prepublication galleys. Pays overseas writers complimentary copies.** Send SASE (or SAE with IRC) for rules for their open biennial competitions (£750 in prizes) and for ***Staple First Editions*** monographs (sample postpaid: £3). Recently published monographs include ***The Half-Acre Ranch*** by Jennifer Olds and ***Fen Poems*** by Peter Cash. They now also produce (to order) poetry postcards of poetry *published* in the magazine. The editor says, "We get too many short minimalist pieces from America. More developed pieces of up to 40-80 lines preferred."

STAR BOOKS, INC. (V); STARLIGHT MAGAZINE (I, IV-Spirituality/inspirational), 408 Pearson St., Wilson NC 27893, phone (919)237-1591, founded 1983, president Allen W. Harrell, who says they are **"very enthusiastically open to beginners. All of our poetry is specifically Christian, in line with the teachings of the Bible. We're looking for the fresh and the new. Can't use avant-garde and/or esoteric. For us the impact of the *thought* of a poem is paramount. Need more short poems, with short lines."** They have published books of poetry by Marilyn Phemister, Norma Woodbridge and Charlotte Carpenter. "Contributors to our ***StarLight*** magazine are largely previously unpublished." As a sample these lines were selected from Gennet Emery's "Lament for a Child" in her **Wayfarer**:

Some thought the pain was less
Because I never saw you

But oh, I did!
My heart and mind wove textured skin,
Caressed your cheeks, touched finespun hair
And smelled sweet breath.

The book is 128 pgs., trade paperback size, flat-spined, professionally printed, with glossy card cover: $8. ***StarLight*** is a quarterly, digest-sized, 60 pgs., saddle-stapled, professionally printed, with matte card cover. The inspirational verse it contains is largely rhymed and free style (some of surprising good quality, considering this is billed mainly as a beginner's market). Some poems are illustrated with Bible excerpts, and the publication includes long bio notes about contributors. Subscription: $15. **Sample postpaid: $4. Guidelines available for SASE. Submit 5-6 poems, one poem/page, no cursive type, no erasable bond, no simultaneous submissions or previously published poems. Name and address on each page. "Don't submit poems in booklet form or center the lines. Title every poem. Include SASE." Reports in 2-4 months. Pays 3 copies of magazine; books pay 10% or more royalties. Acquires first serial rights for *StarLight*; all rights for Star Books. Not currently accepting book mss. Catalog available for #10 SAE with 2 first-class stamps.**

STARMIST BOOKS (V), Box 12640, Rochester NY 14612, founded 1986, president Beth Boyd, publishes 2-4 paperbacks/year. They publish **"poetry that comes from the heart . . . that has the depth of true feeling. No pornography." They are currently not accepting poetry submissions: "We have reached our quota into 1996."** As a sample the editor selected these lines from "blurrings" by jani johe webster:

how is it that you remember a thing
memories turned into dustballs
rolling along the mind's floor

people turned into shadows
and faces blurred photographs
taken years ago

Replies to queries in 2 weeks, to mss (if invited) in 3 weeks. Sometimes sends prepublication galleys. Pay is negotiable. Inquire about samples. The editor advises poets, "To feel always the poetry within – to know it all about us."

STATE STREET PRESS (II), P.O. Box 278, Brockport NY 14420, phone (716)637-0023, founded 1981, poetry editor Judith Kitchen, "publishes **chapbooks of poetry (20-24 pgs.) usually chosen in an anonymous competition.** State Street Press hopes to publish emerging writers with solid first collections and to offer a format for established writers who have a collection of poems that work together as a chapbook. We have also established a full-length publication – for those of our authors who are beginning to have a national reputation. We want **serious traditional and free verse. We are not usually interested in the language school of poets or what would be termed 'beat.' We are quite frankly middle-of-the-road. We ask only that the poems work as a collection, that the chapbook be more than an aggregate of poems – that they work together.**" They have recently published poetry by Naomi Shihab

ALWAYS include a self-addressed, stamped envelope (SASE) when sending a ms or query to a publisher within your own country. When sending material to other countries, include a self-addressed envelope and International Reply Coupons (IRCs), available for purchase at most post offices.

Nye, Dionisio Martinez, Diane Swan, Cecile Goding and William Greenway. As a sample the editor selected these lines from "Botany" by Kathleen Wakefield:

Each day I watch the blossoms close,
then open skyward, as if aspiring to something.
By night, the moth mullein, named
for beast and flower, practices its cool white deceit
by which its stationary blooms in darkness
endlessly repeat.

Chapbooks are beautifully designed and printed, 6×9, 30 pgs., with textured matte wrapper with art. **Send SASE for guidelines and chapbook contest rules. There is a $5 entry fee, for which you receive one of the chapbooks already published. Simultaneous submissions encouraged. Always sends prepublication galleys. Pays copies and small honorarium. Authors buy additional copies at cost, sell at readings and keep the profits.** Judith Kitchen comments, "State Street Press believes that the magazines are doing a good job of publishing beginning poets and we hope to present published and unpublished work in a more permanent format, so we do reflect the current market and tastes. We expect our writers to have published individual poems and to be considering a larger body of work that in some way forms a 'book.' We have been cited as a press that prints poetry that is accessible to the general reader."

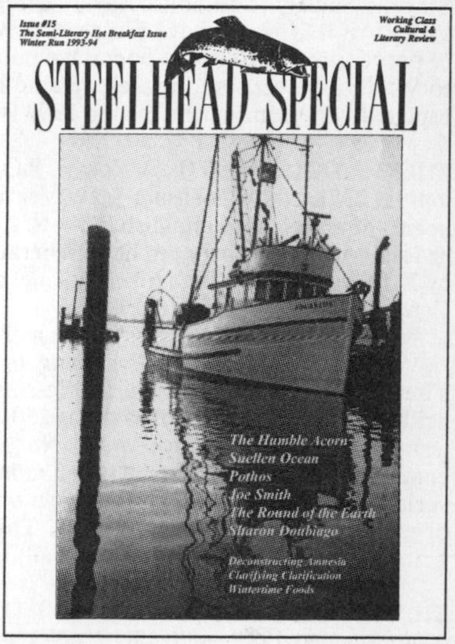

"The rather striking photograph of the boat Aquarius serves as a good solstice image, besides being a classic symbol of the culture we deal with most intimately," says Editor Crawdad Nelson about this cover of **The Steelhead Special*, a quarterly cultural and literary review published in Bayside, California. "We're a community-oriented, regional journal and crabbing is a typical regional means of economic survival. Also, the structural beauty of the boat and its setting stand well for the nobility of human endeavor in a natural setting, a big part of our general philosophy."*** **SS** ***publishes 10-20 poems per issue. Nelson says, "We use poems to help our readers enlarge their view of poetry and see instances of life beyond the mainstream press/pop culture homogenized view." Cover photo: Crawdad Nelson.***

THE STEELHEAD SPECIAL (I), P.O. Box 219, Bayside CA 95524, phone (707)445-1907, founded 1991, editor Crawdad Nelson, is a bimonthly "Northwest working-class cultural and literary review." They want "**fresh, working-class, rugged, bold poetry. Nothing weepy, clichéd, sentimental.**" They have recently published poetry by Joe Smith, Sharon Doubiago and John Colburn. As a sample the editor selected these lines from "The Throat" by L.J. Cirino:

This morning, walking down the ridge,
the throat of the river, beautifully
bloody, washed out and purpled the sea . . .

It is 40 pgs., 8½×11, newsprint, saddle-stapled, with art and graphics. They receive 500-600 poems a year, accept 10-20/issue. Press run is 3,500 for 200 subscribers, rest distributed free to the general public and fishermen. Single copy: $1; subscription: $12. **Sample postpaid: $2. Previously published poems and simultaneous submissions OK. Often comments on rejections. Publishes theme issues. Reports in 1-8 weeks. Sometimes sends prepublication galleys. Pays 1-2 copies; "discounts to poets on larger orders."** Open to unsolicited reviews. Poets may also send books for review consideration. Crawdad Nelson says, "We see lots of good poetry. Hope to see more. Nothing bogged down in bourgeois ennui, please. Vitality helps, but stay alert. We need more *lyrical*, less broken prose. We plan a literary anthology for late 1994, hopefully more in future. Subscriptions encouraged."

THE WALLACE STEVENS JOURNAL (II, IV-Specialized), Liberal Studies, Clarkson University, Box 5750, Potsdam NY 13699-5750, founded 1977, poetry editor Prof. Joseph Duemer, appears biannually using **"poems about or in the spirit of Wallace Stevens or having some relation to his work. No bad parodies of Stevens' anthology pieces."** They have published poetry by Elizabeth Spires, Jorie Graham, Charles Wright, X.J. Kennedy and Robert Creeley. As a sample the editor selected these lines from "A World Without Desire" by Michael G. Gessner:

Occurred tonight for an hour only,
An hour spent around the back porch
Where I was sent from the family, exiled
From myself. It was a world of order,
Order and presence, the final meaning
Of forms conversing through the night
As large as all thought must be
This house a ragged piece of locale
Torn adrift in the space of a dark mind.

The editor describes it as 80-120 pgs., 6×9, typeset, flat-spined, with cover art on glossy stock. They accept 10-15 poems of 50-75 received. Press run is 900 for 600 subscribers of which 200 are libraries. Subscription: $15. **Sample postpaid: $4. Reports in 2-8 weeks. Always sends prepublication galleys. Pays 2 copies. Acquires all rights. Returns rights with permission and acknowledgment.** Staff reviews books of poetry. Send books for review consideration "only if there is some clear connection to Stevens." ***The Wallace Stevens Journal*** is published by the Wallace Stevens Society. The editor says, "Brief cover letters are fine, even encouraged. Please don't submit to ***WSJ*** if you have not read Stevens. We like parodies, but they must *add* a new angle of perception. Most of the poems we publish are not parodies but meditations on themes related to Wallace Stevens and those poets he has influenced. Those wishing to contribute might wish especially to examine the Spring 1993 issue, devoted to prose and poetry by American poets."

STICKS; STICKS PRESS (V, IV-Form), P.O. Box 399, Maplesville AL 36750-0399, press founded 1989, journal 1991, editor/publisher Mary Veazey. ***Sticks***, appearing irregularly, **publishes "the best short poems of experienced/established poets. All styles, subjects. But no haiku. Preferred length: 10 lines or less; width: 50 spaces per line. Generally, no unsolicited manuscripts."** She has published poetry by X.J. Kennedy and Richard Kostelanetz. As a sample the editor selected this poem, "One Way to Carry the Dead," by Robert Barth:

A huge shell thundered: he was vaporized
And, close friends breathing, then internalized.

The magazine is a 4¼×5½, saddle-stapled or saddle-sewn booklet, professionally printed on acid-free paper, 24 pgs. Press run is 250. "Permanent mailing list in lieu of subscriptions. **Sample issue $1; sewn binding by request. No guidelines, just be a master of the short poem." Does not comment on rejections. Reports in 3 months or less. Pays 2 copies. Acquires first North American serial rights.** The editor says, "***Sticks*** will appear *only* when money for printing and a number of excellent small poems converge. **The Oxford Book of Short Poems** is my touchstone here; write the poem that will outlast us all; many such poems have historically been brief."

STILL WATERS PRESS (II, IV-Women), 112 W. Duerer St., Galloway NJ 08201-9402, phone (609)652-1790, founded 1989, editor Shirley Warren, is a "small press publisher of poetry chapbooks, short fiction chapbooks and poet's handbooks (contemporary craft). Especially interested in **works by, for and about women. We prefer poetry firmly planted in the real world, but equally mindful of poetry as art. The transformation from pain to perseverance, from ordinary to extraordinary, from defeat to triumph, pleases us. But we reject Pollyanna poetry immediately. Nothing sexist, in either direction, nothing sexually erotic. No rhymed poetry unless you're a master of form who can meticulously avoid strange manipulations of syntax simply to achieve end-rhyme. No patriarchal religious verse. Preferred length: 4 lines to 2 pages per poem. Form: no restrictions—we expect content to dictate the form."** They have recently published poetry by Charles Rafferty. As a sample the editor selected these lines from "Harvest" in Rafferty's chapbook **The Wave That Will Beach Us Both:**

Recall just this, the day we sat to shuck
the corn: the ripping of leaves, the tangled silks,

the ears combed clean of weevils. The cobs were plump
and smutless, sweet enough to leave us dumb

there in the late summer of our lives.
We ate that corn. It tasted raw like love.

She publishes 4-8 chapbooks a year, averaging 28 pgs. Sample chapbooks: $5; writer's guide booklets: $3. **Send SASE for guidelines, then query. Simultaneous submissions and previously published poems OK. Always sends prepublication galleys. Pays 10% of the press run. Royalties on 2nd and subsequent press runs. Acquires first or reprint rights.** They hold 2 annual contests, each with $10 reading fee; send SASE for detailed guidelines. The editor says, "Read other poets, contemporary and traditional. Attend workshops, establish rapport with your local peers, attend readings. Keep your best work in circulation. Someone out there is looking for you."

STONE SOUP, THE MAGAZINE BY CHILDREN; THE CHILDREN'S ART FOUNDATION (IV-Children), P.O. Box 83, Santa Cruz CA 95063, founded 1973, editor Ms. Gerry Mandel. *Stone Soup* publishes **writing and art by children through age 13; they want to see free verse poetry but no rhyming poetry, haiku or cinquain.** The editor chose as a sample this poem, "Nightfall," by 7-year-old Jaiva Larsen:

When the blackberry moon rises
And the sky flies by like ocean waves
And the chill of the evening
Flies through your heart
Run home
Run home

Stone Soup, published 5 times a year, is a handsome 6×8¾ magazine, professionally printed on heavy stock with 4 full-color art reproductions inside and a full-color illustration on the coated cover, saddle-stapled. A membership in the Children's Art Foundation at $24/year includes a subscription to the magazine, each issue of which contains an Activity Guide. The editor receives 5,000 poetry submissions/year and only uses 20. There are 4 pgs. of poetry in each issue. Circulation is 18,000, all by subscription; 2,000 go to libraries. **Sample postpaid: $4.50. Submissions can be any number of pages, any format, but no simultaneous submissions. Criticism will be given when requested. Guidelines are available for SASE. Reports in 1 month. Pays $10 and 2 copies plus discounts. Buys all rights. Returns rights upon request.** Open to reviews by children. Children through age 13 may also send books for review consideration. ***Stone Soup*** has received both Parents' Choice and Edpress Golden Lamp Honor Awards.

STONEVALE PRESS (II), P.O. Box 484, Burkittsville MD 21718, phone (301)834-9380, founded 1991, editor Helen Vo-Dinh, publishes 2 paperbacks and 1 chapbook/year. **No specifications as to form, length, subject matter, style or purpose, "except no 'inspirational' verse or pornography."** They have published books of poetry by Mary Azrael and Kendra Kopelke. As a sample the editor selected these lines from "Girl Asleep At A Table" in Kopelke's book **Eager Street:**

You see she is asleep
so you want to turn away, embarrassed
yet you feel

strangely welcome, as if you
are the subject of her inner gaze
the stone that holds the plum . . .

That book is about 80 pgs., 5½×9, flat-spined with matte card cover, $8.95. **Query first with 10-15 pgs. of typed material and a cover letter with brief bio and publication credits. Previously published poems and simultaneous submissions OK, if indicated. Replies to queries in 1 month, to mss (if invited) in 2-3 months.** Time between acceptance and publication is 6 months to 1 year. **Occasionally comments on rejections. Pays 10% royalties after expenses and 25 author's copies. Co-op publishing is also an option. Sample book: $7.**

STORMLINE PRESS, INC. (V), Box 593, Urbana IL 61801, phone (217)328-2665, founded 1985, publisher Ray Bial, is an independent press publishing fiction, poetry and photography, **"only by invitation. Do not send unsolicited manuscripts. Query in November and December only with SASE. We publish both established and new poets, but in the latter case prefer to publish those poets who have been working some years to master their craft."** The press publishes 1-2 books each year with an average page count of 48-64. They are 6×9, some flat-spined paperbacks and some hardcover.

STORY LINE PRESS (V); NICHOLAS ROERICH POETRY PRIZE FOR FIRST BOOK OF POETRY (II), Three Oaks Farm, 27006 Gap Road, Brownsville OR 97327-9718, phone (503)466-5352, Story Line Press founded 1985, poetry editor Robert McDowell. Story Line Press publishes each year the winner of the Nicholas Roerich Poetry Prize for a First Book of Poetry ($1,000 plus publication and a paid reading at the Roerich Museum in New York City; a runner-up receives a full Story Line Press Scholarship to the Wesleyan Writers Conference in Middletown, CT; $15 entry and handling fee). Deadline for submissions: October 15. Send SASE for complete guidelines. The press also publishes books about poetry and has published collections by such poets as Colette Inez, Rita Dove, Bruce Bawer and George Keithley. **They consider unsolicited mss only for the Nicholas Roerich Poetry Prize competition. Always sends prepublication galleys.**

STRAIGHT; STANDARD PUBLISHING CO. (IV-Religious, teens), 8121 Hamilton Ave., Cincinnati OH 45231, editor Carla J. Crane. Standard is a large religious publishing company. ***Straight*** is a weekly take-home publication (digest-sized, 12 pgs., color newsprint) **for teens. Poetry is *by* teenagers, any**

style, religious or inspirational in nature. No adult-written poetry. As a sample the editor selected "A New Understanding" by Carla McKenzie:

Then how am I ever to find it?
When will I?
Someday will it just dawn on me,
And then I'll feel it and say,
"Oh, now I have faith?"

Teen author must include birthdate. Simultaneous submissions OK. Publishes theme issues. Guidelines and upcoming themes available for SASE. Reports in 4-6 weeks, publishes acceptances in 9-12 months. Pays $10/poem plus 5 copies. Buys first or reprint rights. The editor says, "Many teenagers write poetry in their English classes at school. If you've written a poem on an inspirational topic, and your teacher's given you an 'A' on it, you've got a very good chance of having it published in ***Straight***."

THE STRAIN (II), Box 330507, Houston TX 77233-0507, poetry editor Michael Bond, editor Norman C. Stewart, Jr. ***The Strain*** is a monthly magazine using **"experimental or traditional poetry of very high quality."** They do not include sample lines of poetry here as they "prefer not to limit style of submissions." **Simultaneous submissions and previously published poems OK. Guidelines issue: $5 and 8 first-class stamps. Pays "no less than $5.** We would **prefer you submit before obtaining the guidelines issue which mostly explains upcoming collections and collaborations."** Send books for review consideration.

STREET PRESS (V), P.O. Box 772, Sound Beach NY 11789-0772, founded 1974, editor Graham Everett. Street Press publishes an occasional limited edition book of poetry. Recent publications: **Much Cry Little Wool** by Ray Freed, **Limousine to Nowhere** by Jim Tyack and **Endless Staircase** by Sandy McIntosh. **They are currently not accepting poetry submissions.** Send SASE for a list of available titles.

STRIDE PUBLICATIONS; TAXUS PRESS; APPARITIONS PRESS; TROMBONE PRESS (II), 11 Sylvan Rd., Exeter, Devon EX4 6EW England, founded 1980, editor R.M. Loydell. Stride Publications publishes poetry, poetry sequences, prose and novels, and an occasional arts magazine. **The editor wants to see any poetry that is "new, inventive, nothing self-oriented, emotional, no narrative or fantasy."** He has published work by Peter Redgrove, Alexis Lykiard, Sheila E. Murphy and David Miller. Stride Publications publishes paperbacks 60-100 pgs. of poetry, plus a few novels and anthologies. **Unsolicited submissions for book publication are accepted. Authors should query first, sending sample poems with return postage. Cover letter required with bio, summary and review quote. Queries will be answered in 3 weeks and mss reported on in 3 months or more. Pays author's copies.** Magazine reviews books and tapes of poetry in 100-200 words, multi-book format. Send books etc. for review consideration.

STRUGGLE: A MAGAZINE OF PROLETARIAN REVOLUTIONARY LITERATURE (I, II, IV-Political, science fiction/fantasy, workers' social issues, women/feminism), Box 13261, Detroit MI 48213-0261, founded 1985, editor Tim Hall, is a "literary quarterly, content: the struggle of the working people against the rich. Issues such as: racism, poverty, aggressive wars, workers' struggle for jobs and job security, the overall struggle for a non-exploitative society, a genuine socialism." The **poetry and songs they use are "generally short, any style, subject matter must criticize or fight against the rule of the billionaires. We welcome experimentation devoted to furthering such content."** They have recently published poetry by Tamar Diana Wilson, Lynda G. Anaya, Cindy Hasio, Willie Abraham Howard Jr. and Ernie Hilbert, Jr. As a sample the editor selected "Economics" by Michael Ceraolo:

A free marketer is one who would command the carpenter
who built the cross upon which Christ was crucified:
after all, he was responding to market forces.

Struggle is 24-40 pgs., digest-sized, printed by photo offset using drawings, occasional photos of artwork, short stories and short plays as well as poetry and songs (sometimes with their music). Subscription: $10 for 4 issues. **Sample postpaid: $2.50. Checks must be payable to "Tim Hall—Special Account." Accepted work usually appears in the next issue. Editor tries to provide criticism "with every submission." Tries to report in 1-3 months. Pays 2 copies.** Tim Hall says, "Show passion and fire. Formal experiments, traditional forms both welcome. Especially favor works reflecting rebellion by the working people against the rich, against racism, sexism, militarism, imperialism; works critical of our exploitative culture, or works showing a desire for—or fantasy of—a non-exploitative society."

STUDENT LEADERSHIP JOURNAL (IV-Students, religious), Dept. PM, P.O. Box 7895, Madison WI 53707-7895, phone (608)274-9001, editor Jeff Yourison, is a **"magazine for Christian student leaders on secular campuses. We accept a wide variety of poetry. Do not want to see trite poetry. Also, we**

accept little rhymed poetry; it must be very, very good." As a sample the editor selected the last stanzas of "A bird in the church" by Luci Shaw:

and high and low and up again, through the sun's
transfixing shafts, her wings test gravity
in a bewilderment of interior air, opening
and closing on her feathered restlessness
until, as though coming home, she settles

on the arm of the crucifix. Having found
a nesting tree (even thine altars, O Lord!),
she lodges at last, at the angle
where vertex and horizon meet, resting
in the steady pain of Christ's left eye.

Student Leadership is a quarterly, magazine-sized, 32 pgs., 2-color inside, 2-color covers, with no advertising, 70% editorial, 30% graphics/art. Press run is 8,000 going to college students in the US and Canada. Subscription: $16. **Sample postpaid: $3. No simultaneous submissions. Previously published poems OK. "Would-be contributors should read us to be familiar with what we publish." Best time to submit mss is March through July ("We set our year's editorial plan"). Editor "occasionally" comments on rejections. Send SASE for guidelines. Reports in 2-3 months, 1-24 months to publication. Pays $25-50/poem plus 2 copies. Buys first or reprint rights.** He says, "Try to express feelings through images and metaphor. Religious poetry should not be overly didactic, and it should never moralize!"

STUDIO, A JOURNAL OF CHRISTIANS WRITING (II, IV-Religious, spirituality), 727 Peel St., Albury, New South Wales 2640 Australia, founded 1980, publisher Paul Grover, is a small press literary quarterly "with contents **focusing upon the Christian striving for excellence in poetry,** prose and occasional articles relating Christian views of literary ideas." **In poetry, the editors want "shorter pieces but with no specification as to form or length (necessarily less than 3-4 pages), subject matter, style or purpose. People who send material should be comfortable being published under this banner: *Studio, A Journal of Christians Writing.*"** They have published poetry by John Foulcher and other Australian poets. ***Studio*** is 36 pgs., digest-sized, professionally printed on high-quality recycled paper, saddle-stapled, matte card cover, with graphics and line drawings. Circulation is 300, all subscriptions. Subscription: $40 (Aud) for overseas members. **Sample available (airmail from US) for $8 (Aud). Submissions may be "double-spaced, typed copy or simultaneous." Name and address must appear on the reverse side of each page submitted. Cover letter required; include brief details of previous publishing history, if any. Reporting time is 2 months and time to publication is 9 months. Pays 1 copy. Acquires first Australian rights.** Reviews books of poetry in 250 words, single format. Open to unsolicited reviews. Poets may also send books for review consideration. The magazine conducts a biannual poetry and short story contest. The editor says, "Trend in Australia is for imagist poetry and poetry exploring the land and the self. Reading the magazine gives the best indication of style and standard, so send a few dollars for a sample copy before sending your poetry. Keep writing, and we look forward to hearing from you."

‡STUDIO ONE (II), P.O. Box 1558, St. Joseph MN 56374, founded 1976, editor changes yearly. ***Studio One*** is an annual literary visual arts magazine designed as a forum for local, regional and national poets/writers. **They have no specifications regarding form, subject matter or style of poetry submitted. However, they say shorter poems stand a better chance of publication. Also, they do not want to see poetry from beginners—"meaning cliché, rhyming poetry."** They have recently published poetry by Bill Meissner and Larry Schug. As a sample the editor selected these lines from Schug's "Firemaker":

Twenty-five below zero this morning,
Firewood splits easy.
Even the twisted elm snaps,
Oak pops like a gunshot.
My breath coalesces into iceballs
That ornament my mustache,
Glisten in horizontal winter light.

The editor says ***Studio One*** is 50-80 pgs., soft cover, typeset. It includes 1-3 short stories, 22-30 poems and 10-13 visual art representations. They receive 250-400 submissions a year, accept about 30-40. **Previously published poems and simultaneous submissions OK. Deadline: February 24 for spring publication. Reads submissions February 1 through March 31. Seldom comments on rejections. Send SASE for guidelines.**

SUB-TERRAIN; ANVIL PRESS (II, IV-Social issues, political, form/style), P.O. Box 1575, Station A, Vancouver, British Columbia V6C 2P7 Canada, phone (604)876-8710, founded 1988, poetry editor Paul Pitre. Anvil Press is an "alternate small press publishing ***Sub-Terrain***—a socially conscious literary quarterly whose aim is to produce a reading source that will stand in contrast to the trite and pandered — as well as broadsheets, chapbooks and the occasional monograph." They want **"work that has a point-of-view; work that has some passion behind it and is exploring issues that are of pressing importance; work that challenges conventional notions of what poetry is or should be; work with a social conscience. No bland, flowery, uninventive poetry that says nothing in style or content."** As a sample the editor selected these lines from "amber drive" by Pat McKinnon:

he must've carried some terrible sadness in his face
which i was too young or too stoned to see
some 8-legged hell crawling down his throat
like maybe his dad held a magnifying glass
between him & the blister sun or maybe
he killed his sister or fucked his brother
or his mom or the dog or . . .

Sub-Terrain is 32 pgs., 7×10, offset, with a press run of 2,000. Subscription: $10. **Sample postpaid: $3. They will consider simultaneous submissions, but not previously published poems. Reports in 8-10 weeks. Pays money only for solicited work; for other work, 4-issue subscription. Acquires one-time rights for magazine. "If chapbook contract, we retain right to publish subsequent printings unless we let a title lapse out-of-print for more than 1 year."** Staff occasionally reviews small press poetry chapbooks. Sponsors Last Poems Poetry Contest; information for SASE. **For chapbook or book publication submit 4 sample poems and bio, no simultaneous submissions. "We are willing to consider mss. But I must stress that we are a co-op, depending on support from an interested audience. New titles will be undertaken with caution. We are not subsidized at this point and do not want to give authors false hopes — but if something is important and should be in print, we will do our best." Editor provides brief comment and more extensive comments for fees.** He says, "Poetry, in our opinion, should be a distillation of emotion and experience that is being given back to the world. Pretty words and fancy syntax are just that. Where are the modern day writers who are willing to risk it all, put it all on the line? Young, new writers: Show it all, bare your guts. The last thing the world needs is soppy, sentimental fluff that gives nothing and says nothing."

THE SUCARNOCHEE REVIEW (II), Station 22, Livingston University, Livingston AL 35470, founded 1985, editor Joe Taylor, is an annual literary magazine which accepts poetry and fiction. "Sucarnochee (suke'nachi) is the Choctaw word for 'hog river' or 'a place where hogs bathe.'" **The editors have no specifications as to form, length, subject matter or style.** They have published poetry by R.T. Smith, Peter Huggins, Lewis Turco and Joseph Powell. As a sample the editor selected these lines from "Van Gogh at Saint Remy" by Wayne Cox:

Today, the poplars were on fire
With autumn; tonight
I see only an abyss of stars.

Once again, I must point myself
And take stock like a farmer
At the end of another bad year.

The editor says it is 70 pgs., perfect-bound. They receive about 500 poems a year, use approximately 10%. Press run is 500. Subscription: $10. **Sample postpaid: $5. No previously published poems; simultaneous submissions OK. Cover letter with short bio required.** Time between acceptance and publication is 6 months. **Seldom comments on rejections. Reports in "one week to four months." Pays 3 copies. Acquires first North American serial rights.** They award $50 for the best poem in each issue. Winning poems are chosen by the editors. You may want to order a sample copy of this magazine because its poetry, mostly structured free verse with emphasis on voice, has wide appeal. We found this a good read (with several poems as fine as what you might find in the best journals).

SULFUR MAGAZINE (II, IV-Translations), %Dept. of English, Eastern Michigan University, Ypsilanti MI 48197, phone (313)483-9787, founded 1981, poetry editor Clayton Eshleman, is a physically gorgeous and hefty (250 pgs., 6×9, flat-spined, glossy card cover, elegant graphics and printing on quality stock) biannual that has earned a distinguished reputation. They have published poetry by John Ashbery, Ed Sanders, Gary Snyder, Jackson MacLow, Paul Blackburn and the editor (one of our better-known poets). As a sample the editor selected "Irish" by Paul Celan, translated by Pierre Joris:

Give me the right of way
across the grain ladder of your sleep,
the right of way
across the sleep trail,
The right, for me to cut peat
along the heart's hillside,

tomorrow.

Published at EMU, ***Sulfur*** has a circulation of 2,000, using approximately 100 pgs. of poetry in each issue. They use 5-10 of 600-700 submissions received/year. Free verse dominates here, much of it leaning toward the experimental. Subscription: $14. **Sample postpaid: $6. "We urge would-be contributors to *read* the magazine and send us material only if it seems to be appropriate." Editor comments "sometimes, if the material is interesting." Reports in 2-3 weeks. Pays $35-45/contributor.** Reviews 10-20 poetry books/issue. Open to unsolicited reviews. Poets may also send books for review consideration. ***Sulfur*** ranked #5 in the "Nontraditional Verse" category of the latest ***Writer's Digest*** Poetry 60 list. Clayton Eshleman says, "Most unsolicited material is of the 'I am sensitive and have practiced my sensitivity' school—with little attention to language as such, or incorporation of materials that lead the poem into more ample contexts than 'personal' experience. I fear too many young writers today spend more time on themselves, without deeply engaging their *selves*, in a serious psychological way—and too little time breaking their heads against the Blakes, Stevens and Vallejos of the world. That is, writing has replaced reading. I believe that writing is a form of reading and vice versa. Of course, it is the quality and wildness of imagination that finally counts—but this 'quality' is a composite considerably dependent on assimilative reading (and translating, too)."

SULPHUR RIVER LITERARY REVIEW (II), P.O. Box 402087, Austin TX 78704-5578, founded 1978, reestablished 1987, editor/publisher James Michael Robbins, is a semiannual of poetry, prose and artwork. They have **"no restrictions except quality." They do not want poetry that is "trite or religious or verse that does not incite thought."** They have recently published poetry by Walt McDonald, Lyn Lifshin, Laurel Speer, Albert Huffstickler and Gerald Burns. As a sample the editor selected these lines from "The Small Credo" by Harland Ristau:

living
is believing
what we did
what is not done.
believing wrapped
with ribbons of hope,
the dream we wake from,
living is believing
spirit will mend,
mend all things,
bandaged by mercy,
with time moored
to a heart knowing
when to come home.

SRLR is digest-sized, perfect-bound, with glossy cover. They receive about 500 poems a year, accept about 10%. Press run is 400 for 200 subscribers, 100 shelf sales. Subscription: $8. **Sample postpaid: $4.50. No previously published poems or simultaneous submissions. Often comments on rejections. Reports in 1 month. Sometimes sends prepublication galleys. Pays 2 copies.** The editor says, "Poetry is, for me, the essential art, the ultimate art, and any effort to reach the effect of the successful poem deserves some comment other than 'sorry.' This is why I try to comment as much as possible on submissions, though by doing so I risk my own special absurdity. So be it. However, there can be no compromise of quality if the poem is to be successful or essential art."

SUMMER STREAM PRESS (II), P.O. Box 6056, Santa Barbara CA 93160-6056, phone (805)962-6540, founded 1978, poetry editor David D. Frost, publishes a series of books (Box Cars) in hardcover and softcover, each presenting 6 poets, averaging 70 text pgs. for each poet. "The mix of poets represents many parts of the country and many approaches to poetry. The poets previously selected have been published, but that is no requirement. We welcome traditional poets in the mix and thus offer them a chance for publication in this world of free-versers. The **six poets share a 15% royalty. We require rights for our editions worldwide and share 50-50 with authors for translation rights and for republication of our editions by another publisher. Otherwise all rights remain with the authors."** They have published poetry by Virginia E. Smith, Sandra Russell, Jennifer MacPherson, Nancy Berg, Lois Shapley Bassen and Nancy J. Wallace. To be considered for future volumes in this series, **query with about 12 samples, no cover letter. Replies to query in 3 months, to submission (if invited) in 1 year. Previously published poetry and simultaneous submissions OK. Editor usually comments on rejections. Always sends prepublication galleys.** He says, "We welcome both traditional poetry and free verse. However, we find we must reject almost all the traditional poetry received simply because the poets exhibit little or no knowledge of the structure and rules of traditional forms. Much of it is rhymed free verse."

THE SUN (II), 107 N. Roberson St., Chapel Hill NC 27516, phone (919)942-5282, founded 1974, editor Sy Safransky, is "a monthly magazine of ideas. **We avoid traditional, rhyming poetry, as well as limericks, haiku and religious poetry. We're open to almost anything else: free verse, prose poems, short and long poems."** They have recently published poetry by Alison Luterman, David Budhill, Chris Bursk, Lyn Lifshin, Robert Bly and Dina Ben-Lev. ***The Sun*** is magazine-sized, 40 pgs., printed on 50 lb. offset, saddle-stapled, with b&w photos and graphics, circulation 20,000, 10,000 subscriptions of which 50 are libraries. They receive 3,000 submissions of poetry/year, use 25, have a 1- to 3-month backlog. Subscription: $32. **Sample postpaid: $3.50. Submit no more than 6 poems. Send SASE for guidelines. Reports within 3-5 months. Pays $25 on publication and in copies and subscription. Buys first serial or one-time rights.** ***The Sun*** received an ***Utne Reader*** Award for General Excellence.

SUN DOG: THE SOUTHEAST REVIEW (II), 406 Williams Bldg., English Dept., Florida State University, Tallahassee FL 32306, phone (904)644-4230, founded 1979, poetry editors Nancy Applegate and Karen Janowsky. "The journal has a small student staff. We publish two flat-spined, 100-page magazines per year of poetry, short fiction and essays. As a norm, we usually accept about 12 poems per issue. **We accept poetry of the highest caliber, looking for the most 'whole' works. A poet may submit any length, but because of space, poems over 2 pages are impractical. Excellent formal verse highly regarded."** They have published poetry by David Bottoms, David Kirby, Peter Meinke and Leon Stokesbury. ***SD*** is 6×9 with a glossy card cover, usually including half-tones, line drawings and color art when budget allows. Press run is 1,250. Subscription: $8 for 2 issues. **Sample postpaid: $4. Poems should be typed single-spaced. Send 2-5 submissions at a time. If simultaneous submission, say so. No previously published poems. Editor will comment briefly on most poems, especially those which come close to being accepted. Send SASE for guidelines. Reports in 3 months. Pays 2 copies. Acquires first North American serial rights.** ***SD*** sponsors the Richard Eberhart Prize in Poetry. This is an annual award given to the best unpublished poem of no fewer than 30 lines and no more than 100. The winner receives $300 and publication in ***Sun Dog***. Submit 1 poem only and SASE for results to the Richard Eberhart Prize at the above address. No entry fee or form is required. Submission deadline: September 15. Winner will be announced on December 31.

SUPERINTENDENT'S PROFILE & POCKET EQUIPMENT DIRECTORY (IV-Specialized), 220 Central Ave., Box 43, Dunkirk NY 14048, phone (716)366-4774, founded 1978, poetry editor Robert Dyment, is a "monthly magazine, circulation 2,500, for town, village, city and county highway superintendents and Department of Public Works directors throughout New York State," and uses **"only poetry that pertains to New York highway superintendents and DPW directors and their activities." Submit no more than one page double-spaced.** They receive about 50 submissions of poetry/year, use 20, have a 2-month backlog. Subscription: $10. **Sample: 80¢ postage. Reports within a month. Pays $5/poem.**

SYCAMORE REVIEW (II), Dept. of English, Purdue University, West Lafayette IN 47907, phone (317)494-3783, founded 1988 (first issue May, 1989), editor-in-chief M.S. Manley, poetry editor changes each year; submit to Poetry Editor. "We accept personal essays, short fiction, translations and **quality poetry in any form. There are no official restrictions as to subject matter or style."** They have recently published poetry by Elizabeth Dodd, Stuart Friebert, Lee Upton, Brigit Pegeen Kelly, Donald Hall, Laura Muller and Colette Inez. The magazine is semiannual in a digest-sized format, 150 pgs., flat-spined, professionally printed, with glossy, color cover. Press run is 650 for 300 subscribers of which 50 are libraries. Subscription: $9. **Sample postpaid: $5. Cover letters not required but invited; include phone number, short bio and previous publications, if any. "We read August 15 through May 1." Guidelines available for SASE. Reports in 4 months. Pays 2 copies.** Staff reviews books of poetry. Send books to editor-in-chief for review consideration. The editor says, "Poets who do not include SASE do not receive a response."

TAILS OF WONDER (IV-Science fiction/fantasy), P.O. Box 23, Franklin Park NJ 08823, founded 1992, publisher Nicolas Samuels, editor Maritza DiSciullo, is a biannual science fiction and fantasy literary magazine featuring short stories, poetry, reviews, articles, art and illustrations. As for poetry, they say, **"Length isn't so important, but poems must have some connection to science fiction or fantasy. Prefer poems under 40 lines." They do not want "anything overly erotic or religious."** They have published poetry by Troy Leaver and Peter Huge. The editor says ***Tails*** is 40-50 pgs., 8½×11, high quality paper, glossy color cover, b&w illustrations and ads. They receive 5-10 poems/month, accept 4-6/issue. Press run is 500 for 200 subscribers, 50 shelf sales. Subscription: $18. **Sample postpaid: $5. Previously published poems and simultaneous submissions OK, if indicated. Cover letter required.** Time between acceptance and publication is 6-8 months. **Seldom comments on rejections. Send SASE for guidelines. Reports within 2 months. Pays 10¢/line ("no less than $1") plus 1 copy. Buys first North American serial or reprint rights.** Plans poetry contest. Send SASE for information. They say, "We love nothing better than great literary work, which is what we expect. Be innovative, challenge the 'cutting edge' and, above all else, write from your heart."

TAK TAK TAK (V, IV-Themes), BCM Tak, London WC1N 3XX England, founded 1986, editors Andrew and Tim Brown, appears occasionally in print and on cassettes, and, in addition, sometimes publishes flat-spined paperback collections of poetry averaging between 40 and 130 pgs. **"No restrictions on form or style. However, we are currently not accepting poetry submissions. Each issue of the magazine is on a theme (i.e., 'Mother Country/Fatherland,' 'Postcards from Paradise'), and *all* contributions must be relevant. If a contribution is long it is going to be more difficult to fit in than something shorter. Write for details of subject(s), etc., of forthcoming issue(s)."** They have published poetry by Michael Horowitz, Karl Blake, Keith Jafrate, Ramona Fotiade and Paul Buck. The editors describe it as "100 pgs., A5, photolithographed, board cover, line drawings and photographs, plus cassette of poetry, music, sounds. Of about 100 poems received in the past year we have used about 25." Press run is 1,000. **Sample postpaid to US: £7.06 airmail (without cassette), £8.11 airmail (with cassette).** The editors say, "Poetry is just one of the many creative forms our contributions take. We are equally interested in prose and in visual and sound media."

TALISMAN: A JOURNAL OF CONTEMPORARY POETRY AND POETICS (III), P.O. Box 1117, Hoboken NJ 07030, phone (201)798-9093, founded 1988, editor Edward Foster, appears twice a year. "Each issue centers on the poetry and poetics of a *major* contemporary poet and includes a selection of new work by other important contemporary writers. **We are particularly interested in poetry in alternative (*not* academic) traditions. We don't want traditional poetry."** They have published poetry by William Bronk, Robert Creeley, Ron Padgett, Anne Waldman, Alice Notley, Edouard Roditi and Rosmarie Waldrop. As a sample the editor selected the following lines from "Opening Day" by Ann Lauterbach:

Locally a firm disavowal within the drift.
Shaman of discourse said
Or could have said
These logics go teasingly forward
Into capacities, and then the then.

Talisman is 268 pgs., digest-sized, flat-spined, photocopied from computer printed Baskerville type, with matte card cover. "We are inundated with submissions and lost track of the number long ago." Their press run is 1,000 with "substantial" subscriptions of which many are libraries. Subscription: $11 individual; $15 institution. **Sample postpaid: $6. Reports in 2 months. Always sends prepublication galleys. Pays 1 copy. Acquires first North American serial rights.** Reviews books of poetry in 500-1,000 words, single format.

‡TAMAQUA (II), C120, Parkland College, 2400 W. Bradley Ave., Champaign IL 61821-1899, phone (217)351-2445, founded 1989, editor-in-chief James McGowan, is a biannual literary/arts journal **"of *high* quality. No restrictions on poetry, but it must be intelligently and professionally done."** They have recently published poetry by Joy Harjo, Ray Young Bear and Lucia Cordell Getsi. As a sample we selected the opening lines of "The Expulsion from Paradise" by Deborah DeNicola:

Between the orange blossoms and the fig trees
an anorexic angel with xanthous wings
shoves Adam, pulling his gaze
from some daisyish flowers, rubbing fire
from flexed pectoral to shoulder

as Eve looks over
a little sheepishly,
already checking her own way out. . . .

Tamaqua is 160-256 pgs., digest-sized, offset and perfect-bound with 4-color coated card cover, b&w (and occasional color) art and photos inside. They receive 3,000-5,000 poems/year, accept approximately 100. Press run is 2,000 for 800 subscribers of which 20 are libraries, 900 shelf sales. Subscription: $10/year. **Sample postpaid: $6. Prefers poems typed on bonded paper. No previously published poems; simultaneous submissions OK. Cover letter required. "All submissions are juried anonymously; only managing editor knows identity of writer before selection." Seldom comments on rejections. Send SASE for guidelines. Reports in 4 months. Pays $10-75/poem plus 2 copies. Acquires first North American serial rights.** Reviews books of poetry in both single and multi-book format, no minimum length. Open to unsolicited reviews, but prefers "meditative review." Poets may also send books for review consideration, attn. Sue Kuykendall. The editor says, "Nothing replaces knowledge of your market; hence *study* ***Tamaqua*** and similar magazines to discern the difference between good, solid, intelligent literature/art and that which is not."

TAMPA REVIEW (III), Dept. PM, University of Tampa, 401 W. Kennedy Blvd., Tampa FL 33606-1490, phone (813)253-3333, ext. 3621, founded 1964 as ***UT Poetry Review,*** became ***Tampa Review*** in 1988, editor Richard Mathews, poetry editors Kathryn Van Spanckeren and Donald Morrill, is an elegant semiannual of fiction, nonfiction, poetry and art (not limited to US authors) wanting **"original and**

well-crafted poetry written with intelligence and spirit. We do accept translations, but no greeting card or inspirational verse." They have published poetry by Alberto Rios, Paul Mariani, Mark Halliday, Denise Levertov and Stephen Dunn. As a sample, the editors selected these lines from "Afternoon" by Jorge Teillier, translated by Carolyne Wright:

The afternoon is a song
hummed now and then
by a lonely traveler.
When the song is extinguished
the wind brings words
that the trees don't understand.

TR is 78-96 pgs., flat-spined, 7½×10½ with a matte card color cover. They accept about 50-60 of 2,000 poems received a year. Their press run is 500 with 175 subscriptions of which 20 are libraries. **Sample postpaid: $5. Unsolicited mss are read between September and December. Reports by mid-February. Sometimes sends prepublication galleys. Pays $10/printed page plus 1 copy and 40% discount on additional copies. Buys first North American serial rights.**

TANGRAM PRESS (III), Dept. PM, P.O. Box 2249, Granbury TX 76048, phone (817)579-1777, contact June Ford. This very small press would like to publish more books such as their handsome coffee-table volume, 12×12, hardback, **Where Rainbows Wait for Rain: The Big Bend Country**, combining poems by Sandra Lynn and b&w photographs by Richard Fenker Jr., but "we have a limited staff. **While we do not discourage submissions, we cannot guarantee comments on same. We are not your standard poetry publisher. Send SASE with submission if you want it returned."**

‡TANTRA PRESS (I, II), P.O. Box 4334, Parkersburg WV 26104, phone (304)422-3112, founded 1993, editors David B. Prather and David W. Carvell, is a quarterly journal of poetic verse. **"We want to see all work—no restrictions, but we do look for detailed imagery and a sensitivity to language. We stay away from singsong and work with little substance."** They have recently published poetry by Susan Sheppard and Kenneth Pobo. As a sample the editors selected these lines from "Ollala: A Meditation on a Name" by Jane Somerville:

She lifts a fleshy finger
and makes a room,
her own, accoutered in gold
and looped in blue
and every line of all that loot
laid out to follow her body.

Tantra Press is 60 pgs., 5½×8½, saddle-stapled with colored card cover with art. They receive 300-500 poems a year, accept 20-30%. Press run is 200. Subscription: $14. **Sample postpaid: $4. No previously published poems; simultaneous submissions OK. Cover letter required. "Please include biographical information. We read all year long with deadlines for submissions on March 15, June 15, September 15 and December 15."** Time between acceptance and publication is 3-6 months. **Seldom comments on rejections. Reports within 2 months. Pays 1 copy. All rights revert to authors.**

TAPJOE: THE ANAPROCRUSTEAN POETRY JOURNAL OF ENUMCLAW (II, IV-Nature, social issues), P.O. Box 632, Leavenworth WA 98826, founded 1987, is a biannual. **"We try to be very open-minded but have a definite preference for free verse poems, 10-50 lines, which yield a sense of place. 'Bioregionalism' and 'deep ecology' describe themes and ideals we hold close."** They have published poetry by David Edelman, Ron McFarland, Jess Mills and Linda Curtis Meyers. As a sample the editor selected these lines from "Pilotfish" by Catherine Carter:

The urge to take and have
and know is terrible,
the dry grasping hunger
of the opposable thumb . . .

The magazine is 28-35 pgs., digest-sized, saddle-stapled, offset from desktop with matte card cover. Accepts about 60 poems/year with 1,000 submissions. Press run is 150-300. Subscription: $10 for 4 issues. **Sample postpaid: $3. "Cover letters appreciated but not necessary. Prefer 4-5 poems per submission." No simultaneous submissions or previously published poems. Final selections may take 6 months or so. Pays 1 copy for each accepted poem.** They say, "Submissions are circulated among several editors living hundreds of miles apart and working hectic jobs; sometimes this makes our responses very slow but we do the best we can. We appreciate purchases of our magazine—but mostly we enjoy receiving submissions of 'good' poetry! Read and buy poetry. The kinds of poets we admire: Gretel Ehrlich, Mary Oliver, Richard Blessing, Robert Sund, John Haines, Linda Hogan."

TAPROOT LITERARY REVIEW (I), 302 Park Rd., Ambridge PA 15003, phone (412)266-8476, founded 1986, editor Tikvah Feinstein, is an annual contest publication, very open to beginners. In addition to contest, each year a guest poet is selected; payment in copies. Writers recently published include Daniel James Sundahl, B.E. Stock, Ida Barton, Mary Donovan Vish, B.Z. Niditch and Lyn Lifshin. As a sample the editor selected the following lines from "Childhood is Cancelled" (Bosnia 1992-93) by Elizabeth A. Bernstein:

The hounds of terror hold
us in hungry jaws,
Feasting on death
Growing in heaps

While innocence withers
Like stricken vines . . .

The review is approximately 80 pgs., printed by offset on white stock with one-color glossy cover, art and no ads. Circulation is 500, sold at bookstores, readings and through the mail. Single copy: $5.50. **Sample postpaid: $5. There is a $5 entry fee for up to 5 poems, "no longer than 30 lines each." Nothing previously published or pending publication will be accepted. Cover letter with general information required. Submissions accepted between September 1 and December 31. Publishes theme issues. Send SASE for upcoming themes. Sometimes sends prepublication galleys. All entrants receive a copy of *Taproot*; enclose $2 for postage and handling.** Send books for review consideration. The editor says, "We want short poems with strong narratives."

TAR RIVER POETRY (II), English Dept., East Carolina University, Greenville NC 27858-4353, phone (919)752-6041, founded 1960, editor Peter Makuck, associate editor Luke Whisnant. **"We are not interested in sentimental, flat-statement poetry. What we would like to see is skillful use of figurative language."** They have recently published poetry by William Matthews, William Stafford, Susan Ludvigson, Susan Elizabeth Howe, A.R. Ammons, Naomi Shihab Nye, Peter Davison, Margaret Gibson, Brendan Galvin and Sharon Bryan. As a sample the editors selected these lines from "Poem for Dizzy" by Betty Adcock:

Sweet and sly, you were all business when that bent-skyward
old horn went up. Sometimes it went up like a rocket,
sometimes like a gentle-turning lark
high in a summer day. Or like an island wind
snapping a line of red and yellow clothes
hard against blue . . . .

Tar River appears twice yearly and is digest-sized, 60 pgs., professionally printed on salmon stock, some decorative line drawings, matte card cover with photo. They receive 6,000-8,000 submissions/year, use 150-200. Press run is 900 for 500 subscribers of which 125 are libraries. Subscription: $10. **Sample: $5.50. "We do not consider simultaneous submissions. Double or single-spaced OK. We prefer not more than 6 pgs. at one time. We do not consider mss during summer months." Reads submissions September 1 through April 15 only. Send SASE for guidelines. Reports in 4-6 weeks. Pays copies. Acquires first rights. Editors will comment "if slight revision will do the trick."** Reviews books of poetry in 4,000 words maximum, single or multi-book format. This is an especially good market for intelligent, concisely written book reviews. Poets may also send books for review consideration. ***Tar River*** is an "all-poetry" magazine that accepts dozens of poems in each issue, providing the talented beginner and experienced writer with an excellent forum that features all styles and forms of verse. Frequently contributors' works are included in the **Anthology of Magazine Verse & Yearbook of American Poetry**. Poetry published in ***Tar River*** has also been selected for inclusion in **The Best American Poetry 1994.** The editors advise, "Read, read, read. Saul Bellow says the writer is primarily a reader moved to emulation. Read the poetry column in ***Writer's Digest***. Read the books recommended therein. Do your homework."

TEARS IN THE FENCE (II), 38 Hodview, Stourpaine, Nr. Blandford Forum, Dorset DT11 8TN England, phone 0258-456803, founded 1984, general editor David Caddy, poetry editor Sarah Hopkins, is a "small press magazine of poetry, fiction, interviews, articles, reviews and graphics. **We are open to a wide variety of poetic styles. Work of a social, political, ecological and feminist awareness will be close to our purpose. However, we like to publish a balanced variety of work." The editors do not want to see "didactic rhyming poems."** They have published poetry by Gerald Locklin, Ann Born, Sheila E. Murphy and Catherine Swanson. As a sample, they selected the following lines from "The Invisible Children" by Andrew Jordan:

we found a well without a cover—its hollowness
echoed with the movements of lost children,

we heard their whisperings. There was a screaming

in the rookery trees that leaned about the house

Tears in the Fence appears 3 times/year. It is 52 pgs., A5, desktop-published on 90 gms. paper with b&w art and graphics and matte card cover. It has a press run of 400, of which 213 go to subscribers. Single copy: $5; **sample available for same price. Writers should submit 5 typed poems with IRCs. Cover letter with brief bio required. Publishes theme issues. Send SASE (or SAE and IRC) for upcoming themes. Reports in 3 months.** Time to publication is 8-10 months "but can be much less." **Pays 1 copy.** Reviews books of poetry in 200-250 words, single or multi-book format. Open to unsolicited reviews. Poets may also send books for review consideration. The magazine is informally connected with the East Street Poets literary promotions, workshops and publications. The editor says, "I think it helps to subscribe to several magazines in order to study the market and develop an understanding of what type of poetry is published. Use the review sections and send off to magazines that are new to you."

10TH MUSE (II), 33 Hartington Rd., Newtown, Southampton, Hants SO2 0EW England, founded 1990, editor Andrew Jordan, is a biannual of poetry, prose, book reviews and b&w artwork. "Generally radical rather than reactionary." They are **"particularly interested in human relationship stuff—sexuality/politics—wider subjects, too. No occasional verse."** They have published poetry by Peter Redgrove, Sheila E. Murphy and Belinda Subraman. As a sample the editor selected these lines from "Aliens" by Jeremy Reed:

leaving a wife, a job, ditching a car
to embrace the vision—holding to that
and how its light breaks open like a star.

10th Muse is 48 pgs., A5, photocopied, saddle-stapled, with card cover, no ads. Press run is 200 for 20 subscribers of which 3 are libraries. Single copy: £2; subscription: £4 for 2 copies. **Send a maximum of 6 poems. No previously published poems or simultaneous submissions. Often comments on rejections. Reports in 2-3 months. Pays 1 copy.** Staff reviews books of poetry. Send books for review consideration. The editor says, "Poets should read a copy of the magazine first. A subscription taken out from a U.S. bank by check would have to be £12 for 2 issues or £6 for one issue. This is because of high bank charges levied in U.K. when cashing foreign currency checks. Alternatively people could send dollar notes equivalent to £4 (2 issues) or £2 (1 issue) plus IRCs to cover the number of issues ordered."

TESSERA (IV-Women, regional, bilingual, translations), 350 Stong, York University, 4700 Keele St., North York, Ontario M3J 1P3 Canada, founded 1984, revived 1988, appears twice a year: **"feminist literary theory and experimental writing by women in French and English, preference to Canadians."** It is 94 pgs., digest-sized, professionally printed, with glossy card cover. Subscription: $18. **Sample postpaid: $10. Submit 4 copies. Deadlines are currently March 31 and August 31. Simultaneous submissions and previously published poems ("sometimes") OK. Editor comments on submissions "sometimes." Pays $10/page.**

TESSERACT PUBLICATIONS (I), P.O. Box 505, Hudson SD 57034-0505, phone (605)987-5070, founded 1981, publisher Janet Leih. **"All my books are subsidized publications. Payment is ⅓ in advance, ⅓ when book goes to printer, balance when book is complete. I help my poets with copyright, bar codes, listings and whatever publicity I can get for them. I have a number of mailing lists and will prepare special mailings for them, work with competent proofreaders, artists and a capable reviewer. Sometimes sends prepublication galleys."** They have helped publish books of poetry by Helen Eikamp, Gertrude Johnson, Fern Stuefen and Ellis Ovesen. As a sample Janet Leih selected these lines from **Love's Subtle Signature** by Maria Bakkum:

Love is
a daughter's deserted room
smiling back
from love-worn Teddy bears
and old doll faces.

They also hold occasional contests. Send SASE for information. Janet Leih adds, "I publish a catalog of books by South Dakota writers and take their books on consignment to fill orders. The catalog is new and modest at this time but the hope is to expand to a larger catalog and distribute it more widely."

TEXAS TECH UNIVERSITY PRESS (III, IV-Series), Lubbock TX 79409-1037, phone (806)742-2982, founded 1971, editor Judith Keeling, considers volumes of poetry in 3 categories only: **First-Book Poetry Series**: "Winning and finalist mss in an annual competition conducted by Poetry Editor Walter McDonald, who surveys some 20 literary journals throughout the year and invites up to 12 poets to submit mss for consideration in the competition"; **Invited Poets Series**: "Collections invited from established poets whose work continues to appear in distinguished journals"; and **TTUP Contemporary Poetry Series**: "Winning and finalist works in current national competitions." **Mss for the TTUP**

Contemporary Poetry Series should be submitted with cover letters and attachments to verify eligibility. Editors never comment on rejections. Books published on royalty contracts.

TEXTILE BRIDGE PRESS; MOODY STREET IRREGULARS: A JACK KEROUAC NEWSLETTER (IV-Specialized), P.O. Box 157, Clarence Center NY 14032, founded 1978, poetry editor Joy Walsh. **"We publish material by and on the work of Jack Kerouac, American author prominent in the fifties. Our chapbooks reflect the spirit of Jack Kerouac. We use poetry in the spirit of Jack Kerouac, poetry of the working class, poetry about the everyday workaday life.** Notice how often the work people spend so much of their life doing is never mentioned in poetry or fiction. Why? **Poetry in any form."** They have published poetry by Joseph Semenovich, Marion Perry, Bonnie Johnson, Boria Sax and Michael Basinski. ***Moody Street Irregulars*** is a 28-page, magazine-sized newsletter, biannual, circulation 700-1,000 (700 subscriptions of which 30 are libraries), using 3-4 pgs. of poetry in each issue. They receive about 50 submissions of poetry/year, use half of them. Subscription: $7. **Sample postpaid: $3.50. Reports in 1 month. Pays copies.** Textile Bridge Press also publishes collections by individuals. For book publication, **query with 5 samples. "The work speaks to me better than a letter." Replies to query in 1 week, to submission (if invited) in 1 month. Simultaneous submission OK for "some things yes, others no." Pays copies. Send SASE for catalog to buy samples. Editor comments on rejections if asked.**

THALIA: STUDIES IN LITERARY HUMOR (I, IV-Subscribers, humor), Dept. of English, University of Ottawa, Ottawa, Ontario K1N 6N5 Canada, editor Dr. J. Tavernier-Courbin, appears twice a year using **"humor (literary, mostly). Poems submitted must actually be literary parodies."** The editor describes it as 7×8½, flat-spined, "with illustrated cover." Press run is 500 for 475 subscribers. Subscription: $20 for individuals, $22 for libraries. **Sample postpaid: $8 up to volume 11, $15 and $20 for volumes 12 and 13 respectively (double issues). Contributors must subscribe. Simultaneous submissions OK but *Thalia* must have copyright. Will authorize reprints. Editor comments on submissions.** Reviews books of poetry. "Send queries to the editor concerning specific books."

THEMA (II, IV-Themes), Thema Literary Society, P.O. Box 74109, Metairie LA 70033-4109, founded 1988, editor Virginia Howard, is a triannual literary magazine **using poetry related to specific themes. "Each issue is based on an unusual premise. Please, please send SASE for guidelines before submitting poetry to find out the upcoming themes. For example: 'Three by a Tremor Tossed' is the theme for November 1, 1994 (submission deadline), 'Laughter on the Steps' is the theme for March 1, 1995 and 'A Solitary Clue' is the theme for July 1, 1995. No scatologic language, alternate life-style, explicit love poetry."** They have recently published poetry by Annie Silverman, Elayne Clift, James Penha and Marilyn Johnston. As a sample the editor selected these lines by Nora Ruth Roberts:

The dust of her kindergarten giggles
rose like petals in my mind.
How she had loved the sea,
clamming and scrabbling and toe-digging
into the swirly dunelets.

Thema is digest-sized, 200 pgs., professionally printed, with matte card cover. They accept about 10% of 320 poems received/year. Press run is 500 for 250 subscribers of which 30 are libraries. Subscription: $16. **Sample postpaid: $8. Submissions are accepted all year, but evaluated after specified deadlines. Editor comments on submissions. Pays $10/poem plus 1 copy. Buys one-time rights only.**

THEMATIC POETRY QUARTERLY (I, IV-Themes), 4444 River Forest Rd., Marianna FL 32446, phone (904)482-3890, editor Wilbur I. Throssell, publishes loose-leaf portfolios **of poetry on specific themes, limit 30 lines. Send SASE for list of themes.**

THE THIRD HALF LITERARY MAGAZINE; K.T. PUBLICATIONS (I, II), 16, Fane Close, Stamford, Lincolnshire PE9 1HG England, founded 1987, editor Mr. Kevin Troop. ***TTH*** appears 3 times/year. K.T. Publications also publishes up to 6 other books, with a Minibooks Series, for use in the classroom. The editor wants **"meaningful, human and humane, funny poems up to 40 lines. Work which actually *says* something without being obscene."** They have published poetry by Lee Bridges (Holland), Ann Keith (Amsterdam), Toby Litt (Prague) and Edmund Harwood, Michael Newman, Louise Rogers and Steve Sneyd (Britain). As a sample the editor selected this poem, "Fly," by Esther Gress (Denmark):

Like a butterfly

Market categories: (I) Beginning; (II) General; (III) Limited; (IV) Specialized; (V) Closed.

we often fly in vain
against the window pane
and see not
like the butterfly
the open door
to the sky

TTH is 44 pgs., A5, printed on white paper with glossy cover. Press run is 200. Individual booklets vary in length and use colored paper and card covers. **Cover letter required. Reports ASAP. Pays 1 copy. "Procedure for the publication of books is explained to each author; each case is different.** *The Third Half* is priced at £2.25 each; 2 issues for £4.25 and all three issues a year for £6.25, including postage and handling."

13TH MOON (II, IV-Women), English Dept., SUNY-Albany, 1400 Washington Ave., Albany NY 12222, phone (518)442-4181, founded 1973, editor Judith Johnson, is a feminist literary magazine appearing yearly (one double issue) in a 6×9, flat-spined, handsomely printed format with glossy card cover, using photographs and line art, ads at $200/page. Beyond a doubt, a real selection of forms and styles is featured here. For instance, in recent issues free verse has appeared with formal work, concrete poems, long poems, stanza patterns, prose poems, a crown of sonnets and more. Press run is 2,000 for 690 subscriptions of which 61 are libraries, 700 shelf sales. Subscription: $10. **Sample postpaid: $10. Reads submissions September 1 through May 30 only. Publishes theme issues. Send SASE for guidelines and upcoming themes. Themes include "special issues on women's poetics, one focusing on poetry, one on narrative forms." Pays 2 copies. Acquires first North American serial rights.** Staff reviews books of poetry in 1,500 words "more or less." Send books to Sue Shaferzak, review editor, for review consideration.

‡THIS: A SERIAL REVIEW (II), 6600 Clough Pike, Cincinnati OH 45224-4090, founded 1993, editor (Mr.) Robin Yale Bergstrom, appears 3 times/year "to give voice to underdogs and established writers and artists. We enjoy writers and artists taking risks—whether in poetry, fiction, prose, artistry or photography. **We seek strong, effective poetry as well as today's ground-breaking styles of craft. No trite rhyme, sentimental or inspirational poetry."** The editor says *This* is about 120 pgs., 8×8, perfect-bound, with 2-color cover, art and graphics and exchange ads. Press run is 2,000. Subscription: $18 (3 issues), $38 (6 issues), $54 (9 issues). **Sample postpaid: $7/each. Submit no more than 10 poems at a time. Previously published poems and simultaneous submissions OK, if notified. Cover letter required.** Time between acceptance and publication is 4-6 months. **Seldom comments on rejections. Send SASE for guidelines. Reports in 2-3 months. Pays 2 copies. Acquires one-time rights.** Reviews books of poetry. Open to unsolicited reviews. Poets may also send books for review consideration. The editor says, "Our publication seeks what is definitive in *today's* poetic craft. We encourage all poets to add their voice. Advice for beginners? Read, read, and read some more."

THISTLEDOWN PRESS LTD. (IV-Regional), 633 Main St., Saskatoon, Saskatchewan S7H 0J8 Canada, phone (306)244-1722, fax (306)244-1762, founded 1975, editor-in-chief Patrick O'Rourke, is "a literary press that specializes in **quality books of contemporary poetry by Canadian authors. Only the best of contemporary poetry that amply demonstrates an understanding of craft with a distinctive use of voice and language. Only interested in full-length poetry mss with 53-71 pgs. minimum."** They have recently published books of poetry by Glen Sorestad, George Whipple, Rhona McAdam, Doug Beardsley, Gary Hyland and John V. Hicks. **Do not submit unsolicited mss.** Canadian poets must **query first with letter, bio and publication credits. Poetry ms submission guidelines available upon request. Replies to queries in 2-3 weeks, to submissions (if invited) in 3 months. No authors outside Canada. No simultaneous submissions. "Please submit quality dot-matrix, laser-printed or photocopied material." Always sends prepublication galleys. Contract is for 10% royalty plus 10 copies.** They comment, "Poets submitting mss to Thistledown Press for possible publication should think in 'book' terms in every facet of the organization and presentation of the mss: Poets presenting mss that *read* like good books of poetry will have greatly enhanced their possibilities of being published. We strongly suggest that poets familiarize themselves with some of our poetry books before submitting a query letter."

THORNTREE PRESS (II), 547 Hawthorn Lane, Winnetka IL 60093, founded 1986, contact Eloise Bradley Fink. This press publishes professionally printed, digest-sized, flat-spined paperbacks, 96 pgs., selected through competition January 1 through February 14 in odd-numbered years. **Sample postpaid: $7.95.** "Included in our 16 books are 21 poets." From **Troika IV** Helen Reed writes:

> *"The trap shuddered with blows of hissing prehistoric snouts, snapping turtles, heads big as knotted fists. They carried their past with them in mossy gouts of green and lightning-forked white scars on plated shells, pale markings of dark water gods . . . . We hid our eyes, shrank from monsters that could swim into our dreams that night . . ."*

Submit a stapled group of 10 pages of original, unpublished poetry, single or double-spaced, photocopied, with a $4 reader's fee. Mss will not be returned. (A SASE for winners' names may be included.) "The top fifteen finalists will be invited to submit a 30-page manuscript for possible publication in **Troika VI.**"

THOUGHTS FOR ALL SEASONS: THE MAGAZINE OF EPIGRAMS (IV-Form, humor), % editor Prof. Em. Michel Paul Richard, 478 NE 56th St., Miami FL 33137-2621, founded 1976, "is an irregular serial: **designed to preserve the epigram as a literary form; satirical.** All issues are commemorative." **Rhyming poetry will be considered although most modern epigrams are prose.** Prof. Richard has published poetry by Jack Hart and offers this sample:

Beware a cause: it is our fate
To turn into the things we hate

TFAS is 84 pgs., offset from typescript on heavy buff stock with full-page cartoon-like drawings, card cover, saddle-stapled. The editor accepts about 20% of material submitted. Press run is 500-1,000. There are several library subscriptions but most distribution is through direct mail or local bookstores and newsstand sales. Single copy: $4.75 plus $1.50 postage. **Simultaneous submissions OK, but not previously published epigrams "unless a thought is appended which alters it." Editor comments on rejections. Publishes one section devoted to a theme. Send SASE for guidelines. Reports in 1 month. Pays 1 copy.**

THREE CONTINENTS PRESS INC. (III, IV-Ethnic, translations), P.O. Box 38009, Colorado Springs CO 80937-8009, phone (719)579-0977, founded 1973, poetry editor Donald Herdeck. **"Published poets only welcomed and only non-European and non-American poets . . . We publish literature by creative writers from the non-western world (Africa, the Middle East, the Caribbean and Asia/Pacific) – poetry *only* by non-western writers or good translations of such poetry if original language is Arabic, French, African vernacular, etc."** They have recently published poetry by Derek Walcott, Khalil Hawi, Mahmud Darwish, Julia Fields, Hillary Tham, Houda Naamani and Nizar Kabbani. They also publish anthologies focused on relevant themes. As a sample the editor selected these lines from "Fear," published in **Fan of Swords** by Muhammad al-Maghut:

On these cloudy days
I am afraid to awaken one morning and find no birds left,
no single flower tucked into a braid,
no friend in any coffee house.
I fear being chained to the wash-stand
or chimney
being sprayed by bullets
while the toothbrush is still in my mouth.
Hurry up, Mother, ask the bedouins
for a leatherbound charm or special weed
to protect me from this fear.

Query with 4-5 samples, bio, publication credits. Replies to queries in 5-10 weeks, to submissions (if invited) in 4-5 weeks. Sometimes sends prepublication galleys. Offers 10% royalty contract (5% for translator) with $100-200 advance plus 10 copies. Buys worldwide English rights. Send SASE for catalog to buy samples.

THE THREEPENNY REVIEW (II), P.O. Box 9131, Berkeley CA 94709, phone (510)849-4545, fax (510)849-4551, founded 1980, poetry editor Wendy Lesser, "is a quarterly review of literature, performing and visual arts, and social articles aimed at the intelligent, well-read, but not necessarily academic reader. Nationwide circulation. **Want: formal, narrative, short poems (and others); do not want: confessional, no punctuation, no capital letters. Prefer under 50 lines but not necessary. No bias *against* formal poetry, in fact a slight bias in favor of it."** They have recently published poetry by Thom Gunn, Frank Bidart, Seamus Heaney, Czeslaw Milosz and Louise Glück. There are about 9-10 poems in each 36-page tabloid issue. They receive about 4,500 submissions of poetry/year, use 12. Press run is 10,000 for 8,000 subscribers of which 300 are libraries. Subscription: $16. **Sample: $6. Send 5 poems or fewer/submission. Send SASE for guidelines. Reports in 2-8 weeks. Pays $100/poem. Buys first serial rights.** Open to unsolicited reviews. "Send for review guidelines (SASE required)." ***The Threepenny Review*** ranked in the "Top Pay" category of the latest ***Writer's Digest*** Poetry 60 list. Work published in this review has also been included in the 1993 and 1994 volumes of **The Best American Poetry.**

THRESHOLD BOOKS (IV-Spirituality, translations), RD #4, Box 600, Dusty Ridge Rd., Putney VT 05346, phone (802)254-8300, fax (802)257-2779, founded 1981, poetry editor Edmund Helminski, is "a small press dedicated to the publication of quality works in metaphysics, poetry in translation and literature with some spiritual impact. **We would like to see poetry in translation of high literary merit with spiritual qualities, or original work by established authors."** Recently published books of poetry include **Love Is A Stranger** by Rumi and **Doorkeeper Of The Heart** by Rabia. As a sample the editor selected these lines by Jelaluddin Rumi, translated by John Moyne and Coleman Barks:

We've given up making a living.
It's all this crazy love poetry now.

It's everywhere. Our eyes and our feelings
Focus together, with our words

That comes from a collection, **Open Secret, Versions of Rumi**, published in a beautifully printed, flat-spined, digest-sized paperback, glossy color card cover, 96 pgs. Per copy: $9. **Query with 10 samples, bio, publication credits and SASE. Simultaneous submissions OK; disks compatible with IBM, hard copy preferred. Replies to queries and submissions (if invited) in 1-2 months. Publishes on 7% contract plus 10 copies (and 50% discount on additional copies). Send SASE for catalog to buy samples.**

THUMBPRINTS (I, IV-Writing, regional), 928 Gibbs, Caro MI 48723, phone (517)673-5563, founded 1984, editor Janet Ihle, is the monthly 8-page Thumb Area Writers' Club newsletter. They want **poetry about writers and writing, nothing "vulgar." Maximum 32 lines.** As a sample, the editor selected the last stanza of "My Pen's Words" by I. Wright:

Sometimes my pen is full of wit
Sometimes it surprises me
Sometimes its words become a poem
For one and all to see.

Press run is 45 for 30 subscriptions. **Sample postpaid: 75¢. Simultaneous submissions and previously published poems OK. Send SASE for guidelines. Editor comments on submissions "sometimes." Reports in about 3 months. Pays 1 copy.** They sponsor seasonal contests for Michigan amateur writers.

TIA CHUCHA PRESS (III, IV-Ethnic, regional, social issues), P.O. Box 476969, Chicago IL 60647, founded 1989, president Luis J. Rodriguez. Tia Chucha **generally discourages unsolicited mss.** They publish 2-4 paperbacks a year, **"multicultural, lyrical, engaging, passionate works informed by social, racial, class experience. Evocative. Poets should be knowledgeable of contemporary and traditional poetry, even if experimenting."** They have published poetry by David Hernandez, Michael Warr and editor Luis J. Rodriguez. As a sample the editor selected these lines from "The Poetry Widow" by Patricia Smith:

Tonight, I wished I was one of your poems;
strong syllables curled in your throat
awaiting a joyous delivery. I wished I
was that clever, stilted script on the
paper in your hand, words you sweat over.

That's from her collection, **Life According to Motown**, published in a 6×9, flat-spined, professionally printed paperback, 74 pgs. with glossy card cover, $6.95. "We usually 'select' poets we'd like to publish, those active in a poetry environment (i.e., bar and cafe scene, magazines, etc.). We believe poetry matters. Although we publish in English, we do not limit our traditions to Western Culture. Poetry should draw on the richness of human cultures, with roots in African, Native American, Asian and Latin sensibilities. We believe in engaging poetry, socially necessary and shaped by political, economic and class realities. Redemptive and relevant. We believe poetry is an art. It needs to be crafted, thought-out and knowledgeable of contemporary and traditional poetics."

TICKLED BY THUNDER: WRITER'S NEWS & ROUNDTABLE (I, II, IV-Subscribers), 7385 129th St., Surrey, British Columbia V3W 7B8 Canada, founded 1990, publisher/editor Larry Lindner, appears 3 times/year, using poems about **"fantasy particularly, about writing or whatever. Keep them short—not interested in long, long poems. Nothing pornographic, childish, unimaginative. Welcome humor and inspirational verse."** They have published poetry by Stephen Gill, Helen Singh, Victoria Collins and John Grey. As a sample the editor selected these lines (poet unidentified):

So she put a monkee in his tea
marshmallows on the side . . .

It is 16-20 pgs., digest-sized, published on Macintosh. Press run is 150 for 100 subscribers. Subscription: $12 for 4 issues. **Sample postpaid: $2.50. Send SASE for guidelines. Include samples of writing with queries. Cover letter required with submissions. Reports in 2-3 months. Pays 1 copy plus cash. Buys first rights. Editor comments on rejections "99% of the time."** Reviews books of poetry in up to 300 words. Open to unsolicited reviews. Poets may also send books for review consideration. They also offer a poetry contest 3 times/year. Deadlines: the 15th of March, July and November. Entry fee: $2 for 3 poems; free for subscribers. Prize: cash, publication and subscription. Send SASE for details.

TIDEPOOL (I, IV-Form), 4 E. 23rd St., Hamilton, Ontario L8V 2W6 Canada, phone (416)383-2857, founded 1984, publisher Herb Barrett, who says, **"We charge $10 entry fee. Money returned if poetry not used." Send SASE for guidelines for details.** He wants to see **"haiku and contemporary short verse, any style or theme (maximum 34 lines). No scatological vulgarity."** He has published poetry by Chris Faiers, Dorothy Cameron Smith and Jeff Seffinga. ***Tidepool***, published each October, is 80 pgs., digest-sized, saddle-stapled, professionally printed with matte card cover. Press run is 400 for 150 subscribers of which 60-70 are libraries. **Sample postpaid: $5. "Prefer unpublished material." Cover letter required. Submit mss in May and June only. Sometimes comments on rejections. Reports on submissions in 2-3 weeks. Pays copies.**

TIGHT (II), P.O. Box 1591, Guerneville CA 95446, founded 1990, editor Ann Erickson, appears 5 times/year. **"*tight* uses immediate poetry—favoring fragmented, condensed, vivid form—direct subjective experience or dream, also preferring poetry which is experimental in sight, sound."** They have recently published poetry by Lisa Kucharski, Sesshu Foster, Marcia Arrieta, Steve Tills, andrew urbanus, Kay Renz, Peter Layton, Patti Sirens, Michael Brownstein, Joel Dailey, Mike Tuggle, Sheila E. Murphy and Monique Avakian. As a sample the editor selected these lines from "Fledgling" by Mary Rudbeck Stanko:

> *Morning is abrupt*
> *and ignites in a globe of grain*
> *while the bird traces a blaze where its wings*
> *leave circles in the sky.*

tight is 72 pgs., 7×8½, photocopied from typescript with 60 lb. matte cover. Press run is 200 for 25 subscribers, 50 shelf sales. **Sample postpaid: $4.50. Checks payable to Ann Erickson. Submit poetry for spring and summer of 1995. Reports in 2 months or sooner. Pays 1 copy. Acquires one-time rights.**

TIGHTROPE (II); SWAMP PRESS (V), 323 Pelham Rd., Amherst MA 01002, founded 1977, chief editor Ed Rayher. Swamp Press is a small press publisher of poetry and graphic art in limited edition, letterpress chapbooks. ***Tightrope***, appearing 1-2 times a year, is a literary magazine of varying format, circulation 300, 150 subscriptions of which 25 are libraries. Subscription: $10 for 2 issues. **Sample of *Tightrope* postpaid: $6. No simultaneous submissions. Sometimes comments on rejections. Send SASE for guidelines. Reports in 2 months, 6-12 months until publication. Pays "sometimes" and provides 2 contributor's copies. Acquires first rights.** Reviews books of poetry in one paragraph, single format. Swamp Press has published books by Edward Kaplan, editor Ed Rayher, Alexis Rotella (miniature, 3×3, containing 6 haiku), Sandra Dutton (a 4 foot long poem), Frannie Lindsay (a 10×13 format containing 3 poems), Andrew Glaze, Tom Haxo, Carole Stone and Steven Ruhl. **Not presently accepting unsolicited submissions for chapbook publication but when he publishes chapbooks he pays 5-10% of press run and, if there is grant money available, an honorarium (about $50).** Send SASE for catalog.

TIMBER CREEK REVIEW (II, IV-Humor), (formerly *Words of Wisdom*), 612 Front St. East, Glendora NJ 08029-1133, founded 1981, editor J.M. Freiermuth, appears monthly using **"short, pithy poetry, the stuff that brings a smile to the reader's face on first reading. No religious."** They have recently published poetry by Darcy Cummings, Gail Zwirn, Alice Zegers, Virginia Hlavsa and Richard Davignon. It is 40-48 pgs., photocopied with plain paper cover. They publish about 75 of 400 submissions received. Press run is 150 for 110 subscribers. Subscription: $15. **Sample postpaid: $2. Make checks payable to J.M. Freiermuth. Will publish simultaneous and previously published material. OK to submit on DOS floppy disk in ASCII format. Cover letter required with submissions; include "names of lit mags author subscribes to." No submissions accepted December 1 through January 31. Reports usually within 2 months. Pays 1 copy. Acquires one-time rights.**

TIMBERLINE PRESS (V), 6281 Red Bud, Fulton MO 65251, phone (314)642-5035, founded 1975, poetry editor Clarence Wolfshohl. "We do limited letterpress editions with the goal of blending strong poetry with well-crafted and designed printing. We lean toward **natural history or strongly imagistic nature poetry but will look at any good work. Also, good humorous poetry. Currently, still not accepting submissions because we have a good backlog of mss to publish—enough for the next 2-3 years."** They have recently published the books **Pigeons in the Chandeliers** by Judy Ray and **Monsoon** by William Hart. As a sample the editor selected these lines from "Morning News" published in Ray's **Pigeons in the Chandeliers** (1993):

> *Trees obscured the thunderheads*
> *so yesterday's bolt came from*
> *sunshine, flinging racquets from*
> *startled tennis grip,*
> *whipcrack*
> *breaking sky-blue china.*

Sample copies may be obtained by sending $5 requesting sample copy and noting you saw the listing in Poet's Market. Reports in under 1 month. Pays "50-50 split with author after Timberline Press has recovered its expenses."

TIMBERLINES (III), % Lake City Writers Forum, P.O. Box 578, Lake City CO 81235, founded 1990, contact Peter Elliot, is an annual literary journal. They **"prefer poetry dealing with nature-man, out-of-doors, but not essential. Shorter poems have better chance of acceptance due to space limitations."** As a sample they selected these lines (poet unidentified):

When I was
little, days were bright yellow blankets
that warmed my words. Clouds were crowns
that blessed mountain tops and brothers
scrambled my eyes with mysteries. Night
held the song of crickets in its palm . . .

Sample postpaid: $5. Poems should be typed exactly as they should appear on the page if accepted. Deadline: March 1. Reads submissions September 1 through April 1 only. Seldom comments on rejections. Pays 1 copy.

‡TIME OF SINGING, A MAGAZINE OF CHRISTIAN POETRY (I, IV-Religious, themes), P.O. Box 211, Cambridge Springs PA 16403, founded 1958-1965, revived 1980, editor Charles A. Waugaman. "The viewpoint is **unblushingly Christian—but in its widest and most inclusive meaning.** Moreover, it is believed that the vital message of Christian poems, as well as inspiring the general reader, will give pastors, teachers, and devotional leaders rich current sources of inspiring material to aid them in their ministries. We tend to have a Fall/Christmas issue, a Lent/Easter one, and a Summer one. But **we do have themes quite often. We tend to value content, rather than form; prefer short poems for practical reasons."** They have recently published poetry by Elva McAllaster, Ralph Seager, Ken Siegelman, Frances P. Reid, Tony Cosier, Mary Balazs, Edith Lovejoy Pierce and Nancy James. The editor selected these sample lines from "Wrestlers" by H. Edgar Hix:

Our God is a wrestler who throws us to our knees
again and again. He is a bruised and bruising God
with strong, quick hands; a Master who understands
how we must wrestle, who gives us purple knees
and strengthened souls.

The triquarterly is digest-sized, 40 pgs., offset from typescript with decorative line drawings scattered throughout. They receive over 500 submissions/year, use about 210. Circulation is 350 with 150 subscriptions. Subscription: $12; per copy: $6. **Sample: $3. Prefer about 5 poems, double-spaced, no simultaneous submissions.** Time between acceptance and publication is 6 months to 1 year. **Editor frequently comments with suggestions for improvement for publication. Send SASE for guidelines and upcoming themes. Reports in 1-2 months. Pays 1 copy. Reserves right to reprint poems in other formats. "We tend to be traditional. We like poems that are aware of grammar. Collections of uneven lines, series of phrases, preachy statements, unstructured 'prayers,' and trite sing-song rhymes usually get returned. We look for poems that 'show' rather than 'tell.' "** They also publish chapbooks of poets of the editor's selection and offer contests, "generally one for each issue on a given subject related to our theme. Send SASE for rules."

TIN WREATH; TEN:BY:SIX (III), P.O. Box 13401, Albany NY 12212-3401, founded 1985, "editor/janitor" David Gonsalves. "*Tin Wreath* is a triquarterly (March, July and November) gathering of writers and writing from the social, political, psychological, spiritual and linguistic margins of late 20th century America." **The editor is looking for poetry "that makes contact with the deeper forces at work in the world and poetry that explores the musical and sculptural qualities inherent in the language; I'd prefer to see abstract, minimalist, non-discursive or otherwise counter-traditional poetry."** He has published work by Geof Huth, Deborah Meadows, N. Sean William and Sheila E. Murphy. As a sample, he chose these lines from "The Lynching of J. Bro" by Michelle Perez:

quick his bonnet
stepped, disrobed
the wife
half silent
stately shook,
a pattern, body
as firm displayed—
the patrons laughed.

David Gonsalves is also the "editor/janitor" of ***ten:by:six***, a bimonthly founded in 1993 with **"poetry that more-or-less directly addresses the social concerns of the community at large." The editor is looking for "straightforward poetic 'snapshots' of people and their world."** He has recently published works by Hya Laurel, Walter Kuchinski, Gina Rocca and Paul Weinman. As a sample, he chose "Falsehood" by Walt Phillips:

the sun tells the building
this is taos
two trees
are laughing
they know where they are

Tin Wreath consists of 12, 8½×11, photocopied pages. ***ten:by:six*** consists of 16, 5½×8½, photocopied pages. Circulation is 150. Subscription for either: $9 individuals, $15 institutions. **Sample postpaid: $3, includes a sample of both publications plus guidelines. Checks must be made payable to David Gonsalves. Writers should send 3-5 poems. Simultaneous submissions are OK. Reporting time is "13 days to 13 weeks" and time to publication is 4-12 months. Pays 3 copies. Acquires first North American serial rights.**

TOAD HIGHWAY (II), 178 E. Main St. B, Lansdale PA 19446, founded 1988, editor Grant Clauser. *Toad Highway* is a small magazine appearing irregularly using "all types of artwork, poetry and reviews. **We want poetry which proves that the poet is obsessed by each sound, each stress, each image, each line. No 'happy poems' or work which shows that the poet has not studied contemporary poetry."** They have recently published work by Peter Wild, Harry Humes, William Heyen and Simon Perchik. As a sample the editor selected these lines from "Hubbel Trading Post" by Robert Edwards:

The first time was the dust,
bolts of calico and velvet,
and Hopi and Pima baskets hanging
by a shadow from the rafters.
There were Navajo rugs of Ganado red,
like flexible iron, on the floor,
and the smell of dark leather
glossed on the salt of many hands.

TH is a 52-page pamphlet, saddle-stapled. "We accept about one in every 100 poems received." Their press run is 250 with 20 subscriptions. **Single copy: $2. Make checks payable to Grant Clauser. Submit maximum of 5 poems, single-spaced. Simultaneous submissions OK. Editor "seldom" comments on rejections. Responds to submissions "when I get to it." Pays 1 copy (discount on others).** "We will review books sent to us." He says, "We want to see strong imagistic narrative or descriptive meditation. Nothing experimental just for the sake of being different. No L.A. type poems. The poem must say something real, not just sit there and wet itself. ***Toad Highway*** aims to be an outlet for quality contemporary poetry at a low budget. I sometimes like to print short prose bits by the authors about their poetry."

‡TOMORROW MAGAZINE (II), P.O. Box 148486, Chicago IL 60614, founded 1982, editor Tim W. Brown, is a biannual magazine appearing in January and July. "We focus roughly half on poets from Chicago, half from elsewhere. We prefer work that falls between the 'academic' and 'saloon' extremes of the literary spectrum." **They want "free verse strong in image and emotion. No formalist and academic poetry, Hallmark verse, or religious poetry."** They have recently published poetry by Richard Kostelanetz, Lyn Lifshin, Hugh Fox and Kay Murphy. As a sample, the editor selected these lines from "Poem" by Jim Tyack:

. . . Who else could live in those eyes
they are quite unhouse-like and I plod and sweep fluttering
insects and leaves off the water's shimmering surface
as you drift away somewhere praying to the snow-covered

Andes or a tree in the backyard where you become an expert
at divining deeper meaning from the common place.

TM is 32 pgs., 8½×11, custom-bound, with card stock cover, b&w cover photo. They receive about 300 mss/year, usually accept 10-12%. Press run is 300 for 200 shelf sales. **Sample postpaid: $5. Send no more than 5-6 poems at one time. No previously published poems; simultaneous submissions OK.** Time between acceptance and publication is 6-9 months. **Seldom comments on rejections. Send SASE for guidelines. Reports in 3 weeks to 3 months. Pays 1 copy. Acquires first rights. Requests acknowledgment when reprinting in anthologies or collections.** The editor says, "There are too many tribes in poetry. At ***Tomorrow*** we like to think we have a pluralistic outlook."

TOUCH (IV-Religious, teens, themes), P.O. Box 7259, Grand Rapids MI 49510, phone (616)241-5616, founded 1970, poetry editor Carol Smith: "Our magazine is a 24-page edition written **for girls 7-14 to show them how God is at work in their lives and in the world around them. *Touch* is theme-orientated. We like our poetry to fit the theme of each issue. We send out a theme update biannually**

CLOSE-UP

Relationships and Reading Spark Translation

For Albert C. Todd, becoming a translator was a matter of "being in the right place at the right time." Todd, who is the chair of Slavic Languages at Queens College in Flushing, New York, is well-known for his translations of Russian poetry. He edited and provided many of the translations for a recently released anthology selected by Russian poet Yevgeny Yevtushenko, **Twentieth Century Russian Poetry: Silver and Steel** (Doubleday, 1993).

Todd's initial interest was in history and politics. However, a 1958 visit to the Soviet Union as a graduate student exposed him to popular readings of traditional poets such as Alexander Blok and Sergei Yesenin, and he became "mesmerized by Russian poetry. I just wandered in from history to literature, and was happy to make the change," he says. Work with the Harvard Cultural Center brought him into contact with contemporary Russian writers, like Yevtushenko. Although he began doing translations as part of his academic work, his interest in translating grew out of personal friendships with the poets he met.

"Poetry has been something of interest to me all of my life. But the idea of translating only came with my friendship with Yevtushenko." Todd helped the poet schedule a tour of the United States in 1966 and accompanied him to some of the readings. "Along the way, the need would arise to translate a poem, and there I was," he laughs. Later, he met other Russian poets through Yevtushenko, and he began doing translations for them as well. As he became better known, other poets and editors approached him. He says that becoming known as a translator was largely a matter of coincidence, "usually somebody who needed a translation knew me, and I just fell into it."

Todd says many translators face the same uncertain path. "Translation is an accidental profession in America. We don't have regular systems of training translators. There is no necessary measurement of qualification, no necessary discipline of training." The opposite is true in the former Soviet Union, he says, where translation is "very highly respected and very well disciplined."

Part of the problem facing translators in America, Todd says, is the lack of emphasis on foreign language skills. "If you're a child in Europe, you realize that if you're going to get any place in the world you'll have to know languages other than your own." As a consequence, children begin studying language, and translation, as early as grade school. By the time they reach college, they are usually proficient in one or more foreign languages. Americans, on the other hand, usually learn languages much later in life.

Becoming a translator is not easy, even for those who have the language skills, Todd cautions. Perhaps because it is not a widely acknowledged field, translators often come to an editor's attention indirectly. Some of Todd's early published translations appeared in articles he wrote about Russian literature. One article discussed the use of religious imagery in contemporary Russian poetry and

Yevgeny Yevtushenko and Albert C. Todd

featured selections from Yevtushenko and others. Rather than use someone else's translation, Todd did the work himself. "If you've done translations, sometimes they [editors] will get back to you in the future."

He admits, though, that it can be difficult to find publishers for translations, especially translations of poetry. "American editors of publishing houses are not always the best at judging poetry," he says, "and if they're not comfortable about judging American poetry, then they are even more reluctant to make decisions about foreign language translations."

The best way to become a successful translator, Todd says, is to become an educated translator. "Read widely in your own field," he advises. Successful translation comes from "relationships, reading, and your own knowledge, following journals and writers in your own field."

He is optimistic about the future need for translators. Americans are becoming increasingly interested in other languages and cultures. Business ties with the rest of the world, particularly with Eastern Europe and the former Soviet bloc countries are growing, he says. "Contacts require communication, communication requires language skills," which means a greater need for translators.

Yet Todd doesn't think translators will be limited to business documents. In the case of Eastern Europe, he says "there is a resurgence in interest in and value for these cultures" and cites the growing number of Americans in cities like Prague. "I think the admiration for that world is going to have its impact on the West," he says. As Americans become more familiar and appreciative of other cultures, there will be a greater demand for translations of literature.

Todd sees the increase in global communications as good for the future of translation and is positive about the role of new technologies. "My own computer is set up with bilingual dictionaries," he notes, "and it's not difficult to imagine that soon entire libraries will be available on CD-ROM. This is going to change the way we think, the way we do things, very dramatically."

While Todd believes computers can aid translators, he's not worried about being replaced. "Translation is a craft," he says, "It's a skill, an art form. And that's something that can't be made rigid."

—Alison Holm

to all our listed freelancers. We prefer short poems with a Christian emphasis that can show girls how God works in their lives." They have published poetry by Janet Shafer Boyanton and Iris Alderson. As a sample we selected "Shall I Compare Myself to Others?" by May Richstone:

Better not. Such comparisons
Most likely would become a strain—
My betters could make me envious,
The lesser tend to make me vain.

Much better compare
Yesterday's me
With the tomorrow's
I hope to be.

Touch is published 10 times a year, magazine-sized, circulation 15,800 with 15,500 subscriptions. They receive 150-200 freelance submissions of poetry/year, use 2 poems in each issue, have a 6-month backlog. Subscription: $9 US, $10.50 Canada, $15 foreign. **Sample and guidelines free with 8×10 SASE. Poems must not be longer than 20 lines—prefer much shorter. Simultaneous submissions OK. Query with SASE for theme update. Themes for September 1994 through March 1995 are as follows: Anticipation (Hope)—September; Prayer—October; Nature—November; Promises—December; Endurance (Physical Fitness)—January; Future—February; Wind Under My Wings (Heroes)—March. Reports in 2 months. Pays $10-15 and copies.**

TOUCHSTONE (I, II), Viterbo College, La Crosse WI 54601, phone (608)791-0271, founded 1950, moderator Richard Ruppel, is a literary quarterly using mostly poetry, short stories and artwork. **"Any form but no longer than 50 lines/poem."** As a sample the editor selected these lines from "Outbound" by Kate Larkin:

Beware of the Park Street exit
Where corners cross
And weepy people
Stare, pasty-faced.

The magazine is digest-sized, 48 pgs., saddle-stapled, with semi-glossy card cover. Press run is 800 for 100 subscribers of which 25 are libraries. Subscription: $5. **Sample postpaid: $2.50. Submit 3-5 poems. Cover letter required; include "a note of origination" (i.e. that the work is original). Reads submissions August 1 through March 1 only. Send SASE for guidelines. Reports in 2 months. Best poem gets $20. All get 1 copy.** The editor says, "Write poetry that is rich in visual imagery. Strive to make your reader *see* what you are talking about. Do not philosophize. Do not moralize. Let the imagery carry the message."

TOUCHSTONE LITERARY JOURNAL; TOUCHSTONE PRESS (II), P.O. Box 8308, Spring TX 77387-8308, founded 1975, poetry editor William Laufer, is an annual publishing **"experimental or well-crafted traditional form, including sonnets, and translations. No light verse or doggerel."** They have published poetry by Walter Griffin, Sheila Murphy, Michael L. Johnson, Walter McDonald and Joyce Pounds Hardy. As a sample the editor selected these lines from "Sackcloth and Ashes" by Gary J. Whitehead:

There will always be those autumn trees,
even when they've become some parking lot,
the blinding sunlit tops of oak and birch
hiding bleeding squirrels and the rip of BB's . . .

Touchstone is digest-sized, flat-spined, 100 pgs., professionally printed in small, dark type with glossy card cover. Subscription: $7. **Sample postpaid: $4. Sometimes sends prepublication galleys. Pays 1 copy.** Reviews books of poetry. Open to unsolicited reviews. Poets may also send books for review consideration, to Review Editor. Touchstone Press also **publishes an occasional chapbook. Send SASE for submission guidelines.** "This year we will also publish a book-length epic, **Kingdom of the Leopard: An Epic of Old Benin** by Nigerian poet chi chi layor. We are open to new projects. Query first, with SASE."

TOWER POETRY SOCIETY; PINE TREE SERIES; TOWER (II), Dundas Public Library, 18 Ogilvie St., Dundas, Ontario L9H 2S2 Canada, founded 1951, editor-in-chief Joanna Lawson. "The Tower Poetry Society was started by a few members of McMaster University faculty to promote interest in poetry. We publish ***Tower*** twice a year and a few chapbooks. We want **rhymed or free verse, traditional or modern, but not prose chopped into short lines, maximum 40 lines in length, any subject, any comprehensible style."** They have recently published poetry by June Walker and Helen Fitzgerald Dougher. The editor selected these sample lines by Tony Cosier:

From forging brass he took to forging soul,
gave up plowing soil to plow his skull,
ripped open the eye that never closed again

and took for tongue the howl of the beast in pain.

Tower is digest-sized, 40 pgs., circulation 250, 60 subscriptions of which 8 are libraries. They receive about 400 unsolicited submissions of poetry/year, use 30, no backlog. Subscription: $6 including postage; $7.50 abroad. **Sample postpaid: $2. Limit submissions to 4 poems. Submit during February or August. Reports in 2 months. Pays 1 copy.** The editor advises, "Read a lot of poetry before you try to write it."

TOWNSHIPS SUN (IV-Rural/ecological, regional), 7 Conley St., P.O. Box 28, Lennoxville, Quebec J1M 1Z3 Canada, phone (819)566-7424, founded 1972, editor Patricia Ball, is a monthly newspaper in English "concerned with **history of townships, English community, agriculture and ecology and using poetry on these themes. Only poems about the area and people of Quebec ever accepted. Others need not submit.**" The tabloid has a press run of 1,500 for 1,200 subscribers of which 20 are libraries, and 280 shelf sales. Subscription: $15/year Canada, $20/year outside Canada. **Sample postpaid: $2. Pays $10-30 plus 1 copy. "Will publish poems specifically about townships, townshippers, or of specific interest to townshippers."** Staff reviews books of poetry.

TRADESWOMEN MAGAZINE (IV-Women, specialized), P.O. Box 2622, Berkeley CA 94702, founded 1982, poetry editor Sue Doro, editor Janet Scoll Johnson, is a national quarterly **"particular to women in blue collar non-traditional work" and uses poetry "pertaining to women in trades, tradeswomen as mothers, family and co-worker relationships."** Subscription: $35. **Sample postpaid: $2. Guidelines available for SASE. They consider simultaneous submissions and previously published poems. Cover letter with short bio—particularly about work history—required. Reports in 1 month. No backlog.** Open to unsolicited reviews. Poets may also send books for review consideration.

TRANSNATIONAL PERSPECTIVES (III), CP161, 1211 Geneva 16 Switzerland, founded 1975, editor René Wadlow, is a "journal of world politics with some emphasis on culture that crosses frontiers." Uses 4-6 poems/issue, usually illustrated by drawing or photo. They want **"poems stressing harmony of nature, human potential, understanding of other cultures—relatively short. No humor, nationalistic themes, nothing 'overly' subjective."** They have published poetry by Verona Bratesch and Janet Pehr. As a sample the editor selected these lines from "1989, A Pivot Year" by Brian Walker:

This year, all bets are off.
Unpredictable chances,
expectations jilted;
adepts will learn new dances.
Watch old system hiccough,
welcome new solutions
in native phrase unstilted:
in apt thoughts, revolutions.

TP appears 3 times a year; it "is oriented toward making policy suggestions in international organizations, especially in the United Nations." It is 48 pgs., handsomely produced, magazine-sized, saddle-stapled with coated color paper cover. They receive about 100 poems/year, use 16. Press run is 5,000 for 4,000 subscribers of which half are libraries. **Sample back issue free on request. Simultaneous submissions OK. No previously published poems. Editor comments "rarely on quality, only why not for *TP*." Reports in 1 month. Pays 5 copies, more if desired.** René Wadlow says, "Poems in ***TP*** come from many countries, especially Eastern Europe, Scandinavia and India, often translated into English, usually 'upbeat' since most articles are on political and economic difficulties of the world."

TRESTLE CREEK REVIEW (II), 1000 West Garden, Coeur d'Alene ID 83814, phone (208)769-3300, ext. 384, founded 1982-83, poetry editor Chad Klinger et al, is a "2-year college creative writing program production. Purposes: (1) expand the range of publishing/editing experience for our small band of writers; (2) expose them to editing experience; (3) create another outlet for serious, beginning writers. **We favor poetry strong on image and sound, the West and country vs. city; spare us the romantic, rhymed clichés. We can't publish much if it's long (more than 2 pgs.).**" They have published poetry by Jesse Bier, Lowell Jaeger, Reja-e Busailah, Ray Mizer and Julia Thomas. As a sample Chad Klinger selected these lines by Ron McFarland:

All around you the furious mines are closing
like angry fists,
their galvanized shells rusting too slowly
to be a tourist attraction.
Outside town a black bronze miner drills the sky.

TCR is a digest-sized, 57-page annual, professionally printed on heavy buff stock, perfect-bound, matte cover with art, circulation 500, 6 subscriptions of which 4 are libraries. This publication is well-designed and features both free and formal verse by relative newcomers. The editors receive unsolicited poetry submissions from about 100 persons/year, use 30. **Sample: $4. Submit**

before March 1 (for May publication), no more than 5 pgs., no simultaneous submissions. Reports by March 30. Pays 2 copies. The editor advises, "Be neat; be precise; don't romanticize or cry in your beer; strike the surprising, universal note. Know the names of things."

TRIQUARTERLY MAGAZINE; THE TERRENCE DES PRES PRIZE FOR POETRY (II), 2020 Ridge Ave., Evanston IL 60208, phone (708)491-7614, founded 1964, editors Reginald Gibbons and Susan Hahn, is one of the most respected and visually appealing journals produced in the United States. Editors accept a wide range of verse forms and styles of verse (long poems, sequences, etc.) **with the emphasis solely on excellence,** and some issues are published as books on specific themes. They have published poetry by Tom Sleigh, Albert Goldbarth, Linda McCarriston, Pattiann Rogers and Theodore Weiss. ***TriQuarterly***'s three issues per year are 6×9, 200 pgs., flat-spined, professionally printed with b&w photography, graphics, glossy card cover. There are about 40 or more pgs. of poetry in each issue. They receive about 3,000 unsolicited submissions of poetry/year, use 60, have about a year backlog. Press run is 4,500 for 2,000 subscribers of which 35% are libraries. Subscription: $20; single copy: $9.95. **Sample postpaid: $5. No simultaneous submissions. Reads submissions October 1 through March 31 only. Sometimes works with poets, inviting rewrites of interesting work. Reports in 3 months. Always sends prepublication galleys. Payment varies. Acquires first North American serial rights. "We *suggest* prospective contributors examine sample copy before submitting."** Reviews books of poetry "at times." Send books for review consideration. ***TriQuarterly*** sponsors The Terrence Des Pres Prize for Poetry. This is awarded every 2 years to a book-length ms of original poems or translations. The prize includes a $2,000 cash award and publication by Northwestern University Press/TriQuarterly Books. Runners-up will be considered for publication. The ms should be at least 48 pgs. in length, in typed or clearly photocopied form. Entry fee: $15, includes a 1-year subscription; send $5 for each additional ms. Send SASE after January 1, 1996, for guidelines and submission deadline. Work appearing in ***TriQuarterly*** has been included in **The Best American Poetry** (1993 and 1994) and the **Pushcart Prize** anthology.

TROUT CREEK PRESS; DOG RIVER REVIEW; DOG RIVER REVIEW POETRY SERIES; BACKPOCKET POETS (II), 5976 Billings Rd., Parkdale OR 97041-9610, founded 1981, poetry editor Laurence F. Hawkins, prefers **"shorter poems (to 30 lines) but will consider longer, book or chapbook consideration. No restrictions on form or content. No pornography or religious verse."** They have recently published poetry by Judson Crews, Gerald Locklin, Arthur Winfield Knight, Wilma Elizabeth McDaniel, Nathaniel Tarn and Sam Silva. As a sample the editor selected these lines from "Madison Buffalo Jump" by Douglas Myers:

Monument to a time large scale dying and inefficient
injury were still pardoned
through ritual apology and prayer,
sixty inches of chipped bone debris

and weathered stone age points
lie under crumbling sandstone cliffs.

Dog River Review is a semiannual, digest-sized, 60 pgs., saddle-stapled, offset from computer typescript with b&w graphics. They receive about 500 submissions of poetry/year, use 40-50. Press run is 300 for 40 subscribers of which 7 are libraries. Single copy: $4; subscription: $8. **Sample postpaid: $2.50. Send SASE for guidelines. Reports in 1 week to 3 months. Pays in copies. Acquires first North American serial rights. *Dog River Review*** is open to unsolicited reviews. Poets may also send books for review consideration. Backpocket Poets is a series of 4×5¼ chapbooks, professionally printed, 26 pgs., saddle-stapled or perfect-bound with matte card cover, selling for $2.50 each, a drawing or photo of the author on the back. The Dog River Review Poetry Series consists of digest-sized, professionally printed, saddle-stapled chapbooks with matte card covers. **For book publication by Trout Creek Press, query with 4-6 samples. Replies to queries immediately, to submissions in 1-2 months. No simultaneous submissions. Editor sometimes comments on rejections. Always sends prepublication galleys for chapbooks. No payment until "material costs recovered. We also publish individual authors on cassette tape."** Send SASE for catalog to buy samples.

TUCUMCARI LITERARY REVIEW (II), 3108 W. Bellevue Ave., Los Angeles CA 90026, founded 1988, editor Troxey Kemper, assistant editor Neoma Reed, appears every other month. **"Prefer rhyming and established forms, 2-100 lines, but the primary goal is to publish good work. No talking animals. No haiku. The quest here is for poetry that will be just as welcome many years later as it is now. Preference is for readable, understandable writing of literary and lasting quality."** They have recently published poetry by Kenneth W. Johnson, Wilma Elizabeth McDaniel, Marian Ford Park, Andy Peterson, Edward Locke, Karin Lindgren, William J. Middleton and Dawn Zapletal. As a sample the editor selected these lines from "Courage Defined," a 52-line poem by Harvey Stanbrough:

Circling, zeroing in on infinity,

soar ever higher on gossamer wings
over the boundaries into eternity;
leave all the nightmares and live in your dreams.
Gently and silently, seek out the reasoning
ones in the manifest mis'ry below;
whisper true courage deep into the hearts of them:
he is courageous who withholds the blow.

The magazine is digest-sized, 48 pgs., saddle-stapled, photocopied from typescript, with card cover. Their press run is 150-200. Subscription: $12, $20 for overseas. **Sample: $2, $4 for overseas. Submit no more than 4 poems at a time. Considers simultaneous submissions and previously published poems. Send SASE for guidelines. Reports within 1 month. Pays 1 copy. Acquires one-time rights.** This magazine is inexpensively produced but contains some good formal poems. If you're looking to place a particular sonnet or villanelle, try Troxey Kemper's magazine. He reports quickly, by the way, and may comment on rejections.

TURBULENCE (IV-Form/style), P.O. Box 40, Hockessin DE 19707, founded 1993, editor David Nemeth, aims to publish 4 times a year to provide an independent voice for poets. They are interested in both poetry and essays on poetics. **"I want to see poetry that goes along with the magazine's title: avant-garde, language, experimental poetry."** They have recently published poetry by John M. Bennett, Charles Bernstein, Sheila E. Murphy and Joe Banford. As a sample we selected these lines from "migration of birds and butterflies" by Deborah Meadows:

moral laws
(Confucian, Hammurabi,
Ecclesiastes, EPA, etc.)
form long after
primeval and molten
elements coalesce
to protein soup

Turbulence is 32 pgs., digest-sized, professionally printed and saddle-stapled with colored card cover. **No previously published poems or simultaneous submissions. Cover letter required. Send SASE for guidelines. Reports in 1-3 months. Always sends prepublication galleys. Pays 1 copy. Acquires first-time rights.** Reviews books, chapbooks and other mags. The editor says, "I want poets to push themselves to their limit and then some."

TURKEY PRESS (V), 6746 Sueno Rd., Isla Vista CA 93117, founded 1974, poetry editor Harry Reese along with his wife, Sandra Reese, "is involved with publishing contemporary literature, producing traditional and experimental book art, one-of-a-kind commissioned projects and collaborations with various artists and writers. **We do not encourage solicitations of any kind to the press. We seek out and develop projects on our own."** They have published poetry by Thomas Merton, James Laughlin, Sam Hamill, Edwin Honig, Glenna Luschei, Tom Clark, Michael Hannon, Keith Waldrop, David Ossman, Peter Whigham, Jack Curtis, Kirk Robertson and Anne E. Edge.

‡TURNSTILE (II), Suite 2348, 175 Fifth Ave., New York NY 10010, founded 1988, is a biannual literary magazine publishing poetry, fiction, essays, art, interviews, novel excerpts and plays. **They want poetry that is "well-crafted, with a strong sense of line, form and sound."** They have published poetry by James Applewhite, Kevin Pilkington, Robert Morgan and Dabney Stuart. The editors describe it as 128 pgs., 6×9, 55 lb. paper. Circulation: 1,500. Subscription: $12. **Sample postpaid: $6.50. "Send no more than 4 poems at one time. Refer to the guidelines in the front of our magazine." Often comments on rejections. Reports in 2-3 months. Pays 5 copies.** In 1993, *Turnstile* received grants from the NEA and the New York State Council on the Arts.

TURNSTONE PRESS (II, IV-Regional), 607-100 Arthur St., Winnipeg, Manitoba R3B 1H3 Canada, phone (204)947-1555, founded 1975, is a "literary press publishing quality contemporary fiction, non-fiction, poetry and criticism by **Canadian citizens and permanent residents of Canada"** in flat-spined books (8/year). They want **"writing based on contemporary poetics, but otherwise wide-ranging. Welcome experimental, graphic, long poems, the unusual. Nothing overly concerned with traditional rhyme and meter."** They have published poetry by Di Brandt, Maara Haas and Kristjana Gunnars. **Submit complete ms with cover letter including bio and other publications. Poems previously published in magazines OK. Reports in 2-3 months. Pays $100-200 advance, 10% royalties and 10 copies. Editor comments on rejections "if we believe it has promise." Send 9×12 SASE (or, from the US, SAE with IRCs) for catalog to buy samples.**

TWISTED (IV-Horror, fantasy), P.O. Box 1249, Palmetto GA 30268-1249, phone (404)463-1458, founded 1985, editor/publisher Christine Hoard, uses **poetry of "horror/dark fantasy; humor OK. Form and style open. Not more than 1 page long."** They have published poetry by John Grey, Lisa

Lepovetsky and Jeffery Lewis. As a sample the editor selected these lines by Jana Hakes:

As a child takes
to puddles of mud
for play,
I prefer puddles
of blood
every day;
horror that stains
the mind,
never washes away.

Christine Hoard describes ***Twisted*** as "150 pgs., magazine-sized, offset, vellum bristol cover, much art, some ads, 60 lb. matte paper. I receive a lot of poetry submissions, use 30-50 per issue." Press run is 300 for single-copy sales. **Sample postpaid: $6, payable to Christine Hoard. "Don't submit more than four poems at a time. You should see a sample copy to get a 'feel' for what we publish." No simultaneous submissions, but previously published poems are sometimes accepted. Editor often comments on rejections. Send SASE for guidelines. Reports within 3 months. "We sometimes close when we are preparing next issue or are overstocked." Pays 1 copy.** She says, "Poets of science fiction, horror, fantasy will be pleased to know there are several markets in the small press and some organizations are available to offer support and market information."

‡TWISTED NIPPLES (I), 544 NW Fourth, Corvallis OR 97330, phone (503)753-8439, founded 1993, editor Mark Hadley, is a monthly publication designed "to give creative people a chance to see their work in print without hassle." They want **poetry that is "humorous, raw, dark, observational. *TN*'s motto is 'Frustration with a smile.' No simple rhyme, epic death poetry, Rush Limbaugh/Geraldo-type logic, racist/sexist crap.** All contributors are real people who have a creative bent." As a sample the editor selected this poem, "Irving Street," by Cristen H. Jaynes:

The bookstore light
Enters the night street
Like an ambush
And the soldiers
Bleed in
To read about themselves

TN is 20-24 pgs., 7 × 8½, typeset, photocopied and saddle-stapled with card cover, b&w drawings, clip art and computer-generated graphics. They receive more than 30 pieces each month, use approximately 99%. Press run is 250 for 10 subscribers, a few shelf sales. "Most are given away locally." Subscription: $12. **Sample postpaid: $1. Previously published poems and simultaneous submissions OK. "Typewritten copies only. Include phone number and I will confirm receiving your submission." Often comments on rejections. Send SASE for guidelines. Reports "same day with phone number." Pays 2 copies. Rights revert to authors.** The editor says, "If I have the money I will also publish chapbooks. If you have a collection of poems that frightens your mother, confuses your father, speaks from the heart and soul of creative frustration, send it." He adds, "I want to see the stuff written late at night, when no one was looking—poetry, stories, articles, cartoons, drawings, computer art—that had to be let out or kill you—because they will. I don't have rules . . . but simple poems bug me . . . don't send 7,000 lines either. I love to laugh. If you can make me smile, you'll get in each month. Be bold, raw, scabby-kneed and unsure."

2 AM MAGAZINE; 2 AM PUBLICATIONS (IV-Science fiction/fantasy, horror), P.O. Box 6754, Rockford IL 61125-1754, founded 1986, editor Gretta McCombs Anderson, is a quarterly that wants **"fantasy, science fiction, heroic fantasy, horror, weird; any form, any style; preferred length is 1-2 pgs. We want poetry that leaves an after-image in the mind of the reader."** They have published poetry by Mark Rich, G.N. Gabbard, Bruce Boston and Robert Frazier. The editor describes it as 68 pgs., magazine-sized, offset on 60 lb. stock, cover printed on glossy stock, illustrations "by leading fantasy artists" and ads. Circulation 2,000 with 350 subscriptions. Single copy: $4.95; subscription: $19/year. **Sample postpaid: $5.95. Submit no more than 5 poems at a time. "Prefer poems no more than 2 pages in length." Editor "sometimes" comments on rejections. Send SASE for guidelines. Reports in 2 months, 6-12 months to publication. Always sends prepublication galleys. Pays 5¢/line or $1 minimum plus 1 copy, 40% discount for more. Buys one-time rights.** Reviews books of poetry in 250 words, single format. Open to unsolicited reviews. Poets may also send books for review consideration, attn. Irwin Chapman. Gretta M. Anderson advises, "Read widely, be aware of what's already been done. Short poems stand a good chance with us. Looking for mood-generating poetry of a cosmic nature, poems with extended imagery that work on multiple levels. Not interested in self-indulgent poetry."

‡**TYRANNOSAURUS POETRY MACHINE; IMPOVERISHED POETS PRESS (I)**, Box 414, 20384 Fraser Highway, Langley, British Columbia V3A 4G1 Canada, founded 1994, editors Robert Ivins and Jamie Scott, appears quarterly. "*TPM* is a forum for bold new artists and poets. We plan to publish each issue in a different format. Our first issue should be printed on milk cartons. We also plan on publishing an issue on a t-shirt." They want **"poetry that pushes boundaries; nothing flowery or fuzzy; just concrete and asphalt. No sexist, racist or pornographic material."** As each issue will be in a different format, there are no subscription rates. **Query for cost of sample. Previously published poems and simultaneous submissions OK. Often comments on rejections. Send SASE (or SAE and IRC) for guidelines. Reports within 6 months. Usually pays 1 copy. Acquires first North American serial or one-time rights.** Impoverished Poets Press also plans to begin publishing 1 chapbook/year. **Query first with sample poems and cover letter with brief bio and publication credits. Replies to queries in 1-2 months, to mss in up to 6 months. Pays author's copies.** Robert Ivins says, "We are in need of short poems but will publish epics if of outstanding quality. We are seeking poets who are unafraid to overturn a few stones in the search for the grotesque, the beautiful and the sublime."

TYRO PUBLISHING (I, II), (formerly Tyro Writers' Group), 194 Carlbert St., Sault Ste. Marie, Ontario P6A 5E1 Canada, phone (705)253-6402, founded 1984, editor Stan Gordon. They only consider full-length mss for book publication. Published works include: **The Book of Cries** by Bruce Bedell, **On a Mound a Sleeping Leopard** by Anna Livig, and **Insight Into Mind of a Schizophrenic Friend** by Gordon Stone and Joan Neimi. **Query first with at least 6 sample poems. Mss should be in standard format. Send SASE for guidelines and further information. Always sends prepublication galleys.**

‡**UGLY PUBLICATIONS; UGLY REVIEW (I, II)**, P.O. Box 4853, Richmond VA 23220, founded 1992, editors Max and Patrick. The *Ugly Review* is a quarterly tabloid. "We publish enough writing by each writer to express personality and voice. **Rather than publishing 50 poems by 50 poets, we publish 8 or 9 pieces from each writer. We also accept anything that goes on a piece of paper."** They have recently published poetry by Bill Sheilds, Dave McCord and Dave Saulnier. Press run is 5,000, all distributed free. **Sample available for "stamps." Send at least 8 poems. Previously published poems and simultaneous submissions OK. Cover letter required.** Time between acceptance and publication is included in acceptance letter. **Often comments on rejections. Send SASE for guidelines. Reports in 1 month. Pays copies.** "We review mags, chapbooks and books." Open to unsolicited reviews. Poets may also send books for review consideration. Ugly Publications also publishes 2 paperbacks and 5 chapbooks of poetry/year. **Query first with sample poems and cover letter with brief bio and publication credits. Replies to queries in 1 week, to mss in 1 month. Pays author's copies.**

ULTRAMARINE PUBLISHING CO., INC. (II), P.O. Box 303, Hastings-on-Hudson NY 10706, founded 1974, editor C.P. Stephens, who says, "We mostly distribute books for authors who had a title dropped by a major publisher—the author is usually able to purchase copies very cheaply. We use existing copies purchased by the author from the publisher when the title is being dropped." Ultramarine's list includes 250 titles, 90% of them cloth bound, one-third of them science fiction and 10% poetry. **The press pays 10% royalties. "Distributor terms are on a book-by-book basis, but is a rough split." Authors should query before making submissions; queries will be answered in 1 week. Simultaneous submissions OK, but no disks.**

UNDERPASS; UNDERPASS PRESS (II), #574-21, 10405 Jasper Ave., Edmonton, Alberta T5J 3S2 Canada, founded 1986, editors Barry Hammond and Brian Schulze. *Underpass* is a literary annual. The press publishes chapbooks and flat-spined paperbacks of poetry. They want **"contemporary, urban, avant-garde, concrete or discursive prose poems. Any length. No religious or nature poetry."** They have published poetry by Brian Burke, Errol Miller and Sheila E. Murphy. As a sample the editors selected these lines from "Dark Horses" by Stan Rogal:

> *American media continues to love*
> *what it cannot possess*
> *& kill what it cannot love.*
> *Romancing the dark horse, always . . .*

Underpass is digest-sized. Their sixth issue was 80 pgs., but they hope to increase size and continue the flat-spined format. It is offset printed with a laminated card cover using b&w and color graphics inside. "This year we received about two hundred and fifty submissions and only used twenty-six poets." Press run is 100-300. **Sample postpaid: $6.95. No simultaneous submissions or previously published poems. Cover letter required; include one-paragraph bio. Reads submissions January 31 through August 31 only. Editor sometimes comments on rejections. Publishes in late fall. Send SASE for guidelines. Always sends prepublication galleys. Pays $5/poem plus 2 copies. All rights remain with authors.** Barry Hammond says, "We would like to receive more prose poetry."

UNITED METHODIST REPORTER; NATIONAL CHRISTIAN REPORTER; UNITED METHODIST REVIEW; UNITED METHODIST RECORD (IV-Religious), Box 660275, Dallas TX 75266-0275, phone (214)630-6495, founded "about 1840." ***UMR*** is a weekly broadsheet newspaper, circulation 400,000, "aimed at United Methodists primarily, ecumenical slant secondarily." They use at most one poem a week. **The poetry "must make a religious point – United Methodist or ecumenical theology; short and concise; concrete imagery; unobtrusive rhyme preferred; literary quality in freshness and imagery; not trite but easy to understand; short enough to fill 1- to 3-inch spaces. Do not want to see poems by 'my 13-year-old niece,' poems dominated by 'I' or rhyme; poems that are too long, too vague or too general; poems without religious slant or point."** Editor John A. Lovelace says they use about 50 of 1,000 poems received/year. Poems may appear in all publications. **No simultaneous submissions or previously published poems. Send no more than 3-4 poems at a time.** Time to publication can be up to a year. **Editor comments on rejection "if it is promising." Send SASE for guidelines. Pays $2/poem and 1 copy.**

UNITY; DAILY WORD (IV-Religious), Unity School of Christianity, Unity Village MO 64065, founded 1889. "Unity periodicals are devoted to spreading the truth of practical Christianity, the everyday use of Christ's principles. The material used in them is constructive, friendly, unbiased as regards creed or sect, and positive and inspirational in tone. We suggest that prospective contributors study carefully the various publications before submitting material. **Sample copies are sent on request. Complimentary copies are sent to writers on publication. We accept mss only with the understanding that they are original and previously unpublished. Mss should be typewritten in double space. Unity School pays on acceptance, buying first North American serial rights.** ***Unity Magazine*** is a monthly journal that publishes "articles and **poems that give a clear message of Truth and provide practical, positive help in meeting human needs for healing, supply and harmony. Only 1 or 2 poems are published each month. We pay a $30 minimum."** ***Daily Word*** is a "monthly manual of daily studies" which "buys a limited number of short devotional articles and poems. **We pay a $30 minimum for poetry and $30 a page for prose.**

UNMUZZLED OX (IV-Themes, bilingual/foreign language), 105 Hudson St., New York NY 10013 or Box 550, Kingston, Ontario K7L 4W5 Canada, founded 1971, poetry editor Michael Andre, is a tabloid literary biannual. **Each edition is built around a theme or specific project.** The editor says, "The chances of an unsolicited poem being accepted are slight since I always have specific ideas in mind." He is assembling material for issues titled ***Poems to the Tune***, "simply poems to old tunes, a buncha contemporary ***Beggar's Opera***. The other is tentatively called ***The Unmuzzled Ox Book of Erotic Verse***. **Only unpublished work will be considered, but works may be in French as well as English."** Subscription: $20.

URBANUS/RAIZIRR; URBANUS PRESS (III), P.O. Box 192561, San Francisco CA 94119, founded 1987, editors Peter Drizhal and Rose Mok, is a biannual journal of fiction and poetry. **"Seeks post-modernist, experimental and mainstream poetry – with a social slant."** They have recently published poetry by Mark Jarman, Yusef Komunyakaa, Amy Gerstler, Ursula K. LeGuin, Charles Bukowski and Heather McHugh. As a sample the editors selected "Selling My Poems on the Street" by William Joyce:

For the most part my buyers
bought as quietly as I wrote.
They smiled, they paid, they left
with hardly a glance over their
shoulders – the same way I wrote.
It was the noisy ones – the ones
who spouted all sorts of appreciation
but who didn't put money on the table
who are so typical of the people
who fuck up our lives irrevocably.

The digest-sized, 64-page, perfect-bound magazine uses approximately 40 of the 2,000 submissions they receive annually. Circulation is 800. Subscription: $8 ($10 institutions). **Sample postpaid: $5. Reports in 2-8 weeks, 6-12 months till publication. Pays 2 copies.** Poetry published in ***Urbanus*** has been selected for inclusion in **The Best American Poetry 1994.**

Use the General Index to find the page number of a specific publisher. If the publisher you are seeking is not listed, check the " '94-'95 Changes" list at the end of this section.

US1 WORKSHEETS; US1 POETS' COOPERATIVE (II), %Postings, P.O. Box 1, Ringoes NJ 08551-0001, founded 1973, is a literary biannual, 20-25 pgs., 11½ × 17, circulation 500, which uses **high quality poetry and fiction. Sample: $4. "We use a rotating board of editors; it's wisest to query when we're next reading before submitting. A self-addressed, stamped postcard to the secretary will get our next reading period dates."** They have published poetry by Alicia Ostriker, Toi Derricotte, Elizabeth Anne Socolow, Jean Hollander, Grace Cavalieri, Geraldine C. Little and David Keller. **"We read a lot but take very few. Prefer complex, well-written work. Requests for sample copies, subscriptions, queries, information about reading periods and all manuscripts should be addressed to the secretary, % POSTINGS (address at beginning of listing)." Sometimes sends prepublication galleys.**

UTAH STATE UNIVERSITY PRESS (V), Logan UT 84322-7800, phone (801)750-1362, founded 1972, editor John R. Alley, publishes poetry but is **not open for submissions.**

THE VANITAS PRESS (I, IV-Specialized, children), Platslagarevägen 4E1, 22730, Lund, Sweden, founded 1978, publisher (Mr.) March Laumer, who says, "The press is the shoestringyest in existence. We publish to an extremely enthusiastic but equally extremely tiny market. **No royalties can be paid, as we distribute volumes at rock-bottom cost of production/mailing (even then subscribers must pay circa $15 a volume; we just can't ask for more to cover royalties)**. But it is your chance to reach an audience of up to 2,000 readers. **Currently we issue only 'latter-day novels' of the 'Oz' saga.** Please read the Oz books in your local public library, then send us short stories, outlines for novels, and/or Oz-oriented art; you're virtually certain to be published if material is promising at all." As a sample he selected these lines from **Charmed Gardens of Oz**:

Well said, indeed,
And when you feed
On things that bleed
I hope you'll heed
What Dot's decreed:
It's only when you talk of flesh that's edible
That you can mention 'meat' and still be credible!

VEGETARIAN JOURNAL; THE VEGETARIAN RESOURCE GROUP (IV-Specialized, children/teens), P.O. Box 1463, Baltimore MD 21203, founded 1982. The Vegetarian Resource Group is a small press publisher of nonfiction, sometimes incorporating poetry. *VJ* is a bimonthly, 36 pgs., 8½ × 11, saddle-stapled and professionally printed with glossy card cover. Circulation is 20,000. **Sample: $3.** The Vegetarian Resource Group offers an annual contest for ages 18 and under, $50 savings bond in 3 age categories for the best contribution on any aspect of vegetarianism. "Most entries are essay, but we would accept poetry with enthusiasm." Deadline: May 1 postmark. Send SASE for details.

VEHICULE PRESS; SIGNAL EDITIONS (V, IV-Regional), Box 125 Station Place du Parc, Montreal, Quebec H2W 2M9 Canada, phone (514)844-6073, fax (514)844-7543, poetry editor Michael Harris, publisher Simon Dardick, is a "literary press with poetry series, Signal Editions, **publishing the work of Canadian poets only.**" They publish flat-spined paperbacks and hardbacks. Among the poets recently published are Peter Dale Scott, Don Coles, David Solway, Susan Glickman and Jan Conn. As a sample they selected these lines by Gérald Godin:

"What, you've forgotten my telephone number?"
"Listen, old friend, I think you know
they removed a tumour from my brain
as big as a mandarine orange
and I'm afraid
your telephone number was in it . . . "

They publish Canadian poetry which is **"first-rate, original, content-conscious." However, they are currently not accepting poetry submissions. "Booked until 1997."**

VERANDAH (II), c/o TAS, Deakin University, Toorak Campus, 336 Glenterrie Rd., Malvern, Victoria, Australia 3144, founded 1986. ***Verandah* seeks poetry of a "high literary standard."** They have published poetry by Lisa Dionofrio, Peter Bakowski, Adrian D'Ambra and Javant Biarujia. As a sample, here is a haiku by Duncan Richardson:

Along the cream
beach they came four pelicans
playing soft biplanes.

It is flat-spined with full-color glossy card cover, professionally printed on glossy stock, 90 pgs. **Sample postpaid: A$10.50. Annual deadline: May 31. Pays A$5-10 plus 2 copies. Buys first Australian publishing rights.**

VERSE (III), English Dept., College of William and Mary, P.O. Box 8795, Williamsburg VA 23187-8795, founded 1984, editors Henry Hart, Robert Crawford and David Kinloch, is "a poetry journal which also publishes interviews with poets, articles about poetry and book reviews." They **want "no specific kind; we only look for high quality poetry."** They have published poetry by A.R. Ammons, James Merrill, James Dickey, Galway Kinnell, Richard Kenney, John Hollander, Charles Wright, Robert Pinsky, Charles Simic and Wendell Berry. ***Verse*** is published 3 times/year. It is digest-sized, 90 pgs., saddle-stapled with card cover, using small type, professionally printed. They accept about 100 of 3,000 poems received. Press run is 700 for 600 subscribers of which 150 are libraries, 100 shelf sales. Subscription: $15 for individuals, $21 for institutions. **Sample postpaid: $5. Simultaneous submissions OK. Reports in 2 months, usually 4-5 months to publication. Sometimes sends prepublication galleys. Pays 2 copies.** Open to unsolicited reviews. Poets may also send books for review consideration. Poetry published in this journal has appeared in **The Best American Poetry 1992**. In addition, ***Verse*** itself ranked #7 in the "Open Markets" category of the latest ***Writer's Digest*** Poetry 60 list. This category ranks those publications most open to both free and formal verse. The editor says, "We would like to receive more narrative poetry."

VERVE (II, IV-Themes), P.O. Box 3205, Simi Valley CA 93093, founded 1989, editor/publisher Ron Reichick, editor Marilyn Hochheiser, associate editors Virginia Anderson and Margie Davidson, is now published twice a year and is **"open to contemporary poetry of any form which fits the theme of the issue; we look for fresh metaphor, unique ideas and language and imagery that informs."** They have recently published poetry by Marge Piercy, Carol Muske, Denise Levertov, Alberto Rios and Quincy Troupe. As a sample the editors selected these lines from "House Ghosts" by Phyllis Janowitz:

What dissonant rules, sent from Kyoto
andante cantabile, *am I to follow,*
which footpath of particular harmony
now that summer is here again. Oh, oh, oh!
A troubled bird whistles outside my window.

Verve is digest-sized, 40 pgs., saddle-stitched, using bios of each contributor. Press run is 750 for 100 subscribers of which 3 are libraries. **Sample postpaid: $3.50. Submit up to 5 poems, 2 pgs. maximum/poem; "36 lines or less has best chance." Simultaneous submissions, if noted, OK. Publishes theme issues. Send SASE for guidelines and upcoming themes. Sometimes sends prepublication galleys. Pays 1 copy. Acquires first rights.** Staff reviews books of poetry in 250 words, single format. Send books for review consideration. They also sponsor 2 annual contests, each having prizes of $100, $50 and $25. Entry fee: $2/poem. The editor advises, "Read a copy of ***Verve*** before you submit. Read good contemporary poetry—then write. Listen to criticism, but follow your instinct *and* the poem. *Then*—keep submitting."

VIET NAM GENERATION; BURNING CITIES PRESS (II, IV-Themes), 18 Center Rd., Woodbridge CT 06525, phone (203)387-6882, fax (203)389-6104, e-mail kalital@minerva.cis.yale.edu, founded 1988, editor Kali Tal, is a quarterly that publishes "the best current fiction, poetry and nonfiction dealing with the Viet Nam War generation." **Poetry should deal with issues of interest to the Viet Nam War generation. "No POW/MIA poems, unless written by POWs. No racist or sexist poetry."** They have published poetry by W.D. Ehrhart, Maggie Jaffe, Gerald McCarthy and Jon Forrest Glade. As a sample the editor selected "Ralphie" by Leroy Quintana:

Ralphie was signed up at seventeen
by a fast-talking sergeant.
Instead of the world got Georgia,
"Airborne" tattooed on his scrawny biceps,
the clap, and caught breaking into footlockers,
another discharge, dishonorable.

The editor says it is 120-220 pgs., $8\frac{1}{2} \times 11$, perfect-bound, with photos and graphics, no ads. They receive 200-300 submissions a year, accept about 40. Press run is 1,000 for 400 subscribers of which 200 are libraries. Subscription: $40. **Sample postpaid: $10 for single issues, $20 for double. Previously published poems OK; no simultaneous submissions. Often comments on rejections. Reports within 3-4 months. Pays 2 copies. Acquires "reprint rights for our own publications."** The Burning Cities Poetry Series publishes 6 paperbacks and **4 chapbooks/year. Query first with sample poems and a cover letter with brief bio and publication credits. Replies to queries and submitted mss in 6-8 weeks. Pays 10% of press run. Sample book or chapbook: $10.**

‡VIGIL; AMMONITE; VIGIL PUBLICATIONS (II), 12 Priory Mead, Bruton, Somerset BA10 ODZ England, founded 1979, poetry editor John Howard Greaves. ***Vigil*** appears 3 times a year. They want **"poetry with a high level of emotional force or intensity of observation. Poems should normally be no longer than 35 lines. Color, imagery and appeal to the senses should be important features. No whining self-indulgent, neurotic soul-baring poetry."** They have recently published poetry by Claudette Bass,

Bettie Anne Doebler, Joseph Farley, Mario Petrucci, Patrick Cauchi and Tom Farbman. As a sample we selected the poem "Night's Colours" by Hilary Mellon:

You make me dress
and leave this naked darkness
before green shades of day
can wake your fears

though knowing that for you
I'll wear night's colours
my stockings shiny as tears

The digest-sized magazine is 40 pgs., saddle-stapled, photoreduced typescript, with colored matte card cover. They accept about 60 of 200 submissions received. Press run is 250 for 85 subscriptions of which 6 are libraries. Subscription: £4.50. **Sample postpaid: £2. Submit no more than 6 poems at a time. Sometimes sends prepublication galleys. Pays 2 copies. Editor sometimes comments on rejections.** *Ammonite* appears twice a year with **"myth, image and word towards the secondary millenium . . . a seedbed of mythology for our future, potently embryonic."** Single copy: £1.75 (UK), £2.50 (overseas); subscription: £3.50 (UK), £5 (overseas). **Query regarding book publication by Vigil Publications.** The editor offers "appraisal" for £7.50 for a sample of a maximum of 12 poems.

VIKING PENGUIN, 375 Hudson St., New York NY 10014. Prefers not to share information.

THE VILLAGER (II), Dept. PM, 135 Midland Ave., Bronxville NY 10708-1800, phone (914)337-3252, founded 1928, editor Amy Murphy, poetry editor M. Josephine Colville, a publication of the Bronxville Women's Club for club members and families, professional people and advertisers, circulation 750, in 9 monthly issues, October through June. **Sample postpaid: $1.25. They use one page or more of poetry/issue, prefer poems less than 20 lines, "in good taste only," seasonal (Thanksgiving, Christmas, Easter) 3 months in advance. SASE required. Pays 2 copies. They copyright material but will release it to author on request.**

THE VINCENT BROTHERS REVIEW (II, IV-Themes), 4566 Northern Circle, Riverside OH 45424-5733, founded 1988, editor Kimberly A. Willardson, is a journal appearing 3 times a year. **"We look for well-crafted, thoughtful poems that shoot bolts of electricity into the reader's mind, stimulating a powerful response. We also welcome light verse and are thrilled by unusual, innovative themes/styles. We do not accept previously published poems, simultaneous submissions or any type of bigoted propaganda. Sloppy mss containing typos and/or unintentional misspellings are automatically rejected.** ***TVBR*** publishes 2 theme issues/year—poets should send us a SASE to receive details about our upcoming themes." They have recently published poetry by G.O. Clark, Michelle Perez and Matthew J. Spireng. As a sample the editor selected these lines from "The Bus to Opacity" by Richard McNally:

we come to realize our destinations—
triple-locked boxes filled with chilled
animal remains, grossly indecent VISA bills,
bleeding TVs beaming political piffle
(property never even mentioned),
couches that eat more of us each night

TVBR is digest-sized, 60-80 pgs., saddle-stapled, professionally printed, with matte card cover. Press run is 350. "We have 100 subscribers, 10 of which are libraries." Subscription: $12. **Sample postpaid: $4.50. Submit no more than 6 poems at a time, name and address on each page. Cover letter preferred; include recent publication credits and note "where author read or heard about *TVBR*. We do not read in December." Editor "often" comments on rejections. Send SASE for guidelines. Reports in 6-8 months (after readings by editor and 2 associate editors). Always sends prepublication galleys. Pays 2 copies for poems printed inside the journal. Pays $5 for each poem printed on "Page Left" (the back page). "For 'Page Left,' we look for the unusual—concrete poems, wordplay, avant-garde pieces, etc." Acquires one-time rights.** Reviews books of poetry in 3,500 words maximum, single or multi-book format. Open to unsolicited reviews. Poets may also send books for review consideration. The editor advises, "*Don't* send your poetry to a magazine you haven't read. Subscribe to the little magazines you respect—they contain the work of your peers and competitors. Proofread your poetry carefully and read it aloud before sending it out."

‡VIOLETTA BOOKS (I, IV-Anthologies), P.O. Box 15191, Springfield MA 01115, founded 1983, editor Kathleen Gilbert, seeks poems of a spiritual, not religious, nature for an anthology to be published in mid to late 1995. The editor notes, "I generally look for understandable writing, unordinary insights into daily life and mystical feeling rising from everyday experiences. In this anthology, especially, I seek **poems about such things as guardian angels, insights from vivid dreams and a feeling of ap-**

proaching the Deity or universal mind, all in a positive vein." She does not want poetry that is "cutely sentimental, trite, tightly rhymed or overly negative." The editor has recently published poetry by Teresa Burleson, Janice H. Brazil and Elaine Thomas. As a sample she selected these lines from "The Garden of Night" by Laurie Lessen:

Luminous and radiant
The moonbeams warm our desperate
Souls, white stairways
To our vast and blinding
Dreams of other worlds.

The anthology is digest-sized, 35-40 pgs., offset from typescript, with matte card cover. **Sample postpaid: $3.50. (Make checks payable to Kathleen Gilbert.) Submit poems of up to 40 lines. Reading fee: $1/submission (unlimited number of poems accepted). Send 1 copy of each poem with name and address. Previously published poems OK, as long as poet holds rights. Pays 1 copy/each poem used; "additional copies will be available for purchase." Acquires one-time rights.** Kathleen Gilbert says, "My purpose in publishing poetry is to encourage poets of all ability levels to write accessible and yet individualistic poetry. I also offer how-to books on poetry marketing and independent publishing. Send SASE for details."

VIRGIN MEAT (IV-Horror), 2325 West Ave. K-15, Lancaster CA 93536, phone (805)722-1758, founded 1986, editor Steve Blum, appears irregularly with fiction, poetry and art. "Fiction is non-violent gothic horror. Subjects range from vampires and ghosts to magic and the occult. **Poetry: Similar subjects, short, emotionally dark and depressing. No rhyming poetry."** The editor describes it as digest-sized. Press run is 300. **Sample postpaid: $2 or $7/4 issues. "No longer reading anything by anyone who has not sent a SASE for guidelines and/or purchased a recent sample copy." Send no less than 4 poems at a time. Simultaneous submissions and previously published poems OK. Reports in 2 months. Pays 1 copy for each poem printed.** Reviews books of poetry "only if it has a cover price."

THE VIRGINIA QUARTERLY REVIEW (III), 1 West Range, Charlottesville VA 22903, founded 1925, is one of the oldest and most distinguished literary journals in the country. **It uses about 15 pgs. of poetry in each issue, no length or subject restrictions.** Recent issues largely include lyric and narrative free verse, most of which features a strong message or powerful voice. The review is 220 pgs., digest-sized, flat-spined, circulation 4,000. **Pays $1/line.** Poetry published here has been included in **The Best American Poetry 1993.**

VIRTUE: THE CHRISTIAN MAGAZINE FOR WOMEN (IV-Religious), P.O. Box 850, Sisters OR 97759-0850, founded 1978, editor Marlee Alex, is a slick magazine, appearing 6 times a year, which **"encourages and integrates biblical truth with daily living." As for poetry, they look for "rhythmic control and metric effects, whether free or patterned stanzas; use of simile and metaphor; sensory perceptions, aptly recorded; and implicit rather than explicit spiritual tone."** As a sample the editor selected these lines from "Bending" by Barbara Seaman:

Down on my knees again, Lord
and undignified as ever,
(how to mop mud with grace?)
attempting to confine the exuberance
of yesterday's rain to the kitchen only . . .

Virtue is magazine-sized, 80 pgs., saddle-stapled, with full-color pages inside as well as on its paper cover. Press run is 150,000. Single copy: $2.95; subscription: $16.95. **Sample postpaid: $3. Submit "no more than 3 poems, each on separate sheet, typewritten; notify if simultaneous submission." Send SASE for guidelines. Reports in 6-8 weeks, time to publication 3-9 months. Pays $20-40/poem and 1 copy. Buys first rights.**

VIVO (II), 1195 Green St., San Francisco CA 94109, phone (415)885-5695, founded 1991, editor/publisher Carolyn Miller, is "an eclectic magazine of poetry, fiction, essays and art that combines humor and serious work," appearing irregularly, about once a year. **"We are open to almost any kind of poetry except the extremes of traditional and experimental work. We like poems that are fresh and alive and that show a love of language. We are interested in both unpublished and published poets." They do not want to see "poems that don't care about either depth of meaning or love of craft."** As a sample the editor selected these lines from "The Origin of Music" by Melissa Kwasny:

So much time,
there must be another life
being lived here,
off the deerless trails,
the cluttered, lower
paths of our narration.

VIVO is 16 pgs., 11×17, printed web offset and unbound, with 2-color cover and centerfold, graphics and ads. You want to be seen in a cafe reading this artsy tabloid. Poetry competes with fiction and prose, but it gets the center spread and features all styles. Press run is 1,400 for 100 subscribers, 450 shelf sales. Single copy: $3; subscription: $8 for 2 issues. **Sample postpaid: $4. Previously published poems and simultaneous submissions OK, but not preferred.** Time between acceptance and publication is 12-18 months. **Seldom comments on rejections. Send SASE for guidelines. Reports in 6 weeks to 3 months. Sends prepublication computer printouts. Pays 2 copies. Rights revert to author on publication.** Reviews books of poetry. Open to unsolicited reviews. Poets may also send books for review consideration. Carolyn Miller says, "The true goal is to live a creative life, to respond to the world as a poet. If you do this honestly and faithfully, and want your poems to have a larger life, keep sending them out, for their sake, not your own."

VOICES INTERNATIONAL (II), 1115 Gillette Dr., Little Rock AR 72207, editor Clovita Rice, is a quarterly poetry journal. **"We look for poetry with a new focus, memorable detail and phrasing, and significant and haunting statement climax, all of which impel the reader to reread the poem and return to it for future pleasure and reference."** As a sample the editor selected these lines from "The Crack Lines" by Marian W. Hurst:

I dreamt you sent me roses.
Three apricot-colored roses
In a blue vase.

On the kitchen table I found
Three withered, moldy apricots
In a delft bowl . . .

It is 32-40 pgs., 6×9, saddle-stapled, professionally printed with b&w matte card cover. Subscription: $10/year. **Sample postpaid (always a back issue): $2. Prefers free verse but accepts high quality traditional. Limit submissions to batches of 5, double-spaced, 3-40 lines (will consider longer if good). Cover letter preferred; include personal data.** Publishes an average of 18 months after acceptance. **Send SASE for guidelines. Pays copies.** The editor says, "Too many poets submit poetry without studying a copy to become familiar with what we are publishing. Our guidelines help poets polish their poems before submission."

VOICES ISRAEL (I, IV-Anthology); REUBEN ROSE POETRY COMPETITION (I); MONTHLY POET'S VOICE (IV-Members), P.O. Box 5780, 46157 Herzlia Israel, founded 1972, ***Voices Israel*** editor Mark L. Levinson, with an editorial board of 7, is an annual anthology of poetry in English coming from all over the world. **You have to buy a copy to see your work in print. Submit all kinds of poetry (up to 4 poems), each no longer than 40 lines, in seven copies.** They have published poetry by Yehuda Amichai, Eugene Dubnov, Alan Sillitoe and Gad Yaacobi. As a sample the editor selected these lines from "What Sort of Beauty Was It?" by Avital Talmor:

But what sort of beauty
that could burn away his one and only dream
until, as if to make sure he wasn't dreaming,
he reached to touch her coal black hair as soft as air,
her eyes so clear like when the day was severed from the night.

The annual ***Voices Israel*** is 6¼×8, offset from laser output on ordinary paper, approximately 121 pgs., flat-spined with varying cover. Circulation 350. Subscription: $13.50. **Sample back copy postpaid: $10. Contributor's copy: $13.50 airmail. Cover letter with brief biographical details required with submissions. Deadline end of February each year; reports in fall. Acquires first publication rights.** Sponsors the annual Reuben Rose Poetry Competition. Send poems of up to 40 lines each, plus $2/poem to P.O. Box 236, Kiriat Ata, Israel. Poet's name and address should be on a separate sheet with titles of poems. ***The Monthly Poet's Voice***, a broadside edited by Ezra Ben-Meir, **is sent only to members of the Voices Group of Poets in English.** The ***Voices Israel*** editor advises, "Never let the reader guess what your next two or three words will be. We would like to see more humorous but well constructed poetry."

‡VOL. NO. MAGAZINE (II, IV-Themes), 24721 Newhall Ave., Newhall CA 91321, phone (805)254-0851, founded 1983, poetry editors Richard Weekley, Jerry Danielsen, Tina Landrum and Don McLeod. "***Vol. No.*** publishes lively and concise works. Vivid connections. **Each issue has a theme. Send SASE for details. No trivial, clichéd or unthoughtout work. Work that penetrates the ozone within. One-page poems have the best chance.**" They have published poetry by Octavio Paz, Anne Marple, Jane Hirshfield and Julian Pulley. The editors selected these sample lines by William Stafford:

We stand for hours where sunlight tells us
it forgives. A golden shaft pours down.
The air waits. A cardinal sings and sings.
We stand for hours.

Vol. No. is a digest-sized, saddle-stapled, 32-page annual, circulation 300. They receive about 600 unsolicited submissions of poetry/year, use 60, have a 6-month backlog. Subscription: $10 (2 issues). **Sample postpaid: $3. Submit limit of 6 poems. Simultaneous submissions OK. Reports in 1-5 months. Pays 2 copies.**

W.I.M. PUBLICATIONS (WOMAN IN THE MOON) (IV-Gay/lesbian, women/feminism), Dept. PM, P.O. Box 2087, Cupertino CA 95015-2087, phone (408)253-3329, founded 1979, poetry editor SDiane Bogus, who says, "We are a small press with trade press ambitions. We publish poetry, business and writing reference books. We generally run 250-1,000 per press run and **give the author half or a percentage of the books. We pay royalties to our established authors. We prefer a query and a modest track record."** She wants poetry by **"gay, black, women, prison poets, enlightened others—contemporary narrative or lyric work, free verse OK, but not too experimental for cognition. We prefer poems to be a page or less if not part of long narrative. No obviously self-indulgent exercises in the psychology of the poet. No sexual abuse themes. No gross sexual references. No hate poems." Send 2 first-class stamps for guidelines/catalog.** In addition to her own work, she has published poetry by Adele Sebastian. As a sample she selected these lines from "His Life" in **The Book of Lives** by Sherrylynn Posey:

> *I had 4 maybe 5 lovers*
> *in my life*
> *one of them*
> *lied to me*

SDiane Bogus publishes 2-4 chapbooks and flat-spined paperbacks a year each averaging 40-100 pages. **Submit 6 sample poems. Include cover letter with statement of "vision and poetics, theme selection of the work, poetic mentors, track record and $7 reading fee. New poets must take poetry test ($10 plus free critique). Submit between January 1 and April 30 each year. We acknowledge submissions upon receipt. We report at end of reading season, July through August 7. Simultaneous submissions and previously published poems OK. Authors are asked to assist in promo and sales by providing list of prospective readers and promotional photos. To established authors we pay 5-10% royalties after costs; others half press run in copies. We may take advanced orders; no subsidy. We will accept subscriptions for a book in production at retail price. We fill orders author has provided and others our promo has prompted."** They sponsor 3 poetry contests/year: The Woman in the Moon Poetry Prize (January 1 through May 31), Pat Parker Memorial Poetry Award (March 1 through May 31) and the Poetry Lottery (one poet wins every 3 months; submissions are good for two chances). Write for guidelines. W.I.M. also offers a self-publishing and consultation criticism service for a fee. Bogus says, "W.I.M. promotes readings for its poets and encourages each poet who submits with a personal letter which discusses her or his strengths and weaknesses. Often we allow repeat submissions. Also, we welcome a tape of the poet reading from the submitted manuscript."

WAKE FOREST UNIVERSITY PRESS (IV-Bilingual/foreign language, ethnic/nationality), P.O. Box 7333, Winston-Salem NC 27109, phone (910)759-5448, founded 1976, director and poetry editor Dillon Johnston. **"We publish only poetry from Ireland and bilingual editions of French poetry in translation. I am able to consider only poetry written by Irish poets or translations of contemporary French poetry. I must return, unread, poetry from American poets."** They have recently published poetry by John Montague, Derek Mahon, Richard Murphy, Michael Longley, Paul Muldoon, Thomas Kinsella, Eilean N. Chuilleanain, Ciaran Carson and Nuala Ni Dhumhnaill. **Query with 4-5 samples and cover letter. No simultaneous submissions. Replies to queries in 1-2 weeks, to submissions (if invited) in 2-3 months. Sometimes sends prepublication galleys. Publishes on 10% royalty contract with $500 advance, 6-8 author's copies. Buys North American or US rights.** They say, "Because our press is so circumscribed, we get few direct submissions from Ireland. Our main problem, however, is receiving submissions from American poets, whom we do not publish because of our very limited focus here. I would advise American poets to read listings carefully so they do not misdirect to presses such as ours work that they, and I, value."

WARTHOG PRESS (II), 29 S. Valley Rd., West Orange NJ 07052, phone (201)731-9269, founded 1979, poetry editor Patricia Fillingham, publishes books of poetry **"that are understandable, poetic."** They have published poetry by Barbara A. Holland, Penny Harter and Marta Fenyves. **Query with 5 samples, cover letter "saying what the author is looking for" and SASE. Simultaneous submissions OK. Ms should be "readable." Comments on rejections, "if asked for. People really don't want criticism." Pays copies, but "I would like to get my costs back."** Patricia Fillingham feels, "The best way to sell poetry still seems to be from poet to listener."

‡WASCANA REVIEW (II), Dept. of English, University of Regina, Regina, Saskatchewan S4S 0A2 Canada, phone (306)585-4311, fax (306)585-4827, founded 1966, editor Kathleen Wall, appears twice a year publishing contemporary poetry and short fiction along with critical articles on modern and post-modern literature. **"We look for high-quality literary poetry of all forms, including translations.**

No haiku or doggerel. No long poems. No concrete poetry." They have recently published poetry by Stephen Heighton, Robert Cooperman, Cornelia Hoogland and Eugene Dubnov. The editor says ***WR*** is a trade-sized paperback, 75-100 pgs., no art/graphics, no ads. They receive about 200-300 submissions a year, accept under 10%. Press run is 400 for 192 subscribers of which 134 are libraries, 100 shelf sales. Subscription: $7/year, $8 outside Canada. **Sample postpaid: $4. No previously published poems or simultaneous submissions. Cover letter required. SASE or SAE and IRCs necessary for return of mss. "Poems are read by at least two individuals who make comments and/or recommendations. Poetry editor chooses poems based on these comments." Often comments on rejections. Reports within 6 months. Pays $10/page and 2 copies. Buys all rights; does not return them.** Reviews books of poetry in both single and multi-book format. The editor says, "***WR*** will be featuring special issues from time to time. Poets should watch for news of these in upcoming editions."

WASHINGTON REVIEW; FRIENDS OF THE WASHINGTON REVIEW OF THE ARTS, INC. (II), P.O. Box 50132, Washington DC 20091-0132, phone (202)638-0515, founded 1974, literary editor Joe Ross, is a bimonthly journal of arts and literature published by the Friends of the Washington Review of the Arts, Inc., a nonprofit, tax-exempt educational organization. ***WR*** is tabloid-sized, using 2 of the large pgs. per issue for poetry, saddle-stapled on high-quality newsprint, circulation 2,000 with 700 subscriptions of which 10 are libraries. **They publish local Washington metropolitan area poets as well as poets from across the US and abroad. "We have eclectic tastes but lean with more favor toward experimental work." Sample postpaid: $2.50. Cover letter with brief bio required with submissions. Pays 5 copies.** Reviews books of poetry in 1,000-1,500 words, single format—multi-book "on occasion." Open to unsolicited reviews. Poets may also send books for review consideration.

WASHINGTON WRITERS' PUBLISHING HOUSE (IV-Regional), P.O. Box 15271, Washington DC 20003, phone (202)543-1905, founded 1975. An editorial board is elected annually from the collective. "We are a poetry publishing collective that publishes outstanding poetry collections in flat-spined paperbacks by **individual authors living in the greater Washington, DC area (60-mile radius, excluding Baltimore) on the basis of competitions held once a year."** They have published poetry by Myra Sklarew, Ann Darr, Barbara Lefcowitz, Maxine Clair, Ann Knox, Nan Fry and Naomi Thiers. The editors chose this sample from "The Kidnapping of Science" in **From the Red Eye of Jupiter** by Patricia Garfinkel:

> *Conception had been a quiet event, not*
> *the harsh strike of steel to flint,*
> *but an easing into fertile corners,*
> *patient as bacteria for the right conditions.*

Submit 50-60 pgs. with SASE only between July 1 and September 30. $5 reading fee. Pays copies. Poets become working members of the collective. "Interested poets may write for a brochure of published poets and sheet of guidelines."

WATER MARK PRESS (V), 138 Duane St., New York NY 10013, founded 1978, editor Coco Gordon, proposes "to publish regardless of form in archival editions with handmade paper and hand done elements in sewn, bound books, broadsides, chapbooks and artworks. **I use only avant-garde material." Currently they do not accept any unsolicited poetry.** They have published poetry by Barbara Roux and Alison Knowles. The editor selected this sample from "After Eden" by Michael Blumenthal:

> *Once again the invasion of purpose*
> *into gesture: the stem towards the vase,*
> *the hands towards the dreaded morning music*
> *of predictability, Indian paintbrush fades*

That's from a collection of his poetry, **Sympathetic Magic**, published in 1980, 96 pgs., flat-spined, with art by Theo Fried, printed on archival, matte card cover with colored art, $9. **Note: Please do not confuse Water Mark Press with the imprint Watermark Press, used by other businesses.**

WATERWAYS: POETRY IN THE MAINSTREAM; TEN PENNY PLAYERS; BARD PRESS (I, IV-Themes, children/teen/young adult, anthologies), 393 St. Paul's Ave., Staten Island NY 10304, founded 1977, poetry editors Barbara Fisher and Richard Spiegel, "publishes **poetry by adult poets in a magazine that is published 11 times a year. We do theme issues** and are trying to increase an audience for poetry and the printed and performed word. The project produces performance readings in public spaces and is in residence year round at our local library with workshops and readings. We publish the magazine, ***Waterways***; anthologies and chapbooks. **We are not fond of haiku or rhyming poetry; never use material of an explicit sexual nature.** We are open to reading material from people we have never published, writing in traditional and experimental poetry forms. While we do 'themes,' sometimes an idea for a future magazine is inspired by a submission so we try to remain open to poets' inspirations. Poets should be guided however by the fact that we are children's and animal rights advocates and are a NYC press." They have published poetry by Arthur Knight and Kit Knight. As a sample, the editors chose these lines from "The Way of Art" by Albert Huffstickler:

It seems to me that,
paralleling the paths of action, devotion, etc.,
there is a path called Art
and that the sages of the East would have recognized
Faulkner, Edward Hopper, Beethoven, William Carlos Williams,
and addressed them as equals.

Waterways is published in a 40-page, 4¼×7 format, saddle-stapled, photocopied from various type styles, using b&w drawings, matte card cover. They use 60% of poems submitted. Circulation 150 with 58 subscriptions of which 12 are libraries. Subscription: $20. **Sample postpaid: $2.60. Submit less than 10 poems for first submission. Simultaneous submissions OK. Send SASE for guidelines for approaching themes.** "Since we've taken the time to be very specific in our response, writers should take seriously our comments and not waste their emotional energy and our time sending material that isn't within our area of interest. Sending for our theme sheet and for a sample issue and then objectively thinking about the writer's own work is practical and wise. Without meaning to sound 'precious' or unfriendly, the writer should understand that small press publishers doing limited editions and all production work in house are working from their personal artistic vision and know exactly what notes will harmonize, effectively counterpoint and meld. Many excellent poems are sent back to the writers by *Waterways* because they don't relate to what we are trying to create in a given month or months. Some poets get printed regularly in *Waterways*; others will probably never be published by us, not because the poet doesn't write well (although that too is sometimes the case) but only because we are artists with opinions and we exercise them in building each issue. Manuscripts that arrive without a return envelope are not sent back." **Reports in less than a month. Pays 1 copy. Acquires one-time publication rights. Editors sometimes comment on rejections.** They hold contests for children only. **Chapbooks published by Ten Penny Players are "by children and young adults only—and not by submission; they come through our workshops in the library and schools. Adult poets are published by us through our Bard Press imprint, by invitation only. Books evolve from the relationship we develop with writers who we publish in *Waterways* and whom we would like to give more exposure."** The editors advise, "We suggest that poets attend book fairs. It's a fast way to find out what we are all publishing."

WAYNE LITERARY REVIEW (II), Dept. of English, Wayne State University, 51 W. Warren, Detroit MI 48202, faculty consultant M.L. Liebler. Appears twice a year using **any kind of poetry except "inspirational and light verse. Footnotes OK. Some preference given to experimental writing and the small personal voice."** They have recently published poetry, prose and "sudden fictions" by Ed Sanders, John Donlan, Dennis Teichman, Faye Kicknosway, Barbara Henning, Andrei Codrescu, Bob Hicok, Kofi Natambu, Lolita Hernandez and many others. As a sample the editors selected these lines by Miriam Jones:

i want a cigarette   want to talk
the way i think
and have you get it
handfuls of crayons then the walls
out into the street   all the wax
this fly motions with its
wings,
tries to tell you why

WLR is published in a flat-spined, 5½×8½ format of about 60 pgs. and is distributed throughout the Detroit/Ann Arbor area free of cost. **Sample postpaid: $2 (checks payable to WSU Dept. of English). Submit 3-5 poems, no more than 6 pgs. in all. Publishes theme issues. Send SASE for upcoming themes. Reports in 3 weeks to 3 months. Pays 1 copy and "eternal gratitude."** The editor says, "We always like to see a fresh perspective, new ideas, whether these are in form or content. We do receive a high percentage of traditional verse, but have no qualms about accepting the best examples of this form."

‡WAYNE STATE UNIVERSITY PRESS (V), 5959 Woodward Ave., Detroit MI 48202, phone (313)577-4606, fax (313)577-6131, founded 1941, director Arthur B. Evans, publishes 1 paperback book of poetry/year. They have recently published poetry by Ruth Whitman and Jim Daniels. **However, they are currently not accepting unsolicited submissions. Query first with sample poems and cover letter with brief bio and publication credits. Previously published poems OK; no simultaneous submissions.** They currently have a 2- to 3-year backlog. **"Two peer reviews are required. If favorable, the project is recommended to an edit board, which must approve all books published." Seldom comments on rejections. Replies to queries in 1 week, to mss (if invited) in 2 months. Pays 6-10% royalties and 6 author's copies.**

WEBSTER REVIEW (II, IV-Translations), English Dept., St. Louis Community College—Meramec, 11333 Big Bend Rd., St. Louis MO 63122, founded 1974, poetry editors Robert Boyd and Greg Marshall, is a literary annual. They want **"no beginners. We are especially interested in translations of foreign contemporary poetry."** They have published poetry by Georgi Belev, Antony Oldknow, Bruce Bond, Jane Schapiro and Ernest Kroll. As a sample the editor selected these lines from "That Day I Died" by James Finnegan:

This is my story of how I died and didn't.
My body paralyzed suddenly
while swimming in the Black River,
you can find it on any map of Missouri,
I sank on my back to the riverbed. Eyes open
awash with all of the world above and around me, . . .

Webster Review is 128 pgs., digest-sized, flat-spined, professionally printed with glossy card cover. They receive about 1,500 poems/year, use 90. Press run is 1,000 with 500 subscribers of which 200 are libraries. Single copy/subscription: $5. **Sample free for SASE. Editors comment on rejections "if time permits." Reports "within a month, usually." Contributors receive 2 copies.**

WELTER (I, II), English Dept., University of Baltimore, 1420 N. Charles St., Baltimore MD 21201, founded 1963, is a literary annual **"extremely interested in beginners and lesser known writers.** Let us know if you're a student." It is flat-spined, digest-sized. Press run is 500. **Sample postpaid: $2. Submit 3-5 poems no more than 30 lines each. Reads submissions September through January only; makes decisions in February through March. Send SASE for guidelines. Pays 2 copies. Acquires first-time rights.**

THE WESLEYAN ADVOCATE (IV-Religious), P.O. Box 50434, Indianapolis IN 46250-0434, phone (317)595-4156, founded 1843, contact Jerry Bricheisen, is a monthly magazine using **"short religious poetry only; no long free verse or secular."** The editor describes it as 36 pgs., magazine-sized, offset, saddle-stapled, with 4-color cover. They use 10-15% of 100-200 poems received/year. Press run is 20,000 with "some" subscriptions of which 50 are libraries, no shelf sales (so it must be distributed free). Subscription: $12.50. **Sample: $2. Reports in 2 weeks. Pays $5-10 plus 4 copies on request. Buys first and/or one-time rights.**

WESLEYAN UNIVERSITY PRESS (III), 110 Mt. Vernon, Middletown CT 06459, phone (203)344-7918, founded 1957, editor Susanna Tammenin, is one of the major publishers of poetry in the nation. They publish 4-6 titles/year. They have published poetry by James Dickey, Joy Harjo, James Tate and Yusef Komunyakaa. **Send query and SASE. Considers simultaneous submissions. Responds to queries in 6-8 weeks, to mss in 2-4 months. Send SASE for guidelines. Pays royalties plus 10 copies.** Poetry publications from Wesleyan tend to get widely (and respectfully) reviewed.

WEST ANGLIA PUBLICATIONS (III), P.O. Box 2683, La Jolla CA 92038, phone (619)453-0706, founded 1982 by editor Helynn Hoffa, is a publishing company that **assumes the cost of putting out a book and pays author in royalties or in books. Author retains rights.** They have published poetry by Wilma Lusk, John Theobald and Gary Morgan, among others. As a sample the editor chose lines from "Approach of Winter" in Kathleen Iddings' **Selected & New Poems, 1980-1990**:

We sit on the ancient porch swing, an eighty
year old father and an aging daughter.
I've never noticed how fast October's wind
could strip an elm; leaves wing by like mallards
heading south. I study the ancient barn,
your escape that held a workshop, tractors, herds—
and wonder when the snows will bring it down.

To query send 6 pgs. of your work, a cover letter, bio and SASE.

WEST BRANCH (II), English Dept., Bucknell Hall, Bucknell University, Lewisburg PA 17837, founded 1977, is a literary biannual, using **quality poetry.** Free verse is the dominant form—lyric, narrative and dramatic—occasionally longer than one page, much of it accessible with the emphasis on voice and/or powerful content. They have published poetry by D. Nurkse, Deborah Burnham, Jim Daniels, Anneliese Wagner, Betsy Sholl, David Citino, Barbara Crooker and David Brooks. It is 100-120 pgs., digest-sized, circulation 500. One-year subscription: $7. Two years (4 issues): $11. **Sample: $3. "We do not consider simultaneous submissions. Each poem is judged on its own merits, regardless of subject or form. We strive to publish the best work being written today." Reports in 6-8 weeks. Pays copies and subscription to the magazine. Acquires first rights.** Reviews books and chapbooks of poetry but only those by writers who have been published in *West Branch*.

‡WEST COAST LINE (II, IV-Regional), 2027 EAA, Simon Fraser University, Burnaby, British Columbia V5A 1S6 Canada, phone (604)291-4287, editor Roy Miki, founded 1965. *West Coast Line* is published 3 times a year and **"favors work by both new and established Canadian writers, but it observes no borders in encouraging original creativity.** Our focus is on contemporary poetry, short fiction, criticism and reviews of books." They have recently published poetry by Bruce Andrews, Dennis Cooley, Ian Wedde, Lydia Kwa, Normand de Bellefeuille, Jean-Paul Daoust, Louise Bouchard and Dinah Hawken. The editor chose these sample lines from "table of contents" by Lazer Lederhendler:

the poem has a table at its heart
a kitchen table, the hardest
things are said at kitchen tables
hard as glass is, full
of holes. the silence each word
travels in. . . .

The magazine is handsomely printed on glossy paper, 6×9, flat-spined, 144 pgs. They accept about 20 of the 500-600 poetry mss received each year. Approximately 26 pages of poetry/issue. Press run is 800 for 500 subscriptions of which 350 are libraries, 150 shelf sales. Subscription: $20. Single copy: $10. **No simultaneous submissions or previously published poetry. Publishes theme issues. Recently published a double issue entitled "Colour—An Issue," on race in Canada. Send SASE for guidelines. Pays approximately $8 (Canadian)/printed page plus a one-year subscription. Reports in 6-8 weeks.** Time between acceptance and publication is 2-8 months. **Sends prepublication galleys on request. Mss returned only if accompanied by sufficient Canadian postage or IRC.**

‡WEST END PRESS (IV-Political, women, foreign language), P.O. Box 27334, Albuquerque NM 87125, founded 1976, publisher John Crawford, publishes 6 paperbacks/year. **They want "political or personal experience, any style. Nothing self-indulgent, 'objective,' or purely descriptive, racist, sexist, elitist, etc. Normally we publish literature of a progressive political orientation. This includes working class literature, literature with political themes and multicultural literature. A majority of our books are written by women. We have also published bilingual and intertextual books containing Spanish and Navajo."** They have published poetry by Margaret Randall, Adrian Louis, Ana Castillo and Wendy Rose. As a sample the editor selected these lines from "The Great Pat Smith American Dreampoem" by Pat Smith:

One day my customer is Busby Berkeley
He leans on my counter, lights his cigar
likes what he sees
and says in a wise voice
Girlie, can you swim?

Editor often comments on rejections. "Reporting time 3 months, no panel review, at least a year backlog." Sometimes sends prepublication galleys. Pays maximum of 6% royalties, but payment is usually in copies, 10% of press run.

WEST OF BOSTON; MENKE KATZ POETRY AWARDS (II), Box 2, Cochituate Station, Wayland MA 01778, phone (508)653-7241, press founded 1983, poetry editor Norman Andrew Kirk, wants to see **"poetry of power, compassion, originality and wit—and talent, too. Poetry that reveals the nature of life from the religious to the sensual, from personal exposures to universal truths. No subject is taboo so long as it is authentic and/or passionate."** They have recently published poetry by Mary K. Leen, R. Nikolas Macioci, Errol Miller, Lyn Lifshin and Barry Spacks. As a sample the editor selected these lines from "Leaves of an Autumn Past" by Lynda S. Silva:

you remember . . .

we had that old
painted-lady house
with a bathroom
red tile and chrome,

an Indian woman, nude,
touched with silver,. . .

They are now accepting submissions for a new publication of previously unpublished poems, also called *West of Boston*. Depending on submissions, it will be an annual or semiannual, perfect-bound on high quality paper. **Include a brief bio and SASE with submission. All contributors will receive 1 copy.** (Subscription available for $10/issue.) **For book or chapbook submission, query with 5-10 sample poems, credits and bio. Simultaneous submissions and previously published poems OK. Editor "sometimes" comments on rejected mss. Sometimes sends prepublication galleys. Pays 10% of press run.** Sponsors the Menke Katz Poetry Awards for a poem of merit by a poet who has not had a volume of poetry published and a poem of merit by a poet with at least 1 published book. Each poet will receive a $250 award. All submissions will be eligible. Some poets will be invited to submit their work. Only subscribers will receive cash awards. Non-subscribers will receive 10 issues when their poem is selected.

WEST WIND REVIEW (II, IV-Anthology), English Dept., Southern Oregon State College, Ashland OR 97520, phone (503)552-6181, founded 1982, is an annual **"looking for sensitive but strong verse that celebrates all aspects of men's and women's experiences, both exalted and tragic. We are looking to print material that reflects ethnic and social diversity."** As a sample the editor selected these lines by Eve Sutton:

Soft mud, gray clay
Pressed in my hands on a whim
Inspired by Michelangelo,
Sculpts itself, becomes surprisingly familiar
All right, mother, now that you've dared me . . .

WWR is handsomely printed, flat-spined, 140-160 pgs., digest-sized, appearing each spring. They receive about 200 submissions/year, publish 40-50 poems and 10 short stories. Press run is 500. **Sample "at current year's price. We take submissions – limit of 5 poems not exceeding 50 lines. Manuscripts should have poet's name and address on each page." No previously published poems or simultaneous submissions. Cover letter required; include brief bio and publication credits. Deadline: January 1 for publication in late May or early June. Send SASE for guidelines. Reports in 2-3 months after deadline. Pays 1 copy.** Offers awards for each category.

WESTERLY; PATRICIA HACKETT PRIZE (II), Centre for Studies in Australian Literature, University of Western Australia, Nedlands 6009, Australia, phone (09) 380-2101, email westerly@uniwa.uwa.edu.au, founded 1956, editors Dennis Haskell and Delys Bird. ***Westerly*** is a literary and cultural quarterly publishing quality short fiction, poetry, literary critical, socio-historical articles and book reviews. **"No restrictions on creative material. Our only criterion [for poetry] is literary quality. We don't dictate to writers on rhyme, style, experimentation, or anything else. We are willing to publish short or long poems. We do assume a reasonably well read, intelligent audience. Past issues of *Westerly* provide the best guides. Not consciously an academic magazine."** They have recently published work by Edwin Thumboo, Jean Kent, Diane Fahey, Brian Turner and Kirpal Singh. The quarterly magazine is 7×10, "electronically printed," 96 pgs., with some photos and graphics. Press run is 1,000. Single copy: $6 (Aus.) plus overseas postage via surface mail; subscription: $24 (Aus.)/year or $10 by email. **Sample: $7 (Aus.) surface mail, $8 (Aus.) airmail. "Please do not send simultaneous submissions." Reporting time is 2-3 months and time to publication approximately 3 months. Minimum pay for poetry is $30 plus 1 copy. Buys first publication rights; requests acknowledgement on reprints.** Reviews books of poetry in 500-1,000 words. Open to unsolicited reviews. Poets may also send books to Reviews Editor for review consideration. The Patricia Hackett Prize (value approx. $500) is awarded in March for the best contribution published in ***Westerly*** during the previous calendar year. The advice of the editors is: "Be sensible. Write what matters for you but think about the reader. Don't spell out the meanings of the poems and the attitudes to be taken to the subject matter – i.e. trust the reader. Don't be swayed by literary fashion. Read the magazine if possible before sending submissions. Read, read, read literature of all kinds and periods."

‡WESTERN HUMANITIES REVIEW (II), Dept. of English, 341 OSH, University of Utah, Salt Lake City UT 84112, phone (801)581-6070, fax (801)581-3392, founded 1947, managing editor Dawn Corrigan, is a quarterly of poetry, fiction and a small selection of nonfiction. **They want "quality poetry of any form, including translations."** They have recently published poetry by Sandra McPherson, Albert Goldbarth, Rachel Hadas, Bruce Bond, T.R. Hummer, Debora Greger, David Lehman, Robert Phillips and Geraldine C. Little. As a sample we selected these lines from "Storm on Fishing Bay" by John Drury:

What's hard to explain
darkens the prospect of happiness—
like wind picking up off shore
where four people retreat, separately.

Darkened, the prospect of happiness
falls back to a hunting lodge
where four people retreat, separately
latching shutters, brewing coffee, gazing.

WHR is 96-125 pgs., 6×9, professionally printed on quality stock and perfect-bound with coated card cover. They receive about 700 submissions a year, accept less than 10%, publish approximately 60 poets. Press run is 1,100 for 1,000 subscribers of which 900 are libraries. Subscription: $20 to individuals in the US. **Sample postpaid: $6. "We do not publish writer's guidelines because we think that the magazine itself conveys an accurate picture of our requirements." No previously**

published poems; simultaneous submissions OK. Reads submissions September 1 through May 31 only. Time between acceptance and publication is 1-3 issues. **Managing editor Dawn Corrigan makes an initial cut ("eliminating only a few submissions"), then Richard Howard, the poetry editor, makes the final selections. Seldom comments on rejections. Occasionally publishes special issues. Reports in 1-6 months. Pays $50/poem and 2 copies. Acquires first serial rights.** They also offer an annual spring contest for Utah poets. Prize is $250. Poetry published in this review has been selected for inclusion in the 1992 and 1993 volumes of **The Best American Poetry.**

WESTERN PRODUCER PUBLICATIONS; WESTERN PEOPLE (IV-Regional), Box 2500, Saskatoon, Saskatchewan S7K 2C4 Canada, phone (306)665-3500, founded 1923, managing editor Michael Gillgannon. *Western People* is a magazine supplement to *The Western Producer*, a weekly newspaper, circulation 100,000, which uses **"poetry about the people, interests and environment of rural Western Canada."** As a sample the editor selected the entire poem "sky so heavy and low" by Marilyn Cay:

it is November in Saskatchewan
the sky so heavy and low
I can feel the weight of it
on my chest
the days so short and getting shorter
I can touch the sides of them
at midday

The tabloid-sized supplement is 8 pgs., newsprint, with color and b&w photography and graphics. They receive about 600 submissions of poetry/year, use 40-50. **Sample free for postage (2 oz.) – and ask for guidelines. One poem/page, maximum of 3 poems/submission. Name, address and telephone number in upper left corner of each page. Publishes theme issues. Reports within 2 weeks. Pays $15-50/poem.** The editor comments, "It is difficult for someone from outside Western Canada to catch the flavor of this region; almost all the poems we purchase are written by Western Canadians."

WESTVIEW: A JOURNAL OF WESTERN OKLAHOMA (II), 100 Campus Dr., SOSU, Weatherford OK 73096, phone (405)774-3168, founded 1981, editor Fred Alsberg, is a quarterly that is **"particularly interested in writers from the Southwest; however, we are open to work of quality by poets from elsewhere. We publish free verse and formal poetry."** They have recently published poetry by Mark Sanders, Michael McKinney, Holly Hunt, Alicia Ostriker and Norman Arrington. As a sample the editor selected these lines from "Outlaw on Holiday" by Richard Plant:

Palmer said that his hands looked like a millionaire's,
so fine and hairless. He worked his spoon in that
glass dish like you or I might play piano
if only we knew how.

Westview is 44 pgs., magazine-sized, saddle-stapled, with glossy card cover in full-color. They use about 25% of 100 poems received/year. Press run is 1,000 for 500 subscribers of which about 25 are libraries, 150 shelf sales. Subscription: $10. **Sample postpaid: $4. Cover letter including biographical data for contributor's note required with submissions. "Poems on computer disk are welcome so long as they are accompanied by the hard copy and the SASE has the appropriate postage." Editor comments on submissions "when close." Publishes theme issues. Send SASE for upcoming themes. "Mss are circulated to an editorial board; we usually respond within 2 months." Pays 1 copy.**

WEYFARERS; GUILDFORD POETS PRESS (II), 9, White Rose Lane, Woking, Surrey GU22 7JA United Kingdom, founded 1972, administrative editor Margaret Pain, poetry editors Margaret Pain, Martin Jones and Jeffery Wheatley. They say, "We publish *Weyfarers* magazine three times a year. All our editors are themselves poets and give their spare time free to help other poets." They describe their needs as **"all types of poetry, serious and humorous, free verse and rhymed/metered, but mostly 'mainstream' modern. Excellence is the main consideration. NO hard porn, graphics, way-out experimental. Any subject publishable, from religious to satire. Not more than 40 lines."** They have published poetry by Susan Skinner, David Schaal, John Gallas and Michael Henry. As a sample the editors chose this extract from "Haldacama" by David Critchard:

Spined flowers
as red & cruel as soldiers
crucify the setting sun
upon a tree of thorns.
The parched earth
sucks the blood.
No ear of wheat
was reaped in silence . . . .

The digest-sized, saddle-stapled format contains about 28 pgs. of poetry (of a total of 32 pgs.).

They use about 125 of 1,200-1,500 submissions received each year. The magazine has a circulation of "about 300," including about 190 subscriptions of which 5 are libraries. **Sample (current issue) postpaid: $5 in cash USA or £1.60 UK. Submit no more than 6 poems, one poem/sheet. No previously published or simultaneous submissions. Closing dates for submissions are end of January, May and September. Sometimes comments briefly, if requested, on rejections. Pays 1 copy.** Staff reviews books of poetry briefly, in newsletter sent to subscribers. "We are associated with Surrey Poetry Center, which has an annual Open Poetry Competition. The prize-winners are published in ***Weyfarers***." Their advice to poets is, "Always read a magazine before submitting. And read plenty of modern poetry."

WHETSTONE (I, II), Dept. of English, University of Lethbridge, 4401 University Drive, Lethbridge, Alberta T1K 3M4 Canada, is a biannual encouraging all forms of submissions. They predominantly publish poetry and short fiction, but are also open to "essays, artwork and other forms of expression. **All submissions must be original and unpublished."** ***Whetstone*** is digest-sized, 80 pgs., perfect-bound professionally printed in boldface type with 2-color matte card cover. Circulation 500 with 200 subscriptions of which 25 are libraries. Subscription: $12 for 1 year, $22 for 2 years (Canadian funds only). **Sample postpaid: $7. Submit up to 6 poems, any length of poetry OK. Cover letter including brief bio required. Editor sometimes comments on rejections. "Submissions which do not have a SASE, or SAE with IRC, will not be returned or commented on." Send SASE for guidelines. Pays 1 copy. "*Whetstone*** also runs periodic features and contests. Regulations are specific and writers should request information before submitting."

WHETSTONE; WHETSTONE PRIZE (II), P.O. Box 1266, Barrington IL 60011, phone (708)382-5626, editors Sandra Berris, Marsha Portnoy, Jean Tolle and Julie Fleenor, is an annual. **"We emphasize quality more than category and favor the concrete over the abstract, the accessible over the obscure. We like poets who use words in ways that transform them and us."** They have recently published poetry by Jackie Bartley, Nancy Cherry, Bruce Guernsey, Peyton Houston and Louis Phillips. As a sample an editor selected these lines by Helen Reed:

I know the corpse inside.
It has my face,
as did each of the others
before it.

It is digest-sized, 96 pgs., professionally printed, flat-spined with matte card cover. Press run is 600 for 100 subscribers of which 5 are libraries, 350 shelf sales. **Sample postpaid: $3. Reports in 1-4 months. Always sends prepublication galleys. Buys first North American serial rights. Pay varies,** with Whetstone Prize of $500 awarded for best poetry or fiction in each issue, and additional prizes as well.

Whisper's central focus is poetry, but it also publishes short stories, art, photographs, recipes and reviews. As Editor Anthony Boyd says, "The stories and interviews are just the bait I use to lure people into reading what's primarily a poetry zine." The California-based quarterly promotes new and established writers, and seeks work that is readable, thoughtful and moving. "I chose this cover just because it's really good and I knew it would entice people to read the issue," says Boyd. "I like the thick lines. The picture is clear, strong, definitive. I wish I had more poetry like that." Cover illustration: Eugene Gryniewicz, Tinley Park IL.

WHISPER; BROADSHEETS; ETHEREAL DANCES; SCREAM PRESS, 509 Enterprise Dr., Rohnert Park CA 94928, founded 1987, editor of ***Whisper*** and ***Broadsheets*** Anthony Boyd, editor of ***Ethereal Dances*** Sara Boyd. All are "publications promoting new and established literary thinkers. **Interested in any**

poetry well done, 40 lines or less, free verse, villanelles, haiku, etc. No 'guy' poems about beer, bars, hookers, etc. No juvenile love poetry. No 'shock value' poetry. We would like to see more traditional forms and more humorous verse." They have recently published poetry by Cheryl Townsend, Errol Miller and Kathleen Iddings. As a sample the editors selected these lines from "the winter of '52" by Will Thompson (published in ***Whisper***):

my father never dreamed that he would die out
his whole life remembered
in a mind's eye snapshot of jet #247 over north korea
and a fading photograph that refuses to answer my questions

and these lines from "war paint" by Jenifer Bartels (published in ***Ethereal Dances***):

Earth's paint splatters and splashes
drips and dribbles
and the Artist made a wonderful mistake
when he spilled the ocean blue into your eyes.

Whisper is a quarterly publication, 20 pgs., 8×11, web offset, saddle-stapled, with art, ads. ***Ethereal Dances*** is a triannual, 20 pgs., 5½×8½, photocopied, saddle-stapled, color paper, cover artwork. ***Broadsheets*** are 4×8, laser printed on special paper, some art, ad for press on back. Anthony Boyd says he receives about 500 submissions a year for ***Whisper*** and ***Broadsheets***. He accepts approximately 9%. Sara Boyd receives about 300 poems from 75 poets for ***Ethereal Dances***. She accepts approximately 15%. Press run for ***Whisper*** is 1000. Subscription: $10. **Sample postpaid: $3 (*Whisper*), $2 (*Ethereal Dances*). *Broadsheets* are available free for 6×9 SASE. Submit 1 poem to a page. Previously published poems OK if noted; no simultaneous submissions. Often comments on rejections. Send SASE for guidelines. Reports in 1 month. Pays 1-2 copies. Acquires first or one-time rights.** Anthony Boyd reviews books of poetry in ***Whisper***. Send books for review consideration to his attention. They say, "Anyone can send anything, but the acceptance rate for those who have seen a sample of our publications is double the rate for those who have not. ***Whisper*** is also available as a freeware program for Macs; email tonyboyd@aol.com for more information, or send for guidelines."

WHITE EAGLE COFFEE STORE PRESS (II); FRESH GROUND (IV-Anthology), P.O. Box 383, Fox River Grove IL 60021-0383, phone (708)639-9200, founded 1992, is a small press publishing 5-6 chapbooks/year. **"Alternate chapbooks are published by invitation and by competition. Author published by invitation becomes judge for next competition."** They are **"open to any kind of poetry. No censorship at this press. Aesthetic values are the only standard. Generally not interested in sentimental or didactic writing."** They have recently published poetry by Annie Davidovicz, Peter Blair, Martha Vertreace and James Plath. As a sample the editor selected these lines from "Hot Saws" by Paul Andrew E. Smith:

It's a metallic taste she has, sweet,
my teeth are numb, my cheek bones.
Yes, by God in the treetops,
I'm beginning to see how these are
necessary skills, this lumberjacking.

Sample postpaid: $5. Submit complete chapbook ms (20-24 pgs.) with a brief bio, 125-word statement that introduces your writing and $10 reading fee. Previously published poems and simultaneous submissions OK, with notice. Competition deadlines: March 30 for spring contest; September 30 for fall contest. Send SASE for guidelines. "Each competition is judged by the author of the most recent chapbook published by invitation." **Seldom comments on rejections. Reports 8-10 weeks after deadline. All entrants will receive a copy of the winning chapbook. Winner receives $150 and 25 copies.** ***Fresh Ground*** is an annual anthology that features "some of the best work of poets who have submitted chapbook manuscripts during the previous year. ***Fresh Ground*** is published in September. Poems for this annual are accepted during May." They say, "Poetry is about a passion for language. That's what we're about. We'd like to provide an opportunity for poets of any age who are fairly early in their careers to publish something substantial. We're excited by the enthusiasm shown for this new press and by the extraordinary quality of the writing we've received."

WHITE PINE PRESS (V), Suite 28, 10 Village Square, Fredonia NY 14063, phone (716)672-5743, founded 1973, editor Dennis Maloney, managing director Elaine LaMattina. White Pine Press publishes poetry, fiction, literature in translation, essays—perfect-bound paperbacks. **"At present we are not accepting unsolicited mss or queries."** They have published poetry by William Kloefkorn, Marjorie

Agosin, Miguel Hernandez, Peter Blue Cloud, Basho, Pablo Neruda, Maurice Kenny and James Wright. **Send $1 for catalog to buy samples.**

JAMES WHITE REVIEW: A GAY MEN'S LITERARY QUARTERLY (IV-Gay), Box 3356, Butler Quarter Station, Minneapolis MN 55403, phone (612)339-8317, founded 1983, poetry editor Clif Mayhood, **uses all kinds of poetry by gay men.** They have published poetry by Robert Peters, Jonathan Bracker and Joel Zizik. They receive about 1,400 submissions/year, use 100, have a 6-week backlog. Press run is 4,000 for 1,500 subscribers of which 50 are libraries. Subscription: $12/year (US). **Sample postpaid: $3. Submit a limit of 8 poems or 250 lines. A poem can exceed 250 lines, but it "better be very good." Send SASE for guidelines. Reports in 4 months. Pays $10/poem.** Reviews books of poetry.

WHITE SANDS POETRY REVIEW (II), P.O. Box 10488, Pensacola FL 32524-0488, founded 1992, editor Sharon Noland Norred, appears 6 times/year. "Our purpose is to showcase the best poems we receive whether they come from new or established poets. **No restrictions on form, length, style, etc. We are looking for poetry with strong imagery that seems to pull us into the poet's heart and mind, evoking the same feelings in the reader that compelled the poet to write the poem. Nothing contrived. No occult. No sing-song rhyme."** They have recently published poetry by Michael McNeilly, Richard Davignon, Lyn Lifshin, Diane L. Krueger and Scott C. Holstad. As a sample the editor selected these lines from "Continuance" by Jim Mikoley:

The misunderstanding called love
is an honest mistake, to be sure,
like the sparrow sure
of continuance
smashing into the picture window:
you don't avoid
the ending
that you can't imagine,
the invisible wall across the flight path.

The editor says it is 20-32 pgs., digest-sized, saddle-stapled with matte cover. They receive 1,000 poems a year, use approximately 150. Press run is 150-200 for 97 subscribers of which 2 are libraries, few shelf sales. Single copy: $2.50; subscription: $12. **Sample postpaid: $3. Previously published poems and simultaneous submissions OK. "Though a cover letter is not required, we appreciate one giving info on previous publications and interesting details for contributor's notes."** Time between acceptance and publication is 2-3 months. **Often comments on rejections. Send SASE for guidelines. Reports in 4-6 weeks. Pays 1 or 2 copies. Acquires one-time rights.** They also sponsor 1 or 2 poetry contests each year. No entry fees. First prize receives $25 (minimum) and publication in the magazine. Other top entries are also published. Send SASE for contest deadlines and guidelines (including special cover sheet to be completed by author and submitted with previously unpublished poems). The editor says, "Submit, submit, submit! Support the small presses who love poetry as much as you do and exist with the sole purpose of getting your poetry into the hands of the general public."

WHITE WALL REVIEW (I), 63 Gould St., Toronto, Ontario M5B 1E9 Canada, phone (416)977-1045, founded 1976, editors change every year, is an annual using **"interesting, preferably spare art. No style is unacceptable. Should poetry serve a purpose beyond being poetry and communicating a poet's idea? Nothing boring, self-satisfied, gratuitously sexual, violent or indulgent."** They have recently published poetry by C.M. Buckaway and Shirley Vogler Meister. As a sample the editor selected this poem, "Magnolia Angel," by Susan McCaslin:

astir, compacted in bud
or loosened from the twig
in tincture of rose-to-white
fleshy aromatic petals

How easily
you unwing yourself before us.
Only a brief fluttering
gives you away.

WWR is between 144-160 pgs., digest-sized, professionally printed, perfect-bound, with glossy

The Subject Index, located before the General Index, can help you narrow down markets for your work. It lists those publishers whose poetry interests are specialized.

card cover, using b&w photos and illustrations. Press run is 500. Subscription: $8 in Canada, $8.50 in US and elsewhere. **Sample postpaid: $8. "Please do not submit between January and August of a given year." Cover letter required; include short bio. Reports "as soon as we can (usually in April or May). We comment on all mss, accepted or not." Pays 1 copy.** They say, "Poets should send what they consider *their best work*, not everything they've got."

TAHANA WHITECROW FOUNDATION; CIRCLE OF REFLECTIONS (IV-Ethnic), Box 18181, Salem OR 97305, phone (503)585-0564, founded 1987, executive director Melanie Smith. The Whitecrow Foundation conducts **one spring/summer poetry contest on Native American themes in poems up to 30 lines in length. Deadline for submissions: May 31. No haiku, Seiku, erotic or porno poems. Fees are $2.75 for a single poem, $10 for 4.** Winners, honorable mentions and selected other entries are published in a periodic anthology, **Circle of Reflections.** Winners receive free copies and are encouraged to purchase others for $4.95 plus $1 handling in order to "help ensure the continuity of our contests." As a sample Melanie Smith selected these lines by David E. Sees:

Alas . .
I see
I hear . .
my grandchild
move and speak . .
the only thing native
is the complexion
of his skin . . his eyes and hair . .
alas . . forgive
this lonely tear

Reviews books of poetry for $10 reading fee (average 32 pages). Melanie Smith adds, "We seek unpublished Native writers. Poetic expressions of full-bloods, mixed bloods and empathetic non-Indians need to be heard. Future goals include chapbooks and native theme art. Advice to new writers: Keep writing, honing and sharpening your material; don't give up—keep submitting."

WHOLE NOTES; WHOLE NOTES PRESS (I, II, IV-Children, translations), P.O. Box 1374, Las Cruces NM 88004, phone (505)382-7446, *WN* founded 1984, Whole Notes Press founded 1988, editor Nancy Peters Hastings. *WN* appears twice a year. Whole Notes Press publishes 1 chapbook/year by a single poet. **"All forms will be considered."** They have published poetry by Stuart Friebert. As a sample the editor selected these lines from "Stone with Horseshoe" by Judita Vaiciunaite:

. . . and again through fog I hear
the horseshoe, hammered out on stone,
the wind in the rye,
the steed barely tamed, neighing in the distance . . .

WN is 32 pgs., digest-sized, "nicely printed," staple bound, with a "linen 'fine arts' cover." They accept about 10% of some 800 submissions/year. Press run is 400 for 200 subscriptions of which 10 are libraries. Subscription: $6. **Sample postpaid: $3. They prefer submissions of 3-7 poems at a time. Some previously published poems used. "We prefer not to receive simultaneous submissions." Reports in 2-3 weeks. Pays 2 copies. For 20-page chapbook consideration, submit 3-15 samples with bio and list of other publications. Pays 25 copies of chapbook. Editor sometimes comments on rejections.** The editor says, "In the fall of each even-numbered year I edit a special issue of *WN* that features writing by young people (under 21). Overall, we'd like to see more translations and more poems about rural experiences."

THE WICAZO SA REVIEW (IV-Ethnic), R.R.#8, Box 510, Rapid City SD 57702, phone (605)341-3228, founded 1985, poetry editor Elizabeth Cook-Lynn, is a "scholarly magazine, appearing twice a year, devoted to the developing of Native American Studies as an academic discipline and using **poetry of exceptional quality."** They have published poetry by Simon Ortiz, Joy Harjo, Gray Cohoe and Earle Thompson. As a sample the editor chose these lines by Ray Young Bear:

With the Community's great "registered" Cottonwood
Smoldering under an overcast sky
no one will believe we are here
in the middle & deepest part
of the flood

TWSR is magazine-sized, 40-46 pgs., saddle-stapled, professionally printed on heavy glossy stock with b&w glossy card cover, press run 600, using only 3-4 poems/issue. Once in a while they "feature" an exceptional poet. **Sample postpaid: $10. Cover letter required including credits and tribal enrollment affiliation. Pays 3 copies.** Reviews books of poetry. Open to unsolicited reviews. Poets may also send books for review consideration.

WICKED MYSTIC (IV-Horror), Dept. WD, P.O. Box 3087, Astoria NY 11103-0087, phone (718)545-6713, founded 1990, editor Andre Scheluchin, is a quarterly of hardcore horror poetry and short stories. They want **"psychological horror, splatter-gore, erotic, death, gothic themes, etc. No safe, conventional, conservative poetry."** They have recently published poetry by Michael A. Arnzen, John Grey and James S. Dorr. As a sample the editor selected this poem, "Alcohol," by Jonathan Yungkans:

In a giant glass vat, a man
hangs by his ankles, drinks beer
into his lungs. A child watches,
walled in a block of ice
stabbed many times, the reddened
pieces dropped into the vat
to keep the man's drink cold.

Wicked Mystic is 100 pgs., magazine-sized, perfect-bound, with heavy stock colored cover and display ads. They receive about 1,000 poems a year, use approximately 5%. Press run is 2,000 for 1,000 subscribers of which 50 are libraries. Subscription: $24 for 4 issues. **Sample postpaid: $6.50 made payable to Andre Scheluchin. Submit typed poems, no longer than 30 lines. No previously published poems or simultaneous submissions. Cover letter required. Often comments on rejections. Reports within 2-8 weeks. Pays 1 copy. Acquires first North American serial rights.**

‡WILDE OAKS (I, IV-Gay/lesbian/bisexual), 175 Stockton Ave., San Jose CA 95126, phone (408)293-2429, founded 1992, editor Bill Olver, is a biannual publication of the Billy DeFrank Lesbian and Gay Community Center. *Wilde Oaks* publishes **"lesbian/gay/bisexual/transgender material only—open to all forms, themes, styles and tones. We get a lot of free verse, but do not want to see 'greeting card verse.' "** They have recently published poetry by Lisa Vice, Shelley Adler and Louie Crew. As a sample the editor selected these lines from "Headless Chickens" by Mark Hallman:

The woman who chops off
chickens' heads is my favorite
Joan Didion character,
not because I have anything
against chickens, but because
this well-bred lady swings
her axe without a flinch . . .

Wilde Oaks is 108-120 pgs., 5½×8½, perfect-bound with b&w or 3-color cover and b&w interior art, photos and cartoons. They receive 150-200 poems a year, accept approximately 50%. Press run is 300 for 20 subscribers. Single copy: $7.95; subscription: $15/year. **Sample postpaid: $8. Previously published poems OK with notation of where published. No simultaneous submissions. Cover letter with brief bio required. "Submissions on 3.5 (non-returnable) Macintosh format diskettes are greatly appreciated." Deadlines are May 1 and November 1. Often comments on rejections. Send SASE for guidelines. Reports within 1 month of deadlines. Pays 1 copy. Acquires one-time rights.** They also publish a bimonthly newsletter of "news, reviews and items of interest." It is free to subscribers and contributors. Poets may send books for review consideration. The editor says, "Our writers in the San Jose area are encouraged to attend our workshops and parties. Others can send a nice note or Christmas card. We really do like to hear from people. We would particularly like to see more work from people of color, of different backgrounds and ability. However, even if you are God's gift to poetry, please refrain from identifying yourself as such. Remember, the editors are poets, too, and God has probably saved the receipt. As for new writers, be sincere, be honest and be diligent and eventually you will be brilliant."

WILDERNESS (II, IV-Nature/ecology), 23030 W. Sheffler Rd., Elmira OR 97437 (poetry submissions only should be sent to this address), founded 1935, poetry editor John Daniel, is a slick quarterly magazine of "The Wilderness Society, one of the oldest and largest American conservation organizations." Requests for sample and subscriptions should go to *Wilderness*, 900 17th St. NW, Washington DC 20006. They want **"poetry related to the natural world. Shorter poems stand a better chance than longer, but all will be read. Poetry in any form or style is welcome."** They have recently published poetry by Pattiann Rogers, W.S. Merwin, Russell Kesler, Ann Fisher-Wirth, Paul Anderson and Jane Hirshfield. The magazine is published on slick stock, full-color, professionally printed, with full-color paper cover, saddle-stapled, 76 pgs. Their press run is 260,000 with 255,000 subscriptions. Subscription: $15. **Sample postpaid: $3.50. No simultaneous submissions or previously published material. Prefers cover letter with submissions indicating that "a human being has sent the poems." Editor comments on rejections "occasionally. Please understand that we have room for only about 15 poems a year." Responds in 2 months. Always sends prepublication galleys. Pays $100 plus 2 copies on publication. "We buy one-time rights and the right to anthologize the poem without further compensation."** *Wilderness* ranked #8 in the "Top Pay" category of the latest *Writer's Digest* Poetry 60 list.

‡WILDWOOD JOURNAL (IV-Specialized: college affiliation); THE WILDWOOD PRIZE IN POETRY (II), T.H.S. Wallace, Arts 213, 1 HACC Dr., Harrisburg PA 17110-2999, phone (717)780-2487. ***Wildwood Journal***, an annual, is **open only to students, alumni and faculty of Harrisburg Area Community College. Sample copy: $5.** The Wildwood Prize, however, is open to any poet, $500 annually, $5 reading fee made payable to HACC. Final selection for the prize is made by a distinguished poet (in 1994: Len Roberts) who usually remains anonymous until the winner is announced. Poems are accepted between October 15 and November 30. Rules available for SASE.

THE WILLIAM AND MARY REVIEW (II), Campus Center, College of William and Mary, P.O. Box 8795, Williamsburg VA 23187-8795, phone (804)221-3290, founded 1962, editor Andrew Zawacki, poetry editors Brian Henry and Stephanie Jones, is a 112-page annual, **"dedicated to publishing new work by established poets as well as work by new and vital voices."** They have recently published poetry by Dana Gioia, Robert Morgan, Cornelius Eady, Amy Clampitt, Elizabeth Alexander, Robert Hershon, Diane Ackerman, Agha Shahid Ali, Bruce Weigl, Judson Jerome and Phyllis Janowitz. They accept 15-20 of about 5,000 poems submitted/year. Press run is 3,500. They have 250 library subscriptions, about 500 shelf sales. **Sample postpaid: $5.50. Submit 1 poem/page, batches of no more than 6 poems. Cover letter required; include address, phone number, past publishing history and brief bio note. Reads submissions September 15 through February 15 only. Reports in approximately 4 months. Always sends prepublication galleys. Pays 5 copies.** Open to unsolicited reviews. Poets may also send books to poetry editors for review consideration.

WILLOW REVIEW; COLLEGE OF LAKE COUNTY READING SERIES (II), 19351 W. Washington St., Grayslake IL 60030-1198, phone (708)223-6601, ext. 2956, fax (708)223-9371, founded 1969, edited by Paulette Roeske. **"We are interested in poetry and fiction of high quality with no preferences as to form, style or subject."** They have recently published poetry by Lisel Mueller, Lucien Stryk, David Ray and Garrett Hongo and interviews with Gregory Orr and Diane Ackerman. As a sample the editor selected these lines from "The Remedy" by Richard Jones:

I pour my bowl of soup,
and recite this poem,
this magic,
this incantation cleaving sickness from
health. I fold the two knives of my hands
in prayer and say grace,
asking to live
a while longer in this body,
which I bless at every meal,
crossing it with one hand
and feeding it with another.

The review is an 88-page, flat-spined annual, 6×9, professionally printed with a 4-color cover featuring work by an Illinois artist. Editors are open to all styles, free verse to form, as long as each poem stands on its own as art and communicates ideas. Circulation is 1,000, with distribution to bookstores nationwide. Subscription: $13 for 3 issues, $20 for 5 issues. **Sample back issue: $4. Submit up to 5 poems or short fiction/creative nonfiction up to 4,000 words. Cover letter required; include name, address, SS#, and information for contributor's notes. "We read year round but response is slower in the summer months." Sometimes sends prepublication galleys. Pays 2 copies. Acquires first North American serial rights. Prizes of $100 are awarded to the best poetry and fiction/creative nonfiction in each issue, with additional prizes totaling $350.** The reading series, 4-7 readings/academic year, has included Angela Jackson, Ellen Bryant Voigt, Thomas Lux, Charles Simic, Gloria Naylor, David Mura, Galway Kinnell, Lisel Mueller, Amiri Baraka, Stephen Dobyns, Heather McHugh, Linda Pastan, Katha Pollitt, Tobias Wolff, William Stafford and others. One reading is for contributors to ***Willow Review***. Readings are usually held on Thursday evenings, for audiences of about 150 students and faculty of the College of Lake County and other area colleges and residents of local communities. They are widely publicized in Chicago and suburban newspapers.

WILLOW SPRINGS (II, IV-Translations), MS-1, Eastern Washington University, Cheney WA 99004, phone (509)458-6429, founded 1977. "We publish quality poetry and fiction that is imaginative, intelligent, and has a concern and care for language. **We are especially interested in translations from any language or period."** They have published poetry by Denise Levertov, Carolyn Kizer, Michael Burkard, Russell Edson, Dara Wier, Thomas Lux, Madeline DeFrees, Hayden Carruth, Al Young, Odysseas Elytis, W.S. Merwin, Olga Broumas, Kay Boyle and Lisel Mueller. ***Willow Springs***, a semiannual, is one of the most visually appealing journals being published. It is 98 pgs., 6×9, flat-spined, professionally printed, with glossy 4-color card cover with art. Circulation is 1,000, 500 subscriptions of which 30% are libraries. They use 1-2% of some 4,000 unsolicited poems received each year. Editors seem to prefer free verse with varying degrees of accessibility (although an occasional formal poem has appeared in recent issues). **Sample postpaid: $4. Submit September 15 through May 15 only. "We do not read in the summer months." Include name on every page, address on first page of each poem. Brief cover letter saying how many poems on how many pages preferred. No simultaneous submissions. Send SASE for guidelines. Reports in 1-3 months. Pays 2 copies, others at half price, and cash when funds available. Acquires all rights. Returns rights on release.** Reviews books of poetry and short fiction in 200-500 words. Open to unsolicited reviews. Poets may also send books for review consideration. They have annual poetry and fiction awards ($100 and $250 respectively) for work published in the journal.

WIND PUBLICATIONS; WIND MAGAZINE (II), P.O. Box 24548, Lexington KY 40524, phone (606)885-5342, ***Wind Magazine*** founded in 1971, editors/publishers Steven R. Cope and Charlie G. Hughes. "Although we publish poets of national repute, we are friendly toward beginners who have something to say and do so effectively and interestingly. **No taboos, no preferred school, form, style, etc. Our interests are inclusive.** Competition is keen; send only your best." ***Wind*** appears twice a year and is about 100 pgs., digest-sized, perfect-bound, containing approximately 40% poetry, also short fiction, essays and reviews ("Editor's Choice"). "We accept about 1% of submissions." Subscription: $10/year. **Sample postpaid: $3.50. Submit no more than 5 poems. No simultaneous submissions. "Cover letter optional; short bio desirable." Editor comments on submissions which are near misses. Reports in 1 month, publication within 1 year. Sometimes sends prepublication galleys. Pays 1 contributor's copy plus discount on extras. "Your submission is understood to guarantee Wind Publications first North American serial rights and anthology reprint rights only."** Wind Publications sponsors a yearly chapbook competition. Reading fee: $10. Send SASE for chapbook guidelines. Also publishes periodic anthologies; the **Best of Wind** anthology is $11.95 plus $1.50 p&h, $8 plus $1.50 p&h to subscribers.

THE WINDLESS ORCHARD; THE WINDLESS ORCHARD CHAPBOOKS (II), English Dept., Indiana University, Fort Wayne IN 46805, phone (219)481-6841, founded 1970, poetry editor Robert Novak, is a "shoestring labor of love—chapbooks only from frequent contributors to magazine. Sometimes publish calendars." They say they want **"heuristic, excited, valid non-xian religious exercises. Our muse is interested only in the beautiful, the erotic and the sacred."** ***The Windless Orchard*** appears irregularly, 50 pgs., digest-sized, offset from typescript, saddle-stapled, with matte card cover with b&w photos. The editors say they have 100 subscriptions of which 25 are libraries, a press run of 300, total circulation: 280. There are about 35 pgs. of poetry in each issue. They receive about 3,000 submissions of poetry/year, use 200, have a 6-month backlog. Subscription: $10. **Sample postpaid: $4. Submit 3-7 pgs. Considers simultaneous submissions. Reports in 1 day to 4 months. Pays 2 copies. Chapbook submissions by invitation only to contributors to the magazine. Poets pay costs for 300 copies, of which The Windless Orchard Chapbook Series receives 100 for its expenses. Sample: $4. Editors sometimes comment on rejections.** They advise, "Memorize a poem a day, do translations for the education."

‡THE WIND-MILL (IV-Specialized: genealogy, ethnic), % Rainbow City, P.O. Box 8447, Berkeley CA 94707-8447, editor Helen B. Harvey, is a semiannual publication featuring articles, poetry, reviews, art and photos relating to genealogy and family history. "The purpose of ***Wind-Mill*** is to provide a friendly, relaxed forum for sharing information about family history research and, in particular, information about German/Dutch (Ostfriesen, East Frisian/North German) culture, history and ethnic traditions." Subscription: $12/year. **Sample postpaid: $6 plus SASE. Submit up to 3 poems, 30 lines maximum each. "Send SASE along with any material that you wish to be returned to you or if you want a response." Submission deadlines: March 1 for Spring/Summer issue; September 1 for Autumn/Winter issue. Pays 1 copy.** They are also interested in reviews of computerized genealogy software; beginning German or Plattdeutsch language instruction programs; reviews of books, tapes and other items related to genealogy research; German/Ostfriesen immigration patterns; amusing anecdotes about ancestors; and specific biographies of or details about individuals. Send SASE for details. The editor advises, "Please obtain and study a sample issue prior to submitting anything for publication."

UNIVERSITY OF WINDSOR REVIEW (II), University of Windsor, Windsor, Ontario N9B 3P4 Canada, phone (519)253-4232, ext. 2303, founded 1966, poetry editor John Ditsky, appears twice a year. **"Open to all poetry but epic length."** They have published poetry by Ben Bennani, Walter McDonald, Larry Rubin and Lyn Lifshin. As a sample the editor selected these lines (poet unidentified):

talking to white wolves
talking to the first
white wolves ever
telling of how things are
in his world.

It is professionally printed, 100 pgs., digest-sized. They accept about 15% of 500 poems received/year. Press run is 400. Subscription: $19.95 (+7% GST) individuals, $29.95 (+7% GST) institutions (Canadian); $19.95 individuals, $29.95 institutions (US). **Sample postpaid: $10. Reports in 6 weeks. Pays $10/poem.**

WINEBERRY PRESS (V, IV-Regional), 3207 Macomb St. NW, Washington DC 20008, phone (202)363-8036 or (416)964-2002, founded 1983, founder and president Elisavietta Ritchie, publishes anthologies and chapbooks of poems by **Washington area poets but is not currently accepting unsolicited mss.** She has published poetry by Judith McCombs, Elizabeth Follin-Jones and Beatrice Murphy. As a sample Elisavietta Ritchie selected these lines from "Through The Looking Glass" by Maxine Combs, included in **Swimming Out Of The Collective Unconscious:**

I drop a carton
in someone else's shopping cart,
kneel to comfort a weeping child
I mistake for my own . . . . We start
swimming out of the collective unconscious
and end by resembling our lovers.

WISCONSIN ACADEMY REVIEW (IV-Regional), 1922 University Ave., Madison WI 53705, phone (608)263-1692, founded 1954, poetry editor Faith B. Miracle, "distributes information on scientific and cultural life of Wisconsin and provides a forum for **Wisconsin (or Wisconsin background) artists and authors." They want "good lyric poetry; traditional meters acceptable if content is fresh. No poem over 65 lines."** They have recently published poetry by Credo Enriquez, Jean Feraca, Felix Pollak, Ron Wallace, Sara Rath and Lorine Niedecker. As a sample we selected these lines from "J L Jones" by Art Madson:

Running before the wind
on canvas wings,
on lifting hands, empty spirits,
I try, like flying fish
sailing the Pacific,
to transcend my element.

Wisconsin Academy Review is a magazine-sized, 52-page quarterly, professionally printed on glossy stock, glossy card color cover. Press run is 1,700 for 1,300 subscribers of which 109 are libraries. They use 3-6 pgs. of poetry/issue. Of over 150 submissions of poetry/year, they use about 24, have a 6- to 12-month backlog. **Sample postpaid: $3. Submit 5 pgs. maximum, double-spaced, include SASE. Must include Wisconsin connection if not Wisconsin return address. Editor sometimes comments on rejections. Reports in 4-6 weeks. Always sends prepublication printouts. Pays 3 copies.** Staff reviews books of poetry with Wisconsin connection only. Send related books for review consideration. The editor says, "We would like to receive good traditional forms—not sentimental rhymes."

UNIVERSITY OF WISCONSIN PRESS; BRITTINGHAM PRIZE IN POETRY; FELIX POLLAK PRIZE IN POETRY (II), 114 N. Murray St., Madison WI 53715-1199, Brittingham Prize inaugurated in 1985, poetry editor Ronald Wallace. The University of Wisconsin Press publishes primarily scholarly works, but they offer the annual **Brittingham Prize and now the Felix Pollak Prize, both $1,000 plus publication. These prizes are the only way in which this press publishes poetry. Send SASE for rules. For both prizes, submit between September 1 and October 1, unbound ms volume of 50-80 pgs., with name, address and telephone number on title page. No translations. Poems must be previously unpublished in book form. Poems published in journals, chapbooks and anthologies may be included but must be acknowledged. There is a non-refundable $15 reading fee which must accompany the ms. (Checks to University of Wisconsin Press.) Mss will *not* be returned. Enclose SASE for contest results.** Qualified readers will screen all mss. Winners will be selected by "a distinguished poet who will remain anonymous until the winners are announced in mid-February." Past judges include C.K. Williams, Maxine Kumin, Mona Van Duyn, Charles Wright, Gerald Stern, Mary Oliver, Donald Finkel, Donald Justice and Lisel Mueller. Winners include Jim Daniels, Patricia Dobler, David Kirby, Lisa Zeidner, Stefanie Marlis, Judith Vollmer, Renée A. Ashley, Tony Hoagland and Stephanie Strickland. The editor says, **"Each submission is considered for both prizes (one entry fee only)."**

THE WISCONSIN RESTAURATEUR (IV-Specialized: food service), #300, 31 S. Henry, Madison WI 53703, phone (608)251-3663, founded 1933, poetry editor Jan LaRue, is a "trade association monthly (except November-December combined), circulation 4,200, for the promotion, protection, and improvement of the Wisconsin foodservice industry." They use **"all types of poetry, but must have food service as subject. Nothing lengthy or off-color (length 10-50 lines)." They buy 6-12 poems/year. Sample: $1.75 plus postage. Send SASE for guidelines. Reports in 1-2 months. Pays $2.50-7.50/poem. Editor sometimes comments on rejections.** She advises, "Study copies of the magazine before submitting."

WISCONSIN REVIEW; WISCONSIN REVIEW PRESS (II), Box 158, Radford Hall, University of Wisconsin-Oshkosh, Oshkosh WI 54901, phone (414)424-2267, founded 1966, editor Troy Schoultz, is published 3 times/year. **"In poetry we publish mostly free verse with strong images and fresh approaches. We want new turns of phrase."** They have published poetry by Laurel Mills, Joseph Bruchac, Kenneth Frost, Paul Marion, Dionisio Martinez, Stephen Perry, Margaret Randall, David Steingass, Brian Swann and Peter Wild. As a sample the editor selected these lines from "Early Morning of Another World" by Tom McKeown:

After squid and cool white wine there is
no sleep. The long tentacles uncurl
out of the dark with all that was left behind.
Promises expand promises. A frayed mouth
loses its color in the dawn.

The ***Review*** is 48-64 pgs., 6×9, elegantly printed on quality white stock, glossy card cover with color art, b&w art inside. They receive about 1,500 poetry submissions/year, use about 75. They use 30-40 pgs. of poetry in each issue. Press run is 2,000, for 50 subscribers, 30 of which are libraries. Single copy: $3; subscription: $8. **Sample postpaid: $2. Submit mss September 15 through May 15. Offices checked bimonthly during summer. Editor requests no more than 4 poems/submission, one poem/page, single-spaced with name and address of writer on each page. Simultaneous submissions OK, but previously unsubmitted works preferable. Cover letter also preferred; include brief bio. Send SASE for guidelines. Reports within 1-4 months. Pays 2 copies.**

THE WISE WOMAN (I, IV-Feminist), 2441 Cordova St., Oakland CA 94602, founded 1980, editor and publisher Ann Forfreedom, is a quarterly journal **"focusing on feminist issues, feminist spirituality, Goddess lore and Feminist Witchcraft." They want "mostly shorter poetry—by both women and men—dealing with these themes."** They have published poetry by Maura Alia Bramkamp and Viviane Lerner. As a sample the editor selected these lines from "Arise O Women" by Kathleen Weinschenk:

O Women of the world,
Catch a vision
Of your own true self.
Discover the power
Within . . .

TWW is magazine-sized, approximately 52 pgs., offset. "At least 20 poems received/year; accept about 30% of appropriate poems." Subscription: $15. **Sample postpaid: $4. Ms should be typed, double-spaced, with writer's name and address on each page. They will consider previously published poems. Cover letter not required, "but it is appreciated." Usually sends typeset copy for review. Pays 1 copy.** Ann Forfreedom says, "I prefer poems that are active, come from the writer's deep experiences or feelings, are brief and are applicable to many kinds of people. A focus on Goddess culture, nature or feminist issues is helpful. Good spelling is deeply appreciated."

WITHOUT HALOS; OCEAN COUNTY POETS COLLECTIVE (II), P.O. Box 1342, Point Pleasant Beach NJ 08742, founded 1983, editor-in-chief Frank Finale, is an annual publication of the Ocean County Poets Collective; it prints "good contemporary poetry." The magazine **"accepts all genres, though no obscenity. Prefers poetry no longer than 2 pages. Wants to see strong, lucid images ground in experience." They do not want "religious verse or greeting card lyrics."** They have recently published poetry by Robert Cooperman, John Dickson, Gayle Elen Harvey and Jean Hollander. "Issue XI features Ted Weiss with a long poem and a short essay." As a sample, the editor selected these lines from "The Road to Chrétien Point" by Marvin Solomon:

Talk about washboards—that road
was chicken bones and ribs even our careful glide

of driving couldn't flesh. She
came out of the wooden general store by

the side of the road to give us directions,
gesturing with an expressive half-emptiness

of Coke bottle sipping the heated air.

Without Halos is 112 pgs., digest-sized, handsomely printed with b&w artwork inside and on the glossy card cover, flat-spined. Circulation is 1,000, of which 100 are subscriptions and 100 are sold on newsstands; other distribution is at cultural events, readings, workshops, etc. Single copy: $5. **Sample (back issue) postpaid: $4. The editors "prefer letter-quality printing, single or double-spaced, no more than 5 poems. Name and address should appear on each page. Reads submissions January 1 through June 30 only. No manuscript returned without proper SASE. Sloppiness tossed back." Reports in 2-4 months and all acceptances are printed in the next**

annual issue, which appears in the winter. Sends prepublication galleys only if requested by the featured poet. Pays 1 copy; discount on extras. Acquires first North American serial rights. For the last seven years, ***Without Halos*** has received modest grants from the New Jersey State Council on the Arts. The editor says, "We would like to receive more poems with some humor."

WOLSAK AND WYNN PUBLISHERS LTD. (II), Box 316, Don Mills Post Office, Don Mills, Ontario M3C 2S7 Canada, phone (416)222-4690, founded 1982, poetry editors Heather Cadsby and Maria Jacobs, publishes 5 flat-spined literary paperbacks/year (56-100 pgs.). They have recently published collections of poetry by Ted Plantos and Carol Malyon. Here is a sample from **Cantos From A Small Room** by Robert Hilles:

Some mornings I wake to an opera on the radio
and I think of her hand raised to me
and how small I was as I kissed it and she
smiled and I knew that her defeat was mine too that
there is little that the living can share with the dying.

The books are handsomely printed. **Sample: $8 US or $10 Canadian. Send sample poems with query, bio, publications. No simultaneous submissions. Reports on queries in 4 months. Always sends prepublication galleys. Pays 10% royalties. Buys first rights.** Maria Jacobs says, "W&W prefers not to prescribe. We are open to *good* writing of any kind."

WOMEN'S EDUCATION DES FEMMES (IV-Regional, women/feminism), 47 Main St., Toronto, Ontario M6J 2G6 Canada, phone (416)960-4644, founded 1982, editor Christina Starr, is a quarterly using **"feminist poetry, about women, written by Canadian women only."** They have recently published poetry by Anne le Drenay and Diane Driedger. As a sample the editor selected these lines from "Girl Lost on the Ice, 1914" by Leslie Smith Dow:

into the foaming drifts
of dairy cream
I sink
at last in sleep enfolded
in your strong arms of birch.

The editor describes it as 48 pgs., magazine-sized, web offset, saddle-stapled, with one-color cover. Subscription: $17 individual, $30 institution. **Sample postpaid: $2.50. Publishes theme issues. Send SASE for upcoming themes. Reports in 2-3 months. Pays $25/poem plus 2 copies.** Occasionally reviews books of poetry. Open to unsolicited reviews.

WOMEN'S PRESS (CANADA) (IV-Women/feminism, lesbian), #233, 517 College St., Toronto, Ontario M6G 4A2 Canada, founded 1972, co-managing editors Ann Decter and Martha Ayim, publishes **"minimum ms 48 pgs. Women of colour, feminist, political content, lesbian, modern or post-modern form. No haiku."** They have recently published poetry by Carmen Rodríguez, Betsy Warland, Cherríe Moraga and Lillian Allen. As a sample the editor selected these lines by Dionne Brand:

this is you girl, this is the poem no woman
ever write for a woman because she 'fraid to touch

They publish 1 flat-spined paperback/year. **Query first with cover letter and sample poems. Reports in 6 months. Always sends prepublication galleys. Pays 10% royalties, $150 advance, 6 copies.**

WOMEN'S STUDIES QUARTERLY; THE FEMINIST PRESS AT CUNY (IV-Women, feminist, bilingual), Dept. PM, 311 E. 94th St., New York NY 10128, phone (212)360-5790. ***Women's Studies Quarterly***, founded 1972, publisher Florence Howe, is a nonfiction quarterly using **"poetry that focuses on current issues of importance to women; emphasis on education or activism preferable."** They have published poetry by Mila Aguilar. The editor describes it as 5½ × 8½, 150-200 pgs. They use 1-5 poems in each issue. Their press run is 1,500. **Sample postpaid: $13. Simultaneous submissions and previously published poems OK. Editor rarely comments on rejections. Pays 1 copy.** The Feminist Press publishes primarily both historical and contemporary fiction and nonfiction (12-15 titles/year), but it also publishes some poetry, such as the series, **The Defiant Muse,** bilingual volumes (Hispanic, French, Italian and German) of poetry by women from the Middle Ages to the present.

WOMENWISE (III, IV-Women/feminism, specialized: health issues), 38 S. Main St., Concord NH 03301, phone (603)225-2739, founded 1978, run by an editorial committee, is "a quarterly newspaper that deals specifically with issues relating to women's health – research, education, and politics." They want **"poetry reflecting status of women in society, relating specifically to women's health issues." They do not want "poetry that doesn't include women or is written by men; poetry that degrades women or is anti-choice."** As a sample we selected these lines from "Two Days Before My Stroke" (poet unidentified):

Whatever happens, we'll always have this, *I said,*

wondering at the melodrama of my words.
We stood at the boat rail, eyes filled with ocean.
Neither of us understood the dream that had waked her
in the night, with a voice that said: Tell Margaret
to feel the energy that spirals through you, into her
and back again. This will be only for a little while . . .

WomenWise is a tabloid newspaper, 12 pgs., printed on quality stock with b&w art and graphics. Press run is 3,000. Subscription: $10/year. **Sample: $2.95. Submissions should be typed double-spaced. Reads submissions March, June, September and December only. Publishes theme issues. Send SASE for upcoming themes. Themes for winter 1994, spring 1995, summer 1995 and fall 1995 are menopause, abortion, lesbian health and cervical health, respectively. Reporting time and time to publication varies. Pays 1-year subscription. Acquires first North American serial rights.** Staff reviews books of poetry in "any word count," single format. They say they often receive mss with no SASE. "We throw them away. Please remember that we are a nonprofit organization with limited resources." The editor adds, "We receive a great deal of badly written free verse. We would appreciate receiving more poetry in traditional form, as well as more poetry in free verse written with skill and care."

WOODLEY MEMORIAL PRESS; THE ROBERT GROSS MEMORIAL PRIZE FOR POETRY (IV-Regional), English Dept., Washburn University, Topeka KS 66621, phone (913)231-1010, ext. 1448, founded 1980, editor Robert Lawson, publishes 1-2 flat-spined paperbacks a year, **collections of poets from Kansas or with Kansas connections, "terms individually arranged with author on acceptance of ms."** They have published poetry by Craig Goad, Michael L. Johnson, Bruce Bond and Harley Elliott. As a sample the editor selected these lines from "In the Old House" by William Stafford:

Inside our Victrola a tin voice, faint
but somehow both fragile and powerful, soared
and could be only Caruso, all the way from
Rome: I traced my fingers on the gold letters
and listened my way deeper and deeper

"We charge $5 reading fee for unsolicited mss." Replies to queries in 2 weeks, to mss in 2 months, published 1 year after acceptance. Samples may be individually ordered from the press for $5. Send SASE for guidelines for Robert Gross Memorial Poetry and Fiction Prize ($100 and publication).

WORCESTER REVIEW; WORCESTER COUNTY POETRY ASSOCIATION, INC. (II, IV-Regional), 6 Chatham St., Worcester MA 01609, phone (508)797-4770, founded 1973, managing editor Rodger Martin. *WR* appears annually with emphasis on poetry. **New England writers are encouraged to submit, though work by other poets is used also. They want "work that is crafted, intuitively honest and empathetic, not work that shows the poet little respects his work or his readers."** They have recently published poetry by Kathleen Spivack, William Stafford and Walter McDonald. As a sample the editor selected these lines from "At the Conservatory of Flowers" by Chris Gompert:

In the snug greenhouse air, water drips down leaves
of Quisqualis Indicia—*Rangoon Creeper vine*
that rambles overhead. Lapping at my feet
are heart-shaped Brazilian Prayer Plants. I stop,
(To be a real flower, you must be a sunflower) . . .

WR is 6×9, flat-spined, 64 pgs., professionally printed in dark type on quality stock with glossy card cover. Press run is 1,000 for 300 subscriptions (50 of them libraries) and 300 shelf sales. Subscription: $15 (includes membership in WCPA). **Sample postpaid: $4. Submit maximum of 5 poems. "I recommend 3 or less for most favorable readings." Simultaneous submissions OK "if indicated." Previously published poems "only on special occasions." Editor comments on rejections "if ms warrants a response." Send SASE for guidelines. Reports in 4-6 months. Pays 2 copies. Buys first rights.** They have an annual contest for poets who live, work, or in some way (past/present) have a Worcester County connection. The editor advises, "Read some. Listen a lot."

‡THE WORD WORKS; THE WASHINGTON PRIZE (II), P.O. Box 42164, Washington DC 20015, founded 1974, poetry editors Karren Alenier, J.H. Beall, Barbara Goldberg and Robert Sargent, "is a nonprofit literary organization publishing contemporary poetry in single author editions usually in collaboration with a visual artist. We sponsor an ongoing poetry reading series, educational programs and the Washington Prize—an award of $1,000 for a book-length manuscript by a living American poet." Previous winners include **Tipping Point** by Fred Marchant, **Stalking the Florida Panther** by Enid Shomer, **Farewell to the Body** by Barbara Moore, **Sun, Moon, Salt** by Nancy White and **Love in Idleness** by John Bradley. Submission open to any American writer except those connected with Word Works. Send SASE for rules. Entries accepted between February 1 and March 1. Deadline is March

1 postmark. They publish perfect-bound paperbacks and occasional anthologies and want **"well-crafted poetry, open to most forms and styles (though not political themes particularly). Experimentation welcomed."** As a sample the editors chose "Wings" from **Blameless Lives** by Elaine Magarrell:

Why are the children careless with their wings?

. . . Next time
they want to fly, the children will wish
they had borne the weight. One day they'll be

able to throw out parts of their lives like us
deliberately with no remorse—smoke a cigarette,
entertain a little death wish. My father once
put out a fire in my hair with his bare hands

never to touch me again.

"We want more than a collection of poetry. We care about the individual poems—the craft, the emotional content and the risks taken—but we want manuscripts where one poem leads to the next. We strongly recommend you read the books that have already won the Washington Prize. Buy them, if you can, or ask for your libraries to purchase them. (Not a prerequisite.) **Currently we are only reading unsolicited manuscripts for the Washington Prize." Simultaneous submissions OK if so stated. Always sends prepublication galleys. Payment is 15% of run (usually of 500). Send SASE for catalog to buy samples. Occasionally comments on rejections.** Their anthology, **The Stones Remember: Native Israeli Poetry**, was a recipient of the Witter Bynner Foundation Award and was selected as an "Outstanding Book" by ***Choice*** magazine. The editors advise, "Get community support for your work, know your audience and support contemporary literature by buying and reading the small press."

WORDSONG; BOYDS MILLS PRESS (IV-Children), 815 Church St., Honesdale PA 18431, phone (717)253-1164, founded 1990, editor-in-chief Dr. Bernice E. Cullinan, is the imprint under which Boyds Mills Press (a ***Highlights for Children*** company) publishes books of poetry for children of all ages. **"Wordsong encourages quality poetry which reflects childhood fun, moral standards and multiculturalism. We are not interested in poetry for adults or that which includes violence or sexuality or promotes hatred."** They have recently published poetry by Jane Yolen, Beverly McLoughland and John Ciardi. As a sample the editor selected these lines from **Somebody Catch My Homework** by David L. Harrison:

Billy brought his snake to school
For show and tell today.
"This snake belongs to me," he said.
"It's gentle as can be," he said.
"It wouldn't hurt a flea," he said.
But it swallowed him anyway.

"Wordsong prefers original work but will consider anthologies and previously published collections. We ask poets to send collections of 30-50 poems with a common theme; please send complete book manuscripts, not single poems. We buy all rights to collections and publish on an advance-and-royalty basis. Wordsong guarantees a response from editors within one month of our receiving submissions or the poet may call us collect to inquire. Please direct submissions to Beth Troop, manuscript coordinator." Always sends prepublication galleys. Wordsong's **Inner Chimes** received the International Reading Association Teachers' Choice Award. Dr. Cullinan says, "Poetry lies at the heart of the elementary school literature and reading program. In fact, poetry lies right at the heart of children's language learning. Poetry speaks to the heart of a child. We are anxious to find poetry that deals with imagination, wonder, seeing the world in a new way, family relationships, friends, school, nature and growing up."

WORKS MAGAZINE (IV-Science fiction), 12 Blakestones Rd., Slaithwaite, Huddersfield, Yorks HD7 5UQ United Kingdom, founded 1989, editor Dave W. Hughes, is a biannual using "speculative and imaginative fiction and poetry favoring science fiction." They want **"surreal/science fiction poetry. Nothing more than 50 lines. No romance or general work."** They have published poetry by Andy Darlington, Steve Sneyd, Paul Weinman and Brian Aldiss. The editor says ***Works*** is 40 pgs., A4, stitched with glossy cover. They receive about 150 poems/year, use 36. Press run is 400 for 200 subscribers of which 4 are libraries, 50 shelf sales. Single copy: £2 (£4.50 for US); 4-issue subscription: £7.50 (£14 US). **No simultaneous submissions. Cover letter required. Disk submissions acceptable: IBM (5¼ or 3½-inch) or Atari 520ST (3½-inch); ASCII files only. Seldom comments on rejections. Send SASE (or SAE and IRC) for guidelines. Reports within a month. Pays 1 copy.** The editor says, "Study the market."

WoRM fEASt!; TAPE WoRM; KNIGHTMAYOR PRODUCTIONS (III, IV-Horror, occult), P.O. Box 519, Westminster MD 21158-0519, *WoRM fEASt!*, an underground monthly, founded 1989, editors Llori Steinberg and Blaire Presley. *Tape WoRM* is an audio magazine with music, poetry, comedy and more. For *Wf* they want **"as strange as humanoids can get; no traditional verse, no rhyme (unless it's way off the keister), no haiku, no love poems unless one-sided and morbid/dark and unusually sickening; and no Christian poetry."** They have recently published poetry by Gregory K.H. Bryant, Robert Howington, C.F. Roberts, Bill Shields and Vinnie Van Leer. The editors say *Wf* is usually 32 pgs., saddle-stitched, format size varies, with artwork and photos (from subscribers). Press run is 500. "The digest is different colors every time." Subscription: $25 for *Tape WoRM;* $20 for *WoRM fEASt!*, when available. **Sample postpaid: $5 (make all checks and any other forms of payment to Llori Steinberg). Previously published poems OK. Cover letter required; "don't have to be professional, just state the facts and why you're interested in submitting; include a picture please." Always comments on rejections. Publishes theme issues. Send SASE for guidelines and upcoming themes. "We report as quickly as we can." Sometimes sends prepublication galleys. Pays 1 copy of *WoRM fEASt!* No payment on *Tape WoRM*; contact for submission guidelines.** Reviews books of poetry. Open to unsolicited reviews. Send books to Llori Steinberg for review consideration. "Sometimes we publish chapbooks for poets' personal use. They buy and they sell." The editors say, "We want weird, shock therapy art and literature; politics, drugs, insanity. Your writing must show depth, must shock us into a coma."

WORMWOOD REVIEW PRESS; THE WORMWOOD REVIEW; THE WORMWOOD AWARD (II), P.O. Box 4698, Stockton CA 95204-0698, phone (209)466-8231, founded 1959, poetry editor Marvin Malone. "The philosophy behind *Wormwood:* (i) avoid publishing oneself and personal friends, (ii) avoid being a 'local' magazine and strive for a national and international audience, (iii) seek unknown talents rather than establishment or fashionable authors, (iv) encourage originality by working with and promoting authors capable of extending the existing patterns of Amerenglish literature, (v) avoid all cults and allegiances and the you-scratch-my-back-and-I-will-scratch-yours approach to publishing, (vi) accept the fact that magazine content is more important than format in the long run, (vii) presume a literate audience and try to make the mag readable from the first page to the last, (viii) restrict the number of pages to no more than 40 per issue since only the insensitive and the masochistic can handle more pages at one sitting, (ix) pay bills on time and don't expect special favors in honor of the muse, and lastly and most importantly (x) don't become too serious and righteous." They want **"poetry and prose poetry that communicate the temper and range of human experience in contemporary society; don't want religious poetry and work that descends into bathos; don't want imitative sweet verse. Must be original; any style or school from traditional to ultra experimental, but *must* communicate; 3-600 lines."** They have published poetry by Ron Koertge, Gerald Locklin, Charles Bukowski, Edward Field and Lyn Lifshin. As a sample the editor selected these lines from "Where Art & Life Meet" by John Levin:

> *so very silly of me*
> *to believe*
> *that immersion in the former*
> *would smooth out*
> *the infinite kinks*
> *of the latter*

Wormwood is a digest-sized quarterly, offset from photoreduced typescript, saddle-stapled. Yellow pages in the center of each issue feature "one poet or one idea." Press run is 700 for 500 subscribers of which 210 are libraries. Subscription: $8. **Sample postpaid: $4. Submit 2-10 poems on as many pages. Send SASE for guidelines. Reports in 2-8 weeks. Pays 2-10 copies of the magazine or cash equivalent ($6-30). Acquires all rights. Returns rights on written request, without cost, provided the magazine is acknowledged whenever reprinted.** Reviews books of poetry. **For chapbook publication, no query; send 40-60 poems. "Covering letter not necessary—decisions are made solely on merit of submitted work." Reports in 1-2 months. Pays 35 copies or cash equivalent ($105). Send $4 for samples or check libraries.** They offer the Wormwood Award to the Most Overlooked Book of Worth (poetry or prose) for a calendar year, judged by Marvin Malone. Comments on rejections if the work has merit. The editor advises, "Have something to say. Read the past and modern 'master' poets. Absorb what they've done, but then write as effectively as you can in your own style. If you can say it in 40 words, do *not* use 400 or 4,000 words."

WRIT (II, IV-Translations), 2 Sussex Ave., Toronto, Ontario M5S 1J5 Canada, phone (416)978-4871, founded 1970, editor Roger Greenwald, associate editor Richard Lush, is a "literary annual publishing new fiction, poetry, and translation of high quality; has room for unestablished writers." **No limitations on kind of poetry sought; new forms welcome. "Must show conscious and disciplined use of language." They do not want to see "haiku, purely formal exercises, and poetry by people who don't bother reading."** They have recently published poems by Rolf Jacobsen, Paavo Haavikko, Adelia Prado, J.

Bernlef, Nils Aslak Valkeapää and Marcelijus Martinaitis. As a sample the editor selected these lines from "Nineteen Poems" by Charles Douglas:

But even underground our journey will observe

laws of topography, until an eruption
becomes like a wart, a small disturbance
of physiognomy, and each of our acts the weight

of a stone on the hillside, under the freedom system.

The magazine is 6×9, 96 pgs., flat-spined and sewn, professionally printed on heavy stock, matte card cover with color art. Circulation is 700, 125 subscriptions of which 75 are libraries, about 125 store and direct sales. **Sample postpaid: $7.50. Poems must be typed and easily legible, printouts as close to letter quality as possible. No simultaneous submissions. Reads submissions September 1 through April 30 only. Editor "sometimes comments on rejections." Reports in 2-3 months. Acceptances appear in the next issue published. Pays 2 copies, nominal fee and discount on bulk purchases. Buys first North American serial rights.** Staff reviews books of poetry. Send books—"but not self-published books"—for review consideration. The editor advises, "Read a copy of the magazine you're submitting to. Let this give you an idea of the quality we're looking for. But in the case of ***WRIT***, don't assume we favor only the styles of the pieces we've already published (we can only print what we get and are open to all styles). Enclose phone number and SASE with Canadian stamps or SAE with International Reply Coupons."

THE WRITE WAY (I, IV-Writing); TAKING CARE OF YOURSELF (I, IV-Specialized: health issues); ANN'S ENTERPRISES, 810 Overhill Rd., Deland FL 32720, phone (904)734-1955, founded 1988, editor Ann Larberg. ***TWW*** is a quarterly using **poems of up to 20 lines on the theme of writing.** As a sample the editor selected "Limerick Lamentation" by Donna Bickley:

Composing a limerick's not easy
Although my attempts make me queasy,
I jot down a line, I stretch for a rhyme.
Reaching as far as it pleases me.

TWW is an 8-page newsletter with articles on writing and ads. Single copy: $3; subscription: $12. **Sample free with SASE. Must include $1 reading fee and SASE with submissions (up to 5 poems). Do not submit in summer. Reads submissions January 1 through June 30. Publishes theme issues. Send SASE for upcoming themes. Themes for 1995 include limericks (spring) and love poems (summer). Reports in 6 weeks. Pays 2 copies.** Open to unsolicited reviews. Poets may also send books for review consideration. They hold contests quarterly and publish an annual holiday poetry edition with cash awards. ***Taking Care of Yourself***, a 4-page newsletter of well-being, is also published quarterly and **accepts 1-2 short poems/issue on the theme of health. Sample free with SASE. Pays copies.**

THE WRITER; POET TO POET (I, II), 120 Boylston St., Boston MA 02116-4615, founded 1887. This monthly magazine for writers has a quarterly instructional column, "Poet to Poet," to which poets may submit work for possible publication and comment. **Readers may find suggestions in the column for possible themes or types of poems.** As a sample the editor selected this poem, "Desert Love," by Sheila Golburgh Johnson:

shrike struck
shrike spiked
desert rat
long haunched
limp dangled
thorn tree impaled
so stuck am I
on sharp spined love
arms legs head
adangle
sun splintered
seared scorched
shrike shriven

Subscription: $27 (introductory offer: 5 issues for $10). Single copy: $3. **Submit no more than 3 poems, no longer than 30 lines each, not on onion skin or erasable bond, name and address on each page, one poem to a page. There is no pay and mss are not acknowledged or returned. Acquires first North American serial rights.**

WRITERS' CENTER PRESS; THE FLYING ISLAND; WRITERS' CENTER OF INDIANAPOLIS (II, IV-Regional), P.O. Box 88386, Indianapolis IN 46208, phone (317)929-0625, founded 1979, executive director Jim Powell. Writers' Center Press publishes ***The Flying Island***, a biannual of fiction, poetry, reviews and literary commentary by those **living in or connected to Indiana. They want poetry of high literary quality; no stylistic or thematic restrictions.** They have published poetry by Jared Carter, Alice Friman, Yusef Komunyakaa and Roger Mitchell. As a sample the editor selected these lines from "Snapshot: Father Washing the Dog" by Karen I. Jaquish:

The reek of Sergeant's Flea Soap stings.
Our dog is lathered into placid acceptance.
You glance up, toss that famous grin
given to stangers and Kodak cameras.

TFI, a 24-page tabloid, includes artwork, graphics and photography. They receive about 1,000 poems a year, accept approximately 5%. Press run is 1,000 for 500 subscribers. **Previously published poems OK, but not encouraged. Simultaneous submissions OK, if so advised. Brief bio required. Often comments on rejections. Send SASE for guidelines. Reports in 3-6 months. Pays $5 minimum for previously unpublished work. Buys first North American serial rights.** Staff reviews books of poetry. Send books for review consideration. The center sponsors frequent contests for members through its quarterly newsletter and open readings. They advise, "Balance solitary writing time by getting involved in a writing community. We frequently recommend rejected writers join a poetry workshop."

WRITER'S DIGEST (IV-Writing, humor); WRITER'S DIGEST WRITING COMPETITION (II), 1507 Dana Ave., Cincinnati OH 45207, phone (513)531-2222, founded 1921, associate editor Angela Terez, is a monthly magazine for freelance writers—fiction, nonfiction, poetry and drama. "All editorial copy is aimed at helping writers to write better and become more successful. **Poetry is included in 'The Writing Life' section of *Writer's Digest* only. Preference is given to short, light verse concerning 'the writing life'—the foibles, frenzies, delights and distractions inherent in being a writer. Serious verse is acceptable; however, no poetry unrelated to writing. We're looking for more serious poems on the joys and foibles of the writing life, but avoid the trite or maudlin." Preferred length: 4-20 lines.** The magazine has published poetry by Charles Ghigna. As a sample, the editors selected this poem, "Mixed Messages," by Lois McBride Terry:

"As a poet, you're no Poe."
"At prose, you're certainly not a pro."
"Your movie script is nondescript.
(And sadder still, your comic strip.)"
The only line they don't reject:
"Enclosed is my subscription check."

They use a maximum of 2 short poems/issue, about 15/year of the 1,500 submitted. ***Writer's Digest*** has a circulation of 225,000. Subscription: $27. **Sample postpaid: $3. Do not submit to Michael Bugeja, poetry columnist for the magazine. Submit to Angela Terez, associate editor, each poem on a separate page, no more than 8/submission. Previously published poems and simultaneous submissions OK if acknowledged in cover letter. Editor comments on rejections "when we want to encourage or explain decision." Send SASE for guidelines. Reports in 1-4 weeks. Always sends prepublication galleys. Pays $15-50/poem.** Poetry up to 16 lines on any theme is eligible for the annual Writer's Digest Writing Competition. Watch magazine for rules and deadlines, or send a SASE for a copy of the contest's rules. They also publish a biennial list of the top markets for poets, The ***Writer's Digest*** Poetry 60. This list contains the top 10 publishers of nontraditional verse, traditional verse, both free and formal verse, publishers that pay the most, those that publish the most new poets and those respected by well-published poets. Watch for a new Poetry 60 in the June 1995 issue. (Also see Writer's Digest Books under Publications Useful to Poets.)

WRITER'S EXCHANGE; R.S.V.P. PRESS (I, IV-Humor, writing), Box 394, Society Hill SC 29593, phone (803)378-4556, founded 1983, editor Gene Boone, is a digest-sized newsletter of articles on any aspect of writing, poetry and artwork with a special emphasis on beginners. He wants **"poetry to 24 lines, any subject or style. I also consider short poems such as haiku, tanka, senryu and other fixed forms. I like writing that is upbeat, positive, enlightening or inspiring, especially humorous poetry. I will not consider material that is anti-religious, racist or obscene."** He has published poetry by Victor Chapman, Winnie E. Fitzpatrick, Violet Wilcox and Mary Ann Henn. As a sample he selected these lines (poet unidentified):

A hurried world, spinning too fast
Modern technology replaces dreams
With skyscraper nightmares
God watches as we dance at Satan's feet.

WE is 12-20 pgs., saddle-stitched, with a colored paper cover. It is published quarterly. He accepts about half or more of the poetry received. Press run is 250. Subscription: $10. **Sample postpaid: $2. "I prefer typed mss, one poem per page, readable. Poets should always proofread mss before sending them out. Errors can cause rejection." No simultaneous submissions. Pre-**

viously published poetry OK. Cover letter required; list "prior credits, if any, and other details of writing background." Send SASE for guidelines. Responds in 2-4 weeks, usually 4 months until publication. Pays 1 copy. Acquires one-time rights. Staff reviews books of poetry. Send books for review consideration. They offer cash awards for quarterly contests sponsored through the magazine. Send SASE for current rules. ***Writer's Exchange*** ranked #9 in the "New Poets" category of the latest *Writer's Digest* Poetry 60 list. This category ranks those markets who often publish poets whose work is new to their publication. The editor says he comments on rejections, "if I feel it will benefit the poet in the long run, never anything too harsh or overly discouraging." His advice to poets: "Support the small press publications you read and enjoy. Without your support these publications will cease to exist. The small press has given many poets their start. In essence, the small press is where poetry lives!"

WRITERS' FORUM (II, IV-Regional), Dept. PM, University of Colorado, Colorado Springs CO 80933-7150, founded 1974, poetry editor Victoria McCabe. ***Writers' Forum***, an annual, publishes both beginning and well-known writers, giving **"some emphasis to contemporary Western literature**, that is, to representation of living experience west of the 100th meridian in relation to place and culture. We collaborate with authors in the process of revision, reconsider and frequently publish revised work. We are open to **solidly crafted imaginative work that is verbally interesting and reveals authentic voice. We would like to see more formal work, nicely executed."** They have published poems by William Stafford, David Ray, Kenneth Fields, Harold Witt and Judson Crews. The annual is digest-sized, 225 pgs., flat-spined, professionally printed with matte card cover, using 40-50 pgs. of poetry in each issue. They use about 25 of 500 submissions of poetry/year. Circulation 800 with 100 subscriptions of which 25 are libraries. **The list price is $8.95 but they offer it at $5.95 to readers of *Writer's Digest*. Simultaneous submissions OK if acknowledged. Send 3-5 poems. Reads submissions September 1 through March 15. Reports in 3 months. Pays 1 copy. Acquires all rights; returns rights.**

WRITERS FORUM; AND; KROKLOK (IV-Form), 89A Petherton Rd., London N5 2QT England, founded 1963, editor Bob Cobbing, is a small press publisher of experimental work including sound and visual poetry in cards, leaflets, chapbooks, occasional paperbacks and magazines. **"Explorations of 'the limits of poetry' including 'graphic' displays, notations for sound and performance, as well as semantic and syntactic developments, not to mention fun."** They have recently published poetry by Bruce Andrews, Maggie O'Sullivan, Paul Dutton, Betty Radin, Pierre Garnier and Bill Keith. As a sample the editor selected these lines by Nicholas Johnson:

out to see thi snow rub yor fore
head in it
till it smart llit
bar now hit ees tuary
eels hoy hoy
braun snowgape

The magazines are published "very irregularly" and use "very little unsolicited poetry; practically none." Press run "varies." **Payment is "by arrangement." Work should generally be submitted camera-ready.** Under the imprint Writers Forum they publish 12-18 books a year averaging 28 pgs. **Samples and listing: $5. For book publication, query with 6 samples, bio, publications. Pays "by arrangement with author."** The editor says, "We publish only that which surprises and excites us; poets who have a very individual voice and style."

WRITER'S GUIDELINES: A ROUNDTABLE FOR WRITERS AND EDITORS (I, IV-Writing), Box 608, Pittsburg MO 65724, founded 1988, poetry editor Susan Salaki, is "an open forum market news magazine, publishing down-to-earth comments and suggestions from editors and writers who want to help close the gap between these two professions, find less expensive ways of marketing work and help each other keep their fingers on the pulse of the buying markets. **Only poetry that can elicit strong emotions and vivid images from the reader is accepted. No vague, abstract poetry. All poetry must somehow pertain to publishing, editors or writing."** They receive about 100 poems a year, accept 6. **Sample postpaid: $4. No simultaneous submissions or previously published works. Send #10 SASE for guidelines**, free Guideline List and Market Barometer, and brochure. **Reports in 1 week. Pays $1 or 1 copy. Acquires first rights.** The editor says, "If your poetry moves us emotionally, we'll buy it."

WRITER'S JOURNAL (I, II), incorporating *Minnesota Ink*, Suite 328, 3585 N. Lexington Ave., Arden Hills MN 55126, phone (612)486-7818, ***Writer's Journal*** founded 1980, poetry editor Esther M. Leiper. ***Writer's Journal*** is a bimonthly magazine "for writers and poets that offers advice and guidance, motivation, inspiration, to the more serious and published writers and poets." Esther Leiper has 2 columns: "Esther Comments," which specifically critiques poems sent in by readers, and "Every Day with Poetry," which discusses a wide range of poetry topics, often—but not always—including readers' work. She says, **"I enjoy a variety of poetry: free verse, strict forms, concrete, Oriental. But we take nothing vulgar, preachy or sloppily written. Since we appeal to those of different skill levels, some**

poems are more sophisticated than others, but those accepted must move, intrigue or otherwise positively capture me. 'Esther Comments' is never used as a negative force to put a poem or a poet down. Indeed, I focus on the best part of a given work and seek to suggest means of improvement on weaker aspects. **Short is best: 25-line limit, though *very* occasionally we use longer. 3-4 poems at a time is just right."** They have published poetry by Lawrence Schug, Diana Sutliff and Eugene E. Grollmes. As a sample the editor selected these lines from "an unidentified author we'd love to hear from":

I am with Haysie again on God's ranch,
It is not yet dawn; we ride west
over the mountains. His face is in shadow
but I know it is Haysie because
I have loved his shadow so.

Writer's Journal is magazine-sized, professionally printed, 60 pgs. (including paper cover), using 4-5 pgs. of poetry in each issue, including columns. Press run is 49,000. They receive about 400 submissions/year of which they use 30-40 (including those used in Esther's column). **Sample postpaid: $4. No query. Reports in 4-5 months. Pays 25¢/line. The section *Minnesota Ink*** began as a separate magazine in 1987. "We are **open to style, prefer light-hearted pieces and of good taste." Payment varies. *Writer's Journal*** has Spring and Fall poetry contests for previously unpublished poetry. Deadlines: April 15 and November 30. ***Minnesota Ink*** has Summer and Winter poetry contests. Deadlines: August 15 and February 28. Reading fee for each contest: $2 first poem, $1 each poem thereafter.

WRITER'S LIFELINE (I), P.O. Box 1641, Cornwall, Ontario K6H 5V6 Canada, phone (613)932-2135, fax (613)932-7735, founded 1974, editor Stephen Gill, published 3 times a year, containing articles and information useful to writers, **poetry** and book reviews. **"We prefer poems on social concerns. We avoid sex."** As a sample the editor selected these lines from his poem, "Bigotry":

It grows
on the babel of confusion
in the lap of
the blinding dust of vanity
by the arrogant prince of ignorance.

WL is 36-40 pgs., digest-sized, saddle-stitched with 2-color paper cover, printed in small type, poems sometimes in bold or italics. Circulation is 1,500. Subscription: $18. **Sample postpaid: $3. Publishes theme issues. Send SASE for guidelines and upcoming themes. Responds in 1 month. Pays 3 copies. Acquires first North American serial rights.** Reviews books of poetry in 500-1,500 words. "We need book reviews." Query if interested.

‡WRITER'S WORLD; MAR-JON PUBLICATIONS (I), 204 E. 19th St., Big Stone Gap VA 24219, phone and fax (703)523-0830, founded 1990, editor Gainelle Murray, poetry editor Diane L. Krueger (**and submissions should go directly to her at 17 Oswego Ave., Rockaway NJ 07866**). ***Writer's World*** is a bimonthly literary publication presenting poetry, articles and columns on writing. **They want "avant-garde, free verse, light verse, traditional, 12-16 lines. No erotica nor anything mentioning violence or drug abuse."** They have recently published poetry by Joyce Carbone, Denise Martinson, William J. White and Arthur C. Ford. As a sample the editor selected the opening lines of "The Poet" by Linda J. Crider:

Bits of memory
Ideas and dreams,
Running in sunlight
Dancing in moonbeams
Floating through tomorrow
On gossamer wings.

WW is 20 pgs., 8½×11, typeset and saddle-stapled with glossy paper cover, clip art and ads. They receive 300-500 poems a year, accept approximately 15%. Press run is 3,600 for 3,100 subscribers of which 2% are libraries. Single copy: $4.50; subscription: $15. **Sample: $3.50 and 9×12 SAE with 98¢ postage. Submit 3-5 poems, none untitled. Previously published poems OK; no simultaneous submissions. Cover letter required. "Submissions without a SASE will not be read or returned."** Time between acceptance and publication is 6-12 months. **Often comments on rejections. Send SASE for guidelines. Reports in 2 months. Pays $5 for poetry used on the front cover; all others receive 2 copies. Buys one-time rights.** The editor says, "We have a critique

‡ ***The double dagger before a listing indicates that the listing is new in this edition. New markets are often the most receptive to submissions.***

service with subscribers given reduced rates. Write for more information."

WRITING FOR OUR LIVES; RUNNING DEER PRESS (I, II, IV-Women), 647 N. Santa Cruz Ave., The Annex, Los Gatos CA 95030, phone (408)354-8604, founded 1991, editor/publisher Janet McEwan, appears twice a year. "*Writing For Our Lives* serves as a vessel for poems, short fiction, stories, letters, autobiographies and journal excerpts from the life stories, experiences and spiritual journeys of women." They want **poetry that is "personal, women's real life, life-saving, autobiographical, serious—but don't forget humorous, silence-breaking, many styles, many voices. Women writers only, please."** They have recently published poetry by tere carranza, Hema Nair, Lesléa Newman, Priscilla Tallsalt and Sondra Zeidenstein. As a sample the editor selected these lines from "Precious" by Joyce E. Young:

You gently wooed my woolly plaits
Chubby legs, dark chocolate skin and wide feet

Now, when you grow weary of my threats
To split nails with my teeth
Slit my wrists, and not bleed
You whisper, gently, "Beloved"

Writing For Our Lives is 64-80 pgs., 5¼×8¼, printed on recycled paper and perfect-bound with matte card cover. They receive about 400 poems a year, accept approximately 5%. Press run is 1,000. Subscription: $11.50 individuals, $14 institutions. **Sample postpaid: $7. Submit typed poems with name and phone number at top of each page. Previously published poems ("sometimes") and simultaneous submissions OK. Include a self-addressed, stamped postcard "so I can promptly acknowledge receipt of your work." A SASE should also be included for reply and return of ms. Closing dates are February 15 and August 15. "I read, make selections and send notification letters as soon as possible after the closing dates." Seldom comments on rejections. Send SASE for guidelines. Pays 2 copies, discount on additional copies and discount on 1-year subscription. Acquires first world-wide English language serial (or one-time reprint) rights.** "Our contributors and circulation are international."

XANADU (II), P.O. Box 773, Huntington NY 11743, founded 1979, editors Mildred Jeffrey, Lois V. Walker, Sue Kain, Mitzie Grossman and Weslea Sidon, is an annual publishing "serious poems and an occasional, adventuresome essay on contemporary poetry or critical theory." They want **"well-crafted quality poems. Nothing inspirational, obscene or from beginners."** They have recently published poetry by Jill Bart, Diana Chang, Simon Perchik, Louis David Brodsky and Aaron Kramer. As a sample the editors selected these lines from "Sex, Genetics, The Sea" by Charles Entrekin:

Like falling backwards in time
toward something I don't comprehend,
if I run forward, if I stand still,
what I see has no name,
slouches away if I look at it,
yet feel in the touch of bones . . .

The editors describe the journal as 55-65 pgs., no ads, no graphics. Press run is 300 for 100 subscribers of which 5 are libraries. **Sample postpaid: $7. No previously published poems; simultaneous submissions OK. Poems must be typed. Seldom comments on rejections. Send #10 SASE for guidelines. Reports in 2 weeks to 3 months. Pays 1 copy. Acquires first North American serial rights.** They say, "We would be glad to look at more quality post-modernist and formalist poetry."

XAVIER REVIEW (II), Box 110C, Xavier University, New Orleans LA 70125, phone (504)486-7411, founded 1961, editor Thomas Bonner, Jr., is a biannual that publishes poetry, fiction, nonfiction and reviews (contemporary literature) for professional writers, libraries, colleges and universities. Press run is 500. Subscription: $10. **Sample postpaid: $5. No submission information provided.**

XENOPHILIA; OMEGA CAT PRESS (II, IV-Themes, science fiction/fantasy), 904 Old Town Ct., Cupertino CA 95014, founded 1990, editor Joy Oestreicher. *Xenophilia* appears twice a year using **poetry on "geo-cultural topics; 'xenology'—alien or other cultures, or our society from other's view; exotic rituals, mythic traditions; surreal, beat, punk, fantasy/science fiction, humor and speculative works (to 20 pgs.). No forced rhymes, unfocused or pointless poems, limp endings."** They have published poetry by Denise Dumars, David Kopaska-Merkel, David Lincoln Fisher, Bruce Boston and Wendy Rathbone. As a sample the editor selected these lines from "An Evening with Aldous Huxley" by Keith Allen Daniels:

. . . Expanding impossibly,
their humors filled the room with sudden

darkness, and then the lamplight shone
once more, but only on the walls and floor
and ceiling of our days.

The magazine is digest-sized, 60 pgs., saddle-stapled with glossy card cover, professionally printed. This small press product packs many poems (and punch) into each issue. Free verse is the norm. Subscription: $7. **Sample postpaid: $4. Publishes theme issues. Send SASE for guidelines and upcoming themes. Reports in 1 month, longer in December. Sometimes sends prepublication galleys. Pays $5/page plus 1 copy. Buys first North American serial rights. Editor comments on rejections "often. I occasionally ask for rewrites."** Reviews books of poetry, 10-100 pgs., single format. Query regarding reviews.

XIB; XIB PUBLICATIONS (II), P.O. Box 262112, San Diego CA 92126, phone (619)298-4927, founded 1990, editor tolek, appears irregularly, usually 2 times/year, publishing poetry, short fiction and b&w artwork and photos. They want **poetry of any form, length, subject, style or purpose. "Prefer 'quirky' things, however."** They have recently published poetry by Robert Nagler, John M. Bennett and Christina C. Brown. As a sample the editor selected these lines from "Monkey House" by Lyn Stefenhagens:

I am not gloss,
nor long of leg
nor food for lions,

so I extract
the gorged ticks,
pop them like grapes
for school children.

xib is 50 pgs., 6½×8½, photocopied on heavy bond, saddle-stapled, 10 pt. gloss mimeo cover, 80% illustrated with art and photos, some ads. They receive about 3,000 poems a year, use approximately 3%. Press run is 500 for 50 subscribers of which a third are libraries, 350 shelf sales. Subscription: $10 for 2 issues and a chapbook. **Sample postpaid: $5, back issues $4; make checks payable to tolek. Previously published poems and simultaneous submissions OK. Cover letter preferred. "Work sent without a cover letter will be read but may be returned without comment." Often comments on rejections. "Guidelines, broadsides and tearsheets available for SASE." Reports in 2-4 weeks. Pays 1 copy. Acquires one-time rights.** xib publications **publishes 1-2 chapbooks/year, "irregularly and arbitrarily. Please do not query or submit with chapbook intent. Most chaps form out of friendly joint-efforts."** Press run for chapbooks is about 75-100. Authors receive half; the rest goes to subscribers, reviewers and trades.

XIQUAN PUBLISHING HOUSE; THE PARADOXIST LITERARY MOVEMENT JOURNAL; THE PARADOXIST MOVEMENT ASSOCIATION (IV-Form), P.O. Box 42561, Phoenix AZ 85080, founded 1990, editor Florentin Smarandache. ***The Paradoxist Literary Movement Journal*** is an annual journal of "avant-garde poetry, experiments, poems without verses, literature beyond the words, anti-language, non-literature and its literature, as well as the sense of the non-sense; revolutionary forms of poetry." They want **"avant-garde poetry, 1-2 pages, any subject, any style (lyrical experiments). No classical, fixed forms."** They have published poetry by Teresinka Pereira, Paul Courget, Ion Rotaru, Michèle de LaPlante and Claude LeRoy. As a sample here is "Dear Deer" from **Nonpoems** by the editor:

\- *Hear, here!*
Buy, by
our hour,
four fore
pears pairs!
\- *Sun son,*
no! Know
two, too!
\- *Hi! Hie!*

The editor says ***TPLM*** is 52 pgs., digest-sized, offset, soft cover. Press run is 500. "It is distributed to its collaborators, U.S. and Canadian university libraries and the Library of Congress as well as European, Chinese, Indian and Japanese libraries." **No previously published poems or simultaneous submissions. Do not submit mss in the summer. "We do not return published or unpublished poems or notify the author of date of publication." Reports in 3-6 months. Pays 1-2 copies.** Xiquan Publishing House also publishes 2 paperbacks and **1-2 chapbooks/year, including translations. The poems must be unpublished and must meet the requirements of the Paradoxist Movement Association. Replies to queries in 1-2 months, to mss in 3-6 months. Pays 50 author's copies. Inquire about sample books.** They say, "We mostly receive traditional or modern verse, but not avant-garde (very different from any previously published verse). We want anti-literature and its literature, style of the non-style, poems without poems, non-words and non-sentence poems, very upset free verse, intelligible unintelligible language, impersonal texts personalized, transformation of the abnormal to the normal. Make literature from everything; make literature from nothing!"

THE YALE REVIEW (II), Yale University, P.O. Box 208243, New Haven CT 06520-8243, phone (203)432-0499, founded 1911, editor J.D. McClatchy, is a "quarterly general magazine of intellectual distinction and literary excellence." It is known for publishing all forms and styles of poetry, and issues reviewed verify that fact. Both formal and free verse, marked by excellence, seems welcome. They have published poetry by John Ashbery, W.S. Merwin and Amy Clampitt. Press run is 6,000 for 2,000 subscribers of which 1,000 are libraries. Single copy: $7; subscription: $22. **No previously published poems or simultaneous submissions. Reads submissions September 1 through June 30 only.** Time between acceptance and publication is 9 months to 1 year. **Seldom comments on rejections. Reports within 2 months. Always sends prepublication galleys. Pays $100-300.** "Volumes of poetry reviewed in a regular essay." Send books for review consideration. Poetry published in ***The Yale Review*** was also selected for inclusion in the 1992, 1993 and 1994 volumes of **The Best American Poetry.**

YALE UNIVERSITY PRESS; THE YALE SERIES OF YOUNGER POETS (III), 92A Yale Station, New Haven CT 06520, phone (203)432-0900, founded 1908, poetry editor (Yale University Press) Jonathan Brent. The Yale Series of Younger Poets is one of the most prestigious means available to launch a book publishing career. It is **open to poets under 40 who have not had a book previously published—a book ms of 48-64 pgs. Entry fee: $8. Submit February 1-28 each year. Send SASE for rules and guidelines.** Poets are not disqualified by previous publication of limited editions of no more than 300 copies or previously published poems in newspapers and periodicals, which may be used in the book ms if so identified. Previous winners include Richard Kenney, Julie Agoos, Pamela Alexander and George Bradley. Publication of the winning volume each year is on a standard royalty contract plus 10 author's copies, and the reputation of the contest guarantees more than the usual number of reviews.

YANKEE MAGAZINE; YANKEE ANNUAL POETRY CONTEST (II), Main St., Dublin NH 03444, phone (603)563-8222, founded in 1935, poetry editor (since 1955) Jean Burden. Though it has a New England emphasis, the poetry is not necessarily about New England or by New Englanders, and it has a national distribution of more than a million subscribers. They want to see **"high quality contemporary poems in either free verse or traditional form. Does not have to be regional in theme. Any subject acceptable, provided it is in good taste. We look for originality in thought, imagery, insight—as well as technical control." They do not want poetry that is "cliché-ridden, banal verse."** They have published poetry by Maxine Kumin, Liz Rosenberg, Josephine Jacobsen, Nancy Willard, Linda Pastan, Paul Zimmer and Hayden Carruth. As a sample the editor selected these lines from "Waking" by Joan LaBombard:

But blood's in thrall to the world
and the body's bound
by its clocks and invisible pulleys—
sun plucking at bedclothes,
a mockingbird's ultimatum.
I reenter the world's cage, the house
of my daylight body.
My blood discovers its old riverbed,
and my name remembers me.

The monthly is 6×9, 170 pgs., saddle-stapled, professionally printed, using full-color and b&w ads and illustrations, with full-color glossy paper cover. They receive over 30,000 submissions a year, accept about 50-60 poems, use 4-5 poems/monthly issue. Subscription: $22. **Submit poems up to 30 lines, free verse or traditional. No simultaneous submissions or previously published poems. Submissions without SASE "are tossed." Editor comments on rejections "only if poem has so many good qualities it only needs minor revisions." Reports in 2-3 weeks. Approximately 18-month backlog. Pays $50/poem, all rights; $35, first magazine rights.** Sponsors an annual poetry contest judged by a prominent New England poet and published in the February issue, with awards of $150, $100 and $50 for the best 3 poems in the preceding year. ***Yankee*** ranked #9 in the "Top Pay" category of the latest ***Writer's Digest*** Poetry 60 list. Jean Burden advises, "Study previous issues of ***Yankee*** to determine the kind of poetry we want. Get involved in poetry workshops at home. Read the best contemporary poetry you can find."

YARROW, A JOURNAL OF POETRY (II), English Dept., Lytle Hall, Kutztown State University, Kutztown PA 19530, founded 1981, editor Harry Humes, appears twice a year. They have published poetry by Gibbons Ruark, Jared Carter, William Pitt Root and Fleda Brown Jackson. It is 40 pgs., 6×9, offset. Press run is 350. Subscription: $5/2 years. **Reports in 1-2 months. Pays 2 copies plus 1-year subscription.** Poetry published in ***Yarrow*** was also selected for inclusion in a **Pushcart Prize** anthology.

‡YEFIEF (II), P.O. Box 8505, Santa Fe NM 87504, founded 1993, editor Ann Racuya-Robbins, is an annual designed "to construct a narrative of culture at the end of the century." **They want "innovative visionary work of all kinds."** They have recently published poetry by Michael Palmer, Simon Perchik and David Shaddock. As a sample we selected these lines from "Agua Negra" by Leo Romero:

Within the mountains
darkness poured like syrup
poured into that black
which filled the valley
like the deepest ocean . . .

Yefief is 176 pgs., 7×9, offset and perfect-bound with color coated card cover and b&w photos, art and graphics inside. Press run is 1,000. Single copy: $7.95. **Previously published poems and simultaneous submissions OK. Reports in 6-8 weeks. Pays 2-3 copies.** Open to unsolicited reviews. Poets may also send books for review consideration.

YELLOW SILK: JOURNAL OF EROTIC ARTS, Verygraphics, P.O. Box 6374, Albany CA 94706. Prefers not to share information.

YESTERDAY'S MAGAZETTE (I, IV-Senior citizens), Independent Publishing Co., P.O. Box 15126, Sarasota FL 34277, editor and publisher Ned Burke, founded 1973. This bimonthly magazine is for **"*all* nostalgia lovers.** ***YM*** believes that everyone has a yesterday and everyone has a memory to share. Nothing fancy here . . . just 'plain folks' relating their individual life experiences. **We are always seeking new and innovative writers with imagination and promise, and we would like to see more 40s, 50s and 60s pieces."** As a sample here are lines from "The Backyard Pump" by J.E. Coulbourn:

With two small hands you'd
grasp the monster's tail
And try to pump the water in the pail,
But if his darned esophagus got dry
No water came no matter how you'd try.

YM is 28 pgs., magazine-sized, saddle-stapled, professionally printed on good stock with glossy color cover. A year's subscription is $14 or 2 years for $25. **Sample: $3. Submissions for "Quills, Quips, & Quotes" (their poetry page) should be "thoughtful, amusing, or just plain interesting for our 'plain folks' readers. No SASE is required as short items are generally not returned nor acknowledged, unless requested by the contributor." Pays copies.**

THE YOUNG CRUSADER (IV-Children), National Woman's Christian Temperance Union, 1730 Chicago Ave., Evanston IL 60201, is a monthly publication for members of the Loyal Temperance Legion and young friends of their age – **about 6-12 years.** They want **"short poems appropriate for the temperance and high moral value and nature themes and their young audience."** It is a 12-page, digest-sized leaflet. **Pays 10¢/line for poetry.**

YOUNG VOICES MAGAZINE (IV-Children), P.O. Box 2321, Olympia WA 98507, phone (206)357-4683, founded 1988, founder/publisher Steve Charak, editor Char Simons, is "a magazine of **creative work of elementary through high school students. The age limit is rigid."** It appears every other month. Press run is 2,000 for 1,000 subscribers of which 100 are libraries. Subscription: $15 for 1 year, $28 for 2. **Sample postpaid: $4. Editor comments "definitely, on every piece of writing accompanied by a SASE." Send SASE for guidelines. Pays $3/poem plus 1 copy (3 copies if you are a subscriber). Buys one-time rights.** Steve Charak says, "Revise. Remember that in a poem, every word counts. Forget about the need to rhyme. Instead, put feeling into each word. We would like to see more non-traditional forms of poetry."

ZEITGEIST (II), P.O. Box 1006, Kalispell MT 59903, founded 1990, publisher/editor John S. Slack, appears 4 times/year. For poetry, **"best is 1 page or less dealing with personal relationships to world and others. Focused ideas. Disturbing or provocative imagery welcomed. No same old love-death-suicide stuff, graphic sex and/or gratuitous profanity. No blatantly didactic stuff. We want poems that provide a bit of the truth."** They have published poetry by Adrian C. Louis, Gina Bergamino and Tom Caufield. As a sample the editor selected these lines by Pete Lee:

You bring it
Back. It
Never really
Leaves you
The habit

Zeitgeist is 20-28 pgs., 8½×11, photocopied, edge-stapled. They accept about 10% of poems submitted. Press run is 50 for 40 subscribers of which 3 are libraries. Subscription: $10. **Sample postpaid: $3. Previously published poems and simultaneous submissions OK. "A 3-line bio would help us get a feel of who you are." Editor often comments on rejections. Send SASE for**

guidelines. Reports in 1-4 months. Sometimes sends prepublication galleys. Pays "each issue in which poet appears." Open to unsolicited reviews. They offer free space for self-publishers. The editor says, "Write often. Sometimes raw is better. Keep your eyes, ears and nose open, along with your mind. Don't take rejection personally. Sometimes it takes a while to find your audience. Write lots and send the best."

ZEPHYR PRESS (III, IV-Translations), 13 Robinson St., Somerville MA 02145, founded 1980, editors Ed Hogan and Leora Zeitlin. "We accept about 1% or less of the mss we receive. **We are now publishing very little poetry, except some Russian and Eastern European poetry in translation."** A recent publication is **The Complete Poems of Anna Akhmatova**, translations by Judith Hemschemeyer. Their catalog lists books of poetry by Sue Standing, Anne Valley Fox and Miriam Sagan. **Query with 5 sample poems. Simultaneous submissions OK. "We will respond only if interested." Pays 10% of press run or by royalty, depending upon the particular project.**

ZOLAND BOOKS INC. (III), 384 Huron Ave., Cambridge MA 02138, phone (617)864-6252, founded 1987, publisher Roland Pease, is a "literary press: fiction, poetry, photography, gift books, books of literary interest." They want **"high-quality" poetry, not sentimental.** They have recently published poetry by William Corbett, Karen Fiser, Marge Piercy, Patricia Smith, Gary Fincke, Alice B. Fogel, Sam Cornish and Kim Vaeth. They publish 8-10 books/year, flat-spined, averaging 104 pgs. **Query with 5-10 sample poems, bio, publications. Editor does not comment on submissions. Sometimes sends prepublication galleys. Pays 5-10% royalties plus 5 copies. Buys all rights.** Zoland's **Big Towns, Big Talk** by Patricia Smith won the Carl Sandburg Award for poetry, sponsored by the Friends of the Chicago Public Library.

ZUZU'S PETALS QUARTERLY (II), P.O. Box 4476, Allentown PA 18105, phone (610)821-1324, founded 1992, editor T. Dunn. "We publish high quality fiction, essays, poetry and reviews. As a journal of both the written and visual arts, we provide a home for outstanding works of postmodern creativity. **Free verse, blank verse, experimental, etc. are all welcome here. We're looking for a freshness of language, new ideas and original expression. No 'June, moon and spoon' rhymed poetry. No light verse. I'm open to considering more feminist, ethnic, alternative poetry."** They have recently published poetry by Max Greenberg, Gayle Elen Harvey, Jean Erhardt and Sandra Nelson. As a sample the editor selected these lines from Jean-Paul DeVellard:

Now I must learn to draw
all over again
struggle to lay claim
to the perfect and last
for all time depiction
of your soft and faithful
universal mouth

ZPQ is 50 pgs., 8½×11, side-stapled, matte card cover, b&w graphics and artwork throughout. They receive about 2,000 poems a year, accept approximately 10%. Press run is 300. Subscription: $17 US, $25 international. **Sample postpaid: $5. Previously published poems and simultaneous submissions OK. Electronic submissions in ASCII (DOS IBM) format on 3½ or 5¼ disks OK. Seldom comments on rejections. Send SASE for guidelines. Reports in 2 weeks to 2 months. Pays 1 copy. Acquires one-time rights.** Staff reviews books of poetry and audiotapes of poetry readings in approximately 200 words. Send books or galleys for review consideration. They also sponsor twice-yearly poetry contests. Entry fee: $2/poem, any style, length or subject. Deadlines are the first of March and September. 40% of proceeds goes to prize winners: 25% to first prize, 10% to second, 5% to third. Free critiques to honorable mentions. The remaining 60% of proceeds goes towards the magazine and keeps it ad-free. ***Library Journal*** described ***ZPQ*** as "an exciting new little." The editor says, "Read as much poetry as you can. Support the literary arts: Go to poetry readings, read chapbooks and collections of verse. Eat poetry for breakfast, cultivate a love of language, then write!"

ZYZZYVA, Suite 1400, 41 Sutter St., San Francisco CA 94104. Prefers not to share information. Editor Howard Junker says, "We publish very few unsolicited poems."

Publishers of Poetry/'94-'95 Changes

Each year we contact all of the publishers listed in **Poet's Market** to request updated information for our next edition. The following magazine and book publishers were listed in the 1994 edition of **Poet's Market** but are not in the 1995 edition because either they did not respond to our request to update their listing (these names appear without further explanation) or their listing was deleted (for the reason indicated in parentheses).

While many of these publishers have ceased operation, the reasons some of them are not included this year are temporary (e.g., overstocked, temporarily suspending publication, etc.) *If you're interested in any of the following, first research the publisher and then write a brief letter (enclosing a SASE) inquiring as to whether they are now interested in receiving submissions.*

Above the Bridge Magazine
Absolute Interzone Bizarre (temporarily suspended publication)
Agassiz
Aileron Press
Aireings
The Alchemist (ceased publication)
Alphabox Press
Ambit
American Dane (requested deletion)
American Knight (temporarily suspending publication)
Americas Review
The Amherst Review
Antaeus (ceasing publication)
The Arizona Unconservative
Arrowood Books, Inc.
Arte Publico Press
Atalantik (future uncertain)
Atlantis
Aura Literary/Arts Magazine
Awede Press (requested deletion)
The Baby Connection News Journal (overstocked)
Ball Magazine
Barnwood Press (requested deletion)
The Barrelhouse (ceased publication)
Beer & Pub Poetry
The Big Now
Big Rain (ceased publication)
Black Fly Review
Black Mountain Review (ceasing publication)
Blind Alleys
Blue Ryder
Boomtown
Boston Literary Review
Brilliant Star
Brooding Heron Press
Cadmus Editions
The California Quarterly (suspended publication)
Canal Lines (ceased publication)
Carousel Magazine (requested deletion)
Chalk Talk
Chaminade Literary Review
Changing Men
Chicory Blue Press
Chimera Poetry Magazine for Children
City Scriptum (ceased publication)
Cochran's Corner
Colorado North Review (ceased publication)
The Columbus Literary Gazette
The Cool Traveler
Cross Roads
Cyanosis
Dialogue
Dickinson Studies (suspended publication)
Dionysos (no longer publishes poetry)
Druid Press (requested deletion)
El Tecolote
Eldritch Tales Magazine of Weird Fantasy
Emrys Journal
Evangel
Experiment in Words (ceased publication)
Experimental Basement Press
Fellowship in Prayer
Figment (ceased publication)
For Poets Only (ceased publication)
Gavea-Brown Publications
Giants Play Well in the Drizzle (ceased publication)
Going Down Swinging
Graven Images
Great Lakes Poetry Press (ceased publication)
Green World Press
Gulf Coast
Heart Attack Magazine (ceased publication)
His Garden Magazine (ceased publication)
Hobo Stew Review
Hold the Pickle (ceased publication)
Hudson Valley Echoes (ceased publication)
Illuminations
Indigo Magazine
Inkshed—Poetry and Fiction
International Poets of the Heart (ceased publication)
Interstate Religious Writers Association (IRWA) Newsletter and Workshops (ceased publication)
Iron Press
Issues
Jeopardy
Joe Soap's Canoe
The Johns Hopkins University Press
Journeys (responded too late)
Judi-isms (requested deletion)
La Bella Figura
La Carta De Oliver
Lake Shore Publishing
Landfall
Lighthouse
The Lockhart Press
Los Hombres Press (ceasing publication)
Luna Ventures
Manushi
Maroverlag
Memes (future uncertain)
Metropolitain (ceasing publication)
Midnight Zoo
Midwest Villages & Voices (requested deletion)
Miriam Press (ceased publication)
Mulberry Press
New Chicana/Chicano Writing (ceased publication)
New Cicada
New Mexico Humanities Review (ceased publication)
New Welsh Review
Nexus (Canada)
The North Carolina Haiku Society Press
Northern Perspective
Notus (ceased publication)
Nutshell
Oasis Books
Occident Magazine
Orphic Lute
Out Loud
Oxford Magazine
Pandora
Panjandrum Books

Paper Radio
Paranoia Press
Pennine Ink
The Pet Gazette
Petronium Press
The Phlebas Press
Poet Papers
The Poetry Connexion
Poetry Nippon Press
University of Portland Review
Poultry (ceased publication)
Printed Matter
Quick Brown Fox (ceased publication)
Rainbow City Express (suspending publication)
The Raven
Revista/Review Interamericana
River Rat Review
Rohwedder
The Rolling Coulter (future uncertain)
Rope Burns
Sacred River
Sacrifice the Common Sense
Scarp
Secrets from the Orange Couch
Skoob Books Publishing Ltd.
The Snail's Pace Review
Sonoma Mandala
Spectrum/Old Times
Spit
Spokes
The Stevan Company
Stohlmberg Publishers
Stone Circle Press
Stone Press (ceased publication)
Street News
Takahe
Tal
Talisman Literary Research
Taproot
Team (no longer publishes poetry)
Texas Poet Series (ceased publication)
A Theater of Blood (now a serial fiction anthology)
Tiger Moon Press (temporarily suspending publication)
Times Change Press (no longer publishes poetry)
Times Literary Supplement
Tornado Alley Quarterly
Translucent Tendency Press
The Twopenny Porringer
Underwhich Editions
Utah Holiday Magazine
Vandeloecht's Fiction Magazine (ceased publication)
The Village Idiot
Widener Review (suspended publication)
Wild East
Willamette River Books
The Windhorse Review (ceased publication)
The Windhover Press (requested deletion)
The Wire
Witwatersrand University Press
Wordsmith
Yammering Twits (ceased publication)

State and Provincial Grants

Arts councils in the United States and Canada provide assistance to artists (including poets) in the form of fellowships or grants. These grants can be substantial and confer prestige upon recipients; however, **only state or province residents are eligible.** Because deadlines and available support vary annually, query first (with a SASE).

United States Art Agencies

Alabama State Council on the Arts
Barbara George, Programs Manager
1 Dexter Ave.
Montgomery AL 36130
(205)242-4076

Alaska State Council on the Arts
Jean Palmer, Grants Officer
Suite 1-E, 411 W. Fourth Ave.
Anchorage AK 99501
(907)279-1558

Arizona Commission on the Arts
Tonda Gorton, Public Information Officer
417 W. Roosevelt
Phoenix AZ 85003
(602)255-5882

Arkansas Arts Council
Sally Williams, Artists Program Coordinator
1500 Tower Bldg., 323 Center St.
Little Rock AR 72201
(501)324-9150

California Arts Council
Carol Shiffman, Individual Fellowships
2411 Alhambra Blvd.
Sacramento CA 95817
(916)227-2550

Colorado Council on the Arts and Humanities
Daniel Salazar, Director
Individual Artists Program
750 Pennsylvania St.
Denver CO 80203-3699
(303)894-2619

Connecticut Commission on the Arts
Linda Dente, Grants Information
227 Lawrence St.
Hartford CT 06106
(203)566-7076

Delaware State Arts Council
Barbara King, Coordinator
Individual Artist Fellowships
State Office Building, 820 N. French St.
Wilmington DE 19801
(302)577-3540

District of Columbia Commission on the Arts and Humanities
Diem Jones, Literature Grants and Aid
5th Floor, Stables Art Center
410 Eighth St. NW
Washington DC 20004
(202)724-5613

Florida Arts Council
Valerie Ohlsson, Arts Consultant
Division of Cultural Affairs
Florida Dept. of State, The Capitol
Tallahassee FL 32399-0250
(904)487-2980

Georgia Council for the Arts
Ann Davis, Grant Manager
Community Arts Development
Suite 115, 530 Means St. NW
Atlanta GA 30318
(404)651-7920

Hawaii State Foundation on Culture & Arts
Wendell P.K. Silva, Executive Director
Room 202, 335 Merchant St.
Honolulu HI 96813
(808)586-0300

Idaho Commission on the Arts
Diane Josephy Peavey, Literature Director
304 W. State St.
Boise ID 83720
(208)334-2119

Illinois Arts Council
Richard Gage, Director
Communication Arts
Suite 10-500, 100 W. Randolph
Chicago IL 60601
(312)814-6750

Indiana Arts Commission
Julie Murphy, Interim Director
Room 072, 402 W. Washington St.
Indianapolis IN 46204-2741
(317)232-1268

Iowa Arts Council
Julie Bailey, Grants Coordinator
Capitol Complex, 600 E. Locust
Des Moines IA 50319
(515)281-4451

Kansas Arts Commission
Tom Klocke, Program Coordinator
Jay Hawk Tower
Suite 1004, 700 Jackson
Topeka KS 66603
(913)296-3335

Kentucky Arts Council
Al Smith, Fellowship Program

31 Fountain Pl.
Frankfort KY 40601
(502)564-3757

Louisiana State Arts Council
Gerri Hobdy, Interim Director
P.O. Box 44247
Baton Rouge LA 70804
(504)342-8180

Maine State Arts Commission
Alden C. Wilson, Director
State House, Station 25
55 Capitol St.
Augusta ME 04333-0025
(207)287-2724

Maryland State Arts Council
Charles Camp, Grants Officer
601 N. Howard St.
Baltimore MD 21201
(410)333-8232

Massachusetts Cultural Council
80 Boylston St.
Boston MA 02116
(617)727-3668

Arts Foundation of Michigan
Kim Adams, Program Director
Suite 2164, 645 Griswold
Detroit MI 48226
(313)964-2244

Minnesota State Arts Board
Karen Mueller, Program Associate
432 Summit Ave.
St. Paul MN 55102-2624
(612)297-2603

Mississippi Arts Commission
Cindy Harper, Program Director
Suite 207, 239 N. Lamar St.
Jackson MS 39201
(601)359-6030

Missouri Arts Council
Michael Hunt, Program Administrator
Wainwright State Office Complex
Suite 105, 111 N. Seventh St.
St. Louis MO 63101
(314)340-6845

Montana Arts Council
Fran Morrow, Dir. of Art Services/Progs.
Suite 252, 316 N. Park Ave.
Helena MT 59620
(406)444-6430

Nebraska Arts Council
Nancy Quinn, Grants Officer
3838 Davenport
Omaha NE 68131-2329
(402)595-2122

Nevada State Council on the Arts
Susan Bofkoff, Executive Director
Capitol Complex, 100 Stewart St.
Carson City NV 89710
(702)687-6680

New Hampshire State Council on the Arts
Audrey Sylvester, Artists Services Coordinator
Phoenix Hall, 40 N. Main St.
Concord NH 03301
(603)271-2789

New Jersey State Council on the Arts
Steve Runk, Grants Coordinator
CN 306, 3rd Floor, Roebling Bldg.
Trenton NJ 08625
(609)292-6130

New Mexico Arts Division
Randy Forrester, Operation Director
228 E. Palace Ave.
Santa Fe NM 87501
(505)827-6490

New York State Council on the Arts
Jewelle Gomez, Director, Literature Program
915 Broadway
New York NY 10010
(212)387-7020

North Carolina Arts Council
Deborah McGill, Literature Director
Department of Cultural Resources
221 E. Lane St.
Raleigh NC 27601-2807
(919)733-2111

North Dakota Council on the Arts
Mark Schultz, Arts Education, Artists Services
Suite 606, Black Bldg., 118 Broadway
Fargo ND 58102
(701)239-7150

Ohio Arts Council
Bob Fox, Literature Coordinator
727 E. Main St.
Columbus OH 43205
(614)466-2613

State Arts Council of Oklahoma
Betty Price, Executive Director
P.O. Box 52001-2001
Oklahoma City OK 73152-2001
(405)521-2931

Oregon Arts Commission
Vincent Dunn, Assistant Director
775 Summer St. NE
Salem OR 97310
(503)378-3625

Pennsylvania Council on the Arts
Marsha Salvatore, Literature Program Director
Room 216, Finance Bldg.
Harrisburg PA 17120
(717)787-6883

Puerto Rican Foundation of the Arts
G.P.O. 4184
San Juan PR 00902-4184
(809)723-2115

Rhode Island State Council on the Arts
Iona B. Dobbins, Executive Director
Suite 103, 95 Cedar St.
Providence RI 02903
(401)277-3880

South Carolina Arts Commission
Steve Lewis, Literary Arts Director
1800 Gervais St.
Columbia SC 29201
(803)734-8696

South Dakota Arts Council
Dennis Holub, Director
Suite 204, 230 S. Phillips Ave.

Sioux Falls SD 57102
(605)339-6646

Tennessee Arts Commission
Alice Swanson, Director of Literary Arts
Suite 100, 320 Sixth Ave. N.
Nashville TN 37243-0780
(615)741-1701

Texas Commission on the Arts
Rita Starpattern, Program Director
Visual and Communication Arts
P.O. Box 13406
Austin TX 78711-3406
(512)463-5535

Utah Arts Council
G. Barnes, Literary Coordinator
617 E. South Temple
Salt Lake City UT 84102
(801)533-5895

Vermont Council on the Arts
Cornelia Carey, Grants Officer
Drawer 33, 136 State St.
Montpelier VT 05633-6001
(802)828-3291

Virgin Islands Council on the Arts
Marie Daniel, Grants Officer
41-42 Norve Gada
St. Thomas VI 00802
(809)774-5984

Virginia Commission for the Arts
Susan FitzPatrick, Program Coordinator
223 Governor St.
Richmond VA 23219
(804)225-3132

Washington State Arts Commission
Awards Department
Artist Fellowship Awards in Literary Arts
110 9th and Columbia Bldg., P.O. Box 42675
Olympia WA 98504-2675
(206)753-3860

West Virginia Arts and Humanities Division
Jill Ellis, Grants Coordinator
1900 Kanawha Blvd. E.
Charleston WV 23505
(304)558-0220

Wisconsin Arts Board
Beth Malner, Individual Artists Program Dir.
1st Floor, 101 E. Wilson St.
Madison WI 53702
(608)266-0190

Wyoming Council on the Arts
Guy Lebea, Literary Arts Coordinator
2320 Capitol Ave.
Cheyenne WY 82002
(307)777-7742

Canadian Provinces Art Agencies

Alberta Arts and Cultural Industries Branch
Clive Padfield, Director
3rd Floor, 10158 - 103 St.
Edmonton, Alberta T5J 0X6
(403)427-6315

British Columbia Arts Council
Cultural Services Branch
Walter Quan, Coord. of Arts Awards Prog.
5th Floor, 800 Johnson St.
Victoria, British Columbia V8V 1X4
(604)356-1728

Manitoba Arts Council
Pat Sanders, Writing/Publishing Off.
525 - 93 Lombard Ave.
Winnipeg, Manitoba R3B 3B1
(204)945-0422

New Brunswick Department of Tourism, Recreation and Heritage
Arts Branch
Bruce Dennis, Program Officer
P.O. Box 6000
Fredericton, New Brunswick E3B 5H1
(506)453-2555

Newfoundland Department of Municipal and Provincial Affairs
Cultural Affairs Division
Elizabeth Batstone, Director of Cultural Affairs
P.O. Box 1854
St. John's, Newfoundland A1C 5P9
(709)729-3650

Nova Scotia Department of Tourism and Culture
Cultural Industries/Research Officer
P.O. Box 578
Halifax, Nova Scotia B3J 259
(902)424-5000

The Canada Council
General Information Officer
P.O. Box 1047, 350 Albert St.
Ottawa, Ontario K1P 5V8
(613)566-4365

Ontario Arts Council
Lorraine Filyer, Literature Officer
Suite 500, 151 Bloor St. W.
Toronto, Ontario M5S 1T6
(416)961-1660

Prince Edward Island Council of the Arts
Judy McDonald, Executive Director
P.O. Box 2234
Charlottetown, Prince Edward Island C1A 8B9
(902)368-4410

Saskatchewan Arts Board
Gail Paul Armstrong, Literary Arts & Multi-disciplinary Consultant
3475 Albert St.
Regina, Saskatchewan S4S 6X6
(306)787-4056

Government of Yukon Arts Branch
Laurel Parry, Arts Consultant
Box 2730
Whitehorse, Yukon Y1A 2C6
(403)667-5264

Contests and Awards

Though considerably smaller than Publishers of Poetry, this section of **Poet's Market** also contains "markets" for your work. Here you will find various contests and awards whose offerings may include publication of your poetry in addition to their monetary prizes. And even if publication is not included, the publicity generated upon winning some of these contests can make your name more familiar to editors.

Listed in this section is a wide range of competitions – everything from contests with modest prizes sponsored by state poetry societies, colleges or even cities to prestigious awards offered by private foundations. What you will not find, however, is any contest or award associated with publishers or organizations listed elsewhere in this directory. For those, you should refer to the list of Additional Contests and Awards at the end of this section and consult the listings mentioned there for information.

Selecting contests

Whether you're reading the listings in this section or referring to those in other sections, you should never submit to contests and awards blindly. Since many contests require entry fees, blind submissions will just waste your money. As in the Publishers of Poetry section, each listing here contains one or more Roman numerals in its heading. These "codes" will not only help you narrow the list of contests and awards, but they can also help you evaluate your chances of winning (and recouping your expenses).

The **I** code, for instance, is given to contests that are very open to beginners. While these contests may require small fees, or membership in the sponsoring organization, they typically are not exploitive of poets, beginning or otherwise. Keep in mind, however, that if a contest charges a $5 entry fee and offers $75 in prizes, then the organizers only need 15 entries to cover the prizes. Even though fees may also go toward providing a small honorarium for the judge, 100 entries will surely net the organizers a neat profit – at the expense of the participating poets. Be careful when deciding which of these contests are worth your money.

The **II** code follows the name of general literary contests, usually for poets with some experience. This code may also follow awards for recently published collections, such as The Poets' Prize and the Kingsley Tufts Poetry Award (which is new to this edition), or fellowships designed for poets of "demonstrated ability," such as the Guggenheims. If you're just beginning, start building a reputation by having your work accepted by periodicals, then try your hand at these competitions.

Of all the codes, however, perhaps the most useful is **IV**, which designates specialized contests and awards. That is, you – or your poetry – must meet certain criteria to be eligible. Some contests, for instance, are regional, so only poets from a certain area can enter. Others are limited to certain groups, such as women or students. A few are for translations only. Still others are limited to poets writing in certain forms. If you write sonnets, for example, consider the Poets Club of Chicago International Shakespearean Sonnet Contest or the Salmon Arm Sonnet Contest. Competitions that primarily consider themselves specialized are often open to both beginning and established poets.

While most of the contests and awards in this section are open to entries, there are a few to which you cannot apply. These are coded **V**, indicating that the winners are chosen by nomination – often by an anonymous committee. See the listing for The Whiting Writers' Awards, for example. We include such awards because winning one is a very high honor and it is not only helpful to know that these awards exist, but it is also important to know that you should not attempt to apply for them.

Once you've narrowed down the contests and awards you want to enter, treat the submission process just as you would if you were submitting to a magazine: Always send a SASE for more information. Many contests want you to submit work along with their specific entry form or application. Others offer guidelines that detail exactly how they want poetry submitted. Also, deadlines for entries are often subject to change and if your work arrives after the deadline date, it may automatically be disqualified.

Finally, if you're considering a contest which publishes an anthology of entrants' work, first read the special sidebar about evaluating anthologies on pages 12 and 13 of Charting Your Path to Poetry Publication.

AAA ANNUAL NATIONAL LITERARY CONTEST; ARIZONA LITERARY MAGAZINE (I), Suite 117-PM, 3509 Shea Blvd., Phoenix AZ 85028-3339, sponsoring organization Arizona Authors' Association, award director Gerry Benninger. 42 lines maximum, $5 entry fee, submit between January 1 and July 29. Prizes are $125, $75, $40, 6 honorable mentions $10 each. Include SASE with entry for contest results; no material will be returned. Winners are announced and prizes awarded in October. Winning entries are published in a special edition of ***Arizona Literary Magazine***. Entries must be typed, double-spaced on 8½×11 paper. Write for more information and entry rules; enclose SASE.

MILTON ACORN POETRY AWARD; PRINCE EDWARD ISLAND LITERARY AWARDS (IV-Regional), The Prince Edward Island Council of the Arts, P.O. Box 2234, Charlottetown, Prince Edward Island C1A 8B9 Canada. Awards are given annually for poetry. Writers must have been resident at least 6 of the 12 months before the contest. Submit October 1 through February 15. For the Milton Acorn Poetry Award, participants may submit as many entries as they wish, each of no more than 10 pgs. Entry fee: $5. Prizes: A trip for 2 via Air Nova to Montreal or Ottawa, first prize; $200 and $100, second and third prizes.

ACTS INSTITUTE, INC. (II), P.O. Box 30854, Palm Beach Gardens FL 33420, contact Charlotte Plotsky. Publishes an anthology of works created by former residents of artists/writers colonies/communities. Net proceeds go to ACTS's Colony Grant Fund (money grants to those individuals/teams/groups accepted by artists/writers colonies who need financial assistance to be able to attend). Finalists in ACTS's Anthology project get their own publication, ***Impressions***. Also, ***Havens for Creatives***, 8th edition, and a new ***Havens for Creatives*** reference edition for libraries are now available. Write for information on these and other publications. ACTS's Artist Residency Program has been moved to P.O. Box 1121, Sacramento CA 95814. For other information, contact ACTS, P.O. Box 10153, Kansas City MO 64123.

THE AIR CANADA AWARD (IV-Regional), % Canadian Authors Association, Suite 500, 275 Slater St., Ottawa, Ontario K1P 5H9 Canada. The Air Canada Award is an annual award of two tickets to any Air Canada destination, to a Canadian author, published or unpublished, under 30 who shows the most promise. Nominations are made before April 30 by Canadian Authors Association branches or other writers' organizations and the award is given at the CAA banquet in June.

AMERICAN-SCANDINAVIAN FOUNDATION TRANSLATION PRIZE; SCANDINAVIAN REVIEW (IV-Translation), 725 Park Ave., New York NY 10021, for the best translation into English of a work (which may be poetry) of a Scandinavian author after 1800; $2,000, publication in the ***Scandinavian Review***, and a bronze medallion. To enter, first request rules. Deadline: June 1.

ARIZONA STATE POETRY SOCIETY ANNUAL CONTEST (I, II, IV), 4805 S. Birch St., Tempe AZ 85282, award director Dorothy Greenlee. Contest for various poetry forms and subjects. Prizes range from $10-75; first, second and third place winners are published in the winter edition of ***The Sandcutters***, the group's quarterly publication, and name and entries are listed for honorable mention winners. Contest information available for SASE. Fees vary. Deadline: August 31.

ARKANSAS POETRY DAY CONTEST; POETS' ROUNDTABLE OF ARKANSAS (I), over 25 categories, many open to all poets. Brochure available in June; deadline in September; awards given in October. For copy send SASE to Verna Lee Hinegardner, Apt. 109, 605 Higdon, Hot Springs AR 71913.

ARTIST TRUST; ARTIST TRUST GAP GRANTS; ARTIST TRUST FELLOWSHIPS (IV-Regional), Suite 415, 1402 Third Ave., Seattle WA 98101, phone (206)467-8734. Artist Trust is a nonprofit arts organization that provides grants to artists (including poets) who are residents of the state. It also publishes a 16-page quarterly tabloid of news about arts opportunities and cultural issues.

‡ARVON INTERNATIONAL POETRY COMPETITION (I, II), Kilnhurst, Kilnhurst Rd., Todmorden, Lancashire OL14 6AX England, phone 0706 816582, fax 0706 816359, jointly sponsored by Duncan Lawrie Limited and ***The Observer***. Poems (which may be of any length and previously unpublished) must be in English. First prize is £5,000 ($8,425), and other cash prizes. The competition is biennial. Distinguished poets serve as judges. Though the contest (which raises funds by entry fees) may be better known internationally, the major function of the Arvon Foundation is to offer writing courses at three retreats: at Totleight Barton, Sheepwash, Beaworthy, Devon EX21 5NS, phone (040923) 338; at Lumb Bank, Hebden Bridge, West Yorkshire HX7 6DF, phone (0422) 843714; and at Moniack Mhor, Teavarran, Kiltarlity, Beauly, Inverness-shire 1V4 7HT, phone (0463) 74675. These are residential programs at attractive country retreats, offered by established writers in subjects such as poetry, playwriting, short fiction, radio drama, and words and music. The tuition is £245 for, typically, 5 days, which includes tuition, food and accommodations, and there is scholarship available from the foundation for those who cannot otherwise afford to attend.

GEORGE BENNETT FELLOWSHIP (II), Phillips Exeter Academy, Exeter NH 03833, provides a $5,000 fellowship plus room and board to a writer with a ms in progress. The Fellow's only official duties are to be in residence while the academy is in session and to be available to students interested in writing. The committee favors writers who have not yet published a book-length work with a major publisher. Send SASE for application materials. Telephone calls strongly discouraged. Deadline: December 1.

BOLLINGEN PRIZE (V), Beinecke Rare Book and Manuscript Library, Yale University, New Haven CT 06520, prize of $10,000 to an American poet for the best poetry collection published during the previous two years, or for a body of poetry written over several years. **By nomination only.** Judges change biennially. Announcements in January of odd-numbered years.

BUCKNELL SEMINAR FOR YOUNGER POETS; STADLER SEMESTER FOR YOUNGER POETS (IV-Students), Bucknell University, Lewisburg PA 17837, phone (717)524-1853, director John Wheatcroft, includes the Stadler Semester for Younger Poets, the Seminar for Younger Poets and the Poet-in-Residence Series. The Stadler Semester is distinctive in allowing undergraduate poets almost four months of concentrated work centered in poetry. Guided by practicing poets, the apprentice will write and read poetry and will receive critical response. The two Fellows selected will work with Bucknell's writing faculty. The visiting Poet-in-Residence also will participate in the program. Fellows will earn a semester of academic credit by taking four units of study: a tutorial or individual project with a mentor poet, a poetry-writing workshop, a literature course, and an elective. Undergraduates from four-year colleges with at least one course in poetry writing are eligible to apply; most applicants will be second-semester juniors. Send a 12- to 15-page portfolio and a letter of presentation (a brief autobiography that expresses commitment to writing poetry, cites relevant courses and lists any publications). Also include a transcript, two recommendations (at least one from a poetry-writing instructor), and a letter from the academic dean granting permission for the student to attend Bucknell for a semester. Application deadline for the Stadler Semester is November 1. Students chosen for the fellowhips will be notified by November 25. The Bucknell Seminar For Younger Poets is not a contest for poems but for 10 fellowships to the Bucknell Seminar, held for 4 weeks in June every year. Seniors and juniors from American colleges are eligible to compete for the 10 fellowships, which consist of tuition, room, board, and spaces for writing. Application deadline for each year's seminar is March 10 of the previous year. Students chosen for fellowships will be notified on April 8.

THE BUNTING FELLOWSHIP PROGRAM (IV-Women), Radcliffe College, 34 Concord Ave., Cambridge MA 02138, phone (617)495-8212, supports women of exceptional promise and demonstrated accomplishment who want to pursue independent study in the creative arts (among other things). The stipend is $30,000 for a fellowship fulltime September 10 through August 15, requiring residence in the Boston area. Applicants in creative arts should be at the equivalent stage in their careers as women who have received doctorates two years before applying. Deadline is early October.

BUSH ARTIST FELLOWSHIPS (IV-Regional), E-900 First National Bank Bldg., 332 Minnesota St., St. Paul MN 55101, open to South and North Dakota, western Wisconsin and Minnesota residents over 25 years of age; helps published writers (poetry, fiction, literary nonfiction, playwriting and screenwriting), visual artists, choreographers and composers to set aside time for work-in-progress or exploration of new directions. Maximum of 15 awards of a maximum of $26,000 (and up to $7,000 additional for production and traveling expenses) are awarded each year for 6- to 18-month fellowships. Deadline is late October.

CALIFORNIA WRITERS' ROUNDTABLE POETRY CONTEST (I), under the auspices of the Los Angeles Chapter, Women's National Book Association, Lou Carter Keay, chairman, Suite 807, 11684 Ventura Blvd., Studio City CA 91614-2652. Annual contest with $50, $25 and $10 cash prizes for unpublished poems on any subject, in various forms, not more than 42 lines in length. WNBA members may submit free; nonmembers pay $3/poem entry fee. Send SASE for guidelines. Deadline: September 30.

CANADIAN AUTHORS ASSOCIATION LITERARY AWARDS; CANADIAN AUTHORS ASSOCIATION (IV-Regional), Suite 500, 275 Slater St., Ottawa, Ontario K1P 5H9 Canada, $5,000 in each of 4 categories (fiction, poetry, nonfiction, drama) to Canadian writers, for a published book in the year of publication (or, in the case of drama, first produced), deadline December 15. Nominations may be made by authors, publishers, agents or others. (Also see The Air Canada Award in this section.)

‡CAPRICORN POETRY AWARD (II); OPEN VOICE AWARDS (I, II); THE WRITER'S VOICE, Writer's Voice, 5 W. 63rd St., New York NY 10023. Capricorn Poetry Award, a cash prize of $1,000 and a reading at The Writer's Voice, limited to writers over 40. $15 entry fee. December 31 deadline. Send SASE for application guidelines. Open Voice Awards, annual awards, $500 honorarium and a reading at The Writer's Voice, open to both published and unpublished poets who have not previously read at The Writer's Voice. $10 entry fee. December 31 deadline. Send SASE for application form. The Writer's Voice is a literary center sponsoring weekly readings, writing workshops, writing awards and other activities.

CINTAS FELLOWSHIP PROGRAM (IV-Regional), Arts International, Institute of International Education, 809 United Nations Plaza, New York NY 10017, makes awards of $10,000 to young professional writers and artists of Cuban lineage living outside of Cuba. Call (212)984-5370, ext. 5514, for applications and guidelines. Deadline for applications: March 1.

CLARK COLLEGE POETRY CONTEST (I), % Arlene Paul, 4312 NE 40th St., Vancouver WA 98661, jointly sponsored by Clark College, Oregon State Poetry Association and Washington Poetry Association. $3/poem entry fee (checks payable to Clark College Foundation), prizes of $50, $75 and $100, for poems up to 25 lines, unpublished, not having won another contest. Entries in triplicate, not identified. Type name, address and phone number on a 3×5 card, include title and first line on card. May purchase book of winners' poems for $3 postpaid. Deadline: February 15.

INA COOLBRITH CIRCLE ANNUAL POETRY CONTEST (IV-Regional), Audrey Allison, Treasurer, #54, 2712 Oak Rd., Walnut Creek CA 94596, has prizes of $10-50 in each of several categories for California residents only. Poems submitted in 3 copies, no names on copies. Enclose a 3×5 card with name, address, phone number, category, title, first line of poem and status as member or nonmember. Members of the Ina Coolbrith Circle pay no fee; others pay $5 for 3 poems (limit 3). For further information contact Audrey Allison. Deadline is August.

ABBIE M. COPPS POETRY COMPETITION; GARFIELD LAKE REVIEW (I, II), contest chairperson Linda Jo Scott, Dept. of Humanities, Olivet College, Olivet MI 49076, phone (616)749-7683. Annual contest awarding $150 prize and publication in the ***Garfield Lake Review***. $2/poem entry fee for unpublished poem up to 100 lines. Submit unsigned, typed poem, entrance fee, and name, address and phone number in a sealed envelope with the first line of the poem on the outside. Judge to be announced. Deadline: February 15.

‡COUNCIL FOR WISCONSIN WRITERS, INC.; PAULETTE CHANDLER AWARD (IV-Regional), Box 55322, Madison WI 53705. The Paulette Chandler Award, $1,500, is given annually to a poet (even years) or short story writer (odd years). Wisconsin residents only. Submit letter of application and 5 poems, published or unpublished, by January 15. "Award is based on ability and need." Send SASE for rules. The Council also offers annual awards of $500 or more for a book of poetry by a Wisconsin resident, published within the awards year (preceding the January 15 deadline). Entry form and entry fee (free for members of the Council, $15 for others) required.

CREATIVE ARTIST PROGRAM (IV-Regional), Cultural Arts Council of Houston, Suite 224, 1964 West Gray, Houston TX 77019-4808, phone (713)527-9330. Offers annual awards of $4,000 to Houston visual artists and writers. Unless funding prohibits, choreographers and composers are also included in the competition. Deadline for entry is in the fall.

DALY CITY POETRY AND SHORT STORY CONTEST (I), Daly City History, Arts & Science Commission, Serramonte Library, 40 Wembley Dr., Daly City CA 94015. Contest held annually, awarding prizes of $30, $25, $15 and $10 in various categories and $5 for honorable mention. Entry fee of $1/poem or $2/story. Stories must be unpublished. Send SASE for rules; attn: Ruth Hoppin, coordinator. Deadline: January 4.

BILLEE MURRAY DENNY POETRY AWARD (II), % Janet Overton, Lincoln College, Lincoln IL 62656. Annual award with prizes of $1,000, $500 and $250. Open to poets who have not previously published a book of poetry with a commercial or university press (except for chapbooks with a circulation of less than 250). Enter up to 3 poems, 100 lines/poem or less at $10/poem. Poems may be on any subject, using any style, but may not contain "any vulgar, obscene, suggestive or offensive word or phrase." Entry form and fees payable to Poetry Contest, Lincoln College. Winning poems are published in **The Denny Poems**, a biennial anthology, available for $4 from Lincoln College. Send SASE for entry form. Deadline: May 31 postmark.

MILTON DORFMAN NATIONAL POETRY PRIZE (II), % Rome Art & Community Center, 308 W. Bloomfield St., Rome NY 13440. Annual award for unpublished poetry. Winners for 1993 were Lisa Chun, first place; Heather Davis, second place; and Peter S. Fendrick, third place. Judge for 1993 was Stephen Dobyns. Prizes: $500, $200 and $100. Entry fee $3/poem (American funds only; $10 returned check penalty); checks made payable to: Rome Art & Community Center. Include name, address and phone number on each entry. Poems are printed in Center's Newsletter. Contest opens July 1. Deadline: November 1. Winners are notified by December 1. Send SASE for results.

ERGO!; BUMBERSHOOT (II), Box 9750-0750, Seattle WA 98109, phone (206)622-5123, founded 1973, producing director Louise DiLenge, an annual publication ***ERGO!*** is issued in conjunction with Bumbershoot, a multi-arts festival at the Seattle Center on Labor Day weekend. "Fifteen hundred will be published for distribution prior to and at the Festival. Included will be selected works by the Writers-in-Performance invitational participants and winners of the Written Works Competitions in addition to the official literary arts program schedule." Twenty-four honoraria will be awarded for written works. Considers simultaneous submissions. Applications must be submitted by February 1. For application forms and further details write Bumbershoot at the address above. ***ERGO!* sample available for $9 postpaid. Competition guidelines available with a SASE.**

FEDERATION INTERNATIONALE DES TRADUCTEURS; UNESCO-CARL-BERTIL NATHHORST TRANSLATION PRIZE; ASTRID LINDGREN TRANSLATION PRIZE (IV-Translation), Dr. Heinrich Maierstrasse 9, A 1180 Wien, Austria, or, for American applicants: American Translators Association, Suite 903, 1735 Jefferson Davis Highway, Arlington VA 22202. The Unesco-Carl-Bertil Nathhorst Prize is awarded once every 3 years for "promoting translation, improving the quality thereof and drawing attention to the role of the translator in bringing the people of the world together." The Astrid Lindgren Prize is awarded every 3 years for "promoting the translation of works written for children."

FLORIDA STATE WRITING COMPETITION; FLORIDA FREELANCE WRITERS ASSOCIATION (I), Cassell Network of Writers, Maple Ridge Rd., North Sandwich NH 03259-9999, is an annual contest with categories in free verse and traditional. Awards prizes up to $100 in each category. Entry fees are $2/poem for members of the FFWA, $2.50 for others. Guidelines available each fall through March for #10 SASE. Deadline: March 15.

FOSTER CITY WRITERS' CONTEST (II), F.C. Committee for the Arts, 650 Shell Blvd., Foster City CA 94404, phone (415)345-5731. Yearly competition for previously unpublished work. $10 entry fee, $250 prize. Send SASE for instructions. Deadline: October 1.

‡FRIENDS OF DOG WATCH OPEN POETRY COMPETITION (I), 267 Hillbury Rd., Warlingham, Surrey CR6 9TL England, phone 0883-622121, contact Michaela Edridge. Annual competition for poems up to 40 lines. Cash prizes. Entry fees: £1/poem. Contest information available for SASE (or SAE and IRCs). Deadline: January 1.

‡ROBERT FROST CHAPTER: CALIFORNIA FEDERATION OF CHAPARRAL POETS ANNUAL POETRY COMPETITION ANNUAL POETRY COMPETITION (I, IV-Students), % Vivian Moody, 342 S. Redwood Ave., San Jose CA 95128. This annual contest has 6 categories with annual changes as to form or fee, limited to 2 entries per category. Prizes are $25, $15 and $10 in each category. Entry fee $2, plus $1/poem for nonmembers. Submissions may be previously published. Award poems not eligible. Open to residents of Canada and US. Deadline first half of August. The parent federation also sponsors monthly contests listed in the Chapter's ***Frostorial N/L*** published since 1963. Affiliation through the chapter includes state activities with yearly convention/award banquet in which the Golden Pegasus is awarded, terminating competitions since 1940.

GEORGIA STATE POETRY SOCIETY, INC.; BYRON HERBERT REECE AND EDWARD DAVIN VICKERS INTERNATIONAL AWARDS; THE REACH OF SONG ANNUAL ANTHOLOGY; ANNUAL CHAPBOOK COMPETITION (IV-Membership); GEORGIA STATE POETRY SOCIETY NEWSLETTER (I, IV-Anthologies, form), P.O. Box 120, Epworth GA 30541. The society sponsors a number of contests open to all poets, described in its quarterly newsletter (membership $20/year). Sponsors an annual anthology, **The Reach of Song**, and an annual chapbook (for members only) competition. The Byron Herbert Reece and the Edward Davin Vickers International Awards have prizes of $250, $100, $50, $25, $15 and $10. Entry fee: $5 first poem, $1 each additional. Deadline: January 31, Reece Awards; April 30, Vickers Awards. Send SASE for guidelines. Sample newsletter: $2; **Reach of Song:** $10.

JOHN GLASSCO TRANSLATION PRIZE (IV-Translation, regional), Literary Translators' Association of Canada, 3492, rue Laval, Montreal, Quebec H2X 3C8 Canada. $500 awarded annually for a translator's first book-length literary translation into French or English, published in Canada during the previous calendar year. The translator must be a Canadian citizen or landed immigrant. Eligible genres include fiction, creative nonfiction, poetry, published plays and children's books. Write for application form. Deadline: February 15.

GREEN RIVERS WRITERS' CONTESTS (I, IV-Themes, forms), Contest Chairman, 1043 Thornfield Lane, Cincinnati OH 45224, offers 6 contests for poetry on various themes and in various forms. Send SASE for rules. Entry fee $3/poem for nonmembers, prizes from $5-75. Deadline: October 31.

GROLIER POETRY PRIZE; ELLEN LA FORGE MEMORIAL POETRY FOUNDATION, INC. (II, IV-Themes), 6 Plympton St., Cambridge MA 02138. The Grolier Poetry Prize is open to all poets who have not published either a vanity, small press, trade or chapbook of poetry. Two poets receive an honorarium of $150 each. Four poems by each winner and 2 by each of 4 runners-up are chosen for publication in the *Grolier Poetry Prize Annual*. Opens January 15 of each year; deadline May 1. Submit 5 poems, not more than 10 double-spaced pages. Submit one ms in duplicate, without name of poet. On a separate sheet give name, address, phone number and titles of poems. $5 entry fee, checks payable to the Ellen La Forge Memorial Poetry Foundation, Inc. Enclose self-addressed stamped postcard if acknowledgement of receipt is required. For update of rules, send SASE to Ellen La Forge Memorial Poetry Foundation before submitting mss. The Ellen La Forge Memorial Poetry Foundation sponsors intercollegiate poetry readings and a reading series, generally 5/semester, held on the grounds of Harvard University. These are generally poets who have new collections of poetry available for sale at the Grolier Poetry Book Shop, Inc., which donates money toward costs (such as rental of the auditorium). They pay poets honoraria from $100-400 and occasionally provide overnight accommodations (but not transportation). Such poets as Mark Strand, Philip Levine, Robin Becker, Donald Hall and Brigit Pegeen Kelly have given readings under their auspices. The small foundation depends upon private gifts and support for its activities.

GUGGENHEIM FELLOWSHIPS (II), John Simon Guggenheim Memorial Foundation, 90 Park Ave., New York NY 10016. Approximately 145 Guggenheims are awarded each year to persons who have already demonstrated exceptional capacity for productive scholarship or exceptional creative ability in the arts. The amounts of the grants vary. The average grant is about $26,900. Application deadline: October 1.

HACKNEY LITERARY AWARDS; BIRMINGHAM-SOUTHERN COLLEGE WRITER'S CONFERENCE (II), Birmingham-Southern College, Box A-3, Birmingham AL 35254. This competition, sponsored by the Cecil Hackney family since 1969, offers $4,000 in prizes for novels, poetry and short stories as part of the annual Birmingham-Southern Writer's Conference. Poems must be postmarked by December 31. Send SASE for Hackney guidelines. Winners are announced at the conference, which is held in the spring. (Also see Writing Today in Conferences and Workshops.)

THE HODDER FELLOWSHIP (II), The Council of the Humanities, 122 E. Pyne, Princeton University, Princeton NJ 08544, is awarded for the pursuit of independent work in the humanities. The recipient is usually a writer or scholar in the early stages of his or her career, a person "with more than ordinary learning" and with "much more than ordinary intellectual and literary gifts." Traditionally, the Hodder Fellow has been a humanist outside of academia. **Candidates for the Ph.D. are not eligible.** The Hodder Fellow spends an academic year in residence at Princeton working independently. He or she may choose to present a lecture to students and faculty in the humanities. **Applicants must submit a résumé, a sample of previous work (10 pgs. maximum, not returnable), a project proposal of 2 to 3 pgs., and a SASE.** The announcement of the Hodder Fellow is made in February by the President of Princeton University. Deadline: November 15.

HENRY HOYNS FELLOWSHIPS (II), Dept. of English, University of Virginia, Charlottesville VA 22903, are fellowships in poetry and fiction of varying amounts for candidates for the M.F.A. in creative writing. Sample poems/prose required with application. Deadline: February 15.

IRISH-AMERICAN CULTURAL INSTITUTE LITERARY AWARDS (IV-Ethnic, foreign language), Mail #5026, 2115 Summit Ave., St. Paul MN 55105, for Irish writers who write in Irish or English, **resident**

in Ireland, with published work. A total of $10,000 in prizes awarded every year.

JOHANN-HEINRICH-VOSS PRIZE FOR TRANSLATION (V), German Academy for Language and Literature, Alexandraweg 23, D-6100 Darmstadt, Germany, is an annual award of DM 20,000 for outstanding lifetime achievement for translating into German, by nomination only. 1993: Roswitha Matwin-Bŭschmann. 1994: Werner Von Koppenfels.

THE CHESTER H. JONES FOUNDATION NATIONAL POETRY COMPETITION (II), P.O. Box 498, Chardon OH 44024, an annual competition for persons in the USA, Canadian and American citizens living abroad. Prizes: $1,000, $500, $250, and $50 honorable mentions. Winning poems plus others called "commendations" are published in a chapbook available for $3.50 from the foundation. Entry fee $2 for the first poem, $1 each for others, no more than 10 entries, no more than 32 lines each. Distinguished poets serve as judges. Deadline: March 31.

LAMPMAN AWARD (IV-Regional); OTTAWA INDEPENDENT WRITERS/LES ECRIVAINS INDEPENDANTS D'OTTAWA, 265 Elderberry Terrace, Orleans, Ontario K1E 1Z2 Canada, phone (613)841-0572, is a $400 award for a published book of English-language poetry by writers in the National Capital region. Submit 3 copies of each title by February 28. Membership in Ottawa Independent Writers is $50/year, and offers their newsletter, programs, an entry in the OIW Directory and registration at reduced fees for their annual conference.

THE STEPHEN LEACOCK MEDAL FOR HUMOUR (IV-Humor, regional), Mrs. Jean Bradley Dickson, award chairman, Stephen Leacock Associates, P.O. Box 854, Orillia, Ontario L3V 3P4 Canada, phone (705)325-6546, for a book of humor in prose, verse, drama or any book form—by a Canadian citizen. Submit 10 copies of book, 8×10 b&w photo, bio and $25 entry fee. Prize: Silver Leacock Medal for Humour and Manulife Bank cash award of $5,000. Deadline: December 31. The committee also publishes ***The Newspacket*** 3 times/year.

THE LEAGUE OF MINNESOTA POETS CONTEST (I, IV-Members, students), % Barbara Sherrard Morgan, 3738 NW Barbeau Rd., Brainerd MN 56401. Offers 20 different contests in a variety of categories and prizes of $5-75 for poems up to 55 lines, fees of $3 to enter all categories for members and $1/category for non-members. There is one category for students in grades 7 through 12 and one category for elementary students through grade 6. July 31 deadline. Winners are not published. Write for details.

LETRAS DE ORO SPANISH LITERARY PRIZES (IV-Foreign language), Iberian Studies Institute, North-South Center, University of Miami, P.O. Box 248123, Coral Gables FL 33124, fax (305)284-4406. Awards include a general prize of $2,500 and publication of the book-length entry. For creative excellence in poetry written in the Spanish language. Write for guidelines. Deadline: October 12.

AMY LOWELL POETRY TRAVELLING SCHOLARSHIP (II), Trust u/w/o Amy Lowell, Exchange Place, 35th Floor, Choate, Hall & Stewart, Boston MA 02109-2891, award director F. Davis Dassori, Jr., Trustee, is an annual award of $29,000 (more-or-less: the amount varies annually), to an American-born "advanced" poet who agrees to live outside of North America for the year of the grant. Deadline for application: October 15.

MASSACHUSETTS STATE POETRY SOCIETY, INC.; ANNUAL NATIONAL POETRY DAY CONTEST; ANNUAL GERTRUDE DOLE MEMORIAL CONTEST (I), %Jeanette C. Maes, President, 64 Harrison Ave., Lynn MA 01905, both contests are open to all poets. The National Poetry Day Contest, with a August 15 deadline, offers prizes of $25, $15 and $10 (or higher) for each of 18 or more categories; $3 fee for entire contest. The Gertrude Dole Memorial Contest, deadline March 15, offers prizes of $25, $15 and $10; $1 entry fee, one poem/poet. Send SASE for contest flyer.

‡FREDERIC G. MELCHER BOOK AWARD (V, IV-Religious), 25 Beacon St., Boston MA 02108, is an annual $1,000 prize for a book making a significant contribution to religious liberalism. Books are nominated by Melcher judges.

MILFORD FINE ARTS COUNCIL NATIONAL POETRY CONTEST (I, II), 5 Broad St., Milford CT 06460. An annual contest open from September 15 to January 29. Send SASE for details.

MISSISSIPPI VALLEY POETRY CONTEST (I, II, IV), sponsored by North American Literary Escadrille, P.O. Box 3188, Rock Island IL 61204, director S. Katz, annually offers prizes of approximately $1,200 for unpublished poems in categories for students (elementary, junior and senior high), adults, Mississippi Valley, senior citizens, jazz, religious, humorous, rhyming, haiku, ethnic and history. Fee: $5 for 1-5 poems; 50 lines/poem limit. Fee for children: $3 for 1-5 poems. Professional readers read winning poems before a reception at an award evening each October. Deadline: September 15.

MONEY FOR WOMEN (IV-Women/feminism), Barbara Deming Memorial Fund, Inc., Box 40-1043, Brooklyn NY 11240-1043, award director Pam McAllister, sponsors a semiannual contest for small grants to feminists in the arts. Subjects include women, peace, justice issues. Send SASE for application form. Applicants must be citizens of US or Canada. Deadlines: December 31 and June 30.

MONTANA ARTS FOUNDATION POETRY CONTEST; MARY BRENNEN CLAPP MEMORIAL AWARD (IV-Regional, membership), P.O. Box 1872, Bozeman MT 59771, annual contest with a March 31 deadline. Open to Montana poets only, for unpublished poems up to 100 lines, in a group of 3. Mary Brennen Clapp Memorial Award of $50 and prizes of $40, $30 and $20. Must submit 3 poems and cover letter. Send SASE for guidelines.

JENNY MCKEAN MOORE FUND FOR WRITERS (II), Dept. of English, George Washington University, Washington DC 20052, provides for a visiting lecturer in creative writing for about $40,000 for 2 semesters. Apply by November 15 with résumé and writing sample of 25 pgs. or less. Awarded to poets and fiction writers in alternating years.

NASHVILLE NEWSLETTER POETRY CONTEST (I), P.O. Box 60535, Nashville TN 37206-0535, Roger Dale Miller, editor/publisher. Founded 1977. Reporting time 6-10 weeks. Published quarterly. Sample copy: $3. Any style or subject up to 40 lines. One unpublished poem to a page with name and address in upper left corner. Entry fee of $5 for up to 3 poems. Must be sent all at once. Prizes of $50, $25 and $10 with at least 50 Certificates of Merit.

NATIONAL ENDOWMENT FOR THE ARTS; FELLOWSHIPS FOR CREATIVE WRITERS; FELLOWSHIPS FOR TRANSLATORS (II), Literature Program, Room 722, Nancy Hanks Center, 1100 Pennsylvania Ave. NW, Washington DC 20506, phone (202)682-5451. Fellowships for Creative Writers is the largest program of individual grants for American writers of poetry, fiction and creative nonfiction. Awards of $20,000 are made each year to published writers. Applications are reviewed and recommendations for funding are made by an advisory panel composed of experts from the literature field. In reviewing applications, advisory panelists consider solely the literary quality of the manuscripts submitted. To be eligible, a poet must have in publication a volume of at least 48 pages, or 20 or more poems or pages of poetry in five or more literary publications in the last 10 years. A limited number of $10,000 fellowship grants are awarded to published translators of creative literature for translation projects from other languages into English. Matching grants are also available to nonprofit organizations for publishing and audience development projects, residencies and reading series, and services to writers and literary organizations. Phone or write for guidelines and application for ms for 1996. Anticipated deadlines: January 1995 for 1996 translation fellowships; March 1995 for 1996 poetry fellowships.

NATIONAL WRITERS ASSOCIATION ANNUAL POETRY CONTEST (I), Suite 424, 1450 S. Havana, Aurora CO 80012, award director Sandy Whelchel, an annual contest with prizes of $100, $50 and $25. Entry fee $8/poem; additional fee charged if poem is longer than 40 lines. All subjects and forms are acceptable. Deadline: October 1.

NATIONAL WRITERS UNION ANNUAL NATIONAL POETRY COMPETITION (II), P.O. Box 2409, Aptos CA 95001, phone (408)457-7488. See National Writers Union listing under Organizations Useful to Poets. The Santa Cruz/Monterey Local 7 chapter at this address sponsors an annual competition with entry fee: $3/poem; prizes of $200, $100 and $50, with prominent poets as judges. Send SASE for rules beginning in April.

THE NATIONAL WRITTEN & ILLUSTRATED BY . . . AWARDS CONTEST FOR STUDENTS; LANDMARK EDITIONS (IV-Students), P.O. Box 4469, Kansas City MO 64127, award director David Melton, is an annual contest for unpublished work for a book written and illustrated by a student. Three books published, one from each of 3 age categories (6-9; 10-13; 14-19). Send #10 SAE with 60¢ postage for rules.

NEUSTADT INTERNATIONAL PRIZE FOR LITERATURE; WORLD LITERATURE TODAY (V), University of Oklahoma, Room 110, 630 Parrington Oval, Norman OK 73019. Award of $40,000 given every other year in recognition of life achievement or to a writer whose work is still in progress; nominations from an international jury only.

NEW YORK FOUNDATION FOR THE ARTS (IV-Regional), 14th Floor, 155 Avenue of Americas, New York NY 10013, phone (212)366-6900, ext. 217, offers fellowships of $7,000 every other year for poets who are at least 18 and have resided in New York State for 2 years prior to application. Submit up to 10 pages of poetry (at least 2 poems), 3 copies of a 1-page résumé, and an application form. Call for application form in June. Deadline is October.

NORDMANNS-FORBUNDET TRANSLATION GRANT (IV-Translation), NORLA, P.O. Box 239 Sentrum, N-0103 Oslo, Norway. In its desire to make Norwegian culture known abroad, the Nordmanns-Forbundet awards an annual grant (maximum 15,000 Norwegian crowns) to one or more publishing houses introducing Norwegian fiction or poetry in translation (preferably contemporary). Applications should be sent to NORLA (The Office for Norwegian Literature Abroad), and future decisions will be made by NORLA's Literary Advisory Board. Mark the application "Nordmanns-Forbundet's translation grant." Deadline: December 15.

THE NORTH CAROLINA POETRY SOCIETY ZOE KINCAID BROCKMAN MEMORIAL BOOK AWARD CONTEST (IV-Regional), % Kay Nelson, #1911, 2205 New Garden, Greensboro NC 27410, is an annual contest for a book of poetry (over 20 pages) by a North Carolina poet (native-born or current resident for 3 years). Send SASE for details. $100 cash prize and a Revere-style bowl awarded.

NORTHWEST POETS & ARTISTS CALENDAR (IV-Regional), Bainbridge Island Arts and Humanities Council, 261 Madison S., Bainbridge Island WA 98110, links literary and visual work by contemporary NW artists. Each year 12 poets are selected by jury for inclusion in this full-color wall calendar and receive cash awards. Recognition given to runners-up. $6 fee for up to 6 poems, June 1 deadline. Send #10 SASE in spring for required entry form. Calendar can be obtained by sending $12.95 plus $2.50 p&h (WA residents add 8.1% sales tax) to the above address.

OHIOANA BOOK AWARDS; OHIOANA KROUT MEMORIAL AWARD FOR POETRY; OHIOANA QUARTERLY; OHIOANA LIBRARY ASSOCIATION (IV-Regional), Ohioana Library Association, Room 1105, 65 S. Front St., Columbus OH 43215. Ohioana Book Awards given yearly to outstanding books published each year. Up to 6 awards may be given for books (including books of poetry) by authors born in Ohio or who have lived in Ohio for at least 5 years. The Ohioana Poetry Award of $1,000 (with the same residence requirements), made possible by a bequest of Helen Krout, is given yearly "to an individual whose body of work has made, and continues to make, a significant contribution to the poetry of Ohio, and through whose work as a writer, teacher, administrator, or in community service, interest in poetry has been developed." Nominations to be received by December 31. ***Ohioana Quarterly*** regularly reviews Ohio magazines and books by Ohio authors. It is available through membership in Ohioana Library Association ($20/year).

NATALIE ORNISH POETRY AWARD (IV-Regional); SOEURETTE DIEHL FRASER TRANSLATION AWARD (IV-Translations, regional); TEXAS INSTITUTE OF LETTERS, % James Hoggard, T.I.L., P.O. Box 9032, Wichita Falls TX 76308-9032. The Texas Institute of Letters gives annual awards for books by Texas authors in 8 categories, including the Natalie Ornish Poetry Award, a $1,000 award for best volume of poetry. Books must have been first published in the year in question, and entries may be made by authors or by their publishers. Deadline is January 4 of the following year. One copy of each entry must be mailed to each of three judges, with "information showing an author's Texas association . . . if it is not otherwise obvious." Poets must have lived in Texas for at least two consecutive years at some time or their work must reflect a notable concern with matters associated with the state. Soeurette Diehl Fraser Translation Award ($1,000) is given for best translation of a work into English. Same rules as those for Natalie Ornish poetry award. Write during the fall for complete instructions.

OZARK CREATIVE WRITERS, INC. CONFERENCE AWARDS (IV-Membership), 6817 Gingerbread Lane, Little Rock AR 72204, phone (501)565-8889, conference director Peggy Vining. Registrants ($30 prior to September 1) for the annual writers' conference may enter various writing contests with prizes of $25, $15 and $10 ("some higher"). Deadline for entry is August 31 postmark. Conference is held in Eureka Springs, Arkansas, at the Inn of the Ozarks in October. Register early for housing. Send SASE (#10 envelope) for brochure after April 1.

PACIFIC NORTHWEST WRITERS CONFERENCE ADULT LITERARY CONTEST (I), Suite 804, 2033 Sixth Ave., Seattle WA 98121, phone (206)443-3807, contest for at least 1 but no more than 5 complete poems for a 5 page maximum length. Complete entry form must accompany entry. Prizes: Distinguished, $300; Excellence, $200; Merit, $150 plus certificates of recognition. Fees are $20 for PNWC members, $30 for nonmembers. Contest deadline: March 15.

‡PANHANDLE PROFESSIONAL WRITERS (I), % Contest Chairman, P.O. Box 19303, Amarillo TX 79114, open to all poets, any subject or form, 50 line maximum, awards of $25, $20 and $15, fee $5 for 2 poems. Deadline: June 15.

PAUMANOK POETRY AWARD COMPETITION; THE VISITING WRITERS PROGRAM (II), SUNY College of Technology, Farmingdale NY 11735, phone (516)420-2031, director Dr. Charles Fishman. The Paumanok Poetry Award Competition offers a prize of $750 plus expenses for a reading in their 1995-96 series. They will also award two runner-up prizes of $300 plus expenses. Submit cover letter, 1 paragraph bio, 5-7 poems, published or unpublished, and $10 entry fee by September 15. Check payable to SUNY Farmingdale Visiting Writers Program (VWP). Poets who have read in their series include Hayden Carruth, Allen Ginsberg, Linda Pastan, Marge Piercy, Joyce Carol Oates, Louis Simpson and David Ignatow. The series changes each year, so entries in the 1994 competition will be considered for the 1995-96 series, entries in 1995 for the 1996-97 series, and so on.

PENNSYLVANIA POETRY SOCIETY ANNUAL CONTEST; WINE AND ROSES POETRY CONTEST; PEGASUS CONTEST FOR STUDENTS, 623 N. Fourth St., Reading PA 19601, award director Dr. Dorman John Grace. The deadline for the society's annual contest, which has 11 categories open to nonmembers and 5 to members only, is January 15. Grand prize in category 1 (open) will be $100 in 1995; prizes in other categories range from $10-25, plus publication. Entry fees are $1.50/poem for nonmembers except for the grand prize, which requires an entry fee of $2/poem for everybody. For information regarding the Pennsylvania Poetry Society Contest contact Dr. Dorman John Grace, (610)374-5982. The Wine and Roses Poetry Contest, sponsored by the Wallace Stevens Chapter for unpublished poems in serious and light verse, has prizes of $50, $25, and $15 plus publication and telecast; entry fee $1/poem; deadline June 1; write to Dr. Dorman John Grace. For information about the Pegasus Contest for Students, write to Anne Pierre Spangler, contest chairman, 1685 Christian Dr., R.D. #2, Lebanon PA 17042. The Pennsylvania Poetry Society publishes a quarterly newsletter and an annual **Prize Poems** soft cover book, containing 69 prize and honorable mention award poems. Prize poems in the Wine and Roses and Pegasus contests are published in ***PPS Newsletter.***

THE RICHARD PHILLIPS POETRY PRIZE (II), 719 E. Delaware, Siloam Springs AR 72761, award director Richard Phillips, Jr. Annual award of $1,000 open to all poets. Submit 40-page ms, published or unpublished poems, any subject, any form. Include $10 reading fee/ms, payable to Richard Phillips Poetry Prize. Postmark deadline: September 5. "Winner will be announced and check for $1,000 presented October 15." Publication is the following year. Mss are not returned. Send SASE for guidelines.

POETIC PERSPECTIVE, INC. (I), 110 Onieda St., Waxahachie TX 75165, founded in 1989 by Pat Haley, editor. Sponsors one annual poetry contest through the Poetry Society of Texas and one through PPI. Send SASE (#10 envelope) for themes and guidelines.

THE POETRY CENTER BOOK AWARD (II), 1600 Holloway Ave., San Francisco CA 94132. Method for entering contest is to submit a published book and a $10 entry fee. "Please include cover letter noting author name, book title(s), name of person or publisher issuing check and check number." Book must be published and copyrighted during the year of the contest and submitted by December 31. "Beginners may enter but in the past winners have published several previous books." Translations and anthologies are not accepted. Books should be by an individual living writer and must be entirely poetry. Prize (only one) is $500 and an invitation to read for the Poetry Center. No entry form is required.

POETRY OF HOPE AWARD (II, IV-Themes, young adult), P.O. Box 21077, Piedmont CA 94620, awarded annually, $200 first prize ($100 for junior division) for a poem up to 100 lines expressing "the spirit of hope" using inspirational themes. Themes should speak to the "healing" of social problems (i.e., war/peace, human rights, the homeless, the earth/ecology, etc.), hope for the highest good for all of creation. Application needed. No fee. Send SASE. Deadline: December 30.

POETRY SOCIETY OF MICHIGAN ANNUAL CONTESTS; THE PSM OPEN; SCHNEIDER MEMORIAL NARRATIVE; MARGARET DRAKE ELLIOTT CONTEST; EDWARD VAN LEISHOUT MEMORIAL CONTEST; KENNETH HEAFIELD CONTEST FOR YOUNG ADULTS (I, IV-Children), 1051 Fox Hills Dr., East Lansing MI 48823, contest coordinator Ben Bohnhorst. Sponsors 5 annual contests open to nonmembers: The PSM Open, any subject, form or length; Schneider Memorial Narrative, any form or length; Margaret Drake Elliott Contest, poetry for children, 20-line limit; Edward Van Leishout Memorial Contest, for poets age 16-25, 30-line limit; Kenneth Heafield Contest, for college students age 18-24, any subject or form, 60-line limit. Various entry fees. Prizes range from $5-100, some include publication. Also sponsors 10 contests for PSM members only. Send SASE for guidelines on all contests and membership information. Deadline for all contests is November 15.

THE POETRY SOCIETY OF VIRGINIA ANNUAL CONTEST (IV-Forms), 2305 Maiden Lane SW, Roanoke VA 24015, phone (703)343-7790, contest chairperson Elisabeth Drewry. Offers 14 contests with 32 cash prizes for various categories including haiku, sonnet, limerick and popular song lyric. Contest information available for SASE. Fees: Adults, $2/poem; $1/high school entry; no fee for elementary school entries.

POETS CLUB OF CHICAGO INTERNATIONAL SHAKESPEAREAN SONNET CONTEST (II, IV-Form), chairman June Shipley, 2930 Franklin St., Highland IN 46322. Write for rules, include SASE, not earlier than March. No entry fee. Prizes of $50, $35 and $15. Deadline: September 1 postmark.

POETS' DINNER CONTEST (IV-Regional), 2214 Derby St., Berkeley CA 94705. Since 1926 there has been an annual awards banquet sponsored by the ad hoc Poets' Dinner Committee, usually at Spenger's Fish Grotto (a Berkeley Landmark). Three typed copies of poems in not more than 3 of the 8 categories are submitted anonymously without fee, and the winning poems (grand prize, 1st, 2nd, 3rd) are read at the banquet and honorable mentions awarded. **Contestant must be present to win.** Prizes awarded cash; honorable mention, books. The event is nonprofit. Deadline: January 15.

POETS OF THE VINEYARD CONTEST (I), P.O. Box 12154, Santa Rosa CA 95406, an annual contest sponsored by the Sonoma County Chapter (PofV) of the California Federation of Chaparral Poets with entries in 7 categories. These include traditional forms, free verse, haiku/senryu and tanka and a themed category on grapes, vineyards, wine, viticulture. For a copy of the current contest rules send SASE. Prizes in each category are $20, $15 and $10, with a grand prize chosen from category winners ($50). Entry fee $2/poem. Prize winning poems will be published in the annual anthology, **Vintage.** Every winning poet will receive a complimentary copy of the anthology in which his/her poem appears. Deadline: March 1.

THE POETS' PRIZE (II), The Poets' Prize Committee, % the Nicholas Roerich Museum, 319 W. 107th St., New York NY 10025, phone (212)864-7752, award directors Robert McDowell, Frederick Morgan and Louis Simpson. Annual cash award of $3,000 given for a book of verse by an American poet published in the previous year. The poet must be an American citizen. Poets making inquiries will receive an explanation of procedures. Books may be sent to the committee members. A list of the members and their addresses will be sent upon request with SASE.

‡POETS RENDEZVOUS CONTEST; INDIANA STATE FEDERATION OF POETRY CLUBS (I), % Dottie Mack, 14915 Gemini Dr., Huntertown IN 46748. The Poets Rendezvous Contest offers $1,030 in prizes for poems in 24 categories, $5 fee covers 24 categories in different forms and subjects, September 1 deadline. The Indiana State Federation of Poetry Clubs also has contest with January 15 and July 15 deadlines for poems no longer than 1 page, $1/poem fee, prizes of $25, $15 and $10 with 3 honorable mentions.

PRESIDIO LA BAHIA AWARD; SUMMERFIELD G. ROBERTS AWARD (IV-Regional), Sons of the Republic of Texas, Suite 222, 5942 Abrams Rd., Dallas TX 75231. Both may be awarded for poetry. The Presidio La Bahia Award is an annual award or awards (depending upon the number and quality of entries) for writing that promotes research into and preservation of the Spanish Colonial influence on Texas culture. $2,000 is available, with a minimum first prize of $1,200. Entries must be in quadruplicate and will not be returned. Deadline: September 30. The Summerfield G. Roberts Award, available to US citizens, is an annual award of $2,500 for a book or manuscript depicting or representing the Republic of Texas (1836-46), written or published during the calendar year for which the award is given. Entries must be submitted in quintuplicate and will not be returned. Deadline: January 15.

‡PRO DOGS CREATIVE WRITING & PHOTOGRAPHIC COMPETITION (I), Pro Dogs National Charity, 267 Hillbury Rd., Warlingham, Surrey CR6 9TL England, phone 0883-622121, award director Michaela Edridge. Biennial contest (1994) for poems up to 32 lines with prize of £250. Contest information available for SASE (or SAE and IRCs). Fees: £2 for first entry; £1 for subsequent entries. Deadline: October 1.

PULITZER PRIZE IN LETTERS (II), % The Pulitzer Prize Board, 702 Journalism, Columbia University, New York NY 10027, offers 5 prizes of $3,000 each year, including 1 in poetry, for books published in the calendar year preceding the award. Submit 4 copies of published books (or galley proofs if book is being published after November), photo, bio, entry form and $20 entry fee. July 1 deadline for books published between January 1 and June 30; November 1 deadline for books published between July 1 and December 31.

REDWOOD ACRES FAIR POETRY CONTEST (I), P.O. Box 6576, Eureka CA 95502, offers an annual contest with various categories for both juniors and seniors with entry fee of 50¢/poem for the junior contests and $1/poem for the senior contests. Deadline: May 18.

REGIONAL ARTISTS' PROJECTS GRANT (I, IV-Regional), Randolph Street Gallery, 756 N. Milwaukee Ave., Chicago IL 60622, phone (312)666-7737, RAP coordinator Kapra Fleming. Offers grants up to $4,000 maximum for regional artists working in interdisciplinary or innovative ways. Must be 1-year resident of Indiana, Illinois, Ohio, Missouri or Michigan. Application available for SASE. Deadline: March 11.

RHYME INTERNATIONAL COMPETITION FOR RHYMING POETRY (IV-Form), 199 The Long Shoot, Nuneaton, Warwickshire CV11 6JQ England, has 2 categories (open class, up to 50 lines, rhymed poetry; strict form class) with prizes averaging £500 in each class each year (at least 60% of fees received); minimum entry fee £5 (or $10). Ajudication takes place during a special workshop weekend in England under the supervision of a well-known poet. They claim to be "the only competition in the world exclusively for rhymed poetry." Write for entry form. Deadline: September 30.

MARY ROBERTS RINEHART FOUNDATION AWARD (II), Mail Stop Number 3E4, English Dept., The Mary Roberts Rinehart Award, George Mason University, 4400 University Dr., Fairfax VA 22030-4444. Two grants are made annually to writers who need financial assistance "to complete work definitely projected." The amount of the award depends upon income the fund generates; in the past the amount was approximately $950 in each category. Poets and fiction writers should submit work in odd numbered years, e.g., 1995, 1997. A writer's work must be nominated by an established author or editor; no written recommendations are necessary. Nominations must be accompanied by a sample of the nominee's work, up to 25 pgs. of poetry and 30 pgs. of fiction. Deadline: November 30.

ANNA DAVIDSON ROSENBERG AWARD (IV-Ethnic), Judah L. Magnes Museum, 2911 Russell St., Berkeley CA 94705, offers prizes of $100, $50 and $25, as well as honorable mentions, for up to 10 pgs. of 1-4 unpublished poems (in English) on the Jewish Experience. There is also a Youth Commendation for poets under 19 and a Senior Award if 65 or over. Do not send poems without entry form; write between April 1 and July 15 for form and guidelines (enclose SASE). Deadline: August 31.

SALMON ARM SONNET CONTEST (IV-Form), Salmon Arm & Dist. Chamber of Commerce, Box 999, Salmon Arm, British Columbia V1E 4P2 Canada. An annual contest for unpublished sonnets. Prizes: $100-300 and books. Entry fee: $6/poem. Limit 2 entries. New juvenile category for 18 and under. Entry fee: $2/poem plus $6 to enter the main contest. Deadline: June 1. Copies of winning entries will be sent to all entrants.

SAN FRANCISCO FOUNDATION; JOSEPH HENRY JACKSON AWARD; JAMES D. PHELAN AWARD (IV-Regional), % Intersection for the Arts, 446 Valencia St., San Francisco CA 94103. The Jackson Award ($2,000) will be made to the author of an unpublished work-in-progress in the form of fiction (novel or short stories), non-fictional prose, or poetry. Applicants must be residents of northern California or Nevada for three consecutive years immediately prior to the deadline date of January 31, and must be between the ages of 20 and 35 as of the deadline. The Phelan Award ($2,000) will be made to the author of an unpublished work-in-progress in the form of fiction (novel or short stories), non-fictional prose, poetry or drama. Applicants must be California-born (although they may now reside outside of the state), and must be between the ages of 20 and 35 as of the January 31 deadline. Mss for both awards must be accompanied by an application form, which may be obtained by sending a SASE to the above address. Entries accepted November 15 through January 31.

CARL SANDBURG AWARDS (IV-Regional), sponsored by Friends of the Chicago Public Library, 9S-7, 400 S. State St., Chicago IL 60605, are given annually to native-born Chicago authors or present Chicago-area writers for new books in 4 categories, including poetry. Each author receives $1,000. Publisher or authors should submit 2 copies of books published between June 1 of one year and May 31 of the next. Deadline: August 1.

SCHOLASTIC WRITING AWARDS (IV-Teens), 555 Broadway, New York NY 10012, phone (212)343-6893, program manager Diane McNutt, director Susan Ebersole, annual award established 1923. Purpose: Encouragement and recognition of young writers. Open to students in grades 7-12. Group I- grades 7, 8, 9. Group II- grades 10, 11, 12. There are 7 categories: short story, short short story, essay/nonfiction/persuasive writing, dramatic script, poetry, humor and science fiction. Seniors only may submit portfolios representing their best group of writing. Awards consist of cash awards, scholarships and prizes. Selected works will be published in Scholastic magazines. Unpublished submissions only. Entries must be postmarked by January 13, 1995, except those from central Pennsylvania; Houston, Texas; and New York City. (Deadlines are indicated on entry forms.) Send SASE for guidelines and entry forms by December 1 to address above. The Scholastic Writing Awards hold all publishing rights for winning entries for two years.

SOCIETY OF MIDLAND AUTHORS AWARD (IV-Regional), % Phyllis Ford-Choyke, 29 E. Division St., Chicago IL 60610, is for authors from Midland states: IL, IN, IA, KS, MI, MN, MO, NE, ND, SD, OH, WI. It is an annual cash award and a plaque given at a dinner. Books in each calendar year are eligible, not self-published. Deadline January 15 of award year. Send SASE for entry form; books must be submitted to each of 3 judges, not to Phyllis Ford-Choyke.

SOUTH DAKOTA POETRY SOCIETY CONTESTS (I), Present Chairman of S.D. State Poetry Society Contests Audrae Visser, 710 Elk, Elkton SD 57026, 10 categories. Deadline: August 31.

SPARROWGRASS POETRY FORUM (I), Dept. HM, 203 Diamond St., Box 193, Sistersville WV 26175, offers 6 annual free contests, each of which has $1,000 in prizes, including a $500 grand prize. Entrants are solicited to buy an anthology, but you do not have to buy the anthology to win. Send 1 original poem, no longer than 20 lines. Name and address at the top of the page. Any style, any subject. Contest deadlines are the last day of every other month.

SPRINGFEST AND WINTERFEST POETRY CONTESTS; MILE HIGH POETRY SOCIETY (I), P.O. Box 21116, Denver CO 80221, phone (303)426-8214, award director Jane C. Schaul. Each spring and fall they offer a contest with $300 1st prize, $100 2nd prize, and two 3rd prizes of $50 each for maximum 36-line poems. Entry fee $3/poem. Deadlines: June 30 and December 31.

WALLACE E. STEGNER FELLOWSHIPS (II), Creative Writing Program, Stanford University, Stanford CA 94305, 4 in poetry, $12,000 plus tuition of $4,800, for promising writers who can benefit from 2 years instruction and criticism at the Writing Center. Previous publication not required, though it can strengthen one's application. Deadline: Postmarked by the first working day after January 1.

THE TRANSLATORS ASSOCIATION; JOHN FLORIO PRIZE; SCHLEGEL-TIECK PRIZE; SCOTT-MONCRIEFF PRIZE; BERNARD SHAW PRIZE (IV-Translation), 84 Drayton Gardens, London SW 10 9SB England. The first three of these prizes are all for translation of 20th century literature published in the United Kingdom. The John Florio Prize of £1,000 is for the best translation from Italian, awarded every other year. The annual Schlegel-Tieck Prize of £2,000 is for translation from German. The biannual Scott-Moncrieff Prize of £1,000 is for translation from French. The association also administers the Bernard Shaw Prize (£1,000 every 3 years), for translations from any period from Swedish into English and published in the United Kingdom.

TRILLIUM BOOK AWARD; PRIX TRILLIUM (IV-Regional), Ministry of Culture, Tourism and Recreation, 3rd Floor, Libraries Branch, 77 Bloor St. W, Toronto, Ontario M7A 2R9 Canada, is given annually for a book by an Ontario author. Submissions of published books are by publishers. Award given in April. Deadline: December 31.

‡KINGSLEY TUFTS POETRY AWARD; KATE TUFTS DISCOVERY AWARD FOR POETRY (II), The Claremont Graduate School, 160 E. Tenth St., Claremont CA 91711, phone (909)621-8974, award director Murray M. Schwartz. The Kingsley Tufts Poetry Award is a $50,000 prize awarded annually to a book-length ms that has been published during the previous year. Subject and form are open. No translations. Submit 3 copies with entry form. Deadline: Dcecember 15. The Kate Tufts Discovery Award for Poetry is an annual $5,000 prize awarded to "first books" only. Submission requirements and deadline are the same as Kingsley Tufts Poetry Award. Both awards are presented at a ceremony in April. Entrants to the Kingsley Tufts Award must "agree to reproduction rights, be present at the award ceremony and spend a week in residence at the Claremont Graduate School." Send SASE for rules and entry forms.

LAURA BOWER VAN NUYS CREATIVE WRITING CONTEST (I, II), Black Hills Writers Group, P.O. Box 1539, Rapid City SD 57709-1539. **"We will be holding the contest in even-numbered years only."** Professional and nonprofessional categories in fiction, articles and poetry. Guidelines available after January 1 of contest year.

‡THE W.D. WEATHERFORD AWARD (IV-Regional), Berea College, CPO 2336, Berea KY 40404, for the published work (including poetry) which "best illuminates the problems, personalities, and unique qualities of the Appalachian South." The award is for $500 and sometimes there are special awards of $200 each.

‡WEST HAVEN COUNCIL OF THE ARTS, 201 Noble St., West Haven CT 06516. An annual national poetry contest open April 15 to September 15. Small fee. Send SASE for guidelines.

WESTERN HERITAGE AWARDS (IV-Specialized), National Cowboy Hall of Fame and Western Heritage Center, 1700 NE 63rd St., Oklahoma City OK 73111. Since 1960, this national museum has awarded excellence in western literature, music, television and film. Principle creators of winning entries in 15 categories receive the bronze "Wrangler," an original sculpture by artist John Free, during special awards ceremonies held at the museum each March. The 1993 award for poetry went to Walter McDonald for his book **All That Matters**, published by Texas Tech University Press. Entry forms are mailed annually in September for works published between January 1 and November 30 of that year. Deadline for entries: November 30.

WESTERN STATES BOOK AWARDS; WESTERN STATES ARTS FEDERATION (IV-Regional), Dept. PM, 236 Montezuma Ave., Santa Fe NM 87501, presents annual book awards to outstanding authors and publishers. The awards include cash prizes, $5,000, for writers for their respective publishers. Mss must be written by an author living in Alaska, Arizona, California, Colorado, Idaho, Montana, Nevada, New Mexico, Oregon, Utah, Washington or Wyoming. Award given to books to be published in fall of 1995. Work must already have been accepted for publication by a publisher in one of these states. Work must be submitted by the publisher, submitted in ms form (not previously published in book form). Publisher must have published at least 3 books. Write for more information.

WFNB ANNUAL LITERARY CONTEST; THE ALFRED G. BAILEY AWARD; WRITERS' FEDERATION OF NEW BRUNSWICK (IV-Regional), P.O. Box 37, Station A, Fredericton, New Brunswick E3B 4Y2 Canada, offers prizes of $200, $100, $30, for unpublished poems of up to 100 lines (typed, double-spaced). The Alfred G. Bailey Award is a $400 prize given annually for poetry mss of 48 pgs. or more. May include some individual poems that have been published. Entry fee: $10 for members, $15 for nonmembers. Send SASE for guidelines. Deadline: February 14.

WHITE RABBIT POETRY CONTEST; THE HARBINGER (II), P.O. Box U-1030 USAL, Mobile AL 36688, is an annual, the winners and honorable mentions being virtually the only poetry published by ***The Harbinger***. Awards are $100, $50 and $25. Send SASE for entry form, which must accompany submissions (2 copies, author's name on 1 only). Deadline: March 31.

WHITING WRITERS' AWARDS; MRS. GILES WHITING FOUNDATION (V), Room 3500, 30 Rockefeller Plaza, New York NY 10112, director Gerald Freund. The Foundation makes awards of $30,000 each to up to 10 writers of fiction, nonfiction, poetry and plays chosen by a selection committee drawn from a list of recognized writers, literary scholars and editors. Recipients of the award are selected from nominations made by writers, educators and editors from communities across the country whose experience and vocations bring them in contact with individuals of unusual talent. The nominators and selectors are appointed by the foundation and serve anonymously. **Direct applications and informal nominations are not accepted by the foundation.**

OSCAR WILLIAMS & GENE DERWOOD AWARD (V), Community Funds, Inc., 2 Park Ave., New York NY 10016, is an award given annually to nominees of the selection committee "to help needy or worthy artists or poets." Selection Committee for the award does not accept nominations. Amount varies from year to year.

WORLD ORDER OF NARRATIVE AND FORMALIST POETS (II, IV-Subscription, form), P.O. Box 174, Station A, Flushing NY 11358, contest chairman Dr. Alfred Dorn. This organization sponsors contests in at least 15 categories of traditional and contemporary poetic forms, including the sonnet, blank verse, ballade, villanelle, free verse and new forms created by Alfred Dorn. Prizes total at least $4,000 and range from $20 to $200. Only subscribers to ***The Formalist*** will be eligible for the competition, as explained in the complete guidelines available from the contest chairman. "We look for originality of thought, phrase and image, combined with masterful craftsmanship. Trite, trivial or technically inept work stands no chance." Postmark deadline for entries: October 26, 1995.

WORLD'S WORST POETRY CONTEST (IV-Regional), Pismo Beach Hardware and Nursery, 930 Price St., Pismo Beach CA 93449, phone (805)773-NAIL, fax (805)773-6772, award directors "Pismo Bob" Pringle and Rudy Natoli. Contest for "bad" poetry that mentions Pismo Beach. The contest is simple to enter. Just send a poem or poems to "Pismo Bob" Pringle, originator of the contest. The poems must include the word "Pismo," but aside from that there are no literary requirements. "In addition to the sheer pride of being the world's worst bard, the Chosen One will also win a free round trip on American Airlines to the wonderful shores of Pismo Beach, California." Deadline: June 15.

WRITERS' GUILD OF ALBERTA BOOK AWARD (IV-Regional), Writer's Guild, 10523 100th Ave., Edmonton, Alberta T5J 0A8 Canada, phone (403)426-5892, awarded in six categories, including poetry. Eligible books will have been published anywhere in the world between January 1 and December 31. Their authors will have been resident in Alberta for at least 12 of the 18 months prior to December 31. Contact the WGA head office for registry forms. Unpublished manuscripts are not eligible. Except in the drama category, anthologies are not eligible. Four copies of each book to be considered must be mailed to the WGA office no later than December 31. Submissions postmarked after this date will not be accepted. **Exceptions will be made for any books *published* between the 15th and 31st of December. These may be submitted by January 15.** Three copies will go to the three judges in that category; one will remain in the WGA library. Works may be submitted by authors, publishers, or any interested parties.

‡WRITERS UNLIMITED (I), %Herbert C. Corben, 4304 O'Leary Ave., Pascagoula MS 39581-2352, offers an annual literary competition, deadline September 1. There are up to 20 categories with cash prizes up to $50 and other prizes. Do not use the same poem for more than one category. $5 entry fee covers entries in all categories up to 20. Send SASE for contest rules.

THE YORKSHIRE OPEN POETRY COMPETITION (II), Ilkley Literature Festival, 9A Leeds Rd., Ilkley, W. Yorkshire LS29 8DH England, administrator J. Davidson. Offers prizes of £250, £150, £75 and 10 prizes of £10 for any style of poetry. Fees are £2.50/poem, £6 for 3. Deadline: July 31.

Additional Contests and Awards

The following listings also contain information about contests and awards. See the General Index for page numbers, then read the listings and send SASEs for specific details about their offerings.

Advocate, The
Aguilar Expression, The
Albatross
Alicejamesbooks
Alms House Press
Amelia
America
American Literary Review
American Poetry Review
American Tolkien Society
Analecta
Anhinga Press
Appalachian Heritage
Apropos
Arc
Arkansas Press, The University of
Bay Area Poets Coalition (BAPC)
Bell's Letters Poet
Beloit Poetry Journal, The
Black Bear Publications
Blue Unicorn, A Triquarterly of Poetry
Bohemian Chronicle
BOOG Literature
Borderlands: Texas Poetry Review
Brussels Sprout
Byline Magazine
Calapooya Collage
Canadian Writer's Journal
Cape Rock, The
Center Press
Chelsea
Chips Off the Writer's Block
Chiron Review
Cincinnati Poetry Review
Cleveland State University Poetry Center
Climbing Art, The
Columbia University Translation Center
Connecticut River Review
Copper Canyon Press
Country Woman
Cover Magazine
Crazyhorse
Cream City Review
Creativity Unlimited Press
Cricket
Crucible
Cumberland Poetry Review
Cutbank
Defined Providence
Devil's Millhopper Press, The
Different Drummer, A
Dream Shop, The
1812
Eighth Mountain Press, The
Elk River Review
Embers
En Plein Air
Envoi
Epoch
Equinox Press
Explorations
Explorer Magazine
Expressions Forum Review
Feelings: America's Beautiful Poetry Magazine
Filling Station
Fine Madness
First Time
Flume Press
Folio: A Literary Journal
Footwork: The Paterson Literary Review
Formalist, The
Frogmore Papers
Frogpond: Quarterly Haiku Journal
Fudge Cake, The
Gaia: A Journal of Literary & Environmental Arts
Georgetown Review
Geppo Haiku Worksheet
Golden Isis Magazine
Grain
Greensboro Review, The
Haiku Headlines: A Monthly Newsletter of Haiku and Senryu
Half Tones to Jubilee
Harp-Strings
Heaven Bone Press
Helicon Nine Editions
Hellas: A Journal of Poetry and the Humanities
Hippopotamus Press
Hob-Nob
Home Planet News
Hopewell Review
Hopewell Review
Housewife-Writer's Forum
Hubbub
Hudson Review, The
Hyacinth House Publications
Icon
Imago: New Writing
International Black Writers
Iowa Press, University of
Iowa Woman
Kalliope, a journal of women's art
Kansas Quarterly
Keystrokes
Ledge Poetry and Fiction Magazine, The
Light and Life Magazine
Lines n' Rhymes
Lite Magazine: The Journal of Satire and Creativity
Literary Focus Poetry Publications
Literary Olympics, Inc.
Literature and Belief
Long Island Quarterly
Lotus Poetry Series
Louisiana Literature
Lucidity
Lyric, The
MacGuffin, The
Madison Review, The
Malahat Review, The
Maryland Poetry Review
Massachusetts Press, The University of
Mid-American Review
Midwest Poetry Review
Minority Literary Expo
Mirrors
Misnomer
Missouri Press, University of
Missouri Review
Mr. Cogito Press
Modern Haiku

Montana Poet Magazine, The
Moving Out: A Feminist Literary and Arts Journal
My Legacy
Mystery Time
Nation, The
Nebraska Review, The
Negative Capability
New Delta Review
New Era Magazine
New Horizons Poetry Club
New Letters
New Poets Series, Inc., The
New Press Literary Quarterly, The
New Voices in Poetry and Prose
Nimrod International Journal of Contemporary Poetry and Fiction
North, The
Northeastern University Press
Nostalgia: A Sentimental State of Mind
Oak, The
Odradek
Ogalala Review, The
Ohio State University Press/ Journal Award in Poetry
Olympia Review
Onionhead
Orbis: An International Quarterly of Poetry and Prose
Oregon Review
Owl Creek Press
Oxalis
Painted Hills Review
Palanquin/TDM
Panhandler, The
Paris Review, The
Parnassus Literary Journal
Pasque Petals
Peace and Freedom
Pearl
Perivale Press
Peterloo Poets
Phoebe
Piedmont Literary Review
Pig Iron
Pikeville Review
Pitt Poetry Series
Pittsburgh Quarterly, The
Plainsongs
Plowman, The
Plum Review, The
Poems & Plays
Poet
Poetic Eloquence
Poetic Page
Poetpourri
Poetry
Poetry & Audience
Poetry Forum
Poetry Harbor
Poetry Kanto
Poetry Northwest
Poetry Nottingham
Poetry Plus Magazine
Poets at Work
Poet's Fantasy
Poet's Review
Poets' Roundtable
Potpourri
Prairie Schooner
Princeton University Press
Pudding House Publications
Purdue University Press
Pygmy Forest Press
Quarterly Review of Literature Poetry Series
Radcliffe Quarterly
Rambunctious Press
Red Cedar Review
Renegade
Rhino
Rio Grande Press
River City
Rockford Review, The
Rose Shell Press
Salmon Run Press
San Diego Poet's Press
San Jose Studies
Saturday Press, Inc.
Scavenger's Newsletter
Sewanee Review, The
Sheila-na-gig
Signpost Press, The
Silver Apples Press
Silver Wings
Silverfish Review
Slate & Style
Slipstream
Smith Publisher, Gibbs
Society of American Poets, The
Sonora Review
Sophomore Jinx
South Coast Poetry Journal
Southern California Anthology, The
Southern Humanities Review
Southern Poetry Review
Southwest Review
Sow's Ear Poetry Review, The
Spitball
Staple
State Street Press
Still Waters Press
Story Line Press
Studio, A Journal of Christians Writing
Sub-Terrain
Sucarnochee Review, The
Sun Dog: The Southeast Review
Tails of Wonder
Taproot Literary Review
Tesseract Publications
Texas Tech University Press
Thorntree Press
Thumbprints
Tickled by Thunder: Writer's News & Roundtable
Time of Singing, A Magazine of Christian Poetry
TriQuarterly Magazine
Vegetarian Journal
Verve
Voices Israel
W.I.M. Publications (Woman in the Moon)
Washington Writers' Publishing House
Waterways: Poetry in the Mainstream
West of Boston
West Wind Review
Westerly
Western Humanities Review
Weyfarers
Whetstone (Canada)
Whetstone (IL)
White Sands Poetry Review
Whitecrow Foundation, Tahana
Wildwood Journal
Willow Review
Willow Springs
Wind Publications
Wisconsin Press, University of
Woodley Memorial Press
Worcester Review
Word Works, The
Wormwood Review Press
Write Way, The
Writers' Center Press
Writer's Digest
Writer's Exchange
Writer's Journal
Yale University Press
Yankee Magazine
Zuzu's Petals Quarterly

Resources

Conferences and Workshops

Conferences and workshops are valuable resources for many poets, especially those just beginning. A conference or workshop serves as an opportunity to learn about specific aspects of the craft, gather feedback from other poets and writers, listen to submission tips from editors, and/or revel in a creative atmosphere that may stimulate one's muse.

In this section you'll find listings for 48 conferences and workshops—more than a dozen of which are new to this edition. Some, such as the Festival of Poetry in Franconia, New Hampshire, are specifically geared to poets. Most, however, are more general conferences with offerings for a variety of writers, including poets.

A "typical" conference may have a number of workshop sessions, keynote speakers and perhaps even a panel or two. Topics may include everything from writing fiction, poetry and books for children to marketing one's work. Often a theme, which may change from year to year, will be the connecting factor. Other conferences and workshops cover a number of topics but have an overriding focus. For example, you'll find two gatherings for Appalachian writers. There are also events geared to women writers and Christian writers. And the Writing Workshop for People Over 57 is specifically designed to aid older adults.

Despite different themes or focuses, each listing in this section details the offerings available for poets. Each also includes information about other workshops, speakers and panels of interest. It is important to note, however, that conference and workshop directors were still in the organizing stages when contacted. Consequently, some listings include information from last year's events simply to provide an idea of what to expect this year. For more up-to-date details, including current costs, send a SASE to the director in question a few months before the date(s) listed.

Benefiting from conferences

Without a doubt, attending conferences and workshops is beneficial. First, these events provide opportunities to learn more about the poetic craft. Some even feature individual sessions with workshop leaders, allowing you to specifically discuss your work with others. If these one-on-one sessions include critiques (generally for an additional fee), we've included this information.

Besides learning from workshop leaders, you may also benefit from conversations with other attendees. Writers on all levels enjoy talking to and sharing insights with others. A conversation over lunch can reveal a new market for your work, or a casual chat while waiting for a session to begin can acquaint you with a new resource. If a conference or workshop includes time for open readings and you choose to participate, you may gain feedback from both workshop leaders and others.

Another reason conferences and workshops are worthwhile is the opportunity they provide to meet editors and publishers who often have tips about marketing work.

The availability of these folks, however, does not necessarily mean they will want to read your latest collection of poems (unless, of course, they are workshop leaders and you have an individual meeting scheduled with them). Though editors and publishers are glad to meet poets and writers, and occasionally discuss work in general terms, they cannot give personal attention to everyone they meet.

Selecting a conference or workshop

When selecting a conference or workshop to attend, keep in mind your goals. If you want to learn how to improve your craft, for example, consider one of the events entirely devoted to poetry or locate a more general conference where one-on-one critique sessions are offered. If you're looking for more informal feedback, choose an event which includes open readings. If marketing your work seems like an ominous task, register for a conference that includes a session with editors. And if you also have an interest in other forms of writing, an event with a wide range of workshops is a good bet.

Of course, take into consideration your own resources. If both your time and funds are limited, search for a conference or workshop within your area. Many events are held during weekends and may be close enough to enable you to commute. On the other hand, if you want to combine your vacation with time spent meeting other writers and working on your craft, consider workshops such as those sponsored by The Writers' Center at Chautauqua. In either case, it is important to at least consider the conference location and be aware of activities to enjoy in the area.

Still other factors may influence your decision when selecting a workshop or conference. For instance, events that sponsor contests may allow you to gain recognition and recoup some of your expenses. Similarly, some conferences and workshops have financial assistance or scholarships available. Finally, many are associated with colleges and/or universities and may offer continuing education credits. You will find all of these options included here. Again, send a SASE for more details.

For other conferences and workshops, see **The Guide to Writers Conferences** (ShawGuides, Inc., Dept. 1406W, 625 Biltmore Way, Coral Gables FL 33134) and/or the May issue of ***Writer's Digest*** magazine (available on newsstands or directly from the publisher at 1507 Dana Ave., Cincinnati OH 45207).

AMERICAN CHRISTIAN WRITERS CONFERENCES, P.O. Box 5168, Phoenix AZ 85010, phone (800)21-WRITE, director Reg Forder. Annual 3-day events founded in 1981. Held throughout the year in cities such as Houston, Dallas/Ft. Worth, Boston, Minneapolis, New York, St. Louis, Detroit, Pittsburgh, Atlanta, Miami and Phoenix. Usually located at a major hotel chain like Holiday Inn. Average attendance is 300. **Open to anyone. Conferences cover fiction, poetry, writing for children.** Cost is $119, extra for beginning writers day; participants are responsible for their own meals. Accommodations include special rates at host hotel. Send SASE for brochures and registration forms.

‡ANTIOCH WRITERS' WORKSHOP, P.O. Box 494, Yellow Springs OH 45387, phone (513)767-7068, director Susan Carpenter. Annual 7-day event founded in 1986. Usually held in July at Antioch College in the village of Yellow Springs. "The campus is quiet, shady, relaxed. The village is unusual for its size: a hotbed of artists, writers and creative people." Average attendance is 70. **Open to everyone. "We create an intense community of writers and cover fiction, poetry and writing for children plus playwriting, screenwriting and mystery. Also talks by editors, agents, and others in the industry."** Offerings specifically available for poets include an introductory class in writing poetry, an intensive seminar, night sessions for participants to share poetry, and critiquing. Speakers for the 1995 conference will include Sue Grafton. She will also be teaching a class in novel writing and reading mss. Cost for 1994 conference was $450; scholarships and some work-study fellowships are available (including the Judson Jerome Scholarship sponsored by ***Writer's Digest*** magazine). Both graduate and undergraduate credit is available for an additional fee. Campus dining room meal ticket is $105 (for 20 meals); must be purchased in advance. Transportation from airport is provided. Information on overnight accommodations is available and includes housing in campus dorms. Individual critiques are also available. Submit work for critique in advance with $35 fee for poetry; $60 fee for story, book or script.

Send SASE for brochures and registration forms. Antioch Writers' Workshop is supported in part by Poets & Writers, Inc.

APPALACHIAN WRITERS' ASSOCIATION CONFERENCE, Dept. of English, WCU, Cullowhee NC 28723, phone (704)227-7264, program chair Steve Eberly. Annual 3-day event founded in 1980. 1995 dates: July 7-9. Location: Madison Dorm and Conference Center on the campus of Western Carolina University. Average attendance is 65 members. **Open to Appalachian writers, "including any interested writers in Kentucky, Tennessee, Georgia, South Carolina, North Carolina, Virginia, West Virginia and other kindred spirits." The conference is designed "to share readings, workshops, marketing tips and skills relating to poetry, fiction and essays; to celebrate the successes, common bonds and concerns of writers in the Appalachian region."** Special features include "Readings by the Creek," a picnic and open readings, at WCU picnic grounds. Cost for conference is $100, including room (2 nights), meals and registration. Local accommodations on campus are arranged by AWA. A list of other accommodations is available on request. On-site rooms: $29/night, single or double occupancy. Poetry, fiction and essay contests are sponsored as part of the conference. Entry requirements: $10/year membership fee. Judges are published regional writers. Send SASE for brochures and registration forms.

APPALACHIAN WRITERS WORKSHOP, Box 844, Hindman KY 41822, phone (606)785-5475, director Mike Mullins. Annual 5-day event founded 1977. Usually held at the end of July or beginning of August. Location: Campus of Hindman Settlement School in Knott County, KY. "The campus is hilly and access for housing is limited for physically impaired, but workshop facilities are accessible." Average attendance is 60-70. **Open to "anyone regardless of sex, age or race." Conference is designed to promote writers and writing of the Appalachian region. It covers fiction, poetry, writing for children, dramatic work and nonfiction.** Offerings specifically available for poets include daily sessions on poetry, individual critique sessions and readings. All of the staff for 1994 were featured readers, including James Still, Lee Smith, Robert Morgan, John Edgerton, Jim Wayne Miller, George Ella Lyon and Barbara Smith. Cost for workshop is approximately $300 for room, board and tuition. Information on overnight accommodations is available for registrants. Accommodations may include special rates at area hotels "once our facilities are filled." Submit mss for individual critiques in advance. Send SASE for brochures and registration forms. They have published **A Gathering At The Forks**, an anthology "of the best of the past 15 workshops." Write for information.

ARKANSAS WRITERS' CONFERENCE, 1115 Gillette Dr., Little Rock AR 72207, phone (501)225-0166, director Clovita Rice. Annual 2-day event founded 1944. "In 1994 we celebrated our 50th anniversary." Always 1st weekend of June at the Holiday Inn West in Little Rock. Average attendance is 200. **Open to all writers. The conference is designed to "appeal both to beginning and already active writers with a varied program on improving their writing skills and marketing their work."** Offerings specifically available for poets include a poetry workshop offering critiques and poetry contests. In 1994, the guest speaker was Sharon Linnea, former associate editor of ***Guideposts Magazine***. Other special features include an awards luncheon (door prizes such as **Writer's Market** and **Poet's Market**) and banquet, and the announcement of the person selected for Arkansas Writers' Hall of Fame. Cost for 1994 conference was $10 registration for 2 days, $5 for 1 day. Five dollar fee to cover entry to 36 contests. Limousine service from airport to Holiday Inn West is provided. Accommodations include special rates at host hotel. Individual critiques are available. Bring one poem, 20-line limit, to workshop. Thirty-six contests (4 require attendance and 8 are limited to Arkansas residents) are sponsored as part of the conference. Each contest has a chairman who will judge or secure a judge. Send SASE for brochures and registration forms after February 1 each year. Clovita Rice, conference director, is editor of ***Voices International*** (see listing in the Publishers of Poetry section).

‡AUSTIN WRITERS' LEAGUE SPRING AND FALL WORKSHOPS, Suite E-2, 1501 W. Fifth St., Austin TX 78703, phone (512)499-8914, executive director Angela Smith. Biannual workshops founded 1982. "Each workshop series has 12-18 workshops. Workshops are usually 3- or 6-hour sessions." Usually held weekends in March, April, May and September, October, November. Location: St. Edward's University Moody Hall. Average attendance is 15 to 200 per workshop. **Open to all writers, beginners and advanced. Workshops cover fiction, poetry, writing for children, nonfiction, screenwriting, book promotion and marketing, working with agents and publishers, journal writing, special interest writing, creativity, grantwriting, copyright law and taxes for writers.** Offerings specifically available for poets include at least 2 workshops during each series. Poetry presenters have included Lorenzo Thomas, Laurel Ann Bogen, Bobby Byrd and Benjamin Saenz. 1994 presenters included Sandra Scofield, Lars Eighner, Sue Grafton, Peter Mehlman and Carol Leifer (top writers from "Seinfeld"), Gregg Levoy, Michael Hague, Lee Merrill Byrd and several New York agents and editors. "Occasionally, presenters agree to do private consults with participants. Also, workshops sometimes incorporate hands-on practice and critique." Cost is $35-75. Members get discount. Cost includes continental breakfast and refreshments for breaks. Meals not included. Arrangements can be made in advance for airport transportation. Information on overnight accommodations is available for registrants. Accommodations include special rates at area hotels. Requirements for critiques are posted in workshop brochure. Send SASE for brochures and registration forms. The Austin Writers' League publishes **Poetography**, an anthology of poems selected by jury, and ***The Austin Writer***, a monthly publication of poetry selected from submissions each month. These poems are eligible for six $100 Word Is Art awards presented in December of each year. Poetry guidelines for other publications, awards and grants programs, and market listings are available through the League library.

AUTUMN AUTHORS' AFFAIR, 1507 Burnham Ave., Calumet City IL 60409, phone (708)862-9797, president Nancy McCann. Annual 3-day event founded 1983. Usually held during the 4th weekend in October at the Hyatt Lisle in Lisle, IL. Average attendance is 200-275. **Open to anyone. Conference covers fiction, but every year Professor Charles Tinkham of Purdue University-Calumet, called "the poet of the people," gives a poetry workshop "covering the entire realm" of writing poetry. "We usually have between 40-75 published authors at the conference each year."** Saturday-only and weekend packages, including most meals, are available. Information on overnight accommodations is also available. Send SASE for brochures and registration forms which include the cost of each package, special hotel rates and itinerary.

BAY AREA WRITERS WORKSHOP, % Poetry Flash, P.O. Box 4172, Berkeley CA 94704, phone (510)525-5476, fax (510)540-1057, co-director Joyce Jenkins. Annual 2-day events founded in 1988. Usually held 4-5 summer weekends at various workshop settings. Average attendance is 15 for workshops. **Open to literary writers. Workshops cover poetry, novel and short story.** In 1994 the weekend intensive workshops were led by Brenda Hillman, Yusef Komunyakaa, James Salter and Dorothy Allison. Cost for workshop is $250; participants are responsible for their own meals. Full scholarships are awarded to 10-15% of participants. Information on overnight accommodations and transportation is available for participants. Workshop evaluations are included. All participants receive manuscripts prior to weekend. Bay Area Writers also sponsor a biennial 1-day literary publishing conference for 300 participants. Cost of conference was $45. Send SASE for brochures and registration forms.

‡BREAD LOAF WRITERS' CONFERENCE, Middlebury College, Middlebury VT 05753, phone (802)388-3711, ext. 5286, administrative coordinator Carol Knauss. Annual 12-day event founded 1926. Usually held in mid-August. Average attendance is 230. **Conference is designed to promote dialogue among writers and provide professional critiques for students. Conference usually covers fiction, nonfiction and poetry.** Cost for 1994 conference was $1,525, including tuition, room and board. Fellowships and scholarships for the conference are available. "Candidates for fellowships must have a book published. Candidates for scholarships must have published in major literary periodicals or newspapers. One letter of nomination required by March 1; applications and supporting materials due by April 1. Awards are announced in June for the conference in August." Taxis to and from the airport or bus station are available. Individual critiques are also available. Send for brochures and registration forms.

CAPE COD WRITERS CONFERENCE OF CAPE COD WRITERS' CENTER, c/o Cape Cod Conservatory, Rte. 132, West Barnstable MA 02668, phone (508)775-4811, director Marion Vuilleumier. Annual week-long event founded in 1963. Usually held the 3rd week of August at the Tabernacle, Craigville Conference Center. Average attendance is 150. **Open to everyone. Conference covers poetry, fiction, nonfiction, mystery/suspense and writing for children.** In 1994 the poetry teacher was Carol Dine. Cost is $80 registration, $60 each course (full time); $25 registration, $20 each course (one day); 4 scholarships available. Participants are responsible for their own meals. "It is recommended that participants stay at the Craigville Conference Center (early registration necessary)." Other housing information available from Bed & Breakfast Cape Cod. Manuscript evaluations ($60) and personal conferences ($30) are also available. Send SASE for brochures and registration forms.

CAPE LITERARY WORKSHOPS OF CAPE COD WRITERS' CENTER, c/o Cape Cod Conservatory, Rte. 132, West Barnstable MA 02668, phone (508)775-4811, director Marion Vuilleumier. Annual week-long event founded 1985. Usually held the 2nd week of August at the Parish House, St. Mary's Church, Barnstable. Average attendance is 10/workshop. **Open to everyone. Workshops usually cover poetry, fiction, scriptwriting, travel, science fiction, magazine article writing and children's book writing and illustration.** Cost is $410; participants are responsible for meals although "plentiful snack spreads" are included. "Twenty hours of practically individual attention is given, including one personal critique." Private transportation recommended. Contact Bed & Breakfast Cape Cod for housing information. Send SASE for brochures and registration forms.

‡CHARLESTON WRITERS' CONFERENCE, Lightsey Conference Center, College of Charleston, Charleston SC 29424-0001, phone (803)953-5822, fax (803)953-1454, director Paul Allen. Annual 4-day event founded 1989. Usually held in March at the College of Charleston, founded 1770, in historic downtown Charleston, South Carolina, "a setting renowned for its beauty, history and intimacy." Average attendance is 150. **Open to everyone. Conference covers fiction, poetry and nonfiction.** Offerings specifically available for poets in 1994 included readings by Scott Cairns and Yusef Komunyakaa; seminars covering topics such as balancing writing and living, submitting your work and discussing the strengths and weaknesses of selected poems; and workshops covering various subjects and exercises. Speakers at previous conferences have included Marvin Bell, Toi Derricotte, Pattiann Rogers, Ellen Bryant Voigt, Nicholas Delbanco and William Stafford. Cost for 1994 conference was $95 ($70 for students); participants are responsible for their own meals. Information on overnight accommodations is available for registrants. Accommodations include special rates at hotels within walking distance of conference. Individual critiques are also available. Submit up to 3 poems, not to exceed 7 pgs., typed and single-spaced with $35 fee. Send SASE for brochures and registration forms or call Judy Sawyer at phone number above.

‡**COOS BAY WRITERS WORKSHOP**, P.O. Box 4022, Coos Bay OR 97420, phone (503)756-7906, director Mary Scheirman. Annual 4-day event founded 1987. Usually held the last Thursday through Sunday in August. Location: University of Oregon Biological Research Station at Charleston Harbor on the beach. Average attendance is 40. **Open to everyone. Workshop usually covers poetry and prose.** Special features include a " 'walking workshop'—an 8-mile hike on wilderness beach with two practicing writers who lead exercises and discussions along the way." Cost for conference is $275, including room, board, tuition and meals. Information on overnight accommodations is available for registrants. Individual critiques are also available. "Submit ms with registration prior to the workshop." Send SASE for brochures and registration forms.

‡**FEMINIST WOMEN'S WRITING WORKSHOPS, INC.**, P.O. Box 6583, Ithaca NY 14851, co-director M.B. O'Connor. Annual 8-day event founded 1974. 1994 dates: July 10-17 (1995 around same time). Location: Hobart and William Smith Colleges, Geneva, New York. Average attendance is 25. **Open to "feminist women writers." Workshop usually covers fiction, poetry, journal writing, screenwriting, personal essay, autobiography, journalism and drama.** Offerings specifically available for poets include daily workshops, critiques and readings. Guest writer for 1995 is poet Ruth Stone. Cost for 1994 workshop was $495, including tuition, room, board and all events. "Limousine service available from nearby airports for an extra fee. We try to help arrange car pools." Participants are housed in a campus residence. Individual critiques while at the conference are optional. "We require a work sample for first-time attendees prior to acceptance." Submit "writing sample (nonreturnable) of up to 10 pgs. Type of sample is your choice. Work in progress, autobiographical writing, nonfiction prose or experimental writing are as welcome as fiction, poetry or drama." Send SASE for brochures and registration forms.

FESTIVAL OF POETRY, Robert Frost Place, Franconia NH 03580, phone (603)823-5510, executive director Donald Sheehan. Annual week-long event founded in 1978. Usually held first week of August at Robert Frost's mountain farm (house and barn), made into a center for poetry and the arts. Average attendance is 50-55. **Open to poets only.** Recent faculty included Hayden Carruth, Amy Clampitt, Donald Hall, Brad Leithauser and Alicia Ostriker. Cost is $350-360 tuition, plus a $25 reading fee. "Room and board available locally; information sent upon acceptance to program." Application should be accompanied by 3 pages of poetry. Send SASE for brochures and registration forms.

THE FLIGHT OF THE MIND, WOMEN'S WRITING WORKSHOPS, 622 SE 29th Ave., Portland OR 97214, phone (503)236-9862, director Judith Barrington. Annual events founded 1983. Usually held at the end of June, beginning of July. Two workshops in summer for 7 days each at "a rustic retreat center (Dominican owned) right on the wild McKenzie River in the foothills of the Oregon Cascades." Average attendance is 65 women/workshop in 5 different classes. **Open to women writers. Workshops cover fiction, poetry, essays, screenwriting, special-topic classes (e.g. "landscape and memory") with a feminist philosophy.** In 1994 workshop leaders included Elizabeth Woody, Naomi Shihab Nye and Terri de la Peña. Cost for workshop (including tuition, all meals and room) was $550 and up depending on accommodations chosen. Scholarships available. Transportation to and from the event is provided. Participants are selected on the basis of work submitted. Peer critique groups form at workshop. "Competition is discouraged." Send first-class stamp for brochures and registration forms.

‡**HAYSTACK WRITING PROGRAM**, School of Extended Studies, Portland State University, P.O. Box 1491, Portland OR 97207, phone (503)725-4186, fax (503)725-4840, contact Maggie Herrington. Annual summer program founded 1968. One-week courses over the six weeks of the program. 1994 dates: June 28-August 5. "Classes are held in the local school of this small coastal community; beach activities are also scheduled and some evening lectures and other entertainment." Average attendance is 10-15/class; 300 total. **Open to all writers. One-week workshops cover fiction, poetry, mystery, radio essay and nonfiction.** Cost for workshop is $295-320; participants pay for their own lodging and meals.

Accommodation options range from camping to luxury hotels. Write for brochures and registration forms (no SASE necessary).

HOFSTRA UNIVERSITY SUMMER WRITERS' CONFERENCE, 110 Hofstra University, Hempstead NY 11550, phone (516)463-5997, fax (516)564-0061, director Lewis Shena. Annual 10-day event founded 1972. Usually starts the Monday after July 4th. Location: Hofstra University. Average attendance is 50-60. **Open to all writers. Conference covers fiction, nonfiction, poetry, children's writing, stage/screenwriting and one other area (science fiction, mystery, etc.). "Every year we offer a poetry workshop."** Guest speakers (other than the workshop leaders) "usually come from the world of publishing." There are also "readings galore and various special presentations." Cost for 1994 conference was $621 (non-credit). Additional fee of $285 for air-conditioned dorm room, one dinner and coffee/tea on a daily basis. For those seeking credit, other fees apply. Individual critiques are also available. "Each writer gets a half hour one-on-one with the poetry workshop leader." They do not sponsor a contest, but "we submit exceptional work to the ***Paris Review***." Send SASE for brochures and registration forms (available as of April).

IOWA SUMMER WRITING FESTIVAL, University of Iowa, 116 International Center, Iowa City IA 52242, phone (319)335-2534, fax (319)335-2740, coordinators Karen Burgus Schootman and Peggy Houston. Annual event founded in 1987. Held each summer in June and July for six weeks, includes one week, two week and weekend workshops at the University of Iowa campus. Average attendance is 125/week. **Open to "all adults who have a desire to write." Conference offers courses in most all writing forms. In 1994, offerings available for poets included 10 poetry classes for all levels.** Speakers were Joy Harjo, Susan Power, Elizabeth Benedict, Michael Martone, Abraham Verghese, Gish Jen and Robert Dana. Cost for 1994 conference was $335 for 1 week and $150 for a weekend; discount available for early payment. Participants are responsible for their own meals. Accommodations available at the Iowa House and the Holiday Inn. Housing in residence hall costs about $25/night. Participants in week-long workshops will have private conference/critique with workshop leader. Send for brochures and registration forms.

THE IWWG SUMMER CONFERENCE, The International Women's Writing Guild, P.O. Box 810, Gracie Station, New York NY 10028, phone (212)737-7536, executive director Hannelore Hahn. Annual week-long event founded 1978. 1995 dates: August 11-18. Location: Skidmore College in Saratoga Springs, NY. Average attendance is 400. **Open to all women. Fifty-six workshops offered. "At least four poetry workshops offered for full week."** Cost is $600 for conference program and room and board. "Critiquing available throughout the week." Send SASE for brochures and registration forms. The International Women's Writing Guild's bimonthly newsletter publishes and features hundreds of outlets for poets. See listing in Organizations Useful to Poets.

LIGONIER VALLEY WRITERS CONFERENCE, Box 8, RR 4, Ligonier PA 15658, phone (412)238-5749, fax (412)238-5190, president E. Kay Myers. Annual 3-day event founded 1986. 1995 dates: July 7-9. "This is a relaxing, educational, inspirational conference in a scenic, small town." Average attendance is 80. **Open to anyone interested in writing. Conference covers fiction, creative nonfiction, poetry, writing for children and screenwriting.** Poetry workshops each day. 1994 workshops conducted by Judy Vollmer. Cost for conference is approximately $200, including some meals and picnic. Participants are responsible for their own dinner and lodging. Information on overnight accommodations is available for registrants. Individual critiques are also available. Must send samples in advance. Send SASE for brochures and registration forms. "We also publish ***The Loyalhanna Review***, a literary journal, which is open to participants."

LITTLE SMOKIES OF OHIO FALL POETRY WORKSHOP, 403 S. Sixth St., Ironton OH 45638, phone (614)858-6621 or contact D.H. Spears at (614)533-1081. Annual 3-day event founded 1992. Usually held during a weekend in September, beginning on Friday night with a campfire reading. Saturday morning is writing on the trails, Saturday afternoon includes time for editing workshops and Saturday evening is an awards banquet. Sunday morning is for evaluation and wrap-up. Average attendance is 22. **Open to anyone interested in the writing of poetry. The workshop "is designed to promote the writing of poetry and to celebrate the poetic achievements of the workshop participants.** The writing 'charge' changes each year and is kept secret until time to head for the trails." Cost is $12 registration; participants are responsible for their own meals and lodging. Information on overnight accommodations is available for registrants. Shawnee Lodge offers rooms that sleep 4; cost is $75/night. Cabins at Shawnee State Park sleep 6; cost is $99/night. A poetry contest is sponsored in conjunction with the workshop. Theme changes yearly. Judge is Harding Stedler, workshop conductor. Send SASE for brochures and registration forms. The event is sponsored by the Phoenix Writers of Portsmouth, Ohio in affiliation with Shawnee State University.

MIDLAND WRITERS CONFERENCE, Grace A. Dow Memorial Library, 1710 W. St. Andrews, Midland MI 48640, phone (517)835-7151, fax (517)835-9791, conference co-chairs Margaret Allen and Eileen

Finzel. Annual 1-day event founded 1979. Usually held the second weekend in June at the Grace A. Dow Memorial Library in Midland, MI. Average attendance is 100. **Open to any writer, published or unpublished. Conference usually includes six sessions that vary in content. "We always have one session on poetry and one session on writing for children. The other four sessions cover other subjects of interest to writers."** In 1994, John Palen presented a session on "Polishing the Poem," and the keynote speaker was P.J. O'Rourke. "We always have a well-known keynoter. In the past we have had Judith Viorst, Kurt Vonnegut, Andrew Greeley, Mary Higgins Clark and David McCullough." Cost for 1994 conference was $45 until 2 weeks prior to the event ($55 after that). For students, senior citizens and handicapped participants, cost was $35 until 2 weeks prior to the event ($45 after that). Information on overnight accommodations is available for registrants. Send for brochures and registration forms.

MIDWEST WRITERS' CONFERENCE, 6000 Frank Ave. NW, Canton OH 44720-7599, phone (216)499-9600, fax (216)494-6121, coordinator of continuing studies Debbie Ruhe. Annual weekend event founded 1968. 1995 dates: October 6-7. Location: Kent State University Stark Campus in Canton, Ohio. Average attendance is 250. **Open to aspiring writers in any category, but the writing contest is directed toward fiction, nonfiction, juvenile literature and poetry. "The conference provides an atmosphere in which aspiring writers can meet with and learn from experienced, established writers through lectures, workshops, competitive contests, personal interviews and informal group discussions."** Offerings specifically available for poets include a lecture session in the poetry area and a contest. Past panelists have included Joyce Carol Oates, Edward Albee, Kurt Vonnegut and Lee Abbott. One special feature of the conference is an all day book fair which includes several Ohio small presses. Cost for 1994 conference was $65, including conference registration, workshops, keynote address, lunch and ms entry fee. Contest entry fee exclusively: $40 for two mss and $10 for each additional ms. Participants are responsible for other meals. Information on overnight accommodations is available for registrants. Special conference rates are available through the Parke Hotel, and there is a special shuttle between the university and the hotel. Individual critiques are also available in the areas of poetry, fiction, nonfiction and juvenile literature. Submit one individual poem up to 200 lines. Contest sponsored as part of conference. "Work must be original, unpublished and not a winner in any contest at the time of entry." Judging is performed by local professionals in their appropriate categories. Send SASE for brochures and registration forms. Kent State University offers submissions to the annual publication of ***Canto***. For more information, call (216)499-9600, ext. 365. Co-sponsor of the Midwest Writers' Conference is the Greater Canton Writers' Guild, 919 Clinton Ave. SW, Canton OH 44706-5196.

MISSISSIPPI VALLEY WRITERS CONFERENCE, Augustana College, Rock Island IL 61201, phone (309)762-8985, founder/director David R. Collins. Annual week-long event founded in 1973. Usually held the second week in June at the Liberal Arts College of Augustana College. Average attendance is 80. **Open to all writers, "beginning beginners to polished professionals." Conference provides a general professional writing focus on many genres of writing. Offers week-long workshop in poetry.** Evening programs as well as daily workshops are included. Cost for 1994 conference was $25 registration, $40 one workshop, $70 two workshops, $30 each additional workshop. Conferees may stay on campus or off. Board and room accommodations are available at Westerlin Hall on Augustana campus, 15 meals and 6 nights lodging approximately $200. Individual critiques are also available. Submit up to 10 poems. Awards presented by workshop leaders. Send SASE for brochures and registration forms.

‡MOUNT HERMON CHRISTIAN WRITERS CONFERENCE, P.O. Box 413, Mount Hermon CA 95041, phone (408)335-4466, fax (408)335-9218, director of public affairs David R. Talbott. Annual 5-day event founded 1970. Always held Friday through Tuesday over Palm Sunday weekend. 1995 dates: April 7-11. Location: Full hotel-service-style conference center in the heart of the California redwoods. Average attendance is 150-200. **Open to "anyone interested in the Christian writing market." Conference is very broad-based. Always covers poetry, fiction, article writing, writing for children, plus an advanced track for published authors.** In 1994, offerings specifically available for poets included "Poetry Forum: The Small Necessity"; "What Makes Poetry Sing?, Poetry People Won't Forget"; "Poetry: The Craft and Marketing of the Art"; and "Self-Publishing for Poets." "We had 34 teaching faculty for 1994—will probably be similar for 1995. Faculty was made up of publishing reps of leading Christian book and magazine publishers, plus selected freelancers." Other special features included an advance critique service (no extra fee); residential conference, with meals taken family-style with faculty; private appointments with faculty; and an autograph party. "High spiritual impact." Cost for 1994 conference was $625 deluxe; $525 standard; $450 economy; including 13 meals, snacks, housing and $275 tuition fee. No-housing fee: $425. All housing on grounds. $15 airport, Greyhound or Amtrack shuttle from San Jose, CA. Send SASE for brochures and registration forms.

NAPA VALLEY WRITERS' CONFERENCE, 2277 Napa-Vallejo Highway, Napa CA 94558, phone (707)253-3070, fax (707)253-3015, managing director Sherri Hallgren. Annual week-long event founded 1981. Usually held the last week in July or first week in August on the grounds of Napa Valley College, 50 miles northeast of San Francisco. Average attendance is 36 in poetry and 36 in fiction. **"The conference has maintained its emphases on process and craft, featuring a faculty as renowned for the quality of their teaching as for their work. It has also remained small and personal, fostering an unusual rapport between faculty writers and conference participants. The poetry session provides the opportunity to work both on generating new poems and on revising previously written ones. Participants spend time with each of the staff poets in daily workshops that emphasize writing new poems - taking risks with new material and forms, pushing boundaries in the poetic process."** The 1994 poetry staff was Garrett Hongo, Jane Hirshfield and David St. John. "Participants register for either the poetry or the fiction workshops, but panels and craft talks are open to all writers attending. Evenings feature readings by the faculty that are open to the public and hosted by Napa Valley wineries." Cost is $450, not including meals or housing. There are some limited partial scholarships, depending on donations. Shuttle service from the San Francisco Airport is available for a nominal fee. "Participants usually find it helpful to have a car during the week, but car pools can be arranged for those who need rides to conference events. A list of valley accommodations is mailed to applicants on acceptance and includes at least one reduced-rate package. Through the generosity of Napa residents, limited accommodations in local homes are available on a first-come, first-served basis." All applicants are asked to submit a qualifying ms with their registration (no more than 5 pgs. of poetry or 12 pgs. of fiction) as well as a brief description of their background as a writer. Send SASE for brochures and registration forms.

THE NAROPA INSTITUTE WRITING & POETICS SUMMER PROGRAM, 2130 Arapahoe Ave., Boulder CO 80302, phone (303)444-0202, director of writing & poetics Anne Waldman, assistant director Andrew Schelling. Annual month-long summer program founded in 1974. Usually held every July; participants may attend from 1-4 weeks. "We are located on 3.7 acres in the center of Boulder, Colorado. The campus houses a performing arts center, meditation hall, classrooms, offices and library. Many of the summer lectures are held under a huge tent on our back lawn." Average attendance is 100-120. **Open to anyone; students attending for credit must obtain department's permission. "It is a convocation of students, scholars, fiction writers, poets and translators. In dialogue with renown practitioners of verbal arts, students confront the composition of poetry and prose."** Theme for 1993 was Deeper into America, "a counter-celebration challenging the Euro-American way of life that has ignored and oppressed certain cultures and forms of life." Theme for 1994 was Beat Reunion, "a tribute to Allen Ginsberg." Offerings specifically available for poets include lectures, readings (both student and faculty), workshops and one-on-one interviews with guest faculty. Conference speakers have included Allen Ginsberg, Anselm Hollo, Bobbie Louise Hawkins, Jack Collom, Bernadette Mayer, Michael McClure, Ron Silliman, Michael Ondaatje, Nathaniel Mackey and Eagle Cruz. Cost for 1 week is $375 (non credit), for 2 weeks $630 (non credit) and $750 (BA credit). Cost of 4 weeks is $1,260 (non credit), $1,500 (BA credit) and $2,000 (MFA credit). Lab fees are $10/week. Four scholarships are available for minority students. Participants are responsible for their own meals. "Student services can help find places to stay." Work to be critiqued does not need to be sent in advance. "During the weekly workshops and personal interviews, every writer will have a chance to be critiqued by professional poets/fiction writers." Write for brochures and registration forms. "We also sponsor student readings and have an informal summer magazine and two other (more formal) school sponsored magazines, ***Bombay Gin*** and ***Exit Zero***."

‡PENNWRITERS CONFERENCE, 841 Tenth St., Oakmont PA 15139, phone (412)828-4468, coordinator Cyndi Bowan. Annual 2-day event founded 1988. Usually held the second weekend in May at a hotel in the Pittsburgh area. Average attendance is 200. **Open to "all levels of writers from novice to multi-published." Conference covers all genres of fiction, also poetry and nonfiction.** In 1994, Poet David K. Harford conducted a workshop on how to use poetry, along with short fiction and nonfiction, to diversify one's writing. Other special features included a social time for guest speakers with conferencees. Cost for conference will be available in brochure. Saturday continental breakfast and Saturday lunch are included in the conference fee. All other meals are a separate expense. Information on overnight accommodations is available for registrants. Send SASE for brochures and registration forms.

‡PORT TOWNSEND WRITERS' CONFERENCE, c/o Centrum, P.O. Box 1158, Port Townsend WA 98368, phone (206)385-3102, fax (206)385-2470, director Carol Jane Bangs. Annual 10-day event founded 1974. Usually held the second week in July at a 400-acre state park at the entrance to Puget Sound. Average attendance is 160. **Open to "all serious writers who pass our preliminary manuscript screening." Conference usually covers fiction (no genre fiction), poetry, creative nonfiction, and writing for children.** Offerings specifically available for poets include "three limited-enrollment workshops, private manuscript conference, open-mike readings, faculty readings and technique classes." Speakers at the last conference were Jane Hirshfield, Garrett Hongo, Pattiann Rogers, Valerie Miner, David Long, Ron Carlson, Robert Pyle, Jane Yolen, Bruce Coville and Marvin Bell. Cost for the 1994 conference was $365 tuition including workshop, ms conference, classes, readings, lectures; $250 tuition without workshop or ms conference; plus $315 optional for dormitory housing and 3 meals per day. Information on overnight accommodations is available for registrants. Individual critiques are also available, however "you must be enrolled in a manuscript workshop." Send SASE for brochures and registration forms.

‡ST. DAVIDS CHRISTIAN WRITERS CONFERENCE, 1775 Eden Rd., Lancaster PA 17601-3523, phone (717)394-6758, address Registrar. Annual 5-day event founded 1957. 1995 dates: June 25-30. Location: campus of Eastern College in St. Davids, PA. Average attendance is 100-120. **Open to "anyone interested in writing." Conference is designed to "train and develop skills of writers for Christian and secular markets."** In 1994, offerings specifically available for poets included "Poetry: Breaking the Silence," taught by Shirley Stevens, board member of the International Poetry Forum. Speakers at last conference were Evelyn Minshull, renowned novelist, and David Page, poet and dramatist. Other special features included personal market consultant and daily tutorial for in progress projects: books, drama, poetry. Cost for conference is $400-500, including classes, room and board. Price varies according to choice of study packages. Transportation to and from the conference includes a commercial airport shuttle plus pickup from St. Davids train station. Housing in on-site facilities costs $200-230. Individual critiques are also available. "Must have a body of work to submit." Contest sponsored as part of conference. "Must be a conference attendee. Faculty members judge contest." Send SASE for brochures and registration forms.

SANTA BARBARA WRITERS' CONFERENCE, P.O. Box 304, Carpinteria CA 93014, phone (805)684-2250, fax (805)684-2250 (after recorded message), conference director Barnaby Conrad. Annual week-long event founded in 1973. Held the last Friday to Friday in June at the Miramar Hotel in Montecito. 1995 dates: June 23-30. Average attendance is 350 people. **Open to everyone. Covers all genres of writing.** Workshops in poetry offered. In 1994, speakers included Ray Bradbury, Sue Grafton, Perie Longo, W.R. Wilkins, Jules Feiffer, Charles Schulz and Julie Smith. Cost for 1994 conference, including all workshops and lectures, 2 al fresco dinners and room (no board), was $955 single, $690 double occupancy, $335 day students. Individual critiques are also available. Submit 1 ms of no more than 3,000 words in advance with SASE. Competitions with awards sponsored as part of conference. Send SASE for brochures and registration forms.

SEWANEE WRITERS' CONFERENCE, 310 St. Luke's Hall, Sewanee TN 37375, phone (615)598-1141, fax (615)598-1145, conference administrator Cheri B. Peters. Annual 12-day event founded 1990. Usually held the last 2 weeks in July at The University of the South ("dormitories for housing, Women's Center for public events, classrooms for workshops, student union building for dining, etc."). Attendance is about 105. **Open to poets, fiction writers and playwrights who submit their work for review in a competitive admissions process. "Genre, rather than thematic, workshops are offered in each of the three areas."** In 1994, poetry workshops were lead by Rachel Hadas, Anthony Hecht, Andrew Hudgins and Maxine Kumin. Other speakers included editors who are also poets who read from their work and responded to questions on the editorial process. Readings have been given by Richard Wilbur and Anthony Hecht. Cost for 1994 conference was $1,150, including room and board. Each year scholarships and fellowships based on merit are available on a competitive basis. "We provide bus transportation from the Nashville airport on the opening day of the conference and back to the airport on the closing day at no additional cost." Individual critiques are also available. "All poets admitted to the conference will have an individual session with a member of the poetry faculty." A ms should be sent in advance after admission to the conference. Write for brochure and application forms. No SASE necessary.

SHAWNEE HILLS SPRING POETRY WORKSHOP, HC 60, Box 562, Greenbo Lake State Park, Greenup KY 41144, phone (800)325-0083, contact D.H. Spears. Annual 3-day event founded 1983. Usually held during a weekend in April, beginning with a keynote speaker on Friday night. Saturday morning is for writing on the trails, Saturday afternoon includes editing workshops and Saturday evening is an awards banquet. Sunday morning is for evaluation and wrap-up. Average attendance is 40. **Open to practicing poets. The workshop is designed "to promote the writing of poetry and to celebrate the poetic achievements of workshop participants.** What varies from year to year are the keynote speaker and the writing 'charge' for going out on the trails. The 'charge' is kept secret until departure time." Cost is $12 registration; participants are responsible for their own meals and lodging. Information on overnight accommodations is available for registrants. The Jesse Stuart Lodge has 37 guest rooms, available at special rates. Rooms are also available at area hotels. The Phoenix Writers sponsor a poetry contest (32-line limit) in conjunction with the workshop. Theme changes yearly. Deadline: March 31. Judge is Harding Stedler, workshop conductor. 1st prize: $50, 2nd: $30, 3rd: $20. Send SASE for brochures and registration forms. For information about The Phoenix Writers, contact Harding Stedler, 307 Tanglewood Dr., Wheelersburg OH 45694. Also see the listing for Little Smokies of Ohio Fall Poetry Workshop.

SINIPEE WRITERS WORKSHOP, P.O. Box 902, Dubuque IA 52004-0902, phone (319)556-0366, director John Tigges. Annual 1-day event founded 1986. Usually held the 3rd or 4th Saturday in April on the campus of Clarke College, Dubuque, Iowa. Average attendance is 50-100. **Open to anyone, "professional or neophyte," who is interested in writing. Conference covers fiction, poetry and nonfiction.** As for offerings specifically available for poets, in 1994, poet Patricia Wild showed how designs in poetry can enhance description in prose. Other speakers in 1994 included literary agent Jodi Jill, off-Broadway playwright Rebecca Christian, romance novelist Pam Dalton, and children's nonfiction author Janet Pack. Cost for 1994 workshop was $60 pre-registration, $65 at the door. Scholarships covering half of the cost are traditionally available to senior citizens and to full-time students, both college and high school. Cost included handouts, coffee and donut break, lunch, snacks in afternoon and book fair with authors in attendance available to autograph their books. Information on overnight accommodations is available for out-of-town registrants. Annual contest for both fiction and poetry sponsored as part of workshop. There is a $5 reading fee for each entry (short story of 1,500 words or poetry of 40 lines). Entrants in the contest may also ask for a written critique by a professional writer. The cost for critique is $15/entry. Send SASE for brochures and registration forms.

SOUTHWEST FLORIDA WRITERS' CONFERENCE, P.O. Box 60210, Ft. Myers FL 33906-6210, phone (813)489-9226, fax (813)489-9051, director Joanne Hartke. Annual event founded 1980. Usually held the 4th Friday and Saturday in February on the campus of Edison Community College. Average attendance is 150-200. **Open to anyone interested in writing, including full-time high school and college students. "We cover many areas; in 1994 our offerings included true crime, poetry and writing for children. Sessions are usually varied to provide something for both beginning and published writers."** The 1994 poetry session was with Ruth Moon Kempher. Cost for the 1994 Friday sessions was $25; the Saturday conference was $49, including a continental breakfast and lunch. Limited scholarships are usually available and full-time students can attend the conference for only $15. "We do arrange for a block of rooms at a local hotel. Rooms are available to conference attendees at a special rate. In 1994 it was $55 per night. We also provide a listing of several area hotels if the conference block is full or not their choice." An annual contest (including poetry) is sponsored as part of the conference. Judges are published authors and writers in the Ft. Myers community. Send SASE for brochures and registration forms.

STATE OF MAINE WRITERS' CONFERENCE, P.O. Box 296, Ocean Park ME 04063, phone (207)934-5034, fax (207)934-2823 (summer), phone (413)596-6734, fax (413)782-1746 (winter), director Dick Burns. Annual August event founded 1941. Usually runs from Tuesday evening to Friday noon. 1995 dates: August 22-25. Average attendance is 50-75. **Open to any interested person. Conference is "very eclectic, covers writing to publishing."** Every year there is a poetry tournament including a poetry booklet, Poems to be Put on Trees Contest and Beach Inspiration Poetry. Cost is $75. Those 21 and under may attend at half price. Information on overnight accommodations is available for registrants. "Local accommodations are reasonable." There are many contests, 15-20/year. Separate contest announcement is available in advance to registrants. Send SASE for brochures and registration forms.

TRENTON STATE COLLEGE WRITERS CONFERENCE, Trenton State College, Hillwood Lakes CN 4700, Trenton NJ 08650-4700, phone (609)771-3254, director Jean Hollander. Annual 1-day event founded 1981. Usually held the beginning of April at Trenton State College Campus. Average attendance is about 800. **Open to anyone. Conference covers all genres of writing. "We usually have a special presentation on breaking into print." 12-15 separate poetry and fiction workshops as well as readings are offered.** In 1994 the speakers were Tama Janowitz and Ken Kesey. Cost in 1994 was $40 for day session; additional cost for workshops and evening session. Discounts available for students. Information on overnight accommodations is available for registrants. Poets and fiction writers may submit ms to be critiqued in writing by workshop leaders. Poetry and short story contest sponsored as part of conference. 1st prize: $100; 2nd prize: $50. Judges are workshop leaders and a special panel from the English Dept. Send SASE for brochures and registration forms.

UNIVERSITY OF MASSACHUSETTS LOWELL WRITERS' CONFERENCE, 1 University Ave., Lowell MA 01854, phone (508)934-2405, fax (508)934-3008, special program coordinator John Hurtado. Annual event founded in 1988. Usually held the 3rd week of June at Lowell Library Complex on the campus of the University of Massachusetts. Average attendance is 80. **Aimed at regional writers but open to everyone. Conference covers fiction, poetry, writing for children and publishing opportunities. Poetry workshops, readings and individual conferences are included.** In 1994 speakers included Carolyn Wright, poet and award-winning author of several books, chapbooks and collections of poetry translations; Tim O'Brien, author of **The Things They Carried** and recipient of several awards including the National Book Award in Fiction; and Bruce Smith, co-editor of ***Graham House Review*** and senior editor of Sheep Meadow Press. Cost for the 1994 conference was $100, including readings, 1 workshop and open microphone readings. Additional workshops available for $50 each. Information on overnight accommodations is available for registrants. Accommodations include special rates at area hotels and B&B's. Individual critiques are also available. Submit no more than 4 poems or 6 pages with $50 fee. Send SASE for brochures and registration forms.

‡**WESTERN RESERVE WRITERS AND FREELANCE CONFERENCE**, #110, 34200 Ridge Rd., Willoughby OH 44094, phone (216)943-3047, coordinator Lea Leever Oldham. Annual 1-day event founded 1983. Usually held the second Saturday in September. Average attendance is 150. **Open to "writers, published and aspiring." Conference usually covers fiction; nonfiction; poetry; articles; books; sometimes photography and other freelance subjects; copyright; writing for children; etc.** "We always include a presentation specifically for poetry." Cost for conference is about $44, including lunch. Participants can make arrangements one-on-one for possible time with guest speakers. Send SASE for brochures and registration forms.

‡**WESTERN RESERVE WRITERS MINI CONFERENCE**, #110, 34200 Ridge Rd., Willoughby OH 44094, phone (216)943-3047, coordinator Lea Leever Oldham. Annual ½-day conference founded 1991. Usually held the last Saturday in March. Average attendance is 100. **Open to "published and aspiring writers." Conference usually covers fiction, nonfiction, poetry, writing for children, articles and romance writing.** "We always have a session with a published poet." Cost for conference is $25, including morning refreshments. Attendees can make their own arrangements with presenters for possible critiques. Send SASE for brochures and registration forms.

WILDACRES WRITERS WORKSHOP, c/o 233 S. Elm St., Greenboro NC 27401, phone and fax (919)273-4044, director Judith Hill. Annual week-long event founded 1983. Usually held the 2nd week in July at "a beautiful retreat facility in the Blue Ridge Mountains of North Carolina." Average attendance is 100. **Open to all "serious adult writers." Conference covers fiction, poetry, screen and play writing, and nonfiction. "We have two poetry workshops with a limit of twelve to a class.** In total, we have eleven writers on staff who read and give programs. Plus we have an agent in residence." Cost is $360, including a double room, all meals and ms critique. Van transportation to and from the Asheville Airport is provided. Send SASE for brochures and registration forms. Some years they also publish ***The Wildacres Review***.

WISCONSIN REGIONAL WRITERS' ASSOCIATION, 912 Cass St., Portage WI 53901, phone (608)742-2410, president Elayne Clipper Hanson. Biannual conferences founded in 1948. Usually held first Saturday in May and last weekend in September at various hotel-conference centers around the state. Average attendance is 100-130. **Open to all writers, "aspiring, amateur or professional." All forms of writing/marketing rotated between conferences. "The purpose is to keep writers informed and prepared to express and market their writing in a proper format." Poetry covered once a year.** In 1994, spring speakers included Ruth Wucherer, discussing travel writing, and Colleen Sutherland, discussing storytelling and writing for children. Other workshops included "Dissecting a Magazine: How to Research Your Market" by Sylvia Bright Green and "The Inner Writer," writing exercises to free up creativity, by Laurel Mills. A book fair is held at both conferences where members can sell their published works. A banquet is held at the fall conference where writing contest winners receive awards. Spring conference is approximately $30-35, fall conference approximately $35-40. Spring conference includes coffee and sweet rolls, lunch and hors d'oeuvres at book fair. Fall conference also includes dinner and entertainment. Information about overnight accommodations is available for registrants. "Our organization 'blocks' rooms at a reduced rate." Sponsors 2 writing contests/year plus a "Yarns of Yesteryear" contest. Membership and small fee are required. Send SASE for brochures and registration forms. "We are affiliated with the Wisconsin Fellowship of Poets, the Wisconsin Authors and Publishers Alliance and the Council of Wisconsin Writers. We also publish a newsletter four times a year for members."

THE WRITERS' CENTER AT CHAUTAUQUA, Box 408, Chautauqua NY 14722, phone (716)357-2445 (June-August) or (717)872-8337, director Mary Jean Irion. Annual event founded 1988. Usually held 9 weeks in summer from late June to late August. Participants may attend for one week or more. "We are an independent, cooperative association of writers located on the grounds of Chautauqua Institution." Average attendance is 30 for readings and speeches, 10 for workshops. **Readings and speeches are open to anyone; workshops are open to writers (or auditors). The purpose is "to make creative writing one of the serious arts in progress at Chautauqua; to provide a vacation opportunity for skilled artists and their guests (one each); and to help learning writers improve their skills and vision."** Workshops are available all nine weeks. Poetry Works meets two hours each day offering one hour of class for every hour of workshop. In 1994, leaders included Michael Waters, Stephanie Strickland and Richard Foerster. Prose Works offers two hours a day in fiction and nonfiction, writing for children and Young Writers' Workshops. Poets are welcome to explore other fields. Other special features include two speeches a week and one reading, usually done by the Writers-In-Residence. Cost is $55/week with price breaks for each additional week. Participants are responsible for gate fees, housing and meals. "A week's gate ticket to Chautauqua is $150 (less if ordered early); housing cost varies widely, but is not cheap; meals vary widely depending on accommodations—from fine restaurants to cooking in a shared kitchen." Access is best by car or plane to Jamestown, NY, where a limousine service is available for the 14 miles to Chautauqua ($18). Phone number for Accommodations Directory Service is available for registrants. Individual critiques are also usually available. Information published in spring mailing. The Director's Prize is given for the best poem handled in the workshops. Send SASE for brochures and registration forms.

WRITERS' FORUM, Community Education Dept., Pasadena City College, 1570 E. Colorado, Pasadena CA 91106-2003, phone (818)795-5592, fax (818)585-7910, contact Meredith Brucker. Annual 1-day event founded 1954. Usually held all day Saturday in mid-March at Pasadena City College. Average attendance is 200. **Open to all. Conference covers a wide variety of topics and always includes one poet.** Recent speakers have included poet Ron Koertge, ***ONTHEBUS*** editor Jack Grapes and Philomene Long speaking on "Poetry for Non-poets." Cost for the 1994 conference was $75, including lunch. Write for brochures and registration forms. No SASE necessary.

‡WRITING TODAY, BSC A-3, Birmingham AL 35243, phone (205)226-4921, fax (205)226-4931, director of special events Martha Andrews. Annual 2-day event founded 1978. 1995 dates: March 10-11. Location: Birmingham-Southern College campus. Average attendance is 400-500. **Open to "everyone interested in writing—beginners, professionals and students. Conference topics vary year to year depending on who is part of the faculty."** In 1994, offerings specifically available for poets included a workshop by the Poet Laureate of Illinois, Gwendolyn Brooks. Speakers at last conference were Willie Morris, Bharati Mukherjee, Barbara Park and Howell Raines. Cost for 1994 conference was $85 before deadline ($90 after deadline), including lunches and reception. Cost for a single day's events was $45, including luncheon. Either day's luncheon was only $20. $10 cancellation fee. Information on overnight accommodations is available for registrants. Accommodations include special rates at area hotels. Individual critiques are also available. In addition, the Hackney Literary Awards competition is sponsored as part of the conference. The competition, open to writers nationwide, offers $2,000 in prizes for poetry and short stories and a $2,000 award for the novel category. Entry requirements for poetry include: Poems not to exceed 50 lines/entry. More than 1 poem may be submitted, but all poems together must not exceed the 50-line limit. Postmark deadline: December 31. Fee: $5/entry. Send SASE to Hackney Literary Awards at above address for complete guidelines. Also send SASE for conference brochures and registration forms.

WRITING WORKSHOP FOR PEOPLE OVER 57, % Donovan Scholars Program, University of Kentucky, Ligon House, 658 S. Limestone St., Lexington KY 40506-0442, phone (606)257-2657, fax (606)258-4940, director Roberta H. James. Annual event founded 1966. Usually held in June, the workshop runs from Sunday afternoon to Friday afternoon. Location: Carnahan House Conference Center, "a beautiful, restored mansion which sits on a former horse farm." Average attendance is 35-50 (maximum). **Open to "adults aged 57 or older who share an interest in writing and wish to learn more about how to express their thoughts in the written form. We offer classes in fiction, nonfiction, children's literature/juvenile novel and poetry."** Offerings specifically available for poets include "classes instructed by established writers in the field of poetry, whether local or elsewhere." Cost is $125/person. Information on overnight accommodations is available for registrants. "We offer four hotels, all within close proximity to Carnahan, and offer the hotel rates at a slight discount to workshop participants. Carnahan House itself offers a shuttle service to and from the various hotels." Writers may register as full-student status, which requires a ms to be submitted for critique, or as auditor status, which does not require a ms. Send SASE for brochures and registration forms. ***Second Spring***, their yearly publication, contains the written work of past workshop participants.

YELLOW BAY WRITERS' WORKSHOP, Center for Continuing Education, The University of Montana, Missoula MT 59812, phone (406)243-6486, fax (406)243-2047, program manager Judy Jones. Annual week-long event founded 1988. Usually held mid-August at the University of Montana's biological research station which includes informal educational facilities and rustic cabin living on Flathead Lake in western Montana. Average attendance is 60. **Open to all writers. Conference offers two workshops in fiction, one in nonfiction and one in poetry.** In 1994, Carol Houck Smith, senior editor and vice president of W.W. Norton & Company, was joined by editors of regional literary and environmental journals for a forum on publishing. In addition, Keith Buckley, British actor, drama coach and stage director, conducted a workshop on how writers can give more effective public readings. Workshop faculty included Edward Hirsch (poetry), Gretel Ehrlich (nonfiction), Earl Ganz and Beverly Lowry (fiction). Cost for 1994 workshop was $425, commuter fee; $725, tuition and single lodging/meals; $695, tuition and double lodging/meals. Round-trip shuttle from Missoula to Yellow Bay (85 miles) is available for $40. Applicants must send a writing sample. Send SASE for brochures and registration forms.

Additional Conferences and Workshops

The following conferences and workshops either did not respond in time to receive a full listing in this section or their offerings for poets were more limited than those listed above. We have included contact names and addresses, however, so that you may write for details. Remember to always include a SASE with any requests for information.

CRAFT OF WRITING, Box 830688 CN 1.1, Richardson TX 75083, (214)690-2207, director Janet Harris. Conference held 4th weekend in September.

HIGHLIGHTS FOUNDATION WRITERS WORKSHOP AT CHAUTAUQUA, c/o 814 Court St., Honesdale PA 18431, (717)253-1192, director Jan Keen. Usually held 4th week of July.

NEBRASKA WRITERS GUILD SPRING/FALL CONFERENCE, Suite 1012, 941 "O" St., Lincoln NE 68508, president Linda Dageforde. One-day conferences held in spring and fall.

PROFESSIONALISM IN WRITING SCHOOL, Suite 701, 4308 S. Peoria, Tulsa OK 74105, (918)749-5588, coordinator Norma Jean Lutz. Usually held last weekend in March.

THUNDER BAY LITERARY CONFERENCE, 211 N. First Ave., Alpena MI 49707, project director Judi Stillion. Usually held Thursday and Friday, last week in September.

UNIVERSITY OF WISCONSIN-MADISON'S SCHOOL OF THE ARTS AT RHINELANDER, 726 Lowell Hall, 610 Langdon St., Madison WI 53703, (608)263-3494, coordinator Kathy Berigan. Usually held last week in July.

WESLEYAN WRITERS CONFERENCE, Wesleyan University, Middletown CT 06457, (203)343-3938, director Anne Greene. Conference held last week in June.

Writing Colonies

Writing colonies are places for writers (including poets) to find solitude and spend concentrated time focusing on their work. While a residency at a writing colony may offer participation in seminars, critiques and/or readings, the atmosphere of a colony or retreat is much more relaxed than that of a conference or workshop. Also, a writer's stay at a colony is typically anywhere from one to twelve weeks (sometimes longer), while time spent at a conference or workshop may only run from one to fourteen days.

Like conferences and workshops, however, writing colonies and retreats span a wide range. Yaddo, perhaps the most well-known colony, primarily offers residencies to writers "who have already achieved some recognition in their field and have new work under way." The Dobie-Paisano Project, on the other hand, limits its fellowships and residencies to writers with an identifiable Texas connection. Also, in addition to listings for colonies across the United States, this section contains listings that offer residencies in Canada, France, Ireland and the Italian Alps.

Despite different focuses and/or locations, all writing colonies and retreats have one thing in common: They are places where you may work undisturbed, usually in very nature-oriented and secluded settings. A colony serves as a place for rejuvenation, a place where you may find new ideas for poems, rework old ones or put the finishing touches to a collection.

Selecting a writing colony

When selecting a colony or retreat, the primary consideration for many writers is cost, and you'll discover that these arrangements vary. The Millay Colony for the Arts, Inc., for instance, has no fee. Other colonies provide residences as well as stipends for personal expenses. Some suggest donations of a certain amount. Still others offer residencies for tidy sums but have financial assistance available.

When investigating the various options, consider the meal and housing arrangements and your own family obligations. Some colonies provide meals for residents, while others require residents to pay for meals. Some colonies house writers in one main building; others provide separate cottages. (In both cases, you are given private work space, although you must usually bring along your own reference materials and typewriter or personal computer.) A few writing colonies have provisions for spouses and/or families. Others prohibit families altogether.

Overall, residencies at writing colonies and retreats are competitive. Since only a handful of spots are available at each place, you must often apply months in advance for the time period you desire. A number of locations are open year-round, and you may find that planning to go during the "off-season" lessens your competition. Other colonies, however, are only available during certain months. In any case, be prepared to include a sample of your best work with your application. Also, know what project you'll work on while in residence (many places request this information) and have alternative projects in mind in case the first one doesn't work out once you're there.

Of course, before making a final decision, send a SASE to the colonies or retreats that interest you to receive the most up-to-date details. All of the above factors—particularly costs, application requirements and deadlines—are subject to change.

For other listings of writing colonies, see **The Guide to Writers Conferences** (available from ShawGuides, Inc., Dept. 1406W, 625 Biltmore Way, Coral Gables FL 33134), which not only provides information about conferences, workshops and seminars but also residencies, retreats and organizations. Another resource is ***Havens for Creatives***, available from ACTS Institute, Inc. (see the listing in the Contests and Awards section).

THE EDWARD F. ALBEE FOUNDATION, INC.; THE WILLIAM FLANAGAN MEMORIAL CREATIVE PERSONS CENTER ("THE BARN"), 14 Harrison St., New York NY 10013, phone (212)226-2020, for information and application forms. The Albee Foundation maintains the center (better known as "The Barn") in Montauk, on Long Island, offering 1-month residencies for writers, painters, sculptors and composers, open June 1 through October 1, accommodating 6 persons at a time. Applications accepted at the above address by regular mail only January 1 through April 1. Fellowship announcements by May 15. "Located approximately 2 miles from the center of Montauk and the Atlantic Ocean, 'The Barn' rests in a secluded knoll that offers privacy and a peaceful atmosphere. The foundation expects all those accepted for residence to work seriously and to conduct themselves in such a manner as to aid fellow residents in their endeavors. The environment is simple and communal. Residents are expected to do their share in maintaining the condition of 'The Barn' as well as its peaceful environment."

ATLANTIC CENTER FOR THE ARTS, 1414 Art Center Ave., New Smyrna Beach FL 32168, phone (904)427-6975. The center was founded in 1979 by sculptor and painter Doris Leeper, who secured a seed grant from The Rockefeller Foundation. That same year the center was chartered by the state of Florida and building began on a 10-acre site. The facility now covers 67 acres. The center was officially opened in 1982. Since 1982, 57 Master Artists-in-Residence sessions have been held. At each of the 3-week sessions, internationally known artists from different disciplines conduct interdisciplinary workshops and lectures and critique works in progress. They also give readings and recitals, exhibit their work and develop projects with their "associates"—mid-career artists who come from all over the US to work with them. The center is run by an advisory council which chooses Master Artists for residencies, helps set policies and guides the center in its growth. The process of becoming an associate is different for each Master Artist. Recent poets in residence at the center include Amy Clampitt (January 1992), John Yau (March 1993), Richard Howard (March 1994) and Diane di Prima (May-June 1994).

BANFF CENTRE FOR THE ARTS WRITING STUDIO; ACTION POETRY, Box 1020, 107 Tunnel Mountain Dr., Banff, Alberta T0L 0C0 Canada, offers 4-6 weeks of residence between October 23 and November 24 to writers "who already have a body of work (some of it preferably, but not necesssarily, published) attesting to their commitment and talent. Applicant should have a project in progress . . . . Enrollment is limited to 20 participants—10 in poetry, 10 in prose. Full scholarships for fee and room are offered to all successful candidates." Located in an inspirational mountain setting, The Banff Centre for the Arts is a unique Canadian institution. Participants are housed in single rooms that also serve as their private work spaces. Application deadline: mid-July. Action Poetry will be held April 10 to April 28, 1995. "This workshop reflects the re-emergence of spoken word performance as a vital expressive medium and catalytic social agent." Professional rappers, storytellers, poets, performance artists and other oral performers will gather to advance their work and to share ideas, techniques and performance strategies. Musicians will act as collaborators. Application deadline: January 2, 1995.

BELLAGIO STUDY AND CONFERENCE CENTER, The Rockefeller Foundation, 420 Fifth Ave., New York NY 10016, manager Susan Garfield. Offers 1-month individual or parallel residencies from February 1 through December 15 for artists, scholars, scientists, policy makers and practitioners with significant publications, compositions, exhibitions, productions or other accomplishments. Applications are considered 4 times/year on a competitive basis. Approximately 140 residencies are awarded annually. The Center is located on Lake Como in the Italian Alps. Room available for spouses. Residents must pay their own travel costs. Write for application and guidelines.

CENTRUM, % Sarah Muirhead, coordinator, Residency Program, P.O. Box 1158, Port Townsend WA 98368, offers 1-month residencies, September through May, for architects, writers, musicians and printmakers. Centrum provides individual cottages, a stipend of $75/week and solitude. Families welcome. Located in Fort Worden State Park on the Strait of Juan de Fuca. Also sponsors the Port Townsend Writers' Conference (see Conferences and Workshops) and other seminars. Contact Carol Jane Bangs, Literature Program Manager, for more information on these events.

CHATEAU DE LESVAULT, 58370 Onlay, France, phone and fax (33)86-84-32-91. This French country residence is located in the national park "Le Morvan" of western Burgundy, halfway between Nevers and Autun and is surrounded by green hills and forests. The chateau accommodates 5 residents at a time in 5 large rooms with private baths, fully furnished and equipped for working. The facilities of the chateau are at the disposal of residents, including the salon, library and grounds. Requests for residencies from October through April should be made at least 3 months in advance. The cost is 4,500 FF per month for room, board (5 days a week) and utilities.

THE CLEARING, Box 65, Ellison Bay WI 54210, phone (414)854-4088, resident managers Donald and Louise Buchholz, "is first a school, then a place of self-discovery." Made up of cabins and lodges in a rustic setting overlooking Green Bay, it offers a variety of courses, including courses in writing and poetry, May through October. Fees include tuition, room (dormitory or twin-bedded room) and board.

COLONYHOUSE: OREGON WRITERS COLONY, c/o Sue Bronson, P.O. Box 15200, Portland OR 97215, phone (503)771-0428, is a log cabin owned and operated by Oregon. It sleeps 8 and is available for weekly and weekend rentals at (Fall-Winter) $350/week, $150/weekend or (Spring-Summer) $450/week, $275/weekend. For colony members only. Membership is $20/year. Membership and newsletter information available through Robert Zimmer at the above address.

DOBIE-PAISANO PROJECT, Attn: Audrey N. Slate, Main Building 101, The University of Texas, Austin TX 78712. Offers two annual fellowships of $7,200 and 6-month residency at Frank Dobie's ranch, Paisano, for Texans, Texas residents or writers with published works about Texas. Write for application and guidelines. Application deadline: January 27, 1995.

DORLAND MOUNTAIN ARTS COLONY, P.O. Box 6, Temecula CA 92593, established 1979. A 300-acre nature preserve which offers 2-week to 2-month residences for writers, visual artists and composers in a rustic environment with no elecricity, propane appliances (refrigerator, water heater, cooking stove, some lights) and oil lamps. Residents provide their own meals. A donation of $150/month is requested. Send SASE for application form and guidelines. Deadlines are the first of September and March.

DORSET COLONY HOUSE RESIDENCIES; AMERICAN THEATRE WORKS, INC., Box 519, Dorset VT 05251, director John Nassivera. Residencies available to writers fall and spring for periods of 1 week to 2 months for intensive work. Requested fee of $85/week, but ability to pay is not a criterion in awarding residencies.

‡FINE ARTS WORK CENTER IN PROVINCETOWN, Box 565, 24 Pearl St., Provincetown MA 02657, provides monthly stipends of $375 and studio/living quarters for 7 uninterrupted months for 20 young artists and writers (10 of each) who have completed their formal training and are capable of working independently. The center has a staff of writers and artists who offer manuscript consultations, arrange readings and slide presentations and visits from other distinguished writers and artists. Each year writing fellows publish ***Shankpainter***, a magazine of prose and poetry. Sessions run from October 1 through May 1. Applications, accompanied by a $25 processing fee, must be received by February 1. To receive an application and program brochure, send a SASE to Writing Fellowship.

GREEN RIVER WRITERS RETREAT, Shelbyville Campus, University of Louisville, Green River Writers, 403 S. Sixth St., Ironton OH 45638, secretary D.H. Spears, phone (614)533-1081, provides a 2-day workshop, then 5-day retreat. Rooms are available at the conference center per night stayed plus registration fee. Beginning writers are furnished with advisors. Details available for SASE.

THE TYRONE GUTHRIE CENTRE, Annaghmakerrig, Newbliss, Co. Monaghan, Ireland, phone (353)47-54003, resident director Bernard Loughlin. Offers residencies, normally 3 weeks to 3 months, for artists, including poets. "Each resident has a private apartment within the house . . . and all the centrally heated comfort an Irish Big House can afford. It is set on a wooded estate of 400 acres and overlooks a large lake. The house is surrounded by gardens and a working dairy farm. Couples or small groups of artists may stay for up to a year in Maggie's Farm, a cottage on the estate, and have use of studios at the Big House. Five newly built, self-contained farmyard cottages are also available for individuals and couples for longer stays. To qualify for residence it is necessary to show evidence of a significant level of achievement in the relevant field. Once accepted, Irish artists are asked to contribute what they can afford toward the cost of their stay. Overseas artists are expected to pay the whole cost of a residency."

HAMBIDGE CENTER FOR CREATIVE ARTS AND SCIENCES, P.O. Box 339, Rabun Gap GA 30568, phone (706)746-5718. The center is located on 650 acres of unspoiled wooded slopes, mountain meadows and streams, near Dillard, Georgia. It is listed on the National Register of Historic Places. Resident Fellowships of 2 weeks to 2 months are awarded to individuals engaged in all artistic disciplines for the purpose of solitude and the pursuit of creative excellence. Those accepted are given a private cottage equipped with a kitchen, living and studio/work space. Center is open from May through October with limited winter fellowships available. For more information and application forms send SASE. Application review begins in March.

HAWK, I'M YOUR SISTER; WOMEN'S WILDERNESS CANOE TRIPS; WRITING RETREATS, Beverly Antaeus, P.O. Box 9109, Santa Fe NM 87504-9109. This organization offers wilderness retreats for women, many of them with writing themes, including A Writing Retreat with Sharon Olds in Utah and A Writing Retreat with Deena Metzger in Baja California, Mexico. The canoe trips are held all over North America and typically last 8-10 days with fees of $895-1,895. Write for annual listing of specific trips.

THE MACDOWELL COLONY, 100 High St., Peterborough NH 03458, founded 1907, offers residencies to established writers, composers, visual artists, filmmakers, architects and interdisciplinary artists. Over 3,000 artists have stayed here, many of them producing major works. Apply about 8 months before desired residency. Application deadlines: January 15 for May through August; April 15 for September through December; September 15 for January through April. Private studio, room and meals provided. Accepted artists are asked to contribute toward residency costs. Current application form is necessary; write address above or call (603)924-3886. Average residency is 6 weeks. Professional work samples required with application.

THE MILLAY COLONY FOR THE ARTS, INC., Steepletop, P.O. Box 3, Austerlitz NY 12017-0003, founded in 1974, assistant director Gail Giles. Provides work space, meals and sleeping accommodations at no cost for a period of 1 month. Send SASE for brochure and application forms and apply with samples of your work before February 1 for June through September; before May 1 for October through January; before September 1 for February through May.

MONTALVO CENTER FOR THE ARTS; MONTALVO BIENNIAL POETRY COMPETITION (IV-Regional), Box 158, Saratoga CA 95071, presents theatre, musical events and other artistic activities. They have an Artist-in-Residence program which has 5 apartments available for artists (including poets) for maximum 3-month periods. (No children or pets.) Limited financial assistance available. Deadlines: March 1 and September 1 of every year. They offer a biennial poetry competition open to residents of Oregon, Nevada, Washington and California, with a prominent judge, with a first prize of $1,000 (and artist residency), other prizes of $500, $300 and 8 honorable mentions. Submit 3 poems in duplicate with $5 entry fee. Deadline: October 1, 1995. Send SASE for rules.

THE NORTHWOOD UNIVERSITY ALDEN B. DOW CREATIVITY CENTER, Midland MI 48640-2398, phone (517)837-4478, fax (517)837-4468, founded 1979, director Carol Coppage. Offers fellowships for 2-month summer residencies at the Northwood University Campus. Travel, room and board plus $750 stipend for personal expenses and/or project materials. No families/pets. Applicants can be undergraduates, graduates, or those without any academic or institutional affiliation, including citizens of other countries (if they can communicate in written and spoken English). Projects may be in any field, but must be new and innovative. Write for application. Annual deadline is December 31 for the following summer.

PALENVILLE INTERARTS COLONY, 2 Bond St., New York NY 10012. Offers 1- to 8-week residencies in Palenville, New York, for seclusion or for interaction among artists of various disciplines in a relaxed and creative atmosphere. Fee (negotiable): $200/week. Open June 1 to September 30. Application deadline: April 1.

PUDDING HOUSE PUBLICATIONS, 60 N. Main St., Johnstown OH 43031. See listing in Publishers of Poetry section.

RAGDALE FOUNDATION, 1260 N. Green Bay Rd., Lake Forest IL 60045, founded 1976, director Michael Wilkerson, provides a peaceful place and uninterrupted time for 12 writers, composers and artists. Meals, linen and laundry facilities are provided. Each resident is assigned private work space and sleeping accommodations. Couples are accepted if each qualifies independently. Residents may come for 2 weeks to 2 months. The fee is $70/week. Some full and partial fee waivers available. The foundation also sponsors poetry readings, concerts, workshops and seminars in writing. Ragdale is open year-round except for two weeks in the late spring and at Christmas. Send SAE for application. Apply by January 15 for residencies in June through December and June 1 for January through May. Application fee: $20.

THE ROCKY MOUNTAIN WOMEN'S INSTITUTE, 7150 Montview Blvd., Denver CO 80220, phone (303)871-6923, founded 1976, executive director Cynthia A. Stone, a nonprofit organization located at the University of Denver. Offers office or studio space, stipends and support services for one year to local artists, writers and scholars chosen from applications. They also offer continuing support for former associates, and they sponsor exhibits, workshops, lectures and performances to highlight and promote the work of current and past associates. Terms begin each September. Applicants should have a specific project. Applications ($5 processing fee) are available beginning each January. Deadline: March 15. Write for further information.

SPLIT ROCK ARTS PROGRAM, University of Minnesota, 306 Wesbrook Hall, 77 Pleasant St. SE, Minneapolis MN 55455. The program is a summer series of week-long workshops in the visual and literary arts and in the nature and applications of creativity, on the Duluth campus of UM "in the green hills overlooking Lake Superior." The 1994 faculty included Paulette Bates Alden, Christina Baldwin, Sandra Benitez, Carol Bly, Michael Dennis Browne, Marisha Chamberlain, Toi Derricotte, Sharon Doubiago, Carolyn Forché, Myra Goldberg, Kate Green, Phebe Hanson, Alexs Pate, Jane Resh Thomas, Roberta Whiteman and Al Young. Tuition is $346-366 with an additional charge for graduate credit. Housing ranges from $168-246, depending on type of accommodation. Most students choose single or double rooms in 2-bedroom apartments on campus. Other housing options also available. Meals are in UMD's cafeteria, cooked by participants in their apartments, or in Duluth restaurants. Complete catalog available in March by mail or phone: (612)624-6800.

UCROSS FOUNDATION RESIDENCY PROGRAM, 2836 US Hwy. 14-16, Clearmont WY 82835, phone (307)737-2291, executive director Elizabeth Guheen. There are 8 concurrent positions open in various disciplines, including poetry, each extending from 2 weeks to 2 months. No charge for room, board or studio space, and they do not expect services or products from guests. Send SASE for information and application guidelines. Residents are selected from a rotating panel of professionals in the arts and humanities. Semiannual application deadlines are March 1 and October 1.

VERMONT STUDIO CENTER; VISUAL ARTISTS AND WRITERS RESIDENCIES, P.O. Box 613NW, Johnson VT 05656, phone (802)635-2727, founded 1984. Offers 2-week Writing Studio Sessions led by prominent writers/teachers focusing on the craft of writing. Independent Writers' Retreats for 2, 4 or more weeks are also available year-round for those wishing more solitude. Room, working studio and meals are included in all programs. Generous work-exchange Fellowships are available. Write or call for more information and application.

VIRGINIA CENTER FOR THE CREATIVE ARTS, Mt. San Angelo, Sweet Briar VA 24595, director William Smart. Provides residencies for 12 writers (and 9 visual artists and 3 composers) for 2 weeks to 2 months at the 450-acre Mt. San Angelo estate. All accommodations provided. The normal fee is $30/day. Financial assistance is available.

THE WRITERS COMMUNITY OF THE WRITER'S VOICE, West Side YMCA, New York NY 10023, phone (212)875-4124. Offers an advanced 3-month master writing program in poetry, October through December and March through May (application deadline mid-September, mid-January), working with a writer-in-residence. Tuition: $95. Submit cover letter and a minimum of 10 pgs. of poetry, which may be published material. All material should be typed or printed and copies should be retained. Mss cannot be returned. Call for application deadlines.

THE HELENE WURLITZER FOUNDATION OF NEW MEXICO, Box 545, Taos NM 87571. Offers residencies to creative, *not* interpretive, artists in all media, for varying periods of time, usually 3 months, from April 1 through September 30, annually. Rent free and utilities free. Residents are responsible for their food. No families. No deadlines on application.

YADDO, Box 395, Saratoga Springs NY 12866-0395, phone (518)584-0746, founded 1900, offers residencies to writers, visual artists, composers, choreographers, film/video artists and performance artists who have already achieved some recognition in their field and have new work under way. During the summer 35 guests can be accommodated, 14 during the winter, approximately 200/year. The hours 9-4 are a quiet period reserved for work. There is no fixed charge for a guest stay, but voluntary payment in the suggested amount of $20/day to help defray costs of the program is accepted. However, no qualified artist is denied admission based on inability to pay. Write for applications to: Admissions, Yaddo, address above; enclose SASE. Application deadlines are January 15 and August 1. A $20 application fee is required.

Organizations Useful to Poets

The organizations listed in this section offer encouragement and support to poets and other writers through a wide variety of services. They may sponsor contests and awards, hold regular workshops or open readings, or release publications with details about new opportunities and/or area events. Many of these groups provide a combination of these services to both members and others.

The PEN American Center, for instance, holds public events, sponsors literary awards, and offers grants and loans to writers in need. Poets seeking financial assistance should also refer to the listing for the Authors League Fund or contact the arts council in their state or province (see State and Provincial Grants on pages 441-443).

Many organizations provide opportunities to meet and discuss work with others. Those with access to computers and modems can connect with poets around the world through either CompuServe or GEnie. The National Federation of State Poetry Societies, Inc. and the Canadian Poetry Association are both national organizations with smaller affiliated groups which may meet in your state or province. And for those seeking gatherings more local or regional in focus, there are organizations such as the Burnaby Writers' Society, The Lane Literary Guild and the Pittsburgh Poetry Exchange.

For organizations even closer to home, check for information at the library or contact the local college English department. Better yet, if you are unable to find a local writer's group, start one by placing an ad in your community newspaper or posting a notice on the library bulletin board. There are sure to be others in your area who would welcome the support, and the library might even have space for your group to meet on a regular basis.

To locate some of the larger organizations (or representative samples of smaller groups) read through the listings that follow and refer to Additional Organizations Useful to Poets at the end of this section. Then send a SASE to those groups that interest you to receive more details about their services and/or membership fees.

THE ACADEMY OF AMERICAN POETS; FELLOWSHIP OF THE ACADEMY OF AMERICAN POETS; WALT WHITMAN AWARD; THE LAMONT POETRY SELECTION; HAROLD MORTON LANDON TRANSLATION AWARD; PETER I.B. LAVAN YOUNGER POET AWARDS, Suite 1208, 584 Broadway, New York NY 10012-3250, founded 1934, executive director William Wadsworth. Robert Penn Warren wrote in **Introduction to Fifty Years of American Poetry**, an anthology published in 1984 containing one poem from each of the 126 Chancellors, Fellows and Award Winners of the Academy: "What does the Academy do? According to its certificate of incorporation, its purpose is 'To encourage, stimulate and foster the production of American poetry. . . .' The responsibility for its activities lies with the Board of Directors and the Board of 12 Chancellors, which has included, over the years, such figures as Louise Bogan, W.H. Auden, Witter Bynner, Randall Jarrell, Robert Lowell, Robinson Jeffers, Marianne Moore, James Merrill, Robert Fitzgerald, F.O. Matthiessen and Archibald MacLeish – certainly not members of the same poetic church." They award fellowships, currently of $20,000 each, to distinguished American poets (no applications taken) – 59 to date – and other annual awards. The Walt Whitman Award pays $1,000 plus publication of a poet's first book by a major publisher. Mss of 50-100 pgs. must be submitted between September 15 and November 15 with a $20 entry fee. Entry form required. Send SASE. The Lamont Poetry Selection, for a poet's second book, is again a prize of $1,000. Submissions must be made by a publisher, in ms form, prior to publication. The Academy distributes 2,000 copies to its members. Poets entering either contest must be American citizens. The Harold Morton Landon Translation Award is for translation of a book-length poem, a collection of poems or a verse-drama translated into English from any language. One award of $1,000 each year to a US citizen. Only publishers may submit the book. Write for guidelines. The Peter I.B. Lavan Younger Poet Awards of $1,000 each are given annually to three younger poets selected by Academy Chancellors (no applications taken). ***Poetry Pilot*** is an informative periodical sent to those who contribute $25 or more/year or who are members. Membership: $45/year. The Academy sponsors a national series of poetry readings and panel discussions.

ASSOCIATED WRITING PROGRAMS; AWP CHRONICLE; THE AWP AWARD SERIES, Old Dominion University, Norfolk VA 23529-0079, founded 1967. Offers a variety of services to the writing community, including information, job placement assistance, publishing opportunities, literary arts advocacy and forums. Annual individual membership is $45; placement service extra. For $18 you can subscribe to the ***AWP Chronicle*** (published 6 times/year), containing information about grants and awards, publishing opportunities, fellowships, and writing programs. They have a directory, **The Official Guide to Writing Programs**, of over 250 college and university writing programs for $20.95 (includes shipping). The AWP Award Series selects a volume of poetry (48 pg. minimum) each year ($10 entry fee for members; $15 for nonmembers) with an award of $1,500 and publication. Deadline: February 28. Send SASE for submission guidelines. Query after November. Their placement service helps writers find jobs in teaching, editing and other related fields.

THE AUTHORS GUILD, INC., 330 W. 42nd St., New York NY 10036, phone (212) 563-5904, executive director Robin Davis Miller, "is an association of professional writers which focuses its efforts on the legal and business concerns of published authors in the areas of publishing contract terms, copyright, taxation and freedom of expression. We do not work in the area of marketing mss to publishers nor do we sponsor or participate in awards or prize selections." Send SASE for information on membership.

AUTHORS LEAGUE FUND, 234 W. 44th St., New York NY 10036. Makes interest-free loans to published authors in need of temporary help because of illness or an emergency. No grants.

BEYOND BAROQUE LITERARY/ARTS CENTER, 681 Venice Blvd., Venice CA 90291, phone (310)822-3006, director Tosh Berman. A nonprofit arts center established in 1968 that has been funded by the NEA, state and city arts councils and corporate donations. Members get a calendar of events, discounts on regularly scheduled programs, discounts in the bookstore, and borrowing privileges in the small press library of 3,000 volumes of poetry, fiction and reference materials, including audiotapes of Beyond Baroque readings. Beyond Baroque contains a bookstore open 5 days a week, including Friday evenings to coincide with regular weekly readings and performances. About 130 writers are invited to read each year; there are also open readings and poetry and fiction workshops.

BLACK CULTURAL CENTRE FOR NOVA SCOTIA, Box 2128, East Dartmouth, Nova Scotia B2W 3Y2 Canada, phone (902)434-6223, fax (902)434-2306. Founded in 1977 "to create among members of the black communities an awareness of their past, their heritage and their identity; to provide programs and activities for the general public to explore, learn about, understand and appreciate black history, black achievements and black experiences in the broad context of Canadian life. The centre houses a museum, reference library, archival area, small auditorium and studio workshops."

BURNABY WRITERS' SOCIETY, 6450 Deer Lake Ave., Burnaby, British Columbia V5G 2J3 Canada, contact person Eileen Kernaghan. Corresponding membership in the society, including a newsletter subscription, is open to anyone, anywhere. Yearly dues are $20. Sample newsletter in return for SASE with Canadian stamp. The society holds monthly meetings at The Burnaby Arts Centre (address at beginning of listing), with a business meeting at 7:30 followed by a writing workshop or speaker. Members of the society stage regular public readings of their own work.

THE WITTER BYNNER FOUNDATION FOR POETRY, INC., P.O. Box 10169, Santa Fe NM 87504, phone (505)988-3251. The foundation awards grants exclusively to nonprofit organizations for the support of poetry-related projects in the area of: 1) support of individual poets through existing nonprofit institutions; 2) developing the poetry audience; 3) poetry translation and the process of poetry translation; and 4) uses of poetry. The foundation "may consider the support of other creative and innovative projects in poetry." Grant applications must be received by February 1 each year; requests for application forms should be submitted to Steven Schwartz, executive director, at the address above.

THE CANADA COUNCIL; GOVERNOR GENERAL'S LITERARY AWARDS; INTERNATIONAL LITERARY PRIZES, P.O. Box 1047, 99 Metcalfe St., Ottawa, Ontario K1P 5V8 Canada, phone (613)566-4365/6. Established by Parliament in 1957, it "provides a wide range of grants and services to professional Canadian artists and art organizations in dance, media arts, music, opera, theater, writing, publishing and the visual arts." The Governor General's Literary Awards, valued at $10,000 (Canadian) each, are given annually for the best English-language and best French-language work in each of seven categories, including poetry. Books must be first-edition trade books written, translated or illustrated by Canadian citizens or permanent residents of Canada and published in Canada or abroad during the previous year (September 1 through September 30). In the case of translation, the original work must also be a Canadian-authored title. Books must be submitted by publishers with a Publisher's Submission Form, which is available from the Writing and Publishing Section. All entries (books and galleys) must be received at the Canada Council by August 31. If the submission is in the form of a bound galley, the actual book must be published and received at the Canada Council no later than September 30. The Canada Council administers three International Literary Prizes (Canada-Australia, Canada-French Community of Belgium, Canada-Switzerland) of $2,500-3,500 (Canadian) and the Canada-Japan Book Award worth $10,000 (Canadian). Winners are selected by juries. Except for the Canada-Japan Book Award, applications are not accepted.

CANADIAN CONFERENCE OF THE ARTS (CCA), 189 Laurier Ave. E., Ottawa, Ontario K1N 6P1 Canada, phone (613)238-3561, fax (613)238-4849, is a national, non-governmental, not-for-profit arts service organization dedicated to the growth and vitality of the arts and cultural industries in Canada. The CCA represents all Canadian artists, cultural workers and arts supporters, and works with all levels of government, the corporate sector and voluntary organizations to enhance appreciation for the role of culture in Canadian life. Each year, the CCA presents awards for contribution to the arts. Regular meetings held across the country ensure that members' views on urgent and ongoing issues are heard and considered in organizing advocacy efforts and forming Board policies. Members stay informed and up-to-date through ***Proscenium***, a news magazine, which is published 5 times a year, and receive discounts on conference fees and on all other publications. Membership is $25 (plus GST) for Canadian individual members, $35 for US members and $45 for international members.

CANADIAN POETRY ASSOCIATION; POEMATA, 340 Station B, London, Ontario N6A 4W1 Canada. A broad based umbrella organization that aims to promote the reading, writing, publishing, purchasing and preservation of poetry in Canada through the individual and combined efforts of its members; to promote and encourage all forms and styles of poetry; to promote communication among poets, publishers and the general public; to promote the establishment and maintenance of poetry libraries and archives in educational institutions across Canada; and to develop an international connection for Canadian poets through ***Poemata,*** its quarterly newsletter, and events organized by independent, locally-run chapters. Through its 6 autonomous local chapters, CPA organizes poetry readings, literary and social events, and runs a book club. Membership is open to anyone with an interest in poetry, including other literary organizations, for $20/year. Sample newsletter: $3.

CANADIAN SOCIETY OF CHILDREN'S AUTHORS, ILLUSTRATORS & PERFORMERS, #103, 542 Mount Pleasant Rd., Toronto, Ontario M4S 2M7 Canada, is a "society of professionals in the field of children's culture. Puts people into contact with publishers, offers advice to beginners, and generally provides a visible profile for members; 365 professional members and over 1,000 associates who are termed 'friends.' An annual conference in Toronto the last week of October provides workshops to people interested in writing, illustrating, and performing for children." Membership is $60 for professional members (and a free copy of the Membership Directory); $25 for associates/year. Both include a subscription to the quarterly ***CANSCAIP News***.

COMPUSERVE INFORMATION SERVICE, 5000 Arlington Centre Blvd., P.O. Box 20212, Columbus OH 43220, phone (800)848-8199 from outside Ohio or (614)457-8600 from within Ohio or outside the US, fax (614)538-1780. An international online information service available via modem from any computer. On CIS are many forums on specialized topics of interests, including Litforum. This has been described as a 24-hour nonalcoholic cocktail party: basically a bulletin board where various members post and respond to public messages (though you may communicate with them privately, too, either through the CompuServe Mail system or by leaving private messages in Litforum). It costs $49.95 to join CIS. When you join, you get a $25 online credit, so joining is practically free. Electronic mail is now included in the $7.95 monthly flat rate service fee. All CompuServe membership kits also contain the CompuServe Information Manager, customized software designed for IBM compatible, Mac and Windows platforms to make CompuServe easy to use. There are many services available through CIS (in addition to electronic mail), but most of the action is in the forums. In Litforum sometimes the talk is quite funny, often bawdy, and far-ranging, though there is a lot of practical, professional communication, too, and many people make contact via Litforum with agents, editors, other writers, researchers, and so on, that prove quite useful. You join Litforum (anyone can join; a number of the regulars are not even writers—just people interested in literature, writing, publication, chitchat), read the messages posted in some or all of the 17 sections (on such things as poetry and lyrics, fiction, nonfiction, speculative fiction, and so on), respond to any that you wish to, or just lurk.

Each section has a library where you can post material you have written or download material by others, and comment if you wish. There is also a workshop for which you can request admission (and you're in automatically) where each writer has a turn to have material criticized by the other workshop members.

COSMEP, THE INTERNATIONAL ASSOCIATION OF INDEPENDENT PUBLISHERS; COSMEP NEWSLETTER, P.O. Box 420703, San Francisco CA 94142-0703. If you are starting a small press or magazine or are embarking on self-publication, you should know about the advantages of membership in COSMEP. Write for information. It is the largest trade association for small press in the US. Included among membership benefits is the monthly ***COSMEP Newsletter***, which prints news and commentary for small publishers. It also sponsors publishing conferences, stages exhibits at booksellers' and librarians' conventions and has insurance and cooperative advertising programs.

COUNCIL OF LITERARY MAGAZINES AND PRESSES, Suite 3-C, 154 Christopher St., New York NY 10014-2839. Publishes an annual directory useful to writers: The **Directory of Literary Magazines**, which has detailed descriptions of over 500 literary magazines, including type of work published, payment to contributors and circulation. The directory is $13.50 postage paid and may be ordered by sending a check to CLMP.

COWBOY POETRY GATHERING; COWBOY MUSIC GATHERING; WESTERN FOLKLIFE CENTER, 501 Railroad St., Elko NV 89801. Both of these gatherings are sponsored by Western Folklife Center, Box 888, Elko NV 89803, phone (702)738-7508, fax (702)738-2900. There is an annual 6-day January gathering of cowboy poets in Elko. The Cowboy Music Gathering is held annually the last weekend in June. The Western Folklife Center publishes and distributes books and tapes of cowboy poetry and songs as well as other cowboy memorabilia. The well-established tradition of cowboy poetry is enjoying a renaissance, and thousands of cowboy poets participate in these activities. Catalog and brochure available by calling (800)748-4466.

FAIRBANKS ARTS ASSOCIATION; FAIRBANKS ARTS, P.O. Box 72786, Fairbanks AK 99707, phone (907)456-6485, fax (907)456-4112, editor Heather Robertson. FAA publishes a bimonthly magazine, ***Fairbanks Arts***, which covers interior Alaskan arts and cultural events, organizations and people (artists, writers, musicians, actors, etc.), plus provides how-to information, market tips for Alaskan writers, humor and personal experiences pertaining to writing, marketing and lifestyles. Articles run 800-1,300 words. **Accepts all forms of poetry; limit submissions to 3 poems with maximum 40 lines each. Pays 5 contributor copies.** Subscription: $15. **Sample and guidelines: $3.** The FAA sponsors a Community Reading Series for Alaskan and visiting writers.

FEDERATION OF BRITISH COLUMBIA WRITERS, M.P.O. Box 2206, Vancouver, British Columbia V6B 3W2 Canada, manager Corey Van't Haaff. The federation "is a nonprofit organization of professional and emerging writers in all genres." They publish a newsletter of markets, political reports, awards and federation news; act as "a network centre for various other provincial writer's organizations; host, promote and organize workshops, readings, literary competitions and social activities; publish directories which are distributed to schools, businesses, and organizations which may request the services of writers; and represent writers' interests to other professionally related organizations."

FESTIVAL OF POETS AND POETRY AT ST. MARY'S; EBENEZER COOKE POETRY FESTIVAL, St. Mary's College of Maryland, St. Mary's City MD 20686, phone (301)862-0239. An annual event held during the last two weekends in May of each year. Approximately 18 guest poets and artists participate in and lead workshops, seminars and readings. Concurrent with the festival, St. Mary's College offers a 2-week intensive poetry writing workshop and a 10-day writer's community retreat. The poetry workshop engages the participants in structured poetry writing experiences. Intended for anyone with a serious interest in writing poetry, it offers four college credits or may be taken as a non-credit course. The retreat, designed for the serious writer, offers individual plans for writing alone or in conjunction with other participants. Three 90-minute workshop sessions are organized for participants. There is also a 12-day fiction writing workshop offered during the festival. For applications or more information on these workshops or the festival, please write to Michael S. Glazer at the above address. The Ebenezer Cooke Poetry Festival is a biennial event in August of even numbered years, held in the name of the first Poet Laureate of Maryland. Poets from Maryland and the surrounding areas are invited to give 5-minute readings, enjoy a crab feast and otherwise celebrate together.

GENIE SERVICE; WRITERS' INK, 401 N. Washington St., Rockville MD 20850, phone (800)638-9636, provides news, research information and entertainment to individuals throughout the US, Canada and numerous foreign countries. "There are dozens of areas of interest to poets, from workshops to an electronic encyclopedia. The heart of the writing community on GEnie is Writers' Ink, an electronic association of poets, authors, illustrators, screenwriters and others interested in all aspects of writing for enjoyment and/or publication. Members 'meet' using their computer and a modem (for most, it's a local phone call). The Writers' Ink Bulletin Board is filled with discussions and information on a wide variety of subjects—from publishing your first poem to working with imagery. Writers' Ink conducts frequent electronic meetings where people from all over the world can gather and discuss poetry and writing. There are also weekly online poetry readings where members share and discuss their work. Poets will find the Writers' Ink Libraries full of useful software, helpful articles and interviews as well as poems and stories by members. Poets can even find market information as well as tips for dealing with editors." Cost is $8.95 for 4 hours of standard time; then cost is $3/hour. This fee includes electronic mail, an encyclopedia and access to many bulletin boards (including Writers' Ink). Other areas of GEnie are available for $6/hour (during non-prime time which is 6 p.m. to 8 a.m. local time).

INTERNATIONAL WOMEN'S WRITING GUILD, P.O. Box 810, Gracie Station, New York NY 10028, phone (212)737-7536, founded 1976, "a network for the personal and professional empowerment of women through writing." The Guild publishes a bimonthly 28-page newsletter which includes members' needs, achievements, contests, and publishing information. A manuscript referral service introduces members to literary agents. Other activities are 13 annual national and regional events, including a summer conference at Skidmore College (see listing under Conferences and Workshops); "regional clusters" (independent regional groups); job referrals; round robin manuscript exchanges; sponsorship of the "Artist of Life" award; group health and life insurance. Membership in the nonprofit Guild costs $35/year in the US and $45/year foreign.

JUST BUFFALO LITERARY CENTER, Suite 209, 493 Franklin St., Buffalo NY 14202, phone (716)881-3211, fax (716)881-3552, founded 1975 by executive director Debora Ott, has two part-time program coordinators, executive assistant, coordinator of community resources, an administrative assistant, and a radio producer and interdisciplinary program consultant. They offer readings, workshops, master classes, residencies, an annual Western New York Writers-in-Residence competition, an annual Labor-in-Literature competition open to WNY union members, Spoken Arts Radio broadcasts on National Public Radio affiliate WBFO, and Writers-in-Education for school-age populations. Just Buffalo acts as a clearinghouse for literary events in the Greater Buffalo area and offers diverse services to writers and to the WNY region. "Although we are not accepting submissions for publication at this time, we will review works for possible readings."

THE LANE LITERARY GUILD, Lane Regional Arts Council, 164 W. Broadway, Eugene OR 97401-3004. The guild is "a volunteer organization dedicated to encouraging and supporting poets and writers in Lane County, Oregon. We hold monthly readings featuring new and established poets and writers. Our readers are drawn from talent locally as well as from other cities and parts of the country. We also hold workshops, symposia and literary contests. Our funding comes from membership fees, donations at readings and from grant support by the Cultural Services Division of the City of Eugene, by the Oregon Arts Commission and by the Lane Regional Arts Council. We are interested in hearing from poets and writers from around the country who will be in our neighborhood and might be interested in being one of our readers."

THE LEAGUE OF CANADIAN POETS; WHEN IS A POEM; WHO'S WHO IN THE LEAGUE OF CANADIAN POETS; HERE IS A POEM; POETRY MARKETS FOR CANADIANS; NATIONAL POETRY CONTEST; GERALD LAMPERT AWARD; PAT LOWTHER AWARD, 3rd Floor, 54 Wolseley, Toronto, Ontario M5T 1A5 Canada, phone (416)504-1657, founded 1966, contact Sandra Drzewiecki. The league's aims are the advancement of poetry in Canada and promotion of the interests of professional, Canadian poets. Information on full and associate membership can be obtained by writing for the brochure, League of Canadian Poets: Services and Membership. The league publishes a biannual **Museletter** (30 pgs., magazine-sized) plus six 4-page issues; **When is a Poem**, on teaching poetry to children; a directory volume called **Who's Who in The League of Canadian Poets** that contains 1 page of information, including a picture, bio, publications and "what critics say" about each of the members; **Here is a Poem**, a companion anthology to **When is a Poem**, featuring the work of Canadian poets; and **Poetry Markets for Canadians** which covers contracts, markets, agents and more. The league's members go on reading tours, and the league encourages them to speak on any facet of Canadian literature at schools and universities, libraries or organizations. The league has arranged "thousands of readings in every part of Canada"; they are now arranging exchange visits featuring the leading poets of such countries as Great Britain, Germany and the US. The league sponsors a National Poetry Contest with prizes of $1,000, $750 and $500; the best 50 poems published in a book. Deadline: January 31. Entry fee: $6/poem. Poems should be unpublished, under 75 lines and typed. Names and addresses should *not* appear on poems but on a separate covering sheet. Please send SASE for complete rules, info on judges, etc. Open to Canadian citizens or landed immigrants only. The Gerald Lampert Award of $1,000 is for a first book of poetry written by a Canadian, published professionally. The Pat Lowther Award of $1,000 is for a book of poetry written by a Canadian woman and published professionally. Write for entry forms. It is also the address of Writers Union of Canada which provides services and information to members, including a writer's guide to Canadian publishers ($3) and a variety of other publications to assist writers.

THE LOFT; LOFT-MCKNIGHT AWARDS, Pratt Community Center, 66 Malcolm Ave. SE, Minneapolis MN 55414, phone (612)379-0754, founded 1974, executive director Susan Broadhead. The Loft was started by a group of poets looking for a place to give readings and conduct workshops and has evolved into a sophisticated hub of activity for creative writing in all genres managed by an 19-member board of directors and staff of 12. This past year 2,000 members contributed $30/year to the Loft; it was further supported by $56,000 from individuals, plus government, foundation and corporate grants. The Loft offers over 75 6- and 12-week courses each year, in addition to 30 workshops and panels. Its publication readings and emerging voices readings are meant for Minnesota writers whereas the Mentor Series and Creative Non-fiction residency feature nationally known writers. The Loft publishes a monthly newsletter called ***A View from the Loft***. The Loft-McKnight Awards are offered annually to Minnesota writers: 8 awards of $7,500 each, 3 in poetry, 5 in creative prose; 2 Awards of Distinction, $10,500 each.

MAINE WRITERS & PUBLISHERS ALLIANCE; MAINE IN PRINT; MAINE WRITERS CENTER, 12 Pleasant St., Brunswick ME 04011-2201, phone (207)729-6333, founded 1975, membership coordinator Paul Doiron. This organization is "a nonprofit organization dedicated to promoting all aspects of writing, publishing, and the book arts. Our membership currently includes over 1,450 writers, publishers, librarians, teachers, booksellers and readers from across Maine and the nation. For an individual contribution of $25 per year members receive a range of benefits including ***Maine in Print***, a monthly compilation of calendar events, updated markets, book reviews, grant information, interviews with Maine authors and publishers, articles about writing and more. The alliance distributes selected books about Maine and by Maine authors and publishers, and it maintains a bookstore, reference library, performance space and word processing station at the Maine Writers Center in Brunswick. MWPA regularly invites writers to read from their works and to conduct Saturday workshops." Reviews books of poetry only by Maine-based presses and poets. "We also have extensive on-going workshops in fiction and poetry and offer an annual fall writing retreat."

NATIONAL FEDERATION OF STATE POETRY SOCIETIES, INC. Membership Chairperson: Barbara Stevens, 909 E. 34th St., Sioux Falls SD 57105; Contest Chairperson: Amy Jo Zook, 3520 State Route 56, Mechanicsburg OH 43044. "NFSPS is a nonprofit organization exclusively educational and literary. Its purpose is to recognize the importance of poetry with respect to national cultural heritage. It is dedicated solely to the furtherance of poetry on the national level and serves to unite poets in the bonds of fellowship and understanding." Any poetry group located in a state not already affiliated but interested in affiliating with NFSPS may contact the membership chairperson. Canadian groups may also apply. "In a state where no valid group exists, help may also be obtained by individuals interested in organizing a poetry group for affiliation." Most reputable state poetry societies are members of the National Federation and advertise their various poetry contests through the quarterly bulletin, ***Strophes***, available for SASE and $1, editor Kay Kinnaman, Route 3, Box 348, Alexandria IN 46001. Beware of organizations calling themselves state poetry societies (however named) that are not members of NFSPS, as such labels are sometimes used by vanity schemes trying to sound respectable. Others, such as the Oregon State Poetry Association, are quite reputable, but they don't belong to NFSPS. NFSPS holds an annual meeting in a different city each year with a large awards banquet, addressed by an honorary chairperson. They sponsor 50 national contests in various categories each year, including the NFSPS Prize of $1,500 for first place; $500, second; $250, third; with entry fees ($3 for the entire contest for members, $5 for NFSPS Award; $1/poem for nonmembers and $5 for NFSPS Award up to 4 poems/entry). All poems winning over $10 are published in an anthology. Rules for all contests are given in a brochure available from Kay Kinnaman at ***Strophes*** or Amy Jo Zook at the address above; you can also write for the address of your state poetry society. Scholarship information is available from Golda Walker, 915 Aberdeen Ave., Baton Rouge LA 70808 for a #10 SASE.

THE NATIONAL POETRY FOUNDATION; SAGETRIEB; PAIDEUMA, University of Maine, Orono ME 04469, publications coordinator Marie M. Alpert. "The NPF is a nonprofit organization concerned with publishing scholarship on the work of 20th century poets, particularly Ezra Pound and those in the Imagist/Objectivist tradition. We publish ***Paideuma***, a journal devoted to Ezra Pound scholarship, and ***Sagetrieb***, a journal devoted to poets in the imagist/objectivist tradition, as well as one other journal of contemporary poetry and comment—***The New York Quarterly***. [See separate listing for ***New York Quarterly*** in the Publishers of Poetry section.] NPF conducts a conference each summer and celebrates the centennial of an individual 20th century poet." Sample copies: $8.95 for ***Paideuma*** or ***Sagetrieb***; $6 for ***New York Quarterly***.

NATIONAL WRITERS UNION, Room 203, 873 Broadway, New York NY 10003. Offers members such services as a grievance committee, contract guidelines, health insurance, press credentials, car rental discounts, and caucuses and trade groups for exchange of information about special markets. Members receive ***The American Writer***, the organization's newsletter. Membership is $75 for those earning less than $5,000/year; $125 for those earning $5,000-25,000; and $170 for those earning more than $25,000.

NORTH CAROLINA WRITERS' NETWORK; THE NETWORK NEWS; HARPERPRINTS POETRY CHAPBOOK COMPETITION; THE RANDALL JARRELL POETRY PRIZE, P.O. Box 954, Carrboro NC 27510, established 1985. Supports the work of writers, writers' organizations, independent bookstores, little magazines and small presses, and literary programming statewide. A $25 donation annually brings members ***The Network News***, a 24-page bimonthly newsletter containing organizational news, national market information and other literary material of interest to writers, and access to the Resource Center, other writers, workshops, conferences, readings and competitions, and a critiquing service. 1,600 members nationwide. Annual fall conference features nationally-known writers, publishers and editors. It is held in a different North Carolina location each year in November. Also sponsors competitions in short fiction, one-act plays and nonfiction essays for North Carolinians and members.

THE OREGON STATE POETRY ASSOCIATION, % Linda Smith, 471 NW Hemlock, Corvallis OR 97330, phone (503)753-3335; newsletter editor Elizabeth Bolton, P.O. Box 219006, Portland OR 97225. Founded for "the promotion and creation of poetry," the association has over 200 members, $12 dues, publishes a quarterly ***OSPA Newsletter***, and sponsors contests twice yearly, October and April, with total cash prizes of $300 each (no entry fee to members, $2/poem for nonmembers; out of state entries welcome). Themes and categories vary. For details write to OSPA, P.O. Box 219006, Portland OR 97225 after August 1 and February 15 each year. The association sponsors workshops, readings and seminars around the state.

PEN AMERICAN CENTER; PEN WRITERS FUND; PEN TRANSLATION PRIZE; RENATO POGGIOLI AWARD; GRANTS AND AWARDS, 568 Broadway, New York NY 10012, phone (212)334-1660, "is the largest of more than 100 centers which comprise International PEN, founded in London in 1921 by John Galsworthy to foster understanding among men and women of letters in all countries. Members of PEN work for freedom of expression wherever it has been endangered, and International PEN is the only worldwide organization of writers and the chief voice of the literary community." Its total membership on all continents is approximately 10,000. The 2,700 members of the American Center include poets, playwrights, essayists, editors, novelists (for the original letters in the acronym PEN), as well as translators and those editors and agents who have made a substantial contribution to the literary community. Membership in American PEN includes reciprocal privileges in foreign centers for those traveling abroad. Branch offices are located in Cambridge, Chicago, Portland/Seattle, Baton Rouge and San Francisco. Among PEN's various activities are public events and symposia, literary awards, assistance to writers in prison and to American writers in need (grants and loans up to $1,000 from PEN Writers Fund). Medical insurance for writers is available to members. The quarterly ***PEN Newsletter*** is sent to all members and is available to nonmembers by subscription. The PEN Translation Prize is sponsored by the Book-of-the-Month Club, 1 prize each year of $3,000 for works published in the current calendar year. The Renato Poggioli Award, $3,000 annually, is designed to encourage a promising translator from the Italian who has not yet been widely recognized. Candidates with a project in literary translation planning a journey to Italy will be favored. Submit résumé, sample translation and description of project before January 15. They publish **Grants and Awards** biennially, containing guidelines, deadlines, eligibility requirements and other information about hundreds of grants, awards and competitions for poets and other writers: $8 postpaid. Send SASE for booklet describing their activities and listing their publications, some of them available free.

PERSONAL POETS UNITED, Villa B-7, 16591 Perdido Key Dr., Pensacola FL 32507, % Jean Hesse, who started a business in 1980 writing poems for individuals for a fee (for greetings, special occasions, etc.). Others started similar businesses, after she began instructing them in the process, especially through a cassette tape training program and other training materials. She then organized a support group of poets around the country writing poetry-to-order, Personal Poets United. Send SASE for free brochure or $19.50 plus $4.50 p&h for training manual, "How to Make Your Poems Pay."

PITTSBURGH POETRY EXCHANGE, P.O. Box 4279, Pittsburgh PA 15203, phone (412)481-POEM. Founded in 1974 as a community-based organization for local poets, it functions as a service organization and information exchange, conducting ongoing workshops, readings, forums and other special events. No dues or fees. "At our open workshop we each drop a dollar into the basket which we turn over to City Books as 'rent' for use of the space. Any other monetary contributions are voluntary, often from outside sources. We've managed not to let our reach exceed our grasp." Their reading programs are primarily committed to local and area poets, with honorariums of $25-60. They sponsor a minimum of three major events each year in addition to a monthly workshop. Some of these have been reading programs in conjunction with community arts festivals, such as the October South Side Poetry Smorgasbord—a series of readings throughout the evening at different shops (galleries, bookstores). Poets from out of town may contact the exchange for assistance in setting up readings at bookstores to help sell their books. Contact Michael Wurster at the above address or phone number.

THE POETRY COMMITTEE OF THE GREATER WASHINGTON AREA, % The Folger Shakespeare Library, 201 E. Capitol St. SE, Washington DC 20003, phone (202)544-7077, executive director Saskia Hamilton. An independent, nonprofit group, the membership (by invitation) consists of about 60 people who represent major and minor poetry organizations in the metropolitan area. Annual sponsors of Celebration of Washington Poetry, a reading and book sale highlighting area poets and presses, the Columbia Book Award for best book of poetry by Washington area poet within the past calendar year and the Columbia Merit Award for service to area poetry.

THE POETRY PROJECT AT ST. MARK'S CHURCH IN THE BOWERY, 131 E. 10th St., New York NY 10003, phone (212)674-0910, was established in 1966 by the US Dept. of H.E.W. in an effort to help wayward youths in the East Village. It is now funded by a variety of government and private sources. Artistic Director: Ed Friedman. Program Coordinator: Gillian McCain. From October through May the project offers workshops, talks, staged readings, performance poetry, lectures, an annual 4-day symposium, literary magazines and a series of featured writers who bring their books to sell at the readings. If the reading is a publication party, the publisher handles the sales.

POETRY RESOURCE CENTER OF MICHIGAN, %English Dept., Wayne State University, 51 W. Warren, Detroit MI 48202, phone (313)754-9645, president Cindi St. Germain, "is a nonprofit organization which exists through the generosity of poets, writers, teachers, publishers, printers, librarians and others dedicated to the reading and enjoyment of poetry in Michigan." The ***PRC Newsletter*** and ***Calendar*** is available by mail monthly for an annual membership donation of $20 or more, and is distributed free of charge at locations throughout the state. To obtain copies for distribution at poetry functions, contact the editor or any member of the PRC Board of Trustees.

POETRY SOCIETY OF AMERICA; POETRY SOCIETY OF AMERICA AWARDS, 15 Gramercy Park, New York NY 10003, phone (212)254-9628, is a nonprofit cultural organization in support of poetry and of poets, member and nonmember, young and established, which sponsors readings, lectures and workshops both in New York City and around the country. Their Peer Group Workshop is open to all members and meets on a weekly basis. They publish a newsletter of their activities and sponsor a wide range of contests. The following are open to members only: Gordon Barber Memorial Award ($200); Gertrude B. Claytor Award ($250); Gustav Davidson Memorial Award ($500); Mary Carolyn Davies Memorial Award ($250); Alice Fay Di Castagnola Award ($2,000); ***Writer Magazine***/Emily Dickinson Award ($100); Consuelo Ford Award ($250); Cecil Hemley Memorial Award ($300); Lucille Medwick Memorial Award ($500). Nonmembers may enter as many of the following contests as they wish, no more than 1 entry for each, for a $5 fee: Ruth Lake Award, $100 for a poem of retrospection any length or style; Elias Lieberman Student Poetry Award, $100 for students in grades 9-12; John Masefield Memorial Award for a narrative poem in English up to 300 lines, $500, translations ineligible; Celia B. Wagner Award, $250 any form or length; George Bogin Memorial Award, $500 for a selection of 4 to 5 poems which take a stand against oppression; Robert H. Winner Memorial Award, $2,500 for a poem written by a poet over 40, still unpublished or with one book. (All have a deadline of December 22; awards are made at a ceremony and banquet in late spring.) The Society also has 3 book contests open to works submitted by publishers only. They must obtain an entry form, and there is a $10 fee for each book entered. Book awards are: Melville Cane Award, $500 in even-numbered years awarded to a book of poems, in odd years to prose work on poetry; Norma Farber Award, $1,000 for a first book; William Carlos Williams Award, $1,250 for a book of poetry published by a small, nonprofit or university press, by a permanent resident of the US—translations not eligible. The Shelley Memorial Award of $6,486 is by nomination only. For necessary rules and guidelines for their various contests send SASE between October 1 and December 22. Membership: $40.

POETS & WRITERS, INC., See listing under Publications Useful to Poets.

POETS' CORNER, THE CATHEDRAL CHURCH OF ST. JOHN THE DIVINE, Cathedral Heights, 1047 Amsterdam Ave. at 112 St., New York NY 10025, initiated in 1984 with memorials for Emily Dickinson, Walt Whitman, Washington Irving, Robert Frost, Herman Melville, Nathaniel Hawthorne, Edgar Allan Poe, Henry James, Henry David Thoreau, Mark Twain, Ralph Waldo Emerson, William Faulkner, Wallace Stevens, Willa Cather, T.S. Eliot, Marianne Moore, Henry Wadsworth Longfellow, Stephen Crane and Edwin Arlington Robinson. It is similar in concept to the British Poets' Corner in Westminster Abbey, and was established and dedicated to memorialize this country's greatest writers. A Board of Electors comprised of thirteen eminent poets and writers chooses two deceased authors each year for inclusion in The Poets' Corner.

POETS HOUSE; THE REED FOUNDATION LIBRARY; THE POETRY PUBLICATION SHOWCASE; DIRECTORY OF AMERICAN POETRY BOOKS, 72 Spring St., New York NY 10012, phone (212)431-

7920, founded 1985, executive director Lee Ellen Briccetti, "is a comfortable, accessible place for poetry—a library and meeting place which invites poets and the public to step into the living tradition of poetry." It is the home of the Reed Foundation Library, a 30,000 volume poetry collection open to the public, as well as over 25 public events each year, and a variety of programs for students and educators. In addition, Poets House hosts the annual Poetry Publication Showcase, a festival of events organized around a comprehensive exhibit of the year's new poetry releases from commercial, independent and university press publishers. The **Directory of American Poetry Books** is compiled through the Poetry Publication Showcase. Poetry publishers are urged to send review copies to Poets House care of the "Showcase," or to call for more information. Poets House also welcomes membership, donations of books to its library, and visits to its comfortable loft space.

‡POETS THEATRE, RD 2, Box 155, Cohocton NY 14826. In its 14th year of sponsoring readings and performances with limited funding from Poets & Writers. For a mostly conservative, rural audience. A featured poet, followed by open reading, monthly.

POETS-IN-THE-SCHOOLS. Most states have PITS programs that send published poets into classrooms to teach students poetry writing. If you have published poetry widely and have a proven commitment to children, contact your state arts council, Arts-in-Education Dept., to see whether you qualify. Three of the biggest programs are Poets in Public Service, Suite 3B, 154 Christopher St., New York NY 10014, phone (212)206-9000; California Poets-in-the-Schools, 2845 24th St., San Francisco CA 94110, phone (415)695-7988; and COMPAS, Landmark Center, #308, 75 W. Fifth St., St. Paul MN 55102.

SCOTTISH POETRY LIBRARY; SCHOOL OF POETS; CRITICAL SERVICE, Tweeddale Court, 14 High St., Edinburgh EH1 1TE Scotland, phone (031)557-2876, director Tessa Ransford, librarian Penny Duce. It is a central information source and free lending library, also lending by post. The library has a computerized catalogue allowing subject-based searches. The collection has over 12,000 items and consists of Scottish and international poetry. The School of Poets is open to anyone; "at meetings members divide into small groups in which each participant reads a poem which is then analyzed and discussed." Meetings normally take place at 7:30 p.m. on the first Tuesday of each month at the library. They also offer a Critical Service in which groups of up to 6 poems, not exceeding 200 lines in all, are given critical comment by members of the School: £15 for each critique (with SAE).

THE SOCIETY OF AUTHORS, 84 Drayton Gardens, London SW10 9SB England. Advises members on business matters, takes up their complaints and institutes legal proceedings, sends them a quarterly journal, ***The Author***, publishes guides regarding agents, copyright, income tax, contracts, etc., offers members retirement and medical insurance programs, administers trust funds as well as a number of literary awards, organizes special interest groups (e.g., broadcasters, children's writers, etc.), and pursues campaigns on behalf of the profession (e.g., for legislative changes).

SONGWRITERS AND POETS CRITIQUE, 11599 Coontz Rd., Orient OH 43146, phone (614)877-1727, founded in 1985 by Ellis Cordle. A nonprofit association whose purpose is to serve songwriters, poets and musicians in their area. The president of the organization says, "We have over 200 members from over 16 states at several levels of ability from novice to advanced, and try to help and support each other with the craft and the business of poetry and songs. We have published writers and recorded artists. We share information about how to pitch, send and package a demo and who to send it to. We also have a songwriting contest for member writers." Annual dues are $25.

SOUTHERN POETRY ASSOCIATION; THE POET'S VOICE, P.O. Box 524, Pass Christian MS 39571, founded 1986, poetry editor Mildred Klyce. SPA offers networking, publishing, free critique service for members through Round Robin Groups and assistance in publishing chapbooks. $10 annual membership fee includes ***The Poet's Voice*** quarterly newsletter. The association sponsors a number of contests, including Voices of the South, Yarn Spinner, Poetry in Motion, Special People; some are for members only; some, such as the Voices of the South Contest, are open to all. Prizes total $200 with $3 entry fee/poem (28-line limit). June 1 deadline. High scoring poems are published in an anthology (which the poet is not required to purchase). Send 9×12 SAE with 58¢ postage for details. ***The Poet's Voice*** contains poetry book reviews, articles on great poets of the past, current activities and input from SPA members.

THE THURBER HOUSE; JAMES THURBER WRITER-IN-RESIDENCE, 77 Jefferson Ave., Columbus OH 43215, phone (614)464-1032, officially opened in 1984. It is "one of the most diversely active of all restored writer's homes." The Thurber House has a staff of 8, over 50 volunteers and 22 board members. Its budget comes from state, local and national arts councils; foundations; corporate, business and individual sponsors; and sales. Listed on the National Register of Historic Places, The Thurber House is a literary center, bookstore and museum of Thurber materials. Programs include writing classes, author readings, Thurber celebrations, events for children and an art gallery. The

Thurber House sponsors a writer-in-residence program where 2 journalists, a playwright, a poet and a fiction writer are invited to spend a season living and writing in The Thurber House while teaching a course at The Ohio State University. Each writer will receive a $5,000 stipend and housing in the third-floor apartment of Thurber's boyhood home. Please call or write to The Thurber House for application information.

THE UNTERBERG POETRY CENTER OF THE 92ND STREET Y; "DISCOVERY"/THE NATION POETRY CONTEST, 1395 Lexington Ave., New York NY 10128, phone (212)415-5760. Offers annual series of readings by major literary figures (36 readings September through May), writing workshops, master classes in fiction and poetry, and lectures. Also co-sponsors the "Discovery"/***The Nation*** Poetry Contest. Deadline early February. Send SASE for information.

WALT WHITMAN CULTURAL ARTS CENTER; CAMDEN POETRY AWARD, 2nd and Cooper St., Camden NJ 08102, executive director René L. Huggins, program coordinator J. Daniel Johnson, phone (609)964-8300. A writers' center, founded 1975, it offers a variety of programs such as Notable Poets and Writers Series, Walt Whitman Poetry Series, school programs, adult and children's theater, musical presentations, Fine Art Exhibitions and the Camden Poetry Award. Their regular season runs September through June. During the summer months they provide a 1-month Creativity Camp and a children's theater series entitled "10 Fridays of Fun."

WOODLAND PATTERN, Box 92081, 720 E. Locust St., Milwaukee WI 53202, phone (414)263-5001. Executive director Anne Kingsbury calls it "a semi-glamorous literary and arts center." Kingsbury regards the center as a neighborhood organization; it includes a bookstore that concentrates on contemporary literature, much of it small press, much of it poetry, and also on multicultural children's literature. It also incorporates a multipurpose gallery/performance/reading space, where exhibitions, readings, a lecture series, musical programs and a reading and study group are held. The ***Woodland Pattern Newsletter***, mailed free to 2,500 people, contains an annotated calendar and pieces about visiting writers.

WORLD-WIDE WRITERS SERVICE, INC.; WRITERS INK; WRITERS INK PRESS; WRITERS UNLIMITED AGENCY, INC.; WESTHAMPTON WRITERS FESTIVAL; JEANNE VOEGE POETRY AWARDS, P.O. Box 698, Centereach NY 11720-0698, phone (516)736-6439, founded in 1976, Writers Ink Press founded 1978, director Suk-Hang Chin, poetry editor Dr. David B. Axelrod. "World-wide Writers Service is a literary and speakers' booking agency. With its not-for-profit affiliate, Writers Unlimited Agency, Inc., it presents literary workshops and performances, conferences and other literary services, and publishes through Writers Ink Press, chapbooks and small flat-spined books as well as arts editions. **We publish only by our specific invitation at this time."** ***Writers Ink*** is "a sometimely newsletter of events on Long Island, now including programs of our conferences. We welcome news of other presses and poets' activities. Review books of poetry. We fund raise for nonprofit projects and are associates and sponsors of Westhampton Writers Festival and Jeanne Voege Poetry Awards. Arts Editions are profit productions employing hand-made papers, bindings, etc. We have editorial services available at small fees ($50 minimum), but only after inquiry and if appropriate. We are currently concentrating on works in translation, particularly Chinese."

THE WRITER'S CENTER; CAROUSEL; POET LORE, 4508 Walsh St., Bethesda MD 20815, phone (301)654-8664, founder and artistic director Allan Lefcowitz, director Jane Fox. This is an outstanding resource for writers not only in Washington DC but in the wider area ranging from southern Pennsylvania to North Carolina and West Virginia. The center offers 200 multi-meeting workshops each year in writing, word processing, and graphic arts, and provides a research library. It is open 7 days a week, 10 hours a day. Some 2,300 members support the center with $30 annual donations, which allows for 4 paid staff members. There is a book gallery at which publications of small presses are displayed and sold. The center's publication, ***The Carousel***, is a 24-page magazine that comes out 6 times a year. They also sponsor 40 annual performance events, which include presentations in poetry, fiction and theater. The center is publisher of ***Poet Lore***—100 years old in 1989 (see listing in the Publishers of Poetry section). Reviews books of poetry.

THE WRITERS ROOM, 5th Floor, 153 Waverly Pl., New York NY 10014, phone (212)807-9519, provides a "home away from home" for any writer "with a serious commitment to writing," who needs a place to work. It is open 24 hours a day, 7 days a week, offering desks, storage space and "an alternative to isolation" for up to 150 writers. Space is allotted on a quarterly basis (which may be extended indefinitely) and costs $165/quarter. "We now offer in-house scholarships for one-quarter year to writers in financial need." It is supported by the National Endowment for the Arts, the New York State Council on the Arts and other public and private sources, and it encourages applications. The Writers Room also offers monthly readings and workshops for its residents and has occasional exhibits on "writerly" subjects, such as revision.

Additional Organizations Useful to Poets

The following listings also contain information about organizations useful to poets. See the General Index for page numbers.

Publications Useful to Poets

The publications in this section are designed to help poets with all aspects of poetry writing and publishing. While few are actual markets for poetry, many detail new publishing opportunities in addition to providing information on writing poetry, advice on marketing or interviews with poets and writers.

Poets & Writers Magazine, in fact, is one of the most useful resources for both poets and fiction writers. In addition to informative articles and interviews, it includes calls for submissions and contests and awards. ***Writer's Digest***, on the other hand, covers the entire field of writing and features various market listings as well as a monthly poetry column by Michael J. Bugeja, author of **The Art and Craft of Poetry** (Writer's Digest Books, 1994).

Other publications, such as ***Dusty Dog Reviews***, ***Small Press Review*** (which now incorporates ***Small Magazine Review***) and ***Literary Magazine Review***, include reviews of poetry books and chapbooks and/or reviews of small press magazines. These reviews provide insight into the different markets you are considering.

Finally, for those interested in further exploring various publishing opportunities, this section also includes information about other market directories as well as materials on self-publishing. And, in addition to the listings that follow, you will find other useful publications, such as ***Canadian Author*** and ***New Writer's Magazine***, under Additional Publications Useful to Poets at the end of this section.

To determine which of these publications may be most useful to you, read sample issues. Many of these books and periodicals may be found in your local library or located on newsstands or in bookstores. If you are unable to locate a certain magazine, order a copy directly from the publisher. For books, send a SASE with a request for the publisher's current catalog and/or further information.

R.R. BOWKER; LITERARY MARKET PLACE; BOOKS IN PRINT, 121 Chanlon Rd., New Providence NJ 07974, phone (908)464-6800. **LMP** is the major trade directory of publishers and people involved in publishing books. It is available in most libraries, or individual copies may be purchased (appears in December each year; standing order price: $165). **BIP** is another standard reference available in most libraries and bookstores. Bowker publishes a wide range of reference books pertaining to publishing. Write for their catalog.

CANADIAN POETRY, English Dept., University of Western Ontario, London, Ontario N6A 3K7 Canada, phone (519)661-3403, founded 1977, editor Prof. D.M.R. Bentley. A biannual journal of critical articles, reviews and historical documents (such as interviews). It is a professionally printed, scholarly edited, flat-spined, 100-page journal which pays contributors in copies. Subscription: $15. **Sample: $7.50. Note that they publish no poetry except as quotations in articles.**

DUSTBOOKS; INTERNATIONAL DIRECTORY OF LITTLE MAGAZINES AND SMALL PRESSES; DIRECTORY OF POETRY PUBLISHERS; SMALL PRESS REVIEW; SMALL MAGAZINE REVIEW, P.O. Box 100, Paradise CA 95967. Dustbooks publishes a number of books useful to writers. Send SASE for catalog. Among their regular publications, **International Directory** is an annual directory of small presses and literary magazines, over 5,000 entries, a third being magazines, half being book publishers, and the rest being both. There is very detailed information about what these presses and magazines report to be their policies in regard to payment, copyright, format and publishing schedules. **Directory of Poetry Publishers** has similar information for 2,000 publishers of poetry. ***Small Press Review*** is a monthly magazine, newsprint, carrying current updating of listings in **ID**, small press needs, news, announcements and reviews—a valuable way to stay abreast of the literary marketplace. ***Small Magazine Review***, which began publication in June, 1993, is now included within ***Small Press Review*** and covers small press magazines in a similar fashion.

DUSTY DOG REVIEWS, 1904-A Gladden, Gallup NM 87301, phone (505)863-2398, founded 1990, editor/publisher John Pierce. ***Dusty Dog Reviews*** is a review magazine appearing 3 times/year, reviewing small press poetry books and chapbooks, 60-80/issue, average length 200 words. Subscription: $4.50. Sample: $2. Open to unsolicited reviews. Poets may also send books for review consideration to Dave Castleman, 512 Tamalpais Dr., Mill Valley CA 94941. "All editors and publishers whose poetry books/chapbooks get reviewed will receive one copy of the issue in which the review appears." The editor advises, "Become very familiar with **Poet's Market** and what is said at the beginning of the book. The small press magazines are often 1 person staff and work very hard for you, the poet. Be patient with them, and support the magazines you like. If poets don't subscribe to the magazines that publish them, it is very hard for the magazine to continue publishing."

LAUGHING BEAR NEWSLETTER; LAUGHING BEAR PRESS (V), P.O. Box 36159, Denver CO 80236, phone (303)744-3624, founded 1976, editor Tom Person. ***LBN*** is a monthly publication of small press information for writers and publishers containing articles, news and reviews; it was named one of the 9 best publishing and marketing newsletters in the 1992 ***Small Press*** Newsletter Awards. Cost: $10/year. Send SASE for sample copy. ***LBN*** is interested in short (200- to 300-word) articles on self-publishing and small press. Pays copies.

THE LETTER EXCHANGE, published by The Readers' League, % Stephen Sikora, P.O. Box 6218, Albany CA 94706. Published 3 times each year, ***The Letter Exchange*** is a digest-sized magazine, 36 pgs., that publishes 4 types of listings: regular (which are rather like personal classifieds); ghost letters, which contain lines like "Send news of the Entwives!"; amateur magazines, which publicizes readers' own publishing ventures; and sketch ads, in which readers who would rather draw than write can communicate in their chosen mode. All ads are coded, and readers respond through the code numbers. Subscription to ***The Letter Exchange*** is $20/year, and sample copies are $9 postpaid for current issue. Poets who are so inclined often exchange poems and criticism with each other through this medium.

LITERARY MAGAZINE REVIEW, English Dept., Kansas State University, Manhattan KS 66506, founded 1981, editor G.W. Clift. A quarterly magazine (digest-sized, perfect-bound, about 60 pgs.) that publishes critiques, 2-5 pgs. long, of various literary magazines, plus shorter "reviews" (about ½ page), directories of literary magazines (such as British publications) and descriptive listings of new journals during a particular year. Single copies are available for $5 or subscriptions for $12.50 year.

OPEN HORIZONS, P.O. Box 205, Fairfield IA 52556-0205, phone (515)472-6130, publisher John Kremer, publishes how-to books about book publishing and self-publishing, such as **1001 Ways to Market Your Books, Directory of Book Printers**, and **Book Publishing Resource Guide** (also available on IBM PC or Macintosh disk as a database). Send SASE for catalog.

PARA PUBLISHING, Box 4232-880, Santa Barbara CA 93140-4232, phone (805)968-7277, orders (800)727-2782, fax (805)968-1379. Author/publisher Dan Poynter publishes how-to books on book publishing and self-publishing. **Is There a Book Inside You?** shows you how to get your book out. **The Self-Publishing Manual, How to Write, Print and Sell Your Own Book** is all about book promotion. **Publishing Short-Run Books** shows you how to typeset and lay out your own book. Poynter also publishes **Publishing Contracts on Disk, Book Fairs** and 19 Special Reports on various aspects of book production, promotion, marketing and distribution. *Free* book publishing information kit. Newly available through Para Publishing is a 24-hour fax service called Fax-On-Demand. This service enables you to obtain free documents on book writing and publishing; and lists of workshops and presentations offered by Dan Poynter. Call (805)968-8947 from your fax machine handset, then follow the voice prompts to hear a list of documents and to order. The fax machine will retrieve the documents and print them instantly. This is a good way to sample Para Publishing's offerings.

POETRY BOOK SOCIETY, 10 Barley Mow Passage, London W4 4PH England. A book club with an annual subscription rate of £28, which covers 4 books of new poetry, the ***PBS Bulletin***, a premium offer (for new members) and free surface postage and packing to anywhere in the world. The selectors also recommend other books of special merit, which are obtainable at a discount of 25%. The Poetry Book Society is subsidized by the Arts Council of Great Britain. Please write for details or phone 081-995-3635 (24-hour fax/answer service).

THE POETRY CONNECTION, 13455 SW 16 Court #F-405-PM, Pembroke Pines FL 33027, phone (305)431-3016, editor/publisher Sylvia Shichman. ***The Poetry Connection*** provides information in flyer format. Poets, writers and songwriters receive information on how to sell their poetry/books, poetry and musical publications and contests, and obtain assistance in getting poetry published. *TPC* has information on writing for greeting card companies, poetry publications and songwriting directories. Sample issue: $5 plus 5 first-class stamps.

POETRY EXCHANGE, P.O. Box 85477, Seattle WA 98145-1477. A monthly newsletter, circulation 1,600, $12/year, to which you may subscribe or in which you can buy ads. It has listings of workshops, "manuscripts wanted," and a calendar of regional poetic events. It is 4 to 8 magazine-sized pages.

POETS & WRITERS, INC.; A DIRECTORY OF AMERICAN POETS AND FICTION WRITERS; WRITER'S GUIDE TO COPYRIGHT; AUTHOR & AUDIENCE; LITERARY AGENTS; LITERARY BOOKSTORES; POETS & WRITERS MAGAZINE, 72 Spring St., New York NY 10012, phone (212)226-3586 or (800)666-2268 (California only), is our major support organization. Its many helpful publications include ***Poets & Writers Magazine***, which appears 6 times a year ($18 or $3.95 for a single copy), magazine-sized, 88 pgs., offset, has been called ***The Wall Street Journal*** of our profession, and it is there that one most readily finds out about resources, current needs of magazines and presses, contests, awards, jobs and retreats for writers, and discussions of business, legal and other issues affecting writers. P&W also publishes a number of valuable directories such as its biennial **A Directory of American Poets and Fiction Writers** ($24.95 paperback), which editors, publishers, agents and sponsors of readings and workshops use to locate over 7,000 active writers in the country. (You may qualify for a listing if you have a number of publications.) They also publish **A Writer's Guide to Copyright; Author & Audience**, a list of over 400 organizations which sponsor readings and workshops involving poets and fiction writers, including a section on how to organize and present a reading or workshop; **Literary Agents: A Writer's Guide; Literary Bookstores: A Cross-Country Guide**, for people who travel; and a new series of eight chapbooks, "Into Print: Guides to the Writing Life," that includes **Out of the Slush Pile and Into Print; Contracts and Royalties: Negotiating Your Own; On Cloud Nine: Writers' Colonies, Retreats, Ranches, Residencies, and Sanctuaries**; and **Helping Writers Help Themselves: A National Guide to Writers' Resources.** The new chapbooks are available from P&W for $6 each plus p&h.

POETS' AUDIO CENTER; THE WATERSHED FOUNDATION, P.O. Box 50145, Washington DC 20091. This is an international clearinghouse for ordering any poetry recording available, from both commercial and noncommercial producers. Catalog available free ("an introduction to our collection"); they stock over 500 titles. **Foundation not accepting applications at this time.**

BERN PORTER INTERNATIONAL, 22 Salmond Rd., Belfast ME 04915, founded 1911. A monthly journal that both reviews books of poetry and publishes poetry. Also provides sleeping bag space for poets and writers May 1 through November 1 for the cost or freewill contribution. No smoking. No drugs. No telephone.

PUSHCART PRESS, P.O. Box 380, Wainscott NY 11975. Publishes a number of books useful to writers, including the Pushcart Prize Series—annual anthologies representing the best small press publications, according to the judges; The Editors' Book Award Series, "to encourage the writing of distinguished books of uncertain financial value"; The Original Publish-It-Yourself Handbook; and the Literary Companion Series. Send SASE for catalog.

SIPAPU; KONOCTI BOOKS, 23311 County Rd. 88, Winters CA 95694, phone (916)662-3364, founded 1970, editor/publisher Noel Peattie. ***Sipapu*** consists of reviews of small press publications, interviews and conference news, but publishes no new poetry. Konocti Books has published poetry but is now publishing by invitation only.

THE WASHINGTON INTERNATIONAL ARTS LETTER, P.O. Box 12010, Des Moines IA 50312, phone (515)255-5577 or P.O. Box 2908, Sausalito CA 94966-2908, phone and fax (415)331-0441. Appears 10 times/year, 6- to 8-page newsletter on grants and other forms of assistance for the arts and humanities—mostly lists various programs of support to artists, including many for poets. Reviews books of poetry. Subscription: $124 full rate; $55 for individuals; $82 for institutions. Send all orders and requests for information to the California address.

WORDWRIGHTS CANADA, P.O. Box 456 Station O, Toronto, Ontario M4A 2P1 Canada, director Susan Ioannou, publishes "books on poetics in layman's, not academic terms, such as **Writing Reader-friendly Poems: Over 50 Rules of Thumb for Clearer Communication** and **Literary Markets that Pay.**" They consider manuscripts of such books for publication, paying $50 advance, 10% royalties and 5% of press run. They also conduct a "Manuscript Reading Service." Request order form to buy samples.

WRITER'S DIGEST BOOKS; WRITER'S DIGEST, 1507 Dana Ave., Cincinnati OH 45207, phone (800)289-0963 or (513)531-2222. Writer's Digest Books publishes a remarkable array of books useful to all types of writers. In addition to **Poet's Market**, books for poets include **The Poet's Handbook** by Judson Jerome, **Creating Poetry** by John Drury and **The Art and Craft of Poetry** by Michael J. Bugeja. Call or write for a complete catalog. ***Writer's Digest*** is a monthly magazine about writing with frequent articles and market news about poetry, in addition to a monthly poetry column. See the listing in the Publishers of Poetry section.

WRITERS NEWS; WRITERS LIBRARY, P.O. Box 4, Nairn, 1V12 4HU Scotland, phone 0667-454441, fax 0667-454401. The monthly magazine ***Writer's News***, 48 pgs., is chock-full of announcements of markets, competitions, opportunities and news of the writing world. A regular feature is their Poetry Workshop, discussing the writing of poetry. Writers Library distributes books on writing, including many published by Writer's Digest Books, as is also the case with the UK book club, the Writers Book Society. Subscription to the magazine: £39.90 or £34.90 if you pay by "direct debit" (charge card). Write for their book catalog.

Additional Publications Useful to Poets

The following listings also contain information about publications useful to poets. See the General Index for page numbers.

Aardvark Enterprises
Academy of American Poets, The
American Poetry Review
Anterior Poetry Monthly
Artist Trust
Associated Writing Programs
Black Bear Publications
Black Buzzard Press
Borealis Press
Byline Magazine
Canadian Author
Canadian Conference of the Arts
Canadian Poetry Association
Canadian Writer's Journal
Chips Off the Writer's Block
COSMEP, The International Association of Independent Publishers
Council of Literary Magazines and Presses
Emerald Coast Review
Fairbanks Arts Association
Federation of British Columbia Writers
Frank: An International Journal of Contemporary Writing and Art
Insight Press
International Women's Writing Guild
IWWG Summer Conference, The
Keystrokes
Laureate Letter, The
Leacock Medal for Humour, The Stephen
League of Canadian Poets, The
Ligonier Valley Writers Conference
Loft, The
Maine Writers & Publishers Alliance
Midwest Writers' Conference
My Legacy
Naropa Institute Writing & Poetics Summer Program, The
National Federation of State Poetry Societies, Inc.
National Poetry Foundation, The
National Writers Union
New Horizons Poetry Club
New Writer's Magazine
North Carolina Writers' Network
Northwoods Press
Oak, The
Oregon State Poetry Association, The
Parnassus: Poetry in Review
PEN American Center
Pequod: A Journal of Contemporary Literature and Literary Criticism
Piedmont Literary Review
Poetry London Newsletter
Poetry Plus Magazine
Poetry Resource Center of Michigan
Poetry Society of America
Poets House
Poets' Roundtable
Quarry Magazine
Rio Grande Press
Scavenger's Newsletter
Seneca Review
Small Press Genre Association
Smith, The
Society of Authors, The
Southern Poetry Association
Thumbprints
University of Massachusetts Lowell Writers' Conference
Verse
Violetta Books
Wisconsin Regional Writers' Association
World-wide Writers Service, Inc.
Write Way, The
Writer, The
Writer's Center, The
Writer's Digest
Writer's Exchange
Writers Forum (England)
Writer's Guidelines: A Roundtable for Writers and Editors
Writer's Journal
Writer's Lifeline

U.S. and Canadian Postal Codes

United States

AL Alabama
AK Alaska
AZ Arizona
AR Arkansas
CA California
CO Colorado
CT Connecticut
DE Delaware
DC District of Columbia
FL Florida
GA Georgia
GU Guam
HI Hawaii
ID Idaho
IL Illinois
IN Indiana
IA Iowa
KS Kansas
KY Kentucky
LA Louisiana
ME Maine
MD Maryland
MA Massachusetts
MI Michigan
MN Minnesota
MS Mississippi
MO Missouri
MT Montana
NE Nebraska
NV Nevada
NH New Hampshire
NJ New Jersey
NM New Mexico
NY New York
NC North Carolina
ND North Dakota
OH Ohio
OK Oklahoma
OR Oregon
PA Pennsylvania
PR Puerto Rico
RI Rhode Island
SC South Carolina
SD South Dakota
TN Tennessee
TX Texas
UT Utah
VT Vermont
VI Virgin Islands
VA Virginia
WA Washington
WV West Virginia
WI Wisconsin
WY Wyoming

Canada

AB Alberta
BC British Columbia
LB Labrador
MB Manitoba
NB New Brunswick
NF Newfoundland
NT Northwest Territories
NS Nova Scotia
ON Ontario
PEI Prince Edward Island
PQ Quebec
SK Sasketchewan
YT Yukon

ALWAYS include a self-addressed, stamped envelope (SASE) when sending a ms or query to a publisher within your own country. When sending material to other countries, include a self-addressed envelope and International Reply Coupons (IRCs), available for purchase at most post offices.

Glossary

A3, A4, A5. Metric equivalents of 11¾ × 16½, 8¼ × 11¾ and 5⅞ × 8¼ respectively.

Bio. Some publishers ask you to send a short biographical paragraph with your submission; it is commonly called a "bio." They may also ask for your important previous publications or "credits."

Chapbook. A small book of approximately 20-25 pages of poetry. Such a book is less expensive to produce than a full-length book collection, though it is seldom noted by reviewers.

Cover letter. Letter accompanying a submission giving brief account of publishing credits and biographical information. See the advice and sample in Charting Your Path to Poetry Publication.

Digest-sized. Approximately 5½ × 8½, the size of a folded sheet of conventional typing paper.

Flat-spined. What many publishers call "perfect-bound," glued with a flat edge (usually permitting readable type on the spine).

Galleys. Typeset copies of your poem(s). You should proofread and correct any mistakes and return the galleys to editors within 48 hours of receipt.

IRC. International Reply Coupon, postage for return of submissions from another country. One IRC is sufficient for one ounce by *surface mail.* If you want an airmail return, you need one IRC for each half-ounce. Do not send checks or cash for postage to other countries: The exchange rates are so high it is not worthwhile for editors to bother with. (Exception: Many Canadian editors do not object to U.S. dollars; use IRCs the first time and inquire.)

Magazine-sized. Approximately 8½ × 11, the size of conventional typing paper unfolded.

ms, mss. Manuscript, manuscripts.

Multi-book review. Also known as an omnibus or essay review. A review of several books by the same author or by several authors, such as a review of four or five political poetry books.

Multiple submission. Submission of more than one poem at a time; most poetry publishers *prefer* multiple submissions and specify how many poems should be in a packet. Some say a multiple submission means the poet has sent more than one manuscript to the same publication before receiving word on the first submission. This type of multiple submission is generally discouraged.

p. Abbreviation for pence.

pg., pgs. Page, pages.

Perfect-bound. See Flat-spined.

Query letter. Letter written to a publisher to elicit interest in a manuscript or to determine if submissions are acceptable.

Rights. First North American serial rights means the publisher is acquiring the right to publish your poem first in a U.S. or Canadian periodical. All rights means the publisher is buying the poem outright. Selling all rights usually requires that you obtain permission to reprint your work, even in a book-length collection.

Saddle-stapled. What many publishers call "saddle-stitched," folded and stapled along the fold.

SAE. Self-addressed envelope.

SASE. Self-addressed, stamped envelope. *Every* publisher requires, with any submission, query or request for information, a self-addressed, stamped envelope. This requirement is so basic it is typically excluded from individual listings but repeated in bold type at the bottom of many pages throughout this book. The return envelope (usually folded for inclusion) should be large enough to hold the material submitted or requested, and the postage provided—stamps if the submission is within your own country, IRCs if it is to another country—should be sufficient for its return.

Simultaneous submission. Submission of the same manuscript to more than one publisher at a time. Most magazine editors *refuse to accept* simultaneous submissions. Some book and chapbook publishers do not object to simultaneous submissions. In all cases, notify them that the manuscript is being simultaneously submitted elsewhere if that is what you are doing.

Slush pile. Unsolicited manuscripts, usually hundreds each year, cluttering an editor's desk.

Status. The current situation concerning a particular manuscript: 1) The manuscript was never received. 2) We received the manuscript but cannot locate it. 3) We received and rejected said manuscript. 4) We are still considering it. 5) We are in the process of accepting your manuscript.

Subsidy press. See Vanity press.

Tabloid-sized. 11 × 15 or larger, the size of an ordinary newspaper folded and turned sideways.

Vanity press. A slang term for a publisher that requires the writer to pay publishing costs, especially one that flatters an author to generate business. These presses often use the term "subsidy" to describe themselves. Some presses, however, derive subsidies from other sources, such as government grants, and do not require author payment. These are not considered vanity presses.

Visual poetry. A combination of text and graphics usually only reproduced photographically.

Indexes

Chapbook Publishers

A chapbook is a slim volume of a poet's work, usually 20-25 pages (although page requirements vary greatly). Given the high cost of printing, a publisher is more apt to accept a chapbook than an entire book from an unproven poet.

Some chapbooks are published as inserts in magazines. Others are separate volumes. Whenever possible, request submission guidelines and samples to determine the quality of the product.

You'll find many presses charge reading fees. Avoid any over $10. (Some folks go as high as $15 for book-length manuscripts, but chapbooks are easier to process.)

If your chapbook is published, by the way, you may still participate in "first-book" competitions. For more information about both chapbook and book publishing, read Charting Your Path to Poetry Publication, beginning on page 5.

Following are publishers who consider chapbook manuscripts. See the General Index for their specific page numbers.

Geographical Index

Use this index to locate small presses and magazines in your region. Much of the poetry published today reflects regional interests; also publishers often favor poets (and work) from their own areas.

The U.S. listings are arranged alphabetically by state/territory; refer to the General Index for specific page numbers. Also check your neighboring states for other opportunities. The last sections are publishers in Canada, the United Kingdom and other countries. Remember to always include a SAE and IRCs for replies from countries outside your own.

North Carolina

North Dakota

Ohio

Oklahoma

Oregon

Pennsylvania

Rhode Island

South Carolina

South Dakota

Tennessee

Texas

Utah

Vermont

Virgin Islands

Virginia

Washington

West Virginia

Wisconsin

Other Countries

Subject Index

Use this index to save time in your search for the best markets for your poetry. The categories are listed alphabetically and contain the magazines, publishers, contests and awards that buy or accept poetry in these special categories. Most of these markets are coded **IV** in their listings.

Check through the index first to see what subjects are represented. Then look at the listings in the categories you're interested in. For example, if you're seeking a magazine or contest for your poem about "the great outdoors," look at the listings under **Nature/Rural/Ecology**. After you've selected a possible market, refer to the General Index for the page number. Then read the listing *carefully* for details on submission requirements.

This year we've added a few new categories, including **Mystery** and **Writing**. Also, if you're a beginning cowboy poet, you can now easily find markets for your work under the category **Cowboy**. And those who write about ghoulish topics will discover that **Horror** has been separated from **Science Fiction/Fantasy**.

Under **Themes**, we now list those book and magazine publishers that regularly publish anthologies or issues on announced themes (if interested, send a SASE to these publishers for details on upcoming topics). **Regional** includes those outlets which publish poetry about or by poets from a certain geographic area; and the category **Form/Style** contains those magazines and presses that seek particular poetic forms or styles, such as haiku or sonnets or experimental work. Finally, those publishers listed under **Specialized** are very narrow in their focus—too narrow, in fact, to be listed in one of our other categories.

We do not recommend you use this index exclusively in your search for a market. Most magazines, publishers and contests listed in **Poet's Market** are very general in their specifications and don't choose to be listed by category. Also, many specialize in one subject but are open to others as well. Reading *all* the listings is still your best marketing strategy.

Children/Teen/Young Adult

Cowboy

Ethnic/Nationality

Essence (African-American women)
European Judaism
Firebrand Books
Four Directions, The (Native American)
Gairm (Scottish Gaelic)
Gentle Survivalist, The (Native American)
Guernica Editions Inc. (Italian, Italian-Canadian, Italian-American)
Guild Press (minorities)
Ice Cold Watermelon (African-American)
India Currents
International Black Writers
Irish-American Cultural Institute Literary Awards
Israel Horizons
Italian Americana
Japanophile
Kitchen Table: Women of Color Press
Kuumba (African-American)
Kwibidi Publisher (minorities)
Language Bridges Quarterly (Polish)
L'Apache: An International Journal of Literature & Art
Lilith Magazine (Jewish)
Living Poets Society (African-American)
Middle East Report
Midstream: A Monthly Jewish Review
Minority Literary Expo
Miorita: A Journal of Romanian Studies
Obsidian II: Black Literature in Review
Oracle Poetry (African)
Path Press, Inc. (African-American, Third World)
Poetry Wales Press (Welsh, Welsh-American)
Rarach Press (Czech)
Rashi (Jewish)
Reconstructionist (Jewish)
Response (Jewish)
Review: Latin American Literature and Arts
Rosenberg Award, Anna Davidson (Jewish)
Sandberry Press (Caribbean)
Shamal Books (African-American, Caribbean)
Shofar (American Jewish)
Shooting Star Review (African-American)
Sister Vision Press (women of color)
Soleil Press (Franco-American)
Three Continents Press Inc. (non-Western; Asian/Pacific; Africa; Middle East; Caribbean)
Tia Chucha Press (African, Asian, Latin, Native American)
Wake Forest University Press (Irish French)
Whitecrow Foundation, Tahana (Native American)
Wicazo SA Review, The (Native American)
Wind-Mill, The (German, Dutch)

Form/Style

Alpha Beat Soup (Beat)
Amelia (all forms)
American Writing: A Magazine (experimental)
Asylum (prose poems)
Bennett & Kitchel
black bough (haiku, senryu, tanka, haibun)
Bouillabaisse
Brussels Sprout (haiku, senryu, tanka)
Damaged Wine (free verse)
dbqp (short language, visual)
Dead Rebel News, The (language poetry)
Drop Forge (experimental, visual)
Epigrammatist, The
Equinox Press (haiku, senryu)
Formalist, The (metrical)
Frank: An International Journal of Contemporary Writing and Art
Free Focus
Frogpond: Quarterly Haiku Journal
Generator (language, concrete, visual)
Georgia State Poetry Society, Inc.
Geppo Haiku Worksheet
Green Rivers Writers' Contests
Haiku Headlines: A Monthly Newsletter of Haiku and Senryu
Hellas: A Journal of Poetry and the Humanities
High/Coo Press (haiku)
Hippopotamus Press
Hrafnhoh (metrical Christian)
Imploding Tie-Dyed Toupee, The (Dada, surrealism, experimental, visual)
Inkstone: A Magazine of Haiku
Japanophile
Juniper Press
Kaldron: An International Journal of Visual Poetry and Language Art
Lamp-Post, The (formal Christian)
Lilliput Review (no longer than 10 lines)
Lizard's Eyelid, The (short, witty, shocking, bizarre)
Luna Bisonte Prods (experimental, visual, collaboration)
Lynx, A Journal for Linking Poets (renga)
Lyric, The (traditional)
M.A.F. Press (13 lines only)
Malahat Review, The (long poems)
Mirrors (haiku)
Modern Haiku
Nada Press (objectivist-based, short)
9th St. Laboratories (experimental, graphic)
Penny Dreadful Review, The (dark, erotic, experimental)
Piedmont Literary Review (oriental, haiku)
Plains Poetry Journal (rhyme, meter)
Pleiades Magazine (rhyme)
Poetical Histories (British, modernist)
Poetry Society of Virginia Annual Contest, The

Gay/Lesbian/Bisexual

Horror

Humor

Love/Romance/Erotica

Religious

Science Fiction/Fantasy

Senior Citizen

Social Issues

Specialized

Spirituality/ Inspirational

Women/Feminism

Writing

General Index

B

Can't find a poetry publisher's listing? Check Publishers of Poetry/'94-'95 Changes on pages 439-440 for information about other publishers.

Can't find a poetry publisher's listing? Check Publishers of Poetry/'94-'95 Changes on pages 439-440 for information about other publishers.

Can't find a poetry publisher's listing? Check Publishers of Poetry/'94-'95 Changes on pages 439-440 for information about other publishers.

Can't find a poetry publisher's listing? Check Publishers of Poetry/'94-'95 Changes on pages 439-440 for information about other publishers.

Can't find a poetry publisher's listing? Check Publishers of Poetry/'94-'95 Changes on pages 439-440 for information about other publishers.

Can't find a poetry publisher's listing? Check Publishers of Poetry/'94-'95 Changes on pages 439-440 for information about other publishers.

Can't find a poetry publisher's listing? Check Publishers of Poetry/'94-'95 Changes on pages 439-440 for information about other publishers.

Can't find a poetry publisher's listing? Check Publishers of Poetry/'94-'95 Changes on pages 439-440 for information about other publishers.

Can't find a poetry publisher's listing? Check Publishers of Poetry/'94-'95 Changes on pages 439-440 for information about other publishers.

T

Can't find a poetry publisher's listing? Check Publishers of Poetry/'94-'95 Changes on pages 439-440 for information about other publishers.

Can't find a poetry publisher's listing? Check Publishers of Poetry/'94-'95 Changes on pages 439-440 for information about other publishers.

Can't find a poetry publisher's listing? Check Publishers of Poetry/'94-'95 Changes on pages 439-440 for information about other publishers.

Before Submitting Your Poetry:

1. *Read widely to discover where your work fits into the general poetry scene.*
2. *Learn about the organizations and publications readily available to poets—and get to know the people involved in them.*
3. *Explore* Poet's Market *subject and geographical indexes to locate the publishers closest to your interests and area.*
4. *Use the market codes in each listing to help you select the best publishers for your work.*
5. *Avoid inappropriate submissions by studying market listings for information about the type, form and number of poems a publisher seeks.*
6. *Obtain available guidelines and sample copies of the publications you're interested in* before *sending your work to those markets.*
7. *Proofread your work carefully; make sure it is exactly as you would like it to appear.*
8. *Keep cover letters brief and informative.*
9. *Inform editors if you're submitting simultaneous or previously published poems. (Note: Some editors will not consider such submissions.)*